Ireland

Tom Smallman
Pat Yale.
Steve Fallon

Ireland

3rd edition

Published by
Lonely Planet Publications
Head Office: PO Box 617, Hawthorn, Vic 3122, Australia
Branches: 155 Filbert St, Suite 251, Oakland, CA 94607, USA
               10a Spring Place, London NW5 3BH, UK
               71 bis rue du Cardinal Lemoine, 75005 Paris, France

Printed by
The Bookmaker Pty Ltd
Printed in Hong Kong

Photographs by

Mark Daffey	Tom Smallman	Pat Yale
John Murray	Tony Wheeler	

Front cover: Brightly coloured cafe (Grant V Faint, The Image Bank)

First Published
January 1994

This Edition
March 1998

National Library of Australia Cataloguing in Publication Data

Smallman, Tom
Ireland

3rd ed.
Includes index.
ISBN 0 86442 530 9

1. Ireland – Guidebooks. I. Yale, Pat, 1954-. II. Fallon, Steve. III. Title. (Series: Lonely Planet travel survival kit)

914.1504

text & maps © Lonely Planet 1998
photos © photographers as indicated 1998
Donegal and Limerick climate charts compiled from information supplied by Patrick J Tyson, © Patrick J Tyson, 1998

Tom Smallman

Tom lives in Melbourne, Australia, and had a number of jobs before joining Lonely Planet as an editor. He now works full time as an author and has worked on Lonely Planet guides to *Canada*, *Dublin*, *New South Wales*, *Sydney*, *New York*, and *New Jersey & Pennsylvania*.

Pat Yale

Pat spent several years selling holidays before throwing up sensible careerdom to head overland from Egypt to Zimbabwe. She then mixed teaching tourism with travel in Europe, Asia and Central and South America, before becoming a full-time writer. She has worked on LP's guides to *Dublin*, *Britain*, *London* and *Turkey*, and has contributed to *Walking in Britain*. After stints in London, Cambridge and Cirencester, she currently lives in Bristol.

Steve Fallon

Steve, whose grandparents left counties Roscommon and Cork for America at the end of the last century, was born in Boston, Massachusetts, and graduated from Georgetown University with a Bachelor of Science in modern languages. After stints teaching English at the University of Silesia near Katowice, Poland, and working for a Gannett newspaper in the USA, his fascination with the 'new' Asia took him to Hong Kong, where he lived and worked for 13 years for a variety of publications and was editor of *Business Traveller* magazine. In 1987, he put journalism on hold when he opened Wanderlust Books, Asia's only travel bookshop. Steve lived in Budapest for 2½ years from where he wrote LP's guides to *Hungary* and *Slovenia* before moving to London in 1994. He has written or contributed to a number of other LP titles, including *France* and the forthcoming *Germany*.

From the Authors

Tom Smallman My thanks to Sue Graefe for her enduring patience and tolerant support; to Arthur and Liz who made it all possible; to Lindy Mark for her invaluable information; to Eileen Maguire, Siobhan, Brendan and Darragh for their hospitality in Dublin; to Kathleen, Christy and Christy junior for doing the same in Tipperary (Roger, we must talk about the photoluminescence of nano-structures sometime); to Kathleen for the coffee and chats in Dublin; to Mike and Mike for the meal and the Guinness in Carnlough; to Tricia and Brian for a great weekend and putting up with my driving; to Cyril in Belfast; to Colette at the NITB office in Belfast; to Vivian at the NITB office and Phil at the marine biology centre, both in Portaferry; to all those other people in the travel industry who patiently answered my questions; to the hard-working Lonely Planet staff in Melbourne; to my co-researchers Pat and Steve; and to all those readers who wrote in with comments on the previous edition.

Pat Yale Of the many people who were generous with their time and information I would particularly like to thank Damien and Marian Smyth in Tralee; Diane Hyde in Waterford; Jim Maher in Killarney; Liam and Kay Maher in Cork City; Lisa O'Shea in Kenmare; Mick Murphy at Skibbereen; Vari Finlay at Schull; Eddie McCarthy at Kinsale; Ian O'Leary in Kilkenny; Helen Monaghan at the James Joyce Centre in Dublin; Laura Gilfoyle at the IHH in Dublin; John Bolton at Bus Éireann; Craig, Charlie, Casey and Noel of Slow Coach for their stream of anecdotes; and particularly Michael, Clare and Shane Campbell and all the staff at the wonderful Globetrotters in Dublin who took in a wet and downhearted author and sent her on her way with a spring in her step again. Others who helped me through my time away from home were Jamie who provided inspirational conversation at Gannares on the Beara; and Sara Hayes who showed up just in time to celebrate Bloomsday with me. Thanks, too, to Tracy and Ellen for their house-sitting efforts and to Neil Cossor for remembering to send me his notes.

Steve Fallon *Go raibh maith agat* to tourist office staff throughout Ireland, especially in Ennis, Boyle, Oughterard, Omagh and Enniskillen, for their assistance, and to Joan Pyne of Derry, Mr & Mrs Sexton of Galway, Denise Callan at the King House Interpretive Centre in Boyle, and IHH owners almost everywhere for their warmth and hospitality. A *póg* for my much missed aunt Alice M Murphy for putting some Irish language and music in my head, and one again for Michael Rothschild, who likes Ireland and the Irish almost as much as I do.

This Book

The 1st edition of this book was written by John Murray, Sean Sheehan and Tony Wheeler. The 2nd edition was updated by Tom Smallman, Sean Sheehan and Pat

Yale. The 3rd edition was updated by Tom Smallman, Pat Yale and Steve Fallon.

From the Publisher

This book was edited at the Lonely Planet office in Melbourne, Australia, by Chris Wyness with the help of John Atwood, Miriam Cannel, Jane Fitzpatrick, Martin Hughes, Sarah Mathers, and Steve Womersley. Piotr Czajkowski was responsible for the mapping and design, while Jenny Jones and Michelle Lewis were responsible for the layout of this edition. The cover was designed by David Kemp and Adam McCrow.

Warning & Request

Things change – prices go up, schedules change, good places go bad and bad places go bankrupt – nothing stays the same. So, if you find things better or worse, recently opened or long since closed, please tell us and help make the next edition even more accurate and useful.

We value all of the feedback we receive from travellers. Julie Young coordinates a small team who read and acknowledge every letter, postcard and email, and ensure that every morsel of information finds its way to the appropriate authors, editors and publishers.

Everyone who writes to us will find their name in the next edition of the appropriate guide and will also receive a free subscription to our quarterly newsletter, *Planet Talk*. The very best contributions will be rewarded with a free Lonely Planet guide.

Excerpts from your correspondence may appear in new editions of this guide; in our newsletter, *Planet Talk*; or in updates on our Web site – so please let us know if you don't want your letter published or your name acknowledged.

Thanks

Many thanks to the travellers who used the last edition and wrote to us with helpful hints, useful advice and interesting anecdotes. Your names appear on page 760.

Contents

Boxed Asides

Map Legend

BOUNDARIES

.... International Boundary
.... Provincial Boundary

ROUTES

..... Freeway, with Route Number **A25**
.... Major Road
.... Minor Road
.... Minor Road - unsealed
.... City Road
.... City Street
.... City Lane
.... Steps on Street
.... Train Route, with Station
.... Path thru a Park
.... Ferry Route
.... Walking Tour
.... Walking Track

AREA FEATURES

.... Building
.... Cemetery
.... Beach
.... Market
.... Park, Gardens
.... Pedestrian Mall
.... Reef
.... Urban Area

HYDROGRAPHIC FEATURES

.... Canal
.... Coastline
.... Creek, River
.... Lake, Intermittent Lake
.... Rapids, Waterfalls
.... Salt Lake
.... Swamp

SYMBOLS

○	**CAPITAL**	........National Capital	✈	.... Airport	▲	.... Mountain or Hill
◉	**CAPITAL**	......Provincial Capital		... Ancient or City Wall	⌒⌒	.... Mountain Range
●	**CITY**	.... City	∴	.... Archaeological Site	🏛	....................Museum
●	**Town**	.... Town	Ө	.... Bank	←	........One Way Street
●	Village	.... Village	↗	.... Beach	🅿	.... Parking
			⅋	.... Bicycle Track	)(	.... Pass
■		.... Place to Stay	☗	.... Castle or Fort	℗	.... Petrol Station
🏕		.... Camping Ground	⌒	.... Cave	★	.... Police Station
🏕		.... Caravan Park	▭ 🛈	.... Church	✉	.... Post Office
🏠		.... Hut or Chalet	⌒⌒⌒	.... Cliff or Escarpment	❖	.... Shopping Centre
			⊘	.... Embassy	🏊	.... Swimming Pool
▼		.... Place to Eat	⊕	.... Hospital	☎	.... Telephone
🍷		.... Pub or Bar	※	.... Lookout	❶	....Tourist Information
☕		.... Cafe	⛩	.... Lighthouse	⊖	.... Transport
			⚔	.... Mine	🐘	.... Zoo
			⚱	.... Monument		

Note: not all symbols displayed above appear in this book

Map Index

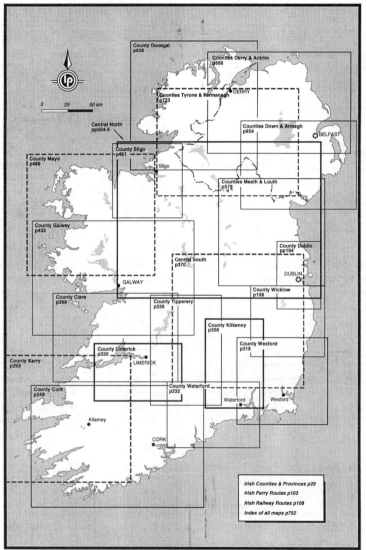

County Donegal p538

Counties Derry & Antrim p686

Counties Tyrone & Fermanagh p723

●DERRY

Counties Down & Armagh p654

✪BELFAST

Central North pp504-5

County Sligo p491

County Mayo p469

Sligo

Counties Meath & Louth p578

County Galway p433

County Dublin pp194

Central South p370

DUBLIN ✪

GALWAY

County Wicklow p198

County Clare p398

County Tipperary p339

County Kilkenny p356

County Wexford p218

County Limerick p330

LIMERICK

County Kerry p293

County Waterford p232

County Cork p248

Waterford

Wexford

Killarney

CORK

0   25   50 km

Irish Counties & Provinces p29

Irish Ferry Routes p103

Irish Railway Routes p108

Index of all maps p752

Introduction

Ireland is one of Western Europe's most lightly populated, least industrialised and, in a word, least 'spoilt' countries. It also has one of the longest and most tragic histories in Europe.

That long history is easy to trace, from Stone Age passage tombs and ring forts, through ancient monasteries and castles, down to the great houses and splendid Georgian architecture of the 18th and 19th centuries. The tragic side of that history is equally easy to unearth. The destruction wrought by the Vikings from the end of the 8th century AD onwards is still visible in the ruins of once-great monasteries. The country's history since the arrival of the English in the 12th century is punctuated with rebellion and repression. Oliver Cromwell's visit in 1649-50 is still remembered with horror; and the Irish population is only now recovering from the mass starvation and emigration resulting from the Famine in the mid-19th century. The 20th century has been no less turbulent, and the

Troubles have continued in Northern Ireland up to today. There are, however, hopeful signs of a permanent, though fragile, peace.

Travellers could be forgiven for forgetting this sad history when facing the peaceful green landscape of the centre, with its lakes and mountains, or the magnificent cliffs of the wild Atlantic coast, and the offshore islands which have been inhabited for millennia. Many traces of traditional culture survive in these remote western areas, and there are still communities in which Irish is the first language.

In cities such as Dublin, Cork and Galway, you can still find narrow, medieval streets – a traffic planner's nightmare. Dublin was at its architectural peak in the 18th century, and many of those fine buildings have lasted for over 200 years almost unchanged. But these aren't museum cities: they're friendly places with great pubs, live music, good theatres and – when it's not raining – cheerful street life. In the North, Belfast and Derry are also remarkably welcoming places. It's worth

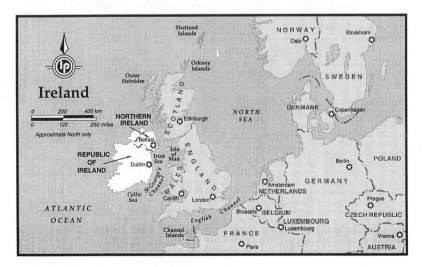

emphasising that they're probably safer for visitors than most other European cities!

When the distinction between Ireland the island and Ireland the state needs to be made in this book, the state is referred to as the Republic of Ireland, the Republic or 'the South'. You may also hear Ireland (the state) referred to as Éire, Southern Ireland or the Free State. In this book Northern Ireland is either referred to as such or as 'the North'. You may also hear it dubbed Ulster or 'the six counties'. Prior to the division of Ireland, the old province of Ulster actually comprised nine counties. Six of these went into Northern Ireland and the other three into the Republic of Ireland.

Facts about Ireland

HISTORY
First Settlers

Ireland was probably first settled by humans about 10,000 years ago, at the end of the last Ice Age. This is relatively late in European prehistory, as Palaeolithic or Old Stone Age people were living in southern England 400,000 years ago and in Wales 250,000 years ago.

With the low sea levels of the last Ice Age, there were land or ice bridges between Ireland and Britain and between Britain and mainland Europe. But conditions in Ireland would have been hostile until the glaciers receded between 12,000 and 10,000 years ago, and prey animals such as deer and boar would have been scarce. These increased in numbers as the climate warmed. Around 12,000 years ago, the Irish giant elk flourished, and there were probably no humans around to hunt it.

As the ice caps melted, there was an enormous rise in the sea level, and about 9000 years ago Ireland was cut off from Britain. It was around this time that the first humans seem to have reached Ireland (landing in the north-east near the modern-day town of Larne) from Britain, possibly across the land bridge or in small hide-covered boats. These people were Middle Stone Age (Mesolithic) hunter-gatherers. They lived in small family or tribal groups collecting fruit and nuts and hunting any animals they could tackle. Their lifestyle would have been similar to that of the Australian Aborigines or the Kalahari Bushpeople.

Traces of these first Irish men and women are faint – just a few scattered rubbish dumps or middens, containing shells and the bones of small animals. Their weapons and tools included flint axes and slivers of flint called microliths, which were used as blades set in a bone or wooden handle. They hunted boar, kept dogs and had a fondness for eels and salmon. The richest concentration of these early sites are in Northern Ireland, including one at Mountsandel Mount near Coleraine, and date from around 8000 to 6000 BC.

First Farmers

While the first settlers were busy discovering Ireland, the greatest revolution in human history had already taken place in the fertile crescent of the Middle East. It was another 2000 or 3000 years before farming reached Ireland, around 4000 BC. Farming marked the arrival of New Stone Age or Neolithic times, and archaeologists can't be certain whether a new wave of farmers colonised Ireland or whether the concept of farming filtered through with just a few immigrants.

A settlement from this era was discovered at Lough Gur near Grange in County Limerick. The traces of pottery, wooden houses and implements indicated a much more prosperous and settled way of life than before. At Céide Fields, near Ballycastle in north Mayo, a remarkable complex of intact stone field walls dating from these times was discovered hidden under a vast blanket of bog. Also around this time was born one of the first Irish exports. Tievebulliagh Mountain near Cushendall in County Antrim has an outcrop of remarkably hard stone called porcellanite, and it formed the basis of a thriving stone-axe industry. Tievebulliagh stone axes have been found as far away as the south of England.

These farmers had enormous respect for ✓ the dead and, from about 3000 BC, built the extraordinary passage graves at Newgrange, Knowth and Dowth in the Boyne Valley. Over 1000 megalithic tombs survive from the Neolithic period, and two large Neolithic settlements have been discovered in the Six Mile Water Valley in County Antrim.

The Bronze Age

The next great human revolution was the ability to work metal and track down the tin and copper ores which could be amalgamated to produce bronze. This heralded the

Bronze Age, which in Ireland is characterised by a reduction in the scale and number of stone tombs, but which produced a truly wonderful legacy of gold and bronze metalwork.

The Bronze Age started in Ireland about 2500 BC, and the early prospectors were amazingly astute at finding sources of metal. Almost everywhere that modern geologists have discovered traces of copper and other metals, they have also discovered that someone else was there some 4000 years previously, without the help of modern equipment and mapping. Bronze Age mine workings can still be seen on Mt Gabriel near Schull in County Cork, and St Kevin's Bed or Cave in Glendalough is thought by many to be an early mine.

Gold-working flourished during the Bronze Age, and the quality of the craftwork and the quantity of metal used say something about the wealth of Ireland at this time. The National Museum in Dublin contains the finest collection of prehistoric goldwork in Europe. Some of the gold may have come from the Wicklow Mountains. (A gold rush took place in the area much later, in 1795.)

Through the Bronze and Iron Ages, the tentacles of trade spread farther and farther out from Ireland. Blue faience beads manufactured in Egypt have turned up in graves on the Hill of Tara in County Meath, as did amber from Scandinavia. The skeleton of a Barbary ape from Spain or Portugal was discovered in a site dating from 200 BC on Emain Macha or Navan Fort in County Armagh.

The Celts

The Celts were Iron Age warrior tribes from eastern Europe who conquered large sections of central and southern Europe between 800 and 300 BC. The Romans called them 'Galli' or Gauls and the Greeks used the term 'Keltoi' or Celts. Both societies had cause to fear the Celts, who plundered Rome in the 4th century AD and were described by contemporary scholars as fierce and dashing warriors. The use of iron was by now widespread throughout Europe, although bronze weapons continued to be used for quite some time.

Celtic warriors and adventurers probably reached Ireland around 300 BC, and were certainly well ensconced by 100 BC. In relatively small numbers, they moved in, controlled the country for 1000 years, and left a legacy of language and culture that survives today.

The Celts also had a common code of law called the Brehon Law and their religion was druidism. They had a distinctive style of design, and its swirls and loops are seen on many Irish artefacts from the 2nd and 1st centuries BC. Some good examples are the Broighter Collar in the National Museum and the Turoe Standing Stone near Loughrea in County Galway. The Irish language is Celtic in origin.

There are no written records for the early Celtic period. Chieftains ensured their immortality through heroic deeds and actions, which were passed down the generations in songs and stories. The epic tales of *Cúchulainn* and the *Táin Bó Cuailnge* are believed to have come from this period. Cúchulainn is the consummate Celtic hero warrior; similar figures appear in Homer's *Iliad* and in the *Mahabharata* poem from India. The *Táin Bó Cuailnge* may not be historically accurate, but the stories may give some idea of Irish society in the first couple of centuries AD.

The country was divided into five provinces: Leinster, Meath, Connaught, Ulster and Munster. Meath later merged with Leinster. The principal struggle for power as reflected in the *Táin Bó Cuailnge* was between Connaught and Ulster. Emain Macha (now called Navan Fort) in County Armagh, mentioned in the *Táin Bó Cuailnge*, is recorded in the map of Ireland drawn in the 2nd century AD by the Egyptian scholar Ptolemy. He called it Isamnium. Within the provinces there were perhaps 100 or more minor kings and chieftains controlling sections (known as *Tuatha)* of the country, and Tara in County Meath became the base for some of the most powerful leaders.

Some of the many door knockers and brightly painted doors found in Dublin

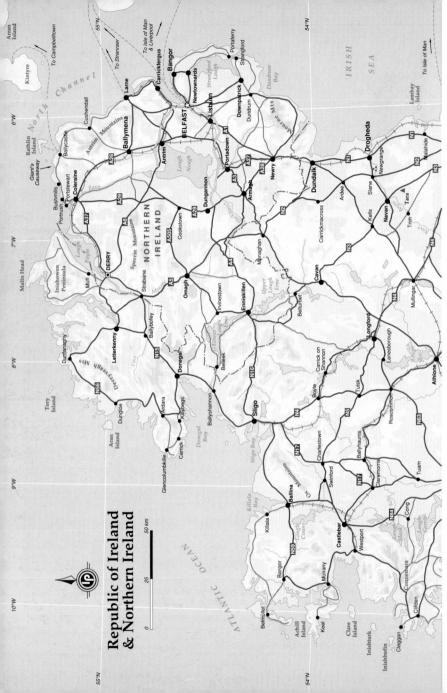

Republic of Ireland & Northern Ireland

0   25   50 km

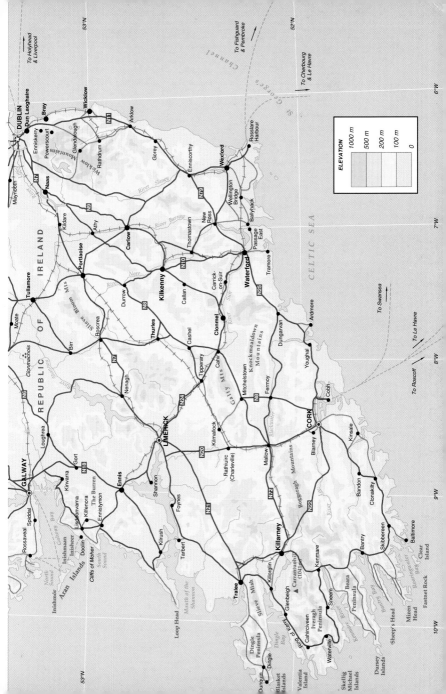

TONY WHEELER

PAT YALE

PAT YALE

Busking in Grafton Street, Dublin

St Patrick & Christianity

The westward march of the Roman empire came to a halt in England. As the empire declined and the Dark Ages began to engulf much of Europe, Ireland became an outpost of European civilisation.

Christianity arrived sometime between the 3rd and 5th centuries, and while St Patrick is given the credit for proselytising the native Irish, there were certainly earlier missionaries. Some scholars dispute that there was a St Patrick at all, and claim the stories about him are really about these early clerics, or later inventions. However, the evidence suggests that there was a St Patrick who lived in the 5th century, and that at the age of 16 he was kidnapped from Britain by Irish pirates. During six years in Ireland as a slave tending sheep, Patrick found religion.

After escaping back to Britain, he was instructed by powerful visions to return to Ireland. Patrick first went to Europe to train as a cleric, and from around 432 AD spent the rest of his life converting the Irish to Christianity. His base was Armagh in County Down, probably chosen because of the symbolic pagan significance of nearby Emain Macha (Navan Fort).

Much of our knowledge of Patrick comes from his own writings. St Patrick's *Confession* is a copy of one such account from the 9th century 'Book of Armagh' (held in Trinity College, Dublin).

As Europe sank into the Dark Ages, Ireland in the 7th and 8th centuries became a 'land of saints and scholars', with thriving monasteries where monks wrote in Latin and illuminated manuscripts, including the world-famous 'Book of Kells' (also in Trinity College). Outstanding among the monasteries were Clonmacnois in County Offaly and Glendalough in County Wicklow. Monks such as Colmcille and Columbanus founded monasteries abroad.

The Vikings

During the 8th century, however, Vikings in their slim powerful boats began to appear off the north and east coasts of Ireland attacking settlements, plundering monasteries and

ushering in a new, more turbulent period of Irish history. In passing, it must be said that the local Irish clans were just as fond of raiding the monasteries as the Vikings were. Monasteries were places of wealth and power, and were often caught in intertribal squabbles. But the increasingly frequent Viking raids burned into the consciousness of Irish monks, and into their accounts of these times. Round towers were built to act as lookout posts and places of refuge in the event of an attack.

In 795 AD, a Viking fleet sailed down the west coast of Scotland, raiding St Colmcille's monastery on Iona before turning their attentions to the east coast of Ireland. They came ashore either at Rathlin Island off the Antrim coast or Lambay Island near Dublin. Irish weapons and soldiers were no match for the superbly armed and ferocious Norsemen. During the 9th century the Vikings started to settle in Ireland and form alliances with native families and chieftains. They established many settlements which bear Viking names today including Wicklow, Waterford and Wexford. They founded Dublin, which in the 10th century was a small Viking kingdom.

The struggles continued between the Vikings and the native Irish, who learned many lessons in the art of warfare. The most decisive defeat for Viking ambitions was at the Battle of Clontarf in 1014, by Irish forces led by Brian Ború, king of Munster, who was aided in the fight by other Vikings from Waterford and Limerick. The elderly Brian Ború was killed by retreating Vikings and subsequent divisions among his chieftains meant the victory wasn't consolidated, but Viking military power in Ireland had been broken. Large numbers of Vikings, however, remained in Ireland, marrying with the native Irish, converting to Christianity and joining in the struggle against the next wave of invaders – the Normans.

The Norman Conquest

In 1066 the Normans under William the Conqueror invaded and conquered England. They were former Vikings themselves, who had settled in northern France 150 years previously, had come to terms with the French king, and had adopted the country's language, religion and military technology. They made no immediate effort to involve themselves in Ireland, but this could only be a matter of time. When they did go over, they were, ironically, responding to an invitation by an Irish chief.

This came about because the king of Leinster, Dermot MacMurrough, and the king of Connaught, Tiernan O'Rourke, were arch rivals. Their relationship was not improved by MacMurrough's kidnapping of O'Rourke's wife in 1152 (although it appears she went willingly). O'Rourke defeated MacMurrough, who fled abroad in 1166 to search for foreign allies. After arguing his case in France, MacMurrough obtained a hearing with the astute Henry II of England, who at first was much too busy to get involved himself, but encouraged MacMurrough to seek help elsewhere among his subjects.

MacMurrough went to Wales, where he met Richard FitzGilbert de Clare, earl of Pembroke, better known as Strongbow, who agreed to muster an army to send to Ireland. In return Strongbow demanded Mac-Murrough's daughter in marriage and the inheritance of the kingship of Leinster once MacMurrough was dead. MacMurrough accepted his proposal, and the stage was set for more than 800 years of English involvement in Ireland.

In May 1169, the first Norman forces arrived in Bannow Bay, County Wexford. MacMurrough joined them and they took Wexford Town and Dublin with ease. The next group of Normans arrived in Bannow Bay in 1170 led by Strongbow's lieutenant, Raymond le Gros, and defeated a considerably larger Irish and Viking army at Baginbun Head on the Hook Peninsula.

In August 1170, Strongbow himself arrived, and with le Gros took Waterford after a fierce battle. A few days later MacMurrough arrived and handed his daughter Aoife to Strongbow. After MacMurrough's death the following year,

Strongbow set about consolidating his new position as king of Leinster.

Meanwhile in England, Henry II was watching events in Ireland with growing unease. In 1754 Henry II had been recognised by the pope as Lord of Ireland and technically Strongbow was one of his subjects. But Strongbow's independence of mind and action was worrying him. In 1171, Henry II sailed from England with a huge naval force, landed at Waterford and declared the place a royal city. He took a semblance of control, but the new Norman lords still did pretty much as they pleased.

Just as the Vikings first settled and were then absorbed so were the new Anglo-Norman intruders. Barons like de Courcy and de Lacy set up power bases very similar to native Irish kingdoms, outside the control of the English king. Over the next two hundred years integration between the Anglo-Normans and native Irish was so successful that in 1336 the English crown introduced the Statutes of Kilkenny which made intermarriage and the use of Irish language and customs illegal. It was too late, and assimilation had gone too far. Over the centuries English control gradually retreated to an area around Dublin known as 'the Pale'. Hence the expression 'beyond the Pale' for an area beyond control.

Henry VIII

In the 16th century, Henry VIII moved to reinforce English control over his unruly neighbour. He was particularly worried that France or Spain might use Ireland as a base from which to attack England. The principal power brokers in Ireland, the Anglo-Norman Fitzgeralds, earls of Kildare, and nominally the representatives of the English crown in Ireland, were in open rebellion. Henry sought their downfall.

In 1534, Garret Óg, the reigning earl, was meeting with Henry in London. The story goes that his 27-year-old son Silken Thomas heard rumours that his father had been executed. Silken Thomas gathered his father's forces and attacked Dublin and the English garrisons. In London, Garret Óg was, however, very much alive and well, and Henry packed off a large army to Ireland which easily crushed Silken Thomas's rebellion. The Fitzgeralds may have been trying to prove they were still a force to be reckoned with in Ireland.

Thomas and his followers surrendered, but they were subsequently executed in what became known as the 'pardon of Maynooth'. This pattern of retribution was to become familiar in following centuries. The Fitzgerald estates were divided among English settlers, and an English viceroy was also appointed.

Meanwhile Henry was involved in a separate battle – with the pope, over the difficult matter of his divorce from Catherine of Aragon. In 1532 he broke with the Catholic Church. With the downfall of the earls of Kildare in 1535, Henry was also able to launch an assault on the property of the Catholic Church in Ireland, which had encouraged rebellion. The wealthy Irish monasteries were dissolved – at considerable profit to the crown – over the next few years. In 1541 Henry ensured that the Irish Parliament declared him king of Ireland.

Elizabeth I

Under Elizabeth I, the English consolidated their power in Ireland. The forests of Ireland were proving invaluable as a source of wood for shipbuilding, and oak was turned into charcoal for smelting ores. Strategically, too, Ireland was important as a possible back door for an invasion from England's enemies in mainland Europe.

English jurisdiction was established in Connaught and Munster despite a number of rebellions by the local ruling families. The success of Elizabeth's policies was borne out when survivors of the 1588 Spanish Armada were washed up on the west coast of Ireland and were mostly massacred by the local sheriffs and their forces.

The thorn in Elizabeth's side was Ulster, the last outpost of the Irish chiefs. Hugh O'Neill, earl of Tyrone, was the prime mover in the last serious assault on English power in Ireland. O'Neill had been educated in

Hugh O'Neill, earl of Tyrone

London, and Elizabeth believed that he would be loyal. A story is told of O'Neill ordering lead from England to re-roof his castle; in reality the lead was for bullets. From 1594, O'Neill moved into open conflict with the English and thus began the Nine Years War (1594-1603). He proved a courageous and crafty foe, and the English forces stepped up their campaign against him, but met with little success until 1601.

In September of that year, a Spanish force landed in Ireland to join O'Neill. Unfortunately, the Spanish anchored at Kinsale in County Cork, almost 480km from O'Neill's territory. O'Neill was forced to march south to join them, and after an exhausting journey ended up fighting just outside Kinsale in unfamiliar country. The Irish were defeated by the English forces under Lord Mountjoy, while the Spanish army was pinned down in Kinsale.

The Battle of Kinsale was the end for O'Neill and for Ulster. Although O'Neill and his forces made it back to Ulster, their power was broken, and 15 months later in 1603 he surrendered and signed the Treaty of Mellifont, handing over power and authority to the English crown. O'Neill was allowed to stay on in Ulster on condition that he pledge allegiance to the crown, which he did. But, in 1607, after a number of frustrating years of subjugation and harassment, O'Neill and 90 other Ulster chiefs boarded a ship in Lough Swilly for Europe, leaving Ireland for ever. This was the 'Flight of the Earls', and it left Ulster leaderless and open to English rule.

With the native chiefs gone, Elizabeth and her successor, James I, pursued a policy of colonisation known as 'plantation' – an organised and ambitious expropriation of land which sowed the seeds for the division of Ulster that we see today. Huge swathes of land were confiscated from the Irish and large numbers of new settlers came from Scotland and England. They brought a new way of life and a different religion. Unlike most previous invaders, they didn't intermarry with the native Irish, and kept their culture and religion very much to themselves. And so, living among these new Protestant landowners was an impoverished and very angry population of native Irish and Old English Catholics.

Oliver Cromwell

In 1641, worried by developments in England and Ireland and believing Charles I to be pro-Catholic, these Irish and Old English Catholics took up arms. What happened subsequently is a matter of debate: certainly a considerable number of the new settlers were killed, but modern historians have revised the likely number of deaths down to perhaps 2000, from earlier widely exaggerated estimates; and many Catholics were also killed, in revenge. Stories of the 1641 atrocities have been used in anti-Catholic propaganda ever since.

The English Civil War kept most of the English busy at home for much of the 1640s. In Ireland, the native Irish and Old English Catholics, allied under the 1641 Confederation of Kilkenny, supported Charles I against the Protestant parliamentarians in the hope of restoring Catholic power in the country. After Charles' execution, the victorious Oliver Cromwell, leader of the parliamentarians, decided to go to Ireland and sort them out.

He arrived in 1649, and rampaged through the country, leaving a trail of death behind him and shipping many of the defeated as slaves to the Caribbean. Under the Act of Settlement (1652) others were dispossessed and exiled to the harsh and infertile lands in the west of Ireland, in the province of Connaught. Two million hectares of land were confiscated – more than a quarter of the country – and handed over to Cromwell's supporters many of whom remained to settle the land. Cromwell's tour of Ireland has never been forgotten.

Battle of the Boyne

The 1660 Restoration saw Charles II, who kept his Catholic sympathies in check, on the English throne. In 1685 his brother James succeeded him. James II's more open Catholicism raised English ire. He was forced to flee the country at the beginning of 1689, intending to raise an army in Ireland and regain his throne from the Protestant William of Orange who had been invited to sit on the English throne by Parliament.

In late 1688, with rumours spreading among Irish Protestants that Irish Catholics were about to rise in support of James II, the Protestant citizens of Derry heard that a Catholic regiment was to be stationed in their city. After furious debate among the local worthies, 13 apprentice boys purloined the keys to the city and slammed the gates in the face of James's soldiers.

In March 1689 James II himself arrived from France at Kinsale, and marched north to Dublin, where the Irish parliament recognised him as king and began to organise the return of expropriated land to Catholic landowners. The siege of Derry began in earnest in April, and ended after mass starvation with the arrival of William's ships in July. The Protestant slogan 'No Surrender!' dates from the siege, which acquired mythical status among Irish Protestants over the following centuries.

William of Orange landed in 1690 at Carrickfergus, just north of Belfast, with an army of up to 36,000 men, and the Battle of the Boyne took place on 12 July. It was fought between Irish Catholics (led by James

II, a Scot) and English Protestants (led by William of Orange, a Dutchman). To make things more complicated, James was William's uncle and his father-in-law. James II's principal supporter was Louis XIV of France, and fear of growing French power led both the Catholic king of Spain and the pope himself to back William and the Protestant side!

William's victory was a turning point, and is commemorated to this day by northern Protestants as a pivotal victory over 'popes and popery'. The final surrender of the Irish came in 1691, when the Catholic leader Patrick Sarsfield signed the Treaty of Limerick. He and thousands of his troops went into exile in France where they served in the French army.

Penal Times

The Treaty of Limerick contained quite generous terms of surrender for the Catholics, but these were largely ignored, and replaced by a harsh regime of penal laws a few years later in 1695. They were passed by a Protestant gentry anxious to consolidate their powers and worried that Louis XIV of France might attempt an invasion of Ireland. Also known as a 'popery code', these laws forbade Catholics from buying land, bringing their children up in their own religion, and from entering the army, navy or legal profession. All Irish culture, music and education was banned. There were also lesser restrictions imposed on Presbyterians and other nonconformists.

The Catholics organised open-air masses at secret locations usually marked by a 'mass rock', and illegal outdoor schools known as 'hedge schools' continued to teach the Irish language and culture. Among the educated classes, many Catholics converted to Protestantism to preserve their careers and wealth.

From around 1715, strict enforcement of the religious sections of the penal laws eased off, although many of the restrictions to do with employment and public office still held. A significant majority of the Catholic population were now tenants living in wretched conditions. By the mid-18th century, Catho-

lics held less than 15% of the land in Ireland, and by 1778 barely 5%. Many middle-class Catholics went into trade.

The 18th Century

Meanwhile Dublin thrived, ranking as Europe's fifth-largest city. The Irish ruling class were members of the established Protestant Episcopalian Church, and were descendants of Cromwellian soldiers, Norman nobles and Elizabethan settlers. They formed a new and prosperous upper class known as the Protestant Ascendancy. There was a Protestant-only parliament, but laws still had to be approved by the British crown and parliament. It was from these Protestants that pressure first came for Ireland to be treated on an equal footing with Britain.

A strong 'Patriot' party calling for independence developed under the leadership of Henry Grattan and Henry Flood. When the American War of Independence broke out in 1776, Britain was in a difficult position. The majority of her forces had to be withdrawn from Ireland to fight in the colonies, leaving security in Ireland largely at the hands of Protestant 'volunteer' forces under the control of the landowners and merchant classes. To avoid further clashes with the increasingly independent Irish parliament, the British government in 1782 allowed the Irish what it considered to be complete freedom of legislation. The new Irish governing body was known as Grattan's parliament. However, London still controlled much of what went on in Ireland through royal patronage and favours and the crown still had the power of veto.

To achieve prosperity in Ireland, Grattan had espoused improved conditions and rights for Catholics. Henry Flood and the majority of other Protestant members were not as sympathetic, and in the life of the parliament – nearly 20 years – little progress was made.

The French Revolution

With the American War of Independence and – much more shocking to Britain – the

French Revolution of 1789, the aristocracy and entrenched politicians could no longer be complacent about the poverty-stricken masses.

In Ireland, an organisation known as the United Irishmen had been formed by Belfast Presbyterians, but its most prominent leader was a young Dublin Protestant and republican, Theobald Wolfe Tone (1763-98). The United Irishmen started out with high ideals of bringing together men of all creeds to reform and reduce England's power in Ireland. Their attempts at gaining power through straightforward politics were fruitless, and when war broke out between Britain and France the United Irishmen found they were no longer being tolerated by the establishment. They reformed themselves as an underground organisation committed to bringing change by any means, violent or otherwise. Tone was keen to enlist the help of the French, who, fresh from their European victories, were easily persuaded.

At the same time, loyalist Protestants were worried by the turn of events and prepared for possible conflict by forming the Protestant Orange Society, which later became known as the Orange Order.

In 1796, a French invasion fleet with thousands of troops approached Bantry Bay in County Cork. On shore the local militia were ill-equipped to repel them. On board one of the French ships was Wolfe Tone, decked out in a French uniform and itching to get into action. However, a strong offshore wind repelled every attempt by the fleet to sail up the bay to a safe landing spot. A few attempted to drop anchor, but as the wind strengthened into a full gale, the ships were forced to head for the open Atlantic and back to France. A disappointed Wolfe Tone went back with them.

Saved by the weather, the government in Ireland woke up to the serious threat posed by the United Irishmen and similar groups. A nationwide campaign got underway to hunt them out and it proved extremely effective. Meanwhile another group of United Irishmen led by Lord Edward Fitzgerald tried to mount a rebellion, which also failed because of informers and poor communications between the rebels. After uncovering this attempted rebellion, the government and army really got stuck into the population in search of arms and rebels. Floggings and indiscriminate torture sent a wave of panic through the country and sparked off the 1798 Rising. Wexford, a county not noted for its rebellious tendencies, saw the fiercest fighting, with Father John Murphy leading the resistance. After a number of minor victories the rebels were finally and decisively defeated at Vinegar Hill just outside Enniscorthy.

Meanwhile the French had been planning another invasion, and a few months after Vinegar Hill a small fleet landed in County Mayo and achieved some minor successes but was soon defeated. Wolfe Tone himself arrived later in the year with another French fleet which was defeated at sea. Wolfe Tone was captured and brought to Dublin where he committed suicide in his prison cell. It was the end for the United Irishmen and ironically led to the demise of the independent Irish parliament.

The Protestant gentry, alarmed at the level of unrest, was much inclined to cuddle back up to the security of Britain. In 1800, the Act of Union, uniting Ireland politically with Britain, was passed, taking effect from 1

Theobald Wolfe Tone

January 1801. Many of the wealthier Irish Catholics supported the Act, especially after the British prime minister, William Pitt, promised to remove the last of the penal laws, most of which had been repealed by 1793. The Irish parliament voted itself out of existence, and around 100 of the MPs moved to the House of Commons in London.

As if to remind them of the rebellious nature of the country, a tiny and completely ineffectual rebellion was staged in Dublin in 1803, led by a former United Irishman, Robert Emmet (1778-1803). Less than 100 men took part and Emmet was caught, tried and executed. He gave a famous speech from the dock which included the oft-quoted words: 'Let no man write my epitaph ... When my country takes her place among the nations of the earth, then and not till then let my epitaph be written'.

The Great Liberator

While Emmet was swinging from the gallows, a 28-year-old Kerry man called Daniel O'Connell (1775-1847) was set on a course that would make him one of Ireland's greatest leaders. The O'Connell family were from Caherdaniel in County Kerry and had made their money from smuggling. Remarkably, the family managed to hang onto their house and lands through penal times.

In 1823, O'Connell founded the Catholic Association with the aim of achieving political equality for Catholics. The association soon became a vehicle for peaceful mass protest and action, and in an 1826 general election it first showed its muscle by backing Protestant candidates in favour of Catholic emancipation. The high point was in the election of 1828 when O'Connell himself stood for a seat in County Clare, even though being a Catholic he could not take the seat. O'Connell won easily, putting the British parliament in a quandary. Although William Pitt had promised to repeal the last of the penal laws, this hadn't happened. The remaining laws denied Catholics the right to sit in parliament and take important offices. If the British parliament didn't allow O'Connell to take his seat, there might be a

popular uprising. Many in the House of Commons favoured emancipation, and the combination of circumstances led them to pass the 1829 Act of Catholic Emancipation allowing Catholics limited voting rights and the right to be elected as MPs.

After this great victory, O'Connell settled down to the business of securing further reforms. Ten years later he turned his attentions to repeal of the Act of Union and re-establishing an Irish parliament. Now that Catholics could become MPs, such a body would be very different to the old Protestant-dominated Irish parliaments.

In 1843 the campaign really took off, with O'Connell working alongside the young Thomas Davis. His 'monster meetings' attracted up to half a million supporters, and took place all over Ireland. O'Connell exploited the threat that such gatherings represented to the establishment, but he baulked at the idea of a genuinely radical confrontation with the British. His bluff was called when a monster meeting at Clontarf was prohibited and O'Connell called it off.

He was arrested in 1844 but went out of his way to avoid any kind of violent clash. After he served a short spell in prison, O'Connell returned to Derrynane. He quarrelled with the Young Ireland movement (which, having seen pacifism fail, favoured the use of violence) and never again posed a threat to the British. He died four years later in 1847, as his country was being devoured by famine.

The Great Famine

Ireland suffered its greatest tragedy in the years 1845-51. The potato was the staple food of a rapidly growing but desperately poor population. From 1800 to 1840 the population had rocketed from four to eight million, putting even greater pressure on the land. Then between 1845 and 1851 a succession of almost complete failures of the potato crop resulted in mass starvation, emigration and death.

During this time, there were excellent harvests of other crops such as wheat, but these were too expensive for the poor to purchase.

While millions of its citizens were starving, Ireland continued to export food. Some landlords did their best for their tenants, but many others ignored the situation from their homes in Britain.

As a result, about one million people died, many of disease rather than straight starvation, and about another million emigrated. Emigration continued to reduce the population during the next 100 years. Huge numbers of Irish settlers who found their way abroad, particularly to the USA, carried with them a lasting bitterness. Irish-American wealth would later find its way back to Ireland to finance the independence struggle.

Parnell & the Land League

In spite of the bitterness aroused by the Famine, there was hardly any challenge to Britain's control of Ireland for quite some time. The abortive Fenian rising in March 1867 had its most publicised action in Manchester, England, when 30 Irishmen attempted to free two of their leaders. In so doing they killed an English policeman, either by accident or design. Three of them were executed and became known in nationalist circles as the 'Manchester Martyrs'.

In the 1870s and 1880s, Charles Stewart Parnell (1846-91) appeared on the political scene. The son of a Protestant landowner from Avondale in County Wicklow, he had much in common with other members of the Anglo-Irish ascendancy. But there were differences. Parnell's mother was American, and her father had fought the British in America. Parnell's family supported the principle of Irish independence from Britain.

Charles was a boisterous young man, educated in England, and he attended Cambridge before becoming an MP for County Meath. He quickly became noticed in the House of Commons as a passionate and difficult member who asked all the wrong questions.

In 1879 Ireland appeared to be facing another famine as potato crops were failing once again and evictions were becoming widespread. Cheap corn from America had pushed grain prices through the floor and

with it the earnings of the tenants who paid their rent from grain they grew on their plots. A Fenian called Michael Davitt began to organise the tenants, and early on found a sympathetic ear in the unlikely person of Parnell. This odd pair were the brains behind the Land League, which initiated widespread agitation for reduced rents and improved working conditions. The conflict heated up and there was violence on both sides. Parnell instigated the strategy known as 'boycotting' against tenants, agents and landlords who didn't adhere to the Land League's aims and were thus treated as lepers by the local population. Charles Boycott was a land agent in County Mayo and one of the first people the new strategy was used against.

The 'land war', as it became known, lasted from 1879 to 1882 and was a momentous period. For the first time, tenants were defying their landlords en masse. An election in 1880 brought William Gladstone to power in Britain. In the face of the situation in Ireland, he introduced his Land Act of 1881, which improved life immeasurably for tenants, creating fair rents and the possibility of tenants owning their land.

A crisis threatened in 1882 when two of the crown's leading figures in Ireland were murdered in Phoenix Park, Dublin. However, reform had been achieved, and Parnell now turned his attentions to achieving a limited form of autonomy for Ireland called Home Rule. Parnell had an extraordinary ally in William Gladstone, who in 1886 became prime minister for the third time and was dependent on Parnell for crucial support in parliament. But Gladstone and Parnell were defeated partly as a result of defections from Gladstone's own party.

The end was drawing near for Parnell. For 10 years he had been having an affair with Kitty O'Shea, who was married to a member of his own party. When the relationship was exposed in 1890, Parnell refused to resign as party leader, and the party split. Parnell was deposed as leader and the Catholic Church in Ireland quickly turned against him. The 'Uncrowned king of Ireland' was no longer welcome. Parnell's health deteriorated rapidly and he died less than a year later, aged just 45.

Home Rule Beckons

Gladstone was elected as prime minister for a fourth term in 1892 and this time managed to get his 'Home Rule for Ireland' bill through the House of Commons, but it was thrown out by the House of Lords. The Protestant community in Ireland, most numerous in the north-east, were becoming more and more alarmed at Gladstone's support for Home Rule, which might threaten their status and privileges.

By now eastern Ulster was quite a prosperous place. It had been spared the worst effects of the Famine, and heavy industrialisation meant the Protestant ruling class was doing nicely.

While Gladstone had failed for the time being, the Ulster Unionists (the Unionist party had been formed in 1885) were now acutely aware that Home Rule could surface again. They were determined to resist it, at least as far as Ulster was concerned. The unionists, led by Sir Edward Carson, a Dublin lawyer, formed a Protestant vigilante brigade called the Ulster Volunteer Force (UVF), and it held a series of mass paramilitary rallies. The UVF was formed to fight should Home Rule become law and in 1911 their worst nightmare seemed ready to unfold.

In Britain a new Liberal government under Prime Minister Asquith had removed the House of Lords' power to veto bills, and began to put another Home Rule for Ireland bill through Parliament – the political price being demanded by Irish Home Rule MPs for their support. The bill was put through in

---

Edward Carson

It was Edward Carson (1854-1935), a Protestant lawyer from Dublin, who spearheaded the Ulster opposition to Home Rule and led the movement which eventually resulted in Ireland's partition. Carson's career in law included numerous successful prosecutions of Irish tenants on behalf of British absentee landlords, and he played a leading role in the conviction of Oscar Wilde for homosexuality in 1895.

Carson was elected to the British House of Commons in 1892 and was solicitor general for Britain from 1900 to 1905. He was in line for the leadership of the Conservative Party until, in 1910, his fervent distaste for Home Rule and Irish independence led him to take the leadership of the Irish Unionists. Carson believed that without Belfast's heavy industries an independent Ireland would be economically unviable, and that he could frustrate Irish independence simply by keeping the North separate. The British Liberal government's determination to enact Home Rule was frustrated by Carson's parliamentary manoeuvres in 1912, and a year later he actually established a provisional government for the North in Belfast.

Carson threatened an armed struggle for a separate Northern Ireland if independence was granted to Ireland. By 1913 he had established a private Ulster army, and weapons were landed from Germany at Larne in 1914, shortly before the outbreak of WWI. The British began to bend before this Ulster opposition and, in July 1914 Carson agreed that Home Rule could go through for Ireland, so long as Ulster was kept separate. The events of WWI and the 1916 Easter Rising in Dublin shifted the whole question from Home Rule to complete independence. By 1921, however, the Ulster opposition which Carson had nurtured was so strong that the country was carved up.

A statue of Carson defiantly fronts Stormont, the now unused parliament building which remains a symbol of Loyalist opposition to a united Ireland. Carson himself is buried in St Anne's Cathedral in central Belfast. ∎

1912 against strident unionist and conservative British opposition, which mounted in ferocity.

As the UVF grew in strength, a republican group called the Irish Volunteers, led by the academic Eoin MacNeill, was set up in the south to defend Home Rule for the whole of Ireland. They lacked the weapons and organisation of the UVF, however, which succeeded in large-scale gun-running in 1914. There was widespread support for the UVF among officers of the British army.

Despite opposition, the Home Rule Act was passed, but suspended at the outbreak of WWI in August 1914. The question of Ulster was left unresolved. Many Irish nationalists believed that Home Rule would come after the war and that by helping out they could influence British opinion in their favour. John Redmond, the leader of the Irish Home Rule party, actively encouraged people to join the British forces to fight Germany.

The Gaelic Revival

While all of these attempts at Home Rule were being shunted about, something of a revolution was taking place in Irish arts, literature and identity.

The Anglo-Irish literary revival was one aspect of this, championed by the young William Butler Yeats. The poet had a coterie of literary friends such as Lady Gregory, Douglas Hyde, John Millington Synge and George Russell. They unearthed many of the Celtic tales of Cúchulainn, and wrote with fresh enthusiasm about a romantic Ireland of epic battles and warrior queens. For a country that had suffered centuries of invasion and deprivation, these images presented a much more attractive version of history. Yeats and his friends were decidedly upper-crust themselves, and pursued the new literature and poetry primarily through the English language, aiming at the educated classes. A national theatre, later to become the Abbey Theatre, was born in Dublin from their efforts.

At the same time, people like Douglas Hyde and Eoin MacNeill were doing their best to ensure the survival of the Irish language and the more everyday Irish customs and culture. They formed the Gaelic League in 1893 which, among other aims, pushed for the teaching of Irish in schools. The Gaelic League stressed the importance of the Irish language and culture to the Irish identity. In the 1890s it was primarily a cultural outfit and only assumed a nationalistic aura later on.

There were many other forces at work. The Gaelic Athletic Association, initially founded in 1884 to promote Irish sport and culture, was by the turn of the century a thriving and strongly politicised organisation. A small pressure group called *Sinn Féin* ('We Ourselves') was set up under the leadership of Arthur Griffith, founder of the *United Irishmen* newspaper. He proposed that all Irish MPs should abandon the House of Commons in London and set up a parliament in Dublin (a similar strategy to that employed by Hungary in gaining its independence from Austria). Another group, the Fenians, also called the Irish Republican Brotherhood (IRB), believed in independence through violence if necessary.

Socialism was gaining support in Dublin amongst the hungry tenement dwellers who had to endure some of the worst urban housing conditions in Europe. In 1913 Jim Larkin and James Connolly called the transport workers out on strike. Although the strike ended in a return to work, the employers failed to break the union and Larkin and Connolly had created the Irish Citizens' Army for self-defence. It now joined forces with the Irish Volunteers.

It must be said, however, that the majority of Dubliners were probably more concerned with WWI, and while some might have believed independence from Britain was a good idea, their passions went no further than that.

The Easter Rising

Many Irishmen with nationalist sympathies went off to the battlefields of Europe believing their sacrifice would ensure that Britain stood by its promise of Home Rule for Ireland. The Home Rule Act was passed just before war broke out and would in theory be put into action once the war was over. However, a minority of nationalists in Ireland were not so trusting of Britain's resolve. The Irish Volunteers split into two groups, those under John Redmond who adopted this wait-and-see approach and a more radical group which believed in a more revolutionary course of action.

Two small groups – a section of the Irish Volunteers under Patrick Pearse and the Irish Citizens' Army led by James Connolly – staged a rebellion that took the country by surprise. On Easter Monday 1916, they marched into Dublin and took over a number of key positions in the city. Their headquarters was the General Post Office on O'Connell St, and from its steps Pearse read out to nonplussed passers-by a declaration that Ireland was now a republic and that his band were the provisional government. Less than a week of fighting ensued before the rebels surrendered in the face of superior British forces and firepower. The rebels were not popular, and as they were marched to jail they had to be protected from angry Dubliners.

The leader of the Irish Volunteers was Eoin MacNeill, and the rising had been planned by Pearse and others without his knowledge. When he discovered the plans at the last minute, MacNeill attempted to call the rebellion off, resulting in very few turning up on the day. The Germans were also supposed to arrive in U-boats and this didn't happen. So what might have been a real threat to British authority fizzled out completely. Many have said that Pearse knew they didn't stand a chance, but was preoccupied with a blood sacrifice, a noble gesture by a few brave souls that would galvanise the nation. Whether he believed this or not, a blood sacrifice was on the way.

The Easter Rising would probably have had little impact on the Irish situation, had the British not made martyrs of the leaders of the rebellion. Of the 77 given death sentences, 15 were executed. Pearse was shot three days after the surrender, and nine days later James Connolly was the last to die, shot

in a chair because he couldn't stand on a gangrenous ankle. The deaths provoked a sea change in public attitudes to the republicans, whose support climbed from then on.

Countess Markievicz was one of those not executed, because she was female and there had been a recent outcry in Britain over the execution by the Germans of Edith Cavell, a nurse, in Belgium. Countess Markievicz was later to be the first woman elected to the British parliament (preceding Nancy Astor), but she refused to take up her seat. Eamon de Valera's death sentence was commuted to life imprisonment because of his US citizenship.

In the 1918 general election, the republicans stood under the banner of Sinn Féin and won a large majority of the Irish seats. Ignoring London's parliament, where technically they were supposed to sit, the newly elected Sinn Féin deputies – many of them veterans of the 1916 Easter Rising – declared Ireland independent and formed the first *Dáil Éireann* (Irish assembly or lower house), which sat in Dublin's Mansion House under the leadership of Eamon de Valera. While the Irish had declared independence, the British had by no means conceded it, and a confrontation was imminent.

The Anglo-Irish War

The day the Dáil convened in Dublin in January 1919, two policemen were shot dead in County Tipperary. This was the beginning of the bitter Anglo-Irish war, which lasted from 1919 to the middle of 1921. This was the period when Michael Collins came to the fore, a charismatic and ruthless leader who masterminded the campaign of violence against the British while at the same time serving as minister for finance in the new Dáil.

The war quickly became entrenched and bloody. On the Irish side was the Irish Republican Army (IRA), successor to the Irish Volunteers, and on the other a coalition of the Royal Irish Constabulary, regular British-army soldiers and two groups of quasi-military status who rapidly gained a vicious reputation: the Auxiliaries and the

Black & Tans. Their use of violence crystallised resentment against the British and support for the nationalist cause. The death from hunger strike of Terence Mac-Swiney, the mayor of Cork, further crystallised Irish opinion. The IRA created 'flying columns', small groups of armed volunteers to ambush British forces, and on home ground, they operated successfully. A truce was eventually agreed in July 1921.

After months of negotiations in London, the Irish delegation signed the Anglo-Irish Treaty on 6 December 1921, which gave 26 counties of Ireland independence and allowed six largely Protestant Ulster counties the choice of opting out. If they did (a foregone conclusion), a Boundary Commission would then decide on the final frontiers between north and south. The Treaty might have seemed the answer to Ireland's problems, but it wasn't to be.

The Civil War
The negotiations on the Treaty had been largely carried on the Irish side by Michael Collins and Arthur Griffith. Both men knew that many Dáil members wouldn't accept the loss of the north, or the fact that the British king would still be head of the new Irish Free State and Irish MPs would still have to swear an oath of allegiance to the crown. Under pressure from Britain's Lloyd George and after a spell of exhausting negotiations, they signed the Treaty without checking with de Valera in Dublin.

Collins regarded the issue of the monarchy and the oath of allegiance as largely symbolic; he hoped that the north-eastern six counties wouldn't be a viable entity and would eventually become part of the Free State. During the treaty negotiations he had been encouraged to think that the Border Commission would decrease the size of that part of Ireland remaining outside the Free State. He hoped that he could convince the rest of his comrades, but he knew the risks and declared, 'I have signed my death warrant'.

In the end Collins couldn't persuade his colleagues to accept the Treaty. De Valera

was furious, and it wasn't long before a bitter civil war broke out between comrades who, a year previously, had fought alongside each other.

Ireland Since Partition
For the history of Ireland since partition, see the introductions to the Republic of Ireland and Northern Ireland.

GEOGRAPHY & GEOLOGY
Ireland is an island lying off the north-western edge of the Eurasian landmass, separated from Britain by the Irish Sea and the St George and North channels. The area of the island is 84,421 sq km: 14,139 sq km in the North and 70,282 sq km in the South. It stretches nearly 500km north to south and just over 300km east to west, and the convoluted coastline extends for 5631km.

Political Geography
Ireland is divided into 32 counties. The Republic of Ireland (also called the South) consists of 26 counties, and Northern Ireland of six. The northernmost point in the South is actually farther north than anywhere in the North! To confuse things further the island has traditionally been divided into four provinces: Leinster, Ulster, Connaught and Munster. Northern Ireland is often loosely referred to as Ulster, but three of the Republic's counties – Donegal, Cavan and Monaghan – were also in the old province of Ulster, which, with the six counties of Northern Ireland, makes a total of nine.

Landscape
It can be as little as 50km from the heart of one of Ireland's major cities through the midland plains to an isolated sweep of mountains and bogland. Most of the higher ground is close to the coast, while the central regions or midlands are largely flat. Almost the entire western seaboard from Cork to Donegal is a continuous bulwark of cliffs, hills and mountains with few safe anchorages. The only significant breaches in the chain are the Shannon estuary and Galway Bay.

The western mountain ranges aren't particularly high but they're often beautiful. The highest mountains are in the south-west; the tallest mountain in Ireland, at just only 1041m, is Carrantuohill in Kerry's Magillicuddy Reeks.

The Shannon is the longest river in Ireland or Britain. It runs for 259km from its source in Cavan's Cuilcagh Mountains down through the midlands before emptying into the wide Shannon estuary west of Limerick City. Lough Neagh in Northern Ireland is the island's largest lake, covering 396 sq km.

The midlands of Ireland lie above Carboniferous limestone deposited between 300 and 400 million years ago. On the surface, the flat landscape is mostly rich farmland or raised bogs, huge swathes of brown peat rapidly disappearing under the machines of the Irish Turf Board, Bord na Móna.

As you travel west from the midlands, the soil becomes poorer and the fields smaller, and stone walls more numerous. The Cromwellian cry, 'to hell or to Connaught', wasn't without foundation, as the land west of the Shannon can't compare with fertile counties like Meath and Tipperary. On the western seaboard, small farmers struggle to make a living by raising sheep, potatoes and some cattle.

Before the Famine, the pressure on land was enormous; eight million people had to be fed and they farmed in the most inaccessible places. Up the hillsides above today's fields, you may see the faint regular lines of pre-Famine potato ridges called 'lazy beds'.

Ice Age The last Ice Age had a huge impact on the Irish landscape. It lasted from 100,000 to just over 10,000 years ago, and most of the country was glaciated. Characteristic U-shaped valleys were carved out by glaciers, as were the small deep-set corrie lakes high on the mountainsides. The receding ice left behind many shallow lakes mainly in the centre of Ireland. Most of the baked sedimentary rocks covering the Wicklow Mountains were stripped away, exposing the underlying granite. In County Clare, lime-stone appeared when a layer of waterproof shale and sandstone was removed.

Many of Ireland's mountains and hills have a round, smooth profile, formed by the abrasive effect of moving ice. The ice also deposited soil in its wake, leaving a layer of boulder clay on many parts of the country. *Drumlins* are small round hills of boulder clay that were dropped and shaped by the passing ice, and there is a large belt of them across the country from County Cavan to Clew Bay in County Mayo. The result is the characteristic 'basket of eggs' topography.

Often pieces of rock were picked up and dropped a long way from their source, and so you find granite 'glacial erratics' as they are called on the limestone desert of Clare's Burren region. Here the ice polished the limestone to mirror smoothness, and in some places you can see deep scratches on the surface of the stone, engraved by harder stones embedded in the moving ice.

CLIMATE

Ireland is farther north than either Newfoundland or Vancouver yet the climate is mild with a mean annual temperature of around 10°C. The temperature only drops below freezing intermittently during the winter and snow is scarce – perhaps one or two brief flurries every year. The coldest months of the year are January and February, when daily temperatures range from 4°C to 8°C with 7°C the average. During the summer, temperatures during the day are a comfortable 15°C to 20°C. During the warmest months of July and August the average is 16°C. A hot summer's day in Ireland is 22°C to 24°C although it can sometimes reach 30°C. There are about 18 hours of daylight during July and August, and it's only truly dark after about 11 pm. In May and June, Ireland has an average of five to six hours of sunshine a day, while in the southeast during July and August the average is seven hours.

The reason Ireland has such a mild climate is the moderating effect of the Atlantic Ocean and particularly the Gulf Stream. This is an enormous current which moves clockwise

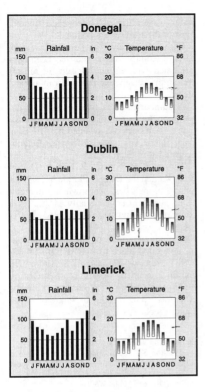

Donegal

Dublin

Limerick

clouds from the Atlantic which dump their loads as soon as they meet high ground.

The heaviest rain usually falls where the scenery is best. The mountains of south-west Kerry are the wettest part of the country. The south-east, particularly Counties Wexford and Waterford, is the driest area, enjoying something like a more southern continental climate.

If you do find the rain getting you down you might find some comfort in the Irish saying: 'It doesn't rain in the pub'!

ECOLOGY & ENVIRONMENT

Ireland has long been associated with the colour green, but the rise in environmental awareness has given this association an added significance.

Ireland has experienced limited industrialisation compared to other developed countries and much of the beautiful Irish countryside that we see today has been formed by hundreds of years of agricultural practice and change.

In the 1970s, the EU encouraged intensive, specialised farming and the use of pesticides and chemical fertilisers. These caused serious pollution and land degradation. More recently, the EU and the Irish government have been promoting environmental protection, less-intensive farming methods and the adoption of alternative practices or crops. The result has been a reduction in pollution, though it continues to occur in rivers and lakes, and fish kills are not uncommon.

In the same period the trend toward larger farms (although small farms are still in the majority) led, in places like the Burren in County Clare, to the destruction of many ring forts and stone walls which have disappeared forever.

At one time Ireland was largely covered by forests. Then about 6000 years ago, the first farmers cleared small areas for their crops, the beginning of a long process of deforestation. Substantial tracts of natural oak wood survived until the mid-16th century. The next 200 years saw the country stripped of its oak for ship timbers, charcoal,

around the Atlantic bringing warm water up to Western Europe from the Caribbean. Often the Gulf Stream brings Caribbean sea life with it, and turtles and triggerfish are commonly washed up on the west coast of Ireland.

One thing you can be sure about Irish weather is how little you can be sure of. It may be shirtsleeves and sunglasses in February, winter woollies in March and even during the summer.

And then there's the rain. Ireland does get a lot of rain – about 1000mm a year, ranging from 750mm in the midlands to over 1300mm in the south-west. Certain parts get rain on as many as 270 days of the year. The prevailing winds over Ireland come from the south-west, and they bring in rainbearing

tanning and barrels. So extensive was the clearance that by the mid-18th century almost all the country's timber was being imported, right down to the staves for barrels.

Pine plantations were born in the 20th century out of the need for local timber and the desire to do something with what many people considered to be wasteland. There are still state subsidies for plantations, although the most widely used species – sitka spruce and lodgepole pine – are so fast growing and so soft as to be unsuitable for high-quality wood products.

Today forests cover about 5.5% of the country and although the percentage is slowly increasing, much of it is for commercial purposes. Recognition of the need for native forest is found in places such as Glencree in County Wicklow where there's a project to reforest part of the area with oak trees.

Since the mid-1960s well over half the Irish population has lived in urban areas. Dublin in particular has grown enormously. Extensive housing estates built on its periphery and the decentralisation of industry, spread the city's influence not only into County Dublin but into surrounding counties. For a long time little was done to tackle the problems of inner-city decay and population decline, but recent urban renewal programmes are beginning to turn things around. The emergence of Temple Bar as a living, cultural and entertainment centre is one example of this. To retain the city's unique character much of this redevelopment is in the form of refurbishment and restoration of existing buildings rather than the construction of new ones. Aided by finance from the EU and the International Fund for Ireland, this urban renewal is also happening in other towns and cities across Ireland.

Dublin's famous river, the Liffey, may no longer smell (that was gotten rid of in 1985) but its water quality has deteriorated as the city has developed. About 32 rivers and streams feed into the Liffey catchment, which supplies much of the region's drinking water. According to Greenpeace Ireland, most of these rivers are polluted.

We've also received a report that in remote parts of County Mayo water has been contaminated with *E. coli* caused by run-off containing sheep excrement from upland areas.

A number of Irish beaches suffer from pollution, but as part of a scheme to improve them, clean ones are awarded the EU Blue Flag. Taisce An (National Trust for Ireland) keeps a list of them.

The town of Skerries in County Dublin was awarded the Entente Florale in 1996 for being Europe's best kept town, but in many other places litter, especially plastic, is a common sight and waste is disposed of carelessly.

To find out more about Ireland's environment, a good place to start is Enfo (☎ 01-679314, fax 01-679 5204), 17 St Andrew St, Dublin 2, near the Dublin Tourism Centre. It's a public information service and opens 10 am to 5 pm, Monday to Saturday. Other sources include:

Conservation Volunteer Ireland
    PO Box 3837, Ballsbridge, Dublin 4 – runs a number of volunteer conservation projects around the country (☎ 01-668 1844)
Dúchas (Office of Public Works)
    51 St Stephen's Green, Dublin 2 – Dúchas is the government body that oversees many parks, gardens, monuments, inland waterways and sites of natural, historical and cultural importance; it was formerly known as the Office of Public Works (OPW); the staff wear Dúchas badges but you'll still see OPW on many of the signs (☎ 01-661 3111)
Greenpeace Ireland
    44 Upper Mount St, Dublin 2 – a nonprofit organisation that campaigns on a diverse range of environmental issues (☎ 01-6619836, fax 01-6606258)
Irish Wildlife Federation
    3 Lower Mount St, Dublin 2 – non-government organisation, focussed on protection of wilderness and the designation of wilderness areas (☎ 01-676 8588)
National Trust (Northern Ireland)
    Public Affairs Manager, Rowallane, Saintfield BT24 7LH – a non-profit organisation dedicated to the preservation of historical buildings and

important natural sites like the Giant's Causeway (☎ 01238-510721)

Taisce An (National Trust for Ireland)
The Tailors Hall, Back Lane, Dublin 8 – performs a similar function to its Northern Ireland counterpart (☎ 01-454 1786)

FLORA & FAUNA
Flora

After the end of the last Ice Age 10,000 years ago, a shrubby flora similar to that found in modern Arctic tundra took hold. This was eventually replaced by oak forest, which established itself on most of the island. In the upland regions and on more exposed hillsides, the oak was mixed with or replaced by birch and pine. In the lower regions where the soil was richer there was also elm, alder, hawthorn and ash. Underneath the oak trees were smaller plants like holly, hazel, ferns, mosses and brambles, which provided a rich habitat for animals.

Today, however, the Irish landscape and predominant flora that you see are almost wholly the result of human influence (see the previous Ecology & Environment section). Only 1% of genuine native oak forest survives. There are remnants in Killarney National Park and in south Wicklow near Shillelagh, and smaller fragments near Tullamore and Abbeyleix.

Regular dull columns of pine plantations are a major feature of the Irish countryside and don't add much in the way of beauty. Pine species include sitka spruce, lodgepole pine, Douglas fir, Norway spruce and Scots pine.

Many native plants survive in the hedgerows and in the wilder parts of the country. Because intensive agriculture has only arrived comparatively recently, the range of surviving plant and animal species is much larger than in many other European countries. Irish hedgerows are a blaze of colour in spring and summer.

The Burren limestone region in Clare was covered in light woodland before the early

Ireland's Disappearing Bogs

There are two types of bogs – raised bogs and blanket bogs. Raised ones are formed when sphagnum moss gains a foothold in a low-lying, waterlogged area. The moss accumulates as it dies, retaining a lot of water, and the bog starts to form. The centres of these bogs are higher than the edges, hence the term 'raised bog'. These are mostly found in flat areas such as the midlands; the most famous example in Ireland is the Bog of Allen, which once covered as much as 100,000 hectares. The bogs of the midlands have been worked by the Bord na Móna (Irish Turf Board) since 1932. A whole range of enormous machines does the job.

The bogs found covering hills and valleys are known as blanket bogs, and they develop on acid soil in a very wet climate, which usually means 240 days of rain a year or more. There are good examples of blanket bogs still surviving in Wicklow, Sligo, Antrim and the Slieve Bloom Mountains.

About 17% of Ireland's landscape was once made up of bogs, but it's now thought that at the present rate of destruction they could all be gone within a few years, wiping out 10,000 years of accumulation. Bog conservation is a recent phenomenon, as bogs have always been seen either as large tracts of potential fuel or as useless and dangerous ground. On top of this they were closely tied to the stereotype of the bog Irishman, so no-one had much affection for them. Now that these great raised bogs have been almost obliterated, there is an urgent need to conserve some of what's left – it has been suggested that 4% should be earmarked for protection. Some argue that it should all be conserved, especially since bogs are home to their own unique family of plants and insects and provide habitation for birdlife.

The preservation properties of bogs are seen as another reason to conserve them. Due to the acidity and lack of oxygen in the peat, fragile organic artefacts are occasionally preserved, which would have disintegrated long ago in any other environment. The countless relics, some of them 5000 years old, include Iron Age wooden highways, preserved bodies and wooden wheels and buckets. Among more recent items found were 300-year-old packets of cheese and butter.

For more information contact the Irish Peatland Conservation Council (☎ 01 660 2511, email ipcc@indigo.ie), St Martin's House, Waterloo Rd, Dublin 4. ∎

settlers arrived. However, many of the original plants live on, a remarkable mixture of Mediterranean and alpine species.

The bogs of Ireland are home to a unique flora adapted to wet, acidic and nutrient-poor conditions. Sphagnum moss is the key bogplant and is joined by plants such as the sundew, which uses its long hairs covered in sweet sticky stuff to catch insects.

Fauna

Mammals The most common native land mammals of any size are foxes and badgers and while there are plenty about you're unlikely to see any on a casual visit. Smaller mammals include rabbits – introduced by the Normans for food – hares, hedgehogs, red and grey squirrels, shrews and bats. Red deer roam the hillsides in many of the wilder parts of the country, particularly the Wicklow Mountains, and in Killarney National Park, which holds the country's only herd of native red deer. Sika deer and other red deer have been introduced from abroad.

Less common in Ireland are the elusive otters, stoats and pine martens which are usually found in remote areas such as the Burren in County Clare or Connemara in County Galway.

Sea mammals include grey and common seals which are found all around the coastline and can often be seen if you keep quiet and know where to look. There are some substantial colonies of grey seals living on uninhabited islands off County Mayo and around the shores of Strangford Lough in Northern Ireland. Dolphins often swim close to land, particularly in the bays and inlets off the west coast, and for many years Dingle Harbour has had a famous resident bottle-nosed dolphin called Fungie. There are whales in the sea off Ireland, but they tend to be so dispersed and stay so far out to sea that they are rarely sighted.

Birds Ireland is home to a wide range of migrating and locally breeding birds. Many birds that breed in the Arctic areas of Canada, Greenland, Iceland and elsewhere fly to Ireland to pass the milder winters there, while others use it as a stopover as they migrate north or south. Brent, barnacle and Greenland white-fronted geese and also Bewick's swans, are seasonal visitors. They winter in Ireland in places like the Wexford North and South Slobs, and Dublin's North Bull, Ireland's Eye and Lambay islands, Tyrone's Lough Neagh and Down's Strangford Lough. Also found during the winter are teal, redshanks and curlews. April to May and September to October are the main migration periods.

The coastlines are home to a huge variety of seabirds – kittiwakes, razorbills, puffins, Manx shearwater, storm petrel etc – and most of them breed in the late spring and early summer, the best time to view them. Little Skellig out in the Atlantic Ocean off Kerry is the second largest gannet colony in the world, with some 25,000 pairs breeding annually on the rock. Old Head of Kinsale, County Cork, is the nesting place for thousands of fulmars and guillemots. Other good locations for seabirds are Clear Island in Cork, Hook Head and the Saltee Islands in Wexford, the Burren in Clare, Malin Head in Donegal and Rathlin Island in Antrim.

Birds of prey include hen harriers, sparrow hawks, falcons and the odd buzzard. The magnificent peregrine falcon has been

Puffins nest in large colonies on seaside cliffs

making something of a recovery and can be found nesting on cliffs in Wicklow and elsewhere.

Fish The main fish to be found in Ireland are salmon and varieties of trout (brown, rainbow and sea), but there are other species including mackerel and pollack off the coast and pike, bream, perch and roach in lakes and rivers.

Other Fauna The spotted Kerry slug is found, as the name suggests, in Kerry. So are natterjack toads, Ireland's only species of toad, which live in sandy areas behind Inch Strand and near Castlegregory on the north side of the Dingle Peninsula.

In the Burren, County Clare, you'll find 28 of Ireland's 33 species of butterfly.

Rare & Endangered Species
All species native to Ireland's raised bogs are threatened with extinction if their habitat disappears in the next few years.

One of Ireland's rarest native birds is the corncrake, which used to be common in grasslands and meadows, but whose numbers have been slowly diminishing. Corncrakes can still be found in some remote and undisturbed areas, such as the low-lying flooded grasslands of the Shannon Callows and parts of Donegal.

Also rare, choughs – unusual crows with bright red feet and beaks – can be seen in the west, particularly along coastlines with extensive sand-dune complexes.

In the Ring of Kerry, the Kerry Bog pony is officially designated a rare breed.

The Burren in County Clare is a stronghold of Ireland's most elusive mammal, the weasel-like pine marten.

National Parks
Ireland has four national parks – Connemara (Galway), Glenveagh (Donegal), Killarney (Kerry) and Wicklow Mountains (Wicklow). These have been developed to protect, preserve and make accessible areas of significant natural heritage and the number is growing. Camping isn't allowed in any of the

parks. The parks open year round and each has its own information office, but for general information you can contact Dúchas (☎ 01-661 3111), 51 St Stephen's Green, Dublin 2.

Forests & Forest Parks
Coillte Teoranta (Irish Forestry Board) administers about 400,000 hectares of forested land which includes designated picnic areas and 12 forest parks. These parks open all year and feature a range of wildlife and habitats. Some also have chalets and/or caravan parks, shops, cafés and play areas for children. For further information contact Coillte Teoranta (☎ 01-661 5666), Leeson Lane, Dublin 2.

National Nature Reserves
In Northern Ireland there are over 40 National Nature Reserves (NNRs), which are leased or owned by the Department of the Environment. These reserves are defined as areas of importance for their special flora, fauna or geology and include the Giant's Causeway and Glenariff Glen in Antrim, Marble Arch in County Fermanagh and North Strangford Lough in County Down. More information is available from the Senior Warden (☎ 01232-230560), Department of the Environment for Northern Ireland, Countryside & Wildlife Branch, Calvert House, 23 Castle Place, Belfast BT1 1FY.

POPULATION & PEOPLE
The total population of Ireland is around 5.2 million. This figure is actually lower than it was 150 years ago. Prior to the 1845-51 Famine the population was around eight million. Death and emigration reduced the population to around six million, and emigration continued at a high level for the next 100 years. It wasn't until the 1960s that Ireland's population finally began to increase again.

The Republic's population is 3.6 million. Dublin is the island's largest city and capital of the Republic with up to 1.5 million people – about 40% of the population – living within commuting distance of the city centre. In order of size the Republic's next largest cities are Cork with 174,400, Limerick with 75,400 and Galway with 50,850. A high proportion of the population is in the younger age groups with 53.4% under the age of 25.

Northern Ireland has a population of about 1.6 million and Belfast, the principal settlement, around 279,200.

Though a mixture of many races, genetically the Irish are remarkably homogenous. If you can make generalisations, the Irish are a fair-skinned, dark-haired race with quite a number of redhaired, freckled members thrown in for good measure. Invaders such as the Vikings, Normans and British have added to the gene pool, but their characteristics have been diluted through the whole population.

Even the Catholics and Protestants of Northern Ireland are more closely related than they might imagine. Settlers from both Scotland and England have produced a distinctive Protestant culture which has remained separate to this day. But scholars suggest that Catholics and Protestants are genetically almost identical.

EDUCATION

With such a young population it's not surprising that over 25% of Ireland's populace is in full-time education. Attendance at school is compulsory and free up to and including the age of 15. Most schools at primary and secondary levels are run by religious denominations and receive state aid. Secondary schools are for children 12 and over and those who successfully complete their education at this level receive the Leaving Certificate. There are also state-run vocational schools.

At the tertiary level there are four universities. Dublin University is housed in Trinity College; the National University of Ireland (NUI) has colleges in Dublin, Maynooth (Kildare), Cork and Galway: the two other universities are Dublin City University and the University of Limerick. Regional techni-

cal colleges provide tertiary vocational training.

Irish is a compulsory subject in primary and secondary schools and the growth of interest in the Irish language and traditional culture has led to the creation of a number of Irish-medium schools *(gaelscoileanna)*, mostly at the primary level.

In Northern Ireland, education is modelled on the British system though here, too, many schools are operated by religious denominations. There are two universities: Queen's University in Belfast and the University of Ulster with colleges in Belfast, Coleraine, Derry and Jordanstown.

ARTS & CULTURE
Literature

Of all the arts, the Irish have probably had the greatest impact on literature. English may be an adopted language but the Irish truly have a way with it!

If you took all the Irish writers off the university reading lists for English Literature the degree courses could probably be shortened by a year! Jonathan Swift (1667-1745), William Congreve (1670-1729), George Farquhar (1678-1707), Laurence Sterne (1713-68), Oliver Goldsmith (1728-74), Richard Sheridan (1751-1816), Oscar Wilde (1854-1900), George Bernard Shaw (1856-1950), WB Yeats (1856-1939), John Millington Synge (1871-1909), Sean O'Casey (1880-1964) and James Joyce (1882-1941) are just some of the more famous names born before 1900.

Ireland can boast four winners of the Nobel Prize for Literature – George Bernard Shaw in 1925, WB Yeats in 1938, Samuel Beckett in 1969 and Seamus Heaney in 1995.

Fiction & Drama James Joyce and WB Yeats, along with Samuel Beckett (1906-89), have achieved the highest status on the stage of world literature; out of the three Joyce is the most obviously 'Irish' and, despite the awesome difficulty of his last work *Finnegans Wake*, remains accessible as well

James Joyce

Regarded as probably the most significant writer of literature in the 20th century, James Joyce (1882-1941) had a strange and singular life. He was born into a fairly well-off family and at the age of 'half past six' became the youngest-ever pupil at Ireland's most prestigious school – Clongowes Wood School, run by the Jesuits.

By the time he entered University College Dublin, at the age of 16, his family had fallen into hard times and Joyce was a poor but brilliant student. He paid little attention to the formal syllabus and formed few close relationships. He was downright antagonistic to the increasingly popular Irish cultural nationalism and, while WB Yeats was writing books like *The Cultural Twilight*, Joyce was learning Norwegian so that he could read Henrik Ibsen in the original. He scorned what he later called the 'cultic twalette' of Irish nationalism, but was never really apolitical.

After leaving Ireland with Nora Barnacle he spent the next 10 years in Trieste. Apart from odd jobs in language schools and giving private lessons when strapped for cash, Joyce never worked for anyone else again after leaving his job as a bank clerk in Rome. He lived through WWI in neutral Zürich and after a short return to Trieste spent most of the rest of his life in Paris. When WWII broke out he fled back to Zürich, where he died two years later.

Joyce constantly spurned the idea of returning to live in Ireland. When he first left, his motives were a mixture of economic and ideological ones, but his refusal to return was basically ideological. He certainly didn't lack the money, for Harriet Weaver, editor of the *Egoist* magazine and publisher of *A Portrait of the Artist as a Young Man*, gave him today's equivalent of at least half a million pounds through a series of grants. As well as being an admirer, Weaver also felt sympathetic towards Joyce's problems which included eye diseases. From 1917 to 1930, Joyce underwent a series of 25 operations for glaucoma, iritis and cataracts, which sometimes left him totally blind for short intervals.

Joyce despised the way the Catholic Church maintained its hold over the hearts and minds of his newly independent country and the thought of returning to that conservatism and repression was anathema to him. Joyce was always political in the broad sense of the word and when he moved to Paris in 1920 he left behind in Trieste a library of books that included classic anarchist texts. His refusal to marry was a political statement and when he finally agreed to a registry-office marriage in 1931, it was purely to protect his family.

Joyce was frequently asked why he didn't return to Ireland and one of his few recorded replies was 'Have I ever left it?' All his writing bears this out. Ireland's attitude to Joyce, on the other hand, has been a flagrant case of cultural expropriation, and the benign face that now graces the country's IR£10 note has been craftily doctored to present a kindly old gent, smiling indulgently. It conveys nothing of the man who always refused to change his British passport for an Irish one or the angry young man who left Ireland in 1904 with Nora Barnacle, not to mention the author of a series of thoroughly pornographic letters to his wife. ∎

---

as rewarding for anyone wanting a window on the Irish soul. *Dubliners* (1914) is a collection of remarkable short stories, especially the final story *The Dead*, which John Huston turned into an equally memorable film. *A Portrait of the Artist as a Young Man* (1914) is, for the most part, a semi-autobiographical tale of a young man coming to realise his artistic vocation.

Ulysses (1922) has such topographical realism that it has produced a spate of Dublin guides based on the events in the novel. See the Dublin chapter for suggestions of *Ulysses* walking guides. Although much has changed in 90 years there is still enough left to sustain a steady flow of Joyce admirers,

bent on retracing the events of Bloomsday – 16 June 1904.

A recommended read for anyone who wants to know more about Joyce's life is *Nora: A Biography of Nora Joyce* by Brenda Maddox (1988). It complements Richard Ellmann's more reverential biography (1982) of James Joyce himself.

Samuel Beckett is probably best known for his play *Waiting for Godot* (1956) but his unassailable reputation is based on a number of novels and plays. His writing doesn't seem so 'Irish' when compared with Joyce or Yeats (which can be a help for the reader new to his work) and a good place to start is with *Murphy* and *Watt*.

A funny post-Joyce novelist is Flann O'Brien, real name Brian O'Nuallain and second pseudonym Myles na Gopaleen, whose novels include *The Third Policeman*, *At Swim-Two-Birds* and *The Dalkey Archive*.

CS Lewis (1898-1963), from Belfast, is best known for *The Chronicles of Narnia*, a series of children's stories.

Playwright, Brendan Behan (1923-64), expelled from school, a member of the IRA, imprisoned in Britain then deported back to Ireland, and an alcoholic, died in a Dublin hospital at the height of his fame. His most enduring works are *The Quare Fellow*, *Borstal Boy* and *The Hostage*. John Banville has written a succession of excellent novels including *Long Lankin* and *Book of Evidence*.

Despite (or maybe because of) Ireland's tragic history, the comic vision has always been a characteristic of Irish writers and it features in the work of Roddy Doyle, one of the most successful writers currently achieving fame and fortune because of his way with words. His stories, set in the working class world of north Dublin, won him the Booker prize in 1993 with his *Paddy Clarke Ha Ha Ha*. Earlier, *The Commitments* was made into an internationally successful film. *The Snapper* and *The Van* also trace the trials and tribulations of the Rabbitt family. His new book *The Woman who Walked into Doors* is about domestic violence and growing up white and female in working class Dublin.

Christy Brown's marvellous autobiographical novel, *Down all the Days*, summed up Dublin's back street energy in a slightly earlier era with equal abandon. JP Donleavy's *The Ginger Man* was another high-energy excursion around Dublin, this time from the Trinity College perspective. It received the church's seal of approval by lingering on the Irish banned list for many years.

The legacy of the past – centuries of fighting the British and then a destructive civil war just when victory was at hand – continues to affect Irish writers. *The Informer* (1925) by Liam O'Flaherty (1896-1984) was the classic book about the divided sympathies which plagued Ireland throughout its struggle for independence and the ensuing civil war. John McGahern is well worth reading as his fiction is never just narrowly political: *The Barracks* (1963), and especially *Amongst Women* (1990), are recommended. Gerry Conlon was one of the Guildford Four who, like the Birmingham Six, suffered years in prison accused of IRA bombings in Britain of which he was completely innocent. His true story *Proved Innocent* (1990) was made into the film *In the Name of the Father*.

John Banville is an important contemporary writer whose novels like *The Book of Evidence*, *Ghosts* and *Athena* (1995) are notable for the quality of their prose.

A New Book of Dubliners (1988) edited by Ben Forkner is a fine collection of Dublin-related short stories, stretching from James Joyce through to stories from the 1980s and including works by Liam O'Flaherty, Samuel Beckett, Oliver St John Gogarty, Flann O'Brien, Sean O'Faolain, Benedict Kiely and others.

The prolific Anglo-Irish playwright, Martin McDonagh is still in his 20s but has had his work performed by Britain's National Theatre and received critical praise in the US. *The Leenane Trilogy* is set in Leenane in Galway.

The Irish way with words applies just as strongly north of the border as south – in fact it's astonishing how many good writers a place as small as Northern Ireland manages to turn out. The Troubles feature in much of their writing.

Bernard MacLaverty's *Cal* (1983) traces a life where the choices are miserable and the consequences terrible and inevitable. *Cal* and McLaverty's other novel, *Lamb*, were both made into films. Those no-win political situations are also seen in Brian Moore's *Lies of Silence* (1990), which was shortlisted for the Booker Prize. Moore is a prolific writer, but not all his books are about Ireland.

In Glenn Patterson's amusing first novel *Fat Lad* (1992) the political situation is a backdrop to a story which captures the feel of life in Belfast today. And the title? It's an

Ulster children's mnemonic for learning the names of the six counties: Fermanagah-Armagh-Tyrone (FAT) and Londonderry-Antrim-Down (LAD).

Republished, after being out of print, *Call My Brother Back* (1939) by Michael McLaverty recounts growing up on Rathlin Island and the Falls Rd, Belfast, in the 1920s; much of the feel of his Belfast survives to this day.

Belfast-born Robert McLiam Wilson is at the forefront of modern Irish writing. His first novel was the award-winning *Ripley Bogle* (1989) which follows 'the prince of the Pavements ... the Parkbench King', a West Belfast tramp, through London, with flashbacks to his youth. *Eureka Street*, set in Belfast, is his third novel.

The work of playwright and poet, Damian Gorman, has received considerable praise. *Broken Nails*, his first play, received four Ulster Theatre awards. He is presently involved in the *An Crann* (Irish for 'tree') project to collect stories from Northern Irish people of their experience of the Troubles, which it's hoped will form part of a museum.

Best-selling *Angela's Ashes* by New York-based retired school teacher, Frank McCourt, is about growing up in Limerick and won the 1997 Pulitzer prize. Another best seller is *The Untouchable* by John Banville.

Ireland has produced its share of women writers. Notable among them is Edna O'Brien. She explores the smallminded, hypocritical side of Irish life and early enjoyed the accolade of having her *The Country Girls* (1960) banned. Not afraid to confront contemporary issues, her latest novel, *Down by the River*, is based on the real-life controversy of the 14-year-old Dublin girl who was raped and went to England for an abortion. O'Brien adds incest to the mix by making the girl's father the rapist.

Iris Murdoch is an internationally recognised author, although she lives in England and isn't noted for using Ireland in her books. Her *The Sea, The Sea* won the Booker Prize.

Jennifer Johnston's *The Old Jest* (1979)

goes back to Ireland between the wars. The protagonist is an Anglo-Irish girl growing up in the South at a time when change is about to sweep through the country, with a sense that the Anglo-Irish ascendancy is in its final days.

Clare Boylan's books include *Holy Pictures*, *Concerning Virgins* and *Black Baby*. Molly Keane wrote several books in the 1920s and 30s under the pseudonym MJ Farrell, then had a literary second life in her seventies when *Good Behaviour* and *Time After Time* came out under her real name.

Maeve Binchy, the Jackie Collins of Irish popular fiction, is *the* writer of blockbusters which just rise above the sex and shopping genre. They have lots of Irish settings and *Circle of Friends*, set in Dublin, was made into a film. Her latest novel, *Evening Class*, is also set in Dublin, and centres on the characters attending an Italian evening class in a grim part of the city.

Emma Donoghue's *Stirfry* deals with lesbianism.

Poetry WB Yeats was a playwright and poet, but it's his poetry that has the greatest appeal and, being out of copyright, countless editions are available. His *Love Poems*, edited by Norman Jeffares (1988) makes a suitable introduction for anyone new to his writing. A collected edition, *The Poems*, in the Everyman series edited by Daniel Albright, includes a useful set of notes.

Patrick Kavanagh (1904-67), one of Ireland's most respected poets, was born in Inniskeen, County Monaghan. *The Great Hunger* (1942) and *Tarry Flynn* (1948) evoke the atmosphere and often grim reality of life for the poor farming community. You'll find a bronze statue of him in Dublin, sitting beside his beloved Grand Canal.

For a taste of modern Irish poetry try *Contemporary Irish Poetry* edited by Fallon and Mahon (1990). Seamus Heaney, winner of the 1995 Nobel Prize for Literature, is there of course, and so are a host of other poets from both the North and the Republic. In 1997 Heaney added the Whitbread Book of the Year to his accolades for *The Spirit*

Level; some of the poems reflect the hope, disappointment and disillusionment of the peace process. *A Rage for Order* (1992) edited by Frank Ormsby is a vibrant collection of the poetry of the North.

Cork-born, Irish-language poet Louis de Paor, has had two of his collections win Ireland's prestigious Sean O'Riordan prize. Although he now bases himself in Australia, he continues to write poetry in Irish.

Tom Paulin writes memorable poetry about the North; try *The Strange Museum*. Other notable contemporary poets are Eavan Boland, Paul Muldoon and Derek Mahon.

Music

The rock band U2 may still be Ireland's biggest musical export, but when people talk about Irish music they are generally referring to a much older, more intimate style of traditional/folk music whose most prominent contemporary face belongs to Christy Moore.

For the visitor, the joy of Irish music lies in its sheer accessibility. The biggest names may play the same big venues as the rock stars, but almost every town and village seems to have a pub renowned for its music where you can show up and find a session in progress, even join in if you feel so inclined.

Most traditional music is performed on the fiddle, the tin whistle, the *bodhrán* (a goatskin drum) and the *uileann* pipes. Unaccompanied music fits into five main categories – jigs, reels, hornpipes, polkas and slow airs. There are two main styles of song: *sean nós*, old-style tunes often sung in Gaelic either unaccompanied or with the backing of a bodhrán; and more familiar ballads. Traditional music has its strongest following in the Republic, but that's not to say you can't find it in Northern Ireland. Nor should it be thought of as the 'possession' of one side of the sectarian divide.

Of the Irish music groups, perhaps the best known is The Chieftains who've been going since the 1960s and have taken their mainly instrumental music as far afield as China and South America. Adding the words come bands like The Dubliners with their notorious drinking songs (like *Seven Drunken Nights)*, the Wolfe Tones who've been described as 'the rabble end of the rebel song tradition', and the Fureys, who have achieved success despite their Traveller origins. Younger groups like Clannad from Donegal, Altan, Dervish and Nomos espouse a quieter, more mystical style of singing, while the London-Irish band The Pogues, led by Shane MacGowan, helped to keep things wild.

Christy Moore is king of the contemporary singer-songwriter tradition, whose songs include controversial political subjects.

Moore's younger brother, Luka Bloom, has carved out a solo career for himself too

---

Songs with Bite

Of all the popular musicians playing in a broadly traditional idiom, the most successful must be singer-songwriter Christy Moore who is guaranteed to pack out Dublin's Point Theatre for six nights in a row.

Moore has been performing since the mid-60s and was a pivotal member of the influential bands Planxty and Moving Hearts. But he's probably best known for solo albums which mix his own songs with renditions of music by everyone from Jackson Browne to Shane McGowan.

While not all Moore's songs are political, most of his albums contain lyrics guaranteed to raise the hackles of someone in authority. The latest, *Graffiti Tongue*, is no exception, with its musical memorial to the horrors of Bloody Sunday *Minds Locked Shut*; its yearning plea for understanding between Ireland's divided communities in *North and South of the River*; and his dig at the Brits who happily claim Nobel-prizewinning poet Seamus Heaney as one of their own, while disowning less celebrated Northerners in *On the Mainland*. ■

as has Andy Irvine who, like Moore, was once member of the folk group Planxty.

Other male singer-songwriters to listen out for include Finbar Furey, Mick Hanly, Jimmy MacCarthy, Kieran Goss, Strabane-born Paul Brady, Davy Spillane and Christie Hennessy.

Female singer-songwriters have an equally strong following. The mystical voice of Donegal's Enya, formerly of Clannad, has penetrated to a wider audience, as has that of the more controversial Sinéad O'Connor who drew opprobrium by ripping up a picture of the pope before one of her concerts. Amongst the best known contemporary female singers to look out for are sisters Mary and Frances Black, smoky-voiced Mary Coughlan, wild melodion-player Sharon Shannon, Dolores Keane and Eleanor McEvoy.

If you can't get to hear these singers performing live, it's worth buying either of the two *Women's Heart* albums or *Four for the Road* as general introductions to the singer-songwriter scene. It's also worth listening to Bill Whelan's idiosyncratic *Riverdance* which leapt to fame on the unlikely back of the Eurovision Song Contest.

Of course Ireland also has its pop and rock music scene, exemplified in the 1970s and 80s by bands like Thin Lizzy and the Boomtown Rats and by singers like Bob Geldof, Elvis Costello and Chris de Burgh. U2, whose albums include *Unforgettable Fire, The Joshua Tree, Rattle & Hum, Achtung Baby* and *Zooropa*, are the biggest of them all, but they're being challenged by the group Ash from Downpatrick who had huge success with their album *1977*. Then there's The Cranberries who are the cutting-edge band to watch out for.

On the pop scene, The Corrs, from North Dublin, combine a touch of the traditional with American pop rhythms and harmonies. Their album *Forgiven not Forgotten*, went quadruple platinum in Ireland. Teen idols Boyzone and OTT attract crowds of screaming girl fans.

In a class of his own is Van Morrison, who seems to have been going forever. In the 1960s he was lead singer with Them whose anthem *Gloria* was a Beatles-era classic. 'Van the Man' moved onto a solo career in the USA, and his *Astral Weeks* is regularly listed by critics as one of the seminal records of the 1960s. Although he has never generated a mass audience, Van Morrison has always attracted a cult following. His continuing relevance was highlighted in 1995 when the wonderful *Brown Eyed Girl* was used as the backing track for peace adverts in Belfast cinemas.

No account of contemporary Irish music could close without reference to the popularity of country music and to singer Daniel O'Donnell, the Barry Manilow of the Irish music scene, with millions of album sales (mainly to the over-forties) under his belt. Like him or loathe him, he certainly can't be ignored.

Cinema

Ireland and Dublin have made numerous movie appearances and many Irish people have achieved international success in the film industry.

Hollywood came to Ireland in 1952 when John Ford filmed John Wayne as the *The Quiet Man*, wooing Maureen O'Hara in Cong, County Sligo. You can take Quiet Man tours in Cong today. The 1970 David Lean epic *Ryan's Daughter* with Sarah Miles, Robert Mitchum, Trevor Howard and John Mills was filmed on the Dingle Peninsula in County Kerry and the place and the film have been inextricably linked ever since. The Dingle Peninsula has simply become 'Ryan's Daughter country'.

The Field, with Richard Harris, was filmed around Leenane in County Galway. *Hear My Song* about the Irish tenor, Joseph Locke, was a surprise success in the early 90s, as was *Into the West*, a delightful story of two children and a mythical white horse.

The Tom Cruise and Nicole Kidman vehicle *Far & Away* (1991) provided some picturesque views of the west coast region, and Dublin's Temple Bar district stood in for late 19th-century Boston! The 1994 *Secret of*

Roan Innish is a mystical tale set off the west coast of Ireland.

Ireland has also been a pure and straightforward backdrop. Youghal in County Cork was Captain Ahab's port in John Huston's 1956 *Moby Dick*. The Irish countryside was used for the WWI aerial epic *The Blue Max* (1966), and *Educating Rita* (1982) used Trinity College as its quintessentially English university! Mel Gibson's Oscar-winning *Braveheart* (1994) was filmed in Ireland.

The Powerscourt Estate near Enniskerry in County Wicklow was the setting for films such as Laurence Olivier's *Henry V* (1943) and John Boorman's *Excalibur* (1980).

Many films have featured Dublin. Joseph Strick attempted the seemingly impossible task of putting *Ulysses* on screen in 1967. The film was promptly banned in Ireland. John Huston's superb final film was *The Dead*, released in 1987 and based on a story from James Joyce's *Dubliners*.

Noel Pearson and Jim Sheridan's *My Left Foot* (1989) tells the true story of Dublin writer Christy Brown, who was crippled with cerebral palsy. The film managed to make some interesting peregrinations around Dublin including visits to John Mulligan's, the pub reputed to pull the best Guinness in Ireland.

The Commitments (1990), by the English director Alan Parker, was a wonderful, bright and energetic hit about a north Dublin soul band. Dublin audiences (well, north Dublin ones at least) were amused by some of the geographical jumps around the city which the characters managed to make! *The Snapper* (1992) and *The Van* (1995), the next two of Roddy Doyle's trilogy, were also made into films.

A Man of no Importance (1994) starring Albert Finney is set in Dublin in the early 1960s and tells the story of a gay bus conductor who runs an amateur theatre group. *Circle of Friends* (1994) uses bits of Dublin, especially the interior of the Museum Building of Trinity College. It's based on Maeve Binchy's novel, but changes the book's strong feminist end into Hollywood schlock!

The Troubles have spawned a number of films, including the *Odd Man Out* (1947), *Angel* (1982) and *Cal* (1984). It has been said with some justification that the IRA gets all the best films. The IRA featured in the British film *The Long Good Friday* starring Bob Hoskins. Harrison Ford's thriller *Patriot Games* is the story of a man who thwarts an IRA assassination attempt in London and is then hunted by IRA agents seeking revenge. *The Crying Game* (1992) is perhaps the most intriguing commercial film to feature the IRA.

In the Name of the Father (1993), filmed in Kilmainham Jail in Dublin, starred Daniel Day-Lewis as Gerry Conlon and Emma Thompson as his lawyer. Beginning with powerful scenes of rioting in Belfast in the early 1970s, it tells the story of the arrest and conviction of the Guildford Four for a pub bombing in England; then of the struggle to clear their names and their subsequent release.

Neil Jordan's powerful *Michael Collins* (1996), stars Liam Neeson and Stephen Rea. It follows the life of Collins from the Easter Rising, through the creation of the IRA, to the Anglo-Irish war, civil war and his death in 1922 at the hands of his former comrades.

Some Mother's Son (1996), starring Helen Mirren, deals with events surrounding the hunger strike of 1981 and the election of Bobby Sands as MP for Tyrone & Fermanagh shortly before his death. Two other films are Channel 4's *A Further Gesture* (1996), about an IRA man (Stephen Rea) escaping to Paris; and *Devil's Own* (1996), with Brad Pitt as an IRA gunrunner unwittingly harboured by New York cop, Harrison Ford.

Neil Jordan is one of the most talented writers and directors working today and has built up an impressive body of work. Jordan's films include *Mona Lisa* starring Bob Hoskins, *Cal*, *The Company of Wolves*, *The Miracle*, *The Crying Game* (Jordan won an Oscar for the script) and *Michael Collins*. Other important film-makers are Noel Pearson and Jim Sheridan who worked together on *My Left Foot* and *The Field*; Pat

O'Connor whose first film as director was of Bernard MacLaverty's *Cal*, and more recently *Circle of Friends*.

Irish actors like Liam Neeson, Patrick Bergin, Gabriel Byrne, Pierce Brosnan, Fionnula Flanagan, Aidan Quinn and Stephen Rea pursue successful careers, following in the footsteps of Barry Fitzgerald, Greer Garson, Maureen O'Hara, Richard Harris and Peter O'Toole. Some Irish actors have successfully combined a film and TV career. Brenda Fricker won an Oscar for her role in *My Left Foot* and appeared in the Australian TV mini-series, *Brides of Christ*. Colm Meaney played the father in the Roddy Doyle trilogy and appears in the action film *Con Air*. He has guaranteed his immortality, however, by his role as Starfleet officer, O'Brien, in Star Trek's *The Next Generation* and *Deep Space Nine*.

Architecture

Ireland is packed with prehistoric graves, ruined monasteries, crumbling fortresses and many other solid reminders of its long and often dramatic history. The buildings used in the country over the last few thousand years fall into a number of groups and you're likely to come across examples of some or all of them on your travels.

The simplest structures are standing stones and stone circles which in Ireland date from the Stone or Bronze Ages and were erected all the way up to Christian times.

The earliest settlers built houses of wood and reeds, of which nothing survives except the faint traces of post-holes. The principal surviving structures from Stone Age times are the graves and monuments the people built for their dead, usually grouped under the heading of megalithic tombs, or 'great stone' tombs.

Megalithic Tombs Among the most easily recognisable megalithic tombs are *dolmens*, massive three-legged structures rather like giant stone stools, in which a number of bodies were interred before the whole structure was covered in earth. Most are 4000 to 5000 years old. Usually the earth eroded away leaving the standing stones. There are good examples at Poulnabrone in Clare, Proleek near Dundalk, and at Browne's Hill near Carlow Town; the capstone at Browne's Hill weighs more than 100 tonnes. Dolmens are the best known type of chambered tomb or gallery graves; similar but more complex are wedge tombs, cist graves and court cairns.

Passage graves such as Newgrange and

A typical dolmen, at Kilclooney, north of Ardara in County Donegal

Knowth in Meath are huge mounds with entrances through narrow stone-walled passages leading to burial chambers. They're surrounded by stone circles of unknown significance. Some passage graves were made from piles of stones erected near or on hill tops, sometimes called *cairns*. Good examples are on the Slieve na Calliaghe hills in Meath and Seefin in County Wicklow.

Ogham Stones These are peculiarly Irish standing stones dating from the 4th to 7th centuries AD. *Ogham* (pronounced 'o-am') was an early form of Irish script using a variety of notched strokes placed above, below or across a keyline, usually on stones. The stones mainly indicate graves and are inscribed with the name of the deceased. The majority are found in counties Cork, Kerry and Waterford, and many have been moved; you may find them incorporated in walls, buildings or gateposts.

Forts Ring forts, 'fairy rings' and raths are all one and the same. The Irish names for forts – *dun*, *rath*, *caiseal/cashel* and *caher* – have ended up in the names of countless towns, villages and townlands. The Irish countryside is peppered with the remains of over 30,000. The earliest known examples date from the Bronze Age, and ring forts have been built and used for many thousands of years since. Some were lived in as late as the 17th century. Wooden and other types of houses were built within the forts' protective confines.

The most common type was the ring fort, with circular earth and stone banks topped by a wooden palisade fence to keep intruders out and surrounded on the outside by a moat-like ditch. Ring forts are found everywhere and were the basic family or tribal enclosure in Ireland for thousands of years. They may have protected anything from one family to the entire court of a tribal chieftain. Ring forts may have up to three earthen ramparts surrounding them; Mooghaun Fort near Dromoland Castle in County Clare is a particularly fine example. Outside Clonakilty in County Cork, Lisnagun ring fort has been

reconstructed to give some idea of its original appearance.

Some forts were constructed entirely of stone; Staigue Fort in Kerry and Cathair Dhún Iorais on Clare's Black Head are fine examples. Promontory forts were built on headlands or on cliff edges, which gave natural protection on one side. The Iron Age fort of Dún Aengus on the Aran Islands is a superb example.

The Normans used many ring forts to their full advantage by building inside them. A characteristic Norman fort was the motte-and-bailey. The motte was a small flat-topped hill surrounded by a ditch and earthen banks at the base for further protection; attached to and surrounding the motte was the bailey, an enclosure for animals and their keepers. These forts were largely military in purpose, built to protect and secure the Normans' newly conquered territory.

Crannógs Crannógs are artificial islands found in many Irish lakes and are the equivalent of a ring fort on water. Many of them were built completely by humans: wooden piles were driven into the lake floor and the structure built up with wood, stone, earth and anything else the builders could lay their hands on. After the island had been built, the occupants built wooden fences and a house to live in. The Craggaunowen Project in Clare has a reconstructed example, and the lake near Fair Head in County Antrim has an easily spotted original.

The midland lakes have many crannógs, which today are usually overgrown with little evidence betraying their artificial origins, except perhaps the too-perfect circular outline. Sometimes they were built in bogs, or the original lake has since become a bog; and many are now hidden below the water level.

Estimates put the number of crannógs in Ireland at over 250. Crannógs date back to the Bronze Age and like the ring forts were used by humans right up to the 16th and 17th centuries. Often there was a secret causeway leading out to the crannóg, just under the surface of the water, and it twisted and turned so that ignorant intruders would have difficulty using it.

Monasteries & Churches The vast majority of early monasteries were built of perishable materials, particularly wood. Sometimes the central church or chapel was stone and these are often the only structures that survive. The early stone churches were often very simple, some roofed with timber like Teampall Benen on the Aran Islands or built completely of stone like Gallarus Oratory on the Dingle Peninsula. Early hermitages include the small beehive huts and buildings on the summit of Skellig Michael off County Kerry.

As the monasteries grew in size and stature so did the architecture. The 'cathedrals' at Glendalough and Clonmacnois are good examples, although they're tiny compared with modern cathedrals.

Round towers have become symbols of Ireland, and these tall, stone needle-like structures were built largely as lookout posts and refuges in the event of Viking attacks. The earliest round towers were built in the late 9th or early 10th centuries.

That other great Irish symbol, the Celtic cross, comes from these Christian times. Some suggest that the circle imposed on the arms of the cross represents pagan sun worship being incorporated into the new faith. They developed from simple crosses with rough designs to complex works decorated with high-relief scenes, usually of Biblical characters and tales.

Ireland's early church architecture really developed in isolation, as Europe was experiencing the Dark Ages. However, foreign influences began to take effect in the 11th and 12th centuries, and the Cistercians, a European order of monks, established their first Irish monastery at Mellifont, County Louth, in 1141. The strict and formal layout of these new establishments was radically different to the simple and relatively random layout of the traditional Irish monastery as exemplified by nearby Monasterboice, Glendalough in Wicklow and Clonmacnois in Offaly. Cormac's Chapel at the Rock of Cashel shows strong foreign influence, and elements of European Romanesque design became common in Irish monasteries and buildings. Elaborately carved doorways are common, with human and animal heads intricately interwoven into the stone patterns.

With the Normans came the Gothic style of architecture: tall vaulted windows and soaring V-shaped arches were incorporated in the churches and cathedrals of this period.

Castles & Mansions The Normans first built temporary motte-and-bailey forts (see Forts above). Once they had established themselves, however, they built more permanent stone castles. The great castle at Trim, County Meath, is the best example. Castles and cathedrals were built in Dublin and the other large towns.

Many of the castles you see today are the tall, thin tower houses built between the 14th and 17th centuries for local landlords or chieftains. They're often inside a protective wall called a *bawn*. The earliest forms of these are simple, small keeps with few embellishments, while the later forms became more like large, fortified stone houses with sophisticated features, bigger windows, and less emphasis on security.

From the 17th century on, as the established landowning families became wealthier and felt more secure, they built great mansions, particularly in the less rebellious parts of the country around counties Kildare, Meath, Dublin and Wicklow. Castletown House near Celbridge, Russborough House near Blessington and Carton House in Maynooth are good examples.

Georgian Houses In Georgian times, Dublin became one of the architectural glories of Europe, with simple and beautifully built Georgian terraces of red brick, with delicate glass fanlights over large, elegant, curved doorways. From the 1960s Dublin's Georgian heritage suffered badly but many, in places like Mountjoy Square, are being restored. You can see fine examples around Merrion and Fitzwilliam squares. Georgian architecture wasn't confined to

Dublin and you'll see other fine examples in places like Limerick.

Cottages The traditional Irish thatched cottage, built to suit the elements and the landscape, has become rare.

Painting

Although Ireland doesn't have a tradition of painting anything like its literary history, the National Gallery does have an extensive Irish School collection, much of it chronicling the personages and pursuits of the Anglo-Irish aristocracy. Just as WB Yeats played a seminal role in the Celtic literary revival, his younger brother Jack Butler Yeats (1871-1957), inspired an artistic surge of creativity. Their father, John Butler Yeats, was also a noted portrait painter.

Earlier noted portrait painters were Garrett Murphy (1680-1716) and James Latham (1696-1747). Important 18th and 19th-century landscape painters were George Barret, Robert Carver, William Ashford, Roderick O'Connor and Thomas Roberts. James Malton captured 18th-century Dublin on canvas in a number of paintings.

SOCIETY & CONDUCT

Ireland's economic success, social changes and cultural resurgence are dispelling old stereotypes of the country as a predominantly poor, rural, agrarian backwater unable to stop the exodus of its children. It has a booming economy that has embraced high technology, with a young population and flourishing arts.

There are few of the class distinctions so prevalent in England, and while advertising and marketing people divide the population into wealth and class brackets, the boundaries of these are quite fluid. Movement between social classes is common and more to do with personal wealth than birth or background. There are vestiges of an upper class made up of the descendants of the Protestant landed gentry, but their status and their houses are being taken over by the newer business elite.

That said there's a growing division between the 'haves' and 'have nots'. Many people may be enjoying their share of Ireland's new-found economic success, but it hasn't reached areas like the Dublin housing estates where drugs and crime are rife. Those living below the poverty line (set at 60% of the average national wage) rose from 31% in 1989 to 35% in 1996. It's paradoxical that there should be a rise in the number of poor at a time of unprecedented national wealth.

Religion and politics are inextricably mixed, especially in the North, but on the whole, Irish of all political or religious persuasions are friendly and accommodating towards foreigners. Whenever these subjects come up, as a visitor it's probably a good idea to make this a time to practise your listening skills – at least until you're sure of the situation.

As the number of pubs attest, the Irish are a social, gregarious people, but in rural Ireland, introductions and conversations are usually low key until some mutual respect is established. If you want to get on with people, don't crash into a B&B or a country pub and make lots of noise. Go quietly, say hello and let conversation arise naturally.

RELIGION

The Republic of Ireland is 95% Roman Catholic, 3.4% Protestant and 0.1% Jewish. The remaining 1.5% either have no religious beliefs or belong to other religious groupings including Islam and Buddhism. In the North the breakdown is about 60% Protestant, 40% Catholic. Most Irish Protestants are members of the Church of Ireland, an offshoot of the Church of England, and the Presbyterian and Methodist churches.

The Catholic Church has always taken a strong line on abortion, contraception and divorce, and opposed attempts to liberalise the laws on these matters. But today only abortion is still forbidden by law. The Church is treated with a curious mixture of respect and derision by various sections of the community.

Despite its declining power, the Catholic

To Catch a Leprechaun

Now you see him, now you don't. The leprechaun is a little man no more than 150cm tall with a jaunty feather sticking out of his green cap. Of course he's at pains to hide from you because, as everyone knows, the leprechaun carries a crock of gold. Catch him and you can force him to give it to you. Take your eyes off him for a second and he'll vanish into thin air.

That's the blarney which has spawned many an Irish teatowel. In reality scholars believe the leprechaun is a reminder of the days when the early Christians neutralised the power of the pagan gods by turning them into 'little people'. ■

Church still wields considerable influence in the South especially in rural areas. Large numbers attend mass every Sunday as part of the weekly social round. It's probably still too early to talk of a post-Catholic Ireland.

Oddly enough, the primates of both the Roman Catholic Church and the Church of Ireland sit in Armagh, the traditional base of St Patrick, which is in Northern Ireland. The country's religious history clearly overrides its current divisions.

LANGUAGE

Although English is the main language of Ireland, it's spoken with a peculiar Irish flavour and lilt. Indeed the Irish accent is one of the most pleasant varieties of English to be heard. Some of the peculiarly Irish sentence constructions in English are closely related to the Irish language; for instance, the usual word order in Irish sentences is verb, subject, object. The present participle is also used more frequently in constructions like 'Would you be wanting a room for the night, then?' Another peculiarity is the use of 'after' as in 'I'm just after going to the shop' meaning 'I have just been to the shop'. The Irish also have a notable bias towards the use of scatological speech.

English is spoken throughout Ireland, but there are still parts of western and southern Ireland known as *Gaeltacht* areas where Irish is the native language – Kerry, Galway, Mayo, the Aran Islands, Donegal and Ring, County Waterford; there's also a small pocket in Meath. The number of native speakers is around 83,000. Irish is a Celtic language, probably first introduced to Ireland by the Celts in the last few centuries BC. Irish is similar to Scottish Gaelic, and has much in common with Welsh and Breton.

Officially the Republic of Ireland is bilingual, and many official documents and road signs are printed in both Irish and English. The reality, however, is a little bit more complex.

Until the time of the plantation in the late 16th and early 17th centuries, successive invaders had been assimilated and adopted the Irish language. From the time of the plantation Irish was seen as the language of the old Irish aristocracy, the poor and dispossessed, and strenuous efforts were made by the English to wipe it out. Social advancement meant giving up Irish. When independence was achieved in 1921 efforts were made to revive the language but progress has been slow.

Irish is compulsory in both primary and secondary schools, and most colleges and universities require prospective students to pass the subject in their school-leaving exams. Despite this – partly because too much emphasis is placed on the complex grammar and too little on speaking the language – most Irish school leavers would be hard pressed to hold a simple conversation in Irish despite having just completed 13 years of daily classes in the subject. Many complain that it's a waste of time studying a difficult language that's not in everyday use.

However, attitudes are changing; it no longer carries a stigma and even in Dublin there's a revival with several Irish-medium infant and junior schools. An Irish-language radio station, Radio na Gaeltachta, broadcasts from Connemara; Telefis na Ghaelige is a national Irish-language TV station; and RTE, the Irish national broadcaster, has daily news bulletins and programmes in Irish. An increasing number of people derive intense satisfaction from speaking and keeping alive an ancient aspect of Ireland's culture.

Irish is one of the official languages of the European Union.

Lonely Planet's *Western Europe Phrasebook* devotes a chapter to the Irish language.

Pronunciation

There are three main varieties of pronunciation of Irish in the Gaeltacht areas. These are: Connaught Irish (Galway and north Mayo), Munster Irish (Cork, Kerry, Waterford) and Ulster Irish (Donegal). The pronunciation guidelines given here are an anglicised-spelling version of the 'standard' form, an amalgam of the three dialects.

a   as the 'a' in 'cat'
á   as the 'a' in 'saw'
e   as the 'e' in 'bet'
é   as the 'a' in 'day'
i   as the 'i' in 'sit'
í   as the 'i' in 'fine'
o   as the 'u' in 'sun'
ó   as the 'o' in 'cow'
u   as the 'u' in 'but'
ú   as the 'oo' in 'cook'

c   as the 'k' in 'key'
ch as the 'ch' in the Scottish 'loch'
d   as the 'j' in 'jug' when followed by 'e' or 'i'; as the 'd' in 'door' when followed by 'o' or 'u'
dh as the 'y' in 'young' when followed by 'e' or 'i'; like the 'g' in 'huge' when followed by 'o' or 'u'
t   as the 'ch' in 'church' when followed or preceded by 'e' or 'i'; like the 't' in 'toast' when followed or preceded by 'o' or 'u'
th like the 'h' in 'house'; sometimes at the end of a word it is silent

s   like the 'sh' in 'shirt'

Greetings & Civilities

Hello.	Dia Dhuit. (lit. 'God be with you') *dee-a-gwit*
Goodbye.	Slán Agat. *slawn aguth*
Good night.	Oiche mhaith. *eeheh woh*
Welcome.	Fáilte. *fawlcha*
Welcome.	Céad mhíle fáilte. (100,000 welcomes) *kade meela fawlcha*
Thank you.	Go raibh maith aguth. *goh rev moh aguth*
Thank you very much.	Gur a mhíle maith agat. *gur a mila moh agut* Go raibh mhíle maith agat. *goh rev meela moh aguth*
Please.	Le do thoil. *le do hull*
Excuse me.	Gabh mo leiscéil. *gawv mo lesh scale*
How are you?	Conas a tá tú? *kunas a thaw two*
I am fine.	Táim go maith. *thawm gohmoh*
What is your name?	Cad is anim duit? *cod is anim dit*
Sean Frayne is my name.	Sean Frayne is anim dom *Sean Frayne iss anim dumb*
another/one more	ceann eile *keown ella*
good, fine, OK	go maith *go moh*
nice	go deas *goh dass*
yes	tá/sea *thaw/shah*
no/it is not	níl/ní hea *knee hah*

Questions & Comments

Why?	Cén fáth?
	kane faw
What is this?	Cad é seo?
	kod ay shawh
What is that?	Cad é sin?
	kod ay shin
How much/how many?	Cé mhéid?
	kay vaid
expensive – very dear	ana dhaor
	ana gare
where is ...?	cá bhfuil ...?
	kaw will
which way?	cén slí?
	kane shlee
I don't understand.	Ní thuigim.
	nee higgim
this/that	é seo/é sin
	ay shoh/ay shin
big/small	mór/beag
	moor/beeugh
open/closed	oscailte/dúnta
	uskulta/doonta
slowly/quickly	go mall/go tapaidh
	guh mowl/guh topigg

Getting Around

I would like to go to ...	Ba mhaith liom dul go dtí ...
	baw woh lum dull go dee
I would like to buy ...	Ba mhaith liom cheannach ...
	bah woh lumb kyarok
ticket	ticéid
	tickaid
boat/ship	bád/long
	bawd/lung
car/bus	gluaisteáin/bus
	glooshtawn/bus
here/there	anseo/ansin
	anshuh/onshin
stop/go	stad/ar aghaidh
	stod/err eyeg
town square	lár an baile
	lawr an vollyeh
street/road	sráid/bóthar
	sroyed/bowher

town/city	baile/cathair
	bollyeh/kawher
bank/shop	an banc/siopa
	an bonk/shuppa

Useful Signs

MEN	FIR
	(FEAR)
WOMEN	MNÁ
	(ME-NAW)
TOILET	LEITHREAS
	(LEHRASS)
POLICE	GARDAÍ
	(GARDEE)
POST OFFICE	OIFIG AN PHOIST
	(IF-IG ON PWIST)
TELEPHONE	TELEFÓN
	(TAY LAY FOAN)
TOWN CENTRE	AN LÁR
	(AN LAAH)

Accommodation

one night	oíche amháin
	eeheh a woin
one person	aon duine
	ayn dinnah
bed/room	leaba/seomra
	leeabah/showmra
hotel	óstán
	oh stahn
bed & breakfast	loístín oíche
	leestin eeheh

Time & Dates

today/tomorrow	inniu/amárach
	innyuv/amawrok
hour/minute	huair/noiméid
	oor/nomade
week/month	seachtain/mí
	shocktin/mee
What time is it?	Cén tam é?
	kane towm ay
7 o' clock	seacht a chlog
	shocked ah klug

Monday	dé luan *day loon*	9	naoi *nay*
Tuesday	dé máirt *day mawrt*	10	deich *jeh*
Wednesday	dé céadaoin *day kaydeen*	11	aon deag *ayen deeuct*
Thursday	déardaoin *daredeen*	12	dó deag *doe dayugg*
Friday	dé haoine *day heena*	20	fiche *feekh*
Saturday	dé sathairn *day saheren*	21	fiche aon *feekh-ayn*
Sunday	dé domhnaigh *day downick*	30	tríocha *chree-okha*

Numbers

½	leath *lah*	40	daichead *daykh-ayd*
1	aon *ayn*	50	caoga *ka-uga*
2	dó *doe*	60	seasca *shay-ska*
3	trí *three*	70	seachtó *shocked-ow*
4	cathar *kahirr*	80	ochtó *ukth-ow*
5	cúig *koo-ig*	90	nócha *now-kha*
6	sé *shay*		
7	seacht *shocked*	and so on...	
8	ocht *ukth*	100	céad *kade*
		1000	míle *meal-ah*

Facts for the Visitor

PLANNING
When to Go
The weather is generally warm in July and August and the daylight hours are long, but the crowds will be greater, the costs higher and accommodation harder to come by. Although the winter months are quieter, you may get miserable weather, the days are short and many tourist facilities are shut. It's worth considering visiting Ireland April to June or in September when the weather can be better than at other times of year, it's less crowded then and most attractions and tourist offices are open.

What Kind of Trip?
Your particular interests will have a large bearing on the kind of trip it'll be, as will the amount of time and money at your disposal. The longer you stay, the more likely you'll step outside the often-superficial world of the tourist, and the lower your relative daily expenses will be.

If your holiday is limited, try to leave enough time to walk one or two way-marked trails (at least part of them, anyway) or to do some cycle touring somewhere off the beaten track. Some visitor attractions have no public transport so walking or cycling may be your only way to see them.

You may also want to consider hiring a car for part of the trip to visit some out of the way places. However, most attractions can be visited as part of a guided tour. This is often a good way to get a quick overview of areas you're unfamiliar with and allows you to consider your options should you want to return.

Travelling alone is fine provided you follow the normal precautions and is a great way to meet new people. Hostels and camp grounds are good places to meet fellow travellers, and B&Bs allow you to meet locals who may offer the kind of insights unavailable at the local tourist office.

Maps
There are numerous good-quality maps of Ireland. The Michelin Map of Ireland No 405 (1:400,000) has most of the scenic roads accurately highlighted in green. The four maps – North, South, East and West – that make up the Ordnance Survey Holiday Map series are useful if you want something more detailed than a whole Ireland map. Their scale is 1:250,000.

For greater detail the Ordnance Survey covers the whole island in 25 sheets with a 1:126,720 scale (half an inch to one mile). This series, however, is gradually being replaced by the Discovery series of 89 Ordnance Survey maps with a 1:50,000 scale (2cm to 1km). The new maps are a pleasure to use and it's always worth checking to see if the area you want is available in the new series. They can be obtained from the Government Publications Sales Office bookshop (☎ 01-661 3111), Sun Alliance House, Molesworth St, Dublin 2.

Special maps for the Kerry Way, Dingle Way and other trails are available from tourist offices, and at a pinch they'll suffice. For the Ulster Way, section maps are available from the Sports Council for Northern Ireland (☎ 01232-381222), House of Sport, Upper Malone Rd, Belfast BT9 5LA.

Tim Robinson of Folding Landscapes, Roundstone, County Galway, produces superbly detailed maps of the Burren, the Aran Islands and Connemara; also, his and Joss Lynam's *Connemara: A Hill Walker's Guide* contains a useful detailed map.

What to Bring
A travelpack – a combination of backpack and shoulder bag – is the most popular item for carrying gear. A travelpack's straps zip away inside the pack when not needed, making it easy to handle in airports and on crowded public transport. They also look better than a hiking pack and can be made

reasonably thief-proof with small combination locks.

A raincoat or an umbrella is a necessity, as are some warm clothes – even during good summer weather it gets chilly in the evenings. Walkers should be well prepared if they're crossing exposed country. Dress is usually casual, and you're unlikely to come across many coat-and-tie-type regulations.

Bear in mind the strict regulations about birth control in Ireland. Condoms aren't always easily available in rural areas, though they're becoming more common in pharmacies and pub vending machines in the cities.

A sleeping bag is useful in hostels and when visiting friends; get one that can be used as a quilt. A sleeping sheet with a pillow cover is necessary if you plan to stay in hostels, though you can buy or hire one if you don't bring your own.

Other possible items include a Swiss Army knife or equivalent, a compass (to help orient yourself on walks), a torch (flashlight), an alarm clock or watch with an alarm function, an adapter plug for electrical appliances, a universal bath/sink plug, sunglasses and an elastic clothesline.

SUGGESTED ITINERARIES

Depending on the length of your stay, you might want to see and do the following:

Three days
> Visit Dublin and perhaps a couple of places nearby – Powerscourt and Glendalough to the south, or perhaps Newgrange, Mellifont and Monasterboice to the north.

One week
> Visit Dublin, then Newgrange, Mellifont, Kilkenny, Killarney, Dingle and the Burren.

Two weeks
> As above, plus the Ring of Kerry and Cork.

One month
> With a car or motorcycle you'd have time to explore Ireland's main attractions but you'd be moving quite fast. This would be more difficult to achieve within a month on public transport. You could fit in some walking and cycling too.

HIGHLIGHTS
Scenery, Beaches & Coastline

The scenery is one of Ireland's major attractions, whether it's those soft green fields, awesome cliffs tumbling into a ferocious Atlantic, or rocky, barren areas in the far west. Highlights include the beautiful scenery around the Ring of Kerry and the Dingle Peninsula, the barren stretches of the Burren, the rocky Aran Islands and the beautiful lake areas south and north.

Favourite stretches of Ireland's 3200km coastline include the wildly beautiful Cliffs of Moher, the Connemara and Donegal coasts and the wonderful Antrim coast road of Northern Ireland. There are some fine beaches (and marginally warmer water) around the south-east coast, and some great surfing around the west and north-west coasts.

The EU Blue Flag flies over the cleanest and safest beaches of Ireland. If a beach doesn't have a Blue Flag it's best to enquire locally before venturing out for a swim.

Museums, Castles & Houses

Trinity College Library with the ancient 'Book of Kells' is on every visitor's must-see list, but Dublin also has the fine National Museum and National Gallery. Belfast has the excellent Ulster Museum and, just outside the city, the extensive Ulster Folk & Transport Museum.

Ireland is littered with castles and forts of various types and sizes and in various stages of ruination. The Stone Age forts on the Aran Islands are of particular interest, but there are other ancient ring forts all over Ireland. Castles are numerous and prime examples are Dublin Castle, Charles Fort at Kinsale and Kilkenny Castle, not forgetting Blarney Castle with its famous stone!

The Anglo-Irish aristocracy left a good selection of fine stately homes, many of which are open to the public like Castletown House, Malahide House, Westport House, Bantry House and Mt Stewart, and the beautiful gardens at Powerscourt Estate.

Religious Sites

Stone rings, portal tombs or dolmens and passage graves are reminders of an earlier pre-Christian Ireland. The massive passage grave at Newgrange is the most impressive relic of that time. Early Christian churches, many well over 1000 years old, are scattered throughout Ireland, and ruined monastic sites, many with round towers, are also numerous. Clonmacnois, Glendalough, Mellifont Abbey, Grey Abbey, Inch Abbey and Jerpoint Abbey are particularly interesting monastic sites. The rock-top complex at Cashel is one of Ireland's major tourist attractions, and the beehive huts built by monks on Skellig Michael, off the coast of Kerry, are well worth visiting.

Islands

Lying off Ireland's coast are all sorts and shapes of islands, some inhabited by humans, others inhabited only by migrating birds, some easily accessible, others requiring the private hire of a boat.

The Aran Islands in County Galway and Achill Island in County Mayo are the most touristy, but it's not difficult to find more isolated ones. A boat trip to the Skelligs is one of the highlights of a visit to Ireland, and their wildlife is fascinating. The Blaskets, off the Dingle Peninsula in County Kerry, are glorious on a fine day. Tory Island, off the Donegal coast, is a wild place and is the home of a group of local artists. County Cork has a number of accessible islands, of which Clear Island is famous for its birdlife and scenery and nearby Sherkin Island has sandy and safe beaches.

TOURIST OFFICES

Bord Fáilte (Irish Tourist Board) and the Northern Ireland Tourist Board (NITB) operate separate tourist offices but produce some joint brochures and publications.

They also administer a computerised tourist information and accommodation reservation service known as Gulliver. Anyone intending to visit Ireland can go to a travel agent and access this information and make reservations from anywhere in the world. Within Ireland call ☎ 800 600800.

Bord Fáilte can be contacted at its Information Service (☎ 01-602 4000; fax 602 4100; http://www.ireland.travel.ie), PO Box 273, Dublin 8.

The head office of the NITB (☎ 01232-246609; fax 240960; http://www.nitourism.com) is at St Anne's Court, 59 North St, Belfast BT1 1NB.

Local Tourist Offices

Dublin has Bord Fáilte, Dublin Tourism and NITB offices. Belfast has NITB and Bord Fáilte offices. Elsewhere in Ireland and Northern Ireland there is a tourist office in almost every town big enough to have half a dozen pubs (it doesn't take much population to justify half a dozen pubs in Ireland).

However, no doubt as a result of pressures to be self-financing, some local Bord Fáilte offices have become almost indistinguishable from souvenir shops, with little information available free. Since they can only book Bord Fáilte approved accommodation and often know little about public transport it may not always be worth joining queues at busy times. Some tourist offices also open for such limited periods that other enterprises are stepping in to fill the gap. Often, hostel owners (and some B&B owners) are more useful sources of local information for those on limited budgets.

In the bigger towns and more touristed areas opening hours are usually Monday to Friday, 9 am to 5 pm, Saturday 9 am to 1 pm, but the hours are often extended in summer. In other areas offices only open seasonally (from April, May or June to September) or for much shorter hours from October to April. These offices will find you tourist board approved accommodation and book it – for a IR£1 charge (£1 in the North) if it's local, IR£2 (£2) elsewhere.

Tourist Offices Abroad

Some of the offices of Bord Fáilte include:

Australia
  5th Floor, 36 Carrington St, Sydney, NSW 2000 – also has information on Northern Ireland (☎ 02-9299 6177)
Belgium
  Ave de Beaulieu 25, 1160 Bruxelles (☎ 02-673 9940)

Canada
>160 Bloor St East, Suite 1150, Toronto, Ontario M4W 1B9 (☎ 416-929 2777)

Denmark
>Amagertory 29/3, 1160 Kobenhavn K (☎ 033-15 8045)

France
>33 rue de Miromesnil, 75008 Paris (☎ 01 47 42 03 36)

Germany
>Untermainanlage 7, 60329 Frankfurt Main 1 (☎ 069-23 64 92)

Italy
>Via S Maria Segreta 6, 20123 Milano (☎ 02-869 0541)

Netherlands
>Spuistraat 104, 1012 VA Amsterdam (☎ 020-622 3101)

New Zealand
>Dingwall Building, 87 Queen St, Auckland 1 (☎ 09-379 3708)

Northern Ireland
>53 Castle St, Belfast BT1 1GH (☎ 01232-327888)

Spain
>Claudio Coello 73, 28001 Madrid (☎ 91-577 1787)

Sweden
>Sibyllegatan 49, 114 42 Stockholm (☎ 08-662 8510)

UK
>Ireland House, 150 New Bond St, London W1Y 0AQ (☎ 0171-493 3201)

USA
>345 Park Ave, New York, NY 10154 (☎ 212-418 0800)

Tourist information for Northern Ireland is handled by the British Tourist Authority, although you may also find offices of the Northern Ireland Tourist Board in some locations:

Canada
>111 Avenue Rd, Suite 450, Toronto, Ontario M5R 3J8 (☎ 416-925 6368)

France
>3 rue de Pontoise, 78100 St Germain-en-Laye (☎ 01 39 21 93 80)

Germany
>Taununstrasse 52-60, 60329 Frankfurt/Main, (☎ 069-23 45 04)

Ireland, Republic of
>16 Nassau St, Dublin 2 (☎ 01-679 1977, 1850 230 230)

New Zealand
>Dingwall Building, 87 Queen St, Auckland 1 (☎ 09-379 3708)

UK
>British Travel Centre, 12 Lower Regent St, London SW1Y 4PQ (☎ 0171-839 8416)
>135 Buchanan St, Glasgow G1 2JA (☎ 0141-204 4454)

USA
>551 5th Ave, Suite 701, New York, NY 10176 (☎ 212-922 0101, 1800-282662)

VISAS & DOCUMENTS

Passport

Your most important travel document is a passport, which should remain valid for at least six months after your intended stay. If it's about to expire, renew it before you go. This may not be easy to do away from your home country. Applying for or renewing a passport can take from a few days to several months, so don't leave it till the last minute. Things will probably happen faster if you do everything in person, but check first on what you need to take with you. Once you start travelling, carry your passport at all times and guard it carefully.

UK nationals born in Britain or Northern Ireland don't require a passport to visit the Republic, but may need some form of identification, for example when changing travellers' cheques or hiring a car.

Visas

For citizens of the EU and most other western countries, including Australia, Canada, New Zealand, South Africa and the USA, no visa is required to visit either the Republic or Northern Ireland. Visas are required from citizens of India and Pakistan, from Hong Kong citizens who don't hold a UK passport and citizens of some African states. EU nationals are allowed to stay indefinitely, while other visitors can usually remain for three to six months. If you want to stay longer contact the Department of Justice (☎ 01-678 9711), 72 St Stephen's Green, Dublin 2.

Photocopies

It's sensible to keep photocopies of important documents (passport, visa, driver's licence, airline ticket, travel insurance policy, travellers' cheque serial numbers) in a separate place in case of theft. It might be wise to stash IR£50 with the photocopies just in case. Ideally, leave a second set of copies with a responsible person in your home country. If your documents are lost or stolen, replacing them will be much easier.

Onward Tickets
Although you don't need an onward or return ticket to enter Ireland, this could help if there's any doubt that you have sufficient funds to support yourself or to buy an onward ticket in Ireland.

Travel Insurance
This not only covers you for medical expenses and luggage theft or loss, but also for cancellations or delays in your travel arrangements under certain circumstances (you might fall seriously ill two days before departure, for example). There's a wide variety of policies and your travel agent will have recommendations. Cover depends on your insurance and type of ticket, so ask both your insurer and your ticket-issuing agency to explain where you stand.

Some policies offer lower and higher medical-expense options, but the higher one is chiefly for countries like the USA which have extremely high medical costs. Everyone should be covered for the worst possible case, such as an accident requiring an ambulance, hospital treatment and an emergency flight home. If you have to stretch out you'll need two seats and somebody has to pay for them! You may prefer a policy which pays doctors or hospitals direct rather than you having to pay on the spot and claim later.

Ticket loss is also (usually) covered by travel insurance. Buy travel insurance as early as possible. If you buy it the week before you fly, you may find, for example, that you're not covered for delays to your flight caused by strikes or industrial action.

Check the fine print: some policies exclude 'dangerous activities' like scuba diving or motorcycling. If such activities are on your agenda, you don't want that policy. A locally acquired motorcycle licence may not be valid under your policy.

Finally, make sure the policy includes health care and medication in the countries you may visit to/from Ireland.

Driving Licence & Permit
Your normal driving licence is valid for 12 months from the date of entry to Ireland, and you should have held it for two years. If you don't hold a European licence and plan to drive in other parts of Europe, obtain an International Driving Permit (IDP) from your home automobile association before you leave. While you're at it, ask for a Card of Introduction, which entitles you to services offered by sister organisations (maps and information, help with breakdowns, legal advice etc), usually free of charge.

Hostel Card
If you're travelling on a budget, membership of Hostelling International will give you access to An Óige hostels in the South and YHANI in the North (see Accommodation later), though you can usually get temporary membership if you just turn up at one of the hostels. A hostel card also entitles you to an impressive array of discounts.

Student & Youth Card
The most useful is the International Student Identity Card (ISIC), a plastic ID-style card with your photograph. With it you can get all sorts of discounts on transport, commercial goods and services, and entry to museums and sights. If you're under 26, but not a student, you can apply for a European Youth Card (EYC), also called a Euro<26 Card, which offers similar discounts to an ISIC. (See also Bus & Train Discount Deals in the Getting Around chapter.)

EMBASSIES
Irish Embassies Abroad
Irish diplomatic offices overseas include:

Australia
20 Arkana St, Yarralumla, Canberra, ACT 2600
(☎ 02-6273 3022)

Canada
> 130 Albert St, Ottawa, Ontario K1A 0L6 (☎ 613-233 6281)

Denmark
> Ostbanegade 21, 2100 Copenhagen (☎ 31-42 32 33)

France
> 12 Ave Foch, 75116 Paris (☎ 1-44 17 67 00)

Germany
> Godesberger Allee 119, 53175 Bonn (☎ 228-95 92 90)

Italy
> Piazza di Campitelli 3, 00186 Rome (☎ 6-697 91211)

Japan
> 2-10-7 Kojimachi, Chiyoda-ku, Tokyo 102 (☎ 3-3263 0695)

Netherlands
> Dr Kuyperstraat 9, 2514 BA The Hague (☎ 70-363 0993)

Portugal
> Rua da Imprensa a Estrela 1-4, 1200 Lisbon (☎ 1-396 1569)

South Africa
> Delheim Suite, Tulbach Park, 1234 Church St, 0083 Colbyn, Pretoria (☎ 12-342 5062)

Spain
> 1st Floor, Claudio Coello 73, 28001 Madrid (☎ 1-576 3500)

Sweden
> Östermalmsgatan 97, PO Box 10326, 100 55 Stockholm (☎ 8-661 8005)

Switzerland
> Kirchendfeldstrasse 68, 3005 Berne (☎ 31-352 1442)

UK
> 17 Grosvenor Place, London SW1X 7HR (☎ 0171-235 2171)

USA
> 2234 Massachusetts Ave NW, Washington, DC 20008 (☎ 202-462 3939). In addition there are consulates in Boston, Chicago, New York and San Francisco.

Foreign Embassies in Ireland

See the Dublin and Belfast chapters for diplomatic offices in those cities.

CUSTOMS

There is a two-tier system: the first for goods bought duty free, the second for goods bought in an EU country where taxes and duties have been paid.

The second is relevant because a number of products (including alcohol and tobacco) are much cheaper on the continent. Under the rules of the single market, however, as long as duty or taxes have been paid somewhere in the EU there are no additional taxes if the goods are exported within the EU – provided they're for personal consumption. There's no customs inspection apart from those concerned with drugs and national security.

But while you can bring vast quantities of cheap wine purchased, for example, in France to Ireland, wine purchased duty free on board a ferry from France or at an airport remain subject to the normal restrictions. You're allowed to import 200 cigarettes, one litre of spirits, two litres of wine, 60mls of perfume, 250mls of toilet water, and other dutiable goods to the value of IR£73.

MONEY
Costs

Ireland is expensive, but costs vary around the country. A hostel bed in a dormitory will cost IR£6 to IR£13 a night. If you're not staying in a hostel your costs increase dramatically by having to eat out. A modest meal at lunch time costs IR£3 to IR£5 and in the evening this can easily double. A cheap B&B will cost about IR£15 to IR£22 per person while a more luxurious B&B or guesthouse with attached bathroom would be anything from about IR£18 to IR£45. Dinner in a reasonable restaurant with a glass of wine or a beer costs from IR£10 to IR£15.

Assuming you stay at a hostel, eat a light pub lunch and cook your own meal in the evening, you could get by on IR£18 to IR£20 a day. In practice you usually spend more and when you move around the country you'll need to factor in transport.

Many places to stay have different high and low season prices. In this book, unless it says otherwise, the prices quoted are for the high season. Some places may have not just a high season but a peak high season price. Entry prices are often lower for children or students than for adults.

It's also more economical, in terms of accommodation, to travel with another person since many places charge a single-occupancy supplement. This means that solo

Sightseeing Discounts

Many parks, monuments and gardens in the South are operated by Dúchas (formerly the Office of Public Works). From any of its sites, for IR£15 (children and students IR£6) you can get a Heritage Card giving you free access to all these sites for one year – worthwhile if you're planning a serious onslaught on Ireland's plentiful supply of castles, monasteries etc. The child/student card in particular can pay for itself in three or four visits. For more information contact the Heritage Service (☎ 01-661 3111), Dúchas, 51 St Stephen's Green, Dublin 2.

In Northern Ireland, membership of the National Trust entitles you to free entry to its properties, but because there are fewer sites it really only makes economic sense if you're going to be doing some touring in Britain as well. The cost of membership is £27, under-26 £13, family £51. For more information contact the Public Affairs Manager (☎ 01238-510721), National Trust, Rowallane, Saintfield BT24 7LH. ■

travellers often pay more than half the double or twin rate.

At busy times of year, B&Bs may add a few pounds to their price. Watch out for the awful practice of charging an extra 50p or IR£1 for a bath.

A pint of Guinness is usually at least IR£1.85 and the rounds system – where you take your turn in buying drinks for the assembled company – is a good way of spending a remarkable amount of money in a remarkably short space of time.

Car hire is extremely expensive, and unleaded petrol costs about 60p a litre, leaded four to five pence more.

Carrying Money

Carry your money (and only the money you'll need for that day) somewhere inside your clothing (in a money belt, a bra or your socks) rather than in a handbag or an outside pocket. You might want to stitch an inside pocket into your skirt or trousers to keep an emergency stash; keep something like IR£50 separate from the rest of your cash in case of emergency. Put the money in several places. Most hotels and hostels provide safekeeping, so you can leave money and other valuables with them. Hide, or don't wear, any valuable jewellery.

Cash & Travellers' Cheques

Most major currencies and brands of travellers' cheques are readily accepted in Ireland, but carrying them in pounds sterling has the advantage that in Northern Ireland or Britain you can change them without exchange loss or commission.

Nothing beats cash for convenience or ... risk. It's still a good idea, though, to travel with some local currency in cash, if only to tide you over till you get to an exchange facility.

American Express and Thomas Cook travellers' cheques are widely recognised and don't charge commission for cashing their own cheques. Eurocheques can be cashed in Ireland. Keeping a record of the cheque numbers and the cheques you have cashed is vital in case of loss. Keep this list separate from the cheques themselves. Travellers' cheques are rarely accepted outside banks or used for everyday transactions (as in the USA) so you need to cash them beforehand.

Take most cheques in large denominations. It's only towards the end of a stay that you may want to change a small cheque to make sure you don't get left with too much local currency.

ATMs & Credit/Charge Cards

Plastic cards are ideal for major purchases and can allow you to withdraw cash (using a personal identification number or PIN) from selected banks and automatic teller machines (ATMs). The Allied Irish Bank (AIB) ATMs, called Passpoints, are particularly useful. Many ATMs are linked to international money systems such as Cirrus, Maestro or

Plus, so you can get instant cash. But ATMs aren't fail-safe, especially if the card was issued outside Europe, and it's safer to go to a human teller – it can be a headache if an ATM swallows your card.

Credit cards aren't usually linked to an ATM network unless you specifically ask your bank to do this. You should also ask which ATMs abroad accept your particular card.

Charge cards like American Express and Diners Club don't have credit limits but may not be accepted in small establishments or off the beaten track. Credit cards like Visa, MasterCard or Access are more widely accepted, though many B&Bs and some smaller or remote petrol stations only take cash.

International Transfers

You can instruct your bank back home to send you a draft. Specify the city, bank and branch to which you want your money directed, or ask your home bank to tell you where a suitable one is, and make sure you get the details right. The procedure is easier if you've authorised someone back home to access your account.

Money sent by telegraphic transfer should reach you within a week; by mail allow at least two weeks. When it arrives it will most likely be converted into local currency – you can take it as it is or buy traveller's cheques.

You can also transfer money by American Express or Thomas Cook.

Currency

In Ireland the Irish pound or punt (IR£) is used, and like the British pound sterling it's divided into 100 pence (p). Irish banknotes come in denominations of IR£100, IR£50, IR£20, IR£10 and IR£5. Coins come in the form of IR£1, 50p, 20p, 10p, 5p, 2p and 1p.

The British pound sterling (£) is used in Northern Ireland and comes in the same banknote and coin denominations as the Irish punt. Don't confuse Northern Irish pounds (issued by the First Trust Bank, Ulster Bank, Northern Bank and Bank of England) with Republic of Ireland pounds (issued by the

Central Bank of Ireland). 'Sterling' or 'Belfast' are giveaway words on the Northern Irish notes. The Northern Irish pound sterling is worth the same as the British variety. Northern Irish notes are not readily accepted in Britain, but British banks will swap them for normal sterling notes.

The Republic's currency is not legal tender in the North and vice versa, though some businesses may accept the other country's notes at a one-for-one exchange.

Currency Exchange

The Irish punt (IR£1) is worth about 95 UK pence.

Australia	A$1	= IR£0.47	= £0.45
Canada	C$1	= IR£0.56	= £0.45
France	10 FF	= IR£1.30	= £1.15
Germany	DM1	= IR£0.50	= £0.40
Japan	¥100	= IR£0.65	= £0.55
New Zealand	NZ$1	= IR£0.40	= £0.41
South Africa	SAR1	= IR£0.15	= £0.14
USA	US$1	= IR£0.72	= £0.64

Changing Money

The best exchange rates are obtained at banks. In the Republic they normally open from 10 am to 3 pm, though most also stay open till 5 pm at least one day a week, usually a Thursday or a Friday. In Dublin they stay open until 5 pm on Thursday. In Northern Ireland banks open weekdays 9.30 am to 4.30 pm and most stay open until 5 pm on Thursday. In rural areas some banks close for lunch from 12.30 to 1.30 pm and some may only open two or three days a week, so it's best to change money in larger towns. Most banks remain open at lunch time in larger urban centres. In the North the Halifax Bank opens Saturday 9 am to noon.

Bureaux de change and other exchange facilities usually open longer hours than banks, but the rate and/or commission will be worse. Building societies often handle foreign exchange and are open longer hours than the banks. Many post offices in both the Republic and Northern Ireland have a currency-exchange facility and have the advantage of opening on Saturday morning.

If you've not obtained some currency in advance there are unofficial moneychangers near the border between the North and South, often at petrol stations.

Tipping

Fancy hotels and restaurants usually add a 10% or 15% service charge and no additional tip is required. Simpler places usually don't add a service charge; if you decide to tip, just round up the bill or add at most 10%. For taxi drivers a tip of 10% is fine, while porters should get 50p per bag. Tipping in bars isn't expected, but the distinction between pubs and restaurants is blurred by bars becoming more like restaurants at meal times.

Taxes & Refunds

Value-added tax (VAT) is a sales tax that applies to most goods and services in Ireland, excluding books and children's clothing or footwear. Residents of the EU are not entitled to VAT refund. On large purchases which they subsequently export outside the EU, other visitors can claim back the VAT (minus an administration fee).

If you buy something from a store displaying the sign 'Tax Free for Tourists' you'll be given a Europe Tax Free Shopping (ETS) cheque which can be cashed at Dublin or Shannon airports. If the value of the refund is IR£200 or more you'll first need to go to customs in the arrivals hall to have the cheque stamped, before cashing it at the ETS desk. If you're leaving Ireland from elsewhere the cheques can be stamped at customs and mailed back for a refund.

In Northern Ireland, shops participating in the refund scheme will give you a form/invoice on request. This must be presented with the goods and receipts to customs when you leave. After customs have certified the form, it should be returned to the shop for a refund.

POST & COMMUNICATIONS
Post

Post offices in the South open weekdays 8.30 am (9.30 am on Wednesday) to 5.30 pm, Saturday 9 am to noon; smaller offices close for lunch. Postcards cost 28p to EU countries, 38p outside Europe. Airmail letters cost 32p to EU countries, 52p outside Europe. All mail to Britain goes by air so there is no need to use airmail envelopes or stickers.

Post office hours in the North are weekdays 9 am to 5.30 pm, Saturday 9 am to 1 pm. Postal rates are as in Britain – 26p for letters by 1st-class mail, 20p 2nd-class, 26p to EU countries, and 43p for letters and postcards to the Americas and Australasia.

Mail to both the North and the Republic can be addressed to poste restante at post offices but is officially only held for two weeks. Writing 'hold for collection' on the envelope may have some effect.

Over 95% of letters within the country are delivered the next working day. To North America it's about 10 days, Britain and the rest of Europe three to five days and Australia a week to 10 days.

Telephone

Telecom Éireann, the Republic's state-owned telecommunications company, has one of the most up-to-date digital telephone systems in the world. In the North most public phones are owned by the privately run British Telecom (BT), but other companies compete for its business.

Phonecards (Callcards in the South), which save fishing for coins and give you a small discount, are worth having. International calls can be dialled directly from pay phones.

Phone calls between the Republic and the North are classified as international calls.

Calls from Ireland To call a UK number (except for Northern Ireland) from the South dial 0044 plus the area code (minus the 0) plus the number. Thus an 0171 number in London would start 0044-171. To call elsewhere overseas dial 00 then the international code for that country (1 for the USA or Canada, 61 for Australia, 64 for New Zealand, 65 for Singapore etc) then the area code (dropping any leading 0) and then the number. The one variation is that to call Northern Ireland from the South you dial 08 and then the Northern Irish area code *without* dropping the leading 0.

For enquiries about calls to Northern Ireland dial 1190, to Britain dial 1197, to elsewhere dial 1198. For operator-assisted calls dial 10; for international reverse-charge (collect) calls dial 114.

Calls from Northern Ireland From Northern Ireland dial 00 for international access followed by the country code. The country code for the Republic is 353. Dial 155 for the BT international operator, or 153 for international directory assistance.

Call Costs In the South the standard rate for a three-minute local call is 11.5p. When making a long-distance phone call from a hotel room bear in mind that the cost will be at least doubled.

The cost of a direct-dial international call from Ireland varies according to the time of day. Reduced rates are available after 6 pm and before 8 am; between midnight and 8 am and between 2 and 8 pm to Australia and New Zealand. Standard charges for one minute are:

Australia	88p
France	39p
Germany	48p
North America	48p
New Zealand	88p
UK	29p

Direct Home Calls Rather than placing reverse charge (collect) calls through the operator in Ireland you can dial direct to your home country operator and then reverse charges or charge the call to a local phone credit card. To use the direct home service, dial the following codes followed by the area code and number you want. Your home country operator will then come on the line before the call goes through:

Australia	1800 5500 61 + number
France	1800 5500 33 + number
New Zealand	1800 5500 64 + number
UK – BT	1800 5500 44 + number
UK – Mercury	1800 5500 04 + number

USA – AT&T	1800 5500 00 + number
USA – MCI	1800 5510 01 + number
USA – Sprint	1800 5520 01 + number

Pay Phones & Phonecards Local calls from pay phones cost 20p per three-minute unit; STD calls cost IR£1.30 for the first three minutes. You can make local calls from street phone booths and from public phones in hotels, shops, pubs etc.

Callcards are available in 10 (IR£2), 20 (IR£3.50), 50 (IR£8) and 100 (IR£16) unit versions in the Republic. Each unit gives you one local phone call. BT phonecards cost £2 to £20. Card-operated phones are useful for making international calls since you don't have to carry a sack of coins to the phone booth. Bear in mind that you can't make operator-assisted international calls from a card-operated phone.

Fax, Telegraph & Email

Faxes can be sent from post offices or other specialist offices. Most hotels now have faxes. Phone the operator on ☎ 196 in the South to send international telegrams; in the North call BT on ☎ 0800 190 190.

If you want to send or receive email, there are service providers which can allow you access to your existing POP email account and to other Internet services. A few of the current major players are:

Connect Ireland
☎ 01-670 6701; www.connect.ie
EuNet Ireland
☎ 01-679 0832; www.eunet.ie
Ireland On Line
☎ 01-855 1739; www.iol.ie
Telecom Internet
☎ 1850 203204; www.tinet.ie

If you don't have your own hardware you can log on at some public libraries, or at one of the growing number of cybercafés for around IR£5 per hour.

BOOKS

A glance in almost any bookshop in Ireland will reveal huge Irish-interest sections: fiction, history, current events, and other numerous local and regional guidebooks. Many larger cities have more than one good bookshop, Waterstone's and Eason's being familiar names, and many small towns will also have a small but well-stocked bookshop. Most, if not all, of the books below should be available in bookshops and libraries across Ireland. They're all paperback unless stated otherwise.

Lonely Planet

The information in Lonely Planet's *Dublin city guide* is an expansion of information in this guidebook, but if you're reading this in a bookshop and plan to visit only Dublin (and/or its environs), check it out. If you're going to be spending time in Britain, then take a look at Lonely Planet's *Britain – a travel survival kit* or *London city guide*. *Walking in Britain* outlines Britain's national trails, long-distance footpaths and other interesting walking possibilities.

Guidebooks

Insight Guides' *Ireland* is a collection of essays and photographs which offer a preview of what you'll encounter, as well as a reasonable introduction to history and culture. Blue Guide's *Ireland* has detailed, scholarly information on history, art and architecture, including good maps.

Ireland, and Dublin in particular, have produced so many writers that you could easily plan a literary holiday or just a Dublin literary holiday. The *Oxford Literary Guide to Great Britain and Ireland* details the writers who have immortalised various towns and villages. *A Literary Guide to Dublin* (1995) by Vivien Igoe includes detailed route maps, a guide to cemeteries and an eight-page section on literary and historical pubs.

James Joyce is, of course, the most Dublin-oriented of Irish writers, and serious Joyce groupies can make their own Bloomsday tour of the city with a number of books which follow the wanderings of *Ulysses*'s characters in minute detail. *Joyce's Dublin – A Walking Guide to Ulysses* (1988) by Jack McCarthy traces the events chapter by chapter with very clear maps. *The Ulysses Guide – Tours through Joyce's Dublin* (1988) by Robert Nicholson concentrates on certain areas and follows the events of the various related chapters. Again there are clear and easy-to-follow maps.

The *Irish Pub Guide* lists and describes a number of pubs across Ireland that are of particular interest. *The Hidden Gardens of Ireland* (1994) by Mariane Heron is an informative guide to its more sober subject.

See the Activities chapter for details of cycling and walking guidebooks and books on tracing your ancestors.

For specialist books on accommodation and food see those sections later in this chapter.

Visitors' & Residents' Accounts

To understand the Anglo-Irish, read *Woodbrook* (1994) by David Thomson, who, when a young man, went to the north-west as tutor to an Anglo-Irish family. The book maps his gradual awakening to the reality around him.

For cycling visitors, Eric Newby's *Round Ireland in Low Gear* is a Newby classic of travel masochism complete with lousy weather, steep hills, high winds and predatory trucks.

The nature of life in the North has attracted writers to the region and compelled residents to write about it. *Titanic Town* (1992) is subtitled *Memoirs of a Belfast Girlhood*, and Mary Costello manages to make growing up in the tough Andersonstown area of West Belfast funny and sad in equal measures. From Sinn Féin president Gerry Adams, *The Street* (1992) is a collection of stories dealing with life in West Belfast where he grew up.

The Crack – A Belfast Year (1987) by Sally Belfrage, is a reporter's accounts from a series of visits to Belfast in the 1980s.

In the mid-1970s Irish travel writer Dervla Murphy jumped on her faithful bicycle Roz, the same one she had taken to India in the 1960s, and rode off to explore Northern Ireland. The result was *A Place Apart* (1978). It's a highly readable book and so makes an accessible introduction to things such as

Orangeism, Paisleyism, the problems in South Armagh etc.

US travel writer Paul Theroux included Northern Ireland on his UK itinerary for *Kingdom by the Sea* (1983). Travelling round most of Britain made the famously sour Theroux even more dyspeptic than usual, but he warmed towards the Ulster people. PJ O'Rourke gave Belfast a chapter in his book *Holidays in Hell* (1988), but, like many other visitors, he found Belfast altogether too tame for its reputation. Where are the appalling slums?

History & Politics

The three volumes that make up *The Green Flag* (1989) by Robert Kee offer a useful introduction although the emphasis is more on narrative than analysis. The focus of interest in Kee's books is the 19th and 20th centuries. For an introduction to earlier times try *The Course of Irish History* (1987) by Moody & Martin which has been reprinted many times.

A Concise History of Ireland (revised 1985) by Máire & Conor Cruise O'Brien is a readable and comprehensively illustrated short history of Ireland. *Ireland – A History* (updated 1995) by Robert Kee covers similar ground in a similar format in a book developed from a BBC/RTE TV series.

The classic study of the 1845-51 Famine when some two million Irish either emigrated overseas or perished through lack of food is *The Great Hunger* (1985) by Cecil Woodham Smith. Liam O'Flaherty used the catastrophe as the basis for his novel *Famine* (1988). A more recent novel on the Famine is *The Hanging Gale* based on the BBC Northern Ireland/RTE TV series.

There is a range of books on Michael Collins including *Michael Collins – The Man who Won the War*, by T Ryle Dwyer, *Michael Collins – the path to freedom*, and *The Troubles* by Ulick O'Connor about Michael Collins and the volunteers struggle for independence 1912-22.

The Begrudger's Guide to Irish Politics (1986) by Breandán O'hEithir is a semi-humorous account of the 1980s political

scene. He has also written *A Pocket History of Ireland* (1989), which gives a concise account of Irish history.

Ireland: Anatomy of a Changing State (1995) by Gemma Hussey is a useful, though perhaps too uncontroversial, guide to various social and political issues that bedevil the country. *The Long War* (1995) traces the evolution of Sinn Féin and the IRA up to the period before the first IRA (1994) ceasefire.

Since the mid-1990s commentators have been talking of a post-Catholic Ireland. Given the crowds outside many churches on Sunday it's probably too early to read the last rites over Catholicism. However, journalist Mary Kenny's *Farewell to Catholic Ireland* (1997) traces how attitudes have changed during the 20th century. It highlights the shock felt by many ordinary people as one clergy scandal followed another in the 1990s.

Stephen Conlin's *Dublin – One Thousand Years* (1988) is an evocative collection of watercolour views recreating Dublin over the centuries.

If you're heading for the Skelligs, try reading Geoffrey Moorhouse's *Sun Dancing* (1997). It's a two-part book which attempts an imaginative recreation of medieval monastic life over the centuries, then provides the back-up evidence in a sequence of short essays on everything from Brendan the Navigator to Skellig birdlife.

The North The problem with books about Northern Ireland's recent confused history is that they're in constant need of updating and it's difficult to find a truly impartial account of what has been happening.

A serious and far-reaching attempt to get to grips with Ulster's story is *A History of Ulster* (1992) by Jonathan Bardon. It's a thorough but readable account stretching from prehistoric Ulster up to the early 1990s.

German academic Sabine Wichert, a Belfast resident since the early 1970s, managed to bring an outsider's inside view to the question in *Northern Ireland Since 1945* (1991). Patrick Buckland's *A History of Northern Ireland* (1981) is concise but somewhat out of date. *The Troubles* (1980), edited by Taylor Downing, was written to accompany a TV series on the conflict but also suffers from being dated. J Bowyer-Bell's *The Troubles – A Generation of Violence* (1993) is a more recent account. Gerry Adams, the president of Sinn Féin, gives his version of the Troubles in *The Politics of Irish Freedom* (1986) and more recently in *Free Ireland: Towards a Lasting Peace* (1995), which came out after the first ceasefire.

The Dispossessed (1992) investigates the background and reality of poverty in Britain through the 1980s. Writer Robert Wilson and photographer Donovan Wylie are both Belfast-born and the book concentrates on the story in London, Glasgow and Belfast.

Paisley (1986) by Ed Moloney & Andy Pollack is a compelling account by two Irish journalists of the rise to power of the charismatic leader of the Democratic Unionist Party (not the Unionist Party) and the Free Presbyterian Church of Ulster (not the Presbyterian Church). If nothing else read the introduction with its astonishing Paisley speech. *Despatches from Belfast* (1989), by David McKittrick the Irish correspondent for the UK newspaper the *Independent*, covers 1985-89 with well-informed articles from a liberal point of view.

Two books that get inside the minds of paramilitaries on both sides and try to explain what motivates them are *25 Years of Terror* (1995), by Martin Dillon, and *We Wrecked the Place* (1996), by Jonathan Stevenson.

Eyewitness Bloody Sunday (1997) edited by Don Mullan contains harrowing accounts by ordinary people caught up in the violent events of 30 January 1972 in Derry/Londonderry.

General

Culture Shock! Ireland (1996) by Patricia Levy is recommended as an up-to-date introduction to aspects of Irish culture and will help the visitor understand the country and its people. A good reference book, with lots of information on many different aspects of Irish life is the *Irish Almanac & Yearbook of Facts*.

May the Lord in his Mercy be kind to Belfast (1996) by Tony Parker is a collection of interviews with Belfast people expressing their point of view about life in the troubled city.

ONLINE SERVICES

The World Wide Web is a major source of information, although sites vary widely in accuracy and reliability and things on the Internet change rapidly. Nevertheless, there's a range of sites which provide useful information on Ireland. Bord Fáilte and the NITB have their own web sites (see Tourist Offices earlier); some others are:

Lonely Planet
> Lonely Planet's site on travel in Ireland is definitely worth a look. Well, we would say that, wouldn't we?
> www.lonelyplanet.com.au/dest/eur/ire.htm

Aer Lingus
> The Irish airline's site gives details of services, flight schedules, special offers and links to other related sites
> www.aerlingus.ie

Best of Ireland
> This site provides detailed descriptions of various destinations in the country.
> internet-ireland.ie/boi

Hedonist's Guide to Dublin
> Aimed at young people this is a fun look at pubs, clubs, cafés, shopping and what's on in the capital
> shaw.iol.ie/smytho/dublin

Ireland Online
> This site has information on sights, transport, accommodation, visas, events etc
> www.iol.ie/discover

World Wide Web Virtual Library: Ireland
> There's lots of information here on government, arts, media, education, business recreation, travel etc
> www.itw.ie/wwwlib.html

NEWSPAPERS & MAGAZINES

The daily *Irish Times* is a bastion of liberal opinion and good journalism and is often mentioned as being up there with the world's best newspapers. The biggest seller is the *Irish Independent* which tends to be lighter in content, with more features and gossip. Both also have Sunday versions. *The Examiner*, published in Cork, has a good journalistic reputation and *The Star* is the country's daily tabloid. The two main evening papers are the *Evening Herald*, published in Dublin, and Cork's *Evening Echo*. There are also sanitised Irish versions of the British daily tabloids.

The *Sunday Tribune* has a liberal approach and claims to be good at investigating and breaking stories. One of the biggest sellers on Sunday is the *Sunday World* with plenty of titillation. The *Sunday Business Post* concentrates on financial matters.

In the North you'll find the evening *Belfast Telegraph* and the tabloid and staunchly Protestant *News Letter*. The *Irish News* is a pro-Nationalist daily newspaper, while *An Phoblacht* (Republican News) is published weekly by Sinn Féin.

Ireland has a growing number of magazines that cater for almost any interest, but the most popular is the *RTE Guide*, the weekly radio and TV guide.

British papers and magazines are readily available in both the North and the South. They sell at a slightly higher price in the South than in the North but still undercut the Irish ones. The main European and US newspapers and magazines, including *Time* and *Newsweek*, are sold in the larger newsagents in Dublin, Belfast and Cork.

RADIO & TV

The Republic has two state-controlled TV channels and three radio stations. Irish radio, AM or FM, varies in quality. Many of the morning programmes consist of phone-ins. RTE Radio One (88-90 FM or 567/729 MW) has a good mix of documentaries, music and talk shows. Broadcasters like Gay Byrne, Pat Kenny and Marion Finucane give an insight into the country's foibles. RTE's 2FM (92-93 FM or 612/1278 MW) is the national pop music station and does what pop stations do. Mind you, it's a good forum for upcoming Irish rock talent and is where U2 got their first airing. The *Gerry Ryan Show* in the morning is worth listening to. Radió na

Gaeltachta (92.5-96 FM or 540/828/963 MW) is the national Irish-language service.

There is a host of regional radio stations, offering good local services. The best of them are LM FM in counties Louth and Meath broadcasting on 95.8 FM, Radio Kerry on 97.6 FM and Clare FM on 96.4 FM. In Dublin 98 FM and FM 104 stations offer an unending diet of classic international rock and pop tunes. It's possible to tune into British BBC radio and independent channels, though the further west you go the weaker the signal.

The state-controlled TV channels are RTE 1 and 2, and the Irish language Telefis na Ghaelige. British BBC and independent TV programmes can be picked up in many parts of the country and offer a welcome substitute for the sometimes dreary Irish programming. In its defence, RTE isn't that bad by international standards. It may appear parochial but local topics are always of limited interest to outsiders.

A programme worth watching is *The Late Late Show*, the longest-running chat show in the world, hosted by Gay Byrne, Ireland's top media personality. The show has a good mix of celebrities and current affairs, and is often an interesting window into Irish life. Current affairs programmes such as *Tuesday File* and *Prime Time* are also worth a look. Watch out for Gaelic football and hurling matches broadcast on weekends. Many hotels and pubs have satellite TV from the European Astra satellite.

In Northern Ireland, there are two TV stations – BBC NI and Ulster TV, which mix their own programming with input from their parent companies in the UK – BBC and ITV respectively. Channel 4 and Channel 5 also broadcast in Northern Ireland.

VIDEO SYSTEMS

Overseas visitors thinking of purchasing videos as souvenirs should remember that Ireland, like Britain and much of Europe, uses the Phase Alternative Line (PAL) system which isn't compatible with other standards unless converted.

PHOTOGRAPHY & VIDEO
Photography

Ireland has enough spectacular seascapes, ancient ruins, picturesque villages and interesting faces to keep any photographer happy. But almost always it's the mood that makes the shot and Ireland is noted for its rapidly changing and unusual light. In bright sunlight, west coast beaches can look like the tropics, and then a couple of hours and a few clouds later, Arctic Norway. Try and be imaginative with monuments and Celtic crosses, get the sun behind or at the side of your subject, use fill flash, get low with a wide-angle lens and put some plants or other points of interest in the foreground.

The best times for pictures are early morning and late evening when the sunlight is low and warm. If you are keen and using slide film, the slower the film the better, eg Fuji Velvia 50 ASA or Ektachrome 64 or 100 ASA. However, Irish light can be very dull, so to capture the sombre atmosphere you may need faster film, eg 200 or 400 ASA, and a small tripod will be useful. In good weather a polariser is terrific for cutting out haze and giving punchy primary-green fields and blue skies with cotton-puff clouds. A plastic bag is handy to stop your camera getting wet.

In the North, if you want to take photos of fortified police stations or army posts and other military or quasi-military paraphernalia, ask first to be on the safe side.

Some tourist attractions either charge for taking photos or prohibit it altogether. Use of flash is often forbidden to protect delicate pictures and fabrics. Video cameras are often disallowed because of the inconvenience they can cause other visitors.

Film & Processing

There are plenty of camera shops in the cities and bigger towns, but in smaller towns and villages it's the chemists or pharmacies that stock film and arrange for processing. They'll usually have Fuji or Kodak print film. Slide film is usually Fujichrome or Ektachrome, but don't depend on them having any in stock. Kodachrome is scarce and has to be sent to France for processing. Chemists and many of the smaller camera shops are expensive so stock up beforehand.

In Dublin you can buy reasonably priced film at LSL Photolabs (☎ 01-478 1078) at 25 Lennox St, Dublin 8, or at Quirke Lynch (☎ 01-496 4666), 41 Lower Rathmines Rd, Dublin 6. Most towns and cities have good quality one-hour processing shops. Developing and printing a 24-exposure print film typically costs IR£4 to IR£5 for one-hour service. Slide processing costs about IR£6 a roll and takes a few days, though the Film Bank (☎ 01-660 6082), 102 Lower Baggot St, Dublin 2, has a same-day service for about IR£9.

Photographing People

You can't generalise about how Irish people will react to having their photographs taken. As always, being courteous and having a chat beforehand will make things a lot easier for the photographer.

Airport Security

You'll have to put your camera and film through the X-ray machine at all airports. The machines are supposed to be film-safe, but you may feel happier if you put exposed films in a lead-lined bag to protect them.

TIME

Ireland is on Greenwich Mean Time (GMT), otherwise referred to as Universal Time Coordinated (UTC), the same as Britain. Without making allowances for daylight-saving time changes, when it's noon in Dublin or London it's 8 pm in Singapore, 10 pm in Sydney or Melbourne, 7 am in New York and 3 am in Los Angeles or Vancouver.

As in Britain, clocks are advanced by one hour from mid-March to the end of October. During the summer it stays light until late at night, particularly on the west coast where in June you could still just about read by natural light at 11 pm. In the middle of November it's dark from 5 pm to 8 am.

ELECTRICITY

Electricity is 220V, 50 cycles AC, and plugs

are usually flat three-pin, as in Britain. Some older buildings may still have the older round-pin plugs, but adapters are available from electrical stores. Apart from shavers, if you have a round two-pin plug bring with you a plastic converter that plugs into the three-pin plug. Many bathrooms have a two-pin 110V to 120V AC source for shavers which is useful if you have any 110V gadgets.

WEIGHTS & MEASURES

As in Britain, progress towards metrication in Ireland is slow and piecemeal. On road signs distances are measured in miles and km; food in shops is priced and weighed in metric; petrol is sold in litres but beer in pubs is served in pints. To help you out of your confusion there's a conversion table at the back of this book.

LAUNDRY

Most hostels and some cheaper hotels have self-service laundry facilities, while the more expensive hotels will return your clothes washed, dried and neatly folded. Otherwise there are self-service laundrettes or dry-cleaning places, many of which open daily. Washing a load costs about IR£2.50 and drying it another IR£1 or so. Laundrettes sometimes have attendants who wash, dry and fold your clothes for around IR£4.50.

HEALTH

Apart from cholesterol, Ireland poses no serious threats to health. The Catholic distaste for contraception doesn't prevent condoms being sold through pharmacies, if the pharmacist isn't personally opposed! Condoms are also available from vending machines in some pubs and nightclubs. The pill is available only on prescription.

Citizens of EU countries are eligible for medical care; other visitors should have medical insurance or be prepared to pay. There are various regional health boards whose services are listed at the front of the white pages phone book.

Predeparture Preparations

Health Insurance A travel insurance policy to cover theft, loss and medical problems is a wise idea. See Travel Insurance earlier under Documents for details of the types of cover available, and always read the fine print.

Medical Kit A small, straightforward medical kit is a wise thing to carry. A kit should include:

- Aspirin or paracetamol (acetaminophen in the US) – for pain or fever.
- Antihistamine (such as Benadryl) – useful as a decongestant for colds and allergies, to ease the itch from insect bites or stings, and to help prevent motion sickness. Antihistamines may cause sedation and interact with alcohol so care should be taken when using them.
- Loperamide (eg Imodium) or Lomotil for diarrhoea; prochlorperazine (eg Stemetil) or metaclopramide (eg Maxalon) for nausea and vomiting. Antidiarrhoea medication shouldn't be given to children under the age of 12.
- Antiseptic such as Betadine, which comes as impregnated swabs or ointment, and an antibiotic powder or similar 'dry' spray – for cuts and grazes.
- Bandages and Band-aids – for minor injuries.
- Scissors, tweezers and a thermometer (note that mercury thermometers are prohibited by airlines).
- Sun block, chapstick

Health Preparations If you wear glasses, take a spare pair and your prescription. Losing your glasses can be a real problem, although in many places you can get new spectacles made up quickly, cheaply and competently. If you require a particular medication or a specific oral contraceptive take note of the generic name rather than the brand name as it may not be available locally. It's wise to have a legible prescription or a letter from your doctor to show that you legally use the medication.

Immunisations These aren't necessary for Ireland unless you're stopping over on the way and arrive from an infected area. If you're going to Europe with stopovers in Asia, Africa or Latin America, check with your travel agent and doctor. Don't leave it till the last minute, as the vaccinations may have to be spread out a bit.

Vaccinations should be recorded on an International Health Certificate, which is available from your physician or government health department.

Basic Rules
Care in what you eat and drink and maintenance of personal hygiene are the most important health rules, wherever you travel.

Water Tap water is normally safe but don't drink straight from a stream: you can never be certain there are no people or animals upstream. It has been reported that there is some water pollution in remote rural areas of County Mayo in the north-west.

Water Purification The simplest way of purifying water is to boil it thoroughly. Vigorously boiling for five minutes should be satisfactory; however, at high altitude water boils at a lower temperature, so germs are less likely to be killed.

Filtering won't remove all dangerous organisms, so if you can't boil water it should be treated chemically. Chlorine tablets (Puritabs, Steritabs or other brand names) will kill many but not all pathogens. Iodine is very effective in purifying water and is available in tablet form (such as Potable Aqua). If you can't find tablets, tincture of iodine (2%) or iodine crystals can be used. Four drops of tincture of iodine per litre or quart of clear water is the recommended dosage; the treated water should be left to stand for 20 to 30 minutes before drinking.

Everyday Health Normal body temperature is 98.6°F or 37°C; more than 2°C higher indicates a 'high' fever. The normal adult pulse rate is 60 to 80 per minute (children 80 to 100, babies 100 to 140). You should know how to take a temperature and a pulse rate. As a general rule the pulse increases about 20 beats per minute for each °C rise in fever.

The breathing rate is also an indicator of illness. People with a high fever or serious respiratory illness breathe more quickly than normal. Count the number of breaths per minute: between 12 and 20 is normal for adults and older children (up to 30 for younger children, 40 for babies).

Many health problems can be avoided by just taking care of yourself. Wash your hands frequently.

Medical Problems & Treatment
Sunburn Even in Ireland, and even through cloud cover it's possible to get sunburnt surprisingly quickly – especially if you're on water, snow or ice. Use a 15+ sunscreen, wear a hat and cover up with a long-sleeved shirt and trousers.

Heat Exhaustion Dehydration or salt deficiency can cause heat exhaustion. In hot conditions (they do happen!) and if you're exerting yourself make sure you get sufficient nonalcoholic liquids. Salt deficiency is characterised by fatigue, lethargy, headaches, giddiness and muscle cramps. Vomiting or diarrhoea can deplete your liquid and salt levels.

Fungal Infections To prevent fungal infections wear loose, comfortable clothes, avoid artificial fibres, wash frequently and dry carefully. Always wear thongs (flip-flops) in shared bathrooms. If you do get an infection, consult a chemist. Try to expose the infected area to air or sunlight as much as possible and wash all towels and underwear in hot water as well as changing them often.

Cold Hypothermia occurs when the body loses heat faster than it can produce it and the core temperature of the body falls. It's easy to progress from very cold to dangerously cold due to a combination of wind, wet clothing, fatigue and hunger, even if the air temperature is above freezing.

Walkers in Ireland should always be prepared for difficult conditions. It's best to dress in layers and a hat is important, as a lot of heat is lost through the head. A strong, waterproof outer layer is essential. Carry basic supplies, including food containing simple sugars to generate heat quickly.

Symptoms of hypothermia are exhaustion, numb skin (particularly toes and fingers), shivering, slurred speech, irrational or violent behaviour, lethargy, stumbling, dizzy spells, muscle cramps and violent bursts of energy.

To treat mild hypothermia, first get the person out of the wind and/or rain, remove their clothing if it's wet and replace it with dry, warm clothing. Give them hot liquids – not alcohol – and some high-calorie, easily digestible food. This should be enough to treat the early stages of hypothermia, but if it has gone further, it may be necessary to place victims in warm sleeping bags and get in with them. Don't rub patients, place them near a fire or remove their wet clothes in the wind. If possible, place a sufferer in a warm (not hot) bath.

Motion Sickness Eating lightly before and during a trip reduces the chances of motion sickness. If you're prone to motion sickness, try to find a place that minimises disturbance, for example, near the wing on aircraft, near the centre on buses. Fresh air usually helps, while reading or cigarette smoke doesn't. Commercial motion sickness preparations, which can cause drowsiness, have to be taken before the trip begins; when you're feeling sick it's usually too late. Ginger (available in capsule form) and peppermint (including mint-flavoured sweets) are natural preventatives.

Jet Lag Jet lag is experienced when a person travels by air across more than three time zones (each time zone usually represents a one hour time difference). It occurs because many functions of the human body (such as temperature, pulse rate and emptying of the bladder and bowels) are regulated by internal 24-hour cycles called circadian rhythms. When we travel long distances rapidly, our bodies take time to adjust to the 'new time' of our destination, and we may experience fatigue, disorientation, insomnia, anxiety, impaired concentration and loss of appetite. These effects are usually gone within three

days of arrival, but there are ways of minimising the impact of jet lag:

- Rest for a couple of days prior to departure; try to avoid late nights and last-minute dashes for travellers' cheques, passport etc.
- Try to select flight schedules that minimise sleep deprivation; arriving late in the day means you can sleep soon after you arrive. For long flights, try to organise a stopover.
- Avoid excessive eating (which bloats the stomach) and alcohol (which causes dehydration) during the flight. Instead, drink plenty of noncarbonated, nonalcoholic drinks such as fruit juice or water.
- Avoid smoking (even if the airline permits it), as this reduces the amount of oxygen in the aeroplane cabin even further and causes greater fatigue.
- Make yourself comfortable by wearing loose-fitting clothes and perhaps bringing an eye mask and ear plugs to help you sleep.

Sexually Transmitted Diseases (STDs)

Sexual contact with an infected sexual partner spreads these diseases. While abstinence is the only 100% preventative, using condoms is also effective. Gonorrhoea and syphilis are the most common of these diseases; sores, blisters or rashes around the genitals, discharges or pain when urinating are common symptoms. Symptoms may be less marked or not observed at all in women. Syphilis symptoms eventually disappear completely, but the disease continues and can cause severe problems in later years. The treatment of gonorrhoea and syphilis is by antibiotics.

There are numerous other sexually transmitted diseases, for most of which effective treatment is available. However, there is no cure for herpes and there is also currently no cure for AIDS.

HIV/AIDS The Human Immunodeficiency Virus (HIV), may develop into Acquired Immune Deficiency Syndrome (AIDS). Exposure to blood, blood products or bodily fluids may put the individual at risk. In countries like Ireland transmission is mostly through contact between homosexual or bisexual males, or via contaminated needles shared by IV drug users. Apart from abstinence, the most effective preventative is always to practise safe sex using condoms. It's impossible to detect the HIV-positive status of an otherwise healthy-looking person without a blood test.

HIV/AIDS can also be spread through infected blood transfusions, but in Ireland these are safe. It can also be spread by dirty needles – vaccinations, acupuncture, tattooing and ear or nose piercing can potentially be as dangerous as intravenous drug use if the equipment isn't clean. In Ireland, although there may be a risk of infection, it's very small. Fear of HIV infection should never preclude treatment for serious medical conditions.

TOILETS

Many Irish restaurants and bars display notices asserting that toilets are reserved for customers only. Given this fact and the money Ireland makes from visitors it wouldn't seem unreasonable to expect that decent facilities would be available elsewhere. Instead, public toilets are often fairly sordid. Even places like Kinsale, Blessington and Enniskerry with a large throughput of visitors seem to regard keeping their facilities clean as a low priority.

Most toilets have signs indicating gender in English and Irish, but some may only have a sign in Irish. To avoid any confused embarrassment (and any unwanted delay) be warned that the Irish word *mná* which looks a lot like the English word 'man' does in fact mean 'women'; the Gaelic word for men is *fir*. The Irish word for toilet is *leithreas*.

WOMEN TRAVELLERS

Women travellers will find Ireland a blissfully relaxing experience, with little risk of hassle on the street or anywhere else. Nonetheless, you still need to take elementary safety precautions. Walking alone at night, especially in certain parts of Dublin, is probably unwise. Since a young woman disappeared while hitchhiking in County Kildare this means of getting around the country has looked less wise, even though hitching in Ireland is probably still safer than

hitching pretty well anywhere else in Europe.

One or two hostel owners let the side down when it comes to bothering female guests. Keep your ears pinned to the ground and heed any warnings that come your way. Should you have any problems, be sure to report them to the local tourist authorities ... and to us!

There's little need to worry about what you wear in Ireland, and the climate is hardly conducive to controversial topless sunbathing. Nor is finding contraception the problem it once was, although anyone on the pill should bring adequate supplies with them.

GAY & LESBIAN TRAVELLERS

Despite the 1993 decriminalisation of homosexuality for those over the age of 17 in the Republic (1982 in Northern Ireland), gay life is generally not acknowledged or understood in most parts of conservative Ireland. Only Dublin and to a certain extent Belfast and Cork have openly gay communities. The *Gay Community News*, a free tabloid published monthly in Dublin, is the only publication with Ireland-wide information on gay and lesbian services, organisations and entertainment. In Dublin it's available from the *Gay Community News* office at 10 Fownes St, from Condompower at 57 Dame St, and from bars and cafés. Information is also available from the following:

National Lesbian & Gay Federation (NLGF)
    Hirschfield Centre, 10 Fownes St, Dublin 2
    (☎ 01-671 0939)
Northern Ireland Gay Rights Association (NIGRA)
    Cathedral Buildings, Lower Donegall St, Belfast
    (☎ 01232-664 111)

The following helplines can be called from anywhere in Ireland:

Gay Switchboard Dublin
    ☎ 01-872 1055 (Sunday to Friday 8 to 10 pm;
    Saturday 3.30 to 6 pm)
Lesbian Line Dublin
    ☎ 01-872 9911 (daily 7 to 9 pm)

Cara-Friend Belfast
☎ 01232-322 023 (Monday to Wednesday 7.30 to 10 pm)
Lesbian Line Belfast
☎ 01232-238 668 (Thursday 7.30 to 10 pm)

DISABLED TRAVELLERS

If you have a physical disability, get in touch with your national support organisation (preferably the travel officer if there is one) and ask about the countries you plan to visit. They often have complete libraries devoted to travel, and can put you in touch with travel agents who specialise in tours for the disabled.

Guesthouses, hotels and sights in Ireland are gradually being adapted for people with disabilities though there is still a long way to go. Bord Fáilte's annual *Accommodation Guide* indicates which places are wheelchair accessible. The NITB publishes *Accessible Accommodation in Northern Ireland*. Your travel agent may have access to the most recent details (see Gulliver under Tourist Offices earlier) about facilities available for disabled people. Alternatively, you can obtain information on individual counties in the Republic by contacting the National Rehabilitation Board (☎ 01-874 7503), 44 North Great George's St, Dublin 1. In Northern Ireland contact Disability Action (☎ 01232-491011), 2 Annadale Ave, Belfast BT7 3JH.

SENIOR TRAVELLERS

Senior citizens are entitled to many discounts in Europe on things like public transport, museum admission fees etc, provided they show proof of their age. In some cases they might need a special pass. The minimum qualifying age is usually 60 to 65 for men, and 55 to 65 for women.

In your home country, a lower age may already entitle you to all sorts of interesting travel packages and discounts (on car hire, for instance) through organisations and travel agents that cater to senior travellers. Start hunting at your local senior citizens' advice bureau.

Some car rental companies won't rent to drivers over 70 or 75.

TRAVEL WITH CHILDREN

Successful travel with young children requires effort, but can certainly be done. Try not to overdo things and consider using some sort of self-catering accommodation as a base. Include children in the planning process; if they've helped to work out where you'll be going, they will be much more interested when they get there. Include a range of activities – balance a visit to Trinity College for example with one to the National Wax Museum. For more information see Lonely Planet's *Travel with Children* by Maureen Wheeler.

USEFUL ORGANISATIONS
Union of Students in Ireland (USIT)

USIT (☎ 01-679 8833, 677 8117), 19 Aston Quay, O'Connell Bridge, Dublin 2, is the Irish youth and student travel association. It has offices in most major cities in Ireland, including Belfast, Waterford, Cork and Galway. It issues the International Student Identity Card (ISIC) and the European Youth Card (EYC), and also organises cheap fares to Ireland for students. Its overseas offices include:

France
    USIT Voyages, 12 rue Vivienne, 75002 Paris (☎ 1-42 44 14 00)
UK
    Campus Travel, 52 Grosvenor Gardens, London SW1W OAG (☎ 0171-730 3402)
USA
    New York Student Center, 895 Amsterdam Ave (at West 103rd St), New York, NY 10025 (☎ 212-663 5435)

DANGERS & ANNOYANCES

See also Car & Motorcycle in the Getting Around chapter.

Crime

Ireland is safer than most countries in Europe but the usual precautions should be observed. Drug-related crime is quite common and Dublin has its fair share of pickpockets and sneak thieves waiting to relieve the unwary of unwatched bags. See the Dublin chapter for more details.

If you're travelling by car don't leave valuables on view inside when the car is parked. Dublin is particularly notorious for car break-ins, and foreign-registered cars and rent-a-cars are prime targets. Cyclists should always lock their bicycles securely and be cautious about leaving bags on the bike, particularly in larger towns or more touristy locations.

The police in the Republic are called by their Irish name of Garda Síochána, or just garda for one police officer and gardaí (gard-ee) for more than one. In Northern Ireland the police are called the Royal Ulster Constabulary (RUC) and ☎ 999 is the emergency number in both the North and the South; in the South you can also dial ☎ 112. After dialling the emergency number, specify whether you want the police (gardaí), fire, ambulance or boat or coastal rescue.

The Troubles

Obviously, there's a certain amount of danger in Northern Ireland but it's small and if the second ceasefire and the peace process continue this will diminish. That said, it's probably best to make sure your visit to Northern Ireland doesn't coincide with the climax of the Orange marching season on 12 July. Many Northern Irish, both Protestant and Catholic, leave the province for a few days either side of that date.

If you confine yourself to the Antrim coast you may well never see the British army, but in Derry or South Armagh, on the other hand, its presence is more obvious. Tourists are treated with courtesy by the security forces, but you may be asked for some form of identification. Don't leave a bag unattended: apart from the risk of theft it could be the subject of a security alert.

A British accent can be a help or a hindrance, depending on who you're dealing with.

Racism

Racially, the Irish people are very homogeneous and most have had little experience of those with different coloured skin. Some prejudice – and curiosity – is therefore inevitable, but most unlikely to reach the level of personal hostility that's so common in parts of Britain.

On the other hand, Ireland has absorbed a number of refugees largely from Eastern Europe, and some, particularly if they can't speak English, have been subject to abuse. The widely proclaimed strength of the Irish economy has also attracted illegal immigrants whose presence (though quite small in number) fans racist intolerance.

LEGAL MATTERS

If you need legal assistance contact the Legal Aid Board whose head office (☎ 01-661 5811) is at St Stephens Green House, Dublin 2. It has a number of local law centres which are listed in the phone book.

Drugs

The importation of illegal drugs is prohibited and could result in prison. The possession of small quantities of marijuana attracts a fine or warning, but harder drugs are treated more seriously.

Drinking & Driving

The legal drinking age is 18 and you may need a photo ID to prove your age. Although there's some tolerance toward drink driving (in the South at least), stiff fines, jail or other penalties could be incurred if you're caught driving under the influence. In the South the legal limit is 80mg of alcohol per 100ml of blood, in the North it's 35mg/100ml. The safest approach is not to drink anything if you're planning to drive.

Traffic offences (illegal parking, speeding etc) usually incur a fine for which you're normally allowed 30 days to pay.

See also Road Rules under Car & Motorcycle in the Getting Around chapter.

BUSINESS & PUB HOURS
Business Hours

Offices open Monday to Friday 9 am to 5 pm, shops to 5.30 pm or 6 pm. On Thursday and/or Friday shops stay open later. Many also open on Saturday or Sunday. In winter, tourist offices and attractions often open shorter hours or fewer days per week, or shut completely.

Outside the cities, shops and businesses often close for one afternoon in the week. It varies from region to region. In small towns most shops are also likely to close for an hour or so at lunch time.

In Northern Ireland the main thing to remember is that many tourist attractions close Sunday morning, rarely opening until around 2 pm, well after church finishing time.

For banking hours see Changing Money earlier; for post office hours see Post earlier.

Pub Hours

In the Republic pubs open 10 am to 11.30 pm Monday to Saturday between June and September. The rest of the year closing time is 11 pm. In Dublin, pubs close for a 'holy hour' which may be one or more hours in the afternoon. On Sunday the opening hours are 12.30 to 2 pm and 4 to 11 pm. The only days when pubs definitely close are Christmas Day and Good Friday.

In the North pubs open 11.30 am to 11 pm, Monday to Saturday. On Sunday the hours are 12.30 to 2 pm and 7 to 10 pm, but pubs in Protestant areas often stay closed all day.

PUBLIC HOLIDAYS & SPECIAL EVENTS

Bear in mind that Northern and Southern public holidays (bank holidays) don't always coincide, which can have a bearing on the availability of beds in border resorts like Newcastle. In the North most shops open on Good Friday, but close on the Tuesday following Easter Monday.

Public holidays in the Republic of Ireland (IR), Northern Ireland (NI) or both are:

New Year – 1 January
St Patrick's Day (IR) – 17 March
Easter Monday
May Holiday (IR) – 1 May
May Holiday (NI) – first Monday in May
June Holiday (IR) – first Monday in June

The 12th (NI) – 12 July (next day if 12 July is a Sunday)
August Holiday (IR) – first Monday in August
August Holiday (NI) – last Monday in August
October Holiday (IR) – last Monday in October
Christmas Day – 25 December
St Stephen's Day/Boxing Day – 26 December

The St Patrick's Day and St Stephen's Day/Boxing Day holidays are taken on the following Monday should they fall on a weekend, Christmas Day on the following Tuesday. Banks and many shops and offices close Good Friday even though it isn't an official public holiday.

Following is a list of the more major events and festivals held around the country during the year.

January
> There are regular horse races at a number of tracks throughout the country, including Leopardstown in County Dublin and Naas in County Kildare. The international rugby season usually begins in January.

February
> In Dublin the International Film Festival begins at the end of the month. International rugby games for the Five Nations Championship (between Ireland, England, Scotland, Wales and France) take place throughout the month, two of them being held at Lansdowne Park. In Belfast there's a music festival.

March
> Dublin has a St Patrick's Day parade on March 17 as does Armagh and smaller celebrations take place in the other cities. Although Dublin's parade doesn't compare with the razzmatazz in New York, it's a much bigger celebration than it used to be. St Patrick's Day is a national holiday so shops and businesses close and the day passes off unostentatiously in the countryside, apart from the traditional wearing of a ribbon or shamrock leaf in one's lapel. In Dublin, the World Irish Dancing Championship take place.

April
> Two major sporting events take place: the Irish Grand National at Fairyhouse, County Meath, and the final of the Gaelic football league competition in Dublin. At the World Irish Dancing Championship in Cork, Irish dancers gather to compete against each other.

May
> The Royal Dublin Society Showground hosts the Spring Show featuring agricultural and farming pursuits. Dublin also sees the Irish soccer final this month. At Ennis in County Clare, the Fleadh

Nua is a festival of traditional music and dance, while Cork has the International Choral & Folk Dance Festival. At Bantry, in the same county, there's a Mussel Festival. Belfast has its annual marathon.

June

In Dublin, 16 June is Bloomsday when Leopold Bloom's Joycean journey around the city is re-enacted and various readings and dramatisations take place around the city. More bookish events can be found in Listowel in County Cork with its Writers' Week literary festival. Some 48km from the capital the Irish Derby takes place at the Curragh. Up in Donegal, at Rathmullen, an international fishing festival takes place. June to the middle of August pilgrims leave Pettigo in County Donegal for the boat trip to Lough Derg and the penitential Stations of the Cross. Across the border in Belleek there's a small Fiddle Stone festival while Belfast hosts a Jazz & Blues Festival.

July

Fishing events get under way in Athlone and in Mayo, while on the last Sunday of the month there's a mass pilgrimage to the top of Mayo's Croagh Patrick. The Galway Arts Festival begins in late July.

August

The second week sees the annual Dublin Horse Show at the Royal Dublin Society Showground (Ireland's answer to Wimbledon and Ascot when it comes to showing off one's social status). Horse racing takes place in Tralee in County Kerry, and for the last week of the month Tralee has the Rose of Tralee Festival. In the same county at Killorglin the ancient Puck Fair heralds unrestricted drinking for days and nights. Kilkenny has an Arts Week and Clifden in County Galway has the Connemara Pony Show. In Ballycastle in County Antrim the Oul' Lammas Fair occurs over the last weekend of the month and attracts holiday-makers as well as enterprising traders. The August Bank Holiday weekend (the first Monday in August and the Saturday and Sunday that precede it) is the time for Ireland's major annual rock festival known as Féile, at Thurles in County Tipperary. The Belfast Folk Festival also takes place this month.

September

The All-Ireland Hurling and Football finals both take place in September. In Lisdoonvarna, County Clare, the Matchmaking Festival gets down to business. Cork has its Film Festival, Sligo its Arts Week, Waterford its International Festival of Light Opera, and Dublin its Theatre Festival. Belfast has its own Folk Festival.

October

An International Jazz Festival takes over the city of Cork, with special boat trains bringing audiences from Britain and elsewhere. The Dublin Theatre Festival takes place over two weeks in October. On the last Monday of the month Dublin has its marathon, while Ballinasloe in County Galway hosts the country's biggest cattle and horse fair. Kinsale in County Cork is home to Ireland's Gourmet Festival.

November

In Wexford the Opera Festival is a prestigious event attracting audiences and participants from all parts of the world. In the North the Belfast Festival takes place at Queen's University.

December

Christmas is a quiet affair in the countryside though on 26 December the ancient practice of Wren Boys is re-enacted, when groups of children dress up and expect money at the door after singing a few desultory hymns.

LANGUAGE COURSES

Irish

With the revival of the Irish language there is a growing number of courses in the language and culture, particularly in the Gaeltacht-speaking areas.

University College, Galway, runs intensive one/two week courses for IR£150/250; contact the Irish Language Centre (☎ 091-595101), or Áras Mháirtín Uí Chadhain, University College Galway, Galway City. In Glencolumbcille, Donegal, weekend and week-long courses in Irish and Irish culture are provided late March to October by Oideas Gael (☎ 073-30248) at the Foras Cultúir Uladh (Ulster Cultural Foundation).

Contact Bord Fáilte for more information.

English

Given Ireland's significant contribution to English literature it's probably not surprising that it has become a centre for the learning of English, particularly for people from other Catholic countries, mainly Spain, Italy, France and Portugal. There are some English-language schools in other parts of the country but most are in and around Dublin.

Bord Fáilte publishes a list of schools that have been recognised by the Department of Education for the teaching of English as a foreign language. Some schools run summer programmes and provide specialised courses (eg for business people); the schools can arrange accommodation and organise sporting and cultural activities.

Some of the approved schools in Dublin are:

Academy of English Studies Ireland
    33 Dawson St, Dublin 2 (☎ 01-679 6464)
Dublin School of English
    11 Westmoreland St, Dublin 2 (☎ 01-677 3322)
English Language Institute
    99 St Stephen's Green, Dublin 2 (☎ 01-475 2965)
Language Centre of Ireland
    The Language School, 45 Kildare St, Dublin 2 (☎ 01-671 6266)

WORK

Despite Ireland's economic upturn, unemployment remains high so this isn't a good country for finding casual work. Lowly paid seasonal work is available in the tourist industry, usually in restaurants and pubs, and hostel noticeboards sometimes advertise casual work. Without skills, though, it's difficult to find a job that pays sufficiently well to enable you to save money. You're almost certainly better off saving in your country of origin.

Ireland is a member of the EU so citizens of other EU countries can work in Ireland. If you have an Irish parent or grandparent, it's fairly easy to obtain Irish citizenship without necessarily renouncing your own nationality, and this opens the door to employment throughout the EU. Obtaining citizenship isn't an overnight procedure, so enquire about the process at an Irish embassy or consulate in your own country.

Citizens of Commonwealth countries aged 17 to 27 can apply for a Working Holiday Entry Certificate that allows them to spend two years in the UK and to take work that's 'incidental' to a holiday. Commonwealth citizens with a UK-born parent may be eligible for a Certificate of Entitlement to the Right of Abode, which entitles them to live and work in the UK free of immigration control. Commonwealth citizens with a UK-born grandparent, or a grandparent born before 31 March 1922 in what's now the Republic, may qualify for a UK Ancestry-Employment Certificate, allowing them to work full time up to four years in the UK.

Visiting full-time US students, aged 18 and over, can get a six-month work permit for Ireland and the UK through the Council on Educational Exchange (☎ 212-822 2600; http://www.ciee.org), 205 East 42nd St, New York, NY 10017.

ACCOMMODATION

Bord Fáilte's annual *Accommodation Guide* costs IR£5 and has an awesome list of B&Bs, hotels, campsites and other accommodation. It far from exhausts the possibilities, however, as there are also a great many places which aren't 'tourist board approved'. This doesn't necessarily mean they're in any way inferior to the approved places. The NITB publishes its own *Where to Stay* book (£3.99) which covers the same ground. Gulliver (☎ 800 600800) is the name of their combined computerised accommodation reservation service.

Bord Fáilte offices book local accommodation for a fee of IR£1, or IR£2 in another town. All this really involves is phoning a place on their list; but in high summer, when it may take numerous phone calls to find a free room, that can be a pound or two well spent. The NITB provides a similar booking service.

Camping & Caravanning

Camping and caravan parks aren't as common as in Britain or on the continent, but there are still plenty of them around Ireland. Some hostels also have camping space for tents and usually offer the use of the kitchen and shower facilities, which often makes them better value than the main campsites. At commercial parks, tent sites typically cost IR£4 to IR£8 and many have coin-operated showers. Parks usually have different rates depending on the type of tent (a two-person tent as opposed to a family tent being the usual distinction) and whether you arrive by bike or car. Site rates for caravans cost around IR£6 to IR£8

Free tent camping is often available as

long as you ask permission from the farmer. Around the touristy parts of Kerry and Cork, farmers may ask for a pound or two, but it shouldn't be too difficult to find one who'll let you camp for nothing.

An alternative to normal caravanning is to hire a horse-drawn caravan with which to wander the countryside. In the high season you can hire one for around IR£550 a week.

Hostels

If you're travelling on a tight budget, the numerous hostels – both official and independent – offer cheap accommodation and are also great centres for meeting fellow travellers. May to September and on public holidays, hostels can be heavily booked but so is everything else.

An Óige (the Irish Youth Hostel Association) and the Youth Hostel Association of Northern Ireland (YHANI) are the two associations that belong to Hostelling International (HI). An Óige and YHANI hostels have been changing a lot for the better. They operate a fax-a-bed-ahead facility that books accommodation in advance. Bookings can be made by credit card at many of the larger hostels and some hostels have family and smaller rooms. And these days you can take a car to a hostel.

An Óige has 37 hostels scattered round the South and YHANI has seven in the North. Annual membership is IR£7.50 (£7.50). Overseas visitors who aren't members can stay at the hostels and may join by obtaining a 'guest card' and paying IR£1.25 for a stamp on top of the nightly charge. If they buy six stamps (total IR£7.50) they become a HI member.

Nightly costs vary with the time of year but June to September are usually IR£6 to IR£7 except for the more expensive Galway and Dublin hostels. Rates are cheaper if you're under 18. To use a hostel you must also have or rent a sleeping sheet. Prices quoted are high season and for those over 18.

The addresses are:

An Óige
  61 Mountjoy St, Dublin 7

(☎ 01-830 4555; fax 830 5808; email anoige@iol.ie, http://www.irelandyha.org)
Youth Hostel Association of Northern Ireland
  22-32 Donegall Rd, Belfast BT12 5JN (☎ 01232-315435; fax 01232-439699)

Ireland has seen independent hostels pop up like toadstools after rain. With no membership requirements, they emphasise their easy-going ambience and lack of rules, but while most have no curfew, others don't allow you access to your room for a part of the day. Not all are of a high standard; some are cold in winter, stuffy in summer and often cramped, with up to 20 people in a room sleeping on flimsy metal bunk beds. Associations with usually reliable accommodation are:

Independent Holiday Hostels (IHH)
  57 Lower Gardiner St, Dublin 1 – a cooperative group with hostels in both the North and the South (☎ 01-836 4700; fax 01-836 4710, email ihh@iol.ie)
Independent Hostel Owners in Ireland (IHO)
  Dooey Hostel, Glencolumbeille, County Donegal – a 'back to basics' association (☎ 073-30130; fax 073-30339)
Celtic Budget Accommodation Ireland
  13 South Leinster St, Dublin 2 (☎ 01-662 1991; fax 01-678 5011)

B&Bs

If you're not staying in hostels you are probably staying in a B&B. It sometimes seems every other house in Ireland is a B&B and you'll stumble upon them in the most unusual and remote locations.

The typical cost is IR£15 to IR£20 a night, and you rarely pay less or more than that, except in the big towns where some luxurious B&Bs can cost IR£25 to IR£30 or more a night. A number don't have private bathrooms but where they do the cost is usually IR£2 higher. At some places costs are higher for a single room. Prices in the North are similar. Most B&Bs are small, just two to four rooms, so April to September they can quickly fill up. Outside the big cities, most B&Bs only accept cash.

Breakfast at a B&B is almost inevitably cereal followed by 'a fry', which means fried eggs, bacon and sausages, plus toast and brown bread. A week of B&B breakfasts exceeds every known international guideline for cholesterol intake, but if you decline fried food you're left with cereal and toast. If your bloodstream can take the pressure, you'll have eaten enough food to last you till dinnertime, but it's a shame more places don't offer alternatives like fruit, yoghurt or the delicious variety of Irish breads and scones which are widely available. In Northern Ireland you may meet the awesome 'Ulster Fry', which adds fried bread, blood sausage, tomatoes and assorted other fried foods to the basic version.

Hotels

Accommodation in a hotel can range from the local pub to a medieval castle. It's often possible to negotiate better deals than the published rates, especially out of season. Ask if any discounts are given and try to think of a reason why you in particular merit one. Out of the main holiday season, hotels often have special deals for certain days of the week, but these are usually quite flexible and can often be extended to whatever days you want. Payment for a night's stay usually includes breakfast.

Self-Catering

Self-catering accommodation is often on a weekly basis and usually means an apartment or house where you look after yourself. The rates vary from one region and season to another. A smart cottage in Schull (County Cork) in August is around IR£575 a week, sleeping six people, while the equivalent in Banagher (County Offaly) in April is about IR£180.

Other Accommodation

In Dublin during summer there's accommodation at Trinity College and University College Dublin.

Guesthouses are often just like larger and more expensive B&Bs, but sometimes they're more like small hotels with a restaurant, sitting room and telephone and TV in the rooms. Farmhouse accommodation usually means it's a B&B on a farm; they're sometimes excellent value and you may get a chance to see how the farm works. Country houses are rural B&Bs, usually costing a fair bit more and in a rather grander than usual house.

Another option is to hire a boat, on which you can live aboard while cruising Ireland's many inland waterways.

FOOD

Irish cooking once had a poor reputation, but things have improved enormously and you can generally eat very well. Readily available high-quality produce, the influence of international cuisines, a growing awareness of healthy eating and the higher expectations of Ireland's numerous visitors have combined to produce what is called by some, new Irish cuisine. Of course, if you want meat or fish cooked until it's dried and shrivelled and vegetables turned to mush, there are still enough places that can perform the feat.

Irish meals are usually meat-based, with beef, lamb and pork common options. A really traditional meal is bacon and cabbage, a delicious combination that should be tried at least once.

Seafood, long neglected, is finding a place on the table in Irish homes, and is widely available in restaurants. It's often excellent especially in the west; trout and salmon are delicious.

Irish bread has a wonderful reputation and indeed it can be very good, but, unfortunately, there's a tendency to fall back on the infamous white-sliced bread, *pan* in Irish. B&Bs are often guilty of this. Try some soda bread, made from flour and buttermilk. Irish scones are a delight; tea and scones is a great snack at any time of day. Even pubs often offer tea and scones.

Traditional foods include:

Bacon & Cabbage
   a stew consisting simply of its two named ingredients: bacon and cabbage
Barm Brack
   an Irish cake-like bread
Boxty
   rather like a filled pancake

Champ
  Northern Irish dish of potatoes mashed with spring onions
Colcannon
  mashed potato, cabbage and onion fried in butter and milk
Crubeens
  pig's trotters
Dublin Coddle
  a semi-thick stew made with sausages, bacon, onions and potatoes
Dulse
  a dried seaweed that's sold salted and ready to eat, mainly in Ballycastle, County Antrim
Guinness Cake
  a popular fruitcake flavoured with Guinness beer
Irish Stew
  this quintessential Irish dish is a stew of mutton, potatoes and onions, flavoured with parsley and thyme and simmered slowly
Soda Bread
  Belfast is probably the place in Ireland for bread at its best, but soda bread in particular, white or brown, is found throughout the country
Yellowman
  a hard, chewy toffee available in County Antrim

It's common for Irish people to eat their main meal of the day at lunch time, and every town has at least one hotel or restaurant, offering special three-course meals for around IR£5. A similar meal in the evening may be at least double the cost.

The main alternatives to Irish food are provided by Italian and Chinese restaurants. In the bigger cities like Dublin, Belfast and Cork you'll also find a cosmopolitan range of cuisines including French, Indian, Middle Eastern, Mexican and other choices.

Fast food is well established, from traditional fish & chips to more recent arrivals like burgers, pizzas, kebabs and tacos. Pubs are often good places to eat, particularly at lunch time when a bowl of the soup of the day (usually vegetable) and some good bread can make a fine, economical meal.

There are some superb vegetarian places and frequently they turn out to be run by British or other Europeans who have settled in Ireland. Hotels and restaurants often feature a vegetarian dish on their menus, though they can sometimes be bland and unimaginative. At the more expensive restaurants it's always a good idea to inform

them in advance that you want a vegetarian meal. If you're vegetarian then staying at a B&B can be a bad deal. The best excuse for the high prices charged by most B&Bs is the huge breakfast they serve. The vegetarian alternative will usually be just cornflakes and toast, but the charge will be the same. Some are happy to serve baked beans on toast if you ask. See the earlier B&B section for information on the famous Irish breakfast.

There are several specialist food and restaurant guides to Ireland. The Bridgestone *100 Best Restaurants in Ireland* and the Bridgestone *Vegetarians' Guide to Ireland* are both by Sally & John McKenna and are practical, independent guides to their subject. Bord Fáilte has its own publication of recommended restaurants but the restaurants concerned simply pay for their entry and submit their own write-up. The NITB has its own *Where to Eat* book for £2.99 and lists everything from the very expensive to the local Chinese takeaway.

DRINKS
In Ireland a drink means a beer – either lager or stout. Stout usually means Guinness, the famous black beer of Dublin, although in Cork it can mean a Murphy's or a Beamish. If you don't develop a taste for stout (and you should at least try) a wide variety of lager beers are available including Irish Harp (brewed 'by Guinness') and many locally brewed 'imports' such as Budweiser, Fosters or Heineken. For British-style bitter try Smithwicks (the 'w' isn't pronounced) or Caffrey's. Simply asking for a Guinness or a Harp will get you a pint (570 ml, IR£1.80 to IR£2.30 in a pub). If you want a half pint (85p to IR£1.35) ask for a 'glass' or a 'half'. Children are allowed in pubs until 7 or 8 pm and in smaller towns this restriction is treated with customary Irish flexibility.

Irish coffee is something you'll see marketed in touristy hotels and restaurants, but it's not a traditional drink. It's a modern phenomenon and was considered a bit of a novelty when served to the first trans-Atlantic passengers arriving at Shannon airport

Whiskey, Beer & Wine

Apart from imbibing large quantities of alcoholic refreshments, the Irish have also been responsible for some important developments in the field. They were pioneers in the development of distilling whiskey (distilled three times and spelt with an 'e' as opposed to the twice-distilled Scotch whisky) and also adopted the dark British beer known as stout or porter (since it was particularly popular with the porters who worked around Covent Garden market in London). Promoted by the Guinness family, it soon gained an enduring stranglehold on the Irish taste for beer. In neighbouring Britain, lager wines have taken a slice of the market from the traditional British bitter, but in Ireland Guinness still reigns.

In an Irish pub, talk is just as important an ingredient as the beer, though the conversation will often turn to the perfect Guinness. Proximity to the St James's Gate Brewery is one requirement for perfection, for although a Guinness in Kuala Lumpur can still be a fine thing, Guinness is at its best in Ireland. The perfect Guinness also requires expertise in its 'pulling'. If you want a perfect pint, you do not simply hold the glass under the tap and slosh it in. The angle at which the glass is held, the point at which the pouring is halted, the time that then passes while the beer settles and the head subsides and the precision with which the final top-up is completed, are all crucial in ensuring satisfaction. It's worth the wait.

Guinness may still be *the* drink in Ireland, but Irish drinking patterns are changing. The imbibing of ales is in steady decline. On the other hand, even though Ireland doesn't have any vineyards and the Irish are still way behind their continental neighbours in consumption of wine (a mere 5.7L per head per year), recent years have seen a rapid rise in wine sales.

With alcohol such an important social lubricant, it's not surprising that the 1994 drink-driving laws reducing the permitted blood-alcohol level weren't met with much enthusiasm. The government minister responsible for the legislation even had his home telephone number written up as a 24 hour taxi service in public telephone booths in his Tipperary constituency.

All of this said, however, it is interesting to note that a 1995 report on health commissioned by the EU found that the per capita consumption of alcohol in Ireland was the lowest in the EU. The Irish drank an average 7.4L of alcohol each in 1994 compared with 12.6L in France and 10.5L in Germany. The EU average is 9.9L. An EU official observed that these statistics may be a result of an increasing awareness of health, or it could reflect the fact that Ireland's child population is greater than in other EU countries. ■

(though some say it was invented in San Francisco). It's a mixture of coffee and whiskey served in a heated glass and topped with cream.

When ordering a whiskey, the Irish people never ask for a Scotch (though Scotch whisky is available); they use the brand name of an Irish whiskey instead: Paddy's, Powers, Bushmills or whatever. It may seem dear but the Irish measure is generous, by law.

Nonalcoholic drinks in pubs and hotels consist of soft drinks and brand-named fizzy ones (called 'minerals'). To judge by the prices they charge you might think they were

deliberately discouraging customers from drinking them.

Coffee is available in nearly all pubs, from 45p to 80p usually, but don't expect a smile if you order one at 10.30 pm on a busy night. If you ask for cream with your coffee, cream is what you'll get, a big dollop of it.

The Irish drink lots of tea and this is usually served black, in a small teapot, with milk in a separate jug.

ENTERTAINMENT

Listening to traditional music while nursing a pint of Guinness is the most popular form of entertainment in Ireland. If someone should suggest visiting a particular pub for its 'good crack' *(craíc* in Irish), don't think you've just found the local dope dealer. 'Crack' is Irish for a good time – convivial company, sparkling conversation and rousing music. Pubs offer a variety of music from traditional to rock.

Theatre is popular, especially in the summer when a number of touring groups travel around the country. Dublin, particularly, is renowned for its excellent theatres and there's always a broad range of plays and shows on. Most famous is the Abbey Theatre, which was founded by WB Yeats, Lady Gregory and other writers and artists behind the Anglo-Irish literary revival. The Gate Theatre is a much smaller company but puts on a remarkable variety of new and unusual work. Both the Gaiety and Olympia theatres are beautifully preserved old showhouses which host a mix of plays, pantomimes and shows.

A 'medieval banquet' finds its way on to many tourist itineraries, with the banquet at Bunratty Castle in County Clare probably being the best known. They tend to be expensive and the food is often disappointing. May to September, local festivals and concerts are a common event and it's always worth calling in at the local tourist office to check on what's coming up.

SPECTATOR SPORT
Gaelic Football & Hurling Ireland has a couple of native games with a large and enthusiastic following – Gaelic football and hurling.

Gaelic football is a fast and exciting spectacle. The ball is round like a soccer ball, but the players can kick, handle and run with it as in rugby. They can pass it in any direction but only by kicking or punching. The goalposts are similar to rugby posts, and a goal, worth three points, is scored by putting the ball below the bar, while a single point is awarded when the ball goes over the bar. Gaelic football is popular in both the South and the North.

Hurling is Ireland's most characteristic sport. It's a ball-and-stick game something like hockey, but much faster and more physical. Visitors are often taken aback by the crash of players wielding what look like ferocious clubs, but injuries are infrequent. The goalposts and scoring method are the same as Gaelic football, but the leather ball or *sliotar* is the size of a baseball. A player can pick the ball up on his stick and run with it for a certain distance. Players can handle the ball briefly and pass it by palming it. The players' broad wooden sticks are called hurleys.

Hurling has an ancient history and is mentioned in many old Irish tales. Cúchulainn was a legendary exponent of the game. Today hurling is played on a standard field, but in the old days the game might have been played across country between two towns or villages, the only aim being to get the ball to a certain spot or goal.

Both Gaelic football and hurling are played nationwide by a network of town and country clubs and under the auspices of the Gaelic Athletic Association (GAA). The most important competitions are played at county level, and the county winners out of each of the four provinces come together in the autumn for the All-Ireland finals, the

Hurling is a fast and physical game

climax of Ireland's sporting year. Both finals are played in September at Dublin's Croke Park in front of huge crowds.

Soccer & Rugby Soccer and rugby union enjoy considerable support all over the country, particularly around Dublin, and soccer is very popular in Northern Ireland.

The international rugby team consists of members from the North and the Republic and has a tremendous following. The highlights of the rugby year are the international matches played against England, Scotland, Wales and France between January and March. Home matches are played at Lansdowne Rd in Dublin.

The North and the Republic field separate soccer teams and both have a good record in international competitions. Many of the home players from North and South play professional soccer in Britain and the most successful ones have the status of pop or movie stars. British club teams like Arsenal, Liverpool and Manchester United have strong followings in Ireland. Such is the popularity of Manchester United, that an opposition organisation has sprung up called ABU – Anyone But United!

Athletics, Boxing & Swimming Athletics is also popular, and the Republic usually has a few international athletes, particularly in middle and long-distance events. In 1995, Cork athlete, Sonia O'Sullivan, won the 5000m outdoor final at the world championships in Gothenberg. Main events are held at Morton Stadium in Dublin. Boxing has traditionally had a strong working-class following, and Irish boxers have often won Olympic medals or been world champions. Barry McGuigan (former world featherweight champion), Michael Carruth and Wayne MacCullough are some recent heroes. The principal venue is Dublin's National Stadium.

Ireland hasn't had a strong tradition in swimming, but Michelle Smith raised its profile when she won three gold medals and one bronze at the 1996 Atlanta Olympics.

Horse Racing Horses have played a big role in Irish life over the centuries and Ireland has produced a large number of internationally successful racing horses. The Irish love of horse racing can be appreciated at various courses around the country, including Leopardstown in County Dublin and Naas, Punchestown and the Curragh in County Kildare.

Golf Golf is enormously popular in Ireland and there are many fine golf courses. If you prefer to spectate rather than participate, the annual Irish Open takes place in June.

Road Bowling The object of this sport is to throw a cast-iron ball along a public road (normally one with little traffic) for a designated distance, usually one or two miles. The person who does it in the least number of throws is the winner. The main centres are Cork and Armagh and competitions take place throughout the year, attracting considerable crowds.

Handball Handball is another Irish sport with ancient origins and is also governed by the GAA.

THINGS TO BUY
Clothing

All over the country, but especially in County Galway, it's possible to purchase Aran sweaters. The name derives from the islands where they were first made by the women as working garments for their husbands. Hand-knitted ones, not unnaturally, cost a lot more than machine-made ones. County Donegal is famous for its tweeds and Magee's in Donegal Town has a large selection. It can be purchased in lengths or finished as jackets, skirts or caps. Tweed is also produced in County Wicklow and County Dublin. Hand-woven shawls and woollen blankets make lovely presents.

Irish linen is of high quality and comes in the form of everything from blouses to handkerchiefs. The Irish produce some high quality outdoor activities gear – they have plenty of experience with wet weather. Irish lace is another fine product, at its best in Limerick, or Carrickmacross in County Monaghan.

Crystal

Waterford crystal is world famous and is obtainable throughout Ireland, although the company has reduced its workforce in Waterford and moved some business overseas. Smaller manufacturers of crystal produce fine work and at prices that are far more attractive. In the North, Tyrone Crystal is based outside Dungannon and the factory can be toured, with no obligation to purchase from the showroom.

Pottery

All over the country there are small potteries turning out unusual and attractive work. The village of Belleek in County Fermanagh straddles the Northern Ireland border with Donegal and produces delicate bone china. In the South the area around Dingle in County Kerry has superb pottery. Enniscorthy in County Wexford, and Kilkenny and Thomastown in County Kilkenny, also stand out in this regard. Generally, throughout west Cork and Kerry there are countless small workshops that open in the summer

with their stocks of pottery and other craftwork.

Food & Drink

Irish whiskey is not just spelt differently; it also has its own distinctive taste. The big names are Paddy, Jameson, Powers, Bushmills and Tullamore Dew, and they're not always readily available in other parts of the world. Two Irish liqueurs are very well established: Irish Mist and Bailey's Irish Cream. Some excellent handmade cheeses are worth considering as a gift to take home. Two from west Cork are particularly worth mentioning: Gubbeen is a soft cheese from Schull while Mileens is more spicy. Tipperary has its own Cashel Blue and Cooleeny cheeses.

Other Items

Other possibilities include jewellery, especially *Claddagh rings* (see the Glossary for a description), enamel work and baskets woven of willow or rush. Connemara marble is a natural green stone found in the west of Ireland and is often cunningly fashioned into Celtic designs. Plenty of stores sell CDs of Irish music, traditional and modern.

Activities

Ireland is a great place for doing things and, although it's expensive to travel in, many activities not only open up some of the most beautiful and fascinating corners of the island, they're also within the reach of the tightest budget. In fact, those on a shoestring budget may find themselves hiking or cycling out of necessity. Fortunately, a walk or ride in the countryside will almost certainly be a highlight – as well as the cheapest part – of an Irish holiday. For those who have the money, other activities like golf or fishing are available as part of holiday packages that include bed, board and transportation.

Most activities are well organised and have clubs and associations (some of which are listed here) that can give visitors invaluable information and sometimes substantial discounts. Many of these clubs have national or international affiliations, so check with clubs before leaving home.

The tourist boards put out a wide selection of information sheets and brochures covering just about every activity and these can be a starting point for further research.

WALKING

There are many superb walks in Ireland and walking has become increasingly popular since the early 1980s when the Wicklow Way, the country's first way-marked trail, was established. There are now over 25 waymarked trails varying in length from the 26km Cavan Way to the more than 900km of the Ulster Way. The network of trails is growing all the time and the eventual aim is to link them all up.

The energetic and the impecunious should definitely consider some long-distance overnight walks. Civilisation is never far away so it's generally easy to follow walks that connect with public transport and link hostels, B&Bs and villages. Some walkers might opt to walk the entire length of a way,

but others might just choose a section that meets the constraints of ability, time or transport.

In most cases, a tent and cooking equipment isn't necessary. Warm and waterproof clothing (including a hat and gloves), sturdy footwear, lunch and some high-energy food (for emergencies), a water bottle (with purification tablets), a first-aid kit, a whistle and torch (flashlight), and a map and compass are all that you need.

The countryside can look deceptively gentle but, especially in the hills or on the open moors, the weather can turn nasty very quickly at any time of year. Although Ireland has a relatively mild climate there is one aspect of the weather that will affect the walker and that is the rain. As well as getting you wet, it causes the ground underfoot to be slippery, and low clouds in the hills make navigation problematic. It's vital if you're walking in upland areas to be well equipped and to carry (and know how to use) a compass, good maps and/or a walking guidebook. This is important even though at frequent intervals along the ways there are signposts usually marked with a yellow arrow and walking figure – sometimes the signs are hidden by leafage or simply just missing.

Always leave details of your route with someone trustworthy and let them know when you should be back; never walk alone in isolated areas.

The ways mainly follow old, disused roads, *boreens* (small lanes or roadways) and forest trails. Ireland has a tradition of relatively free access to open country and through privately owned land, but the growth in the number of walkers and the carelessness of a few have made some farmers less obliging. Walkers can help by taking out all litter, not damaging fences or walls and minimising disturbance to farm animals; if you're in doubt ask permission, especially if you plan to pitch a tent.

Information

The maintenance and development of the ways is administered in the South by the Long-Distance Walking Routes Committee (☎ 01-873 4700), Cospóir (National Sports Council), 11th Floor, Hawkins House, Hawkins St, Dublin 2, and in the North by the Sports Council for Northern Ireland (☎ 01232-381222), House of Sport, Upper Malone Rd, Belfast BT9 5LA.

For Mountain Rescue, ring ☎ 999.

Guides & Maps A useful general walking guidebook is *Irish Long Distance Walks* by Michael Fewer. It is a practical and up-to-date guide for anyone contemplating one or more walks. Joss Lynam has put together a collection of 76 shorter walks in *Best Irish Walks*. There are also regional and individual-trail walking guidebooks available. A visit to a good bookshop like Eason's in Dublin is recommended or you could contact Gill & Macmillan Publishers (☎ 01-453 1005), Goldenbridge, Inchicore, Dublin 8, for a list of their walking guide titles.

Bord Fáilte's booklet *Walking Ireland* (IR£1) gives a brief description of the waymarked trails in the South. The tourist boards also have free information and maps on popular walks, but if you're planning more than one day's walking it's worth investing in one of the route maps available. Ordnance Survey maps cover the whole island in 25 sheets with a 1:126,720 scale (half an inch to one mile); this series, however, is gradually being replaced by the Ordnance Survey Discovery series of 89 maps with a 1:50,000 scale (2cm to 1km). It's worth checking to see if there's a new map (or maps) available for the walk you're doing. The addresses are:

Ordnance Survey Service
    Phoenix Park, Dublin 8 (☎ 01-820 6100)
Ordnance Survey of Northern Ireland
    Colby House, Stranmillis Court, Belfast BT9 5BJ
    (☎ 01232-661244)

They can also be obtained from the Government Publications Sales Office bookshop (☎ 01-661 3111), Sun Alliance House, Molesworth St, Dublin 2.

Organised Walks If you don't have a travelling companion one option is to join an organised walking group.

Organised walks are offered by the Irish Walking Holidays Association (☎ 055-27479), Old Rectory, Ballycanew, Gorey, County Wexford. For details of hiking tours in the North contact Mary Doyle (☎ 01232-624289 in the evenings), Ulster Federation of Rambling Clubs, 27 Slievegallion Drive, Belfast BT11 8JN. Go Ireland (☎ 066-62094, email goireland@fexco.ie), Killorgin, County Kerry, offers tours of the west and Donegal.

Joyce's Ireland offers walking tours for groups of no more than 14 people, taking in both the Republic and the North. These tours have the added advantage that your luggage (including musical instruments) is carried by minibus. Individual walks take from a couple of hours to a full day, perfect for anyone reasonably fit. For more information contact Joyce's Ireland (☎ 0117-946 7903, http://www.minkcheck.co.uk/joycesireland) 70 West St, Banwell, Somerset BS24 6DE, England.

Kerry Way

The 215km Kerry Way is the Republic's longest marked footpath and is usually walked anticlockwise. It starts and ends in Killarney and stays inland for the first three days, winding through the spectacular Macgillycuddy's Reeks and past 1041m Carrantuohil, Ireland's highest mountain, before continuing around the coast through Cahirciveen, Waterville, Caherdaniel, Sneem and Kenmare. You could complete the walk in about 10 days, provided you're up to walking a good 20km a day. With less time it's worth walking the first three days as far as Glenbeigh from where a bus or a lift could return you to Killarney.

The tourist board map guide (IR£2.50) divides the Kerry Way into 12 sections, but more useful is the 1:50,000 Ordnance Survey Discovery series; map No 78 covers the first three days but No 83 is also necessary for completing the whole walk. *New Irish Walk Guides: Southwest* also covers the entire way with maps and detailed notes although *Irish Long Distance Walks* by Michael Fewer is more up-to-date.

Accommodation isn't a problem, with hostels in Killarney and Glenbeigh, and B&Bs fairly thick on the ground – the proviso being the need to book ahead in July and August. In contrast, places to eat are thin on the ground so consider carrying your own food for much of the way.

Beara Way

This moderately easy, 197km walk forms a loop around the delightful Beara Peninsula in West Cork. The peninsula is relatively unused to mass tourism and makes a pleasant contrast with the Iveragh Peninsula to the north.

Part of the walk, between Casteltownbere and Glengarriff, follows the route taken by Donal O'Sullivan and his band after the English took his castle after an 11 day siege in 1602. At Glengarriff, O'Sullivan met up with other families and set out on a journey north, hoping to reunite with other remaining pockets of Gaelic resistance. Of the thousand men who set out in winter, only 30 completed the trek.

The Beara Way mostly follows old roads and tracks and rarely rises above 340m. There's no official start or finish point and the route can be walked in either direction. It could easily be reduced to seven days by skipping Bere Island and Dursey Island, and if you start at Castletownbere you could reach Kenmare in five days or less.

There are hostels at Glengarriff, Adrigole, Allihies and Eyeries but outside April to September you'll have problems finding much open. Even B&B places tend to shut, so make sure you plan ahead. Bere Island only has a B&B and Dursey Island has no accommodation at all. Packed lunches will be needed for most days of the walk and there are few shops west of Castletownbere, necessitating some advance planning.

Both the Glengarriff (☎ 027-63084) and

Castletownbere (☎ 027-70344) tourist offices only open in July and August, but Kenmare (☎ 064-41233) is open throughout the summer. If you want to visit Bere Island, check the ferry times before reaching Castletownbere.

The tourist board's Beara Way map would do at a pinch, but much better is the new Ordnance Survey 1:50,000 map. The old Ordnance Survey 1:126,720 map No 24 covers the complete Beara Way.

Ulster Way: North-Eastern Section

The Ulster Way makes a circuit round the six counties of Northern Ireland and Donegal. In total the footpath covers just over 900km, so walking all of it might take five weeks. However, it can easily be broken down into smaller sections which could more realistically be attempted during a short stay. The scenery along the way varies enormously, encompassing dramatic coastal scenery, gentler lakeside country and the mountainous inland terrain of the Mountains of Mourne.

Some of the most spectacular scenery lies along the north-eastern section which follows the Glens of Antrim and then the glorious Causeway Coastline, a UNESCO-recognised World Heritage Site. The 165km north-east section begins unpromisingly in Belfast's western suburbs, heads north-eastward to meet the coast at Glenarm then follows the coast round to the Giant's Causeway; this can be completed in six or seven days. The stretch of coast immediately surrounding the Giant's Causeway is likely to be busiest, especially in high summer when you should book accommodation well ahead.

Walking this stretch of coast shouldn't be beyond most averagely fit and sensibly equipped people, but rockfalls along the coast can occasionally obstruct stretches of it.

The Northern Ireland Tourist Board can supply *An Information Guide to Walking* which includes basic details of 14 walks along the Ulster Way. *The Ulster Way: A Guide to the Route and its Facilities* by

Paddy Dillon gives details of the entire trail together with extracts from the relevant Ordnance Survey maps. You might also look at *Ulster Rambles* by Peter Wright or *Walking the Ulster Way* by Alan Warner. You'll need Ordnance Survey 1:50,000 maps Nos 5, 9 and 15 to do the walk.

While some stretches of this walk can seem wonderfully wild, you're never going to be that far from civilisation. There are tourist offices at Cushendall (☎ 012667-71180), Ballycastle (☎ 012657-62024) and the Giant's Causeway (☎ 012657-31855) and they can book accommodation for you (a good idea in summer). There are plenty of campsites; hostels in Cushendall, Ballycastle and White Park Bay; and a reasonable number of B&Bs.

Ulster Way: Donegal Section

The main Ulster Way crosses into Donegal at the small pilgrimage town of Pettigo on Lough Erne, but then circles straight back to Rosscor in Northern Ireland. A spur – also confusingly called the Ulster Way – cuts north across the central moorlands of Donegal to Falcarragh on the north coast. In all, this stretch of walk is only 111km long which means it can be walked in four or five days. Bear in mind, however, that much of central Donegal is bleak, boggy terrain where walking can be tough going, especially if the weather's bad – which it often is!

This stretch of the Ulster Way is intended for wilderness-lovers, and although the walking-man symbol sometimes appears on markers, in general you'll be looking out for white-painted posts which simply tell you that you're heading in the right general direction. Some of the scenery en route is truly magnificent, as you pass the Blue Stack and Derryveagh Mountains and Errigal Mountain, Donegal's highest at 752m. The route also skirts the glorious Glenveagh National Park where you might want to divert and break your journey. There are few dramatic historical remains to distract you, but plenty of minor prehistoric burial sites en route.

Tourist offices are thin on the ground, and unlikely to be open when you want them

anyway. Outside mid-June to September almost all tourist offices are closed, although you should still be able to find places to stay. The tourist office (☎ 074-21160), on the Derry road outside Letterkenny, can provide information in the summer season. Midway along the way, the Dunlewy Lakeside Centre (☎ 075-31699) and Glenveagh National Park Visitor Centre (☎ 074-37090) are likely to prove more helpful.

The Ulster Way: A Guide to the Route and its Facilities by Paddy Dillon gives details of the spur route. Ordnance Survey 1:50,000 maps Nos 1, 6 and 11 should do you.

Places to stay and eat are few and far between, so forward planning is essential. There are no official campsites, although most farmers will probably let you pitch a tent if you ask. There are two useful hostels, at Fintown and Dunlewy, and just enough B&Bs to see you through.

Wicklow Way

Opened in 1982, the popular, 132km Wicklow Way was Ireland's first long-distance trail. Despite its name it actually starts in south Dublin and ends in Clonegal in County Carlow although most of the way is through County Wicklow. From its beginnings in Marlay Park, Rathfarnham, in south Dublin, about 13km from the city centre, the trail quickly enters a mountain wilderness (the highest point is Mt Mullaghmór at 661m) though you're never far from a public road. Forest walks, sheep paths, bog roads and mountain passes join up to provide a spectacular walk which passes by Glencree, Powerscourt, Djouce Mountain, Luggala, Lough Dan, Glenmacnass, Glendalough, Glenmalure and Aghavannagh.

Especially south of Laragh, some sections are desolate, with much of the trail above 500m. The weather can change quickly so good hiking boots, outdoor gear and emergency supplies are essential. There are many worthwhile detours: up Glenmacnass to the waterfall, down to the shores of Lough Dan, up to the summit of Lugnaquilla Mountain.

For the entire trail allow eight to 10 days, plus time for diversions. It's easy to pick up sections and it can be done in either direction, though most walkers start in Dublin. Breaking the journey at Laragh, just under half way, would let you visit the monastic site at Glendalough and do some local walks.

Dublin Tourism Centre in St Andrew's St, Dublin, should be able to supply Bord Fáilte Information Sheet No 26B. The small national park information office (☎ 0404-45425) at Glendalough's Upper Lake may also be able to help you; it's open daily from late April to late August.

The Complete Wicklow Way by JB Malone or *The Wicklow Way, from Marlay to Glenmalure* by Michael Fewer are good trail guides. For other detailed information, check *Hill Walker's Wicklow* or *New Irish Walk Guides, East & South East* both by David Herman. Also useful is *The Wicklow Way – a Natural History Field Guide* by Ken Boyle and Orla Burke. The Wicklow Way Map & Guide contains a series of six strip 1:50,000 maps and is produced by East West Mapping (☎ 054-77835), Ballyredmond, Clonegal, Enniscorthy, County Wexford.

The Ordnance Survey 1:50,000 Wicklow Way map covers the trail to south of Aghavannagh (about 50km from the finish). The newer map No 56 (same scale) also includes much of this section of the way. The older Ordnance Survey 1:126,720 maps Nos 16 and 19 cover the whole route.

There are An Óige hostels at Glencree, Knockree, Glendalough, Glenmalure and Aghavannagh, plus two private hostels in Laragh. These hostels remain open all year, as do some of the B&Bs. Most of the B&Bs are in and around Laragh close to Glendalough, but there are others in Enniskerry, Roundwood, Tinahely, Shillelagh, and in County Wexford at Bunclody a few km south of the end of the walk. South of Laragh accommodation becomes scarcer. Camping is possible along the route, but you'll need to ask permission from local farmers. Roundwood also has an official campsite.

Because of the way's popularity, walking outside the busy June to August period is advisable. In peak season you should certainly book accommodation in advance.

If you're hostelling you'll need to carry food with you. Enniskerry, Laragh and Roundwood have good places to eat. Stock up with food at Laragh; from there to Clonegal even shops are rare.

If you're a glutton for punishment, the South Leinster Way starts a couple of km south-west of Clonegal in Kildavin.

South Leinster Way

The tiny village of Kildavin in County Carlow just south-west of Clonegal, on the slopes of Mt Leinster, is the northern starting point of the 100km South Leinster Way which winds through counties Carlow and Kilkenny. It follows remote mountain roads and river towpaths through the medieval villages of Borris, Graiguenamanagh, Inistioge, Mullinavat and Piltown to the finish post at Carrick-on-Suir just inside the Tipperary border. The southerly section is not as scenic as the rest, but the low hills have their own charm, and on a sunny day they offer fine views south over the Suir Valley and Waterford Harbour.

The way heads in a generally south-west direction from Kildavin to Carrick-on-Suir but could easily be done in the opposite direction. It should take you four or five days depending on whether you stop over in Graiguenamanagh.

The route is marked so you should have no difficulty finding your way. Ask for Bord Fáilte Information Sheet No 26D, with details of the route, at the tourist offices in Carlow Town (☎ 061-317522; open all year), or Kilkenny City (☎ 056-51500; open all year).

Much of the trail is above 500m and the weather can change quickly. Good hiking boots, outdoor gear and emergency supplies are essential.

East West Mapping publishes *South Leinster Way – Walkers Guide*. The way is also included in *Irish Long Distance Walks* by Michael Fewer. The Ordnance Survey 1:126,720 maps Nos 19, 22 and 23 cover the whole trail.

There are no official campsites but it's possible to camp on farmland provided you obtain permission. There's an IHH hostel in Bunclody and, except for Kildavin, plenty of B&Bs in the villages along the route. Food is available in pubs, while Borris and Inistioge have small restaurants. A packed lunch is needed most days, but you can stock up at grocery stores as you go.

Other Long Walks

East Munster Way This 63km walk travels along forestry roads, open moorland, small country roads and a river towpath. It's clearly laid out with black markers bearing yellow arrows and could be managed in three days, starting from Carrick-on-Suir in County Tipperary and finishing at Clogheen in County Waterford. The first day of 26km takes you to Clonmel, the second day of 16km on to Newcastle and the last day another 21km to Clogheen which, although 5km beyond the official end of the way at the Vee Gap, is where accommodation and transport can be found.

There's a hostel in Clonmel and B&B accommodation elsewhere along the way. The route is covered by the Ordnance Survey 1:126,720 map No 22, or Bord Fáilte Information Sheet No 26J. The walk is also covered in Michael Fewer's *Irish Long Distance Walks*.

Dingle Way This 153km walk in County Kerry loops round one of the most beautiful peninsulas in the whole country. It would take eight days to complete the way, beginning and ending in Tralee, with an average daily distance of 22km. The first three days offer the easiest walk but the first day, from Tralee to Camp, is the least interesting; it could be skipped by taking the bus to Camp and starting from there. You could also walk 8km from Camp to the Bog View hostel, and then the next day 15km on to Lispole and on the third day a mere 9km to Dingle. This would also allow for a lovely 15km return trip from the Bog View hostel to Lake Annascaul.

See the Dingle Peninsula section of the Kerry chapter for details of where to stay and eat. The route is covered by the Ordnance Survey 1:126,720 map No 20, but infinitely better is map No 83 in the 1:50,000 series which covers most of the walk although you'll need map No 78 as well to cover the whole way. The Dingle Way is also covered in *New Irish Walk Guides – Southwest* by Seá Ó Súilleabháin and *Irish Long Distance Walks* by Michael Fewer, both published by Gill & Macmillan. Bord Fáilte's own map guide costs IR£1.95.

Burren Way This 45km walk traverses the limestone plateau in County Clare that presents a strange, unique landscape to the walker. There's very little soil and few trees but a surprising abundance of flora. The way stretches between Ballyvaughan, on the north coast of County Clare, and Liscannor to the south-west and it takes in the village of Doolin, famous as a traditional music centre. The highlight of the route is the track along the dramatic heights of the Cliffs of Moher.

The best time for this walk is late spring or early summer. The route is pretty dry, but walking boots are useful as the limestone is sharp.

The best map is No 51 in the 1:50,000 Ordnance Survey Discovery series, but Tim Robinson's *Burren Map & Guide* is much more useful. Shannon Development, 62 O'Connell St, Limerick, County Limerick, publishes *The Burren Way Mapguide* which describes the way. It's also covered in *The Waymarked Trails of Ireland* by Michael Fewer. See the Burren Area section of the Clare chapter for information on where to stay and eat and details on some parts of the way.

Royal Canal Way It's possible to walk along the towpath of the Royal Canal (constructed between 1789 and 1801) all the way from Spencer Dock in Dublin to the 40th lock at Mullawomia, a distance of 125km, without the need to slog up any hills. Eventually, it'll be possible to continue all the way to Shannon and Longford.

For the first 6.5km to Reilly's Bridge, the path runs through grotty, run-down urban scenery, but from then on it becomes much more rural and enjoyable (after the interruption of the M50 bridges). There are signposts at every bridge between Clonsilla and Mullingar but not, as yet, all the way along the route. To ensure you don't go wrong you need Ordnance Survey 1:50,000 maps Nos 12, 13 and 16. There's also a good *Guide to the Royal Canal of Ireland*, published by Dúchas (formerly the OPW), which shows the stretches of the towpath that are overgrown, as well as highlighting important things like pubs! To find out about activities along the Royal Canal, contact the Royal Canal Amenity Group (☎ 01-629 0980), Main St, Maynooth, County Kildare.

Mourne Trail The Mourne Trail is actually the south-eastern section of the Ulster Way, south of Belfast, and runs from Newry, round the Mourne Mountains, to the seaside resort of Newcastle and then on to Strangford where you can take a ferry across to Portaferry and continue north to Newtownards. From Newry to Strangford is a distance of 106km and could probably be managed in four days. Route details are given in *The Ulster Way: A Guide to the Route and its Facilities* by Paddy Dillon. Ordnance Survey of Northern Ireland Discovery maps Nos 21 and 29 have all the necessary data for planning a walk. For other information contact the Mourne Countryside Centre (☎ 013967-24059), 91 Central Promenade, Newcastle, County Down.

There's gorgeous mountain, forest and coastal scenery along the way and, once you've left Newry, not much in the way of built-up towns to spoil the views. Provided you're reasonably fit and well-shod, this is not an especially difficult route to walk although it does climb as high as 559m at Slievemoughanmore, the highest point on the Ulster Way. There aren't many B&Bs in this part of Ireland, so it's as well to book ahead. There's a YHANI hostel (☎ 013967-22133) in Newcastle (the biggest accommodation hub in the area) and another (☎ 012477-29598) in Portaferry if you make it as far as Strangford.

Lough Derg Way This 52km walking trail begins in Limerick City and ends in County Tipperary at the village of Dromineer on the eastern shore of Lough Derg, one of three lakes along the Shannon and the Republic's largest lake. Eventually it will extend as far as Portumna in Galway, north of Lough Derg. The 35km from Limerick to Ballina via O'Brien's Bridge has been fully marked and signposted; it starts outside the Limerick City tourist office and follows the old city canal, the first of the old Shannon navigation canals.

Trail details are given in the *Lough Derg Way* guide and Ordnance Survey 1:126,720 scale maps Nos 15 and 18.

The only drawback is the lack of accommodation along the route. One possibility would be to walk a part of the trail and then catch a bus back to Limerick City. Enquire at the Limerick City or Killaloe/Ballina tourist office for information and a walk leaflet (40p).

Cavan Way In the north-west of County Cavan the villages of Blacklion and Dowra are the ends of the 26km Cavan Way. The way runs in a north-east to south-west direction past a number of Stone Age monuments – court cairns, ring forts, tombs – and this area is said to be one of the last strongholds of druidism. At the midpoint is the Shannon Pot, a pool on the boulder-strewn slopes of the Cuilcagh Mountains and the source of the River Shannon, which from there flows into Lough Allen. The Shannon Pot divides the walk into two parts: from Blacklion it is mainly hill walking; from Shannon Pot to Dowra it's mainly by road. The highest point on the walk is Giant's Grave (260m).

The way is covered by Bord Fáilte information sheet No 26I and Ordnance Survey 1:50,000 map No 26 and the *Cavan Way Mapguide*. Blacklion has several B&Bs. A Bus Éireann bus stops once daily in Blacklion between Westport and Belfast; call ☎ 049-31353 in Cavan Town for details.

Dowra joins up with the Leitrim Way which runs between Manorhamilton and

Drumshanbo. Blacklion is also on the Ulster Way.

Wexford Coastal Path Developed in 1993, the Wexford Coastal Path (Slí Charman) follows the county's coastline for 221km from Ballyhack in the south-east on Waterford Harbour to Kilmichael Point in the north-east corner near the border with County Wicklow. As well as passing through the main coastal settlements of Kilmore Quay, Rosslare Harbour and Wexford Town, the path also takes you past areas of great natural beauty popular with birdwatchers including the North and South Slobs and Hook Peninsula. The terrain varies from rocky headlands to sandy beaches.

The path is marked by signs showing a man with a walking stick walking on water. For more information contact Wexford Town tourist office.

St Declan's Way This 94km walk, mostly tracing an old pilgrimage way from Ardmore to the Rock of Cashel in Tipperary, traverses the Knockmealdown Mountains. Its highest point is the Bearna Cloch an Bhuideal Pass (537m) but for the most part the trail is gently undulating. The walk can be done in stages and public transport is available from a number of places along the way – Cappoquin, Ardfinnan, Cahir and Newinn. If you are heading through the pass call the mountain rescue base (☎ 058-54404) at Mt Melleray before and after. Ardmore tourist office (☎ 024-94444) sells a good 1:50,000 map in strips (IR£4) which also shows circular routes off the way, or you can use Ordnance Survey maps – Nos 18 and 22 of the 1:26,720 series or Nos 66, 74, 81 and 82 of the 1:50,000 series. There are B&Bs and hotels along the route; and camping is possible, though you'll need to ask permission from local farmers.

Slieve Bloom Way Close to the geographical centre of Ireland, the Slieve Bloom Way is a 77km signposted trail which does a complete circuit of the Slieve Bloom Mountains taking in most major points of interest.

The trail follows tracks, forest firebreaks and old roads, and crosses the Mountrath to Kinnitty and Mountrath to Clonaslee roads. Its highest point is at Glendine Gap (460m). The recommended starting point is the car park at Glenbarrow, 5km from Rosenallis. Bord Fáilte Information Sheet No 26F is available from any tourist office; the way is also covered by Ordnance Survey 1:126,720 map No 15 and 1:50,000 map No 54.

Camping in state forests is forbidden, but there's plenty of open space outside the forest for tents; otherwise, accommodation en route is almost nonexistent. Nor is there any public transport to the area, though buses stop in the nearby towns of Mountrath and Rosenallis.

Kildare Way The 150km Kildare Way connects a series of canal towpaths in the north of the county. Killed off as transport routes by the advent of the railway, these have been revived by people seeking leisure activities like walking, cruising, canoeing and fishing. The walk is mainly flat with few hills and the highest point is at Glenaree Lock (92m). At the hub of the Kildare Way is Robertstown from where trails radiate out to Naas, Kildare, Edenderry and Celbridge.

For more information ask for Bord Fáilte Information Sheet No 26E; the Ordnance Survey maps are Nos 16 and 19 in the 1:126,720 series. There's accommodation at the places mentioned above and buses go to most access points.

CYCLING
Many visitors explore Ireland by bicycle. The most interesting areas can be hilly, some of the roads have poor surfaces and the weather is often wet, but despite these drawbacks it's a great place for bicycle touring. The facilities are good, distances are relatively short, roads off the main highways have relatively little traffic, the scenery is beautiful, and you're never too far from a pub. If you intend to cycle in the west, bear in mind that because of the direction of the prevailing winds, it's easier to cycle south to north.

Information

You can either bring your bike with you or rent one in Ireland. Ferries transport bicycles for free or a small fee and airlines will usually accept them as part of your 20kg luggage allowance. When buying your ticket check with the ferry company or airline about any regulations or restrictions on the transportation of bicycles.

Bicycles can be transported by bus provided there's enough room in the luggage compartment. With Bus Éireann the charge varies; on Ulsterbus the cost is half the adult one-way fare with a minimum charge of 80p. By train the cost varies from IR£2 to IR£6 for a one-way journey depending on the distance. Bicycles are not allowed on certain rail routes including the Dublin Area Rapid Transit (DART); you can check with Iarnród Éireann.

Typical rental costs are IR£7 to IR£10 a day or IR£30 to IR£35 a week plus a deposit of around IR£40 which is refunded when the bicycle is returned. Bags and other equipment can also be rented. Several dealers have outlets around the country; the dealers and their head offices are:

Irish Cycle Hire
    Drogheda, County Louth (☎ 041-41067, 35369)
Raleigh Ireland
    Raleigh House, Kylemore Rd, Dublin 10 – Ireland's biggest rental dealer (☎ 01-626 1333)
Rent a Bike Ireland
    58 Lower Gardiner St, Dublin 1 (☎ 01-872 5399)

There are also many local independent outlets.

Regional and national tour operators organise cycling holidays and the tourist boards can supply you with a list of their names. Irish Cycling Safaris (☎ 01-260 0749, email ics@ucd.ie), 7 Dartry Park, Dublin 6, organises tours for groups of cyclists in the south-west, the south-east and Connemara, with bikes, guides, a van that carries luggage, and B&B accommodation. Go Ireland (see Organised Walks earlier) provides cycling tours of the west and Donegal.

Numerous tourist-office publications on cycling exist and there are a number of books and guides on the subject. Good maps are available (see Maps in the Facts for the Visitor chapter). You might also want to get in touch with the Federation of Irish Cyclists (☎ 01-855 1522), Kelly Roche House, 619 North Circular Rd, Dublin 1.

Where to Cycle

South-West Most of West Cork is ideal cycling territory and examples of local cycling tours for Clonakilty and Schull can be found under those sections in the Cork chapter, but the whole region could be explored on bike. One recommended route is west from Cork City to Kinsale, then on through Timoleague, Butlerstown, Clonakilty, Rosscarbery and down to Baltimore and Clear Island. Another route is down the Mizen Head Peninsula (starting from Skibbereen where you can hire bikes), looping around the village of Toormore to take in the south and north coasts. A third route would be a circular one of the Sheep's Head Peninsula, starting and finishing in Bantry (where bikes can be hired).

In Kerry, a wonderful tour would be around the starkly beautiful Beara Peninsula from either Kenmare, Glengarriff or Bantry and taking in the spectacular Healy Pass either down from Lauragh to Adrigole (good brakes are absolutely essential) or with a herculean slog in the other direction. Killarney makes a good base for cycling trips into (but not *around*, unless you want car and coach fumes in your lungs) the Iveragh Peninsula where many of the sights are only accessible by bike or on foot. Examples of two such tours are the 30km ride via the Gap of Dunloe and the 80km trip via Lake Acoose and Moll's Gap.

In Clare the Burren region is good for mountain-biking.

North-West The Lough Gill tour in the Yeats country outside Sligo Town lends itself to cycling. So, too, do many historic and prehistoric sites in the county – as well as other places of interest associated with Yeats – because most of them are in the vicinity of Sligo Town (where you can hire bikes).

Achill Island has largely flat roads which makes cycling an easy way of travelling around the whole island. Bikes can be hired at Achill Sound and returned there after cycling west to Keel, turning north up to Dugort and then back south on another road.

In County Galway, Clifden is the best base for cycling tours of Connemara and takes you through some superb scenery.

In Donegal you can follow the road west of Donegal Town along the coast road via Killybegs to Malin More. North of Killybegs, past Ardara to Dunfanaghy the coast is absolutely superb and there are wonderful cycling tours to be enjoyed around Bloody Foreland and Horn Head. The peninsula that extends west from Ardare is well worth cycling too. North-east of Donegal Town the loop around Lough Eske is a pleasant shorter trip on roads surrounded by the Blue Stack Mountains.

North-East In County Down, Bangor is a good base from which to cycle the reasonably flat Ards Peninsula: you could follow the coast road south via Donaghadee to Portaferry, from where the A2 heads back north skirting Strangford Lough. Alternatively, Newcastle is a good spot from which to explore the valley routes through the Mourne Mountains in south County Down.

In Antrim the scenic route along the coast north from Belfast to the Giant's Causeway passes through the foothills of the Antrim Mountains. From Enniskillen in Fermanagh you can hire bikes to visit ancient religious sites and antiquities, following roads along the shores of Lower Lough Erne to Belleek on the Donegal border and back.

South-East Just south of Dublin, the varied scenery of Wicklow – moors, bogs, mountains, lakes, valleys and forests – provides some beautiful but strenuous cycling. From Wicklow Town south to Wexford the weather is warmer and the landscape flatter. Between Wexford and Waterford, by taking the Ballyhack to Passage East ferry you avoid the longer route north via New Ross.

In Waterford the relatively flat Hook Pen-

insula – out to the lighthouse at the tip of the head and back along the west side to Duncannon – is a good area to explore. In the west of the county the route through the Knockmealdown Mountains offers magnificent views.

Tipperary and Kilkenny have rich, rolling farmland interspersed with ancient monuments like the Rock of Cashel and fine architectural remains. From Kilkenny City there's a beautiful excursion to Kilfane, Jerpoint Abbey, Inistioge and Kells.

Centre In Westmeath, from Athlone north into Longford east of Lough Rea is Goldsmith Country (named after the 18th century poet, playwright and novelist, Oliver Goldsmith) and the gentle terrain is great for cycling. A cycle tour of the *drumlins* (rounded hills formed by retreating glacier) and lakes of Cavan, Monaghan and southern Leitrim along the quiet country roads is very pleasant.

FISHING
Ireland is renowned for its fishing and many visitors come to Ireland for no other reason. Fishing is divided into several categories, topped by dry-fly fishing, where an artificial lure, made to imitate a small insect, is gently dropped on the surface in order to deceive and catch the fish. Fish are described as coarse or game fish, the latter because they vigorously struggle against capture.

In the South, on private stretches of rivers a permit is usually required and the average price is IR£5 a day. In addition a state national licence is required for salmon and sea trout fishing. This costs IR£25 annually, IR£10 for three weeks, IR£3 for one day and can be purchased from a local tackle shop or direct from the Central Fisheries Board (☎ 01-837 9206), Balngowan House, Mobhi Boreen, Glasnevin, Dublin 9.

It is not necessary to have any licence for brown trout, rainbow trout or coarse fish, nor for general sea angling. However, there is a system of share certificates (issued to help raise funds) for trout and coarse fishing, which you purchase beforehand; in most regions payment is voluntary. The certificates cost IR£12 for a year, IR£5 for three weeks or IR£3 for three days.

In the North, you need a rod licence (£9.35 for eight days) which is obtainable from the Foyle Fisheries Commission (☎ 01504-42100), 8 Victoria Rd, Derry BT47 2AB, for the Foyle area, and from the Fisheries Conservancy Board (☎ 01762-334666), 1 Mahon Rd, Portadown, Craigavon, County Armagh, for all other regions. You also require a permit from the owner, which is usually the Department of Agriculture, Dundonald House, Upper Newtownards Rd, Belfast BT4 3SB. Call ☎ 01232-520100 and ask for the fisheries division. It charges £8/32.50 for one/eight days.

Bord Fáilte and the Northern Ireland Tourist Board produce several information leaflets on fishing. Bord Fáilte annually publishes *The Anglers' Guide*, which lists accommodation, major fishing events and charter-boat operators. Three good books are *Game Angling Guide*, *Coarse Angling Guide* and *Sea Angling Guide* from the Central Fisheries Board and published by Gill & Macmillan (☎ 01-435 1005), Goldenbridge, Inchicore, Dublin 8. They're full of practical information and details of the permits and licences required.

WATER SPORTS

Ireland's more than 5630km coastline, its rivers and numerous lakes provide plenty of opportunities for a range of water sports.

Swimming & Surfing

The climate and the water temperature are good reasons why Ireland isn't the first place you'd think of for swimming or surfing. On the other hand, it has some magnificent coastline and some great sandy beaches. Sadly, a number of Irish beaches suffer from pollution, but the cleaner, safer ones have been awarded the EU Blue Flag and you can get a list of these from Taisce An (☎ 01-454 1786), The Tailors Hall, Back Lane, Dublin 8.

Following is a list of Ireland's major surfing spots.

North-West
Easkey in the west of County Sligo is known locally as a surfing haunt and is highly regarded by surfers, but by international standards is uncrowded. Achill Island in County Mayo has surfing beaches and there's an Activity & Leisure Centre on the Keel road where you can get information and equipment.

South-West
Barley Cove beach on the Mizen Head Peninsula is the only surfing beach in County Cork, but it isn't crowded. In Kerry, around Caherdaniel on the Iveragh Peninsula it's possible to hire equipment at the local beach; the broad, empty beaches around Castlegregory on Castlegregory Peninsula are perfect for surfing; at Inch on the Dingle Peninsula the waves average 1m to 3m.

West
Spanish Point near Miltown Malby and Lahinch in west Clare are good for surfing.

South-East
In Wexford, equipment is available for hire at Rosslare Strand. In County Waterford, Ballinacourty, Dunmore East, Tramore and Dungarvan are all worth considering for surfing. Equipment and advice is available in Dunmore East.

North
Portrush on the north coast in County Antrim is a popular surfing centre; you can hire equipment in town.

The Irish Surfing Association (☎ 073-21053), Tirchonaill St, Donegal Town, County Donegal can supply you with more details.

Scuba Diving

Ireland has some of the best scuba diving in Europe, almost entirely off the west coast; visibility averages over 12m but can increase to 30m on good days. A number of centres around the country offer equipment and training. Oceantec Adventures (☎ 01-280 1083) in Dun Laoghaire, County Dublin, is a five-star PADI centre with a dive shop and school and it can arrange dive vacations on the west coast. For more details about scuba diving in Ireland write to or phone the Irish Underwater Council (☎ 01-284 601), 78A Patrick St, Dun Laoghaire, County Dublin. The council publishes Ireland's dive magazine, *Subsea*.

Following are some favourite dive sites.

South-West

Bantry Bay and Dunmanus Bay in County Cork are good sites and they are serviced by Bantry Bay Divers in Glengarriff; the area is largely virgin territory – a major draw with divers. The Iveragh Peninsula in Kerry has two main bases: Valentia Island and Caherdaniel.

West

The Connemara coastline and surrounding islands in County Galway are serviced by Scubadive West, a local company based at Glassillaun Beach. In County Clare, Kilkee is a popular diving centre and equipment is locally available. Ballyreen, near Lisdoonvarna, is less well known, as are Doolin and Fanore.

South-East

Around Hook Head in County Wexford is popular and facilities are available.

East

From Dun Laoghaire scuba divers head for the waters around Dalkey Island.

Sailing

Sailing has a long heritage in Ireland and the country has over 120 yacht and sailing clubs including the Royal Cork Yacht Club at Crosshaven, which, established in 1720, is the world's oldest. The most popular areas for sailing are the west coast especially between Cork Harbour and the Dingle Peninsula, the coastline north and south of Dublin, the coast of Antrim and some of the larger lakes like Lough Derg, Lough Erne and Lough Gill.

For more information contact the Irish Sailing Association (☎ 01-280 0239), 3 Park Rd, Dun Laoghaire, County Dublin, which is the national body governing the sport. Ireland has a number of professional training schools catering for people of varying degrees of expertise and which operate under the auspices of the Irish Association for Sail Training (☎ 01-660 1011), Irish Marine Federation, Confederation House, 84-86 Baggott St Lower, Dublin 2.

A recommended publication is the *Irish Cruising Club Sailing Directions* available from booksellers, which contains details of port facilities, harbour plans and coast and tidal information.

Windsurfing

The windsurfer has plenty of locations, along the coast and on rivers and lakes, to indulge this popular sport, with the west coast facing the Atlantic being the most challenging. Even the Grand Canal in Dublin is used by windsurfers. The bay at Rosslare is ideal for windsurfing and you can obtain equipment and tuition there from the Rosslare Windsurfing Centre (☎ 053-32101). The Irish Sailing Association (see above) is the governing authority of the sport and has details of other centres offering the same.

Canoeing

There are many opportunities for canoeing and it's a great way to travel round the country. The Liffey Descent in September is a major international competition. The type of canoeing in Ireland and degree of difficulty varies from gentle paddling to white-water canoeing and canoe surfing. Information on locations and conditions can be obtained from the Irish Canoe Union (☎ 01-450 9838), House of Sport, Long Mile Rd, Walkinstown, Dublin 12; it also runs training courses on the River Liffey. Tiglin Adventure Centre (☎ 0404-40169), Ashford, County Wicklow, runs courses and organises canoeing trips.

Water Skiing

There are water-ski clubs all over Ireland offering tuition, equipment and boats. Bord Fáilte provides the names of some of these clubs, but a full list and other details are available from the Irish Water-Ski Federation (☎ 01-624 0526), 29 Hermitage Rd, Lucan, County Dublin.

BIRDWATCHING

Ireland's location on the north-western edge of Europe and the variety and size of the flocks that visit or breed there make it of particular interest to birdwatchers. It's also home to some rare and endangered species. For a description of some of the birds and where to find them see under Fauna in the Facts about the Country chapter.

There are more than 70 reserves and sanctuaries in Ireland, but some aren't open to visitors and others are privately owned so you'll need permission from the proprietors before entering them. It's also illegal to interfere with wild birds, their nests and eggs. Information can be obtained from:

National Parks & Wildlife Service
    Dúchas, 51 St Stephen's Green, Dublin 2 (☎ 01-661 3111)
Irish Wildbird Conservancy
    Ruttledge House, 8 Longford Place, Monkstown, County Dublin (☎ 01-280 4322)
Royal Society for the Protection of Birds
    Belvoir Park Forest, Belfast BT8 4QT (☎ 01232-491547)
National Trust
    Rowallane House, Saintfield, County Down BT24 7LH (☎ 01238-510721)

Some useful publications on birdwatching are *Where to Watch Birds in Ireland* by CD Hutchinson, *The Birds of Ireland* by G D'Arcy and *Complete Guide to Ireland's Birds* by E Dempsey & M O'Cleary.

GOLF
There are around 350 golf courses in Ireland, South and North, often in beautiful settings. They range from illustrious and expensive ones at Killarney, Portmarnock near Dublin and Royal County Down, to more modest places like the one at Castletownbere on the Beara Peninsula.

Bord Fáilte and the Northern Ireland Tourist Board produce information leaflets, plus brochures on customised golfing holidays with descriptions of courses and local accommodation. You could also try contacting the Golfing Union of Ireland (☎ 01-269 4111), 81 Eglington Rd, Dublin 4, or the Irish Ladies Golf Union (☎ 01-269 6244), 1 Clonskeagh Square, Clonskeagh Rd, Dublin 14.

Green fees, usually based on a per day rather than a per round basis, start from IR£10 on weekdays (more on weekends) but the top-notch places will charge more than three times this. Fees are about the same in the North.

Courses are tested for their level of difficulty and many are playable year round. It's always advisable to book in advance. Most clubs give members priority in booking tee-off times; it's usually easier to book a tee-off time on a public course but on weekends, public holidays and days when the weather is good, it's often busy on all courses. You should also check whether there's a dress code, and whether the course has golf clubs for hire (not all do) if you don't have your own.

HANG GLIDING
Some of the finest hang gliding can be found at Mt Leinster in Carlow, Great Sugar Loaf Mountain in Wicklow, Benone/Magillan Beach in Derry and Achill Island in Mayo. Contact the Irish Hang-Gliding Association (☎ 01-450 9845), AFAS House of Sport, Longmile Rd, Dublin 12, for general information. For tuition contact the Irish Paragliding Centre (☎ 01-276 0456), 21 St Cronan's Rd, Bray, County Wicklow.

ROCK CLIMBING
Ireland's mountain ranges aren't high – Carrantuohill in Kerry's Macgillycuddy's Reeks at only 1041m is the tallest in Ireland – but they're often beautiful and offer some excellent climbing possibilities. For further information get in touch with the Mountaineering Council of Ireland (☎ 01-450 9845), AFAS House of Sport, Longmile Rd, Dublin 12, which also publishes a number of climbing guides.

The highest mountains are in the southwest. Cork has a number of easy climbs, including Mt Gabriel (407m) on the Mizen Head Peninsula, Seefin (528m) on the Sheep's Head Peninsula and Sugarloaf Mountain (574m) on the Beara Peninsula; Hungry Hill (686m), also on the Beara Peninsula is more demanding. The Iveragh Peninsula in County Kerry is the place to head for if you want to be surrounded by mountains just waiting to be climbed. Macgillycuddy's Reeks are here.

In the north-west Knocknarea (328m) outside Sligo Town is an easy climb and so, too, is Croagh Patrick (763m), in west Mayo, although it takes a lot longer. On Achill Island in Mayo are some of the highest cliffs in Europe. In Galway, Clifden makes a good base for climbing in Connemara, and in Clare there's excellent rock climbing at Ballyreen near Fanore. Errigal Mountain (752m) in Donegal is popular with climbers when the weather allows.

At the northern end of Lough Tay in the Wicklow Mountains are some spectacular cliffs popular with rock climbers. Also popular are the large crags in Glendalough, at the western end of the valley not far from the Upper Lake. Tiglin Adventure Centre (☎ 0404-40169), near Ashford, runs rock-climbing courses in the Wicklows.

The Mourne Mountains in County Down, Northern Ireland, have steep, craggy granite peaks including Eagle Mountain, Pigeon Rock Mountain and Slieve Donard which, at 850m, is the highest peak in the range. You can base yourself in nearby Newcastle.

HORSE RIDING

Not surprisingly this is a popular pastime and there are literally dozens of centres through-out Ireland offering horses or ponies for riding along beaches, country lanes, mountain and forest trails and over farmland. Possibilities range from hiring a horse for an hour (from IR£10) to fully packaged residential equestrian holidays; in some places you can even combine it with English-language tuition. Bord Fáilte and the Northern Irish Tourist Board have full details.

The lovely wooded valleys and heathery mountains of north County Waterford are good for horse riding as are the Wicklow Mountains. Kildare is an equestrian paradise. Other areas include the Dingle Peninsula in Kerry, Connemara in Galway, around Bundoran and the Finn Valley in Donegal and near Clonakilty and Killarney in Cork.

SCENIC ROUTES

If you're only visiting Ireland for a short time then touring by car or motorcycle will help you to fit in a lot more. Following are some scenic routes, though the list is by no means exhaustive. The west of Ireland has the most dramatic scenery, but there are many other

---

Tracing your Ancestors

Many visitors to Ireland have ancestors who once lived in this country. Your trip would be a good chance to find out more about them and their lives; you may even find relatives you never even knew you had. The Irish diaspora is huge with more than 40 million people of Irish descent in the USA, over five million in Canada, a similar figure in Australia, hundreds of thousands in South America, nobody knows quite how many millions in Britain, plus many in other countries.

To achieve the most success from your visit you should begin researching in your home country, by finding out, if possible, the date and point of arrival of your ancestor(s).

If you contact the Genealogical Office (☎ 01-603 0200), 2 Kildare St, Dublin 2, or the Public Record Office of Northern Ireland (PRONI; ☎ 01232-251318), 66 Balmoral Ave, Belfast BT9 6NY, they'll be able to provide you with information on what to do. They can also provide you with a list of local research centres in Ireland, so if you know which county your ancestors came from you can then write to the centres directly. Much of the data of civil and church records is computerised and many local genealogy centres are connected to a computer network.

If you can't or don't want to undertake the research yourself there are numerous commercial agencies that will do it for you for a fee. For information on these contact the Association of Professional Genealogists in Ireland (APGI), c/o the Genealogical Office in Dublin, and the Association of Ulster Genealogists & Record Agents (AUGRA), Glen Cottage, Glenmachan Rd, Belfast BT4 2NP.

A huge number of books is available on the subject. *The Irish Roots Guide* by Tony McCarthy serves as a useful introduction. Other publications include *Tracing Your Irish Roots* by Christine Kinealy and recommended is *Tracing Your Irish Ancestors: A Comprehensive Guide* by John Grenham. All these publications, and other items of genealogical concern, may be obtained from the Genealogy Bookshop (☎ 01-679 5313), 3 Nassau St, Dublin 2; in Belfast the place to go is the Familia bookshop (☎01232-235392), 64 Wellington Place. ■

parts of the country where the landscape is also stunningly beautiful.

South-West

The routes that use the main roads to loop around the lush, green peninsulas of Mizen Head and Sheep's Head and the more desolate Beara in West Cork are all scenic. The north coast of the Beara, the Healy Pass that cuts through the peninsula, and the Goat's Path along the north side of the Sheep's Head are the most spectacular parts of these routes.

The road from Bantry to Kenmare and on to Killarney is an attractive drive as is the one from Bantry east to Macroom. The Ring of Kerry, the road that loops around the Iveragh Peninsula, is justly famous and attracts a lot of vehicles.

From Tralee in County Clare there are two routes into the Dingle Peninsula, but the more beautiful is the one that follows the northern coastline and crosses over the Slieve Mish Mountains via Connor Pass to the town of Dingle and onto the western headlands.

Following Clare's Atlantic coastline offers dramatic views while the road that follows the south-western shores of Lough Derg passes through gentle countryside and picturesque villages.

West & North-West

In County Mayo the road between Louisburg and Delphi is one of the most scenic anywhere in the west of Ireland; it works its magic on motorists who all seem unusually willing to slow down. The route in north Mayo that passes Ballycastle has magnificent views.

In Galway the Lough Inagh Valley in Connemara between the Maumturk Mountains and the Twelve Bens is one of the most scenic in the country. There are marvellous views along the road between Recess and Clifden to the south of the Twelve Bens.

Donegal has many scenic routes and one of the best is the road from Glencolumbcille to Ardara by way of the visually striking Glengesh Pass. From Ballyliffin to Buncrana there is a scenic coastal road via the Gap of Mamore and Dunree.

North-East

The A2 road east out of Belfast is a pleasant route to Bangor and the eastern coastline of the Ards Peninsula then south to Portavogie and Portaferry. You can return to Belfast north along the A20 following the eastern shoreline of Strangford Lough.

North of Belfast the A2 will take you to the Giant's Causeway following the magnificent Antrim coast, with the Antrim Mountains to the west; between Cushendun and Ballycastle you can follow an alternative road that loops around the headland and rejoins the A2 at Ballyvoy.

The road that circles Lough Erne from Enniskillen in County Fermanagh is interesting historically as well as visually.

East & South-East

South of Dublin there are several routes into the Wicklow Mountains. The most scenic begins at Glencree, leads south over the Sally Gap to Glendalough, continues to Avoca and then on to Arklow on the coast. The Wicklow coast between Greystones and Rathnew has some lovely countryside too.

In southern County Carlow quiet roads connect picturesque villages like Leighlinbridge and Borris, with other villages in neighbouring counties Wexford and Kilkenny. Borris is also one starting point for a scenic drive up to nearby Mt Leinster.

In Waterford the coast road between Tramore and Dungarvan has lots of panoramic views and attractive villages. In the west of the county there are signposted scenic drives round the Knockmealdown Mountains with some terrific views.

Getting There & Away

Whichever way you're travelling to Ireland, make sure you take out travel insurance (see Documents in the Facts for the Visitor chapter).

For information about cheap deals to Ireland, students and young people should contact the Union of Students in Ireland Travel (USIT), – see Useful Organisations in the Facts for the Visitor chapter.

AIR
Airports & Airlines

Dublin (☎ 01-844 4900) is the Republic's major international airport, but Cork (☎ 1800-626747) and Shannon (☎ 061-471444) also have international airports. There are flights from these to the UK, Europe and the USA. Some smaller airports, including Galway (☎ 091-755569) and Waterford (☎ 051-875589), have direct flights to the UK. Aer Lingus is the Irish national airline and Ryanair is the next largest Irish airline. Both have international connections to the UK, Europe and the USA.

Belfast has two airports. Most flights go to the international airport (☎ 01849-422888) 30km north of town, but there's also the more central Belfast city airport (☎ 01232-457745), which has flights to some regional airports in Britain. City of Derry airport (☎ 01504-810784) has flights to Britain, Dublin and Paris. The main carriers to the North are British Airways Express and Jersey European.

Buying Tickets

If you're flying to Ireland from outside Europe, the plane ticket will probably be the single most expensive item in your budget, and it's worth taking some time to research the current state of the market.

Start early: some of the cheapest tickets have to be bought well in advance, and some popular flights sell out early. Have a talk to recent travellers, look at the ads in newspa-

> **Warning**
> The information in this chapter is particularly vulnerable to change: prices for international travel are volatile, routes are introduced and cancelled, schedules change, special deals come and go, and rules and visa requirements are amended.
> Airlines and governments seem to take a perverse pleasure in making price structures and regulations as complicated as possible. Check directly with the airline or a travel agent to make sure you understand how a fare (and ticket you may buy) works. In addition, the travel industry is highly competitive and there are many lurks and perks.
> Before you part with your hard-earned cash you should get opinions, quotes and advice from as many airlines and travel agents as possible. The details given in this chapter should be regarded as pointers and are not a substitute for your own careful, up-to-date research.

pers and magazines including any catering specifically to the Irish community in your country, and watch for special offers. Then phone round travel agents for bargains. Find out the fare, the route, the duration of the journey and any restrictions on the ticket, then decide which is best for you.

Cheap tickets are available in two categories: official and unofficial. Official ones have a variety of names including advance purchase tickets, advance purchase excursion (Apex) fares, super-Apex or whatever name the airlines care to use. Unofficial tickets are discounted tickets that airlines release through selected travel agents. Airlines can supply information on routes and timetables, and their low-season, student and senior citizens' fares can be competitive, but they don't sell discounted tickets. Normal, full-fare airline tickets sometimes include one or more free side trips to Europe, and/or fly-drive packages which can make them good value.

Return (round-trip) tickets usually work

Air Travel Glossary

Apex Apex, or 'advance purchase excursion' is a discounted ticket which must be paid for in advance. There are penalties if you wish to change it.

Baggage Allowance This will be written on your ticket: usually one 20kg item to go in the hold, plus one item of hand luggage.

Bucket Shop An unbonded travel agency specialising in discounted airline tickets.

Bumped Just because you have a confirmed seat doesn't mean you're going to get on the plane – see Overbooking.

Cancellation Penalties If you have to cancel or change an Apex ticket, there are often heavy penalties involved – insurance can sometimes be taken out against these penalties. Some airlines impose penalties on regular tickets as well, particularly against 'no show' passengers.

Check In Airlines ask you to check in at a certain time ahead of the flight departure (usually 1½ hours on international flights). If you fail to check in on time and the flight is overbooked, the airline can cancel your booking and give your seat to somebody else.

Confirmation Having a ticket written out with the flight and date you want doesn't necessarily mean you have a seat. Until the agent has checked with the airline that your status is 'OK' or confirmed, you could just be 'on request' (RQ), this being the code that would be written in place of OK on your ticket.

Discounted Tickets There are two types of discounted fares – officially discounted (see Promotional Fares) and unofficially discounted. The lowest prices often impose drawbacks like flying with unpopular airlines, inconvenient schedules, or unpleasant routes and connections. A discounted ticket can save you other things than money – you may be able to pay Apex prices without the associated Apex advance booking and other requirements. Discounted tickets only exist where there is fierce competition.

Full Fares Airlines traditionally offer 1st class (coded F), business class (coded J) and economy class (coded Y) tickets. These days, there are so many promotional and discounted fares available from the regular economy class that few passengers pay full economy fare.

Lost Tickets If you lose your ticket an airline will usually treat it like a travellers' cheque and, after enquiries, issue you with another one. Legally, however, an airline is entitled to treat it like cash and if you lose it then it's gone forever. Take good care of your tickets.

No Shows No shows are passengers who fail to show up for their flight, sometimes due to unexpected delays or disasters, sometimes due to simply forgetting, sometimes because they made more than one booking and didn't bother to cancel the one they didn't want. Full-fare passengers who fail to turn up are sometimes entitled to travel on a later flight. The rest of us are penalised (see Cancellation Penalties).

On Request An unconfirmed booking for a flight, see Confirmation.

Open Jaws A return ticket where you fly out to one place but return from another. If available, this can save you backtracking to your arrival point.

---

out cheaper than two one-way fares. In some cases, a return ticket can even be cheaper than a one-way.

Round-the-World (RTW) tickets can also be great bargains, and can work out to be no more expensive or even cheaper than an ordinary return ticket. Standard fares in the high season are about UK£1550, US$3350, A$3500. An RTW might take you directly to Dublin, Shannon or Belfast or as a side trip from London.

Official airline RTW tickets are usually put together by a combination of two or more airlines, and permit you to fly anywhere you want on their route systems so long as you don't backtrack. Other restrictions are that you (usually) must book the first sector in advance and cancellation penalties then apply. There may be restrictions on how many stops you're permitted and usually the tickets are valid for 90 days up to a year from the date of the first outbound flight. Travel agents put together unofficial RTW tickets by combining a number of discounted tickets.

Discounted tickets are usually available at prices as low as or lower than the official Apex or budget tickets. When you phone around, find out the fare, the route, the duration of the journey, the stopovers allowed and any restrictions on the ticket, and ask about cancellation penalties.

Overbooking Airlines hate to fly empty seats and, since every flight has some passengers who fail to show up (see No Shows), they often book more passengers than they have seats. Usually the excess passengers balance those who fail to show up, but occasionally somebody gets bumped. If this happens, guess who it is most likely to be? The passengers who check in late.

Promotional Fares Officially discounted fares like Apex fares which are available from travel agents or direct from the airline.

Reconfirmation At least 72 hours prior to departure time of an onward or return flight you should normally contact the airline and 'reconfirm' that you intend to be on the flight. If you don't do this the airline can delete your name from the passenger list and you could lose your seat. You don't have to reconfirm the first flight on your itinerary or if your stopover is less than 72 hours. It doesn't hurt to reconfirm more than once.

Restrictions Discounted tickets often have various restrictions on them – advance purchase is the most usual one (see Apex). Others are restrictions on the minimum and maximum period you must be away, such as a minimum of 14 days or a maximum of one year. See Cancellation Penalties.

Standby A discounted ticket where you only fly if there is a seat free at the last moment. Standby fares are usually only available on domestic routes.

Tickets Out An entry requirement for many countries is that you have an onward or return ticket, in other words, a ticket out of the country. If you're not sure what you intend to do next, the easiest solution is to buy the cheapest onward ticket to a neighbouring country or a ticket from a reliable airline which can later be refunded if you do not use it.

Transferred Tickets Airline tickets cannot be transferred from one person to another. Travellers sometimes try to sell the return half of their ticket, but officials can ask you to prove that you are the person named on the ticket. This is unlikely to happen on domestic flights, but on international flights tickets may be compared with passports.

Travel Agencies Travel agencies vary widely and you should ensure you use one that suits your needs. Some simply handle tours, while full-service agencies handle everything from tours and tickets to car rental and hotel bookings. A good one will do all these things and can save you a lot of money, but if all you want is a ticket at the lowest possible price, then you really need an agency specialising in discounted tickets. A discounted ticket agency, however, may not be useful for other things, like hotel bookings.

Travel Periods Some officially discounted fares, Apex fares in particular, vary with the time of year. There is often a low (off-peak) season and a high (peak) season. Sometimes there's an intermediate or shoulder season as well. At peak times, when everyone wants to fly, not only will the officially discounted fares be higher, but so will unofficially discounted fares; or there may simply be no discounted tickets available. Usually, the fare depends on your outward flight – if you depart in the high season and return in the low season, you pay the high-season fare. ■

You may discover that the cheapest flights are 'fully booked', but the agency happens to know of another one that 'costs a bit more'. Or that the flight is on an airline notorious for its poor safety standards and leaves you in the world's least favourite airport in mid-journey for 14 hours (where you're confined to the transit lounge because you don't have a visa). Or that the agents have the last two seats available for Ireland for the whole of July, which they'll hold for a maximum of two hours. Don't panic – keep ringing around.

If you're flying to Ireland from the UK, USA or South-East Asia you'll probably find that the cheapest flights are being advertised by small and obscure agencies – the proverbial 'bucket shops'. Many such firms are honest and solvent, but there are a few rogues who'll take your money and disappear. If you feel suspicious about a firm, don't give them all the money at once – leave a 20% deposit or so and pay the balance when you get the ticket. You could phone the airline direct to check you actually have a booking before you pick up the ticket. If the agent insists on cash in advance, go somewhere else or be prepared to take a big risk.

You may decide to pay more than the rock-bottom fare by opting for the safety of a better-known travel agent. Firms such as STA Travel (which has offices worldwide),

USIT (with offices in Britain, Europe, New Zealand and New York), Trailfinders (in Britain), Council Travel (in the USA) or Travel CUTS (in Canada) offer good prices to most destinations, and are competitive and usually reliable.

Once you have your ticket, write its number down, together with the flight number and other details, and keep the information somewhere separate. If the ticket is lost or stolen, this will help you get a replacement.

Use the fares quoted in this book as a guide only. They're likely to have changed by the time you read this.

Travellers with Special Needs

If you have special needs of any sort – you've broken a leg, you require a special diet, you're travelling in a wheelchair, taking a baby, terrified of flying, or whatever – let the airline staff know as soon as possible so that they can make the necessary arrangements. Remind them when you reconfirm your booking and again when you check in at the airport. It may also be worth ringing round the airlines before you make your booking to find out how they can handle your particular needs. If necessary, also discuss your travel needs with your doctor.

Children under two travel for 10% of the standard fare (or free on some airlines) as long as they don't occupy a seat, but they don't get a baggage allowance. 'Skycots', baby food and nappies (diapers) should be provided by the airline if requested in advance. Children aged two to 12 years can usually occupy a seat for half to two-thirds of the full fare, and get a baggage allowance.

The UK

Aer Lingus and Ryanair are the main operators between the UK and the Republic of Ireland. British Airways Express flies to Belfast and Derry in Northern Ireland and to Dublin in the South. Dublin is linked by a variety of airlines to several cities in the UK.

Trailfinders (☎ 0171-938 3939), 194 Kensington High St, London W8 6FT (tube station: High St Kensington), produces an illustrated brochure which includes air-fare details. STA Travel (☎ 0171-361 6262), 74 Old Brompton Rd, London SW7 (tube station: South Kensington) has a number of branches in the UK. Council Travel (☎ 0171-437 7767), 28 Poland St, London W1V 3DB (tube station: Oxford Circus), is the USA's largest student and budget travel agency. USIT/Campus Travel (☎ 0171-730 3402), 52 Grosvenor Gardens, London SW1W 0AG (tube station: Victoria) has offices in large YHA Adventure Shops.

Look in the listings of magazines like *Time Out*, plus the Sunday papers and *Exchange & Mart* for ads. Also look out for the free magazines widely available in London – start by looking outside the main railway stations and the tube stations.

There's a £5 departure tax from Britain to Ireland (and to other countries in the European Union), which is added to the price of your ticket.

Republic of Ireland There are flights between Dublin and all the major London airports. Aer Lingus and British Midland Airways fly from Heathrow, Aer Lingus and British Airways Express fly from Gatwick, Ryanair flies from Gatwick, Luton and Stansted, Virgin Atlantic flies from London city airport, Britannia Airways flies from Luton and Air UK flies from Stansted. Connections are generally frequent; in the summer Aer Lingus has nearly 20 Heathrow-Dublin services daily and British Midland another 10.

The regular one-way economy fare from London to Dublin is £99, but advance-purchase fares are available offering round-trip tickets for as low as £60 to £100. These should be booked well in advance as seats are often limited.

Heathrow can be reached by airport bus or by the tube (underground railway). There are regular train services to Gatwick from Victoria station; there are also regular trains between Stansted and Liverpool St station. From London city airport there are shuttlebuses to Liverpool St station and to Canary Wharf.

UK addresses and phone numbers are:

Aer Lingus
 64 Conduit St, London W1R 0AJ (☎ 0181-899 4747)
Air UK
 Stansted House, Stansted Airport, Essex (☎ 0345-666777)
British Airways
 156 Regent St, London W1R 5TA
 Victoria Station Concourse, London SW1V 1JT
 Plus other British Airways Travel Shops in London and throughout Britain (☎ 0345-222111)
British Midland Airways
 PO Box 60, Donington Hall, Castle Donington, Derby DE7 2SB (☎ 0345-554554)
Ryanair
 116-18 Finchley Rd, London NW3 5HT (☎ 0171-435 7101)
Virgin Atlantic
 London City Airport, Royal Docks, London E16 2PX (☎ 01293-747146)

Other places in Britain with flights to Dublin are:

Birmingham:	Aer Lingus, Ryanair
Bristol:	Aer Lingus, Ryanair
Cardiff:	Manx Airlines, Ryanair
East Midlands:	British Midland
Edinburgh:	Aer Lingus
Glasgow:	Aer Lingus, Ryanair (to Prestwick)
Isle of Man:	Manx Airlines
Jersey:	Manx Airlines, Aer Lingus, Jersey European
Leeds/Bradford:	Aer Lingus, Ryanair
Liverpool:	Ryanair
Luton:	Ryanair
Manchester:	Aer Lingus, Ryanair
Newcastle-upon-Tyne:	Aer Lingus

Fares between Manchester and Dublin are similar to London-Dublin fares but other connections can be much more expensive.

Other cities in Ireland with air connections from the UK include Cork, Galway, Killarney, Shannon, Sligo and Waterford.

Northern Ireland There are flights from some regional airports in Britain to the convenient Belfast city airport (☎ 01232-457745), virtually in the centre of the city, but everything else goes through to Belfast

international airport (☎ 01849-422888), in Aldergrove 30km north of the city.

Belfast has a regular Cityflyer/British Airways Express shuttle service from London Heathrow. Costs on the shuttle range from as low as £82 for a saver off-peak one-way or £139 for an advance-purchase return, to as high as £130 for a regular one way with no restrictions.

British Midland Airways offers similar fares, but Britannia Airways (Belfast international) and Manx Airlines/British Airways Express (Belfast city) fly from Luton to Belfast from £46. Luton airport is only 45 minutes north of London. There are also connections between Belfast and other centres including flights to and from the convenient Belfast city airport.

Europe
Discount charter flights are often available to full-time students aged under 30 and all young travellers aged under 26 (you need an ISIC or EYC card; see Documents in the Facts for the Visitor chapter) and are available through large student travel agencies.

Dublin is connected with major centres in Europe. From Paris, the standard return fare to Dublin is FF1690, to Belfast (via London) FF2090. Places in Europe with connections to Dublin are:

Amsterdam, Netherlands:	Aer Lingus
Barcelona, Spain:	Iberia
Brussels, Belgium:	Aer Lingus, Sabena (both to National); Ryanair (to Charleroi)
Cologne, Germany:	Lufthansa
Copenhagen, Denmark:	Aer Lingus, SAS
Dusseldorf, Germany:	Aer Lingus
Frankfurt, Germany:	Aer Lingus, Lufthansa
Lisbon, Portugal:	TAP
Madrid, Spain:	Aer Lingus, Iberia
Milan, Italy:	Aer Lingus, Alitalia
Moscow, Russia:	Aeroflot
Munich, Germany:	Lufthansa
Paris, France:	Aer Lingus, Air France, Cityjet (all to Charles de Gaulle); Ryanair (to Beauvais)
Rome, Italy:	Aer Lingus, Alitalia
Zurich, Switzerland:	Aer Lingus, Crossair

North America

Flights from North America put down in Dublin and Shannon, but because competition on flights to London is so much fiercer it's generally cheaper to fly to London first. From Ireland to the USA, Virgin Atlantic via London is often the cheapest option.

Aer Lingus connects Dublin, Belfast and other Irish cities with many US cities including Boston, Chicago, Dallas, Denver, Detroit, Los Angeles, New Orleans, New York, Philadelphia, San Francisco, Seattle and Washington DC. Its New York office (☎ 212-557 1110 or 1-800-223 6537) is at 122 East 42nd St, New York. In Canada, Aer Lingus can be contacted by calling ☎ 1-800 223 6537, although it doesn't actually fly to Canada. The only other US operator with direct connections to Ireland is Delta Airlines (☎ 1-800 2414141), which operates Atlanta-Shannon-Dublin, linking into its huge US network. From Vancouver, Montreal and Toronto in Canada there are direct flights to Ireland on Air Canada and Canadian Airlines.

During the summer high season the round trip between New York and Dublin with Aer Lingus costs US$800 midweek or US$996 at weekends. Usually there are advance-purchase fares offered early in the year which allow you to fly from New York to Dublin for just under US$600 return.

In the low season, discount return fares from New York to London will be in the US$450 to US$500 range, in the high season US$800 to US$900. From the west coast fares to London will cost from around US$200 more.

Check the Sunday travel sections of papers like the *New York Times, Los Angeles Times, Chicago Tribune* or *San Francisco Chronicle-Examiner* for the latest fares. The *Globe & Mail, Toronto Star* or *Vancouver Sun* have similar details from Canada. Offices of Council Travel or STA Travel in the USA or Travel CUTS in Canada are good sources of reliable discounted tickets. The *Travel Unlimited* newsletter, PO Box 1058, Allston, MA 02134, publishes details of the cheapest air fares and courier possibilities for destinations all over the world from the USA and other countries.

Australia & New Zealand

STA Travel and Flight Centres International are major dealers in discounted airfares from Australia or New Zealand. Shamrock Travel (☎ 03-9602 3700), Level 9, 310 King St, Melbourne, Victoria, specialises in flights to Ireland.

The Saturday travel sections of the *Sydney Morning Herald* and Melbourne *Age* newspapers have many ads offering cheap fares, but don't be surprised if they're sold out when you contact the agents: they're usually low-season fares on obscure airlines with conditions attached.

Excursion or Apex fares from Australia or New Zealand to Britain can have a return flight to Dublin tagged on at no extra cost. Return fares from Australia vary from around A$1600 (low season) to A$2900 (high season) but there are often short-term special deals available.

The cheapest fares from New Zealand will probably take the eastbound route via the USA but a Round-the-World ticket may be cheaper than a return.

For information about Aer Lingus flights contact World Aviation Systems (☎ 02-9321 9123), 64 York St, Sydney 2000 (it also has offices in Adelaide, Brisbane, Canberra, Melbourne and Perth). In New Zealand, World Aviation Systems (☎ 09-379 4455) is at Trustbank Building, 229 Queen St, Auckland.

SEA

There's a great variety of services from France and Britain to Ireland using modern ferries and catamarans. There are often special deals, return fares and other money-savers which compare favourably with the cheaper air fares.

Want to travel free? On some routes the cost for a car includes up to four or five passengers at no additional cost. If you can hitch a ride in a less than full car, it costs the driver nothing extra.

The UK

Numerous services operate from ports in England, Scotland, Wales and the Isle of Man to the Republic and the North. It's wise to plan ahead because fares vary considerably depending on the season, time of day, length of stay and day of the week. Some return fares aren't much more than one-way fares. Companies also provide special deals which it's worth keeping an eye out for and offer reductions to ISIC cardholders and HI/YHA members.

The shipping lines are:

Argyll & Antrim Steam Packet Company
    A subsidiary of Sea Containers Ferries Scotland (see below) – for services from Campbeltown (Scotland) (☎ 0345-523523)
Irish Ferries
    150 New Bond St, London W1Y 0AQ – for services from Holyhead, Pembroke and Cairnryan (☎ 0990-171717)
Isle of Man Steam Packet
    PO Box 5, Douglas, Isle of Man, IM99 1AF – for services from Douglas (☎ 0345-523523)
Norse Irish Ferries
    North Brocklebank Dock, Bootle, Merseyside L20 1BY – for services from Liverpool to Belfast (☎ 0151-944 1010)
P&O
    Cairnryan, Stranraer, Wigtownshire DG9 8RF – for services from Cairnryan to Larne (☎ 0990-980777)
Sea Containers Ferries Scotland
    SeaCat Terminal, West Pier, Stranraer – for services from Stranraer to Belfast by catamaran, and Liverpool to Dublin (☎ 0345-523523)
Stena Line
    Charter House, Park St, Ashford, Kent TN24 8EX – for services from Holyhead, Fishguard and Stranraer (☎ 0990-707070)
Swansea Cork Ferries
    Ferryport, Kings Dock, Swansea, West Glamorgan SA1 SRU – for services from Swansea (☎ 01792-456116)

There are some interesting possibilities for those who are also touring the UK. Except for the Cairnryan-Line route, the figures quoted below are one-way fares for a single adult, for two adults with a car and for four adults with a car.

Irish Ferry Routes

The Republic of Ireland The following are routes to the Republic:

Fishguard & Pembroke to Rosslare These popular short crossings take 3½ hours (from Fishguard) or 4½ hours (from Pembroke) and cost as much as £35/229/229 on peak season weekends; at other times of year the cost drops to as low as £20/119/119. The high-speed catamaran crossing from Fishguard takes just over 1½ hours and costs £35/229/229 on peak-season weekends.

Holyhead to Dublin & Dun Laoghaire The crossing takes 3½ hours and costs £33/224/224 at peak-season weekends. The high-speed catamaran crossing from Holyhead to Dun Laoghaire takes a little over 1½ hours and costs £33/236/236.

Liverpool to Dublin This new daily service takes 6½ hours and costs £25/129/179 at peak times.

Swansea to Cork The 10-hour crossing costs £30/185/185 at peak times; the ferry doesn't operate in February.

Northern Ireland The following routes are to the North:

Campbeltown to Ballycastle The three-hour crossing from Campbeltown in Argyll to Ballycastle in Antrim costs £25/163/179.

Liverpool to Belfast The Norse Irish Ferries overnight service is not heavily promoted but it's easy to get to Liverpool from London. The trip costs £53/189/283 at peak times. There are also Isle of Man Steam Packet services from Liverpool via Douglas (Isle of Man). From Douglas a small car costs £77 in the peak season, passengers £36 each.

Stranraer to Belfast The SeaCat service uses a high-speed catamaran to race across in just 1½ hours at a cost of £26/198/218 at peak times. Stena Line also has a catamaran and ferry service on this route.

Cairnryan to Larne This service takes 2¼ hours and costs £27/182/209 at peak times down to £22/122/144.

France

Le Havre to Rosslare takes 22 hours and in the peak season costs as much as IR£90/300/370 (or the equivalent in French francs). Cherbourg to Rosslare is faster at 18½ hours but the cost is the same. May to September there are ferries from Le Havre to Cork taking 20½ hours, again at the same fare. There are also Roscoff to Cork services May to August, taking 15 hours and once again at the same price.

These services are operated by Irish Ferries and some can be used (with pre-booking) by Eurail pass holders. In France contact Transports et Voyages (☎ 1-42 66 90 90), 8 rue Auber, 75009 Paris. Inter-Rail passes also give reductions on these routes.

LAND & SEA

The relatively low cost of air fares from Britain make taking the bus or train hardly worth the hassle. Bus Éireann buses are old and cramped, and there are frequent delays. Unless you go from London, the train usually involves horrific connections and hanging around in the dead of night.

Bus Éireann and National Express operate Eurolines and Supabus services direct from London and other UK centres to Dublin, Belfast and other cities. For details in London contact Eurolines (☎ 0171-730 8235), 52 Grosvenor Gardens, Victoria, London SW1W 0AU or National Express

(☎ 0990-808080), Victoria coach station, Buckingham Palace Rd, London SW1W. Slattery's (☎ 0171-730 3666), 28 Elizabeth St, beside Victoria coach station, is an Irish bus company with routes from Bristol, Leeds, London, Liverpool, Manchester and north Wales to Dublin, Galway, Limerick, Tipperary, Tralee, Waterford, Ennis and Listowel. It has another office (☎ 0171-482 1604) at 162 Kentish Town Rd, London NW5 2AG. With Bus Éireann, London to Dublin takes about 12 hours and costs £36 return off-peak.

Ulsterbus (with National Express and Scottish Citylink) has express services to major cities in Britain. London to Belfast takes about 13 hours and the standard weekend fare is £42 one way (£44 return).

It's also possible to combine a rail and ferry ticket. London to Dun Laoghaire takes 9½ hours and costs £69 return (or £59 if you do the overnight crossing) at peak times.

DEPARTURE TAXES

There's an Irish government travel tax of IR£5 which is built into the price of an air ticket. You also pay this tax if you leave by ferry. See under Money in the Facts for the Visitor chapter for details of how to reclaim value-added tax (VAT) when you depart.

ORGANISED TOURS

There are numerous companies offering general or special-interest tours of Ireland. See your travel agent, check the small ads in newspaper travel pages or contact Bord Fáilte (Irish Tourist Board) and the Northern Ireland Tourist Board (or the British Tourist Authority) for the names of tour operators. See Tourist Offices in the Facts for the Visitor chapter.

In the USA there are a number of companies offering whirlwind coach tours of Ireland. American Express Vacations (☎ 1-800-446-6234, 770-368 5100), Box 1525, Fort Lauderdale, Florida 33302, has 10 and 12-day packages. Similar deals can be found with TWA Getaway Vacations (☎ 1-800-438 2929; fax 1-609-985 4125), 28 South 6th St, Philadelphia, Pennsylvania 19106. More-expensive tours are operated by Abercrombie & Kent (☎ 1-800-323 7308, 708-954 2944), 1520 Kensington Rd, Oak Brook, Illinois 60521, and include accommodation in castles and country houses.

From the UK, CIE Tours International (☎ 0990-143910; fax 0800-838814), 183-85 London Rd, Croydon, London CR0 2RJ, does four-day to 10-day coach tours, two of which include the North.

Getting Around

On the map, travelling around Ireland looks simple enough – the distances are short and there's a network of roads and railways – but in practice there are a few problems. In Ireland, from A to B is never a straight line and there are always a great many intriguing diversions to make. Public transport is often expensive (particularly train services), infrequent or both. Plus, public transport simply does not reach many of the interesting places so having your own transport can be a major advantage – though trying to follow the road signs has its own difficulties.

It's worth considering car rental for at least a part of your trip. However, even if you're not driving, with a mix of buses, the occasional taxi, plenty of time, walking and sometimes hiring a bicycle, you can get to just about anywhere.

AIR

Ireland's size makes flying unnecessary, but there are flights between Dublin and Belfast, Cork, Derry/Londonderry, Galway, Knock, Shannon, Sligo, Waterford and other centres. Most flights within Ireland take between 30 and 40 minutes.

Aer Rianta, the Republic's national airport authority, publishes a guide to airport services and flight schedules. Its head office (☎ 01-844 4900) is at Dublin airport.

As well as handling international flights, Aer Lingus and Ryanair are the two main domestic airlines. Aer Lingus' head office (☎ 01-705 2222) is at Dublin airport with ticket offices in Dublin, Cork, Belfast, Limerick and Shannon. For bookings call ☎ 01-705 3333 between 7.30 am and 9.30 pm; for flight information call ☎ 01-705 6705.

Ryanair's head office is in Dublin airport, with ticket offices in Dublin, Cork, Shannon, Waterford, Galway, Knock and Kerry airports. For bookings call ☎ 01-609 7800; for flight information call ☎ 1550 500 500.

One useful air service is the short flight across to the Aran Islands. See the Galway chapter for details.

BUS

Bus Éireann (☎ 01-836 6111), Busáras, Store St, Dublin 1, is the Republic's bus line, with services throughout the South and to the North. All services are nonsmoking. Fares aren't much more than one-third the regular railway fares, and special deals are often available such as cheaper midweek return tickets (see also Bus & Train Discount Passes). Bear in mind that the winter bus schedule is often drastically reduced and many routes simply disappear after September. The national timetable only costs 80p, but doesn't list fares.

Private buses compete with Bus Éireann, and sometimes run where the national buses are irregular or absent. The larger ones usually carry bikes free but you should always check in advance. Most private companies are properly licensed and all passengers are insured, but if this is going to worry you then ask beforehand.

Ulsterbus (☎ 01232-351201), Milewater Rd, Belfast BT3 9BG, is the service in the North. Call ☎ 01232-333000 for timetable information weekdays 7.30 am to 7.30 pm, Saturday 9 am to 5 pm, Sunday 9 am to 4 pm. Ulsterbus also produces a series of four regional timetables (25p each). For tickets call ☎ 01232-320011.

There are no private bus companies in the North (partly for fear of possible paramilitary extortion rackets).

Return fares are often the same as or little more than a one-way fare. Sample one-way bus fares, travelling times and frequency Monday to Saturday (services are fewer on Sunday) are:

Dublin-Belfast
    £10.50, 3 hours, 4 daily
Dublin-Cork
    IR£12, 3½ hours, 5 daily

Dublin-Donegal
   IR£10, 4¼ hours, 5 daily
Dublin-Limerick
   IR£10, 3¼ hours, 5 daily
Dublin-Tralee
   IR£14, 6 hours, 5 daily
Killarney-Cork
   IR£8.80, 2 hours, 5 daily
Derry-Belfast
   £6.10, 1 hour 40 minutes, over 20 daily
Derry-Galway
   £14, 6 hours 30 minutes, 3 daily
Killarney-Wexford
   IR£15, 5½ hours, 2 daily

Local country buses can work out quite expensive, and services are usually infrequent. From Bantry in south-west Cork, for example, there's only one bus a week

running the 26km journey to Kilcrohane, the last village on the Sheep's Head Peninsula, and the half-hour journey costs over IR£6. The private buses in County Donegal are a notable exception; Feda O'Donnell buses, for example, charges IR£3 to IR£4 for any journey within the county, though these journeys can be very time-consuming.

TRAIN

Iarnród Éireann (Irish Rail; ☎ 01-836 6222), Connolly station, Amiens St, Dublin 1, operates trains in the Republic on routes which fan out from Dublin. Enquiries can also be made at Iarnród Travelcentre, 35 Lower Abbey St, Dublin 1.

   Although trains get you to the major urban

Ferry, Bus & Train Discount Deals

Eurail passes are valid for train travel in the Republic of Ireland – but not in Northern Ireland – and entitle you to a reduction on Bus Éireann's three-day Irish Rambler ticket (see below). They're also valid on Irish Ferries between France (Cherbourg and Le Havre) and the Republic (Rosslare and Cork), but you must book. The Eurail pass is only usable by non-Europeans who have been in Europe for less than six months. Eurail passes can be bought within Europe, as long as your passport proves you've been there for less than six months. The outlets where you can do this are limited and the passes are more expensive than buying them outside Europe. The Rail Shop (☎ 0990-300003), 179 Piccadilly, London W1V 0BA, is one such outlet.

   If you've been in Europe for more than six months you're eligible for an Inter-Rail pass. This gives you a 50% reduction on train travel within Ireland and discounts on Irish Ferries and Stena Sealink connecting ferries.

   For IR£7 (£5.50 in Northern Ireland) full-time students can have a Travelsave stamp affixed to their ISIC card. This gives a 50% discount on Iarnród Éireann (Irish Rail) and Northern Ireland Railways (NIR), and 15% on Bus Éireann services for fares over IR£1. Holders of an EYC (or Euro<26) card can get up to 30% discount on Iarnród Éireann with a Fairstamp attached to their card. The stamps are available from USIT offices (see Useful Organisations in the Facts for the Visitor chapter).

   There's a variety of unlimited-travel tickets for buses and trains, in the North and South. Irish Rambler tickets are available from Bus Éireann for bus-only travel within the Republic of Ireland. They cost IR£28 (three days out of eight consecutive days), IR£68 (eight days out of 15 consecutive days) or IR£98 (15 days out of 30 consecutive days).

   Iarnród Éireann's Faircard (IR£8.50) gives up to 50% reduction on any intercity journey to people under 26, while the Weekender gives up to 30% off (Friday to Tuesday) to people 26 and over. For train and bus travel within the Republic, the Irish Explorer ticket allows you eight days travel out of 15 consecutive days (IR£90).

   In Northern Ireland the Freedom of Northern Ireland pass allows unlimited travel on Ulsterbus, Citybus and Northern Ireland Railways services for £9 for one day or £32 for seven consecutive days.

   The Irish Rover ticket combines services on Bus Éireann and Ulsterbus. This costs IR£36 (or pounds sterling equivalent) for three days, IR£85 for eight days and IR£130 for 15 days.

   The Emerald Card gives you unlimited travel throughout Ireland on all scheduled services of Iarnród Éireann, Northern Ireland Railways, Bus Éireann, Dublinbus, Ulsterbus and Citybus. The card costs IR£105 (or pounds sterling equivalent) for eight days or IR£180 for 15 days.

   Children under 16 pay half fare on all these passes.

   You can buy the passes after you arrive in Ireland, but they only make economic sense if you're planning to travel around Ireland at the speed of light. ■

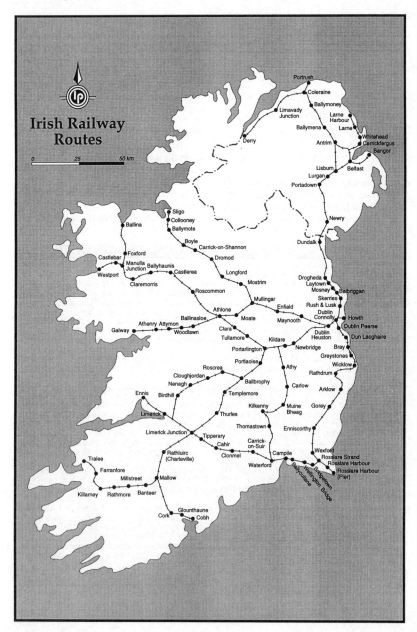

Irish Railway Routes

0   25   50 km

centres faster than buses, the rail system is not as extensive. There are, for example, no direct connections between Waterford and Cork, or Limerick and Galway. Distances, however, are short in Ireland and the longest trip you can make by train from Dublin is just over four hours to Tralee in County Kerry.

Regular one-way fares from Dublin include Belfast IR£15 (2¼ hours, six daily), Cork IR£33 (3¼ hours, up to eight daily), Galway IR£14 (three hours, four daily) and Limerick IR£25 (2¼ hours, up to 13 daily). The Dublin-Belfast route is the only direct rail link between North and South. Travelling by train on a one-way ticket is expensive, and it's worth considering how to use a return ticket; a midweek return ticket is often the same as or not much more than a one-way fare. A same-day return from Dublin to Belfast costs IR£15, the same as a one-way ticket! As with buses, special fares are often available (see the Bus & Train Discount Deals boxed aside). First-class tickets cost IR£5 to IR£15 more than the standard fare for a single journey. Ordinary seats can be reserved for IR£1.

Northern Ireland Railways (NIR; ☎ 01232-899411), Belfast Central station, East Bridge St, Belfast BT1 3PB, has four routes from Belfast. One links with the system in the South via Newry to Dublin; the other three go east to Bangor, north-east to Larne and north-west to Derry/Londonderry via Coleraine.

CAR & MOTORCYCLE

Petrol is a few pence cheaper in the North. Unleaded petrol is available throughout the North and South. Most service stations accept payment by credit card, but some smaller, remote ones will only take cash.

Road Rules

As in Britain, driving in the Republic and the North is on the left and you should only overtake on the outside (to the right) of the vehicle ahead of you. Safety belts must be worn by the driver and all passengers. Children under 12 aren't allowed to sit on the front seats. Motorcyclists and their passengers must wear helmets. Minor roads may sometimes be potholed and will often be very narrow, but the traffic is rarely heavy except as you go through popular tourist or busy commercial towns.

When entering a roundabout, give way to traffic already on the roundabout.

Speed limits in the North and South are generally the same as in Britain: 70 mph (112 km/h) on motorways, 60 mph (96 km/h) on other roads and 30 mph (48 km/h) or as signposted in towns. These limits tend to be treated with some disdain in the South. On the quiet, narrow, winding rural roads it's advisable to stick to the speed limit: head-on collisions aren't unheard of and there may be a person walking or an animal grazing beside the road just around the next bend.

The Irish can't seem to make up their minds on metrication. In the Republic, speed limits are in miles per hour (though in some areas they are in km, including from Dublin airport to the city), distance signs appear in either km or miles, and most car speedometers are imperial rather than metric. Green signposts give distances in km. The older white signs use miles, but there are also newer white signs using km as well!

In the North, speed limits and other laws are as in Britain.

There are parking meters in Dublin and a handful of other cities, but usually parking in car parks or other specified areas is regulated by 'pay and display' tickets or disc parking (you have a disc, available from newsagencies, which rotates to display the time you park your car).

Never leave valuables unattended or visible in your car in Dublin, and see the Dublin chapter for further parking warnings.

In the North, some town centres have Control Zones (though these are gradually being withdrawn), where, for security reasons, cars absolutely must not be left unattended. You can also be fined for not locking your car. Double yellow lines by the roadside mean no parking at any time, and single yellow lines warn of restrictions – the only way to establish the exact restrictions is to find the nearby sign that spells them out.

Red, white and blue kerbstones mean you're in a Loyalist area; green, white and orange mean it's Republican!

Rental

Car rental in Ireland is expensive so you'll often be better off making arrangements in your home country with some sort of package deal, and in the high season it's wise to book ahead. Off season some companies simply discount all rates by about 25%; there are often special deals and the longer you hire the car the lower the relative daily rent. Some smaller companies make an extra daily charge if you go across the border, North or South. Most cars are manual; automatically operated ones are available at a greater fee.

In the Republic of Ireland typical weekly high-season (July and August) rental rates with insurance, collision-damage waiver (CDW), value-added tax (VAT) and unlimited distance are around IR£250 for a small car (Ford Fiesta), IR£330 for a medium-sized car (Toyota Corolla 1.3) and IR£360 for a larger car (Ford Mondeo). In the North, similar cars would cost about 10% more. Check that the posted price includes insurance, CDW and VAT. If you are travelling from the Republic into Northern Ireland it's important to be sure that your insurance covers journeys to the North.

People under 21 aren't allowed to hire a car; for the majority of rental companies you have to be at least 23 and to have had a valid driving licence for a minimum of 12 months. Some companies will not rent to you if you're over 70 or 75. Your own licence is usually enough to hire a car for three months.

The international rental companies Avis, Budget, Hertz, Thrifty and the major local operators, Murray's Europcar and Dan Dooley, have offices all over Ireland. There are many smaller and local operators.

Motorbikes or mopeds are not available for rent.

Automobile Clubs

The Automobile Association (AA) has

Roadsigns

When you're travelling around Ireland you'll need a good road map because, as you'll soon come to realise, roadsigns have to be treated with a certain amount of healthy scepticism – particularly once you get off the motorways and main highways into more remote areas.

There are three main kinds of roadsigns. Those with white lettering on a green background are found on all major routes, with distances given clearly in kilometres. Brown signs with white lettering are used to indicate local tourist offices, sights, accommodation and other facilities. Black-on-white signs are the most problematical for visitors – the older ones give distances in miles, while the newer ones give distances in kilometres; you can usually tell which is which because the newer ones have 'km' after the number while the older ones just have the number.

Sometimes you'll see a sign for your destination, then, as you travel further, you'll see signs to other places at road junctions, but not to where you want to go. At some road junctions there may be no sign at all. This is when a good map comes in handy. As you continue, you may see another sign to your destination – or you may not. Assuming you've gone in the right direction, you could arrive at your destination without having seen another sign for it.

Occasionally, when you do find a sign, it could be pointing the wrong way. This is sometimes the work of pranksters, but another explanation is that these signposts are so close to the road that heavy vehicles have hit the signs as they passed and twisted them around. ■

offices in Belfast (☎ 0990-989 989), Dublin (☎ 01-677 9481) and Cork (☎ 021-505155). The AA breakdown number in the Republic is ☎ 1800-667788; in the North ☎ 0800-887766. In the North, members of the Royal Automobile Club (RAC) call ☎ 0345-331133 for information; its breakdown number is ☎ 0800-828282.

WALKING & BICYCLE

Walking and cycling are two popular, rewarding ways to explore Ireland, both South and North. For information see the Activities chapter.

HITCHING

While Lonely Planet doesn't recommend hitching – it's never entirely safe in any country, and the local maniac may not carry an identifying badge – hitching in Ireland is generally easy. The major exceptions are in heavily touristed areas where the competition from other hitchers is severe and the cars are often full with families. In the Republic there are usually large numbers of Irish hitchhikers on the road who use hitching as an everyday means of travel.

For visitors the usual hitching rules apply. Carry cardboard and a marker pen so you can make a sign showing where you're going. Try to look like a visitor and put your backpack out on view, ideally with a flag on it. Making yourself an obvious tourist is especially important in the North, and if the subject of the Troubles should come up in conversation it's probably best to exercise some diplomatic caution. Cross-border roads are open and hitching between the Republic and the North presents few if any problems.

Women hitching on their own should be extremely careful when choosing lifts – if in doubt, don't. Many local women hitch alone without serious problems, but a tourist is likely to be more at risk.

Sea Legs: Hitch-hiking the Coast of Ireland Alone by Rosita Boland tells the tale of an Irish woman's solo (yes, the Irish are always doing things against the rules) exploration of Ireland by thumb.

BOAT

There are many boat services to islands lying off the coast including to the Aran and Skellig islands to the west, the Saltee Islands to the south-east and Rathlin Island to the north. Ferries also operate across rivers and loughs. Some river services make interesting short cuts, particularly for cyclists: these include the ferry across the River Suir from Ballyhack (County Wexford) to Passage East (County Waterford), and across the Shannon Estuary from Killimer (County Clare) to Tarbert (County Kerry).

The only ferry between the Republic and the North is the limited service across Carlingford Lough from Omeath on the Cooley Peninsula in County Louth to Warrenpoint in County Down.

Cruises are very popular on the 258km Shannon-Erne Waterway – combining rivers, lakes and canals – from County Leitrim to Lough Erne in Northern Ireland. There are also a variety of cruises on lakes and loughs.

If you ask at the tourist offices you won't always get the full information on boats because they won't recommend, or sometimes even mention, operators who don't fulfil all their regulations. Many of the various boats from Portmagee, Ballinskelligs or Derrynane to the Skellig Islands off the Kerry coast, for instance, don't exist as far as official tourist literature is concerned. Details of unofficial boat trips are given under the relevant sections.

LOCAL TRANSPORT

There are comprehensive local bus networks in Dublin (Bus Átha Cliath), Belfast (Citybus) and some other larger towns. The Dublin Area Rapid Transport (DART) line in Dublin is the only local railway line. In the North, Northern Ireland Railways (NIR) operates all rail services.

Taxis in Ireland tend to be expensive, but in Belfast and Derry there are share-taxi services operating rather like buses. There are metered taxis in Belfast, Cork, Dublin, Galway and Limerick, but in other places you'll need to agree on the fare beforehand.

Slow Coach

A popular way to get round Ireland is to take the Slow Coach, a hop-on, hop-off service which runs between Dublin, Athlone, Galway, Clifden, Tralee, Dingle, Killarney, Kenmare, Bantry, Schull, Cork, Cashel, Kilkenny and back to Dublin. You can get on where you like, but must keep moving in an anticlockwise direction with no backtracking. The buses drop you at hostels along the way, saving all that baggage humping. Tickets cost IR£99 if bought in Ireland, slightly less if bought overseas at branches of STA Travel. They're valid more or less indefinitely. To buy one you need a passport-sized photo.

If Slow Coach had a drawback at the time of writing it was that services ran three or four times weekly rather than daily. With plenty of time that doesn't matter, but if you're pressed for time it can mean spending two or three days somewhere you'd rather spend one or two. While you're not obliged to book each leg of the journey in advance you're certainly advised to do so in July and August.

It's not a coach tour in the conventional sense, but Slow Coach does build in some sightseeing en route, with breaks to take in Trim Castle, the Cliffs of Moher, and Torc Waterfall near Killarney. The drivers' commentary mixes history with anecdotes and general advice for visitors.

Slow Coach is particularly popular with women who can make up to 75% of the clientele. Although the service operates year-round, the number of departures drops between November and April. A conventional tour may be substituted in winter.

Slow Coach (☎ 01-679 2684, fax 670 7740, email slocoach@star.co.uk) is at 1st Floor, 6 South William St, Dublin 2. ■

If you book a taxi by telephone there may be a small pick-up charge.

ORGANISED TOURS

If your time is limited it might be worth considering an organised tour, though it's cheaper to see things independently and Ireland is small enough that you can get to even the most remote places in a few hours. Tours can be booked through travel agencies, tourist offices in the major cities, or directly through the tour companies themselves.

CIE Tours International (☎ 01-703 1888), 35 Lower Abbey St, Dublin 1, has coach tours of the South and North all departing from Dublin; the tours include accommodation, breakfast, dinner and discounts for people aged 55 and over. Its four-day 'Taste of Ireland' tour takes in Blarney, the Ring of Kerry, Killarney, the Cliffs of Moher and the region around the River Shannon for IR£239 (in the high season). Its other tours are from six to eight days in length.

March to September, Bus Éireann (☎ 01-836 6111) has 'minibreaks', which include overnight accommodation, to various parts of the South and to Belfast, departing from Dublin's Busáras. Ulsterbus Tours (☎ 01232-337004) has a large number of day trips throughout the North. Call for information and bookings or visit the Ulsterbus Travel Centre (open weekdays 8.45 am to 5.25 pm, Saturday 9 am to noon) in the Europa Buscentre, Glengall St, Belfast.

Gray Line Tours (☎ 01-670 8822), The Mill House, Grand Canal Quay, Dublin 2, has half-day, day and extended trips from Dublin and Limerick which can be booked through the tourist offices in those cities.

Tir na nÓg ('The Land of Eternal Youth') offers a choice of two six-day tours of Ireland. The northern one travels from Dublin through County Louth to Derry, Donegal, Mayo and Galway before returning to Dublin. The southern one travels through County Wicklow to West Cork, the Ring of Kerry, Tralee and Galway before returning to Dublin. To take one tour costs IR£169, to combine both costs IR£319. Buses take no more than 20 people and fill up fast so book ahead. Tours start picking up from Dublin hostels at 10 am every Monday throughout the year. Overnights are spent at IHH hostels along the way. Tir na nÓg (☎ 01-836 4684; fax 836 4710; e-mail tnn@indigo.ie) is at 57 Lower Gardiner St, Dublin 1.

See also Organised Walks under Walks – Information in the Activities chapter.

The Republic of Ireland

The Irish Free State, as it was known until 1949, was established after the signing in December 1921 of the Anglo-Irish Treaty, between the British government and an Irish delegation led by Michael Collins. Eamon de Valera had been elected president of the new self-proclaimed republic in August, and he remained in Dublin during negotiations. He wasn't consulted before the signing and was outraged when the delegates returned with what he and many other republicans regarded as a betrayal of the IRA's principles.

The Treaty was ratified in the Dáil (Irish assembly or lower house) in January 1922, and in June the country's first general election resulted in victory for the pro-Treaty forces. Fighting broke out two weeks later.

Amazingly, the Civil War was primarily about the oath of allegiance to the crown, rather than the exclusion of the six counties from the Irish Free State. Of the 400 or more pages of Dáil records on the Treaty debate, only seven deal with the issue of Ulster. The rest focus on the oath and the crown.

Collins was ambushed and shot dead in Cork by anti-Treaty forces, and de Valera was imprisoned by the new Free State government, under its prime minister William Cosgrave, which went so far as to execute 77 of its former comrades. The Civil War ground to an exhausted halt in 1923.

After boycotting the Dáil for a number of years, de Valera founded a new party called Fianna Fáil ('Warriors of Ireland') which won nearly half the seats in the 1927 election. De Valera and the other new teachta Dála (TDs, members of the Dáil) managed within weeks to enter the Dáil by the simple expedient of not taking the oath but signing in as if they had.

Fianna Fáil won a majority in the 1932 election, and remained in power for 16 years. De Valera introduced a new constitution in 1937, doing away with the oath and claiming sovereignty over the six counties of the North. In 1938 the UK renounced its right to use certain Irish ports for military purposes, which it had been granted under the Treaty. The South was therefore able to remain neutral in WWII.

In 1948 Fianna Fáil lost the general election to Fine Gael – the direct descendants of the first Free State government – in coalition with the new republican Clann an Poblachta. The new government declared the Free State to be a republic at last. Ireland left the British Commonwealth in 1949. In 1955 it became a member of the United Nations.

When Sean Lamass came to power in 1959 as successor to de Valera he sought to stem the continuing serious emigration by improving the country's economic prospects. By the mid-1960s his policies had been successful enough to reduce emigration to less than half what it had been in the mid-50s, and many who had left began to return. He also introduced free secondary education.

In 1972 the Republic (along with Northern Ireland) became a member of the European Economic Community (EEC). At first, membership brought some measure of prosperity, but by the early 1980s Ireland was once more in economic difficulties and emigration rose again. By the early 1990s the Irish economy began to recover and is now one of the strongest in Europe, though unemployment remains high.

The results of referenda in the 1980s on abortion and divorce left both illegal in the South. But socially, things are changing fast. While single mothers might still have a tough time in remote rural areas, in Dublin they're almost as commonplace as in London and no one bats an eyelid. The abortion debate rages on and people get steamed up about it, but many Irish women quietly go to Britain to terminate their pregnancies every year. Divorce is now legal.

In 1991 Mary Robinson was elected as

Abortion Debate

Ireland continues to do its best to tie itself into knots over the thorny issue of abortion.

Prior to 1983, therapeutic abortions were legal, and doctors could use their discretion as to whether or not a pregnancy was 'life-threatening' for the woman. Abortion for any other reason, including severe malformation or pregnancy due to rape, was, and still is, not permitted.

In 1983, the law was tightened and incorporated into the constitution, but in such woolly terms that things went on much as before, with one remarkable exception: women could no longer be given information about seeking abortions abroad. British phone books were duly taken out of libraries, and women's magazines were impounded or censored at the airports.

While trips to British abortion clinics continued unabated, Ireland held the moral high ground of protecting the unborn child at any cost – until 1992, when parents whose 14-year-old daughter had allegedly been raped by her friend's father took her to England for an abortion. But when they contacted the gardai to ask if tissue from the foetus could be collected and used in the prosecution of the alleged rapist they were issued with an injunction ordering them to bring the girl back, foetus intact, or face prosecution. All hell broke loose. The matter went to the High Court, which fudged the issue by saying that the girl could travel to the UK for an abortion since she was suicidal.

Anti-abortion campaigners demanded that the High Court prevent women leaving the country to seek abortions abroad, opening up the prospect of pregnancy tests at airports. Others interpreted the High Court ruling to mean that abortion had become legal if the woman was suicidal.

A referendum on the issue took place in 1992, on the same day as the general election. A clear majority supported the right to travel abroad for an abortion, but the option of making abortion available to all women in Ireland wasn't offered.

In 1995 a new law allowed doctors and pregnancy counselling services to give a pregnant woman the names and phone numbers of British abortion clinics. However, they're still barred from making appointments or arrangements with the clinics.

The contentious issue of permitting abortion continues to be debated. In the meantime, as Mary Harney, leader of the Progressive Democrats, once pointed out, although abortion is illegal in Ireland, an Irish woman is more likely to have an abortion than a woman in the Netherlands, where it's freely available. ■

president. Although the president's power is limited she wielded considerable informal influence on social policies, contributing to a shift in attitudes away from the traditionally conservative positions on issues such as divorce, abortion and gay rights. In 1997 Mary McAleese was elected president.

In 1994 the Fine Gael party, under John Bruton, came to power in coalition with the Labour Party and the Democratic Left, after a crisis over the appointment of a president to the High Court had destroyed the previous coalition and forced the resignation of the then Taoiseach, Albert Reynolds. Bruton's government was the first to take office without a general election.

When it did face one in 1997 it was ousted by Fianna Fáil under Bertie Ahern, in coalition with the Progressive Democrats and a number of independents. Mary Harney became Ireland's first female Tánaiste (deputy prime minister).

GOVERNMENT & POLITICS

The Republic has a parliamentary system of government loosely based on the British model. The parliament (Oireachtas) has a lower house known as the Dáil (pronounced 'doyle') which has 166 elected members who sit in Leinster House on Dublin's Kildare St. Dáil members are known as teachta Dála (TDs), the prime minister as Taoiseach (roughly pronounced 'teashock'; the plural is Taosigh) and the deputy prime minister as Tánaiste. The Dáil has a relatively high percentage of female members.

The upper house is the Senate or Seanad and senators are nominated by the Taoiseach or elected by university graduates and councillors from around the country. The Senate's functions are limited; senators debate on and pass legislation framed in the Dáil, but many critics claim it is merely a happy hunting ground for failed TDs.

The country's constitutional head of state

Taking Ireland by Storm – Ireland's First Female President

The 7th of November 1990 was a red letter day for Irish women when Mary Robinson, a barrister associated with all sorts of liberal causes (including the rights of single mothers, gays, travellers and students) was elected president of Ireland.

Born in 1944 in Ballina in County Mayo, Mary Robinson studied at Trinity College, Dublin, and at Harvard University in the USA, later becoming a barrister and Trinity's youngest ever Professor of Law. She was elected to the Senate in 1969.

Once appointed to the presidency, Robinson set about modernising the institution, raising its profile in a relentless tour of the country – there's hardly a tourist attraction in Ireland that doesn't boast a plaque commemorating her visit.

Almost single-handedly Robinson has dispelled old ideas of a backward Ireland dominated by a reactionary church which kept women tied to the home. In 1997 she was appointed the United Nations High Commissioner for Human Rights. Ireland's loss should be very much the world's gain. ■

is the president (An tUachtaran), who is elected by popular vote for a seven-year term, but has little real power.

The national flag is the tricolour of green, white and orange, and the national symbol is the harp.

The Republic's electoral system is proportional representation, a complex but fair system where voters mark the electoral candidates in order of preference. As the first-preference votes are counted and candidates are elected, the voters' second and third choices are passed on to the various other candidates.

The principal political parties are Fianna Fáil and Fine Gael, although the Labour Party has made great strides in recent years.

Founded by Eamon de Valera and other notables, Fianna Fáil has been the driving force in Irish politics since the early years of the state. Fianna Fáil has almost always won the greatest number of seats in general elections, and has usually been either in government or barely out of it. Fianna Fáil has always been a catch-all party, claiming to be the voice of the rural populace, urban workers and business community in turn with no apparent difficulty.

Many of Ireland's most notable leaders have come from the party's ranks, including Eamon de Valera, Sean Lemass, Jack Lynch, and more recently the colourful and wily Charles Haughey and Albert Reynolds. The current party leader is Bertie Ahern. Fianna

Fáil has in the past usually taken an extremely conservative line on social matters, particularly when it came to divorce, abortion and contraception.

Founded in 1933, Fine Gael is the second largest party and promotes enterprise; its image has been clean-cut, worthy, middle-class and university-educated.

Labour has been on the fringes of power for most of its existence, but has shared in various coalition governments with Fine Gael. The Labour Party, under the leadership of Dick Spring since 1982, occupies the middle ground and attracts support from all classes of voters.

In 1985 a split in Fianna Fáil resulted in the formation of the small Progressive Democrats now led by Mary Harney. Ironically, its two periods of power have been in coalition with Fianna Fáil. The only other party of consequence is the left-wing Democratic Left whose leader is Proinsias de Rossa and was part of John Bruton's coalition government.

Coalition has been a feature of most recent governments in the Republic, as the once mighty Fianna Fáil has found itself less able to muster the parliamentary majorities it used to command.

Unfortunately, Irish politics has a reputation for corruption, but it's not just disillusioned voters who say this. Former Israeli ambassador to Ireland, Benjamin Netanyahu, once declared that if Richard Nixon had been president of Ireland he would never have lost office the way he did. One of the biggest scandals of 1997 was the disclosure that Charles Haughey, a hero to many, had received IR£1.3 million in 1983 from Ben Dunne, owner of Dunne's Stores, while the former was still Taoiseach.

ECONOMY

The Irish economy is one of Europe's most buoyant and has overtaken Britain in growth and per capita income. Pundits often refer to it as the Celtic or Emerald tiger in reference to the successful 'tiger' economies of Asia.

Inflation is low, running at around 2%. Exports continue to reach record levels. Ireland is second only to the US in the export of computer software, and information technology is now contributing more to the economy than agriculture. In 1995 the economy grew by an annual average of 10.1%, in 1996 by 7.25%, and is expected to grow for the next few years at an average of 6%. It's true that Ireland has been one of the main beneficiaries of EU investment, but that investment only accounts for about 1% of recent growth. The national debt is at a sustainable level and in 1996 fell for the first time in nearly 40 years.

One of the reasons for Ireland's success is the high quality of education and the encouragement by successive Irish governments of educational concentration on computer technology. Another is the inducement to foreign investors of only 10% corporate tax on their profits for the first 10 years.

The trade surplus for the Republic as a percentage of GDP is one of the largest in the developed world. This also means that Ireland's small open economy is heavily dependent on the state of the world economy. Although Ireland has reduced its dependence on Britain, the latter is still its main trading partner followed by the EU and the USA.

Despite a steady fall in unemployment, it's still 11.5% of the workforce. Many of the unemployed are the unskilled who live on inner-city housing estates where drugs and crime are endemic. This situation and the incredible costs of welfare and unemployment payments are problems that look set to continue.

Taxes are high in the Republic, and petrol, alcohol, tobacco, cars and luxury items are particularly expensive. Tourism is enormously important, and Ireland attracts visitors from all over Western Europe as well as from the English-speaking nations.

Dublin

DUBLIN

Ireland's capital and its largest, most cosmopolitan city, Dublin is a city of great contrasts. Prosperous Georgian squares can quickly give way to blighted crime-and-drug-ridden housing estates where the unemployment is high. Still one of the smallest European Union (EU) capitals, it's growing and modernising fast. The transformation of Dublin is best exemplified by Temple Bar, which, once decayed and earmarked to be flattened to make way for a bus station, is now one of the city's main attractions.

In spite of the rapid changes, Dublin still manages to remain a place with soul: the city's literary history seems to bump against you at every corner and the pubs are open to everyone. An evening with a succession of pints of Guinness, that noble black brew, is as much a part of the Dublin experience as the Georgian streets and the fine old buildings.

It's not only the pubs which are easily accessible. Dublin is a city on a human scale so it's easy to get around on foot. Accommodation is varied, ranging from cheap and cheerful backpacker hostels to elegant five-star hotels. The food is also surprisingly varied and good, with dishes from every corner of the world as well as down-to-earth local specialities such as Irish stew or Dublin coddle.

There's little modern architecture of any note, but the city has maintained much of its Georgian character. Dublin is a curious, colourful place, an easy city to like and a fine introduction to Ireland.

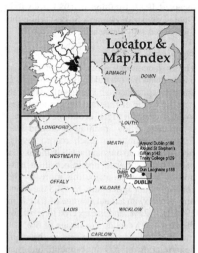

Locator & Map Index

Highlights

- Take in a Dublin pub crawl
- Explore the many delights of Temple Bar
- Visit Trinity College and the 'Book of Kells'
- See the treasures of the National Museum
- Learn about the tragedy of Irish history in Kilmainham Jail
- Be amused by one man's folly – the Casino at Marino
- Find salvation in St Patrick's Cathedral
- Tour the corridors of power at Dublin Castle
- Taste the 'perfect Guinness' in the Guinness Hop Store
- Relax in St Stephen's Green, especially on a sunny Sunday

HISTORY

Dublin officially celebrated its millennium in 1988 but there were settlements here long before 988 AD. The first early Celtic habitation was on the banks of the River Liffey, and the city's Irish name, Baile Átha Cliath, 'the Town of the Hurdle Ford', comes from an ancient river crossing that can still be pinpointed today. St Patrick's Cathedral is said to be built on the site of a well used by Ireland's patron saint for early conversions in the 5th century.

It wasn't until the Vikings turned up that Dublin became a permanent fixture. By the 9th century, raids from the north had become a fact of Irish life, but some of the fierce

118

Danes chose to stay rather than simply rape, pillage and depart. They intermarried with the Irish and established a vigorous trading port at the point where the River Poddle joined the Liffey in a black pool, in Irish a *dubh linn*. Today there's little trace of the Poddle, which has been channelled underground and flows under St Patrick's Cathedral to dribble into the Liffey by the Capel St (or Grattan) Bridge.

Norman and then early English Dublin was still centred around the black pool which gave the city its name. The boom years came with the 18th century, the period of the Protestant Ascendancy when, for a time, London was the only larger city in the British Empire. As the city expanded, the nouveaux riches abandoned medieval Dublin and moved north across the river to a new Dublin of stately squares surrounded by fine Georgian mansions. The planning of this magnificent Georgian Dublin was assisted by the establishment in 1757 of the Commission for Making Wide & Convenient Streets!

The city's slums soon spread north in pursuit of the rich, who turned back south to new homes in Merrion Square, Fitzwilliam Square and St Stephen's Green.

In 1745 when James Fitzgerald, the earl of Kildare, began building Leinster House, his magnificent mansion south of the Liffey, he was mocked for this foolish move away from the centre into the wilds. 'Where I go society will follow,' he confidently predicted and was soon proved right. Today Leinster House is home to the Irish parliament and is right in the centre of modern Dublin.

The Georgian boom years of the 18th century were followed by more trouble and unrest, and the union with Britain in 1801, ending the separate Irish parliament, spelt the end of Dublin's century of dramatic growth. Dublin entered the 20th century a downtrodden, dispirited place.

The 1916 Easter Rising caused considerable damage to parts of central Dublin, particularly along O'Connell St where the GPO was gutted. The struggle between British forces and the IRA led to more damage to Dublin including the burning of the Custom House in 1921. A year later Ireland was independent, but then tumbled into the Civil War which inflicted still more damage on the city, including the burning of the Four Courts in 1922 and a further bout of destruction for O'Connell St.

When peace finally came to Ireland, Dublin was exhausted – a shadow of its Georgian self. Until the 1970s it was a city in decay, but Ireland's membership of what was then the European Economic Community (now the European Union) in 1973 held the prospect of better times to come. Today, Ireland's economic turn around and cultural resurgence is helping to transform the city.

Dublin's expansion has continued south to Dun Laoghaire and beyond, but the River Liffey remains a rough dividing line between southern 'haves' and northern 'have-nots'.

ORIENTATION

Greater Dublin sprawls around the arc of Dublin Bay, bounded to the north by the hills at Howth and to the south by the Dalkey headland.

North of the River Liffey the important streets for visitors are O'Connell St, the major shopping thoroughfare, and Gardiner St, with many B&Bs. At the northern end of O'Connell St is Parnell Square. Many hostels are in and around Gardiner St, which becomes rather run down as it continues north. The main bus station, Busáras, and Connolly station, one of the city's two main railway stations, are near the southern end of Gardiner St.

Immediately south of the river, over O'Connell Bridge, is the intriguing Temple Bar area and the expanse of Trinity College. Nassau St, along the southern edge of the campus, and pedestrianised Grafton St are the main shopping streets. At the southern end of Grafton St is St Stephen's Green. About 2km west beside the river, is Heuston station, the city's other main railway station.

The post codes for central Dublin are Dublin 1 immediately north of the river and Dublin 2 immediately south. The posh Ballsbridge area south-east of the centre is Dublin 4.

DUBLIN

DUBLIN

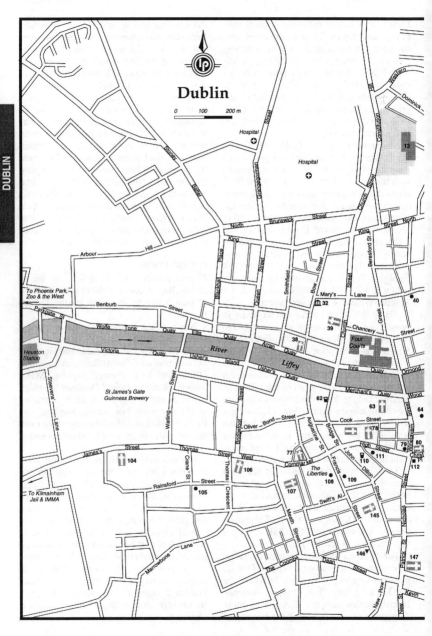

Dublin

0   100   200 m

Hospital

Hospital

To Phoenix Park,
Zoo & the West

Heuston
Station

St James's Gate
Guinness Brewery

To Kilmainham
Jail & IMMA

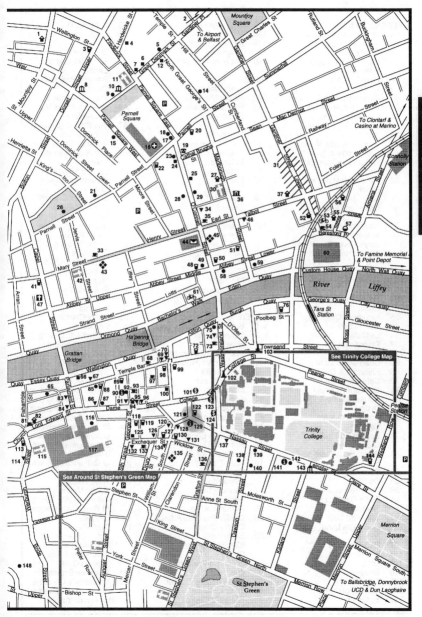

PLACES TO STAY
1 Dublin International Youth Hostel
2 Cheap B&Bs
4 Waverley House & Sinclair House
6 Barry's Hotel
7 Castle Hotel
12 Belvedere Hotel
24 Royal Dublin Hotel
25 Gresham Hotel
27 Marlborough Hostel
31 B&Bs
37 Cardijn House Hostel
52 Globetrotters Tourist Hostel/The Townhouse
55 Isaac's Hostel/Isaac's Hotel
56 Jury's Inn
66 Clarence Hotel
82 Kinlay House
94 Strollers Hostel
100 Bloom's Hotel
112 Jury's Christ Church Inn
125 Central Hotel

PLACES TO EAT
33 Bewley's Oriental Café
34 Beshoff's Fish & Chips
35 Kylemore Café
46 101 Talbot
54 Le Café
67 Planet Web Restaurant
68 Chameleon Café
69 Elephant & Castle
70 Café Gertrude
71 Gallagher's Boxty House, Alamo & Dyflin
73 Bewley's Oriental Café
74 Beshoff's Fish & Chips
81 Wood Quay Café & Bar
83 Poco Loco
84 Da Pino
86 Les Frères Jacques
91 Fan's Cantonese Restaurant
93 Well Fed Café
95 La Mezza Luna
96 Nico's
97 Bad Ass Café
114 Leo Burdock's
120 QV.2
126 Boulevard Café
128 Trocadero
131 Cornucopia
132 Shalimar

133 Wed Wose Café
134 Munchies
136 Bewley's Oriental Café
137 Judge Roy Bean's
146 Old Dublin Restaurant

PUBS
3 Joxer Daly's
20 Fibber McGee's
22 Patrick Conway
41 Slattery's
48 Oval
50 Madigan's
51 Sean O'Casey's
62 The Brazen Head
72 Palace Bar
76 John Mulligan's
88 Bad Bob's
89 Norseman
98 The Auld Dubliner
99 Oliver St John Gogarty
110 Mother Redcap's Tavern & Market
113 Lord Edward
118 Dame Tavern
119 Stag's Head
122 O'Neill's
127 Old Stand
130 International Bar
144 Kennedy's

OTHER
5 Belvedere College
8 National Wax Museum
9 Municipal Gallery of Modern Art (Hugh Lane Gallery)
10 Dublin Writers' Museum
11 Abbey Presbyterian Church
13 King's Inns
14 James Joyce Centre
15 Sinn Féin Bookshop
16 Rotunda Hospital
17 Ambassador Cinema
18 Gate Theatre
19 Telecom Éireann Telecentre
21 Laundry Shop
23 Aer Lingus
26 Parnell Centre
28 Dublin Bus (Bus Átha Cliath) Office
29 Exclusively Irish (Dublin Tourism Shop)
30 St Mary's Pro-Cathedral
32 Irish Whiskey Corner
36 Tyrone House
38 St Paul's Church

39 St Michan's Church
40 Corporation Fruit Market
42 St Mary's Church
43 Jervis Shopping Centre
44 General Post Office
45 Clerys
47 St Mary's Abbey
49 Eason's Bookshop
53 Rent-a-Bike
57 Bus Station (Busáras)
58 Irish Rail (Iarnród Éireann) Office
59 Abbey & Peacock Theatres
60 Custom House
61 C Harding Bicycle Shop
63 St Francis' Church (Adam & Eve's Church)
64 Dublin Corporation Civic Offices
65 Dublin's Viking Adventure
75 USIT Travel Office
77 Church of St John & Augustine
78 St Audoen's Churches
79 Dublinia
80 Christ Church Cathedral
85 Project Arts Centre
87 Olympia Theatre
90 Temple Bar Information Centre
92 Cyberia Café & Arthouse Multimedia Centre for the Arts
101 Bank of Ireland
102 Thomas Moore Statue
103 Steyne Sculpture
104 St James's Church
105 Guinness Hop Store
106 St Catherine's Church (Protestant)
107 St Catherine's Church (Catholic)
108 Tivoli Theatre
109 Iveagh Market
111 Tailor's Hall/An Taisce
115 St Werburgh's Church
116 City Hall
117 Dublin Castle
121 Enfo - Government Environmental Information Office
123 Thomas Cook
124 American Express
129 St Andrew's Church & Dublin Tourism Centre
Continued on next page

135	Powerscourt Townhouse Shopping Centre	141	Northern Ireland Tourist Board	145	St Nicholas of Myra Church
138	Hodges Figgis Bookshop	142	Kilkenny Shop	147	St Patrick's Cathedral
139	Fred Hanna's Bookshop	143	Heraldic Museum, Genealogical Office & Alliance Française	148	Marsh's Library
140	Waterstone Bookshop				

DUBLIN

Finding Addresses

Finding addresses in Dublin can be complicated by the tendency for street names to change every few blocks and for streets to be subdivided into upper and lower or north and south parts. It doesn't seem to matter if you put the definer in front of or behind the name – thus you can have Lower Baggot St or Baggot St Lower, South Anne St or Anne St South. Street numbering often runs up one side of a street and down the other, rather than having odd numbers on one side and even on the other.

INFORMATION
Tourist Offices

Dublin Tourism and Bord Fáilte offer more or less identical services.

If you arrive by air or sea, you'll find tourist offices at the airport and on the waterfront at Dun Laoghaire. In the city, the Dublin Tourism Centre is at St Andrews Church in Suffolk St near Trinity College. In summer it's open 8.30 am to 8 pm Monday to Saturday and 10.30 am to 2 pm on Sunday, 9 am to 5 pm Monday to Saturday in winter. As well as information it provides accommodation and tour bookings; there's also car rental and currency exchange facilities, a bookshop and café. All three offices have the same 24-hour phone number: ☎ 1550 112 233 which costs 58p per minute.

Dublin Tourism operates a shop called Exclusively Irish, at 14 O'Connell St Upper, selling guides, maps, T-shirts etc.

The head office of Bord Fáilte (☎ 676 5871, 602 4000) at Baggot St Bridge has an information desk and although it's inconveniently located – well to the south of the city centre, beyond St Stephen's Green – it's also much less crowded. The entrance is in Wilton Terrace.

Foreign Embassies & Consulates

You'll find embassies of the following countries in Dublin. For citizens of New Zealand and Singapore, the closest embassies are in London.

Australia
    6th Floor, Fitzwilton House, Wilton Terrace, Dublin 2 (☎ 676 1517)
Canada
    65-68 St Stephen's Green, Dublin 2 (☎ 478 1988)
Denmark
    121 St Stephen's Green, Dublin 2 (☎ 475 6404)
France
    36 Ailesbury Rd, Dublin 4 (☎ 260 1666)
Germany
    31 Trimleston Ave, Booterstown, Dublin 4 (☎ 269 3011)
Italy
    63 Northumberland Rd, Dublin 4 (☎ 660 1744)
Japan
    Nutley Building, Merrion Centre, Nutley Lane, Dublin 4 (☎ 269 4244)
Netherlands
    160 Merrion Rd, Dublin 4 (☎ 269 3444)
New Zealand
    (in London) New Zealand House, Haymarket, London SW1Y 4QT (☎ 0171-930 8422)
Norway
    34 Molesworth St, Dublin 2 (☎ 662 1800)
Portugal
    Knocksinna House, Foxrock, Dublin 18 (☎ 289 4416)
Singapore
    (in London) 2 Wilton Crescent, London SW1X 8RW (☎ 0171-235 8315)
Spain
    17A Merlyn Park, Dublin 4 (☎ 269 1640)
Sweden
    Sun Alliance House, Dawson St, Dublin 2 (☎ 671 5822)

Switzerland
    6 Ailesbury Rd, Dublin 4 (☎ 269 2515)
UK
    31 Merrion Rd, Dublin 4 (☎ 205 3700)
USA
    42 Elgin Rd, Dublin 4 (☎ 668 8777)

Money

The currency exchange counter at Dublin airport is in the baggage collection area and opens for most flight arrivals. There are numerous banks around the centre with exchange facilities; the Bank of Ireland operates a bureau de change in Westmoreland St Monday to Saturday 9 am to 9 pm, Sunday 10 am to 7 pm.

American Express (☎ 01-677 2874), 116 Grafton St, and Thomas Cook (☎ 01-677 1721/1307), at No 118, are across the road from the entrance to Trinity College. Thomas Cook opens Monday to Saturday 9 am to 5.30 pm (from 10 am Wednesday), while American Express opens Monday to Friday 9 am to 5 pm, Saturday 9 am to noon (the foreign exchange desk stays open until 5 pm). American Express also has a desk in the Dublin Tourism Centre.

Post & Communications

Dublin's famed GPO, on O'Connell St, north of the river, opens 8 am to 8 pm Monday to Saturday, 10.30 am to 6 pm Sunday and holidays. Here you'll find the poste restante, a philatelic counter and a bank of telephones. South of the river the handy post office in Anne St South, just off Grafton St, is well patronised by foreign visitors and is used to dealing with their curious requests.

Telecom Éireann Telecentre (☎ 01-661 1111), Findlater House, O'Connell St Upper, has public phones that use cash or phonecards; the staff there will also help with any queries or problems you may have. It's open Monday to Thursday 9.30 am to 5 pm, Friday to 4.45 pm.

The telephone code for Dublin is ☎ 01.

Online Services

A number of cafés/restaurants offer access to the Internet including Planet Web Restaurant (☎ 677 2727), 3 The Cobbles, Essex St East, in Temple Bar, which charges IR£5 per hour and offers pizzas and pastas. Also in Temple Bar, Cyberia Café (☎ 679 7607) in the Arthouse Multimedia Centre for the Arts, on Curved St, charges the same.

At the Internet Exchange (☎ 475 8788), Drury Hall, around the corner from South Great George's St, you can play chess while you're waiting to download.

Travel Agencies

American Express and Thomas Cook both have offices in the centre of Dublin (see Money earlier). The office of the Union of Students in Ireland Travel (USIT; ☎ 679 8833), 19 Aston Quay, south of O'Connell Bridge, is open Monday to Friday 9 am to 6 pm (Thursday until 8 pm), Saturday 10 am to 5.30 pm.

Bookshops

Given Dublin's strong literary tradition it's not surprising that the city has some good bookshops.

Directly opposite Trinity College is the excellent Fred Hanna (☎ 677 1255), 27-29 Nassau St. Around the corner is the large, well-stocked Hodges Figgis (☎ 677 4754), 56-58 Dawson St, with a large selection on things Irish. Facing it across the road is Waterstone (☎ 679 1415), 7 Dawson St, which also carries a wide range of books. The Dublin Bookshop (☎ 677 5568), 24 Grafton St, has a particularly good selection of books of Irish interest.

North of the Liffey, Eason's (☎ 873 3811), 40 O'Connell St, near the post office, has a wide range of books and one of the biggest selections of magazines in Ireland. The Winding Stair (☎ 873 3292), 40 Lower Ormond Quay, does new and second-hand books and has a café upstairs.

A number of bookshops cater to special interests. Forbidden Planet (☎ 671 0688), 36 Dawson St, Dublin 2, is a wonderful science fiction and comic-book specialist. The Sinn Féin Bookshop (☎ 872 7096) is at 44 Parnell Square West, Dublin 1. An Siopa Leabhar (☎ 478 3814), in Harcourt St, just off St

Stephen's Green, has books in Irish. The Irish Museum of Modern Art (IMMA), at the Royal Hospital Kilmainham and the National Gallery in Merrion Square, both have bookshops offering a good range of art books and books on Ireland generally.

There is an excellent bookshop in the Dublin Writers' Museum, 18 Parnell Square North, Dublin 1. The Library Book Shop at Trinity College has a wide selection of Irish interest books, including, of course, various titles on the 'Book of Kells'. For all kinds of official publications and maps, there's also the Office of Public Works bookshop (☎ 661 3111), Sun Alliance House, Molesworth St, Dublin 2.

George Webb (☎ 677 7489), 5 Crampton Quay, Dublin 2, has old books of Irish interest as do Greene's Bookshop (☎ 873 3149), 16 Clare St, Dublin 2, and Cathach Books (☎ 671 8676), 10 Duke St, Dublin 2.

Cultural Centres

Dublin has an international selection of cultural centres. The city is a popular centre for English-language instruction, particularly for students from Spain who flock to Dublin every summer and have become a colourful part of the city scene. The city's cultural centres include:

Alliance Française
    1 Kildare St, Dublin 2 (☎ 676 1732)
British Council
    Newmount House, 22-24 Mount St Lower, Dublin 2 (☎ 676 4088)
Goethe Institute
    37 Merrion Square, Dublin 2 (☎ 661 1155)
Instituto Cervantes (Spanish Cultural Institute)
    58 Northumberland Rd, Dublin 4 (☎ 668 2024)
Italian Cultural Institute
    11 Fitzwilliam Square, Dublin 2 (☎ 676 6662)

Useful Organisations

Enfo (☎ 679-3144), opposite the Dublin Tourism Centre, is a government body with useful information on the environment; it has videos, brochures and a library and opens weekdays 10 am to 5 pm.

Travellers with disabilities can get help and advice from the National Rehabilitation Board (☎ 668 4181), 25 Clyde Rd, Ballsbridge, Dublin 4, or at 44 North St George's St (☎ 874 7503).

The Gay Switchboard (☎ 872 1055) is in Carmichael House, North Brunswick St, Dublin 7.

The Automobile Association (AA; ☎ 677 9481) is at 23 Suffolk St, Dublin 2.

Laundry

Convenient laundries in north Dublin include the Laundry Shop (☎ 872 3541), 191 Parnell St, Dublin 1, off Parnell Square, and the Laundrette (☎ 830 0340), 110 Dorset St Lower near the An Óige Hostel.

Near Trinity College and Temple Bar is the cheerful All American Laundrette (☎ 677 2779), 40 South Great George St. South of the centre and just north of the Grand Canal is Powders Laundrette (☎ 478 2655), 42A Richmond St South.

If you're staying north-east of the centre at Clontarf there's the Clothes Line (☎ 833 8480), 53 Clontarf Rd.

Medical Services

The Eastern Health Board Dublin Area (☎ 679 0700), Doctor Steevens Hospital, Dublin 8, has a Choice of Doctor Scheme which can advise you on a suitable doctor from 9 am to 5 pm Monday to Friday. It also provides services for the physically and mentally handicapped. There are Well Women clinics at 35 Lower Liffey St (☎ 872 8051) and 73 Lower Leeson St (☎ 661 0083). Both can help with female medical problems and can supply contraceptives, including the 'morning-after' pill.

Emergency

For emergency assistance phone ☎ 999 or ☎ 112 (both free) for gardai (police), ambulance or fire brigade. Other useful numbers include:

Poisons Information Service
    Beaumont Hospital, Beaumont Rd, Dublin 9 (☎ 837 9964/9966)

Rape Crisis Centre
70 Leeson St Lower, Dublin 2 (☎ 661 4911, 1800 778 888)
Samaritans
112 Marlborough St, Dublin 1 – for people who are depressed or suicidal (☎ 1850 609 090, 872 7700)
Drugs Advisory & Treatment Centre
Trinity Court, 30-31 Pearse St, Dublin 2 (☎ 677 1122)

Dangers & Annoyances

Dublin was once regarded as a very safe city, and although this is still largely true, a continuing drug problem means there's a fair amount of petty (and not so petty) crime. In 1996 journalist Veronica Guerin was murdered while investigating Dublin's drugs trade. More recently, there have been hold-ups by thieves brandishing used syringes.

Notices alert you to the risk of pickpockets and sneak thieves, many of them unusually young. If you have a car, don't leave valuables inside it when it's parked; Dublin is notorious for car break-ins, and foreign registered cars and rental cars are a particular target. Cyclists should always lock their bicycles securely and remove anything removable. Certain areas of Dublin, particularly north of the Liffey, aren't safe at night. Visitors should avoid run-down, deserted-looking and poorly lit areas. Camping in Phoenix Park is a very bad idea indeed.

As in other parts of Europe, beggars, some of them alarmingly young, are commonplace. If you don't want to give them money, but would like to do something to help the homeless and long-term unemployed, you could buy a copy of the magazine *The Big Issues* (IR£1), some of the proceeds of which go to them.

Like all big cities, Dublin is choking on traffic fumes. Nor has smoking died the social death it has in other western countries; cinemas may be smoke-free zones, but not even all the expensive restaurants have designated nonsmoking areas. Consequently, after a few days here you may feel your lungs need a burst of fresh air.

ALONG THE LIFFEY

The River Liffey comes down to Dublin from the Wicklow Hills, passing the open expanse of Phoenix Park and flowing under 14 city bridges before reaching Dublin Harbour and Dublin Bay. In a straight line it's only about 20km from its source to the sea, but the Liffey meanders for over 100km along its route and changes remarkably in that distance. Well into the city, around Phoenix Park, the Liffey is still rural-looking, and if you're waiting for a train at Heuston station you can wander over to the riverside and watch the fish in the clear water below.

The Liffey isn't a notable river, although Joyce immortalised its spirit as 'Anna Livia', the woman you see lying in sculpted form ('the floozy in the jacuzzi') in the middle of O'Connell St and on thousands of Dublin doorknockers. The best Liffey views are from O'Connell Bridge or, just upstream, from the pedestrian Ha'penny Bridge of 1816 which leads into the colourful Temple Bar.

Although there have been bridges over the Liffey for nearly 800 years, the oldest exist-

---

Death of a Drugsbuster

In June 1996 Dublin's image as one of Europe's safest cities suffered a fatal blow with the shooting of Veronica Guerin as she sat in her car at the traffic lights on a busy main road.

A journalist on the *Sunday Independent*, Guerin had devoted herself to exposing the men behind Ireland's burgeoning drugs trade, and she persisted in her pursuit even after she was shot in the leg by a gunman on her own doorstep.

Guerin's death galvanised the police into a less defeatist attitude to the dealers. A Criminal Assets Board was set up to try and freeze the proceeds of drugs deals; at the time of writing an estimated IR£10 million had been seized and the particular Mr Big she had been pursuing had been put out of business. Several high-profile sweeps have driven dealers out of O'Connell St. Communities are said to be doing their bit by effectively ostracising known drug dealers.

Look out for a spate of books and films immortalising Guerin, widely seen as Public Heroine Number One. ■

ing bridge is the Liam Mellows Bridge which was originally built as Queen's Bridge in 1768. It's still popularly known as the Queen St Bridge, for the simple reason that Queen St runs down to it.

The River Poddle originally joined the Liffey near the Grattan Bridge, better known as the Capel St Bridge, which crosses the river from Capel St. The black pool or *dubh linn* at this point gave the city its name, but today the miserable Poddle runs its final 5km in an underground channel and trickles into the Liffey through a grating on the south side of the river just downstream from the bridge.

The Liffey does more than divide Dublin into northern and southern halves – it also marks a psychological and social break between north and south.

Although Liffey water was once a vital constituent in Guinness, you'll be relieved to hear that this is no longer the case.

Dublin Harbour

In medieval times the River Liffey spread out into a broad estuary as it flowed into the bay. That estuary has long since been reclaimed (Trinity College has stood on it for 400 years) and the Liffey is embanked as far as the sea.

Dublin Harbour first came into existence in 1714, when the Liffey embankments were built. North Wall Quay was then built, and later a 5km breakwater known as the South Wall was added, followed by the North and South Bull Walls. The South Wall starts at Ringsend, where Oliver Cromwell first set foot in Ireland in 1649. From there it runs out to the Pigeon House Fort, built from 1748 and now used as a power station, and from there continues a further 2km out to the 1762 Poolbeg Lighthouse at the end of the breakwater. It's a pleasant, though long stroll out to the lighthouse.

Four Courts

On Inns Quay beside the river the extensive Four Courts with its 130m-long facade was one of James Gandon's masterpieces. James Gandon was 18th century Dublin's pre-eminent architect. Construction, which

began in 1786 and soon engulfed the Public Offices (built a short time before at the western end of the same site), continued through to 1802. By then it included a Corinthian-columned central block connected to flanking wings with enclosed quadrangles. The ensemble is topped by a diverse collection of statuary.

The original four courts – Exchequer, Common Pleas, King's Bench and Chancery – branch off the central rotunda. The 1224 Dominican Convent of St Saviour formerly stood on the site, but was replaced first by the King's Inns and then by the present building. The last parliament of James II was held here in 1689.

The Four Courts played a brief role in the 1916 Easter Rising, without suffering damage, but the events of 1922 were not so kind. When anti-Treaty republicans seized the building and refused to leave, it was shelled from across the river; as the occupiers retreated, the building was set on fire and many irreplaceable early records were burnt. This event sparked off the Civil War. The building wasn't restored until 1932.

Visitors are allowed to wander through, but not to enter courts or other restricted areas. In the lobby of the central rotunda you'll see bewigged barristers conferring and police officers handcuffed to their charges waiting to enter court.

Custom House

The Custom House, the Four Courts building farther up the river, the King's Inns and some elements of the parliament building (now the Bank of Ireland) are among James Gandon's masterpieces.

The Custom House, his first great building, was constructed between 1781 and 1791 just past Eden Quay, in spite of vociferous local opposition.

In 1921, during the independence struggle, the Custom House was set alight and completely gutted in a fire that burned for five days. The interior was later extensively redesigned, and a further major renovation took place between 1986 and 1988.

The glistening white building stretches

114m along the Liffey. The best complete view is obtained from across the river, though a close-up inspection of its many fine details is also worthwhile. The building is topped by a copper dome with four clocks. Above that stands a 5m statue of Hope.

In the visitor centre (☎ 878 7660) there's an exhibition on the history of the building. Mid-March to October it's open weekdays 10 am to 5 pm, weekends 2 to 5 pm; call for opening times the rest of the year. Entry is IR£2/1.

Famine Memorial
Beside the river, east of the Custom House, in the old docklands area that's now being redeveloped, is this memorial to the people who died or emigrated as a result of the Famine. It was unveiled by Mary Robinson in 1997, 150 years after the Famine began and consists of seven tall, gaunt, bronze figures 'walking' along the quay towards Dublin harbour. The memorial was donated by Norma Smurfit, an Englishwoman who has lived in Ireland for more than 30 years.

SOUTH OF THE LIFFEY
South Dublin has the fanciest shops, almost all the restaurants of note and a majority of the hotels, as well as most of the reminders of Dublin's early history and the finest Georgian squares and houses.

Trinity College
Ireland's premier university was founded by Elizabeth I in 1592 on grounds confiscated from a monastery. By providing an alternative to education on the Continent, the queen hoped that the students would avoid being 'infected with popery'. The college is in the centre of Dublin though at the time of its foundation it was outside the city walls. Archbishop Ussher, whose scientific feats included the precise dating of the act of creation to 4004 BC, was one of the college's founders.

Officially, the university's name is the University of Dublin, but Trinity College is the institution's sole college. Until 1793 Trinity College remained completely Protes-

tant apart from one short break. Even when the Protestants allowed Catholics in, the Catholic Church forbade it, a restriction which wasn't completely lifted until 1970. To this day Trinity College is still something of a centre of British and Protestant influence even though the majority of its 9500 students are Catholic. Women were first admitted to the college in 1903, earlier than at most British universities.

In summer, walking tours depart regularly from the main gate on College Green, Monday to Saturday 9.30 am to 4.30 pm, Sunday noon to 4 pm. The IR£3.50 cost of the walking tour is good value since it includes the fee to see the 'Book of Kells'.

Main Entrance Facing College Green (the street in front of the college), the 'Front Gate' or Regent House entrance to the college grounds was built in 1752-59 and is guarded by statues of the poet Oliver Goldsmith (1730-74) and the orator Edmund Burke (1729-97).

Around the Campanile The open area reached from Regent House is divided into Front Square, Parliament Square and Library Square. The area is dominated by the 30m Campanile, designed by Edward Lanyon and erected in 1852-53 on what was believed to be the centre of the monastery that preceded the college. To the left of the Campanile is a statue of George Salmon, the College Provost from 1888 to 1904, who fought bitterly to keep women out of the college. He carried out his threat to permit them 'over his dead body' by promptly dropping dead when the worst came to pass.

Chapel & Dining Hall Clockwise around the Front Square from the entrance gate, the first building is the chapel, built from 1798 by the architect Sir William Chambers (1723-96) and since 1972 open to all denominations. It's noted for its extremely fine plasterwork by Michael Stapleton, its Ionic columns and its painted, rather than stained-glass

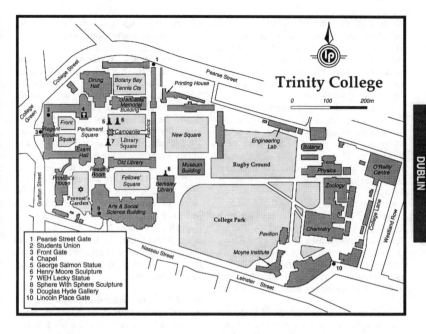

1 Pearse Street Gate
2 Students Union
3 Front Gate
4 Chapel
5 George Salmon Statue
6 Henry Moore Sculpture
7 WEH Lecky Statue
8 Sphere With Sphere Sculpture
9 Douglas Hyde Gallery
10 Lincoln Place Gate

windows. The main one is dedicated to Archbishop Ussher.

Next to the chapel is the dining hall, originally designed in 1743 by Richard Castle, but dismantled only 15 years later because of problems caused by inadequate foundations. The replacement was completed in 1761 and may have retained elements of the original design. It was extensively restored after a fire in 1984.

Graduates' Memorial Building & the Rubrics The 1892 Graduates' Memorial Building forms the north side of Library Square. Behind it are the tennis courts in the open area known as Botany Bay. The popular legend behind this name is that the unruly students housed around the square were suitable candidates for the British penal colony at Botany Bay (Sydney) in Australia. At the east side of Library Square, the red-brick Rubrics Building dates from around 1690, making it the oldest building in the college.

It was extensively altered in an 1894 restoration and then underwent major structural modifications in the 1970s.

Old Library To the south of the square is the Old Library, which was built in a rather severe style by Thomas Burgh between 1712 and 1732. The Old Library's 65m Long Room contains numerous unique ancient texts and the 'Book of Kells' is displayed in the Library Colonnades.

Despite Ireland's independence, the Library Act of 1801 still entitles Trinity College Library, along with three libraries in Britain, to a free copy of every book published in the UK. Housing this bounty requires nearly another km of shelving every year and the collection amounts to around three million books. Of course these cannot all be kept at the college library, so there are now additional library storage facilities dotted around Dublin.

The Long Room is mainly used for about

200,000 of the library's oldest volumes. Until 1892 the ground floor Colonnades was an open arcade, but it was enclosed at that time to increase the storage area. A previous attempt to increase the room's storage capacity had been made in 1853, when the Long Room ceiling was raised.

As well as the world-famous 'Book of Kells', on display is the so-called harp of Brian Ború, which was definitely not in use when the army of this early Irish hero defeated the Danes at the Battle of Clontarf in 1014. It does, however, date from around 1400, making it one of the oldest harps in Ireland.

Other exhibits in the Long Room include a rare copy of the Proclamation of the Irish Republic, which was read out by Patrick Pearse at the beginning of the Easter Rising in 1916. The collection of 18th and 19th century marble busts around the walls features Jonathan Swift, Edmund Burke and Wolfe Tone, all former members of Trinity College.

The Long Room and 'Book of Kells' are open Monday to Saturday 9.30 am to 5 pm, Sunday noon to 4.30 pm. Entry is IR£3.50/3 (children under 12 free). In high season it gets packed out, so try and come out of season. The Colonnades also houses a busy book and souvenir shop and a temporary exhibition hall.

Reading Room, Exam Hall & Provost's House Continuing clockwise around the Campanile there's the Reading Room and the Public Theatre or Exam Hall, which dates from 1779-91. Like the Chapel building which it faces and closely resembles, it was the work of William Chambers and also has plasterwork by Michael Stapleton. The Exam Hall has an oak chandelier rescued from the Houses of Parliament (now the Bank of Ireland) across College Green and an organ said to have been salvaged from a Spanish ship in 1702, though the evidence indicates otherwise.

Behind the Exam Hall is the 1760 Provost's House, a particularly fine Georgian house where the provost or college head

still resides. The house and its adjacent garden are not open to the public.

Berkeley Library To one side of the Old Library is Paul Koralek's 1967 Berkeley Library. This solid square brutalist-style building has been hailed as the best example of modern architecture in Ireland, though it has to be admitted the competition isn't great. It's fronted by Arnaldo Pomodoro's 1982-83 sculpture *Sphere with Sphere*. The library isn't open to the public.

George Berkeley was born in Kilkenny in 1685, studied at Trinity when he was only 15 years old and went on to a distinguished career in many fields, but particularly in philosophy. His influence spread to the new English colonies in North America where, among other things, he helped to found the University of Pennsylvania. Berkeley in California, and its namesake university, are named after him.

Arts & Social Science Building & Douglas Hyde Gallery South of the old library is the 1978 Arts & Social Science Building, which backs on to Nassau St and forms the alternative main entrance to the college. Like the Berkeley Library it was designed by Paul Koralek; it also houses the Douglas Hyde Gallery of Modern Art (☎ 608 1116). Fellows Square is surrounded on three sides by the two library buildings and the Arts & Social Science Building.

The Dublin Experience After the 'Book of Kells' the college's other big tourist attraction is the Dublin Experience, a 45 minute audiovisual introduction to the city. Daily shows take place at the back of the Arts & Social Science Building on the hour from 10 am to 5 pm, late May to early October. Entry is IR£3/2.75. Combined tickets to the 'Book of Kells' and the Dublin Experience are available.

Around New Square Behind the Rubrics Building, at the eastern end of Library Square, is New Square. The highly ornate 1853-57 **Museum Building** (☎ 608 1477)

Book of Kells

For visitors, Trinity College's prime attraction is the magnificent 'Book of Kells', an illuminated manuscript dating from around 800 AD – one of the oldest books in the world. Although the book was brought to the college for safekeeping from the monastery at Kells in County Meath in 1654, it undoubtedly predates the monastery itself. It was probably produced by monks at St Columcille's Monastery on the remote island of Iona, off the west coast of Scotland. When repeated Viking raids made their monastery untenable, the monks moved to the temporary safety of Kells in Ireland in 806, taking their masterpiece with them. In 1007, the book was stolen, then rediscovered three months later, buried in the ground. Some time before the dissolution of the monastery, the metal shrine or *cumdach* was lost, possibly taken by looting Vikings who wouldn't have valued the text itself. About 30 of the beginning and ending folios have also disappeared.

The 'Book of Kells' contains the four gospels of the New Testament, written in Latin, as well as prefaces, summaries and other text. If it were merely words, the 'Book of Kells' would simply be a very old book – it's the extensive and amazingly complex illustrations which make it so wonderful. The superbly decorated opening initials are only part of the story, for the book also has numerous smaller illustrations between the lines.

St John the Eagle, Book of Kells

The 680 page (340 folio) book was rebound in four calfskin volumes in 1953. Two volumes are usually on display, one showing an illuminated page and the other showing text. The pages are turned over regularly, but you can acquire your own reproduction copy for a mere US$19,800. If that's too steep, the library bookshop has various lesser books, including *The Book of Kells*, a paperback with some attractive colour plates and text for IR£10.95.

The 'Book of Kells' is usually on display in the East Pavilion of the Colonnades library, underneath the actual library. As well as the 'Book of Kells', the 807 'Book of Armagh' and the 675 'Book of Durrow' are on display in the East Pavilion. ■

has the skeletons of two enormous giant Irish deer just inside the entrance and the Geological Museum upstairs. It's open by prior arrangement only.

The 1734 **Printing House**, designed by Richard Castle to resemble a Doric temple and now used for the microelectronics and electrical engineering departments, is at the north-west corner of New Square.

At the eastern end of the college grounds are the rugby ground and College Park, where cricket games are often played. There are a number of science buildings at the

eastern end of the grounds. The Lincoln Place Gate at this end is usually open and makes a good entrance or exit from the college, especially if you're on a bicycle.

Bank of Ireland

The imposing Bank of Ireland building (☎ 677 6801), on College Green directly opposite Trinity College, was originally built in 1729 to house the Irish Parliament. When the parliament voted itself out of existence by the Act of Union in 1801, it became a building without a role. It was sold with instructions that the interior be altered to prevent it from being used as a debating chamber in the future. Consequently, the large central House of Commons was re-modelled but the smaller chamber of the House of Lords survived. After independence the Irish government chose to make Leinster House the new parliamentary building and ignored the possibility of restoring this fine building to its original use.

Over a long period of time, a string of architects worked on the building, yet it somehow manages to avoid looking like a hotchpotch of styles. Edward Lovett Pearce designed the circular central part which was constructed between 1729 and 1739, and the east front was designed by James Gandon in 1785. Other architects involved in its construction were Robert Park and Francis Johnston, who converted it from a parliament building to a bank after it was sold in 1803.

Inside, the banking mall occupies what was once the House of Commons, but offers little hint of its former role. The Irish House of Lords is much more interesting with its Irish oak woodwork, late 18th century Dublin crystal chandelier and 10kg silver-gilt mace. The tapestries date from the 1730s and depict the Siege of Derry in 1689 and the Battle of the Boyne in 1690, the two great Protestant victories over Catholic Ireland.

The building can be visited during banking hours, Monday to Friday from 10 am to 4 pm, Thursday to 5 pm. Free tours of the House of Lords take place Tuesday at 10.30, 11.30 am and 1.45 pm.

Nearby, the Bank of Ireland Arts Centre, Foster Place, houses the **Story of Banking Museum**, which has an exhibition on the history of the bank. It's open Tuesday to Friday 10 am to 4 pm, Saturday 2 to 5 pm, Sunday 10 am to 1 pm; entry is IR£1.50/free.

Around the Bank of Ireland
The area between the Bank and Trinity College, today a constant tangle of traffic and pedestrians, was once a green swathe and is still known as College Green. In front of the bank stands a statue of Henry Grattan

(1746-1820), a distinguished parliamentary orator.

The traffic island where College Green, Westmoreland St and College St meet houses public toilets (no longer in use) and a statue of the poet and composer Thomas Moore (1779-1852), renowned for James Joyce's comment in *Ulysses* that standing atop a public urinal wasn't a bad place for the man who penned the poem 'The Meeting of the Waters'. The other end of College St, where it meets Pearse St, is topped by a 1986 sculpture known as *Steyne*. It's a copy of the *steyne* (the Viking word for stone), erected on the riverbank in the 9th century to stop ships from grounding, and not removed until 1720.

Temple Bar
West of College Green and the Bank of Ireland, the maze of streets that make up Temple Bar are sandwiched between Dame St and the river. This is one of the oldest areas of Dublin and has numerous restaurants, pubs and trendy shops.

Dame St, which forms the southern boundary of the Temple Bar area, links new Dublin (centred around Trinity College and Grafton St) and old (stretching from Dublin Castle to encompass the two cathedrals). Along its route Dame St changes name to become Cork Hill, Lord Edward St and Christ Church Place.

Information The Temple Bar Information Centre (☎ 671 5717), 18 Eustace St, has information on the area and an exhibition on its development and publishes the useful *Temple Bar Guide*. It opens Monday to Friday 9 am to 6 pm all year, plus from June to August, Saturday 11 am to 4 pm and Sunday noon to 4 pm.

The notice board in the Resource Centre/ Well Fed Café on Crow St displays a useful round-up of local goings-on.

Temple Bar History This stretch of riverside land was owned by Augustinian friars from 1282 until Henry VIII's dissolution of the monasteries in 1537 when Sir William

Temple (1554-1628) acquired the land which bears his name. The term 'bar' referred to a riverside walkway, so this area was called Temple's Bar. Until 1537, Temple Lane was known as Hogges Lane and gave access to the friars' house. During its monastic era the Temple Bar area was marshy land that had only recently been reclaimed from the river. Much of it was outside the city walls and the River Poddle flowed through it, connecting the black pool with the Liffey.

The narrow lanes and alleys of Temple Bar started to take form in the early 18th century when this was a disreputable area of pubs and brothels. Through the 19th century it developed a commercial character with many small craft and trade businesses, but in the first half of the 20th century it went into decline, along with most of central Dublin.

In the 1960s it was decided to demolish the area to build a major bus station, but these plans took a long time to develop and meanwhile the area became a thriving countercultural centre. In the 1980s the bus station plan was abandoned and Temple Bar was encouraged to develop as a centre for arts, restaurants, shops and entertainment instead. The area now boasts two public squares, residential apartments, centres for film, art and photography, a student housing centre and a Viking museum.

Exploring Temple Bar The western boundary of Temple Bar is formed by Fishamble St, the oldest street in Dublin, dating back to Viking times – not that you'd know that to see it now. Christ Church Cathedral, beside Fishamble St, dates from 1170, but there was an earlier Viking church on this site. Brass symbols in the pavement direct you towards a mosaic laid out to show the ground plan of the sort of Viking dwelling excavated here in 1980-81.

Another Viking area is being excavated closer to Parliament St. Nearby is **Dublin's Viking Adventure** (☎ 679 6040), Essex St West, where there's an entertaining 40 minute tour of Viking Dublin, then known as Dyflin. You take a simulated ride on a Viking ship, land at the village of Dyflin (complete with smells) which you then walk through. Actors play the parts of villagers and tell you about their way of life. It's not often you get to talk to exhibits in a museum. It's open Monday to Saturday, 10 am to 4.30 pm, Sunday 11.30 am to 5.30 pm and the tour costs IR£4.75/2.95.

In 1742 Handel conducted the first performance of his *Messiah* in the Dublin Music Hall, which stood at that time behind what is now Kinlay House. The Music Hall, which had opened a year earlier in 1741, was designed by Richard Castle; the only reminder of it today is the entrance and the original door, which stand to the left of Kennan's engineering works.

Parliament St, which runs straight up from the river to the City Hall and Dublin Castle, has, at No 4, Read's Cutlers, the oldest shop in Dublin, having operated under the same name since 1760. At the bottom of the street, beside the river, the Sunlight Chambers have a beautiful frieze running round the facade. Sunlight was a brand of soap manufactured by the Lever Brothers, who were responsible for the turn-of-the-century building. The frieze shows the Lever Brothers' view of the world and soap: men make clothes dirty, women wash them!

Eustace St is particularly interesting, with the popular Norseman pub at the river end and the 1715 Presbyterian Meeting House. The Dublin branch of the United Irishmen, who set themselves up to campaign for both parliamentary reform and equality for Catholics, was first convened in 1791 in the Eagle Tavern, now the Friends Meeting House.

Merchant's Arch leads to the Ha'penny Bridge. If you cross to the north side of the Liffey, pause to look at the statue of two stout Dublin matrons sitting on a park bench with their shopping bags, dubbed 'the hags with the bags'. The Stock Exchange lives on Anglesea St, in a building dating from 1878. The Bank of Ireland also occupies a corner of Temple Bar.

Dublin Castle

The centre of British power in Ireland and originally built on the orders of King John in

1204, Dublin Castle (☎ 677 7129) is more palace than castle. Only the Record Tower, completed in 1258, survives from the original Norman castle. Parts of the castle's foundations remain, and a visit to the excavations is the most interesting part of the castle tour. The castle moats, which are now completely covered by more modern developments, were once filled by the River Poddle.

Dublin Castle enjoyed a relatively quiet history despite a siege by Silken Thomas Fitzgerald in 1534, a fire which destroyed much of the castle in 1684, and the events of the 1916 Easter Rising. The castle was used as the official residence of the British viceroys of Ireland, until the Viceregal Lodge was built in Phoenix Park. Earlier it had been used as a prison, though not always with great success. Red Hugh O'Donnell, one of the last of the great Gaelic leaders, escaped from the Record Tower in 1591, was recaptured, and escaped again in 1592.

The castle tops Cork Hill, behind the City Hall on Dame St, and, provided it's not in use for important state business, tours are held weekdays 10 am to 5 pm, weekends 2 to 5 pm. Tours cost IR£2/1. Friday morning isn't a good time to visit because that's when the Peace & Reconciliation Forum meets.

The visitor centre in the south-east corner of the Lower Yard has a gift shop and café.

Castle Tour The main **Upper Yard** of the castle with the entrance underneath the **Throne Room** is reached either directly from Cork Hill or via the Lower Yard. From the main entrance, the castle tour takes you around the state chambers, developed during Dublin's British heyday and still used for official state occasions. The sequence of rooms the tour takes you through may vary.

From the entrance you ascend the stairs to the **Battle-Axe Landing**, where the viceroy's guards once stood, armed with battle-axes.

Turning left you pass through a series of drawing rooms, formerly used as visitors' bedrooms. One contains a Van Dyck painting of Elizabeth, second Viscountess of

Southampton, at the age of 17, another a book painted on vellum between 1989 and 1991 as a sort of latterday 'Book of Kells'. The castle gardens, visible from the windows of these rooms, end in a high wall said to have been built for Queen Victoria's visit to block out the distressing sight of the Stephen St slums. James Connolly was detained in the first of these rooms after the siege of the GPO in 1916, before being taken to Kilmainham Jail to face a firing squad.

From the long **State Corridor** you enter the **State Drawing Room**, which was seriously damaged by a fire in 1941. It has been restored with furniture and paintings dating from 1740. From there you enter the ornate **Throne Room**, built in 1740.

The long **Portrait Gallery** has portraits of some of the British viceroys and ends at an anteroom from which you enter George's Hall, added to the castle in 1911 for George V's visit to Ireland.

From these rooms you return through the anteroom to the blue **Wedgwood Room** (yes, the whole room does look like Wedgwood china), which in turn leads to the **Bermingham Tower**, originally dating from 1411 but rebuilt in 1775-77. The tower was used as a prison on a number of occasions, particularly during the Anglo-Irish War from 1918 to 1920.

Leaving the tower you pass through the 25m-long **St Patrick's Hall**. The Knights of St Patrick, an order created in 1783, were invested here and their standards are displayed around the walls. These days Irish presidents are inaugurated here and it is used for receptions. The huge painting on the ceiling shows St Patrick lighting the fire on Slane Hill; the Irish chieftains handing over power to the Anglo-Normans; and the coronation of George III who created the Order of St Patrick.

St Patrick's Hall ends back on the Battle-Axe Landing but the tour now takes you down to the **Undercroft** where remnants of the earlier Viking fort, the 13th century Powder Tower and the city wall can be seen. This excavation of the original moat is now well below street level.

Bedford Tower & Genealogical Office
Other points of interest in the castle include the Bedford Tower and the Genealogical Office, directly across the Upper Yard from the main entrance. In 1907 the collection known as the Irish Crown Jewels was stolen from the tower and never recovered.

The entranceway to the castle yard, beside the Bedford Tower, is topped by a figure of justice which has always been a subject of mirth. She faces the castle and has her back to the city – seen as a sure indicator of how much justice the average Irish citizen could expect from the British. The scales of justice also had a distinct tendency to fill with rain and tilt in one direction or the other, rather than assuming the approved level position. Eventually a hole was drilled in the bottom of each pan so the rainwater could drain out.

Royal Chapel The Church of the Holy Trinity, previously known as the Royal Chapel, which was built in Gothic style by Francis Johnston in 1807-14, is in the Lower Yard. Decorating the cold grey exterior are over 90 heads of various Irish personages and assorted saints carved out of Tullamore limestone. The interior is wildly exuberant, with fan vaulting alongside quadripartite vaulting, wooden galleries, stained-glass and lots of lively looking sculpted angels.

Record Tower Rising over the chapel is the Record Tower, which was used as a storage facility for official records from 1579 until they were transferred to the Record Office in the Four Courts building in the early 19th century. (When the Four Courts was burnt out at the start of the Civil War in 1922, almost all these priceless records were destroyed.) Although the tower was rebuilt in 1813 it retains much of its original appearance, including the massive 5m-thick walls.

City Hall & Municipal Buildings
Fronting Dublin Castle on Lord Edward St, the City Hall was built by Thomas Cooley in 1769-79 as the Royal Exchange and later became the offices of the Dublin Corporation. It stands on the site of the Lucas Coffee

House and The Eagle Tavern in which Dublin's infamous Hell Fire Club was established in 1735. Founded by Richard Parsons, earl of Rosse, it was one of a number of gentlemen's clubs in Dublin where less than gentlemanly conduct took place. It (has) gained a reputation for debauchery and black magic, but there's no evidence that such things took place. Parliament St (1762), which leads up from the river to the front of City Hall, was the first of the wide boulevards to be laid out by the Commission for Wide & Convenient Streets.

The 1781 Municipal Buildings, immediately west of the City Hall, were built by Thomas Ivory (1720-86), who was also responsible for the Genealogical Office in Dublin Castle. The Genealogical Office, as an institution, dates from 1552, but where it's now housed dates from the 18th century and was built by Ivory.

Christ Church Cathedral
Christ Church Cathedral (Church of the Holy Trinity) (☎ 677 8099) is on Christ Church Place, just south of the river and west of the city centre and Temple Bar. Dublin's original Viking settlement stood between the cathedral and the river. This was also the centre of medieval Dublin, with Dublin Castle nearby and the Tholsel or town hall (demolished in 1809) and the original Four Courts (demolished in 1796) both beside the cathedral. Nearby, on Back Lane, is the only remaining guildhall in Dublin. The 1706 **Tailor's Hall** was due for demolition in the 1960s, but survived to become the office of An Taisce (National Trust for Ireland).

Originally built in wood by the Danes in 1038, the cathedral was subsequently rebuilt in stone from 1172, by Richard de Clare, earl of Pembroke (better known as Strongbow), the Anglo-Norman noble who invaded Ireland in 1170. The archbishop of Dublin at that time, Laurence (Lorcan in Irish) O'Toole, later become St Laurence, the patron saint of Dublin. Strongbow died in 1176 and Laurence O'Toole in 1180, before the church was complete. Nor was their cathedral destined to have a long life: the foundations were essentially a peat bog and the south wall collapsed in 1562, though it was soon rebuilt. Most of what you see from the outside dates from architect GE Street's major 1871-78 restoration. Above ground, the north wall, the transepts and the western part of the choir are almost all that remain from the original.

Through much of its history, Christ Church vied for supremacy with nearby St Patrick's Cathedral, but, like its neighbour, it fell on hard times in the 18th and 19th centuries and was virtually derelict by the time restoration took place. Earlier, the nave had been used as a market and the crypt had housed taverns. Today both Church of Ireland cathedrals are outsiders in a Catholic nation.

From the south-east entrance to the churchyard you walk past the ruins of the chapter house, dating from 1230. The entrance to the cathedral is at the south-west corner and as you enter you face the north wall. This survived the collapse of its southern counterpart, but has also suffered from subsiding foundations; from the eastern end it leans visibly.

The south aisle has a monument to the legendary Strongbow. The armoured figure on the tomb is unlikely to be of Strongbow (it's more probably the earl of Drogheda) but his internal organs may have been buried here. A popular legend relates that the half-figure beside the tomb is of Strongbow's son, who was cut in two by his father when his bravery in battle was suspect.

The south transept contains the superb Baroque tomb of the 19th earl of Kildare (died 1734). His grandson, Lord Edward Fitzgerald, was a member of the United Irishmen and died in the abortive 1798 Rising. The entrance to the Chapel of St Laurence is off the south transept and contains two effigies, one of them reputed to be that of either Strongbow's wife or sister. Laurence O'Toole's embalmed heart was placed in the Chapel of St Laud.

At the east end of the cathedral is the Lady Chapel or Chapel of the Blessed Virgin Mary. Also at the east end is the Chapel of St Edmund and the chapter house, the latter closed to visitors. Parts of the choir, in the centre of the church, and the north transept are original, but the baptistry was added during the 1871-78 restoration.

An entrance just by the south transept descends to the unusually large arched crypt which dates back to the original Viking church. Curiosities in the crypt include a glass display case housing a mummified cat chasing a mummified mouse that were trapped inside an organ pipe in the 1860s! From the main entrance a bridge, part of the 1871-78 restoration, leads to Dublinia (see next section).

The cathedral opens daily 10 am to 5 pm and entry is IR£1/50p.

Dublinia

Inside what was once the Synod Hall attached to Christ Church Cathedral, the Medieval Trust has created Dublinia, a lively attempt to bring medieval Dublin to life. The ground floor has several models of episodes in Dublin's history which are explained through headsets as you walk around. On the 1st floor, finds from medieval excavations are displayed alongside a large model of the city. There are also models of the medieval quayside and of a cobbler's shop. On the top floor a multimedia show runs every half-hour. Finally you can climb neighbouring St Michael's Tower for views over the city to the Dublin Hills.

Dublinia is open April to September daily, 10 am to 5 pm, October to March 11 am to 4 pm Monday to Saturday, 10 am to 4.30 pm Sunday. Admission costs IR£3.95/2.90 which gets you into Christ Church Cathedral free (via the link bridge).

St Patrick's Cathedral

St Patrick himself is said to have baptised converts at a well within the cathedral grounds, so the cathedral (☎ 475 4817) stands on one of the earliest Christian sites in the city. Like Christ Church Cathedral it was built on unstable ground, with the subterranean River Poddle flowing under its foundations. Because of the high water table St Patrick's doesn't have a crypt.

Its current form dates mainly from some rather over-enthusiastic restoration in 1864 which included the addition of the flying buttresses. St Patrick's Park, the expanse of green beside the cathedral, was a crowded slum until it was cleared and its residents evicted in the early years of the 20th century.

Although a church stood on the Patrick St site from as early as the 5th century, the present building dates from 1190 or 1225 – opinions differ. The stone Norman construction was rebuilt in the early 13th century in a style mimicked by the present form.

Like Christ Church Cathedral, the building has suffered a rather dramatic history. A storm brought down the spire in 1316 and soon after, the building was badly damaged in a fire. Another more disastrous fire followed in 1362 which required the addition of Archbishop Minot's west tower in 1370. For some reason it was built at a slight angle to the rest of the cathedral. In 1560 one of the first clocks in Dublin was added to the 43m tower, and a 31m spire in 1749. Oliver Cromwell, during his 1649 visit to Ireland, converted St Patrick's to a stable for his army's horses, an indignity to which he also subjected numerous other Irish churches. Jonathan Swift was the dean of the cathedral from 1713 to 1745, but prior to its mid-19th century restoration it became very neglected.

Entering the cathedral from the southwest porch you come almost immediately, on your right, to the graves of Swift and Esther Johnson or Stella, Swift's long-term companion. On the wall nearby are Swift's own Latin epitaphs to the two of them, and a bust of him.

The huge dusty Boyle Monument to the left was erected in 1632 by Richard Boyle, the earl of Cork, and is decorated with numerous painted figures of members of his family. It stood beside the altar until, in 1633, Dublin's viceroy, Thomas Wentworth, the future earl of Strafford, had it shifted. Wentworth won this round in his bitter conflict with the earl of Cork, but the latter had the final say when he contributed to Went-

---

Chancing One's Arm

Leaning against a column at the west end of the cathedral is an old door with a rectangular hole cut through it, which was once the entry to the chapter house. In 1492, the year in which Columbus was busy landing in the New World, a furious argument took place within the cathedral between the earl of Kildare and the earl of Ormond.

Each was supported by his armed retainers, but when strong words were about to lead to heavy blows, the earl of Ormonde retreated to the chapter house. The earl of Kildare, realising that the dispute was pointless wanted to end it but Ormond didn't respond. Using a spear, Kildare cut a hole in the door and thrust his hand through to show his good faith. It was clasped by another hand, the door was opened and the two men embraced thereby ending the dispute.

In extending his arm through the door, the earl of Kildare added the phrase 'chancing one's arm' to the English language. ■

---

worth's impeachment and execution. The figure in the centre on the bottom level is of the earl's five-year-old son, Robert Boyle (1627-91), who became a noted scientist. His contributions to physics include Boyle's Law, which relates the pressure and volume of gases.

In the north-west corner of the church is a cross on a stone slab, which once marked the position of St Patrick's original well. The south transept was formerly a separate chapter house.

During the cathedral's decay in the 18th and 19th centuries the north transept was virtually a separate church. It now contains memorials to the Royal Irish Regiments. The Swift corner, in the north transept, features Swift's pulpit, his chair and a book-filled glass cabinet containing his death mask.

The Guinness family were noted contributors to the cathedral's restoration and a monument to Sir Benjamin Guinness's daughter stands in the Chapel of St Stephen beneath a window bearing the words 'I was thirsty and ye gave me drink'! The chapel also has a chair used by William of Orange at a service in the cathedral after his victory at the Boyne.

The cathedral is open 9 am to 6 pm Monday to Friday, 9 am to 5 pm Saturday (to 4 pm November to April), and 10 to 11 am and 12.45 to 3 pm Sunday (10.30 to 11 am, 12.45 to 3 pm November to April). Entry is IR£1.20/50p. The cathedral's choir school dates back to 1432 and the choir took part in the first performance of Handel's *Messiah* in 1742. You can hear the choir sing Thursday to Tuesday in July and August.

Bus Nos 50, 50A or 56A from Aston Quay or Nos 54 or 54A from Burgh Quay run to the cathedral.

Marsh's Library

In St Patrick's Close, beside St Patrick's Cathedral, is Marsh's Library (☎ 454 3511), founded in 1701 by Archbishop Narcissus Marsh (1638-1713) and opened in 1707. It was designed by Sir William Robinson, who was also responsible for the Royal Hospital, Kilmainham. The oldest public library in the country, it contains 25,000 books dating from the 16th to the early 18th centuries, as well as maps, numerous manuscripts and a collection of incunabula, the technical term for books printed before 1500. One of the oldest and finest books in the collection is a volume of Cicero's *Letters to his Friends* printed in Milan in 1472. The manuscript collection includes one in Latin dating back to 1400.

The three alcoves where scholars were once locked in to peruse rare volumes still stand in the virtually unchanged interior. The skull lurking in the furthest one doesn't, however, belong to some poor forgotten scholar. Instead it's a cast taken of Swift's Stella's head. A bindery to repair and restore rare old books operates from the library, which makes an appearance in Joyce's *Ulysses*.

The library has regular exhibits and is open weekdays (not Tuesday), 10 am to 12.45 pm and 2 to 5 pm, Saturday 10.30 am to 12.45 pm. Entry is IR£1. You can reach the library by taking bus No 50, 50A or 56A

from Aston Quay or bus No 54 or 54A from Burgh Quay.

St Werburgh's Church

In Werburgh St, just south of Christ Church Cathedral and beside Dublin Castle, St Werburgh's stands on ancient foundations. Its early history, however, is unknown. It was rebuilt in 1662, in 1715 and again in 1759 (with some elegance) after a fire in 1754. It is linked with the Fitzgerald family; Lord Edward Fitzgerald, who joined the United Irishmen and was a leader of the 1798 Rising, is interred in the vault. In what was an unfortunately frequent theme of Irish uprisings, compatriots betrayed him and he died from wounds received while being captured. Major Henry Sirr, his captor, is buried in the graveyard.

Despite its long history, fine design and interesting interior, the church is run-down and rarely used except for Sunday morning mass. A note at the front directs you around the corner to 8 Castle St if you want to have a look inside (between 10 am and 4 pm). If you can't raise anybody, try phoning ☎ 478 3710.

Werburgh St was also the location of Dublin's first theatre and Jonathan Swift was born just off the street in Hoey's Court in 1667.

St Audoen's Churches

Lucky St Audoen has two churches to his name, both just west of Christ Church Cathedral. The Church of Ireland church is the older and smaller building, and is the only surviving medieval parish church in the city. Its tower and door date from the 12th century, the aisle from the 15th century and various other bits and pieces from early times, but the church today is mainly a 19th century restoration. The tower's bells include the three oldest bells in Ireland, all dating from 1423.

There are several entries to the church grounds including via an arch beside Cook St, to the north of the church. Part of the old city wall, this arch was built in 1240 and is the only surviving reminder of the city gates.

Parts of an even earlier Viking church of St Colmcille may be included in the later constructions.

Joined onto the older Protestant St Audoen's is the newer and larger Catholic St Audoen's, which was completed in 1846. The dome was replaced in 1884 after it collapsed, and the front, with its imposing Corinthian columns, was added in 1899. Unfortunately, you're unlikely to find either church open, except during weekend services.

National Museum

The National Museum (☎ 661 8811), on Kildare St, was designed by Sir Thomas Newenham Deane and completed in 1890. The star attraction is the Treasury, which has two superb collections and an accompanying audiovisual display.

One of the collections is of Bronze and Iron Age gold objects, including a magnificent gold collar and a delicate little gold model of a galley, both from the Broighter Hoard (1st century BC). Most of the hoards displayed were discovered by railway workers, ploughmen and peat cutters – rarely by archaeologists.

The other Treasury collection is from medieval times. Outstanding among the objects on display are the 8th century silver Ardagh Chalice, the 12th century Cross of Cong, which once enshrined a supposed fragment of the True Cross, and the beautiful 8th century Tara Brooch, made of gold, enamel and amber.

Upstairs, Viking Age Dublin tells the story of Dublin's Viking era, with exhibits from the excavations at Wood Quay – the area between Christ Church Cathedral and the river, where Dublin City Council plonked its new headquarters. Other exhibits focus on the 1916 Easter Rising and the independence struggle between 1900 and 1921. Numerous interesting displays relate to this important period of modern Irish history. Frequent short-term exhibitions are also held.

The museum's collections of Irish decorative arts, ceramics, musical instruments and Japanese decorative arts are housed in the annex at Collins Barracks in Benburb St, off Ellis Quay.

The museum is open Tuesday to Saturday 10 am to 5 pm, Sunday 2 to 5 pm. Entry is free. Guided tours are available daily June to September for IR£1.

National Gallery

Opened in 1864, the National Gallery (☎ 661 5133) looks out on Merrion Square. Its excellent collection is strong in Irish art, but there are also high-quality collections of every major school of European painting.

On the lawn in front of the gallery is a statue of the Irish railway magnate, William Dargan, who organised the 1853 Dublin Industrial Exhibition at this spot; the profits from the exhibition were used to found the gallery. Nearby is a statue of George Bernard Shaw, a major benefactor of the gallery.

The gallery has three wings: the original Dargan Wing, the Milltown Rooms and the North Wing. The Dargan Wing's ground floor has the imposing Shaw Room, lined with full-length portraits and illuminated by a series of spectacular Waterford crystal chandeliers. Upstairs, a series of rooms is dedicated to the Italian early and high Renaissance, 16th century north Italian art and 17th and 18th century Italian art. Fra Angelico, Titian and Tintoretto are among the artists represented.

The central Milltown Rooms were added in 1899-1903 to hold Russborough House's art collection presented to the gallery in 1902. The ground floor displays the gallery's fine Irish collection plus a smaller British collection, with works by Reynolds, Hogarth, Gainsborough, Landseer and Turner. One highlight is the room at the back of the gallery displaying works by Jack B Yeats (1871-1957), younger brother of WB Yeats. Other rooms relate to specific periods and styles of Irish art, including one room of works by Irish artists painting in France.

Upstairs are works from Germany, the Netherlands and Spain. There are rooms full of works by Rembrandt and his circle and by the Spanish artists of Seville. The Spanish collection features works by El Greco, Goya and Picasso.

The North Wing was only added in 1964-68 but has undergone extensive refurbishment. It houses works by British and European artists. The gallery also has an art reference library, a lecture theatre, a good bookshop and the deservedly popular Fitzers Café. The gallery hours are Monday to Saturday 10 am to 5.30 pm (to 8.30 pm Thursday), Sunday 2 to 5 pm. Entry is free and there are guided tours Saturday at 3 pm, Sunday at 2.30, 3.15 and 4 pm.

Leinster House – Irish Parliament

The Dáil (lower house) and the Seanad (upper house) of Ireland's parliament, the Oireachtas na hÉireann, meet in Leinster House on Kildare St. The entrance to Leinster House from Kildare St is flanked by the National Library and the National Museum. Originally built as Kildare House in 1745-48 for the earl of Kildare, the name of the building was changed when he also assumed the title of Duke of Leinster in 1766. One of the members of the Fitzgerald family who held the title was Lord Edward Fitzgerald, who died of wounds he received in the abortive 1798 Rising.

Leinster House's Kildare St frontage was designed by Richard Castle to look like a town house, whereas the Merrion Square frontage was made to look like a country house. The lawn in front of the Merrion Square country-house frontage was the site for railway pioneer William Dargan's 1853 Dublin Industrial Exhibition, which in turn led to the creation of the National Gallery. There's a statue of him at the National Gallery end of the lawn. At the other end of the lawn is a statue of Prince Albert, Queen Victoria's consort. Queen Victoria herself was commemorated in massive form on the Kildare St side from 1908 until the statue was removed in 1948. The obelisk in front of the building is dedicated to Arthur Griffith, Michael Collins and Kevin O'Higgins, architects of independent Ireland.

The Dublin Society, later named the Royal Dublin Society, bought the building in 1814 but moved out in stages between 1922 and 1925, when the first government of independent Ireland decided to establish the parliament there.

The Seanad meets in the north-wing saloon, while the Dáil meets in a less interesting room that was originally a lecture theatre added to the original building in 1897. When parliament is sitting, visitors are admitted to an observation gallery. You get an entry ticket from the Kildare St entrance on production of some identification. Bags can't be taken in, or notes or photographs taken. Parliament sits for 90 days a year, usually November to May, on Tuesday (2.30 to 8.30 pm), Wednesday (10.30 am to 8.30 pm) and Thursday (10.30 am to 5.30 pm).

Government Buildings

On Merrion St Upper, the domed Government Buildings were opened in 1911, in a rather heavy-handed Edwardian interpretation of the Georgian style. On Saturday, 40-minute tours are conducted 10.30 am to 3.30 pm. Tickets are available free from the National Gallery ticket office. Only 16 people can join each tour, so if a group has just arrived you may have to wait; although you can't book in advance, you can go along in the morning and put your name down for later in the day. You get to see the Taoiseach's office, the ceremonial staircase with stunning stained-glass window, the cabinet room and innumerable fine examples of Irish arts & crafts on loan from the Arts Council. Bags can't be taken into the building.

Across the road at 24 Merrion St Upper, **Mornington House** is a Georgian mansion thought to be the birthplace of the Duke of Wellington, who was somewhat ashamed of his Irish origins. It's possible that his actual birthplace was Trim in County Meath. The mansion is being renovated to become part of a new hotel, the Merrion.

National Library

Flanking the Kildare St entrance to Leinster House is the National Library, which was built in 1884-90, at the same time and to a similar design as the National Museum by

Sir Thomas Newenham Deane and his son Sir Thomas Manly Deane. Leinster House, the library and museum were all part of the Royal Dublin Society (formed in 1731), which aimed to improve conditions for poor people and to promote the arts and sciences. The library's extensive collection has many valuable early manuscripts, first editions, maps and other items. Temporary displays are often held in the entrance area and the library's reading room featured in *Ulysses*. The library is open Monday 10 am to 9 pm, Tuesday and Wednesday 2 to 9 pm, Thursday and Friday 10 am to 5 pm, Saturday 10 am to 1 pm.

Heraldic Museum & Genealogical Office

On the corner of Kildare and Nassau Sts, the former home of the Kildare St Club (an important right-wing institution during Dublin's Anglo-Irish heyday) is shared by the Heraldic Museum and Genealogical Office and the Alliance Française. It's a popular destination for visitors intent on tracing their Irish roots. Note the whimsical though rather worn stone carvings of animals that decorate the building's windows, including monkeys playing billiards.

The Heraldic Museum's displays follow the story of heraldry in Ireland and Europe. It's open Monday to Friday 10.30 am to 12.30 pm and 2 to 4.30 pm; entry is free.

Natural History Museum

Just as the National Library and the National Museum flank the entrance to Leinster House on the Kildare St side, the National Gallery and Natural History Museum perform the same function on the Merrion St Upper/Merrion Square side.

The Natural History Museum (☎ 661 8811) has scarcely changed since 1857 when Scottish explorer Dr David Livingstone delivered the opening lecture. It's known as the Dead Zoo, but despite that disheartening appellation it's well worth a visit, for its collection is huge and well kept. That moth-eaten look which afflicts neglected collections of stuffed animals has been kept at

bay and children in particular are likely to find it fascinating.

On the ground floor, the collection of skeletons, stuffed animals and the like covers the full range of Irish fauna. It includes three skeletons of the Irish giant deer, which became extinct about 10,000 years ago. On the 1st and 2nd floors are fauna from around the world.

The museum is open Tuesday to Saturday 10 am to 5 pm, Sunday 2 to 5 pm. Entry is free.

Grafton St & Around

Grafton St was the major traffic artery of south Dublin until it was turned into a pedestrian precinct in 1982. It's now Dublin's fanciest and most colourful shopping centre with plenty of street life and the city's most entertaining buskers. The street is equally lively after dark as some of Dublin's most interesting pubs are clustered around it.

Apart from fine shops, like the Brown Thomas (opened in 1848) department store, Grafton St also boasts Bewley's Oriental Café. This branch of the chain has memorabilia upstairs relating to the company's history.

Johnson's Court leads off Grafton St to the elegantly converted Powerscourt Townhouse Shopping Centre on William St South. Built between 1771 and 1774, this grand house has a balconied courtyard and, following its conversion in 1981, now shelters three levels of shops and restaurants. The Powerscourt family's principal residence was Powerscourt House in County Wicklow and this city mansion was soon sold for commercial use. It survived that period in remarkably good condition and in its present incarnation forms a convenient link from Grafton St to the South City Market on South Great George's St. The building features plasterwork by Michael Stapleton, who also worked on Belvedere House in north Dublin.

At the College Green end of Grafton St is the modern statue of Molly Malone of song fame, rendered in such extreme *déshabillée* that she's nicknamed the 'tart with the cart'.

Dublin Civic Museum

Located in the 18th century Assembly House beside the Powerscourt Townhouse, the Dublin Civic Museum (☎ 679 4260), 58 William St South, is a stone's throw from Grafton St. It has changing exhibitions relating to the history of the city. In particular, look out for the head from Nelson's Pillar on O'Connell St which was toppled by the IRA in 1966.

The small museum is open Tuesday to Saturday 10 am to 6 pm, Sunday 11 am to 2 pm; entry is free. It's worth popping in just to see the architecture.

Mansion House

Mansion House on Dawson St was built in 1710 by Joshua Dawson, after whom the street is named. Only five years later the house was bought as a residence for the Lord Mayor of Dublin. The building's original brick Queen Anne style has all but disappeared behind a stucco facade tacked on in the Victorian era. The building was the site for the 1919 Declaration of Independence, but isn't generally open to the public. Next door is the **Royal Irish Academy**, also generally closed to visitors.

St Stephen's Green

On warm summer days the nine hectares of St Stephen's Green provide a popular lunchtime escape for city office workers. The green was originally an expanse of open common land where public whippings, burnings and hangings took place. The green was enclosed by a fence in 1664 when Dublin Corporation sold off the surrounding land for buildings. A stone wall replaced the fence in 1669 and trees and gravel paths soon followed within. By the end of that century restrictions were already in force prohibiting buildings of less than two storeys or those constructed of mud and wattle. At the same time Grafton St, the main route to the green from what was then central Dublin, was upgraded from a 'foule and out of repaire' laneway to a crown causeway.

The fine Georgian buildings around the square date mainly from Dublin's mid to late 18th century Georgian prime. At that time the north side was known as the Beaux' Walk and it's still one of Dublin society's most esteemed meeting places. Some further improvements were made in 1753, with seats being put in place, but in 1814 railings and locked gates were added and an annual fee

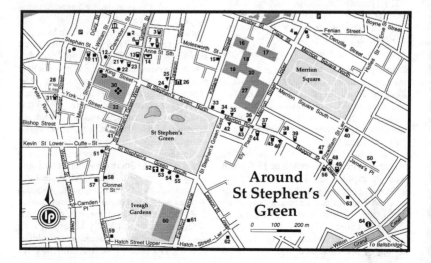

of one guinea was charged to use the green. This private use continued until 1877 when Sir Arthur Edward Guinness, later Lord Ardilaun, pushed an act through parliament once again opening the green to the public. He also financed the central park's gardens and ponds, which date from 1880.

Across the road from the west side of the green are the 1863 **Unitarian Church** and the **Royal College of Surgeons**, the latter with one of the finest facades around St Stephen's Green. It was built in 1806 and extended in 1825-27 to the design of William Murray. Forty years later Murray's son, William G Murray, designed the Royal College of Physicians building on Kildare St. In the 1916 Easter Rising, the Royal College of Surgeons was occupied by the colourful Countess Markievicz (1868-1927), an Irish nationalist married to a Polish count. The columns still bear bullet marks.

The main entrance to the green was once on this side, but now it's through the **Fusiliers' Arch** at the north-west corner of

the green from Grafton St. Modelled on the Arch of Titus in Rome, the arch commemorates the 212 soldiers of the Royal Dublin Fusiliers who died in the Boer War (1899-1902).

A path from the arch passes by the duck pond while around the fountain in the centre of the green are a number of statues, including a bust of Countess Markievicz. The centre of the park also has a garden for the blind, complete with signs in Braille and plants which can be handled.

On the eastern side of the green there's a children's play park and to the south is a fine old **bandstand**, erected for Queen Victoria's jubilee in 1887. Concerts often take place here in the summer.

Just inside the green at the south-east corner, near Leeson St, is a statue of the Three Fates, presented to Dublin in 1956 by West Germany in gratitude for Irish aid immediately after WWII. The north-west corner, opposite the Shelbourne Hotel and Merrion Row, is marked by the Wolfe Tone

DUBLIN

PLACES TO STAY
2 Westbury Hotel
4 Mont Clare Hotel
5 Davenport Hotel
11 Grafton Plaza
15 Buswell's Hotel
31 Avalon House
33 Shelbourne Hotel
38 Georgian House
47 Longfield's
53 Staunton's on the Green
56 Fitzwilliam
57 Russell Court Hotel
58 Albany House
59 Harcourt Hotel
61 Hotel Conrad
62 Leeson Court
63 Latchford's

PLACES TO EAT
7 Eddie Rocket's, Café Java & Gotham Café
21 Pasta Fresca
25 La Stampa
35 Galligan's Restaurant
42 Pierre Victoire

46 Ayumi-ya & Hanna's Kitchen
50 Restaurant Patrick Guilbaud

PUBS
3 Davy Byrne's
6 Bruxelles
8 John Kehoe's
10 Break for the Border
13 McDaid's
23 Neary's
37 Doheny & Nesbitt's
39 Maguire's Pub
43 O'Donoghue's
44 Big Jack's Baggot Inn
45 James Toner's
48 Larry Murphy's
49 Henry Grattan

OTHER
1 Dublin Civic Museum
9 Internet Exchange
12 Dublin Arts Centre
14 Post Office
16 National Library
17 National Gallery
18 Leinster House (Irish Parliament)

19 National Museum
20 Natural History Museum
22 Gaiety Theatre
24 Aer Lingus
26 Mansion House
27 Government Buildings
28 Whitefriars Carmelite Church
29 Major Tom's Nightclub
30 St Stephen's Green Shopping Centre
32 Royal College of Surgeons
34 Huguenot Cemetery
36 Irish Ferries
40 No 29 Fitzwilliam St Lower
41 Unitarian Church
51 An Siopa Leabhar Bookshop
52 Catholic University Church
54 Newman House
55 Iveagh House
60 National Concert Hall
64 Bord Fáilte (Irish Tourist Board)

Monument to the leader of the abortive 1796 invasion. The vertical slabs which serve as a backdrop for Wolfe Tone's statue have been dubbed 'Tonehenge'. Just inside the park at this entrance is a memorial to the victims of the Famine.

Notable buildings around the green include the imposing old 1867 **Shelbourne Hotel** on the north side, with statues of Nubian princesses and their ankle-fettered slave girls decorating the front. Just beyond the Shelbourne is a small **Huguenot cemetery** dating from 1693, when many French Huguenots fled here from persecution under Louis XIV.

At No 80-81 on the south side of the green is **Iveagh House**, where the Guinness family was once domiciled; today Telecom Éireann has offices there. Designed by Richard Castle in 1730, this was his first project in Dublin. He went on to create many more buildings, including Leinster House and the Rotunda Hospital.

At 85-86 St Stephen's Green on the south side is **Newman House** (☎ 475 7255), now part of University College Dublin. These buildings have some of the finest plasterwork in the city. No 85 was built between 1736 and 1738 by Richard Castle for Hugh Montgomery MP. The particularly fine plasterwork was by the Swiss stuccodores Paul and Philip Francini (also known as Paolo and Filippo Lafranchi) and can be best appreciated in the wonderfully detailed Apollo Room on the ground floor.

Richard Chapel Whaley MP had taken possession of No 85 in 1765 but decided to display his wealth by constructing a much grander home next door at No 86.

Whaley's son Buck contrived to become an MP while still a teenager and also one of the more notorious members of Dublin's Hell Fire Club. He was also a noted gambler, once walking all the way to Jerusalem to win a bet.

The Catholic University of Ireland, predecessor of University College Dublin, acquired the building in 1865, with the Jesuits following in their footsteps. Some of the plasterwork was a little too detailed for

Jesuit tastes, however, so cover-ups were prescribed. On the ceiling of the upstairs Saloon, previously naked female figures were clothed in what can best be described as furry swimsuits. One survived the restoration process.

The Catholic University named Newman House after its first rector, John Henry Newman. Gerard Manley Hopkins, professor of classics at the college from 1884 until his death in 1889, lived upstairs at No 86. It wasn't until some time after his death that his innovative if rather depressive poetry was published. His room is now preserved as it was during his residence. Among former students of the college are James Joyce, Patrick Pearse, leader of the 1916 Easter Rising, and Eamon de Valera.

The restoration of Newman House has been going on since 1990 and will continue for some time. The house is open for 40-minute conducted tours June, July and August, Tuesday to Friday noon to 5 pm, Saturday 2 to 5 pm, Sunday 11 am to 2 pm. The IR£2/1 fee includes a video about the building.

Next to Newman House is the **Catholic University Church** or Newman Chapel, built in 1854-56 with a colourful neo-Byzantine interior that attracted a great deal of criticism at the time. Today this is one of the most fashionable churches in Dublin for weddings.

Grafton St runs from the north-west corner of the green, while Merrion Row, with its popular pubs, runs from the north-east. At the south-east is Leeson St, the nightclub centre of Dublin. The Hotel Conrad, Dublin's Hilton Hotel, is just off the square from this corner on Earlsfort Terrace, as is the National Concert Hall.

Harcourt St, from the south-west corner, was laid out in 1775. Well-known names associated with the street include Edward Carson, who was born at No 4 in 1854. As the architect of Northern Irish 'unionism', he makes an easy scapegoat for many of the problems caused by Ireland's division. Bram Stoker, author of *Dracula*, lived at No 16 and George Bernard Shaw at No 61. For 99 years from 1859 to 1958 the Dublin-Bray railway line used to terminate at Harcourt St station, which was then at the bottom of this road. From Harcourt St, Clonmel St leads to the pleasant **Iveagh Gardens**, which provide a tranquil respite from the city.

Merrion Square

Merrion Square, with its well-kept Archbishop Ryan Park and elegant Georgian buildings, dates back to 1762 and has the National Gallery on its west side. Around this square you can find some of the best of Dublin's Georgian entrances, with fine doors, peacock fanlights, ornate door knockers and more than a few foot scrapers where gentlemen removed mud from their shoes before venturing indoors.

Oscar Wilde's parents, the surgeon Sir William Wilde and the poet Lady Wilde, who wrote under the pseudonym Speranza, lived at 1 Merrion Square North. Oscar was born in 1854 at 21 Westland Row, just north of the square. WB Yeats (1865-1939) lived first at 52 Merrion Square East and later, in 1922-28, at 82 Merrion Square South. George (AE) Russell (1867-1935), the 'poet, mystic, painter and co-operator', worked at No 84. Daniel O'Connell (1775-1847) was a resident of No 58 in his later years. The Austrian Erwin Schrödinger (1887-1961), co-winner of the 1933 Nobel Prize for physics, lived at No 65 between 1940 and 1956. Dublin seems to attract the writers of horror stories: Joseph Sheridan Le Fanu (1814-73), who penned the vampire classic *Carmilla*, was a former resident of No 70.

The UK Embassy was at 39 Merrion Square East until it was burnt out in 1972 in protest against Bloody Sunday in Derry, Northern Ireland. The Architectural Association is at 8 Merrion Square North, a few doors down from the Wilde residence.

The Leinster Lawn at the western end of the square has the 1791 **Rutland Fountain** and an 18m obelisk honouring the founders of independent Ireland.

Merrion Square hasn't always been merely graceful and affluent, however. During the 1845-51 Famine, soup kitchens were set up in the gardens, which were crowded with starving rural refugees.

Damage to fine Dublin buildings hasn't always been the prerogative of vandals, terrorists or protesters. Merrion Square East once continued into Fitzwilliam St Lower in the longest unbroken series of Georgian houses anywhere in Europe. In 1961 the Electricity Supply Board (ESB) knocked down 26 of the houses to build an office block.

At the south-east corner of Merrion Square the ESB had the decency to preserve one of the fine old Georgian houses at **No 29 Fitzwilliam St Lower** (☎ 702 6165) which has been restored to give a good impression of genteel home life in Dublin between 1790 and 1820. The house is open Tuesday to Saturday 10 am to 5 pm, Sunday 2 to 5 pm, and an audiovisual display on its history is followed by a 30 minute guided tour. Entry is IR£2.50/free.

Merrion St Upper & Ely Place

Merrion St Upper was built around 1770, and runs south from Merrion Square towards St Stephen's Green. The Duke of Wellington was probably born at 24 Merrion St Upper. On the other side of Baggot St, Merrion St becomes Ely (pronounced 'e-lie') Place.

John Philpot Curran (1750-1817), a great advocate of Irish liberty, once lived at No 4, as did the novelist George Moore (1852-1933). The house at No 6 was the residence of the earl of Clare. Better known as Black Jack Fitzgibbon (1749-1802), he was a bitter opponent of Irish political aspirations, and in 1794 a mob attempted to storm the house. Ely House at No 8 is one of the city's best examples of a Georgian mansion. The plasterwork is by Michael Stapleton and the staircase, which illustrates the Labours of Hercules, is one of the finest in the city. At one time the surgeon Sir Thornley Stoker (whose brother Bram Stoker wrote *Dracula*) lived here. Oliver St John Gogarty (1878-1957) lived for a time at No 25, but the art gallery of the Royal Hibernian Academy now occupies that position.

Fitzwilliam Square

South of Merrion Square and east of St Stephen's Green, the original and well-kept Fitzwilliam Square is a centre for the Dublin medical profession. Built between 1791 and 1825, it was the smallest and the last of Dublin's great Georgian squares. It's also the only square where the central garden is still the private domain of residents of the square. William Dargan (1799-1861), the railway pioneer and founder of the National Gallery, lived at No 2, and Jack B Yeats (1871-1957) at No 18. Look out for the attractive 18th and 19th century coal hole covers.

Other South Dublin Churches

St Andrew's Church The Protestant St Andrew's Church, on St Andrew's St near Trinity College, the Bank of Ireland and Grafton St, is now the home of the Dublin Tourism Centre. Designed by Charles Lanyon, the Gothic-style church was built in 1860-73 on the site of an ancient nunnery. Across the street, on the corner of Church Lane and Suffolk St, there once stood a huge Viking ceremonial mound or *thingmote*. It was levelled in 1661 and used to raise the level of Nassau St, which had previously been subject to flooding.

Whitefriars Carmelite Church Next to the popular Avalon House backpackers hostel on Aungier St, the Carmelite Church stands on the former site of the Whitefriars Carmelite monastery. The monastery was founded in 1278 but, like other monasteries, was suppressed by Henry VIII in 1537 and all its lands and wealth seized by the Crown. Eventually the Carmelites returned to their former church and re-established it, dedicating the new building in 1827.

In the north-east corner of the church, the 16th century Flemish oak statue of the Virgin & Child escaped destruction during the Reformation; it probably once belonged to St Mary's Abbey in north Dublin. The church's altar contains the remains of St Valentine, of St Valentine's Day fame, donated to the church in 1836 by the pope.

St Ann's Church St Ann's, on Dawson St near Mansion House, was built in 1720 but is now lost behind an 1868 neo-Romanesque facade. There's a fine view of it looking down Anne St South from Grafton St, and it is noted for its lunch-time recitals.

St Stephen's Church Built in 1824 in Greek Revival style, St Stephen's, complete with cupola, is at the far end of Mount St Upper from Merrion Square and has been converted into business units. Because of its appearance, it was nicknamed the 'Peppercanister Church'. You can visit inside 12.30 to 3.20 pm Monday to Friday.

NORTH OF THE LIFFEY

Though south Dublin has the lion's share of the city's tourist attractions, there are still many reasons to head across the Liffey, starting with Dublin's grandest avenue.

O'Connell St

O'Connell St is the major thoroughfare of north Dublin and probably the most important and imposing street in the city. Its earlier glory has gone, but city authorities have slated it for 'rejuvenation'. It started life in the early 18th century as Drogheda St, named after Viscount Henry Moore, the earl of Drogheda. There are still a Henry St, a Moore St and an Earl St nearby. The earl even managed to squeeze in an Of Lane! At that time Capel St, farther to the west, was the main traffic route and Drogheda St, lacking a bridge to connect it with south Dublin, was of little importance.

In the 1740s, Luke Gardiner, later Viscount Mountjoy, widened the street to 45m to turn it into an elongated promenade bearing his name. However, it was the completion of Carlisle Bridge across the Liffey in 1794 which quickly made it the city's most important street. In 1880, Carlisle Bridge was replaced by the much wider O'Connell Bridge which stands today.

Gardiner's Mall soon became Sackville St, but was renamed again in 1924 after Daniel O'Connell, the Irish nationalist leader whose 1854 bronze statue surveys the avenue from the river end.

O'Connell St has certainly had its share of drama; its high-speed redevelopment began during the 1916 Easter Rising when the GPO building became the starting point for, and main centre of, the abortive revolt. Only six years later in 1922, the unfortunate avenue suffered another bout of destruction when it became the scene of a Civil War clash that burnt down most of the eastern side of the street. The bullet marks on the GPO and O'Connell's statue are a legacy of this period.

The street's once most famous monument, Nelson's Pillar, was a victim of 'explosive' redesign. In 1815 O'Connell St was graced with a Doric column topped by a statue of Nelson, the British naval captain who defeated the French at Trafalgar. It predated his column in Trafalgar Square (London) by 32 years. In 1966, however, to mark the 50th anniversary of the 1916 Easter Rising, this symbol of British imperialism was damaged by an IRA explosion and subsequently demolished. The head can be seen in the Dublin Civic Museum. Nelson's demise put an end to the quip that the main street of the capital city of this most piously Catholic of countries had statues honouring three noted adulterers: O'Connell at the bottom of the street, Parnell at the top and Nelson in the middle.

Poor O'Connell St suffered more damage in the 1960s and 1970s, when parts of Dublin went through a period of rampant redevelopment under lax government controls. Today's tacky fast-food and cheap-office-block atmosphere is a legacy of that era.

The site of Nelson's demolished column is halfway up the street, between Henry and Earl Sts, opposite the GPO. Nearby, a figure of James Joyce stands nonchalantly outside the Café Kylemore on the corner of pedestrianised Earl St North. South of the former site of the column is a fountain figure of Anna Livia, Joyce's spirit of the Liffey – a 1988 addition to the streetscape. It was almost immediately dubbed the 'floozy in the jacuzzi'.

Gresham Hotel is on the right before the figure of Father Theobald Mathew (1790-1856), the 'apostle of temperance', a hopeless role in Ireland. This quixotic task, however, also resulted in a Liffey bridge bearing his name. The northern end of the street is completed by the imposing statue of Charles Stewart Parnell (1846-91), Home Rule advocate and victim of Irish morality.

Just to the west of O'Connell St, on Moore St, is an energetic and colourful open-air market area. The Abbey Theatre and the Catholic St Mary's Pro-Cathedral are to the east. North of O'Connell St is Parnell Square.

General Post Office

The GPO building on O'Connell St is an important landmark physically and historically. The building, designed by Francis Johnston and opened in 1818, was the focus for the 1916 Easter Rising when Patrick Pearse, James Connolly and the other leaders read their proclamation from the front steps. In the subsequent siege the building was completely burnt out. The facade with its Ionic portico is still pockmarked from the 1916 clash and from further damage wrought at the start of the Civil War in 1922. The GPO wasn't reopened until 1929. Its central role in the history of independent Ireland has made it a prime site for everything from official parades to personal protests.

Abbey Theatre

Opened in 1904, the Abbey Theatre (☎ 878 7222), on the corner of Marlborough St and Abbey St Lower, is just north of the Liffey. The Irish National Theatre Society soon made a name not only for playwrights like JM Synge and Sean O'Casey but also for Irish acting ability and theatrical presentation. The 1907 premiere of JM Synge's *The Playboy of the Western World* brought a storm of protest from theatregoers, and Sean O'Casey's *The Plough & the Stars* prompted a similar reaction in 1926. On the latter occasion WB Yeats himself came on stage after the performance to tick the audience off!

The original theatre burnt down in 1951.

It took 15 years to come up with a replacement and the dull building fails to live up to its famous name or the company's continuing reputation. The smaller Peacock Theatre at the same location presents new and experimental works.

St Mary's Pro-Cathedral

On the corner of Marlborough and Cathedral Sts, just east of O'Connell St, is Dublin's most important Catholic church, built between 1816 and 1825. Unfortunately, the cramped Marlborough St location makes it difficult to stand back far enough to admire the front with its six Doric columns, modelled on the Temple of Theseus in Athens.

The 1814 competition for the church's design was won by John Sweetman, a former owner of Sweetman's Brewery. And who organised the competition? Why William Sweetman, John Sweetman's brother. And did John Sweetman design it himself? Well, possibly not. He was living in Paris at the time and may have bought the plans from a French architect who designed the remarkably similar Notre Dame de Lorette in northern France.

Tyrone House

On Marlborough St, opposite the Pro-Cathedral, the sombre Tyrone House, built in 1740-41, was designed by Richard Castle and features plasterwork by the Francini brothers. It's occupied by the Department of Education. On the lawn is a marble *Pietà* (statue of the Virgin Mary cradling the dead body of Jesus Christ) sculpted in 1930 and given to Ireland by the Italian government in 1948 in thanks for Irish assistance immediately after the war. You wouldn't know it now, but this area was once a busy red-light district known as Monto and featured in Joyce's *Ulysses* as Nighttown.

Parnell Square

The principal squares of north Dublin are poor relations of the great squares south of the Liffey, though they do have their points of interest.

Parnell Square's north side was built on lands acquired in the mid-18th century by Dr Bartholomew Mosse, founder of the Rotunda Hospital, and was originally named Palace Row. The terrace was laid out in 1755 and Lord Charlemont bought the land for his home at No 22 in 1762. Charlemont's home was designed by Sir William Chambers, who also designed Lord Charlemont's extraordinary Casino at Marino. Today, the building houses the Municipal Gallery of Modern Art. The street was completed in 1769 and the gardens were renamed Rutland Square in 1786, before acquiring their current name.

Next to the gallery is the Dublin Writers' Museum and on the north-east corner is the Abbey Presbyterian Church. In 1966 the northern slice of the square was turned into a Garden of Remembrance for the 50th anniversary of the 1916 Easter Rising. Its centrepiece is a sculpture by Oisin Kelly depicting the myth of the Children of Lir.

There are some fine, though rather rundown, Georgian houses on the east side of the square. Oliver St John Gogarty, immortalised as Buck Mulligan in Joyce's *Ulysses*, was born at No 5 in 1878. On the other side of the square, at 44 Parnell Square West, you'll find the Sinn Féin Bookshop. The square also contains the Gate Theatre, Ambassador Cinema and Rotunda Hospital.

Rotunda Hospital In 1757, Dr Bartholomew Mosse opened the Rotunda Hospital, the first maternity hospital in Ireland or Britain. It was built at a time when Dublin's burgeoning urban population suffered horrific levels of infant mortality. The hospital shares its basic design with Leinster House because Richard Castle reused the floorplan as an economy measure.

To his Leinster House design Castle added a three storey tower which Mosse had intended to use as a lookout to raise funds for the hospital's operation. The Rotunda Assembly Hall, now occupied by the Ambassador Cinema, was built as an adjunct to the hospital as another fundraiser. The Rotunda Chapel is over the main entrance of the hospital and was built in 1758 with superb coloured plasterwork by Bartholomew Cramillion.

The Rotunda Hospital still functions as a maternity hospital. The Patrick Conway pub opposite the hospital dates from 1745 and has been hosting expectant fathers since the day the hospital opened.

Gate Theatre At the top end of O'Connell St, in the south-east corner of Parnell Square, is the Gate Theatre, opened in 1929 by Micheál MacLiammóir and Hilton Edwards. MacLiammóir continued to act at his theatre until 1975, when he retired at the age of 76 after making his 1384th performance of the one-man show *The Importance of Being Oscar* (Oscar being Oscar Wilde, of course). The Gate Theatre was also the stage for Orson Welles's first professional appearance. The building dates from 1784-86 when it was constructed as part of the Rotunda Maternity Hospital complex.

The Municipal Gallery of Modern Art The Municipal Gallery of Modern Art or Hugh Lane Gallery (☎ 874 1903), 22 Parnell Square North, has a fine collection of work by French Impressionists and by 20th century Irish artists.

The gallery was founded in 1908 and moved to its present location in Charlemont House, formerly the earl of Charlemont's town house, in 1933. The gallery was established by wealthy Sir Hugh Lane, who died in the 1915 sinking of the *Lusitania*, which was torpedoed off the southern coast of Ireland by a German U-boat. The Lane Bequest pictures, which formed the nucleus of the gallery, were the subject of a dispute over Lane's will between the gallery and the National Gallery in London. A settlement was finally reached in 1959 which split the collection.

The gallery opens, free, Tuesday to Friday 9.30 am to 6 pm, Saturday 9.30 am to 5 pm, Sunday 11 am to 5 pm.

Dublin Writers' Museum This museum (☎ 872 2077), 18 Parnell Square North, next to the Hugh Lane Gallery, celebrates the city's long and continuing history as a literary centre. The Gallery of Writers upstairs houses busts and portraits of some of Ireland's most famous writers; their letters, photographs and first editions are downstairs. The museum also has a bookshop and the Chapter One restaurant.

Entry is IR£2.90/1.20 (students IR£2.40) and it's open Monday to Saturday 10 am to 5 pm, Sunday 11.30 am to 6 pm. In June, July and August it stays open until 7 pm Monday to Friday. If you plan to visit the James Joyce Tower and the George Bernard Shaw Museum, bear in mind that combined tickets are cheaper than three separate ones.

While the museum concerns itself primarily with dead authors, next door at No 19 the **Irish Writers' Centre** provides a meeting and working place for their living successors.

Abbey Presbyterian Church The soaring spire of this church, at the corner of Frederick St and Parnell Square North, overlooking Parnell Square, is a convenient landmark. Dating from 1864 the church was financed by the Scottish grocery and brewery magnate Alex Findlater and is often referred to as Findlater's Church.

National Wax Museum
Every city worth its tourist traps has a wax museum. Dublin's National Wax Museum (☎ 872 6340) is on Granby Row, north of Parnell Square. Along with the usual fantasy and fairy-tale offerings, the inevitable Chamber of Horrors and a rock music 'megastars' area, there are also figures of Irish heroes like Wolfe Tone, Robert Emmet and Charles Parnell, the leaders of the 1916 Easter Rising, and Taoisigh (prime ministers, plural of Taoiseach). Prominent literary and political figures also get a look in. Recorded commentaries help to explain each individual's role in Irish history. The museum is open Monday to Saturday 10 am to 6 pm, Sunday noon to 6 pm. Entry is IR£3.50/2 (family IR£10).

Great Denmark St

From the north-east corner of Parnell Square, Great Denmark St runs eastwards to Mountjoy Square, passing by the 1775 Belvedere House which has been used since 1841 as the Jesuit **Belvedere College**. James Joyce was a student here between 1893 and 1898 and describes it in *A Portrait of the Artist as a Young Man*. The building is renowned for its magnificent plasterwork by the master stuccodore Michael Stapleton and for its fireplaces by the Venetian artisan Bossi. It's not open to the public.

Mountjoy Square

Built between 1792 and 1818, Mountjoy Square was a fashionable and affluent centre at the height of the Protestant Ascendancy. Today it's a run-down symbol of north Dublin's urban decay, though redevelopment is beginning to happen. Viscount Mountjoy, after whom the square was named, was that energetic developer Luke Gardiner, who briefly gave his name to Gardiner Mall before it became Sackville St and then O'Connell St. The square was in fact named after him twice, as it started life as Gardiner Square.

Legends relate that this was where Brian Ború pitched his tent at the Battle of Clontarf in 1014. Residents of the square have included Sean O'Casey, who set his play *The Shadow of a Gunman* here, though he referred to it as Hilljoy Square. As a child James Joyce lived just off the square at 14 Fitzgibbon St.

St George's Church

St George's Church, on Hardwicke Place off Temple St, was built by Francis Johnston from 1802 in Greek Ionic style and has a 60m-high steeple modelled after that of St Martin-in-the-Fields in London. The church's bells were added in 1836. Although this was one of Johnston's finest works and the Duke of Wellington was married here, the church is no longer in use.

St Mary's Abbey

Despite the intriguing history of St Mary's Abbey, there's little to see, and even finding the abbey is tricky; it's just west of Capel St in Meetinghouse Lane, which runs off a street named Mary's Abbey.

When the abbey was founded in 1139 by Benedictine monks this was a rural location, far from the temptations of city life. In 1147, it was taken over by the Cistercians. Until its suppression in the mid-16th century this was the most important monastery within English-controlled Ireland. St Mary's property was confiscated by Henry VIII in 1537; it turned out to be the most valuable in all of Ireland, at a total of £537. Mellifont Abbey, north of Dublin, came in second at £352, but no other Irish monastery was worth over £100.

By the end of the century the abbey was virtually derelict. In 1676, stones from the abbey were used to construct the Essex Bridge. Using the abbey as a quarry soon removed all visible traces of the monastery and not until comparatively recently were the remaining fragments rediscovered.

The chapter house, where monks gathered after morning mass, is the only surviving part of the abbey which, in its prime, encompassed land stretching as far east as Ballybough. The floor level in the abbey is 2m below street level – a clear indication of the changes wrought over eight centuries.

At the time of writing the abbey was closed indefinitely.

St Mary's Church

In Mary St, between Capel and Liffey Sts, St Mary's was designed in 1697 by Sir William Robinson, who was also responsible for the Royal Hospital Kilmainham. The church was completed in 1702 and a roll call of famous Dubliners were baptised here. In this church John Wesley, the founder of Methodism, preached for the first time in Ireland in 1747. Today, it's no longer used as a church but as a store selling decorating goods.

Irish patriot Wolfe Tone was born on the adjacent Wolfe Tone St.

St Michan's Church

Named after a Danish saint, St Michan's

Church on Church St Lower, near the Four Courts, was founded by Danes in 1095, though there's little trace of the original. The battlement tower dates from the 15th century, but otherwise it was rebuilt in the late 17th century and considerably restored in the early 19th century and again after the Civil War during which it had been damaged.

The church contains a 1724 organ which Handel may have played for the first-ever performance of his *Messiah*. The organ case is distinguished by a fine oak carving of 17 entwined musical instruments on its front. A skull on the floor on one side of the altar is said to represent Oliver Cromwell. On the opposite side, a penitent's chair was for people to make public confessions. But the church's main 'attraction' lies in the subterranean crypt where a group of bodies have been preserved to varying degrees, not by mummification, but by the constant dry atmosphere. You can visit the church any time during opening hours, but you can only see the crypt as part of a tour.

Tours of the church and crypt are conducted Monday to Friday 10 am to 12.45 pm, 2 to 4.45 pm, Saturday 10 am to 12.45 pm. The cost is IR£1.20/50p.

Irish Whiskey Corner
Just north of St Michan's Church, the Irish Whiskey Corner (☎ 872 5566) is in an old warehouse on Bow St, Dublin 7, and the admission charge of IR£3 includes entry to the museum, a short film and a sample of Irish whiskey. May to October there are tours Monday to Friday at 11 am, 2.30 and 3.30 pm; the rest of the year, only the 3.30 pm tour operates.

James Joyce Centre
North Great George's St was a fashionable address in 18th century Dublin, but like so much of north Dublin, it fell on hard times when the Act of Union turned the city into a backwater. James Joyce's family lived in north Dublin for a time and he would have been familiar with the street. The dancing instructor, Denis Maginni, who taught in the front room of No 35, appears several times in *Ulysses*. In the 20th century many of the houses became run-down tenements with as many as 70 people living in each one.

Then in 1982 Senator David Norris, a charismatic Joycean scholar and gay-rights activist, moved into the street and took over No 35, now restored and a centre for the study of James Joyce and his books.

Visitors see the room where Maginni taught and a collection of pictures of the 17 different Dublin addresses occupied by Joyce's family and of the real individuals fictionalised in his books. Some of the fine plaster ceilings are restored originals, others careful reproductions of Michael Stapleton's designs.

Admission is IR£2.75/0.70. The house opens Monday to Saturday 9.30 am to 5 pm, Sunday 12.30 to 5 pm. Tours of north Dublin depart from here Monday to Saturday (see Walking Tours below).

Incidentally, North Great George's St as a whole has had a facelift and boasts some fine Georgian doorways and fanlights.

King's Inns & Henrietta St
King's Inns, home of the Dublin legal profession, is north of the river on Constitution Hill and Henrietta St. This classical building by James Gandon suffered many delays between its design in 1795 and its completion in 1817. Several other architects lent a hand along the way, including Francis Johnston, who added the cupola. The building is normally open only to members of the Inns.

Henrietta St, along the south side of the building, was Dublin's first Georgian street and has buildings dating from 1720 but is unfortunately now in a state of disrepair. These early Georgian mansions were large and varied in style and for a time Henrietta St rejoiced in the name Primate's Hill, as the archbishop of Armagh and other high church officials lived there. Luke Gardiner, who was responsible for so much of the early development of Georgian north Dublin, lived at 10 Henrietta St.

OTHER SIGHTS
There's still much more to see in Dublin. To

DUBLIN

DUBLIN

Bloomsday

Six days after meeting her, the writer James Joyce had his first date with Nora Barnacle, the woman he was to marry, on 16 June 1904. Later, when he came to write his masterpiece *Ulysses*, which describes a single day in the life of Dubliner Leopold Bloom, the date he chose for this latterday odyssey was 16 June 1904. Now Dublin duly celebrates 'Bloomsday' on 16 June each year, with a range of entertainment, some serious, some less so, at venues all round the city. Serious Bloomsdayers don Edwardian costume for the day.

In general, events are designed to follow Bloom's progress round town. You can kick things off with breakfast either at the James Joyce Centre (☎ 878 8547), 35 Great George's St North or at the South Bank Restaurant (☎ 280 8788), 1 Martello Terrace, Dun Laoghaire. In both cases, the 'inner organs of beast and fowl' come accompanied by celebratory readings, a fact reflected in the prices.

In the morning, guided tours of Joycean sites usually leave from the GPO and the James Joyce Centre. Lunch-time activity focuses on Davy Byrne's, Joyce's 'moral pub' in Duke St, where Bloom paused to dine on a glass of Burgundy and a slice of Gorgonzola (IR£4 at today's prices). Street entertainers are likely to keep you amused as you eat.

In the afternoon, the guided walks are topped up with animated readings from *Ulysses* and Joyce's other books at appropriate sites and times: Ormond Hotel, Ormond Quay, at 4 pm and *Harrison's* restaurant in Westmoreland St later in the day.

Should you have any energy left, you can spin things out to the early hours, perhaps in *Bewley's* in Grafton St where animated performances of Molly Bloom's closing (and at one time controversial) soliloquy take place.

Events also take place in the days leading up to and following Bloomsday. The best source of information about what's on in any particular year is likely to be the James Joyce Centre, although the *Dublin Event Guide* also publishes outline details in advance. Popular events sell out quickly; advance booking, especially for the breakfasts, is essential.

You don't have to know anything about Joyce or his books to enjoy the day, although it certainly helps! ∎

the west are the Guinness Brewery in the colourful Liberties area, Kilmainham Jail and Phoenix Park. To the north and north-east are the Royal Canal, Prospect Cemetery, the Botanic Gardens, the Casino at Marino and Clontarf.

To the south and south-east are the Grand Canal, Ballsbridge, the Royal Dublin Society Showground and the Chester Beatty Library.

St Catherine's Church

Westward from St Audoen's Churches, towards that more recent Dublin shrine, the Guinness Brewery, is St Catherine's Church, whose huge front faces Thomas St. The church was built on the site of St Thomas Abbey, which Henry II built in honour of Thomas à Becket, the Archbishop of Canterbury, after having him killed. The church was completed in 1769 and is now used as a community centre. After being hanged, the corpse of patriot Robert Emmet was put to

the further indignity of being beheaded outside the church in 1803.

Guinness Brewery

West of St Audoen's churches, Thomas St metamorphoses into James's St in the area of Dublin known as the Liberties. Along James's St stretches the historic St James's Gate Guinness Brewery (☎ 453 6700, ext 5155) where 2½ million pints of stout are brewed daily. From its foundation by Arthur Guinness in 1759, the operation has expanded down to the Liffey and across both sides of the street. It covers 26 hectares and for a time was the largest brewery in the world. The oldest parts of the site are south of James's St; at one time there was a gate spanning the street.

In the **Guinness Hop Store**, on the corner of Sugar House Lane (the southern extension of Crane St) and Rainsford St, visitors can watch a Guinness audiovisual display and inspect an extensive Guinness museum. It

may not be a tour of the brewery, but your entry fee includes a pint of the black stuff.

In its early years Guinness was only one of dozens of Dublin breweries, but it outgrew and outlasted all of them. At one time a Grand Canal tributary was cut into the brewery to enable special Guinness barges to carry consignments onto the Irish canal system or to the Dublin port. When the brewery extensions reached the Liffey in 1872, the fleet of Guinness barges became a familiar sight. There was also a Guinness railway on the site, complete with a spiral tunnel. Guinness still operates its own ships to convey the vital fluid to the British market. Over 50% of all the beer consumed in Ireland is brewed here.

Opening hours are Monday to Saturday 9.30 am to 5 pm. Entry is IR£3/1. To get there take bus No 21A, 78 or 78A from Fleet St. The upper floors of the building house temporary art exhibits.

Round the corner at No 1 Thomas St, a plaque marks the house where Arthur Guinness (1725-1803) lived. In a yard across the road stands **St Patrick's Tower**, Europe's tallest smock windmill, which was built about 1757.

IMMA & Royal Hospital Kilmainham

The Irish Museum of Modern Art (IMMA; ☎ 671 8666) at the old Royal Hospital Kilmainham is close to Kilmainham Jail. The permanent collection and regular temporary exhibitions display a range of 20th century Irish and international art.

The Royal Hospital Kilmainham was built in 1680-87 but not as a hospital. It was in fact a home for retired soldiers and continued to fill that role until after Irish independence. It preceded the similar Chelsea Hospital in London and inmates were often referred to as 'Chelsea Pensioners' although there was no connection. At the time of its construction, it was one of the finest buildings in Ireland and there was considerable muttering that it was altogether too good a place for its residents. The building was designed by William Robinson, whose other work included Marsh's Library.

There's a good café and bookshop. The IMMA is open Tuesday to Saturday 10 am to 5.30 pm, Sunday noon to 5.30 pm. Entry is free and there are guided tours Sunday between 2 and 4.30 pm. You can get there on bus Nos 24, 79 or 90 from Aston Quay outside Virgin Megastore.

Kilmainham Jail

Built in 1792-95, Kilmainham Jail (☎ 453 5984) on Inchicore Rd, Dublin 8, is a solid, grey, threatening, old building. During each act of Ireland's long, painful path to independence, at least one part of the performance took place at the jail.

The uprisings of 1798, 1803, 1848, 1867 and 1916 ended with the leaders' confinement here. Robert Emmet, Thomas Francis Meagher, Charles Stewart Parnell and the 1916 Easter Rising leaders were all visitors, but it was the executions in 1916 which most deeply etched the jail's name into the Irish consciousness. Of the 15 executions that took place between 3 and 12 May after the rising, 14 were conducted here. As a finale, prisoners from the Civil War struggles were held here from 1922. The jail closed in 1924.

An excellent audiovisual introduction to the building is followed by a thought-provoking tour. Incongruously sitting outside in the yard is the *Asgard*, the ship which successfully ran the British blockade to deliver arms to nationalist forces in 1914. The tour finishes in the gloomy yard where the 1916

DUBLIN

executions took place. There's also an exhibition area on the history of the jail.

Opening hours are 10 am to 6 pm daily May to September; and 1 to 4 pm Monday to Friday and 1 to 6 pm on Sunday, October to April. Entry is IR£2/1 and you can get there by bus No 23, 51, 51A, 78 or 79 from the city centre.

Phoenix Park

The 700-plus hectares of Phoenix Park make it one of the world's largest city parks, dwarfing Central Park in New York (a mere 337 hectares) and all the London parks – Hampstead Heath is only 324 hectares. There are gardens and lakes, a host of sporting facilities, the second-oldest public zoo in Europe, a visitor's centre and castle, various government offices, the Garda Síochána (police) Headquarters, the residences of the US ambassador and the Irish President, and even a herd of deer.

Lord Ormonde turned this land into a park in 1671, but it wasn't opened to the public until 1747 by Lord Chesterfield. The name Phoenix is actually a corruption of the Irish words for clear water, *fionn uisce*. The park played a crucial role in Irish history, as Lord Cavendish, the British Chief Secretary for Ireland, and his assistant were murdered here in 1882 by an Irish nationalist group called the National Invincibles. Lord Cavendish's home is now Deerfield, the US ambassador's residence, and the murder took place outside what is now the Irish president's residence.

Near the Parkgate St entrance to the park is the 63m-high **Wellington Monument** obelisk. This took from 1817 to 1861 to build, mainly because the Duke of Wellington fell from public favour during its construction. Nearby are the **People's Garden**, dating from 1864 and the bandstand in the **Hollow**. Just north of the Hollow is **Dublin Zoo**. Chesterfield Ave separates the Hollow and the zoo from the Phoenix Park Cricket Club of 1830 and from **Citadel Pond**, usually referred to as the Dog Pond. Behind the zoo, on the edge of the park, the Garda Síochána Headquarters has a small **police museum**.

Going north along Chesterfield Ave is Áras an Uachtaráin, the Irish President's residence, on the right. On the left, a white cross marks the site where Pope John Paul II preached to 1¼ million people in 1979. In the centre of the park the **Phoenix Monument**, erected by Lord Chesterfield in 1747, looks very unphoenix-like and is often referred to as the Eagle Monument.

North-west of the monument stands the **Phoenix Park Visitor Centre & Ashdown Castle**. The southern part of the park is given over to a large number of football and hurling pitches, and, though they occupy about 80 hectares (200 acres), the area is known as the Fifteen Acres.

White's Gate, the park exit from its northwest side, leads to Castleknock College and Castleknock Castle. Near White's Gate and Quarry Pond, at the north-west end of the park, are the offices of the **Ordnance Survey**, the government mapping department. South of this building is the attractive rural-looking Furry Glen and Glen Pond corner of the park.

Back towards the Parkgate entrance is **Magazine Fort**, on Thomas's Hill. The fort took from 1734 to 1801 to build and never served any discernible purpose although it was a target in the 1916 Easter Rising.

Dublin Zoo Established in 1830, the 12-hectare Dublin Zoo (☎ 677 1425), in the south-east corner of Phoenix Park, is one of the oldest in the world, but is mainly of interest to children. The lion-breeding programme dates back to 1857 and includes among its offspring the lion that roars at the start of MGM films. Entry is IR£5.80/3.10 and it's open March to October, Monday to Saturday, 9.30 am to 6 pm, and Sunday from 10.30 am; November to February it closes at 4.30 pm. The zoo can be reached by bus No 10 from O'Connell St or bus No 25 or 26 from Abbey St Middle.

Áras an Uachtaráin The residence of the Irish president was built in 1751 and enlarged in 1782 then again in 1816 on the latter occasion by the noted Irish architect,

Francis Johnston, who added the Ionic portico. From 1782 to 1922 it was the residence of the British viceroys or lord lieutenants. After independence it became the home of Ireland's governor-general until Ireland cut the ties with the British crown and created the office of president in 1937.

Phoenix Park Visitor Centre & Ashtown Castle The Phoenix Park Visitor Centre (☎ 677 0095) is in what were the stables of the Papal Nuncio. A video outlines the history of the park and there are two floors of exhibits. Visitors are taken on a tour of neighbouring Ashtown Castle, a 17th century tower house which had been concealed inside the Papal Nuncio until its demolition in 1986; box hedges pick out the ground-plan of the old building. The visitor centre is open daily April to May 9.30 am to 5.30 pm, June to September 9.30 am to 6.30 pm; in late March and in October it closes at 5 pm; November to mid-March it opens weekends only, 9.30 am to 4.30 pm. Admission is IR£2/1.

The Royal Canal
Constructed from 1790, by which time the older Grand Canal was already past its prime, the Royal Canal, which encircles Dublin to the north, was a commercial failure, but its story is certainly colourful. It was founded by Long John Binns, a Grand Canal director who quit the board because of a supposed insult over his being a shoemaker. He established the Royal Canal principally for revenge but it never made money and actually became known as the Shoemaker's Canal. In 1840 the canal was sold to a railway company and tracks still run alongside much of the canal's route through the city.

The Royal Canal towpath makes a relaxing walk through the heart of the city. You can join it beside Newcomen Bridge at Strand Rd North, just north of Connolly station, and follow it to the suburb of Clonsilla and beyond, over 10km away. The walk is particularly pleasant beyond Binns Bridge in Drumcondra. At the top of

Blessington St, near the Dublin International Youth Hostel, a large pond which was used when the canal also supplied drinking water to the city, now attracts waterbirds.

National Botanic Gardens
Founded in 1795, the National Botanic Gardens, directly north of the centre on Botanic Rd in Glasnevin, were used as a garden before that time, but only the Yew Walk, also known as Addison's Walk, has trees dating back to the first half of the 18th century.

The 19.5 hectare gardens are flanked to the north by the River Tolka and in the gardens is a series of curvilinear glasshouses dating from 1843-69. The glasshouses were created by Richard Turner who was also responsible for the glasshouse at Belfast Botanic Gardens and the Palm House in London's Kew Gardens. Dublin's gardens also have a palm house, built in 1884. Among the pioneering botanical work conducted here was the first attempt to raise orchids from seed, back in 1844. Pampas grass and the giant lily were first grown in Europe in these gardens.

The gardens are open March to October, Monday to Saturday 9 am to 6 pm, Sunday 11 am to 6 pm; November to February, Monday to Saturday 10 am to 4.30 pm, Sunday 11 am to 4.30 pm. The conservatories have shorter opening hours; in particular, on Sunday they only open 2 to 4.15 pm. Entry is free. You can get there on bus Nos 13 or 19 from O'Connell St or Nos 34 or 34A from Abbey St Middle.

Prospect Cemetery
Prospect or Glasnevin Cemetery, Finglas Rd, north-west of the city centre, is the largest in Ireland. It was established in 1832 as a cemetery for Roman Catholics who faced opposition when they conducted burials in the city's Protestant cemeteries. Many monuments and memorials have staunchly patriotic overtones with numerous high crosses, shamrocks, harps and other Irish symbols. The single most imposing memorial is the colossal monument to Cardinal

McCabe (1837-1921), Archbishop of Dublin and Primate of Ireland.

A modern replica of a round tower acts as a handy landmark for locating the tomb of Daniel O'Connell, who died in 1847 and was reinterred here in 1869, when the tower was completed. Charles Stewart Parnell's tomb is topped with a huge granite rock. Other notable people buried here include Sir Roger Casement, who was executed for treason by the British in 1916 and whose remains weren't returned to Ireland until 1964; the republican leader Michael Collins who died in the Civil War; the docker and trade unionist Jim Larkin, a prime force in the 1913 general strike; and the poet Gerard Manley Hopkins. There's also a poignant 'class' memorial to the men who have starved themselves to death for the cause of Irish freedom over the century, including 10 of them in the 1981 H Block hunger strikes.

The most interesting parts of the cemetery are at the south-eastern Prospect Square end. The cemetery watchtowers were once used to keep watch for body snatchers. *Ulysses* pauses at the cemetery and there are several clues for Joyce enthusiasts to follow.

Casino at Marino

The Casino at Marino (☎ 833 1618), just off Malahide Rd, north of the junction with Howth Rd in Clontarf, about 5km north-east of the city centre, isn't a casino at all. It's a pleasure house built for the earl of Charlemont in the grounds of Marino House in the mid-18th century. Although Marino House itself was demolished in the 1920s the casino survives as a wonderful folly.

Externally, the building, with its 12 Tuscan columns forming a temple-like facade and its huge entrance doorway, creates the expectation that inside it will be a simple single open space. But the interior is an extravagant convoluted maze: flights of fancy include chimneys for the central heating which are disguised as roof urns, downpipes hidden in columns, carved draperies, ornate fireplaces, beautiful parquet

---

The Earl & the Casino

The somewhat eccentric James Caulfield (1728-99), later to become the earl of Charlemont, set out on a European grand tour in 1746 at the age of 18. The visit lasted nine years, including a four-year spell in Italy. He returned to Ireland with a huge art collection and a burning ambition to bring Italian style to the estate he acquired in 1756. He commissioned Sir William Chambers to design the casino, a process which started in the late 1750s, continued into the 1770s, and never really came to a conclusion, in part because Lord Charlemont frittered away his fortune.

When Lord Charlemont married, the casino became a garden retreat rather than a bachelor's quarters. It's said that a visit from Charlemont's mother-in-law would send him scuttling down a 400m-long underground tunnel that joined the main house to the casino. Another building would have housed the art and antiquities he had acquired during his European tour, so it's perhaps fitting that his town house on Parnell Square, also designed by Sir William Chambers, is now the Municipal Gallery of Modern Art.

Despite his wealth, Charlemont was a comparatively liberal and free-thinking aristocrat. He never fenced in his demesne and allowed the public to use it as an open park.

He wasn't the only local eccentric; in 1792 a painter named Folliot took a dislike to the lord and built Marino Crescent at the bottom of Malahide Rd purely to block his view of the sea. Bram Stoker (1847-1912), author of *Dracula*, was born at 15 Marino Crescent.

After Charlemont's death his estate, crippled by his debts, collapsed and the art collection was dispersed. ■

floors constructed of rare woods and a spacious wine cellar. A variety of statuary adorns the outside but it's the amusing fakes which are most enjoyable. The towering front door is a sham, and a much smaller panel opens to reveal the secret interior. The windows have blacked-out panels to hide the fact that the interior is a complex of rooms, not a single chamber.

In 1870 the town house was sold to the government. The Marino estate followed in 1881 and the casino in 1930 though it was decrepit by then. Restoration is continuing and although the casino grounds are only a tiny fragment of the Marino estate, trees and planting help to hide the surrounding houses.

The casino opens daily mid-June to September 9.30 am to 6.30 pm, October 10 am to 5 pm; February to mid-June and in November it opens Sunday and Wednesday noon to 4 pm. You can only visit the building on a guided tour; entry is IR£2/1.

Bus Nos 20A, 20B, 27, 27A, 27B, 32A, 42 and 42B will take you there from the city centre.

Clontarf & North Bull Island

Clontarf, a bayside suburb 5km north-east of the city centre, takes its name from *cluain tarbh*, the bull's meadow. Here, in 1014, Brian Ború defeated the Danes at the Battle of Clontarf, though the Irish hero was killed along with his son and grandson. The Normans later erected a castle here which was handed on to the Knights Templar in 1179, rebuilt in 1835 and later converted into a hotel.

The North Bull Wall, extending from Clontarf about a km into Dublin Bay, was built in 1820 at the suggestion of Captain William Bligh of HMS *Bounty* mutiny fame, in order to stop Dublin Harbour from silting up. Many birds migrate here from the Arctic in winter, and at times the bird population can reach 40,000. You reach the interpretive centre on the island via the northern causeway which is a good 1.5km to walk across. Bus Nos 30 and 32X run to the start of the causeway on James Larkin Rd. The Royal

Dublin and St Anne's golf courses are also on the island.

The Grand Canal

Built to connect Dublin with the River Shannon, the Grand Canal makes a graceful 6km loop around south Dublin. At its eastern end the canal forms a harbour connected with the Liffey at Ringsend. True Dubliners, it's said, are born within the confines of the Grand and Royal Canals.

History Although Parliament proposed the canal in 1715, work didn't begin until 1756. Construction was slow but by 1779 the first cargo barges started to operate to Sallins, about 35km west of Dublin. Passenger services began a year later, when the terminus of the canal was the James's St Harbour, near the Guinness Brewery. By 1796 it was the longest canal in Britain or Ireland. It extended for 550km, of which about 250km were along the Shannon and Barrow rivers.

Railways started to spread across Ireland from the mid-19th century and the canal went into decline. WWII provided a temporary respite, but the private canal company folded in 1950 and the last barge carried a cargo of Guinness from Dublin in 1960.

The canal fell into disrepair and, in the early 1970s, the St James's St Harbour and the stretch of canal back from there to the Circular Line were filled in. The canal is now enjoying a modest revival as a tourist attraction. Despite the limited number of boats that ply the canal, all the locks are in working order.

Along the Canal The Grand Canal enters the Liffey at **Ringsend**, through locks that were built in 1796. The large **Grand Canal Dock**, flanked by Hanover and Charlotte quays, is now used by windsurfers and canoeists.

At the north-west corner of the dock is **Misery Hill**, once the site for the public execution of criminals. It was once the practice to bring the corpses of those already hung at Gallows Hill, near Baggot St Upper, to this spot, to be strung up for public display for anything from six to 12 months.

DUBLIN

Upstream from the Grand Canal Dock is the **Waterways Visitors' Centre** (☎ 677 7510). It's run by Dúchas (OPW) and houses an exhibition and interpretation centre on the construction and operation of Irish canals and waterways. From its roof you can get your bearings and try and imagine what the grim surroundings will look like when/if redevelopment plans get into their stride. The centre is open daily June to September 9.30 am to 6.30 pm; October to May, Wednesday to Sunday 12.30 to 5 pm. The last admission is one hour before closing; entry costs IR£2/1.

A memorial to the 1916 Easter Rising can be seen on the **Mount St Bridge**. A little farther along, Baggot St crosses the canal on the 1791 **Macartney Bridge**. The main office of Bord Fáilte is on the north side of the canal, and Bridge House and Parson's newsagency are on the south side.

This lovely stretch of the canal with its grassy, tree-lined banks was a favourite haunt of the poet Patrick Kavanagh. Among his compositions is the hauntingly beautiful *On Raglan Road*, a popular song which Van Morrison fans can find on the album *Irish*

Poet Patrick Kavanagh loved the Grand Canal

Heartbeat featuring the Chieftains. One Kavanagh poem requested that he be commemorated by 'a canal bank seat for passersby' and Kavanagh's friends obliged with a seat beside the lock on the south side of the canal. A little farther along on the north side you can sit down by Kavanagh himself, cast in bronze, comfortably lounging on a bench and watching his beloved canal.

The next stretch of the canal has some fine pubs, such as the *Barge Inn* and the *Porto Bello*, both right by the canal. The Porto Bello is a fine old-fashioned place with music on weekend evenings and Sunday mornings. The *Lower Deck*, on Richmond St, is also near the canal. You could also pause for a meal at the *Locks Restaurant*, on Windsor Terrace. The Institute of Education Business College by the Porto Bello was built in 1807 as Portobello House; as the Grand Canal Hotel, it was the Dublin terminus for passenger traffic on the canal. The artist Jack B Yeats lived there for seven years until his death in 1957.

Farther west from here, the **Circular Line** isn't so interesting and is better appreciated by bicycle rather than on foot. The spur running off the Circular Line alongside Grand Canal Bank to the old St James's St Harbour is filled in and is now a park and bicycle path.

Ballsbridge & Donnybrook

South-east of central Dublin, the suburb of Ballsbridge was principally laid out between 1830 and 1860 and many streets have British names with a distinctly military flavour. Many embassies, including the US Embassy, are in Ballsbridge. It also has some middle-bracket B&Bs and several upper-bracket hotels. The main attractions are the Royal Dublin Society Showground, the Chester Beatty Library and the Lansdowne Rd rugby stadium.

Adjoining Ballsbridge to the south is Donnybrook, at one time a village on the banks of the River Dodder. For centuries it was famous for the Donnybrook Fair which was first held in 1204. By the 19th century it had become a 15-day event centred around horse dealing, which was such a scene of drunkenness and sexual debauchery that the increasingly sedate residents of Donnybrook had it banned in 1855.

Royal Dublin Society (RDS) Showground

On Merrion Rd in Ballsbridge, the Royal Dublin Society Showground is used for various exhibitions throughout the year. The society was founded in 1731 and had its headquarters in a number of well-known Dublin buildings, including, from 1814 to 1925, Leinster House. The society was involved in the foundation of the National Museum, Library, Gallery and Botanic Gardens. The most important annual event at the showground is the August Dublin Horse Show which includes an international showjumping contest.

You can book tickets for the horse show from the Ticket Office (☎ 668 0866), Royal Dublin Society, PO Box 121, Ballsbridge, Dublin 4. Ask at the tourist office or consult a listings magazine for other events.

Chester Beatty Library & Gallery of Oriental Art

This library and gallery (☎ 269 2386), 20 Shrewsbury Rd, Dublin 4, just south of Ballsbridge, houses the collection of the mining engineer Sir Alfred Chester Beatty (1875-1968). It includes over 20,000 manuscripts, numerous rare books, miniature paintings, clay tablets, costumes and other objects, predominantly from the Middle East and Asia.

The gallery includes a reference library and a bookshop, but unfortunately only a tiny fraction of the total can be shown at any one time. This situation should change when it moves into new premises in the old Barracks of Dublin Castle; while the move takes place the library and gallery will close. In the meantime opening hours are Tuesday to Friday 10 am to 5 pm, Saturday 2 to 5 pm. Entry is free and there are guided tours Wednesday and Saturday at 2.30 pm.

Bus No 5, 7, 7A, 7X or 8 from Burgh Quay, No 46 or 46A from College St or No 10 from O'Connell St drop you nearby.

Alternatively, take the DART to Sandymount station, Sydney Parade.

Pearse Museum

Patrick (or Padráig in the Irish he worked so hard to promote) Pearse was a leader of the 1916 Easter Rising and one of the first to be executed at Kilmainham Jail. St Enda's, the school he established with his brother Willie to further his ideas of Irish language and culture, is now a museum and memorial to the brothers.

The Pearse Museum (☎ 493 4208) is at the junction of Grange Rd and Taylor's Lane in Rathfarnham, south-west of the city centre. It is open daily May to August 10 am to 5.30 pm. February to April and in September and October it closes half an hour earlier. November to January it closes at 4 pm. Entry is free and you can get there on bus No 16 from the city centre.

Other Museums

Apart from the museums described in the north and south Dublin sections, there are a number of other smaller museums or museums of specialist interest.

The **George Bernard Shaw House** (☎ 872 2077) at 33 Synge St, Dublin 2, opens May to October, Monday to Saturday 10 am to 6 pm, Sunday and holidays 11.30 am to 6 pm. Entry is IR£2.40/1.15 (students IR£2).

The **Irish Traditional Music Archive** (☎ 661 9699), 63 Merrion Square South, collects, preserves and organises traditional Irish music. The archive is open to the public by appointment.

The **Geological Survey of Ireland** (☎ 670 7444), Beggars Bush, Haddington Rd, Dublin 4, has exhibits on the geology and mineral resources of Ireland. It's open Monday to Friday 2.30 to 4.30 pm.

The **Irish Jewish Museum** (☎ 453 1797), 3-4 Walworth Rd, off Victoria St, Portobello, Dublin 8, is housed in what was once a synagogue and relates the history of Ireland's Jewish community. It's open May to September, Sunday, Tuesday and Thursday 11 am to 3 pm; October to April, Sunday 10.30 am to 2.30 pm.

The main display at the **Museum of Childhood** (☎ 497 8696), The Palms, 20 Palmerston Park, Rathmines, Dublin 6, south of the centre, is a collection of dolls, some nearly 300 years old. It opens Sunday 2 to 5.30 pm; entry is IR£1/75p.

The **Irish Architectural Archive & Architecture Centre** (☎ 676 3430), 73 Merrion Square South, Dublin 2, traces Dublin's architectural history from 1560 to the current day. The archive is housed in a fine 1793 town house. The Royal Institute of the Architects of Ireland (☎ 676 1703), has its headquarters across the square at 8 Merrion Square North, and exhibitions and displays are also held there.

Other Galleries

As well as the National Gallery and the IMMA, south of the river, and the Hugh Lane Municipal Gallery of Modern Art north of the river, there are a great many private galleries, arts centres and corporate exhibition areas.

The **Douglas Hyde Gallery** (☎ 608 1116) is in the Arts Building in Trinity College, and the entrance is on Nassau St. The **City Arts Centre** (☎ 677 0643), 23-25 Moss St, has changing exhibitions in its two galleries which open free weekdays 11 am to 5.30 pm, Saturday noon to 4 pm.

In the **Bank of Ireland** building (☎ 661 5255) on Baggot St Lower, just past Fitzwilliam St towards the Bord Fáilte office and Ballsbridge, there are usually changing displays of contemporary Irish art.

ACTIVITIES

Dublin offers plenty of sporting opportunities for both spectators and participants.

Jogging & Cycling

Away from the traffic fumes, the large Phoenix Park offers the best opportunity for jogging or cycling.

Beaches & Swimming

Dublin is hardly the sort of place to work on your suntan and even a hot Irish summer day is unlikely to raise the water temperature much above freezing. However, there are some pleasant beaches and many Joyce fans feel compelled to take a dip in the Forty Foot Pool at Dun Laoghaire. Sandy beaches near the centre include Sutton (11km), Portmarnock (11km), Malahide (11km), Claremount (14km) and Donabate (21km). Although the beach at Sandymount is nothing special, it is only 5km from central Dublin. There are outdoor public pools at Blackrock, Clontarf and Dun Laoghaire.

Scuba Diving

The Irish Underwater Council (☎ 284 4601), 78A Patrick St in Dun Laoghaire, publishes the quarterly magazine *Subsea*. Oceantec (☎ 280 1083) is a dive shop in Dun Laoghaire that organises local dives and runs courses. See the Dun Laoghaire section for more information.

Sailing, Windsurfing & Canoeing

Howth, Malahide and Dun Laoghaire are the major sailing centres in the Dublin area, but you can also go sailing at Clontarf, Kilbarrack, Rush, Skerries, Sutton and Swords. See the Dun Laoghaire section for details of the sailing clubs there. The Irish Sailing Association (☎ 280 0239) is at 3 Park Rd, Dun Laoghaire.

Dinghy sailing courses are offered by the Irish National Sailing School (☎ 284 4195), Marine Activity Centre, West Pier, Dun Laoghaire, and by the Fingall Sailing School (☎ 845 1979) Upper Strand Rd, Broadmeadow Estuary, Malahide.

In Dublin itself, the Surfdock Centre (☎ 668 3945), Grand Canal Dock, Dock Rd South, Ringsend, runs sailing, windsurfing and canoeing courses. Windsurfing courses cost IR£90 for four three-hour sessions. You can also rent sailboards for IR£7 an hour, canoes for IR£5 and boats for IR£10.

Fishing

Fishing tackle shops in Dublin can supply permits, equipment, bait and advice. Check the Golden Pages phone directory under Fishing Gear & Tackle. Sea fishing is popular at Howth, Dun Laoghaire and

Greystones. The River Liffey has salmon fishing (only fair) and trout fishing (good). Brown trout are found between Celbridge and Millicent Bridge, near Clane, 20km from the city centre. The Dublin Trout Anglers' Association has fishing rights along parts of this stretch of the Liffey and on the River Tolka.

Hang-Gliding & Paragliding
In County Wicklow, south of Dublin, Great Sugar Loaf Mountain and Mt Leinster are popular locations for these sports, though you need to bring your own equipment. Phone ☎ 831 4551 for information or contact the Irish Hang-Gliding Association (☎ 450 9845), AFAS House of Sport, Longmile Rd, Dublin 12.

Golf
Public courses include Corballis (☎ 843 6583) at Donabate (24km north) and Deer Park (☎ 832 2624) at Howth (15km north). There are more than 20 private nine-hole and 18-hole courses in and around Dublin as well as a great many short pitch & putt courses.

ORGANISED TOURS
Many Dublin tours operate only during the summer months but at that time you can take bus tours, and walking tours. You can book these tours directly with the operators or through your hotel front desk, at the various city tourist offices or with a travel agent or American Express.

Bus Tours
Gray Line (☎ 605 7705), Dublin Tourism, Suffolk St, has tours around Dublin and farther afield but only March to November. Different morning and afternoon tours are available, each costing IR£14.50, including any admission charges, and lasting 2¾ hours. There's a variety of half-day tours out of Dublin to Newgrange, Malahide Castle, Powerscourt Gardens or Newbridge House, each costing IR£14.50. Day-long tours out of Dublin cost IR£27 and include tours to Glendalough and the Wicklow Mountains, to

the Boyne Valley and various combinations of the half-day tours.

Gray Line also has nightlife tours to Jury's Irish Cabaret (IR£22 with two drinks or IR£35 with dinner) or to Doyle's Irish Cabaret (IR£19.50 with two drinks or IR£34.50 with dinner). See the Irish Entertainment section under Entertainment for more details.

Dublin Bus (☎ 873 4222) tours can be booked at its office, 59 O'Connell St Upper, or at the Dublin Tourism office. The 2¾ hour Grand Dublin Tour uses an open-top double-decker bus (weather permitting) and operates twice daily throughout the year. The tour costs IR£8/4.

Dublin Bus also operates a hop-on hop-off service which does a 1¼ hour city tour, with commentary, 11 times daily mid-April to late September. There are eight additional daily circuits during the peak summer months. The IR£5/2 ticket lets you travel all day, getting on or off at the eight stops. The Old Dublin Tour/Gray Line (☎ 458 0808) does similar city sightseeing tours.

You can book Bus Éireann tours directly at Busáras (☎ 836 6111), or through the Bus Éireann desk at the Dublin Bus office, 59 O'Connell St Upper, or the Dublin Tourism office. It has a day tour out of the city to Glendalough and Wicklow which operates April to September Saturday to Thursday and costs IR£10/6. It does a similar tour of the Hill of Tara, Newgrange and the Boyne Valley for IR£16/9.

In the summer months there are also day tours farther afield to places such as Kilkenny, the River Shannon, Waterford, the Mountains of Mourne, Armagh and Navan, and Lough Erne.

Mary Gibbons Tours (☎ 283 9973) also does half-day Dublin city tours (IR£12) and tours to the Boyne Valley (IR£15) and Powerscourt/Glendalough (R£16). A full-day Dublin and Boyne Valley tour costs IR£27.

Walking Tours
During summer there are various walking tours which are a great way to explore this

very walkable city. A Trinity College historical walking tour departs frequently from Front Square just inside the college and costs IR£4 (free for children under 12), including entry to the 'Book of Kells' exhibit. See the Trinity College section for more details.

Dublin Footsteps Walking Tours (☎ 496 0641) operates two-hour walks at 11 am and 2.30 pm daily. The tours start from Bewley's Café on Grafton St, and explore medieval Dublin or 18th century Georgian Dublin and literary Dublin. The cost is IR£5 which includes a coffee or tea.

One-hour walking tours of north Dublin, focusing on sites associated with James Joyce, depart from the James Joyce Centre at 35 North Great George's St at 2.30 pm Monday to Saturday; phone ☎ 873 1984 to check for tours outside the summer months. The cost of a tour of the centre and the walk is IR£6.

Historical Walking Tours (☎ 845 0241) are conducted by Trinity College history graduates, take two hours and depart from the front gates of Trinity College. The walks take place several times daily mid-May to September (weekends only the rest of the year) and cost IR£5/4.

The Dublin Literary Pub Crawl (☎ 454 0228) operates daily, starting at 7.30 pm from The Duke on Duke St, just off Grafton St. May to September there are also tours at 3 pm (and at noon on Sunday as well). The walk is great fun and costs IR£6/5, though Guinness consumption can quickly add a few pounds to the figure. Indeed the emphasis seems more on drinking than literature. The actors leading the tour put on a theatrical performance appropriate to the various places and pubs along the way. The particular pubs chosen vary each night.

The Dublin Musical Pub Crawl (☎ 478 0191) leaves from upstairs in St John Gogarty's pub in Temple Bar every night Saturday to Thursday at 7.30 pm. Two musicians take you to McDaids and The Clarendon and put on sample traditional music sessions with a commentary. You wind up in O'Donoghue's for a final session around 10 pm. Once again this is great fun and a good

intro to traditional music if you're interested but ignorant. Tours cost IR£6.

Carriage Tours
You can pick up a horse and carriage with a driver/commentator at the junction of Grafton St and St Stephen's Green. Half-hour tours cost IR£20 and the carriages can take four or five people. Tours of different lengths can be negotiated with the drivers.

Tour Guides
The Federation of Irish Guiding Interests (FIGI; ☎ 278 1626), 24 Main St, Blackrock, can put you in touch with approved guides. The recommended fees for a full-day guide in Dublin are IR£45 to IR£65 in English, IR£80 in a foreign language.

SPECIAL EVENTS
Highlights of the Dublin year include:

February/March
> *Dublin Film Festival* – showcases Irish and foreign films

March
> *St Patrick's Day Parade* – 17 March, with an international marching band competition and up to a quarter of a million spectators

May
> *The Irish Football Association Cup Final*

June
> *Bloomsday* – on 16 June Dublin celebrates the day immortalised in James Joyce's classic, *Ulysses*.

August
> *Dublin Horse Show* – second week, at the Royal Dublin Society Showground

September
> *All Ireland Hurling Final* – first Sunday in September at Dublin's Croke Park; attracts 60,000 to 80,000 spectators; *All Ireland Football Final* – at Croke Park on the third Sunday in September

October
> *Dublin Theatre Festival* – takes place over two weeks

PLACES TO STAY
Dublin has a wide range of accommodation possibilities, but April to September finding a bed can be difficult in anything from the cheapest hostel to the most expensive five-star hotel. If you can, book your room in

advance. The alternative is to head for one of the tourist offices at the airport, by the harbour in Dun Laoghaire or in Dublin itself and ask them to book you a room. For a flat fee of IR£1 they'll find you somewhere in Dublin to stay. If it takes a lot of phoning around this can be a pound very well spent.

Another option is Bed Finders (☎ 6704 704), 8 Dawson St next to Waterstone, a private company offering a computerised accommodation reservation service.

Accommodation in central Dublin can be neatly divided into areas north and south of the River Liffey. The south side is generally neater, cleaner and more expensive than the north side. Prices drop as you move away from the centre. The seaside suburbs of Dun Laoghaire, Howth and Bray are also within easy commuting distance of central Dublin on the convenient DART rail service.

Camping
There's no convenient central campsite in Dublin. *Do not* try to camp in Phoenix Park: a German cyclist camping there was murdered in 1991. At the *Shankill Caravan & Camping Park* (☎ 282 0011), 16km south of the centre on the N11 Wexford Rd, a site for two costs IR£6 in summer. You can get there on bus No 45 or 84 from Eden Quay, bus No 45A from Dun Laoghaire. About 25km north of Dublin, near Rush, is *North Beach Caravan & Camping Park* (☎ 843 7131) with sites for IR£7 for two. Take bus No 33 from Eden Quay.

Hostels
Since there are no conveniently central campsites in Dublin, budget travellers usually head for one of Dublin's numerous hostels, one operated by An Óige, the national youth hostel association, the others independently. Hostels offer the cheapest accommodation and are also great for meeting other travellers and exchanging information. In spring and summer (late April to late September) they can be heavily booked but then so is everything else.

North of the Liffey The An Óige *Dublin International Youth Hostel* (☎ 830 1766), 61 Mountjoy St, is a big, well-equipped hostel in a restored, converted old convent. From Dublin airport, bus No 41A drops you in Dorset St Upper, a few minutes' walk away. It's a longer walk from the bus and railway stations but it's signposted. The hostel is in the run-down northern area of the city centre; security at the hostel is good but keep an eye on your bags in adjacent streets. The nightly cost for HI members is IR£9.50, non-members IR£10 including continental breakfast; there's an overflow hostel for the height of the summer crush.

The IHH *Cardijn House Hostel* (☎ 878 8091), aka 'Goin' My Way', is a smaller, older hostel at 15 Talbot St, east of O'Connell St. The nightly cost is IR£8 plus 50p for a shower. Breakfast is included and there are good, clean cooking facilities. The IHH *Marlborough Hostel* (☎ 878 7629), at 81-82 Marlborough St, next to the Pro-Cathedral, has dorms accommodating four to 10 people and the weekday cost is IR£7.50 per person irrespective of the dorm size; Friday and Saturday it's IR£8.50. Double rooms cost IR£13 per person. Rates include breakfast and cooking facilities are available.

For convenience you can't beat the big IHH *Isaac's Hostel* (☎ 874 9321), 2-5 Frenchman's Lane, or *Jacobs Inn* (☎ 855 5660), 21-28 Talbot Place, both a stone's throw from the Busáras or Connolly railway station, and not far from popular restaurants and pubs on either side of the Liffey.

Isaac's Hostel has cooking facilities and a small café, but is run along lines that make old-fashioned An Óige hostels look positively laid-back: no one can get into the dorms between 11 am and 5 pm, and baggage put into the locker-room can only be retrieved on the hour and half-hour. Trains also pass close to some rooms. Dorm beds are cheap at IR£6.95 to IR£8.50 and there are singles/doubles at IR£18.50/31. Jacobs Inn has similar facilities but is more expensive with dorm beds for IR£10.25 and singles/doubles for IR£29/36.

Nearby, at 46-48 Gardiner St Lower, is the

much more relaxed and welcoming IHH *Globetrotter's Tourist Hostel* (☎ 873 5893) where dorm beds cost IR£10 including continental breakfast. With 10 people to a dorm there's bound to be some disturbance, but this is a clean, modern place with good security. Breakfasts are in a pleasant dining room overlooking a small garden.

A little further down Gardiner St Lower at No 82-83 is IHH *Abraham House* (☎ 855 0600) where beds in the largest dorms cost IR£8, or IR£10 in four-bed dorms; rates include breakfast.

South of the Liffey South of the Liffey, the big, well-equipped IHH *Kinlay House* (☎ 679 6644), beside Christ Church Cathedral at 2-12 Lord Edward St, is central, but some rooms can suffer from traffic noise. Kinlay House costs from IR£12 per person in four-bed dorms, IR£13 for dorms with bathrooms and IR£18/28 a single/double. Continental breakfast is included and cooking facilities are available. Bus Nos 54A, 68A, 78A and 123 stop outside.

IHH *Avalon House* (☎ 475 0001), 55 Aungier St, in a comprehensively renovated old building, is nicely positioned just west of St Stephen's Green. It's well equipped and some of the cleverly designed rooms have mezzanine levels, which are great for families. The basic nightly cost in dorms is IR£7.50 to IR£10.50 including a continental breakfast. A bed in a four-bed room with attached bathroom costs IR£12; in a twin it's IR£14. Take bus No 16, 16A, 19 or 22 to the door or bus No 11, 13 or 46A to nearby St Stephen's Green. From the Dun Laoghaire ferry terminal you can take bus No 46A to St Stephen's Green or the DART to Pearse station.

Right in the lively (and noisy) Temple Bar area is *Strollers* (☎ 677 5614), 29 Eustace St, with dorm beds IR£11 to IR£13, twins IR£15 per person. Prices include breakfast. There's no common room or cooking facilities, but there's a public car park nearby.

Further out but with a good range of sleeping set-ups is *Morehampton House* (☎ 668 8866), 78 Morehampton Rd, Donnybrook,

Dublin 4. The cheapest beds, at IR£7.95, are in 10-bed basement dorms. For bigger, lighter eight and four-bed rooms you pay IR£11.95; IR£15 per person in twins and triples. Breakfast is another IR£1.50, but there are clean, spacious cooking facilities and a garden for alfresco picnics. Bus Nos 10, 46A and 46B pass by.

Student Accommodation
In the summer months you can stay at *Trinity Hall* (☎ 497 1772), Dartry Rd, Rathmines; rates are from IR£20 for singles or IR£15 per person if you share a twin. There are some family rooms where children aged under 10 can stay for IR£3 with two adults. To get there, take bus No 14 or 14A from D'Olier St beside the O'Connell Bridge.

University College Dublin's *UCD Village* (☎ 269 7696) is 6km south of the centre, en route to Dun Laoghaire. Accommodation here is in apartments, with three single rooms sharing a bathroom and a kitchen/meals/living area. It's modern and well appointed but way out and, at IR£22, rather expensive. For a family a three-room apartment at IR£66 could be good value. If you have a car, the ease of parking may compensate for the distance and the soulless surroundings; if you don't, bus No 10 departs every 10 minutes from O'Connell St/St Stephen's Green and goes direct to the campus. The fare is IR£1.

B&Bs
B&Bs, the backbone of cheap accommodation in Ireland, are well represented in Dublin and typically cost IR£18 to IR£22 per person per night. The cheaper B&Bs usually don't have private bathrooms, but where they do the cost is often just a pound or two more. Dublin also has some more luxuriously equipped B&Bs costing around IR£30 per person, but this category is usually monopolised by the smaller hotels and guesthouses. Most of these places levy single supplements.

If you arrive when accommodation is tight and don't like the location offered, the best advice is to take it and then try to book something better for subsequent nights. Booking just one or two days ahead can often turn up a much better choice.

If you want something cheap but close to the city, Gardiner St Upper and Lower in Dublin 1 on the north side of the Liffey is the place to look. It's a rather grubby, run-down area, but is cheap and convenient.

Further out, you can find a better price and quality combination north of the centre at Clontarf or in the seaside suburbs of Dun Laoghaire or Howth. The Ballsbridge embassy zone, just south of the centre, offers convenience and quality but you pay more for the combination. Other suburbs to try are Sandymount (immediately east of Ballsbridge) and Drumcondra (north of the centre en route to the airport).

Gardiner St There's a large collection of places on Gardiner St Lower, near the bus and railway stations, and another, cheaper, group on Gardiner St Upper, farther north past Mountjoy Square. The B&Bs on Gardiner St Upper are respectable if rather basic.

North of Mountjoy Square at the renovated, friendly *Harvey's Guesthouse* (☎ 874 8384), 11 Gardiner St Upper, singles with shared facilities are IR£18, doubles with bath IR£22.50 per person. There are several more B&Bs nearby, including *Stella Maris* (☎ 874 0835), next door at No 13, *Flynn's B&B* (☎ 874 1702), at No 15, *Carmel House* (☎ 874 1639) at No 16 and *Fatima House* (☎ 874 5410) at No 17. The cheapest is *Marian Guest House* (☎ 874 4129), at No 21, with rooms for IR£15 per person, though the plumbing can be a little loud at times. Just

off Gardiner St Upper from Mountjoy Square, at 4 Gardiner Place, is the *Dergvale Hotel* (☎ 874 4753). Regular rooms are more expensive; singles/doubles with attached bathroom cost IR£30/54.

Hardwicke St, only a short walk from Gardiner St Upper, has a couple of B&Bs that will do at a pinch – *Waverley House* (☎ 874 6132), at No 4 and *Sinclair House* (☎ 855 0792), next door at No 3. Singles cost IR£21 to IR£23, doubles IR£31 to IR£35.

Clontarf There are numerous places along Clontarf Rd, about 5km from the city centre. One of these is the friendly *Ferryview* (☎ 833 5893) at No 96. Farther along there's the slightly more expensive *White House* (☎ 833 3196) at No 125, *San Vista* (☎ 833 9582) at No 237, *Bayview* (☎ 833 9870) at No 265 and *Sea Breeze* (☎ 833 2787) at No 312. These Clontarf Rd B&Bs typically cost IR£20 to IR£26 for singles, IR£33 to IR£40 for doubles. Bus No 130 from Abbey St will get you there for IR£1.10.

Ballsbridge & Donnybrook Ballsbridge isn't only the embassy quarter and the site for a number of upper bracket hotels but is also the locale for a number of better quality B&Bs. Not to be confused with the nearby Morehampton House, which is a hostel, *Morehampton Townhouse* (☎ 660 8630), 46 Morehampton Rd, Donnybrook, is directly opposite Sachs Hotel. Singles/doubles are IR£45/60. All rooms are centrally heated and have bathrooms and the excellent breakfast proves that there can be more to life than just bacon and eggs.

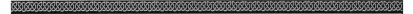

Some B&Bs for Gay & Lesbian Travellers
Dublin has several gay B&Bs; if your punt is pink, they're there and very central. The largest, the none-too-salubrious *Horse & Carriage* (☎ 478 3537; fax 478 4010), 15 Aungier St, adjoins the Incognito sauna. Singles/doubles (none with bathrooms) start at IR£35/50; single bookings aren't accepted on weekends. *Frankies* (☎ 478 3087), a friendly place on narrow Camden Place between Camden and Harcourt Sts, has a dozen smallish rooms (three with showers) for IR£25 per person. *Inn on the Liffey* (☎ 677 0828), 21 Upper Ormond Quay, and convenient to the Out on the Liffey pub, charges the same. ■

Farther south at No 113, the traditional *Morehampton Lodge* (☎ 283 7499) has rooms for IR£47.50/60.

Middle-Range Guesthouses & Hotels
The line dividing B&Bs from guesthouses and cheaper hotels is often a hazy one. Places in this middle-range bracket usually cost from IR£30 to IR£60 per night per person. Some of the small, central hotels in this category are among the most enjoyable places to stay in Dublin.

These middle-range places are a big jump up from the cheaper B&Bs in facilities and price but still cost a lot less than Dublin's expensive hotels. Breakfast is usually provided (it usually isn't in the top-notch hotels) and it's very good (unlike that offered by some cheap B&Bs). Many of these hotels offer fruit, a choice of cereals, croissants, scones and other morning delights to supplement the inevitable bacon and eggs.

North of the Liffey – Dublin 1 Just north of the Liffey is *Wynn's Hotel* (☎ 874 5131), 35-39 Abbey St Lower. Only a few steps from the Abbey Theatre, this older hotel has 66 rooms, all with attached bathroom, which cost IR£45/54 for singles/doubles with reductions at weekends. Right by the river, the *Ormond Hotel* (☎ 872 1811), Ormond Quay Upper, Dublin 1, has 55 rooms with attached bathroom for IR£92. A plaque outside notes its role in *Ulysses*.

At 47-48 Gardiner St Lower, *The Townhouse* (☎ 878 8808), next to the Globetrotter's Tourist Hostel and sharing with it a breakfast room, has singles/doubles for IR£30/60, or IR£35/65 with ensuite; tariffs include a good breakfast. This is a pleasingly decorated and furnished and safety-conscious guesthouse with a small Japanese garden and a car park – an excellent choice. Across the road at No 75 is the family-run *Maple Hotel* (☎ 874 0225/5239) which has singles/doubles for IR£45/70 with attached bathroom. Round the corner on Frenchman's Lane next to Isaac's Hostel is *Isaac's Hotel* (☎ 855 0667), with an Italian restaurant and ensuite rooms for IR£50/70.

Farther from the river is the *Castle Hotel* (☎ 874 6949), at 34 Gardiner Row, with 35 rooms. It's just off Parnell Square, only a few minutes' walk from O'Connell St but on the edge of the better part of north Dublin, before the decline sets in. Rooms cost IR£39/72 including breakfast. Further along on the same side of the road is *Barry's Hotel* (☎ 874 9407), 1-2 Great Denmark St. The hotel's 29 rooms cost IR£30/51, or IR£33/54 with attached bathroom. Across the road is the cheaper *Belvedere Hotel* (☎ 872 8522) opposite Belvedere College, which James Joyce attended as a boy. The 45 rooms, all with attached bathroom, cost IR£27.50/49.

South of the Liffey – Dublin 2 Good value for its location, the central *Fitzwilliam* (☎ 662 5155; fax 676 7488), 41 Fitzwilliam St Upper, is on the corner of Baggot St Lower, but is still quiet at night. The 12 rooms in this small hotel all have ensuite and cost IR£45/80 for singles/doubles during summer.

Even more central is *Georgian House* (☎ 661 8832) at 20-21 Baggot St Lower, equally close to St Stephen's Green or Merrion Square. Once again this is a fine old Georgian building in excellent condition. Its 47 rooms have attached bathrooms and cost IR£75/98 in summer. The breakfast is excellent. There's also a car park.

At St Stephen's Green South, *Staunton's on the Green* hotel (☎ 478 2133) is in a Georgian house in an excellent position. Rooms cost IR£96, including breakfast.

Close to the green, in another magnificent Georgian building at 21-25 Harcourt St, is the *Russell Court Hotel* (☎ 478 4991) with 42 rooms, all with attached bathroom and costing IR£65/87. Across the road at No 84 the elegant *Albany House* (☎ 475 1092) has singles/doubles for IR£60/90. Further down at No 60-61, in another Georgian building where George Bernard Shaw lived from 1874 to 1876, is the *Harcourt Hotel* (☎ 478 3677) with 40 rooms from IR£70/90 to IR£75/100.

Another place off St Stephen's Green is *Leeson Court* (☎ 676 3380), 26-27 Leeson

St Lower, at the start of Dublin's nightclub block. There's a warm open fire in the lobby, and its 20 ensuite rooms cost IR£55/78. The modern *Grafton Plaza* (☎ 475 0888), Johnsons Place, next to Break for the Border, behind the St Stephen's Green Shopping Centre, looks as if it should be more expensive than it is. In fact a single/double costs IR£90/105 in high season, with continental breakfast an extra IR£4.75.

Latchford's (☎ 676 0784), 99-100 Baggot St Lower, offers serviced rooms with self-catering facilities in an impressive Georgian house with fine plaster ceilings in some bedrooms. Prices range from IR£49/75 to IR£65/105 a single/double, with reductions for week-long stays. There's an excellent bistro attached.

Immediately opposite Christ Church Cathedral, in Christ Church Place, the big *Jury's Christ Church Inn* (☎ 475 0111) has rooms for IR£55. Unfortunately it lacks a car park.

At 21-22 Wellington Quay, overlooking the River Liffey and backing on to the fascinating Temple Bar area, the renovated *Wellington Hotel* (☎ 677 9315) charges IR£50/90 for a single/double.

Elsewhere in Dublin *Ariel Guesthouse* (☎ 668 5512) is at 52 Lansdowne Rd, Dublin 4, 2km south-east of the centre in the Ballsbridge area. It's conveniently close to Lansdowne Rd station and the big Berkeley Court Hotel. The 28 ensuite rooms cost IR£75 per person, with breakfast extra; out of season you may be able to negotiate a discount.

Further down, Lansdowne Rd changes its name to Herbert Rd, where you'll find the *Mt Herbert* (☎ 668 4321), 7 Herbert Rd, Dublin 4, about 3km from the centre. This larger hotel was once the Dublin residence of an English lord. The 155 ensuite rooms cost IR£75/85; breakfast costs extra.

The well-equipped *Ashling Hotel* (☎ 677 2324/2783) is on Parkgate St, Dublin 8, 2.5km west of the centre and directly across the river from Heuston station. Beds in its 54 rooms cost IR£62.50/96 for singles/doubles including breakfast.

Expensive Hotels
Hotels in this price range cost from IR£75 per person or IR£110 for a double. There are two categories: the top bracket with five or four-star ratings and those which fall just below the top bracket in standards and price but are more expensive than the middle range.

Almost Top Bracket At the top end of O'Connell St in north Dublin, farther up from the Gresham Hotel, is the *Royal Dublin Hotel* (☎ 873 3666; fax 873 3120), with 117 rooms at IR£95/120 for singles/doubles.

Bloom's Hotel (☎ 671 5622; fax 671 5997), on Anglesea St, in the colourful Temple Bar district, has 86 rooms costing IR£65/110 for singles/doubles. Just south of Dame St is the *Central Hotel* (☎ 679 7302; fax 679 7303), 1-5 Exchequer St, which has 70 rooms from IR£75/110 without breakfast. Though the rooms are rather small it's well located.

Close to the National Museum, *Buswells* (☎ 676 4013, 661 3888; fax 676 2090), 23-27 Molesworth St, is closed for complete refurbishment. The small *Longfield's* (☎ 676 1367; fax 676 1542), 9-10 Fitzwilliam St Lower, between Merrion and Fitzwilliam squares, has 26 rooms at IR£85/105 for singles/doubles.

Stephen's Hall (☎ 661 0585; fax 661 0606) is just a stone's throw from the south-east corner of St Stephen's Green at 14-17 Leeson St Lower. The 37 rooms, all with attached bathroom, cost IR£145.

About 3km south-east of the centre in Donnybrook, just beyond Ballsbridge, is *Sachs Hotel* (☎ 668 0995; fax 668 6147) at 19-29 Morehampton Rd, Dublin 4. This small but elegant and expensive place has 20 rooms, all ensuite, costing IR£110/160.

Top Bracket Even a single room at these hotels can cost IR£140 or more, though most guests will have probably booked through an agency or as part of a package and obtained

DUBLIN

some sort of discount from the rack (published) rates.

The only top-bracket hotel north of the Liffey is the long-established *Gresham Hotel* (☎ 874 6881; fax 878 7175), on O'Connell St Upper, which has 208 rooms for IR£180 to IR£250.

The city's best known hotel is the elegant 160-room *Shelbourne Hotel* (☎ 676 6471; fax 661 6006) strategically placed overlooking St Stephen's Green and indubitably the best address in Dublin to meet. Singles cost IR£154, doubles from IR£182. Despite the prices the rooms are a little cramped, but afternoon tea (IR£9, 3 to 5.30 pm) at the hotel is something all Dublin visitors should experience, regardless of whether they stay there.

The *Hotel Conrad* (☎ 676 5555; fax 676 5424), Earlsfort Terrace, Dublin 2, south of St Stephen's Green, is a popular business and showbusiness hotel run by the Hilton group. Rates in its 191 rooms are IR£175/200.

Also close to St Stephen's Green, the modern 203-room *Westbury Hotel* (☎ 679 1122; fax 679 7078) is in the narrow Balfe St just off Grafton St, south Dublin's pedestrianised main shopping street. Rooms on the upper floors offer views of the Dublin hills. Rates start at IR£175/195.

Mont Clare Hotel (☎ 661 6799; fax 661 5663) is a classic old hotel on elegant Merrion Square with 74 rooms for IR£120 to IR£850. The *Davenport Hotel* (☎ 661 6800; fax 661 5663) on Westland Row opposite the Mont Clare, is housed inside what was once Merrion Hall, built in 1863 for the Plymouth Brethren (a puritanical religious sect). It has 120 rooms with singles/doubles for IR£120/150.

Berkeley Court Hotel (☎ 660 1711; fax 661 7238), on Lansdowne Rd 2km southeast of the centre in Ballsbridge is in a quiet, relaxed location. It offers 187 spacious rooms at IR£185 and has a fitness centre.

Ireland's largest hotel (451 rooms), the modern *Burlington Hotel* (☎ 660 5222; fax 660 8496), is on Leeson St Upper, Dublin 4, 2km south of the centre, overlooking the Grand Canal. Rooms cost IR£139. In the same general area is *Jury's Hotel & Towers*

(☎ 660 5000; fax 660 5540), a large, modern hotel on Pembroke Rd in Ballsbridge, Dublin 4, 2.5km south of the centre. Rooms are IR£176/196. It has a swimming pool and in summer the Irish cabaret here is very popular (see Entertainment later).

The *Clarence Hotel* (☎ 662 3066; fax 662 3077), 6-8 Wellington Quay, is a completely renovated, old hotel owned by the rock band U2. It has a large clientele among the cultural and showbiz elite and in 1997 David Bowie stayed three weeks in the penthouse suite for a mere IR£1500 a night. Most rooms though cost (only?) IR£165 to IR£535.

Airport Hotels There are several hotels near Dublin airport, including the large *Forte Posthouse Hotel* (☎ 844 4211; fax 842 5874), off the N1 motorway beside the airport. It has 188 rooms costing IR£110.

PLACES TO EAT

Restaurants are divided into three popular zones. There are limited possibilities north of the Liffey, but the trendy Temple Bar enclave and Dame St, along its southern boundary, are packed with restaurants of all types. There are also numerous restaurants on both sides of busy Grafton St and along Merrion Row and Baggot St.

North of the Liffey

Dining possibilities north of the Liffey essentially consist of fast food, cheap eats or chains. Which isn't to say that you'll eat badly here, just that the choice of restaurants is much better to the south.

Fast Food & Cafés O'Connell St is the fast-food centre of Dublin; most are clustered toward the bridge. The Irish fast-food chain *Abrakebabra* (☎ 878 6499), has a branch at No 34; it serves a varied menu from burgers to baguettes. Nearby at No 14 is *La Pizza* (☎ 878 8010), another local chain; it also offers home delivery.

Isaac's Hostel, *Jacobs Inn* and *Dublin International Youth Hostel* (see Hostels under Places to Stay) have good cafeteria-style facilities. At 1-2 O'Connell St, *Café*

Kylemore is a big, somewhat impersonal but always busy fast-food place; it's good for a cup of tea or coffee or a snack any time of day. Alternatively, on the 1st floor of *Clerys* department store, you can get afternoon tea complete with cucumber sandwiches in stylish surroundings for IR£3.95.

Ireland's most famous purveyor of fish & chips from IR£3, *Beshoff's* has a branch in O'Connell St with great views from the upstairs windows.

There's a branch of *Bewley's Oriental Café* at 40 Mary St.

In the Corporation Fruit Market, between Chancery St and Mary's Lane, is *Paddy's Place* (☎ 873 5130) where the food is as staunchly Irish as the name. It's open 7.30 am to 3 pm Monday to Friday so you can go there for an early breakfast (IR£2 to IR£3.50, served all day) or a filling lunch time Irish stew.

For good coffee visit *Ernest's Coffee House* (☎ 878 1143), on the ground floor of the Jervis Shopping Centre on Mary St.

Restaurants Restaurant possibilities north of the Liffey are limited, but *Chapter One* (☎ 873 2266), below the Dublin Writers' Museum on the north side of Parnell Square, is worth a look even though the food is resolutely conservative. The fillet steak is IR£14.25.

Closer to the river, *101 Talbot St* (☎ 874 5011), at, funnily enough, 101 Talbot St, opens for lunch Monday to Saturday and dinner Tuesday to Saturday in an attempt to bring good food north of the river. The prices are reasonable, the food moderately adventurous and well prepared. Filling pasta mains cost IR£8.95.

Residents of the Gardiner St hostels and B&Bs can also eat at *Le Café* (☎ 855 2424), 5 Beresford Place. It serves pastas (IR£6) and burgers and is also open for breakfast. Prints of angels and cherubim adorn the walls.

Il Vignardo (☎ 855 2798), in Isaac's Hotel on Frenchmans Lane, serves Italian food from noon onwards.

Temple Bar

The old, interesting and rapidly revitalising Temple Bar area is Dublin's most concentrated restaurant area. It's bounded by the river to the north, Westmoreland St to the east and Christ Church Cathedral to the west. The southern boundary is Dame St and its extension, Lord Edward St, but for convenience's sake restaurants on both the northern and southern side of Dame St are listed in this section.

Fast Food & Cafés *Abrakebabra* has a branch (☎ 671 9248) at the O'Connell Bridge end of Westmoreland St. *Beshoff's* has a second branch (☎ 677 8026) with waiter service upstairs at 14 Westmoreland St, also just south of O'Connell Bridge.

Beside Kinlay House hostel, is *Wood Quay Café & Bar* (☎ 679 8428), on the corner of Lord Edward and Fishamble Sts. It serves modern Irish food mixing traditional dishes with influences from the Mediterranean and other parts of the world. Mains cost IR£7 to IR£9. It's open from noon and has brightly painted abstract paintings on the walls. The vegetarian *Well Fed Café* (☎ 677 2234), 6 Crow St, is a big, busy, alternative-style place, great for lunch or a snack with large servings. Mexican taco is IR£2.60. It's open noon to 8 pm Monday to Saturday.

At *Cyberia Café* (☎ 679 7607), on the corner of Temple Lane and Curved St, and part of the Arthouse Multimedia Centre, you can have coffee and a salsa bagel melt (IR£2.50) while you surf the Internet.

The newest branch of *Fitzers* (a local chain), on Fownes St Upper, beside Temple Bar Square, has BLT sandwiches with fries and salad for IR£6.25 and mains for IR£8 to IR£15.

Italian Restaurants Temple Bar has all sorts of restaurants but the Irish passion for pasta and pizza comes through loud and clear.

The popular *Bad Ass Café* (☎ 671 2596), 9-11 Crown Alley, is a bright, cheerful, warehouse-style place just south of Ha'penny Bridge. It offers pretty good pizzas for IR£6 to IR£8.25 in a rather convivial studentish atmosphere with pulleys to whip orders to the kitchen at busy times, but doesn't open for breakfast. One of its claims to fame is that Sinéad O'Connor once worked here as a waitress. A couple of doors up, *Garibaldi's* (☎ 671 7288), 15-16 Crown Alley, does burgers and steaks to complement its pizzas and pastas.

Nico's (☎ 677 3062), 53 Dame St on the corner of Temple Lane, offers conservative Italian food with a strong Irish influence. It's solidly popular, has a piano player, opens for dinner Monday to Saturday, and also for lunch on weekdays. Pastas cost IR£6.50, fish mains IR£11.50 to IR£12. Despite being called after the ancient name for Dublin, *Dyflin* (☎ 677 8528), 23 Temple Bar on the corner of Bedford Row, serves mostly Italian dishes, including pizzas for under IR£6. *Café Gertrude* (☎ 677 9043), 3-4 Bedford Row, down a side turning and therefore likely to have tables when other places are full, does pizza at reasonable prices (IR£4.25 to IR£5.50).

You can also find pizza at the fancier *Da Pino* (☎ 671 9308), 38-40 Parliament St on the corner of Dame St. This spacious and bright restaurant has pizzas for IR£4.30 to IR£6.70, and three-course lunch specials for IR£3.90. *La Mezza Luna* (☎ 671 2840) is also on Dame St. This slightly more up-market restaurant is enormously popular, and you may have to book a table or be prepared to wait. The pasta dishes are great value at IR£3.50 to IR£7. It's open daily 10 am to 5 pm.

Il Pasticcio (☎ 677 6111), 12 Fownes St, does wood-baked pizzas and good pasta in a rather cramped setting with paintings on the walls by up-and-coming artists. Pasta main dishes range from IR£5.50 to IR£6.95, pizzas from IR£5 to IR£7.

Other Restaurants Despite the number of trattorias, ristorantes and pizzerias, there's more to Temple Bar than pasta and pizza. At the *Eamonn Doran Imbibing Emporium* (☎ 679 9773), 3A Crown Alley, directly across from The Bad Ass Café, you can get burgers for IR£5.95. It has a similar venue in New York City.

Omelettes (from IR£5.75) are a speciality at the popular and bustling, but somewhat overpriced *Elephant & Castle* (☎ 679 3121), 18 Temple Bar; how 'free' are coffee fill-ups when the first cup is IR£1.50? It stays open until midnight on Friday and Saturday, until 11.30 pm on other days. Right next door at 20-21 Temple Bar is the equally popular *Gallagher's Boxty House* (☎ 677 2762). A boxty is rather like a stuffed pancake and tastes like a bland Indian masala dosa. Real Irish food isn't something that's widely available in Dublin so it's worth trying. Main dishes are IR£6 to IR£9. Next to that is the *Alamo* (☎ 677 6546) where you can get good reasonably priced Mexican dishes.

The Chameleon (☎ 671 0362), 1 Fownes St, just off Wellington Quay, specialises in Indonesian dishes such as rijstaffel or gado gado. It's only open in the evenings.

Poco Loco (☎ 679 1950), 32 Parliament St, offers straightforward Tex-Mex interpretations of Mexican food but they do have Corona beer (cerveza if you wish!) and their combination plates are great value at IR£6.25. It's open daily for dinner.

Rebel with Several Causes

For some years it looked as if motherhood had tamed the bad girl of Irish pop. Then Sinéad O'Connor released a new single. *This is a Rebel Song* took the British government to task for not admitting Sinn Féin to the Northern Ireland peace talks and was judged too controversial to be released in England.

Controversy has dogged Sinéad's footsteps ever since she burst onto the world's consciousness as the shaven-headed, doe-eyed singer of *Nothing Compares 2 U*. At a New Jersey concert she refused to have the US flag flown; she has confessed to an abortion; she has detailed her abused childhood; and she has even admitted IRA sympathies (since retracted).

Ironic, then, to find the woman who ripped up the Pope's picture on the US television show *Saturday Night Live* cropping up as the Virgin Mary in Neil Jordan's film of Pat McCabe's *The Butcher Boy*. ∎

Dame St's international mix of restaurants includes Chinese possibilities like *Fan's Cantonese Restaurant* (☎ 679 4263/73) at No 60. *Les Frères Jacques* (☎ 679 4555) at No 74 is one of Temple Bar's fancier places with three-course lunches for IR£13.50. The food is as French as the name would indicate, the mood is slightly serious, and the bill can make quite a dent in your budget. It's open Monday to Friday for lunch, Monday to Saturday for dinner.

Turn off Dame St into Crow St where you'll find *Tante Zoé's* (☎ 679 4407) at No 1. It's open Monday to Saturday for lunch, Monday to Sunday for dinner and is more proof of how cosmopolitan Dublin dining can be, since Cajun and Creole food is the speciality with a four-course lunch for IR£6.50. The next lane again is Fownes St Upper, where your taste buds can continue their travels to Cuba at *Café Havana* where tortillas cost IR£4.50 to IR£5.90.

Around Grafton St

Pedestrianised Grafton St is the No 1 shopping street in south Dublin and notably lacking in restaurants and pubs. The streets to the east and west of Grafton St are more promising. Dame St restaurants are covered in the Temple Bar section.

Fast Food & Cafés Grafton St is the fast-food centre south of the Liffey. *Captain America* (☎ 671 5266), 44 Grafton St, has burgers until midnight every night; last food orders are about 11.30 pm. The singer Chris de Burgh performed here in his post-student days. Round the corner at 1 St Stephen's Green North is a branch of *La Pizza* (☎ 671 7175).

There are three branches of *Bewley's Oriental Cafés* around the centre. Bewley's is something of a Dublin institution and its huge cafeteria-style places offer good-quality food, including breakfast, lunch time sandwiches (IR£1.65 to IR£3) and complete meals (IR£3.95 to IR£5). They are equally good for a quick cup of tea or coffee and actually offer a choice of teas. Watch the price of cakes though.

The 78 Grafton St branch is the flagship, with company memorabilia displayed upstairs. It's open Sunday to Thursday 7.30 am to 1 am, Friday and Saturday to 5 am, Sunday 9.30 am to 7 pm. The branch at 11-12 Westmoreland St opens Monday to Saturday 7.30 am to 9 pm, Sunday 9.30 am to 9 pm. There's also a branch at 13 South Great George's St.

Round the corner from Dublin Castle at 2 Werburgh St *Leo Burdock's* (☎ 54 0366), next to the Lord Edward Pub, is said to dole out the best fish & chips in Dublin. You can eat them down the road in the park beside St Patrick's Cathedral.

The Grafton St area has office workers, Trinity College students and tourists to feed and there are plenty of cafés and restaurants to keep them happy at lunch time. Backpackers staying at *Avalon House* on Aungier St (see Hostels under Places to Stay) can take advantage of the most stylish hostel café in town.

Subway, on Anne St South, just off Grafton St, turns out filling sandwiches, baps (a soft Irish version of a bread roll) and rolls for around IR£2 to IR£4. Eat there or even better, if it's a sunny day, have a picnic in nearby St Stephen's Green. There are pizzas and pasta dishes to go with the coffee. *Café Java* (☎ 670 7239), 5 Anne St South, does excellent three-course weekday lunches of soup, a sandwich and tea or coffee for IR£3.95. There's a second branch (☎ 660 0675) at 145 Upper Leeson St.

Munchies, on the corner of Exchequer St and William St South, just west of Grafton St, claims to produce the best sandwiches in Ireland. For IR£1.70 to IR£2.50 you can check if it's true.

A little closer to Grafton St at 19 Wicklow St is *Cornucopia* (☎ 677 7583), a popular wholefood café turning out all sorts of goodies for those trying to escape the Irish cholesterol habit. There's even a hot vegetarian breakfast for IR£2.65 as an alternative to muesli. It's open for breakfast and lunch Monday to Saturday and until 8 pm on weekday evenings, 9 pm on Thursday. Head the other way along Exchequer St to try the

Wed Wose Café at No 18 which has sandwiches and burgers (from IR£1.60).

The Powerscourt Townhouse Shopping Centre is stuffed with eating places and makes a great place for lunch. They include *Blazing Salads II* (☎ 671 9552), a popular vegetarian restaurant on the top level, with a variety of salads for 80p each. It's open Monday to Saturday 9.30 am to 6 pm. *La Piazza*, next door, does pizzas for IR£4.75. On the 1st floor, *Chompy's* (☎ 679 4552) boasts a Grand Slam breakfast for IR£5, salads for IR£4 and lunches for IR£4.50 to IR£5.50. In the open central ground floor area is *Mary Rose*, a good place for breakfast (IR£2.95). On the ground floor you will find the *Whistlestop Café* and *Fair City Sandwich Bar*, serving everything from soups to burgers. *Twisted Lemon* does crêpes and pancake pizzas and you can round off with a coffee at *Coffee Roastery*.

For sizeable sandwiches for under IR£3 there are branches of *O'Brien's* at 54 Mary St and on the 1st floor of the St Stephen's Green Shopping Centre.

Other places to eat in St Stephen's Green Shopping Centre include a branch of *Café Kylemore* on the 1st floor and the *Pavlova Pantry* on the 2nd, which serves sandwiches and snacks as well as the Australian-invented cake.

Just beside the centre is a branch of *Chicago Pizza Pie Factory* (☎ 478 1233), where pizzas cost IR£7.25 to IR£13.95. Nearby, in Clarendon Market, the new *Kaffeemoka* does large delicious sandwiches for IR£2.30 to IR£3.75, and has a variety of good coffees and teas.

The large *Kilkenny Restaurant* (☎ 677 7066) is on the 1st floor of the Kilkenny Shop at 6 Nassau St. The generally excellent food is served cafeteria-style and at times the queues can be discouragingly long. There's a simpler food counter which can be faster. It's open Monday to Saturday 9 am to 5 pm, Sunday noon to 5 pm.

There's a large cafeteria at the *Alliance Française* on the corner of Kildare and Nassau Sts, also opposite Trinity. From the windows you can gaze across to the college grounds. Nearby is the *Leinster Coffee House* for good, strong coffee.

Fitzers' slick outlets are great places for lunch or early evening meals on weekdays. There's a Fitzers (☎ 677 1155) at 51 Dawson St with tables outside, towards the Trinity College and Nassau St end. The best Fitzers, however, is in the National Gallery, and is covered under Merrion Row, Baggot St & Beyond later in this section.

For an excellent cheap lunch, look for *Marks Bros Café* (☎ 677 0185), 7 South Great George St. It's been there for over a decade now, turning out big, filling sandwiches, tasty soups, meals and scrumptious carrot cake. Mains are IR£5 to IR£8.25.

Restaurants St Andrew's St, just west of Grafton St's northern end, is packed with good restaurant possibilities. The excellent *Trocadero* (☎ 677 5545, 679 9772), 3 St Andrew's St, offers no culinary surprises which is why it's so popular. Simple food, straightforward preparation, large helpings and late opening hours are the selling points. Irish stew is IR£9. The Troc, as it's locally known, opens past midnight every night except Sunday, when it closes just a little earlier.

Across the road, *QV.2* (☎ 677 3363), 14-15 St Andrew's St, manages to look more expensive than it is. There are good pasta dishes for IR£8.50 and main courses for IR£9.50 to IR£15, but vegetables cost extra. It offers good, mildly adventurous food, pleasant surroundings and a dessert called Eton Mess (IR£3.95), that shouldn't be missed. It's open Monday to Saturday for lunch and dinner until after midnight.

Still on St Andrew's St the *Cedar Tree* (☎ 677 2121) at No 11A is a Lebanese restaurant with a good selection of vegetarian dishes; felafel is IR£7.50. Or turn left at the corner to *Taverna* (☎ 677 3665), 33 Wicklow St. Open daily for lunch and dinner, it combines sunny Greek food with an equally sunny atmosphere; moussaka is IR£6.50. It has a good vegetarian selection. Opposite at No 12A, the *Imperial Chinese Restaurant* (☎ 677 2580) opens daily and is notable for its lunch time dim sums. Most mains are IR£8.50 to IR£9.50.

The modern, cheerful *Pasta Fresca* (☎ 679 2402/8965), 3-4 Chatham St, just off Grafton St's southern end, proves once again that the Irish really like their Italian food. It has authentic pasta dishes for IR£5.50 to IR£6.95 and opens from 8 am until reasonably late Monday to Saturday. Sundays it opens noon to 8.30 pm. Just off Chatham St, *Pizza Stop* (☎ 679 6712), 6 Chatham Lane, is a popular pizzeria with pizzas for IR£6 to IR£7, but also does pastas for under IR£6. Alternatively, at 27 Exchequer St, a bit to the north, there's the fashionable *Boulevard Café* (☎ 679 2565) with pasta dishes for IR£5 to IR£6.20. It's open daily 10 am to midnight.

There are several pubs with good food close to Grafton St. The *Stag's Head* (☎ 679 3701) is on Dame Court, and, apart from being an extremely popular drinking spot during summer (see Entertainment later), also turns out simple, well-prepared, economical meals. At 37 Exchequer St on the corner of St Andrew's St is the *Old Stand*, another popular place for pub food with meals from IR£5.

Davy Byrne's, 21 Duke St, has been famous for its food ever since Leopold Bloom dropped in for a sandwich. It's now a swish watering hole but you can still eat there. Farther west, the *Lord Edward Restaurant* (☎ 454 2420), upstairs in the Lord Edward Pub, 23 Christ Church Place opposite Christ Church Cathedral, is Dublin's oldest seafood restaurant. It's open Monday to Friday for lunch and Monday to Saturday for dinner. Even farther west, *The Brazen Head*, in Bridge St is always packed at lunch time. It has a variety of menus offering everything from sandwiches to a carvery.

The Tex-Mex *Judge Roy Bean's* (☎ 679 7539), 45-47 Nassau St, on the corner of Grafton St, serves whopping helpings of tacos for IR£7.95 and has a popular bar with music. *Eddie Rocket's* (☎ 679 7340), 7 Anne St South, is a 1950s-style American diner ready to dish out anything from breakfast at 7.30 am to an excellent late-night hot dog for IR£3.25. Friday and Saturday nights it's open to 4 am. Next door is the trendy, popular *Gotham Café* (☎ 679 5266), 8 Anne St South, with pizzas prepared with some pizzazz for IR£4.95 to IR£8.95. If you can stand the smell, the *Periwinkle Seafood Bar* (☎ 679 4203) in the Powerscourt Townhouse Shopping Centre serves economically priced seafood lunches with the accent on shellfish; seafood salad is IR£5.65.

Regular visitors to India may remember Rajdoot as a popular brand of Indian motorcycle. Those in search of Indian food in Dublin can scoot down to *Rajdoot Tandoori* (☎ 679 4274), 26-28 Clarendon St in the Westbury Centre, behind the Westbury Hotel, for superb North Indian tandoori dishes. Set 'executive lunches' cost IR£6.95. Nearby, and with similarly Mogul-style Indian cuisine, is the large *Shalimar* (☎ 671 0738), 17 South Great George's St on the corner of Exchequer St, which offers a wide variety of delectable Indian breads and *baltis* (IR£7.50 to IR£8.50).

La Stampa (☎ 677 8611), 35 Dawson St, is Dublin's upmarket Italian restaurant with a large and very attractive Georgian dining area, liberally festooned with colourful paintings. It's open from lunch time until late daily and main courses are IR£10.50 to IR£15.

For a French restaurant without the pretentiousness which that sometimes implies, try *Chez Jules* (☎ 677 0499) tucked away at 16A D'Olier St, just north-west of Trinity College. You eat at long benches with red-and-white check cloths. The food is well cooked and not extortionately priced; mains start from around IR£12.

In the basement of Newman House, at 85-86 St Stephen's Green, is *The Commons* (☎ 475 2597), one of Dublin's Michelin-starred restaurants. As you'd expect, the food here is pricey and it would be as well to book ahead, especially for weekends. Chef Michael Bolster's 'tasting menu' of seven courses costs IR£50.

Finally, on Stephen St Lower, behind the big St Stephen's Green Shopping Centre, *Break for the Border* (☎ 478-0300) is a busy, barn-like restaurant, bar-and-entertainment complex serving Tex-Mex food until late. Look for the horse and Indian rider statue out front.

Merrion Row, Baggot St & Beyond

Merrion Row, leading out south-east from St Stephen's Green, and its extension, Baggot St, is a busy boulevard of middle to upper bracket guesthouses, popular pubs and an eclectic selection of restaurants.

Fast Food & Cafés *Fitzers* (☎ 668 6481), inside the National Gallery in Merrion Square, is well worth a detour, particularly at lunch time. The artistic interlude as you walk through makes a pleasant introduction to this slightly pricey but popular restaurant. It has the same opening hours as the gallery and has varied meals for IR£5.25 to IR£6.25, as well as salads, cakes and wine.

Pierre Victoire (☎ 678 5412), 11 Merrion Row, does set lunches for IR£4.90 and set dinners for IR£7.90. Farther along, *Georgian Fare* (☎ 676 7736), 14 Baggot St Lower, has good sandwiches, while *Miller's Pizza Kitchen* (☎ 676 6098), 9-10 Baggot St Lower, is firmly in pastaland. *Hanna's Kitchen*, on the corner of Baggot St Lower and Pembroke St West, next to Ayumi-ya Japanese restaurant, is good for coffee and snacks.

The Coffee Dock (☎ 660 5000), is in Jury's Hotel & Towers, Pembroke Rd, Ballsbridge, 2.5km from the city centre. It's open Monday 7 am to 11.30 pm, Tuesday to Sunday 6 am to 11.30 pm and has four course Irish breakfast for IR£9.25. Mains like mixed grill cost around IR£10.

Restaurants *Galligan's Restaurant* (☎ 676 5955), 6 Merrion Row, past the Shelbourne Hotel, has moved upmarket in recent years but is still a good place for lunch or dinner. It serves pasta for IR£6 or steak for IR£9.

There's an international line-up of restaurants among the colourful Baggot St pubs, one of which is *Ayumi-ya* (☎ 662 0233), in the basement at 132 Baggot St Lower. This is a Westernised Japanese steakhouse offer-

ing good-value set meals comprising a starter, soup, main course (try the Tokyo burger), dessert and tea or coffee for IR£13.95. The food is good. It also has vegetarian dishes. There's a second more formal branch of Ayumi-ya in the suburb of Blackrock, serving more traditional Japanese food.

The *Ante Room* (☎ 660 4716), 20 Baggot St Lower, underneath the popular Maguire's pub, is a seafood specialist with main courses IR£11 to IR£16 and traditional Irish music on most summer nights. *Miller's Pizza Kitchen* (☎ 660 6022), at No 50, has a wine bar and serves decent pizzas for IR£5.50 to IR£8.55.

The elegant Michelin-starred *Restaurant Patrick Guilbaud* (☎ 676 4192), 46 James's Place, just off Baggot St Lower beyond Fitzwilliam St, has a reputation as Dublin's best place for modern French food. Don't come here unless your credit card is in A1 condition. The smooth décor and service is backed up by delicious food. There's nothing overpoweringly fancy about anything, it's just good food, beautifully prepared and elegantly presented. There's a table d'hôte lunch menu for IR£22, and a dinner menu of IR£35, but with drinks and service count on paying at least IR£45 per person. It's open for lunch Monday to Friday and for dinner Monday to Saturday.

The *Old Dublin* (☎ 454 2028), 90 Francis St, makes an interesting departure from most menus, as it specialises in Russian and Scandinavian food. It has a four-course lunch for only IR£12.50.

Out from the centre is the *Lobster Pot Restaurant* (☎ 668 0025), 9 Ballsbridge Terrace, Dublin 4. It's a staunchly old-fashioned place offering substantial and solid dishes in an equally substantial atmosphere. As the name indicates, seafood is the speciality. Prices are fairly high. Next door is *Roly's Bistro* (☎ 668 2611), at No 7, which receives rave write-ups for its food; advance booking is advisable. Close by at 15-17 Ballsbridge Terrace is *Kites Chinese Restaurant* (☎ 660 7415), which serves Chinese food with style and moderate to high prices; most mains are IR£9 to IR£10.

ENTERTAINMENT

Dublin has theatres, cinemas, nightclubs and concert halls, but just as in every village throughout the Emerald Isle, the pubs are the real centres of activity. Dublin has hundreds of pubs and they're great for anything from a contemplative pint of Guinness to a rowdy night out with the latest Irish rock band. For what's-on information get the fortnightly magazine *In Dublin* (IR£1.50) or the giveaway *Dublin Event Guide*.

Pub Entertainment

There's considerable overlap between music styles at the various Dublin pubs – some specialise solely in one type of music, others switch from night to night. Others may have one band on upstairs and another, of an entirely different style, downstairs. Pubs must close at night by 11.30 pm, or by 11 pm in winter.

Rock Music Various pubs specialise in rock music, and some of them charge an entry fee. *Whelan's*, the *Purty Kitchen & Bar* and the *Big Jack's Baggot Inn* have bands playing almost every night. Other pubs/music venues include *Fibber McGee's* and *The Mean Fiddler*. The *Olympia Theatre* has 'Midnight at the Olympia' performances on Friday and Saturday nights, year-round.

Traditional & Folk Music Traditional Irish music and folk music also have big followings in Dublin pubs. Worth trying are *The Auld Dubliner* (when it reopens), the *Brazen Head*, *Harcourt Hotel*, *The Mean Fiddler*, *Mother Redcaps*, *O'Donoghue's*, the *Purty Kitchen & Bar*, *Slattery's* and *Whelan's*.

Country Music Along with all the other popular music forms in Ireland, there's a real passion for country music. Pubs where country music is popular include *Barry's Hotel*, the *Lower Deck* and the *Purty Kitchen & Bar*. *Break for the Border* in Stephen St Lower also hosts regular country music sessions.

Jazz & Blues Jazz and blues are also played at several pubs, including *The Barge Inn*, *Harcourt Hotel*, the *International Bar*, *McDaid's*, *Hotel Pierre*, *Slattery's* and *Whelan's*. *Sachs Hotel* and *Jury's Hotel* also have jazz sessions on Sunday.

Comedy Several pubs have comedy acts from time to time (telephone to find out when), including the *Ha'penny Bridge Inn*, *The Waterfront* and the *Purty Kitchen & Bar*. The *International Bar* has a regular Wednesday night Comedy Cellar, which takes place upstairs, of course.

Venues The phone numbers and locations of the music and entertainment pubs mentioned here are as follows:

The Auld Dubliner
    17 Anglesea St, Dublin 2 (☎ 677 0527)
Bad Bob's Backstage Bar
    East Essex St, Dublin 2 (☎ 679 2992)
The Big Jack's Baggot Inn
    143 Baggot St, Dublin 2 (☎ 676 1430)
The Barge Inn
    42 Charlemont St, Dublin 2 (☎ 475 1869)
Barry's Hotel
    Great Denmark St, Dublin 1 (☎ 874 6943)
The Brazen Head
    Bridge St, Dublin 8 (☎ 677 9549)
Fibber MacGee's
    Gate Hotel, Parnell St, Dublin 2 (☎ 874 5253)
Ha'penny Bridge Inn
    42 Wellington Quay, Dublin 2 (☎ 677 0616); 60 Harcourt St, Dublin 2 (☎ 778 3677)
The Harcourt Hotel
    60 Harcourt St, Dublin 1 (☎ 778 3677)
Howl at the Moon (O'Dwyer's Pub)
    68 Mount St, Dublin 2 (☎ 676 2887)
The International Bar
    23 Wicklow St, Dublin 2 (☎ 677 9250)
Jury's Hotel
    Ballsbridge, Dublin 4 (☎ 660 5000)
The Lower Deck
    Portobello Harbour, Dublin 8 (☎ 475 1423)
McDaid's
    3 Harry St, Dublin 2 (☎ 679 4395)
The Mean Fiddler
    16 Wexford St, Dublin 2 (☎ 475 8555)
Mother Redcaps
    Back Lane, The Liberties, Dublin 8 (☎ 453 8306)
O'Donoghue's
    15 Merrion Row, Dublin 2 (☎ 661 4303)
Hotel Pierre
    Seafront, Dun Laoghaire (☎ 280 0291)

DUBLIN

The Purty Kitchen & Bar
    Old Dunleary Rd, Dun Laoghaire (☎ 284 3576)
Sachs Hotel
    19-29 Morehampton Rd, Dublin 4 (☎ 668 4829)
Slattery's
    129 Capel St, Dublin 1 (☎ 872 7971)
The Waterfront
    14 Sir John Rogersons Quay, Dublin 2 (☎ 677 8466)
Whelan's
    25 Wexford St, Dublin 2 (☎ 478 0766)

Irish Entertainment

Several places in Dublin offer tourists an evening of entertainment, with Irish songs, Irish dancing and probably a few Irish jokes thrown in along the way.

Jury's Irish Cabaret (☎ 660 5000) at Jury's Hotel, Ballsbridge, Dublin 4, features 2½ hours of Irish music, song and dance. This has been a tourist favourite for over three decades. You can either come for dinner and the show (IR£35.50) from 7.15 pm or just for the show (IR£22, including two drinks) from 8 pm. It operates Tuesday to Sunday from the beginning of May to mid-October.

Similar performances are put on at the *Burlington Hotel* (☎ 660 5222), at Upper Leeson St, Dublin 4. The 2½-hour performances take place Monday to Saturday from 8 pm May to October. Dinner starts an hour

A Dublin Pub Crawl

A visit to the city should properly include a walking tour of some of the best of the old pubs. A traditional Irish pub has *snugs*, partitioned-off tables where you can meet friends in privacy. Some snugs even have their own serving hatches, so drinks can be passed in discreetly should the drinkers not want to be seen ordering 'just the one'. Dublin has a huge selection of pubs, so there's no possibility of being unable to find a Guinness should you develop a thirst.

A Dublin pub crawl should start at *The Brazen Head* on Bridge St, just south of the Liffey beyond Christ Church Cathedral. This is Dublin's oldest pub, though its history is uncertain. Its own sign proclaims that it was founded in 1198, but the earliest reference to it is in 1613 and licensing laws didn't come into effect until 1635. Others claim that it was founded in 1666 or 1688, but the present building is thought to date from 1754. The sunken level of the entrance courtyard is a clear indicator of how much street levels have altered since its construction. In the 1790s it was the headquarters of the United Irishmen, who, it would appear, had a tendency to talk too much after a few drinks, leading to numerous arrests being made here. Robert Emmet was a regular visitor at that time. Not surprisingly, James Joyce mentioned it in *Ulysses* with a half-hearted recommendation for the food: 'you get a decent enough do in the Brazen Head'.

From the Brazen Head, walk eastward along the Liffey to the trendy Temple Bar district and dive into those narrow lanes for a drink at popular pubs like the *Norseman*. On summer evenings young visitors to Dublin congregate for a nightly street party that stretches along Temple Bar from one pub to the other.

On Fleet St, in Temple Bar, the *Palace Bar*, with its mirrors and wooden floor, is frequently cited as a perfect example of an old Dublin pub and is popular with journalists from the *Irish Times* nearby. On the corner of Temple Bar and Anglesea St is the *Auld Dubliner*, and on the opposite corner, at the junction of Fleet and Anglesea Sts, is the *Oliver St John Gogarty* where Musical Pub Crawls kick off nightly at 7.30 pm except Friday.

From Temple Bar cross Dame St, itself well supplied with drinking establishments, to the intersection of Dame Court and Dame Lane, where *Dame Tavern* and the *Stag's Head* face each other from opposite corners. Here, too, a street party takes place between the pubs on summer evenings. The *Stag's Head* was built in 1770, then remodelled in 1895 and featured in a postage stamp series on Irish pubs.

With time and energy you could divert down South Great George St to the luxuriant *Long Hall*. Otherwise, continue down Dame Lane past the *Banker's* to *O'Neill's* on Suffolk St. It's only a stone's throw from Trinity College, so this fine old traditional pub has long been a student haunt. A block over on Exchequer St is the *Old Stand*, furnished in hybrid Georgian-Victorian style and renowned for its rugby connections and fine pub food. On the other corner, on Wicklow St, the *International Bar* has blues music weekends.

Emerge on to Grafton St, which, despite being Dublin's premier shopping street, is completely publess. Fear not – there are numerous interesting establishments just off the street, including *Davy*

earlier and the cost for dinner and the show is IR£34.50, or IR£19.50 for the show and two drinks. *Clontarf Castle* (☎ 833 2321) at Castle Ave, Clontarf, Dublin 3, also has shows from 7.30 pm Monday to Saturday.

Cinema

Dublin's restaurants are overwhelmingly south of the river, pubs are more evenly spread between north and south, but city cinemas are more heavily concentrated on the north side.

The first-run cinemas are the *Ambassador* (☎ 872 7000), Parnell St; the five screen *Savoy* (☎ 874 6000), O'Connell St Upper,

and the nine screen *Virgin Mulitplex* (☎ 872 8400) in the Parnell Centre, Parnell St. The three-screen *Screen* (☎ 671 4988, 872 3922), College St, Dublin 2, south of the river, is more arthouse, less big release. Ditto for the *Light House* (☎ 873 0438), 106 Abbey St Middle, Dublin 1.

The *Irish Film Centre* (☎ 679 5744) has two screens at 6 Eustace St in Temple Bar. The complex also has a bar, a café and a bookshop; comedy shows are sometimes staged in the atrium.

Entry prices are generally about IR£4.75, though there are often reduced prices for afternoon shows. Late-night shows take

DUBLIN

Byrne's on Duke St. Davy Byrne's was Bloom's 'moral pub' in *Ulysses* and he stopped there for a Gorgonzola cheese sandwich with mustard washed down with a glass of Burgundy. It also featured in *Dubliners*, but after a glossy refurbishment is now something of a yuppie hang-out which Joyce would hardly recognise.

On Harry St, also off Grafton St, you'll find *McDaid's*, once Brendan Behan's local, now a bit of a tourist trap but still popular, as is the *Bruxelles* across the road. On Anne St South there's *John Kehoe's* with its old snugs, where patrons can still savour their Guinness in relative privacy. Chatham St features *Neary's*, a showy Victorian era pub with a particularly fine frontage, popular with actors from the nearby Gaiety Theatre.

From the end of Grafton St turn along the north side of St Stephen's Green (the 'Beaux' Walk') and continue on past the Shelbourne Hotel to Merrion Row for a drink at *O'Donoghue's*. In the evening you'll probably have traditional music to accompany your pint as this is one of Dublin's most famous music pubs. The folk group the Dubliners started out here. On summer evenings a crowd spills into the courtyard outside.

Merrion Row changes name to become Baggot St Lower and on either side of the street are two traditional old pubs *James Toner's* and *Doheny & Nesbitt's*. Toner's, with its stone floor, is almost a country pub in the heart of the city and the shelves and drawers are reminders that it once doubled as a grocery store. Doheny & Nesbitt's is equipped with antique snugs and is a favourite place for political gossip among politicians and journalists; Leinster House is only a short stroll away. *Big Jack's Baggot Inn*, close to Toner's, is a popular place for rock music. If you continue farther south along Baggot St Lower you'll come to *Larry Murphy's* and the *Henry Grattan*.

Backtrack a few steps to Merrion St Upper and walk north past Merrion Square to *Kennedy's* on Lincoln Place, which is tucked in behind Trinity College and has long been a Trinity student haunt. It's well known for its spontaneous traditional music sessions. Continue round the edge of Trinity College towards the river where you'll come to *John Mulligan's* on Poolbeg St, another pub that has scarcely changed over the years. It featured as the local in the film *My Left Foot*. Mulligan's was established in 1782 and has long been reputed to have some of the best Guinness in Ireland as well as a wonderfully varied crowd of 'regulars'.

No thorough pub crawl should be restricted to pubs south of the Liffey, so head north to try *Slattery's*, 129 Capel St, on the corner of Mary's Lane, and *Sean O'Casey's*, 105 Marlborough St, on the corner of Sackville Place. Both are busy music pubs where you'll often find traditional Irish music downstairs and loud rock upstairs. Other north Dublin pubs to sample are the *Oval* on Abbey St Middle, another journalists' hang-out, and *Madigan's* on Abbey St Lower.

Head farther north to the *Patrick Conway* on Parnell St which has been in operation since 1745; new fathers have been stopping in here for a celebratory pint from the day the Rotunda Maternity Hospital opened across the road in 1757. *Joxer Daly's*, 103-104 Dorset St Upper, is a Victorian-style pub, conveniently close to the Dublin International Youth Hostel. ■

place from time to time, particularly at the Savoy on Saturday nights.

Theatre

Dublin's theatre scene is small but busy. Bookings can usually be made by quoting a credit card number over the phone and the tickets can then be collected just before the performance.

The famous *Abbey Theatre* (☎ 878 7222), Abbey St Lower, Dublin 1, near the river, puts on new Irish works as well as a steady series of revivals of classic Irish works by WB Yeats, JM Synge, Sean O'Casey, Brendan Behan, Samuel Beckett and others. Performances are at 8 pm, with Saturday matinees at 2.30 pm. Tickets cost IR£8 to IR£14, student discounts are available. The smaller *Peacock Theatre* is part of the same complex but ticket prices are lower. Together, the two theatres make up Ireland's National Theatre.

Also north of the Liffey is the *Gate Theatre* (☎ 874 4045), on the south-east corner of Parnell Square, at the top of O'Connell St. It specialises in international classics and older Irish works with a touch of comedy by playwrights such as Oscar Wilde, George Bernard Shaw and Oliver Goldsmith.

South of the river, the *Gaiety Theatre* (☎ 677 1717), on King St South off Grafton St, was built in 1871 and is Dublin's oldest theatre; it hosts a variety of performances including modern plays and TV shows.

Previously known as the Palace Theatre and Dan Lowry's Music Hall, the 1892 *Olympia Theatre* (☎ 677 7744), on Dame St in Temple Bar, is the city's largest and second oldest theatre. Performances include rock concerts as well as plays. Over in the Liberties, the *Tivoli Theatre* (☎ 454 4472) is at 135 Francis St, Dublin 8, opposite the Iveagh Market. Experimental and less-commercial performances take place at the *City Arts Centre* (☎ 677 0643) at 23-25 Moss St, Dublin 2, and at the *Project Arts Centre* (☎ 671 2321), 39 Essex St East, Temple Bar; the Project Arts Centre has another venue

north of the Liffey at the Mint, Henry Place off Henry St.

The *International Bar* (☎ 677 9250), 23 Wicklow St, Dublin 2, sometimes hosts theatrical performances. Puppet performances are put on at the *Lambert Puppet Theatre & Museum* (☎ 280 0974) in Clifton Lane, Monkstown.

Theatrical performances also take place at:

Andrew's Lane Theatre
  9-17 St Andrew's Lane, Dublin 2 (☎ 679 5720)
Eblana Theatre
  Busáras, Dublin 1 (☎ 679 8404)
Focus Theatre
  6 Pembroke Place, Dublin 2 (☎ 676 3071)
Players' Theatre
  Trinity College, Dublin 2 (☎ 677 2941, ext 1239)
Riverbank Theatre
  10 Merchant's Quay, Dublin 8 (☎ 677 3370)

Concerts

Classical concerts are performed at the *National Concert Hall* (☎ 671 1888) in Earlsfort Terrace, Dublin 2, just south of St Stephen's Green. In summer there are lunch time concerts on Fridays with entry prices of around IR£4. Classical performances may also take place at the *Bank of Ireland Arts Centre* in Foster Place, at the *Municipal Gallery of Modern Art (Hugh Lane Gallery)* in Parnell Square or at the *Royal Dublin Society (RDS) Showground Concert Hall*.

Big rock concerts are held at the *Point Depot* (☎ 836 3633) at East Link Bridge, North Wall Quay, by the river and originally constructed as a railway terminus in 1878. The *Lansdowne Rd Stadium*, a mecca for rugby enthusiasts, is also used for big rock performances.

Bookings can be made either directly at the concert venue or through HMV (☎ 679 5334; 24-hour credit card bookings ☎ 456 9569), 65 Grafton St, Dublin 2.

Dance & Nightclubs

Leeson St Lower, to the south-east of St Stephen's Green, is the nightclub quarter of Dublin, with a string of basement clubs. They're easily pinpointed by the black-

Gay & Lesbian Entertainment Venues

Nightly gay venues in Dublin include the multilevel, ever-throbbing *George*, 89 South Great George St, still the most popular place in town for drinking and cruising, especially when it hosts the Block disco on Friday and Saturday nights; *Out on the Liffey*, 27 Upper Ormond Quay, a more relaxed and mixed-age pub; and *O'Looney's*, 13 High St near Christ Church Cathedral.

As in London, other places (including most dance clubs) are gay, lesbian and/or mixed on certain nights of the week only; for more details, consult the *Gay Community News* monthly freebie or the 'Queer' pages of the weekly what's-on magazine *In Dublin* for specific days and times.

Such 'one-off' venues include: Candy Club at the *Kitchen*, East Essex St; Tradespotting at the *Temple of Sound* in the Ormond Hotel on Ormond Quay (Monday); Mildred at the *Da Club* next to the Break for the Border club on Stephen St Lower (Tuesday); Little Green Bag at the *Mean Fiddler*, 26 Wexford St; Muscle at *Tin Pan Alley*, D'Olier St (Thursday); HAM at *POD*, Old Harcourt St railway station; the women-only Aquarium at *Tin Pan Alley* (Friday), and *Stonewallz* at Griffith College on the South Circular Rd (Saturday); the Playground at the *Temple of Sound*; and Cruz at the *Mission* on Eustace St, opposite the Irish Film Centre at No 6. ■

suited bouncers lined up outside, but the currently 'in' clubs change from one year (or even one month) to another. It's probably best just to follow the crowds – if it looks busy it's likely to be good. Leeson St clubs usually stay open until around 4 am or later and there are no admission charges, but drink prices make up for that; count on paying at least IR£15 for a bottle of basic wine.

Other popular venues usually have an entry charge. *Lillie's Bordello* (☎ 679 9204), Adam Court off Grafton St at the Trinity College end, opens daily 10 pm to 2 am. Nearby, young people crowd into *Rasher Geraghty's* (☎ 670 4220), 6 Wicklow St off Grafton St, on weekend nights.

Rather different is *Bad Bob's Big Fun Bar* (☎ 679 2992) in East Essex St in Temple Bar where there's a variety of music nightly, 4 pm to 2.30 am. Monday night offers 70s retro music. Entry ranges from IR£2 to IR£8. Still in Temple Bar, *Club M* (☎ 671 5622) in the Bloom's Hotel basement on Anglesea St is very popular.

In Temple Bar the *Eamonn Doran Imbibing Emporium* (☎ 679 9773), 3A Crown Alley, has food, drink and music nightly.

Break for the Border (☎ 478 0300), on Stephen St Lower, is a huge entertainment complex combining a bar with a Tex-Mex restaurant. *Major Tom's* (☎ 478 3266), on South King St (leading off Stephen's Green

North), is a popular bar and diner, with queues on Friday and Saturday nights. Nearby *Dublin Arts (DA) Club* (☎ 671 1130), 3 Clarendon Market, has an intimate atmosphere with live music (hiphop, blues etc) and comedy. Entry is IR£3.

Howl at the Moon (☎ 676 1717), in O'Dwyer's pub in Mount St, opens nightly 11 pm to 2 am and admission is IR£2 Sunday to Wednesday, IR£5 Thursday to Saturday. The over-30s *Danse Macabre* club upstairs opens Tuesday to Saturday.

Probably Dublin's flashiest nightclub is *The Pod* (☎ 478 0225), in Harcourt St, but don't even think of showing up there unless you've got the clothes to be seen in, and the cash to match.

Buskers

Dublin is well set up for free entertainment in the form of buskers, but contributions are always gratefully accepted. The best of the city's plentiful supply work busy Grafton St, where they're occasionally hassled by shopkeepers (for blocking access to their concerns) and by the police, but are mainly left to get on with it. At the Trinity College end of Grafton St, you'll usually trip over pavement artists, some distressingly young, busily chalking pictures around the statue of Molly Malone. Farther along the street you're likely to meet crooning folk singers, raucous rock bands or classical string quartets.

SPECTATOR SPORT

The Irish love of horse racing can be observed at *Leopardstown Race Course* (☎ 289 3607), about 10km south of the city centre in Foxrock. Greyhound racing takes place at *Harold's Cross Park* (☎ 497 1081), 151 Harold's Cross Rd near Rathmines, and *Shelbourne Park* (☎ 668 3502), Bridge Town Rd, Ringsend. For current information on horse and greyhound meetings call ☎ 1550 11 22 18 (24 hours).

The rugby season is from September to April and the soccer season from August to May; rugby and soccer international matches take place at the *Lansdowne Rd Stadium* (☎ 668 9300) near Ballsbridge. Hurling and Gaelic football games are held February to November at *Croke Park* (☎ 836 3222), headquarters of the Gaelic Athletic Association, north of the Royal Canal in Drumcondra. Call ☎ 1550 11 22 15 (24 hours) for the latest details.

THINGS TO BUY

If it's made in Ireland, you can probably buy it in Dublin. Popular purchases include fine Irish knitwear like the renowned Aran sweaters; jewellery with a Celtic influence, including Claddagh rings with two hands clasping a heart; books on Irish topics; crystal from Waterford, Galway, Tyrone and Tipperary; Irish coats of arms; china from Beleek; Royal Tara chinaware; and linen from Donegal. Citizens of non-EU countries can reclaim the VAT (sales tax) paid on purchases made at stores displaying a Cashback sticker; ask for details.

The bulk of things to buy are found south of the river. Dublin's main shopping street is pedestrianised Grafton St with the big department stores: long-established Brown Thomas/Switzers and the newer Marks & Spencer. At one end of Grafton St is the striking white-balconied St Stephen's Green Shopping Centre, but more interesting is the Powerscourt Townhouse Shopping Centre, a converted 18th century building, between

William St South and Clarendon St, worth visiting for the architecture even if you can't afford the designer wedding dresses. At the Trinity College end of Grafton St is Nassau St, with the House of Ireland (☎ 671 6133), at No 38, and the Kilkenny Shop (☎ 677 7066), at No 6, both selling a variety of Irish crafts. This is also where you'll find Knobs & Knockers (☎ 671 0288), at No 19, if you fancy a Dublin doorknocker to grace your front door.

Grafton St has most of the big, international-name stores, but Temple Bar is the area to head for if you want to find the one-offs. Claddagh Records (☎ 677 0262), 2 Cecilia St, for example, sells a wide range of Irish traditional and folk music, while China Blue (☎ 671 8785), in Merchant's Arch, Eager Beaver (☎ 677 3342), Crown Alley, and Flip (☎ 671 4249), 4 Upper Fownes St, are just a few of the designer clothes shops. Giving the lie to Dublin's squeaky clean image is Condom Power (☎ 677 8963), a sex shop by any other name, in the basement of 57 Dame St.

The Colonnades shop in Trinity College has a range of merchandise linked to 'The Book of Kells', while the Guinness Hop Store can kit you (and your fridge) out in Guinness advertising material. Also worth trying for small gifts and souvenirs is the Irish Celtic Craftshop (☎ 679 9912) at 10-12 Lord Edward St. For woollens, head for the Dublin Woollen Company (☎ 677 5014) at 41 Ormond Quay, The Sweater Shop (☎ 671 3270), 9 Wicklow St, or Blarney Woollen Mills (☎ 677 7066), 21-23 Nassau St. For bookshops, see that section under Information earlier.

Celtic Note (☎ 670 4157), 12 Nassau St, near the Kilkenny Shop, has CDs and tapes on traditional and modern Irish music.

If you're interested in antiques, Francis St (south of the Tivoli Theatre) in the Liberties is the place to go.

Of Dublin's markets, probably the most promising for visitors, with a good selection of second-hand books, crafts, pictures, jewellery and records, is Mother Redcap's (☎ 454 0652) in Back Lane, near Christ

Church Cathedral. It opens Friday to Sunday, 10 am to 5.30 pm.

North of the river, the Jervis Shopping Centre, 125 Abbey St Upper, is a huge mall, with department stores, a food court and the Republic's first branch of Boot's the chemist.

GETTING THERE & AWAY
Air
Dublin is Ireland's major international gateway airport with direct flights from Europe, North America and Asia. See the Getting There & Away chapter for details on flights and fares.

Airline offices in Dublin include:

Aer Lingus
40-41 O'Connell St Upper, Dublin 1; 13 St Stephen's Green (on the corner of Dawson St); Jury's Hotel, Ballsbridge; 12 George's St Upper, Dun Laoghaire; call ☎ 705 3333 for reservations, ☎ 705 6705 for arrival and departure enquiries
Aeroflot
15 Dawson St, Dublin 2 (☎ 679 1453)
Air France
29-30 Dawson St, Dublin 2 (☎ 677 8899)
Alitalia
4-5 Dawson St, Dublin 2 (☎ 677 5171)
British Airways Express
(☎ 1800 626 747)
British Midland
Nutley, Merrion Rd, Dublin 4 (☎ 283 8833)
Delta Airlines
24 Merrion Square, Dublin 2 (☎ 676 8080)
Iberia Airlines
54 Dawson St, Dublin 2 (☎ 677 9846)
Lufthansa
Dublin Airport (☎ 844 5544)
Manx Airlines
c/o British Midland (phone reservations only) (☎ 260 1588)
Qantas
Dublin Airport (☎ 874 7747)
Ryanair
3 Dawson St, Dublin 2 (☎ 677 4422); Dublin Airport (☎ 609 7800)
Sabena: Belgian World Airlines
Dublin Airport (☎ 844 5454)
Scandinavian Airlines (SAS)
Dublin Airport (☎ 844 5440)
Singapore Airlines
3rd Floor, 29 Dawson St, Dublin 2 (☎ 671 0722)
TAP Air Portugal
54 Dawson St, Dublin 2 (☎ 679 8844)
Virgin
30 Lower Abbey St, Dublin 1 (☎ 873 3388); Cityjet to London (☎ 844 5566)

Bus
Busáras, at Store St, just north of the Custom House and the River Liffey, is Bus Éireann's central bus station. Information on buses is available there from the Travel Centre (☎ 836 6111) open Monday to Saturday from 8.30 am to 7 pm, Sunday and public holidays from 9 am to 7 pm.

Standard one-way fares from Dublin include Cork IR£12 (five daily, 3½ hours), Donegal IR£10 (five daily, 4¼ hours), Galway IR£8 (three daily, 3¾ hours), Rosslare Harbour IR£9 (six daily, three hours), Tralee IR£14 (five daily, six hours) and Waterford IR£6 (seven daily, 2¾ hours). These fares are much cheaper than the regular railway fares; return fares are usually only a little more expensive than one way, and special deals are often available.

Buses to Belfast in Northern Ireland depart from Busáras four times a day Monday to Saturday (three times on Sunday).

Services from the Europa Buscentre in Belfast's Glengall St operate with the same frequency. The trip takes about three hours and costs IR£10.50 one way or IR£14 for a return within one month.

Train
For general information contact Iarnród Éireann Travel Centre (☎ 836 6222), 35 Abbey St Lower, open weekdays 9 am to 5 pm, Saturday 9 am to 1 pm. Trains fan out from Dublin. Connolly station (☎ 836 3333), just north of the Liffey and the city centre, is the station for Belfast, Derry, Sligo and other points north. Heuston station (☎ 836 5421), just south of the Liffey and well west of the centre, is the station for Cork, Galway, Killarney, Limerick, Wexford, Waterford and other points west, south and south-west.

See Train in the Getting Around chapter for more information.

Ferry

There are two direct services from Holyhead on the north-west tip of Wales – one to Dublin, and the other to Dun Laoghaire, the port on the southern side of Dublin Bay. A new terminal is being built in Dublin and should be operating by the time you read this.

See the Getting There & Away chapter for details.

Bus & Ferry

There are coaches direct from London and other UK centres to Dublin – see the Getting There & Away chapter for details.

GETTING AROUND
Dublin Airport

Dublin airport (☎ 844 4900) has a currency exchange counter in the baggage arrivals area; a branch of the Bank of Ireland on level 2 which keeps regular banking hours and also offers currency exchange; an Aer Rianta (the Irish airport authority) desk (☎ 704 4222) with information about the airport's facilities; a Bord Fáilte tourist office that also books accommodation; a CIE desk with information on trains and buses; plus shops, restaurants, bars, a hairdresser, a nursery, a church and car-hire counters. There's a post office in the car park atrium, open Monday to Friday 9 am to 5 pm, Saturday 9 am to 12.30 pm, and a left-luggage office (☎ 704 4633), open daily 6 am to 10 pm.

The airport is 10km north of the centre and can be reached from the city by bus or taxi.

Airport Bus Services The Airlink Express Coach (☎ 873 4222), operated by Dublin Bus, runs to/from Busáras (the central bus station north of the River Liffey in central Dublin) for IR£2.50/1.25. It also runs to/from Heuston station for IR£3/1.50. Both journeys take about half an hour. Timetables are available at the airport or in the city. Monday to Saturday, Busáras to airport services go about every 20 to 30 minutes from 7.05 am to 10.25 pm. On Sunday they operate less frequently from 7.35 am to 10.30 pm. Monday to Saturday airport to Busáras services operate 6.40 am to 11 pm.

On Sunday they run 7.10 am to 11 pm. The demand for seats sometimes exceeds the capacity of the bus, in which case it's worth getting a group together and sharing a taxi.

The alternative service is on the slower bus Nos 41 and 41A, which make a number of useful stops on the way, terminate near Eden Quay near O'Connell St and cost IR£1.10. The trip can take up to one hour, but they run more frequently than the express bus.

There are direct buses between the airport and Belfast.

Airport Taxi Services Taxis are subject to additional charges for baggage, extra passengers and 'unsocial hours'. However, a taxi usually costs about IR£10 between the airport and the centre, so between four people it's unlikely to be more expensive than the express bus. There's a supplementary charge of IR£1.30 from the airport to the city, but this charge doesn't apply from the city to the airport. Make sure the meter is switched on, as some Dublin airport taxi drivers can be as unscrupulous as their brethren anywhere else in the world.

Ferry Terminals

Buses go to Busáras from the Dublin Ferryport terminal (☎ 855 2222), Alexandra Rd, after all ferry arrivals. Buses also run from Busáras to meet ferry departures. For the morning ferry departure from Dublin, buses leave Busáras at 8.30 am. For the evening departure, buses leave Heuston station at 10 pm, the Busáras at 10.30 pm.

To travel between Dun Laoghaire's ferry terminal (☎ 880 1905) and Dublin, take bus No 46A to Fleet St in Temple Bar, bus No 7 to Eden Quay, or bus Nos 7A or 8 to Burgh Quay. Alternatively, take the DART (see the Train section later) to Pearse station (for south Dublin) or Connolly station (for north Dublin).

Connolly & Heuston Stations

The bus No 90 Rail Link runs between the two stations up to six times an hour at peak periods and costs a flat 60p. Connolly station is a short walk north of Busáras.

Bus

Dublin Bus (Bus Átha Cliath) information office (☎ 873 4222), 59 O'Connell St Upper, is open Monday 8.30 am to 5.30 pm, Tuesday to Friday 9 am to 5.30 pm, Saturday 9 am to 1 pm. The central bus station, or Busáras, is just north of the river, behind the Custom House and has a left-luggage facility (IR£1.50 per day).

The Dublin Bus Citizone stretches from Swords in the north to Ballybrack in the south. Fares range from 55p to IR£1.10. Outside the Citizone the maximum fare is IR£1.25. Ten-ride tickets offer discounts of between 50p and IR£2. One-day passes cost IR£3.30 for the bus, or IR£4.50 for bus and rail. Other passes include a one-week Citizone bus pass for IR£11 (students IR£9), or a bus and rail pass for IR£14.50 (plus IR£2 for a photo).

Nitelink late-night buses run from the College St, Westmoreland St, D'Olier St triangle hourly midnight to 3 am, Thursday, Friday and Saturday nights. They go as far north as Howth and Swords, and as far south as Dun Laoghaire and Rathfarnam.

Train

The Dublin Area Rapid Transport (DART) provides quick rail access to the coast as far north as Howth and as far south as Bray. Pearse station is convenient for central Dublin south of the Liffey, and Connolly station for north of the Liffey. Monday to Saturday there are services every 10 to 20 minutes, sometimes even more frequently, from around 6.30 am to midnight. Services are less frequent on Sunday. It takes about 30 minutes from Dublin to Bray at one extreme or Howth at the other. Dublin to Dun Laoghaire only takes about 15 to 20 minutes. There are also Suburban Rail services north as far as Dundalk, inland to Mullingar and south past Bray to Arklow.

A one-way DART ticket from Dublin costs IR£1.10 to Dun Laoghaire or Howth, IR£1.30 to Bray. Within the DART region, a one-day, unlimited-travel ticket costs IR£3.20. A ticket combining DART and Dublin Bus services costs IR£4.50 for an adult (IR£2.25 children, IR£6 family), but you can't use this ticket during Monday to Friday peak hours (7 to 9.45 am, 4.30 to 6.30 pm). A weekly DART and bus ticket costs IR£14.50 but requires an ID photo. A Dublin Explorer ticket allows you four days DART and bus travel for IR£10.50 but you can't use it until after 9.45 am Monday to Friday.

Bicycles can't be taken on DART services, but they can be taken on the less-frequent suburban train services, either in the guards' van or in a special compartment at the opposite end of the train from the engine. There's a IR£2 charge for transporting a bicycle up to 56km.

There are left-luggage lockers at Heuston station which cost IR£1.50 (or IR£4 in the large ones) per day. There's a left-luggage office at Connolly station which charges IR£1 per day, or IR£2 for backpacks.

Car & Motorcycle

As in most big cities, having a car in Dublin is as much a millstone as a convenience, though it can be useful for day trips outside the city limits.

There are parking meters around central Dublin and a selection of open and sheltered car parks. You don't have to go far from the centre to find free roadside parking, especially in north Dublin. However, the gardai warn visitors that it's safer to park in a supervised car park, since cars are often broken into even in broad daylight close to major tourist attractions. Cars with foreign number plates, which may contain valuable personal effects, are a prime target. Rental cars are also targeted, but nowadays most have no external indication that they're owned by a rental company.

When you're booking accommodation check on parking facilities. Some B&Bs which claim to offer private parking, especially in the centre, may have a sharing arrangement with a nearby hotel to use its car park – provided the car park hasn't been filled by the hotel patrons' cars.

Car Rental See the Getting Around chapter for information on car rental. A number of

DUBLIN

rental companies have desks at the airport, but other operators are based close to the airport and deliver cars for airport collection. Typical daily high-season rental rates with insurance and unlimited km are IR£45 to IR£90. Argus has particularly competitive prices. There are many smaller local operators with lower prices.

Some of the main rental companies in Dublin are:

Argus Rent-a-Car
    59 Terenure Rd East, Dublin 6 (☎ 490 4444); Dublin Tourism Office, Suffolk St, Dublin 2 (☎ 605 7701); Dublin Airport (☎ 844 4257)
Avis Rent-a-Car
    1 Hanover St East, Dublin 2 & Dublin Airport (☎ 605 7500/7555)
Budget Rent-a-Car
    1 Lower Drumcondra Rd, Dublin 9 (☎ 837 9611); Dublin Airport, Dublin 9 (☎ 844 5919)
Dan Dooley Car & Van Rentals
    42-43 Westland Row, Dublin 2 (☎ 677 2723); Dublin Airport (☎ 844 5156)
Hertz Rent-a-Car
    149 Leeson St Upper, Dublin 2 (☎ 660 2255); Dublin Airport (☎ 844 5466)
Murrays Europcar Car Rental
    Baggot St Bridge, Dublin 4 (☎ 668 1777); Dublin Airport (☎ 0600 2400)
Payless Bunratty Car Rentals
    Dublin Airport (☎ 844 5522)
Practical Car Rental
    545 Howth Rd, Dublin 3 (☎ 831 1944)
Thrifty Rent-a-Car
    14 Duke St, Dublin 2 (☎ 679 9420); Dublin Airport (☎ 844 4199)
Windsor Car Rentals
    Belgard Rd, Dublin 24 (☎ 451 6020, 1800 51 58 00)

Taxi

Taxis in Dublin are expensive with an IR£1.80 minimum price (flagfall) for the first half-mile or four minutes, then 10p for every one-eighth of a mile or one minute. In addition there are a number of extra charges – 40p for each extra passenger, 40p for each piece of luggage, IR£1.20 for telephone bookings and 40p for unsocial hours, which means 8 pm to 8 am and all day Sunday. Public holidays are even more unsocial and require a higher supplement.

Taxis can be hailed on the street and are found at taxi ranks around the city, including on O'Connell St in north Dublin, College Green in front of Trinity College and St Stephen's Green at the end of Grafton St. There are numerous taxi companies that will dispatch taxis by radio. Try City Cabs (☎ 872 2688) or National Radio Cabs (☎ 677 2222).

Phone the Garda Carriage Office on ☎ 475 5888 for complaints about taxis and queries regarding lost property.

Bicycle

Dublin isn't a bad place to get around by bicycle, as it is small enough and flat enough to make bike travel a breeze, but the absence of cycle lanes is a source of considerable local grievance. Many visitors explore farther afield by bicycle, a popular activity in Ireland despite the often less-than-encouraging weather.

All the hostels seem to offer secure bicycle parking areas, but if you're going to have a bike stolen anywhere in Ireland, Dublin is where it would happen. Lock your bike up well. Surprisingly, considering how popular bicycles are in Dublin, there's a scarcity of suitable bicycle parking facilities. Grafton St and Temple Bar are virtually devoid of places to lock a bike. Elsewhere, there are signs on many likely stretches of railing announcing that bikes must not be parked there. Nevertheless, there are places where you can park your bike, such as the Grafton St corner of St Stephen's Green and in Trinity College.

Bicycle Rental Typical rental costs are IR£7 to IR£10 a day or IR£30 to IR£35 a week. Some hostels offer bike rental.

Rent-a-Bike Ireland has a number of offices around the country including Belfast and offers one-way rentals between its outlets for an extra IR£5. The head office is at the Bike Store (☎ 872 5399), 58 Gardiner St Lower, Dublin 1, round the corner from Isaac's Hostel and a stone's throw from Busáras. It can arrange cycling tours staying in either B&Bs or hostels.

Raleigh Rent-a-Bike agencies can be found all over Ireland, north and south of the border. Contact them at Raleigh Ireland (☎ 626 1333), Raleigh House, Kylemore Rd, Dublin 10. Raleigh agencies in Dublin include:

CGL
    9 Townyard Lane, Malahide (☎ 845 4275)
Joe Daly
    Main St Lower, Dundrum, Dublin 14 (☎ 298 1485)
Dublin Bike Hire
    27 North Great Georges St, Dublin 1 (☎ 878 8473)
Hollingsworth Cycle
    14/54 Templeogue Rd, Templeogue, Dublin 6 (☎ 490 5094, 492 0026)

Around Dublin

Although the centre of Dublin is set back from the bay, there are a number of seaside suburbs around the curve of Dublin Bay. Dun Laoghaire to the south and Howth to the north are historic ports and popular day trips from the city. Connected to central Dublin by the convenient DART rail service, they also make interesting alternatives to staying in the city. Malahide with its castle, the imposing Anglo-Irish mansion of Newbridge House, and the village of Swords are other Dublin-area attractions.

DUN LAOGHAIRE
Dun Laoghaire (pronounced 'dun leary'), only 13km south-east of central Dublin, is both a busy harbour with ferry connections to Britain and a popular resort. From 1821, when King George IV departed from here after a visit to Ireland, until Irish independence in 1922, the port was known as Kingstown. There are many B&Bs in Dun Laoghaire, they're a bit cheaper than in central Dublin and the fast and frequent DART rail connections make it easy to stay out here.

History
There was a coastal settlement at the site of Dun Laoghaire over 1000 years ago, but it was little more than a small fishing village until 1767, when the first pier was constructed. Dun Laoghaire grew more rapidly after that time and the Sandycove Martello Tower was erected in the early 19th century, as there was great fear of an invasion from Napoleonic France.

Construction of the harbour was proposed in 1815 to provide a refuge for ships unable to reach the safety of Dublin Harbour in inclement weather. Originally, a single pier was proposed, but engineer John Rennie proposed to build two massive piers enclosing a huge 100 hectare artificial harbour. Work began in 1817 and by 1823 the workforce comprised 1000 men. However, despite huge expenditure, the harbour wasn't completed until 1842, Carlisle Pier wasn't added until 1859 and parts of the West Pier stonework have never been finished. The total cost approached £1 million, an astronomical figure in the mid-19th century.

Shipping services began to/from Liverpool and Holyhead, and the completion of a rail link to Dublin in 1834 made this a state-of-the-art transport centre. The line from Dublin was the first railway anywhere in Ireland. It's only just over 100km from Dun Laoghaire to Holyhead in Wales and a ferry service has operated across the Irish Sea on this route since the mid-19th century.

The first mail steamers took nearly six hours to make the crossing, but by 1860 the crossing time was reduced to less than four hours and, on one occasion in 1887, the paddle steamer the *Ireland* made the crossing in less than three hours. Car ferries were introduced in the early 1960s. During WWI the RMS *Leinster* was torpedoed by a German U-boat 25km from Dun Laoghaire and over 500 lives were lost.

Orientation & Information
George's St Upper and Lower, which runs parallel to the coast, is the main shopping street through Dun Laoghaire. The huge harbour is sheltered by the encircling arms of the East and West Piers. Sandycove with the James Joyce Museum and the Forty Foot

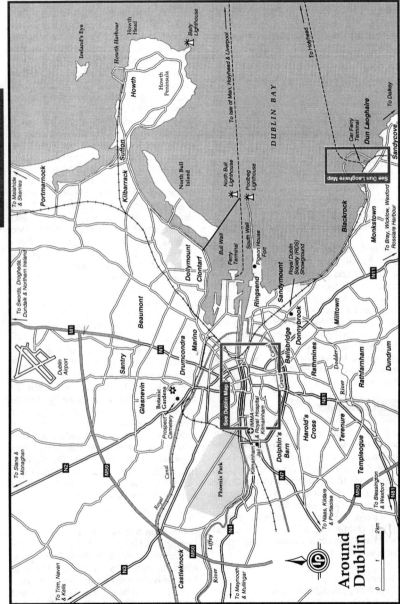

Pool is about a km east of central Dun Laoghaire.

The Dublin Tourism office, in the new ferry terminal, opens daily 10 am to 9 pm. A bureau de change, also in the terminal, opens for ferry arrivals and departures. The older Carlisle Terminal is closed. The post office, on George's St Upper opens Monday and Wednesday 9 am to 6 pm, Tuesday 9.30 am to 6 pm, Thursday and Friday 9 am to 6 pm and Saturday 9 am to 5.30 pm. At 5 George's St Upper, is a branch (☎ 280 5528) of Eason, the newsagent and bookshop chain.

The Harbour

The 1290m East and 1548m West Piers, each ending in a lighthouse from the 1850s, have always been popular for walking (especially the East Pier), bird-watching and fishing (particularly from the end of the West Pier). You can also ride a bicycle out along the piers (bottom level only). In the 19th century the practice of 'scorching' – riding out along the pier at breakneck speed – became so prevalent that bicycles were banned for some time.

The East Pier has an 1890s bandstand and a memorial to Captain Boyd and the crew of the Dun Laoghaire lifeboat who were drowned in a rescue attempt. Near the end of the pier is the 1852 anemometer, one of the first of these wind-speed measuring devices to be installed anywhere in the world. The East Pier ends at the East Pier Battery with a lighthouse and a gun saluting station, which is useful when visiting VIPs arrive by sea.

The harbour has long been a popular yachting centre and the Royal Irish Yacht Club's building, dating from around 1850, was the first purpose-built yacht club in Ireland. The Royal St George Yacht Club's building dates from 1863 and that of the National Yacht Club from 1876. The world's first one-design sailing boat class started life at Dun Laoghaire with a dinghy design known as the *Water Wag*. A variety of specifically Dublin Bay one-design classes still race here, as do Mirrors and other popular small sailing boats.

Carlisle Pier, opened in 1859, is also known as the Mailboat Pier and was modi-fied to handle drive-on/drive-off car ferries in 1970. With the completion of the new ferry terminal in 1995, the terminal here closed. St Michael's Pier, also known as the Car Ferry, was added in 1969. Over on the West Pier side of the harbour are two anchored lightships which have now been replaced by automatic buoys.

National Maritime Museum

Between Haigh Terrace and Adelaide St, the museum (☎ 280 0969) is housed in the Mariner's Church, built in 1837 'for the benefit of sailors in men-of-war, merchant ships, fishing boats and yachts'. The window in the chancel is a replica of the Five Sisters window at York Minster in England. The museum is open May to September 1 to 5 pm Tuesday to Sunday; entry is IR£1.50/80p.

Exhibits include a French ship's longboat captured at Bantry in 1796 from Wolfe Tone's abortive invasion. The huge clock-work-driven Great Baily Light Optic came from the Baily Lighthouse on Howth Peninsula. It operated from 1902 until 1972, when it was replaced with an electrically powered lens.

There's a model of the *Great Eastern* (1858), the early steam-powered vessel built by English engineer Isambard Kingdom Brunel, which proved a commercial failure as a passenger ship but successfully laid the first transatlantic telegraph cable between Ireland and North America. There are various items from the German submarine U19 which landed Sir Roger Casement in Kerry in 1916 (see the Sandycove section). These were donated 50 years after the event by the U-boat's captain, Raimund Weisbach.

Around the Town

Nothing remains of the *dún* or fort that gave Dun Laoghaire its name, as it was totally destroyed during the construction of the railway line. The railway line from Dun Laoghaire towards Dalkey was built along the route of an earlier line known as the Metals. This line was used to bring stone for the harbour construction from the quarries at Dalkey Hill. By means of a pulley system,

DUBLIN

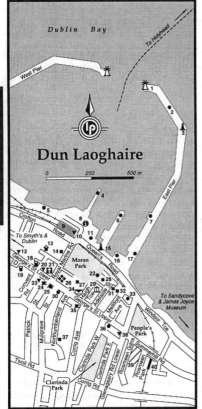

PLACES TO STAY
13   Old School House Hostel
14   Port View Hotel
27   Royal Marine Hotel
28   Bayside B&B
31   Kingston Hotel
32   Hotel Pierre
37   Innisfree B&B
39   Rosmeen Gardens B&Bs

PLACES TO EAT
10   Restaurant Na Mara
12   The Black Tulip
20   Ann's Bakery
23   Lal Qila
24   Ritz Café
35   The Coffee Bean
38   Outlaws Restaurant

PUBS
18   Cooney's
19   Dunphy's

OTHER
1   Lighthouse
2   Anemometer
3   Lifeboat Memorial
4   St Michael's Pier
5   Royal Irish Yacht Club
6   Carlisle Pier
7   Bandstand
8   Ferry Terminal & Dublin Tourism Office
9   Dun Laoghaire DART Station
11   Royal St George Yacht Club
15   King George IV Monument
16   National Yacht Club
17   Compass Pointer
21   St Michael's Church
22   Christ the King Sculpture
25   Eason Bookshop
26   Dun Laoghaire Shopping Centre
29   National Maritime Museum
30   Aer Lingus
33   Oceantec Adventure Dive Shop
34   Post Office
36   Star Laundry
40   Sandycove & Glasthule DART Station

the laden trucks trundling down to the harbour pulled the empty ones back up to the quarry.

On the waterfront is a curious monument to King George IV to commemorate his visit in 1821. It consists of an obelisk balanced on four stone balls, one of which is missing as a result of an IRA bomb attack.

On the other side of the coast road is the *Christ the King* sculpture, which was created in Paris in 1926, bought in 1949 and then put in storage until 1978 because the religious authorities decided they didn't really like it all that much.

Sandycove

Only 1km south of Dun Laoghaire is Sandycove, with a pretty little beach and the Martello Tower that houses the James Joyce Museum. Sir Roger Casement, who attempted to organise a German-backed Irish freedom force during WWI, was born here in 1864. He was captured after being landed in County Kerry from a German U-boat and executed by the British as a traitor in 1916.

James Joyce Museum The Martello Tower, which houses the museum (☎ 280 9265), is where the action begins in James Joyce's epic novel *Ulysses*. The museum was opened in 1962 by Sylvia Beach, the Paris-based publisher who first dared to put *Ulysses* into print, and has photographs, letters, documents, various editions of Joyce's work and two death masks of Joyce on display.

A string of Martello towers were built around the coast of Ireland between 1804 and 1815 in case of invasion by Napoleon's forces. The granite tower stands 12m high with walls 2.5m thick and was copied from a tower at Cape Mortella in Corsica. Originally, the entrance to the tower led straight into what is now the 'upstairs'. Other tower sites included Dalkey Island, Killiney and Bray, all to the south of Dun Laoghaire, and to the north, Howth and Ireland's Eye, the island off Howth.

There are fine views from the tower. To the south-east you can see Dalkey Island with its signal tower and Killiney Hill with its obelisk. Howth Head is visible on the northern side of Dublin Bay. There's another Martello Tower not far to the south near Bullock Harbour.

The tower is open April to October, 10 am to 1 pm and 2 to 5 pm Monday to Saturday, 2 to 6 pm Sunday. Entry is IR£2.40/1.15 (students IR£2); family tickets are IR£7.

You can get to the tower by a 30 minute walk along the seafront from Dun Laoghaire Harbour, a 15 minute walk from Sandycove & Glasthule DART station or a five minute walk from Sandycove Ave West, which is served by bus No 8.

Forty Foot Pool Below the Martello Tower is the Forty Foot Pool, an open-air sea water bathing pool that took its name from the army regiment, the Fortieth Foot, which was stationed at the tower until it was disbanded in 1904. At the close of the first chapter of *Ulysses*, Buck Mulligan heads off to the Forty Foot Pool for a morning swim. A morning wake-up here is still a Dun Laoghaire tradition, winter or summer. In

Holiday in Sandycove

In 1904, Oliver St John Gogarty – the 'stately, plump' Buck Mulligan of *Ulysses* – rented the Martello Tower from the army for the princely sum of £8 a year and James Joyce stayed there briefly. The stay was actually less than a week, as another guest, Samuel Chenevix Trench (who appears in *Ulysses* as the Englishman, Haines), had a nightmare one night and dealt with it by drawing his revolver and taking a shot at the fireplace. Gogarty took the gun from him, yelled 'Leave him to me' and fired at the sauce-pans on the shelf above Joyce's bed. Relations between Gogarty and Joyce had been uneasy after Joyce had accused him of snobbery in a poem, so Joyce, taking this incident as a hint that he wasn't welcome, left the next morning. He was soon to leave Ireland as well, eloping to the Continent with Nora Barnacle in 1904.

Trench's aim didn't improve, as just five years later he shot himself, fatally, in the head. ■

fact, a winter dip isn't much braver than a summer one since the water temperature only varies by about 5°C, winter or summer. Basically, it's always bloody cold.

Originally nudist and for men only, pressure from female bathers eventually opened this public stretch of water to both sexes, despite strong opposition from the 'forty foot gentlemen'. They eventually compromised with the ruling that a 'togs must be worn' sign would now apply after 9 am. Prior to that time nudity prevails and swimmers are still predominantly 'forty foot gentlemen', and the odd brave woman.

Activities

A series of walks in the Dun Laoghaire area make up the signposted Dun Laoghaire Way. The *Heritage Map of Dun Laoghaire* includes a map and notes on the seven separate walks.

Scuba divers head for the waters around Dalkey Island and to Muglands, a small rocky island further out. Oceantec Adventures (☎ 280 1083; fax 284 3885) is a dive shop at 10-11 Marine Terrace. It rents diving equipment at IR£25 a day; a local dive costs

IR£12.50. It's also a fully accredited PADI centre and runs courses year-round.

Places to Stay

As a major ferry port, Dun Laoghaire has plenty of accommodation especially in the form of B&Bs.

Hostel Not far from the ferry terminal, the IHH *Old School House Hostel* (☎ 280 8777), is off Eblana Ave. It has a large kitchen area and lounge, opens all year and charges IR£7.95 to IR£10 for dorm beds, IR£12 per person in private rooms.

B&Bs Rosmeen Gardens is packed with B&Bs. To get there, just walk south along George's St, the main shopping street; Rosmeen Gardens is the first street after Glenageary Rd Lower, directly opposite People's Park. *Mrs Callanan* (☎ 280 6083) is at No 1, *Rathoe* (☎ 280 8070) is at No 12, *Rosmeen House* (☎ 280 7613) is at No 13, *Mrs McGloughlin* (☎ 280 4333) is at No 27, *Annesgrove* (☎ 280 9801) is at No 28 and *Mrs Dunne* (☎ 280 3360) is at No 30. Prices here are IR£20 to IR£25 for singles, IR£35 to IR£44 for doubles.

There are also B&Bs on Northumberland Ave, like *Innisfree* (☎ 280 5598) at No 31. With views of the harbour, *Bayside* (☎ 280 4660) at Seafront, 5 Haddington Terrace just past Adelaide St, is slightly more expensive, with singles/doubles for IR£30/40. Others can be found on Mellifont and Corrig Aves.

Hotels Dun Laoghaire has a number of attractively situated seaside hotels.

The small *Port View Hotel* (☎ 280 1663; fax 280 0447) is on Royal Marine Rd. About half of the 20 rooms have ensuite facilities and these better rooms cost IR£38/59 for singles/doubles. The larger *Hotel Pierre* (☎ 280 0291; fax 284 3332), is also close to the waterfront at 3 Victoria Terrace. There are 36 rooms, almost all of them with ensuite facilities at IR£35/65 including breakfast. Close by, on Haddington Terrace, is the *Kingston Hotel* (☎ 280 1810; fax 280 1237)

with 24 rooms, all with attached bathroom, costing IR£39/63 with breakfast.

The port's premier hotel is the *Royal Marine Hotel* (☎ 280 1911; fax 280 1089) on Royal Marine Rd, only a few minutes' walk from Dun Laoghaire's Carlisle Terminal. There are 104 rooms, all with attached bathroom, costing from IR£90/100.

Places to Eat

Fast Food & Cafés Fast-food outlets including branches of *La Pizza* and *Abrakebabra* can be found on George's St. Just off George's St on Patrick St is the *Ritz Café* for traditional fish & chips.

Everything is baked on the premises at *Ann's Bakery*, which has good tea and snacks during the day. *The Coffee Bean*, on George's St Upper near the corner of Corrig Ave, is popular at lunch times, with good coffee and snacks; quiche is IR£2.45, lasagne IR£3.45.

Restaurants Open in the evenings from 6 pm, *Outlaws* (☎ 284 2817), 62 George's St Upper, offers steak, burgers (including a vegeburger) and Tex-Mex fare; fajitas are IR£6.95. *Lal Qila* (☎ 280 5623), on Convent Rd just off George's St Lower, has a standard Indian menu; chicken masala is IR£6.95.

Near the harbour, *Restaurant Na Mara* (☎ 280 6787), in what used to be the railway station, is more expensive but offers a four-course dinner for IR£17.95; the emphasis is on seafood. Open for lunch and dinner, *The Black Tulip* (☎ 280 5318), 107 George's St Lower, is another fancier restaurant which offers excellent seafood; baked salmon is IR£12.95.

Entertainment

Popular pubs include *Cooney's*, 88 George's St Lower, and *Dunphy's*, right across the road at No 41. Farther out along George's St is *Smyth's*, with its seafaring interior and music five nights a week. *Hotel Pierre* is noted for its jazz performances, and the *Purty Kitchen & Bar* on the Old Dunleary Rd often has traditional Irish music, or rock, country and comedy.

Getting There & Away

See the introductory Getting There & Away chapter for details of the ferries between Dun Laoghaire and Holyhead in the UK.

Bus Nos 7, 7A, 8, or 46A or the DART rail service take you from Dublin to Dun Laoghaire. It only takes 15 to 20 minutes to cover the 12km by DART with a day return fare of IR£2.10.

DALKEY

South of Sandycove is Dalkey (Deilginis), which has the remains of a number of old castles. On Castle St, the main street, two 16th century castles face each other – the **Goat Castle** and **Archbold's Castle**. On the same street is the ancient **St Begnet's Church**, dating from the 9th century. **Bulloch Castle** overlooking Bullock Harbour, north of town, was built by St Mary's Abbey in Dublin in the 12th century.

To the south there are good **views** from the small park at Sorrento Point and from Killiney Hill.

Dalkey Quarry is a popular site for rock climbers, and originally provided most of the granite for the gigantic piers at Dun Laoghaire Harbour.

Dalkey has several holy wells, including **St Begnet's Holy Well** (the waters of which are reputed to cure rheumatism) on nine-hectare Dalkey Island which lies a few hundred metres offshore. There's plenty of birdlife here and the waters around the island are popular with scuba divers.

A number of rocky swimming pools are found along the Dalkey coast.

Dalkey is on the DART suburban line or you can catch bus No 8 from Burgh Quay.

HOWTH

The bulbous Howth Peninsula delineates the northern end of Dublin Bay. Howth (Binn Éadair) town is only 15km from central Dublin and is easily reached by DART train or by simply following the Clontarf Rd out around the north bay shoreline. En route you pass Clontarf, site of the pivotal clash between Celtic and Viking forces at the Battle of Clontarf in 1014. Farther along is North Bull Island, a wildlife sanctuary where many migratory birds pause in winter. Howth is a popular excursion from Dublin and has developed as a residential suburb.

History

Howth's name (which rhymes with 'both') has Viking origins, and comes from the Danish word *hoved* or head. Howth Harbour dates from 1807-09 and was the main Dublin harbour for the packet boats from England. The Howth Rd was built to ensure rapid transfer of incoming mail and dispatches from the harbour to the city. The replacement of sailing packets with steam packets in 1818 reduced the transit time from Holyhead to seven hours, but Howth's period of importance was short because, by 1813, the harbour was already showing signs of silting up. It was superseded by Dun Laoghaire in 1833. Howth's most famous arrival was King George IV, who visited Ireland in 1821 and is chiefly remembered because he staggered off the boat in a highly inebriated state. He did manage to leave his footprint at the point where he stepped ashore on the West Pier.

In 1914 Robert Erskine Childers' yacht, *Asgard*, brought a cargo of 900 rifles in to the port to arm the nationalists. During the Civil War, Childers was court-martialled by his former comrades and executed by firing squad for illegal possession of a revolver. The *Asgard* is now on display at Kilmainham Jail.

Howth Town

Howth is a pretty little town built on steep streets running down to the waterfront. Although the harbour's role as a shipping port has long gone, Howth is now a major fishing centre and yachting harbour.

St Mary's Abbey stands in ruins near the centre and was originally founded in 1042, supposedly by the Viking, King Sitric, who also founded the original church on the site of Christ Church Cathedral in Dublin. It was amalgamated with the monastery on Ireland's Eye in 1235. Some parts of the ruins date from that time, but most of it was built in the 15th and 16th centuries. The tomb of Christopher St Lawrence (Lord Howth), in the south-east corner, dates from around 1470. You can walk around the abbey grounds, but to enter the abbey itself you need to obtain the key (instructions on where to get it are on the inside gate) from the caretaker.

Howth Castle & Demesne

Howth Castle's demesne was acquired by the Norman noble Sir Almeric Tristram in 1177 and has remained in the family ever since, though the unbroken chain of male succession finally came to an end in 1909. The family name was changed to St Lawrence when Sir Almeric won a battle at, so he believed, St Lawrence's behest.

Originally built in 1564, the St Lawrence family's Howth Castle has been much restored and rebuilt over the years, most recently in 1910 by the British architect Sir Edwin Lutyens.

A legend relates that in 1575 Grace O'Malley, the 'Queen' of western Ireland, dropped by the castle on her way back from a visit to England's Queen Elizabeth I. When the family claimed they were busy having dinner and refused her entry, she kidnapped the son and only returned him when Lord Howth promised that in future his doors would always be open at meal times. As a result, so it's claimed, for many years the castle extended an open invitation to hungry passers-by.

Despite Grace O'Malley's actions, the castle is no longer open, but you can visit the gardens in spring and summer and there's a popular golf course beyond the castle.

The castle gardens are noted for their rhododendrons, which bloom in May and June, for their azaleas and for a long stretch of 10m-high beech hedges planted back in 1710. The castle grounds also have the ruins of 16th century **Corr Castle** and an ancient dolmen known as **Aideen's Grave**. It's said that Aideen died of a broken heart after her husband was killed at the Battle of Gavra near Tara in 184 AD, but that's probably mere legend as the dolmen is thought to be much older.

To get to the castle, turn right out of the station, follow the road round then turn left at the sign for the Deer Park Hotel and National Transport Museum.

National Transport Museum

In a green, corrugated-iron, barn-like building, the National Transport Museum (☎ 847 5623) has a variety of exhibits. These include double-decker buses, fire engines and trams including a Hill of Howth tram which operated from 1901 to 1959. June to August it's open daily 10 to 6 pm; and the rest of the year it's open weekends 2 to 5 pm. Entry is IR£1.50/50p. You can reach the museum by entering the castle gates and turning right just before the castle.

Around the Peninsula

The 171m **Summit**, to the south-east of the town, offers views across Dublin Bay to the Wicklow Hills. From the Summit you can walk to the top of the Ben of Howth, which has a cairn said to mark a 2000-year-old Celtic royal grave. The 1814 **Baily Lighthouse** at the south-east corner is on the site of an old stone fort or 'bailey' and can be reached by a dramatic clifftop walk. There was an earlier hilltop beacon here in 1670.

Ireland's Eye

A short distance offshore from Howth is Ireland's Eye, a rocky sea-bird sanctuary with the ruins of a 6th century monastery. There's a **Martello Tower** at the north-west end of the island, where boats from Howth land, while the east end plummets into the sea in a spectacularly sheer rock face. As well as the sea birds overhead, you can see young birds on the ground during the nesting season. Seals can also be spotted around the island.

Doyle & Sons (☎ 831 4200) take boats out to the island from the East Pier of Howth Harbour during the summer, daily if there are enough people from 11 am. The cost is IR£4/2 return. Don't wear shorts if you're planning to visit the monastery ruins, as they're surrounded by a thicket of stinging

TONY WHEELER

TOM SMALLMAN

TOM SMALLMAN

TOM SMALLMAN

PAT YALE

PAT YALE

Dublin
A: Dublin Castle yard entrance
B: The Custom House
C: Georgian houses, Fitzwilliam Square
D: Famine memorial statues
E: James Joyce Centre
F: Bloomsday revellers

TOM SMALLMAN

TONY WHEELER

TONY WHEELER

TONY WHEELER

TONY WHEELER

TOM SMALLMAN

A	B
C	D
E	F

Dublin
A: St Stephen's Green
B: *Sphere with Sphere*
C: The Temple Bar
D: O'Neills Pub
E: Christ Church Cathedral
F: Traditional dancing beside Pearse
   Museum, Rathfarnham

nettles. And take your garbage away with you – too many island visitors don't.

Farther north from Ireland's Eye is **Lambay Island**, a more remote and even more important sea-bird sanctuary.

Places to Stay

There are several B&Bs along Thormanby and Nashville Rds with typical overnight costs of IR£15 to IR£22 per person. *Gleannna-Smol* (☎ 832 2936) is on Nashville Rd, while *Hazelwood* (☎ 839 1391) and *Highfield* (☎ 832 3936) are both on Thormanby Rd.

The *St Lawrence Hotel* (☎ 832 2643), on Harbour Rd directly overlooking the harbour, has 11 rooms, all with attached bathroom. Rooms cost IR£30 per person including breakfast.

By the golf course in the grounds of Howth Castle is the larger *Deer Park Hotel* (☎ 832 2624), charging IR£64/100 a single/double. On the Dublin side of Howth village there are good views of Ireland's Eye from the more upmarket *Howth Lodge Hotel* (☎ 832 1010) where rooms with attached bathroom cost IR£130 per person in the high season.

Places to Eat

If you want to buy food and prepare it yourself, Howth has fine seafood and you can buy it fresh from the string of seafood shops on the West Pier.

Pizza Milano (☎ 839 3045), 53 Harbour Rd, has pizzas for IR£3.95 to IR£7.95 during the day; upstairs, *Porto Fino's Ristorante* (☎ 839 3054) serves Italian food in the evenings with pasta for IR£6.50 to IR£9.50. Other economical alternatives include Howth's plentiful supply of pubs, like *Pier House* (☎ 832 4510) on the East Pier and *Ye Old Abbey Tavern* (☎ 839 0307) near St Mary's Abbey; the *St Lawrence Hotel* (☎ 832 2643) by the harbour has a carvery restaurant that opens daily.

The King Sitric (☎ 32 5235), near the East Pier, is known for its fine seafood and is open for lunch and dinner Monday to Saturday.

Most mains are IR£18 to IR£21; wild Irish salmon costs IR£18.50

Entertainment

Howth's pubs are noted for their jazz performances and some also provide traditional Irish music. You can try *The Cock Tavern*, near the entrance to the abbey grounds, the *Baily Court Hotel*, on Thormanby Rd, the *Waterside Inn*, the *Pier House*, both on Harbour Rd, *Ye Old Abbey Tavern*, on Main St, and others – they're all likely to have something on and are all in the centre.

Getting There & Away

The easiest, quickest way to Howth from Dublin is by the DART, which whisks you there in just over 20 minutes for IR£2.10 return.

SWORDS

The village of Swords (Sord) is 16km north of Dublin and 5km west of Malahide. The Archbishop of Dublin built a fortified palace here in the 12th century, but the castellated walls date from the 15th century and numerous other modifications were made over the centuries. The windows to the right of the main entrance date from around 1250.

Swords also had an ancient monastery, but today only its 23m-high round tower remains and that was rebuilt several times between 1400 and 1700. It stands in the grounds of the Church of Ireland. The body of Brian Ború was kept overnight in the monastery after his death in 1014 at the Battle of Clontarf, when his forces defeated the Vikings.

Bus Nos 33 and 33B depart from Dublin's Eden Quay every half-hour or so and take less than an hour to get to Swords.

MALAHIDE

Malahide (Mullach Ide) is 13km north of Dublin on the coast beyond Howth. It has virtually been swallowed by Dublin's northward expansion, although it still has its own pretty marina. The well-kept 101 hectares of the Malahide Demesne, which contains Malahide Castle, is the town's principal

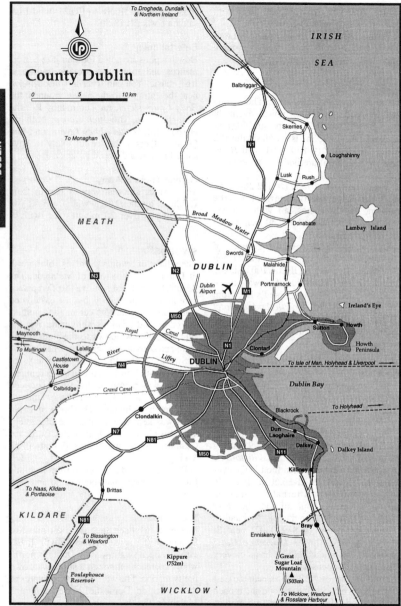

attraction. Talbot Botanic Gardens are next to the castle and the extensive Fry Model Railway is in the castle grounds.

Malahide Castle

Despite the vicissitudes of Irish history, the Talbot family managed to keep Malahide Castle (☎ 846 2184) under their control from 1185 to 1976 apart from a short interlude while Cromwell was around (1649-60). The oldest part of the castle is a three storey, 12th century tower house; otherwise it's the usual hotchpotch of additions and renovations. The facade is flanked by circular towers added in 1765.

The castle is packed with furniture and paintings, and Puck, the family ghost, is still in residence. Highlights include the 16th century oak room with its decorative carvings and the medieval Great Hall with family portraits, a minstrel's gallery and a gigantic painting of the Battle of the Boyne.

The castle's opening hours vary. All year it's open Monday to Friday 10 am to 12.45 pm and 2 to 5 pm. November to March it opens weekends and holidays 2 to 5 pm. April to October weekend hours are 11.30 am to 6 pm. Entry is IR£2.95/1.60 (students IR£2.45). Combined tickets are available for the castle and railway (see below) and for the castle and Newbridge House.

Fry Model Railway

Ireland's biggest model railway layout covers 240 sq metres and authentically displays much of Dublin and Ireland's rail and public transport system, including the DART line and Irish Sea ferry services in O-gauge (track width of 32mm). There's also a separate room exhibiting railway models and other memorabilia.

April to September, it's open Monday to Thursday 10 am to 1 pm and 2 to 6 pm, Saturday 11 am to 1 pm and 2 to 6 pm, Sunday and holidays 2 to 6 pm. June to September, it also opens Friday 10 am to 1 pm and 2 to 6 pm. October to March, it opens weekends and holidays 2 to 5 pm. Entry is IR£2.65/1.50 (students IR£2). You can get

combined castle and railway tickets for IR£4.60/2.50 (students IR£3.50).

Getting There & Away

Bus No 42 from Beresford Place, near Busáras, takes about 45 minutes to Malahide. Alternatively, take a Drogheda suburban train to Malahide station, only 10 minutes' walk from the park.

NEWBRIDGE HOUSE

North of Malahide at Donabate is Newbridge House (☎ 843 6534), a historic 1737 Georgian mansion with fine plasterwork, a private museum, an impressive kitchen and a large traditional farm with cows, pigs and exotic chickens. In the stables look out for the Lord Chancellor's elaborate coach, built in 1790. It was painted black for Queen Victoria's funeral and it wasn't until 1982 that the paint was scraped off to reveal the glittering masterpiece underneath.

Newbridge House is open April to September, 10 am to 1 pm and 2 to 5 pm Tuesday to Friday, 11 am to 6 pm Saturday, 2 to 6 pm Sunday and holidays. October to March, it opens weekends and holidays 2 to 5 pm. Entry is IR£2.75/1.50 (students IR£2.45). Combined Newbridge House and Malahide Castle tickets cost IR£4.70/2.35 (students IR£3.70).

Getting There & Away

Donabate is 19km north of Dublin. Bus no 33B runs from Eden Quay to Donabate village. You can also get there on the suburban rail service from Connolly or Pearse stations.

LUSK HERITAGE CENTRE

On the way to Skerries you'll spot the dominating turrets of Lusk (Lusca) church, where a 10th century round tower stands beside and joined to a medieval tower. The various floors of the tower are now used to display a selection of medieval and later effigies from churches in the County Dublin area.

The much duller 19th century nave contains Willie Monks' dusty, somewhat forlorn collection of household and other items. The heritage centre (☎ 843 7683) only opens mid-June to mid-September, 2 to 5 pm, Wednesday and Sunday (but the last entry is at 4.15 pm). Admission is IR£1/40p. Bus No 33 from Eden Quay takes just under an hour to get there.

SKERRIES

The sleepy seaside resort of Skerries (Na Sceiri) is 30km north of Dublin. St Patrick is said to have made his arrival in Ireland here at what is now called St Patrick's Island which has an old church ruin; he also visited Red Island, now attached to the mainland.

There's a good cliff walk south from Skerries to the bay of Loughshinny.

At low tide you can walk to Shenick's, a small island off Skerries. Colt Island is another small island. Farther offshore is Rockabill with a lighthouse. The 7th century oratory and holy well of St Moibhi and the ruins of Baldongan Castle are all near the town.

Getting There & Away

Bus No 33 departs from Dublin's Eden Quay about every hour and takes just over an hour to reach Skerries. Trains from Connolly station are less frequent but slightly faster.

County Wicklow

Not all of Ireland's impressive landscapes are in the west of the country. Barely 16km south of Dublin, you can drive for an hour through wild and desolate scenery without seeing more than a handful of houses or people. The most beautiful parts of County Wicklow (Cill Mhantáin) fall within a broad north-south swathe running down the centre of the mountains, beginning at Glencree close to Dublin and ending near Avoca. Glendalough has some of the country's best preserved early Christian remains. At 132km, the Wicklow Way is the longest trail in the country, providing good hiking and cycling opportunities.

County Wicklow's rolling granite hills are the source of Dublin's River Liffey. Southern Wicklow was one of the last outposts of the Gaelic Irish: using remote valleys like Glenmalure and the Glen of Imaal as hideouts, families like the O'Tooles and the O'Byrnes would sally forth to attack the English. Such was the Crown's concern that they built an access road from Dublin through the heart of the mountains to the bandits. Thanks to their efforts, the Military Rd still takes you through the finest Wicklow scenery.

In northern Wicklow, the Anglo-Irish gentry felt close enough to the safety of Dublin to build magnificent mansions like those at Russborough near Blessington and Powerscourt near Enniskerry. The exquisite formal gardens of the latter are still one of the county's biggest draws.

Wicklow's highways and main towns, many of them dormitories for Dublin, lie along the relatively narrow coastal strip south to Wexford. Heading south there are pleasant seaside resorts and some fine beaches along the way, especially at Brittas Bay, the first of a chain stretching to County Waterford.

Wicklow is particularly known for its beautiful gardens, and during the Wicklow Gardens Festival in May and June many

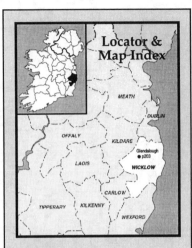

Highlights

- Explore the fine beaches, especially at Brittas Bay
- Travel along Military Rd, which goes through the finest Wicklow scenery
- Visit Russborough House near Blessington, one of the best stately homes in Ireland
- Walk along the Wicklow Way, the longest trail in the country
- Wander around Glendalough, the site of some of the best preserved early Christian remains
- Enjoy Powerscourt Estate, near Enniskerry, and its exquisite formal gardens

gardens not normally open to the public welcome visitors. For details contact Wicklow County Tourism (☎ 0404-66058), St Manntan's House, Kilmantin Hill, Wicklow.

As well as the usual bus and train connections around County Wicklow, *Over the Top and Into the West* offers tours of the county for IR£15 (students IR£13). These depart

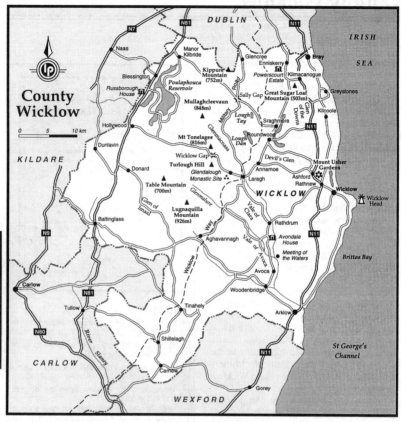

from outside the Dublin Tourism Centre at 9.45 am daily.

Wicklow Mountains

From Killakee, a few km north-west of Glencree, you can turn your back on Dublin's sprawl and travel for 30km across vast sweeps of heather-clad moors, bogs and mountains dotted with small corrie lakes along the Military Rd.

The Wicklow Mountains are a vast granite intrusion, or batholith, a welling up of hot igneous rock which consolidated some 400 million years ago. The heat baked the overlying clays and sedimentary rocks, producing shiny mica schists which can be seen across the county but particularly in the rivers and streams around Glenmalure. The soft metamorphosed rocks have weathered away over the millennia, exposing the granite, but significant traces remain, particularly on top of Lugnaquilla (926m), where a cap of schist remains.

The mountains were rounded and shaped during the Ice Ages, producing the smooth profiles you see today. While flattening the peaks, the ice also created deep valleys like Glenmacnass, Glenmalure and Glendalough. Corrie lakes like Lough Bray Upper and Lower were gouged out by ice at the head of glaciers.

Beginning on Dublin's southern fringes, the narrow Military Rd winds down to the remotest parts of Wicklow. The best place to join it is at Glencree via Enniskerry. It then runs south through the Sally Gap, Glenmacnass, Laragh, Glendalough and on to Glenmalure and Aghavannagh.

The British constructed the road early in the 19th century to get access to the Wicklow rebels, including Michael Dwyer, who were holed up in the southern half of the county, particularly around Glenmalure. It was a considerable feat of engineering, traversing open bog and barren mountainscapes for 50km.

Enniskerry makes a good starting point, and on the trip south, you can divert east at the Sally Gap to look at Lough Tay, Lough Dan and the Luggala Estate. Farther south you pass the great waterfall at Glenmacnass before dropping down into Laragh, with the magnificent monastic ruins of Glendalough nearby. Continue south through the valley of Glenmalure, and if you're fit enough, climb Lugnaquilla, Wicklow's highest peak.

The Sally Gap and the Wicklow Gap farther south are the two principal east-west passes through the mountains. Although the Wicklows' western flanks are less attractive than the centre and east, the Glen of Imaal, north-west of Aghavannagh, is still very remote and scenic.

ENNISKERRY

Enniskerry, south of Dublin on the R117, owes its origin to the adjoining Powerscourt Estate. The landlord built this elegant, picturesque little village to accompany his impressive manor, the entrance to which is just south of the village square. Set round a small triangle, the rows of cottages ooze quiet charm. A number of pleasant cafés make great places to unwind after a foray

into the mountains, for which Enniskerry is an excellent base.

Heading west up the hill takes you through some lovely scenery into Glencree and the hamlet of the same name 10km up at the head of the valley which leads to the Military Rd.

Enniskerry is a popular day trip destination for Dubliners, but the village has so far escaped the blight of modern urban development. Don't miss the small detour to Powerscourt Waterfall & Gardens.

The telephone code is ☎ 01.

Places to Stay

Hostel The An Óige *Lackan House* hostel (☎ 286 4036) is 7km south-west of Enniskerry, in Knockree at the base of Knockree Mountain, right by the Wicklow Way in a converted farm. It's open year round, has 42 beds and charges IR£5.50/4.

B&Bs *Cherbury* (☎ 282 8679) overlooks the valley in Monastery, 1km west of Enniskerry, on the Dublin road. Rooms with bathroom cost from IR£16 per person. In the village are *Corner House* (☎ 286 0149), costing from IR£20/30 for singles/doubles, and *Ferndale* (☎ 286 3518) from IR£27/34.

Hotels The attractively isolated and cosy *Enniscree Lodge Hotel* (☎ 286 3542; fax 286 6037), on the right as you head up into Glencree, offers wonderful views of the valley. B&B is IR£59/80.

The *Powerscourt Arms* (☎ 282 8903) is right in Enniskerry village facing the square. Despite its potential it's rather run-of-the-mill. B&B costs IR£22/40.

Places to Eat

Up the hill past the post office is *Buttercups*, a small deli and bread shop serving delicious takeaway food. Readers have also enjoyed eating at *Poppies*, on the square, which offers an inviting selection of pies, quiches, cakes and main courses in the IR£3.50 to IR£5 range. Also reasonably priced is *Harvest Home*, up the hill past the Glenwood Inn, with meals for around IR£5. A fourth choice is *Stepping Stones* which does breakfast for IR£3.99.

For more luxurious surroundings, you have a couple of choices on the road west leading to Glencree. The first is *Curtlestown House Restaurant* (☎ 282 5803), an up-market restaurant in a farmhouse about 5km along. Its set menu costs IR£18. At *Enniscree Lodge Hotel* (☎ 286 3542) a four-course dinner costs IR£26.

Getting There & Away

Enniskerry is just 3km west of the N11, the main Dublin to Wexford road. Bus Éireann (☎ 836 6111) express buses from the Busáras in Dublin will drop you at the turn-off for Enniskerry. Dublin area bus No 44 goes to Enniskerry from Hawkins St in Dublin, or you can take the DART train to Bray and get bus No 85 from the station.

POWERSCOURT ESTATE

This 64-sq-km estate near Enniskerry, with its magnificent formal gardens, is a major tourist attraction. The main entrance to the house and estate is 500m south of the square in Enniskerry. Continuing past the entrance, you skirt the estate and eventually reach the famous Powerscourt Waterfall.

Powerscourt House (1743) was designed by Richard Castle, who also designed Dublin's Leinster House and Russborough House in Blessington. Unfortunately, a disastrous fire gutted the interior in 1974 just before the house was to be opened to the public. Today it's owned by the Slazenger family. At the time of writing a new visitor centre, restaurant and Avoca Handweavers shop were due to open.

The 20-hectare formal gardens were created in the 19th century, with the Great Sugar Loaf Mountain providing a magnificent natural backdrop to the east. Five terraces drop more than 500m to the lovely Triton Lake. The Italian Gardens alone took 100 men 12 years to complete.

The wilder parts of the estate provided the setting for such films as John Boorman's *Excalibur*, Stanley Kubrick's *Barry Lyndon* and Laurence Olivier's 1943 *Henry V*.

The estate opens March to October, from 9.30 am to 5.30 pm daily. Tickets come with a map laying out a 40-minute and hour-long tour of the gardens. Don't miss the Japanese Gardens or the Pepperpot Tower, supposedly modelled on a three-inch version inside the house. Admission to the gardens and visitor centre is IR£4/3; to the gardens alone it's IR£3/2.

A 6km walk takes you to a separate part of the estate and a lovely ramble down to the **Powerscourt Waterfall**, at 130m the highest in Britain or Ireland and most impressive after heavy rain. You can also get to the falls by road (5km), following the signs from the estate entrance. The waterfall opens daily all year round from 10.30 am to 7 pm or dusk in winter, and admission is IR£1.50/80p. The waterfall road continues along the southern slopes of Glencree and joins up with the Military Rd which goes south to the Sally Gap.

GLENCREE

Just south of the border with Dublin and 10km west of Enniskerry, is Glencree, a leafy hamlet set into the side of the valley of the same name which opens east to give a magnificent view down to the Great Sugar Loaf Mountain and the sea.

The valley floor is home to the Glencree Oak Project, an ambitious plan to reforest part of Glencree with the native oak vegetation which once covered most of the country.

The village, such as it is, has a tiny shop and a hostel but no pub. A small grotto to the Virgin Mary, who is said to have appeared here in the 1980s, is set into the hillside. There's also a poignant German cemetery, dedicated to servicemen who died in Ireland during WWI and WWII, mostly after shipwrecks or plane crashes. Just south of the village, the former military barracks are now a retreat house and reconciliation centre for people of different religions in the Republic and the North.

The Military Rd heads on south to the Sally Gap, one of the two main east-west routes over the Wicklow Mountains.

Places to Stay

The An Óige *Stone House* hostel (☎ 286 4037), just up from the German cemetery, has 40 beds costing IR£5.50/4. It gets busy in summer so be sure to book ahead.

SALLY GAP

The Sally Gap is one of the two main passes across the Wicklow Mountains from east to west. From the turn-off on the lower road between Roundwood and Kilmacanogue near Bray, the narrow road passes above the dark waters of Lough Tay and Lough Dan and the Luggala Estate. It then heads up to the Sally Gap crossroads where it cuts across the Military Rd and heads north-west for Kilbride and the N81, following the young River Liffey, still only a stream. Just north of the Sally Gap crossroads is Kippure Mountain (752m) with its TV transmitter. The surrounding bogs have dark lines incised into them by turfcutters.

Midway along the R759 from the Gap to Sraghmore you'll find *McGuirk's Tearoom* hiding in a clump of rhododendrons. It's been there since 1989 and it's still churning out pleasant cakes and scones.

LOUGH TAY & LOUGH DAN

Lough Tay lies like a spilt pint of Guinness at the bottom of a spectacular gash in the mountains 5km south-east of the Sally Gap crossroads and about the same distance from Roundwood to the south-east. The lake is part of Luggala, an estate owned by Garech de Brun, a member of the Guinness family and an Irish music enthusiast, and it featured in John Boorman's film *Excalibur*. At the north end of the lough above a creamy brown beach sits Luggala House, overlooked by spectacular cliffs popular with rock climbers on the far side of the valley.

Luggala Estate covers almost all of the valley, as far down as Lough Dan, which nestles among lower hills to the south. The road to the Sally Gap skirts the top of the valley on the eastern side and is crossed by the Wicklow Way walking trail, which continues south past Lough Dan.

The valley provides some magnificent walks. A convenient starting point for any of them comes just before the road dips over the southern edge of the valley and down towards Roundwood. Here, a small private road heads down into the valley and you're allowed to walk or cycle (but not drive) down. Along the road you pass the private entrance to Luggala House and a small estate cottage with a sign indicating the distance to Lough Dan as '2 Irish Miles'.

The first and easiest option is to walk part of the Wicklow Way to Lough Dan; from the top of the road this is about four km each way. There's a lovely view of the cliffs and Lough Tay from among the trees at the valley floor. If you look carefully, you can make out traces of old potato furrows (or 'lazy beds') dating back to Famine times on the hills.

Another option is to walk round Lough Tay. As before, follow the private road to the valley floor but then head north-west up the mountain (called Fancy) to the cliffs overlooking the lake. You can continue north from there, meet the road to the Sally Gap and then return to your starting point.

ROUNDWOOD

At 238m above sea level, Roundwood is widely touted as Ireland's highest village, though it's hardly Mont Blanc. The village is essentially one long main street which leads south to Glendalough and southern Wicklow. Turn-offs lead to Ashford to the east and the south shore of Lough Dan to the west. Unfortunately, almost all Lough Dan's southern shoreline is private property and you can't get to the lake on this side. To the north is the turn-off to Bray.

Roundwood's pubs are usually packed with tired walkers on weekend afternoons. There are shops, a post office and a thriving market selling cakes, breads, flowers etc, held every Sunday afternoon, March to December, in the small hall on Main St.

North-west of the village you'll find some of the county's best scenery on the road to the Sally Gap, with a tremendous panorama over Lough Tay and the Luggala Estate.

WICKLOW

Places to Stay & Eat

Roundwood Caravan & Camping Park (☎ 281 8163), within walking distance of the village pubs, has good facilities and pitches for hikers and cyclists for IR£6. It's open from Easter through September. Facing each other at the north end of Main St are the *Roundwood Inn* and the many-gabled *Coach House Inn*. Both do food, and that at the Coach House has been recommended by readers; chicken and chips is IR£4.99.

Getting There & Away

St Kevin's Bus Service (☎ 281 8119) passes through Roundwood on its twice daily run between Dublin and Glendalough (see that section for more details).

GLENMACNASS

The most desolate section of the Military Rd runs through wild bogland between the Sally Gap crossroads and Laragh. Along the way you may catch glimpses of Lough Dan to the east, and until you reach the top of Glenmacnass Valley not a single building breaks the sense of isolation.

The highest mountain to the west is Mt Mullaghcleevaun (848m), and River Glenmacnass flows south and tumbles over the edge of the mountain plateau into Glenmacnass in a great foaming cascade. The drop marks a boundary between granite and metamorphosed schist.

There's a car park near the top. Be careful when walking on rocks near the Glenmacnass Waterfall, as several people have slipped to their deaths. There are fine walks up Mt Mullaghcleevaun or in the hills to the east of the waterfall car park.

THE WICKLOW GAP

Between Mt Tonelagee (816m) to the north-east and Table Mountain (700m) to the south-west, the Wicklow Gap is the second major pass over the mountains. The eastern end of the road begins just to the north of Glendalough (see the following section) and climbs through some lovely scenery north-westward up along the Glendassan Valley. It passes the remains of some old lead and zinc workings before meeting a side road which leads south and up Turlough Hill, the location of Ireland's only pumped storage power station.

A lake was created on the summit and a tunnel was bored down through the hill to the other lake at its base. The water is pumped to the top reservoir at times of low electricity demand and sent down through the turbines in the tunnel at times of high demand. You can walk up the hill to have a look over the top lake.

GLENDALOUGH

Glendalough (Gleann dá Loch), the 'glen of the two lakes', is a magical place – an ancient monastic settlement tucked beside two dark lakes and overshadowed by the sheer walls of a deep valley. It's one of the most picturesque settings in the Wicklow Mountains or for that matter in Ireland, and site of one of

---

Wicklow Mountains National Park

Most of Glendalough is contained within two nature reserves, owned and managed by Dúchas and legally protected by the Wildlife Act. The larger reserve, west of the visitors' centre, conserves the extensive heath and bog of the Glenealo Valley, an important habitat for moorland birds and deer, plus the Upper Lake and valley slopes on either side. The second reserve, Glendalough Wood Nature Reserve, conserves oak woods stretching from the Upper Lake as far as the Rathdrum road to the east.

Together with other state-owned land, the two reserves form the 12,700-hectare heart of the Wicklow Mountains National Park. At Liffey Head, north-east of Sally Gap, 2500 hectares of mountain blanket bog will eventually form part of the national park too. The ultimate aim is to have a park of up to 30,000 hectares of mostly higher ground stretching the length of the Wicklow Mountains. ■

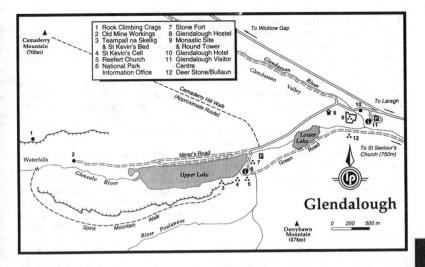

the most significant ancient monastic settlements in the country.

Barely an hour away from Dublin, Glendalough is extremely popular. Visit early or late in the day or out of season to avoid the coach-tour crowds and atmosphere-shattering school parties.

History

Glendalough's past and present status are thanks to St Kevin, an early Christian bishop who established a monastery here in the 6th century. From rough beginnings as a hermitage on the south side of the Upper Lake, only accessible by boat, his monastery began to attract followers. In time it became a monastic city catering to thousands of students and teachers. During the Dark Ages, Glendalough was one of the places that gave Ireland its reputation as the island of saints and scholars.

The main sections of the monastery are thought to have been a few hundred metres west of the round tower, and it must have spread over a considerable area. Most of the present buildings date from between the 10th and 12th centuries. A famous son of Glendalough was St Laurence O'Toole, who studied here and then became Abbot of Glendalough in 1117 and Archbishop of Dublin in 1161.

Glendalough's remote location was still within reach of the Vikings, who sacked the monastery at least four times between 775 and 1071. The final blow came in 1398, when English forces from Dublin almost completely destroyed it. Efforts were made to rebuild, and some life lingered on here as late as the 17th century, when, under renewed repression, the monastery finally died.

Geography

Glendalough Valley was carved out by a series of glaciers, the last one retreating around 12,000 years ago. There was once one long deep lake which was later divided into the two you see today by the delta of the River Poulanass from the southern slopes. The larger Upper Lake is about 35m deep.

The surrounding mountains are formed mostly of 400-million-year-old granite and schist, the remains of earlier sediments cooked by the welling up granite. The granite has a number of mineral veins in it containing white quartz and ores of lead, silver and zinc. There were extensive mining operations here between 1800 and 1920, with as many as 2000 miners working the mines, some of which were known as Van Diemen's mines because of their remote location (a reference to Van Diemen's Land, the original name for Tasmania, Australia, and one of Britain's former penal colonies).

The remains of the buildings and poisonous grey tailings from the mines are clearly visible at the far end of the Upper Lake and on the surrounding slopes. Some of the shafts extended north for nearly 2km through the mountain into the Glendassan Valley, and you can see the remains while driving up the Wicklow Gap.

Information & Orientation

At the valley entrance just before the Glendalough Hotel is the Glendalough Visitor Centre (☎ 0404-45325), which has a good 20-minute audiovisual presentation on the Irish monasteries. It's open daily 9.30 am to 6 pm year round, and admission is IR£2/1.

At the Upper Lake a small information office (☎ 45425) has details of activities in the national park. It's open daily late April to late August, 10 am to 6.30 pm, but if you find it closed the staff may be out running guided walks. *Exploring the Glendalough Valley* (Dúchas) is a good booklet on the trails in the area.

It's important to get your bearings in Glendalough as the ruins and sites are spread out all over the valley. Coming from Laragh you first see the visitors' centre, then the Glendalough Hotel which is beside the entrance to the main group of ruins and the round tower. The Lower Lake is a small dark lake to the west, while farther west up the valley is the much bigger and more impressive Upper Lake, with a large car park (IR£1.50 car, 50p motorbike) and more ruins nearby. Be sure to visit the Upper Lake and take one of the surrounding walks.

A model in the visitor's centre should help you fix where everything is in relation to each other.

The telephone code is ☎ 0404.

The Ruins

The principal remains are of seven churches, a monastic gatehouse (the only one of its kind), a fine round tower and a monastic graveyard.

The original site of St Kevin's settlement is at the base of the cliffs towering over the south side of the Upper Lake and accessible only by boat; unfortunately, there's no regular boat service to the site.

Upper Lake Sites The earliest sites are thought to be those at **Teampall na Skellig**, where St Kevin first lived as a hermit. It's a small platform at the base of the vertical cliffs on the south side of the Upper Lake. It's directly across the lake from the path leading down the north shore to the mining village.

The terraced shelf at Teampall na Skellig has the reconstructed ruins of a church and early graveyard. Rough wattle huts once stood on the raised ground nearby. Scattered around are some early grave slabs and simple stone crosses.

Just east of here and 10m above the lake waters is a little cave 2m deep called **St Kevin's Bed**, said to be where Kevin lived. A local story relates how a woman appeared in the cave to tempt Kevin. The earliest human habitation of the cave was long before St Kevin's era. It may have been the burial chamber of a Bronze Age chief or perhaps even a prehistoric mine as there's evidence that people lived in the valley for thousands of years before the monks arrived.

In the green area just south of the car park is a large **circular wall**, thought to be the remains of an early Christian *caher* or stone fort.

Follow the lakeshore path south-west of the car park until you find the considerable remains of **Reefert Church** above the tiny River Poulanass. This is a small, rather plain, 11th century, Romanesque-style nave-and-chancel church with some reassembled arches and walls. Traditionally, Reefert (which means 'king's burial place') was the burial site of the chiefs of the local O'Toole family, and they probably built the church on

The Saint Who Lived in a Tree

Born around 498 AD, St Kevin was a member of the royal house of Leinster and his name is derived from Cóemgen, meaning the 'fair one' or 'well featured'. As a child he studied under the three holy men Énna, Eoghan and Lochan, and while under their tutelage he supposedly went to Glendalough and lived in a tree. Later he lived as a hermit in the cave that became known as St Kevin's Bed. It was, however, impossible for him to escape the world completely; knowledge of his piety spread and people flocked to Glendalough to share his isolated existence. His monastic settlement spread from the Upper Lake to the site of the town whose remains we see today. St Kevin became abbot of the monastery in 570 and died in 617 or 618 – which would have made him around 120 years old!

In the Middle Ages his shrine was so revered that seven pilgrimages to Glendalough were said to equal one to Rome. ■

the site of an earlier one. The surrounding graveyard has a number of rough stone crosses and slabs, most made of shiny mica schist.

If you climb the steps at the back of the churchyard and follow the path to the west, you'll find, at the top of a rise overlooking the lake, the scant remains of **St Kevin's Cell**, a small bee-hive hut.

Lower Lake Sites While the Upper Lake has the best scenery, the most fascinating buildings lie in the lower part of the valley east of the Lower Lake.

Just round the bend from the hotel is the stone arch of the monastery **gatehouse**, the only surviving example of a monastic entranceway in the country. There used to be another storey and a containing wall. Just inside the entrance is a large slab with an incised cross.

Beyond that lies a graveyard which is still in use. The 10th century **round tower** is 33m tall and 16m in circumference at the base. The upper storeys and conical roof were reconstructed in 1876. Near the tower to the south-east is the **Cathedral of St Peter & St Paul**, with a 10th century nave. The chancel and sacristy date from the 12th century. Inside are some good carvings and early gravestones.

At the centre of the graveyard to the south of the round tower is the **Priest's House**. This odd building dates from 1170 AD but has been heavily reconstructed. It may have been the location of shrines of St Kevin. Later, during penal times it became a burial site for local priests – hence the name. The 10th century **St Mary's Church**, 140m south-west of the round tower, probably stood originally outside the walls of the monastery and belonged to local nuns. It has a lovely western doorway. A little to the east are the scant remains of **St Kieran's Church**, the smallest of Glendalough's churches.

Glendalough's trademark is **St Kevin's Church** or **Kitchen** at the southern edge of the enclosure. This church, with miniature round-tower-like belfry, protruding sacristy and steep stone roof, is a stone masterpiece. How it came to be known as a kitchen is a mystery as there's no indication that it was anything other than a church. The oldest parts of the building and the belfry date from the 11th century and the structure has been remodelled since but it's still a classic early

The 10th century round tower at the Lower Lake is 33m tall

Irish church. It was used by Catholics up to 1850 and now stores miscellaneous carvings and slabs.

At the junction with the green road as you cross the river just south of these two churches is the **Deer Stone** in the middle of a group of rocks. Legend claims that when St Kevin needed milk for two orphaned babies, a doe stood here waiting to be milked. The stone is actually a *bullaun*, used as grinding stones for medicines or food. Many are thought to be prehistoric and they were widely regarded as having supernatural properties; women who bathed their faces with water from the hollow were supposed to keep their looks forever. The early churchmen brought them into their monasteries, perhaps hoping to inherit some of the stones' powers.

The road east leads to **St Saviour's Church** with its detailed Romanesque carvings. To the west a nice woodland trail leads up the valley past the Lower Lake to the Upper Lake.

Walks

Numerous fine walks fan out from Glendalough. The first, easiest and most popular option is the gentle but delightful walk along the north shore of the **Upper Lake** to the lead and zinc mine workings which date from 1800. It's about a 30 minute walk to the mines. The best route is along the lake shore rather than on the road which runs 30m in from the shore. You can continue on up the head of the valley if you wish.

Alternatively you can go up **Spink Mountain**, the steep ridge with vertical cliffs running along the south flanks of the Upper Lake. You can go part of the way and turn back, or complete a circuit of the Upper Lake by following the top of the cliff, eventually coming down by the mine workings and back along the north shore. The circuit takes about three hours.

The third option is a hike up **Camaderry** (700m), a mountain hidden behind the hills that flank the northern side of the valley. It starts on the road just 50m back towards Glendalough from the entrance to the Upper

Lake car park. Head straight up the steep hill to the north and you come out on open mountains with sweeping views in all directions. You can then continue up Camaderry to the north-west or just follow the ridge west looking over the Upper Lake. To the top of Camaderry and back takes about four hours.

If you're intending to go on a serious hike, make sure you take all the usual precautions, have the right equipment and, most importantly, tell someone where you're going and when you should be back. For Mountain Rescue, ring ☎ 999. For more detailed information on walking in the area, check *Hill Walker's Wicklow* or *New Irish Walk Guides, East & South East*, both by David Herman. For walking partners check at the hostels or go on an organised walk with the information office (☎ 45425) or Tiglin Adventure Centre (☎ 40169).

Other Activities

At the west end of the valley beyond the Upper Lake and the mine workings are a couple of large crags, popular with rock climbers. The Mountaineering Council of Ireland publishes a guide to the routes which is available from Joss Lynam (☎ 01-288 4672). Laragh Trekking Centre (☎ 45282), based just outside the village, runs horse trail rides.

Places to Stay

Camping No camping is allowed within the national park. The independent *Old Mill Hostel* (see the following section) will let you pitch a tent for IR£4.50 a night but some readers have been dissatisfied with the facilities. The nearest official camping spot is in Roundwood (see that section earlier).

Hostels There are several hostels near Glendalough. The superior An Óige *Glendalough Hostel* (☎ 45143) is about 300m west of the round tower. The pleasant garden comes in for particular praise although showers are fairly rudimentary. Beds cost IR£6/4.50. Another An Óige hostel, *Tiglin Hostel* (☎ 40259), in Devil's Glen about 10km north-east of Laragh via

Annamoe, has hostel accommodation for IR£5.50/4.

In the village of Laragh, *Wicklow Way Hostel* (☎ 45398), beside Lynham's Bar, charges IR£6 for a dorm bed and opens all year.

Housed in attractive farm buildings 1km south of Laragh on the road to Rathdrum, the IHO's *Old Mill Hostel* (☎ 45156) should be nicer than it is. Dorm beds cost IR£6.50, doubles IR£12.50 a head. Unfortunately, the dorms are pretty dingy and there's no proper reception. New rooms were being added at the time of writing so things may improve.

B&Bs Most B&Bs are in or around Laragh, the village 3km east of Glendalough, or on the road down into Glendalough itself. *Lilac Cottage* (☎ 45574) in Laragh is run by an ex-pat New Zealander and has simple but adequate rooms with separate bathroom for IR£14 a head. Farther down towards Glendalough opposite Trinity Church, *Valeview* (☎ 45292) has well-kept rooms, a great view of the valley and, as well as the normal cooked breakfast, provides the option of yoghurt and fruit. It charges from IR£16/18 per person.

Laragh Trekking Centre (☎ 45282) charges IR£32/44 for singles/doubles with bathroom. The house is in Glenmacnass: turn north at the shop-cum-petrol-station in Laragh on the Dublin side of the bridge, and keep going for almost four km. Five km north-east of Glendalough in Annamoe on the main road to Roundwood is *Carmel's* (☎ 45297), which costs IR£32 for rooms with bathroom. It's open March through October.

Hotel *Glendalough Hotel* (☎ 45135; fax 45142) has one of the country's best locations close to the ruins and with the river running under the restaurant. It's gradually being extended and modernised. B&B costs from IR£46.50/69.

Country House *Derrybawn House* (☎ 45134) stands in wooded grounds just south of Laragh on the road to Rathdrum. B&B costs IR£32/50.

Places to Eat
At Glendalough itself there's surprisingly little to eat. *Glendalough Hotel* has a strictly limited bar menu or a scone and tea for IR£1.80. Otherwise there's a tacky takeaway booth in the Upper Lake car park.

For anything else you need to go into Laragh. About the best place for anything substantial is the *Wicklow Heather Restaurant* (☎ 45157), beside Lilac Cottage. Main courses are around IR£5.50 and it's open for dinner until 8.30 pm. During summer villagers put out signs and serve tea and scones on the village green.

Getting There & Away
All year round, St Kevin's Bus Service (☎ 01-281 8119) runs to Glendalough from outside the College of Surgeons west off St Stephen's Green in Dublin, at 11.30 am and 6 pm daily. Every day except Sunday (5.30 pm) the buses return to Dublin at 4.15 pm, leaving you just three hours at the site; if you can it's much better to stay the night and return on the 7.15 am service (9.45 am on Saturday and Sunday). The one-way/return fare is IR£5/8. From Bray there are services at 12.10 and 6.40 pm (return IR£6).

GLENMALURE
Deep in the mountains, near the southern end of the Military Rd, is Glenmalure, a sombre and majestic blind valley overlooked on its western side by Wicklow's highest peak, Lugnaquilla (926m), and flanked farther up by classic scree slopes of loose boulders. After coming over the mountains into Glenmalure you turn north-west at the Drumgoff bridge. From there it's about 6km up the road beside the Avonbeg River to a car park where trails lead off in various directions.

For a long time, Glenmalure was a stronghold of resistance to the English. Various clans, particularly the O'Byrnes, made forays up into the Pale, harassing the crown's forces and loyal subjects. The most famous clan leader was Fiach MacHugh O'Byrne. In 1580 he defeated an army of 1000 English soldiers led by the Lord Deputy, Lord Grey de Wilton, at Glenmalure; over 800 men died in the battle and English control over Ireland was set back for decades. Fiach was captured in 1597 and his head impaled on the gates of Dublin Castle.

Near Drumgoff is Dwyer's or Cullen's Rock, which commemorates both the Glenmalure battle and Michael Dwyer, another rebel who holed up here. Men were hanged from the rock during the 1798 Rising.

Michael Dwyer, a 1798 leader born in the nearby Glen of Imaal, successfully sustained the struggle against the English for five years from this remote outpost before being captured in 1803 and deported to Australia, where he died in 1825. For more details, see the Glen of Imaal section under West Wicklow later in this chapter.

Walks
You can walk up Lugnaquilla or head up the blind Fraughan Rock Glen east of the car park. Alternatively, you can go straight up Glenmalure passing the small, seasonal An Óige hostel after which the trail divides – heading north-east, the trail takes you over the hills to Glendalough, while going north-west brings you into the Glen of Imaal.

The head of Glenmalure and parts of the neighbouring Glen of Imaal are off-limits – it's military land, well posted with warning signs.

Places to Stay
About 1km up from the car park in Glenmalure is the small 36-bed An Óige *Glenmalure Hostel*. It's open in July and August and on weekends the rest of the year. It has no phone or electricity and dorm beds cost IR£5.50/4 in high season. Much bigger is the An Óige *Aghavannagh House* hostel (☎ 0402-36366), 14km south-west in a former barracks built at the time of the 1798 Rising; it was at one time used as a shooting lodge by Charles Stewart Parnell. Beds cost IR£6/

4.50 in high season. Both hostels make good bases for walking up Lugnaquilla.

WICKLOW WAY
The Wicklow Way was the first trail set up in Ireland in 1981. It's 132km long and neither starts nor finishes within County Wicklow itself. See the Activities chapter for details.

West Wicklow

The western slopes of the Wicklow Mountains were less deeply glaciated than the eastern ones, and the landscape isn't as spectacular. From the Sally Gap crossroads to Kilbride, however, you pass the upper reaches of the River Liffey and some lovely wild scenery. Another picturesque trip passes over the Wicklow Gap from Glendalough.

West Wicklow's most interesting features are the Poulaphouca Reservoir (also known as Blessington Lakes), Russborough House nearby, and, farther south, the lovely Glen of Imaal.

BLESSINGTON
Once an important stop on the stage-coach run between Dublin, Carlow, Waterford and Kilkenny, Blessington is 35km south-west of Dublin on the N81. Its pleasant main street is lined with solid 17th and 18th century town houses and it makes a good base for exploring the surrounding area.

Blessington owes its origins to an archbishop of Dublin, Michael Boyle, who designed it in the 1670s. Boyle's manor, Downshire House, was destroyed by fire in 1760, and the village was all but destroyed by rebels in 1798.

Blessington is near the shores of Poulaphouca Reservoir, created in 1940 to drive the turbines of the local Electricity Supply Board (ESB) power station to the east of town and to supply Dublin with water.

Information
The tourist office (☎ 045-865850) is in the

Blessington Business Centre, across the road from the Downshire House Hotel. It's open Monday to Saturday, June through August, 10 am to 6 pm.

The telephone code is ☎ 045.

Places to Stay & Eat

Hostel Five km from Blessington, the An Óige *Baltyboys Hostel* (☎ 67266), on the peninsula opposite Russborough House, opens March through November and has beds for IR£5.50/4. Take the road south to Poulaphouca and turn east at Burgage Cross towards Valleymount. Dublin bus No 65 passes by.

B&Bs The *Heathers* (☎ 864554) overlooks the reservoir in Poulaphouca, 7km south along the Baltinglass road and only 3km from Russborough House. B&B is from IR£19/28 for singles/doubles. Also in Poulaphouca is the similarly priced *The Conifers* (☎ 864298).

Hotel The prominent *Downshire House Hotel* (☎ 865199), on Main St, charges IR£45/77 without breakfast.

Country Houses The early 19th century *Manor* (☎ 01-458 2105; fax 458 2607) has 18 hectares of gardens with views over the Wicklow Hills. It's about 10km north-west of Blessington, just south of Manor Kilbride and opens April through September. B&B is a hefty IR£45 per person. Even more expensive is the rambling *Rathsallagh House* (☎ 403112; fax 403343), 20km south of Blessington in Dunlavin. B&B is IR£190 in high season, single or double.

Places to Eat

Next to the tourist office, *The Courtyard Restaurant* stays open until 9 pm in high season, serving a range of basic meals. *The Skillet Pot* on Main St does light lunches like shepherd's pie for IR£3.75. For somewhere to drink *Hennessy's Lounge*, also on Main St, deserves credit for its pretty hanging baskets.

Getting There & Away

Blessington has regular daily services by Dublin suburban bus No 65 from Eden Quay. Bus Éireann (☎ 01-836 3111) express bus No 005 to and from Waterford stops in Blessington two or three times a day; from Dublin it's pick up only, from Waterford drop off only.

RUSSBOROUGH HOUSE

Five km south-west of Blessington is one of Ireland's finest stately homes, built for Joseph Leeson later Lord Russborough, whose family were major players in Ireland's 18th century brewing industry.

A truly magnificent Palladian villa, Russborough House was built between 1741 and 1751. It was designed by Richard Castle, at the height of his fame and ability, with the help of another architect, Francis Bindon from County Clare. At the front the granite central building is flanked by two elegant wings connected to the main block by curving, pillared colonnades. This 275m frontage is further extended by granite walls and Baroque gates, and topped off with urns and heraldic lions. The interior has many impressive state rooms and remarkable plasterwork by the Francini brothers, Paul and Philip, whose work can also be seen in Castletown House in Celbridge, County Kildare.

Joseph Leeson filled the house with treasures and the house stayed in the family until 1931. In 1952 it was sold to Sir Alfred Beit, nephew of another Sir Alfred Beit, co-founder, with Cecil Rhodes, of de Beers. The older Sir Alfred had used the wealth from the diamonds to purchase important works of art. The nephew inherited the lot, and paintings by Velasquez, Vermeer, Goya and Rubens now slot comfortably into their grand surroundings. Unfortunately they've attracted some unwanted attention. In 1974 an Englishwoman, Rose Dugdale, stole 16 of the paintings to help the IRA. Those paintings were recovered. Some of those grabbed in 1986 are still missing.

The house was closed to the public until 1976, when Sir Alfred established the Beit

Foundation, making the house a centre for the arts. Paintings from the National Gallery of Ireland are sometimes exhibited here. The house opens daily 10.30 am to 5.30 pm, June through August. In May and September it closes at 2.30 pm except on Sunday. In April and October it's open Sunday and bank holidays only. The main 45-minute tour of the house including all the important paintings costs IR£3/1 (students IR£2). An additional 30-minute tour of the bedrooms upstairs containing more silver and furniture costs IR£1.50, children free.

June through September, Bus Éireann runs an excellent day trip to Russborough House and Powerscourt Gardens leaving the Búsaras in Dublin at 10 am. The IR£16 cost includes admission fees, and the tour takes in Lough Tay and the Sally Gap as well.

GLEN OF IMAAL

Seven km south-east of Donard, the lovely Glen of Imaal is overlooked by Lugnaquilla, about the only scenery of consequence on the western flanks of the Wicklow Mountains. It's named after Mal, a brother of the 2nd century king of Ireland. Cathal Mór. Unfortunately the glen's north-eastern slopes are mostly cordoned off as an army firing range and for manoeuvres. Look out for red danger signs.

The area's most famous son was Michael Dwyer, who led rebel forces during the 1798 Rising and held out for many years in the local hills and glens. On the south-east side of the glen at Derrynamuck is a small whitewashed, thatched cottage where Dwyer and three friends were surrounded by 100 English soldiers. One of his companions, Samuel McAllister, ran out the front, drawing fire and meeting his death, while Dwyer escaped into the night. He was eventually deported and jailed on Norfolk Island, off the east coast of Australia, but became chief constable of Liverpool near Sydney before he died in 1825. The cottage is now a small folk museum.

Donard is a hamlet in the glen about 8km south-east of Dunlavin. The 40-bed An Óige *Ballinclea Hostel* (☎ 045-404657), 5km south-east of Donard on the road to Knockanarrigan and 13km west of Glenmalure, opens March through November. Beds cost IR£5.50/4.

BALTINGLASS

In the far western corner of Wicklow, 27km south-west of Blessington along the N81, is Baltinglass on the banks of the River Slaney. This small town grew up around the Cistercian **Abbey of Vallis Salutis**, founded in 1148 by Dermot MacMurrough as a satellite to Mellifont Monastery in County Louth. It was MacMurrough, as king of Leinster, who 'invited' the Anglo-Normans to Ireland, an offer they gratefully accepted. The rest, as they say, is history. Some locals suggest MacMurrough was laid to rest here in 1171, though he is more probably buried near his base in Ferns, County Wexford. Records suggest that the Irish parliament met in the abbey for three days in 1397.

The ruined nave with several simple Gothic arches and scant remnants of a cloister lie 350m north of the town centre. The eastern section of the structure was used as a Protestant church long after the dissolution of the monasteries in 1541. A Gothic-style bell tower was added in 1815.

A stiff climb to the summit of Baltinglass Hill to the north-east brings you to **Rathcoran**, a large hill fort and a Bronze Age cairn with several passage graves.

The IHH *Rathcoran House* hostel (☎ 0508-81073), in Baltinglass, has dorm beds for IR£8.50 and opens mid-June through August.

At least two buses a day pass through Baltinglass between Dublin and Waterford and vice versa.

The Coast

The main N11 from Dublin to Wexford passes to the west of Bray and then south through Wicklow, keeping a few km inland from the sea. South of Kilmacanogue you see the Great Sugar Loaf Mountain (503m) to the west and pass through a great glacial rift, the Glen of the Downs, carved out of an Ice Age lake by floodwaters and with its slopes covered in native oak and beech. There's a forest walk up to a ruined teahouse on top of the ridge to the east.

If you're travelling farther south, the coastal route through Greystones, Kilcoole and then along country lanes to Rathnew is preferable.

Worth seeing around Wicklow Town are the Mount Usher Gardens near Ashford and the fine beaches of Brittas Bay which stretch south into County Wexford.

BRAY

Bray is a run-down dormitory town on the coast just 19km south of Dublin. In 1854 the railway's arrival turned it into the 'Brighton' of Ireland, a bustling seaside resort with a long promenade, fronted by a beach and backed by hotels and lodging houses, all nicely overshadowed by Bray Head to the south. Unfortunately the seafront which should be modern Bray's glory is now home to cheap hotels, fast-food places, amusement arcades and endless parking space for DART train commuters. The other focal point is Main St, lined with shops and pubs.

The tourist office (☎ 01-286 7128) is in the 19th century courthouse beside the Royal Hotel at the bottom of Main St. It's open 9.30 am to 5 pm Monday to Saturday in June through September, closing at 4.30 pm the rest of the year. Enquire here about Finnegan Bray's (☎ 286 0061) half-day and full-day tours to Glendalough, Dublin and 'Ballykissangel' (aka Avoca).

The excellent Dubray Books, on Main St, sells maps and Wicklow walking guides.

The telephone code is ☎ 01.

Things to See & Do

A fine 8km **cliff walk** winds around Bray Head to Greystones from the south end of the promenade, offering good views south to the Great Sugar Loaf Mountain. Bray Head has many old smuggling caves and rail tunnels including one which is 1.5km long, the second longest in Ireland, built by the engi-

neer Isambard Kingdom Brunel in 1856. The inland rail route was an easier and more obvious choice, but the local earl didn't want the railway cutting through his land. James Joyce lived in Bray from 1889 to 1891 and, as in Sandycove near Dun Laoghaire, there is a **Martello Tower**.

The tourist office houses a small **heritage centre**. At the time of writing the **National Aquarium** on the seafront was closed; check whether it's reopened at the tourist office. **Kilruddery House & Gardens**, about 3km south of Bray, has been home to the Brabazon family since 1618 and has one of Ireland's oldest gardens. It's open daily May, June and September, 1 to 5 pm. Entry to the house and gardens is IR£2.50/1, to the gardens only is IR£1/free.

Kilmacanogue

The biggest and best local craft shop is **Avoca Handweavers** (☎ 286 7466) set in a 19th century arboretum in Kilmacanogue, 4km south on the N11. The showroom has a huge array of hand-made crafts and garments, and a café serves snacks and lunches.

Bray tourist office's *Wicklow Trail Sheet No 4* (IR£1) details a three-hour exploration of the Great Sugar Loaf Mountain (Sliabh Cualann) starting from Kilmacanogue.

To drive to Kilmacanogue from Bray, take the right fork up by the town hall, continue for 3km till you come to the N11 then turn left (south) for 1km. Local bus No 145 sometimes stops in Kilmacanogue; check with the driver.

Places to Stay & Eat

If Dublin is full (not impossible over summer weekends) there are many B&Bs along Bray's sea-facing Strand Rd, just minutes from the DART station. At the north end they tend to overlook parking lots so it's worth continuing south towards Bray Head. Try *Strand House* (☎ 286 8920), right at the end, with singles/doubles for IR£22/36, or more central *Ulysses* (☎ 286 3860) at IR£23/40. The best hotel is the *Esplanade* (☎ 286 2056) which charges IR£80/130.

The delightful *Escape* is a good vegetarian

WICKLOW

restaurant in Albert Ave, just off Strand Rd. Main courses cost IR£6.95 and booking is advisable (☎ 286 6755). *The Tree of Idleness* (☎ 286 3498), also on Strand Rd, serves delicious Greek-Cypriot food; mains start from IR£12.95. The nearby *Porter House* does pub food but its main attraction is the wide variety of beers from around the world.

Getting There & Away
Bus Dublin suburban bus Nos 45 (from Hawkins St) and 84 (from Eden Quay) run every 45 minutes or so between Dublin and Bray. You can also catch them outside Trinity College on Nassau St. Both go past Bray railway station and bus Nos 84 and 84A run on to Greystones and Kilcoole. Bus No 85 runs from the railway station to Enniskerry every 25 to 45 minutes.

On its Dublin to Rosslare Harbour route Bus Éireann (☎ 836 6111) picks up passengers in Bray for destinations south to Rosslare Harbour and drops them off in the reverse direction. You'll be dropped on the highway, 15 minutes' walk from the B&Bs.

St Kevin's Bus Service (☎ 281 8119) has two buses from the town hall daily to Dublin at 8 am and 5 pm. A single fare is IR£1.20.

Train Bray railway station (☎ 236 3333) is 500m east of Main St just before the seafront. There are DART trains into Dublin and north to Howth every five minutes at peak times and every 20 or 30 minutes at quiet times.

The station is also on the mainline from Dublin to Wexford and Rosslare Harbour, with up to five trains daily in each direction Monday to Saturday, four on Sunday.

Getting Around
Bray Sports Centre (☎ 286 3046), 8 Main St, is the Raleigh Rent-a-Bike dealer, with bikes for IR£7/30 a day/week.

GREYSTONES TO WICKLOW
Eight km south of Bray, the resort of **Greystones** was once a charming fishing village, and the seafront around the little harbour is idyllic, with a broad bay and beach sweeping north to Bray Head. In summer, the bay is dotted with dinghies and windsurfers. Sadly, the surrounding countryside is vanishing beneath housing developments.

Kilcoole, 3km south of Greystones, is noteworthy only as the setting for Ireland's leading TV soap opera, *Glenroe*, based on a farm. Bus Éireann runs a couch-potato tour taking in Glenroe and Ballykissangel (Avoca) which leaves the Búsaras in Dublin every Saturday in June through September at 10 am. It costs IR£16/9.

South of Kilcoole, in Ashford, are the eight-hectare **Mt Usher Gardens** (☎ 0404-40205), informally laid out around the River Vartry with rare plants from around the world. The gardens open daily mid-March through October, 10.30 am to 6 pm. Admission is IR£3/2.50. Bus Éireann (☎ 01-836 6111) buses stop outside Ashford House on the three times daily Dublin to Rosslare Harbour route.

West of Ashford the road leads into the Wicklow Mountains through **Devil's Glen** (beginning 3km from Ashford), a beautiful wooded glen with a fine walking trail. **Tiglin Adventure Centre** (☎ 0404-40169), 3km further west, runs courses in rock climbing and canoeing and organises treks throughout the mountains.

WICKLOW TOWN & AROUND
Wicklow Town, 27km south of Bray, is not an exciting county town but does boast a fine big harbour, which hosts the start of the biennial Round Ireland yacht race. The sweep of beach and bay to the north and the bulge of Wicklow Head to the south are the area's best features.

There's not much to see here although Wicklow makes a good base for exploring the surrounding area. Unfortunately, the layout is not very backpacker-friendly, with the bus stop and train station some distance from the hostel and the B&Bs, and from each other.

The helpful tourist office (☎ 0404-69117) in Fitzwilliam Square opens all year. June through September it's open Monday to Saturday 9.30 am to 6 pm.

The telephone code is ☎ 0404.

Things to See & Do

A new **heritage centre** in the Old Gaol on Kilmantin Hill was due to open in 1998; ask at the tourist office for times and prices.

The few remaining fragments of the **Black Castle** are on the shore at the south end of town, with pleasant views up and down the coast. The castle was built by the Fitzgeralds from Wales in 1169 after they were granted lands in the area by Strongbow. It used to be linked to the mainland by a drawbridge, and rumour has it that an escape tunnel ran from the sea cave underneath up into the town. At low tide you can swim or snorkel into the cave.

The walk along the cliffs to **Wicklow Head** offers great views of the Wicklow Mountains.

A string of fine **beaches** – Silver Strand, Brittas Bay and Maheramore – start 16km south of Wicklow; with high dunes, safe shallow bathing and powdery sand, the beaches attract droves of Dubliners in good weather. Caravan parks lurk behind the dunes.

Places to Stay

The very welcoming *Wicklow Bay Hostel* (☎ 69213) may not boast the most scenic surroundings but there are fine sea views from the dorms and the building itself has had an unusually chequered history as, in turn, school, hotel, barracks, orphanage and bottling plant. There's a big, clean kitchen. Dorm beds cost IR£8 and there are some family rooms too.

There's a clutch of B&Bs in and around Dunbur Hill and a few more uphill along St Patrick's Rd. In the town centre the *Bayview Hotel* (☎ 67383) has singles/doubles for IR£21.50/45. The *Bridge Tavern* also does B&B in a building famed as the birthplace of Captain Halpin and for its live music sessions.

Places to Eat

Hannah's in Main St will sort you out for breakfast, light lunches or afternoon tea. *The Old Forge* has a good choice of bar meals. *The Opera House* in Market Square does pasta and pizza from around IR£5.50. *The Bakery Café and Restaurant* (☎ 66770) in Church St is good for vegetarians, with dishes like apple and Camembert strudel for IR£7.50.

Getting There & Away

Up to two Bus Éireann (☎ 01-836 6111) buses a day leave from the Grand Hotel on Main St to Dublin and to Rosslare Harbour. Trains (☎ 836 3333) stop at Wicklow at least four times daily in each direction between Dublin and Rosslare Harbour. The station is 10 minutes' walk from the town centre.

Getting Around

Wicklow Cabs (☎ 66888) in Main St picks up passengers from the 6.30 and 7.30 pm Dublin trains. The fare to anywhere in town is IR£1.50. The same company organises tours to local beauty spots, nightclubs, music pubs, etc.

South Wicklow

RATHDRUM

These days Rathdrum is little more than a few old houses and shops to the south of Glendalough and the Vale of Clara, the pleasant valley leading north to Laragh, but in the late 19th century it could have claimed to be the unofficial capital of Wicklow, with a healthy flannel industry and a poorhouse. The railway and fine aqueduct were built in 1861. More recently Rathdrum provided a setting for parts of the Neil Jordan film *Michael Collins*.

Twisting roads lead to a stone bridge over the Avonmore River which joins with the Avonbeg River at Meeting of the Waters near Avoca.

The telephone code is ☎ 0404.

Avondale House

In 1846 the great Irish politician Charles Stewart Parnell was born in Avondale House, which was designed by James Wyatt in 1779. The house was recently restored to its 1850s splendour and a 20-minute audiovisual tells the story of Parnell. The house is signposted 1.5km south of Rathdrum and opens to the public daily 10 am to 6 pm, May through September; the rest of the year it opens 11 am to 5 pm. Admission to the house is IR£2.75/1.75.

The 209 hectares of woodland incorporate an arboretum and nature walks. You can visit during daylight hours all year. Parking costs IR£2.

Places to Stay

The IHH *Old Presbytery* hostel (☎ 46930) in Rathdrum has dorm beds for IR£8 and private rooms for IR£20. You can camp in the grounds and there's a laundry.

Most of Rathdrum's B&Bs are actually in Corballis, along the road south to Avoca and Arklow. *Beechlawn* (☎ 46474), 500m south on the Avoca road, costs from IR£19/28. At *The Hawthorns* (☎ 46217), also in Corballis, 1km from Rathdrum, B&B costs from IR£23/28. A little farther along the same road is *St Bridget's* (☎ 46477) where B&B is IR£20/31 with separate bathroom.

Getting There & Away

The Bus Éireann (☎ 01-836 6111) Dublin to Wexford and Rosslare Harbour bus stops at Rathdrum twice a day in each direction. Three trains (☎ 836 3333) stop at Rathdrum daily in each direction between Dublin and Rosslare Harbour.

VALE OF AVOCA

The Avonbeg and Avonmore rivers come together to form the River Avoca at Meeting of the Waters, a lovely spot made famous by Thomas Moore's poem of the same name:

There is not in this wide world a valley so sweet
As that vale in whose bosom the bright waters meet;
Oh! the last rays of feeling and life must depart,
'Ere the bloom of that valley shall fade from my heart.

The Vale of Avoca meanders through a gentle, darkly wooded valley which is charming if hardly awe-inspiring. Unfortunately there's some badly scarred landscape

north-west of Avoca village, the legacy of centuries of copper mining which also polluted the river. The last mine closed in 1982. In the 18th century the valley was cut off from the outside world and had its own coinage, the cronbane.

Meeting of the Waters is marked by a pub, called *The Meetings* (☎ 0402-35226) which serves food all day and has music at weekends all year round. From April to October there are also Sunday ceilidhs between 4 and 6 pm. Buses to Avoca also stop at The Meetings, or you can walk up from Avoca.

Avoca

The tiny village of Avoca (Abhóca) shot to fame in 1996 when it was chosen as the location for the unexpectedly popular TV series *Ballykissangel*. The focal point is *Fitzgerald's*, a suitably olde-worlde pub by the river which plays a crucial part in the series. While tucking into pub food here you can admire snapshots of the stars, Stephen Tompkinson and Dervla Kirwan, on the walls.

Also in the village is **Avoca Handweavers** (☎ 0402-35105) which has been in business since 1723 and claims to be Ireland's oldest surviving business. You can look round the weaving sheds and then admire the pricey tweeds, throws and other fabrics in their shop. The excellent café opens for lunches and teas.

There's a seasonal tourist office in the library.

The telephone code is ☎ 0402.

Places to Stay

Camping There are two well-equipped campsites near the village of Redcross, about 7km north-east of Avoca on the R754 country road. *Johnson's* (☎ 0404-48133), just north of Redcross, charges IR£6 per tent, as does the *River Valley Park* (☎ 0404-41647), just south of the village.

B&Bs The Georgian *Riverview House* (☎ 35181), by the bus stop in Avoca, is highly recommended. It's open Easter

The Village of Make Believe

The post office is really a tea shop, the National School a community centre. O'Reilly's provisions shop may say it's open but never actually is. The pub offers accommodation – until you try to book a room. This is *Ballykissangel*, the fictional TV village so popular that it has virtually eclipsed Avoca, the real-life village where much of it takes place.

When the BBC started to film a TV series about an English priest washed up in a small Irish village, they were not to know they had a smash hit on their hands. But with *Ballykissangel* sold to Australia, the USA and Ireland itself, Avoca has rocketed to the top of the tourism pops, so much so, in fact, that the tiny library has had to turn itself into a tourist information office to cope with the 70,000 people streaming off the tour buses annually.

Not everyone is thrilled about this, detractors claiming that the BBC hasn't provided anything in Avoca to enable locals to profit from its sudden popularity. Still, sales at Fitzgerald's bar have never been better. ■

through September and has singles/doubles with separate bathroom for IR£17/29. The *Arbours* (☎ 35294) has great breakfasts and rooms with separate bathroom for IR£19.50/29.

Ashdene (☎ 35327), 2km outside Avoca in Knockanree Lower and open from mid-March through October, offers B&B from IR£19/29. *Greenhills* (☎ 35197), also in Knockanree Lower, charges IR£22/34 with bathroom and opens May through September.

Getting There & Away

Bus No 133 from Dublin to Arklow via Bray, Wicklow and Rathdrum stops in Avoca twice a day (once on Sunday). A day return from Dublin costs IR£6 ... and you get a free cup of tea and a scone at Avoca Handweavers thrown in.

ARKLOW

Besides Bray, Arklow is probably County Wicklow's busiest town. A thriving commercial shopping centre with some light industry, it makes a reasonable base for exploring the Wicklow hills, but is not particularly attractive in its own right.

Once a minor fishing village, Arklow became one of the country's busiest ports and a well-known boat-building centre. Sir Francis Chichester's *Gypsy Moth IV* (now in Greenwich, London) and the Irish training vessel the *Asgard II* were built here. In 1841

the port had 80 schooners working out of the harbour.

During the 1798 Rising, Arklow saw fierce fighting when some 20,000 of the rebels led by Father Michael Murphy tried to storm the town and were defeated by the better equipped and trained British army. Murphy and 700 men died in the battle. A monument to them sits in front of St Mary and St Peter's church today.

The tourist office (☎ 0402-32484) in a portacabin beside the courthouse theoretically opens Monday to Saturday, 9.30 am to 1 pm. The telephone code is ☎ 0402.

The small **maritime museum** in St Mary's Rd traces the town's sea-going past; it's open daily 10 am to 5 pm (closed 1 to 2 pm); admission is IR£2.

Places to Stay & Eat

There are plenty of B&Bs, especially on the south side of town. You could try *Tara* (☎ 39333), about 1km from the town centre on the Gorey road, with singles/doubles for IR£19/28 without bathroom. In Main St *Óstán Beag* (☎ 33044) charges IR£30 a head.

Riverwalk Restaurant by the river offers kippers and smoked haddock to ring the breakfast changes. On Main St *Kitty's* pub-restaurant serves main courses for around IR£5, while *Christy's* also does good food, including vegetarian options. Lunch specials cost IR£4.50.

WICKLOW

Getting There & Away

Bus Éireann has regular services from Busáras in Dublin to Arklow via Wicklow Town. They stop outside the Chocolate Shop.

DART trains run to Dublin via Rathdrum, Wicklow Town, Greystones and Bray six times a day (three times on Sunday). One early morning service continues to Drogheda via Malahide, Rush, Lusk and Skerries. There are five trains a day to Rosslare (three on Sunday) and two to Gorey.

WICKLOW

Counties Wexford & Waterford

The ferries to Rosslare Harbour bring lots of visitors to the counties of Wexford and Waterford who are on their way to other destinations, but there are places here to enjoy in their own right. The coastline offers superb beaches and possibilities for water sports, and Wexford Town and particularly Waterford City make good bases for exploring. Both counties are rich in history, and the countryside, while lacking the rugged splendour of the west and south-west, has an appealing beauty that surprises many visitors.

County Wexford

County Wexford takes up the south-east corner of Ireland and many visitors arrive at Rosslare Harbour on the ferries from Wales and France. Most speed through en route to Dublin, Kilkenny or the west coast, but while Wexford hasn't a huge amount to divert them, there are a few spots worth pausing for.

Geographically, the county is almost entirely flat, except near its western borders with Carlow and Kilkenny where the Blackstairs Mountains rise to 796m at their highest point, Mt Leinster. There are some pleasant routes through these little explored hills, particularly west from Enniscorthy and over the Scullogue Gap.

Wexford Town is pleasant enough, but retains few traces of its Viking past. To its north, a string of fine beaches runs along the coast towards County Wicklow. In the centre, Enniscorthy is an attractive hilly town on the banks of the River Slaney. Farther west, the River Barrow runs right by New Ross, a good base for exploring the river's lovely upper reaches.

On the south coast is the fishing village of Kilmore Quay and farther west the flat and lonely Hook Peninsula, with one of the world's oldest lighthouses.

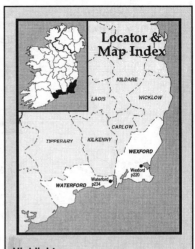

Highlights
- Walk, cycle or drive along the lovely Hook Peninsula in County Wexford
- Watch the birds on the Saltee Islands
- Explore the historic sights of Waterford city

WEXFORD TOWN

Wexford (Loch Garman) vies with Waterford City for the position of principal settlement in the south-east. It was once a thriving port, but over the centuries the slow-moving River Slaney has deposited so much silt and mud in the estuary as to make the channel almost unusable. Now most commercial sea traffic goes through Waterford and all passenger traffic through Rosslare Harbour, 20km to the south-east.

The Vikings arrived in the region around 850 AD, attracted by its handy location near the mouth of the River Slaney. The Viking name Waesfjord means 'harbour of mud flats' or 'sandy harbour'. The Normans captured the town just after their first landings

217

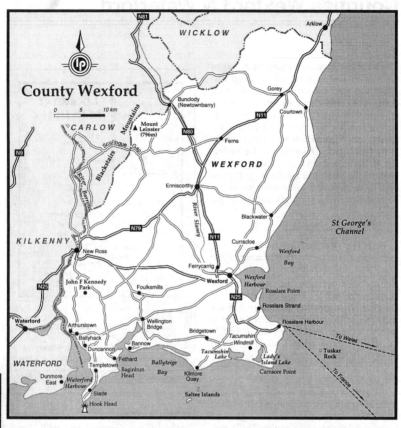

in 1169, and traces of their fort can still be seen in the grounds of the Irish National Heritage Park north of town at Ferrycarrig.

Cromwell included Wexford in his 1649-50 Irish tour. Three-quarters of the 2000 inhabitants were put to the sword, including all the town's Franciscan friars – the standard treatment for towns that refused to surrender. After Wexford, surrender became increasingly popular.

During the 1798 Rising, rebels made a determined stand in Wexford Town before they were defeated.

Modern Wexford is renowned for its opera festival, a good time to visit provided you plan well ahead.

Orientation

From Wexford Bridge at the north end of town, the quays run south-east along the waterfront as Commercial Quay, Custom House Quay and Paul Quay, with the tourist office in the small kink called the Crescent. The quays are of little interest except as a place for an evening stroll but run roughly parallel to North and South Main St, a block inland. Most of the banks, shops and other commercial outlets are along the Main Sts.

Information

The tourist office (☎ 053-23111), is on the waterfront at the Crescent. It's open May to September, 9 am to 6 pm, Monday to Saturday, and Sunday in July and August, 10 am to 5 pm. The rest of the year it's open 9 am to 5.15 pm, Monday to Friday. The Book Centre on North Main St has plenty of books on Irish topics as well as a limited stock of foreign newspapers and magazines. Readers Paradise in North Main St stocks second-hand paperbacks.

Discs for disc parking (30p per hour) can be bought in most newsagents.

The telephone code is ☎ 053.

The Crescent

As well as the Chamber of Commerce building which houses the tourist office, the Crescent is home to a statue of Commodore John Barry, a local seaman born in 1745, who emigrated to America and founded the US navy during the American Revolution.

Bull Ring

Between Commercial Quay and North Main St is the Bull Ring, at one time a centre for bull-baiting but also the site of Cromwell's long-remembered massacre. Nowadays it's just the intersection of several streets. The **Lone Pikeman** statue commemorates the participants in the 1798 Fenian rebellion.

There's usually a market in the New Market beside the Bull Ring on Friday and Saturday mornings.

West Gate

Some stretches of the town walls remain, including a fine section by Cornmarket. Of the six original town gates only the 14th century West Gate, at the north end of town on the corner of Slaney St, survives.

The West Gate Heritage Centre (☎ 46506) beside the gate has a audiovisual display on the history of Wexford. Admission is IR£1.50/1, and it's open Monday to Saturday 9.30 am to 5.30 pm, Sunday 2 to 6 pm in July and August. May, June and September it opens at 11 am.

Selskar Abbey

Selskar Abbey was founded by Alexander de la Roche in 1190 after a crusade to the Holy Land. Its present ruinous state is a result of Cromwell's visit in 1649. Strongbow's sister Bascilla is supposed to have married one of Henry II's brave lieutenants, Raymond le Gros, in the abbey.

The ruins should be unlocked when the Heritage Centre opens. At other times, it's rather hit or miss.

St Iberius' Church

South of the Bull Ring on Main St the existing St Iberius' Church was built in 1760 on the site of several previous churches. The graceful 18th century interior is worth a look, though whether you really need a IR£1 guided tour is debatable. Most noteworthy features are the altar rails from a Dublin church and a set of monuments dating back to the 18th century in the gallery. It's open 10 am to 5 pm.

Organised Tours

Tynan Tours (☎ 65929) runs tours from the tourist office 9.15 am to 4.30 pm Monday to Saturday (from 11 am on Sunday) from June through August. Wexford Historical Society provides free guided walking tours during the summer, Monday to Saturday at 11 am and 2.30 pm from Talbot and White's hotels. For more information contact the tourist office.

Wexford Opera Festival

This 17-day extravaganza in October is an excuse for Wexford townsfolk to shake out their cocktail dresses and dinner jackets and prepare for a huge influx of cultured visitors. The festival began in 1951 and has grown to be the country's premier opera event, presenting many rarely performed operas and shows to packed audiences.

During the festival, the town is transformed, with street theatre, poetry readings and exhibitions every day.

Tickets for the principal operas are hard to come by and pricey. Booking is essential and should be done at least three months in

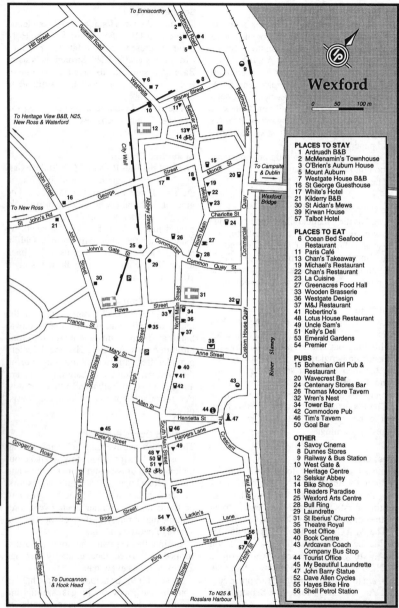

Wexford

0   50   100 m

PLACES TO STAY
1 Ardruadh B&B
2 McMenamin's Townhouse
3 O'Brien's Auburn House
5 Mount Auburn
7 Westgate House B&B
16 St George Guesthouse
17 White's Hotel
21 Kilderry B&B
30 St Aidan's Mews
39 Kirwan House
57 Talbot Hotel

PLACES TO EAT
6 Ocean Bed Seafood
   Restaurant
11 Paris Café
13 Chan's Takeaway
19 Michael's Restaurant
22 Chan's Restaurant
23 La Cuisine
27 Greenacres Food Hall
33 Wooden Brasserie
36 Westgate Design
37 M&J Restaurant
41 Robertino's
48 Lotus House Restaurant
49 Uncle Sam's
51 Kelly's Deli
53 Emerald Gardens
54 Premier

PUBS
15 Bohemian Girl Pub &
   Restaurant
20 Wavecrest Bar
24 Centenary Stores Bar
26 Thomas Moore Tavern
32 Wren's Nest
34 Tower Bar
42 Commodore Pub
46 Tim's Tavern
50 Goal Bar

OTHER
4 Savoy Cinema
8 Dunnes Stores
9 Railway & Bus Station
10 West Gate &
   Heritage Centre
12 Selskar Abbey
14 Bike Shop
18 Readers Paradise
28 Wexford Arts Centre
29 Bull Ring
31 St Iberius' Church
35 Theatre Royal
38 Post Office
40 Book Centre
43 Ardcavan Coach
   Company Bus Stop
44 Tourist Office
45 My Beautiful Laundrette
47 John Barry Statue
52 Dave Allen Cycles
55 Hayes Bike Hire
56 Shell Petrol Station

WEXFORD & WATERFORD

advance. You can write to the Wexford Opera Festival at Theatre Royal, 27 High St, Wexford, or phone the festival office (☎ 22240) or the box office (☎ 22144).

Places to Stay

Camping *Ferrybank Camping & Caravan Park* (☎ 44378) is across the river from the town centre, off the Dublin road. It has good facilities and opens Easter to mid-October. A tent for two people costs IR£6.

Hostel *Kirwan House* (☎ 21208) in Mary St is a new hostel with dorm beds for IR£7.50. The owners may be able to collect you from Rosslare Harbour.

B&Bs *Westgate House* (☎ 22167) near the railway station has rooms from IR£17/32. *Ardruadh* (☎ 23194) is round the corner on Spawell Rd and costs from IR£20/36; set back from the road, it could be a bit quieter.

McMenamin's Townhouse (☎ 46442) is also near the station at 3 Auburn Terrace, off Redmond Rd. The IR£19.50 per head rate includes a particularly good breakfast. Next door at No 2 *O'Brien's Auburn House* (☎ 23605) charges IR£22/36 a single/double. *Mount Auburn* (☎ 24609), at No 1, charges from IR£18 a head.

Half a km from the centre on St John's Rd, *Kilderry* (☎ 23848) has rooms from IR£22/28. Across the road *The St George Guesthouse* (☎ 43474) at the top of George St charges from IR£25/40. On John St, *St Aidan's Mews* (☎ 22691) has rooms from IR£19/34.

Hotels *White's Hotel* (☎ 22311; fax 45000), on the corner of George St and North Main St, is mostly new but incorporates part of an old coaching inn. It's friendly and well run, with B&B from IR£37.50. The *Talbot Hotel* (☎ 22566; fax 23377) in Trinity St has a ghastly exterior but the rooms are good. B&B runs from IR£52/84, with big discounts for children.

The very comfortable *Wexford Lodge* (☎ 23611; fax 23342), over the bridge on the river's east bank, is a bit cheaper, with rooms

from IR£40/70. The top-class, modern *Ferrycarrig Hotel* (☎ 20999; fax 20982), beside the Heritage Park on the banks of the River Slaney, charges from IR£40/71.

Clonard House (☎ 43141) is a 1780s farmhouse 3km from town off the main Waterford road (N25) with B&B for IR£25/40.

Places to Eat

Cafés & Takeaways Downstairs in the marvellous *Westgate Design* shop a café serves breakfast for IR£3.95 right through till 4 pm.

Kelly's Deli, 80 South Main St, does sandwiches and lunches with some vegetarian choices. Similarly *La Cuisine* at 80 North Main St offers soups and toasted sandwiches around the IR£2 mark. Other possible lunch stops include *Wooden Brasserie* on the corner with Rowe St and the *Paris Café* at the top of Selskar St. The *Cellar Bistro* in the Arts Centre is another popular lunch venue.

You can put together a picnic at *Greenacres Food Hall* in North Main St or sit down for a bite and a drink at *Playwrite Tearooms* at the back.

North and South Main Sts cater for most tastes, with fish & chips at the *Premier*, 104 South Main St, or fast food at *Uncle Sam's*, 53 South Main St. *Robertino's*, 19 North Main St, does pizzas from IR£3.90 and pasta from IR£4.95. Also on North Main St is the *M&J Restaurant*, a cafeteria-style place with a long menu and takeaway service. It closes at 7.30 pm Monday to Saturday.

Restaurants Café-ish *Michael's Restaurant*, 94 North Main St, serves omelettes, steak and fish in the IR£4 to IR£10 range. Readers have recommended the *Ocean Bed Seafood Restaurant* in Westgate which will set you back a good IR£9 for a main course.

For Chinese food, try the *Lotus House* (☎ 24273), 70 South Main St, or, for more upmarket European and Chinese food, *Chan's Restaurant* (☎ 22356), 90 North Main St. There's also the *Emerald Gardens* (☎ 24856) further down South Main St.

Entertainment

Pubs Even for Ireland, Wexford has plenty of pubs, many of them strung along North and South Main Sts where you'll find *Tim's Tavern*, the *Commodore* and the *Bohemian Girl*. The *Goal Bar*, on South Main St, should have been completely renovated by the time you read this.

On Cornmarket, towards the abbey ruins, is the atmospheric old *Thomas Moore Tavern*. Music often features at the *Wren's Nest* and the *Tower Bar* on the quay. For the 20s to 30s age group the in pub is the *Centenary Stores*, on Charlotte St just off North Main St, which has Irish music on Wednesday night. The *Wavecrest Bar* on Commercial Quay has Irish music almost every night during the summer.

Theatres & Cinema The *Theatre Royal* (☎ 22144), in High St, hosts drama and opera. The *Wexford Arts Centre* (☎ 23764), in the 18th century Market House and Assembly Room in Cornmarket, caters for exhibitions, theatre, dance and music performances.

The three-screen *Savoy* cineplex is near the railway station. Artier films show at the Arts Centre on Tuesday nights at 8 pm.

Getting There & Away

Continue south from the quays for Rosslare Harbour. For Duncannon or Hook Head, turn west either at the Crescent along Harpers Lane or from Paul Quay along King St.

Note the short cut between counties Wexford and Waterford by taking the Ballyhack to Passage East ferry, avoiding the longer route via New Ross.

Bus Bus Éireann (☎ 22522) is at the railway station on Redmond Place at the north end of the quays. There are buses to Rosslare Harbour (seven daily, 20 minutes, IR£2.50), Dublin (six daily, 2½ hours, IR£7), Killarney (two daily, 5½ hours, IR£15) and all stops en route.

It also operates twice weekly services to Gorey via Courtown Harbour. July and

August, it runs tours of the surrounding areas.

JJ Kavanagh (☎ 0503-43081) has a twice-daily service to Carlow via Enniscorthy from Redmond Place. Ardcavan Coach Company (☎ 22561) operates daily services between Wexford and Dublin. Buses leave from outside Asple's Irish pub in the Crescent at 8 am. A one-way fare is IR£5.

Train The O'Hanrahan railway station (☎ 22522) is at the north end of town in Redmond Place. Wexford is on the Dublin to Rosslare Harbour line and is serviced by three trains daily in each direction (2½ hours, IR£10). There are also three trains daily to Rosslare Harbour (25 minutes, IR£3.50), two daily to Wicklow (IR£8) and frequent services to Enniscorthy (IR£4.50).

Getting Around

The Bike Shop (☎ 22514), 9 Selskar St, and Hayes (☎ 22462), 108 South Main St, have bikes for IR£7/30 a day/week. Dave Allen Cycles (☎ 22516), 84 South Main St, hires out bikes for IR£5 a day.

AROUND WEXFORD TOWN
Irish National Heritage Park

Four km north of Wexford, at Ferrycarrig beside the Dublin to Rosslare N11 road, the Irish National Heritage Park (☎ 41733) is an outdoor theme park which attempts to condense the country's entire history on one site.

A visit takes in recreations of a Mesolithic campsite, a Neolithic farmstead, a dolmen, a cyst burial tomb, a stone circle, a rath or ring fort, a monastery, a *crannóg* or lake settlement, a Viking shipyard, a motte-and-bailey, a Norman castle, a round tower and a couple of other smaller displays. A replica Viking longship is anchored on the River Slaney outside the park.

The entry fee of IR£3/2 includes an informative guided tour. Opening hours are 10 am to 7 pm, March to October, with last admissions at 5.30 pm. A bus goes to the park from Wexford Town; phone Westgate Minitours on ☎ 24655 for details.

Johnstown Castle & Gardens

Seven km south-west of Wexford on the way to Murntown, the former home of the Fitz-gerald and Esmonde families is a splendid 19th century Gothic-style castellated house overlooking a small lake and surrounded by 20 hectares of thickly wooded gardens. The castle and its outbuildings now house an agricultural research centre, the headquarters of the Irish Environmental Protection Agency and an agricultural museum.

The castle itself isn't open to the public, but the gardens are open daily 9 am to 5.30 pm. The museum opens 9 am to 5 pm Monday to Friday, and 2 to 5 pm at week-ends, June through August. Admission costs IR£1.50/50p.

Wexford Wildfowl Reserve

Five km north-east of Wexford Town are the North Slobs, a swathe of low-lying land reclaimed from the sea. In winter, the Slobs are home to half the world's population of Greenland white-fronted geese, numbering some 10,000 birds. It's a great sight to stand on the sea wall and watch the V-shaped formations of geese flying into the darkness of the bay, where they pass the night on sandbanks and islands.

Wintertime is also good for brent geese from Arctic Canada, and throughout the year you'll see mallards, pochards, godwits, mute and bewick swans, redshanks, terns, coots, oystercatchers and many other species.

Wexford Wildfowl Reserve was set up to protect the birds' feeding grounds. Along-side the usual visitor centre, there's also an observation tower and assorted hides. It's open, free, daily mid-April through Septem-ber, 9 am to 6 pm; 10 am to 5 pm for the rest of the year.

To get to the reserve leave Wexford on the Dublin road and head north for 3.5km until you see a signpost pointing to the right.

The Raven

This lovely nature reserve is near Curracloe. A long walk through forest brings you out on dunes where you may see Greenland white-fronted geese and various waders. To get there take the Dublin road out of town, follow the signposts for Curracloe Beach and watch for signs for the Raven off to the right.

Curracloe Beach

Over 11km long, Curracloe is one of a string of magnificent beaches that line the coast north of Wexford Town. Extensive dunes behind the beach provide some shelter, and you can pitch a tent if you're discreet. Curracloe Beach is 15km north-east of Wexford off the Dublin road.

ROSSLARE STRAND

Rosslare Strand is about 8km north of Ross-lare Harbour and 15km south of Wexford Town. The long golden beaches attract huge crowds in summer and there are also good walks north to Rosslare Point. The long shallow bay is ideal for windsurfing, and boards, wetsuits and tuition are available from Kieran Lambert at the Rosslare Windsurfing Centre (☎ 053-32101).

The telephone code is ☎ 053.

Places to Stay

Camping *Burrow Camping & Caravan Park* (☎ 32190), just south of the village, has excellent facilities including a laundry, a games room and tennis courts but charges IR£8 to IR£14 per night depending on the season, regardless of tent size or number of people. *Rosslare Holiday Park* (☎ 32291) has more basic facilities and charges IR£8.

B&Bs *Decca House* (☎ 32410), 1km from Rosslare Strand, charges from IR£20/28 a single/double. *Harbour Lights* (☎ 32295) is 3.5km inland at Grahmorack. Head for Tagoat on the main road to the harbour and turn south; the house is signposted 1km down the road. Singles/doubles cost IR£21/32 but there are only four rooms.

Hotels With every sports and leisure facility in the book, *Kelly's Resort Hotel* (☎ 32114; fax 32222) is popular with families. B&B is from IR£53/100.

Getting There & Away
Trains on the main line between Dublin, Wexford and Rosslare Harbour stop at Rosslare Strand. Only the 11 am bus from Rosslare Harbour and the 11 pm from Wexford to Rosslare Harbour stop there.

ROSSLARE HARBOUR
In the south-eastern corner of the country, Rosslare Harbour (Ros Láir) is 20km southeast of Wexford Town and has busy ferry connections to Wales and France. The harbour surrounds are not particularly pretty or pedestrian-friendly and you might prefer to head straight on to Wexford. If you do need to stay there's plenty of accommodation in what is really a large village.

Information
The tourist office in the ferry terminal building (☎ 053-33622) opens all year while the one by the main Wexford road in Kilrane north of town (☎ 33232) opens June to September.

The telephone code is ☎ 053.

Places to Stay
Camping You might be able to pitch a tent for IR£2 a head at *Foley* (☎ 33522), 3 St Martin's Rd. The nearest official campsites are 8km north in Rosslare Strand (see the previous section).

Hostel The An Óige *Rosslare Harbour Hostel* (☎ 33399), on Goulding St, is up the hill from the ferry terminal; take the flight of steps on the left as you leave the harbour and cut down beside the Hotel Rosslare. It opens early or late for ferry arrivals and departures. Beds in 19-bed dorms cost IR£6 a head.

B&Bs The cheapest place to stay is the basic *Foley* (☎ 33522), 3 St Martin's Rd, which has beds for IR£8. Otherwise one of the cheapest B&Bs is the welcoming *Glenville* (☎ 33142) on St Patrick's Rd (the N25 Wexford road), at IR£15/30. *Carragh Lodge* (☎ 33492) in quieter Station Rd has singles/doubles for IR£21/32. Overlooking the harbour, the big *Ailsa Lodge* (☎ 33230) has

beds for IR£30/40. If these are full there are lots of other B&Bs overlooking the harbour and a km further inland along the Wexford Rd in Kilrane.

Hotels There are several smart hotels in St Martin's Rd overlooking the ferry port. The bright pink *Hotel Rosslare* (☎ 33110) sits on top of the cliff and has plenty of facilities for IR£49/78; ask about special deals for longer stays. The nearby *Tuskar House Hotel* (☎ 33363) charges IR£39/68 in high season. Plushest of all is the *Great Southern Hotel* (☎ 33233) which has an indoor pool and charges IR£80 per room.

Places to Eat
One burger bar aside, there are few places to eat except the hotels. *Hotel Rosslare* does excellent lunches from IR£7; its attractive *Portholes Bar* also serves hefty portions of bar food, with main courses from around IR£5.

Getting There & Away
Ferry Two ferry companies operate to and from Rosslare Harbour and there's a convenient train and bus station by the ferry terminal.

Stena Line (☎ 33115) has day and night crossings to Fishguard in Wales taking around 3½ hours, while Irish Ferries (☎ 33158) has two daily sailings to Pembroke in Wales, taking around 4½ hours. From late March through September, Irish Ferries also has one or two sailings a week to Cherbourg, two or three to Le Havre and one or two to Roscoff in France (late May to mid-September only). Sailings take around 24 hours.

Bus Bus Éireann has services to Wexford (six daily, 20 minutes, IR£2.50) and Dublin (six daily, 3 hours, IR£9), and a single daily service to Galway via Kilkenny in July and August (6½ hours, IR£16).

Ardcavan Coach Company (☎ 22561) operates between Rosslare Harbour and Dublin daily via Wexford, Enniscorthy, Ferns, Gorey and Arklow.

TOM SMALLMAN

MARK DAFFEY

TOM SMALLMAN

County Wicklow
Top Left: Abbey of Vallis Salutis, Baltinglass
Top Right: Glendalough, Wicklow Mountains
Bottom: Saviour's Church, Glendalough

TOM SMALLMAN

JOHN MURRAY

TOM SMALLMAN

County Wexford
Top Left: Statue of Commodore John Barry, Wexford Town
Top Right: The lighthouse, Hook Head
Bottom: Dual-purpose pub in Wexford Town

Train Trains (☎ 33114) operate from Rosslare Europort station at the ferry terminal to Wexford (three daily, IR£2), Dublin (three daily, three hours, IR£10.50), Waterford (two daily except Sunday, 1¼ hours, IR£6) and Limerick (one daily except Sunday, 3½ hours, IR£12).

Car Rental Budget (☎ 33318), Hertz (☎ 23511) and Murrays (☎ 33634) share a desk in the terminal.

SOUTH OF ROSSLARE HARBOUR

Nine km south of Rosslare Harbour is **Carnsore Point**, where Ireland's first nuclear power station was to be built, had cost not killed it off. Carnsore Point was noted as the country's south-easternmost point on the map drawn by Ptolemy in the 2nd century AD. Offshore to the east is Tuskar Rock Lighthouse.

Carne has a fine beach, and *Carne Beach Caravan & Camping Park* (☎ 053-31131) is near the point. There's excellent pub food and seafood in the *Lobster Pot* (☎ 053-31110) bar and restaurant in Carne. A reader rated the mussels but warned that you need to grab a seat by 6.30 pm.

Turning west brings you to **Tacumshin**, where in 1840 Nicholas Moran built the Tacumshin Windmill, one of Ireland's few thatched windmills. The key can be picked up from the shop where you park but you'll probably be charged. Just to the east is **Lady's Island**, site of an early Augustinian priory and still a centre of devotion. Both Tacumshin and Lady's Island have small brackish lakes which are home to migrating and breeding **birds**. Lady's Island is best from autumn to spring, when you may see brent geese, shelducks, redshanks, godwits, mute swans, teals and various terns.

Bridgetown, 12km south-west of Wexford Town on the way to lovely Kilmore Quay, was the first part of Ireland to be colonised by the Anglo-Normans. To the west, en route to Hook Head, the Irish chapter of the Hell's Angels meet at **Wellington Bridge** over the June bank holiday weekend! **Hook Head** is well worth a detour

---

Forth & Bargy is Yola to Me

Faint remnants of a dialect called *yola* still survive in south-eastern County Wexford, which is sometimes called 'Forth & Bargy'. Yola stood for 'ye olde language' and was a mixture of old French, English, Irish, Welsh and Flemish. Examples of the language would be to *curk*, meaning to sit on your thighs, or to be *hachee* or bad-tempered. A *chi o' whate* means a small amount of straw while a *stouk* is a truculent woman. ■

---

and you can save yourself a circuitous trip north by taking a ferry from Ballyhack across to Passage East in Waterford (see Passage East). There's no public transport to this area.

KILMORE QUAY

A small fishing village on the east side of Ballyteige Bay, peaceful Kilmore Quay is noted for its lobsters and deep-sea fishing. The Seafood Festival in the second week of July involves all types of seafood tastings, music and dancing.

Lining the attractive main street up from the harbour are a fair number of whitewashed thatched cottages. The harbour is the jumping-off point for the Saltee Islands, which are clearly visible out to sea. In the harbour the Guillemot Lightship houses a small maritime museum, open during the summer. To the north-west a good sandy beach stretches towards Cullenstown.

The telephone code is ☎ 053.

Places to Stay & Eat

Killturk Hostel (☎ 29883), 2km from Kilmore Quay on the main Wexford road, is a good place to stay. It charges IR£6.50 for a dorm bed or IR£16 for private rooms, and has a low-priced café.

At *Coral House* (☎ 29640), in Grange, Kilmore, 2km along the R739 road, singles/doubles cost from IR£19/28.

Dining possibilities include the *Wooden House Restaurant & Bar*, the *Silver Fox Restaurant* or the *Hotel Saltees* (☎ 29601), which has a good-value tourist menu and B&B for IR£31/52.

Getting There & Away

Public transport to Kilmore Quay is very limited. On Wednesday and Saturday only there are two Bus Éireann services a day from Wexford Town. Every Friday there's also a private bus from Kilmore Quay to Wexford. For details, ask at the post office.

SALTEE ISLANDS

The Saltee Islands are 4km offshore from Kilmore Quay and have some of the oldest rocks in Europe, dating back 2000 million years or more.

Once the haunt of privateers and smugglers, the Saltees are one of Ireland's most important bird sanctuaries, home to over 375 recorded species, principally gannets, guillemots, cormorants, kittiwakes, puffins and Manx shearwaters. The best time to visit is the spring and early summer nesting season, as once the chicks can fly, the birds leave. By early August it's eerily quiet.

The Saltees – nicknamed the 'graveyard of a thousand ships' – were touched by the 1798 Rising, for it was here that two of the Wexford rebel leaders, Bagenal Harvey and Dr John Colclough, were found hiding before they were both brought to Wexford, hanged and beheaded. The Saltees were bought in 1943 by Michael Neale who then crowned himself Prince Michael, the 'First Prince of the Saltees'. He even erected a throne and obelisk in his own honour on the Great Saltee. To book a crossing to the Saltees try local boatmen like Declan Bates (☎ 053-29684) or Tom O'Brien (☎ 053-29727). Depending on the weather, boats leave most days in summer at 10 am and return at about 3 or 4 pm. It's a 30-minute crossing and the fare is IR£12 return. For more on the islands read *The Saltees, Islands of Birds & Legends* (O'Brien Press) by Richard Roche & Oscar Merne.

HOOK PENINSULA

The south-west of the county is dominated by the long tapering finger of Hook Penin-

sula, terminating at Hook Head. Cromwell's statement that Waterford Town would fall 'by Hook or by Crooke', referred to the two possible landing points from which to take the area: here or at Crooke in County Waterford. In good weather, it's a fine journey out to the lighthouse at the tip of the head and back along the west side to Duncannon.

The telephone code is ☎ 051.

On the way out to Hook, **Tintern Abbey** is a 12th century Cistercian abbey in a lovely rural setting near the village of Saltmills. It was founded by William Marshall, earl of Pembroke, after he nearly perished at sea. Following restoration it was expected to reopen to visitors by 1998. Continuing south towards the head, **Fethard-on-Sea** is the largest village in the area.

Just south of Fethard, near Bannow Bay, is **Baginbun Head** where the Anglo-Normans made their first landings in Ireland in 1169. Joining forces with the far larger army of Dermot MacMurrough, they captured Wexford in the same year. Ramparts were built to fortify the headland at Baginbun, until more Normans arrived in 1170 under Raymond le Gros. Shortly after he landed, 3000 Irish-Norse soldiers set out from Waterford City and attacked Baginbun, outnumbering the defenders seven to one.

Le Gros stampeded a herd of cattle onto them and then taught them a lesson in organised warfare. Seventy of Waterford's citizens and soldiers were captured, had their legs broken and were thrown over the cliffs to their death. So it was to be that:

> At the creek of Baginbun,
> Ireland was lost and won.

After the Norman leader Strongbow had landed at Passage East with another 1200 men, the Anglo-Normans gathered their forces and marched on to Waterford City, marking the start of more than 800 years of English involvement in Ireland.

Today a small road leads down to a rather battered memorial overlooking Baginbun Beach. If you look carefully at the headland on the right, you can just make out the overgrown earthen ramparts built by the Normans when they first arrived. The stone **Martello Tower** dates from the early 1800s.

The journey out to **Hook Head** is lovely, the land extremely flat with few houses interrupting the open space. About 2km from the head, turning left at a T-junction brings you down to the odd village of **Slade** where a ruined castle dominates the harbour.

Farther south, Hook Head is crowned by Europe's, and possibly the world's, oldest **lighthouse**. It's said that monks lit a beacon on the head from the 5th century and that the first Viking invaders were so happy to have a guiding light that they left the monks alone. In the 12th century a more solid beacon was erected by Ray-mond le Gros, and 800 years later that is largely the structure you see today.

There are lovely walks both sides of the head, a haunting and beautiful place in the evening. Be careful of the numerous blowholes on the west side of the peninsula. The rocks around the lighthouse are carboniferous limestone, rich in fossil remains. If you search carefully, you may find 350-million-year-old shells and tiny disc-like pieces of crinoids, a type of starfish. Hook Head is also a good vantage point for **bird-watching**; over 200 species have been recorded passing through.

The village of **Duncannon** is a small holiday resort with a lovely sandy beach and a good view over Waterford Harbour. To the west is Duncannon Fort, one of many structures built on this site since pre-Norman times. Admission costs IR£1.50/50p.

Four km to the north of Duncannon is **Ballyhack** where there's a year-round ferry to Passage East in County Waterford (see Getting There & Away under Passage East later). Ballyhack also has a 15th century **Knights Templar castle** overlooking the estuary. It's open 10 am to 6 pm daily in July and August, and from noon Wednesday to Sunday in September and April through June. Admission costs IR£1/50p.

Dunbrody Abbey is a beautiful ruin on the west side of Hook Head near the village of Campile and about 9km north of Duncannon. It was built around 1170 AD by Cistercian monks from Buildwas in Shropshire, England. Most of the structure still survives to make a fine sight among the fields. Nearby are the ruins of **Dunbrody Castle**, with a craft shop and small museum. The site opens 10 am to 6 pm, April through June and in September, staying open until 7 pm in July and August. Admission costs IR£1.50/1, with an additional charge to visit the maze.

Scuba Diving

Hook Head is popular with divers; the best spots are out from the inlet under the lighthouse or from the rocks at the south-west corner of the head. The underwater scenery is pleasant, with lots of caves, crevasses and gullies. The depths are no more than 15m. If it's too rough try Churchtown, about 1km back from the point just before the road goes inland by the ruined church. Follow the path west to some gullies and coves. Otherwise try the rocks south of Slade harbour, a popular area. Tanks can be filled at the Naomh Seosamh Hotel in Fethard and in summer there are often local dive groups here.

Places to Stay

Fethard-on-Sea has most of the local accommodation, but there are a few places on the west side of the peninsula around Duncannon and Ballyhack.

Camping *Fethard Camping & Caravan Park* (☎ 397123) is at the northern end of town, while the *Ocean Island Caravan Park* (☎ 397148) is about a km farther north. Both charge around IR£8 for a tent for two. Your best bet is to stock up and head a farther 12km out to Hook Head where you can camp along the shore. There's a small petrol station and shop about 5km from the headland for replenishing supplies.

Hostel The only hostel in the region is the An Óige *Arthurstown Hostel* (☎ 389411), 1km from Ballyhack on the west side of the peninsula.

B&Bs In Fethard the *Hotel Naomh Seosamh* (☎ 397129), on the main street, is popular and good fun at weekends; it costs from IR£18 a head and has a diving compressor. *Bore-a-Trae House* (☎ 397102), 3km south-west of Fethard on the way to Templetown head, is a good B&B charging IR£17/32.

Places to Eat

Fethard's hotels and pubs are the peninsula's principal eating spots, but nowhere particularly stands out. On the west side of the peninsula, Ballyhack has the *Neptune Bar & Seafood Restaurant* (☎ 389284), a terrific place serving simple but delicious seafood. À la carte dinners cost around IR£17 but you can bring your own bottle (IR£3 corkage charge).

Hopetown House in Foulksmills has the *Cellar Restaurant* (☎ 565771), with dinner from IR£21.50 or an early-bird midweek special until 8 pm for IR£16.95. *Moorings Seafood Bar & Restaurant* (☎ 389242) in Duncannon has very good seafood while *Templar's Inn*, in Templetown, also specialises in seafood.

Getting There & Away

Particularly if you're travelling by bike, it's well worth taking the 10 minute crossing between County Wexford and County Waterford on the Ballyhack to Passage East ferry. For details on fares and times see under Passage East, County Waterford, later in this chapter. Bus services are virtually non-existent, although on Monday and Thursday, Bus Éireann buses from Wexford to Waterford will drop you in Fethard. They leave Wexford Town at 2.50 pm. Return services leave Fethard at 11.26 am.

NEW ROSS

New Ross (Rhos Mhic Triúin), 34km west of Wexford Town, is a sizeable settlement astride the River Barrow. It's not an especially pretty town, with large oil-storage tanks and old warehouses looming over the river banks, but the east bank is better than the west, with some steep, narrow streets and St Mary's Church.

New Ross was the scene of fierce fighting during the 1798 Rising when a group of rebels under Bagenal Harvey and John Kelly tried to take the town. They were repelled by the defending garrison, leaving 3000 people dead and much of the town in ruins.

Information

A tourist office (☎ 051-21857) operates from the refurbished grain store building on the quay from mid-June through August.

The telephone code is ☎ 051.

St Mary's Church

A roofless ruin on Church Lane, St Mary's Church was founded by William and Isabella in the 13th century. Inside is a rough slab with some barely decipherable words, 'Isabel ... Laegn', which translates roughly as 'Isabel of Leinster'. She died around 1220 and was buried in England so this is probably a memorial to her. The church key is available from the caretaker across the road.

Cruises

The Galley Cruising Restaurant (☎ 421723) operates out of New Ross. The lunch time cruise, which sails at 12.30 pm May to October, costs IR£13. A two-hour cruise including afternoon tea leaves at 3 pm from June to August and costs IR£6. Dinner cruises May to September cost from IR£20 and depart at 5.30 pm or 7 pm.

Places to Stay & Eat

The IHH *MacMurrough Farm Hostel* (☎ 421383) is a well thought of place, sleeping 17, 3km north-east of town. A bed costs IR£6.

Katie Pat's (☎ 22404) on the quay is good for cheap sandwiches and lunches. It also has a restaurant upstairs and serves dinner from 5 to 9 pm, with main courses in the IR£6 to IR£12 range. Across the road from Katie Pat's is *John V's* pub which does a good bar lunch, and has a seafood restaurant upstairs.

Getting There & Away

Bus Éireann (☎ 053-22522) has a twice-daily service to Dublin from outside Ryan's on the quay. It also has at least three daily services to Wexford and Rosslare Harbour, and to Waterford. At least one bus a day goes to Duncannon on the Hook.

AROUND NEW ROSS

Five km south of New Ross, **Dunganstown** was the birthplace of Patrick Kennedy, grandfather of John F Kennedy. Patrick left Ireland for the USA in 1858 and JFK visited the town during his presidency. The original Kennedy house no longer exists, but there's a small cottage belonging to the Ryan family who are direct descendants, and a small plaque marks the spot.

A couple of km to the south, the **John F Kennedy Park & Arboretum** (☎ 051-88171) covers 252 hectares of woodlands and gardens with more than 4500 species of trees and shrubs. The park was opened in 1968 in memory of the late US president, and was funded by some prominent Irish-Americans. It's open daily 10 am to 5 pm, October to March, to 6.30 pm in April and September, and to 8 pm from May through August. Admission costs IR£2/1.

Slieve Coillte hill, opposite the park entrance, offers a splendid view of the surrounding countryside and the Saltee Islands.

ENNISCORTHY

Enniscorthy (Inis Coirthaidh) is an attractive hilly little town, on the banks of the River Slaney in the heart of County Wexford, 20km north-west of Wexford Town. It was the site of some of the fiercest fighting of the 1798 Rising.

Information

The tourist office (☎ 054-34699) in the town centre opens mid-June through August only. The main post office is at the bottom of Castle Hill on Abbey Square.

A good time to visit is late June/early July, when Enniscorthy holds its annual Strawberry Fair, a harvest festival with pub extensions, strawberries & cream and the crowning of a 'Strawberry Queen'. For exact dates and details phone ☎ 21688.

The telephone code is ☎ 054.

Enniscorthy Castle & Wexford County Museum

A fine stout building with drum towers at the corners, Enniscorthy's impressive Norman castle dates from 1205 and was a private residence until 1951. The poet Edmund Spenser lived here for a time and locals claim that Queen Elizabeth I gave him the castle in return for the many flattering things he said about her in his great work *The Faerie Queene*.

It was the site of a fierce battle in 1649, and during the 1798 Rising the rebels took control of the town and used the castle as a prison. Today it houses Wexford County Museum (☎ 35926), a mish-mash of bits and pieces, which is sorely in need of an overhaul.

The castle and museum open Monday to Saturday 10 am to 6 pm (closed 1 to 2 pm) and Sunday 2 to 5.30 pm, April through September. The rest of the year it opens afternoons only (in December and January on Sundays only). Admission is IR£2/1.

Potteries

If you fancy a clay plant pot, there are numerous potteries round town including Hillview and Carley's Bridge potteries (which dates back to 1694), both on the road to New Ross;

The Battle of Vinegar Hill

A memorial to Father John Murphy and the band of rebels who stormed Enniscorthy and captured the castle in May 1798 dominates the Market Square. One faction marched under the banner MWS, for 'Murder Without Sin'. The last major battle of the rising took place on Vinegar Hill, to the east of town, where the rebels had set up their headquarters. On 9 June, a force of 20,000 troops led by generals Lake and Johnson almost completely surrounded the rebels, who held out against huge odds for 30 days. The ruined windmill on the hill was once the rebel command post.

The road to Vinegar Hill is signposted from the railway station. It's a half-hour walk, and you'll be rewarded by panoramic views of Enniscorthy. ■

Badger's Hill Pottery, farther along the same road; and Kiltrea Bridge Pottery, north-west of the town.

Places to Stay
B&Bs *Murphy's* (☎ 33522), 9 Main St above a bar and shop, costs from IR£14/28. Also central is *Old Bridge House* (☎ 34222) at Slaney Place. *Murphy Flood's Hotel* (☎ /fax 33413) is conveniently located on Main St just up from Market Square, with B&B from IR£32/54.

Woodville House (☎ 47810), with comfortable rooms from IR£21/32, is 8km south on the minor Ballyhogue road, along the west side of the River Slaney. In Ballycarney, *Oakville Lodge* (☎ 88626) and its fine gardens overlook the Slaney Valley, with B&B from IR£19/32. The house is 9km away, signposted off the N80 road to Bunclody. A lovely mansion dating from 1840, *Ballinkeele House* (☎ 38105) lies 10km to the south-east in Ballymurn. The four elegant rooms cost IR£48/80 a single/double but are only let March through October.

Places to Eat
Concorde at the top of Rafter St has set lunches for IR£4.25 and *Waffle's Bistro* on Castle Hill has lunch specials for IR£6.95. *Rackard's* in Rafter St is also extremely popular at lunch time.

At the monument end of Rafter St try the *Paris Café* or *The Baked Potato* for tea and cakes.

China China dishes up Chinese meals at the top of Rafter St, while *Malocci's* in Slaney St does rather overpriced pizzas as well as full Irish breakfasts for IR£3.95. The restaurant at *Murphy Flood's Hotel* has early evening bar specials for IR£6.50.

The *Antique Tavern*, at the bottom of Slaney St, offers good and affordable lunches (but not to footpads, thimblemen or three-card tricksters), as does the *Tavern* in Templeshannon, on the east bank of the river, which has music on Sunday night.

Getting There & Away
Bus Éireann buses stop on the east bank of the river outside the Bus Stop Shop. There are six daily buses (five on Sunday) to Dublin, as well as to Rosslare Harbour (one hour, IR£5) and Wexford Town.

Enniscorthy is on the Dublin to Rosslare Harbour line with three trains daily in each direction. The station (☎ 33488) is on the east bank of the river.

GOREY
Gorey is a small traffic bottleneck of a town 20km south of Arklow, on the main Dublin to Wexford road and below the foothills of the Wicklow Mountains.

During the 1798 Rising, it was attacked by rebels trying to reach the coast road to Dublin. They camped on Gorey Hill just south-west of the town and there's a memorial to their efforts at one end of Main St. The Church of Ireland parish **church** has some fine stained glass by Michael Healy from around 1904. There's a good ramble out to **Tara Hill** 7km north-east of town.

The tourist office (☎ 055-21248) on Lower Main St opens all year round.

COURTOWN
Seven km south-east of Gorey along the L31 is the small seaside resort of Courtown at the mouth of the River Ounavarra which boasts Ireland's lowest rainfall. The beach to the north of the village is popular with Dublin holidaymakers and has the usual amusement arcades, takeaways and seaside caravan parks and guesthouses. The Bayview Hotel dominates the beachfront.

The telephone code is ☎ 055.

Places to Stay
Camping & Hostel *Courtown Caravan & Camping Park* (☎ 25280) is well signposted just inland from Courtown. It charges IR£10 per tent or IR£5.50 if you are either hiking or cycling, and has excellent facilities. *Parklands Holiday Park* (☎ 25202), just south of Courtown, has only 10 tent pitches and charges IR£12 for a family tent or IR£6.50 for a hiker or cyclist. Otherwise you could find a quiet spot among the dunes and pitch your tent free. The IHO *Anchorage*

Hostel (☎ 25335) is a small place some 5km south of Courtown at Poulshone. Dorm beds are IR£6, doubles IR£14.

B&Bs *Riverchapel House* (☎ 25120), 1km from the harbour charges from IR£28 a double. *Seamount House* (☎ 25128), in the village, costs from IR£19/30.

Places to Eat
Good restaurants include the *Bosun's Chair* in Ardmine, 2km south of Courtown along the coast (☎ 25198), and the *Cowhouse Bistro* (☎ 25219) at Tomsilla Farm, outside town on the Gorey road. A set five-course dinner costs IR£16.

FERNS
Ferns is 17km south-west of Gorey. Most traffic whizzes south for Wexford and Rosslare Harbour, but this sleepy little village was the administrative capital of Leinster and an important diocese for several hundred years. It was the base for the MacMurrough kings of Leinster, and in particular for Dermot MacMurrough, who brought the Normans to Ireland and died here in 1171.

The telephone code is ☎ 054.

Ferns Castle
Dating from around 1220 AD, the remains of this castle at the north-west end of the village are thought to stand on the site of Dermot MacMurrough's old fortress. A couple of walls and part of the moat survive, with good views available from the top of the one complete tower. To the left of the door at the top is a murder hole through which oil or arrows could be dropped on attackers below. Parliamentarians under Sir Charles Coote destroyed the castle and put most of the local population to death in 1649.

Other Attractions
Other antiquities include fragments of the 13th century **Cathedral of St Aidan** (now part of the modern Church of Ireland cathedral) with a graveyard and the remains of a high cross said to mark the grave of Dermot

MacMurrough. Father Redmond, who is buried in the graveyard, is said to have saved the life of a young French student, one Napoleon Bonaparte. Outside the graveyard is **St Moling's Well**. Look also for the remains of an **Augustinian monastery**, founded by Dermot MacMurrough in the 1150s.

Places to Stay & Eat
The friendly *Clone House* (☎ 66113) is a 350-year-old farmhouse 3km from Ferns on the Enniscorthy road, with four bedrooms, three with own bathrooms, from IR£22.50/35.

The *Celtic Arms* (☎ 66490) at the south end of Main St was undergoing restoration at the time of writing but will no doubt resume serving lunches and dinners as soon as possible.

Getting There & Away
Bus Éireann buses on the main Dublin to Wexford route stop in Ferns. There are at least five daily in both directions; contact Wexford bus station (☎ 053-22522) for details.

MT LEINSTER
Bunclody, on the border with County Carlow 16km north-west of Ferns, is a good base from which to climb Mt Leinster, at 796m the highest mountain in the Blackstairs. If you want to drive to the top, take the Borris road out of Ferns for 8km, turn left at the sign for the Mt Leinster Scenic Rd, and continue to the radio mast at the top. The last few km are on narrow, exposed roads with steep fall-offs, so drive slowly and watch for sheep. Mt Leinster provides some of Ireland's best **hang-gliding**.

WEXFORD COASTAL WALK
The Wexford Coastal Walk (Slí Charman) follows the county's coastline for 221km from Ballyhack to Kilmichael Point. See the Activities chapter for more details.

County Waterford

Wedged into Ireland's south-east corner, County Waterford combines the low farmland and sandy coastlines typical of County Wexford with the more rugged landscape common in County Cork.

WATERFORD CITY

Like Kilkenny, Waterford (Port Láirge) feels almost medieval, with narrow alleyways leading off many of the larger streets. Reginald's Tower marks the city's Viking heart and the surrounding area is particularly attractive. Georgian times left a legacy of fine houses and commercial buildings, particularly around The Mall, George's St and O'Connell St.

But Waterford is first and foremost a commercial city and port. The River Suir's estuary is deep enough to allow large modern ships right up to the city's quays and the port is still one of Ireland's busiest. Sadly this means the north bank of the river is marred by industrial development. The Quays Committee is fighting a valiant battle to brighten up the south side, at present little more than a parking lot with bus stops. However, Bus Éireann buses may eventually be allowed to drop off and pick up passengers here instead of across the river.

The hand-blown Waterford crystal made here is one of Ireland's most famous exports.

History

In the 8th century Vikings settled at a riverside site called Port Lairge which they renamed Vadrafjord. Recent excavations suggest the actual city was founded in 914 AD and quickly became a booming trading post.

Waterford's strategic importance ensured that its fortunes were closely linked to those of the country as a whole (see History in the Facts about the Country chapter). In 1170 an

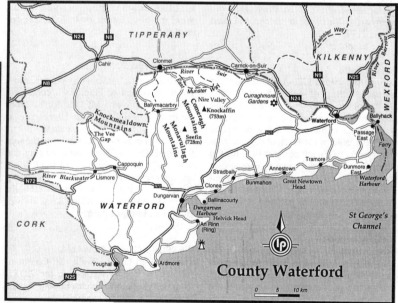

Irish/Viking army was defeated in battle by the newly arrived Anglo-Normans: 70 prominent citizens were thrown to their deaths off Baginbun Head. Later that year the city was besieged by Strongbow, who overcame a desperate defence.

In 1210 King John extended the original Viking city walls and Waterford became Ireland's most powerful city and an important trading centre. In the 15th century, it resisted the forces of two pretenders to the English crown, Lambert Simnel and Perkin Warbeck, thus earning the motto *Urbs intacta manet Waterfordia* ('Waterford City remains unconquered').

The town defied Cromwell in 1649 but in 1650 his forces returned and the city finally surrendered. Although it escaped the customary slaughter, much damage was done and the population declined as Catholics were either exiled to the west or shipped as slaves to the Caribbean.

Orientation

Waterford lies on the tidal reach of the River Suir, 16km inland. The main shopping street runs directly back from the River Suir, beginning as Barronstrand St and changing names as it runs south to become Broad St, Michael St and John St before intersecting with Parnell St. This runs north-east back up to the river, becoming The Mall on the way. Most of the sights and shopping areas lie within this triangle.

Reginald's Tower at the top of The Mall and the Clocktower at the top of Barronstrand St make good landmarks.

Information

The tourist office (☎ 051-875788) is near the river at 41 Merchant's Quay. It's open 9 am to 6 pm daily, June through August, closing an hour earlier and on Sunday in April/May and September/October. It's open 9 am to 5 pm Monday to Friday for the rest of the year.

The excellent Book Centre on Barronstrand St has three floors selling books (including foreign papers and magazines) and records, and there's a café. Gladstone's in Gladstone St does second-hand paperbacks.

Duds 'n' Suds, 6 Parnell St is a laundrette with a rudimentary café. It's open daily 7.30 am to 9 pm. Across the road in Parnell Court off Parnell St, you can send and receive your email messages at Voyager Internet Café (☎ 843843) 11 am to 11 pm daily.

The telephone code is ☎ 051.

City Walls

Waterford's city walls were originally built by the Vikings around 1000 AD, and extended by King John two centuries later. After Derry's, these are Ireland's best surviving city walls. Near the Theatre Royal in the Palace Garden some remnants stretch out near the houses in Spring Garden Alley. Several towers also remain, including one on Patrick St, the Watch Tower near Railway Square, the French and Double Towers in Castle St, and Reginald's Tower on The Mall.

Reginald's Tower

The most interesting relic of the walls is Reginald's Tower, built by the Normans in the 12th century on the site of a Viking wooden tower. With walls 3m to 4m thick, it was the city's key fortification.

Over the years the tower has served as a mint, an arsenal and a prison. Many of Waterford's royal visitors stayed in this 'safe house', including Richard II, Henry II and James II, who took a last look at Ireland from the tower before departing to exile in France.

At the time of writing, the tower was being extensively renovated. It's expected to reopen to the public in 1998. Exhibits should then include artefacts connected to one of Waterford's most famous sons, Thomas Francis Meagher (1823-67).

Behind the tower a section of the **old wall** is incorporated into Reginald's restaurant and pub. The two arches were sallyports, to let boats 'sally forth' onto the inlet which used to flow right by the wall.

The Mall

The Mall is a wide 18th century street

WEXFORD & WATERFORD

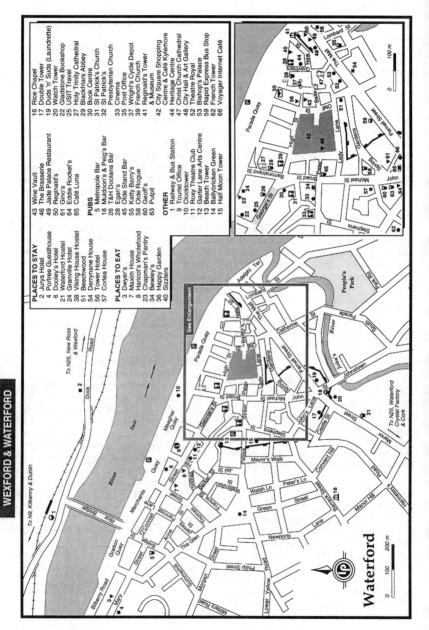

PLACES TO STAY
2 Jurys Hotel
4 Portree Guesthouse
6 Dooley's Hotel
21 Waterford Hostel
24 Granville Hotel
38 Viking House Hostel
51 Beechwood
54 Derrynane House
56 Tower Hotel
57 Corlea House

PLACES TO EAT
3 Dwyer's
7 Maxim House
8 Haricot's Wholefood
23 Chapman's Pantry
34 Bewley's
36 Happy Garden
40 Sizzlers

43 Wine Vault
46 The Brasserie
49 Jade Palace Restaurant
50 Reginald's
61 Gino's
64 Eddie Rocket's
65 Café Luna

PUBS
5 Metropole Bar
18 Muldoon's & Peig's Bar
26 T&H Doolans Bar
28 Egan's
45 Olde Stand Bar
55 Kathy Barry's
58 Olde Rogue
60 Geoff's
63 Pulpit

16 Rice Chapel
17 Double Tower
19 Duds 'n' Suds (Launderette)
20 Watch Tower
22 Gladstone Bookshop
25 USIT Travel
27 Holy Trinity Cathedral
29 Blackfriars Abbey
30 Book Centre
31 St Patrick's Church
32 St Patrick's
33 Cinema
35 Post Office
37 Wright's Cycle Depot
39 French Church
41 Reginald's Tower & Museum
42 City Square Shopping Centre & Café Kylemore
44 Heritage Centre
47 Christ Church Cathedral
48 City Hall & Art Gallery
52 Theatre Royal
53 Bishop's Palace
59 Rapid Express Bus Stop
62 French Tower
66 Voyager Internet Café

OTHER
1 Railway & Bus Station
9 Tourist Office
10 Clocktower
11 Roxy Theatre Club
12 Garter Lane Arts Centre
13 Beach Tower
14 Ballybricken Green
15 Half Moon Tower

Waterford

Thomas Francis Meagher

Born in the Granville Hotel, this Young Ireland leader was captured in Derrynane House (now a B&B) for his part in the 1848 Rising and was shipped to a penal colony in Australia. From there he escaped to the USA, where he became captain of the 'Fighting 69th' Irish Brigade in Fort Sumter and Fredricksburg in the American Civil War. Meagher later became governor of Montana and died in 1867, having tripped on a coil of rope and fallen overboard while spending the night on a Missouri paddle steamer. His body was never recovered. ■

running back from the river and built on reclaimed land which, until 1735, was a tidal inlet running alongside the walls. The **City Hall** was built in 1788 by local architect John Roberts. A remarkable Waterford glass chandelier hangs in the council's meeting room (there's a replica in Philadelphia's Independence Hall in the USA). The City Hall houses Waterford's Municipal Art Gallery but access is only via sporadic guided tours; for details phone ☎ 873501 ext 489.

Also built by John Roberts, the **Theatre Royal** next door is Ireland's finest intact 18th century theatre.

Beyond City Hall is the austere **Bishop's Palace**, begun in 1741 after a stretch of the wall was demolished. One of Ireland's finest townhouses, it was designed by Richard Castle (or Cassels) who was also responsible for Powerscourt House, Westport House and Dublin's Leinster House and Rotunda Hospital. It now acts as the city engineering offices.

Christ Church Cathedral

Behind City Hall is Christ Church Cathedral (☎ 396270) in Cathedral Square, Europe's only neo-classical Georgian cathedral. It was designed by John Roberts and stands on the site of an 11th century Viking church. While the medieval cathedral was being demolished, a remarkable collection of 15th century Italian priests' vestments were uncovered.

Don't miss the tomb of James Rice, seven times Lord Mayor of Waterford, who died in 1469 and is depicted in a state of decay with worms and frogs crawling out of his body. The cathedral also houses several bibles in Irish.

A recorded presentation on the city's history takes place June through September, at 9.30 and 11.30 am, 2.40 and 4 pm Monday to Saturday (afternoons only on Sunday). In April, May and October performances are at 11.30 am and 2.40 and 4 pm Monday to Friday. Admission costs IR£3/2.50. At 45 minutes, it will be about 15 minutes too long for many attention spans.

French Church

The ruins of a French Church built in 1240 by Franciscan monks ('Grey Friars') are on Greyfriars St. It became a hospital after the dissolution of the monasteries and was then occupied by French Huguenot refugees from 1693 to 1815. One of its last leading doctors was TF Meagher's father, Thomas Meagher Senior, Mayor of Waterford. You can pick up the church key across the road at 5 Greyfriars St.

Waterford Heritage Centre

Next to the ruins of the French Church is the small and uninspiring Waterford Heritage Centre (☎ 871277) which exhibits royal charters dating back to 1215 and local Viking artefacts. Entry is IR£1.50/50p. It's open 10 am to 5 pm Monday to Friday, 2 to 5 pm Saturday, staying open until 8.30 pm, June through August.

Other Buildings

The ruins and square tower of the Dominican **Blackfriars Abbey** on Arundel Square date from 1226.

Nearby on Barronstrand St the Catholic **Holy Trinity Cathedral** was built between 1792 and 1796 by John Roberts who also designed the Protestant Christ Church Cathedral. The sumptuous interior boasts a fine carved pulpit, painted pillars with Corinthian capitals and lovely Waterford crystal chandeliers.

A Saint in the Making

Born at Westcourt near Callan in County Kilkenny in 1762, Edmund Rice had a rudimentary education, like most Catholics of that era. At 17 he was apprenticed to his uncle's in Waterford, later inheriting his business.

On the surface Rice appeared a conventional businessman, but behind the scenes he was already helping the poor. In 1802 he established his first school before quitting ship chandlery to become a full-time teacher. In 1804 he opened a new classroom at Mount Sion in Waterford. New schools in Clonmel and Dungarvan soon followed.

In 1820 the Pope approved the Institute of the Brothers of the Christian Schools of Ireland, and Rice remained the 'superior general' until his death in 1838. By then the Christian Brothers had schools in Britain, Gibraltar, Australia, the USA and South Africa.

The Brothers have played an important role in educating Catholic youngsters right through the 20th century. Amongst those to have received their tutelage were broadcaster Gay Byrne, actor Gabriel Byrne, writer Brendan Behan and politicians Patrick Pearse, Eamonn de Valera, Gerry Adams and Bertie Ahern.

Then in the 1990s scandal rocked the movement after men claimed they had been physically and sexually abused by their teachers. Despite the inevitable cloud cast over the movement, Rice himself is still revered and has been beatified by the Pope, the first step towards attaining sainthood. ■

Near Ballybricken Green is the old city wall's **Half Moon Tower** by Patrick St. **St Patrick's Church** on Jenkins' Lane is an atmospheric 18th century Catholic chapel which managed to survive the savage suppression of Catholicism at that time. At the top of Jenkins' Lane is the **Beach Tower**, another remnant of the old city wall.

The **Chamber of Commerce** building on Great George's St was originally built as a town house by John Roberts and has a magnificent staircase.

Edmund Ignatius Rice, founder of the Christian Brothers, established his first school at Mt Sion in Barrack St where the **Rice Chapel** is a delightful combination of red-brick and stained glass, with Rice's tomb in pride of place awaiting the likely canonisation of its occupant. If you phone ☎ 74390 you can also arrange to see an audiovisual presentation on Rice's life and works.

Waterford Crystal

The first Waterford glass factory was established at the west end of the riverside quays in 1783 but closed in 1851 as a result of punitive taxes imposed on the raw materials by the British government. The business wasn't revived until 1947 and the existing factory opened in 1971. Today, it employs 1600 people, amongst them highly skilled glass blowers, cutters and engravers (all men) who take from eight to 10 years to learn their craft. The glass is a heavy lead (over 30%) crystal made from red lead, silica sand and potash.

The visitor centre (☎ 373311) is 2km out on the Cork road. From April through October you can guide yourself round the plant, with staff on hand to explain things; the site opens daily 8.30 am to 4 pm. The rest of the year there are guided tours Monday to Friday 9 am to 3.15 pm. They're worth it if only to see the fountain designed for Harrod's in London in 1971. It's made up of 3034 pieces of glass, weighs 360kg and cost IR£110,000.

A visit costs IR£3.50/1.75. Afterwards you can part with large amounts of money in the Crystal Gallery and then have lunch or tea in the café. Yellow 'Imp' buses run to the factory from Shop 'Round The Clock opposite the clocktower on the quays every 10 minutes (IR£1.40 return). In summer you can buy a ticket in advance from the tourist office to avoid long queues at the factory.

Organised Tours

Walking Tours One-hour guided historic

walking tours (☎ 873711) depart from the Granville Hotel daily, March to October, at noon and 2 pm (IR£3).

Cruises The Galley Cruising Restaurant (☎ 421723) operates out of Waterford from June through August. Morning cruises leaving Meagher Quay at 10.30 am cost IR£5. Two-hour cruises including afternoon tea leave at 3 pm and costs IR£6. Evening cruises leaving at 7 or 8 pm cost IR£5.

Special Events

Waterford's Light Opera Festival takes place in September/October. It's cheaper and more easily accessible than the more famous Wexford Opera Festival but booking is still advisable. Much of the city takes part, and there are pub singing competitions and late bar extensions. Contact the Theatre Royal (☎ 874402), The Mall, Waterford.

Places to Stay

Camping See the Tramore section for details of the nearest campsites.

Hostels The IHH's clean, modern *Viking House* (☎ 853827) is tucked behind the quayside in Coffee House Lane in the city's old quarter. Dorm beds cost from IR£7.50, good doubles cost IR£12 to IR£13.50 and singles cost IR£15. On the down side the door is locked noon to 3 pm. It also seems likely that the Viking will convert to housing students September through to June, so ring to check before showing up.

If you arrive and find the Viking full or closed, women in particular should check at the tourist office before booking any other hostel.

A second May to September only hostel is *Waterford Hostel* (☎ 50163), 70 Manor St, which has beds for IR£9 a head.

B&Bs Waterford is disappointingly lacking in good, centrally positioned, tourist board approved B&Bs. The Mall and Parnell St have several relatively cheap B&Bs, but traffic noise can be a problem. You could try *Derrynane House* (☎ 875179), 19 The Mall,

but ask for a room at the back for a quiet night. *Beechwood* (☎ 876677), attractively positioned at 7 Cathedral Square, has rooms for IR£15/25. The *Portree Guesthouse* (☎ 874574), on Mary St, costs from IR£18/27. Also worth trying is *Corlea House* (☎ 875764), 2 New St, which does B&B for IR£14/25.

Almost 5km from Waterford on the Dunmore East road, *Knockboy House* (☎ 873484) has rooms from IR£19/28.

Hotels Classy *Granville Hotel* (☎ 855111; fax 870307), on Meagher Quay, does B&B for IR£49/88. For a bedside view of Reginald's Tower try the modern *Tower Hotel & Leisure Centre* (☎ 875801; fax 870129), at the north end of The Mall, which has an indoor pool, sauna and gymnasium; B&B is IR£82.50/132. Across the river *Jurys Hotel* (☎ 832111; fax 832863) has much the same facilities for IR£86/106 without breakfast.

Newly restored *Dooley's* (☎ 873531), on The Quay, offers good value with spacious rooms for IR£45/80 from June through September.

Most exclusive of all Waterford's hotels is *Waterford Castle* (☎ 878203; fax 879316), out of town and accessible by ferry just off the Passage East road. If you need to ask about the prices you probably can't afford it!

Places to Eat

Cafés & Snacks *Sizzlers*, near Reginald's Tower, opens 24 hours at weekends and serves some cheapish burger-style meals. *Chapman's Pantry* is a terrific coffee-shop-cum-restaurant next to the Granville Hotel on Meagher Quay. It's open 8 am to 6 pm and the deli in front is good too. At 11 O'Connell St *Haricot's Wholefood* has vegetarian and non-vegetarian dishes for around IR£5 (lunch specials for IR£3.95). It's open Monday to Friday 10 am to 8 pm, Saturday to 5.45 pm.

Bewley's has a coffee house upstairs in the Broad St mall. In the City Square mall there's a branch of *Café Kylemore* for quick coffee fixes. *Pages* in the Book Centre is also good for teas and light lunches.

For coffee and all sorts of sandwiches *Café Luna* (☎ 843539) in John St provides a cool setting with artworks on the walls and Latin sounds in the background. It's open until 4 am Friday and Saturday and to 3.30 am Wednesday, Thursday and Sunday.

A promising newcomer to the city eating scene is *The Brasserie* on the edge of the City Square mall which does moderately priced pizzas, toasted sandwiches and more ambitious dishes like trout with almonds.

The Barronstrand St pubs are locked into healthy competition for lunch specials at around IR£3 to IR£5. *Egan's* serves the food, cafeteria-style, in a separate area at the back.

T&H Doolan, on Great George's St, is good for lunches (roast beef for IR£4.95), as is the *Olde Stand*, in Michael St which serves bar food downstairs and seafood and steaks upstairs for around IR£10.

Restaurants *Gino's*, on Applemarket just off Michael St, does delicious pizzas, including a masterpiece of a vegetarian version for IR£3.75.

For Chinese meals and takeaways, try *Maxim House* on O'Connell St or the *Happy Garden* on High St. More upmarket is the *Jade Palace* (☎ 855611) on The Mall, said to be one of Ireland's best (and most expensive) Chinese restaurants.

Reginald's bar and restaurant (☎ 855087) behind Reginald's Tower does bar meals and a set dinner for IR£14.95. Late-night burger-hunters should head for *Eddie Rocket's* in John St which opens until 4 am at weekends.

One of the best places in town is *Dwyer's* (☎ 877478), 5 Mary St, in an old barracks near the bridge. Sophisticated food comes in generous helpings and there's an early bird menu for IR£15 between 6 and 7.30 pm; later, a full dinner costs more like IR£25 (closed Sunday and bank holidays). Also good is the *Wine Vault* (☎ 853444) in High St where the dinner bill, and the quality of the food, will be about the same.

If you're feeling flush you could head 5km east to Ballinakill and the *Waterford Castle*

restaurant (☎ 878203). Dinner will cost at least IR£30 a head.

Entertainment

Pubs & Clubs Many of the pubs feature live music. The venerable *T&H Doolan* on Great George's St incorporates a remnant of the 1000-year-old city wall. Sinead O'Connor played here before she hit the big time.

Where John St becomes Michael St, *Geoff's* and the *Pulpit* (and its upstairs night-club *Preacher's)* attract a lively young crowd. Across the road is the *Olde Rogue* while just up the road at the junction with Manor Rd there's *Muldoon's* with *Peig's bar* next door; both have regular music sessions. *Egan's*, on Barronstrand St, has the odd karaoke night and a fully fledged nightclub upstairs *(Snags)*. *Reginald's* near the tower has a nightclub and occasional jazz sessions. Nearby, *Katty Barry's* in Mall Lane is rumoured to serve the best Guinness.

The *Roxy Theatre Club* on O'Connell St also has music and discos.

Arts Centres, Theatre & Cinema *Garter Lane Arts Centre* (☎ 855038), 22A O'Connell St, hosts films, exhibitions, poetry readings and theatre. It's open Monday to Saturday 10 am to 6 pm.

The 90-minute Waterford Show (☎ 875788) in the *City Hall* combines music, dancing and wine in a programme about the city's history. From May through September it takes place at 8.45 pm on Thursday, Friday and Sunday. Tickets cost IR£6 and can be booked at the tourist office, Waterford Crystal or City Hall.

The five-screen *Waterford Cineplex* (☎ 74595) is just off Broad St on Patrick St.

Getting There & Away
USIT Travel (☎ 872601) is at 36-7 George's St.

Air Waterford airport (☎ 875589) is 6km south of the city. The daily British Airways Express flight to Stansted can cost as little as IR£89 return. Suckling Airways (☎ 01223-292524) run three daily flights to Luton.

Bus The Bus Éireann station (☎ 879000) is at Plunkett railway station across the bridge to the north of the river. There are plenty of buses daily to Dublin (R£6), Cork (IR£8), Limerick (IR£8) and Rosslare. It's a good 750m walk from here to the hostel and cheap B&Bs.

Rapid Express Coaches (☎ 872149), at Parnell Court in Parnell St, run a service between Waterford/Tramore and Dublin via Dungarvan, Carlow and Naas (at least seven daily, IR£5).

Suirway (☎ 382422) has services to Dunmore East and Passage East. They depart from near the Maxol petrol station and opposite Shop 'Round the Clock on the quay.

Train From the Plunkett railway station (☎ 873401) on the north side of the river, there are regular trains to Dublin (four daily, 2½ hours, IR£11), Limerick (one daily, 2½ hours, IR£10), and Rosslare (twice daily, 80 minutes, IR£6).

Getting Around
Wright's Cycle Depot (☎ 874411) on Henrietta St is a Raleigh Rent-a-Bike outlet, with bikes for IR£7/30 a day/week. BnB Cycles (☎ 870356), 22 Ballybricken, also hires out bikes. There are taxi ranks at Plunkett railway station and outside Penney's department store; fares start at IR£3.

PASSAGE EAST
Heading east from Waterford City on the coast road, your first port of call will probably be Passage East, 11km away, with its little harbour and thatched cottages at the foot of low hills. The Passage East to Ballyhack ferry makes a useful short cut between counties Waterford and Wexford.

Just south of the village is **Crooke** with the remains of the Geneva Barracks nearby. Built in the 18th century as part of a settlement for Swiss refugees, the buildings were turned into barracks after the plan fell through. It was here that a young rebel of the 1798 Rising came to confess his sins to a priest who turned out to be an army officer

in disguise. The lad was arrested and subsequently hanged, a story immortalised in the song *Croppy Boy*.

There are a couple of cheap B&Bs, *Cois Abhann* and *Harbour Lights*.

Getting There & Away
If you're heading to or from Wexford, the car ferry across the estuary from Passage East to Ballyhack in County Wexford can save you an hour's drive via New Ross to the north. The ferry company (☎ 051-382488) is on Barrack St in Passage East and the ferry operates a continuous service 7.20 am to 10 pm, April to September, and 7.20 am to 8 pm the rest of the year. On Sunday, first sailings are at 9.30 am. The cost of the 10 minute crossing for a car is IR£4/6 one way/return, for pedestrians 80p/IR£1, or cyclists IR£1/1.50. Return tickets are valid for an unlimited time.

Suirway (☎ 051-382422) has two buses daily from Waterford City to Passage East (30 minutes, IR£1.50).

DUNMORE EAST
Dunmore East (Dún Mór) is a pretty fishing village strung out along a coastline of low red sandstone cliffs and discreet coves and with thatched cottages, many of them summer homes. Most of the accommodation clusters round Ladies Cove although the hostel is by the busy harbour which is overlooked by an unusual Doric lighthouse built in 1823. There's a good view of Hook Head lighthouse across the water in Wexford. The noisy birds nesting in the cliffs around the harbour are kittiwakes. The most popular beaches are Counsellor's Beach, facing south among the cliffs, and Ladies Cove, right in the village.

Dunmore East Adventure Centre (☎ 051-383783) rents equipment for windsurfing, canoeing, surfing and snorkelling. Short courses in most of these sports are also available.

If you're interested in going fishing for sharks or in exploring old wrecks off the coast contact Dunmore East Angling Charters (☎ 383397).

The telephone code is ☎ 051.

Places to Stay

Camping *Dunmore East Caravan & Camping Park* (☎ 383174) is just south of the village and charges IR£6 per tent.

Hostel The *Dunmore Harbour House* (☎ 383218), overlooking the harbour, has dorm beds for IR£9.50 and singles/doubles for IR£13.50/16 without breakfast. There's a good restaurant as well as the usual kitchen. The hostel was once a hotel servicing passengers on the mail boats between Dunmore East and Milford Haven in Wales.

B&Bs *Church Villa* (☎ 383390) is one of a row of cottages in the town opposite the Protestant Church and near the Ship Restaurant. Its cosy doubles, most with shower, cost IR£32. Elegant *Carraig Laith* (☎ 383273), on the main Harbour Rd, has singles/doubles for IR£21/32 with great sea views. Next to the post office on Harbour Rd *Creaden View* (☎ 383339) charges the same.

Hotels There are three hotels on Harbour Rd. The *Candlelight Inn* (☎ 383215; fax 383289) has doubles from IR£25 while the *Haven Hotel* (☎ 383150; fax 383488) is a black and white Victorian mansion in extensive grounds with B&B from IR£35/60. The shabbier *Ocean Hotel* (☎ 383136; fax 383576) charges from IR£55 per room.

Places to Eat

The *Candlelight Inn* has a good restaurant, with main courses from IR£5.95. The *Ship Inn* also has good food, particularly seafood, both in the bar and restaurant.

The *Strand Inn* (☎ 383174) overlooking Ladies Cove specialises in seafood. A full dinner will cost you around IR£20, but the bar food is more than adequate. It's open for lunch from 12.30 to 2.30 pm and dinner from 7 to 10 pm. The nearby *Anchor Bar* also does bar meals and sometimes has live music.

Dunmore Harbour House (☎ 383218) has

a restaurant specialising in seafood. The set dinner costs IR£18 but you can get by for much less if you go à la carte.

Getting There & Away

There are four daily buses (30 minutes, IR£1.60) from Waterford to Dunmore East in July and August (three for the rest of the year). Contact Suirway (☎ 382422) for timetable details.

TRAMORE & AROUND

The busiest of County Waterford's seaside resorts, Tramore (Trá Mhór) is 12km south of Waterford. A delightful 5km beach is backed with 30m-high dunes at the east end. Tramore itself is fairly tacky, with amusement arcades and fast-food outlets running down to the seafront.

Standing on the shore the bay is hemmed in by **Great Newtown Head** to the southwest and **Brownstown Head** to the north-east, with their standing pillars and the **Iron Man**, a huge painted iron figure of an 18th century sailor in white breeches and blue jacket with his arm pointing seaward to warn approaching ships. These pillars were erected by Lloyds of London in 1816 after 360 lives were lost when a boat mistook Tramore Bay for Waterford Harbour and was wrecked.

The beach aside, Tramore's biggest attraction used to be the Celtworld heritage ride close to the bus stop. At the time of writing this was closed although new owners may yet revive it. Instead you can entertain yourself at the adjacent **Splashworld**, an outsize swimming pool; phone ☎ 051-390176 for details of classes, etc.

The telephone code is ☎ 051.

Places to Stay

Camping There are three caravan and campsites near Tramore. The best facilities are at *Newtown Cove Caravan & Camping Park* (☎ 381979) on the R675 to Dungarvan. It's open from April through September, and costs IR£10 for a tent or caravan or IR£4 per person for hikers and cyclists. Other sites are the *Atlantic View Caravan & Camping*

(☎ 381610) on the seafront, which charges IR£8, and *Fitzmaurice's Caravan Park* (☎ 381968), near the Atlantic View on the inland side of the road, with similar facilities and rates.

Hostel *The Monkey Puzzle* hostel (☎ 386754) is on Upper Branch Rd, not far from the tourist office. Beds are IR£7 and there are two doubles for IR£18. To reach it go up the steep street more or less opposite the bus stop and turn right. It might be wise to phone before arriving.

B&Bs The frequency of buses in and out of Waterford means you could choose to commute to Tramore to sleep.

Cliff Rd is lined with B&Bs offering great sea views. *Church Villa* has beds without bath for IR£13. *The Cliff* (☎ 381497) and *Ard Mor* (☎ 381716) are promising or, just about 1km from the bus stop, there's *Cliff House* (☎ 381497) with singles/double from IR£22/34.

Oban (☎ 381537) to the north-east of town at 1 Eastlands, Pond Rd, charges IR£32 for a double.

For something grander there's the *Majestic Hotel* (☎ 381761) immediately opposite the bus stop. Singles/doubles cost IR£52.50/75. A bit cheaper and less overwhelming is *O'Shea's Hotel* (☎ 381246) on Strand St which charges IR£32.50/60.

At Fenor, 7km west of Tramore heading for Dungarvan, *Mountain View* (☎ 396107) is one of Ireland's few thatched B&Bs and costs from IR£19.50/29.

Places to Eat
Pub food is available at *The Victoria* on Queen St or at *The Seahorse* in Main St.

For something more formal try *Hartley's Bistro* (☎ 390888), 21 Queen St. Early bird menus cost IR£10.50. Expect modern Irish cuisine.

Getting There & Away
Bus Éireann (☎ 873 9000) runs more than 15 buses daily between Waterford and Tramore.

TRAMORE TO DUNGARVAN
The road between Tramore and Dungarvan, 41km to the west along the coast, is punctuated with numerous small villages set in tidy coves. **Annestown**, **Bunmahon** and the picturesque **Stradbally** come in quick succession along a winding road. The *Cove Bar* in Stradbally has reasonable pub food or there's *Ye Olde Bank Restaurant*, 5km from Stradbally in Kilmacthomas.

Eight km to the west of Stradbally is the popular Blue Flag beach at **Clonea**, with the *Clonea Strand Hotel* (☎ 058-42416) and its 10-pin bowling alley and Turkish baths. There's also a campsite here, *Casey's* (☎ 058-41919), charging IR£10 for a family tent but IR£3.75 for hikers or cyclists. There's a surfing beach farther west in **Ballinacourty**.

DUNGARVAN
The small port and market town of Dungarvan (Dún Garbhán), 48km west of Waterford City, grew up in the shelter of an Anglo-Norman castle.

Modern Dungarvan has a lovely setting at the foot of forested hills on the wide bay where the River Colligan meets the sea. Until the river was bridged in the last century this shallow crossing was known as 'Dungarvan's Prospects'; women had to raise their skirts to wade across and the sight was famous among local men. The view aside, Dungarvan is a fairly nondescript town which acts as the administrative centre for County Waterford. The large Harbour Bay complex developing beside the castle ruins could liven things up a bit.

Abbeyside, to the north-east, was birthplace to Ernest Walton, whose work on nuclear fission won the Nobel Prize for physics in 1951.

Dungarvan makes a convenient base for exploring western County Waterford and the Monavullagh, Comeragh and Knockmealdown mountains to the north.

Orientation & Information
The town's central shopping area is centred around the neatly laid out Grattan Square on

WEXFORD & WATERFORD

the south side of the river. Main St (also called O'Connell St) runs along one side of it.

The tourist office (☎ 058-41741) in Grattan Square opens April to the end of August but has little useful information.

The telephone code is ☎ 058.

Things to See & Do

By the quays, **King John's Castle** (1185) is just a collection of rotting walls. The 17th century **Old Market House** has a small museum (admission free), open Monday to Friday 11 am to 1 pm and 2 to 5 pm. As you leave Dungarvan to the west, you'll pass a **monument** to the greyhound Master McGrath which won the Waterloo Cup three times in the 1860s.

Special Events

Over the early May bank holiday weekend 17 Dungarvan pubs and two hotels play host to the Fléile na nDéise, a lively traditional music festival which attracts around 200 musicians. For more information, phone ☎ 42998.

Places to Stay

The small but expanding IHH *Dungarvan Holiday Hostel* (☎ 44340), opposite the Garda station, charges IR£7 for a bed and IR£15 for a double.

Friendly *Abbey House* (☎ 41669), on Friars Walk, Abbeyside, near the church, charges IR£32 for a double. *Fáilte House* (☎ 43216) overlooks the sea from the Youghal road and costs IR£25/36.

The *Old Rectory* (☎ 41394) is just out of town on the Waterford road with rooms around IR£19.50/33. Almost 8km west of Dungarvan on the N25 Youghal road, *Seaview* (☎ 41583) offers sweeping views over Dungarvan and the sea. Rooms cost IR£21/32 a single/double.

At *Lawlor's Hotel* (☎ 41122), on TF Meagher St, just off Grattan Square, B&B costs IR£36 a head.

Places to Eat

An Bialann, in Grattan Square, does popular lunch specials for IR£4. *Flanagan's* in Main St also packs them in at lunchtime. For teas and snacks the upstairs *Koffee Korner*, just off Grattan Square opposite the Lady Belle pub, is comfortable. For reasonably priced pub food cosy *Merry's* (☎ 41974), at the museum end of Main St, makes a good choice.

Entertainment

Molly Molone's and *Downey's* on Main St attract a young crowd, as does the *Buttery Bar*, in Lawlor's Hotel. The *Moorings* and the *Anchor* on the quay have a good atmosphere at weekends; the latter has local bands and traditional Irish music. *Bean a'Leanna* has music on Thursday, Friday and Saturday. For a particularly Irish music scene head out to *Tigh an Cheoil* at Helvick on the Ring peninsula or to *Seanachie*, a few km out on the Cork road.

Getting There & Away

Bus Éireann services run to Dublin, Waterford, Killarney and Cork from the stop on Davitt's Quay. It's IR£6 return from Waterford.

Getting Around

Murphy Cycles (☎ 41376), the Raleigh bike dealer on Main St, has bikes for IR£7/30 a day/week.

AN RINN (RING)

An Rinn, 12km south of Dungarvan on Helvick Head, is a Gaeltacht – an Irish speaking area, with its own special heritage and culture – one of the most famous in Ireland. Many an Irish teenager has studied the language in Ring College on the Helvick Head road. The school runs *ceilís, seisúns* (sessions) of traditional music and dance, most nights during the summer, and there are also evening seisúns in the *Tigh an Cheoil* (☎ 058-46209) bar in an old cottage in Baile Na nGall on the way to Helvick Head. On the road to Youghal, the *Seanchaí* pub, beside the road in the middle of nowhere, also has frequent music sessions. *Mooney's* pub in Ring has excellent sessions every night during the summer.

Aisling B&B (☎ 058-46134) charges IR£14 per person for B&B, as does *Failoeán* (☎ 058-46127) overlooking Helvick Head pier. All households speak Irish and English.

Getting There & Away

The very limited bus service offers one departure a day from Waterford at 1.45 pm on Saturday. This becomes a daily service during July and August.

ARDMORE

South of Helvick Head the coast road veers inland and after 23km brings you back to the sea at Ardmore. A popular seaside resort with a Blue Flag beach, Ardmore has a main street of pretty, pastel-coloured buildings. Don't be put off by the ugly sprawl of caravan parks that spoils the coastal view to the east; this is a nice little place and the beach is lovely.

It is claimed locally that St Declan set up shop here between 350 and 420 AD, well before St Patrick arrived from Britain to convert the heathens.

Information

The locally run tourist office (☎ 024-94444) is in a white sandcastle-shaped building on the seafront. It's open daily May to September and can change money for you.

The telephone code is ☎ 024.

St Declan's Church & Oratory

In a striking position on a hill above the town the ruins of St Declan's Church and a fine slender round tower stand on the site of St Declan's original monastery. The 30m tower dates from the 12th century, relatively late.

The outer west gable wall of the 13th century church has some stone carvings retrieved from an older 9th century church and placed here. They show the Archangel Michael weighing souls, the Adoration of the Magi, Adam and Eve, and a clear depiction of the Judgement of Solomon. Inside the church are two Ogham stones, one of them particularly fine. Look out for the tombstone of a women called Pigeon in the nave.

The smaller building in the compound is the 8th century St Declan's Oratory or Beannachán. It was restored in the 18th century and is traditionally said to be the resting place of St Declan. The depression in the floor is due to worshippers removing earth from the grave site – it was supposed to protect from disease.

St Declan's Well

Overlooking the sea, St Declan's Well is beyond the Cliff House Hotel to the south of the town. Pilgrims once washed in it. Beside it are the ruins of Dysert Church. A fine 5km cliff walk leads from the well; the tourist office stocks a free map. At the south end of the beach is **St Declan's Stone**, said to have arrived on the waves from Wales following St Declan. Crawling under it on St Declan's day (24 July) is said to cure rheumatism and bring spiritual benefits.

St Declan's Way

This 94km walk mostly traces an old pilgrimage way from Ardmore to the Rock of Cashel in Tipperary. The tourist office stocks a map-guide for IR£4.20 which also shows circular routes taking in parts of the Way. See the Activities chapter for more details.

Places to Stay

Hostel The brand-new *Ardmore Beach Hostel* (☎ 94501) in an old stone house near the seafront has dorm beds for IR£8 and family rooms at a discount. Ask at the *The Cup & Saucer* opposite.

B&Bs *Byron Lodge* (☎ 94157) is a Georgian house on the edge of town, with rooms from IR£19/29. To get there find the second thatched cottage on the main street and turn up the road beside it, passing through a crossroads. Byron Lodge is up on your right.

Hotels In the village the *Round Tower Hotel* (☎ 94494) charges IR£25/45 for B&B. The big, white *Cliff House* (☎ 94106), on the low cliffs overlooking the bay, has rooms for IR£25/64 without breakfast.

Places to Eat

Paddy Mac's pub, on Main St, offers good pub snacks and lunches, with jacket potatoes from IR£2.60. Beside the pub the small *Beachcombers Restaurant* serves snacks, soups and spaghetti from IR£1.50 to IR£5. Across the road the *Cup & Saucer Restaurant* offers middle-of-the-road quiche, jacket potatoes and lasagne.

Getting There & Away

Buses stop outside O'Reilly's pub on Main St. There are three services daily to Cork (one on Sunday) all year round, and two to Waterford via Dungarvan in July and August (otherwise it's a Friday and Saturday only service).

NORTH COUNTY WATERFORD

Some of the most scenic parts of County Waterford are in the north of the county around **Ballymacarbry** and in the **Nire Valley** which runs through the heart of the Comeragh Mountains. While not as rugged as the west of Ireland, the mountain scenery has a beauty of its own. The hills form the easternmost extension of a great mass of red sandstone from the Devonian period, some 370 million years ago, which underlies most of the Cork and Kerry scenery.

The lovely wooded valleys and heathery mountains are good for hill walking and pony trekking. Melody's Riding Stables (☎ 052-36147) in Ballymacarbry have horses for half-day (IR£18) or full-day outings (from IR£45) from Easter to October. The Nire Valley area forms part of the East Munster Way from Carrick-on-Suir; for information contact any local tourist office.

Touraneena Heritage Centre, 15km north of Dungarvan on the R672, focuses on showing you a lost way of life, with displays on bread and butter making, and home-curing bacon. There's also a working forge. It's open 10 am to 6 pm, mid-May to October, and admission is IR£3/1.50.

Driving from Waterford to Ballymacarbry you can take in the **Curraghmore Gardens**, 14km north-west of Waterford City. The fine

house dates from the 18th century and is home to the Marquis of Waterford. Although the house is only open to groups by prior arrangement (☎ 051-387102), you can visit the gardens and the 18th century shell grotto on Thursday or bank holidays from Easter to mid-October, 2 to 5 pm. Admission costs IR£2.

Places to Stay & Eat

Hanoras Cottage (☎ 052-36134) in the Nire Valley costs IR£45/70 for B&B; the tearoom-cum-restaurant does some excellent snacks and lunches. From the main Dungarvan to Clonmel road (R672), head to Ballymacarbry then turn east off the T27 to Nire Church.

Nire Valley Farmhouse (☎ 052-36149), just north-west of Ballymacarbry, does B&B at around IR£18/28. Farther north on the same road is *Clonanay Guesthouse* (☎ 052-36141), charging from IR£29/52.

Getting There & Away

There's a Tuesday only bus service from Dungarvan at 2 pm, and two buses from Clonmel on Friday at 1.20 and 5.35 pm.

WEST COUNTY WATERFORD

The small market town of **Cappoquin** is overlooked by the Knockmealdown Mountains. The River Blackwater takes an abrupt turn southwards near the town and the Blackwater Valley to the west is picturesque. There's excellent coarse and game fishing locally and Glenshelane Park, just outside the town, has some lovely forest walks and picnic spots. Salmon-fishing permits are available from the Toby Jug Guesthouse (☎ 058-54317). The Blackwater Valley is also where traces of the earliest Irish peoples have been found – Mesolithic microliths or small stone blades from around 9000 years ago.

Cappoquin is 17km north-west of Dungarvan and is of little note except for **Mt Melleray Cistercian Abbey** (☎ 058-54404), just over 6km to the north. The abbey was founded in 1832 by a group of Irish monks who had been expelled from a monastery near Melleray in Brittany, France. A fully functioning monastery, Mt Melleray opens to visitors seeking quiet reflection and to those who want to see something of the daily routine. They don't charge for a bed in their guesthouse, but it would be bad manners not to make a donation.

Getting There & Away

Twice a week a bus leaves Waterford for Cappoquin travelling via Dungarvan; on Friday it leaves at 8.30 am; on Sunday at 5.30 pm (this service doesn't operate in July and August). On Friday a bus also leaves Cork for Cappoquin at 4.30 pm, travelling via Midleton and Tallow.

LISMORE

Lismore is a small town beautifully situated on the River Blackwater at the foot of the Knockmealdown Mountains. The river rolls on south to Youghal and the sea.

Lismore was the location of a great monastic university first founded by St Cartach or Carthage in the 7th century. In the 8th century, the monastery became a famous centre of learning under St Colman. From the 10th century on, it was sacked many times by the Vikings but hung on as the religious capital of Deise (Deices). Until the 17th century, the remains of eight churches could still be seen.

Information

Lismore has a tourist office (☎ 058-54975), with bureau de change, in Lismore Heritage Centre, in the old courthouse in the town centre. It's open daily April to the end of October and stocks a free town walk map. Ask about guided tours of the town which cost IR£1.50 a head (children free). Alternatively, for IR£1 you can buy *A Walking Tour of Lismore* which describes all the local sights.

The telephone code is ☎ 058.

St Carthage's Cathedral

The striking cathedral (1633) sits among peaceful gardens. Inside are some noteworthy tombs including a MacGrath family

crypt dating from 1557 and the small chapel of St Colmcille.

Lismore Castle

From the Cappoquin road there are fine glimpses of majestic Lismore Castle overlooking the river. In the 12th century Henry II chose this site for a castle, which was eventually erected by Prince John, Lord of Ireland, in 1185. The castle was the local bishop's residence until 1589, when it was presented to Sir Walter Raleigh along with some 200 sq km of the surrounding countryside.

Raleigh, a famous soldier and favourite of Queen Elizabeth I, later sold it to the earl of Cork, Richard Boyle. His 14th child, Robert Boyle (1627-91), was born here and is credited with being the first methodical modern scientist; Boyle's Law is the principle that the pressure of a gas varies with its volume at a constant temperature, a discovery fundamental to modern physics.

Lismore Castle passed to the duke of Devonshire in 1753 and his descendants still own it. The present castle mostly dates from the 19th century, but incorporates small sections of the earlier buildings. During rebuilding, the 15th century *Book of Lismore* and the Lismore Crozier (now in the National Museum, Dublin) were discovered. The book documents the lives of a number of Irish saints, but also holds an account of the voyages of Marco Polo. A more recent castle occupant was Adele Astaire, sister of the famous Fred.

The castle is closed to day trippers but can be rented by seriously rich groups. The gardens (☎ 54424) open May to September 1.45 to 4.45 pm; admission is IR£2.50/1.50.

Lismore Heritage Centre

Lismore Heritage Centre (☎ 54975), in the old courthouse, shows an audiovisual presentation on local history and attractions, legends, follies and walks along the River Blackwater. It's open June through August, Monday to Saturday, 9.30 am to 6 pm, Sunday 10 am to 5.30 pm, closing half an hour earlier in April/May and September/

WEXFORD & WATERFORD

October. The rest of the year it opens Monday to Friday 9 am to 5.30 pm. There are shows every half hour and admission is IR£2.50/1.50.

Places to Stay & Eat
The IHO *Kilmorna Farm Hostel* (☎ 54315) in Lismore has dorm beds for IR£8. There's no official campsite nearby but you could ask local farmers about their fields.

Beechcroft (☎ 54273) on Deerpark Rd, about 1km from the town centre, costs from IR£19/28. *Lismore Hotel* (☎ 54555) is a straightforward hotel charging IR£25 a head for B&B. *Ballyrafter House* (☎ 54002), 1km north of town, has rooms from IR£35/58; an excellent set dinner is IR£22.

Rafters on East Main St above the Roche's supermarket does middle-of-the-road lunches and dinners from IR£5 to IR£10. *Rose's West End* pub on Main St offers soup and toasted sandwiches. Two pubs with food and atmosphere are *Eamon's* and *Madden's*.

Getting There & Away
Buses stop outside O'Dowd's pub on West St. One bus a day leaves Waterford City for Lismore via Dungarvan at 8.40 pm (except Sunday). On Friday there's also a bus at 8.30 am, and Sunday except in July and August there's a bus at 5.30 pm. For details contact Waterford bus station (☎ 051-73401).

EAST MUNSTER WAY
This walking trail covers some 80km between Carrick-on-Suir in County Tipperary and the northern slopes of the Knockmealdown Mountains. East of the Vee Gap the Munster Way crosses a path which marks the ancient Rían Bó Phádraig, or 'track of St Patrick's cow', a highway and pilgrimage route connecting Lismore with Ardfinnan and Cashel. Nearby is a modern memorial to Liam Lynch who was killed during the Irish Civil War in 1922-23.

See the Activities chapter for more information.

County Cork

Ireland's biggest county, County Cork (Corcaigh) has everything which makes Ireland so attractive and a case could be made for arriving here before visiting Dublin. The city of Cork is engagingly small and free of urban stress. The northern part of the county is renowned for fishing while the main tourist trail heads down to Kinsale, Ireland's gourmet capital, and west through the historic towns of Clonakilty and Skibbereen to the peninsulas jutting out into the Atlantic. These underpopulated extremities are rich in history and nature and offer wonderful scenery for walkers, climbers and cyclists. The county's best-known highlight is kissing the Blarney Stone but you'll probably remember just drifting through West Cork for far longer.

Cork

Although hardly exciting, the Irish Republic's second largest city is a pleasant enough place in which to while away a day or so, with a considerable French input as a result of the ferry connections. You should certainly make time to visit the interesting old County Gaol and at night the pubs are as lively as anywhere.

An estimated 35,000 people a year move to Cork and the roads are creaking under the strain of the traffic. When the Lee Tunnel, joining east and west Cork without traversing the centre, is complete (sometime in 1998/9) it should go some way towards easing things.

HISTORY
The city dates back to the 7th century, surviving Cromwell's visit only to fall to King William in 1690. In the 18th century it was an important commercial centre with a major butter market but a century later the Potato

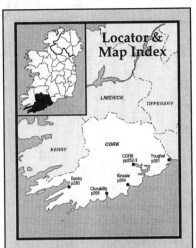

Locator & Map Index

Highlights
- Take the scenic route to West Cork from Kinsale through Clonakilty and Skibbereen to the Mizen Head
- Walk and birdwatch on Clear Island
- Climb Hungry Hill on the Beara Peninsula and relax afterwards in a Castletownbere pub
- Walk all or part of the Beara Way which loops the desolate Beara Peninsula
- Visit Clonakilty and the local historical sights
- Spend time in Kinsale for its picture-postcard charm and gastronomic treats
- Kiss the Blarney Stone to 'gain the privilege of telling lies for seven years'
- See the interior of Bantry House for its eclectic collection of art and artifacts from around the world

Famine reduced Cork to a sorry place, where many disillusioned and dispossessed people bid farewell to their homeland to travel overseas. The port of Cobh remained the major departure point for Irish emigrants right up to 1970; between 1815 and 1970 over three

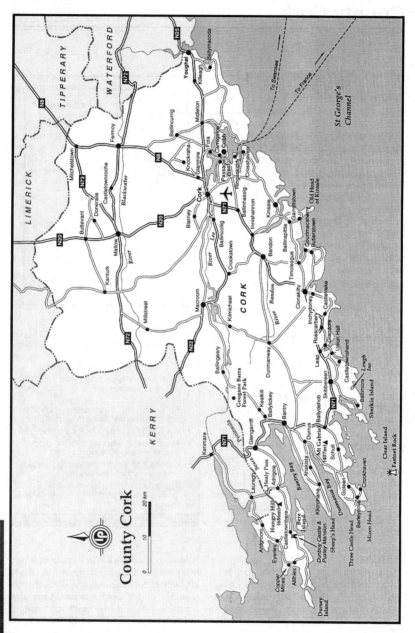

County Cork

The Irish Diaspora

Half the people born in Ireland since 1820 have emigrated. This astonishing statistic accounts for the estimated 60 million people around the world who can claim Irish origins. The most dramatic and tragic period of emigration was precipitated by the Potato Famine of 1845-51 when more than a million left, but the story of Irish emigration goes back much further than this and still continues, albeit on a smaller scale today.

During 1652-53, Oliver Cromwell expelled around 30,000 soldiers and had thousands of civilians transported. The West Indies was a favourite destination because once there they could be sold as slaves. After the Treaty of Limerick in 1691, another 20,000 men and their families fled to France.

Between 1791 and 1853, 39,000 convicts were transported from Cobh to Australia for crimes ranging from theft to murder. Between 1848 and 1850 4000 orphaned females were sent from the workhouses to provide mates for the men.

In the 18th century, emigration to North America began, especially from Ulster where Presbyterians were fed up with being treated as second-class citizens. The Potato Famine accelerated a process that was already well established and, between 1855 and 1914, another four million Irish people left for a new life, mostly in the USA and Britain.

Once a man or woman – and women often outnumbered men in their determination to leave – had decided to book their transatlantic passage it was understood that they were unlikely ever to return, hence the 'American Wake', a farewell party recognised as marking a final parting between emigrants and their families and friends.

Today there are approximately 12 million Americans of Irish origin, with the biggest concentration in New York, Boston and Philadelphia. Some of these people still feel their roots strongly, even contributing financially to the nationalist paramilitaries in Northern Ireland.

Although there is still unemployment in Ireland, the changed economic circumstances of the mid-1990s have seen an end to the routine outflow of citizens. In 1996 for the first time in living memory more people moved to live in Ireland than left for a new life elsewhere. ■

million people are thought to have emigrated from here.

Cork played a key role in Ireland's independence struggle. Thomas MacCurtain, a mayor of the city, was killed by the Black & Tans in 1920. His successor, Terence Mac-Swiney, died in London's Brixton Prison after 75 days on hunger strike. The Black & Tans were at their most brutal in Cork and much of the town was burnt down during the Anglo-Irish War. Cork was also a centre for the Civil War that followed independence, and Irish leader Michael Collins was ambushed and killed nearby.

ORIENTATION

The city centre is an island between two channels of the River Lee . The bridges – and the river smell – are vaguely reminiscent of Amsterdam. The curve of St Patrick's St is the focus of the main shopping precinct, with restaurants and trendy shops crammed into the pedestrianised streets of the Huguenot Quarter to the north. Grand Parade and South Mall boast the finest architecture. Kent

railway station and several hostels are to the north and east where MacCurtain St is the main thoroughfare. On the other side of the city, Washington St leads out to Killarney and West Cork with two more hostels along the way. On a hill to the north, the Shandon area cherishes one or two interesting old buildings but is otherwise somewhat run down.

INFORMATION

The tourist office (☎ 021-273251), on Grand Parade, is open from 9 am to 7 pm and 10 am to 1 pm on Sunday in July and August, and 9 am to 6 pm six days a week in June. Otherwise, it closes at 5.30 pm. Town trail leaflets are on sale here for IR£1.

The telephone code is ☎ 021.

Bookshops

Waterstone's runs between St Patrick's and Paul Sts. Eason's on St Patrick's St has a wide, less academic stock, including French newspapers and magazines. Connolly's, next to the shopping centre in Paul St, has a second-hand selection, as do Vibes & Scribes at 3 Bridge St and The Shelf on George's Quay. For lovers of blood-and-gore literature there's also Mainly Murder, 2A Paul St.

Laundry

There are laundrettes at 14 MacCurtain St across from Isaac's Hostel, and on Western Rd opposite the gates of the University College Cork (UCC).

Camping Equipment

You can hire equipment from The Tent Shop (☎ 278833), 7 Parnell Place, near the bus station. Or just around the corner from Isaac's Hostel in York St, Tents & Leisure (☎ 500702) sells and hires out tents.

Parking

Parking coupons (40p an hour) are obtainable at newsagents and should be displayed inside the car window to park virtually any-

---

Walking Tour of Cork

This tour starts at the eastern end of South Mall, across the river from the grey **City Hall**. On a visit to Ireland in 1963, President John F Kennedy gave an address from the steps of the City Hall. He had returned as a conquering hero to the land his great-grandfather had left, and the city came to a standstill as a massive crowd turned out to welcome him.

Walk west along the river until you reach **Holy Trinity Church**. This was designed by the Pain brothers in 1834 for Father Theobald Matthew, the 'Apostle of Temperance.' He led an effective, but short-lived, crusade against 'the demon drink' which resulted in the production of whiskey more than halving in the early 1840s. On the far side of the river a colourful array of old machinery advertises Fitzpatrick's second-hand shop; unfortunately what's displayed inside is nowhere near as interesting. Take the turning to the right just before the church which brings you out on South Mall. Across the road to the right you'll see the **Imperial Hotel**, dating back to 1816, where Michael Collins, commander-in-chief of the Irish Free State army, slept before setting out on a journey that would end in ambush and his death on 22 August 1922. When he arrived at the Imperial the two sentries in the lobby were asleep and Collins literally knocked their heads together in irritation.

Walk west along South Mall until you reach a small monument to the victims of the Hiroshima and Nagasaki atomic bombs on your left. A few steps further and you'll reach the ornate **Nationalist Monument** in memory of Irish patriots who died between 1798 and 1867.

Turn right along Grand Parade, with the tourist office on your right and three 18th century bow-fronted houses on your left. Between Oliver Plunkett St and Washington St is the small Bishop Lucey Park on the Washington St side. Cross the park to the old church in the right end corner which now houses the Cork Archive Centre. Adjoining it is the **Triskel Arts Centre** – an important arts venue (see Entertainment).

Turn left down South Main St past the Tudor-style Beamish & Crawford brewery. Turn left again down Tuckey St. Go down Tuckey St; at the end on the left, a bollard bears testimony to the days when Grand Parade was an open canal and boats moored by the quayside.

To your right you'll see the single-arched **Parliament Bridge** built, by the British, in 1806 to commemorate the Act of Union which had seen the end of the Irish parliament and the dispatch of its members to Westminster in London six years earlier. Cross the bridge and turn right along Sullivan's Quay. To your right you'll see **South Gate Bridge** (1713), which marks the site of the medieval entrance to the city.

Continue straight ahead along Bishop St to **St Finbarr's Cathedral**. From there it's a short walk west to the **University College Cork** (UCC) where a collection of Ogham stones is housed in the corridor of the quadrangle building facing Western Rd. They're in the corridor of the north wing (the one with a tower), directly behind you as you face the main entrance to the Boole Library.

If you face the front of the Boole Library and walk to the left, you'll see the Department of Plant Science. Behind it is the gorgeous **Honan Chapel**, built in 1915. The stained-glass windows and elaborate mosaic floors are well worth a look.

Return to the quadrangle and follow the path through the north wing by the tower. Follow the road down to the main gate, noting the **Greek Revival portico** originally built for Cork County Gaol on your left. As you emerge on to Western Rd the **Cork Public Museum** is close by, on the other side of the road and to the right in Fitzgerald Park.

Bus No 8 will ferry you back into the town centre. ■

where in the city centre. Alternatively, use the big car park behind Merchant's Quay shopping centre, or park for free in the Shandon area, north of Pope's Quay.

ST FINBARR'S CATHEDRAL

This imposing Protestant cathedral was designed by the Victorian architect William Burges, who was also responsible for Cardiff Castle and Castell Coch in Wales. He beat 67 other entrants in a competition to design a new cathedral to replace the crumbling old one. Work was completed in 1879. The finished building has three spires and a High Victorian interior. Particularly impressive are the huge pulpit and the colourful chancel ceiling.

CORK PUBLIC MUSEUM

The ground floor of this small, rather old-fashioned museum is mostly devoted to Cork's role in the fight for independence, while the 1st floor has archaeological displays. The museum is in pretty Fitzgerald Park behind Western Rd. Get off bus No 8 at the main gates of the university and follow the brown sign pointing the way. Entry is free and it's open Monday to Friday 11 am to 1 pm and 2.15 to 5 pm, to 6 pm in summer, closed on Saturday but open Sunday afternoon 3 to 5 pm.

CRAWFORD ART GALLERY

Crawford Art Gallery is housed in a building which was used partly as the Old Customs House of 1724 and also the Cork School of Art of 1884. It houses an excellent permanent collection, with works by Irish artists like Jack Yeats and Seán Keating as well as works of the British Newlyn and St Ives' schools. There's also an excellent café. It's open Monday to Saturday, 10 am to 5 pm, free.

ST ANNE'S CHURCH, SHANDON

The north side of Cork is dominated by this 18th century church's curious stepped tower, two walls faced with limestone and two with sandstone. The salmon-shaped weathervane was apparently chosen because the local monks reserved for themselves the right to fish for salmon in the river. The church is open 10 am to 5 pm Monday to Saturday. It costs IR£1.50 to climb the tower and ring its bells or IR£1 just to view the interior and its small collection of 17th century books including the letters of poet John Donne.

Nearby is the expensive **Shandon Craft Centre** in what was once the Cork Butter Exchange. Opposite it is the round **Firkin Crane Centre**, which used to house the weighing scales for the butter-casks (firkins) and is now home to a theatre group (see Entertainment).

CORK CITY GAOL

Cork City Gaol received its first prisoners in 1824 and its last in 1923. The 35-minute taped tour, which guides you around the restored and refurnished cells, is very moving and probably more interesting than the 20-minute audiovisual on the prison's history.

Upstairs a new **National Radio Museum** has opened. Alongside collections of beautiful old radios, you can hear the story of Marconi's conquest of the airwaves.

The gaol opens 9.30 am to 5 pm and costs IR£3.50/1.50. It's on Sunday's Well Rd, west of the city. Take bus No 8 from the bus station to the stop for Cork Public Museum and then walk across pretty Fitzgerald Park and over Daly Bridge. Turn right up the hill, left along Convent Ave and you'll see the brown signpost to the gaol.

CORK HERITAGE PARK

Cork Heritage Park is a collection of maritime and other exhibits in landscaped gardens south-east of the city in Bessberro, Blackrock. It's a 5km walk or bus No 2 will drop you off. The park is open Monday to Friday 10.30 am to 6 pm and at weekends noon to 6 pm. Admission costs IR£2.25/1.50.

ORGANISED TOURS

June to September, the tourist office organises free walking tours every Tuesday

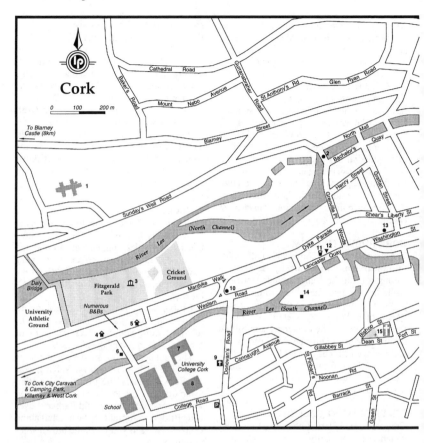

and Thursday at 7.30 pm. Walking tours of the university start at the main gates on Western Rd at 2.30 pm, Monday to Friday, and cost IR£2/75p.

Bus Éireann operates a three-hour open-top bus tour of Cork and Blarney from mid-June to early September (IR£5/3) from the bus station at 10.15 am and 2.45 pm, Monday to Saturday.

From late May through September, Guide Friday (☎ 01-676 5377) operates open-top hop-on, hop-off daily bus tours around Cork City only. In July and August there are 12 departures a day from Grand Parade, which is opposite the tourist office. Tickets cost IR£7/2.

Bus Éireann also offers day trips to Ennis and the Cliffs of Moher (IR£17), the Ring of Kerry (IR£13), the Rock of Cashel (IR£11) etc. Phone ☎ 508188 for more details.

Cork Harbour Cruises can be booked at the tourist office. From June to September, cruises to Cobh, allowing a three-hour visit, leave Penrose Quay at 11 am and cost IR£7.50/4.50. One-hour cruises around the Upper Harbour depart from Penrose Quay at 4.30 pm and cost IR£4/3. For more information phone ☎ 277085.

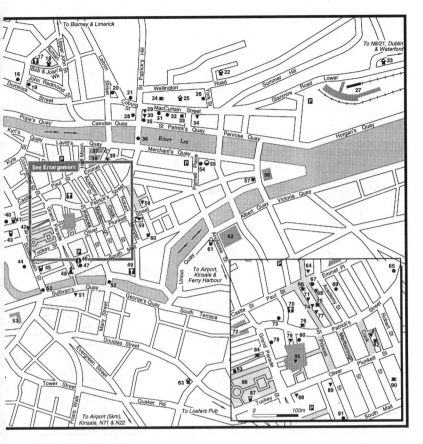

SPECIAL EVENTS

The Cork International Jazz Festival and the International Film Festival both take place in October. Tickets for both can sell out quickly, and programmes are available from the Cork Opera House, Emmet Place (☎ 270022). The International Choral and Folk Dance Festival takes place in late April and early May.

PLACES TO STAY
Camping

Cork City Caravan & Camping Park (☎ 961866) is on Togher Rd quite close to the centre. It's signposted from the Wilton/ city hospital roundabout on the main West Cork road. Bus No 14 from the centre stops outside. The site is conveniently close to the Wilton shopping centre. *Bienvenue Ferry Caravan & Camping Park* (☎ 312711) is on a slip road opposite the entrance to Cork airport off the N27. A tent site for two adults costs IR£5.

Hostels

Three hostels are quite close together, across the river from the bus station. The biggest and most obvious is the IHH's *Isaac's*

PLACES TO STAY
4   Campus House Hostel
5   An Óige Hostel
6   Castlewhite
     Apartments
14   Jury's Hotel
18   Kinlay House
     Shandon Hostel
22   Sheila's Cork Tourist
     Hostel
23   Cork International
     Tourist Hostel
25   Isaac's Hostel/
     Isaac's Hotel &
     Restaurant
33   Metropole Hotel
57   Jury's Cork Inn
60   Imperial Hotel
63   Kelly's Hostel

PLACES TO EAT
12   Café Paradiso
24   O'Briens Café
29   The Boxing Cat
30   Taste of Thailand
     Restaurant
34   Luciano's Pizzeria
39   Pierre Victoire
42   Paddy Garibaldi's
51   Quay Co-Op
     Restaurant
58   The Long Valley
64   Bully's Restaurant
66   Gingerbread House
     Café
68   Meadows & Byrne
71   Singapore Gourmet
     Restaurant
74   Paddy Garibaldi's
     Restaurant
75   An Crêpe
76   Gloria Jeans
77   Café Mexicana

79   Oyster Tavern Pub
     Restaurant
81   Toscani's
82   Bewley's Café
84   O'Briens Café
85   English Market
88   Twomey's Bakery
89   Ivory Tower
90   Java Joe's

PUBS
11   Reidy's Vault Bar
41   Washington Inn
43   Reardens
45   An Spailpín Fánac
     Pub
61   Lobby, Charlie's, An
     Phoenix, Donkey's
     Ears
87   Mollies

OTHER
1   Cork City
     Gaol/National
     Radio Museum
2   North Gate Bridge
3   Cork Public Museum
7   North Wing of
     University College
8   Boole Library
9   Honan Chapel
10   Laundrette
13   Kino
15   St Finbarr's Cathedral
16   Shandon Craft
     Centre/Cork Butter
     Exchange
17   St Anne's Church,
     Shandon
19   Firkin Crane Centre
20   Cork Arts Theatre
21   City Limits
26   Tents & Leisure

27   Kent Railway
     Station
28   Vibes & Scribes
31   Everyman Palace
     Theatre
32   Laundrette
35   Irish Ferries
36   St Patrick's Bridge
37   Cork Opera
     House/Half Moon
     Club
38   Crawford Art Gallery
40   Courthouse
44   Beamish & Crawford
     Brewery
46   Tourist Office
47   Brittany Ferries
48   Nationalist
     Monument
49   Holy Trinity Church
50   South Gate Bridge
52   Parliament Bridge
53   Elizabeth Fort
54   The Tent Shop
55   Bus Station
56   Customs House
59   Post Office
62   City Hall
65   Eason's Bookshop
67   Mostly Murder
69   Aer Lingus Office
70   Church of St Peter &
     St Paul
72   Queen's Old Castle
     Shopping Centre
73   Waterstone's
     Bookshop
78   Capitol Cineplex
80   USIT Travel Office
83   Triskel Arts Centre
86   Bishop Lucey Park
91   Swansea Cork
     Ferries

(☎ 500011) in MacCurtain St, with dorm beds from IR£6.95. It is a rather impersonal place which persists in excluding people from the dorms between 11 am and 5 pm and only lets them collect their baggage on the hour and half-hour.

Back from MacCurtain St at 4 Belgrave Place, off Wellington Rd, is clean, friendly *Sheila's* (☎ 505562) which has bags of facilities: laundry, café, foreign exchange and Western Union link, bike hire, even a sauna. For 50p you can pick up your email here (sheilas@iol.ie). Dorm beds are IR£6.50, private doubles IR£19.

In a more rundown area north of the river is the friendly *Kinlay House Shandon* (☎ 508966) at Bob & Joan's Walk in the old Shandon district immediately behind St Anne's Church. Beds in mixed dorms for up to 12 people cost IR£7.50, twin rooms are IR£22 and singles IR£15, all including light breakfast.

Other fairly central possibilities include the *Cork International Tourist Hostel* (☎ 509089), 100 Glanmire Rd Lower , just beyond the railway station, with beds for IR£6; *Kellys* (☎ 315612), 25 Summerhill South, south of the river, with beds from

IR£6.50; and the new *Island House* (☎ 271716) on Morrison's Quay opposite the Custom House, with dorm beds for IR£10.50 and singles/doubles for IR£26/36.

Out by the university, to the west of the centre, the big An Óige *Cork International Youth Hostel* (☎ 543289), 1-2 Western Rd, has had an expensive makeover and offers excellent value for IR£7.50 a night in a dorm; the kitchen, lounge and dining room are all immaculate for the time being. Should it be full, the much smaller *Campus House* (☎ 343531) is just a few doors further out at 3 Woodland View, Western Rd and has beds for IR£6.50. Bus No 8 from the bus station stops outside the An Óige hostel.

B&Bs

Glanmire Rd Lower beyond the railway station is lined with budget B&Bs. *Kent House* (☎ 504260) at No 47, *Oakland* (☎ 500578) at No 51 and *Tara House* (☎ 500294) at No 52 all have singles for around IR£19, doubles from IR£29.

On the opposite side of town, along Western Rd, there are plenty of B&Bs like *St Kilda's* (☎ 273095), a big blue house with its own car park, close to the gates of the university. Singles/doubles cost IR£40/50. A few doors along is the cheaper *Antoine House* (☎ 273494), at IR£20/35. If you're coming into Cork from the west, these places are on the left after the roundabout at Cork hospital.

Danny's B&B (☎ 503606), a gay guesthouse at 3 St John's Terrace, Upper John St, has rooms from about IR£20/35.

Hotels

Hotel Isaac's (☎ 500011) is centrally positioned at 48 MacCurtain St, attached to the hostel of the same name; newly renovated singles/doubles cost IR£42/56 (self-catering apartments are also available from IR£50). The biggest in the city is the ugly *Jury's* (☎ 276622; fax 276144) on Lancaster Quay to the west. Singles/doubles are an absurd IR£115/135, excluding breakfast, although there's a small outdoor swimming pool. The *Imperial* (☎ 274040; fax 275375) in South

Mall is more central (and more attractive) with rooms at IR£65/85.

Originally a temperance hotel, the *Metropole* (☎ 508122; fax 506450) on MacCurtain St has rooms from IR£60/85.

Good value, especially for families, are two hotels with fixed room rates for up to three adults and two children. *Jury's Cork Inn* (☎ 276444; fax 276144), in the centre on Anderson's Quay, opposite Customs House, charges IR£45; while *Forte Travelodge* (☎ 1800-709709; fax 310707), near the airport at the Kinsale Rd roundabout, charges IR£36.50

At Tivoli, on the road to Waterford, *Lotamore House* (☎ 822344) stands in delightful grounds. Singles/doubles cost IR£27/52.

PLACES TO EAT

Cafés & Takeaways

There's the usual collection of fast-food takeaways, including a branch of *Abrakebabra*, along St Patrick's St.

To put together a picnic, head straight for English Market off the western end of St Patrick's St, which sells all manner of homemade cakes, bagels and West Cork cheeses. *Twomey's*, around the corner in Oliver Plunkett St, is good for fresh bread.

Two of the nicest places for a light lunch or afternoon tea are the *Crawford Gallery Restaurant* in Emmet Place and the upstairs café at the *Triskel Arts Centre*. Alternatively, *O'Briens* at 39 MacCurtain St near Isaac's, is good for tea, scones and sandwiches. It's also one of the few places open early for Sunday breakfasts.

Bewley's Café on Cook St, is a good place for breakfast, as is *Java Joe's* at 14-15 Cook St. *The Long Valley* on Winthrop St, near the post office, is famous for its giant lunch time sandwiches.

Between St Patrick's St and pedestrianised Paul St are several narrow lanes with good places for a sandwich or meal. Try the *Gingerbread House Café* or *Meadows & Byrne* on French Church St for lunch or a coffee or tea. *Gloria Jeans* at 84 Patrick St does great coffee and opens on Sunday at noon, when a lot of other places are closed.

Reidy's Vault Bar, opposite Jury's Hotel on Western Rd, is a comfortable pub serving seafood all day in the IR£6 to IR£11 range.

Restaurants

In the pedestrian area between St Patrick's and Paul Sts, *Bully's* at 40 Paul St does pizza and pasta from IR£2.99. A block away in Carey's Lane *Café Mexicana* has main courses from IR£7 while *Paddy Garibaldi's* serves up fish and burgers as well as pizzas for around the same price (there's another branch in Washington St). Next door *Gambieni's* serves pasta from IR£5.25.

Gino's, at 7 Winthrop St off Oliver Plunkett St, and *Luciano's*, on MacCurtain St, are two good pizzerias. *Toscani* is a comfortable little place in Cook St with main courses from IR£6.

For vegetarians, *Café Paradiso*, opposite Jury's Hotel on Western Rd, has dishes like leek and pinenut timbale for IR£4.20. The *Quay Co-Op*, upstairs at 24 Sullivan's Quay, has soups from IR£1.65 and more elaborate evening menus, again catering for vegetarians too.

Isaac's Restaurant (not run by the MacCurtain St hostel to which it's attached), is deservedly popular and offers some of the best value meals around; menus feature dishes like duck and mushroom pie for IR£5.85. *Taste of Thailand*, 8 Bridge St, has a three-course dinner before 7.30 pm for IR£10. At 4 Bridge St *The Boxing Cat* has dishes like veggie pasta for IR£7.95.

The Ivory Tower, 35 Princes St, serves interesting world food meals, with seafood and vegetarian dishes always available. A set dinner is IR£17.50 but lunch, around IR£8 to IR£11, is better value.

ENTERTAINMENT
Pubs & Traditional Music

Cork's cultural rivalry with Dublin extends to drink. Locally-brewed Murphy's is the stout of choice here, or a Beamish, which is often cheaper. On Union Quay from the corner of Anglesea St, the *Lobby, Charlie's,*

An Phoenix and the *Donkey's Ears* are all side by side, and almost every night one or other will have music.

The *An Spailpín Fánac* on South Main St, ('probably the oldest pub in Ireland' according to the tourist-board pub guide), is fairly atmospheric. To the south, at 48 Barrack St, the arty *Nancy Spain's* has good music. *Mollies*, in Tuckey St, also has music ... and televised football, if that's your scene. In Coburg St, *City Limits* has top comedy on Friday and Saturday from 8.45 pm.

Washington St has a cluster of popular student pubs with music; two of them are near the imposing Court Building – the *Washington Inn* and *Reardens*. The *Half Moon Club*, at the Cork Opera House, has live music Thursday to Saturday from 11.30 pm.

If you're keen on traditional music but pubs aren't your scene, look in at *The Living Tradition* (☎ 502040), 40 MacCurtain St. As well as selling a wide range of tapes and CDs, it also hosts Friday-night music sessions from 8.30 to 10.30 pm.

The *Other Place* (☎ 278745), 8 South Main St, Ireland's only gay community centre, operates a bookshop, café and information line. There's a dance club here on Friday and Saturday nights (one Friday a month is women-only). *Loafers*, 26 Douglas St, is essentially a lesbian pub that attracts male gays at the weekend.

Theatres & Cinema

Cork prides itself on its cultural pursuits. The mainstream theatre is *Cork Opera House* (☎ 270022) in Emmet Place. The *Triskel Arts Centre* (☎ 272022), in Tobin St, off South Main St, is more adventurous, as is *Cork Arts Theatre* (☎ 508398) in Knapps Square to the north. The newly restored *Everyman Palace Theatre* (☎ 501673) is in MacCurtain St. *Firkin Crane Centre* (☎ 507487) has mid-week sessions of traditional song and dance in the summer.

Capitol Cineplex (☎ 278777), in Grand Parade, shows mainstream films, while *Kino* (☎ 271571) in Washington St West is more of an arthouse cinema.

GETTING THERE & AWAY

The USIT Travel Office (☎ 270900) is hidden away at 10-11 Market Parade, an arcade off St Patrick's St near the Grand Parade junction.

Air

Cork airport has direct flights to Dublin, London, Manchester, Exeter, Jersey, Paris, Rennes and Amsterdam. Other overseas flights go via Dublin. For flight information call ☎ 1800-626747 or contact the Aer Lingus office (☎ 327155) in Academy St. The airport is about 8km south of the city centre on the South City Link Rd and takes about 20 minutes to reach by car.

Ferry

The ferry terminal is at Ringaskiddy, about 15 minutes by car south-east from the city centre along the N28. Bus Éireann runs a fairly frequent daily service to the terminal; the journey takes 45 minutes.

Regular ferries link Cork with the UK and France. Swansea Cork Ferries has an office (☎ 271166) at 52 South Mall, and an office (☎ 378036) at the ferry terminal which opens for arrivals and departures only. The return fare in July for a car and passengers ranges from IR£250 (early July) to IR£370 (late July). Before the end of May, return fares are IR£155 midweek or IR£198 at weekends. The single non-motorist fare ranges from IR£21 before 25 May to IR£30 in August. The ferry doesn't operate from the second week of January to the second week of March.

Brittany Ferries (☎ 277801) has an office next to the tourist office; its services to Roscoff (March-October) cost from IR£507 return, high season (car with two people, booked 21 days in advance), or IR£111 for a non-motorist. These prices don't include cabins.

Irish Ferries (☎ 551995), 9 Bridge St, at the corner of St Patrick's Quay, operates services to Le Havre, Cherbourg and Roscoff. The July return fare for a vehicle and two passengers ranges from IR£530 to IR£600; a single non-motorist fare is IR£90.

Bus

The bus station (☎ 508188) is on the corner of Merchant's Quay and Parnell Place. You can get to almost anywhere in Ireland from Cork: Dublin (4½ hours, four daily, IR£12); Killarney (two hours, five daily, IR£8.80); Waterford (2¼ hours, six to eight daily, IR£8); and Wexford (3¾ hours, two daily, IR£12).

Train

Kent railway station (☎ 506766) is across the river on Glanmire Rd Lower . There's a direct train connection to Dublin (2½ hours, eight daily, IR£22) and indirect routes to other towns such as Killarney (two hours, four daily, IR£9.50) and Waterford (3½ to five hours, four daily, IR£17).

An hourly service south to Cobh stops at Fota, enabling you to take in the wildlife park and heritage centre (see Fota Wildlife Park in Around Cork, following) on a round trip.

GETTING AROUND
The Airport

From April through September there are four buses a day from the bus terminal (IR£2.50).

Bus

Most places you'll need to get to are within easy walking distance of the city centre. If you're staying at the An Óige hostel, however, the bus fare from the bus station is 70p; if you're staying a long time it might be worth considering a weekly ticket for IR£9. You'll need a photo to go with it.

Car

Eurodollar (☎ 344884) have cars from IR£30 a day including insurance. You can pick your car up at the airport or they will deliver it to your hotel/hostel.

Bicycle

Bikes can be hired for around IR£6/30 a day/week. Cycle Scene (☎ 301183), 396 Blarney St, and also Kilgrew's Cycles (☎ 276255), at 6/7 Kyle St, handle the Raleigh Rent-a-Bike scheme.

CORK

Around Cork

BLARNEY

Just north-west of Cork, Blarney (An Bhlarna) is a village with one overwhelming drawcard – Blarney Castle. There's a tourist office (☎ 021-381624) near the bus stop. Beside it is **Blarney Woollen Mills**, a giant tourist shop selling everything from quality garments to tacky Ireland-shaped green telephones accompanied by a 'no blarney' guarantee.

The telephone code is ☎ 021.

Blarney Castle

Even the most untouristy visitor will probably feel compelled to kiss the Blarney Stone and get the gift of the gab or, as an 18th century French consul put it, 'gain the privilege of telling lies for seven years'. It was Queen Elizabeth I, exasperated with Lord Blarney's ability to talk endlessly without ever actually agreeing to her demands, who invented the term.

Dating from 1446, the castle is a tower house built on solid limestone in wonderful grounds; remember to pack a picnic.

Bending over backwards to kiss the sacred rock requires a head for heights. You're unlikely to fall since there's someone there to hold you but a word of warning about general safety is in order. The spiral staircases are narrow and the one at the back has no handrail. Ten years ago a child fell through a window and was killed.

The castle (☎ 385252) is open Monday to Saturday 9 am to 6.30 or 7 pm, or to sundown in winter. Sunday it's open 9.30 am to 5.30 pm or sundown. Entry is IR£3/1. Your enjoyment of your visit to Blarney will probably be in inverse proportion to the number of coach tours there at the time. Getting there at opening time is one way of beating the crowds.

The adjacent **Blarney House** is open noon to 6 pm Monday to Saturday in July and August. It's a late 19th century baronial house full of Victorian trappings and chandeliers made of Waterford glass. Entry is IR£2.50/1 but a combined castle and house ticket saves 50p.

Places to Stay

Camping & Hostel *Blarney Caravan & Camping Park* (☎ 385167), 2.5km from town on the R617, is signposted in Blarney. A couple of km outside Blarney, on the road west to Killarney, there's an unaffiliated hostel (☎ 385580) with IR£5 beds and private doubles for IR£14.

B&Bs Blarney has a host of B&Bs, most of them only open from April or May to October or November. Two exceptions, which are open all year, are *Mrs Callaghan* (☎ 385035) and *Killarney House* (☎ 381841) both on Station Rd. More central is *Rosemount* (☎ 385584) with singles/doubles from IR£19.

Hotels There are two big hotels: the *Blarney Park* (☎ 385281; fax 381506) and *Christys* (☎ 385011; fax 385350), costing IR£110 and IR£98, respectively, for a double. The smaller *Blarney Castle* (☎ 385116) is cheaper at IR£32/54 a single/double.

Places to Eat

Blarney has several restaurants and pubs serving food. *Blarney Stone Restaurant* has lunch dishes starting at IR£3 and *Mackey's* next door serves a set menu for IR£10. Bar food at the *Muskerry Arms* opposite is also reasonably priced.

Getting There & Away

Blarney is 8km north-west of Cork and buses run regularly from the Cork bus station (30 minutes; IR£2.60 return).

BALLINCOLLIG

The village of Ballincollig, 8km west of Cork on the main Killarney road, is home to the Royal Gunpowder Mills. Throughout the 19th century this was one of Europe's largest gunpowder manufacturing plants. It's open April to September 10 am to 6 pm, and admission is IR£2.50/1.50. Regular buses run to the village from Cork City bus station (15 minutes, IR£2.30 return).

PASSAGE WEST

If you're travelling from West to East Cork and want to avoid going through Cork City it's worth knowing about the Cross River Ferry which connects Passage West with Carrigaloe daily from 7.15 am to around midnight. The one-way charge for a car is IR£2.50; for a pedestrian 60p; and for a motorcycle IR£1.30.

CROSSHAVEN

The R612 south-west from Cork brings you to pretty little Crosshaven on the Owenboy River. The marina can look delightful on a sunny day. Otherwise the only specific sights are Georgian Crosshaven House, which isn't open to the public, and scant remains of 16th century Fort Camden. The *Grand Hotel* (☎ 021-832270), which briefly operated as an IHH hostel, was for sale at the time of writing. If it reopens as a hotel, expect prices to reflect its striking architecture and views which take in the river.

FOTA WILDLIFE PARK

Fota Wildlife Park (☎ 021-812678), a kind of zoo without bars, is ideal for children of all ages. Giraffes, ostriches, monkeys, kangaroos and penguins wander freely, and lemurs invade the coffee shop. Cheetahs may not have space to hit full speed here but they're bred and exported to countries from where they originated. Look out in particular for the glorious white and brown scimitar-horned onyxes which are believed to be extinct in the wild.

The park opens Easter to October, 10 am to 5 pm (11 am on Sunday). Admission is IR£3.70/2.20. The *Coffee Shop* is pretty average so it might be worth bringing a picnic. A 'gravy train' runs a circuit around the park every 15 minutes for 40p.

With time on your hands it's worth strolling down to look at the graceful exterior of 18th century **Fota House**, once one of Ireland's grandest houses but now sadly neglected, and the 150-year-old **arboretum**, both at the station end of the park.

Getting There & Away

The park is 16km from Cork. Since cars must be left outside (IR£1 parking fee) and visitors walk around the park, it might make better sense to take the hourly Cork to Cobh train which stops here (15 minutes, IR£1.80 return).

COBH

Picturesque Cobh (pronounced 'cove') was for many years the port of Cork, and has always had a strong connection with Atlantic crossings. In 1838 the *Sirius* was the first steamship to cross the Atlantic, sailing from Cobh. The *Titanic* made its last stop here before its fateful Atlantic crossing in 1912 and it was near Cobh that the *Lusitania* was torpedoed in 1915. The world's first yacht club, the Royal Cork Yacht Club, was founded here in 1720, but now operates from Crosshaven on the other side of Cork Harbour. The old building now houses a small tourist information office (☎ 021-813790) and arts centre,

Cobh is on Great Island which fills much of Cork Harbour and is joined to the mainland by a causeway. In the British era it was known as Queenstown, because it was where Queen Victoria arrived in 1849, on her first visit to Ireland.

The telephone code is ☎ 021.

St Colman's Cathedral

Cobh is dominated by the massive but the comparatively new St Colman's Cathedral standing on a huge platform above the town. Construction of the French-Gothic-style cathedral began in 1868 but wasn't completed until 1915. The Irish communities in Australia and the USA contributed much of the construction cost. The cathedral is noted for its 47-bell carillon, the largest in Ireland. The biggest bell weighs 3440 kg. St Colman (522-604) is the patron saint of the local diocese of Cloyne.

Cobh Heritage Centre

The impressive Cobh Heritage Centre ('the Queenstown Story') has interesting displays on the mass emigrations following the Famine, the era of the great liners and the tragedies of the *Titanic* and *Lusitania*. It's in Cobh's old railway station and admission is IR£3.50/2. Opening hours are 10 am to 6 pm, March to December, and there's a craft and coffee shop.

Cobh Museum

There's a small history museum in the 19th century Scots Presbyterian church, open April to September, Monday to Saturday 11 am to 1 pm and 2 to 6 pm, Sunday 3 to 6 pm.

Harbour Cruises

One-hour cruises around Cobh Harbour leave at 12.15 pm and cost IR£4/3. Phone ☎ 277085 for more details.

Places to Stay & Eat

If you don't care for big towns, Cobh might make a pleasant alternative base to Cork. The best B&B is *Westbourne House* (☎ 811391) which costs IR£12 a head and is on the left if you're walking up from the station. If that's full, try *Mrs O'Rourke* (☎ 812450) at Bellavista in Bishop's Rd, with singles/doubles from IR£22/32.

The *Commodore* (☎ 811277) is the premier hotel and features a heated indoor pool. Singles/doubles cost IR£55/90 in July and August. It's also the most reliable place for a decent meal, with set lunches, bar meals and dinner for IR£19.

A couple of cafés in town serve quick meals, as do some of the many pubs.

Getting There & Away

Cobh is 24km south-east of Cork, off the main N25 Cork to Rosslare road. Hourly trains connect Cobh with Cork (½-hr; IR£2.50 return). Alternatively, June through September you can take a passenger cruiser which leaves Cobh at 3.15 pm and costs IR£5.50/3.50.

Another alternative is to take the five-minute Cross River car ferry (☎ 811223) across Cork Harbour from Glenbrook to Carrigaloe. There are daily sailings from 7.15 am to 12.30 am.

MIDLETON

The Jameson Heritage Centre (☎ 021-613594) is the main reason to pause in Midleton (Mainistir na Corann). Whiskey has been distilled here since the early 19th century, and the old works were opened to the public after a new distillery was opened. Twenty-four million bottles of whiskey are produced at this new plant each year.

Forty-five-minute guided tours start with a film show and continue with a walkabout that reveals the whole whiskey-making process. You see the storeroom where local farmers had their barley weighed and deposited, have the malting process explained to you and then see the huge waterwheel that used to power the plant. Don't miss the world's largest copper still here. The tour ends in the bar where two lucky volunteers get to compare assorted Irish whiskies with Scotch and Bourbon. Everyone gets a free tipple and there's a café for snacks and lunches.

From March to October there are regular daily tours 10 am to 4 pm. The rest of the year there are tours Monday to Friday at noon and 3 pm. Admission is IR£3.50/1.50.

If you want to stay, the *An Stor Midleton Tourist Hostel* (☎ 021-633106) in Drury's Ave has dorm beds for IR£7.

Getting There & Away

Some (but not all) buses from Cork to Waterford stop at Midleton.

YOUGHAL

Youghal (pronounced 'yawl') is an interesting little town where the river Blackmore meets the sea. Sir Walter Raleigh was town mayor from 1588-89 and, tradition has it, he planted the first potatoes here after bringing them back from the New World.

Orientation & Information

Youghal (Eochaill) is little more than one long street, appropriately called North Main

St and South Main St and carrying one-way traffic for most of its length. Come through Youghal in the wrong direction (ie from Waterford to Cork) and you could easily miss the lot.

The old Clock Gate at the south end of Main St is Youghal's major landmark. Nearby is the tourist office (☎ 024-92390), sadly moved from the Gate to Market House. It's open all year, daily April to September 10 am to 5.30 pm, Monday to Friday the rest of the year. A small heritage centre, open for the same hours as the tourist office, explains the town's history for IR£1 or else you can buy the Story of Youghal with a town trail map for IR£1.95. Safe beaches stretch away south of town.

The telephone code is ☎ 024.

Things to See & Do

Heading through town from south to north, here are some things to look out for.

The elegant red brick **Town Hall** on the

seafront south of the tourist office was once Mall House, built in 1789 as a place of entertainment, with a ballroom, tea rooms, and space for gambling and reading.

Fox's Lane Folk Museum, signposted down an alley between The Mall and South Main St, displays over 400 bygones and a Victorian kitchen. You're most likely to find it open in July and August, Tuesday to Saturday, 10 am to 1 pm and 2 to 6 pm, and Sunday 2.30 to 6 pm. Admission is IR£2/1.

The curious **Clock Gate** bridges Main St. In 1777 the present building, a combination of clocktower and jail, replaced the medieval Trinity Gate, a key part of the town's fortifications. In 1798 several members of the rebellious United Irishmen were hanged from its walls.

Red House, on Main St, was designed in 1706 by the Dutch architect Leuventhen, with typically Dutch characteristics, like the cornerstones positioned under the triangular gable. Its name comes from its red bricks. A

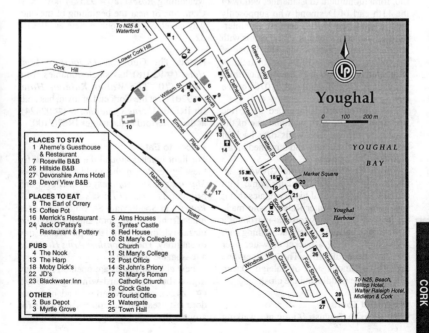

PLACES TO STAY
1 Aherne's Guesthouse & Restaurant
7 Roseville B&B
26 Hillside B&B
27 Devonshire Arms Hotel
28 Devon View B&B

PLACES TO EAT
9 The Earl of Orrery
15 Coffee Pot
16 Merrick's Restaurant
24 Jack O'Patsy's Restaurant & Pottery

PUBS
4 The Nook
13 The Harp
18 Moby Dick's
22 JD's
23 Blackwater Inn

OTHER
2 Bus Depot
3 Myrtle Grove
5 Alms Houses
6 Tyntes' Castle
8 Red House
10 St Mary's Collegiate Church
11 St Mary's College
12 Post Office
14 St John's Priory
17 St Mary's Roman Catholic Church
19 Clock Gate
20 Tourist Office
21 Watergate
25 Town Hall

Youghal

few doors farther up the street are **Alms Houses** built in 1610 by Richard Boyle, the local lord, to house ex-soldiers.

Across the road from the Alms Houses stands 15th century **Tynte's Castle**. Originally it had a defensive riverfront position but as the River Blackwater silted up and changed course it was left high and dry. In 1584 the castle was confiscated and given to Sir Robert Tynte, who married the widow of the poet Edmund Spenser. Today, it's semi-derelict.

Built in 1220, **St Mary's Collegiate Church** incorporates elements of an earlier Danish church dating back to the 11th century. In the late 16th century the earl of Desmond housed his troops here, leading to the destruction of the old chancel roof. Inside there's a monument to Richard Boyle who bought Raleigh's Irish estates and became the first earl of Cork. It shows him with his wife and all 16 of his children, those who died as infants shown lying down. Look out, too, for a monument to Catherine, widow of the 11th earl of Desmond who supposedly died in 1614, aged 140! There are also interesting gravestones to look at here, some with Norman-French inscriptions. This is one of the oldest churches still in use in Ireland, with Sunday services at 11 am. At other times it's usually locked; phone ☎ 91076 for the key.

The **churchyard** is bounded by a fine stretch of the old town wall and one of the remaining turrets. The walls date back at least to the 13th century and remained in use until the 17th century.

Beside St Mary's, **Myrtle Grove** is an interesting house which retains some 16th century features. Local history relates that it was home to Sir Walter Raleigh who made the mistake of smoking tobacco in front of a servant who had never seen such a thing and, accordingly, threw a bucket of water over him to douse the fire. The weathervane depicts the famous story of Raleigh, Queen Elizabeth, the puddle and the cloak.

Organised Tours

From June to August, 90-minute walking tours costing IR£2.50/1.50 leave the tourist office at 11 am and 3 pm Monday to Saturday.

Places to Stay

Camping The *Sonas* campsite (☎ 98132) is about 15km to the south, on the seashore. To get there, take the road off the N25 (west of town) to the village of Ballymacoda, then head west through the village. A tent site for two people with a car costs IR£4.50. The *Summerfield Caravan & Camping Park* (☎ 93537) is just over 1km west of Youghal off the main Cork road. Both campsites are open May to the end of September.

B&Bs Basic accommodation is available for IR£7.50 at *Hillside* (☎ 92468), 6 Strand St, on the one-way road leading to Cork. The elegant Georgian *Devon View* (☎ 92298) is at the Cork end of town, opposite the Devonshire Arms Hotel, and has doubles for IR£29. Coming into town from Waterford, welcoming *Roseville* (☎ 92571) is in New Catherine St near the beginning of the one-way street. Singles/doubles here are IR£18/32.

Hotels The Georgian *Devonshire Arms Hotel* (☎ 92018) has singles/doubles from IR£38/70. The *Walter Raleigh Hotel* (☎ 92011), at the Cork end of town, has beds for IR£30. *Aherne's Guesthouse* (☎ 92424), at the Waterford end, charges IR£70/100.

Places to Eat

For light lunches around the IR£3 mark try the *Coffee Pot* in the middle of town or *Merrick's Restaurant* next door. Bigger and brighter is *Jack O'Patsy's Restaurant & Pottery*, in South Main St, which opens for lunch from noon to 3 pm, and for pasta and pizza-style dinners until 9.30 pm Wednesday to Saturday. The *Devonshire Arms Hotel* has a reasonable bar menu.

Few cheaper places are open on Monday nights but the award-winning *Aherne's* (☎ 92424), at the Waterford end of town, does tasty seafood pies, pizzas and pasta for around IR£7. Splashing out, a full dinner here is IR£23.70. Dinner at *The Earl of Orrery* (☎ 93208) in North Main St is likely to cost at least IR£12.

Entertainment
The *Blackwater Inn*, *JD's*, *The Harp* and *The Nook* on Main St often have music. *Moby Dick's* near the tourist office has little to recommend it beyond being John Huston's port of call during the filming of *Moby Dick* starring Gregory Peck in 1954.

The late August holiday weekend is the occasion for a busking (street music) festival when the pubs are particularly lively.

Getting There & Away
Buses from Cork to Waterford stop in Youghal (1¼ hrs, IR£5.50).

West Cork

KINSALE
Kinsale (Cionn tSáile) has a picture-postcard prettiness reminiscent of Cornwall in England and, like Cornwall, it's blighted by summer traffic jams. The crowds are drawn not just by the scenery and historic buildings but by the fact that Kinsale is the undisputed gourmet capital of Ireland. It's easily reached by car from Cork by taking the route south to the airport.

History
In September 1601, a Spanish fleet anchored at Kinsale was besieged by the English. The Irish army marched the length of the country to attack the English, but were defeated in battle outside Kinsale on Christmas Eve. For the Catholics of Kinsale, the immediate consequence was that they were banned from the town. It was another 100 years before they were allowed to return. Historians now give 1601 as the beginning of the end of Gaelic Ireland.

After 1601 the town developed as a shipbuilding port. In the early 18th century Alexander Selkirk left Kinsale Harbour on a voyage that left him stranded on a desert island, providing Daniel Defoe with the idea for *Robinson Crusoe*.

Orientation & Information
The tourist office (☎ 021-772234) is on the harbourfront, close to the bus stop. There's a laundrette on Main St.

Most of the hotels and restaurants ring the harbour, but some are out at Scilly, a peninsula to the south-east. A path continues from there south-east to Summer Cove and the Charles Fort. To the south-west, Duggan Bridge links Castlepark Marina and the scant ruins of the James Fort to The Pier Rd.

The telephone code is ☎ 021.

Museum
The small museum in the 17th century courthouse in Market Square shows exhibits relating to the 1915 sinking of the *Lusitania*, but you'll be lucky to find it open outside July and August. Admission is 50p/20p.

Charles Fort
Three km east of Kinsale stand the huge ruins of 17th century Charles Fort, one of the best preserved star forts in Europe. Now a Dúchas site, it was built in the 1670s and remained in use until 1921 when much of the fort was destroyed as the British withdrew. Most of the ruins you see inside date to the 18th and 19th centuries. It's open 9 am to 6 pm daily mid-June to mid-September, closing an hour earlier for the rest of the year and completely from November until Easter. Entry is IR£2/1.

Even those not enthralled by military history will enjoy the harbour views from the massive walls. If you follow the signposted Scilly Walk you'll have similar views all the way.

Desmond Castle
This 16th century tower-house on Cork St was occupied by the Spanish in 1601. Since then it has served as a prison for French and American captives and as a workhouse during the Great Famine. In the care of Dúchas, it now houses a small museum on the history of wine. From mid-June to mid-September it's open daily 9 am to 6 pm; from

CORK

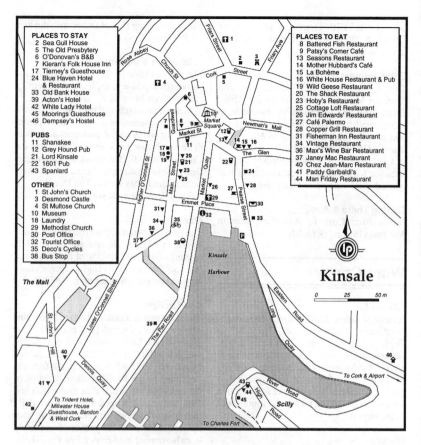

PLACES TO STAY
2 Sea Gull House
5 The Old Presbytery
6 O'Donovan's B&B
7 Kieran's Folk House Inn
17 Tierney's Guesthouse
24 Blue Haven Hotel
& Restaurant
33 Old Bank House
39 Acton's Hotel
42 White Lady Hotel
45 Moorings Guesthouse
46 Dempsey's Hostel

PUBS
11 Shanakee
12 Grey Hound Pub
21 Lord Kinsale
22 1601 Pub
43 Spaniard

OTHER
1 St John's Church
3 Desmond Castle
4 St Multose Church
10 Museum
18 Laundry
29 Methodist Church
30 Post Office
32 Tourist Office
35 Deco's Cycles
38 Bus Stop

PLACES TO EAT
8 Battered Fish Restaurant
9 Patsy's Corner Café
13 Seasons Restaurant
14 Mother Hubbard's Café
15 La Bohème
16 White House Restaurant & Pub
19 Wild Geese Restaurant
20 The Shack Restaurant
23 Hoby's Restaurant
25 Cottage Loft Restaurant
26 Jim Edwards' Restaurant
27 Café Palermo
28 Copper Grill Restaurant
31 Fisherman Inn Restaurant
34 Vintage Restaurant
36 Max's Wine Bar Restaurant
37 Janey Mac Restaurant
40 Chez Jean-Marc Restaurant
41 Paddy Garibaldi's
44 Man Friday Restaurant

Kinsale

mid-April to mid-June it's closed on Monday; the rest of the year it's closed altogether. Admission costs IR£1/70p.

Organised Tours

June to August, one-hour walking tours leave from outside the tourist office at 11.15 am and 2.30 pm. Costing IR£3/1, the tours are available in French, German and Spanish.

Gourmet Festival

This four-day festival in mid-October is organised by the restaurants that make up the

Good Food Circle of Kinsale. Membership for the four days costs around IR£70 and includes entry to various events and a 10% discount in the restaurants. One-day tickets are also available; details and bookings from Peter Barry (☎ 774026), Scilly, Kinsale.

Places to Stay

Kinsale offers few accommodation bargains, particularly if you're travelling alone. You may prefer to make a day trip from Cork.

Camping *Garrettstown House Holiday Park* (☎ 778156) is 10km south-west of town near the village of Ballinspittle from where it's signposted. A tent site for two costs IR£5 in July and August.

Hostel Your best bet is the clean, modern hostel at the *Castlepark Marina Centre* (☎ 774959) although it's a fair walk from the bus stop; from June to September, ferries run on the hour from the Trident Hotel from 8 am; at other times of year call owner Eddie McCarthy and he may be able to collect you. Dorm beds cost IR£8; doubles cost IR£20. There's a small beach immediately behind the hostel, an on-site café and a pub right next door.

Scruffy *Dempsey's Hostel* (☎ 772124) is nearer the centre but its location, behind the Texaco garage on the Cork road, is nothing to write home about. Dorm beds cost IR£5 plus 50p for showers. Two double rooms are IR£12 each.

B&Bs Many of Kinsale's B&Bs are closed from November to March.

One of the few less expensive places is *O'Donovan's* (☎ 772428), centrally located in Guardwell, at the top of Main St, which has singles/doubles from IR£21/34.

On Main St, *Tierney's Guesthouse* (☎ 772205) has singles/doubles for IR£25/35. *Sea Gull House* (☎ 772240) is close to the Desmond Castle in Cork St with singles/doubles for IR£20/34. Nearby the *Old Presbytery* (☎ 772027) is open all year and has singles/doubles from IR£28/40; breakfasts here come highly recommended.

Many Kinsale guesthouses are more like hotels and have prices to match. Friendly *Kieran's Folk House Inn* (☎ 772382), in Guardwell, has good rooms from IR£50/60. Next to the post office in Pearse St, pretty *Old Bank House* (☎ 774075) has rooms from IR£65/100.

All these places could be a bit noisy at night but anything quieter or with sea views attracts a hefty price tag. At the comfortable *Moorings* (☎ 772376), in Scilly, rooms cost from IR£80, with no discounts for singles.

Hotels First choice for sea views and amenities is the ugly *Trident Hotel* (☎ 772301; fax 774173), overlooking the harbour, with singles/doubles from IR£77.50/125 from June to September. Easier on the eye is *Acton's Hotel* (☎ 772135; fax 772231), with singles/doubles from IR£90/120 in July and August. Centrally positioned, in Pearse St, is the even pricier *Blue Haven* (☎ 772209; fax 774268). A bit cheaper is the *White Lady Hotel* (☎ 772737; fax 774641) in Lower O'Connell St with singles/doubles for IR£40/60.

Places to Eat
Bottom End Good places for breakfasts and inexpensive meals are *Mother Hubbard's* at the corner of Pearse St (although a change of ownership was in the pipeline) and *Patsy's Corner* at Market Square.

Café Palermo in Pearse St does reasonably priced pizzas and pasta. The *Wild Geese Restaurant* on Main St has lunch specials from IR£3.25. *The Shack*, just across the road, serves tasty lasagne and other dishes for around IR£5. At the *Battered Fish*, on the corner of Guardwell, you can bring your own wine to wash down pretty average fish and chips. Tucked away in Lower O'Connell St, *Paddy Garibaldi's* serves pizzas and burgers for around IR£7.

In central Kinsale the rather functional *White House* pub is the oldest in town and has a small restaurant behind the bar. Lunch is good value. Other pubs worth frequenting for a drink and a bite are the *1601* in Pearse St and the noisy *Grey Hound* near Market Square.

Some of the upmarket places serve surprisingly affordable lunches and early evening meals. *Seasons*, near Market Square, is worth checking out while *Max's Wine Bar* (☎ 772443) in Main St, has a IR£12 tourist menu before 8 pm. The *Cottage Loft* (☎ 772803) on Main St does early bird menus for IR£13 until 8 pm. *Janey Mac* (☎ 774860) on Main St serves fish dishes in the IR£8 to IR£12 range. *Hoby's*, also on Main St, is small and unpretentious, with a seafood dinner for IR£12.50.

Jim Edwards' (☎ 772541), on Market

Quay, is probably the best place for seafood but *La Bohème* at the top of Pearse St will do you half a dozen oysters for IR£5.50.

Out at Scilly, the *Spinnaker* does cheaper dinners for IR£6 to IR£10.

Top End Expect to pay around IR£25 a head for any à la carte dinner at the more expensive places. The *Blue Haven* (☎ 772209) on Pearse St, as well as the *Vintage Restaurant* (☎ 772502) on Main St, the *Captain's Table* at Acton's Hotel and the *Savannah* at the Trident all have good reputations. Regarded as one of the best is *Chez Jean-Marc* at the bottom of Lower O'Connell St, where you can sample Parisian cuisine with an Irish touch for around IR£25.

Man Friday (☎ 772260), off the beaten track at Scilly, stands out if only because it isn't rubbing shoulders with other prestigious restaurants.

Entertainment
Kinsale has a lively pub scene and music is never difficult to find in summer. The *1601* on Pearse St is always crowded and while you wait to be served you can read up on the finer details of the battle.

Also popular are *Lord Kinsale* on Main St and *The Shanakee* around the corner. Just across the road, *Kieran's Folk House Inn* also has a popular bar. Out at Scilly, the cosy *Spaniard* has traditional music on Wednesdays nights.

The nightclub at the *White Lady Hotel*, on Lower O'Connell St, is popular with the younger crowd, while the *Bacchus Brasserie*, attached to Kieran's Folk House Inn, attracts an older clientele.

Getting There & Away
Bus Éireann buses connect Kinsale with Cork three or four times a day (45 minutes, IR£5.30 return). The bus stops at the Esso garage on The Pier Road near the tourist office.

Getting Around
Bikes can be hired from *Deco's Cycles* (☎ 774884) in Main St. Taxis can be hired locally (☎ 774900 or 772642). It's usually IR£3 to the Castlepark Marina Centre.

KINSALE TO CLONAKILTY
Following the quays west out of Kinsale the main R600 road passes through Ballinspittle and Timoleague before joining the main road from Bandon to reach Clonakilty. Once you're in Timoleague you can detour south to Courtmacsherry and along a small coastal road that goes through Butlerstown to Clonakilty.

Old Head of Kinsale
With time, it's worth diverting along the R604 coast road to Ballinspittle via the Old Head of Kinsale.

Although the headland is given over to a golf course, paths on either side of the entrance lead down to viewpoints overlooking spectacular rocky coastline, the nesting place of thousands of fulmars and penguin-like guillemots. On the way to the headland the *Speckled Door* does pub food.

Road Bowling
You're only likely to encounter this rare sport on a quiet road on a Sunday afternoon in West Cork or County Armagh in Northern Ireland; it's not played anywhere else in the country. A giveaway sign of a game in progress are small groups of men waiting by the side of the road for your vehicle to pass so that the game can resume. Some distance ahead of the main group will be a smaller group, whose task is to chart the distance that a steel ball has been thrown by the two competing sides. The object of the game is to cover a set distance of winding road in as few hurls of the ball as possible. The rules allow for the ball to be lofted over a stretch of field hoping to shortcross a bend. Bets are laid on teams and even individual bowls of the 18cm, 794g ball. ■

Ballinspittle

If you've visited Knock in Mayo you'll appreciate knowing that this village narrowly avoided a similar fate. In the summer of 1985 a grotto outside town with a statue of the Virgin Mary began to attract worshippers after it was reported that the statue had moved. Tens of thousands of people claimed to have seen the same phenomenon, thereby putting Ballinspittle (Béal Átha an Spidéil) on the map. Similar reports came in from other parts of the country but then the whole thing came to a sudden end. The grotto is by the side of the main road before entering Ballinspittle from Kinsale.

TIMOLEAGUE

Once a thriving port, Timoleague is now a sleepy village approached via a causeway across an inlet in Courtmacsherry Bay. The waters and mudflats attract migratory birds from Iceland, Greenland, and the Russian and Canadian Arctic. Most of the time you should be able to see cormorants and herons fishing here but September to May you may also spot golden plovers and rare white egrets.

The telephone code is ☎ 023.

Timoleague Friary

This Franciscan friary was probably founded in the 13th century but the buildings date from various periods with some alterations dating from the early 17th century. In 1642 the English vandalised the friary and smashed the stained glass, but the remains are pretty impressive and clearly visible as you approach Timoleague from Kinsale. Today it serves as the village cemetery.

Timoleague Castle Gardens

Little remains of the 13th century castle that once stood here. However, the attractive gardens are worth visiting. The palm trees, in particular, are a reminder of the mild climate, and there's a superb *Callistemon linearis* (bottlebrush) tree. Admission is IR£2.50/1 and the gardens are usually open from 11 am to 5.30 pm.

Places to Stay

Camping *Sexton's Caravan & Camping Park* (☎ 46347) is signposted off the main road to Clonakilty. A hiker or cyclist pays IR£4.50 for a pitch.

B&Bs Outside Timoleague on the right-hand side of the road to Clonakilty, beautiful *Lettercollum House* was once a convent but is now a restaurant with rooms and spectacular views. Singles/doubles cost from IR£18/24. The decor is wonderfully arty and there are interesting residential courses on everything from Pacific Rim cookery to birdwatching; call ☎ 46251 for details.

In nearby Courtmacsherry, *Travara Lodge* (☎ 46493) is a Georgian house with singles/doubles from IR£25/40. It's open mid-March to October.

Hotel The isolated *Courtmacsherry Hotel* (☎ 46198) is comfortable and friendly, with singles/doubles from IR£45/64.

Places to Eat

In Timoleague village, *Dillon's Bar & Café* serves things like pizza and seafood chowder in pleasant surroundings, while *Graínne's* does soup and sandwiches for lunch and steak-style meals in the evening.

Heading back towards Kinsale, the unmissable *Pink Elephant* (☎ 49608) bar and restaurant offers good bar food all day. On the other side of Timoleague, the restaurant at *Lettercollum House* is in what was once a convent chapel and serves easily the best food in the area. Set lunches cost IR£12 and set dinners IR£18.50.

Getting There & Away

The only bus service to Timoleague from Cork leaves at 5.45 pm, Monday to Friday. Going back to Cork, the bus leaves from outside Pat Joe's pub at 8 am.

CLONAKILTY

This small, pretty town received its first charter in 1292 but was refounded in the early 17th century by the first earl of Cork. He settled it with 100 English families and

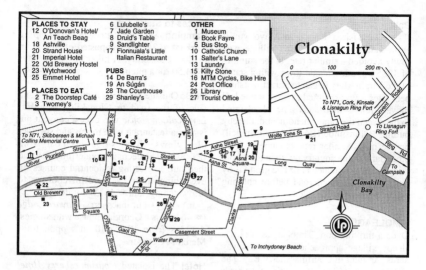

Clonakilty

PLACES TO STAY
12 O'Donovan's Hotel/
   An Teach Beag
18 Ashville
20 Strand House
21 Imperial Hotel
22 Old Brewery Hostel
23 Wytchwood
25 Emmet Hotel

PLACES TO EAT
2 The Doorstep Café
3 Twomey's

6 Lulubelle's
7 Jade Garden
8 Druid's Table
9 Sandlighter
17 Fionnuala's Little
   Italian Restaurant

PUBS
14 De Barra's
19 An Súgán
28 The Courthouse
29 Shanley's

OTHER
1 Museum
4 Book Fayre
5 Bus Stop
10 Catholic Church
11 Salter's Lane
13 Laundry
15 Kilty Stone
16 MTM Cycles, Bike Hire
24 Post Office
26 Library
27 Tourist Office

planned a Protestant town from which Catholics would be excluded. His plan failed; Clonakilty is now very Irish and very Catholic – witness the Presbyterian chapel that has been turned into a post office.

From the mid-18th until the mid-19th century, over 10,000 people worked in the town's linen industry. The bakery by the public water pump was once a linen hall, and the fire station stands on the site of the old linen market. What was once a corn mill driven by the nearby river has been pleasingly converted into a library.

Michael Collins went to school in Clonakilty, a fact of which the community is very proud.

Orientation & Information

All roads converge on Asna Square which is dominated by a statue commemorating local men who died in the 1798 Rising. Also in the square is the Kilty Stone which gave Clonakilty its name. A massive boulder, it probably came from the Norman castle.

The tourist office (☎ 023-33226) in Rossa St is only open during July and August. Your best bet is to buy a copy of the *Historical Walk of Clonakilty and its Sea-Front* booklet

(IR£2) from one of the bookshops. It has a clear illustrated map of the town. Book Fayre in Pearse St stocks second-hand books. Salter's Lane, off Bridge St, shelters a cluster of craft shops.

Five km south of town is Inchydoney, with one of Cork's best beaches, but watch for the dangerous riptide; when lifeguards are on duty a red warning flag indicates danger. Deep-sea fishing and shore angling are possible at Ring; contact P Houlihan at Blackbird's pub in Connolly St for boat hire.

The telephone code is ☎ 023.

West Cork Regional Museum

This small and rather sad museum is, nonetheless, the best Cork has to offer when it comes to material relating to local industrial and social history. It's open May to October, Monday to Saturday, 10.30 am to 5.30 pm; 2.30 to 5.30 pm on Sunday. Admission is IR£1/50p.

Places to Stay

Camping The *Desert House Caravan & Camping Park* (☎ 33331) is 500m from town on the road to Ring and overlooking the river. You can camp from May through September; a tent site for two costs IR£5.

Hostel

The new *Old Brewery Hostel* (☎ 33525) is in a quiet street just off Emmet Square. Beds in six-bed dorms cost IR£7, and there are two doubles for IR£18. There's a small kitchen and dining room, and the hostel offers disabled access.

B&Bs

Opposite the hostel off quiet Emmet Square is the pleasingly decorated *Wytchwood* (☎ 33525), charging from IR£18 a bed in spacious rooms. In Clarke St, *Ashville* (☎ 33125) has four doubles for IR£26. Inquire at the An Súgán pub about rooms in *Strand House* next door, once home to the poetess Mary Jane Irwin who married O'Donovan Rossa, the founder of the Fenian Movement . On the Ring Rd overlooking the river, *Desert House* (☎ 33331) is attached to the campsite and has singles/doubles from IR£19/28.

Hotels

The *Imperial* (☎ 34185), at the Cork end of Wolfe Tone St, has beds in well-equipped rooms from IR£16. A little pricier, but more central and with more facilities, is *O'Donovan's* (☎ 33250) in Pearse St where B&B costs IR£23. The *Inchydoney* (☎ 33143) at the beach charges a flat IR£20 per person, dropping to IR£15 outside July and August.

Places to Eat

Black pudding, made from the blood of pigs and a common ingredient in the full Irish breakfast, is found throughout Ireland but Clonakilty black pudding is particularly renowned. Twomey's Butchers at 16 Pearse St, is reputed to make the best black pudding in Cork.

Even if you're not into black pudding you can eat well in Clonakilty. Starting at the Rosscarbery end of the main street, *The Doorstep* Café, at the junction of Oliver Plunkett and Patrick Sts, serves a West Cork ploughman's lunch featuring three local cheeses for IR£4.25. It closes at 6 pm.

Further along in Pearse St, *Lulubelle's* (☎ 33801) offers an interesting mix of Eastern and European dishes from 7 pm, except on Sunday and Monday. Fairly mild curries cost from IR£6. Across the road, *O'Donovan's Hotel* has a café-style restaurant serving mostly traditional Irish meals during the day.

Fionnuala's Little Italian Restaurant (☎ 34355), on Ashe St, serves pizza and pasta from around IR£5. Out of season it closes on Monday and Tuesday. Across the road the *Druid's Table* opens for a druid's breakfast including black pudding for IR£3.50. In the evening you can bring your own bottle.

An Súgán, on Wolfe Tone St, does popular pub lunches; a vegetable stir fry costs IR£5.50. Set dinners at the upstairs restaurant are pricey unless you catch the early bird tourist menu before 8 pm. Across the road, the *Sandlighter* has lunch specials for IR£4.50. The *Jade Garden* on McCurtain Hill does predictable Chinese meals for middle-of-the-road prices.

Entertainment

Clonakilty has a lively pub scene, especially during its 10-day festival in July. *An Súgán* on Wolfe Tone St and *De Barra's* on Pearse St are crowded at weekends. Other places to try are *The Courthouse* or *Shanley's* in Connolly St. *O'Donovan's Hotel* has music in its lounge bar on Tuesday and Saturday nights, while there's traditional music every Friday and Saturday at *An Teach Beag* in Recorder's Alley through the hotel car park.

Getting There & Away

At least three Cork buses a day stop in Clonakilty, outside the Bank of Ireland on Pearse St. The journey takes 1¼ hours and costs IR£5.90. These buses continue on to Skibbereen and Schull. From late May to mid-September, you can get from Clonakilty to Killarney via Schull once a day including Sunday.

AROUND CLONAKILTY
Lisnagun Ring Fort

Of over 30,000 ring forts scattered across

Ireland, this is the only one that has been reconstructed to give some impression of life in a 10th century defended farmstead. It is complete with a *souterrain* (underground chamber) and a central hut thatched by someone who would have been paid only in food for his months' labours.

In theory the fort is open Monday to Friday 9 am to 5 pm, from 10 am at weekends. In practice if there's no one there to collect the IR£2/1 admission fee you'll only get to see the circular ditch and the encircling wooden palisade. If you're driving, there's a sign to the fort on the N71 outside town on the Cork road opposite Mount Carmel Hospital. Take that turning and keep going until you come to another on the right. The fort is on the left, just past Clonakilty Agricultural College.

If you're walking from Clonakilty and want to avoid traffic, take the turning at the Fax Bridge roundabout at the end of Strand Rd signposted to the Bay View B&B. Follow this road uphill for about 1.5km until you reach a T-junction. Turn right and almost immediately you'll see metal farm gates on your right. Go through the gates and keep

walking straight ahead until you come to a crossroads with a cowshed. Take the track to the left and walk downhill until you reach a minor road. Turn right and the fort is on the left, a stone's throw from the Agricultural College.

Birthplace of Michael Collins

Dúchas manages a small memorial centre to Michael Collins, who was born near Clonakilty in 1890. The old house where he was born and lived for about 10 years is still standing and has been repaired but little remains of the newer house his family later built beside it and where Collins lived until he emigrated to London in 1906. This was burnt down by the Black & Tans in 1921. Despite the meagre remains, the place generates an aura of respect for a man who would have been heartbroken at the consequences of the treaty he signed in 1921.

The birthplace site is signposted on the N71, 5km west of Clonakilty.

ROSSCARBERY TO SKIBBEREEN

You can get from Rosscarbery to Skibbereen along the main N71 via Leap, but far more

---

Michael Collins ... The Big Fella

Michael Collins was born and reared in West Cork. As a young man he left Ireland to work as a civil servant in London. At the age of 26, he returned to take part in the 1916 Easter Rising, and became committed to continued armed struggle against the British. During the War of Independence (1919-21), he earned a reputation as a ruthless organiser of guerilla warfare.

Collins inspired tremendous respect among the Irish and fear among the British, who offered a high reward for his capture. He became a living legend, not least for the ease with which he evaded arrest – seldom bothering to disguise himself and riding freely around Dublin on his bicycle.

Collins infiltrated the British civil and military presence in Ireland, frustrating their efforts to maintain control. His 'flying columns' and assassination squads were clinical and helped drive the British to the negotiating table in 1921.

Eamon De Valera sent Collins to Downing Street to negotiate a truce. Collins resisted the order, to no avail. In going to London, he was forced to give up his most important weapon – his anonymity. Reluctantly, Collins signed a treaty which partitioned Ireland, leaving the six counties of the north under British rule. He considered the partition a stepping-stone to an independent Ireland and believed it was the best deal that could be secured at that time, while prophetically declaring, 'I have signed my own death warrant'.

The treaty split the Irish people and a brutal civil war followed its acceptance, with de Valera heading the anti-Treaty faction. Collins was killed in an ambush near Macroom in Cork, five days short of his 31st birthday.

Much of Neil Jordan's film *Michael Collins* was filmed in West Cork. Despite some inevitable Hollywoodising of the story, it remains a worthwhile and accessible introduction to the 'Big Fella', played by Liam Neeson. ■

enjoyable is the longer route that winds south-west from the end of the causeway at Rosscarbery, taking in the picturesque villages of Glandore and Union Hall and some stunning coastal scenery.

Rosscarbery

Set back from the main N71, Rosscarbery is little more than a village at the head of a landlocked inlet of Rosscarbery Bay with a quiet central square. To reach it when coming from Clonakilty, turn right at the end of the causeway just before the unmissable Celtic Ross Hotel. O'Donovan Rossa was born here in 1831.

St Fachtna's cathedral dates back to the 12th century and has an elaborately carved western doorway, as well as an impressive statue of Lord Carbery (1763-1842) in slashed doublet and hose. The shallow estuary beside the causeway is wonderful for watching wading birds, especially golden plovers in winter.

Rosscarbery Riding Centre (☎ 48232) organises horse trekking. It's signposted opposite the turn-off for Owinhincha Beach.

The telephone code is 023.

Places to Stay & Eat The *Carbery Arms* (☎ 48101), in the square, offers B&B and a shower for IR£18/30 a single/double. *O'Callaghan Walshe's Seafood Restaurant* (☎ 48125) is open Wednesday to Sunday 6.30 to 9.15 pm and serves dishes like seafood tagliatelle for IR£8.95. During the day, the *Carbery Arms* may have bar lunches, or there's the *Country Kitchen* serving teas and coffees across the other side of the square.

Getting There & Away Buses from Clonakilty to Goleen stop in Rosscarbery at least twice a day (15 minutes).

Castle Salem

The most surprising aspect of this 15th century castle, originally called Benduff Castle, is the entrance. In the 17th century, a house was built onto one of the 3m-thick castle walls, and at the top of its carpeted

staircase an ordinary-looking door opens onto the first floor of the castle. Otherwise the castle is slowly crumbling away.

Cromwell gave it to an English soldier, Major Apollo Morris, who later became a Quaker. He renamed it Shalom, Hebrew for peace, which was corrupted into Salem. An old Quaker churchyard is behind the wall on the right immediately after entering the grounds. William Penn (founder of Pennsylvania) is said to have visited Morris in the house.

Castle Salem is signposted off the N71 Skibbereen road west of Rosscarbery. Entry is IR£2/1. You can stay in the 17th century house attached to the Castle. B&B (☎ 48381) is IR£15; ask for the bed that Penn slept in.

Drombeg Stone Circle

Of the many stone circles in West Cork, this particular group of 17 stones dating from around 100 BC is particularly impressive, not least because of its stunning setting. On the south-west side a horizontal stone faces two taller stones on the north-east side. The axis of these two stones and the recumbent one is aligned to the midwinter sunset.

Nearby is a cooking place with a stone trough where hot stones can bring 318.5 litres of water to the boil in 18 minutes and keep it hot for roughly three hours afterwards.

Travelling from Clonakilty the N71 crosses a causeway at Rosscarbery. Just past the end of the causeway, beside the *Orchard* B&B, a road is signposted off to the left for Glandore, Coppinger's Court and assorted B&Bs. Some way along this road the stones are signposted to the left and a rough road continues to a small car park and a path to the circle.

Glandore

This exquisite fishing village bursts into life in summer when well-off boating folk arrive, something that would surely have dismayed William Thompson (1785-1833) who established a commune here as a model for his socialist philosophy. Marx refers to him in *Das Kapital*.

Meadow Camping Park (☎ 028-33280) is 2km outside the village on the Rosscarbery road. Mid-March to September a small tent site costs IR£7. The *Marine Hotel* (☎ 028-33366) charges IR£59/80 so you'll probably prefer just to use its bar. Two km from Glandore, there's B&B at *Kilfinnan Farm* (☎ 028-33233) from IR£20/30 a single/double.

Union Hall

Disappointingly, there's no union hall in this small village, accessible via a narrow road bridge over the estuary. Instead it was named after the 1800 Act of Union, which abolished the separate Irish parliament. Its equally unfortunate Irish name, Brean Traigh, means 'foul beach'. Jonathan Swift came here in 1723 to grieve over the death of his friend Vanessa.

If prizes were being handed out for hostels *Maria's Schoolhouse* (☎ 028-33002) would have to be the front-runner. A stunning conversion of a 19th century National School building on the outskirts of Union Hall, it has a bright, cheerful 10-bed dorm with beds for the usual IR£7, together with private rooms with ensuite facilities from IR£9. The cooking facilities are a bit cramped but the sitting and dining area is a delight, and Maria cooks dinners on request for IR£12 a head (vegetarians catered for). Her breakfasts, if you don't want to rustle up your own, cost IR£3.50 but include local fish and cheese.

Outside Union Hall on the way to Castletownshend a sign points 2km off the road to the small **Ceim Hill Museum** (☎ 028-36280) run by Teresa O'Mahony, who practises folk medicine in her ancient farmhouse. It's recommended for its wonderful mixture of eccentricity and genuine artefacts, not to mention the spectacular views from the winding track. Admission is IR£2/1 and it's open 10 am to 7 pm.

SKIBBEREEN

Traffic-blighted Skibbereen owes its existence to Algerians who raided nearby Baltimore in 1631. The frightened English settlers moved west, establishing two settlements which grew into Skibbereen. For a long time the town was associated with its Protestant founders, but during the Famine years it became known for the sufferings of the local Catholic peasantry. The repercussions were long-lasting: nearly half the local population emigrated in the first half of the 20th century. Some of the shops sell *The Skibbereen Trail* (IR£1) which guides you around local sites with links to the Famine. Today the town prospers from its Friday market (12.30 to 2.30 pm) and a steady influx of tourists on the West Cork trail. For what it's worth, Skib has also produced the largest number of winners of the Lotto – seven at the last count.

Orientation & Information

The main landmark is a statue dedicated to the heroes of the many Irish rebellions against the British which stands at the junction of three roads. Market St heads south past the post office to Lough Ine and Baltimore. The main shopping street, Main St, leads to a junction with Ilen St which heads west over the river to Ballydehob and Bantry. North St heads towards the main Cork road and houses the tourist office (☎ 028-21766), which opens all year.

The telephone code is ☎ 028.

Liss Ard Experience

One km west of Skibbereen on the Castle townshend Rd, the Liss Ard Experience is a 16-hectare expanse of woodland, wild flower meadows and small lakes on the banks of Lough Abisdeasly. It's the work of German Veith Turske who searched Europe for somewhere suitable to create a magical, natural garden. One and two-hour walks are clearly marked out. Don't miss the Irish Sky Garden where you walk across a crater and then into a mound and up steps like a Mayan pyramid to emerge in an amphitheatre with nothing to focus on except the sky.

The gardens open daily from May to September for IR£5/2.

Other Attractions

Along North St, next to the church, the **West Cork Arts Centre** is open 10 am to 6 pm Monday to Saturday. It hosts regular art exhibitions and in summer there's often something theatrical or musical too. The notice board gives useful information about what's happening locally.

Six km out of town on the Baltimore road, you can bathe at tiny **Tragumna**, little more than a pub, a beach and a knitwear shop.

Places to Stay

Camping One km west of town on the Castletownshend road it costs IR£7 to pitch a small tent at *The Hideaway Camp Site* (☎ 33280) from May to mid-September. You can also camp at Russagh Hostel for IR£3.50 a head.

Hostel One and a half km west of town on the Castletownshend road is the *Russagh Mill Hostel & Adventure Centre* (☎ 22451), an old corn mill with much of its machinery still in place. Beds in relatively spacious rooms cost IR£7 and there are nine private rooms for IR£20. Owner Mick Murphy is an experienced mountaineer and canoeist. For IR£8 you can join in a day's canoeing, rock climbing or whatever may be going on. A path leads back to town from behind the hostel, avoiding the main road.

B&Bs The Baltimore road is lined with B&Bs. In town, *The Windmill Tavern* (☎ 21606) in North St has beds from IR£16/20 without/with shower. *Bridge House* (☎ 21273) in Bridge St has pleasing Victorian-style decor; singles/doubles cost IR£20/35.

Six km east of Skibbereen, *Mont Bretia* (☎ 33663) is worth seeking out. Its IR£15 B&B rate includes free use of bicycles, maps and information on cycle/walking routes, and free tea and coffee. Wholefood evening meals start at IR£6.50 (IR£8 with dessert). Although it's nearer Adrigole, the owners will collect guests from Skibbereen or Leap.

Coming from Skibbereen on the N71, take a left turn signposted for Drinagh off the main road. After the Adrigole creamery, take the second left at the fork just past it (signposted for another B&B called Sprucedale). Mont Bretia is on the left.

Hotels The pleasantly balconied *West Cork Hotel* (☎ 21277), opposite the river on Ilen St, is Skibbereen's best at IR£60 a night for two. On Bridge St (the continuation of Main St in the direction of Schull) the *Eldon Hotel* (☎ 21300) has a quiet charm and beds cost from IR£27.

Places to Eat

The *Eldon Hotel* has a good bar menu; meals from IR£4 are available until 9 pm. *Sables Restaurant* across the road does lunch for around IR£6 and dinner for around IR£12, except on Monday.

Also on Bridge St, *Annie May's* pub serves above average bar food for around IR£5. For coffee and snacks, try *O'Donovan's* next door, or *The Stove* which also serves breakfast all day. *Fields Coffee Shop*, near the monument, is popular with local shoppers.

Kalbo's Bistro in North St serves steaks and other fairly standard dishes. Its menu includes a couple of vegetarian dishes for IR£6.95. Further down towards the Arts Centre, the *Ivanhoe Restaurant* does lunches for around IR£3.95 even though its set dinner menu is IR£12.95.

For pub food, *Bernard's Bar*, set back from the road in Main St, is particularly popular. In North St, *The Windmill Tavern* has an extensive lunch menu for around half the price of its dinner menu.

Island Cottage (☎ 38102) is on Hare Island in Roaring Water Bay. Make a reservation, and arrange transport with John O'Neil (☎ 38144) which adds IR£4 per person (IR£2 if he's on a mail trip) to the cost of the IR£16 set dinner. It's good value and good fun.

Entertainment

The *Wine Vaults* in Bridge St is a particularly popular pub with live music on Saturday nights. *Seán Óg's* in Market St, near the square, and *Kearney's Well* in North St also have music most weekends. *Annie May's* hosts some interesting musical evenings. In July and August the *West Cork Hotel* offers a Tuesday night cabaret, costing around IR£4 per person.

Also worth a visit is *The Stag's Head* at Caheragh on the road to Drimoleague. Before dance halls were heard of, music and dance sessions were held on specially surfaced areas outside pubs. The Stag's Head has recreated such a venue and holds Sunday afternoon dancing sessions.

Getting There & Away
Daily buses run to Cork, Baltimore, Schull, Drimoleague and Killarney from outside the Eldon Hotel in Main St. Skibbereen to Schull takes just 30 minutes and costs IR£3 return.

Getting Around
Bicycles can be hired from Roycroft's Cycles (☎ 21235) in Ilen St (the building acted as a soup kitchen during the Famine).

LOUGH INE
Lough Ine, or Hyne, is a saltwater lake connected to the sea by a narrow channel which is now a nature reserve. Lough Ine is 6km due south of Skibbereen and well signposted from the town statue.

Knockomagh Wood, an attractive mixture of deciduous and evergreen trees, is on the right of the road approaching the lough from Skibbereen. You can get to Baltimore by diverting along the seldom-used minor roads around the lough.

Creagh Gardens
Continuing south towards Baltimore you'll come to the eight-hectare organically managed Creagh Gardens on the right. These gardens, set around Creagh House, have a lovely riverside setting and are spectacular in April and May when the rhododendrons are in bloom, and in August and September when the fuchsias and blue hydrangeas are flowering.

The gardens are open daily 10 am to 6 pm and admission costs IR£3/1.50.

BALTIMORE
Just 13km down the River Ilen from Skibbereen, sleepy Baltimore has a population of around 200 which swells enormously during the summer months, as sailing folk, divers and visitors to Sherkin and Clear islands flock in. The harbour is dominated by the remains of Dún na Sead, the Fort of the Jewels, one of nine castles built in the area by the O'Driscoll clan.

Information
The small tourist office (☎ 028-21766) at the harbour opens in high season but lots of useful information is pinned up on a board outside for when it's closed. It can also arrange accommodation on both Clear and Sherkin islands.

The telephone code is ☎ 028.

Activities
The Algiers Inn (☎ 20352) organises sea angling trips, and shorter evening mackerel and pollack fishing trips. The Baltimore Diving Centre (☎ 20300) arranges diving expeditions around Baltimore and off Clear and Sherkin islands for everyone from beginners to experts.

Special Events
Over the third weekend of May, Baltimore stages a seafood festival, with jazz bands performing and mussels and prawns on offer in the pubs. Contact the tourist office for details.

Places to Stay
In a pleasant garden on the edge of Baltimore, *Rolf's Hostel* (☎ 20289) has dorm beds, some of them in a loft, for IR£7 and doubles for IR£23. Camping costs IR£3 a head. The *Algiers Inn* (☎ 20145) opens all year and has beds for IR£15. Next door, *The Old Post Office* (☎ 29155) is slightly more expensive at IR£20 a head. *Corner House* (☎ 20143), on the other side of the pub, has doubles for IR£32.

Places to Eat
One of the best places to eat without busting

the budget is *Café Art*, attached to Rolf's Hostel; salads and more substantial meals are served in a room that doubles as an art gallery; breakfast includes meals like scrambled eggs with salmon for IR£3.50. Otherwise, for light meals try the inexpensive *Lifeboat Restaurant* attached to the post office and bureau de change. The *Algiers Inn* and *McCarthy's Bar* both do reasonably priced pub meals.

Moving up in price, the *Customs House* offers a set seafood dinner for IR£16 from 7 to 10 pm on Thursday to Sunday. Overlooking the harbour, *Chez Youen* does good French-style seafood, with a set dinner for IR£21.50.

Entertainment
There are regular traditional music nights at *McCarthy's Bar* in the Square, although an admission charge of IR£5 can seem a tad steep.

Getting There & Away
Monday to Friday, at least three buses connect Skibbereen and Baltimore. There's a limited Saturday service late May to mid-September. Since Baltimore is only 13km from Skibbereen, you could also cycle or hitch there.

In May and September a boat (☎ 39153) leaves Baltimore for Schull via Heir Island at 2.30 pm, and Schull for Baltimore at 10 am. In June, July and August boats leave Baltimore at 10 am and 1.45 and 4.15 pm, and Schull at 11.30 am and 3 and 5.30 pm. A single crossing costs IR£6.

CLEAR ISLAND
The boat from Baltimore takes 45 minutes to cover the 11km journey to Clear Island and it's a stunning trip on a clear day, retracing the route Algerians took through the harbour when they launched their attack in 1631.

Clear Island is the most southerly point of Ireland apart from the Fastnet Rock, 6km to the south-west. Clear Island is also a Gaeltacht area with about 150 Irish-speaking inhabitants, one shop and three pubs. It's a place for walking and birdwatching; the island is probably the best place in Europe for watching manx shearwaters and other seabirds.

Orientation & Information
The island is 5km long and just over 1.5km wide at its broadest but narrows in the middle where the north and south harbours are divided by an isthmus. There's a tourist information post beyond the pier, open 4 to 6 pm daily in July and August. If it's closed the nearby coffee shop stocks a useful IR£2 *Walkers' Guide*.

A small **heritage centre** has exhibits on the island's history and culture. In summer it's open 3.30 to 5.30 pm. There are fine views looking north across the water to the Mizen Head Peninsula. From the centre it's a short walk downhill to the shop and pubs.

The telephone code is ☎ 028.

Birdwatching
The Bird Observatory is a white-fronted two-storey building by the harbour. Turn right at the end of the pier and it's 100m along. It's worth calling in to ask about any planned birdwatching trips. Clear Island is famous for large movements of seabirds, especially in July and August when manx shearwaters, gannets, fulmars and kittiwakes regularly fly past the south of the island. The guillemot is the only notable seabird that breeds on the island; the others live on the westerly Kerry rocks and, each morning, fly past heading for the Celtic and Irish seas. In the evening they return and the sight is equally amazing; in summer up to 35,000 shearwaters can fly past in an hour, just skimming the surface of the water.

The best place to view the birds is at Blananarragaun, the south-west tip of the island. To reach it from the pier, head up to the shop and turn right, following the sign for the campsite. When the road comes to an end, head due south to the end of the spur of land.

Places to Stay
Signposted from the shop, the campsite

(☎ 39119) costs IR£2.70 per person and opens June through September.

An Óige's pretty basic *Cape Clear Island Hostel* (☎ 39144) costs IR£5.50, is open from Easter until the end of October and is a short walk from the pier. *The Glen* hostel (☎ 39121) is open all year and also does B&B. The *Bird Observatory* (no telephone) has limited hostel accommodation; just turn up and see if a bed is available, least likely at the beginning of October.

B&B is available year round at *Cluain Mara* (☎ 39153) for IR£15; evening meals cost IR£10. The house is signposted behind the last of the three pubs.

Self-catering cottages (☎ 39153) are also available, starting at IR£180 for a week from October to March and rising to IR£360 in July and August.

Places to Eat

Cistin, near the pier, is the only restaurant, so consider a picnic. The one shop near the pier has a limited stock. The café serves light meals. There are three pubs within staggering distance of each other and at night drinking-up time is generous.

Getting There & Away

In June, boats (☎ 28138) leave from Schull pier at 2.30 pm and return at 5.30 pm. In July and August they leave at 10 am, 2.30 and 4.30 pm and return at 11 am, 3.30 and 5.30 pm. The return fare is IR£8/4.

From Baltimore boats leave at 2.15 and 7 pm, Monday to Saturday from June to September, and on Sunday at noon, 2.15, 5 and 7 pm. Coming back they leave Clear Island at 9 am and 6 pm Monday to Saturday and 11 am, 1, 4 and 6 pm on Sunday. The return fare is IR£7/3.50, with no extra charge for bikes.

SHERKIN ISLAND

People visit this minuscule island – 5km long and about the same wide – for the beaches and the two pubs. The three sandy areas – Trabawn, Cow and Silver strands – are all on the far side of the island and reached by road from the pier. All are safe for swimming and

suitable for children. During the annual regatta in late August the pubs stay open even longer than usual. The best place for general information is the post office (☎ 028-20181), which is beside the road running across the island from the pier to the beaches.

The telephone code is ☎ 028.

Places to Stay & Eat

Camping is free; ask permission from the farmer first.

B&Bs on the island include *Garrison House* (☎ 20185), *Island House* (☎ 20314), *Cuina* (☎ 20384), the *Jolly Roger Tavern* (☎ 20379) and *Buggy's* (☎ 20384). They all charge about IR£15 per person.

The Garrison House and the Jolly Roger both serve bar food. The Jolly Roger is the older of the two and near the remains of the old O'Driscoll Castle; to get to either pub, turn right just before the post office.

Getting There & Away

Regular boats leave Baltimore (☎ 20125) for the 10-minute crossing. The service runs seven times a day, starting at 10.30 am and ending at 8.45 pm. The return fare is IR£4. From June through August, boats to Sherkin also depart from Schull at 1.45 pm (IR£6 single).

Mizen Head Peninsula

From Skibbereen the road winds west to Ballydehob. Expatriates from Britain and northern Europe are scattered across West Cork, and while Kinsale attracts the well-heeled, the less economically advantaged, or blow-ins as they are semi-affectionately called, have discovered the land around Ballydehob. From here the road goes west to Schull, with Mt Gabriel (407m) easily identifiable by the two tracking spheres (part of an air-and-sea monitoring system) perched on the summit. The mountain's summit can be reached by road.

From the top of Mt Gabriel, and most high ground on the peninsula, there are views of the Fastnet Lighthouse on a rock 11km off the coast. The first lighthouse was built in 1854 but was replaced in 1906 by a sturdier one which is now fully automated.

The next stop west is Goleen, a small village on the way to Crookhaven, Barleycove and Three Castle Head. Returning from Mizen Head you can take the spectacular coastal road that keeps Dunmanus Bay on the left for most of the way to Durrus. At Durrus, one road heads for Bantry while the other turns west to the Sheep's Head Peninsula.

BALLYDEHOB

This tiny village takes its name from the Irish *Béal an dhá Chab*, meaning 'the ford at the mouth of two rivers'. Approaching from the east, watch for the old 12-arched tramway viaduct.

In late May, Ballydehob stages a procession where villagers decorate their houses, and place religious statuary in their windows and flowers on the pavement. Schull and Ballydehob host the procession in alternate years. It'll be Ballydehob's turn again in 1999.

The telephone code is ☎ 028.

Places to Stay

A small but cosy campsite (☎ 37232) is 200m from the village on the Durrus road. Charges are IR£2.50 per person. B&B is available at the *Ballydehob Inn* (☎ 37139) from IR£15/26. On the road to Schull, *Lynwood* (☎ 37124) has three beds for IR£20/30.

Places to Eat

Ballydehob Inn, on the corner of the road to Durrus, serves bar food and has a restaurant with things like grills from IR£7.50. *Duggan's* in the village centre is the cheapest place for light meals and takeaways. *Hudson's Wholefoods* nearby serves coffee and light lunches but has only two tables. *Annie's*, a few doors down, is renowned for its seafood and steak dinners for IR£22.

Getting There & Away

The twice-daily Clonakilty to Schull bus stops in Ballydehob which is only 8km from Schull.

SCHULL

A small, laidback village at the foot of Mt Gabriel, Schull gets as touristy as anywhere on the Ring of Kerry from June through September but lapses back into peace and quiet for the rest of the year. For good views of Schull harbour and the Fastnet Rock, take the road from Ballydehob to Durrus and Goleen, and turn off for Schull after 5km.

Information

Mizen Computer Services (MCS) operates a seasonal tourist office. Alternatively, pick up the free booklet *Welcome to Schull*, with details of local walks, from Schull Backpackers' Lodge. O'Keeffe's, at 48 Main St, has a bureau de change.

Fuschia Books in the main street sells second-hand books. The Schull Watersports Centre (☎ 028-28554) by the pier offers sailing, windsurfing, diving and other activities.

The telephone code is ☎ 028.

The Planetarium

The Republic's only planetarium (☎ 28552) has an 8m dome and a video and slide show. In July and August it's open Sunday to Thursday 2 to 5 pm and 7 to 9 pm (Sunday afternoon only), with a 45-minute Star Show at 8 pm on Tuesday and Thursday, and at 4 pm Sunday; in June it's open Sunday, Wednesday and Friday 3 to 5 pm with the Star Show at 4 pm;. March to May it's only open Sunday afternoon. Admission is IR£1/50p, IR£3/2 for the Star Show.

The Planetarium is at the Goleen end of the village on the Colla road, just past the hostel. You can also reach it by walking along the Foreshore Path from the pier.

Places to Stay

Hostel & Camping The IHH's excellent *Schull Backpackers' Lodge* (☎ 28681) is on Colla Rd, in a quiet situation a little before

CORK

the Planetarium. Beds in spotless, spacious dorms are IR£7, doubles are IR£20 and camping is sometimes possible.

B&Bs At the Goleen end of the village the *Old Bank House* (☎ 28306) has four doubles for IR£32. More expensive is *Corthna Lodge Country House* (☎ 28517), a little way out of the village at the Goleen end; its rooms are IR£30/40 from June through August. *Adele's* (☎ 28459) also has a few rooms; if you're having trouble finding a single room it's worth asking here.

Hotels The *East End Hotel* (☎ 28101) at the Ballydehob end of Main St has rooms without bath for IR£25/34. *Colla House Hotel* (☎ 28105), at Colla, is similarly priced.

Places to Eat
If you're planning a picnic, stock up at the *Courtyard* in Main St which sells a wide range of West Cork cheeses. There's a small coffee shop at the back and, down an alley beside it, a bar which has tasty seafood. To sample locally baked bread with coffee there's nowhere better than *Adele's* across the road. At night, it reopens as a restaurant (☎ 28459) with main dishes around IR£8. *Cotter's Bar* opposite will rustle up tea and scones if Adele's is full...which it often is.

The longest bar menu is to be found at the popular *Bunratty Inn* at the Goleen end of the village. It doesn't serve lunch on Sunday when the *Waterside Inn* at the other end of Main St fills the gap.

If you would like to visit a local cheese-making farm, contact either *Gubbeen House* (☎ 28231) or *West Cork Natural Cheeses* (☎ 28593) for directions.

Getting There & Away
Buses leave Cork at 11.20 am and 6 pm and travel to Schull via Clonakilty, Skibbereen and Ballydehob. In the other direction, they leave Schull at 8.05 am and 5.50 pm from near the AIB bank at the Goleen end of the village.

Boats for Clear Island and Sherkin Island

leave from the pier (see the Clear Island and Sherkin Island Getting There & Away section for details). See the Baltimore Getting There & Away section for details of the Schull-Baltimore boat service.

Getting Around
Bikes can be hired from Schull Backpacker's Lodge or from Cotter's Yard (☎ 28165) in Main St for IR£7 a day.

In July and August there are cruises around Fastnet (Tuesday and Friday, 7 pm; IR£10) and the islands (Wednesday, 7.30 pm; IR£5).

WEST OF SCHULL TO MIZEN HEAD
The road west from Schull leads to the small village of Goleen. From Goleen, one road runs out to Mizen Head and the other to Crookhaven.

Goleen
If you hanker after artistic creativity it's worth coming to Goleen just to visit **The Ewe** (☎ 028-35492), a magical artists' hide-away with pretty gardens and stunning views. From October to May, Sheena Wood offers one-week creative escapes to let you try out pottery and other handicrafts for IR£150, assuming two people will be staying. Shorter courses may also be possible; ring Sheena to discuss possibilities. Non-artists may be content to check out the small shop where her colourful work is on display. The Ewe is signposted to the right as you enter Goleen.

Mizen Tourism (☎ 028-35255) maintains a small year-round tourist office and foreign exchange just off the main square.

Places to Eat As you drive from Schull to Goleen you'll come to the *Altar Restaurant* (☎ 028-35254) just before the right turn-off to Durrus. At lunch time you can sample dishes like seafood chowder or oysters and stout for around IR£5 to IR£6 in the pleasant slate-floored restaurant. In the evening a set seafood dinner costs IR£23, or you can choose things like crabmeat tagliatelle for IR£13.50. The Altar also has a couple of well-equipped rooms for B&B at IR£16 a head. There are remains of a megalithic tomb on the hillside beside the restaurant.

Heron's Cove Restaurant (☎ 028-35225) in Goleen opens for lunch and dinner daily from June to October.

Getting There & Away The Clonakilty to Goleen bus leaves Clonakilty at 7.05 pm and stops in Rosscarbery, Leap, Skibbereen, Ballydehob and Schull. On Sunday it leaves Clonakilty at 12.25 pm. Returning from Goleen, there are buses at 7.45 am and 5.30 pm Monday to Saturday, and at 5.30 pm on Sunday.

Crookhaven

Crookhaven was built on the far side of a spur of land that runs eastwards enclosing a harbour. The road from Goleen comes down to the north side of the harbour, passing the remains of a once-thriving stone quarry. Crookhaven was once very important as the most westerly harbour along the coast. Mail from America was collected here and it was a busy port for sailing and fishing ships from all over the world.

Today the village still attracts sailors and there are a couple of B&Bs, pubs and seafood restaurants.

Places to Stay & Eat *Marconi House* (☎ 028-35168), on the right when entering the village, was where Guglielmo Marconi (1874-1937), the Italian physicist who developed radiotelegraphy, erected a radio mast in 1902. Singles/doubles cost IR£18/ 34.

The *Crookhaven Inn* serves dishes like steak and stout pie for IR£5.80, while the *Welcome Inn* has the *Ty-ar-Mar* Breton restaurant, serving dinner from 6.30 pm. *Marconi House* also has a small restaurant serving breakfast, lunch and dinner.

Barleycove

This is West Cork's most splendid beach, and because a smaller beach nearer the campsite attracts holidaymakers, Barleycove itself is never crowded. It's a great place for children,

with long stretches of sand and a safe sandy area where a stream flows down to the sea.

The popular *Barleycove Holiday Park* (☎ 028-35302) opens over Easter and from May to September. Family tent sites are IR£8 and bikes can be hired here.

Barley Cove Beach Hotel (☎ 028-35234) does B&B for IR£55/96 in July and August. The restaurant serves bar food, afternoon tea and dinner; dishes like deep fried Mizen scampi cost IR£5.95 but a set dinner is IR£19.

Mizen Head

The Mizen Head Signal Station was completed in 1910, complementing the Fastnet Lighthouse and giving extra protection to Atlantic-bound ships. It's on a small island connected to the mainland by a superb suspension bridge that gives exciting views of the nearby rock formations. Following automation in 1993, the Mizen Head Vision is now open to the public daily from 11 am to 5 pm in April, May and October and 10 am to 5.30 pm June through September. Admission costs IR£2.50/1.25. The rest of the year it's open weekends noon to 4 pm.

Although it's interesting to see how the lighthouse keeper would have lived, on a clear day it's the vision out of the windows that will enthral you. Look out for gannets swirling and diving above the rocks.

Three Castle Head

A prime reason for making the journey to Three Castle Head is to visit the 13th century castle on the headland. According to the *Annals of Innisfallen*, it was built in 1217 and was once a stronghold of the O'Mahoney clan. Today it's a lonely ruin by the side of a supposedly haunted lake, with a sheer drop to the sea behind it.

Leaving the Barley Cove Beach Hotel car park, don't turn left for Mizen Head but go right and then left at the first T-junction. This quickly leads to another junction with a sign pointing left to the Ocean View B&B. Go right instead, follow the road to its end, and go through the farm gate on the right. Take the path to the house, follow the sign to the left and walk north for ten minutes.

Dunmanus & Durrus

The coast road from Mizen Head to Durrus is spectacularly beautiful and takes you past the ruins of another medieval castle at Dunmanus.

In Durrus you could drop into the **Riverock Gardens** which open Monday to Saturday 10 am to 6.30 pm. On the main road *The Long Boat Bar* and *Ivo's* both serve bar meals. Opposite the post office, where the road turns west for Kilcrohane, *Suzanne's* opens for dinner Tuesday to Sunday from 7 to 9 pm. Just outside Durrus, on the cross-peninsula road to Goleen, *Blair's Cove* (☎ 027-61127) serves reputedly wonderful seafood and meat dishes. Dinner is around IR£30.

Dunbeacon Campsite (☎ 027-61246), about 5km from Durrus on the Goleen road, charges IR£2.50 per person plus another 50p for a shower.

BANTRY

Bantry (Beanntraí) narrowly missed fame in the late 18th century, thanks to storms that prevented a French fleet landing to join the United Irishmen's rebellion. A local Englishman, Richard White, was rewarded with a peerage for trying to alert the British military in Cork. His grand home opens to the public and this, along with an exhibition devoted to the events of 1796, is now the town's main attraction.

Before Irish independence, Bantry Bay was a major anchorage for the British navy, and after WWII Spanish trawlers were regular visitors. The bay's deep waters were also exploited by Gulf Oil who built an oil terminal on Whiddy Island, bringing unexpected prosperity.

The island is close to Bantry Harbour and can be seen from the Cork road when entering town. In 1979, 51 lives were lost when fire broke out at the terminal. The disused storage tanks are still visible from the Bantry-Glengarriff road.

Orientation & Information

The two main roads into Bantry converge on the large Wolfe Tone Square, now mostly given over to a free car park. A small market is held here on Friday and some of the region's many expatriates, who are known as

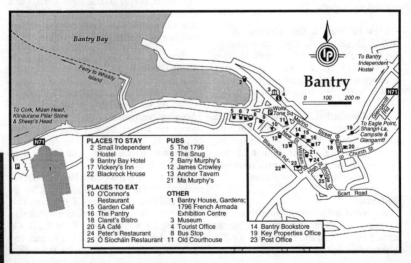

PLACES TO STAY	PUBS
2 Small Independent Hostel	5 The 1796
9 Bantry Bay Hotel	6 The Snug
17 Vickery's Inn	7 Barry Murphy's
22 Blackrock House	12 James Crowley
	13 Anchor Tavern
PLACES TO EAT	21 Ma Murphy's
10 O'Connor's Restaurant	OTHER
15 Garden Café	1 Bantry House, Gardens;
16 The Pantry	1796 French Armada
18 Claret's Bistro	Exhibition Centre
20 5A Café	3 Museum
24 Peter's Restaurant	4 Tourist Office
25 Ó Síocháin Restaurant	8 Bus Stop
	11 Old Courthouse
14 Bantry Bookstore	
19 Key Properties Office	
23 Post Office	

CORK

'blow-ins' or 'hippies' to the locals, come in to sell their wares.

The tourist office (☎ 027-50229) is open late May to September. At the time of writing it was to the south of the square but there are plans to move it into the old courthouse building east of the square sometime soon.

The telephone code is ☎ 027.

Museum

A dejected museum lurks behind the fire station. It's open May to September, Tuesday and Thursday, 10.30 am to 1 pm, Wednesday and Friday 2.30 to 5 pm. Admission costs 50p but until it moves into new premises in the old courthouse you'd be better off buying a cup of tea.

Bantry House & Gardens

Bantry House is superbly situated overlooking the bay. Parts of the house date back to the mid-18th century, but the fine sea-facing north front was added in 1840.

Despite its air of fading gentility, the interior is noted for its French and Flemish tapestries and the eclectic collection of art assembled by the 2nd earl of Bantry during his overseas peregrinations between 1820 and 1850. The old kitchen, with range intact, is now a tearoom serving excellent cakes and light lunches, and a craft shop. The house is open 9 am to 6 pm daily and entry costs IR£5.50 (children free).

But the gardens of Bantry House are its greatest glory and feature in the closing scenes of the film *Moll Flanders*. In front of the house, a well-kept lawn sweeps down towards the sea. Even better is the formal Italian garden at the back with a 'stairway to heaven' offering spectacular views over the bay. Come in May to see the ring of wisteria beautifully in bloom around a fountain. Admission to the gardens costs IR£1.50.

1796 French Armada Exhibition Centre

Considering how Lord Bantry obtained his title it's ironic that the grounds of the house now harbour an exhibition recording the sorry saga of the attempted French landing of 1796. Alongside the history there are a few artefacts rescued from the scuttled French frigate *La Surveillante*, together with a 30-minute video about diving on wrecks. Entry costs IR£3/1.25. Hopefully the old combined house-and-exhibition ticket will soon be reinstated.

Kilnaurane Pillar Stone

This isolated stone is worth seeking out because of its rare depiction of the kind of boat St Brendan is assumed to have used to reach America. To find it, leave Bantry on the N71 Cork Rd. When you reach the Westlodge Hotel, take the turning on the left. After 800m a sign points towards a gate on the right. Go through the gate and walk straight ahead until you spot the stone just over the brow of the hill. On the way back you'll have fine views of Bantry Bay ahead of you.

Cruises

Whiddy Island can be reached by a boat (☎ 50310) which leaves from the pier during the summer for IR£5 return. On the island, the *Bank House* pub and restaurant (☎ 51739) serves bar food and meals, mostly seafood.

Special Events

In the second week of May, Bantry holds a Mussel Fair with various musical events and free mussels distributed around the pubs.

The International Cork Music Festival is held at Bantry House in the first week of July. For details, contact the booking office at Myross Cottage (☎ 028-33757), Union Hall, County Cork.

Places to Stay

Camping The nearest campsite is *Eagle Point* (☎ 50630) in Ballylickey, 6km from town on the Glengarriff road. A tent site for two with a car costs IR£9.50. It's open from late April to September.

Hostel The IHH *Bantry Independent Hostel* (☎ 51050) is off the Glengarriff Rd at Bishop Lucey Place; coming from the town centre, take the fork by the Key Properties office and continue along the rough road to the top of the hill. A dorm bed costs IR£6.50; a double room is IR£18. There's a small kitchen, a cosy sitting room with lots of walking information and a pleasant garden.

The *Small Independent Hostel* (☎ 51140) is right beside the harbour on the north bank. Dorm beds cost IR£6; a double is IR£14.

B&Bs B&Bs are strung out along the Glengarriff Rd. *Shangri-La* (☎ 50244), from IR£19/34, has a good reputation but tends to fill up quickly.

More centrally located, *Blackrock House* (☎ 50432), in Blackrock Terrace beside the post office, has singles/doubles for IR£25/ 34.

In New St near the square, venerable old *Vickery's Inn* (☎ 50006) was once the town's coaching inn and has beds from IR£15 a head. For solo travellers this is a good bet. There's even an Internet connection (email IR£1).

Hotels *Bantry Bay Hotel* (☎ 50062; fax 50261) in Wolfe Tone Square has singles/ doubles for IR£31/55. The charmless *Westlodge* (☎ 50360; fax 50438) is a couple of km outside of town on the Cork road but does boast a swimming pool. Singles/ doubles cost from IR£47/74.

Similar rates are charged at the far superior *Seaview Hotel* (☎ 50073; fax 51555) at Ballylickey. To get there take the Glengarriff road a few km and you'll see it on the right. If you reach a sharp bend where the road to Macroom is signposted, you've passed it.

Romantics will jump at the chance to stay at *Bantry House* (☎ 50047). From May to September beds are IR£60 a head, in April and October IR£50. Dinner costs another IR£20 a head but you get the gardens to yourself after the crowds have gone home.

Another pricey but interesting option is *Ballylickey Manor House* (☎ 50071; fax 50124) which charges a whopping IR£90 a head, plus IR£25 for dinner.

Places to Eat

Best of the few cafés is *The Pantry*, up a

flight of stairs near Vickery's Inn. Alongside the usual salads, soups and sandwiches you can get filled burritos here. A few doors down, *The Garden Café* in the Bakehouse opens for breakfast and lunch. *Peter's* further up New St does grills from IR£3.95.

The *5A Café* in Barrack St does veggie burgers and filled pitta bread but closes at 5 pm, or earlier if trade is slow. Across the road, *Claret's Bistro* serves lunches for around IR£5 until 4 pm, but dinners from 6 to 9.30 pm cost from IR£12 upwards. *Ó Síocháin*, on Bridge St, has a standard café-style menu with specials like spaghetti bolognese for IR£4.50. *Vickery's Inn* does unadventurous but filling three-course lunches for around IR£6; specials cost less and dinner is IR£12.

Several pubs, including *Barry Murphy's* and *The Snug*, serve bar lunches.

O'Connor's (☎ 50221) is an acclaimed seafood restaurant in Wolfe Tone Square. Lunch costs around IR£5-9, dinner from IR£12, and mussels are a specialty. *Bantry Bay Hotel* also has a good, if pricey, menu; vegetarians might fancy the exotic fruit curry with rice for IR£6. Bar meals are also good; try the delicious baked potato stuffed with seafood for IR£3.95.

Entertainment

Barry Murphy's just off the square has music sessions, as does *James Crowley* nearby. *Bantry Bay Hotel* is also worth a look.

Even without music the *Anchor Tavern* is an interesting old pub. Look out, too, for *Ma Murphy's*, an old-style walk-through shop with a pub out the back. Both are in New St.

The 1796, around the corner from the square on the Cork road, is a reliable music and comedy venue.

Getting There & Away

Throughout the year there are three buses a day between Cork and Bantry. During summer the express bus service between Cork and Killarney also stops outside Barry Murphy's in Bantry. It leaves for Glengarriff, Kenmare and Killarney at noon and departs for Skibbereen, Clonakilty and Cork at 6.10

pm. For details phone Bus Éireann on 021-508188.

The private Berehaven bus (☎ 70007) links Castletownbere with Bantry via Glengarriff (IR£3 one way). It leaves the fire station in Wolfe Tone Square at noon on Monday, and 3.45 pm on Tuesday, Friday and Saturday.

Sheep's Head Peninsula

The least visited of Cork's three peninsulas, the Sheep's Head nevertheless has a charm all of its own. There are no substantial antiquities, but a loop road runs close to the sea for most of the way. There are wonderful seascapes to appreciate and country walks where other visitors will be few and far between.

The second turning on the right after leaving Bantry for Cork is the beginning of the **Goat's Path Scenic Route**, which approaches the peninsula from the northern side. The southern part of the loop road begins farther along the main road, just past the Esso garage.

AHAKISTA

Calling Ahakista a village is stretching the meaning of the word: there are two unprepossessing pubs, one shop and an outrageously expensive Japanese restaurant.

Just west of Ahakista a sign points to *Hillcrest* B&B (☎ 027-67045) with singles/doubles from IR£19.50/29. Other B&Bs with almost identical rates are dotted along the road so it's just a matter of picking one that takes your fancy.

If you're looking for something special and don't mind the cost *Shiro* (☎ 027-67030), in beautiful grounds across the road from the Ahakista Bar, serves Japanese meals in a delightfully intimate setting. With just four tables, booking is essential despite the IR£43 a head price tag.

The *Ahakista Bar* has a surprisingly delightful garden at the back and music on

---

Walks on Sheep's Head Peninsula

The start of a walk to the top of Seefin (334m) is at the top of the Goat's Path, about 2km north of Kilcrohane village. Across the road from here, there is a rather forlorn imitation of Michelangelo's *Pietà*, erected by an American with local family roots. While there's no obvious path, it's not difficult to aim for the summit and reach it in less than 45 minutes. There are fine views from the top, and not many people go there.

A good three hour walk could also be started from the top of the Goat's Path. Standing near the *Pietà* and facing Bantry Bay, locate an old road about 100m to the right, recognisable by a low slate wall on the sea-facing side. Follow this remote track until it joins a surfaced road that heads out farther west along the peninsula and eventually crosses to the southern side where the main road leads back to Kilcrohane. A left turn at the village church would bring you back to the start of the walk at the top of the Goat's Path. ∎

Friday nights; otherwise it's sporadically open.

The only bus service leaves Bantry at 8 am on Saturday and returns at 3.25 pm.

KILCROHANE

Cary View Hostel (☎ 027-67035) is a basic bunkhouse with just eight beds for IR£6.50 each. It's signposted off the west end of the village.

Of Kilcrohane's two pubs, *Fitzpatrick's*, just north of the church, makes the most effort with its exterior and serves light refreshments, while the *Bay View Inn* on the main road has music sessions.

The Saturday bus from Bantry to Ahakista continues to Kilcrohane.

Beara Peninsula (Ring of Beara)

The appeal of the Beara Peninsula (Mor Choaird Bheara) lies in its startling natural beauty, best experienced by climbing the hills and cycling the roads. It's a lot bigger and much wilder than the Sheep's Head peninsula to the south. While the Mizen Head and Sheep's Head peninsulas are lush and green, reminiscent of the Ireland imagined by long-departed emigrants, the Beara is desolate, a harsh, rocky landscape which makes wonderful walking country.

The 197km Beara Way is a well signposted long-distance walk linking Glengarriff with Kenmare via Castletownbere, Bere Island, Dursey Island and the north side of the peninsula. Much of the route is along green roads. For more details see the Activities chapter.

The Beara is littered with prehistoric rocks, stone circles and old tombs. If you're interested look for *Beara – An Historical Trail* (IR£1) which describes the sites you'll see indicated by brown and white signs.

ORIENTATION & INFORMATION

A small part of the northern peninsula lies in Kerry but is dealt with here for the convenience of people travelling the Ring of Beara. Castletownbere in Cork or Kenmare in Kerry would make good bases for exploring the peninsula. Small official tourist offices open in Castletownbere and Glengarriff in July and August.

In theory you could drive the 137km around the coast in one day, but at the price of missing a great deal. In particular you would miss the spectacular Healy Pass which cuts across the peninsula to join Adrigole in Cork with Lauragh in Kerry.

The route described below assumes you are starting out from Glengarriff and working your way around the peninsula clockwise to Kenmare.

GLENGARRIFF

A long, thin village, Glengarriff is strung out along the main West Cork to Killarney road with the Eccles Hotel at one end. At the other end, the road divides, with one offshoot leading to Kenmare and the other to the Beara Peninsula. Its sheltered position at the head of Bantry Bay, together with the influence of the Gulf Stream, give it a particularly mild climate, and the local flora is lush and sometimes exotic.

During the second half of the 19th century Glengarriff (An Gleann Garbh) became a popular retreat for prosperous Victorians who would sail from England to Ireland then take the train to Bantry from where a paddle steamer chugged over to Glengarriff. By 1850 the road to Kenmare had been blasted through the mountains and the link with Killarney was established.

A major attraction is the Italianate garden on nearby Garnish Island although it's pleasant just walking in the crassly named Blue Pool Amenity Area which rings the coast in the middle of the village.

Information

The official tourist information office is only open during July and August (☎ 027-63084) and is inconveniently positioned in a portacabin in the Eccles Hotel car park. You'd do better to call into the unofficial version in a shop in the village centre, beside the Blue Pool ferry terminal. Even this is sometimes closed between 1 and 2 pm.

The telephone code is ☎ 027.

Garnish Island

In the early 20th century the English architect, Harold Peto, created an Italianate garden on this 15-hectare island. He planted exotic plants never before seen in Ireland, and they continue to flourish, providing a blaze of colour in a landscape usually dominated by greens and browns. There are panoramic views from the top of the 19th century Martello Tower, built to watch out for a possible Napoleonic invasion.

The gardens are owned by Dúchas which charges a IR£2.50 admission fee. Opening times are April to June and in September, Monday to Saturday 10 am to 6.30 pm and Sunday 1 to 7 pm; July and August, Monday to Saturday 9.30 am to 6.30 pm and Sunday 11 am to 7 pm; March and October, Monday to Saturday 10 am to 4 pm and Sunday 1 to 4.30 pm.

Two ferry companies serve the island. Harbour Queen Ferryboats (☎ 63116) leave from a pier opposite the Eccles Hotel while Blue Pool Ferries (☎ 63333) leave from the centre of the village, near the Quills Woollen Market. Both charge IR£5 return for the 15-minute crossing which will probably pass colonies of seals basking on rocks.

Glengarriff Woods
These 300-hectare oak and pine woods were owned by the White family of Bantry House in the 18th century. After the government took over in the 1950s the range of trees was expanded. The thick tree cover maintains humid conditions that allows ferns and mosses to flourish. Look out especially for tiny white flowers on red stems rising from rosettes of leaves: kidney saxifrage, rare elsewhere.

The woodlands and bogs are also home to the Kerry slug, the 'aristocrat of slugs', found only here and in parts of Kerry and the Iberian Peninsula. It's coffee-coloured with cream spots.

To get to the woods, leave Glengarriff on the N71 Kenmare road. The entrance is about 1km along on the left. A sign, just inside the gate, points across the footbridge to **Lady Bantry's Lookout**. It's a short, steep climb which brings you out seemingly on top of the world.

The tourist information centre in the village sells a 30p leaflet showing routes around the woods.

Scuba Diving
Both Bantry and Dunmanus Bay have exciting sites for scuba diving and a new diving centre *Bantry Bay Divers* (☎ 51310), based at Casey's Hotel in Main St, is recommended for both dedicated and occasional divers. Package trips are arranged and other water activities can be organised. The usual charge for a 2½ hour diving session is IR£30.

Places to Stay
Camping Two km west of Glengarriff on the Castletownbere road, *Dowlings Caravan & Camping Park* (☎ 63154) opens Easter through October. It has a licensed bar and music in the summer. A tent site for two costs

IR£6. *O'Shea's Caravan & Camping Park* (☎ 63140), close by, charges similar rates.

Hostels A brand-new hostel has just opened in the centre of Glengarriff, between the Blue Pool ferry terminal and Casey's Hotel. *Murphy's Village Hostel* (☎ 63555) has dorm beds for IR£7.50 and doubles for IR£20. By the time you read this there should be a café on the ground floor to supplement the 1st-floor cooking facilities. If this is full, scruffy *O'Mahony's* (☎ 63033), at the Bantry end of the village, has beds for IR£6 and two double rooms for IR£14. Two km from the village, signposted along the Kenmare road, *Glengarriff Independent Hostel* (☎ 63211) is an isolated but hardly picturesque bungalow charging the same rates.

B&Bs Bungaloid B&Bs line the road out to Bantry. *Sea Front* (☎ 63079), near the Eccles Hotel, has three beds for IR£14 each and *Island View House* (☎ 63081) has singles/doubles from IR£21/33.

Hotels The grand but fast fading *Eccles* (☎ 63003; fax 63319) boasts past literary guests like Thackeray, Yeats and Shaw but is very much a coach-tour stop-off now. Facing the sea on the main road at the Bantry end of the village, it offers singles/doubles from IR£37/54. *Caseys* (☎ 63010; fax 63072), in the village centre, charges IR£30/50 in peak season.

Places to Eat
Barry's pub beside the post office offers open fish sandwiches for IR£6.50; for more basic sandwiches try the *Blue Loo* pub opposite.

Barry's also boasts a seafood restaurant with main dishes for around IR£12. The *Rainbow Restaurant* nearby has vegetarian curry for IR£5.50. *Caseys* hotel serves pub food all day; fish and chips is IR£4.95.

For coffee and delicious home-made cakes, try the *Café de la Paix* opposite Barry's.

CORK

Getting There & Away

Year-round an express bus travels between Cork and Glengarriff (2½ hours) via Bantry (15 minutes, IR£2.50 midweek return). Coming from Bantry it stops outside the post office; going back to Bantry it stops by the phone boxes across the road.

From late May to September, buses from Cork to Killarney also pass through Bantry and Glengarriff once daily; phone ☎ 021-508188 for details.

The private Berehaven bus (☎ 70007) departs for Bantry at 7.30 am daily and returns at 7.45 pm. This service continues on to Cork.

Getting Around

Jem Creations (☎ 63113), just where the road divides for Castletownbere, is the Raleigh Rent-a-Bike agent, with bikes for IR£7/30 a day/week.

SUGARLOAF MOUNTAIN

Eight km after leaving Glengarriff for Castletownbere look out for a turning on the right; it's half a km after a disused school on the right of the road, opposite a blue sign in the middle of nowhere declaring a Community Alert Area. Follow this road for 1.5km and leave your bicycle or car near the single two-storey house (with pine trees behind it) or near the bungalow just past it.

Sugarloaf Mountain (581m) is best approached by walking up behind the houses and crossing an old road. A steady approach up the side of the mountain would bring you to the triangulation point at the summit in about an hour. There are excellent views from the top: the Caha Mountains to the north, Hungry Hill to the west, Garnish Island to the east and Bantry Bay spread out to the south. On the way up, around the old road, look out for the insectivorous great butterwort in May and June.

ADRIGOLE

The first village you come to on the peninsula is Ardrigole where not a lot happens. *Adrigole Hostel* (☎ 60228), just west of the

village, 16km from Castletownbere on the Glengarriff road, has space for tents too.

HUNGRY HILL

At 686m, Hungry Hill is the highest point on the peninsula. A sign points to one route to the top, 7km west of Adrigole. A longer but more comfortable ascent begins by ignoring this sign, carrying along the road, and turning right just past a church on the right side of the road. This road goes north until blocked by a wire sheep gate. A vehicle could be left just before this or taken past for another km or so. The overgrown road eventually stops near some lakes and from here, keeping the lakes to the left, you head up the east ridge and climb the summit from the north side.

A quicker descent can be made by following the stream down the south-west side to some farmhouses and a road that connects with the one where you began. The whole journey will take at least five hours but the rockscapes are fabulous and the views of West Cork from the stone circle at the top are tremendous. Less arduous would be a walk to the end of the road and a picnic by the lakes.

CASTLETOWNBERE

Castletownbere (Baile Chais Bheara) is Ireland's largest whitefish port and when its full name – Castletownberehaven – is used it shares with Newtownmountkennedy, in County Wicklow, the proud claim of having the country's longest place name. The main town on the peninsula, it originally developed out of the copper mining industry at Allihies and remains little touched by tourism.

Castletownbere is little more than one traffic-choked street with the Bere Island ferry and the harbour at the east and the main square given over to a fire station, garage, car park and fishing suppliers. Tourist information (☎ 027-70344) is available in July and August from a garden shed squeezed in next to the fire station. Otherwise there are supermarkets, a post office with a limited bureau de change, a laundrette and a string of pubs, some with music at night (try Twomey's on Friday nights).

The telephone code is ☎ 027.

Places to Stay

Camping Two km before Castletownbere, the *Wheel Inn Holiday Centre* (☎ 70090) is pleasantly situated with views of Bere Island. You can also camp at the *Beara* and *Adrigole* hostels on the Dursey side of town.

Hostels About 3km west of Castletownbere, just past the sign for Dunboy, the *Beara Hostel* (☎ 70184) on the main road has dorm beds for IR£6 or doubles, some of them in pleasant wooden chalets, for IR£15. *Garranes Hostel* (☎ 73147), between Castletownbere and Allihies, has a superb location overlooking Bantry Bay, a couple of km off the road. It's owned by the Dzogchen Buddhist retreat centre next door and guests have the option of joining in daily meditation sessions, based on Tibetan Buddhist principles. This is a very laidback place; if you're just after the views that's fine as well.

B&Bs The half-dozen B&Bs include *Bay View House* (☎ 70099), along West End, with beds for IR£14, and *The Old Bank Seafood Restaurant* (☎ 70252) right in the centre, with beds for IR£15. *Craigie's Hotel* (☎ 70379) has singles/doubles from IR£51/64.

Places to Eat

Niki's, in the centre of town, has breakfasts for IR£3.95 and seafood dinners for around IR£12. Across the road *Jack Patrick's* also does lunch, with specials for IR£3.50. The *Old Bank Seafood Restaurant*, just west of the main square, is only open in summer; dinner costs around IR£10. Even further west, *The Old Bakery Café and Restaurant* is a cosy place with photos on the wall; mussel soup with soda bread costs IR£2.20.

Getting Around

Bikes can be hired from the SuperValu supermarket (☎ 70020) on the east side of town near the ferry for IR£7/30 a day/week.

BERE ISLAND

This island may be about the same size as Manhattan but has a very different kind of appeal. The deep anchorage helped make it the base for the British navy and the whole Allied fleet spent some time here before the Battle of Jutland in WWI. At the outbreak of WWII, Winston Churchill wanted to continue using it, and a deal for the return of the six northern counties was in the air. However, it wasn't to be.

The Beara Way's 21km walk is the best reason for visiting the island. There are a couple of pubs and small shops but tourist accommodation, April to October only, is limited to four beds at *Harbour View* (☎ 027-75011) from IR£19.50/29. It's best to book in advance.

Late June to late September, a ferry (☎ 027-75009) to Bere Island runs from Castletownbere quay. It costs IR£15 return for a car and driver, IR£3/1.50 for other passengers. July and August there are seven boats a day, 10.30 am to 6 pm.

DUNBOY CASTLE & PUXLEY MANSION

Leaving Castletownbere, you come almost immediately to a sign to Dunboy Castle. Little now remains of the castle, the fortress of the O'Sullivan clan, who ruled supreme for three centuries before succumbing to the English with cannon and 4000 men in 1602. The setting is beautiful.

Don't make the mistake of thinking the grand ruins you come to first are the magnificent remains of a Gaelic stronghold. This is Puxley Mansion, bearing testimony to the vast wealth generated by the copper mined on the Puxley family estate. It was built in the 19th century and burnt down by the old IRA in 1921, but enough remains to show the extravagance of its style. Check out the Italian marble of the columns still standing in what was once the grand hallway.

If you don't mind roughing it, it's possible to camp in the castle grounds for IR£2 a head. Ask at the house on the right after passing the main gate. Horses can also be hired for IR£10 (☎ 70044).

Entry to the castle grounds costs 50p per

CORK

person or IR£2 for a car. On a good day you're much better off walking down. The grounds are open Easter to mid-October; when the gate's not staffed put the fee in the box.

DURSEY ISLAND

At the end of the peninsula is Dursey Island, just 6.5km long by 1.5km wide and 250m offshore. Ireland's only cable car connects the 20 or so inhabitants and their cattle with the mainland. Three hundred people sought refuge here in 1602, when Dunboy Castle was under siege by the English; they were slaughtered and thrown into the sea.

The cable car crosses between 9 and 11 am, between 2.30 and 5 pm, and between 7 and 8 pm, Monday to Saturday. Note that cattle get precedence over humans in the queue for the ride! The two Sunday morning crossings are timed to get people to mass at Cahermore or Allihies, but there are also crossings at 7 pm and 11 pm. From June to August there may also be Sunday crossings between 4 and 5 pm.

While there's no accommodation available on the island it's easy to find somewhere to camp. The Beara Way loops around the island for 11km, and the signal tower is an obvious destination for a shorter walk. Bikes are not allowed on the cable car.

Just before the cable car terminus, *Windy Point House* (☎ 027-73017) does B&B for IR£20/30 and serves tea, coffee and light meals.

ALLIHIES & THE COPPER MINES

Copper was discovered in 1810 and mining quickly brought wealth to the Puxley family who owned the land, but low wages and dangerous, unhealthy work conditions for the workforce, which at one time numbered 1300 men, women and children. Experienced Cornish miners were brought into the area, and the ruins of their stone cottages remain. As late as the 1930s, over 30,000 tonnes of pure copper were being exported but by 1962 the last mine was closed. Daphne du Maurier's novel *Hungry Hill* (Penguin) is based on the Puxley family.

Walks from Allihies

The mines are just north of Allihies village and 19km west of Castletownbere; signs point the way to the remains of an untidy quarry. An old road leads to the ruins of a chimney stack, where the road can be followed up, passing an old reservoir on the right. Mine shafts are scattered around but they're fenced off and the main chimney stack can be approached in relative safety. The track eventually leads to Eyeries and can be followed for as long as you wish. Half an hour's walk leads to a point with a view of Coulagh Bay and Kenmare Bay beyond. You can climb the hills by cutting over the moor to the right, but it's best to consult a local walking guide like *West Cork Walks* by Kevin Corcoran (O'Brien Press, Dublin). ■

Places to Stay & Eat

In Allihies village, there's the IHH *The Village Hostel (Bonnie Braes)* (☎ 027-73107) with dorm beds for IR£7 and private rooms for IR£16 to IR£18. There's limited camping space in the garden for IR£3.50 a head. In amongst the surrounding copper mines is the An Óige *Allihies Hostel* (☎ 027-73014) with beds for IR£5.50/4.

There are also a couple of B&B places: *Sea View Cluin Village* (☎ 027-73004) from IR£15/26, and *Mrs O'Sullivan* (☎ 027-73019) at Glenera for IR£14/24.

Meals are available at the homely *Atlantic Seafood Restaurant*, *O'Neil's* pub does bar food, or there's the *Lighthouse Bar* for a drink.

EYERIES & ARDGROOM

Heading east from Allahies, a 23km coastal road with hedges of fuchsia and rhododendron twists and turns all the way to Eyeries. Look back almost immediately and you'll be able to see the Bull, Cow and Calf Rocks off Dursey Head. Eyries is a village of brightly coloured houses with three pubs, a post office and a church. Beds cost IR£13 at *The Shamrock* (☎ 027-74058), which is along Strand Rd.

The coast road eventually rejoins the main road at Ardgroom, a small village with food

TOM SMALLMAN

TOM SMALLMAN

TOM SMALLMAN

TOM SMALLMAN

County Waterford
A: Red House Inn, Lismore
B: St Carthage's Cathedral, Lismore
C: Rural scene just outside Lismore
D: Lismore Castle

TONY WHEELER

TONY WHEELER

PAT YALE

County Cork
Top Left: Clocktower, Youghal
Top Right: Old town wall, Youghal
Bottom: Art retreat on the Beara Peninsula

available at the *Village Inn* and *The Holly Bar*.

Heading east towards Lauragh look for signs on the right to Ardgroom **stone circle**, a beautifully located Bronze Age monument, the most striking in a valley littered with reminders of prehistory. The ground can be boggy so be careful after rain.

LAURAGH

From Lauragh, a serpentine road travels 11km across the Healy Pass, offering spectacular views of the rocky inland scenery. Lauragh is also home to the century-old **Derreen Gardens** planted by the 5th Lord Lansdowne. An abundance of interesting plants thrive here, including spectacular New Zealand tree ferns and red cedars normally found in rainforests. The gardens are open April to September 11 am to 6 pm and admission is IR£2.50/1.50.

Places to Stay

Creveen Lodge Caravan & Camping Park

Walks from Lauragh

About 1km west of Lauragh on the R572 a road off to the left is marked for **Glanmore Lake**. Take the first turning to the right along this road and follow it until it comes to an end by a couple of farms, the first of which has a stone circle in its back yard. Although the road ends, a path continues across the stream and into the valley until you reach the remains of some stone dwellings. This undemanding walk takes less than an hour from the stone circle.

A more exhilarating walk is to head up behind the house with the stone circle, crossing a sheep fence and keeping to the right of the stream. A stiff climb leads to a hanging valley with mountains on both sides. Avoid the one on the left and head right to climb the shorter summit of **Cummeennahillan** (361m). From here you can walk along the ridge of the mountain and down through holly woods and invasive rhododendrons through another farm to the Glanmore Lake road. The longer trek takes at least a couple of hours, but a wander around the top of Cummeennahillan offers tremendous views and a fine descent along the hanging valley. ∎

(☎ 064-83131), 1.5km south-east of Lauragh on the Healy Pass road, is open Easter to the end of October; a small tent site costs IR£6-7. The An Óige *Glanmore Lake Hostel* (☎ 064-83181), in an old lakeside schoolhouse 5km from Lauragh, is open from Easter to September; beds cost IR£5.50/4.50. *Mountain View* (☎ 064-83143), distinctively located on the Healy Pass, does B&B for IR£20/30 and dinner for IR£12.

North Cork

The chief reasons for visiting north Cork are the fishing and the golf. A few distinguished country houses with fine gardens are open to the public for evening meals and short stays but this is hardly budget traveller's territory: permission to fish for a day on the Blackwater could cost IR£30; a night for two in a country house with dinner could easily approach IR£200. There are no hostels or official campsites, but B&Bs are never far away.

FERMOY

Fermoy is a small town on the River Blackwater at the point where the cross-country roads from Dublin to Cork and from Rosslare to Killarney intersect. There's not a great deal to do here unless you're into fishing, but the sheer number of tea shops makes it a good place to break your journey. The town also hosts a Fishing Festival in the week straddling May and June, in an attempt to lure visitors from England during their Bank Holiday weekend and then Irish anglers for their Bank Holiday weekend the week after.

Information

The tourist office (☎ 025-31811) is in Slattery Travel, facing Pearse Square and to the left of the imposing blue building. It's open all year 9 am to 6 pm.

Any fishing inquiries should be made to

Brian Toomey Sports (☎ 31101), 18 McCurtain St.

The telephone code is ☎ 025.

Places to Stay & Eat

If you need a bed for the night, *St Anne's* (☎ 31205), on the Cahir side of the bridge, does B&B for IR£15 a head.

Beside the bus stops in McCurtain St, *Mary's* and *Partners* both do all-day breakfasts. *Fermoy Tea Rooms*, in Patrick St, has good home-made cakes.

For an unexpectedly interesting dinner try *La Bigoudenne* (☎ 32832), a Breton crêperie at 28 McCurtain St which opens for lunch and again for dinner. Savoury crêpes start at just IR£1.85. There's also a more conventional set dinner menu for IR£16.

Getting There & Away

Fermoy is on the main Dublin to Cork bus route, with three daily services every day except Sunday when there are two.

MALLOW & AROUND

Twice the size of Fermoy, Mallow (Mala) is a prosperous town in the Blackwater Valley that caters for fishing, golfing and horse racing. Nineteenth century visitors to its spa christened it the 'Bath of Ireland' although these days the comparison would seem pretty far-fetched.

The tourist office (☎ 022-42222), on Bridge St near the castle, opens May to September.

From Mallow to Killarney the landscape is pretty nondescript, although you might want to divert to see the well preserved remains of 17th century **Kanturk Castle** – it's said that the mortar was mixed with the blood of the builders who were forced to work on its construction. The English, however, objected to an Irish chief building such a massive mansion and didn't allow it to be roofed.

Kanturk Town has fishing possibilities (☎ 029-50257) and the superior *Assolas Country House* (☎ 029-50015; fax 50795) where you're looking at around IR£70 a head for a bed.

Inland Cork

The most popular westward route from Cork heads south to Kinsale and then along the N71 through Clonakilty and Skibbereen.

An alternative route from Cork to Bantry cuts inland via Macroom, and lets you take in the Gougane Barra Forest Park. The quickest route between Killarney and Cork is also via Macroom.

A quicker inland route to Bantry takes the main road to Bandon and Dunmanway but there are few attractions along the way except the pleasant IHH *Shiplake Mountain Hostel* (☎ 023-45750) where you can hire bikes and find out about local cycling trips. Dorm beds cost IR£6.

BANDON & WEST CORK HERITAGE CENTRE

Twenty km north-east of Clonakilty on the river of the same name, Bandon was a major Protestant settlement in the 17th century, infamous for excluding Catholics. The West Cork Heritage Centre has various exhibits relating to local life through the ages, the most successful being the recreated country shop and bar. Admission is IR£2.50 and it's open from April to October, Monday to Saturday 10 am to 6 pm, and on Sunday 2 to 6 pm.

Getting There & Away

Bus Éireann has at least four buses a day in each direction from Cork to Bandon, continuing to Bantry and Glengarriff. Some also go on to Schull and Skibbereen.

MICHAEL COLLINS AMBUSH SITE

Michael Collins, commander-in-chief of the army of the new Provisional Government that had just won independence from Britain, was killed at Beal-na-Blath, near Macroom, on 22 August 1922, whilst on a quick tour of West Cork. He was recognised by anti-Treaty forces, who were meeting secretly nearby. In the evening they ambushed his car and Collins was shot dead. Collins seems to have ignored advice to drive on after the first shots were fired, choosing instead to make a fight of it.

The site of the ambush is marked by a stone memorial with a Gaelic inscription. Each year, a commemorative service is held on the anniversary of the killing.

Getting There & Away

Leave Macroom on the N22 heading east, then take the left turn towards Crookstown (C590) after roughly 5km. After about one km turn right towards Beal-na-Blath. The ambush site is on the left after another 1.5km.

GOUGANE BARRA FOREST PARK

This is the most picturesque part of inland Cork. The source of the River Lee is a mountain lake, fed by numerous silver streams. St Finbarr, the founder and patron saint of Cork, came here in the 6th century and established a monastery. He had a hermitage on the island in Lough an Ghugain, which is now approached by a short causeway. The small modern chapel on the island has fine stained-glass representations of obscure Celtic saints.

A road runs through the park in a loop and a signboard map shows the meandering paths and nature trails leading off it. It's worth heading for Bealick's summit for the fine views.

Places to Stay & Eat

Seven hundred metres before the main park entrance, the *Gougane Barra Hotel* (☎ 026-47069) overlooks Lough an Ghugain and has singles/doubles from IR£51/68. *Cronin's* bar serves light meals and there's a small gift shop.

Three km before the turn-off to Gougane Barra, to the right of the main road from Macroom, the IHH *Tig Barra Hostel* (☎ 026-47016) has dorm beds for IR£5.50 and one double for IR£14.

B&B is available from IR£22/34 a single/double at *Cois na Coille*, 1km from Ballingeary. As the name might suggest, this is a Gaeltacht area.

Getting There & Away

Driving from Cork to Bantry along the N22 and R584 you'll come to a signpost for the park after Ballingeary. Returning to the main road afterwards and continuing west, you'll pass over the Pass of Keimaneigh and emerge on the N71 at Ballylickey midway between Glengarriff and the Beara Peninsula to the north, and Bantry and the Sheep's Head Peninsula to the south. Opposite this junction is the *Ouvane Falls Hotel* where it's worth stopping for a drink to appreciate the lovely views from the garden at the back.

In July and August there's one Saturday-only bus service which leaves Macroom at 8 am and passes by the Gougane Barra.

County Kerry

While the town of Killarney bursts at the seams and the Ring of Kerry is chock-a-block with tour coaches throughout the summer, the rest of the county is easily big enough for visitors to escape the crowds. The tourist hype does little to detract from the landscape's wild splendour. There are countless opportunities for long and short walks, easy and stiff climbs and bike rides where your only companions will be the birds, the odd cow or sheep and a few like-minded travellers. Especially beautiful is the Dingle Peninsula, but the Iveragh Peninsula to the south has even more opportunities for open-air activities. There's the usual quota of pubs with lively music at night and several small towns of historic interest.

Killarney & Around

KILLARNEY

As tourist towns go Killarney (Cill Airne) is the Numero Uno. There's more registered accommodation here than anywhere else outside Dublin and the shops around the tourist office do a fine line in leprechaun-adorned T-shirts, mugs, towels, you name it. Still, with a National Park and three lakes right on its doorstep, Killarney offers easy escape from the excesses for walkers and cyclists. The town also has its own form of environmentally-friendly transport – the horse-drawn jaunting car – which also give it its distinctive aroma of dung. These carriages have been in use for well over a hundred years so it's a shame the idea of the tail bag hasn't caught on.

Recently Killarney has been doing particularly well economically, so well in fact that the new McDonald's on the outskirts had trouble finding staff. High St's pricey restaurants are testimony to this prosperity. Allow two or three days to do justice to Killarney and the National Park.

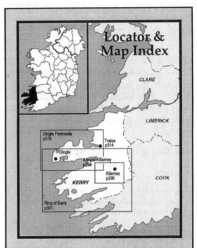

Highlights

- Visit the 9th century Gallarus Oratory on the Dingle Peninsula
- Climb Mt Brandon on the Dingle Peninsula
- Walk the second half of the Dingle Way from Dunquin to Tralee
- Enjoy day-long cycling trips from Killarney
- Row out to Inishfallen Island from Killarney
- Walk all or part of the Kerry Way and escape the brouhaha of Killarney
- Avoid the ritualised Ring of Kerry and cycle or drive through the Ballaghbeama Pass
- Take the boat trip to Skellig Michael, an astonishing 7th century monastery perched on top of a rock in the Atlantic Ocean
- Cycle or drive through the Healy Pass from Lauragh south to County Cork

Information

Killarney's busy but efficient tourist office (☎ 064-31633), in the town hall in Main St, opens 9.15 am to 5.30 pm Monday to Saturday; later in July and August.

A laundrette lurks behind the Spar super-

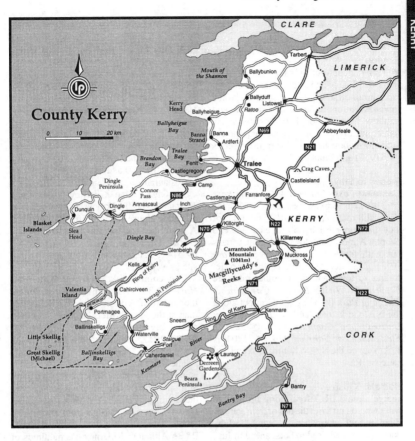

County Kerry

market at the Plunkett St end of College St. The Killarney Bookshop (☎ 34108) is at 32 Main St. Second Editions (☎ 35324), 46 High St, sells second-hand volumes. Irish music is sold at Music Kingdom in Plunkett St. Hillwalkers (☎ 37098) in the covered mall behind the tourist office sells maps and walking gear.

The telephone code is ☎ 064.

St Mary's Cathedral

Built in 1842-55, this cruciform cathedral, at the end of New St, in Cathedral Place, was designed by the architect Augustus Pugin.

During the Famine years it acted as a refuge for the destitute and the huge tree on the front lawn marks the mass grave of women and children who died.

Museum of Irish Transport

This collection of splendid, shiny old cars, bicycles and assorted odds and ends includes an 1844 Meteor Starley Tricycle found in a shop's 'unsold stock' in 1961 and a 1910 Wolseley that belonged to the Gore-Booth family and was also used by Countess Markievicz and WB Yeats.

The museum is in East Avenue Rd. It's

open daily April to October, 10 am to 6 pm.
Entry is IR£2.50/1.

Fishing

You can fish for trout and salmon in the rivers
Flesk and Laune and in the lakes. The small
lakes around the southern side of Killarney
towards Kenmare also have brown and
rainbow trout, although there's no coarse
fishing locally. Permits, licences, equipment
and information are available from O'Neill's
(☎ 31970) at 6 Plunkett St.

Places to Stay

Camping *Fossa Caravan & Camping Park*
(☎ 31497) is 5.6km west of town on the
Killorglin road. A tent is IR£4 per night for
a cyclist or hiker, IR£4.50 for a car and two
people. Almost next door, with similar rates
but with fewer facilities, is *Beech Grove*
(☎ 31727), across from Hotel Europe.
Nearer to town and with similar rates are
*Fleming's White Bridge Caravan &
Camping Park* (☎ 31590), 1.6km out along
the N22 Cork road, and *White Villa Farm
Caravan and Camping Park* (☎ 32456).
Flesk Muckross Caravan Park (☎ 31704) is
1.5km out on the N71 to Kenmare. A tent and
car cost IR£4.

Hostels Killarney's many hostels mostly
charge around IR£7 for a dorm bed. Some
will pick you up from the bus or train station.
Even though there are so many hostels,
you'd be well advised to book ahead in July
and August.

Just off Park Rd and closest to the bus and
rail station, the well-equipped *Killarney
Railway Hostel* (☎ 35299) was about to
acquire a new restaurant and more private
rooms at the time of writing.

Off New St in the town centre a lane leads
to the highly-thought-of and friendly *Neptune's Town Hostel* (☎ 35255), a big place
with some ensuite doubles for IR£17.50 and
a good, big kitchen. You can get your laundry
washed for IR£4.

The small, New Agey *Súgán* (☎ 33104),
in Lewis Rd, gets mixed reviews; friendly,
but noisy and not at all clean (plus an outdoor

shower). At the time of writing the *Four
Winds* (☎ 33094), 43 New St, was for sale.

A little out of town in a quiet setting
Bunrower House Hostel (☎ 33104) is owned
by the same people as the Súgán. Dorm beds
are so-so and although the showers are hot
the washing facilities are pretty basic.
Heading for Kenmare, turn right at the Esso
garage on the road signposted for Ross
Castle. It's a pleasant 20-minute walk across
the park to town but there's also free transport between the two hostels. You can camp
here for IR£3.50 a head. Note that there are
no restaurants or pubs in the vicinity.

An Óige's large *Killarney International
Hostel* (☎ 31240), 2km west of the centre at
Aghadoe House, costs IR£6.50/5 per night.
A hostel bus meets trains from Dublin and
Cork. The IHH *Fossa Holiday Hostel*
(☎ 31497), slightly farther out, has a campsite as well.

The comfortable well-equipped *Atlas
Hostel* (☎ 36144) is 1km from the station off
the Cork road. A dorm bed costs a IR£1 more
than at the other hostels but includes continental breakfast. There are doubles for
IR£22 (IR£25 ensuite) and a triple ensuite
for IR£33.

The IHH *Peacock Farm Hostel* (☎ 33557)
is in Gortdromakiery, Muckross. Take a left
turn on to the Lough Guitane road just after
the jaunting car entrance at Muckross House.
It also offers free pick-ups from town.

B&Bs Although Killarney has hundreds of
B&Bs, finding a room can be tricky in high
season when it's worth paying the IR£1
booking fee to let the tourist office do the
hunting. Along New St *West End House*
(☎ 32271) beside the Shell garage has
singles/doubles for IR£25/35, while the
Killarney Townhouse has beds for IR£20.

Otherwise, Muckross Rd is a particularly
good place to look. Less than 1km from the
centre *Fuchsia House* (☎ 33743) does
singles/doubles from IR£35/50. One km out
Tower House (☎ 33884) has doubles for
IR£34. Two km out *Carriglea Farmhouse*
(☎ 31116) is an elegant house in a quiet
location with doubles for IR£35.

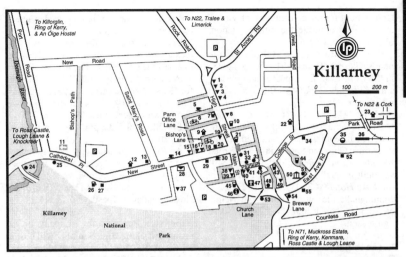

Map of Killarney

PLACES TO STAY
- 9 Neptune's Town Hostel
- 12 Four Winds Hostel
- 13 Killarney Townhouse
- 20 Belvedere Hotel
- 22 Súgán Hostel
- 23 Killarney Railway Hostel
- 27 West End House
- 29 Eviston House Hotel
- 34 Arbutus Hotel
- 52 Great Southern Hotel
- 55 Killarney Park Hotel

PLACES TO EAT
- 1 Gaby's Restaurant
- 2 Bricín Restaurant
- 3 Foley's Restaurant
- 4 Swiss Barn Restaurant
- 5 Green Onion Café
- 8 Allegro Restaurant
- 14 Grunt's Café
- 15 Country Kitchen
- 16 Busy B's Bistro
- 17 Big Ali's Diner
- 19 Sheila's Restaurant
- 30 Caragh Café
- 37 An Taelann Restaurant
- 38 Stella's Restaurant
- 39 Flesk Restaurant
- 40 The Celtic Cauldron
- 41 Strawberry Tree Restaurant
- 49 Kiwi's Restaurant

PUBS
- 7 Courtney's
- 10 O'Connor's
- 21 Laurels
- 43 Kiely's Bar
- 44 Scott's Gardens
- 45 Killarney Grand

OTHER
- 6 O'Sullivan's Bike Hire
- 11 St Mary's Cathedral
- 18 Bike Hire
- 24 Entrance to Killarney National Park & Deenagh Lodge
- 25 Pedestrian Entrance to National Park
- 26 Shell Petrol Station
- 28 Post Office
- 31 Killarney Bookshop
- 32 O'Neill's Fishing Tackle & Bike Hire
- 33 Music Kingdom
- 35 Bus Station
- 36 Railway Station
- 42 Laundrette
- 46 Tourist Office & Town Hall
- 47 St Mary's Church
- 48 American Express
- 50 Museum of Irish Transport
- 51 Destination Killarney, Lake Tours
- 53 Jaunting Cars Pick-up Point
- 54 Cinema

Expect to pay up to IR£60 a double in smarter guesthouses like *Kathleen's Country House* (☎ 32810), 3km out of town on the Tralee road.

Hotels Places costing between IR£60 and IR£90 for a double include *Eviston House* (☎ 31640; fax 33685) and the *Belvedere* (☎ 31133), both in New St. Also central is the *Arbutus* (☎ 31307; fax 34033) on College St, with a friendly atmosphere. The imposing *Great Southern* (☎ 31611; fax

31642), built for the convenience of Victorian travellers opposite the railway station, falls into this price range.

Moving into the IR£100-plus range there's *Killarney Ryan* (☎ 31555; fax 32438) on the Cork road. Even posher and plusher is the *Killarney Park* (☎ 35555; fax 35266) in Kenmare Place.

Along Muckross Rd the *Gleneagle* (☎ 31870; fax 32646) has all sorts of facilities: squash, tennis, pitch & putt, and a range of eateries. Closer to town on the same road the sedate *Cahernane* (☎ 31895; fax 34340) was built in 1877 for the earl of Pembroke. The *Lake Hotel* (☎ 31035; fax 31902) has a stunning lakeside setting and its own Victorian jaunting car. Rooms cost IR£55/80 in high season.

Places to Eat
The more expensive restaurants tend to hug the north end of High St. For cheaper eats, head east to Main St or turn down New St.

Cafés & Takeaways For breakfast, lunchtime sandwiches or a salad try *Grunts Café* on New St or the *Country Kitchen* almost next door.

Near the Neptune Hostel in New St *Big Ali's Diner* is good for pizza, soup and burgers, while *Busy B's Bistro*, above Sheahan's Meat Centre has a long list of cheap dishes such as chicken curry and shepherd's pie, for under IR£5; it stays open until midnight Monday to Wednesday and until 2.30 am for the rest of the week. Duck down Flemings Lane off High St for the *Green Onion Café*, with a good choice of soups, sandwiches and cakes. It opens at 11 am.

Mid-Range Restaurants In High St the *Allegro* does basic pizza, pasta and burgers. Near the tourist office on Main St, *Stella's* is a straightforward '& chips' type place with an IR£9.95 set dinner and main courses around IR£5 to IR£10. Around the corner on New St, the *Caragh Café* is similar. Farther down High St, *Sceilig* is more upmarket, with pizza, pasta and specials at IR£6. A few

doors down, the similarly priced *Sheila's* opens from 6 to 10 pm.

The vegetarian *An Taelann* (☎ 33083) is tucked down Bridewell Lane, off New St, just past the post office. The inviting *Bricín*, above a craftshop in High St, does boxties for IR£8.50 and several vegetarian options. The *Swiss Barn* (☎ 36044) in High St serves good Swiss specialities from IR£12.50 to IR£19.50; until 7.30 pm a set menu costs IR£8.20.

At *Kiwi's Restaurant* (☎ 34694), in the lane that joins East Avenue Rd with College St, you can bring your own wine to accompany tourist meals at IR£11 and IR£13. It's closed Sunday to Tuesday.

Expensive Restaurants At many of the restaurants along High St dinner will cost in excess of IR£15. At the top end of the street *Foley's* (☎ 31217) offers mainly seafood. At nearby *Gaby's* (☎ 32519) a Kerry shellfish platter of oysters, crab claws, lobster and other delicacies costs IR£22.40. The slightly less expensive *Flesk* has an impressively lengthy menu, also concentrating on seafood; eat between 5.30 and 6.30 pm to qualify for a IR£2 discount. The delightful *Strawberry Tree* in Plunkett St does promising organic and wholefood dishes for around IR£16. Almost next door *The Celtic Cauldron* (☎ 36821) does galettes from IR£7.75 and vegetarian and non-vegetarian Celtic platters, with a variety of items culled from the culinary traditions of Scotland, Ireland, Wales and Brittany.

Entertainment
Many Killarney pubs have live music although it's often very tourist-oriented. If you can't bear entertainment of the 'And this is for all the Canadians/Germans/Scots/Australians, in the audience' variety, *The Laurels* on Main St won't be for you. Still, if the mood should so take you, follow the coach-party hordes and expect to pay a IR£3 cover charge. *Scott's Gardens*, between College St and East Avenue Rd, also has music nightly, as does the *Danny Mann Lounge* in Eviston House Hotel.

For something a bit more authentic try *O'Connor's* on High St or *Courtney's*, across the road. Other pubs worth trying include *Charlie Foley's* on New St, *Kiely's Bar* on College St and the *Killarney Grand* on Main St. There's no music at the tiny *Strawberry Tree* in Plunkett St but its spit-and-sawdust appearance makes a pleasant backdrop for a few pints.

From April to October the *Killarney Manor Banquet* (☎ 31551) offers dinner and musical entertainment for around IR£30; reservation is advisable as coach parties often fill the place.

Killarney Cineplex in East Avenue Rd has four screens; for programme details phone ☎ 37007.

Getting There & Away

Air Kerry airport (☎ 066-64644) is at Farranfore, about 15km north of Killarney off the N22. There are direct Aer Lingus flights to Dublin, and Manx Airlines flights to Luton and Manchester.

It's also possible to fly direct from London Stansted to Kerry airport. Call Ryanair (☎ 01-609-7800) for details.

Bus Bus Éireann (☎ 34777) operates from next to the railway station, with regular links to Tralee (IR£4, 30 minutes), Cork (IR£8.80), Dublin (IR£14), Galway (IR£13), Limerick (IR£9.30), Waterford (IR£13) and Rosslare (IR£15). There's also a service to London via Cork and Waterford, leaving at 2.35 pm daily.

From late May to late September, the Ring of Kerry has its own service, departing Killarney at 8.45 am and 1.30 pm (no early bus on Sunday in May or September) for Killorglin, Cahirsiveen, Waterville, Caherdaniel, Sneem and back to Killarney.

Train Travelling by train to Cork involves changing at Mallow, but there's a direct route to Dublin via Limerick. Phone ☎ 31067 for details.

Getting Around

Bicycles are ideal for exploring the scattered sights of the Killarney area, many of them only accessible by bike or on foot. Several places hire bikes at around IR£5 a day. There's O'Sullivan's (☎ 31282) in Pawn Office Lane off High St, and The Laurels pub has its own bike hire (☎ 32578) in Old Market Lane alongside the pub. O'Neill's (☎ 31970) on Plunkett St has children's bikes and will deliver free to your accommodation. Most hostels also do bike hire.

If you're not on two wheels, Killarney's traditional transport is the horse-drawn jaunting car, which comes with a driver known as a *jarvey*. The pick-up point is on East Avenue Rd just past the tourist office but they also congregate in the N71 car park opposite Muckross House and at the Gap of Dunloe. Trips cost IR£12 to IR£35, depending on distance, and the traps carry four people.

AROUND KILLARNEY
Organised Tours

Deros Tours, opposite the Killarney tourist office, does coach trips around the Ring of Kerry (IR£10) and Dingle Peninsula (IR£12); unless you're really pushed for time these make for too rushed a way to do justice to the scenery. For organised horse-riding trips contact O'Sullivan's Killarney Riding Stables (☎ 31686) or Rockland Stables (☎ 32592). For information on tours within Killarney National Park, see that section.

Killarney National Park

Killarney's 10,236-hectare national park extends to the south-west of town, with a pedestrian entrance immediately opposite St Mary's Cathedral and another (for drivers) off the N71. Enclosed within the Park are beautiful Lough Leane (the Lower Lake or 'Lake of Learning'), Muckross Lake and the Upper Lake, as well as the Mangerton, Torc and Shehy peaks and the Purple Mountains. This is wonderful walking and biking country, although there are also specific sights, including the restored Ross Castle, the monastic ruins on Inisfallen Island, and Knockreer and Muckross Houses with their fine gardens. A herd of deer live in the park

KERRY

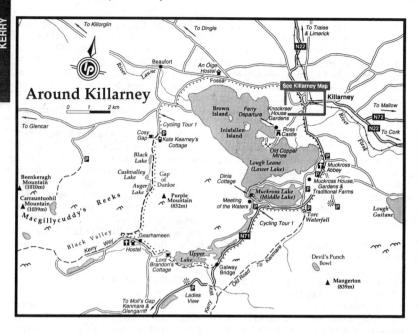

Around Killarney

which is also fun for birdwatchers. In 1981 the park was designated a UNESCO Biosphere Reserve.

Lunches and teas are available at thatched *Deenagh Lodge* just inside the gate opposite St Mary's Cathedral.

Knockreer House & Gardens Just inside the St Mary's Cathedral entrance to the park stands 18th century Knockreer House, surrounded by lovely gardens. The house is not currently open to the public.

Ross Castle Ross Castle dates back to the 15th century when it was a residence of the O'Donoghues. It was the last place in Munster to succumb to Cromwell's forces under the command of Ludlow.

According to prophecy, the castle would only be captured from the water, so in 1652 Ludlow had floating batteries brought upriver from Castlemaine, then transported overland before launching them on to the

lake. Seeing the prophecy about to be fulfilled, the defenders reportedly surrendered promptly.

The castle has been restored by Dúchas and entrance is IR£2.50/1. It's a 2.4km walk from the St Mary's Cathedral park entrance to Ross Castle. If you're driving from Killarney, turn right opposite the Esso garage at the start of the Kenmare road, just past the roundabout. The castle is at the end of the road near the car park.

Hour-long **lake cruises** depart from Ross Castle daily 10.30 am to 5.45 pm. Bookings can be made at the tourist office or with Destination Killarney (☎ 32638) at Scotts Gardens or Killarney Watercoach Cruises (☎ 31068), 3 High St. Out of season you can buy the ticket on the boat.

Inisfallen Island The first monastery on the island is said to have been founded by St Finian the Leper in the 7th century. The island's fame dates from the early 13th century when the *Annals of Inisfallen* were written here. The Annals, now in the Bodleian Library at Oxford, remain a vital source of information for early Irish history. There are ruins of a 12th century oratory with a carved Romanesque doorway and of a later monastery built on the site.

From Ross Castle, boats can be hired to row to the island. Alternatively boatmen charge passengers IR£3 each for the crossing. Some Gap of Dunloe boat and bus tours also stop at the island.

Muckross House, Gardens & Traditional Farms The core of Killarney National Park is the Muckross Estate, donated to the State by Arthur Bourn Vincent in 1932. Muckross House opens to the public and unusually you can walk around the rooms, with their faded 19th century fittings, free of guided tours or over-intrusive custodians. Some of the rooms contain exhibits on 19th century Kerry housing, the Vincent family and once-fashionable bog oak jewellery. You can inspect a variety of crafts including bookbinding and stone-cutting in the basement. It's open daily 9 am to 5.30 pm, November through February, to 6 pm in March through June, and to 7 pm in July and August. Entry is IR£3.30/1.50.

The beautiful gardens laid out by Arthur Bourn Vincent slope down to the lake and incorporate an arboretum. A block behind the house contains a restaurant and craft shop. Jaunting cars wait outside to run you around the park.

Immediately east of Muckross House are the **Muckross Traditional Farms**, reproduction Kerry farmhouses of the 1930s complete with chickens, pigs, cattle and horses. You can walk round the circuit or save your legs and use the 'vintage coach' that shuttles between the buildings. The site opens 1 to 6 pm daily in May, and 10 am to 7 pm June through September. Tickets cost the same as for Muckross House but combined tickets for the two properties work out cheaper at IR£5/2.75.

Muckross House is 5km from town. Vehicle access is about 1km beyond the

Muckross Park Hotel on the N71 Kenmare road. During the summer a tourist bus leaves for the house at 1.45 pm from outside O'Connor's pub, returning at 5.15 pm (IR£4 return). The house is also included in some day tours of Killarney.

If you're walking or cycling to Muckross there's a cycle track alongside the Kenmare Rd for most of the first 2km. A path then turns right into Killarney National Park. Following this path, after 1km you'll come to **Muckross Abbey** which was founded in 1448 and torched by Cromwell's troops in 1652. Look out for fine black Kerry cattle with white horns in fields nearby. Muckross House is another 1.5km from the abbey ruins.

A day trip around Killarney National Park involving a woodland walk and a boat trip on Muckross Lake and Lough Leane leaves from Muckross House at 10.30 am.

From Muckross House, there's a 3.7km walkable or cyclable track round the north shore of Middle Lake to the **Meeting of the Waters**, where it joins the Upper Lake. Nearby *Dinis Cottage* serves teas in a 200-year-old hunting lodge. Check the graffiti etched in the window ... the oldest dates back to 1816. From the Meeting it's another 1.5km back onto the N71 Kenmare Rd.

Warning for Cyclists If you're planning to cycle round Middle Lake, note that you should only do this in an anti-clockwise direction (ie. from Muckross House towards Meeting of the Waters and not vice versa). Nasty accidents involving broken limbs have occurred when two cyclists travelling at speed in opposite directions have collided on corners.

Gap of Dunloe Technically the Gap of Dunloe is outside the national park but as most people start or end their visit to it in the park details are included here.

In high summer, the Gap is Killarney tourism at its worst. Every day cars and buses disgorge countless visitors at Kate Kearney's cottage. They then proceed to pay IR£25 for a one-hour horse-and-trap ride through the

Gap (no cars allowed in summer). You could also walk through the narrow gorge to the Black Valley Hostel at the other end, but don't do this in summer if you want to be alone.

The best way to see the Gap is to hire a bike and cycle to Ross Castle, then take the boat across the lake to Lord Brandon's Cottage and cycle down through the Gap and back into town via the N72 and a path through the golf course. Including bike hire, this should cost you about IR£11.50.

The boat trip alone justifies the trip. It lasts 1½ hours and passes through all three lakes, with lovely views of the surrounding mountains and of the Meeting of the Waters and Ladies View, which was much enjoyed by Queen Victoria's ladies-in-waiting who gave it its name. Lunches and teas are available at *Kate Kearney's Cottage* (or at the *Cosy Gap* café opposite) and at *Lord Brandon's Cottage*.

Organised Gap of Dunloe tours – by bus to Kate Kearney's Cottage, then by horse, bike or jaunting car through the Gap, finishing with a boat trip back to Killarney – can be booked through the tourist office, Castlelough Tours at O'Connor's Pub (☎ 32496), the Killarney Boat & Tour Centre (☎ 31068), or Deros Tours (☎ 31251). The basic trip costs IR£13 return, plus another IR£10 for a seat in a jaunting car or IR£12 for a horse.

Cycling Tours

Two possible cycle tours are marked on the Around Killarney map. One is an adventurous 30km ride via the Gap of Dunloe and Black Valley Hostel, the last third of this journey best undertaken on a dry day. A longer trip is an 80km journey via Lake Acoose and Moll's Gap. Its route is marked on the Ring of Kerry map. See the Activities chapter for more details.

The Ring of Kerry seems the obvious choice for a long cycle but can be busy with traffic. Cutting across the peninsula between Killorglin and Waterville via the Ballaghbeama Pass is highly recommended.

Kerry Way

See the Activities chapter for details of the 215km Kerry Way which starts and ends in Killarney.

Killarney to Kenmare

The N71 links Killarney to Kenmare, with spectacular lake and mountain scenery along the way. Two km from the entrance to Muckross House a path leads 200m to the pretty **Torc Waterfall**. After another 8km you come to **Ladies View**, with fine views along the Upper Lake. There's another fine viewpoint 5km further along at **Moll's Gap**, with a branch of Avoca Handweavers (see Wicklow Town in the County Wicklow chapter). As so often happens, the inviting café buys spectacular views for its diners at the price of inflicting an eyesore on those outside.

Ring of Kerry

The Ring of Kerry, the 179km circuit round the Iveragh Peninsula, is one of Ireland's premier tourist attractions, partly because its width makes it more accessible to coaches than the narrower peninsulas to the north and south. Although it can be 'done' in a day by car or bus, or three days by bike, the more time you take the more you'll enjoy it. Getting off the beaten tourist track is also worthwhile. The Ballaghbeama Pass cuts across the peninsula's central highlands with some spectacular views and remarkably little traffic.

Tour buses approach the Ring in an anticlockwise direction. In high season it's hard to know which is more unpleasant – driving round behind them or travelling in the opposite direction and coming up against them on blind corners. Note that petrol gets more expensive the further west you go; fill up before setting out.

Although the scenery on the Ring is beautiful, some will prefer the Beara or Mizen peninsulas, partly because the views are even more striking, partly because they're so

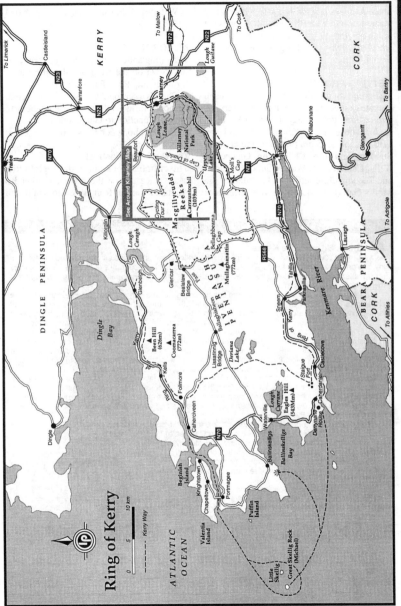

Ring of Kerry

KERRY

much less touristy, with classier hotels and places to eat. It's worth noting that things get much quieter at the west end of the Iveragh, when you leave the Ring of Kerry for the Skerrig Ring.

GETTING AROUND

Mid-May to mid-September Bus Éireann operates a specific Ring of Kerry bus service, two or three times a day (twice on Sunday). In June buses leave Killarney at 8.30 am, 1.30 pm and 3.45 pm (9.40 am and noon on Sunday), and stop at Killorglin, Glenbeigh, Kells, Cahirciveen, Waterville, Caherdaniel and Sneem before returning to Killarney via Moll's Gap (the 3.45 pm service terminates

at Waterville). For more details ring ☎ 064-34777.

KILLORGLIN

Travelling anticlockwise from Killarney, the first town on the Ring is Killorglin, famed for its annual Puck Fair Festival.

There's a seasonal tourist office in a circular booth to the right of the roundabout for the road junction to Glenbeigh.

The telephone code is ☎ 066.

The Puck Fair Festival

This rumbustious three-day celebration takes place during the second weekend in August. It derives from the custom of install-

---

Apartheid Without the Name

As you travel round Ireland, you can hardly help noticing the little huddles of caravans clustered in lay-bys on the outskirts of towns. These are home to many of the country's estimated 30,000 tinkers (or travellers, as many prefer to be called these days), a group so unpopular with society at large that they might as well be lepers.

There are many theories to explain the tinkers' origins. Some suggest that they're descendants of children left orphaned by the Famine of the mid-19th century, others that they're descendants of families driven westwards by Oliver Cromwell in the 17th century. However, study of their language suggests that the tinkers have been around for much longer than this and that they may actually be descendants of Bronze Age tinsmiths and related to Europe's other gypsy and nomadic groups.

Until recently, tinkers had a distinct place in society. Before the days of Tupperware, their tin receptacles had a real value, as did their donkeys and mules before the advent of tractors. Until radio and TV came along, villagers also saw their arrival in the district as a way of keeping in touch with what was happening in the world outside. Now, however, all these roles have vanished.

Despite the apparent poverty of the families you see in the lay-bys and the beggars on the streets, some tinkers actually make a good living from the scrap business or from dealing in secondhand cars. Others sell copper or the lead from old car batteries. A few have even grown wealthy trading in antiques. But even when they own fine houses, most still keep their caravans and spend part of every year on the road.

The tinkers have a dismal reputation for drinking and fighting (although they would argue that this is a fine case of the pot and the kettle), and inevitably there are complaints that they leave sites dirty and strewn with litter. Community ties remain very strong, families of 12 children are still common, and single parents are almost unheard of ... perhaps not surprisingly since many girls are married as soon as they turn 16.

But the tinkers face an uphill struggle to lead worthy lives. Pubs often refuse to serve them and hotels will turn away bookings for wedding receptions if it's suspected that the happy couple are actually travellers. When their children are admitted to mainstream schools, most other parents forbid their offspring to mix with them, thus depriving them of the social benefits of education. As a result, special schools are sometimes set up for travelling children, guaranteeing that integration doesn't take place. ■

ing a billy goat (a puck), horns festooned in ribbons, on a pedestal in the town centre and leaving it there while everyone takes advantage of the special licensing hours. Pubs stay open till 3 am, although it often seems that they simply serve for three days nonstop. Accommodation is hard to come by if you haven't booked in advance.

Places to Stay
Camping Just under 2km from the bridge in Killorglin, on the road to Killarney, is the small family-oriented *West's Holiday Park* (☎ 61240), open from Easter through September. A hiker or cyclist will be charged IR£3.50 for their tent.

Hostel About 2km from the bridge, on the road to Tralee, the IHH's *Laune Valley Farm Hostel* (☎ 61488) comes complete with satellite TV. Dorm beds cost IR£6 or IR£7, doubles from IR£16.

B&Bs *Riverside House* (☎ 61184) has beds for IR£16, or on the Killarney road you could try *Hillcrest* (☎ 61552) with singles/doubles for IR£21/32. Two km out on the Tralee Rd *Hillview Farm* (☎ 67117) has rooms from IR£20/30.

Hotel Centrally placed on Lower Bridge St, *Bianconi* (☎ 61146) has singles without bath from IR£20 and doubles with bath from IR£44 but not all the rooms justify the prices.

Places to Eat
Overlooking the roundabout junction for the road with Glenbeigh, *Bunkers*, a combined pub/restaurant/takeaway, does things like chicken & rice for IR£4.50. Less expensive is the *Starlite Diner* in the town centre, with chicken and chips for IR£3.95. *Nick's Restaurant & Bar* (☎ 61219) in Main St does seafood and steaks in the IR£10 to IR£16 bracket. A more interesting menu is at *Bianconi* (☎ 61146), a cosy pub and restaurant next door, with seafood and meat dinners from IR£13 and bar food available until 9.30 pm.

For something more sedate try a relaxing

dinner, country-house style, 8km out at *Caragh Lodge* (☎ 69115) for around IR£25.

Getting Around
Bikes can be hired from O'Shea's Cycle Centre (☎ 61919) in Lower Bridge St for IR£7/35 a day/week.

KERRY BOG VILLAGE MUSEUM
On the main road between Killorglin and Glenbeigh, the Kerry Bog Village Museum, beside the Red Fox pub, recreates the homes of 19th century turf cutters. Admission is IR£2.50/1 (which some readers have thought too much) and it's open 9 am to 6 pm throughout the tourist season. Look out for rare Kerry Bog Ponies, designated a rare breed in 1994, in a field behind the museum.

The *Red Fox* pub is a real tourist trap but does good pub food (turf cutter's delight is a steak burger for IR£4.75) and has live music every weekend. There's a useful noticeboard just inside the porch, with a phone to follow up interesting leads.

GLENBEIGH
Glenbeigh, 10km west of Killorglin, nestles at the foot of Seefin Mountain and has the attraction of a superb Blue Flag beach (unpolluted and safe for swimming with lifeguards on duty during the day). The 5km of Rossbeigh Strand look across to the Dingle Peninsula and even with a campsite in the vicinity it's easy to find a quiet spot. Swimming is safe and the mud flats off the eastern spit of land make good birdwatching territory. To get there, bear right for 3km at the Y-junction at the Cahirciveen end of town.

Places to Stay
Camping *Glenross Caravan & Camping Park* (☎ 68451) is in town next to the Glenbeigh Hotel; two people with a tent and car will be charged IR£9, two people without a car and with or without a bike IR£7.50.

Hostel At the Killorglin end of town the *Hillside House Hostel* (☎ 68228) is the only available budget accommodation, charging IR£5 per night.

B&Bs In town, *Village House* (☎ 68128) has rooms from IR£25/36 while *Ocean Wave* (☎ 68249), a few doors away, charges from IR£21/32. *Ocean Star* (☎ 68123), 1km out, charges IR£20/30.

Hotels The *Towers Hotel* (☎ 68212), in the town centre, is cosy, relaxed and well used to families. Singles/doubles are from IR£47/64. The *Falcon Inn* (☎ 68215) is at the Cahirciveen end of town, with rooms from IR£25/40, while the *Glenbeigh* (☎ 68333) is by the side of the road to Killarney with rooms from IR£25/42.

Places to Eat

There's very little inexpensive food other than in the pubs. Out at the beach the *Ross Inn* is worth a try.

The three hotels all have restaurants for dinner. The fresh seafood at the *Glenbeigh* is excellent, the atmosphere a little quieter than the others and a set dinner costs IR£18.50. Set dinners are IR£20 at the *Towers* and IR£16.50 at the *Falcon Inn*.

Entertainment

The *Towers* and *Glenbeigh* hotels have music in their bars, while the *Ross Inn* has bands.

KELLS

Near Kells, between Glenbeigh and Cahirciveen, the route of the old Great Southern & Western Railway (a branch line which ran from Killorglin to Valentia Harbour Station, just west of Cahirciveen, and closed in 1960) can be seen on the hillside, with its tunnels and retaining walls. The small beach near Kells is 3km off the road, but doesn't look too clean.

The telephone code is ☎ 066.

Places to Stay

The *Kells Bay Caravan & Camping Park* (☎ 77647) is signposted 1.5km off the road. *Mrs Golden* (☎ 77601) at the post office does B&B as does *Seaview* (☎ 77610) down by the beach. Both charge around £15 a head.

Places to Eat

Thatched *Caitin Beatear's* is a roadside pub and restaurant which draws in the coach parties. All year round it serves soup and sandwich lunches but in July and August Irish stew and seafood feature on the menu. Music sessions are also held throughout the summer. Snacks and tourist information are available at *Pat's* equally touristy craft shop at the Cahirciveen end of Kells.

CAHIRCIVEEN

As late as 1815, Cahirciveen (or Cahirsiveen) only had five houses but this is now one of the larger settlements along the Ring, even if it still remains more or less one long street.

Daniel O'Connell was born near here. The ruins of his home can still be seen to the left of the new bridge coming into town from the Kells end and the large church in the centre of town is called the O'Connell Memorial Holy Cross.

Information

The tourist office (☎ 066-72589) in The Barracks (see below) keeps the same hours as the heritage centre. Coming from the Kells end of town turn right at the junction of Bridge and Church Sts. The tourist office sells an O'Connell Heritage Trail leaflet for IR£1. The four-mile trail should take 2½ hours to complete.

The telephone code is ☎ 066.

Continue across the bridge for White Strand, about 5km away and safe for swimming.

The Barracks

This heritage centre is superbly situated in what was once an intimidating Royal Irish Constabulary (RIC) barracks. The building was burned down in 1922 by anti-Treaty forces but has now been reconstructed to its remarkable state. The story goes that the plans for this building got mixed up with ones intended for India; when you see the place you might believe this particular piece of blarney.

The exhibits concentrate on Daniel

O'Connell, other subjects of local and national interest. June to September a coffee shop serves simple meals. It's open from May through September, Monday to Saturday, 10 am to 6 pm (Sunday from 1 pm); the rest of the year it's open Monday to Friday 9.30 am to 5.30 pm. Admission is IR£3/1.50.

Places to Stay

Camping *Mannix Point Camping & Caravan Park* (☎ 72806), a 15-minute walk from town, is well run and charges a flat rate of IR£3.25 per person, including showers.

Hostel The IHH's *Sive Hostel* (☎ 72717) is at the east end of the long main street. Beds are IR£6.50 and there's one double for IR£16. Skellig trips can be arranged here. There's also the IHO *Mortimer's* (☎ 72338) in the centre with beds for IR£6.

B&Bs *Mount Rivers* (☎ 72509), a striking old house on the road east to Killarney, costs from IR£21.50/32. Close to each other at the Valentia end of town, *Castleview* (☎ 72252) and *San Antoine* (☎ 72521) have beds for around IR£16 a head.

Hotel *Cahirciveen Park* (☎ 72543) in Valentia Rd does singles/doubles for IR£45/70 without breakfast in peak season.

Places to Eat

Grudles in the town centre is a small but cosy café serving fresh fish for IR£5.50. *Red Rose Restaurant* in Church St opposite the O'Connell Memorial Church will do you a salmon sandwich and salad for IR£3.95. *An Cupán* does breakfast for IR£3.75 and stays open for teas and snacks until 5.30 pm (4pm on Saturday).

The *Old School House* (☎ 72426) has a reputation for first-class seafood, at around IR£20 a head. *The Point Bar* restaurant serves excellent seafood and salads with lovely views of Valentia.

Entertainment

At the Glenbeigh end of town the *Shebeen* is pretty touristy so you might prefer *Mike Murt's* virtually next door. The *Sceilig Rock Bar* has traditional music, while the *Harp* has regular discos. Even without music the *Anchor* is pretty atmospheric. If you don't like any of these, there are almost 50 more to choose from!

Getting There & Away

Apart from the regular Ring of Kerry bus service, a private bus (☎ 72249) links Cahirciveen and Killarney, leaving the pier at 5.15 pm. The single/return fare is IR£5/8.

From April through to September ferries (☎ 76141) operate a shuttle service to Valentia Island from Renard Point, just west of Cahirciveen. The five-minute crossing costs IR£3 for a car, IR£2 for a pedestrian or cyclist. Services operate between 7.30 and 10.30 pm Monday to Saturday, between 8.30 am and 10.30 pm Sunday.

Getting Around

Bikes can be hired through the Raleigh scheme from Casey Cycles & Gas Supplies (☎ 72474) in New St.

PORTMAGEE

Portmagee (Port Mhic Aoidh) is a string of houses, restaurants and pubs overlooking the Maurice O'Neill bridge to Valentia Island. Fishing is still an important activity but just as important is the business of ferrying tourists out to the Skellig Islands, with roughly half the licensed boats leaving from here.

If you have to wait around for good enough weather to make the crossing *The Moorings* (☎ 77108) has B&B for IR£21/34 a single/double. The attached restaurant has an early-bird menu from 6 to 7 pm for IR£13. *The Fisherman's Bar* is popular for lunches.

The *Bridge Bar* is also worth checking out and sometimes has free set-dancing lessons.

VALENTIA ISLAND

Valentia may be only 11km long and three wide but it doesn't feel like an island, especially if you come by road. It's a pretty low-key place; unless you're into scuba-diving, the Skellig Experience is about the only real distraction.

KERRY

Most visitors reach the island via the long bridge from Portmagee, turning right at the other end for Chapeltown and Knightstown.

The telephone code is ☎ 066.

The Skellig Experience
Immediately across the bridge you'll see the Skellig Experience on the left-hand side of the road. It contains interesting exhibitions on the life and times of the monks, the history of the lighthouses on Skellig Michael, and the wildlife. A 15-minute audiovisual show describes the monastery's history. If you're planning a trip to the Skelligs it's worth coming here for background info. If the weather's bad this may be as close as you get to the islands.

Admission costs IR£3/1.50. Teas and light meals are available in *Fionan's Kitchen* at the back.

Chapeltown
Chapeltown is just a scattering of houses with a hostel and garage. The *Ring Lyne Hostel* (☎ 76103) has dorm beds for IR£6 and doubles for IR£14. Meals are available in the attached bar and restaurant; mussels in garlic sauce cost IR£5. The *Ring Lyne* also has musical sessions after 9.30 pm most evenings.

KNIGHTSTOWN
Valentia's main population centre is Knightstown, 3km from the Ring of Kerry road and accessible by ferry from near Cahirciveen. It's named after the Knight of Kerry who once owned it.

Heritage Centre
As you leave Knightstown you come to a fork in the road. Take the right fork and almost immediately you'll see the heritage centre in an old National School building on the right. The main item of interest is the history of the Valentia-US cable. Valentia was chosen as the site for the first transatlantic telegraph cable, and when the connection was made in 1858, it put Cahirciveen in direct contact with New York even though it had no connection with Dublin! The link

worked for 27 days before failing, but went back into action some years later. The telegraph station was in operation until 1966.

The centre opens April to September, 11 am to 5 pm. Admission costs IR£1/50p.

Quarry & Grotto
In the 19th century slate quarrying was an important Valentia industry, with boats from the nearby harbour carrying away the roofing slates and flagstones. If you ever wondered what Charing Cross railway station in London and San Salvador station in El Salvador had in common, the answer is that they were both roofed with Valentia slate. A disused quarry tunnel was converted into a religious grotto in 1954, but despite this the place retains a sense of history.

Angling & Diving
For sea angling trips contact Dan McCrohan (☎ 76142). There are three reliable diving centres: Des Lavelle (☎ 76124), the Valentia Hyperbaric Diving Centre (☎ 76225) and the Dive Centre (☎ 76204).

Places to Stay
Hostels The huge, dilapidated *Royal Pier Hostel* (☎ 76144) overlooking the harbour has dorm beds for IR£6.50. You can book Skellig trips here.

The seedy-looking An Óige *Valentia Island Hostel* (☎ 76141) occupies three of the former coastguard station cottages. Beds cost IR£5.50/4.50.

B&Bs Two km out of Knightstown towards Chapeltown, *Glenreen Heights* (☎ 76241) has singles/doubles from IR£19/28. By the waterfront, *Lavelle's* (☎ 76124), once part of the original transatlantic telegraph station, is now a diving centre, with rooms for IR£16/29.

Places to Eat
At the western end of Knightstown the *Islander Café* has a set dinner for IR£13.50 between 6 and 7 pm. Next door the *Gallery Kitchen* (☎ 76105), a combined restaurant, wine bar and sculpture gallery, is more invit-

ing; pastas in interesting sauces cost from IR£6.90.

For pub food, *O'Conaill's/Boston's* serves popular home-cooked dishes and is especially lively on Friday and Sunday.

If you drive out towards the quarry, then turn right downhill for 500m you'll come to the tiny arty *Lighthouse Café* ('the most westerly café in Europe') which does tea and cake. An imaginative dinner menu offers things like chicken kebab and salad for IR£4.50 or vegetable tortilla for IR£5.50 until 8.30 pm

Getting There & Away
The ugly Maurice O'Neill bridge at Portmagee links Valentia Island to the mainland. Pedestrians, cyclists and motorists can also cross by ferry from Renard Point near Cahirciveen (see Getting There & Away in that section for details).

SKELLIG ISLANDS
A boat trip to the Skellig Islands (Oileáin na Scealaga), 12km out in the Atlantic Ocean, is one of the highlights of a trip to Ireland. The 217m jagged rock of Skellig Michael, the larger of the two islands, looks like the last place on earth that anyone would try to land, let alone establish a community. Yet early Christian monks survived here from the 7th until the 12th or 13th century. They were influenced by the Coptic Church founded by St Anthony in the deserts of Egypt and Libya, and their desire for solitude led them to this remote, most westerly corner of Europe.

After the introduction of the Gregorian calendar in 1582, Skellig Michael became a popular spot for weddings. Marriages were forbidden during Lent, but since Skellig used a different calendar, a quick trip over to the islands allowed those unable to wait for Easter to tie the knot. In time these annual pilgrimages became an excuse for other jollifications, and crates of alcohol were hauled over to facilitate the merrymaking. There's even a record of the police being called to a spot of bother on the island.

In the 1820s two lighthouses were built on

Skellig Michael, together with the road that runs around the base.

Birdlife
If you can't get to the Galapagos then a trip to the Skelligs offers a taster of the peculiar pleasure of spying on nesting seabirds. From the boat, look out for diminutive storm petrels, black birds that dart around over the water like swallows, and for yellow-headed gannets with a wingspan of 107 cm. Kittiwakes – lemon-beaked seagulls with black-tipped wings – are easy to see and hear around the covered walkway just after stepping off the boat. They winter at sea but then come to Skellig Michael in their thousands to breed between March and August.

Further up the rock you'll see snub-nosed fulmars, and black and white guillemots and razorbills. Look out, also, for the delightful puffins with their multicoloured beaks and waddling gait. Puffins lay one egg in May at the end of a burrow and parent birds can be seen guarding their nests. Puffins only stay until the first week or two of August.

Skellig Michael
The monastic buildings are perched on a saddle in the rock, some 150m above sea level. The oratories and beehive cells vary in size, the largest cell having a floor space of 4.5m by 3.6m and they're all astounding. The projecting stones on the outside have more than one possible explanation: steps to reach the top and release chimney stones, or maybe holding places for turf that covered the exterior. Some cells have interior rows of stones, and the guides who live on the rock mid-May through September will provide a possible explanation for these as well. They'll also point out the cistern in the rock for storing rainwater.

Little is known about the life of the monastery, but there are records of Viking raids in 812 and 823. Monks were killed or taken away but the community recovered and carried on. In the 11th century a rectangular oratory was added to the site, but although it was expanded in the 12th century, the monks abandoned the rock around this time, perhaps because of more than usually ferocious Atlantic storms.

In the 15th and 16th century the monastery had a brief flurry of new life as a pilgrimage centre.

You're asked to do your picnicking on the way up to the monastery or at Christ's Saddle just before the last flight of steps rather than among the ruins. This is aimed at keeping sandwich-loving birds and their droppings away from the monument.

Small Skellig
While Skellig Michael looks like two triangles linked by a spur, Small Skellig is longer, lower and much craggier. From a distance it looks as if someone had battered it with a feather pillow that burst. Close up you realise you're looking at a colony of 20,000 pairs of breeding gannets. Most boats circle the island so you can see them. Check beforehand if the boat will pause to look for basking seals.

Getting There & Away
Because of concerns for the fragility of Skellig Michael there are limits on how many people can visit on the same day. Nineteen boats are licensed to carry no more than 12 passengers each, so there should never be more than 250 people there at any one time. Because of these limits it's wise to book ahead in July and August, always bearing in mind that if the weather's bad the boats may not be able to sail.

You can depart from either Portmagee (and even Caherciveen), Ballinskelligs or Derrynane and the crossing usually costs IR£20 return. The boat owners will try and restrict you to two hours on the island, the bare minimum, on a good day, to see the monastery, look at the birds and have a picnic. The crossing from Portmagee takes 50 minutes. Bring stout shoes, something to eat and drink, and something waterproof to protect you and your bag from the boat's spray.

Some operators to try include Joe Roddy (☎ 066-74268), Sean Feehan (☎ 066-79182) and JB Walsh (☎ 066-79147) at Ballinskelligs; Brendan O'Keefe (☎ 066-

77103), Michael O'Sullivan (☎ 066-74255), Murphy's (☎ 066-77156) and Casey's (☎ 066-77125) at Portmagee; and Sean O'Shea (☎ 066-75129) at Derrynane, near Caherdaniel. Most pubs and B&Bs in the area will be able to point you in the right direction.

Warning A notice on the island warns of 'an element of danger' in visiting Skellig Michael. Although you could fall on the rocks or stone steps, the biggest element of danger seems attached to getting off the boat at the island. Make sure your shoes have a good grip.

WATERVILLE
This popular resort is a triangle of fairly tacky pubs, restaurants and B&Bs on a narrow bit of land between Ballinskelligs Bay and Lough Currane. Charlie Chaplin was probably the town's most famous visitor, and photographs of him can be seen in the Butler Arms pub.

The telephone code is ☎ 066.

Fishing
There are lots of angling possibilities around Waterville. Lough Currane has free fishing for sea trout while the Inny River is a breeding ground for wild salmon and trout. Sea angling takes in mackerel, pollack and shark. For information ask at O'Sullivan's, a tackle shop between the hostel and Silver Sands on the main street, or at the Lobster Bar (☎ 74183).

Places to Stay & Eat
The IHH's *Waterville Holiday Hostel* (☎ 74644), at the Cahirciveen end of town, has dorm beds for IR£6.50 and doubles for IR£16. *Waterville Caravan & Camping Park* (☎ 74191), 1km north of town off the main Cahirciveen road, is open from late March to mid-September. A hiker or cyclist pays IR£3.50 for their tent.

For B&B you'd be better off stopping before Waterville at the *Scariff Inn* (☎ 75143) on the Coomakesta Pass which boasts 'Ireland's best-known view' from its

Vista Bar. B&B costs IR£25/40 a single/ double and the restaurant serves things like Irish stew and seafood. Alternatively *The Old Cable House* (☎ 74233) is 1km north on the N70 with rooms for IR£20/36.

Most of Waterville's eating places are pretty indifferent but worth giving a whirl is *An Corcán* in Main St which opens until 9.30 pm and serves things like poached salmon as a change from the fry-ups.

The *Sheilin Restaurant* round the corner has a set tourist menu for IR£13.90 between 6 and 8 pm. The *Beachcove Café* beside the post office will do if you just want tea or coffee.

SKELLIG RING

The Skellig Ring is a scenic route that links Waterville with Portmagee via Ballinskelligs. Leaving Waterville, it begins with a turn to the left signposted after the church and a small bridge, and goes down to an unmarked junction: the short potholed road to the left goes to Ballinskelligs Bay, the road straight on goes to the Ballinskelligs departure point for the Skelligs, and a right turn eventually leads to Portmagee and more departures for the Skelligs. It's an enjoyable cycle route, but there are lots of small unmarked roads, making it easy to get lost.

Ballinskelligs Monastery & Bay

The exact relationship between this monastery and the one on Skellig Michael isn't clear. It was probably founded after the monks left Skellig in the 12th or 13th century. The sea is gradually wearing the ruins away and it's the sort of place that children like to explore. Take the road down to Ballinskelligs Bay and walk to the remains from there.

At the western end of this beautiful Blue Flag beach are the last remnants of a 16th century castle stronghold of the McCarthys.

Places to Stay & Eat

The An Oíge *Ballingskelligs Hostel* (☎ 066-79229) is reached by turning right at the small junction after passing the Sigerson Arms on the Skellig Ring; beds here cost IR£5.50/4.50. Overlooking the bay, the *Sigerson Arms* (☎ 066-79104) has half a dozen beds from IR£30 each. This is about the only place to find food before you reach Portmagee.

CAHERDANIEL

Caherdaniel is just a couple of streets but boasts a particularly important historic house and a choice of hostels.

The telephone code is ☎ 066.

Derrynane National Historic Park

Having grown rich on smuggling with France and Spain, the O'Connells bought Derrynane House and the surrounding parkland, evading official restrictions on the purchase of land by Catholics with the help of a co-operative Protestant.

Two km off the main Ring road, the house is largely furnished with items relating to Daniel O'Connell, the campaigner for Catholic emancipation. The dining room is full of early 19th century furniture and silver given to O'Connell by grateful Catholics. The drawing room is renowned for a table which was carved over a period of four years by two men. Upstairs you can view O'Donnell's deathbed. Most amazing of all is the recently restored triumphal chariot in which O'Connell rode around Dublin after his release from prison in 1844.

The adjoining parkland includes a sandy beach and Abbey Island, which can usually be reached on foot across the sand. The **chapel** which O'Connell had added to Derrynane House in 1844 is a copy of the ruined one on Abbey Island.

The house opens May to September, Monday to Saturday, 9 am to 6 pm, Sunday 11 am to 7 pm. It's closed November to March and during the remaining time it's open 1 to 5 pm only and closed Monday. Admission is IR£2/1. There's an excellent café serving scrumptious cakes.

To the left of the road leading down to the house look out for an **Ogham stone**.

Activities

Caherdaniel competes with Valentia as the

KERRY

diving base for the Iveragh Peninsula. Two companies offer courses and equipment hire. Derrynane Diving School (☎ 75110) offers a half-day discovery course for those without certificates. Skellig Aquatics opposite the Village Hostel organise a variety of outdoor courses including diving trips off the Skellig Islands, abseiling, rock climbing and hill walking. Contact Derrynane Sea Sports (☎ 75266) for canoeing, wind-surfing and water-skiing.

Places to Stay

Camping The *Wave Crest Caravan Park* (☎ 75188) has lots of facilities but only 10 tent pitches; with a car you'll pay IR£8.50, without just IR£3. Alternatively try the *Ocean Billow* (☎ 75188).

Hostels In the congested main street the IHH *Village Hostel* (☎ 75227) has dorm beds for IR£6.50. On the main Ring road, the *Traveller's Rest* (☎ 75175) has dorm beds for IR£6.50 and private rooms for IR£16, or there's the *Carrigbeg* (☎ 75229), 1km to the west, with dorm beds for IR£6 and private rooms for IR£14.

B&Bs & Hotels For B&B try *Mrs O'Sullivan* (☎ 75124), with singles/doubles from IR£19/28, or *The Olde Forge* (☎ 75140) for IR£22/32.

The smartest place around is the *Derrynane Hotel* (☎ 75136; fax 75160) with beds for IR£45/70 without breakfast in July and August.

Places to Eat

Across the road from the Village Hostel the *Courthouse Café* serves standard fry-ups. The *Stepping-Stone Restaurant* (☎ 75444) next door does more formal dinners for IR£12.

STAIGUE FORT

This 2000-year-old fort is one of Ireland's finest dry-stone buildings. Its 5m circular wall up to 4m thick is surrounded by a large bank and ditch, rather like at Grianan of Aileach in County Donegal although it hasn't been so thoroughly restored.

The fort probably dates from the 3rd or 4th century AD. Despite having sweeping views down to the coast it can't be seen from the sea. It may have been a communal place of refuge, or a royal residence as the sophisticated staircases incorporated into the walls suggest.

It's about 4km off the main road, reached by a country lane which narrows as it climbs to the site. In summer the road and car park become the scene of absurd traffic jams! An honesty box by the gate demands 50p for access to the land even though the fort is owned by Dúchas.

Where the road to the fort leaves the main road a **Staigue Fort Exhibition Centre** is attached to *Staigue Fort Hotel*. It's open from Easter through September daily 10 am to 9 pm and tells the story of the fort in models and audiovisuals. Admission costs IR£2/1.50.

SNEEM

Visitors have differing reactions to the oddly named town of Sneem (which is pronounced 'shneem', from the Irish *snaidhm*, meaning 'knot' or 'twist', from the snaky river). Some find it quaint, while others think it's sold its soul completely to tourism. Whatever you think, it's an hourglass-shaped village with two greens separated by a small bridge.

The small **museum** in the old courthouse west of the bridge looks like a cluttered antique shop inside. Theoretically it's open daily in summer, 10 am to 5.30 pm (closed 1 to 2 pm) for 50p.

The telephone code is ☎ 064.

Places to Stay

Camping Turn down past the bridge, near the church for the small campsite (☎ 45181). Campers can fish in the river nearby.

Hostel The *Harbour View* (☎ 45276) is a three minute walk from the village at the Kenmare end. Dorm beds are IR£7.50 and ensuite doubles in chalets IR£18; their decor is nothing special but they do boast extras like kettles in the room which not all B&Bs manage.

B&Bs The imposing *Old Convent House* (☎ 45181) next to the campsite is owned by the same family and has a fine riverside setting. Singles/doubles cost IR£21/32. *Derry East Farmhouse* (☎ 45193), 1km out of town on the road to Waterville, has singles/doubles from IR£14.50/33, and an evening meal for IR£13.

Hotel The *Great Southern* (☎ 45122; fax 45323) is a few km out on the Kenmare road at Parknasilla, and costs at least IR£137 for a double. Past guests include Charles de Gaulle, Princess Grace of Monaco and Bernard Shaw (who wrote most of *St Joan* here).

Places to Eat
To the east of the bridge *The Green House* does soup and sandwiches. On the other side *Riverside* and the *Village Kitchen* compete for the lunch trade. *The Blue Bull* facing the eastern green does pub food. *The Hungry Knight* is said to do fish & chips good enough to draw some French customers back year after year.

At the west end of the village *O'Sullivan's Sacre Coeur Restaurant* does seafood for around IR£10, a little less for meat dishes.

The *Pygmalion* at the Great Southern is the most prestigious restaurant on the Ring of Kerry. Set dinners cost IR£25.

Taking the N70 back to Kenmare you'll pass the *Vestry Restaurant* in a converted church off the right-hand side of the road. Dinner costs around IR£20.

Getting There & Away
Apart from the regular Ring of Kerry bus service, a bus links Kenmare to Sneem (35 minutes) twice a day from Monday to Saturday in July and August.

Getting Around
To the west of the bridge, Burns Bike Hire (☎ 45140) hires out bikes for IR£5.50 a day or IR£30 a week.

KENMARE
At the point where the Finnihy, Roughty and Sheen rivers empty into the River Kenmare, the pocket-sized town of Kenmare is ablaze with vivid yellows, greens, reds and blues. Outside July and August it's a sleepy place, its many restaurants and pubs waiting for the tourist onslaught.

For those with their own transport, Kenmare makes a pleasant alternative to Killarney as a base for visiting the Rings of Kerry and Beara.

Orientation & Information
In the 18th century Kenmare was laid out on an X-plan, with a market square in the centre and Fair Green nestling in the upper V. To the south, Henry and Main Sts are the primary shopping and eating/drinking thoroughfares, with Shelbourne St joining them up at the south end. The River Kenmare stretches out to the south, with glorious views in both directions.

The tourist office (☎ 064-41233), near Fair Green, opens Monday to Saturday from 9.15 am to 7 pm from mid-June through August (Sunday too in July and August). The rest of the year it closes at 5.30 pm. Pick up a free heritage trail leaflet showing places of historical interest.

The telephone code is ☎ 064.

Kenmare Heritage Centre
Behind the tourist office and open during the same hours, Kenmare Heritage Centre (☎ 41491) recounts the history of the town from its founding as Neidin by William Petty-Fitzmaurice in 1670. Particularly interesting is the information about the Kenmare Poor Clare Convent (still standing behind Holy Cross Church) which was founded in 1862 and provided local women with work as needlepoint lacemakers. Samples of their work are on display and more can be seen upstairs in the **Kenmare Lace & Design Centre**.

Also interesting is the story of Margaret Anna Cusack (1829-99), the 'Nun of Kenmare', an early advocate of women's rights who was eventually hounded out of

Kenmare as a political agitator, renounced Catholicism in favour of Protestantism and died, embittered, in Leamington, England.

Admission costs IR£2/1.

Other Attractions

South-west along Market Street and Pound Lane is the Bronze Age **Druid Circle**, the largest stone circle in south-west Ireland, with 15 stones ringing a 'boulder dolmen' or burial monument.

Holy Cross Church in Old Killarney Rd was built in 1864 and boasts a splendid wooden roof with 14 angels carved from Bavarian wood. **Our Lady's Well** is a holy well in a pretty flower garden. To find it walk down Pound Lane and turn right along the alley, following it round until it reaches a foot bridge. Cross the bridge, turn right and watch for the sign pointing to the right.

Seafari River Cruises (☎ 83171) depart from the pier near the suspension bridge to the south. Two-hour cruises round Upper Kenmare Bay cost IR£9.50/5. Four-hour cruises to Sneem Harbour or full-day cruises of Kilmakilloge Harbour are also possible.

Kenmare is ringed with lovely scenery and short **walks** can be made along the river or into the hills. The Kerry Way also passes through Kenmare (see the Activities chapter for more details). Kenmare Bookshop on Shelbourne St stocks *A Guide to Kenmare – Tuosist-Sneem* (IR£2), which shows possible walks in the area.

Walking Festival

During the last week of May, Kenmare hosts a Walking Festival when people can undertake a series of walks of varying difficulty around town. To join in you must pay IR£10 and register at a booth in the Square 30 minutes before the walk departs. Two-day classes in mountain skills, costing IR£40, are also organised. Accommodation in town is hard to come by at this time so be sure to book ahead. For more information phone ☎ 41682.

Places to Stay

Camping The *Ring of Kerry Caravan &* *Camping Park* (☎ 41366) is 5km west of town on the Sneem road. Large/small tents are IR£6.50/2 plus IR£1.50 per adult.

Hostels The pleasant IHH *Fáilte Hostel* (☎ 42333), at the junction of Henry and Shelbourne Sts, has a good kitchen and sitting room. Dorm beds cost IR£6.50, private rooms IR£9 a head. To gain access you may need to ring at the side door to Finnegan's Corner across the road. Seven km beyond Kenmare on the road to Killarney, behind a Catholic church, the *Bonane Hostel* (☎ 41098) has beds at IR£6; camping is possible but without the use of the kitchen.

B&Bs South of Kenmare a couple of B&Bs overlook the Kenmare River. *Sallyport House* (☎ 42066) has doubles for IR£60 and some delightful river views. *Ard Na Mara* (☎ 41399) on Pier Rd has similarly good views for IR£31 a double.

Beside Fair Green, *Rose Cottage* (☎ 41330) was where the original Poor Clare nuns stayed when they arrived in Kenmare in 1861. It has three doubles from IR£30 and one rather cramped single for IR£19.

Greenville (☎ 41769) overlooking the Kenmare Golf Club has doubles from IR£32.

Hotels Two of Ireland's most expensive hotels compete for business in Kenmare. The *Park* (☎ 41200; fax 41402) is the oldest with a superb interior full of antiques. *Sheen Falls Lodge* (☎ 41600; fax 41386) is next to the old Kenmare cemetery, with the remains of a 7th century church and a walk down to the sea. A double at either will set you back over IR£200.

The *Wander Inn* (☎ 41038), handily positioned in Henry St, charges from IR£16 a head. Across the road *Foley's* (☎ 41379) has singles/doubles for IR£25/37. The *Lansdowne Arms* (☎ 41368), at the junction of Main and Shelbourne Sts, dates back to the 18th century. It's not the most welcoming place but has rooms from IR£30/50.

Places to Eat

Most of Kenmare's eating places are in Henry and Main Sts. Most serve lunch and dinner, with prices rising considerably in the evening.

Cafés In Henry St, *La Brasserie* opens for uncomplicated breakfasts, lunches and dinners. *The New Delight* further south is a vegetarian café, open only until 5.30 pm, except in June, July and August when it reopens from 6.30 to 9.30 pm for dinner.

Foley's and *The Coachman* in Henry St do pub lunches and pricier dinners.

Restaurants The *Purple Heather Bistro* (☎ 41016) on Henry St does things like open crab sandwiches for IR£5.15. Its partner restaurant *Packies* (☎ 41508), further along the road, opens from 5.30 to 10 pm offering dishes like pasta in a blue cheese and pine nuts sauce for IR£8.90. Near the Fáilte hostel, *Virginia's* (☎ 41021) serves unfussy meals for under IR£10.

An Leath Phingin (☎ 41559) on Main St does hand-made pasta from IR£8.50. Arty *Giuliano's* at the top of Main St has pizzas from IR£4.95 (try the excellent Florence) and pasta from IR£4.50; there's even something for vegans here. Next door *D'Arcy's* (☎ 41589) has main dishes for around IR£13.

The Lime Tree (☎ 41225) is a delightful place in Shelbourne St with main dishes from IR£8.50. The building housing it was once the Lansdowne Estate office. Here 4616 people were given free passage to North America in the 1840s. It later became a school, hence the desks displaying the menus.

The restaurant at the Riversdale House (☎ 41299) hotel overlooks the Kenmare river. Dinner will set you back around IR£20 without wine.

Things to Buy

This is a good place to shop for real Irish crafts as opposed to the usual leprechaunery. Shops in Main, Henry and Shelbourne Sts sell fine knitwear, lace, linen and pottery, often at alarming prices. Sounds of Music in Henry St also has a good range of Irish tapes and CDs.

Getting There & Away

Apart from the main Ring of Kerry bus service there's a July and August service between Sneem and Kenmare. Buses stop outside Brennan's pub on Main St.

Getting Around

Finnegan's Corner (☎ 41083) is the Raleigh bike dealer, with bikes for IR£7/30 a day/week.

Beara Peninsula

Although the small north-eastern corner of this peninsula is in Kerry most of it is in County Cork. For the convenience of people travelling the Ring of Beara it's dealt with altogether in the County Cork chapter.

Tralee & North Kerry

The north Kerry landscape is pretty mediocre and many travellers rush through on their way to Clare via the Tarbert ferry. However, there are some places of historical interest and the coastal strip is popular with Irish holidaymakers.

TRALEE

Tralee (Trá Lí) has enough attractions to occupy a day or so but is also a useful stopover en route to the Dingle Peninsula as it's well stocked with hostels, restaurants and lively music pubs. In the last week of August the Rose of Tralee festival centres on a beauty contest and most B&Bs hike their prices by IR£3 or IR£4 for its duration.

Founded by the Normans in 1216, the town has a long history of rebellion. In the 16th century the last ruling earl of the Desmonds was captured and executed. His head was sent to Elizabeth I, who had it displayed

KERRY

on London Bridge. His property was given to Sir Edward Denny. The Desmond castle once stood at the junction of Denny St and the Mall. Any trace of medieval Tralee that survived the Desmond wars was razed in the Cromwellian period.

Orientation & Information
The tourist office (☎ 066-21288), at the back of Ashe Memorial Hall, opens all year; daily 9 am to 7 pm in July and August (closed Sunday in May and June). The Hall is named after Thomas Ashe, a Kerryman who led the largest Easter Rising action outside Dublin in 1916. He went on a hunger strike in prison but died from medical neglect in 1917 after being forcibly fed.

Tralee is fairly small and you'll find most things you need along The Mall and its continuation Castle St, and in wide, elegant Denny St with the tourist office at its southern end.

The telephone code is ☎ 066.

Kerry the Kingdom
Above the tourist office the Kerry County Museum gives a concise history of Ireland – with the emphasis on Kerry, of course. Downstairs visitors ride around a recreation of the walled town of Tralee in 1450 in time cars. Children love it and a commentary in eight languages is available.

The exhibition opens daily March through October, 10 am to 6 pm (7 pm in August), and 2 to 5 pm in November and December. It's closed in January and February. Admission is IR£5/2.75.

Steam Railway
Between 1891 and 1953 a narrow-gauge railway connected Tralee with Dingle. The first short leg of the journey, from Tralee to Blennerville, has been reopened and operates April to September. The train leaves Ballyard (☎ 27777) on the hour, 11 am to 5 pm, and the 20-minute journey costs IR£2.75/1.50.

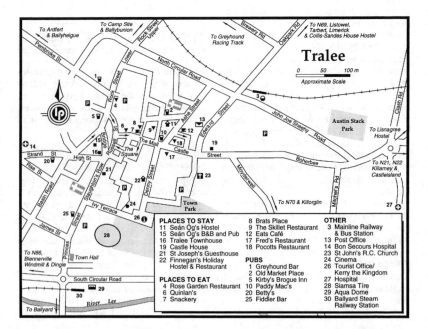

Tralee

0   50   100 m

Approximate Scale

PLACES TO STAY	PLACES TO EAT	OTHER
11 Seán Óg's Hostel	4 Rose Garden Restaurant	3 Mainline Railway
15 Seán Óg's B&B and Pub	6 Quinlan's	& Bus Station
16 Tralee Townhouse	7 Snackery	13 Post Office
19 Castle House	8 Brats Place	14 Bon Secours Hospital
21 St Joseph's Guesthouse	9 The Skillet Restaurant	23 St John's R.C. Church
22 Finnegan's Holiday	12 Eats Café	24 Cinema
Hostel & Restaurant	17 Fred's Restaurant	26 Tourist Office/
	18 Pocotts Restaurant	Kerry the Kingdom
		27 Hospital
	PUBS	28 Siamsa Tíre
	1 Greyhound Bar	29 Aqua Dome
	2 Old Market Place	30 Ballyard Steam
	5 Kirby's Brogue Inn	Railway Station
	10 Paddy Mac's	
	20 Betty's	
	25 Fiddler Bar	

Blennerville Windmill

One km south-west of town, Blennerville used to be the chief port of Tralee although it's long since silted up. A flour mill was built here in 1800 but fell into disuse by 1880. It has now been restored and is the largest working mill in Ireland or Britain. A short video tells its story and there are 40-minute guided tours.

The modern visitor centre detracts from views of the mill but houses an exhibition about the thousands of emigrants who boarded 'coffin ships' for a new life in the USA from what was then Kerry's largest embarkation point. Over the next few years visitors will be able to watch the building of a replica of the *Jeannie Johnston* which ferried several thousand emigrants to Baltimore, New York and Quebec in the mid-19th century without ever losing a single passenger to disease.

The windmill opens daily 10 am to 6 pm, March to early November. Admission is IR£3/1.75. You can take the steam train (combined fare and windmill entry IR£5.50/2.75) or follow the canalside path, looking out for birds as you go.

Places to Stay

Camping The *Bayview Caravan Park* (☎ 26140), 1.6km from town on the Ballybunion road, charges IR£5 for a tent and two people. You can camp at the *Collis-Sandes* hostel.

Hostels Attractively positioned at 17 Denny St, the IHH *Finnegan's Holiday Hostel* (☎ 27610), has IR£7.50 dorm beds and doubles for IR£15; cooking and lounge facilities here are exceptionally good. *Seán Óg's Hostel* (☎ 27199) is tucked away behind the Mall and has beds for IR£6.50, while the brand-new *Atlas Hostel* (☎ 20722) is in McCowans Lane, off Castle St with dorm beds for IR£7.50.

Two other hostels are further from the centre: *Collis-Sandes House* (☎ 28658), a Georgian-style house in Oakpark, is the longest walk away, while *Lisnagree Hostel* (☎ 27133) is on Ballinorig Rd, east of the town centre at Clash Cross. Both charge from IR£6.50 for dorm beds; the Collis-Sandes charges from IR£25 for a private room.

B&Bs & Hotels Centrally placed B&Bs include *Castle House* (☎ 25167) at 27 Upper Castle St and *Seán Óg's* (☎ 28822) at 41 Bridge St ... over a pub so it could be noisy. *St Joseph's Guesthouse* (☎ 21174), 2 Staughton's Row, has beds from IR£16. Nearby in High St the *Tralee Townhouse* (☎ 81111) has the advantage of being newly built so that all its rooms are pristine; beds cost from IR£20.

In Denny St the *Grand Hotel* (☎ 21499; fax 22877) has beds from IR£40/60 and the *Imperial* (☎ 27755; fax 27800) from IR£37/50. Four km out on the Killarney road, the *Earl of Desmond* hotel (☎ 21299; fax 21976), with rooms from IR£34/44, is good value.

Places to Eat

During the day it's not hard finding somewhere reasonable for lunch or a snack. In the evening, however, there are few alternatives to the pubs.

Inexpensive lunches can be had at *Eats* in Ashe St or *O'Brien's* in Tralee Shopping Centre, off Bridge St. The *Snackery* on the Mall does a mini-breakfast for IR£2.25 and fried food for under IR£5. Nearby, *Quinlan's* calls itself a 'select luncheon bar' and is good for light meals until 6 pm when it becomes a conventional bar.

Pocotts Restaurant (☎ 29500) on Ashe St does things like chicken with rice and chips for IR£4.50. *The Skillet* (☎ 24561) on Barrack Lane serves meat and vegetarian dishes for under IR£10. The Chinese *Rose Garden* on Rock St Lower charges around IR£7 a main dish; much less at the takeaway next door. At 18 Milk Market Lane, *Brats Place* opens for vegetarian lunches but not for dinners.

The place to go for Sunday brunch is *Fred's Restaurant* on Castle St, with a choice of sandwiches, burgers and salads for under IR£5. In the evening the actions shifts to

Allegro's on the corner of Denny St and The Mall. The food's nothing to write home about, but the lack of alternatives guarantees queues for tables.

The basement restaurant at *Finnegan's* (☎ 27610), 17 Denny St, brings good food to what can seem like a culinary desert. Tasty continental cuisine is served in cosy surroundings; expect to pay around IR£15 a head without wine. The *Swedish Bistro* (☎ 21711) in McCowans Lane off Castle St offers herrings and other delicacies; prices are cheapest 6 to 8 pm Wednesday to Saturday.

Entertainment
Castle St is thick with pubs, many of them with live entertainment of one kind or another. *Kirby's Brogue Inn* in Rock St, the *Greyhound Bar* in Pembroke St and the *Fiddler Bar* in The Brandon Hotel on Princes St have something every night. *Betty's* on Strand St is recommended for traditional music at weekends. *Paddy Mac's* in the Mall has music every Tuesday night.

The popular *Old Market Place* opposite Seán Óg's hostel has pavement tables in summer.

At Siamsa Tíre (pronounced 'shee-am-sah-tee-reh') the National Folk Theatre of Ireland recreates aspects of Gaelic culture through song, dance and mime. Events take place at 8.30 pm, May through September. The theatre (☎ 23055) is close to the tourist office and tickets cost IR£8/7.

The four-screen Kerry Omniplex cinema is in Ivy Terrace; phone ☎ 23944 for programme details.

The Aqua Dome in an impressive building on the south-western outskirts has water slides, wave pools, the lot, but you pay through the nose to use them. April through September it's open 10 am to 10 pm. For other times phone ☎ 29150.

Getting There & Away
Bus A daily expressway bus connects Dublin and Tralee, via Limerick and Listowel. There's also a daily bus to Rosslare via Killarney, Cork and Waterford. Other services run to Clifden, Ennis, Kenmare, Shannon, Westport and Derry, and locally to Dingle and Dunquin. Contact the bus station (☎ 23566) for times.

Bus Éireann also runs a regular service to London via Limerick, Tipperary and Waterford, departing from the bus station at 2.15 pm. A single fare costs IR£44.

Train There's a regular Dublin to Tralee service. The railway station (☎ 23522) is a 10 minute walk from the town centre.

Getting Around
Bikes can be hired from Tralee Gas & Bicycle Supplies (☎ 22018) in Strand St or E Caball (☎ 22231) in Ashe St.

AROUND TRALEE
The obvious attraction outside Tralee is the Dingle Peninsula but north Kerry has its own modest appeal and the ecclesiastical buildings at Ardfert (Ard Fhearta) are well worth a visit.

Crag Caves
The Crag Caves were only discovered in 1983 when problems with water pollution led to a search for the source of the local river. Although the cave entrance had been known for years the system had never been explored until then.

The caves open March to November, 10 am to 6 pm (closing at 7 pm June through August), with guided tours for IR£3/1.75. Coffee and snacks are available.

To get to the caves, head for Castleisland on the N21 and look for the signs at the Limerick end of town.

Getting There & Away In July and August there's at least one bus a day (except Sunday) between Tralee and Castlemaine that stops in Castleisland.

Ardfert
Most of the present **cathedral** dates back to the 13th century but the Romanesque doorway is 12th century. Set into one of the interior walls is an effigy popularly said to

be of St Brendan the Navigator who was educated in Ardfert and founded a monastery here. There are ruins of two other churches – 12th century Templenahoe and 15th century Templenagriffin – in the grounds.

The cathedral is on the road to Ballyheigue from Tralee. It's owned by Dúchas who run guided tours, opens daily 9.30 am to 6.30 pm and admission is IR£1.50/60p. With luck, work on shoring up the cathedral will be completed by the time you read this.

Turning right in front of the cathedral and going down the road for 500m brings you to the extensive remains of a **Franciscan friary**, dating from the 13th century but with 15th century cloisters. Many will find this the more romantic of the two sites, simply because it's in isolated farmland.

O'Sullivan's does bar food and there's a Spar to stock up on groceries if you're camping on the coast to the north or south.

Getting There & Away In July and August at least one bus a day (except Sunday) stops in Ardfert located between Tralee and Ballybunion.

FENIT

Eight km south-west of Ardfert is the small resort of Fenit, with an offshore lighthouse and a pier running out to an unpromising shed which turns out to contain the rather good **Fenit Seaworld**, one of a new generation of aquaria that uses wave machines and touch pools to make the underwater world more exciting. For the sake of youngsters a story of piracy, complete with sometimes bloodied models, is woven around the fish. It's open daily 10 am to 5.30 pm (until 8 pm in July and August) and admission is IR£4/1.50. There's a café here.

Getting There & Away

On Friday only a bus leaves Tralee for Fenit at 9.45 am and 1.45 pm, returning at 10.15 am and 2.15 pm.

BANNA STRAND & BALLYHEIGUE

This 8km stretch of sandy beach will always be better known for its history than for its recreational qualities. Planning to bring in rifles for the Easter Rising, Sir Roger Casement (1864-1916) was arrested as soon as he landed here in April 1916 from a German submarine. He was tried for treason and executed in London but many years later his body was returned to Ireland. Approaching the beach, a sign points left to the Casement memorial. It's 1km down to the left, past the caravan park.

The beach itself is safe for swimming. You can camp free on the sand dunes at Banna, and there are public toilets, but no showers, at the main entrance to the beach. A couple of caravan parks stretched along the beach attract mainly Irish holidaymakers. The *Banna Beach Hotel* (☎ 066-34103) has rooms from IR£30/50 but it's a tacky motel that won't appeal to everyone. Dinner is around IR£12 but you're better off sticking with bar food.

To the north of Banna Strand is the smaller but equally sandy beach at otherwise uninspiring Ballyheigue. Camping is possible at *Casey's Caravan & Camping Park* (☎ 066-33195), IR£2.50 for a hiker or cyclist and at the IHH *Breakers Hostel* (☎ 066-33242) which is on Cliff Rd amid the B&Bs; dorm beds are IR£6, doubles IR£14.

RATTOO ROUND TOWER & MUSEUM

Kerry's only complete round tower has six floors and is in fine condition. The top windows face the four points of the compass, suggesting that this was an important monastic site in the 9th and 10th centuries. Nothing else remains from that era. To the east are the ruins of a 15th century church.

The tower is visible from the main road before entering the small town of Ballyduff; the turning is signposted.

BALLYBUNION

In June 1834 a longstanding feud between two Ballybunion (Baile an Bhuinneánaigh) families culminated in a brawl on the beach, involving over 3000 combatants. During the summer the beach is still crowded, but only with Irish holidaymakers who have made Ballybunion a popular resort. Apart from the

KERRY

usual seaside attractions there's little to see except the ruins of Ballybunion Castle overlooking the beach. Tourist information is available from a small cubicle, on the left as you enter the Ambassador Golf Hotel.

LISTOWEL
Listowel's main attraction is the annual Writers' Week, although there are some places of interest in the vicinity. The tourist office (☎ 068-22590) in St John's Church opens from June to September. Perhaps surprisingly for a town credited with spawning 360 books by more than 60 writers, McGuire's in Church St is the only bookshop.

The telephone code is 068.

Writers' Week
John B Keane is probably the most famous writer associated with Listowel, especially since the filming of *The Field*. He owns a pub in the town and usually features in Writers' Week. Bryan MacMahon, a short story writer, is another local literary talent.

Now into its 28th year, the literary festival takes place each May – details from Writers' Week, PO Box 147, Listowel, County Kerry. Many events take place in St John's Arts Centre (☎ 22566) in the square.

Getting There & Away
Situated on the Shannon estuary, the town is just south of the car ferry that crosses to County Clare. The car ferry leaves either every hour or every half-hour according to demand.

There are at least three buses a day between Tralee (30 minutes) and Listowel, and two between Limerick and Listowel (one hour 40 minutes). Only one bus travels in either direction on Sunday. In July and August there are also three buses a day to Ballybunion.

AROUND LISTOWEL
Carrigafoyle Castle
The location of this castle, perched above the Shannon estuary, is very attractive. It was probably built at the end of the 15th century

by the O'Connors, who ruled most of northern Kerry. It was besieged by the English in 1580, retaken by O'Connor but fell again to the English under George Carew in 1600, during the suppression of O'Neill's rebellion, and was finally destroyed by Cromwell's forces in 1649. You can climb the spiral staircase 29m to the top for a good view of the estuary.

The castle is 1.5km west of the village of Ballylongford, infrequently accessible by bus from Listowel, Ballybunion or Tarbert.

Lislaughtin Abbey
This Franciscan friary was also founded by the O'Connors in the late 15th century. When the castle was attacked in 1580, the friary was also raided and three elderly friars were murdered in front of the altar. The National Museum in Dublin contains a processional cross (the Ballylongford Cross) from the abbey.

Take the small road to Saleen from the village of Ballylongford and the abbey ruins soon come into view.

Dingle Peninsula

Less touristy and even more beautiful than the Ring of Kerry, the Dingle Peninsula is the Ireland of *Ryan's Daughter* and *Far and Away*, with an extraordinary number of ring forts, high crosses and other ancient monuments. Dingle is the main town. Ferries run from Dunquin to the bleak Blasket Islands, off the tip of the peninsula.

A touring route, the Slea Head Drive, heads west from Dingle to Slea Head, Dunquin, Ballyferriter, Feohanagh, Brandon Creek and back to Dingle. You could drive it in a day but it's more fun to spin it out.

The Dingle Peninsula telephone code is ☎ 066.

TRALEE TO DINGLE VIA CONNOR PASS
There are two routes from Tralee to Dingle, though they both follow the same road out of

Tralee past the Blennerville windmill. Near the village of Camp a right fork heads off to the Connor Pass, while the main road via Annascaul brings you to Dingle more quickly. The Connor Pass route is much more beautiful, and goes past the Castlegregory Peninsula, which divides Brandon and Tralee bays. The broad and empty beaches around Castlegregory are perfect for surfing and those close to the Sandy Bay Caravan Park have been particularly recommended. Bring your own gear.

Castlegregory

A small, traffic-congested village, Castlegregory (Caislean an Ghriare) has a seasonal visitor centre, a couple of hostels and *Barry's* for pizzas and burgers. A road north heads out along a sand-strewn road on a spit of land between Tralee and Brandon bays to Rough Point. It's all very pretty and would be more so were it not for the caravans and bungalows marring the views.

Places to Stay There are two campsites near Castlegregory. The *Anchor Caravan Park* (☎ 39157), 3km before Castlegregory, is signposted on the main road and open Easter through September. There are 30 pitches and a tent for two costs IR£8. *Seaside Caravan & Camping Park* (☎ 30161) is also on the beach.

The *Euro Hostel* (☎ 39133) is above Fitzgerald's pub as you join the road to Rough Point. Beds in six-bed dorms are IR£5.50 and doubles are IR£12. In Main St, *Lynch's Hostel* (☎ 39128), attached to a funeral parlour of all things, charges similar rates. Neither is very exciting.

Griffins Tip Top Farmhouse (☎ 39147), on the main road about 1km from Castlegregory, does B&B from IR£20/36.

Getting There & Away There's a year round bus service which leaves Tralee for Castlegregory on Friday only at 8.55 am and 2 pm and returns at 10.35 am only. In July and early August there are also two services a day on Monday and Wednesday, leaving Tralee at 10.20 am and 4.15 pm, and returning at 11.05 am and 5 pm.

Cloghane & Brandon

At Kilcummin the main N86 cuts over the Connor Pass to Dingle. A fork to the right heads down to the relatively little visited

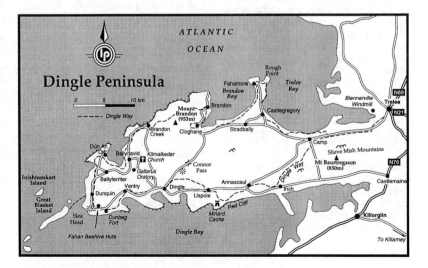

villages of Cloghane and Brandon and on to Brandon Point with fine views of Brandon Bay. The area is one of only three in Ireland that is working towards acquiring an EU 'eco-label', the environmental equivalent of a Blue Flag beach and indicating an area of pristine natural quality.

Cloghane has a helpful information centre (☎ 38277) where you can buy the *Cloghane & Brandon Walking Guide* (IR£3), with details of all the trails you'll see signposted. Those interested in the region's many archaeological sites should ask about guided walks, or buy the *Loch a'Dúin Archaeological & Nature Trail* (IR£3).

Immediately opposite the centre St Brendan's Church has a stained-glass window showing the Gallarus Oratory and Ardfert Cathedral.

Mt Brandon At 953m Mt Brandon is Ireland's second highest mountain. There are two main routes up: a gradual one from the west and a more exciting one from the east; allow at least five hours for the climb.

If you want to climb the mountain, make sure there's no danger of a mist descending, as the top is frequently shrouded in cloud. If you do get caught, you may need a compass to make your way down. The traditional way up the mountain is by way of the Saint's Rd that starts at Kilmakedar Church. The eastern, more demanding, approach starts just beyond Cloghane and is clearly signposted.

The ruins of St Brendan's Oratory mark the summit. The legend is that the navigator saint climbed the mountain with his seafaring monks before they set out in their curraghs for the journey to Greenland and America.

Places to Stay The *Green Acres Caravan & Camping Park* (☎ 39158), close to Crutchs Country House Hotel, charges IR£8 for a tent and two adults.

The inviting *Crutchs Country House Hotel* (☎ 38118) is tucked away on the left almost as soon as you turn down the small road leading to Cloghane. It has singles/

doubles from IR£58/77. *Fermoyle Restaurant* here serves dinner for IR£20 but bar food is also available.

Getting There & Away On Friday only buses leave Tralee at 8.55 am and 2 pm, taking an hour to reach Cloghane. Returning, they leave Cloghane at 10.05 am and 3.10 pm.

Connor Pass
At 456m, the Connor (or Conor) pass is the highest in Ireland and offers spectacular views of Dingle harbour and Mt Brandon to the north. There's a car park near the summit. Take the path up behind it to see the peninsula spread out below you.

Connor Pass Hostel (☎ 39179) is by the main road at Stradbally; the proprietor also runs the pub opposite. Dorm beds are IR£6. *Beenoskee* (☎ 39263) at Cappateigue on the Connor Pass road charges from IR£19/28 for B&B.

TRALEE TO DINGLE VIA ANNASCAUL
For drivers this route has little to recommend it other than being faster than the Connor Pass route. By bike it's less demanding. On foot the journey constitutes the first three days of the Dingle Way.

Dingle Way
This 178km circular route from Tralee passes through Dingle and Dunquin, returning to Tralee via Castlegregory. The whole walk takes eight days but the last four days, from Dunquin to Tralee, are by far the best in terms of scenery. See the Activities chapter for further details.

Tralee to Annascaul
The very friendly IHH *Bog View Hostel* (☎ 58125) is a converted school halfway between Tralee and Dingle. Dorm beds cost IR£6, a private room IR£16. Meals are available, bikes can be hired and there's a free pick-up service.

A few km past the Bog View the well-equipped IHH *Fuschia Lodge Hostel*

MARK DAFFEY

MARK DAFFEY

MARK DAFFEY

MARK DAFFEY

County Kerry
A: Shopfronts, Listowel
B: Outside a pub in Dingle

C: Slea Head, Dingle Peninsula
D: Shopfront mural, Dingle

TONY WHEELER

TONY WHEELER

TONY WHEELER

MARK DAFFEY

Counties Limerick & Tipperary
A: Street sign in Limerick City
B: King John's Castle, Limerick City
C: Cottage in Adare, County Limerick
D: St Patrick's Rock, Cashel, Tipperary

(☎ 57150) has dorm beds from IR£6, doubles from IR£16 and camping space.

Annascaul

The main reason to pause in Annascaul is to visit the *South Pole Inn* which commemorates villager Tom Crean who went to the South Pole with Scott and Shackleton; you can study the memorabilia and read up on his expeditions while tucking into your lunch. Alternatively the *Anchor Restaurant* (☎ 57382) has dishes at IR£10 and *Brackluin House* does evening meals.

CASTLEMAINE TO DINGLE

Travelling from Killarney to Dingle the quickest route is by way of Killorglin and Castlemaine. At Castlemaine a road heads west to Dingle, soon meeting the coast and passing Inch on the way to joining the main Tralee road to Dingle. Apart from the odd pub or two there's little provision for food so bring your own.

Monday to Saturday there's a bus service out of Tralee to Dingle stopping at Annascaul and Lispole on the way. Late May to mid-September it also stops at Castlemaine and Inch and continues to Killarney.

Castlemaine

Six km west of Castlemaine you'll see the *Phoenix Café & Vegetarian Hostel* (☎ 066-66284) beside the road. Beautiful ethnic fabrics and artefacts decorate a hostel with simple dorm beds on the floor for IR£7 and doubles for IR£25. There's a wide choice of books in the lounge but note that even self-caterers must stick with the no-meat rule. The café serves things like filled pitta for IR£4.50. You can camp in the adjoining field for IR£3.50.

Inch

The main attraction locally is the 6km sand spit that runs into Dingle Bay – a location for the film of *The Playboy of the Western World*. The sand dunes were once home to Iron Age settlements. Cars are allowed on the beach but be careful because – and this is supported by personal experience – vehicles

regularly get stuck in the wet sand. Bring your gear for surfing waves which average 1m to 3m.

Places to Stay At the Castlemaine end of Inch, *Waterside* (☎ 58129) has ocean views from some rooms. Rooms are IR£14/16. On the other side of Inch, *Red Cliff* (☎ 57136) was once owned by Dr Eamonn Casey, Bishop of Galway, who used it for a liaison. The mother of his son went public in 1992, and journalists turned up in force. There are some who believe the Catholic church has never really recovered from this and other similar upsets.

Lispole

Blink and you'll miss Lispole but the *Seacrest* hostel (☎ 51390), just over 1km outside, has beds for IR£6 and a double for IR£15. There's a free pick-up service.

Between Annascaul junction and Lispole look out for a turning on the left to 15th century **Minard Castle** which has been in a dangerous condition since its destruction by Cromwellian forces in the 17th century. Children should not be left unsupervised.

DINGLE

The attractive little port of Dingle (An Daingean) makes a good base for exploring the Dingle Peninsula, and has a famous resident dolphin. What saves it from complete surrender to tourism is the continued existence of a large resident fishing fleet. At the time of writing tempers were running hot over whether to replace the old boat yard on the quay with a tourism complex complete with large hotel, restaurant and 'theme' bar.

Information

The town centre tourist office (☎ 066-51188) opens April to October, 9 am to 6 pm Monday to Saturday. One-hour guided walks round Dingle (☎ 51937) depart from outside at 11.30 am and 2.30 pm for IR£2.50.

The telephone code is ☎ 066.

Fungie the Dolphin

In the winter of 1984 fisherfolk began to

notice a solitary bottlenose dolphin that followed their vessels, jumped about in the water and sometimes leapt over their boats. Fungie the dolphin is now an international celebrity.

During the summer, regular boats leave the pier for a one-hour dolphin-spotting trip. The cost is IR£6/3 (free if Fungie doesn't show, but he usually does). A daily boat also leaves at 8 am for those who want to swim with Fungie; the trip lasts two hours and the cost is IR£10/5 (plus IR£14 to hire a wetsuit if necessary). As well as Fungie, you'll get the chance to watch cormorants, guillemots, razorbills and shearwaters on the water.

You can watch Fungie from the shore, although without getting nearly so close. From Dingle take the Tralee road and turn right down a lane about 1.5km from the Esso garage. The turning is easy to miss so look for a set of whitish gateposts beside the lane. At the end of the lane is a tiny parking space (remember that the farmer needs access to his fields). Walk along the sea wall towards the old tower and you'll come to the harbour mouth.

Wetsuits can be hired from Flannery's (☎ 51337) in a house near the pier. Ballin-taggart Hostel also has wetsuits for hire, mainly for residents.

Dingle Oceanworld

A new aquarium (☎ 52111) opposite Dingle Harbour concentrates on showing off the fish and other sealife from the local area; most of the specimens were caught by the local fisherfolk. There's a walk-through tunnel and a touch pool. It's open daily 10 am to 6 pm (later in July and August) and costs IR£4/2.25. The café has fine harbour views.

Activities

The Mountain Man shop (☎ 51868) on Strand St does outdoor equipment and maps, hires out bikes and runs an organised walks programme. Half-day walks in the beautiful countryside west of Dingle cost IR£12, whole-day hikes up Mt Brandon IR£20.

Scuba diving can be arranged in Ventry (☎ 59876) and Ballyferriter (☎ 56105).

Ask at the tourist office for details of sea fishing trips or contact the boatman himself (☎ 51163).

Places to Stay

Camping Three of the hostels provide for

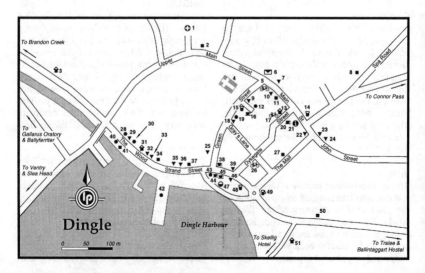

campers: the *Seacrest*, furthest out of town near Lispole, the *Ballintaggart* and the *Rainbow*. Expect to pay around IR£3 a head.

Hostels The going rate for a dorm bed in Dingle is IR£6 to IR£7. The inviting *Grapevine Hostel* (☎ 51434) in Dykegate St has beds in dorms and four-bedded rooms. *Lovett's* (☎ 51903) is a small family house down the road from the Esso garage, less than 100m from the main roundabout.

For a more rural setting try the deservedly popular *Rainbow Hostel* (☎ 51044), just 300m west of town (free pick-ups from the bus stop), with a good, big kitchen. East along the Tralee road the IHH's equally popular *Ballintaggart Hostel* (☎ 51454), in a spacious early 19th century house, also has a free shuttle service to and from town, plus bike hire, a bureau de change and pony trekking.

If all these are full there's also the extremely basic *Marina Hostel* (☎ 51065) near the pier with 20 dorm beds, plus private rooms for IR£15.

B&Bs A few pubs by the pier have gone into B&B; the *Marina Inn* (☎ 51660) offers B&B for IR£12, while *Murphy's* (☎ 51450) has rooms with separate bathroom for IR£16 per person. On the Mall, *Captain's House* (☎ 51531), from IR£25/40, overlooks a beautiful stream and garden.

Main St has several B&Bs, including *Boland's* (☎ 51426), with beds from IR£18/28. The comfortable *Doyle's Townhouse* (☎ 51174) at the bottom of John St costs IR£42/66.

On the Tralee road, just east of the roundabout, the big *Alpine House* (☎ 51250) has singles/doubles from IR£30/37. The sea views are terrific.

Hotels *Benners* (☎ 51638; fax 51412) in a Georgian house on Main St is attractively furnished, with singles/doubles from IR£40/60 without breakfast. Bigger and pricier is the unattractive *Skellig Hotel* (☎ 51144; fax 51501), a 10 minute walk from town, southeast of the roundabout. Doubles cost from IR£86.

The not much prettier *Hillgrove* hotel (☎ 51131) is a five minute walk from town on Spa Rd; rooms cost from IR£25/40.

Places to Eat
Cafés & Pubs The excellent *An Café Liteártha*, on Dykegate St, is a bookshop

PLACES TO STAY		
2	Boland's B&B	
3	Rainbow Hostel	
8	Hillgrove Hotel	
11	Benner's Hotel	
13	Grapevine Hostel	
27	Captain's House B&B	
31	Marina Hostel	
34	Marina Inn	
37	Murphy's Pub/B&B	
41	Ocean View B&B	
50	Alpine House	
51	Lovett's Hostel	

PLACES TO EAT	
7	Adams Restaurant & Bar
9	El Toro Restaurant
10	Lord Baker's Restaurant
16	Café Ceol
18	Beginish Restaurant

20	An Café Literártha
22	Old Smokehouse
23	Half Door
24	Doyle's Seafood Restaurant
25	Fenton's Restaurant
29	Sméara Dubha
32	Waterside
33	Moon Goddess
35	Danno's Restaurant Bar
36	Armada Restaurant
38	Oven Doors Café
39	Forge Restaurant
44	Nell's Coffee Shop
45	Tig Lise
46	Greany's Restaurant

PUBS	
14	Small Bridge Bar
15	Dick Mack's

48	O'Flaherty's

OTHER	
1	Hospital
4	St Mary's Church
5	Foxy John's Bike Hire
6	Post Office
12	Laundrette
17	Bike Hire
19	Lisbeth Mulcahy Shop
21	Tourist Office
26	Bike Hire
28	Craft Village
30	Dingle Oceanworld
40	Brian De Staic Jewellery
42	Pier & Dolphin Boats' Departure Point
43	Mountain Man
47	Bus Stop
49	Esso Petrol Station

with a small inexpensive café with a handy noticeboard at the back.

The pleasant *Oven Doors* at the corner of Green St and Strand St serves pizzas from IR£3.45 until 10.30 pm. Across the road *Tig Lise* does soup for IR£1.80 and tasty cakes. *Greany's* does breakfast from IR£1, lunch specials for IR£4.95 and a set dinner for IR£12.95. Round the corner in Strand St *Nell's Coffee Shop* can fix you an Irish stew for IR£3.45.

The unpretentious *Old Smokehouse*, at the corner of the Mall and Main St, serves pizza, lasagne and the like for around IR£5.

Vegetarians can eat at *Café Ceol*, at the end of the lane opposite the church in Green St or at *Sméara Dubha* (☎ 51465) off The Wood to the west of town. The latter only opens 6 to 10 pm.

Most of the pubs opposite the pier serve bar food all day. *Murphy's* offers a traditional bacon and cabbage meal for IR£4.25 until 9 pm. More upmarket is the *Waterside* where sandwiches with exotic fillings cost from IR£3.75. *Danno's Restaurant Bar* stands on the site of the old Dingle station and offers a fairly standard menu of burgers and pasta.

For Chinese food at around IR£5 a main dish try the *Moon Goddess*, also opposite the pier.

Restaurants The *Forge Restaurant* in the town centre has standard meals in the IR£5 to IR£10 range, including vegetarian choices. The *Armada*, opposite the pier, has seafood and grills for between IR£6 to IR£14.

Opposite St Mary's Church in Green St, *El Toro* (☎ 51820) serves pizzas from IR£6 and seafood for between IR£9 and IR£14 from 5.30 pm. Further down the road *Fenton's Restaurant* has a set dinner for IR£17.95 (IR£5 reduction between 6 and 7 pm). Excellent value for money is the award-winning *Beginish Restaurant* (☎ 51588), also in Green St, which can always be relied on for a good seafood or vegetarian meal.

On Main St, *Adams* has a bar on one side and a small restaurant on the other side serving vegetarian and fish dishes for between IR£4 to IR£8, while *Lord Baker's* (☎ 51277) is a seafood restaurant with a light set dinner from 6 pm for IR£15. *Doyle's Seafood Bar* (☎ 51174), 4 John St, does dinners only, and most main courses are in the IR£12 to IR£15 range. The *Half Door* (☎ 57600) next door is similar.

Entertainment

Many pubs have live music, and three in town are particularly worth checking out: *O'Flaherty's* near the roundabout, *Murphy's*, by the pier, and the *Small Bridge Bar/An Droisead Beag*, at the end of Main St by the bridge. In Green St, *Dick Mack's* is a marvellous old-style pub with a shop on one side and a drinks counter on the other.

Things to Buy

The Craft Village on the Wood has several workshops specialising in leatherware and garments. To have your name inscribed in Ogham script on a piece of jewellery go to Brian de Staic nearby.

Green St is packed with craft shops; look out for Lisbeth Mulcahy with lovely, if pricey, pottery and woven garments. Her husband has a workshop west of Dingle near Ballyferriter (see that section).

Getting There & Away

Buses stop outside the car park at the back of the Super Valu store. Buses leave Tralee at 11 am, 2, 4.15 and 6 pm Monday to Saturday, with an extra morning bus at 9 am from late May to mid-September and an extra evening bus at 8.10 pm, June to September. Two buses daily depart Killarney for Dingle in the summer at 10.30 am and 1.30 pm.

From Dingle (☎ 23566) the earliest daily bus to Tralee leaves at 7.25 am except on Saturday. The 2.45 pm service goes on from Tralee to Killarney. Note that there are even fewer services on Sunday.

An infrequent bus service links Dingle to Ventry, Slea Head, Ballyferriter and Dunquin.

Getting Around

There are several bike-rental places and the

daily rate is IR£5. Foxy John's (☎ 51316) on Main St does the Raleigh Rent-a-Bike scheme.

WEST OF DINGLE

The area west of Dingle has the greatest concentration of ancient sites in Kerry if not the whole of Ireland. To do them justice you should use one of the specialist guides on sale in the An Café Liteártha or the tourist office. The sites listed here are among the most interesting and easiest to find.

The land west of Dingle has some other attractions. It's a Gaeltacht, or genuine Irish-speaking area. The landscape is dramatic, except when it's hidden in mist, and there are striking views of the Blasket Islands from Slea Head. The sandy beach nearby, Coumenole, is lovely to walk along but like most of those in the area it's treacherous for swimming.

Tourism came late to Dingle but the area is handling it well, avoiding the tackiness of Killarney and the Ring of Kerry. In 1971, David Lean filmed *Ryan's Daughter* here. Much of it was shot near Dunquin, and the ruins of the film's schoolhouse can still be found. Film buffs should enquire at Kruger's pub in Dunquin.

Orientation

If you cross the bridge west of Dingle and take the first left with a clutter of signs, you come to a Y-junction after 5km. To the right are Kilmalkedar Church and Brandon Creek; from here you could return to Dingle on a circular route. To the left are the Gallarus Oratory and the Riasc site, from which you can reach Ballyferriter and Dunquin, for boats to the Blasket Islands. The road continues down the coast and back to Dingle, via Ventry.

Kilmalkedar Church

This 12th century church was once part of a complex of religious buildings. The characteristic Romanesque doorway has a tympanum with a head on one side and a mythical beast on the other. There's an Ogham stone, pierced by a hole, in the

grounds. About 50m away is a two-storey building known as St Brendan's House, believed to have been the residence of the medieval clergy. The road connecting these two ruins is the beginning of the Saint's Rd, the traditional approach to Mt Brandon (see the Cloghane & Brandon section).

Brandon Creek

Tradition has it that St Brendan set off from this inlet and sailed to America in the 5th century. As Tim Severin shows in *The Brendan Voyage*, this voyage could indeed have been done hundreds of years before Columbus. The fishing boats add to the creek's atmosphere, and on a warm day the water is inviting.

To get there, carry on along the road that you turned off to reach the church. After a few km turn right at the junction that points to the Tigh A'Phoist hostel, then right at the unmarked T-junction. Carry on this road for nearly 2km until you reach the tiny village of Bothar Bui and the IHO hostel. Carry straight on to the next junction and turn left (signposted for Slea Head Drive) for Brandon Creek at the unnamed pub. A right turn at this junction returns to Dingle.

The basic IHO *Tigh A'Phoist Hostel* (☎ 55109) in Bothar Bui village is attached to a shop and has dorm beds for IR£6.50 and doubles from IR£16. On Tuesday and Friday the Dingle to Ballydavid bus goes close but ask to be dropped off at the Caragh church.

The friendly *An Bothar* (☎ 55342) pub does B&B for IR£13.50 per person and is ideally located if you want to climb Mt Brandon. To get there, continue past the hostel for half a km.

Gallarus Oratory

Simple but stunning, this superb dry-stone oratory is reason enough for visiting the Dingle Peninsula. It's in perfect condition, apart from a slight sagging in the roof, and has withstood the assault of the elements for some 1200 years. Traces of mortar suggest that the interior and exterior walls may have been plastered. Shaped like an upturned boat, it has a doorway on the west side and a

Gallarus Oratory was used for private prayer

small round-headed window on the east side. Inside the doorway are two projecting stones with holes which once supported the door.

Bear left at the Y-junction (see the Orientation section earlier), and after 2km turn left at the sign. The oratory is half a km down the road on the left.

Europe's most westerly campsite is *Teach An Aragail* (Oratory House Camp) (☎ 55143) near the oratory. A tent for two car-occupants costs IR£7 a night; for two cyclists it's IR£6.

On Tuesday and Friday only a bus leaves Dingle at 9 am and drops off at Gallarus 10 minutes later. From Gallarus it picks up for Dingle at 1.25 pm.

Riasc Monastic Settlement
The remains of this 5th or 6th century monastic settlement are impressive. Excavations have revealed, among other finds, the foundations of an oratory first built with wood and later stone, a kiln for drying corn and a cemetery. Most interesting is a pillar with beautiful Celtic designs.

From Dingle a sign points the way from the Y-junction (see Orientation). Follow the road for 4km until you see a sign on the left to the Reask View B&B and the monastic settlement. The site is half a km up this road.

BALLYFERRITER
Heading north on the R559 road out of Dingle and following the Slea Head Drive signs, you'll eventually come to the small village of Ballyferriter, named after Piaras Ferriter, a poet and soldier who emerged as a local leader in the 1641 rebellion and was the last Kerry commander to submit to Cromwell's army. Near the village are the Three Sisters hills, Smerwick Harbour and the remains of Dún An Óir Fort.

Social, cultural and historical aspects of life on the Dingle Peninsula and the Blasket Islands are the main concerns of the small **Ballyferriter Museum** (☎ 56100). It's open over Easter and from June to the end of September, Monday to Friday 10 am to noon and 2 to 4 pm. There's a café here too.

Dún An Óir Fort
During the 1580 rebellion in Munster, the 'Fort of Gold' was held by an international brigade of Italians, Spaniards and Basques. On 17 November, English troops under Lord Grey attacked the fort and the people inside surrendered. 'Then putt I in certeyn bandes who streight fell to execution. There were 600 slayne', said the poet Edmund Spenser, who was secretary to Lord Grey.

To get to Dún An Óir, head west from Ballyferriter. After 1km turn right at a brown sign to Dún An Óir Hotel. After a further 1.5km, take the right fork at a Y-junction. Go straight on, ignoring side tracks, until you come to a T-junction. Turn right and after roughly 300m you'll see a signpost to the fort along a wretchedly surfaced road; do your suspension a favour and walk it. The views alone justify the effort of finding the scant remains of the fort.

Places to Stay & Eat
Free camping is possible near Ferriter's Cove but there are no facilities. The IHO *An Cat Dubh Hostel* (☎ 56286), an ordinary house attached to a shop, is just past the Granville Hotel on the road to Dunquin. Dorm beds cost IR£6. A few B&Bs are dotted around. Three km out, *Mrs Ferris* (☎ 56282) charges IR£19/28.

The *Granville* (☎ 56116) is west of Ballyferriter before the An Cat Dubh Hostel. Singles/doubles here are from IR£18/36. To get to the *Óstan Dún An Óir* (☎ 56133) look for a sign on the right after leaving Bally-ferriter. Rooms are IR£40/60 and there's an outdoor heated swimming pool.

The *Tigh Pheig* pub does everything from burger and chips for IR£4.50 to a seafood platter for IR£10.50. The nearby *Óstan Dún An Óir Hotel* also does food.

DUNQUIN & AROUND
If Ballyferriter is small, it does at least have a centre which is more than can be said for scattered Dunquin, the place you'll need to come to if you want to catch a boat to the Blasket Islands. It's on the Slea Head Drive out of Dingle, roughly the same distance whether you set out to the north via Bally-ferriter or to the west via Ventry.

The Blasket Centre
The wonderful heritage centre at Dunquin celebrates the lost lifestyle of the Blasket Islanders, and the Irish language and culture. The 20-minute audiovisual presentation can be seen in French and German as well as English. The centre cost IR£4 million to build, most of it provided by the EU, and the building provides an incidental showcase for marvellous stained glass, ceramics and weaving. There's a café with Blasket views and a small bookshop selling the various books written by and about the Islanders. Admission to this Dúchas centre is IR£2.50/1 and it's open 10 am to 6 pm daily (to 7 pm in July and August).

Louis Mulcahy Pottery
This is certainly one of the most interesting potteries on the peninsula. Visitors can see the potters at work and the two floors of the shop display a variety of tea sets, bowls, lamps, vases and platters costing from IR£5 to IR£500. Purchases can be mailed overseas from the shop (☎ 56229) which is on the road just north of Dunquin.

Beehive Huts & Dunbeg Fort
The road between Dunquin and Slea Head is dotted with beehive huts, forts and church sites. The **Fahan** huts are accessible from

two points and you'll see signs pointing the way from the road.

Prehistoric Dunbeg Fort, on a clifftop promontory, has a sheer drop to the Atlantic and four outer walls of stone. Inside are the remains of a house and a beehive hut as well as an underground passage. The fort is 8km from Dunquin heading towards Dingle.

To visit any of these sights you'll be charged IR£1, pretty steep given that there's no 'presentation' and other sites on the peninsula are free.

Slea Head
Slea Head offers some of the Dingle Peninsula's best views and is thoroughly popular with coach parties. If you want to stop for something to eat the *Bearfoot Café* across the road from the car park does things like salami sandwiches for IR£3.30. Upstairs the **Enchanted Forest Museum** of toys isn't perhaps the most obvious, or appropriate, development for a beauty spot but parents with children who've had enough of beehive huts may be grateful for the break. It's open noon to 5 pm daily (11 am to 6 pm in July and August); admission costs IR£2.50/1.50 (families IR£7).

Ventry
The small village of Ventry has a marvellous post office-cum-delicatessen-cum-wine-shop. For sit-down dinners there's also the cheerful *Cormorant Restaurant* (☎ 59858) which does things like felafels for lunch but opens for pricier dinners until 10 pm from Easter to October.

Places to Stay
The year-round An Oíge *Dunquin Hostel* (☎ 56121) is conveniently close to the ferry departure point for Great Blasket Island. Beds cost IR£6.50/5.

Krugers Guesthouse (☎ 56127) is within walking distance of the ferry to the Blasket Islands. Despite its promising setting the guesthouse is disappointingly old-fashioned. Beds cost IR£15. You're probably better off continuing east for 1km to *Gleann*

KERRY

Derug where similarly priced beds can be found in more cheerful rooms.

Places to Eat

Despite its dreary decor, *Krugers Pub* near the ferry landing stage is Dunquin's social centre and one of the few places to get an evening meal. When you've seen the photos of people dancing there in its heyday in the Blasket Centre you may feel slightly less inclined to turn up your nose at it.

A better choice is the *Café-Gallery Tigh Aire*, tucked away on the coast side of the road north of Dunquin. Every evening the proprietors dish up one meat (IR£6.50), one fish (IR£5.50) and one vegetarian (IR£5.50) dish from 7 pm onwards but it's also open for breakfasts, lunches and teas.

On the road to Slea Head the *Dunquin Pottery Café* does meals and snacks. The unpromising exterior conceals a thoughtful interior decorated with a fine Irish dresser and old editions of Blasket Island books. Note an upturned Blasket Island boat in the garden.

Getting There & Away

Monday and Thursday only, a bus operates a service from Dingle to Dunquin, via Ventry, Slea Head and Ballyferriter year round. Late May to mid-September the service leaves Tralee at 9.45 am and Killarney at 10.30 am Monday to Saturday. For more details phone Bus Éireann on ☎ 066-23566.

BLASKET ISLANDS

Five km out into the Atlantic, the Blaskets are a group of four big and two smaller islands, the most westerly islands in Europe.

At 6km by 1.2km, Great Blasket is the largest and most visited and is mountainous enough for strenuous walks including a good one detailed in Kevin Corcoran's *Kerry Walks*.

The last islanders left for the mainland in 1953 but lyrical stories of their lives survive. Three books in particular are usually available at the Blasket Centre or An Café Liteártha in Dingle. The best is the English translation of Thomas O'Crohan's *The Islandman*; the other two are Maurice O'Sullivan's *Twenty Years A-Growing* and the translation of Peig Sayers' *Peig*.

Eventually the government hopes to buy all the empty properties on the Great Blasket, renovate some of them and create a National Historic Park, with a new pier allowing larger boats to ferry visitors across.

Places to Stay & Eat

There's no accommodation on the island but camping is free. A café serves snacks and campers could arrange for meals to be cooked.

Getting There & Away

Weather permitting, boats (☎ 56455) operate throughout the summer; the 20-minute crossing costs IR£10 return. Boats leave on the hour 10 am to 3 pm and return on the half-hour.

Monday and Thursday, the first bus for Dunquin leaves Dingle at 8.50 am, giving you 40 minutes before the first boat leaves. Late June to mid-September a bus leaves Dingle at 12.30 and 3.10 pm Monday to Saturday. The last boat from Great Blasket leaves around 3.30 pm.

Counties Limerick & Tipperary

While these counties are outshone by neighbouring Cork, Kerry, Clare and Galway, both County Limerick and Tipperary have places of interest that invite you to pause rather than just tear through en route to somewhere else. Limerick City makes an obvious base for visiting Lough Gur and Adare, while County Tipperary boasts the Rock of Cashel as well as the pleasant towns of Cahir and Carrick-on-Suir and smaller Fethard.

County Limerick

In 1690, the siege of Limerick played centre stage in the struggle between Ireland and England, and the imposing remains of the city's castle bear testimony to this decisive event. Apart from the historical interest and amenities of Limerick City itself, the fascinating historic and prehistoric sites to the south of the city make ideal bicycle excursions. The nearby town of Adare is one of the prettiest in Ireland, in striking contrast with proletarian Limerick City.

LIMERICK

Despite being one of Ireland's largest cities, set on the River Shannon and with a name to set pens in motion, Limerick (Luimneach) used to be regarded as pretty dismal. Fortunately, it's shedding its old 'Stab City' image – it once had a reputation for being a violent city – and things are definitely looking up. With a new visitor centre in King John's Castle, the Hunt Museum's move to the city centre and the fine Georgian architecture getting a lick of paint, Limerick is now a place of interest in its own right, with all sorts of eating establishments and a lively music scene.

History

The Vikings first reached Limerick in the 10th century. From then on they fought over

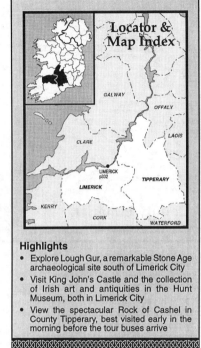

Locator & Map Index

GALWAY

OFFALY

CLARE

LAOIS

LIMERICK p332

TIPPERARY

LIMERICK

KERRY

CORK

WATERFORD

Highlights
- Explore Lough Gur, a remarkable Stone Age archaeological site south of Limerick City
- Visit King John's Castle and the collection of Irish art and antiquities in the Hunt Museum, both in Limerick City
- View the spectacular Rock of Cashel in County Tipperary, best visited early in the morning before the tour buses arrive

the town with the native Irish until Brian Ború's forces defeated the Norsemen at the Battle of Clontarf in 1014. Throughout the Middle Ages the Irish clustered to the south of the Abbey River in Irishtown and the English to the north in Englishtown.

In 1690, Limerick acquired heroic status in the ongoing saga of the English occupation of Ireland. After the Battle of the Boyne, the defeated Jacobite forces withdrew west behind the famously strong walls of Limerick. Surrender seemed inevitable, but the Irish Jacobite leader Patrick Sarsfield escaped with 600 men and launched a surprise

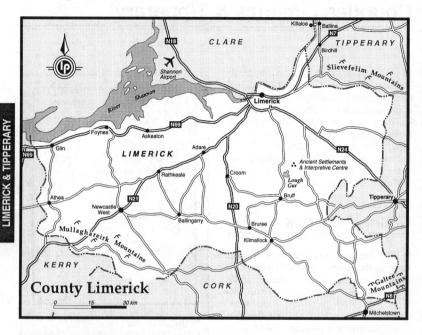

County Limerick

0   15   30 km

attack on the English supply train. Cannons, mortars and 200 wagons of ammunition were destroyed. Sarsfield and his followers returned undetected to Limerick.

Months of bombardment followed and eventually Sarsfield sued for peace. The terms of the Treaty of Limerick were agreed and Sarsfield and 14,000 soldiers were allowed to leave the city for France. The treaty guaranteed religious freedom for Catholics, but the English reneged on it, and enforced fierce anti-Catholic legislation, an act of betrayal which came to symbolise the injustice of British rule.

The new town of Limerick developed and prospered in the 18th century after the old town walls were demolished. However, by the early 20th century that prosperity had passed and in 1919 there was a general strike in protest against British military rule. A Strike Committee took charge of running essential services, and for one week the city of Limerick operated outside all legal struc-

tures. The Strike Committee even issued its own banknotes, becoming known as the Limerick Soviet.

Recently Limerick has revived considerably and although there are still pockets of poverty, a lot of new building has taken place. Many of the old Georgian houses to the south are being restored and 2 Pery Square will eventually become a museum.

Orientation & Information

The main street through town changes name from Rutland St to Patrick St, O'Connell St, The Crescent and Quinlan St as it runs south. Most things of interest are clustered to the north on King's Island, to the south around The Crescent and Pery Square, and along the riverbanks.

The tourist office (☎ 061-317522) is at Arthur's Quay near the river. It's open Monday to Friday 9 am to 6.30 pm in July and August (9.30 am to 5.30 pm on Saturday and Sunday); otherwise it's open 9.30 am to

5.30 pm Monday to Friday (half day on Saturday). The tourist office sells a map of two River Shannon walking trails (IR£1.50) and another of Georgian Limerick (IR£3).

The post office is on Lower Cecil St, and the railway and bus station lie to the southeast, off Parnell St.

Perhaps the best second-hand bookshop is O'Brien's Bookshop (☎ 412833), near the Savoy Centre in Bedford Row. There's a branch of Eason's at 9 O'Connell St but for books on all things Irish try the Celtic Bookshop (☎ 401155), 2 Rutland St.

For walking gear and maps River Deep, Mountain High (☎ 400944) is at 7 Rutland St. USIT (☎ 415064) is at 55 O'Connell St.

The telephone code is ☎ 061.

St Mary's Cathedral

The oldest building in the city but recently restored, the cathedral was founded in 1172 by Donal Mór O'Brien, King of Munster. The original Romanesque west doorway and clerestory survive, but the chancel and chapels were added in the 15th century. There are grand tombs, memorial stones and splendid black oak misericords – support ledges for choristers, dating from around 1489, carved with pictures of animals and other figures. The graveyard boasts many 18th century tombstones.

Visitors are asked to donate IR£1 towards the cathedral's upkeep.

King John's Castle

King John of England had this castle built on the site of an earlier fortification in 1200-12 to guard and administer the rich Shannon region. The new cannon technology necessitated stronger defences than ever before, and the castle became the most formidable bastion of English power in the west of Ireland.

But whoever described the new interpretive centre dumped in the middle as a 'cross-barred horror' hit the nail square on the head – interesting it may be, beautiful it's certainly not. After watching a 20 minute presentation on the castle's history you can descend to inspect the remains of mines and

countermines dug by besiegers and besieged. In the courtyard stand replicas of three engines of early castle warfare: two catapults – a mangonel and a trebuchet, used to hurl weights, burning material and dead animals at the enemy – and a battering ram.

The castle opens daily between April and October, 9.30 am to 5.30 pm (last admission 4.30 pm). Admission is IR£3.80/2.10.

Opposite the castle the **Treaty Stone** marks the spot on the riverbank where the Treaty of Limerick was signed. Before you cross the bridge look out for the 18th century **Bishop's House** and the ancient **tollgate**.

Limerick Museum

At the time of writing this history museum was due to move to purpose-designed premises near the castle. At its old premises it was open Tuesday to Saturday 10 am to 1 pm and 2 to 5 pm, entrance free, but this could change.

Hunt Museum

This wonderful museum, the private collection of John and Gertrude Hunt, is housed in the Palladian Custom House on the banks of the river on Rutland St. It contains probably the finest collection of Bronze Age, Celtic and medieval treasures outside Dublin. Look out in particular for a marvellous 17th century statue of Apollo draped with the tools of assorted trades; for an extraordinary self-portrait of the artist Robert Fagan and his half-naked wife; and for a Syracusan coin thought to have been one of the '30 pieces of silver' paid to Judas to betray Christ.

It's open Tuesday to Saturday 10 am to 5 pm (Sunday 2 to 5pm), and costs IR£3/1.50.

City Art Gallery

At the time of writing this gallery, in a corner of People's Park near the An Óige hostel, was being reorganised. It's to be hoped that more space (and labelling) can be found for an excellent permanent collection which includes work by artists like Jack B Yeats and Sean Keating. It's open, free, 10 am to 1 pm and 2 to 6 pm Monday to Friday (to 7 pm on Thursday); mornings only on Saturday.

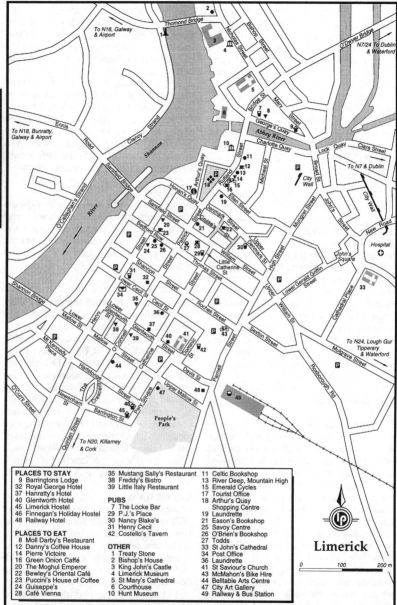

Limerick

PLACES TO STAY
9 Barringtons Lodge
32 Royal George Hotel
37 Hanratty's Hotel
40 Glentworth Hotel
45 Limerick Hostel
46 Finnegan's Holiday Hostel
48 Railway Hotel

PLACES TO EAT
8 Moll Darby's Restaurant
12 Danny's Coffee House
14 Pierre Victoire
16 Green Onion Caffé
20 The Moghul Emperor
22 Bewley's Oriental Café
23 Puccini's House of Coffee
24 Guiseppe's
28 Café Vienna

35 Mustang Sally's Restaurant
38 Freddy's Bistro
39 Little Italy Restaurant

PUBS
7 The Locke Bar
29 P.J.'s Place
30 Nancy Blake's
31 Henry Cecil
42 Costello's Tavern

OTHER
1 Treaty Stone
2 Bishop's House
3 King John's Castle
4 Limerick Museum
5 St Mary's Cathedral
6 Courthouse
10 Hunt Museum

11 Celtic Bookshop
13 River Deep, Mountain High
15 Emerald Cycles
17 Tourist Office
18 Arthur's Quay
    Shopping Centre
19 Laundrette
21 Eason's Bookshop
25 Savoy Centre
26 O'Brien's Bookshop
27 Todds
33 St John's Cathedral
34 Post Office
36 Laundrette
41 St Saviour's Church
44 McMahon's Bike Hire
44 Belltable Arts Centre
47 City Art Gallery
49 Railway & Bus Station

0   100   200 m

St Saviour's Dominican Church

This well-kept 19th century church in Glentworth St contains a statue of Our Lady given to the Dominicans in 1640 by a rich Limerick citizen who wanted to atone for the fact that his uncle had sentenced a man to death for letting a priest say mass in his house. There's some striking modern stained glass.

Organised Tours

Historical walking tours (☎ 318106) depart from 44 Nicholas St at 11 am and 2.30 pm, Monday to Friday, June to August. They cost IR£3.50/1.

May to September, Bus Éireann operates open-top bus tours of the city for IR£3.50 a head.

Places to Stay

Camping *Shannon Cottage Caravan & Camping Park* (☎ 377118) is about 12km from Limerick, reached by turning left at Birdhill – the signpost is easily missed – on the N7 road to Dublin. After Birdhill follow signs to O'Brien's Bridge and turn sharp right after crossing the bridge. Small tents cost IR£9 (IR£3.50 a head for a hiker or cyclist).

Hostels The An Oíge *Limerick Hostel* (☎ 314672), 1 Pery Square, is a short walk across People's Park from the bus and railway station. Beds cost IR£6.50/5. At 6 Pery Square the IHH *Finnegan's Holiday Hostel* (☎ 310308), in a fine Georgian house, has dorm beds for IR£7.50. The large IHH *Barringtons Lodge & Hostel* (☎ 415222) on George's Quay charges IR£7 in rooms for two to four. The bigger single rooms are good value at IR£10 and the riverside situation close to the castle is a distinct plus.

B&Bs *Alexandra* (☎ 318472), 6 Alexandra Terrace, O'Connell Ave, is fairly close to the centre and has singles/doubles from IR£18/34. Otherwise the Ennis Rd (N18) leading from Limerick to Ennis and Galway is lined with B&Bs for several km, including *Clifton House* (☎ 451166), just 1km out, with singles/doubles from IR£25/36. One km further on, *Parkview* (☎ 451505) has good doubles for IR£32.

Hotels Cheapest is the *Railway Hotel* (☎ 413653) on Parnell St opposite the station, with rooms from IR£16/42. The quite comfortable *Royal George Hotel* (☎ 414566; fax 317171) is centrally located on O'Connell St but can be noisy at night. Rooms cost from IR£35/55, excluding breakfast. *Glentworth Hotel* (☎ 413822; fax 413073), in the street of the same name, has rooms from IR£30/48, excluding breakfast. Just down the road *Hanratty's Hotel* (☎ 410999; fax 411077) has rooms from IR£35/65.

Most of the big hotels along the Ennis Rd (N18) are unnecessarily expensive for the average traveller. Just 1km from town on Ennis Rd, *Woodfield House* (☎ 453022; fax 326755) has rooms from IR£40/60. Pushing the boat out, the *Limerick Inn* (☎ 326666; fax 326281), also on Ennis Rd, has rooms from IR£88/100, excluding breakfast.

Places to Eat

Cafés & Takeaways For cheap eats try *Sails* in the modern Arthur's Quay Shopping Centre beside the tourist office; fish & chips, peas, bread & butter, and tea costs IR£4. On O'Connell St *WoKing*, opposite the Royal George Hotel, is a fast Chinese food place with a sit-in counter and takeaway service. Next door *La Romana* does mostly pasta dishes for around IR£6. There's also a branch of *Abrakebabra* here.

At stylish *Danny's Coffee House* on Rutland St, breakfast costs IR£2.95 and tea comes in big mugs. *Café Vienna* on William St is OK for soups, fish & chips, and salads. *Chimes*, in the basement at the Belltable Arts Centre, does good toasted sandwiches for IR£1.30. *Puccini's House of Coffee* in Bedford Row is good for a pre-cinema snack. There's a *Bewley's Oriental Café* along pedestrianised Cruise's St.

Restaurants From 5.30 pm decent meals can be had at *Freddy's Bistro* (☎ 418749), tucked away down Theatre Lane between Lower Mallow and Lower Glentworth Sts; it's open every day except Monday and dishes include steaks for about IR£13 and seafood for IR£11. *Guiseppe's* in Henry St has a wide range of dishes for around IR£6. *The Moghul Emperor*, at the corner of Henry and Sarsfield Sts, does vegetable biryani for IR£5.95 and chicken vindaloo for IR£6.50.

The classy *Hunt Museum restaurant* is a very popular lunch stop; get there early for the tables with river views. Soup and bread costs IR£2.40; cooked meals around IR£5. Across the road *Pierre Victoire* (☎ 400822) in the 19th century Commercial Buildings does set lunches for IR£4.50 and three-course dinners with a French flavour for IR£9.90.

The laid-back *Green Onion Caffé* (☎ 400710) in Ellen St does pasta and pitta dishes from IR£5 to IR£13 from 6 pm; it has a particularly good wine list. *Mustang Sally's*, 103 O'Connell St, is a bright Tex-Mex joint open from 5 pm, with tacos from IR£6.

On George's Quay, just up from Barringtons Lodge hostel, *Moll Darby's* pizzeria (☎ 417270) serves crispy pizzas from IR£5.95 and a scrumptious white chocolate and pecan mousse for IR£2.95. The *Little Italy Restaurant* at the bottom end of O'Connell St does pasta from IR£5.

Entertainment

The music scene shifts by the night but there's something at the popular *Nancy Blake's* on Upper Denmark St. You could also try *Costello's Tavern* on Dominic St or the *Henry Cecil* at the Henry St end of Lower Cecil St. *The Locke Bar* on George's Quay has outdoor tables, immensely popular on mild evenings. *PJ's Place* on Little Catherine St has a mock thatched roof and traditional music.

The *Belltable Arts Centre* (☎ 319866), 69 O'Connell St, hosts travelling theatre companies, and has a small gallery. The *Savoy Centre* off Henry St and Bedford Row has an eight screen cinema.

To dance Saturday night away, try *Strictly Rhythm* at the Savoy Centre in Bedford Row from 11 pm onwards.

Getting There & Away

Air Shannon airport (☎ 471444), just over the border in County Clare, handles both domestic and international flights. The airport is 24km from Limerick; over half an hour by car.

Bus Bus Éireann services operate from the bus and railway station (☎ 313333), a short walk south of the centre. There are regular connections to Dublin (IR£10, 3¼ hours), Tralee (IR£9, two hours), Cork, Galway, Killarney, Rosslare, Donegal, Sligo, Shannon, Derry and most other centres. You can often be dropped outside Todds in O'Connell St.

Train There are services to all the main towns served by rail: eight trains daily to Dublin; two daily to Rosslare Harbour, Cahir and Tipperary; and one to Cork. Other routes involve changing at Limerick Junction, 20km south-east of Limerick. Phone Colbert station (☎ 315555) for details.

Getting Around

Regular buses connect Shannon airport with Limerick bus and railway station.

As Limerick is quite small you can easily get around on foot or by bike. To walk across town from St Mary's Cathedral to the railway station takes about 15 minutes.

Bikes can be hired at Emerald Cycles (☎ 416983), 1 Patrick St and returned at 50 points around Ireland. The rate is IR£7 a day, IR£30 a week plus IR£6 extra if returning outside of Limerick. Bikes can also be hired from An Óige and from McMahons (☎ 415202), 30 Roches St.

AROUND LIMERICK

A few places south of Limerick could be taken in by car in a day or covered by bike over a few days. The R512 road to Lough Gur continues through the village of Bruff to the historic town of Kilmallock. From there, it's a short journey to the pretty village of

Bruree, former home of Eamon de Valera. From Bruree a country road leads to Bruff and the R512 back to Limerick.

Lough Gur

Gathered around a small horseshoe-shaped lake south of Limerick are a number of Stone Age remains. Coming from the city, the first is the 4000-year-old **Grange stone circle**, just past the village of Grange to the left of the road. With its 113 stones it's the largest in Ireland. One km farther along the road a left turn goes up towards Lough Gur; 100m past a ruined 15th century church there's a **wedge tomb** on the other side of the road.

Another 2km along is an **interpretive centre** in a thatched replica of a prehistoric hut where you can see a 12 minute slide presentation on the prehistoric remains. There's also a small **museum** with a few Neolithic artefacts and a replica of the Lough Gur shield that's now in the National Museum in Dublin (although the Lough Gur finds in the Hunt Museum in Limerick are more impressive). The 700 BC shield is 72cm in diameter with six circles of raised bosses designed to weaken the impact of an enemy's sword. The centre opens 10 am to 6 pm, early May to the end of September. Admission is IR£2/1.10.

The lake is set in pleasant parkland, perfect for picnics; look out for the burial mounds, standing stones, ancient enclosures and other remains dotted around. A festival used to be held around the summer solstice (21 June); ask at the interpretive centre in case it's been reintroduced.

To get there, leave Limerick on the N24 road south to Waterford. Look for a sign to Lough Gur indicating a right turn at the roundabout outside town.

Kilmallock

In the Middle Ages, Kilmallock was Ireland's third-largest town after Dublin and Kilkenny. It developed around an abbey founded in the 7th century by St Mocheallóg, hence its Irish name *Cill of Mocheallóg* which means 'church of Mocheallóg'. From the 14th to the 17th centuries it was the seat of the earls of Desmond, in an important defensive position. In the mid-18th century it had a brief flurry of renewed importance with the coming of the railway, but then sank back into the sleepy state it's in today.

Coming into town from Limerick, the first place to see is the four storey **King's Castle**, a 15th century tower house with the street pavement running through it. On the other side of the road a lane leads down to a tiny information centre that houses a ramshackle local collection and a model of the town in 1597. It's open 1.30 to 5.30 pm Monday to Friday, 2 to 5 pm on Saturday and Sunday.

Beyond the museum and across the River Lubagh are the ruins of the 13th century **Dominican Priory**, with an attractive 13th century east window and a tower and south window added in the 15th century. Kilmallock surrendered to Cromwell's forces in 1648 and the priory was sacked and partly destroyed.

Returning to the main street, you'll see a **medieval stone mansion** – one of the 30 or so that once housed the town's prosperous merchants and landowners. Continue along the main street and take the turning on the left that goes down to the 13th century **Collegiate Church**. This has a round tower, which probably belonged to an earlier monastery on the site. The impressively carved door on the south side of the nave dates from the 15th century.

Further along the main street, turn left along Wolfe Tone St. Just before the bridge you'll see a plaque marking the house where the Irish poet Aindrias MacCraith died in 1795. Across the road one of the pretty single-storey cottages leaves its door open so you can pop in and see what a three roomed dwelling used to look like.

Near the junction of Sarsfield St and Lord Edward St is **Blossom's Gate**, the one surviving gate of the original medieval town wall, traces of which can be seen in the vicinity.

If you want to spend a night here, *Deebert House* (☎ 063-98106) is a good B&B, with singles/doubles from IR£20/30. To find it go down Wolfe Tone St and turn right after the bridge.

Bruree

Eamon de Valera was born in New York in 1882, to an Irish mother and Spanish father. His father died when he was two years old, and his mother sent the young Eamon to Ireland in 1885 with his uncle. As a child he lived in a small cottage in Bruree and attended a Christian Brothers school in the nearby town of Charleville. The **cottage** where he spent his formative years is open to the public although there's precious little in it. At the Kilmallock end of the village a sign points to the cottage, just over 1km down the road. The key to the house is available from the next house 200m farther up the road on the right-hand side.

The **Valera Museum & Bruree Heritage Centre** is in the National School attended by de Valera at the other end of the village and contains items associated with de Valera, as well as information on local history. It's open Tuesday to Friday 10 am to 5 pm, 2 to 5 pm at weekends; admission is IR£3/1. The village can be reached off the N20 road connecting Limerick and Cork. If coming from Kilmallock there's a direct road to Bruree.

ADARE & AROUND

This pretty village 16km south-west of Limerick is tourist Ireland at its most sanitised. The charming thatched cottages were created by the third earl of Dunraven in the 1820s; nowadays they're mostly craft shops or restaurants. Coach tours generally stop in Adare (Áth Dara) and its cultivated prettiness means high prices for food and accommodation.

Information

The tourist office (☎ 061-396255) is in

Eamon de Valera

As a young mathematics teacher, de Valera attended a meeting organised to protest at the 1911 visit to Ireland of the British monarchy. Enthused by the idea of an independent Irish republic, he quickly joined the new Irish Volunteers. During the 1916 Easter Rising he ambushed British reinforcements travelling to Dublin, securing the greatest military success of the rebellion.

Like the other leaders, he was sentenced to death for his role in the uprising but his US citizenship helped secure him escape with life imprisonment. After the amnesty of June 1917, he was elected Sinn Féin MP for East Clare, becoming Sinn Féin president from 1917 to 1926. In 1918 he was imprisoned in Lincoln Prison, England, but escaped using a duplicate key.

When the IRA split in 1921 over the Anglo-Irish Treaty, 'Dev' led the anti-Treaty forces in a bitter civil war. After the war he continued to be elected, this time for the Irish parliament (the Dáil), but refused to swear the contentious oath of allegiance to the British king. Eventually he entered the Dáil, skirting round the oath by not taking it but signing in as if he had, and claiming he was entering to ensure its abolition. His new party, Fianna Fáil, established a government in 1932. The new constitution abolished the oath and included a claim to sovereignty over the six northern counties. That claim is still part of the Irish constitution and contributes to the difficulties in reaching a settlement to the Troubles.

In Neil Jordan's film, *Michael Collins*, de Valera is played as an effete idealist by Alan Rickman, which is symptomatic of the recent decline in his reputation. ■

Adare Heritage Centre on the main street. From June to September it's open 9 am to 7 pm Monday to Friday, closing at 6 pm on Saturday and Sunday. The rest of the year it tends to keep standard office hours, although it closes in January and February and in the first two weeks of December.

May to September a costumed guide leads daily walking tours of the village; ☎ 061-396666 for more details.

The telephone code is ☎ 061.

Adare Heritage Centre

In the centre of the village, this surprisingly good heritage centre uses models and a short audiovisual presentation to help you make sense of the ruins scattered about; the model showing the village in 1500 is particularly worth a look. May to September it's open daily 9 am to 5 pm, closing at 1 pm on Saturday and all day Sunday for the rest of the year. Admission costs IR£2.50/1.50.

Desmond Castle

Dating back to around 1200, this photogenically ruined castle was partly rebuilt in the following century and besieged by English forces in 1580. When Cromwell's army took possession in 1657, it had already lost its strategic importance. By the time you read this, restoration work should have been completed and you should be able to view the castle without risking your life on the busy main road.

Adare Manor

When the earl of Dunraven decided to create a new mansion in 1832 he enlisted the architectural help of James Pain and AC Pugin, with quirky details like 52 chimneys and 365 windows. The building work it offered is said to have helped the village survive the Famine of the 19th century rather better than some others. Nowadays the house is an exclusive hotel surrounded by golf courses and you'll be charged IR£2 just to walk round its lovely grounds.

Religious Houses

At the time of the dissolution of the monas-

teries in 1539, Adare had three flourishing religious houses, the remains of which can still be seen.

In the village itself the dramatic tower and south wall of the **Church of the Most Holy Trinity** are the remains of a 13th century Trinitarian monastery (the only one in Ireland) which was restored by the first Earl of Dunraven and is now the Catholic church. There's a restored 14th century dovecot which used to belong to the monastery down the side turning next to the church.

The ruins of a **Franciscan Friary** founded by the earl of Kildare in 1464 stand in the middle of the Adare Manor golf course beside the river Maigue to the south of the village. Ask at the clubhouse for permission to visit but you'll have to walk all the way to the 15th tee. Look out for a well-preserved sedilia (set of seats for priests) in the south wall of the chancel.

Also south of the village on the N20, the Church of Ireland parish church was once the **Augustinian Friary**, founded in 1316. The tower was added in the 15th century, and the church was restored in 1807 by the first earl of Dunraven.

Celtic Park & Gardens

Eight km north-west of Adare in Kilcornan the Celtic Park is a collection of recreated 'Celtic' structures (plus a few originals) on a site known to have been inhabited in Celtic times. There's also an extensive rose garden and tearooms. The site opens daily March to November, 9 am to 7 pm. Admission costs IR£3 (children free).

Matrix Castle

This carefully preserved 15th century Norman tower is full of artefacts and *objets d'art*. Daily tours start at 10.30 am and continue until 6.30 pm. Entry is IR£3/2. The castle is 13km west of Adare on the N21, near Rathkeale.

Places to Stay

There are several B&Bs in the village but single travellers are in for an expensive time; better to stay in Limerick and commute. On

Main St, *Village House* (☎ 396554) charges from IR£27/35. *Elm House* (☎ 396306), Mondellihy, at around IR£34 for a double, has been recommended.

At *Adare Manor* (☎ 396566; fax 396124) a double can cost the best part of IR£400. Compared with that, the *Dunraven Arms* (☎ 396633; fax 396541) on the main street sounds a positive snip at IR£80/110 without breakfast.

Places to Eat

For reasonable pub lunches try *Lena's Bar* or *O'Coileain* in the main street. Alternatively there's the *Abbot's Rest* in the heritage centre; soup for IR£1.80, chicken curry for IR£4.50. Afternoon tea costs IR£5.50 at the *Blue Door* opposite Holy Trinity church. A few doors away at the award-winning *Wild Geese* (☎ 396451) a set meal costs IR£27; it's closed Sunday and Monday. Dinner at *Adare Manor* will set you back IR£32.50.

Entertainment

There's live music at *Bill Chawke*'s pub on Thursday and at *Collins* pub on Tuesday and Saturday.

The International Jazz Festival takes place over St Patrick's weekend in March; phone ☎ 396666 for details.

Getting There & Away

The five daily Dublin to Tralee buses call at Limerick and then Adare (IR£3.50 return to Limerick). For times contact Limerick bus station (☎ 313333).

County Tipperary

County Tipperary occupies a fair chunk of Ireland's south midlands and boasts the sort of limey, fertile soil that farmers dream of owning. Consequently Tipperary is at the heart of Irish farming, particularly around the southern Golden Vale, which has some of the country's richest pastures.

Tipperary is mostly flat in the centre, with hills intruding over the borders from other counties. The River Suir cuts through the heart of the county and every major town lies on the banks of the Suir or one of its tributaries. Some towns have very active animal fairs or marts, especially Tipperary Town which, incidentally, is not the major settlement: Clonmel, Cahir and Nenagh are far larger.

No WWI movie would be complete without some British private singing:

It's a long way to Tipperary,
It's a long way to go...

It was written as a marching song by Englishman Jack Judge in 1912. He had never set foot in Ireland and the word Tipperary was chosen only for its sound.

TIPPERARY TOWN

Originally an Anglo-Norman settlement, Tipperary Town (Tiobrad Árann) is a working town which consists essentially of the long Main St. The tourist office (☎ 062-51457) is off the west end of Main St on James St. It's open May to October, Monday to Saturday 10 am to 6 pm.

The telephone code is ☎ 062.

In the middle of Main St is a statue of Charles T Kickham (1822-82), a local novelist (author of *Knocknagow*) and Young Irelander. The **Sean Treacy Swimming Pool** at the east end of Main St houses a large display cabinet, with letters, photographs and artefacts relating to the War of Independence (1919-21) which had its very first engagement in a quarry a few km north of the town. It's free, but for diehard enthusiasts only.

Tipperary Racecourse is 3km out on the Limerick road with regular weekly meetings during the summer. See the local press for details or phone ☎ 51000.

A lively cattle mart is held at the east end of Main St on Wednesday and Friday.

Places to Stay & Eat

The *Royal Hotel* (☎ 51204) on Bridge St charges IR£20 per person for bed and breakfast. B&Bs can be found either side of town

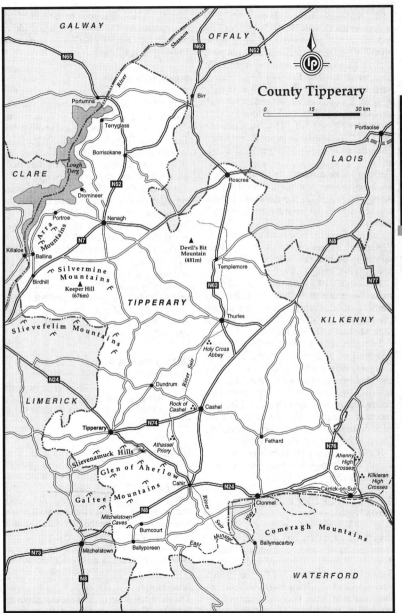

County Tipperary

on the N24 while *Airmont House* (☎ 51231) in Station Rd charges IR£14.50 per person.

Most of the pubs along Main St serve breakfast, tea and coffee, and lunch. In peak season they also do evening meals. In Kickham Place *The Basment Restaurant* is particularly popular for snacks and light lunches. It's open until 5 pm and serves Irish breakfasts for IR£3.10. Hidden in St Michael's St, just off Main St, *Cranley's* (☎ 33917) is an excellent small restaurant doing things like seafood crêpes for IR£5.95.

Getting There & Away
Most buses stop near the Brown Trout on Abbey St, except for the Rosslare Harbour service which stops outside Rafferty's Travel.

There are regular buses on the Limerick to Waterford express route and one daily service in each direction from Tipperary to Shannon in County Clare.

Kavanagh's (☎ 51563) buses travel daily from Tipperary to Dublin via Cahir and Cashel (not on Sunday). They leave at 8 am from outside the Marian Hall at the far end of St Michael's St from Main St.

Tipperary is on the Waterford to Limerick Junction line, with one daily service to Cahir, Clonmel, Waterford and Rosslare Harbour and multiple connections from Limerick Junction (☎ 51406), barely 3km from Tipperary along the Limerick road. Limerick Junction is one of the country's busiest railway stations, with daily services to Cork, Kerry, Waterford, Rosslare and Dublin.

Rafferty's Travel (☎ 51555) on Main St handles bookings for Bus Éireann and Iarnród Éireann.

GLEN OF AHERLOW & GALTEE MOUNTAINS
South of Tipperary Town are the Slievenamuck Hills and then the Galtee Mountains, separated by the gently beautiful Glen of Aherlow. Between Tipperary and Cahir is **Bansha** at the eastern end of the glen, which marks the start of a 20km trip to Galbally, an easy bike ride. It's a pleasant area for low-key hiking, with plenty of country accom-

modation. Cahir is a good base from which to explore the Galtees. The scenic drive through the Glen of Aherlow is signposted from Tipperary Town.

Places to Stay
Ballinacourty House Caravan & Camping Park (☎ 062-56230) has excellent caravan and camping facilities, as well as a fine garden, restaurant, wine bar and tennis court. This oasis is 10km from Bansha on the R663 to Galbally and opens from late March to late October. A tent with car is IR£7 plus IR£1 per adult. Hikers and cyclists pay just IR£4.

An Óige's *Ballydavid Wood House* (☎ 062-54148) is an old hunting lodge in the south-east corner of the glen 3km off the Tipperary to Cahir road on the north slopes of the Galtees. Beds cost IR£6/4.50.

The Georgian *Bansha House* (☎ 062-54194) is only 200m from Bansha village and does B&B from IR£20 a head.

Close by Bansha House is *Bansha Castle* (☎ 062-54187), a lovely castellated 19th century house and former residence of some of the Butlers of Ormond. B&B is from IR£21/32, dinner from IR£15.

Getting There & Away
The express Tipperary Town to Waterford bus stops at Bansha and there are five or six buses daily in both directions. For details, contact Rafferty's Travel (☎ 062-51555) in Tipperary Town.

CASHEL
Cashel (Caiseal Mumhan) is a prosperous market town with a staggering tourist drawcard in the Rock of Cashel. Unfortunately it's right on the main Dublin to Cork road and traffic thunders through at all hours. The good news is that the ruins you've come to admire are well away from the main road and that the high street doesn't feel quite as swamped by tourism as, say, Killarney's.

Information
The town hall in the middle of the main street contains Cashel's seasonal tourist office

(☎ 062-61333), which opens daily April to September.

The telephone code is ☎ 062.

Rock of Cashel

Far and away the most important reason for coming to Cashel is to visit the Rock of Cashel which dominates every viewpoint. The site is so important that it has its own separate entry following on from the Cashel town entry.

Folk Village

A thatched blue building in Dominic St houses this small but interesting Museum of Rural Life, which incorporates old buildings and shopfronts from around the town. Of particular interest are the model Penal Chapel where priests might have said mass in the days when to do so might have put them at risk of imprisonment; the slate-fronted Republican Museum room; and a traditional caravan which was home to a family of 16 until 1986. Take time to read some of the folk remedies such as shamrock and dogfern paste to cure lumbago, and garlic in the shoe to ward off rheumatism.

The museum opens Monday to Saturday 9.30 am to 7.30 pm and costs IR£2/50p.

Other Attractions

Around town there are a number of ruins which are sometimes overlooked. To get your bearings it's worth calling into the small heritage centre attached to the tourist office where a model shows what Cashel looked like in the 1640s. It's open daily April to September, 9.30 am to 5.30 pm, staying open until 8 pm in July and August. Admission costs IR£1/50p.

The first right-hand turn after leaving the Rock leads onto Dominic St with its small **Dominican Friary** ruin from 1243 which, unlike Hore Abbey, has been engulfed by the town.

Up a lane directly opposite the Cashel Palace Hotel is the **GPA Bolton Library** (GPA stands for Guinness Peat Aviation). This small building, once a chapter house in the grounds of the graceful 18th century Protestant cathedral, is now home to valuable manuscripts and first editions. It's open Monday to Friday, June to August, 11 am to 4.30 pm. Admission is IR£2.50/1.50. At other times contact Dr Knowles on ☎ 61232 for an appointment.

The **Cashel Palace Hotel** is a lovely Queen Anne residence built by Edward Lovett Pearce (architect of the Bank of Ireland in College Green, Dublin) for Archbishop Bolton in 1730.

Places to Stay

Camping & Hostels The IHH *O'Brien's Farm Hostel* (☎ 61003), in a converted coach house in Dundrum Rd, is friendly and well equipped, with views of the Rock and Hore Abbey to die for. Beds in reasonably spacious dorms cost IR£7, doubles are IR£20, and camping is IR£3.50 a head. The IHH *Cashel Holiday Hostel* (☎ 62330), at 6 John St, a quiet turning off Main St, also gets good reports. Dorm beds cost IR£6.50 to IR£7.50, the two double rooms IR£18 each.

B&B Dominic St, on the way from Main St to the Rock, has several quiet B&Bs with views of the Rock. The first you'll come to is *Abbey House* (☎ 61104) with good facilities for IR£15 a head. *Maryville* (☎ 61098), a little further along, charges IR£21.50/29 for a single/double without bath. Further still, *Rockville House* (☎ 61760) charges IR£32 for an ensuite double.

In quiet John St, *Ashmore House* (☎ 61286) has rooms from IR£21/29.

On Main St, *Bailey's* (☎ 61937) is a fine Georgian town house with B&B from IR£20 a head. Front rooms scoop Rock views but traffic noise can be irksome. There's a restaurant in the basement. *Ros-Guill House* (☎ 61507), 1km out on the Dualla road, also has Rock views plus exceptionally good breakfasts; rooms are from IR£21.50/31 and it's open mid-April to mid-October.

Hotels *Kearney's Castle Hotel*, (☎ 61044), in Main St, is a 15th century square tower once known as Quirke's Castle, with rooms from as little as IR£25/40.

Cashel Palace Hotel (☎ 61411; fax 61521) on Main St is exquisite, with an unbeatable view of the Rock; a private footpath joins the two. The bad news is that at IR£155 a double from April to October you're talking dreamland for most travellers.

Places to Eat

Despite the number of tourists flowing through, the Cashel eating scene is, with one or two exceptions, pretty basic.

For tea and coffee or a light lunch the best place on Main St is the *Coffee Shop* above the bakery across the road from the tourist office. Just down from the Rock, similar fare is available from the flower-bedecked *Granny's Kitchen* which also sells whiskey cake.

Although there's *O'Dowd's* on Main St for takeaways, none of the fast-food chains have made it this far.

The Spearman's Restaurant, at the Dublin end of Main St, serves things like lamb burgers for IR£6.95. Possibly better, and certainly more prominently positioned near the bus stop, is *Bianconi's Bistro* which does middle-of-the-road-fare but does at least manage one vegetarian dish in a town conspicuously short of these. Better still, *Roasters*, a family restaurant at the Cork end of Main St, has a choice of four non-meat dishes for IR£5.95. *Pasta Milano*, on the terrace in Ladyswell St, does pizza from IR£4 and pasta from IR£5.50; it's open until midnight at weekends.

The best restaurant in town is *Chez Hans* (☎ 61177), inside a converted church to the right at the end of Dominic St. A terrific dinner is likely to set you back a good IR£25 a head, but there's nothing for vegetarians unless they've asked in advance.

Cashel Blue cheese is actually made at Beechmount in Fethard but you can still buy chunks of it in the tourist office.

Entertainment

Down the hill past the Rock car park is *Brú Ború* (☎ 61122), a centre for traditional Irish music which serves it up seven nights a week during the summer season. Starting at 9 pm

there's music, song, dance, storytelling and crack galore. Admission is IR£6 for the night, and there's an optional pre-show banquet.

Irish nights on a smaller scale are held at *Kearney's Castle Hotel* (☎ 61044) every Thursday at 9 pm. Admission is IR£2.

For pub music try *Con Gleeson's*, *Feehan's* or *Alexander Knox & Co*, all along Main St, or the *Moor Lane Tavern*, behind the tourist office.

Getting There & Away

Bus Éireann runs three express buses daily between Dublin and Cork via Cahir and Fermoy and vice versa, with two on Sunday. In July and August there are an extra four buses a day to Cahir for the castle. There's also one bus daily each way on the Cork to Athlone via Thurs, Rescuer and Biro route. Rafferty's Travel (☎ 62121) on Main St handles Bus Éireann tickets and enquiries.

Kavanagh's (☎ 51563) has daily buses to Dublin, leaving Cashel at 8.45 am. Coming back, they leave Dublin (George's Quay near Tara St station) at 6 pm and arrive in Cashel at 8.30 pm. It also does a daily run between Cashel and Clonmel, departing from Cashel at noon, and another to Thurles, departing at 4 pm. None of these buses run on Sunday or bank holidays.

Getting Around

From June to September the Cashel Heritage Tram trundles round town linking up the places of interest. While this is obviously good for people who have trouble walking, it will seem disappointingly Disneyish to others. Tickets cost IR£3/1.50 from the tourist office.

The hostels hire out bicycles. Cahir and Fethard are both within cycling distance.

ROCK OF CASHEL

The Rock of Cashel (☎ 61437) is one of Ireland's most spectacular archaeological sites. For 20km or so in every direction there's a grassy plain, but on the outskirts of Cashel a huge lump of limestone bristling with ancient fortifications rises up. Mighty stone walls encircle a complete round tower, a roofless abbey and the finest 12th century Romanesque chapel in the country. For over a thousand years, the Rock of Cashel was a symbol of power, the base of kings and churchmen who ruled over the region and large swathes of the country.

The word Cashel is an anglicised version of the Irish *caiseal* meaning 'fortress', and it's easy to imagine that the site developed in territory hostile to the Church. From the Dublin road, the Rock is concealed by smaller hills until the last minute. The site is busy, especially in July and August, so go first thing in the morning or in late afternoon.

In the 4th century, the Rock of Cashel was chosen as a base by the Eóghanachta clan from Wales, who went on to conquer much of Munster and become kings of the region. For some 400 years it rivalled Tara as a centre of power in Ireland.

The clan's links with the church started early; St Patrick converted their leader in the 5th century in a ceremony in which he accidentally stabbed the king in the foot with his crozier. Thinking this a painful initiation rite, the king bore the pain with fortitude. Possibly he was afraid to react, considering how St Patrick had reacted to unbelievers on previous occasions.

In the 10th century the clan lost possession of the Rock to the O'Brien, or Dál gCais, tribe under Brian Ború's leadership. In 1101, King Muircheartach O'Brien presented the Rock to the Church, a move designed to curry favour with the powerful bishops and to stop the Eóghanachta ever regaining the Rock, as they could never ask the Church to return such a present. So the Eóghanachta, by now the MacCarthys, moved to Cork; as a sign of goodwill Cormac MacCarthy built Cormac's Chapel in 1127 before leaving.

This chapel proved to be too small. A new cathedral was built in 1169 but was replaced in the 13th century.

In 1647, the Rock fell to a Cromwellian army under Lord Inchiquin which sacked and burned its way to the top. Early in the 18th century the Protestant church took it over for 20 years, but this was the last time

the rock was officially used as a place of worship. The abbey roof only collapsed in the late 18th or early 19th century.

The Rock of Cashel opens year-round: mid-September to mid-March, it's open daily 9.30 am to 4.30 pm; between March and early June it's open daily 9.30 am to 5.30 pm; while June to mid-September it's open daily 9 am to 7.30 pm. Entry costs IR£2.50/1, and final admission is 40 minutes before closing time. There are two parking spaces for disabled visitors on the Rock itself; everyone else should use the car park at the foot which charges 50p.

Hall of the Vicars Choral

The entrance to the Rock is through this 15th century house, which now contains the ticket office. A 20 minute audiovisual presentation runs every half hour, detailing the Rock's history (there are French, German and Italian showings as well as English). The exhibits downstairs include some very rare silverware and **St Patrick's Cross**, a badly worn 12th century crutched cross with a crucifixion scene on the west face and interlacing and animals on the opposite side. Tradition held that the kings of Cashel and Munster – including Brian Ború – were inaugurated at the base of the cross. A replica stands outside. A couple of rooms upstairs contain period furniture, tapestries and paintings.

The Cathedral

This 13th century Gothic structure overshadows the other ruins. Entry is through a small porch facing the Hall of the Vicars Choral. The cathedral's west end is formed by the Archbishop's Residence, a 15th century, four-storey castle which had its great hall built over the nave. Soaring above the centre of the cathedral is a huge, square tower with a turret on the south-west corner.

Scattered throughout are monuments, panels from 16th century altar-tombs and coats of arms of the Butlers. On the north side of the choir is the recess tomb of Archbishop Hamilton. Opposite this is the tomb of Miler Mac Grath, who died in 1621. Miler was Catholic Bishop of Down and Connor until

1569, when he switched to the Protestant faith and ordained himself Protestant Archbishop of Cashel with Elizabeth I's blessing. Her forces were busy at the time torturing and executing his rival, the Catholic Archbishop Dermot O'Hurley.

Round Tower

On the north-east corner of the cathedral is the sandstone 11th or 12th century round tower, the earliest building on the Rock. It's 28m tall and the doorway is 3.5m above the ground – perhaps for structural rather than defensive reasons.

Cormac's Chapel

This is the Rock of Ca-shel's *pièce de résistance*, standing com- pletely intact to the south of the cathedral. Built from 1127, Cormac's Chapel is small, solid, stone-roofed and cruciform-shaped, with an unusual square tower on either side. Compared with other churches of the same era, the chapel is sophisticated in design, and displays influences from Britain and continental Europe – including the square towers.

Outside are impressive Romanesque arches, richly carved. Above the north door (opposite the entrance) in the minute courtyard adjoining the cathedral is a carving of a Norman helmeted figure firing an arrow at a huge lion which has just killed two animals.

The chapel's interior is dark, its windows either blocked up – perhaps to shield the

Carving of a Norman figure above the north door of Cormac's Chapel, Cashel

murals from light – or in the constant shadow of the cathedral.

The barrel-vaulted nave is only 12m long, with a fine archway into the east chancel, boasting many finely carved heads and capitals. The south tower leads to a stone-roofed vault or croft above the nave. Inside the main door to the chapel on the left is the sarcophagus said to house King Cormac, dating from between 1125 and 1150. The deeply cut, interlacing design is highly developed, with motifs more commonly found on metalwork from earlier centuries.

Unfortunately, a 10 year programme aimed at restoring the ancient frescoes in the chancel has left the chapel full of scaffolding, making it impossible to see most of the carvings. There's a chance it will be gone by the time you read this but don't bank on it. Work on the external stonework means yet more scaffolding on the outside ... and some will find the crisp, restored stonework a little harsh. If so, a glance up at the weathered corbel table offers a salutary reminder of why the work needed to be done.

Hore Abbey

The extensive ruins of 13th century Hore Abbey are set in farmland less than 1km north of the base of the Rock. It was the last daughter house – a religious house affiliated to the main monastery – of the Mellifont Cistercians and was a gift from a 13th century archbishop who expelled the Benedictine monks after dreaming that they planned to murder him. A pleasant walk (signposted) from the Rock leads to Hore Abbey, passing O'Brien's Farmhouse Hostel.

ATHASSEL PRIORY

Eight km south-west of Cashel is Athassel Priory. This extensive and long-abandoned Norman monastery sits peacefully on the west bank of the River Suir. It was built around 1200 by William de Burgh, who wanted it to be one of the richest and most important in the country. The native Irish, in the guise of the Earl of Desmond and the O'Briens, burned the priory and its accompanying town in 1319 and again in 1329.

What's left today are the remains of a gatehouse, gateway, surrounding walls and the cloisters or arched passageways where monks would walk in prayer, as well as some foundations of various other monastic buildings, including the chapter house. To get there take the N74 to the village of Golden and then head south for 2km to the priory

CAHIR

Cahir (pronounced 'Care') is 15km south of Cashel, at the eastern tip of the Galtees and on the banks of the River Suir. Dominated by its spectacular castle, Cahir (An Cathair) is on the main Dublin to Cork road, which ensures constant heavy traffic.

Orientation & Information

Buses stop in Castle St by a large car park (50p) beside the tourist office and facing the castle. East of Castle St, the square is ringed with shops, pubs and cafés. The post office is north of the square on Church St.

The tourist office (☎ 052-41453) opens May to September, Monday to Saturday, 9.30 am to 6 pm (closed 1 to 2 pm) and Sunday in July and August, 11 am to 5 pm. Ask for its free leaflet showing walking routes around Cahir Park.

The telephone code is ☎ 052.

Cahir Castle

Cahir's most noteworthy feature is the great 13th and 15th century castle in the town centre. The castle, one of Ireland's largest, was founded by Conor O'Brien in 1142 and passed to the Butler family in 1375. Its occupants surrendered to Cromwell in 1650 without a struggle – memories of the battering the place had suffered at the hands of the earl of Essex and his meagre two cannons in 1599 were still fresh. Consequently the castle is remarkably intact. It was also extensively restored in the 1840s and again in the 1960s when it came into state ownership. Some of John Boorman's *Excalibur* was filmed in Cahir Castle.

The castle sits on a rocky island in the River Suir. It consists of three wards or yards, surrounded by a thick fortifying curtain wall, with the main structural towers and halls around the innermost ward. Entry is along the sloping barbican running parallel to the inner-ward wall, and then through the reception area. This opens into the small middle ward, overshadowed by the large gatehouse and keep to the right. Go through this gatehouse, under the reconstructed and fully functioning portcullis, to reach the inner ward. Its buildings are sparsely furnished although there are small exhibitions on arms, Irish castles and Irish women in Tudor times. Don't miss the 10,000-year-old antlers of a giant Irish deer in the Banqueting Hall.

Beside the north-east tower, the small **well tower** offers the best vantage point over the river (marred, unfortunately, by a hideous grain silo with bright red shutters). The tower spirals down to the river and once provided a vital water supply for any extended siege.

The large garden-like outer ward has a 19th century cottage at the far end. This houses a short audiovisual show on other local sites of historic interest.

Cahir Castle, run by Dúchas, opens daily year-round: April to mid-June and mid-September to mid-October, it's open 10 am to 5.30 pm; mid-June to mid-September, it's open 9 am to 7 pm. The rest of the year it opens 10 am to 4 pm, but closes 1 to 2 pm. Admission is IR£2/1.

Afterwards, cross the bridge beside the castle and follow the road for five minutes until you come to the ruins of the 13th century **Cahir Abbey** on the right.

Swiss Cottage

A pleasant riverside path from behind the car park wanders 2km south to Cahir Park and the Swiss Cottage, also run by Dúchas. The Swiss Cottage is an exquisite thatched *cottage ornée*, the best in Ireland, surrounded by roses, lavender and honeysuckle. It was designed by Regency architect John Nash as a place of retreat for Richard Butler, 12th Baron Caher, and his wife. In accordance with contemporary French ideas, the cottage was supposed to look as if it had sprung fully-formed from the earth; straight lines and symmetry were abhorred and your guide will point out all the tricks used to make it seem more 'natural'. The 30-minute (compulsory) guided tours are thoroughly enjoyable.

The cottage opens daily 10 am to 6 pm between May and September. At other times of the year it closes on Monday and 1 to 2 pm. In April it closes at 5 pm and in late March and October to November at 4.30 pm. Admission is IR£2/1.

John Nash was also responsible for **St Paul's Church** (1820) whose graceful spire is visible from Cahir Bridge in the town centre.

Places to Stay

Camping At Moorstown on the N24 just between Cahir (6km) and Clonmel (9km) you can camp at *The Apple Caravan & Camping Park* (☎ 41459), on a fruit farm. The charge is IR£3.50 per adult and IR£1.75 per child. It's open from May to September.

Hostels Near Cahir there are three independent hostels. The run-of-the-mill IHH *Lisakyle Hostel* (☎ 41963) is 2km south of town on a back road to Ardfinnan past the Swiss Cottage. Dorm beds cost IR£6 and there's one double for IR£16. Maurice Condon's shop opposite the post office in Church St handles enquiries and arranges lifts to the hostel.

The excellent IHO *Kilcoran Farm Hostel* (☎ 41288), on an organic farm, is 6km west of Cahir, signposted 1.6km off the N8 Mitchelstown road at a petrol station. It has free showers, kitchen facilities and donkey rides for kids. Beds cost a flat IR£7 per person.

Five km south-west of Cahir at Ballyea on the Tubbrid road the *Holistic Centre* (☎ 41962) also has a hostel with beds for IR£7. This is the place to come if you want to treat yourself to an aromatherapy session.

The nearest An Óige hostel is *Ballydavid Wood House*, 10km away (see the Glen of Aherlow above).

B&Bs & Hotels On the Cashel road *The Rectory* (☎ 41406) is a lovely Georgian

house with doubles from IR£32. It's only open May to September. One km along the Cashel road is *Ashling* (☎ 41601) with B&B from IR£22/34.

At Cahir you can stay the night in a castle as well as simply view one. The 16th century *Carrigeen Castle* (☎ 41370) on the Cork road is often mistaken for Cahir Castle. It's actually a B&B, with beds from IR£20/30.

In the town centre, the *Castle Court Hotel* (☎ 41210; fax 42333) on Church St is a pleasant family-run hotel costing IR£40/65. Six km along the Cork road, the *Kilcoran Lodge Hotel* (☎ 41288; fax 41994) has a pool and health club. B&B starts at IR£35/60.

Places to Eat

Opposite Cahir Castle car park and above a craft shop is the *Crock of Gold*, a scruffy restaurant which serves breakfasts (IR£3.50) and light meals until 8 pm. Frillier and more inviting is *Kay's Coffee Shop* in the square. The *Galtee Inn*, also in the square, does soup and a roll for IR£1.35 and main courses for IR£4.85.

The *Italian Connection* in Castle St does pizza from IR£3.95 and pasta from IR£5.35. *Roma Café* in The Square does burgers and sandwiches.

Getting There & Away

Cahir is on the Dublin to Cork, Limerick to Waterford, Kilkenny to Cork, and Cork to Athlone express bus routes. Less frequent services run from and to Tralee with connections on the northbound bus to Galway, Sligo, Derry, Drogheda, Dundalk and Belfast. The bus stop is outside the Crock of Gold, across the road from Cahir Castle. For bus times, ring ☎ 062-51555.

Kavanagh's (☎ 062-51563) buses travel daily except Sunday from Tipperary Town to Cahir, Cashel and Dublin.

One train a day on the Waterford to Limerick Junction line stops at Cahir (not Sunday), with connections to Cork and Rosslare. For details, contact Thurles railway station (☎ 0504-21733).

MITCHELSTOWN CAVES

The Galtee Mountains are sandstone, but along the south side runs a narrow band of limestone, which is home to the Mitchelstown Caves. They're near Burncourt, 16km south-west of Cahir and sign-posted off the road to Mitchelstown. Far superior to Kilkenny's Dunmore Caves and yet less developed for tourists, these caves are among the most extensive in the country.

In 1833, Michael Condon was quarrying limestone when he lost his crowbar down a crack in the rock. His efforts to retrieve it opened up the system now called the New Caves. An earlier cave system nearby – now called the Old Caves – was already known to have been used in prehistoric times. Although the Old Caves contain the system's largest chamber, it's the New Caves that form the basis of the tour. Exploration begins through Condon's original opening. Internal temperatures are pretty constant at around 13°C. Underground, there are nearly 2km of passages and spectacular chambers full of text-book formations, inventively labelled from classical and biblical sources.

The caves (☎ 052-67246) are open all year 10 am to 6 pm. Call at the English's farmhouse opposite the car park for tickets and a tour guide. Admission is IR£3/1.

Places to Stay

Six km due north of the caves on the slopes of the Galtees is the An Óige *Mountain Lodge Hostel* (☎ 052-67277), north off the main Mitchelstown to Cahir road. It's open March to September and is a handy base for exploring the Galtees. Beds cost IR£5.50/4.

Getting There & Away

Daily express buses from Dublin to Cork will drop you at the Mountain Lodge hostel. Ring ☎ 062-51555 for details.

CLONMEL

Clonmel (Cluain Meala) is Tipperary's largest, liveliest and most cosmopolitan town. Coming from Carrick-on-Suir look out for the Bulmer's cider orchards alongside the road.

Over the centuries Clonmel's wealth has attracted many business people, one of whom is now synonymous with Clonmel. Charles Bianconi (1786-1875) arrived in Ireland from northern Italy, aged 16 and sent by his father in an attempt to break a liaison with a young lady who was already spoken for. In 1815, he set up a coach service between Clonmel and Cahir, and the company quickly grew, becoming a nationwide passenger and mail carrier. For putting Clonmel on the map, Bianconi was twice elected mayor. The company's former headquarters is now Hearn's Hotel on Parnell St – Hearn was an assistant to Bianconi.

Orientation & Information

Clonmel's heart lies on the north bank of the River Suir. Set back from the quays and running parallel to the river, the main street runs from east to west, starting off as Parnell St and becoming Mitchel St and O'Connell St before passing under West Gate and becoming Irishtown and Abbey Rd. Running north off this long thoroughfare is Gladstone St, with lots of shops and pubs.

The tourist office (☎ 052-22960), in the Chamber of Commerce building opposite the Clonmel Arms Hotel, opens Monday to Friday year-round 9 am to 5 pm. The post office is in a courtyard of the one-time county gaol at the north end of Emmet St, which runs north off Mitchel St.

The telephone code is ☎ 052.

Walking Tour

A good starting point for a whip round town is **Hearn's Hotel**, the former headquarters of Bianconi's coach business.

South of Parnell St in Nelson St is the **County Courthouse** designed by Richard Morrison in 1802. It was here that the Young Irelanders of 1848, including Thomas Francis Meagher, were tried and sentenced to be transported to Australia. From June to September at 8.15 pm on Wednesday, Thursday and Friday it's possible to see some of the most famous trials recreated; phone ☎ 22960 for details.

Back on Parnell St the faded **County Museum** exhibits the shirt worn by Michael Hogan, who was captain of the Tipperary Gaelic Football team in Croke Park when they played Dublin in November 1920. In retaliation for the deaths of 14 British army intelligence officers, the British police auxiliaries (the Black & Tans) opened fire on the crowd and players during a match, killing Hogan and 13 others. This was the first of several Bloody Sundays. The museum opens, free, Tuesday to Saturday 10 am to 1 pm and 2 to 5 pm.

West along Mitchel St (past the pistachio-coloured town hall with its statue commemorating the 1798 Rising) and south down Abbey St, is the **Franciscan Friary**. The 15th century tower is surrounded by newer work dating only from 1848 and 1884. Inside, near the door, is a 1533 Butler tomb depicting a knight and his lady. There's some fine modern stained-glass, especially in St Anthony's Chapel to the north.

Back up on Mitchel St at the junction with Sarsfield St is the **Main Guard**, a Butler courthouse from 1674, based on a design by Christopher Wren. At the time of writing it was undergoing restoration.

Turn south down Bridge St and cross the river, following the road round until it opens out at **Lady Blessington's Bath**, a picturesque stretch of the river, excellent for picnicking.

Return to O'Connell St. Spanning the far end is the **West Gate**, an 1831 reconstruction of an earlier town gate. On the east side is a plaque commemorating Laurence Sterne (1713-68), a native of the town and author of *A Sentimental Journey* and *Tristram Shandy*. Just before the arch is Wolfe Tone St which heads north past **White Memorial Theatre**, once the Wesleyan Chapel, to **Old St Mary's Church**, built in 1204 by William de Burgh and boasting a fine octagonal tower. To the north and west sides are overgrown stretches of the 14th century town wall.

The other side of West Gate is **Irishtown**, named after those native Irish who worked inside the town but were forbidden to live within its walls.

Places to Stay

Camping The *Power's the Pot Caravan & Camping Park* (☎ 23085) has a Clonmel address even though it's 9km to the southeast on the northern slopes of the Comeragh Mountains, well inside County Waterford. To get there, cross south over the river in Clonmel and then follow the road to Rathgormack. It has a good restaurant and 'beds are available in bad weather'. A tent for two costs IR£6; hikers and cyclists pay IR£3.50.

B&Bs & Hotels Many B&Bs are on Marlfield Rd, due west of Irishtown and Abbey Rd. *Benuala* (☎ 22158) charges from IR£16/28 while *Hillcourt* (☎ 21029) is from IR£21/32. *Amberville* (☎ 21470) on Glenconnor Rd, north off Western Rd beside St Luke's Hospital, is within walking distance of the centre. B&B is from IR£19/28.

Hearn's Hotel (☎ 21611; fax 21135), right in the town centre, does singles/doubles for IR£40/70. The fine *Clonmel Arms Hotel* (☎ 211233; fax 21526) is down from the main street towards the river on Sarsfield St and costs from IR£60/90, excluding breakfast.

South of the River Suir, the *Hotel Minella* (☎ 22388; fax 24381) is a three-star hotel with four hectares of gardens, almost 2km east of town on the Coleville road (follow the South Quays east). B&B costs from IR£75/130. Six km from Clonmel *Knocklofty Country House Hotel* (☎ 38222; fax 38300) is set in 42 hectares of parkland – a good choice if you're ready to splash out IR£55/100 a single/double.

Places to Eat

Cosy *Niamh's* is a coffee shop on Mitchel St with dishes like coronation chicken pitta for IR£2.75, while *Angela's* in Abbey St is good for light lunches with things like spinach and mushroom pasta bake for IR£4.40. In the Marystone Centre, *Coyle's Coffee House* is open until 5.30 pm, with snacks like beans on toast for IR£1.40.

Bar food is available in *Tierney's Pub* on O'Connell St while *Barry's* next door serves

Tex-Mex meals. *Mulcahy's*, a vast pub and restaurant on Gladstone St, opens 10 am to 10 pm and serves some Irish dishes – boxties for IR£2.75, coddle for IR£5. The *Clonmel Arms Hotel* on Sarsfield St is one of the best places in town for reasonably priced bar lunches.

The *Emerald Garden* (☎ 24270) Chinese restaurant on O'Connell St is cheaper for lunch than dinner; its takeaway offshoot is across the road. *La Scala* (☎ 24147), on Market St off Gladstone St, has an early bird 'international' menu for IR£10.50 until 9 pm. *Catalpa* in Sarsfield St does pizza from IR£3.95 and pasta from IR£4.25.

Entertainment
Lonergan's on O'Connell St has music on Monday night. Many other bars, like the *Coachman* on Parnell St and *Mulcahy's* on Gladstone St, have local bands and Irish music in the summer.

The River Room in the Clonmel Arms Hotel is a Friday and Saturday nightclub.

South Tipperary Arts Centre (☎ 27877) in Nelson St has temporary art exhibitions.

Spectator Sports
Clonmel is the heartland of Irish greyhound racing and coursing. At the east end of Parnell St on Davis St is the greyhound track which has dog racing on Monday and Thursday at 8 pm. Powerstown Park Racecourse is north of town and has a year-round fixture list – though events may be a few weeks apart. For details of all fixtures call ☎ 21422.

Getting There & Away
Bus Bus Éireann (☎ 051-79000) has two buses daily each way to Dublin and Cork, with a more complicated timetable to Waterford, Limerick and Kilkenny. Rafferty's Travel (☎ 22622) acts as Bus Éireann's ticket agency and the bus stop is at the railway station. Kavanagh's (☎ 062-51563) has daily buses between Cashel and Clonmel, leaving Cashel at noon and Clonmel at 3 pm (not on Sunday).

Train The railway station (☎ 21982) is north of Gladstone St on Prior Park Rd, within walking distance of the town centre. Clonmel is on the Cork-Limerick-Rosslare Harbour line, with one train each way daily except on Sunday. There's no direct rail link to Dublin, but there are connections from Waterford or Limerick Junction.

Getting Around
Classic Cycles, 8 Mary St, is the Raleigh rent-a-bike dealer with bikes for IR£7/30 a day/week.

AROUND CLONMEL
Directly south of Clonmel are the Comeragh Mountains in County Waterford, and there's a fine scenic route south to Ballymacarbry and the Nire Valley. Instead of coming back the same way you can do a circle, heading down to Ballymacarbry from the east and heading back up to Clonmel from the west side. For more details, see the Nire Valley section in County Waterford.

The **East Munster Way** long-distance walk (see the Activities chapter) passes through Clonmel following the old towpath along the River Suir. At Sir Thomas Bridge the trail cuts south away from the river and into the Comeraghs to Harney's Crossroads before rejoining the River Suir again at Kilsheelan Bridge from where it follows the towpath all the way to Carrick-on-Suir. From Clonmel, you can take shorter walks along parts of the trail using the same towpath. The main road between Clonmel and Carrick-on-Suir also follows the river through some lovely countryside dotted with ruined 16th and 17th tower houses and roofless medieval churches.

FETHARD
Fourteen km north of Clonmel on the River Clashawley is Fethard, a sleepy community grown rich from the proceeds of the local stud farm. Like Carlingford in County Louth, Fethard is sprinkled with medieval ruins. Despite this it hasn't really cottoned on to the potential of tourism, making it a pleasant place for those seeking peace and quiet.

A nameless newsagent's in Main St, opposite the entrance to Trinity Church, sells a good guide to the town, incorporating a walking guide, for IR£3.

The telephone code is ☎ 052.

Things to See

The single most striking survivor from medieval times is **Holy Trinity Church**, in Main St, which dates from the 13th century and boasts a sturdy tower that looks as if it was built to defend the church although the clergy probably lived in it. Surrounding the churchyard is a stretch of reconstructed **medieval wall** complete with 15th century turrets. Unfortunately, to get into the churchyard you must collect a key from Whyte's Supermarket in Main St while to get into the church you must collect a separate key from Dr Stoke's surgery at the east end of Main St.

Almost next to the church in Main St is the 17th century **town hall** with some fine coats of arms mounted on the facade.

The greatest concentration of medieval remains can be found south of the church at the end of Watergate St. Beside the Castle Inn are the ruins of several fortified **tower houses** dating from the 17th century. Better still you can see the entire length of the **town wall** dating from the 15th or 16th centuries, although parts are even older. Near Watergate Bridge a **sheila-na-gig** is set into a section of the wall.

East along Abbey St is the 14th century **Augustinian Friary**, now in use as the Catholic church but with some fine medieval stained-glass.

Fethard's only signposted attraction is the small **Folk Museum** in the old railway station on the Cashel road which houses a collection of agricultural appliances and hosts a Sunday market. It's open June to August, daily 10.30 am to 5 pm, and on Sunday for the rest of the year 1 to 5 pm. Admission is IR£1/50p.

Places to Stay & Eat

The Gateway (☎ 31701) is a small B&B in Rocklow Rd, near the ruined 15th century North Gate, with rooms for IR£18/30.

G&T's, at the west end of Main St, will do you a bacon and pancake breakfast for IR£2 and burgers for around IR£5. For something a bit more formal there's *J's Restaurant* (☎ 31176) next door which opens for dinner from 6 to 10 pm Wednesday to Sunday and for Sunday lunch from 12.30 to 2.30 pm.

Getting There & Away

There's no public transport to Fethard but it would make a pleasant cycle ride from Cashel, 15km to the west.

CARRICK-ON-SUIR

The market town of Carrick-on-Suir (Carraig na Siúire), 20km east of Clonmel, grew to considerable importance through the brewing and wool industries during the Middle Ages. For a long time, the seven-arched 15th century bridge was the only crossing point on the river for 40km from the Suir's mouth at Waterford Harbour. In the 18th century, the population was 11,000, almost twice what it is today. Compared to Clonmel, Carrick-on-Suir is quiet and unsophisticated, perhaps because the N24 bypasses the town centre. It's surrounded by rich green farmland with the Comeragh Mountains in the distance.

Most places only make a fuss of their famous inhabitants after their demise, but Carrick-on-Suir was quick to honour Sean Kelly, one of the world's greatest cyclists of the late 1980s. The town square now bears his name, as does the sports centre. There are even plans for a cycling museum.

From Carrick-on-Suir the East Munster Way winds its way west to Clonmel before heading south into Waterford. For more details see the Activities chapter.

Information

An old church off Main St houses the tourist information office (☎ 051-640200) which opens March to October, 9 am to 5 pm Monday to Saturday (closed 1 to 2 pm) and 2 to 5 pm Sunday. There's also a small **heritage centre** here but it makes no attempt to provide a narrative or explain its ragbag of exhibits. Consequently the IR£1/50p charge is hardly worth it.

The telephone code is ☎ 051.

Ormond Castle

Carrick-on-Suir was once the property of the Butlers, the earls of Ormond, who built the 14th century castle on the banks of the river at the east end of Castle St. Anne Boleyn, the second of Henry VIII's six wives, is rumoured to have been born here, though many other castles claim this distinction. She was the great-grand daughter of the 7th earl of Ormond. The Elizabethan mansion next to the castle was built by the 10th earl of Ormond, Black Tom Butler, in anticipation of a visit by his cousin, Queen Elizabeth I, who unfortunately never got round to seeing the result of his efforts.

Some of the rooms have fine 16th century stuccowork, especially the Long Gallery, with its depictions of Elizabeth and the Butler coat of arms. Considering the turmoil of the period, it's interesting to note the house's almost complete lack of defences. Indeed this is Ireland's only example of the sort of Tudor manor house common in more settled England. Unfortunately, the Dúchas-owned castle is only open mid-June to September, daily 9.30 am to 5.45 pm. Admission is IR£2/1.

Places to Stay

Camping The small *Carrick-on-Suir Caravan & Camping Park* (☎ 640461) is at Ballyrichard off the Kilkenny Rd. A tent site plus car costs IR£6; for hikers and cyclists it's IR£3.

B&Bs & Hotels

Centrally located on Sean Kelly Square is *Orchard House* (☎ 641390), with B&B in quiet, comfortable rooms from IR£15 a head. On John St, nor far from the Greenside bus stop, *Fatima House* (☎ 640298) has singles/doubles from IR£15/26.

Carraig Hotel (☎ 641455; fax 641604) on Main St has rooms from IR£35/60 for B&B. More modern is *The Bell & Salmon Arms* (☎ 645555), 95-7 Main St, with rooms for IR£33/55.

Places to Eat

At the Sean Kelly Square end of Main St, *The Weir* is a pleasant tea shop which does soup and good brown bread for IR£1.30 and lunch specials for IR£3.95. Most of the Main St pubs do lunches. The *Carraig Hotel* is probably the best place to eat; there are lunch specials for IR£4.95 and dinner will cost you around IR£12 – the seafood bisque is strongly recommended. The *Europa*, also on Main St, does pizzas and takeaways.

Entertainment

Side by side on Main St, *N Cooney's* and *Just Gerry's* are atmospheric old bars. The *Strand Theatre* by the new bridge doubles as a cinema. There's line dancing at the *Carraigh Hotel* every Wednesday night from 8 to 11 pm.

Getting There & Away

Bus Bus Éireann (☎ 79000) has extensive bus services to and from the town. The Limerick to Waterford express route has five or six daily buses serving Tipperary Town, Cahir, Clonmel and Carrick-on-Suir, and with connections to Galway and Rosslare Harbour. There are also at least three or four daily buses from Clonmel to Dublin via Carrick-on-Suir and Kilkenny, and with connections to Cork. Buses stop at Greenside, the park beside the main N24.

Train There's one train a day, except on Sunday, on the Cork to Rosslare Harbour line via Limerick Junction and Waterford. For information contact Thurles railway station (☎ 0504-21733).

AHENNY & KILKIERAN HIGH CROSSES

Roughly 5km and 8km north of Carrick-on-Suir and signposted off the road to Windgap are the two groups of high crosses at Ahenny and Kilkieran.

The impressive Ahenny crosses are both 4m tall and date from the 8th century. Unusually, they're almost exclusively covered in an interlacing design in high relief. The more typical religious scenes only appear on the base and are said to represent the transition from the older abstract designs of high crosses to the pictorial scenes found on many later crosses. Another odd feature are the removable cap stones, sometimes known as mitres (bishop's hats). Legend has it that these caps can cure migraine headaches if placed on the sufferer's head. Given the size of the stones, the victim would have more than migraine to worry about!

A panel on the base of the north cross depicts seven men, supposedly bishops who had returned from Rome, each carrying a bag of sand as a souvenir. Mistaking their bags for purses, robbers ambushed them, then murdered them, convinced that the bishops had turned their gold into sand to save it from being stolen.

A third cross was reputedly stolen about 200 years ago. The story goes that the ship which was carrying the cross out of Waterford was lost at sea off Passage East, and that the cross lies somewhere on the sea floor.

About 2km nearer Carrick-on-Suir are the three Kilkieran crosses. The west cross is similar to those in Ahenny: 4m tall, richly decorated and with mitre intact. The other is extremely plain. The most interesting is the needle-like Long Shaft Cross, a shape unique in Ireland.

At the far end of the cemetery is St Kieran's well whose waters are said to cure headaches. There must have been a plague of headaches, given the plethora of cures to be found locally.

THURLES

Thurles (Durlas) is a large market town 22km north of Cashel which was founded by the Butlers in the 13th century. Little of note has been built there since and the town square is little more than an ugly car park.

Information

The tourist information desk (☎ 0504-23579) in the Centrefield building on the Slievenamon road, which is north off Liberty Square, opens May to August.

The telephone code is ☎ 0504.

Things to See

The ruins of two square tower houses survive: 15th century **Barry's Castle** by the bridge and **Black Castle** at the opposite end of Liberty Square, behind the shops. An incongruous **bird sanctuary** sits on an island in the middle of the River Suir. A few hundred metres farther on is the **Catholic cathedral**, built in the 1860s in the Italian Romanesque style.

In Liberty Square is **Hayes Hotel** where, as every Irish schoolchild learns, the Gaelic Athletic Association, or GAA, was founded in 1884 to foster the pursuit of Irish sports and pastimes, particularly Gaelic football and hurling, which it continues to oversee. Over the years, the GAA has been the most successful of the Gaelic revivalist groups. The Centrefield building on the Slievenamon road off the Square houses **Lár na Páirce**, a museum of hurling, open 2 to 5 pm daily, with a 20 minute video of game highlights. Admission costs IR£2.50/1.50.

Getting There & Away

Bus Éireann (☎ 051-79000) buses stop at Thurles once daily on the Cork to Athlone route, with connections to Cahir, Roscrea and Birr. There's no Sunday service. In July and August there's also one service a day Monday to Saturday from Waterford to Galway via Thurles.

Thurles is on the Dublin to Limerick and Dublin to Cork railway lines. For details contact Thurles railway station (☎ 21733).

HOLY CROSS ABBEY

Six km south-west of Thurles is the picturesque Cistercian Holy Cross Abbey right beside the River Suir. The abbey was in ruins until the early 1970s, but the cloisters and chapels are now a living church again.

The buildings you see today date from the 15th century, when the abbey was largely remodelled. The ground plan is typically Cistercian: a fine cruciform church with a square tower and cloisters to the east. Inside the church, look out for the small fleurs-de-

A Relic of the True Cross
Holy Cross Abbey was home to a relic of the True Cross, a splinter of wood said to be from Jesus' cross, which attracted pilgrims to the abbey from its foundation in the 1160s. The splinter of wood was said to have been presented by Pope Pascal II to the King of Munster, Murtagh O'Brien, in the early 12th century. It was the only cross relic in the country and was passed on to the nuns of the Ursuline Convent in Cork in the 19th century. ■

lis and other symbols carved on the old stone pillars, the individual trademarks of the stonemasons. There's also a fine medieval fresco showing a hunting scene.

Built into the side of the abbey complex is a pub which does good food. Holy Cross Abbey is signposted from Thurles and Cashel.

ROSCREA

For somewhere to break your journey between Dublin and Limerick, the medium-sized town of Roscrea (Ros Cré) is much more inviting than Nenagh. On the eastern edge of the county, Roscrea, like Mountrath in Laois, can be used as a base for exploring the Slieve Bloom Hills to the north-east. Although the main Limerick to Dublin road cuts through the town, the wide streets are better able than those in smaller towns to cope with the traffic.

Roscrea owes its origin to a 5th century monk, St Crónán, who set up a way station for the travelling poor. Most of the historical structures are on or near the main street.

The telephone code is ☎ 0505.

Things to See

Coming into town from the Dublin side, you're faced with a truncated **round tower** built into the wall of a builder's yard, while across the road are the remains of St Crónán's second monastery: the gable end of **St Crónán's Church** with its finely worked stone Romanesque doorway, and a **high cross** dating from the 12th century. The rest

of the church was torn down in 1812. The site of St Crónán's first monastery is almost 2km east of town and south of the main Dublin road.

The Book of Dímma, a 7th century illuminated manuscript which originated from here can now be seen in Trinity College, Dublin.

In the centre of town is the Dúchas-restored 13th century **Castle**, with the substantial remains of a gatehouse, walls and towers. Inside the courtyard stands austere **Damer House**, the Queen Anne residence of the Damer family, which houses **Roscrea Heritage Centre**. This contains several interesting exhibitions, including one on the medieval monasteries of the midlands and another on early 20th century farming life. It's open June to September, daily 9.30 am to 5.45 pm, and admission is IR£2.50/1. October to May it's open weekends only 10 am to 5 pm.

Abbey St has considerable remains of a 15th century **Franciscan Friary**. Nearby in Rosemary Square don't miss Roscrea's answer to the *Mannequin Pis*, a fountain with four cherubs pouring water out of urns.

Places to Stay & Eat

If you want to stay, *Grants Hotel* (☎ 23300; fax 23209) near the castle has rooms for I£35/60 without breakfast. The *Waterfront Coffee Shop and Gallery*, signed as you walk from the castle to the round tower, does light lunches like soup for IR£1.40 or a spring roll for IR£2.75.

Getting There & Away

Frequent Dublin to Limerick express buses (☎ 01-836 6111) stop at Roscrea (two hours). There are also a couple of daily buses to Limerick and Tralee via Nenagh, but only one on Sunday. Roscrea is also on a daily Cork to Athlone express route which serves Fermoy, Cahir, Cashel, Thurles and Templemore and Birr.

Two Dublin to Limerick trains stop at Roscrea every day. For details ring Thurles railway station (☎ 0504-21733).

LOUGH DERG

Lough Derg marks the border between Counties Tipperary and Clare. The **Lough Derg Way** walking trail begins in Limerick City and ends at the village of Dromineer in County Tipperary. See the Activities chapter for details.

If you're heading north-east from Limerick City towards Nenagh it's much more enjoyable to take the scenic route from Birdhill along the River Shannon to Ballina and then follow the road hemmed in between the edge of Lough Derg and the Arra Mountains rather then to follow the N7 all the way. **Ballina** is joined by a bridge to the heritage town of Killaloe in County Clare; see that section for more details. The tourist office on the Killaloe side of the bridge stocks a free walking tour leaflet which covers Ballina as well.

NENAGH & AROUND

Nenagh (Aonach) is a busy, rather dreary town on the main Dublin to Limerick road and blighted by heavy traffic.

The tourist office (☎ 067-31610) on Connolly St opens Monday to Saturday, May to September, and stocks a good free town trail map.

The telephone code is ☎ 067.

Things to See

Nenagh Castle was the seat of the first Butler of Ireland, Theobald fitzWalter, in the early 13th century and remained in the family's possession for 400 years. The fitzWalters changed their name to Butler and in the late 14th century moved their principal seat of power to Kilkenny Castle (see Kilkenny City and Castle for more details). All that remains of their castle at Nenagh is a striking circular **donjon** or tower dating from 1217. It's over 30m tall; the final 8m was added by the Bishop of Killaloe in 1860.

Across the road is a Doric courthouse and beside it a convent, originally a prison. Some of the buildings now house the **Nenagh Heritage Centre** which is in two parts. The first, and most interesting, is the Gatehouse Gaol where 17 men were hanged between 1842. You can inspect the condemned cells and read about their crimes, before gazing on their last drop. Along the driveway is the octagonal Governor's House, which contains good mock-ups of an old country schoolroom, a pub/shop, a kitchen and a dairy.

The centre opens early May to late September, Monday to Friday 10 am to 5 pm. It's closed on Saturday and opens 2.30 to 5 pm on Sunday. Admission is IR£2/1.

Getting There & Away

Bus Buses to Nenagh stop in Banba Square in the middle of town; some also stop at the railway station. There are frequent buses on the Dublin to Limerick express route. A less frequent daily service runs from Tralee to Roscrea, Birr and Athlone via Nenagh. Another Monday to Saturday service runs from Nenagh to Limerick via Killaloe. From late June to August the Galway to Rosslare Harbour bus also stops at Nenagh.

Rapid Express Coaches (☎ 26266) has daily services to Dublin, leaving from the deserted O'Meara's Hotel in Pearse St from 8.10 am; an extra Monday service leaves at 6 am. These buses travel via Roscrea, Portlaoise and Kildare.

Train Two Dublin to Limerick trains stop at Nenagh every day. For details ring Thurles railway station (☎ 0504-21733).

County Kilkenny

A verdant farming county, Kilkenny is peppered with solid stone walls, medieval ruins and stands of old trees. The Normans liked this part of Ireland and settled here in numbers, leaving their stamp on Kilkenny City which is a league above most midland towns. The county's most attractive areas are along the rivers Nore and Barrow, with charming villages like Inistioge and Graiguenamanagh. Jerpoint Abbey and Kells Priory are two of the country's finest medieval monastic settlements.

Since medieval times, Kilkenny's history has been inextricably linked with the fortunes of one Anglo-Norman family, the Butlers, earls of Ormond. After arriving in 1171, they made the region their own, promoting first the Norman cause and then that of the English royal household. They were based in Kilkenny City.

Walking the stretch of the South Leinster Way that crosses southern Kilkenny offers an opportunity to see rural Ireland at its prettiest.

Kilkenny

Kilkenny is perhaps the most attractive large town in the country although, with just 20,000 people, it's far from being the largest; its status has more to do with its role in the past than in the present.

Despite being ransacked by Cromwell during his 1650 visit, Kilkenny retains some of its medieval ground plan, particularly the narrow streets which can lead to nasty traffic jams. The city's Irish name is Cill Chainnigh after the monastery of St Cainneach which existed here in the 6th century. The saint's name is also attached to the city's splendid medieval cathedral. Overlooking a sweeping bend in the River Nore, Kilkenny Castle is the other 'must' for visitors.

Kilkenny is sometimes called the 'Marble

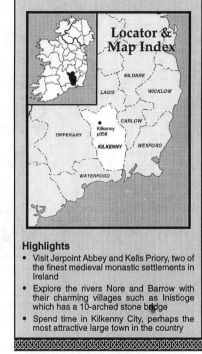

Highlights

- Visit Jerpoint Abbey and Kells Priory, two of the finest medieval monastic settlements in Ireland
- Explore the rivers Nore and Barrow with their charming villages such as Inistioge which has a 10-arched stone bridge
- Spend time in Kilkenny City, perhaps the most attractive large town in the country

City' because of the local black limestone seen to most striking effect in the cathedral.

HISTORY

In the 5th century, St Kieran is said to have visited Kilkenny and, on the present site of Kilkenny Castle, challenged the chieftains of Ossory to accept the Christian faith. St Canice established his monastery in the 6th century.

Kilkenny consolidated its importance in the 13th century under William Marshall, the earl of Pembroke and son-in-law of the Norman conqueror, Strongbow. Kilkenny

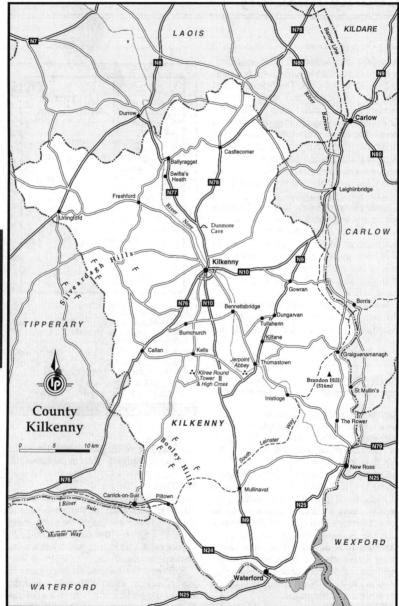

KILKENNY

LAOIS

KILDARE

N7

N8

N78

N80

Barrow Line

N9

River Barrow

Carlow

Durrow

Castlecomer

N80

Ballyragget

Swifte's Heath

N78

Leighlinbridge

Freshford

N77

CARLOW

Urlingford

River Nore

Dunmore Cave

Silveardagh Hills

Kilkenny

N10

N9

Gowran

Borris

TIPPERARY

N76

N10

Bennettsbridge

Dungarvan

Tullaherin

Burnchurch

Kilfane

Graiguenamanagh

Callan

Kells

Jerpoint Abbey

Thomastown

Brandon Hill (516m)

St Mullin's

Kilree Round Tower & High Cross

Inistioge

County Kilkenny

0   5   10 km

KILKENNY

Booley Hills

South Leinster Way

The Rower

N79

New Ross

N25

Carrick-on-Suir

Piltown

Mullinavat

N76

River Suir

N9

East Munster Way

N24

WEXFORD

WATERFORD

Waterford

N25

N25

Castle was built to secure a crossing point on the Nore.

During the Middle Ages, Kilkenny was intermittently the unofficial capital of Ireland, with its own Anglo-Norman parliament. In 1366 the Kilkenny parliament passed a set of laws called the Statutes of Kilkenny, aimed at preventing assimilation of the increasingly assertive Anglo-Normans into Irish society. The Anglo-Normans were prohibited from marrying the native Irish, taking part in Irish sports, speaking or dressing like the Irish or playing any of their music. Although the laws remained theoretically in force for over 200 years, the Anglo-Normans eventually became 'more Irish than the Irish themselves'.

During the 1640s, Kilkenny sided with the royalists in the English Civil War. The 1641 Confederation of Kilkenny, an uneasy alliance of native Irish and Old English, aimed to bring about the return of land and power to the Catholics. After Charles I's execution, Cromwell besieged Kilkenny for five days, destroying much of the south wall of the castle before Ormond surrendered. The city never fully recovered from this defeat.

ORIENTATION

At the junction of several major highways, Kilkenny straddles the River Nore, which flows through much of the county. St Canice's Cathedral sits on the north bank of the River Bregagh (a tributary of the Nore) to the north of the city centre outside the city walls.

From the cathedral, Kilkenny's main thoroughfare runs south-east, past St Canice's Place to Irishtown (where the common folk were once concentrated, outside the city walls) then over the bridge, eventually becoming Parliament St, which then splits in two. The eastern fork, St Kieran's St, meets Rose Inn St which leads north-east to John's Bridge over the River Nore. The western fork, High St, carries on south to Patrick St. South-east from Rose Inn St, the Parade leads up to Kilkenny Castle which dominates the city's southern side.

INFORMATION

At the time of going to press the tourist office (☎ 51500) was in the lovely stone Shee Alms House on Rose Inn St but there are plans to move it to the Quays. It sells excellent guides to the city and walking maps of the county for 40p a sheet.

Upstairs the CityScope Exhibition takes place every half hour. A half-hour commentary on the city's history focusing on a model of medieval Kilkenny is too static to grip the imagination. Admission is IR£1/50p.

The Book Centre, 10 High St, stocks a range of books and maps on Ireland, while farther north, at No 67, the Ossory Bookshop has second-hand books too.

The telephone code is ☎ 056.

KILKENNY CASTLE

The first structure on this strategic site overlooking the River Nore was a wooden tower built in 1172 by Richard de Clare, the Anglo-Norman conqueror of Ireland better known as Strongbow. Twenty years later, his son-in-law William Marshall erected a stone castle with four towers, three of which still survive.

The castle was bought by the powerful Butler family in 1391, and their descendants continued to live there until 1935. Maintaining such a structure became an enormous financial strain and most of the furnishings were finally sold at auction. The castle was handed over to the city in 1967 for the princely sum of IR£50 and is now administered by Dúchas.

Work continues to restore the castle to its Victorian splendour and many of the rooms have only recently been opened to the public. The **Long Gallery** (the wing of the castle nearest the river), with its vividly painted ceiling mixing Celtic and Pre-Raphaelite motifs and portraits of the Butler family members over the centuries, is particularly splendid and forms the focus of the 40 minute guided tour. It was the most significant part of the work carried out in 1826.

The castle (☎ 21450) opens 10 am to 7 pm daily between June and September. October to March, it opens 10.30 am to 12.45 pm and 2 to 5 pm Tuesday to Saturday, while on

KILKENNY

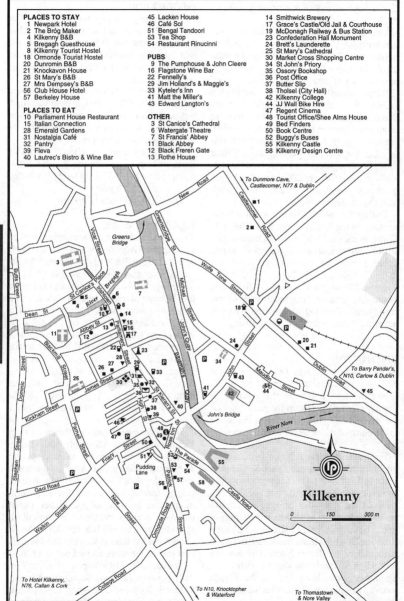

PLACES TO STAY
1 Newpark Hotel
2 The Bróg Maker
4 Kilkenny B&B
5 Bregagh Guesthouse
8 Kilkenny Tourist Hostel
18 Ormonde Tourist Hostel
20 Dunromin B&B
21 Knockavon House
26 St Mary's B&B
27 Mrs Dempsey's B&B
56 Club House Hotel
57 Berkeley House

PLACES TO EAT
10 Parliament House Restaurant
15 Italian Connection
28 Emerald Gardens
31 Nostalgia Café
32 Pantry
39 Fleva
40 Lautrec's Bistro & Wine Bar

45 Lacken House
46 Café Sol
51 Bengal Tandoori
53 Tea Shop
54 Restaurant Rinucinni

PUBS
9 The Pumphouse & John Cleere
16 Flagstone Wine Bar
22 Fennelly's
29 Jim Holland's & Maggie's
33 Kyteler's Inn
41 Matt the Miller's
43 Edward Langton's

OTHER
3 St Canice's Cathedral
6 Watergate Theatre
7 St Francis' Abbey
11 Black Abbey
12 Black Freren Gate
13 Rothe House

14 Smithwick Brewery
17 Grace's Castle/Old Jail & Courthouse
19 McDonagh Railway & Bus Station
23 Confederation Hall Monument
24 Brett's Launderette
25 St Mary's Cathedral
30 Market Cross Shopping Centre
34 St John's Priory
35 Ossory Bookshop
36 Post Office
37 Butter Slip
38 Tholsel (City Hall)
42 Kilkenny College
44 JJ Wall Bike Hire
47 Regent Cinema
48 Tourist Office/Shee Alms House
49 Bed Finders
50 Book Centre
52 Buggy's Buses
55 Kilkenny Castle
58 Kilkenny Design Centre

Kilkenny

0   150   300 m

Sunday it's open 11 am to 12.45 pm and 2 to 5 pm. In April and May it opens 10 am to 5 pm daily. Entry is IR£3/1.25.

The castle also hosts contemporary art exhibitions in the **Butler Gallery**, and in the basement, the castle kitchen houses a popular summertime restaurant (see Places to Eat).

Twenty hectares of **parkland** extend to the north-east, with a Celtic cross-shaped rose garden, a fountain to the north end and a children's playground to the south. Entry to the grounds is free and they're open 10 am to 8.30 pm in summer.

ST CANICE'S CATHEDRAL

St Canice's Cathedral dominates Irishtown at the northern end of Parliament St. The approach on foot from Parliament St leads you over Irishtown bridge and up St Canice's Steps which date from 1614; the wall at the top contains fragmentary medieval carvings. Around the cathedral are a graveyard, a round tower and an 18th century bishop's palace. Although the present cathedral dates from 1251, it has a much longer history and contains some remarkable tombs and monuments which are decoded on a board in the south aisle.

This site may well have had pre-Christian significance. Legend relates that the first monastery was built here by St Cainneach, Canice or Kenneth, Kilkenny's patron saint, who moved here from Aghaboe, County Laois, in the 6th century. There are records of a wooden church on the site, which was burnt down in 1087. The 30m-high **round tower** beside the church is the oldest structure within the cathedral grounds and was built somewhere between 700 and 1000 AD on the site of an earlier Christian cemetery. Apart from missing its crown, the round tower is in excellent condition, and you can admire the fine view from the top for IR£1/50p between 9 am and 12.30 pm and 2 to 5.30 pm. It's a tight squeeze and you'll need both hands to climb the steep ladders.

St Canice's was built in early English Gothic style but suffered a history of catastrophe and resurrection. The first disaster, when the bell tower collapsed in 1332, is connected with the story of Kilkenny's legendary witch, Dame Alice Kyteler. In 1650, Cromwell's forces defaced and damaged the church, even using it to stable their horses. Repairs began in 1661, but there was still much to be done a century later.

On the walls and in the floor are many highly polished ancient **graveslabs**. On the north wall opposite the entrance a slab inscribed in Norman French commemorates Jose de Keteller, who died in 1280; despite

---

The Butler Family

Kilkenny City and castle are intimately associated with the Butler family, the earls of Ormond. This Anglo-Norman clan were originally known as the Walters, but changed their name after Theobald fitzWalter was given the title of Chief Butler of Ireland by Henry II in 1185. With the title came the butlerage or duty charged on all wine imported into Ireland and England. When Walter Butler was strapped for cash in 1811, he sold the right for nearly £216,000, an extraordinary sum in those days. The three wine glasses on the family shield commemorate this important source of family wealth.

The Butlers owned vast tracts of land in Tipperary and Kilkenny. During Henry VIII's reign, their power extended across much of southern Ireland, but they lost out under Cromwell when the earl was exiled. Even so his wife, Lady Ormond, managed to hang on to the estates; because her treacherous husband wasn't in control, Cromwell didn't take away the family's positions or titles.

The Butlers bounced back with the restoration of Charles II in 1660 (James Butler was a great friend of the monarch's) and picked the victorious side at the Battle of the Boyne in 1690, only to go down in flames when they backed a planned Spanish invasion of England in 1714. Although they later reclaimed some of their influence, they never again reached their earlier importance. Both Tipperary and Kilkenny have numerous castles built by the family, including Carrick-on-Suir Castle (in Tipperary), Ireland's finest Elizabethan mansion. ■

the difference in spelling he was probably the father of Kilkenny's witch, Alice Kyteler. The stone chair of St Kieran embedded in the wall dates from the 13th century. Don't miss the fine 1596 monument to Honorina Grace at the west end of the south aisle. It's made of beautiful local black marble.

In the south transept is a beautiful **black tomb** with effigies of Piers Butler, who died in 1539, and his wife Margaret Fitzgerald. Tombs and monuments to other notable Butlers crowd this corner of the church.

Donations of IR£1 towards the cathedral's upkeep are requested.

BLACK ABBEY

The Dominican Black Abbey on Abbey St was founded in 1225 by William Marshall and takes its name from the monks' black habits. After Henry VIII's dissolution of the monasteries in 1543, it was turned into a courthouse. Following Cromwell's visit in 1650, it remained a roofless ruin until restoration in 1866. Much of what survives dates from the 18th and 19th centuries.

Nearby to the south-west, off James St, is the small and less interesting Catholic **St Mary's Cathedral of the Assumption**, founded in 1843. A side altar added to the cathedral during renovations around 1890 was the work of stonemason James Pearse (father of Patrick, a 1916 Easter Rising leader).

ROTHE HOUSE

Rothe House, on Parliament St, is a fine Tudor house, the best surviving example of a 16th century merchant's house in Ireland. The house was built around a series of courtyards and now has a museum with a sparse collection of local items and costumes from various periods displayed in its old timber-vaulted rooms. The fine kingpost roof of the 2nd floor is a meticulous and impressive reconstruction.

In the 1640s, the wealthy Rothe family played a part in the Confederation of Kilkenny, and Peter Rothe, son of the original builder, had all his property confiscated. His sister was able to reclaim it, but just

before the Battle of the Boyne (1690), the family supported James II and so lost the house permanently. In 1850 a confederation banner was discovered in the house. It's now in the National Museum, Dublin.

Rothe House opens April to October, 10.30 am to 5 pm Monday to Saturday, 3 to 5 pm on Sunday. The rest of the year it only opens 3 to 5 pm on Saturday and Sunday. Entry is IR£2/1. A 20 minute audiovisual presentation sets the scene for your visit.

SMITHWICK BREWERY

Founded in 1710 on the site of a Franciscan monastery, the Smithwick Brewery, on Parliament St, is now owned by Guinness and brews Budweiser under licence as well as Smithwick's own brands. From June to August the brewery shows a short video on the production process, more or less as an excuse for the beer tastings that follow. Shows take place at 3 pm Monday to Friday and although they're free you have to collect a ticket from the tourist office first.

St Francis' Abbey was founded by William Marshall in 1232, but desecrated by Cromwell in 1650. The monks were reputed to be expert brewers.

OTHER ATTRACTIONS

Stretches of the old Norman city walls can still be traced, but **Black Freren Gate**, north-east of the Black Abbey on Abbey St, is the only gate still standing.

Shee Alms House, on Rose Inn St, was built in 1582 by local benefactor Sir Richard Shee and his wife to provide help to the poor. It continued as a hospital until 1740 but now houses the tourist office. The **Tholsel**, or city hall, on High St was built in 1761 on the site where Dame Alice Kyteler's maid, Petronella, was burnt at the stake in 1324 (see The Witch of Kilkenny). Just north of the Tholsel is the **Butter Slip**, a narrow alleyway built in 1616 to connect High St with Low Lane (now St Kieran's St) and once lined with the stalls of butter sellers.

On the corner of Parliament St and the road leading down to Bateman's Quay, a **monument** beside the Bank of Ireland

The Witch of Kilkenny
In the Middle Ages, Dame Alice Kyteler went through four husbands, all in suspicious circumstances. Having acquired some powerful enemies, she was charged with witchcraft in 1324. Witnesses claimed to have seen her sweeping dust to the door of her son, William Outlawe, while chanting, 'to the house of William, my son, lie all the wealth of Kilkenny town'. Worse still, she was supposed to have sacrificed cockerels and consorted with the devil. She was duly convicted, along with her sister, her son and her maid, Petronella. Dame Alice managed to escape to England but Petronella was burnt at the stake outside Kilkenny's Tholsel. The sister's fate is unknown.

Alice's son escaped his sentence by offering to reroof part of the cathedral with lead tiles. Unfortunately, the new roof proved too heavy and collapsed in 1332, bringing the church tower down with it.

Dame Alice's former home at 27 St Kieran's St is now Kyteler's Inn, a restaurant and bar. ■

marks the site of the Confederation Hall, where the national parliament met from 1642 to 1649. Nearby is **Grace's Castle** originally built in 1210 but lost to the family and converted into a prison in 1568 and then into a courthouse in 1794 which it remains today. Rebels from the 1798 Rising were executed here. People taking part in one of Tynan's Tours (see Organised Tours) get to see inside the cells.

Across the river stand the ruins of **St John's Priory**, which was founded in 1200 and was noted for its many beautiful windows until Cromwell's visit. Nearby, **Kilkenny College**, at the east end of Lower John St, dates from 1666. Its students included Jonathan Swift and the philosopher George Berkeley but it now houses Kilkenny's county hall.

ORGANISED TOURS
Tynan Tours (☎ 65929) conducts hour-long walking tours of the city six times daily (four on Sunday) March to October starting from the tourist office. They cost IR£2.50/60p (students IR£2). In winter, three tours a day are scheduled for Tuesday to Saturday.

The Old Kilkenny Tour is a hop on, hop off open-top bus tour of the city which departs from Kilkenny Castle every 30 minutes between 10 am and 5 pm. Tickets cost IR£5/2.

SPECIAL EVENTS
The Confederation of Kilkenny Festival, which commemorates Kilkenny's days as the Irish capital, takes place in June, bringing the streets to life, with parades and historic pageantry.

Over the June bank holiday weekend the Cats Laugh Comedy Festival is an increasingly important crowd-puller when beds can be almost impossible to find. For details phone ☎ 51254.

The highlight of the year is the Kilkenny Arts Week Festival in late August, when exhibitions, music, drama and theatrical events take place all over the city. Once again beds will be like gold dust, so book well ahead. Phone ☎ 52175 or email kaw@iol.ie for details.

PLACES TO STAY
Camping
The small *Tree Grove Caravan & Camping Park* (☎ 70302) is 1.5km south of Kilkenny on the New Ross road. A tent for two costs IR£6. Otherwise, the *Nore Valley Caravan & Camping Park* is about 11km away, near Bennettsbridge; see that section later for details.

Hostels
The IHH *Kilkenny Tourist Hostel* (☎ 63541), 35 Parliament St, is clean and central, has a kitchen and laundry (IR£3), and 60 beds at IR£7 a night in dorms or IR£9 in private rooms. The one family room costs IR£32.

Ormonde Tourist Hostel (☎ 52733), John's Green, is close to the railway and bus station and has dorm beds for IR£7, doubles for IR£10 per person. Good facilities include a kitchen, laundry, TV room and plentiful parking space, although it can't quite shake off an institutional air – it was once the county council offices.

The An Óige hostel is beautifully sited in *Foulksrath Castle* (☎ 67144), a 16th century Norman castle 13km north of Kilkenny in Jenkinstown near Ballyragget. Beds cost IR£5.50/4. June to September, it serves reasonably priced meals. Buggy's Buses (☎ 41264) operates a bus service between The Parade in Kilkenny and the hostel, leaving at 11.30 am and 5.30 pm Monday to Saturday; from the hostel it leaves at 8.25 am and 3 pm. The fare is IR£1 and the journey takes about 20 minutes. Some JJ Kavanagh buses also pass near the hostel; call ☎ 31106 for details.

B&Bs

There are plenty of B&Bs, especially south of the city along Patrick St and north of the city on Castlecomer Rd, but accommodation can still be hard to find at weekends and especially during festival times. Bed Finders (☎ 70088), 23 Rose Inn St, undertakes to help you find somewhere to stay without charging a booking fee, a service that could come in handy at busy times.

In the centre, *Mrs Dempsey's* (☎ 21954) and *St Mary's* (☎ 22091) are two small town houses side by side on James St. Mrs Dempsey charges IR£15/34 a single/double with bathroom. St Mary's charges IR£16/18 and has big breakfasts.

Also central is the *Bregagh Guesthouse* (☎ 22315), on Dean St near St Canice's Cathedral, costing from IR£18/24. A few doors down is *Kilkenny B&B* (☎ 64040), with a wide variety of rooms from IR£15 a head.

Knockavon House (☎ 64294), on Dublin Rd quite near the railway station, charges IR£22/32 with bathroom, while nearby *Dunromin* (☎ 61387) charges IR£20/30 which includes a top-notch breakfast. *The Bróg Maker* (☎ 52900), on Castlecomer Rd near the Newpark Hotel, is a cheerful

pub/guesthouse offering B&B for IR£25 a head.

Hotels

The Georgian *Berkeley House* (☎ 64848; fax 64829) at 5 Lower Patrick St charges from IR£25/45 a single/double.

The modern *Newpark Hotel* (☎ 22122; fax 61111), north of the railway station on Castlecomer Rd, has swimming pools, saunas, a gym and 20 hectares of parkland. The cost per person is from IR£45/69 a single/double with bath. The *Kilkenny Hotel* (☎ 62000; fax 65984), about a 10 minute walk from the city centre on College Rd, has excellent facilities and costs from IR£50 a head depending on the season.

Country Houses

Blanchville House (☎ 27197; fax 27636), Maddoxtown, is a lovely 19th century house on its own farm about 8km east of the city. B&B is from IR£30/50 a single/double, and it's open from March to October. To get there, go along the N10 Carlow road and take the first right after the Pike pub. After 3km turn left at a crossroads near Connolly's pub. It's almost 2km down the road on the left.

The highly rated *Lacken House* (☎ 61085; fax 62435), just out of town on Dublin Rd, is more expensive at IR£36/60 (April to October) but has an excellent restaurant.

PLACES TO EAT
Cafés & Takeaways

In summer, *Kilkenny Castle Kitchen* is a good place for lunch or for delicious, if pricey, cakes; you don't have to pay the castle admission charge to eat there. Across the road, the restaurant upstairs in the *Kilkenny Design Centre* (open 9 am to 5 pm daily) is excellent for snacks or lunch but attracts coach parties.

An excellent choice for lunch is *Café Sol* (☎ 64987), tucked away down William St and with the sort of colour scheme to evoke the sunny Med rather than wet and windy Kilkenny. Lunch costs around IR£5.50, dinner more like IR£20 a head. The menu here is very Modern Irish, as it is at *Fleva* upstairs in the High St, near the Tholsel; a baguette filled with hot chicken, dill and lemon costs IR£3.75, Kilkenny meatloaf with potatoes is IR£5.

The *Nostalgia Café* in the High St favours over-the-top kitsch décor as a backing for a good choice of lunch and dinner dishes; roast chicken for IR£4.25, vegetarian pasta for IR£3.55. It stays open until 10 pm. The *Pantry*, a small self-service coffee shop on St Kieran's St, carries things to the other extreme, with a décor verging on the austere. Still, it's very popular for lunch with the locals. The unpretentious *Tea Shop*, on Patrick St, does sandwiches from IR£1.50. There's also a branch of *Bewley's* on the ground floor of the Market Cross Shopping Centre.

Pub Food
Kilkenny has plenty of pubs serving reasonable food. On St Kieran's St, *Kyteler's Inn* (☎ 21604) has a rustic restaurant downstairs and a bar upstairs. While the food isn't brilliant, it's certainly popular. A mixed grill costs IR£6.75, breaded chicken IR£4.25. *John Cleere* and *The Pumphouse* are also well worth trying.

North-east of the river, *Edward Langton's* (☎ 21728), 69 John St, has an award-winning restaurant. Lunch-time meals like roast beef will cost a reasonable IR£5, sandwiches from IR£3.50 including chips. Set dinners, served until 11 pm, cost IR£18.50; à la carte dishes from IR£12.50 to IR£14.

Restaurants
The popular *Italian Connection* (☎ 64225), 38 Parliament St, serves delicious spaghetti in pesto sauce for IR£6.95. More upmarket is *Ristorante Rinucinni* (☎ 61575), a cellar restaurant on The Parade with delicious pastas, all freshly prepared.

Near Kyteler's Inn on St Kieran's St is the late-night *Lautrec's Bistro & Wine Bar* (☎ 62720), which serves an eclectic range of Italian and Mexican dishes costing from IR£3.95 until 1 am.

Parliament House Restaurant, on Parliament St opposite Kilkenny Tourist Hostel,
serves traditional food but is quite expensive; a set lunch is IR£11.50.

On High St, the Chinese *Emerald Gardens* (☎ 61812) does main courses from IR£7. The *Bengal Tandoori* (☎ 64722), on Pudding Lane, does eat-as-much-as-you-like Sunday lunches from 1 to 5 pm for IR£7.95.

Widely regarded as the best local restaurant is *Lacken House* (☎ 61085), just out of town on Dublin Rd. Dinner will cost you IR£22 or more.

ENTERTAINMENT
Pubs
There's no shortage of pubs in Kilkenny and music is often playing in several at the same time.

A string of pubs line the northern end of Parliament St opposite the Kilkenny Tourist Hostel. The *Pumphouse* offers rock and pop, as well as traditional music on Tuesday and Wednesday. *John Cleere* has regular, year-round productions of plays, revues, poetry readings and anything else that's going. Monday night is Traditional Irish Music & Folk night. Spontaneous sessions can happen any time. Other places to try include *Fennelly's* on Monday and Friday nights and *Maggie's* on St Kieran's St on Tuesday and Thursday nights.

Over the river, *Edward Langton's*, on John St, has discos on Tuesday and Saturday nights. The *Flagstone Wine Bar*, in a basement a few doors up from Kilkenny Tourist Hostel, also has weekend discos midnight until 2 am. *Matt the Miller's*, just across the river, is another popular pub for hanging out in.

On Tuesday night in July and August there's live musical entertainment of the more touristy type at the *Club House Hotel* (☎ 21994) on Patrick St. It kicks off at 8.30 pm and admission costs IR£4.

Theatre & Cinema
Watergate Theatre (☎ 61674), on Parliament St, hosts drama, comedy and musical performances by both professional and amateur

KILKENNY

groups. See also the John Cleere pub in the previous section.

The single-screen *Regent* cinema is at the end of William St, a cul-de-sac opposite the Tholsel.

THINGS TO BUY
Across The Parade from Kilkenny Castle are the elegant former Castle Stables (1760) which have been tastefully converted into the Kilkenny Design Centre, with an outstanding collection of Irish goods and crafts for sale. Behind the shop through the arched gateway is the Castle Yard with the studios of various local craftspeople.

GETTING THERE & AWAY
Bus
Bus Éireann (☎ 64933) operates out of the railway station and provides seven services to and from Dublin, Monday to Saturday, with four on Sunday. There are three buses daily to/from Cork City (two on Sunday). Two buses a day (except Sunday) also pass through Kilkenny en route from Dublin to Waterford.

On the Waterford to Longford route, one bus a day passes through in each direction. In July and August one bus a day (except Sunday) links Kilkenny with Galway and Waterford. On Thursday there's also a bus from New Ross to Kilkenny, leaving at 10 am and returning at 1.15 pm.

JJ Kavanagh & Sons (☎ 31106) runs daily buses between Kilkenny and Cashel via Kells and Fethard, as well as buses to Carlow, Portlaoise and Thurles. These buses stop in the Parade.

Train
McDonagh railway station (☎ 22024) is on Dublin Rd, north-east of the town centre via John St. Four trains a day (five on Friday, three on Sunday) link Dublin (Heuston station) with Waterford via Kilkenny; the journey takes just under two hours. For details phone ☎ 01-836 6222.

GETTING AROUND
Buggy's Buses (☎ 41264) has a daily service

Monday to Saturday from The Parade to Foulksrath Castle (and the An Óige hostel), Ballyragget, Dunmore Cave and Castlecomer.

JJ Wall (☎ 21236), 86 Maudlin St, rents bikes at IR£7 a day, plus a deposit of IR£30. The circuit round Kells, Inistioge, Jerpoint Abbey and Kilfane makes a fine day's ride.

Cars can be rented from Barry Pender Motors (☎ 65777), 1.5km out on Dublin Rd, for a steep IR£50 a day.

Central Kilkenny

A tour of the county south of Kilkenny takes in much of the Nore Valley and sections of the Barrow Valley. The most scenic parts are from Graiguenamanagh in the east, down to The Rower and then north on the road to Inistioge, Thomastown, Kells and Callan near the Tipperary border.

BENNETTSBRIDGE
Bennettsbridge, a village south of Kilkenny on the River Nore, has two of Ireland's most renowned potteries and an official camping ground.

In a big mill by the river, **Nicholas Mosse Pottery** (☎ 27126) turns out handmade spongewear – creamy-brown pottery which is covered with sponged patterns. The factory shop opens Monday to Saturday 10 am to 6 pm (and in July and August on Sunday 2 to 6 pm) and there's a café opposite.

Almost 2km north of Bennettsbridge on the minor road to Kilkenny, **Stoneware Jackson Pottery** (☎ 27175) produces a wide variety of chunky pottery. It's open Monday to Saturday 10 am to 6 pm.

Nore Valley Camping & Caravan Park (☎ 27229) is on a farm and charges hikers and cyclists IR£4 to camp. If you're coming into Bennettsbridge from Kilkenny along the R700, turn right just before the bridge and the park is signposted. The site opens from Easter to October.

KELLS

Only 13km south of Kilkenny, Kells is not to be confused with its namesake in County Meath. This is a treat of a hamlet, nestling beside a fine stone bridge on the King's River – a tributary of the Nore. In Kells Priory, the village has one of Ireland's most impressive and romantic monastic sites.

Kells Priory

The earliest remains of the magnificent Kells Priory date from the late 12th century, with the bulk of the present ruins from the 15th century. In a sea of rich farmland, a protective wall, carefully restored, connects seven dwelling towers. Inside the walls are the remains of an Augustinian abbey and the foundations of some chapels and houses. It's unusually well fortified for a monastery, and the heavy curtain walls hint at a troubled history. Indeed, within a single century from 1250, the abbey was twice fought over and burnt down by squabbling warlords.

Extraordinarily there's no charge for visiting and no set opening hours provided you don't mind braving the sheep in the surrounding fields. The ruins are 800m out of Kells on the Stonyford road.

Kilree Round Tower & High Cross

Two km south of Kells (signposted from the priory car park) there's a 29m-high round tower and a simple early high cross, said to mark the grave of a 9th century Irish high king, Niall Caille. He's supposed to have drowned in the King's River at Callan some time in the 840s while attempting to save a servant, and his body washed up near Kells. His final resting place lies beyond the church grounds because he wasn't a Christian.

THOMASTOWN

Thomastown is a small market town, nicely situated by the River Nore. Unfortunately it's also on the main Dublin to Waterford road (N9) and the traffic can be horrific. However, most people ignore this aspect of the town and concentrate on its many drinking establishments, some with music, others with reasonable food.

At the edge of town on the Waterford road, the Grennan Mill Craft School (☎ 24557) has a craft shop open Monday to Saturday from 9 am to 5 pm.

Named after a Welsh mercenary in 1169, Thomastown has some fragments of a medieval wall and the partly ruined 13th century **Church of St Mary** but **Mullin's Castle** down by the bridge is the sole survivor of the original 14 castles. On the outskirts of Thomastown is **Mount Juliet**, a stately home turned hotel with a riverside park and lovely walled gardens. Visits to the grounds are possible at any time but to stay you're looking at more than IR£120 a head (☎ 24455; fax 24766).

Getting There & Away

Bus Éireann (☎ 64933) has up to seven services a day between Dublin and Waterford with stops at Gowran, Thomastown and Mullinavat. One service a day also links Waterford with Longford via Thomastown, Carlow, Kilkenny, Tullamore and Athlone. On Thursday there's also one service from New Ross, leaving at 10 am. Buses stop outside O'Keeffe's Supermarket on Main St.

The town is on the main Dublin to Waterford railway line with the same service as Kilkenny. It's about 15 minutes to Kilkenny, 25 minutes to Waterford and two hours to Dublin. The station is 1km west of town past Kavanagh's Supermarket.

AROUND THOMASTOWN
Jerpoint Abbey

One and a half km south-west of Thomastown on the Waterford road, Jerpoint Abbey was established by a king of Ossory in the 12th century. One of Ireland's finest Cistercian ruins, it has been partially restored. The fine tower and cloister are late 14th or early 15th century. Fragments of the cloister are particularly interesting with a series of often amusing figures carved on the pillars. There are also stone carvings on the church walls and in the tombs of members of the Butler and Walshe families. Faint traces of a 15th or 16th century painting remain on the north wall of the church. This chancel area also

KILKENNY

contains a tomb thought to be that of Felix O'Dullany, Jerpoint's first abbot and bishop of Ossory, who died in 1202.

According to local legend, St Nicholas (or Santa Claus) is buried near the abbey. While retreating in the Crusades, the Knights of Jerpoint removed his body from Myra in modern-day Turkey and reburied him in the Church of St Nicholas to the west of the abbey. The grave is marked by a broken slab decorated with a carving of a monk.

Entry to Jerpoint Abbey (☎ 24623) is IR£2/1. The abbey opens daily mid-June to September, 9.30 am to 6.30 pm; and between the end of September to mid-October, daily 10 am to 1 pm and 2 to 5 pm; and April to mid-June, 10 am to 1 pm and 2 to 5 pm Tuesday to Sunday.

If you want to stay, the attractive Georgian *Abbey House* (☎ 24166), opposite the entrance has singles/doubles from IR£25/33.

Kilfane

Three km north of Thomastown on the Dublin road, the village of Kilfane has a small ruined 13th century church and Norman tower, signposted 50m off the road. The church has a remarkable stone carving of Thomas de Cantwell, called the Cantwell Fada or 'long Cantwell'. It depicts a tall, thin knight in detailed chain mail armour, brandishing a shield decorated with the Cantwell coat of arms.

Another 2km along the road brings you to **Kilfane Glen & Waterfall**, a Romantic period garden with a *cottage ornée*. It's open May to mid-September, 2 to 6 pm except on Monday. Admission is IR£3.

INISTIOGE

Inistioge (pronounced 'Inishteeg') is a delightful little village, with a 10-arched stone bridge spanning the River Nore and a picturesque tree-lined square with many of its original shop and pub fronts. Somewhere so inviting could hardly hope to escape the Hollywood sleuths and Inistioge's film credits include *Widow's Peak* in 1993, *Circle of Friends* in 1994 and *Where the Sun is King* in 1996.

The village is 10km south-east of Graiguenamanagh on the opposite side of Brandon Hill, reached through a gap in the mountains. At the bottom of the hill that leads to Woodstock Park is a pottery which produces lovely work in light pastel colours.

One km south on Mt Alto is **Woodstock Park**. The hike up is well worth the effort for the panorama of the valley below and the demesne itself. The 18th century house was one of the finest in the county, but was destroyed during the Civil War in 1922. The elevated garden and forest are now a state park with picnic areas and trails. For another fine walk, follow the river bank and climb any of the surrounding hills. Inistioge is also on the South Leinster Way.

The *School House Café*, by the river, is a good, if unsophisticated, place to stop for tea, sandwiches and cakes.

Getting There & Away

On Thursday only, a single bus runs between New Ross and Kilkenny, calling at Inistioge en route. It leaves New Ross at 10 am and returns from Inistioge at 1.50 pm.

GRAIGUENAMANAGH

Graiguenamanagh (pronounced 'Greg-na-mana') is a small market town on a lovely stretch of the River Barrow, 23km south-east of Kilkenny at the foot of Brandon Hill (516m). There's no public transport but it is on the South Leinster Way.

Duiske Abbey

Dating back to 1204, Duiske Abbey was once Ireland's largest Cistercian abbey. Today it has been completely restored and its pleasantly simple, whitewashed interior is in everyday use. Its name comes from the Irish Dubh Uisce (Black Water), a tributary of the River Barrow.

Inside the abbey to the right of the main entrance is the Knight of Duiske, a 14th century high-relief carving of a knight in chain mail reaching for his sword. On the floor nearby a glass panel reveals some of the original 13th century floor tiles 2m below the present floor level. To the left of the entrance is the 18th century painted reredos taken from an old mass house which was attached to the ruins before they were restored. The nave has been reroofed in medieval style, without the use of nails.

In the grounds stand two early high crosses, brought here for protection in the last century. The smaller Ballyogan Cross has panels on the east side depicting the Crucifixion, Adam & Eve, Abraham's sacrifice of Isaac, and David playing the harp. The west side shows the Massacre of the Innocents.

Opposite the abbey the *Café Duiske* does things like lasagne for IR£3.90. Round the corner the **Abbey Centre** houses a small exhibition of Christian art, plus pictures of the abbey in its unrestored state.

GOWRAN
The village of Gowran, 12km east of Kilkenny, is famous for its **racecourse** and 13th century **St Mary's Church** which has some fine carvings and Butler family tombs. *Whitethorns* (☎ 26102), 300m off the main Dublin to Kilkenny road, is a pleasant guesthouse offering B&B from IR£19/28 a single/double.

Gowran is on the Dublin to Waterford express bus route, with up to five services a day in each direction.

Southern Kilkenny

Much of southern Kilkenny is sparsely populated with gentle hills separating the valleys of the Nore, Barrow and Suir rivers. Carrick-on-Suir in Tipperary and Waterford City are within easy reach, with a wide choice of accommodation and restaurants. Southern Kilkenny is crossed by the **South Leinster Way**, which runs from Carrick-on-Suir, through Piltown, Mullinavat, Inistioge, Graiguenamanagh and on to Borris in County Carlow. See the Activities chapter for more details.

MULLINAVAT
Twelve km north of Waterford on the Kilkenny road (N9), Mullinavat makes an agreeable spot to spend a relaxing day or two. Two km south of the village, *Tory View* (☎ 051-85513) offers B&B in smallish rooms for IR£13/15 per person without/with bathroom, and evening meals are available. Alternatively, there's the 17th century *Rising Sun* (☎ 051-898173), a beautiful old stone building with an upstairs restaurant in the Main St. All rooms have bathroom, phone and TV but at IR£28/46 a single/double for B&B it's a bit pricey.

Express buses between Dublin and Waterford call at Mullinavat up to five times a day, stopping outside Mulhearn's on Main St. One service a day links Mullinavat with Longford via Thomastown, Carlow, Tullamore and Athlone. In July and August there's also one request service a day linking Mullinavat with Galway, via Kilkenny, Thurles and Nenagh.

Northern Kilkenny

CASTLECOMER & AROUND
An attractive town 18km north of Kilkenny, Castlecomer is on the River Dinin which flows across the Castlecomer Plateau.

The town became a centre for anthracite mining after it was discovered nearby in 1636; the mines only closed for good in the mid-1960s. The anthracite was widely regarded as being Europe's best with very little sulphur and producing almost no smoke. Castlecomer saw action in the 1798 Rising when the Fenian rebels, led by Father John Murphy, captured it en route from Wexford to the midlands. There's little to do here, but the tree-lined square and neat town houses are thoroughly pleasing.

Things to See
Eight km west-south-west of Castlecomer is **Ballyragget**, with an almost intact square tower in the 16th century Butler Castle. Five km south of Castlecomer on the road to

Kilkenny is the markedly similar 16th century square-towered **Foulksrath Castle**.

Almost 2km south of Ballyragget is **Swifte's Heath**, home to Jonathan Swift during his school years in Kilkenny, and now offering B&B accommodation.

Places to Stay

Foulksrath Castle is now a busy An Óige hostel (☎ 67144) with a superb setting. For more details see Places to Stay under Kilkenny.

In Castlecomer, the *Avalon* pub/guesthouse (☎ 41302), on the square near the bridge, is housed in the old mine offices and has B&B for IR£25/40 a single/double. Alternatively, 19th century *Wandesforde House* (☎ 42441) has six rooms, all with a bathroom; B&B is IR£21/36 and dinner is IR£15.

Getting There & Away

Castlecomer is on Bus Éireann's (☎ 64933) route between Cork, Kilkenny and Dublin and is serviced by up to four buses daily Monday to Saturday, three on Sunday. Buses stop outside Houlihan's. JJ Kavanagh (☎ 31555) runs buses twice daily between Clonmel, Kilkenny, Castlecomer, Athy and Dublin (the Gresham Hotel); from Castlecomer it takes 75 minutes to Dublin. Buggy's Buses (☎ 41264) runs a Monday to Saturday service from Kilkenny to Castlecomer.

DUNMORE CAVE

Dunmore Cave, about 10km north of Kilkenny on the Castlecomer road (N78), is a large cave divided into three parts with many limestone formations.

According to some sources, marauding Vikings killed 1000 people at two ring forts near Dunmore Cave in 928 AD. When sur-

vivors hid in the caverns the Vikings tried to smoke them out by lighting fires at the entrance. It's thought that they then dragged off the men as slaves and left the women and children to suffocate.

Excavations in 1973 uncovered the remains of at least 44 people, mostly women and children. They also found coins dating from the 920s but none from any later date. One theory suggests that the coins were dropped by the Vikings (who often carried them in their armpits, secured with wax) while enthusiastically engaged in the slaughter. However, there are few marks of violence on the skeletons, which lends weight to the theory that the people suffocated.

The limestone cave is well lit and spacious. After a steep descent through the large entrance, you enter imaginatively nicknamed caverns full of stalactites, stalagmites and columns, including the 7m Market Cross, Europe's largest freestanding stalagmite. It's damp and cold, so a sweater or coat is advised. The compulsory guided tours are very worthwhile.

The cave opens mid-March to mid-June, 10 am to 5 pm daily; mid-June to mid-September, 10 am to 7 pm daily; mid-September to October, 10 am to 5 pm daily; and November to mid-March, 10 am to 5 pm weekends only. Entry to the cave is IR£2/1.

Buggy's Buses (☎ 056-41264) runs a Monday to Saturday bus from The Parade in Kilkenny which drops you off 1km from the cave. It leaves at 12.30 pm and returns at 4.15 pm (IR£2 return), leaving you more than three hours at the cave where there's not even a café. However, one of the visitors is bound to be able to run you back to town. On Saturday there's a bus back at 2.30 pm, leaving a much more reasonable 1½ hours to inspect the cave.

Central South

The four counties of Carlow, Kildare, Laois and Offaly make up a large portion of the Irish midlands. Sites of archaeological interest include the Rock of Dunamase near Portlaoise, Moone High Cross in Kildare, Kildare Town's cathedral, the Browne's Hill Dolmen just outside Carlow Town, the Rosse Estate and observatory in Birr and, most impressive of all, Clonmacnoise on the banks of the River Shannon, probably Ireland's most important monastic site.

County Kildare

Kildare (Cill Dara), to the west and south-west of Dublin, is mostly rich green farmland in the south, with the extensive Bog of Allen peatland hogging the north-west corner. A limestone plain underlies the pasture and bog.

The main towns are dominated by traffic, a problem which should be alleviated as the local councils finish building bypasses around them. Nearly all the main road and rail arteries cross the county, as do the 18th century Grand and Royal canals, now enjoying a new lease of life. The River Barrow marks the county's eastern border, while the Curragh forms a great sweep of unfenced countryside to the south.

GRAND & ROYAL CANALS
The Grand and Royal canals were built in the 18th century to revolutionise goods and passenger transport, but as the railways superseded them during the 19th century, the canals fell into disuse. Today they're owned by Dúchas and offer a pleasant way of drifting across the country.

Grand Canal
The Grand Canal, opened in 1779, carried passengers until 1852 and goods until 1960. The canal threads its way from Dublin through County Kildare to Robertstown.

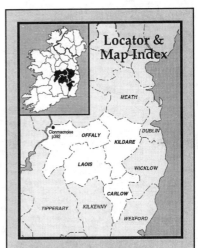

Locator & Map Index

Highlights
- See the High Cross at Moone in Kildare which was erected in the 8th or 9th century and is 6m tall
- Visit St Brigid's Cathedral in Kildare
- Explore the 5000-year-old Browne's Hill Dolmen outside Carlow
- Wander through Birr Castle & Demesne, which are among the finest in Ireland, and visit the Birr Observatory & Telescope, which at one time was the largest in the world
- Enjoy a visit to Clonmacnois, Ireland's most important monastic site, overlooking the River Shannon

From there one branch heads west through Tullamore to join the River Shannon at Shannon Harbour in County Offaly, while the other turns south to join the River Barrow at Athy, providing passage to New Ross in County Wexford and to Waterford Town.

Besides the many finely crafted locks and tiny lock cottages, you will come across treasures like the seven-arched Leinster

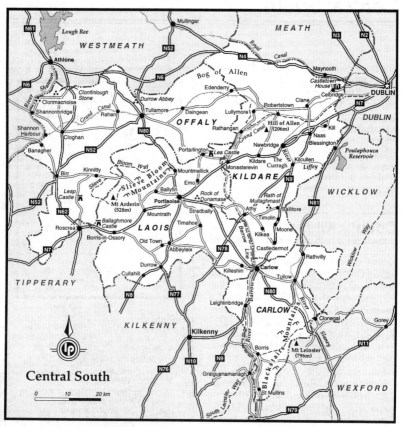

Central South

0   10   20 km

Aqueduct, 5km north of Naas near the village of Sallins, where the canal crosses the River Liffey. Farther south of Robertstown, sections of the River Barrow are particularly lovely.

Royal Canal

The Royal Canal follows Kildare's northern border and also wends its way to the River Shannon, joining it farther north at Cloondara (or Clondra) in County Longford above Lough Ree. However, it's only navigable between Blanchardstown in County Dublin and Mullingar in County Westmeath. It was never as profitable as the Grand Canal, and has aged less gracefully. Restoration work aims to link the Dublin City section with the River Liffey and to improve the section west of Mullingar. The Royal Canal should be fully navigable around the turn of the millennium.

Barges & Boats

Boating facilities are only available on the Grand Canal. Six-berth River Shannon narrowboats can be hired from Lowtown Marine (☎ 045-860427), 13km west of Naas, 1km west along the north bank of the canal over the bridge from Robertstown. The weekly cost is from IR£400 in October to IR£680 in July and August. On Sunday 45-minute trips on the *Eustace*, a refurbished canal barge, depart from the Grand Canal Hotel in Robertstown on the hour between 2 and 6 pm. The trips cost IR£2.50/1.50; for details phone ☎ 045-860260. During the summer there are also day trips from Robertstown.

Walking the Towpaths
The canal towpaths are ideal for walkers, and Robertstown makes a good starting point for many canal walks. Three *Canal Bank Walks* leaflets which detail a 45km trail along the Grand Canal from Edenderry to Celbridge can be picked up at tourist offices. For more information call County Kildare Youth & Sports (☎ 045-879502).

Robertstown is also at the hub of the Kildare Way and River Barrow towpath trails, the latter stretching all the way to St Mullins, 95km south in County Carlow. From there it's possible to connect with the South Leinster Way at Graiguenamanagh or the southern end of the Wicklow Way at Clonegal, north of Mt Leinster.

MAYNOOTH & AROUND
Twenty-four km west of Dublin on the N4, Maynooth (Maigh Nuad) has a tree-lined main street with stone-fronted houses and shops and the Royal Canal passing to the south of the centre. Main St runs east-west. Leinster St runs south off Main St to the canal and the railway station (accessed via a couple of footbridges over the canal).

The telephone code is ☎ 01.

St Patrick's College
St Patrick's College & Seminary (☎ 628 5222), also called Maynooth College, at the western end of town has been turning out Catholic priests since 1795 and became a college of the National University in 1910. Ironically, the seminary was founded by the English, alarmed at the prospect of Irish priests studying in France and picking up ideas about revolution and republicanism.

You enter the college via Georgian Stoyte House which has fine plastered ceilings. Beyond that is St Joseph's Square laid out as a rose garden. Across the square is St Patrick's House, a fine Victorian Gothic building, with the College Chapel looming at one end; this is the world's largest choir chapel, with stalls for more than 450 choristers. Through St Patrick's House is the delightful Bicentennial Garden, with lily ponds and imitation standing stones.

The small visitor's centre shows a video on the College's history and stocks a leaflet for guiding yourself around the buildings. Guided tours cost IR£2/1.50. It's open Monday to Friday 11 am to 5 pm and, Sunday 2 to 6 pm. The small science museum, open on request, costs IR£1/50p.

The college has 4500 students. Over the last two centuries it has trained more than 11,000 Catholic priests. At present 120 men are studying for the priesthood.

Maynooth Castle
The ruined gatehouse, keep and great hall of the 13th century castle stand by the entrance to St Patrick's College. The key can be picked up from 1 Parsons St in return for a deposit.

The castle was home to the Fitzgeralds. After the 1536 rebellion led by Silken Thomas Fitzgerald, the English besieged the castle whose garrison surrendered after being promised leniency. Then, in what became known as the 'Pardon of Maynooth', Thomas and his men were summarily executed. The castle was dismantled in Cromwellian times when the Fitzgeralds moved to Kilkea Castle.

Canoeing
The town of **Leixlip** on the River Liffey between Maynooth and Dublin is an important canoeing centre. It's the starting point of the Irish Sprint Canoe Championships and annual 28km International Liffey Descent Race, when the Electricity Supply Board (ESB) releases 30 million tonnes of water from the Poulaphouca Reservoir in County Wicklow to bring the river up to flood level.

CENTRAL SOUTH

Canoes can be hired from Kilcullen Canoe & Outdoor Pursuits Club (☎ 045-81240), 10km south-west of Naas.

Places to Stay

B&Bs *Park Lodge* (☎ 628 6002), 201 Railpark, 1km south of Maynooth near the bridge, charges IR£16 a head while *Windgate Lodge* (☎ 627 3415), 2km farther south in Barberstown, costs from IR£22/36.

Hotels The attractive old *Leinster Arms* pub (☎ 628 6323), in Main St, has rooms with shower for IR£20 per person. Breakfast is an extra IR£5. If your trunk load of cash is weighing you down, the lovely Georgian *Moyglare Manor* (☎ 628 6351; fax 628 5405) is 3.5km to the north. One of Ireland's best country houses, it charges IR£95/150 a single/double without breakfast.

Places to Eat

For light lunches *Kehoe's Coffee Shop* in Main St is very popular for things like soup and toasted sandwiches. For more substantial meals the *Orange Tree Restaurant*, behind the Mill pub in Mill St, does an early bird two-course dinner for IR£9.95.

The *Leinster Arms* has a carvery restaurant serving food from 12.30 to 9.30 pm; prices are reasonable at IR£4 to IR£6 for a main course.

Getting There & Away

Bus From Middle Abbey St in Dublin, suburban bus Nos 66 and 67 go to Maynooth (one hour). Numerous long-distance buses also pass through en route to Galway and Sligo. For information ring ☎ 873 4222. Bus No 66 stops outside Brady's pub on Main St, while No 67 stops on Leinster St, near the station.

Train Maynooth is linked to Dublin by the Western Suburban line and is on the main Dublin to Sligo line with four to five trains daily in each direction. Call ☎ 836 6222 for details.

CELBRIDGE

Celbridge, 6.5km south-east of Maynooth on the River Liffey, wouldn't have a lot going for it were it not home to the magnificent Palladian Castletown House.

The telephone code is ☎ 01.

Castletown House

This huge Irish mansion, with its tree-lined avenue from the village (continue straight ahead after entering the gate), is said to be Ireland's largest private house. It was built between 1722 and 1732 for William Conolly, who started life as the son of a pub owner and rose to become speaker of the Irish House of Commons. He financed Castletown House from a fortune amassed as a land agent in the chaotic aftermath to the Battle of the Boyne.

Castletown was designed by Alessandro Galilei, and continued by Edward Lovett Pearce (creator of the Bank of Ireland building on College Green, Dublin), who oversaw the building of the two sweeping columned wings. The house remained with the Conolly family until 1965 and is now cared for by Dúchas.

Many of the magnificent rooms were decorated well after the building had been finished. The Italian Francini brothers did the plasterwork in the hall and above the main staircase.

Castletown has two follies, commissioned by William Conolly's wife, Katherine, to provide employment for the poor. The **obelisk**, designed by Richard Castle, can be seen from the Long Gallery at the back of the house. Completed in 1740, it consists of a series of arches piled one upon another and topped by a 40m obelisk.

The even more curious **Wonderful Barn** lies to the north-east on private property just outside Leixlip and dates from 1743. It consists of four domes one on top of another and scaled by a spiral staircase.

At the time of writing Castletown House was closed for restoration. It is worth phoning ☎ 628 8252 to see if it's reopened.

Dublin bus No 67 or 67A to Celbridge will drop you at the gate.

Celbridge Abbey

At the other end of Main St, beside the River Liffey, is Celbridge Abbey, built in the 1690s by Bartholomew van Homrigh, a Dutch merchant who became Lord Mayor of Dublin. His daughter, Vanessa, was a close friend of Jonathan Swift, whose visits to her at the abbey she marked by preparing a bower and planting laurel trees.

The abbey is now owned by the St John of God Brothers but the picturesque grounds are open to the public Monday to Saturday 10 am to 6 pm, and Sunday from noon; admission is IR£2.50/1.50. Facilities include a model railway, river walks, picnic areas and a café.

Places to Stay

One km out on the Dublin road is *Green Acre* (☎ 627 1163), a B&B with beds from IR£16. *Mt Carmel* (☎ 627 3461), a little farther out, has very similar facilities and rooms for IR£20/30; it's open mid-March to October. More expensive is *Setanta House* (☎ 627 1111; fax 627 3387) on Clane Rd, an elegant family-run hotel, with singles/doubles for IR£55/80.

Places to Eat

For tea, coffee or a light meal, head for *Gulliver's* just inside the entrance to the abbey. The *Castletown Inn* has things like burgers from IR£3.25.

Getting There & Away

Bus Nos 67 and 67A go from Middle Abbey St in Dublin to Celbridge, departing every 40 minutes.

STRAFFAN

South-west of Celbridge on the road to Clane, in the village of Straffan, is the **Straffan Steam Museum**, housed in the former church of St Jude in Lodge Park. The museum contains several working steam engines and displays on the history of steam power. It's open April, May and September, Sunday 2.30 to 5.30 pm; and June to August, Tuesday to Saturday, 2 to 6 pm. Admission is IR£3/2.

At the **Straffan Butterfly Farm** in Ovidstown, you can see butterflies flying freely in a tropical greenhouse, as well as stick insects, bird-eating spiders and reptiles safely behind glass. The farm opens May to late August noon to 5.30 pm daily. Admission costs IR£2.50/1.50.

Bus Éireann has five services a day (one on Sunday) to Straffan.

BOG OF ALLEN

The Bog of Allen is Ireland's best known raised bog, a huge expanse of peat that once covered much of the midlands. The bog stretches like a brown desert through Offaly, Laois and Kildare, but like other raised bogs it's rapidly being reduced to potting compost and fuel.

RATHANGAN

The sleepy Victorian village of Rathangan, surrounded by the Bog of Allen, is on the Grand Canal 20km west of Naas but well off the beaten track. For information on coarse fishing and boat hire contact John Conway (☎ 045-524331) at the camping ground.

The telephone code is ☎ 045.

Peatland World

In a converted farm in Lullymore on the R414 9km north-east of Rathangan is Peatland World, an interpretive centre with displays covering flora, fauna, fuel, conservation and archaeological finds, as well as a video presentation and trails through parts of the bog. It's open 9.30 am to 5 pm weekdays, 2 to 6 pm weekends; admission is IR£2/1 (students IR£1.50).

Places to Stay

Carasli Caravan & Camping Park (☎ 524331) on the outskirts of Rathangan charges IR£6 per tent plus IR£1 for power. The entrance is beside the Jet service station.

Milorka (☎ 24544) is 1km along the Portarlington road in Kilnantogue. B&B in excellent rooms costs IR£16 per person, and evening meals are available.

Places to Eat
Tommies, on the main street, does reliable burgers, fish & chips etc for around IR£3. *Dillon's Bar* and the *Village Pump* are worth trying for pub food.

HILL OF ALLEN
The Hill of Allen rises above the flatlands of Kildare, which gradually change from green to the desolate brown of the Bog of Allen. Nine km north-west of Newbridge and marked today by a folly, the hill has been a strategic spot through the centuries with commanding views in all directions. The Iron Age fortifications are said to mark the home of Fionn McCumhaill, the leader of the Fianna, a mythical band of warriors who feature in many tales of ancient Ireland.

ROBERTSTOWN
Tiny Robertstown might have had all passing traffic diverted for the past 100 years. It's 12km north-west of Naas, and its old buildings overlook the Grand Canal, which is spanned by a stone bridge. On summer Sundays, the refurbished barge, *Eustace*, offers short cruises (☎ 045-60808). (See the Grand & Royal Canals section earlier.)

NAAS
Kildare's uninspiring county town of Naas (pronounced 'Nace') is about 27km south-west of Dublin. You're probably unlikely to want to linger unless you're visiting the Naas, Punchestown or Curragh racecourses although Naas (An Nás) does have a cinema, reasonable shops and an array of pubs boasting the Sky sports channel so no one need miss the racing.

Tourist information is available from the Apollo Travel Agency (☎ 045-876934), 19 North Main St.

One km south on the N7 to Kildare Town is **Jigginstown House**, Naas' only notable ruin, which was begun by Thomas Wentworth, Earl of Strafford and Lord Deputy of Ireland from 1632 to 1641. It would have been one of Ireland's largest brick buildings

if he hadn't been executed before it was finished.

The telephone code is ☎ 045.

Places to Stay & Eat
B&B is available at *Avondale* (☎ 876254) on the Dublin road for IR£34 a double, or at *Lucerne* (☎ 897533), further along the Dublin road, for IR£24/40 a single/double. If you want to splash out, a good place to stay would be *Naas Court Hotel* (☎ 866073) on Main St where rooms cost IR£49.50/77.

Opposite the bus stop in Main St, *Hanrahan's* does snacks like chicken vol-au-vents for IR£1.95, while *Alice's Restaurant* does big breakfasts, and tea and cakes. The *Five Lamps* on Main St does pub lunches round a roaring fire. In Kilcullen Rd, the southerly extension of Main St, *Finan's Restaurant & Pizzeria* has set lunches for IR£4.95 and 'Punchestown Special' set dinners for IR£14.95. A good place for a burger is *Jailhouse Diner* in Naas Court Hotel.

Getting There & Away
Bus Éireann has hourly services to Dublin, as well as services to Limerick, Kilkenny, Waterford, Clonmel, Portlaoise, Kildare, Carlow and Newbridge. New Princess Coaches (☎ 01-679 1549) has two services a day from Dublin to Kilkenny and Clonmel via Naas. The bus stop is on Main St opposite the post office; for times ring ☎ 01-836 6111.

NEWBRIDGE & THE CURRAGH
The town of Newbridge (Droichead Nua) is the gateway to the Curragh. At around 20 sq km, it is one of the country's largest pieces of unfenced fertile land and os home to the Curragh Racecourse (☎ 045-41205) and a large military training barracks. Horse trainers use the Curragh's wide open spaces to exercise their thoroughbred charges.

The N7 highway runs through the Curragh between Newbridge and Kildare Town. The No 126 Dublin to Kildare bus service stops in Newbridge and at Curragh Camp. You might want to pause to visit the **Newbridge Cutlery Visitor Centre**.

KILDARE TOWN

Kildare is a small cathedral and market town 24km south-west of Naas. Its busy triangular square with pubs on each side makes a pleasant change from the county's other non-descript urban centres.

Information

The county's main tourist office (☎ 045-522696), in Market House in the centre of the square, opens Monday to Saturday 10 am to 6 pm, June to mid-September.

The telephone code is ☎ 045.

St Brigid's Cathedral

One of the country's best loved saints, St Brigid is remembered by St Brigid's Cross, a simply constructed four-pointed cross woven from reeds and found in many homes and gift shops. In the 5th century she founded a religious centre, unusual in that it was shared by nuns and monks, who were separated by screens in church. A fire, tended only by virgins over the age of 30, was kept burning perpetually in a fire temple, out of bounds to males. It survived until the 16th century dissolution of the monasteries. The restored fire pit can be seen in the grounds of the 13th century Protestant St Brigid's Cathedral, whose solid presence looms over the square.

The 10th century round tower in the grounds is Ireland's second highest at 31.5m. Its original conical top has been replaced with an unusual Norman battlement.

The cathedral theoretically opens 10 am to 5 pm Monday to Friday but don't hold your breath. Should it be open, you may also be able to climb to the top of the round tower on payment of a small fee.

Irish National Stud & Japanese Gardens

More than any other county, Kildare is synonymous with the multimillion-pound bloodstock industry, and Kildare Town is twinned with another famous horse-breeding centre, Lexington-Fayette in Kentucky, USA.

The Irish National Stud (☎ 521617), 1km south of the centre in Tully, was set up in 1900 by Colonel Hall Walker (later Lord Wavertree) who gave it to the Crown in

A Day at the Races

Kildare has more horseflesh per sq km than any other Irish county, and the racecourses are home to some of the biggest meetings of the year. The calcium-rich grass breeds strong-boned horses, while excellent stud facilities and generous tax concessions attract many foreign horse owners.

Travelling through Kildare you'll see plenty of studs, most of them private and not too keen on visitors. You can, however, visit the state-owned National Stud just outside Kildare Town. You could also check out a thoroughbred auction at Goff's Sales (☎ 045-877211), Kildare Paddocks, a huge complex beside the main Dublin road (N7) near Kill, north-east of Naas. There you'll see spindly thoroughbred foals and yearlings change hands for astronomical sums.

Almost everyone in Ireland goes to the races. At meetings you'll see all of Irish society at play: the glitterati swilling champagne in their private boxes and the ordinary punters oblivious to everything except their bets – and, between races, their drink.

With three of Ireland's most famous tracks, Kildare has racing all year round. Best known is the Curragh Racecourse (☎ 045-441205), over 2km south-west of Newbridge on the road to Kildare Town. The March to November Curragh Racecourse season boasts some of the biggest meetings of the country's racing calendar, including the 1000 and 2000 Guineas in May, the Irish Derby in June, the Irish Oaks in July and the St Leger in September. Expect to pay around IR£10 for a ticket.

Four km south of Naas is Punchestown (☎ 045-897704), a top-notch steeplechase course where the Irish National Hunt Festival is held every April; a ticket will cost around IR£10. Finally, just to the north, Naas has its own racetrack (☎ 045-897391), which holds well-attended meetings every two weeks or so.

Special bus services operate from Dublin's Busáras to Curragh, Naas and Punchestown on race days; phone Bus Éireann (☎ 01-873 4222) for details. There are also special rail services to Curragh on race days; phone ☎ 01-836 6222 for details. ■

CENTRAL SOUTH

1915. The site was chosen because the mineral-rich Tully river is especially good for bone formation. Walker was remarkably successful with his horses, although his breeding techniques were notably eccentric; when a foal was born, he drew up its horoscope and used this to decide whether to keep it. In the hands of the Irish government since 1943, the stud's purpose is to breed high-quality stallions to mate with mares from all over the world.

On the hour every hour there are guided tours of the stud which let you see the intensive care unit for newborn foals and to learn about the horse that likes to listen to the radio and the horse with the straw allergy. Afterwards you can walk through the various stables, paddocks and meadows, or pop into the foaling unit and watch a 10 minute video on the birth of a foal. Look out for *Vintage Crop*, the horse who won the Melbourne Cup in 1993 and earned over IR£1 million before coming here to retire.

The small but interesting **Irish Horse Museum** examines the role horses have played in Irish life over the centuries and includes the skeleton of Arkle, who won the prestigious Cheltenham Gold Cup race in Britain three years running in the 1960s. There's also a lengthy video on Arkle's life. Arkle was the object of national adoration and after his death in 1968 the country went into mourning.

Also here are the delightful Japanese Gardens created for Lord Wavertree who brought two superb gardeners, Tasa Eida and his son Minoru, back from a trip to Japan. They acted as overseers to 40 local men for the four years it took to complete the work. The gardens were planted to symbolise the passage through the Life of Man. Pick up a leaflet in reception which explains the symbolism.

The large visitor's centre houses a café, a shop and a children's play area.

The stud and gardens are open daily mid-February to mid-November, 9.30 am to 6 pm. Admission costs IR£5/2 with a IR£1 discount for Bus Éireann ticket holders.

If you walk from Kildare look out for the ruins of the 12th century **Black Abbey** on the left. Shortly afterwards a turn on the right leads to **St Brigid's Well**. It's probably sacrilegious to say so but this quiet spot would make a great place for a picnic.

Places to Stay

In town, *Fremont* (☎ 21604), just south of the town square on the Tully road, charges IR£ for 17/30 singles/doubles. *Catherine Singleton's* (☎ 521964), in a new house at 1 Dara Park off Station Rd, has three rooms at IR£20/32 with bathroom.

The shabby *Lord Edward Guesthouse* (☎ 522389), behind the Silken Thomas pub on the square, has rooms for IR£17/30. On the Dublin road, the *Curragh Lodge Hotel* (☎ 522144) has rooms for IR£27.50 per person.

In Maddenstown, near the Irish National Stud, *St Mary's* (☎ 521243) does B&B for IR£14 per person.

Places to Eat

You needn't move far from the main square for a meal. For fast food there's a branch of *Abrakebabra*. *Simply Gourmet* serves everything from breakfasts through to full dinners, although it can't quite live up to the promise of its name. Nearby *George's* (☎ 521984) offers pasta from IR£5.55 and pizza from IR£4.30. It's closed on Monday.

Silken Thomas (☎ 522232), partly converted out of a cinema, has an unusually impressive, and popular, menu; beef rogan josh costs IR£10.50, seafood from IR£7.50. *Boland's Pub* across the square does dishes like steak and mushroom pie for IR£2.10.

Getting There & Away

The main N7 highway from Dublin to western Ireland passes through Kildare. Bus Éireann has numerous coaches from the Busáras (☎ 01-836 6111) which take about 1½ hours. One bus a day (two on Sunday) stops at the Irish National Stud; a day return costs IR£5/2.75.

Kildare is on the Dublin-Limerick-Ennis, Dublin-Galway and Dublin-Kilkenny-Waterford railway lines. It's 30 minutes from

Dublin (IR£7.50). For other details ring
☎ 01-836 3333.

NAAS TO CARLOW TOWN

The 48km stretch of the N9 between Naas
and Carlow Town offers several interesting
side trips.

Kilcullen

The tiny village of Kilcullen is on the River
Liffey, 12km east of Kildare Town. Nearby
at **Old Kilcullen**, the scant remains of a high
cross and round tower are all that remain of
an early Christian settlement.

On the edge of the Curragh, 4km north-
west of Kilcullen on the west side of the L19,
Donnelly's Hollow was the scene of numerous victories of Dan Donnelly (1788-1820),
Ireland's greatest bare-knuckle fighter of the
last century. It's said he had a reach so long
that he could touch his knees without having
to stoop, and that a fight here attracted about
20,000 spectators. An obelisk at the centre of
the hollow details his glorious career.

Back in Kilcullen his mummified arm can
be seen in **The Hideout** (☎ 045-81232), a
famous and wildly eccentric pub.

Ballitore & Timolin

At Ballitore on the River Greese the **Crookstown Mill & Heritage Centre** (☎ 0507-
23222) has a functioning water mill and a
display covering the history of milling and
baking. It also has a coffee shop and opens
April to September, 10 am to 7 or 8 pm daily,
closing at 4 pm the rest of the year; admission
is IR£2/1. Ballitore was originally settled by
18th century Quakers, whose influence can
be seen throughout the area in the fine buildings and graveyards. One of the settlers was
an ancestor of Ernest Shackleton, the Antarctic explorer, who was born nearby in Kilkea
House.

Two km west is the **Rath of Mullaghmast**, an Iron Age hill fort where Daniel
O'Connell, champion of Catholic emancipation, held one of his 'monster meetings' in
1843.

Three km south of Ballitore and just north
of Moone, the village of Timolin is home to

the **Irish Pewter Mill & Craft Centre**
(☎ 0507-24164). *Woodcourte House*
(☎ 0507-24167) in Timolin has a tennis
court, runs arts & crafts weekends and offers
B&B from IR£15 with bathroom. Take the
turn beside the Sportsman Inn and the house
is about 200m on the right past the Irish
Pewter Mill.

Moone

The barely noticeable village of Moone is
just south of Timolin. One km west in an
early Christian monastic churchyard is the
magnificent **Moone High Cross**. This 8th or
9th century masterpiece is slender and, at
6m, remarkably tall. The numerous crisply
carved panels display biblical scenes including the Loaves & Fishes, the Flight into
Egypt and a wonderful representation of the
Twelve Apostles.

The 18th century *Moone High Cross Inn*
(☎ 045-24112) is a delightful bar and guesthouse about 100m west of the N9, 1km south
of Moone village. It does hefty pub food
including a great Irish stew. B&B costs
IR£35/55 a single/double.

Kilkea Castle

This 12th century castle, completely restored
in the 19th century, is 5km north-west of
Castledermot on the Athy road and was once
the second home of the Maynooth Fitzgeralds. The castle grounds are supposed to be
haunted by the son of Silken Thomas, Gerald
the Wizard Earl, who rises every seven years
from the Rath of Mullaghmast to free Ireland
from its enemies, a neat trick given that the
Wizard Earl was buried in London.

Although the castle is now an exclusive
hotel (☎ 0503-45156; fax 45187) you can
still have a drink in the bar and pick up a
booklet on the building's history. Among its
oddities is an **Evil Eye Stone** set high up on
the exterior wall at the back of the castle.
Thought to date from the 13th or 14th
century, this is a depiction of various half-
human, animal and birdlike figures which
are erotically entwined. The castle has
formal gardens and a forest park.

In case you're interested, accommodation

CENTRAL SOUTH

starts at an unbelievable IR£130/200 a single/double.

Castledermot

Castledermot's ruined Franciscan Friary is right by the road at the south end of town on Abbey St. It dates from the mid-13th century and the key is available from the adjacent cottage.

A little farther north on Main St and back from the road is a churchyard, the site of a monastery founded originally by St Diarmuid in 812 AD. Two fine 9th or 10th century granite high crosses stand beside the remains of a round tower 20m high and topped with a medieval battlement, and a 12th century Romanesque church doorway.

Places to Stay & Eat The old stone *Kilkea Lodge* (☎ 0503-45112) has big open fires and is more expensive than most B&Bs at IR£28 a bed. The small, intimate *Doyle's Schoolhouse Inn* (☎ 0503-44282) is consistently rated as one of Ireland's best restaurants. Dinner will cost around IR£22 and reservations are essential. It also offers B&B at IR£25 per person.

ATHY

Founded in the 12th century, Athy (pronounced 'A-thigh') sits at the junction of the River Barrow and the Grand Canal near the County Laois border. Athy (Áth Í) has the feel of a genuine country town, with a pleasant if somewhat dilapidated old square. The 15th century tower of White Castle, built by the earls of Kildare who once owned the town, is now a private house.

The tourist office (☎ 0507-31859), in the town hall building on Emily Square, opens-year round. The town hall also houses a local museum and library.

There's coarse, salmon and trout fishing on the Grand Canal and the River Barrow. For information check with Kane's pub (☎ 31434).

The telephone code is ☎ 0507.

Places to Stay & Eat

There are several B&Bs in and around Athy.

Forest Farm (☎ 31231), a small country farmhouse 5km out of Athy on the Dublin road, and *Ballindrum Farm* (☎ 26294), a few km farther out in Ballindrum, both have rooms for around IR£21/32 a single/double without bath.

For cheap and cheerful pub food, try the *Castle Inn* on Leinster St, or the *Leinster Arms* on the corner of Emily Square. The *Duck Press Restaurant* (☎ 38952), at the south end of Leinster St over the river, is good for lunch or dinner.

The excellent *Tonlegee House* (☎ /fax 31473), in a beautiful setting beside the remains of an old church south of town on the Kilkenny road, is expensive at about IR£22. It also has guest rooms upstairs for IR£45/65 a single/double.

Getting There & Away

Buses from Dublin to Clonmel stop at Athy and provide connections to Naas, Kilkenny and Carrick-on-Suir. Contact Bus Éireann (☎ 01-836 6111) or JJ Kavanagh (☎ 056-31106) for details.

County Carlow

Carlow (Ceatharlach), Ireland's second-smallest county, has the scenic Blackstairs Mountains to the east, the Killeshin Hills to the west, and sections of the rivers Barrow and Slaney, with quietly picturesque villages like Rathvilly, Leighlinbridge and Borris. The Dublin to Carlow Town route via southwest Wicklow runs through some wild and lightly populated country.

The rest of Carlow is mainly undulating farmland where you will quite often see sugar beet awaiting collection by the roadside. Browne's Hill Dolmen, the county's most interesting archaeological feature, is just outside Carlow Town.

CARLOW

Its strategic location on the River Barrow, on the border with the Pale, made Carlow a frontier town for many centuries. Today, it's a busy market and industrial centre serving a large rural area. Carlow was the first town outside Dublin to have electric street lighting, from power generated downstream at Milford. Railway pioneer William Dargan, who founded the National Gallery in Dublin, was born here. Perhaps the main reason for pausing is to inspect Browne's Hill Dolmen on the outskirts.

Orientation & Information

Dublin St is the city's principal north-south axis, with Tullow St, the main shopping street, running off it at a right angle. The tourist office (☎ 0503-31554), in Kennedy Ave, is theoretically open all year round. The post office is on the corner of Kennedy Ave and Dublin St.

The telephone code is ☎ 0503.

Things to See

In Catle St, **Carlow Castle**, was built by William Marshall in the 12th century on the site of an earlier Norman motte-and-bailey fort. Officials once had to be paid danger money to live here among the native Irish. The castle survived Cromwell's attentions and would be largely intact if a Dr Middleton hadn't decided to turn it into an asylum and blow it up in 1814; the mighty castle was reduced to a single wall flanked by two towers.

It's said that the plans for Carlow and Cork courthouses got mixed up, so this little town ended up with William Morrison's splendid 1830 building, based on the Parthenon in Athens, while Cork had to make do with a less impressive design. The cannon beside the steps was taken from the Russians during the Crimean War. The **courthouse** is at the northern end of Dublin St.

Down College St from the courthouse, the 1833 **Cathedral of the Assumption** has an elaborate pulpit and some fine stained-glass windows. John Hogan's statue of Bishop Doyle, better known as JKL (James of Kildare & Leighin) for his work as a supporter of Catholic Emancipation, includes a woman who represents Ireland rising up against her oppressors.

The small **Carlow County Museum** is currently in the town hall, on Centaur St off the Haymarket. It's open 11 am to 5 pm Tuesday to Friday and 2 to 5 pm at weekends. Admission is IR£1/50p. At the moment it's a dejected place. Should plans for a move into the old Dublin St library come off the contents might get a better showing.

In 1798 640 United Irish rebels were killed in the bloodiest fighting of the rising around what is now Tullow St. A Celtic **high cross** marks the Croppie Grave, across the river, where most of the bodies were buried.

Activities

The River Barrow is popular with canoeists, kayakers and rowers (Carlow Rowing Club has been going since 1859). Otterholt Riverside Lodge (see Places to Stay) can arrange canoeing for around IR£10 for a half-day. Alternatively phone Adventure Canoeing Days on ☎ 0509-31307.

Places to Stay

The IHH's *Otterholt Riverside Lodge* (☎ 30404), on Kilkenny Rd, has delightful gardens and charges IR£8 in a 10-bed dorm. *Red Setter House* (☎ 41848), 14 Dublin St, is a spotless central B&B with a range of rooms, some with shower, some without. Prices start at IR£15/26 a single/double. *Barrow Lodge* (☎ 41173) has a pleasant riverside setting and beds for IR£16 a head.

The *Royal Hotel* (☎ 31621), 8 Dublin St, has rooms for IR£33/60. The modern *Óstan Dinn Rí* (☎ 3311) in Tullow St has singles/doubles for IR£30/50 in a complex with bar, restaurant and nightclub.

Places to Eat

In Tullow St, *Muffins* does 'healthy' breakfasts for IR£1.95. Also on Tullow St, *Bradbury's Coffee Shop* is good for light lunches (soup and a roll for IR£1.20) and is one of the few places other than pubs open on Sunday.

Teach Dolmain in Tullow St has a lengthy bar meals menu; seafood chowder for IR£2.75, and a thoroughly unhealthy vegetarian mix of french fries, onion rings and battered mushrooms in mayonnaise for IR£3.95.

Beams Restaurant (☎ 31824) in Dublin St opens Tuesday to Saturday for meals in the IR£10 to IR£13 price range. Nearby *The Owl* does a range of roast beef and shepherd's pie-style meals, while across the road in the *Royal Hotel Restaurant*, pasta in an asparagus sauce costs IR£5.50

Entertainment

Carlow has wall-to-wall pubs, with something to suit most tastes. The triangular Haymarket is very typical, with *Tormey's*, *Ewing's* and *The Market House Bar* facing each other along the sides. *The Plough* in Tullow St has a few outdoor tables, chickens and a dovecot. Further up the road *Teach Dolmain* makes much of its dolmen décor. *The Castle Inn* has traditional music on Friday night.

Óstan Dinn Rí has a Thursday nightclub with free admission until 2 am. When bands play there's a variable admission charge.

Getting There & Away

Bus Bus Éireann (☎ 01-836 6111) has regular services to Dublin (at least five daily, 1½ hours), Kilkenny (three daily except Sunday, 30 minutes) and Waterford (at least five daily, 1½ hours). Rapid Express Coaches (☎ 43081) has at least seven buses daily to Dublin and Waterford. JJ Kavanagh (☎ 43081) has a twice-daily service to Athy, Monasterevin, Curragh and Kildare; a daily service to Portlaoise; a service to Wexford; a Friday/Sunday service to Cork via Kilkenny, Cashel and Cahir; and a Friday/Sunday service to Limerick. All these buses leave from near the Rapid Express office on Barrack St south of the post office.

Train The station (☎ 31633) is on Railway St to the north-east of town. Carlow is on the Dublin to Kilkenny and Waterford line with at least four trains daily in each direction (three on Sunday). A day return to Dublin or Waterford is IR£5.50.

Getting Around

Coleman's (☎ 31273), 19 Dublin St, is a Raleigh dealer with bikes for IR£7/30 a day/week.

AROUND CARLOW TOWN

There's no public transport to the following sights, but the first two are within easy cycling distance.

Browne's Hill Dolmen

This 5000-year-old granite monster is believed to have the largest capstone in Europe, weighing over 100 tonnes. When complete, the structure would have been covered with a mound of earth. The dolmen is 3km east of town on the R726 Hacketstown road; a path leads around the field to the dolmen.

Milford

One of the nicer drives to the south is via Milford on the minor road that follows the River Barrow valley. The village lies midway between Carlow Town and Leighlinbridge. The old mill at Milford was the site of the turbine which first powered Carlow Town's electric street lighting in the 1890s. John Alexander, the present owner, still runs a turbine and supplies electricity to the Electricity Supply Board (ESB). There's good salmon and trout fishing here.

TULLOW

Tullow is a well-known angling town on the River Slaney in the north of the county. Father John Murphy, a local leader of the 1798 Rising, was captured and executed in the market square in July 1798; a memorial stands in the town centre. Tullow Museum, beside the town bridge, opens on Sunday and Wednesday afternoons.

Five km due east of Tullow on Shillelagh Rd is the Iron Age ring fort of **Rathgall**, dating from the 8th century BC and protected by three overgrown outer ring walls. The final wall is still in good condition, though somewhat lower nowadays. Rathgall is said to be the burial site of the kings of Leinster.

Eleven km south-west of Tullow near

Ballon are the beautiful **Altamont Gardens**, with a lake, bog garden and arboretum. Unfortunately they're only open on Sunday and bank holidays April to October, 2 to 6 pm. Admission is IR£2.

Places to Stay
The early Georgian *Sherwood Park House* (☎ 0503-59117) is south of Tullow in Kilbride just off the N80 between Ballon and Kildavin. B&B costs IR£28/46 a single/double with bathroom.

Getting There & Away
Tullow is on Bus Éireann's (☎ 01-836 6111) Dublin to Waterford route, which also stops at Enniscorthy and New Ross. There are three buses daily in each direction (two on Sunday).

LEIGHLINBRIDGE
Leighlinbridge, just off the main Kilkenny road, 13km south-west of Carlow Town, has one of Ireland's first Norman castles. The rather uninspiring **Black Castle** dates from 1181 and overlooks the first bridge to be built over the River Barrow. This pleasant village also produced Captain Myles Kehoe, the last of General George Custer's men left alive at the 1876 Battle of Little Bighorn in Montana, USA.

Three km west is **Old Leighlin**, the site of a 6th century monastic settlement founded by St Laserian. The small cathedral has some finely carved stonework and a Romanesque doorway although it's not as impressive as Killeshin Church (see the County Laois section for more details).

Places to Stay & Eat
Nevin's (☎ 0503-21202) in the main street has simple rooms for IR£12 per person. The owner, Martin Nevin, is a teacher who's very interested in local history.

Next door, the popular *Lord Bagenal Inn* (☎ 0503-21668) is an inviting place with a big open fire and a restaurant serving excellent steaks, fish and pasta, and good vegetarian food.

Getting There & Away
At least five buses a day in each direction pass through Leighlinbridge on the Dublin to Waterford via Naas and Carlow route.

BORRIS
Sixteen km south of Leighlinbridge, the Georgian village of Borris is overlooked by a disused railway viaduct with 16 arches. **Borris House** is the residence of the MacMurrough Kavanaghs, descendants of the ancient kings of Leinster, and is still in the family's possession, Andrew Mac-Murrough Kavanagh being the present occupant.

A most remarkable MacMurrough Kavanagh was Arthur (1831-89), who was born with only rudimentary limbs yet learned to ride and shoot and later became an MP. Visits to the castle are by appointment only. The entrance is at the north end of town near the White House pub.

Borris is a starting point for the Mt Leinster Scenic Drive (which can also be walked) and is also on the South Leinster Way. Alternatively, there's a lovely 10km walk along a towpath beside the River Barrow to picturesque Graiguenamanagh, just inside County Kilkenny.

The telephone code is ☎ 0503.

Places to Stay & Eat
Breen's (☎ 732318), on Church St, does B&B for IR£13.50/27 a single/double. Half way between Borris and Bagenalstown, the *Lorum Old Rectory* (☎ 75282) is overlooked by the Blackstairs Mountains and charges from IR£30/50, with excellent dinners at IR£20.

Getting There & Away
Foley's (☎ 24641) operates one bus a day (except Sunday) to Borris from Kilkenny, leaving at 5.30 pm.

MT LEINSTER
At 796m, Mt Leinster offers some of Ireland's finest hang-gliding. It's also worth the hike up for the panoramic views over counties Carlow, Wexford and Wicklow. To get

CENTRAL SOUTH

there from Borris, follow the Mt Leinster Scenic Drive signposts 13km towards Bunclody in County Wexford (see the Counties Wexford & Waterford chapter for more details). It takes a good two hours on foot or 20 minutes by car.

SOUTH LEINSTER WAY
South-west of Clonegal, on the north slopes of Mt Leinster, is the tiny village of **Kildavin**, the starting point of the South Leinster Way. Carlow Town and St Mullins are also on the Kildare Trails. See the Activities chapter for details.

County Laois

Laois (pronounced 'Leash') is a 1½ hour drive south-west of Dublin and is the only inland county surrounded on all sides by counties none of which touch the coast. For most visitors it's somewhere to whip through en route to Limerick or Cork, with a fairly uninteresting landscape of raised bogs and poor farms. With time to linger you'll find some pleasant country towns and the unspoiled Slieve Bloom Mountains.

PORTLAOISE
Although founded by the O'Mores just before the 16th century plantations, Portlaoise (Port Laoise) is mostly modern, and only the courthouse by Richard Morrison on the corner of Main and Church Sts is notable. Bristling with wire fencing at the east end of town is a maximum security prison, Portlaoise's main claim to fame for many people. Even before the bypass was built there was little to linger for. Once it's completed you'll probably sweep straight past.

To the west lie the Slieve Bloom Mountains, while to the east is the one historic site worth a special detour, the impressive Rock of Dunamase on the Stradbally road.

Information
The year-round tourist office (☎ 0502-21178), in the shopping centre car park beside the bypass on James Fintan Lawlor Ave, has lots of local information. To get there from Main St, cut through the lane beside Dowling's café.

The telephone code is ☎ 0502.

Places to Stay & Eat
If you need a hotel, *O'Loughlin's* (☎ 21305) on Main St has singles/doubles for IR£25/40. There's also a bar and restaurant downstairs.

Dowling's, also on Main St, serves good hot food (from IR£3.50) and sandwiches during the day.

Getting There & Away
Portlaoise is on one of the busiest main roads in the country at the junction of the N8 and N7, with frequent Bus Éireann (☎ 01-836 6111) buses passing between Dublin and Cashel, Cork, Limerick and Kerry. It is also on the Waterford, Kilkenny, Carlow, Athlone and Longford route. JJ Kavanagh's private bus company (☎ 056-31106) has two buses a day to Carlow.

Just one hour from Dublin on the main line to Tipperary, Cork, Limerick and Tralee, Portlaoise is serviced by numerous daily trains. The station (☎ 21303), on Railway St, is a five-minute walk north of the town centre.

ROCK OF DUNAMASE
Six km east of Portlaoise along the Stradbally road is a dramatic fractured limestone hill covered with the remains of fortifications. It may not be Cashel, but the surrounding countryside is so flat that the summit offers fine views of the Timahoe round tower to the south and of Portarlington power station to the north.

The remains include an Iron Age ring fort and a 12th or 13th century keep. The slopes of Dunamase can be treacherous, particularly on the north side, and these natural barriers would have complicated any assault on its defenders. First sacked by the Vikings in the 840s, Dunamase was later given away by Dermot MacMurrough, king of Leinster, as part of his daughter Aoife's dowry when she married Strongbow, the Norman invader of Ireland. Dunamase was then reinforced by William Marshall, Strongbow's successor, who built three baileys on the spot.

The local clan, the O'Mores, captured the rock from the English near the end of the 14th century and held it until it was retaken by Charles Coote in 1641. He was a leading Parliamentarian and one of Cromwell's most able leaders in Ireland. Recaptured five years later by Catholic forces, it was finally wrecked by Cromwell's henchmen Reynolds and Hewson in 1650.

Hewson gave his name to the hill to the south-west, which has the ruined 9th century church of Dysert. The earth embankments 500m to the east are known as Cromwell's lines, although they're actually the remains of a much older two-ringed fort.

The main ruins consist of a badly shattered 13th century castle on the summit (best seen from the north side) surrounded by an outer wall of which little remains. You enter the complex through the twin-towered gateway, which leads to the outer bailey and fortified courtyard to the south-east.

JJ Kavanagh's (☎ 056-31106) two daily Portlaoise to Carlow buses pass by the rock. Otherwise, it's a good hour's walk from the town centre.

EMO COURT & DEMESNE
Thirteen km north-east of Portlaoise and signposted off the main road to Dublin, Emo Court was the county seat of the 1st earl of Portarlington. The rather unusual house with its prominent green dome was designed by James Gandon (architect of Dublin's Customs House) in 1790 and served as a Jesuit novitiate for many years. The estate offers long walks through forests and by Emo Lake, and is littered with Greek statues. From the Emo village gate it's a 2km walk along the drive to the house.

The house was recently restored by Dúchas and is now open to the public for guided tours daily mid-June to mid-September, 10 am to 6 pm. Admission costs IR£2/1. The grounds are open free during daylight hours.

South of Emo village off the main Portlaoise road is the elegantly simple **St John's Church**, in Coolbanagher, also designed by Gandon in 1786 as a replacement for a thatched church which was destroyed in 1779.

Emo is just off the main Portlaoise to Dublin road, with daily buses in both directions.

STRADBALLY
The village of Stradbally (or Strathbally), 10km south-east of Portlaoise, was once a seat of the mighty O'More clan. Most of the present buildings date from the 17th century.

The O'Mores were the force behind the Franciscan friary established here in 1447. The family were the holders of *The Book of Leinster*, a manuscript compiled between 1151 and 1224 to record all the knowledge of Aéd Crúamthainn, scribe to the high kings of Ireland. This book contained, among other things, vivid descriptions of the banqueting hall at Tara, the seat of the high kings, and is now to be found in Trinity College Library, Dublin.

Stradbally Steam Museum
At the southern end of town, this museum has a collection of fire engines, steam tractors and steamrollers, lovingly restored by the Irish Steam Preservation Society. Housed in a tightly packed warehouse, the prize exhibits include a Merryweather horse-drawn fire engine from 1880.

The 1895 Guinness Brewery steam locomotive in the village is used six times annually for a day trip to Dublin. During the three-day Steam Rally in early August the 40 hectares of Cosby Hall are taken over by steam-operated machines and vintage cars. The museum opens Monday to Friday 11 am to 1 pm and 2 to 4 pm. Admission is IR£1.50 (children free).

Getting There & Away
JJ Kavanagh (☎ 056-31106) has two daily buses from Portlaoise to Carlow via Stradbally. Stradbally is also on Bus Éireann's twice daily Waterford to Longford service

CENTRAL SOUTH

which also passes through Kilkenny, Carlow, Portlaoise and Athlone.

PORTARLINGTON

Portarlington (Cúil an tSúdaire) grew up under the influence of French Huguenot and German settlers introduced by Lord Arlington, who was granted land here after the Cromwellian wars. Some of the finer 18th century buildings are a result of Henry Dawson, earl of Portarlington's efforts to improve the town. Unfortunately, many are terribly neglected.

The 1851 **St Paul's Church**, on the site of the original 17th century French church, was built for the Huguenots some of whose tombstones stand in a corner of the churchyard. Stretches of the River Barrow along the borders with counties Kildare and Carlow are lovely.

The power station's large cooling tower is a local landmark. Built in 1936, it was the first in Ireland to use peat to generate electricity.

Getting There & Away

Portarlington is on the main railway lines between Dublin and Galway, Limerick, Tralee and Cork, with numerous daily trains in both directions. For details contact Portlaoise railway station (☎ 0502-21303). There are no bus services.

LEA CASTLE

On the banks of the River Barrow 4km east of Portarlington, this ivy-clad 13th century ruin was the stronghold of Maurice Fitzgerald, 2nd baron of Offaly. It consists of a fairly intact towered keep with two outer walls running down to the Barrow and a twin-towered gatehouse. It was burned in 1315 by Edward Bruce, the brother of King Robert Bruce of Scotland. In 1315 Edward came to Ireland at the invitation of Irish chieftains to create trouble for the Anglo-Normans/ English. He hoped this would distract the English and lessen their pressure on his brother in Scotland.

Crowned high king of Ireland, Edward Bruce hassled the forces loyal to England,

until he was killed in 1318 at the Battle of Faughart near Dundalk. His remains are said to be buried in a churchyard at Faughart 4km from Castleroche.

In the 16th century Silken Thomas sought refuge here after his failed rebellion against Henry VIII. In 1650 the castle was blown up by Cromwell's forces, fresh from their success at Dunamase. The castle stairways were filled with explosives to maximise the damage. '

In early morning and evening the ruins can be tranquil and evocative. Access is through a farmyard half a km to the north off the main Monasterevin road (R420).

MOUNTMELLICK

Mountmellick is a faded market town with many Georgian houses, 10km north of Portlaoise on the River Owenass. Its fortunes rose with Quaker settlers who produced linen which was exported by barge on a branch of the Grand Canal which runs away to the east. Something of a boom town in the late 18th and early 19th centuries, it was home to Ireland's first sugar-beet factory, built in 1851. The small visitor's centre (☎ 0502-24525) with a display on Quaker life and Mountmellick embroidery opens 10 am to 5 pm Monday to Friday (plus summer weekends 2 to 6 pm).

Getting There & Away

Mountmellick is on Bus Éireann's twice-daily Waterford to Longford (☎ 01-836 6111) route which passes through Kilkenny, Carlow, Stradbally, Portlaoise and Athlone. There's also a daily service to and from Dublin via Naas, Newbridge and Kildare.

MOUNTRATH & AROUND

Like so many other Irish settlements, Mountrath is associated with St Patrick and St Brigid, who are supposed to have established religious houses here, although no trace of either remains. Much of the town and surrounding land belonged to Sir Charles Coote, an ardent supporter of Cromwell during and after the wars of the 1640s. Mountrath's glory days were in the 17th and

18th centuries, when it prospered from the linen industry.

The telephone code is ☎ 0502.

St Fintan's Tree

Three km east on the Portlaoise road, there are scant remains of the 6th century monastery of St Fintan at Clonenagh. St Fintan's Tree is a large sycamore with a water-filled groove in one of its lower branches. Supposedly this never dries out and the tree has long been a place of pilgrimage; the coins embedded in the trunk are offerings by pilgrims who attribute healing powers to the water.

Ballyfin House

Eight km north of Mountrath off the Mountmellick road is Ballyfin House, built by Sir Charles Henry Coote in 1850 to the designs of Richard Morrison (better known for his courthouses). Overlooking a small lake in quiet, rolling countryside, it has been described as Ireland's finest 19th century house. Inside, some of the ornamentation is completely over the top; in the dining room, or 'gold room', someone ran amok with plaster and gold paint, creating something that would look at home in Versailles. Sir Charles reckoned all good houses should have a lake, and the one in front is artificial.

An intriguing piece of contemporary aristocratic eccentricity was megalithomania, or a passion for building imitation Stone Age monuments. Ballyfin has an excellent example in the form of a rough stone shelter hidden among the trees on the far side of the fence to the right of the avenue about 200m short of the house. Such extravagances were still being built just years after the Potato Famine decimated the population. An unattractive modern wing now houses a school.

Places to Stay & Eat

The Lodge (☎ 32756) in Coote Terrace has four rooms with separate bathroom for IR£15 a head. *Phelan's Restaurant*, on Main St by the square, has reasonable burgers and chips.

Getting There & Away

Mountrath is on the main Bus Éireann (☎ 01-836 6111) Dublin to Limerick route, with up to four buses a day in each direction. Buses stop in front of Darcy's.

SLIEVE BLOOM MOUNTAINS

One of the best reasons for visiting Laois is to explore the Slieve Bloom Mountains (Slieve is pronounced 'shleeve'). Their name means Mountains of Bladhma, after a Celtic warrior who used the mountains as a refuge. Though nowhere near as splendid as their cousins in Wicklow and the west, the Slieve Blooms win out for their relative absence of visitors. You can't miss the brown signs on almost every road into the hills.

The highest point is Mt Arderin (528m) south of the Glendine Gap on the Offaly border. On a clear day it's possible to see the highest points of all four of the ancient provinces of Ireland. East is Lugnaquilla in Leinster, west is Nephin in Connacht, north is Slieve Donard in Ulster and south-west is Carrauntuohill in Munster.

Mountrath to the south and lovely **Kinnitty** to the north of the hills make good bases. **Glenbarrow**, south-west of Rosenallis, has a gentle walk by the River Barrow which has its source just a few km farther up in the hills. There are some waterfalls, a large moraine on the north side of the river and unusual local plants, including orchids, butterwort and blue fleabane. Other spots worth checking out are **Glendine Park** near the Glendine Gap, and the **Cut** mountain pass. The road north of the mountains from Mountmellick to Birr via Clonaslee and Kinnitty is particularly scenic.

Slieve Bloom Way

The Slieve Bloom Way is a 70km signposted trail which does a complete circuit of the mountains taking in most major points of interest. See the Activities chapter for more details.

WEST LAOIS

South of the Slieve Bloom Mountains, **Borris-in-Ossory** on the N7, once known as the Gate of Munster, was a major coaching stop in the 18th century before the railways developed. It's on a Bus Éireann express Dublin to Limerick route, with four buses daily in each direction (three on Sunday).

About 3km farther west on the same road, **Ballaghmore Castle** (☎ 0505-21453) controlled the edges of the Fitzpatrick family lands and is one of several small castles open to the public. The square tower fortress dating from 1480 has been faithfully restored. Those with good eyesight might spot the **sheila-na-gig** in the south wall. Ballaghmore Castle opens daily; admission is IR£2.50/1.50.

ABBEYLEIX

Abbeyleix, 14km south of Portlaoise, is as well tended a country town as you will find. It grew up around a 12th century Cistercian monastery in nearby Old Town, though the only traces of this are two ancient monuments. In the 18th century the local landowner, Lord de Vesci, moved the town centre to its present location and supervised the layout of tree-lined streets and neat town houses. During the Famine de Vesci proved a kinder landlord than many and the fountain-obelisk in the square was erected as a thank you from his tenants.

De Vesci's mansion, **Abbeyleix House**, was erected in 1773 from a design by James Wyatt. It's 2km south-west of town on the Rathdowney road, but isn't open to the public.

The old National School building at the Portlaoise end of town is now the **Heritage House** which details the town's history and contains examples of the Turkish-influenced carpets woven in Abbeyleix from 1904 and 1913. It's open Monday to Friday 9 am to 5 pm, opening at 1 am at weekends. Admission costs IR£2/1. A coffee shop in the basement serves breakfast until noon and light lunches.

Morrissey's in the high street is a marvellous old pub/shop which used to act as a travel agency and undertaker's as well. Drinkers down their pints around an old-fashioned stovepipe or perch on stools at a sloping counter gazing on packets of soap powder. At the time of writing it was due to be auctioned and looked vulnerable to a heritage overhaul. It's to be hoped the new owners will leave well alone.

Places to Stay & Eat

Creeper-clad *Preston House* (☎ 0502-31432) offers B&B in what were once the assembly rooms; a double costs IR£50. There's a café here too.

The striking greystone *Hibernian Hotel* (☎ 0502-31252) does beds for IR£35/50 a single/double without breakfast.

Getting There & Away

Abbeyleix is on an express Bus Éireann (☎ 01-836 6111) route between Dublin and Cork, with three buses daily (two on Sunday). JJ Kavanagh's private bus service (☎ 056-31106) has a daily Portlaoise, Abbeyleix, Durrow, Cullahill, Urlingford bus and another Friday-only service between Carlow and Limerick.

TIMAHOE

Tiny Timahoe is just a handful of houses around a grassy square, 10km north-east of Abbeyleix on a minor road (R426). South of the village seven roads converge on a 30m-tall **round tower** with a slight tilt, all that remains of a 12th century monastery. The tower has a beautifully worked Romanesque entrance with carved human faces.

DURROW

In Durrow, about 10km south of Abbeyleix at the junction of the N77 and N8, neat rows of houses surround a manicured green with the imposing gateway to **Castle Durrow** (1716), a large Palladian villa, on the west side. The castle is privately owned and not open to the public.

The *Castle Arms Hotel* (☎ 0502-36117), on the square, charges IR£25 per person for B&B and has entertainment most weekends.

KILLESHIN CHURCH

Killeshin Church is a mere 5km from Carlow Town. Killeshin used to be one of the biggest towns in Laois and had one of the finest round towers in the country. A local farmer is said to have destroyed it in the 18th century in case it collapsed and killed his livestock.

The shattered 11th century church has a steeply arched Romanesque doorway bearing intricately carved patterns and human heads.

County Offaly

Offaly is home to Clonmacnoise, one of Ireland's most extensive and attractive monastic sites. The county has the typical flat, boggy landscape of central Ireland, exemplified by the extensive Bog of Allen and Boora Bog between Ferbane and Kilcormac. The mighty River Shannon forms part of Offaly's border with Galway, while the Grand Canal also threads its way through the county. Offaly shares the Slieve Bloom Mountains with County Laois.

BIRR

On the River Camcor, a small tributary of the River Shannon in the south-west of the county, Birr is Offaly's most attractive town. With formal tree-lined avenues and Georgian terraces, Birr retains much of its 18th and 19th century character. Many traditional shopfronts survive along Connaught and Main Sts, and all the main roads converge on Emmet Square, where a statue of the Duke of Cumberland (victor of the Battle of Culloden) stood on the central column until 1925. In one corner, Dooly's Hotel, dating from 1747, was once a coaching inn on the busy route west.

History

After starting out as a 6th century monastic site founded by St Brendan of Birr, the town acquired an Anglo-Norman castle in 1208. During the plantation of 1620, the castle and estate were given to Sir Laurence Parsons who laid out streets, established a glass factory and issued decrees that anyone who 'cast dunge rubbidge filth or sweepings in the forestreet' was to be fined four pennies.

Any woman caught working as a barmaid was to 'be set in the stocks by the constable for three whole market days'.

Later, the Parsons became earls of Rosse. The present earl and his wife still live on the estate, which has remained in the family for 14 generations.

Orientation & Information

The centre of town is Emmet Square, with the post office in the north-west corner.

The tourist office (☎ 0509-20110) is in Rosse Row, almost directly opposite the castle gates, and opens May to September, 10 am to 5.30 pm daily.

The two finest streets of Georgian houses are tree-lined Oxmantown Mall connecting Rosse Row and Emmet Square, and John's Mall.

The telephone code is ☎ 0509.

Birr Castle & Demesne

Most visitors to Birr come to see the castle and grounds, which are among the finest in Ireland. Most of the present structure dates from around 1620 when Sir Laurence Parsons was granted the estate. A later Laurence presided over alterations in the early 19th century, which left the castle almost exactly as you see it today. In 1820 the castle was fortified again after a local Protestant woman, Mrs Legge, convinced her brethren that the Catholics were going to rise up and kill them in their beds.

The demesne, which runs north from the castle, consists of 50 hectares of magnificent gardens set around a large artificial lake. The gardens hold over 1000 species of shrubs and trees from all over the world including a collection from the Himalayas and China, brought back from the 6th earl's 1935 honeymoon in Peking. The world's tallest box hedges, planted in the 1780s, now stand some 12m high.

Today the castle is the home of Lord and Lady Rosse; group visits are possible if arranged well in advance through the Estate Office (☎ 20056), Rosse Row, Birr, County Offaly. The demesne opens all year 9 am to 6 pm daily, but the exhibitions associated

CENTRAL SOUTH

Birr Observatory & Telescope

The castle grounds hold one of Ireland's most extraordinary scientific structures. The third Earl of Rosse, William Parsons (1800-67), wanted to build the world's biggest telescope. The resulting 'leviathan of Parsonstown', a 72 inch (183cm) reflector telescope completed in 1845, remained the largest in existence for 75 years, attracting astronomers and scientists from all over the world. The instrument was used to map the moon's surface, and made innumerable discoveries including the spiral galaxies. The telescope was built using local engineering and materials.

The telescope is slowly being restored and three times a day there are demonstrations of how it works.

The remarkable Rosse family were not just stargazers. The next Earl of Rosse, Lawrence Parsons, built a device to measure the heat given off by the moon. Charles Algernon Parsons, Lawrence's brother, invented the steam turbine for the earliest British iron battleships, while their mother, Mary Rosse, the third earl's wife, was a pioneer in 19th century photography. ■

with the giant telescope only open May to mid-September, 2.30 to 5.30 pm daily; admission is IR£3.50/1.50.

Other Attractions

A Tourist Trail leaflet is available at the tourist office.

John's Mall has John Henry Foley's statue of the 3rd earl of Rosse and a Russian cannon from the Crimean War. Nearby is the **Birr Stone**, a megalithic stone found in an early Christian monastery and said to have marked the centre of Ireland. Some fine Victorian houses built between 1870 and 1878 are on the side of the square opposite the Birr Heritage Centre. This was closed at the time of writing but the Civic Trust was hoping to reopen it.

South-west of Emmet square are the remains of **Old St Brendan's Church**, reputedly the site of St Brendan's 6th century settlement.

A fine **riverside walk** runs east along the River Camcor from Oxmantown Bridge near the Catholic church to Elmgrove Bridge.

Birr Outdoor Education Centre (☎ 20029), Roscrea Rd, offers courses in walking, sailing, canoeing and rock-climbing in the nearby Slieve Blooms.

Places to Stay

Hostel The nearest hostel is *Crank House* in Banagher, 13km to the north. (See that section later.)

B&Bs B&Bs in town are not particularly cheap. *The Chains* (☎ 21687) in Johns Mall has singles/doubles from IR£22.50/33. *Ard na Gréine* (☎ 20256), in Hillside 1km from Birr along the Roscrea road, is cheaper, with rooms for IR£19/28. The Georgian *Ormond House* (☎ 20291), in Emmet Square, and *Stables* (☎ 20263), in Oxmantown Mall, both charge from IR£20 for a bed.

Hotels The friendly *County Arms Hotel* (☎ 20791; fax 21234) is within walking distance of the centre on Railway Rd, which becomes the road to Roscrea. Rooms are well equipped and B&B costs IR£45/80.

Originally a hunting lodge, *Dooly's* (☎ 20032; fax 21332), on Emmet Square, has 18 comfortable rooms for B&B at IR£33/60.

Country Houses The 18th century *Tullanisk* (☎ 20572; fax 21783), 2km out towards Banagher up a long avenue on the right, has delightful rooms on the Birr Estate. B&B costs from IR£35 to IR£52.

Places to Eat

The pleasant *Castle Kitchen* in the same building as the tourist office does vegetarian dishes as well as the regular food. *Dooly's Hotel* (☎ 20032) in Emmet Square has an excellent cafeteria-style coffee shop (open 8.30 am to 10 pm); lunch is available at the

CENTRAL SOUTH

bar from 12.30 to 2.30 pm, while the restaurant in the front of the hotel serves dinner.

North of the square and near the castle walls is *Stables Restaurant* (☎ 20263), in a converted mews on Oxmantown Mall. It serves good four-course dinners Tuesday to Saturday for IR£16 and lunch on Sunday. The *County Arms Hotel* (☎ 20791) does good bar lunches and more than acceptable dinners in the evenings for around IR£20.

Tullanisk House (☎ 20572) blends old English and Asian influences in a IR£22.50 set dinner (see Places to Stay).

Entertainment
Foster's, on Connaught St at the back of Dooly's, is an old-style pub which gets a good crowd at weekends and usually has music. The *Palace Bar* on O'Connell St often has live bands at weekends. *Kelly's* is a locals' haunt, just off the square towards the castle. *Mary Walshe's Bar* has Irish music on Friday and Saturday nights. In Dooly's Hotel *Melba's Nite Club* opens Friday, Saturday and Sunday nights.

Getting There & Away
A single daily bus passes through on the Dublin to Portumna route and another heading from Athlone to Cork. Call Athlone bus station (☎ 0902-72651) for times.

Kearn's Coaches (☎ 22244) has services from Dublin and Tullamore through Birr to Portumna. Three buses pass through Birr on Sunday, Monday and Friday, two on Saturday and one Tuesday to Thursday. Up to two buses a day go from Portumna to Birr and Dublin. A one-way ticket from Birr to Dublin costs IR£5. All buses stop in Emmet Square.

LEAP CASTLE
South-east of Birr between Kinnitty and Roscrea (in Tipperary) are the remains of Leap Castle, in one of the few areas of Offaly rich in pre-Christian ring forts and burial mounds. It was originally an O'Carroll family residence, keeping guard over a crucial route between Munster and Leinster, and was renowned for a 'smelly ghost';

indeed it was said by locals to be one of the most haunted castles in Europe. It was destroyed in 1922 during the Civil War. The site offers good views of the Slieve Bloom Mountains.

SLIEVE BLOOM MOUNTAINS
It's a bit of an exaggeration to call them mountains, but the Slieve Blooms in the south-east of the county are little visited and yet boast moorlands, pine forests and hidden river valleys. It's a lovely journey from Birr to the hamlet of Kinnitty, the jumping-off point for the mountains. There's also a good trip over the hills to Mountrath (County Laois), and a pleasant drive around the northern flanks of the hills between Kinnitty and Mountmellick (also in County Laois).

For more details see the County Laois section earlier.

RIVER SHANNON & THE BOGS
Dominating the region geographically and commercially, the River Shannon forms the border between Offaly and Galway until it veers off west to Lough Derg south of Banagher. Towns like Banagher grew up beside the river when it was a busier highway than it is today.

The Grand Canal also threads its way through the county, entering to the east near Edenderry and passing through Tullamore

Eskers and the Kings' Road
West Offaly's flat bog lands are often prevented from draining into the River Shannon by *eskers*, long, winding, glacial ridges made up of fossilised coarse sand and gravel deposits from meltwater rivers that ran underneath glaciers. Over time the vegetation built up layers of peat up to 10m deep. The best known esker is Esker Riada ('the Kings' Road') which ran across much of the country, forming the principal highway between Leinster and Connaught. You can still see parts of it near the main road to Dublin. Clonmacnoise sits on part of this esker in the north-west corner of Offaly.

Esker is one of the few Irish words which has entered the English language. ■

before joining the River Shannon at Shannon Harbour, just north of Banagher.

Offaly has two extensive peatlands: the **Bog of Allen** in the east and **Boora Bog** in the west. The Bog of Allen is an enormous brown expanse that stretches over into Kildare and which – along with many other bogs – is being mined by the huge machines of the Bord na Móna (Irish Turf Board) for potting compost and fuel briquettes. However, some of Offaly's bogs, like **Clara Bog**, are remarkably untouched and are recognised internationally for their plant and animal life.

BANAGHER & AROUND

The quiet riverside town of Banagher, 12km north of Birr, is one of the few crossing points of the River Shannon in this area. Heading north, the next crossing point is at Athlone.

While a post office clerk here in 1841, Anthony Trollope wrote his first novels. Charlotte Brontë honeymooned here, and her husband, the Reverend Arthur Bell Nicholls, stayed on after she died in England. Cuba Ave is named after local boy George Frazer who became governor of that island.

There is a tourist information desk (☎ 0509-51458) in Crank House on Main St and some pleasant pubs and restaurants.

The telephone code is ☎ 0509.

Things to See & Do

About 3km south of Banagher and 10km north-west of Birr in Lusmagh near the confluence of the rivers Little Brosna and Shannon is **Cloghan Castle**. The well-preserved keep has an adjoining 19th century house and protective walls.

Cloghan Castle has been in use for nearly 800 years, starting life as a McCoghlan stronghold, and seeing more than its fair share of bloodshed. The present owner, Brian Thompson, has brought together a very interesting and varied assortment of antiques. Pride of place in the main hall goes to the enormous antlers of an Irish elk. At the end of the 45 minute tour, the visitor can examine Cromwellian armaments in the rustic dining room and marvel at just how heavy their breastplates were.

The castle opens May to September, 2 to 6 pm Wednesday to Saturday; admission is IR£3.50/1.50. There's no bus service, but the owners will collect people from Crank House by arrangement.

Seven km north-east of Banagher is **Cloghan village**, where all six roads out of town lead into wide tracts of peat. Five km from Cloghan, on the road north-west to Shannonbridge, 16th century **Clonony Castle's** four-storey square tower is enclosed by an overgrown castellated wall. Stories that Henry VIII's second wife Anne

Antlers of the extinct giant Irish elk in the main hall of Cloghan Castle

Boleyn was born here are unlikely to be true but her cousins Elizabeth and Mary Boleyn are buried beside the ruins.

Eight km south of Banagher on the County Galway side is the delightful **Meelick Church**, one of the oldest still in use in Ireland.

You can hire canoes for trips on the River Shannon or Grand Canal from Shannon Adventure Canoeing Holidays (☎ 51411), 21 Cuba Ave.

In the evening you could do worse than head for pretty, vine-draped *JJ Hough's*, the 'singing pub' in Main St.

Places to Stay & Eat

The only hostel in the region is the excellent IHH *Crank House Hostel* (☎ 51458), Main St, which charges IR£7 a night in two and four-bed rooms and opens all year. Crank House also contains the tourist information desk, an exhibition room for local artists and the office of Crann (☎ 51718), set up to restore some of the deciduous trees that once covered much of Ireland. At the back is *Alma's Traditional Irish Coffee Shop*, open until 6 pm daily.

The cheapest B&B is *Ashling* (☎ 51228), Cuba Ave, which has rooms with bath for IR£15/27 a single/double.

Getting There & Away

Kearns Coaches (☎ 22244) includes Banagher on its daily Portumna to Dublin service. Bus Éireann has one Saturday service to Banagher, leaving Dublin's Busáras at 9.30 am.

SHANNONBRIDGE

At otherwise unremarkable Shannonbridge a narrow bridge crosses the river into County Roscommon. Look for a 19th century **fort** on the west bank just up from the bridge where heavy artillery was placed to bombard Napoleon lest he was cheeky enough to try to invade via the river. Part of the road north towards Clonmacnoise runs along the top of the esker on which Clonmacnoise is also built.

Just south of Shannonbridge, a 45 minute **train tour** on the Clonmacnoise & West Offaly Railway/Blackwater Railway (☎ 0905-74114) takes you through the Blackwater section of the Bog of Allen on the narrow-gauge line which used to transport the peat. During the 9km trip, you'll be told about the bog landscape and its special flora. The journey begins near the Bord na Móna Blackwater peat-fired power station which is visible for km around. Trips leave on the hour from 10 am to 5 pm daily, April to October, and cost IR£3.50/2.30. Tickets are available from the coffee shop.

CLONMACNOISE

Ireland's most important monastic site is superbly placed, overlooking the River Shannon from a ridge. It consists of a walled field containing numerous early churches, high crosses, round towers and graves in remarkably good condition. The site is surrounded by low marshy ground and fields known as the Shannon Callows. These are home to many wild plants and are one of the last refuges of the seriously endangered corncrake.

History

Roughly translated, Clonmacnoise (Cluain Mhic Nóis) means 'Meadow of the Sons of Nós'. The glacial ridge called the Esker Riada on which it stands was once one of the principal cross-country routes between Leinster and Connaught. St Ciarán, the son of a chariot maker, is said to have founded the monastery in 545 AD and died only seven months later after building the first church with the assistance of Diarmuid, the high king of Tara.

The monastery's beginning was humble as only eight followers of Ciarán had set out with him, but it soon became an unrivalled bastion of Irish religion, literature and art. Between the 7th and 12th centuries monks from all over Europe came to study and pray here. Clonmacnoise was one of the reasons Ireland became known as the 'island of saints and scholars' while much of Europe languished in the Dark Ages. Such was its importance that the high kings of Connaught

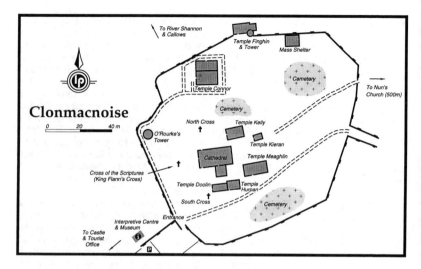

Clonmacnoise

To River Shannon & Callows

Temple Finghin & Tower

Mass Shelter

Temple Connor

Cemetery

To Nun's Church (500m)

Cemetery

North Cross

Temple Kelly

O'Rourke's Tower

Temple Kieran

Cathedral

Temple Meaghlin

Cross of the Scriptures (King Flann's Cross)

Temple Doolin

Temple Hurpan

South Cross

Cemetery

Entrance

Interpretive Centre & Museum

To Castle & Tourist Office

0   20   40 m

and Tara were brought here for burial; many lie in the cathedral, or the Church of Kings, among them the last high king of Tara, Rory O'Connor, who died in 1198.

Most of the remains date from the 10th to 12th centuries; earlier buildings of wood, clay and wattle have long since disappeared. The monks would have lived in small huts scattered in and around the monastery, which would probably have been surrounded by a ditch or rampart of earth. It was recorded that there were 106 houses and 13 churches here in 1179 when the site was ravaged by fire. These scattered Irish sites contrast with the strict layout and planning of monasteries elsewhere in Europe.

The river became a deadly conduit when Viking raiders used it to penetrate into the heart of Ireland. Clonmacnoise was pillaged repeatedly between 830 and 1165 (records suggest on at least eight occasions). Nor were the Vikings the only ones guilty of attacks; the monastery was burned at least 12 times between 720 and 1205 and attacked 27 times by native Irish forces between 830 and 1165. After the 12th century, it fell into decline and by the 15th century it was home to a bishop of only minor importance. The

end came in 1552 when it was plundered by the English regiment based in Athlone: 'Not a bell, large or small, or an image, or an altar, or a book, or a gem, or even glass in a window, was left which was not carried away'.

Among the treasures which survived the continued onslaught are the crozier of the abbots of Clonmacnoise in the National Museum and the *Leabhar na hUidhre* ('The Book of the Dun Cow'), now in the Royal Irish Academy in Dublin.

Information

Dúchas provides a museum, an on-site interpretive centre and coffee shop. The tourist office (☎ 0905-74134) in the car park opens April to September.

Clonmacnoise opens June to mid-September, 9 am to 7 pm daily; mid-September to October and mid-March to May, 10 am to 6 pm; and November to mid-March, 10 am to 5 pm. Visiting early or late will help you avoid the crowds. Admission is IR£2.50/1. The 20 minute audiovisual show provides a good introduction to the site.

There are river cruises to Clonmacnoise

from Athlone in County Westmeath; see the Central North chapter for details.

High Crosses

In the compound are seven church buildings and three replicas of 9th century high crosses (the originals are now in the museum for protection). The sandstone **Cross of the Scriptures** is the most richly decorated and has unique upward-tilted arms. Its west face depicts the Crucifixion, soldiers guarding Jesus' tomb and the arrest of Jesus. On the east face are scenes of St Ciarán and King Diarmuid placing the corner stone of the cathedral. It's also known as King Flann's Cross because a rough inscription on the

Cross of the Scriptures, Clonmacnoise

base is said to attribute it to him. He died in 916 AD.

Nearer the river the **North Cross** dates from around 800 AD. Only the shaft remains, with lions, rich spirals and a single figure, thought to be the Celtic god Cerrunnos or Carnunas, who sits in a Buddha-like position. The two-headed snake is associated with him. The richly decorated **South Cross** has more carvings, including the Crucifixion on the west face.

Cathedral

The biggest building at Clonmacnoise, the cathedral, or MacDermot's Church, was built in the 12th century but incorporates part of a 10th century church. Its most interesting feature is the intricate 15th century Gothic doorway with carvings of St Francis, St Patrick and St Dominic and a badly worn Latin inscription which, roughly translated, says: 'This doorway was erected for the eternal glory of God'.

The door is also known as the Whispering Door because a whisper carries from one side of it to the other. It's said that lepers would come here to confess because the door's acoustics would let the priest hear their confession from a safe distance.

The last high kings of Tara – Turlough Mór O'Connor (died 1156) and his son Ruairí or Rory (died 1198) – are said to be buried near the altar.

Temples

The small churches are called temples, a derivation of the Irish word *teampall*, meaning 'church'. Past the scant foundations of **Temple Kelly** (1167) is the tiny **Temple Kieran**, less than 4m long and 2.5m wide. Also known as St Ciarán's Church, it's believed to be the burial place of St Ciarán, the site's founder; his hand was kept here as a relic until the 16th century, but is now lost. The remarkable Crozier of the Abbots and a chalice are supposed to have been discovered here in the 19th century.

The floor level in Temple Kieran is lower than outside because local farmers have for centuries been taking clay from the church to place in the four corners of their fields, where it's said to protect crops against an eelworm parasite and cattle against red-water disease. The floor was covered in slabs to stop further digging but even today hand-fuls of clay are removed from outside the church in the early spring.

Near the temple's south-west corner is a *bullaun*, or ancient grinding stone, suppos-edly used for making medicines for the monastery's hospital. Today the rainwater which collects in it is said to cure warts.

Continuing round the compound you come to the 12th century **Temple Meaghlin**, with its attractive windows, and the twin structures of **Temple Hurpan** and **Temple Doolin**. Doolin is named after Edmund Dowling, who repaired it in 1689 and made it the family crypt. At the same time he may have restored Temple Hurpan, which is also known as Claffey's Church.

Round Towers
Overlooking the River Shannon is the trun-cated O'Rourke's Tower, a 20m tower named after the high king of Connaught, Fergal O'Rourke (died 964 AD). The top of the tower is said to have been blown apart by lightning in 1135, but the tower was used up to 1552.

Temple Finghin and its round tower are on the northern boundary of the site, also overlooking the Shannon. The quaint build-ing, also known as MacCarthy's Church & Tower, appears in most photographs of Clonmacnoise and dates from around 1160 to 1170. It has some fine Romanesque carv-ings and the unusual miniature tower's cone roof has stones set in a herringbone pattern. This is the only Irish round tower roof that has never been altered. Most such towers were used by monks for protection when their monasteries were attacked, but this one was probably used as a bell tower as the doorway is at ground level.

Other Remains
Still used by Church of Ireland parishioners on the last Sunday of the summer months, **Temple Connor** is a little, roofed church.

Beyond the boundary wall, 500m east through the modern graveyard, is the secluded **Nun's Church** with wonderful Romanesque arches; it's well worth seeking out. West of the church is a cairn said to mark the burial place of a servant of St Ciarán who was supposedly refused burial in the monas-tery graveyard after losing the saint's dun cow.

On the ridge near the car park is a motte with the oddly-shaped ruins of a 13th century **castle**. John de Grey, Bishop of Norwich, is said to have had it built to watch over the Shannon.

Museum
The three beehive-like structures near the entrance are a museum echoing the design of the early monastic dwellings. It contains the originals of the three principal high crosses and various artefacts uncovered during exca-vation, including silver pins, beaded glass and an Ogham stone.

The museum also contains many of Clonmacnoise's 8th to 12th century grave-slabs, the largest collection of early Christian graveslabs in Europe. Many are in remark-able condition with inscriptions clearly visible, often starting with *oroit do* or *ar* meaning 'a prayer for'.

Places to Stay
If you want to stay the night close to the ruins try *Kajon House* (☎ 0905-74191) with singles/doubles from IR£20/30. It's on the road signposted to Tullamore.

Getting There & Away
Clonmacnoise is 7km north of Shannon-bridge and about 24km south of Athlone. Paddy Kavanagh (☎ 0902-74839) runs a minibus to Clonmacnoise from Athlone, departing the castle at 11 am and returning at 4 pm. A ticket costs IR£6. To visit the Clonmacnoise and West Offaly Railway as well costs IR£15 all in.

TULLAMORE
Tullamore (Tulach Mór), Offaly's county town 80km due east of Dublin on the Grand

Canal, is pleasant enough to while away a few hours, with Charleville Castle the main attraction. The market square and some of the old houses are attractive.

Founded in 1750 by the Bury family of Limerick, Tullamore soon superseded Philipstown (now Daingean) as the county capital. In 1785 a hot-air balloon crashed and started a fire that consumed hundreds of homes!

Information

The tourist office (☎ 0506-52617), open Monday to Friday from June to September, is on Bury Quay between the defunct Irish Mist factory and the canal. In the same building is the Offaly Historical Archaeological Society (open from 9.30 am to 4 pm Monday to Friday), which may be able to help when the tourist office is closed. The post office faces O'Connor Square which is little more than a parking lot.

The telephone code is ☎ 0506.

Charleville Forest Castle

The great Gothic structure of Charleville Forest Castle (☎ 21279) sits in a large estate to the west of the town centre. What some call a 'Gothic fantasy castle' with its spires and turrets was the family seat of the Burys, who in 1798 commissioned the design from Francis Johnston, one of Ireland's most famous architects.

From the entrance on Charleville Rd, south of town on the road to Limerick, there's a rough 1.5km lane (take the right fork after you enter the gate) to the castle itself which is popular with joggers. (Tullamore Harriers is one of Ireland's premier running clubs.) The present owners, the Hutton-Burys, intend to restore the property and turn it into a classy hotel.

Thirty-minute tours must be booked in advance and costs IR£3.50/2. If you haven't booked, your best hope of tagging onto a tour is 11 am to 5 pm, Wednesday to Sunday, from June to September or weekends only in April and May. The castle grounds are also worth exploring.

Tullamore Heritage Centre

Since Irish Mist relocated to Clonmel, Tullamore has lost its other main focus. However, at the time of writing the go-ahead had been given for a new Tullamore Heritage Centre attached to the tourist office on Bury Quay. It will concentrate on the history of the Irish Mist and Tullamore Dew whiskies, on the Grand Canal and on Tullamore local history and is expected to open in 1998.

Cruises

Celtic Canal Cruisers (☎ 21861) has boats available by the week from IR£302 for two people in the low season up to IR£1190 for nine people in July. You can cruise west to the River Shannon, joining it at Shannon Harbour, or east to Edenderry, Laytown and down into the Grand Canal and River Barrow systems.

Places to Stay & Eat

Of the two hotels on the main street, *High House* (☎ 51358) is preferable to the *Phoenix Arms Hotel* ☎ 21066),with beds in comfortable rooms for IR£25. Neither is ideal because of the noise of traffic roaring through.

The most popular place to eat seems to be the *Bridge House Inn* on Bridge St which has a familiar mix of grills and steaks. Of the fast food places, the best is the spanking new *Abrakebabra* in Church St.

Getting There & Away

The Bus Éireann (☎ 21431) stop is at the railway station, south of town on Western Relief Rd off Charleville Rd. From Tullamore there is one bus daily each way on the Dublin (1¾ hours) to Portumna (one hour) route, and one daily on the Waterford (3½ hours) to Longford (1½ hours) route. Kearn's Coaches (☎ 20776) has three buses from Tullamore on Monday, Friday and Sunday, two on Saturday and one Tuesday to Wednesday on its Dublin to Portumna route.

There are at least seven trains daily to Dublin (one hour) and Galway (2½ hours) on weekdays, and five at weekends.

CENTRAL SOUTH

DURROW ABBEY

St Colmcille (also known as St Columba) founded a monastery at Durrow Abbey in the 6th century, and the monastery's scriptorium later produced the *Book of Durrow*, a Latin gospel. The book was kept here for over 800 years until the dissolution of the monasteries, when it fell into the hands of a local farmer. The book's bright illustrations survived being immersed in his cattle's drinking water to ward off evil spirits. In 1661 the local bishop gave it to Trinity College, Dublin, where it can be seen today.

The *Book of Durrow* fared better than the rest of the monastery. It was damaged in 1186 by Hugh de Lacy, who literally lost his head in the process when a local man took exception to his using the monastery stones to build a castle on the mound nearby.

Today, the site's only prominent structures are a Georgian mansion and a derelict 19th century Protestant church. Some high kings of Tara are said to have been buried here including Donal (who died in 758) and a grandson of Brian Ború, Murcadh, who died in 1068. The remains include St Colmcille's Well to the north-east of the church and a 10th century high cross. The east face of the cross shows King David, Abraham's sacrifice of Isaac and the Last Judgement, while the west face shows soldiers guarding Jesus' tomb and the Crucifixion.

Durrow Abbey is 7km north of Tullamore down a long lane west off the N52 Kilbeggan road.

EDENDERRY

On the River Boyne bordering County Kildare and the Bog of Allen, Edenderry is 16km north-east of Daingean. Although it sprang to life with the arrival of the Grand Canal in 1802, its origins go back to the 14th century and the de Berminghams, whose ruined **Carrickoris Castle** is 7km north of town on Carrick Hill. Three km north-west on the Rhode road is the scanty monastic site of **Monasteroris**. It was built for the Franciscans by John de Bermingham in 1325 to ease his conscience over his father's massacre of 32 local chieftains 20 years before in Carrickoris Castle. The name Edenderry came from the oak woods that once blanketed the hills around the town. The local O'Connor family used to harry the English and retreat into the bogs that cover the region. There's a pleasant walk from the imposing Georgian town hall along the canal towpath out to the Downshire Bridge.

The post office is in the oddly named JKL St. The telephone code is ☎ 0405.

Places to Stay & Eat

Bellavista (☎ 31179), on St Mary's Rd, has B&B with four rooms (shared bathroom) for IR£14 per person. There isn't much choice for dining but the *Eden Restaurant* and *The Coffee Shop* in O'Connell Square serve plain, dependable food; the latter does breakfast for IR£2.95.

Getting There & Away

Bus Éireann (☎ 01-836 6111) has up to six buses a day to Dublin (three on Sunday). A single daily bus goes to and from Tullamore, Banagher and Birr.

County Clare

County Clare is almost a peninsula, with the Shannon Estuary cutting deep into its southern border and Galway Bay on its northern side. Wedged between Kerry and Galway, Clare's land is mostly poor, with a large sweep of limestone rock in the north of the county forming the unique and interesting Burren region.

Clare (An Clár) doesn't get the attention of either Kerry or Galway, although it has special charms of its own. There's some spectacular scenery, particularly around the Cliffs of Moher, and the attraction of the Burren grows with every visit. This limestone landscape has countless monuments, castles and rare flowers, and there are some wonderful walks.

Many of Clare's towns and villages have resisted both the commercialisation and prettification that you see in many more heavily touristed places in Ireland. Ennis, Clare's county town, retains its charming narrow streets, while villages like Ennistymon have many of their old shops and pubs that host traditional music sessions on summer evenings.

The county has some 250 castles in various stages of preservation; Knappogue near Quin and the famous tower house at Bunratty are fine examples. As for activities, there's scuba diving at Kilkee, Doolin and Fanore, excellent rock climbing at Ballyreen near Fanore, and caving is possible all over the Burren.

A couple of villages have become havens for particular types of visitors. Doolin attracts music lovers and backpackers, while genteel Ballyvaughan has become a weekend seaside retreat for a more well heeled bunch.

The shortest route to Clare if you're travelling up the coast is via the car ferry between Killimer and Tarbert in County Kerry (see the Killimer section for details). Shannon airport in Clare is Ireland's second-largest; for more information see that section.

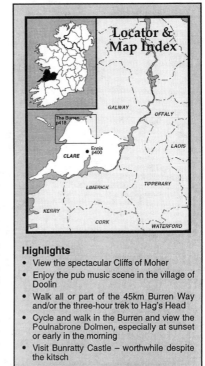

Highlights

- View the spectacular Cliffs of Moher
- Enjoy the pub music scene in the village of Doolin
- Walk all or part of the 45km Burren Way and/or the three-hour trek to Hag's Head
- Cycle and walk in the Burren and view the Poulnabrone Dolmen, especially at sunset or early in the morning
- Visit Bunratty Castle – worthwhile despite the kitsch

Ennis

Ennis (Inis), Clare's principal town, is a busy market centre with a population of just over 16,000, putting it among Ireland's dozen largest towns. It lies on the banks of the River Fergus, which runs east and then south into the Shannon Estuary. The town's medieval origins can be seen in the narrow streets, and there are many old shops and pubs. The

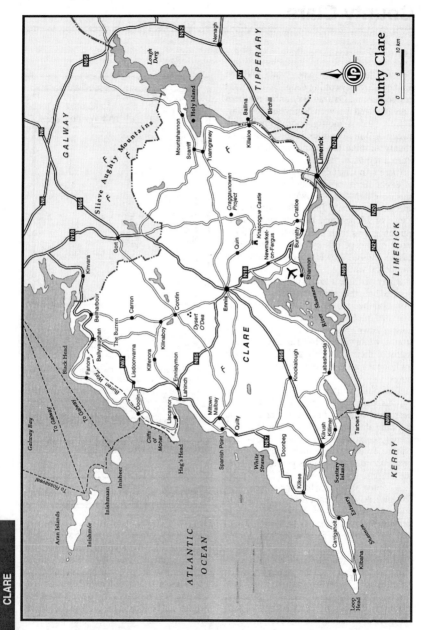

County Clare

friary, founded in the 13th century, is Ennis' most important historical site.

History

The O'Briens, kings of Thomond, built a castle here in the 13th century and were also the force behind the impressive Ennis Friary. Much of the wooden town was destroyed by fire in 1249 and again in 1306 when it was razed by one of the O'Briens.

In the centre of town is a memorial to Daniel O'Connell, whose election to the British Parliament by a huge majority in 1828 forced Britain to lift its bar on Catholic MPs and led to the Act of Catholic Emancipation a year later.

Orientation

The old town centre is on O'Connell Square, and the principal streets – O'Connell St, High St (becoming Parnell St), Bank Place and Abbey St – fan out from here. The large but not particularly attractive cathedral (1843) is at the southern end of O'Connell St.

Information

The excellent tourist office (☎ 065-28366) is a 20-minute walk outside Ennis, on the N18 road to Limerick and Shannon. There's no bus. As you leave town it's on the left side of the road just before the West County Inn. Money can be changed here. Mid-March to the end of September it's open Monday to Saturday, 9 am to 6 pm (plus Sunday from mid-May). The rest of the year the hours are 9.30 am to 5.15 pm, Monday to Saturday and closed 1 to 2 pm. The location suits those with vehicles. Ask for the pamphlet *Ennis: A Walking Trail*.

In town, local tourist information is available from Upstairs Downstairs (☎ 065-41670), a craft shop with a good selection of books and maps at O'Connell Square. They are open Monday to Saturday, 9 am to 9 pm and Sunday 10 am to 6 pm. A walking tour of Ennis leaves from here daily at 11 am and 2.30 pm.

Apart from the banks, including the Bank of Ireland on O'Connell Square and a Trustee Savings Bank on Abbey St, you can also change money at McMahon's newsagents on O'Connell Square. The post office is on Bank Place, north-west of O'Connell Square. Ennis Bookshop on Abbey St is good for maps and books of local interest. The Snow White Laundrette on Abbey St opens Monday to Saturday, 8.30 am to 6.30 pm.

The telephone code is ☎ 065.

Ennis Friary

Ennis Friary was founded by Donnchadh Cairbreach O'Brien, king of Thomond, sometime between 1240 and 1249, though a lot of the present structure was completed in the 14th century. Partly restored, it has a graceful five-section window dating from the late 13th century and a McMahon tomb (1460) with alabaster panels depicting scenes from the Passion, including the Entombment of Christ. At the height of its fame in the 15th century, the friary was one of Ireland's great centres of learning, with

The O'Briens

The eccentric O'Briens, the kings of Thomond, were one of Clare's most important ruling families. The ruined square castle on the point outside Liscannor was built by the O'Connors, taken later by the O'Briens. At the time of the Spanish Armada it was occupied by Turlough O'Brien, who was loyal to the English crown and co-executioner of the Spanish survivors washed up at Spanish Point.

Cornelius O'Brien, a rather idiosyncratic 19th century descendant and MP for Clare, lived in the now ruined manor house north of Liscannor. To the west is a monument to Cornelius, erected in 1853 by his tenants with some persuasion from the man himself. He also erected the viewing tower at the Cliffs of Moher. ■

CLARE

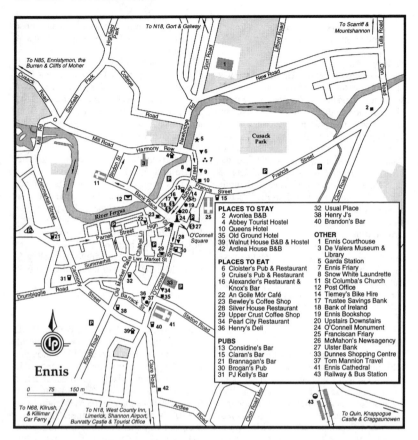

PLACES TO STAY
2 Avonlea B&B
4 Abbey Tourist Hostel
10 Queens Hotel
35 Old Ground Hotel
39 Walnut House B&B & Hostel
42 Ardlea House B&B

PLACES TO EAT
6 Cloister's Pub & Restaurant
9 Cruise's Pub & Restaurant
16 Alexander's Restaurant & Knox's Bar
22 An Goile Mór Café
23 Bewley's Coffee Shop
28 Silver House Restaurant
29 Upper Crust Coffee Shop
34 Pearl City Restaurant
36 Henry's Deli

PUBS
13 Considine's Bar
15 Ciaran's Bar
21 Brannagan's Bar
30 Brogan's Pub
31 PJ Kelly's Bar

32 Usual Place
38 Henry J's
40 Brandon's Bar

OTHER
1 Ennis Courthouse
3 De Valera Museum & Library
5 Garda Station
7 Ennis Friary
8 Snow White Laundrette
11 St Columba's Church
12 Post Office
14 Tierney's Bike Hire
17 Trustee Savings Bank
18 Bank of Ireland
19 Ennis Bookshop
20 Upstairs Downstairs
24 O'Connell Monument
25 Franciscan Friary
26 McMahon's Newsagency
27 Ulster Bank
33 Dunnes Shopping Centre
37 Tom Mannion Travel
41 Ennis Cathedral
43 Railway & Bus Station

Ennis

over 300 monks in residence. They were expelled in 1692. Being an OPW site Ennis Friary (☎ 29100) offers the usual informative guided tours in season. It's open late May to late September daily 9.30 to 6.30 pm. The entrance fee is IR£1/40p.

De Valera Museum
The late President Eamon de Valera was MP for Clare from 1917 to 1959. There's a bronze statue of him near the courthouse and a small museum devoted to his life and work on Harmony Row. The museum also houses esoteric material like the shovel used by

Parnell to turn the first sod of the West Clare Railway in 1885 and a ship's door from the Spanish Armada. The museum (☎ 21616) is in a disused church next to the town library; entry is through the latter. It opens all year 11 am to 5.30 pm on Monday and Thursday, and 11 am to 8 pm on Tuesday, Wednesday and Friday. There's no admission charge.

Places to Stay
Hostels The rule-ridden IHH *Abbey Tourist Hostel* (☎ 22620), in an old hotel on Harmony Row just up from O'Connell Square, has 80 beds (IR£5.90 to IR£6.50)

CLARE

and opens all year. The five private rooms, none with ensuite bathrooms, are priced at IR£7.50 per person, but you may have to pay the double rate if alone. There are plans to open a second hostel on Carmody St; ask the tourist office for details.

The *Walnut House* (☎ 28956), primarily a B&B with doubles for IR£24, has a few dormitory beds in season for IR£8. It's on the corner of O'Connell and Carmody Sts, past the cathedral.

B&Bs Ennis is not short of guesthouses. Near the Quinnsworth shopping centre on Clon Rd is *Avonlea* (☎ 21632). Good rooms, all with bathrooms, are IR£21/32. *Ardlea House* (☎ 20256) on Clare Rd has rooms from IR£16 per person.

Clare Manor House (☎ 20701) is about 2km along the Limerick road. The six rooms, all with bathrooms, are IR£21/33 for singles/doubles. *Laurel Lodge* (☎ 21560) is on the right-hand side along Clare Rd and has doubles for IR£34.

Two km north of Ennis on Tulla Rd, the continuation of Clon Rd, is *Newpark House* (☎ 21233), a 300-year-old country manor with excellent breakfasts and rooms from IR£30/50. To get there go along the Scarriff road and turn right at the Roslevan Arms Travel Lodge.

Hotels The lovely *Old Ground Hotel* (☎ 28127) is on Station Rd near the centre of town, and its 58 rooms are IR£58/83 or IR£78/104, depending on the season. On Abbey St the comfortable 30-room *Queens Hotel* (☎ 28963) is a notch below the Old Ground with rooms from IR£43/76.

Two other good hotels are out of town. *West County Inn* (☎ 28421), just south of Ennis on the road to Limerick (N18), has 98 rooms priced from IR£44/58 or IR£50/72, and the equally large *Auburn Lodge* (☎ 21247), just north of Ennis on the N18, has B&B from IR£40/70.

If you fancy staying at a luxurious manor house in the country, *Carnelly House* (☎ 28442) is 4km north of Ennis in Clarecas-

tle. B&B is a mere IR£96/156 a night, and dinner is IR£28 (or more) per person.

Places to Eat
Cafés & Takeaways *Henry's* on Old Barrack St is an excellent new café/delicatessen; make sure to try the local cheeses in stock. *An Goile Mór* ('the big appetite), at 17 Salthouse Lane running off Parnell St, is another excellent place for lunch or a snack and opens Monday to Friday till 8 pm.

Bewley's has a branch on Bank Place near High St, and the coffee and light meals are of the usual standard. Another good lunch place is the *Upper Crust Coffee Shop* in Lower Market St. Both are closed in the evenings.

Pubs & Restaurants Have a look at *Cruise's Pub & Restaurant* (☎ 41800) near the friary on Abbey St, full of old world charm and an excellent place for a drink and a meal. Bar food is served until late at night, and the restaurant opens for lunch and dinner. Starters are IR£2.50 to IR£5, main course from IR£10 to IR£12.

Brogan's, a pub at 24 O'Connell St, has good bar food; a three-course lunch will cost you IR£5. Nearby, *Brandon's Bar* has similar fare in the IR£5 to IR£10 range. The *Old Ground Hotel* is a huge old place with lunches at tables in the bar. Rock-solid Irish fare – cabbage and piles of spuds etc – costs around IR£5 in a comfortable setting. Farther up O'Connell St, *Pearl City* is a Chinese restaurant with dishes around IR£6 and a three-course dinner for IR£10.95. A distant second choice for rice and noodles is *Silver House*, a few doors to the north on the same street.

Alexander's, upstairs in Knox's Bar on Abbey St, is one of the most popular new eateries in town but the best is *Cloister's Pub & Restaurant* (☎ 29521), farther north on Abbey St near the friary. It's also the most expensive, charging from about IR£25 (including service) per person for dinner. They also do excellent meals in the bar from noon to 10 pm, with main courses costing from IR£6. If you don't mind travelling,

Garvello's (☎ 40011), a short distance past the tourist office on the N18 to Limerick, has superb seafood and Mediterranean specialities.

Entertainment

As the capital of a renowned music county, Ennis is not short of good music pubs. *Cíaran's Bar* is a small but very cosy place near the Queens Hotel at 1 Francis St. It's popular with the local football crowd and has Irish music Thursday to Sunday evenings. *Cruise's* has traditional music nightly. *Brogan's* pub is a big, popular place with frequent live music sessions, especially on Tuesday. *Brannagan's* on Cornmarket St at the western end of Parnell St is a blues and rock place with a trendy following. The *Usual Place* pub in the market is an attractive, old-style local in an ancient stone building. *Henry J's*, a huge modern place nearby with pool tables, couldn't be more different.

Brandon's Bar has live music some nights as does *PJ Kelly's Bar*, 5 Carmody St. *Considine's* on Parnell St has occasional Irish sessions.

One km north of town along the N18 is a low wooden music hall, the *Cois na hAbhna* (☎ 20996), where a *céilí*, a session of traditional music and dancing, is held Wednesday night year round 8.30 to 11 pm (IR£1.50). There's a *oíche céilí* ('music night') most Saturdays, 9.30 to 11.30 pm (IR£4). Cois na hAbhna has a good selection of tapes, books and records for sale.

Things to Buy

On Saturdays, there is a market at the Old Market Place. For general shopping, use the huge Dunnes supermarket, which can be entered half way down O'Connell St. The success of the supermarket might account for all the derelict shops along Parnell St.

Getting There & Away

The Bus Éireann depot (☎ 24177) is at the railway station. Buses run from Ennis to Limerick (40 minutes) about a dozen times daily Monday to Saturday (six on Sunday).

There's a frequent direct service to and from Dublin (four hours) on weekdays (seven on Sunday), five buses seven days a week to and from Galway (two hours) and Cork (three hours), and up to 12 a day (seven on Sunday) to Shannon airport (30 minutes).

Trains leave Ennis railway station (☎ 40444) twice a day Monday to Saturday for Dublin (three hours) via Limerick (one on Sunday). About a dozen trains a day (eight on Sunday) link Dublin and Limerick, 37km south-east of Ennis. Check with Limerick railway station (☎ 061-315555) for times.

Getting Around

You can order a taxi on ☎ 23456 or ☎ 24759.

Tierney Cycles & Fishing (☎ 29433), 17 Abbey St, has well maintained mountain bikes renting for IR£7/30 a day/week plus deposit. Tom Mannion Travel (☎ 24211), 71 O'Connell St, can fix you up with anything from a car to a motor home. King Car Rentals at Concorde Travel (☎ 29989) on Bank Place is another place to try.

Around Ennis

To the north of Ennis is the early Christian site of Dysert O'Dea. To the south-east are castles, theme parks and other attractions. East of Ennis, the countryside rolls gently to the River Shannon and Lough Derg, while to the west the farms get smaller and the land poorer as you approach the Atlantic. Shannon international airport is 23km to the south-east.

GETTING AROUND

There are local and express buses covering most areas around Ennis, but the frequency of service varies widely. Many buses run only in summer and on certain days; it's best to confirm times and destinations with the Ennis bus station (☎ 065-24177) before making plans.

The express service running between Limerick and Galway can be picked up in Ennis between four and six times a day to get to Clarecastle, Newmarket-on-Fergus and Bunratty, but most are 'request only' stops. A bus service also operates to Limerick via Clarecastle, Newmarket-on-Fergus and sometimes Bunratty.

An infrequent weekday service goes north-west to Ennistymon and then south along the coast to Kilkee.

DYSERT O'DEA

Nine km north of Ennis on the road to Corofin (R476) is Dysert O'Dea, where St Tola founded a monastery in the 8th century. The church and high cross – known as the White Cross of St Tola – date from the 12th or 13th centuries. The cross depicts Daniel in the Lions' Den on one side and a crucified Christ above a bishop carved in relief. Look for the carvings of animal and human heads in a semi-circle on the south doorway of the Romanesque church. There are also the remains of a 12m-high round tower.

In 1318, the O'Briens and the Norman de Clares of Bunratty fought a pitched battle nearby, which the O'Briens won, thus postponing the Anglo-Norman conquest of Clare for some two centuries. The 15th century O'Dea Castle nearby houses the Clare Archeology Centre (☎ 065-37722) and opens May to September daily 10 am to 6 pm; admission is about IR£1.80/80p. A 3km history trail around the castle passes some two dozen ancient monuments – from ring forts and high crosses to an ancient cooking site.

Just south of Dysert O'Dea off the N18 is **Dromore Wood** (☎ 065-37166), an OPW nature reserve encompassing some 400 hectares as well as the ruins of the 17th century O'Brien Castle, two ring forts and the site of Kilakee church. The wood opens mid-June to mid-September daily 10 am to 6 pm.

Getting There & Away

In July and August, there is a daily bus Monday to Friday coming from Limerick, which leaves Ennis for Corofin and Ennistymon at 2.15 pm, passing by Dysert O'Dea en route. During the rest of the year, a bus heads out of Ennis on the same route

on weekdays only at 3 pm and on Saturday at 3.50 pm.

QUIN

Quin, a tiny village 11km south-east of Ennis, was the site of the Great Clare Find of 1854, the most important discovery of prehistoric goldwork in Ireland. Sadly, few of the several hundred torcs, gorgets and other pieces, discovered by labourers working on the Limerick-Ennis railway, made it to the National Museum in Dublin; most were sold and melted down. The source of this and much of ancient Ireland's gold may have been the Wicklow Mountains.

Quin Abbey

This Franciscan friary was founded in 1433 using part of the walls of an older de Clare castle built in 1280. An elegant belfry rises above the main body of the abbey, and you can climb the narrow spiral staircase and look down on the fine cloister and surrounding countryside.

Despite many periods of persecution, Franciscan monks lived here until the 19th century. The last friar, Father Hogan, who died in 1820, is buried in one corner. Another occupant is the impressively named Fireballs McNamara, a notorious duellist and member of the region's ruling family. Beside the friary is the 13th century Gothic Church of St Finghin. The abbey (☎ 065-544084 for information) opens daily June to September.

KNAPPOGUE CASTLE

Knappogue Castle, 3km south-east of Quin, was built in 1467 by the McNamaras. They held sway over a large part of Clare from the 5th to mid-15th centuries and built 42 castles in the region. Knappogue's huge walls are intact, and it has a fine collection of period furniture and fireplaces.

When Oliver Cromwell came to Ireland from England in 1649, he used Knappogue as a base while in the area, which is one of the reasons it was spared from destruction. The McNamara family regained the castle after the Restoration in 1660.

Knappogue Castle (☎ 061-368102) opens

April to October, daily 9.30 am to 5 pm, with last entry at 4.30 pm. Admission is IR£2.55/1.55/1.35 for adults/students/children. It has a small souvenir shop in the courtyard. Knappogue also hosts medieval banquets (☎ 061-360788) daily at 5.30 and 8.45 pm May to October, and the cost is IR£31. See the Bunratty section for more details. Knappogue, unlike Bunratty, lays on knives and forks.

CRAGGAUNOWEN PROJECT

Six km east of Quin, the Craggaunowen Project includes recreated ancient dwelling places such as a crannóg and a ring fort; real artefacts like a 2000-year-old oak road, and related items such as Tim Severin's leather boat the *Brendan*, in which he crossed the Atlantic in 1976-77.

Craggaunowen Castle is a small and well preserved McNamara fortified house. The Craggaunowen Project (☎ 061-367178) opens mid-March to October, daily 10 am to 6 pm, with the last admission at 5 pm. Entry is IR£3.50/3/2.60. It has a nice little *restaurant* for light snacks or lunch. Cullaun Lake nearby is a popular boating and picnic spot with forest trails.

DROMOLAND CASTLE

North of Newmarket-on-Fergus is Dromoland Castle (☎ 061-368144), a magnificent building constructed in 1826 and today one of Ireland's finest hotels. It sits in 220 hectares of vast and beautiful gardens by the River Fergus and has an 18-hole golf course. Inside, oak panels and silken fabrics adorn virtually every bit of wall space. B&B at IR£255 to IR£430 (April to September) in one of the hotel's 75 rooms is beyond most travellers' budgets, but venture in for a drink at the bar.

Mooghaun Ring Fort

In Dromoland demesne are the remains of one of Europe's largest Iron Age hill forts: three circular earthen banks enclosing some 13 hectares. The fort's occupants may have been the owners of the huge gold hoard uncovered nearby in Quin in 1854. Access to

the fort is through Dromoland Forest, which is signposted off the Newmarket to Dromoland road (N18).

East & South-East Clare

Clare's eastern boundary is formed by the River Shannon and long, narrow Lough Derg, which stretches some 48km from Portumna in County Galway, to just south of Killaloe. Farther south the road between the two towns swings past the lake through some gentle countryside and picturesque hamlets like Mountshannon. From high ground, there are panoramic views across the lake to the Silvermine Mountains in Tipperary.

East Clare is fishing and shooting country, and the villages on the eastern shores of Lough Derg are favoured by hunting types.

South-east Clare is visually unremarkable compared with the county's Atlantic coastline or the lakeside scenery north of Killaloe. Most people pass through quickly, taking in diversions like Bunratty Castle, Quin Abbey or Cratloe's ancient oak woods. Some 24km west of Limerick is Shannon airport, until recently the arrival and departure point for all transatlantic flights to Ireland.

SHANNON AIRPORT

Shannon, Ireland's second-largest airport, sits in the apparent wilderness of south-east Clare. Like Gander airport in Newfoundland, Shannon airport used to be a vital fuelling stop on the transatlantic air route, as piston-engined planes barely had enough range to make it across the ocean. If you come through Shannon, the extensive runways and numerous departure gates will remind you of its successful past. It's said that Irish coffee (a healthy slug of whiskey in a strong coffee topped with cream) was invented at Shannon airport for early transatlantic passengers.

Information

There's a tourist office (☎ 061-471664) in the arrivals hall, open 6 am (6.30 am in

CLARE

winter) until 6 pm daily. For flight information, phone ☎ 061-471444. The Bank of Ireland counter opens from the first flight (about 6.30 am) until 5.30 pm. In Shannon Town Centre – an American-style glass-enclosed shopping mall – in the town of Shannon, there are three banks (Bank of Ireland, Ulster Bank, AIB) and a post office.

The telephone code is ☎ 061.

Duty-Free

The world's first duty-free when it opened in 1947, Shannon has an enormous stock of Irish and international goods. It's worth a browse and is a good place to rid yourself of any leftover punts. However, prices for international goods – jewellery, perfumes etc – are the same as in any duty-free shop, while Irish tweeds, pottery and crystal cost about the same (if not less) in any high street shop.

Places to Stay

Hostels The closest hostels are in Ennis and Limerick; see those sections for details.

B&Bs There are plenty of B&Bs 5km from the airport in Shannon, Ireland's only 'new town', and 11km away in Bunratty. Only 400m from Shannon Town Centre is *Moloney's B&B* (☎ 364185) down a quiet cul-de-sac at 21 Coill Mhara St, with singles/doubles from IR£19/28. Less than 3km from the airport, on a hill overlooking the estuary is the stylish, modern *Lohan's B&B* (☎ 364268) at 35 Tullyglass Crescent charging IR£17 per person.

Hotels On the road into Shannon town is the 75-room *Oak Wood Arms Hotel* (☎ 361500), with B&B from IR£55/80. The comfortable *Great Southern Hotel* (☎ 471122), directly in front of the airport terminal, costs IR£90 to IR£96 for one of its 115 rooms.

Places to Eat

The airport has the self-service *Courtyard* and the upmarket *Lindbergh Room*, but it's worth going to Shannon Town Centre, where *Mr Pickwick's* is a cheap and cheerful place offering a full Irish breakfast for IR£2.99, a

set lunch for IR£4 and dinner for IR£12. Also in the mall, the *Rineanna Bar* in the Shannon Knights Inn does reasonable bar food.

Getting There & Away

Air For general enquiries, call the airport authority, Aer Rianta (☎ 471444). Aer Lingus (☎ 471666), Delta (☎ 471200), Aeroflot (☎ 472299), AB Shannon (☎ 363636) and the French-carrier Corsair (01-679 1233 in Dublin) fly to and from Shannon.

Bus There are up to 12 Bus Éireann buses a day to Ennis (seven on Sunday). The ticket office (☎ 474311) in the airport opens at 7 am, the first bus leaves at 8 am and the fare is IR£5. There are also services to Limerick (15 daily, 12 on Sunday, 40 minutes), Galway (up to four daily, one on Sunday, two hours) and Dublin (up to five daily, one on Sunday, $3\frac{1}{3}$ hours).

Taxi A taxi to Limerick or Ennis costs about IR£15, with possible extra charges for luggage or 'unsocial hours'.

BUNRATTY

The castle at Bunratty (Bun Raite), which overlooks the Shannon Estuary, is in excellent condition and well worth a look, but it's a prime tourist attraction and is besieged by coach tours in summer. With an attached Folk Park and Durty Nelly's 'auld Oirish' pub nearby, the area is as close as you'll get to a medieval Irish Disneyland. Go early in the day.

Bunratty Castle

The Vikings built a fortified settlement at this spot, a former island surrounded by a moat. Then came the Normans; Thomas de Clare built the first stone structure on the site in the 1270s. The present castle is the fourth or fifth incarnation to occupy the location beside the River Ratty.

The castle was built in the early 1400s by the energetic McNamara family, but it fell shortly thereafter to the O'Briens, kings of Thomond, in whose possession it remained until the 17th century. Admiral Penn, father

CLARE

of William Penn, the Quaker founder of the US state of Pennsylvania and the city of Philadelphia, resided here for a short time.

A complete restoration was carried out in modern times, and today the castle's magnificent Great Hall holds a very fine collection of 14th to 18th century furniture, paintings and wall hangings. Combined admission to the castle (☎ 061-361511) and Folk Park is IR£4.85/3.50/2.40 for adults/students/children. It opens daily June to August 9.30 am to 7 pm and 9.30 am to 5.30 pm the rest of the year.

Medieval Banquets The Great Hall hosts 'medieval banquets' (☎ 061-360788), replete with comely maidens playing the harp, court jesters cracking corny jokes, food à la Middle Ages (a pale imitation) served by wenches and washed down with mead, a kind of honey wine. You eat with your fingers. A seat at the banquet table will set you back IR£31, and they're heavily booked with coach parties. The whole thing is stage Irish but taken in spirit can be quite fun.

The banquets at Knappogue and Dunguaire castles are generally smaller, quieter and often more pleasant. All run two banquets daily at 5.30 pm and 8.45 pm. Bunratty's opens year round, Knappogue's May to October and Dunguaire's May to September.

Bunratty Folk Park

Bunratty Folk Park is a reconstructed traditional Irish village, with cottages, a forge and working blacksmith, weavers weaving and buttermakers making butter. There's a complete village street with post office, pub and small café, some of them transplanted from the site of Shannon airport. Agricultural machinery buffs will find a good collection here in Bunratty House overlooking the Folk Park. Admission to just the Folk Park (not including Bunratty Castle) is IR£3.50/1.90 for adults/children.

Every evening between May and October a **Shannon Céilí** is held in the Folk Park, serving up music, dancing, Irish stew, apple pie and soda bread. It's meant to demonstrate how the peasants passed their time while the gentry gorged themselves in the safety of their castles. The cost is IR£26 per person, and there are céilithe daily at 5.30 pm and 8.45 pm. For bookings ring ☎ 061-360788.

Places to Eat

If you're hungry and looking for quantity at reasonable prices, the *Bunratty Castle Hotel* (☎ 061-362116) does a huge lunch for around IR£10 that will keep you going for the day. *Durty Nelly's* (☎ 061-364861), the 'olde world' pub beside the castle, has fairly good bar food and also houses two restaurants: the *Oyster* downstairs, open 10.30 am to 10.30 pm, and the *Loft* upstairs, open 6 to 10.30 pm. Both are fine, with main courses from IR£12 to IR£15.

In the Folk Park, *Mac's Bar* does light meals as does the tearoom at *Bunratty Cottage* opposite the castle. The *Avoca Cottage Café* beside Durty Nelly's is good for lunch. Meals in all three are around IR£5. *Truffles Restaurant* (☎ 061-361177) in the Fitzpatrick Bunratty Shamrock Hotel is a good hotel restaurant, with dinner costing around IR£20. It opens daily to 10 pm.

MacCloskey's (☎ 061-364082) in the cellars of Bunratty House Mews, a fine Georgian-style house next to the Fitzpatrick Bunratty Shamrock Hotel, is the best and most expensive restaurant in the area. Dinner costs IR£26 (or more), but the food, with mostly Irish ingredients, is top-class.

Entertainment

Durty Nelly's was built in the early 1600s, and the atmosphere is laid on by the shovel load. A peat fire burns in front of rough wooden chairs and benches. But it can be good fun, and the pub does attract a local crowd as well as tourists. There's music most evenings.

Mac's Bar in the Folk Park has Irish music on Wednesday, Friday, Saturday and Sunday evenings June to September (Saturday and Sunday only the rest of the year). It's accessible even after the Folk Park is closed.

Things to Buy

Avoca Handweavers at O'Connor's Duty-Free Shop next to Durty Nelly's has a good selection of tweeds, crafts and woollen suits. Bunratty Mills at Bunratty Cottage opposite the castle stocks every conceivable Irish jumper (sweater). Mike McGlynn Antiques, opposite the Fitzpatrick Bunratty Shamrock Hotel, is worth a look. Along the Limerick to Shannon road is Ballycasey Craft Workshops, home to weavers, silversmiths, leatherworkers and potters.

Getting There & Away

The bus stop for Bunratty is outside the Fitzpatrick Bunratty Shamrock Hotel. Some three to four buses a day on the Limerick to Galway route stop at Bunratty; the first leaves Limerick bus station (☎ 061-313333) at 8.45 am.

Buses travelling south through Bunratty leave Ennis daily from around 10 am onwards. Bunratty is also served by up to a dozen (three on Sunday) daily buses on the Shannon airport to Limerick route.

Getting Around

Bikes can be hired at the Shannon Cycle Centre (☎ 061-364696), 12 Firgrove, Hurlers Cross, almost 4km north of Bunratty on the main road to Ennis.

CRATLOE

Three km east of Bunratty, just north of the main road to Limerick (N18), is Cratloe, a picturesque village overlooking the Shannon Estuary. Nearby are hills covered in oak trees – a rare sight in Ireland today, although such forests once blanketed the island. The oak roof beams of Westminster Hall in London are said to be from Cratloe. To reach the woods, go along the Kilmurry road from Cratloe, under a railway bridge and turn right. There are some fine walks in the area and views over the estuary from Woodcock Hill.

A rare 17th century longhouse called **Cratloe Woods House** (☎ 061-327028) on the N18 opens to the public June to mid-September, Monday to Saturday, 2 to 6 pm and

costs IR£2.50/1.50, including an excellent guided tour.

Places to Stay

Cratloe has a fair selection of guesthouses. *Cratloe Heights* (☎ 061-357253), Ballymorris, charges from IR£19/28. The *Grange* (☎ 061-357389), similarly priced, is on Wood Rd 2km off the main Limerick road; turn north at the Limerick Inn Hotel.

Getting There & Away

While there is no bus service directly to Cratloe, there are plenty of buses passing through Bunratty nearby. Visitors can hire a bike in Bunratty (see the Getting Around section for Bunratty earlier) or walk out to Cratloe.

KILLALOE & AROUND

Killaloe (Cill Dalua) is one of the principal crossings on the River Shannon, and a fine old 13-arched bridge spans the river. Across the river and in County Tipperary, Ballina is Killaloe's other half and some of the better pubs and restaurants are found there. From Killaloe, the Shannon is navigable all the way up to Lough Key in County Sligo, and in summer the town is jammed with weekend sailors.

The town itself has a fine setting, with the Slieve Bearnagh hills rising abruptly to the west, the Arra Mountains to the east and Lough Derg right at the doorstep.

Orientation & Information

The narrow street running from the river on the Killaloe side is Bridge St, which turns right becoming Main St. The tourist office (☎ 061-376866) in the Killaloe Heritage Centre building is right beside Shannon Bridge.

Things to See

Also known as St Flannan's Cathedral, **Killaloe Cathedral** dates from the early 13th century and was built by the O'Brien family on top of an earlier 6th century church. Take a look at the carvings inside around the Romanesque south doorway, which dates

CLARE

from an older chapel; the carvings are among the finest in the country.

Next to the doorway is the early Christian **Thorgrim's Stone**, unusual in that it bears both the old Scandinavian runic and Irish Ogham scripts. It's the shaft of a stone cross and could have been carved by a converted Viking doing penance for his past sins. The runic script reads: 'Thórgrímr carved this cross'. The translation of the Ogham is: 'A blessing on Thórgrímr'. In the cathedral grounds is St Flannan's Oratory, of 12th century Romanesque design.

The modern **Church of St Flannan** up the hill to the west of the river is without interest except for 9th century **St Lua's Oratory** in the churchyard. It was moved here from Friars Island in the Shannon when the island was flooded by a hydroelectric scheme.

Killaloe Heritage Centre in the same building as the tourist office has exhibits dealing with local history and the cathedral. It opens June to mid-September and costs IR£1.50/1.

Mountshannon

North of Killaloe, on the south-western shores of Lough Derg, is the attractive 18th century village of Mountshannon (Baile Uí Bheoláin). Its stone houses overlook the lake, while anglers pass the evenings in pubs, discussing the day's catch. With luck, you'll find Irish music in summer.

The small stone harbour is usually busy with fishing boats and is the main port for trips to Holy Island, one of Clare's finest early Christian settlements.

There's a small seasonal tourist office (☎ 061-927300) next to the post office in Hickey's shop on the main street.

Holy Island

This is the site of a monastic settlement thought to have been founded by St Cáimín in the 7th century. On Holy Island (Inis Cealtra) you'll see a round tower which is over 27m tall (though missing its top storey). You'll also find four old chapels, a hermit's cell and some early Christian gravestones dating from the 7th to the 13th centuries. One

of the chapels has an elegant Romanesque arch; inside the chapel there's an inscription in old Irish, which translates as 'Pray for Tornog, who made this cross'.

The Vikings gave this monastery a rough ride in the 9th century, but under the subsequent protection of Brian Ború and others it flourished. The Holy Well was once the focus for a lively festival, which was banned in the 1830s because a lot of, well, nonreligious behaviour was creeping in.

From Mountshannon, the *Derg Princess* run by R&B Marine (☎ 061-375011) has trips to Holy Island daily May to September at 3 pm for about IR£4/2. Trips can also be arranged June to September through the East Clare Heritage Centre (☎ 061-921351) in Tuamgraney, about 10km to the south-west on the R352.

Other Attractions

The journey north on either side of Lough Derg to Mountshannon or Portroe is very scenic. About 1.5km north of Killaloe, **Beal Ború** is an earthen mound or fort said to have been Kincora, the palace of the famous Irish king, Brian Ború, who defeated the Vikings at the Battle of Clontarf in 1014. Traces of Bronze Age settlement have been found. With its commanding view over Lough Derg, this was obviously a site of strategic importance.

Three km north again is Cragliath Hill which has another fort, **Griananlaghna**, named after Brian Ború's great-grandfather, King Lachtna.

Activities

The Shannonside Activity Centre (☎ 061-376622) is an approved sailing centre, offering sailing, windsurfing, canoeing, pony trekking, hill walking and biking. It's 3km south-west of Mountshannon on the Scarriff road (R352). Also nearby is the Mountshannon Pony Centre (☎ 061-921428), with ponies for hire and riding lessons.

Hickey's (☎ 061-927255), which also functions as the Mountshannon post office, has fishing tackle and equipment as well as boats for hire. In Ballina over the bridge from Killaloe, TJ's Angling Centre (☎ 061-376009) has the same.

Places to Stay & Eat

Killaloe & Ballina The *Lough Derg Holiday Park* (☎ 061-376329) is a campsite 5km north of Killaloe along Scariff road (R463) on the lake shore charging IR£7.50 for a tent and IR£2.50/1 per adult/child. Hikers and cyclists pay IR£3.50. *Kincora Hall* (☎ 061-376000) is a lovely 25-room hotel some 10km from Killaloe on the Scariff road. It opens May to September and costs IR£50/68 or IR£60/78 for singles/doubles.

In Ballina, *Gooser's Pub & Restaurant* has some of the best food in town. The restaurant at the back is fine but expensive at about IR£20 for dinner. *Simply Delicious*, a coffee shop just down from Gooser's, has snacks and lunches for under IR£5. The *Anchor Inn* pub on the Killaloe side does decent bar food.

Lantern House in Ogonnelloe, 10km out along the Scariff road, does simple but wholesome food, including a substantial and reasonable high tea from 6 to 7 pm.

Mountshannon *Lakeside Caravan & Camping Park* (☎ 061-927225), open May to September, charges IR£5 or IR£6 for a tent plus IR£1/50p per adult/child; hostel accommodation may be available on the grounds in mobile homes or chalets. There are boats and equipment for hire for windsurfing, rowing and sailing. To get there, go along the Portumna road (R352) from Mountshannon and take the first turn right.

Derg Lodge (☎ 061-927180) in the village offers B&B from IR£19.50/29 and opens all year. *Oak House* (☎ 061-927185), a country house overlooking the lake 6km from the village, costs from IR£14 per person. In the village, the delightful 14-room *Mountshannon Hotel* (☎ 061-927162) charges IR£32 per person. Dinner is IR£15. *An Cupán Caife* ('the coffee cup'), on the main street, is good for snacks and light meals and opens Easter to November, daily 10 am to 9 pm.

Entertainment

Good pubs in Killaloe/Ballina are *Molly's*, *Gooser's* and *Crotty's Courtyard*; most have traditional music at weekends. In Mountshannon, try *Cois na hAbhna* on the main street.

Getting There & Away

There are regular weekday buses from Killaloe to Limerick bus station (☎ 061-313333) and to Scarriff.

On Saturday only there is a single bus from Limerick to Whitegate via Scarriff and Mountshannon at 1.15 pm. The journey time to Mountshannon is one hour and 25 minutes. A bus leaves Mountshannon for Limerick each Saturday at 8.50 am. The bus stop in Killaloe is outside the cathedral; in Mountshannon it's outside Keane's on the main street.

NORTH TO GALWAY

North of Mountshannon, the road swerves away from the lake and the views are nondescript. Inland is an area known as the Clare Lakelands, based around Feakle. There are numerous lakes with good coarse fishing.

South-West & West Clare

Loop Head at the county's south-western tip is a big wedge splitting the mighty waves of the Atlantic. North of Kilkee, a popular seaside resort, the road (N67) moves inland, but there are some worthwhile detours along the lonely coast and beaches where Spanish Armada ships were wrecked over 400 years ago. The coast between Kilkee and Loop Head has some outstanding cliff scenery. White Strand, Kilkee, Spanish Point and Lahinch all have good beaches.

To the north and north-west of Ennis are a number of small villages, including Corofin and Ennistymon. These are both at the very southern limits of the outstanding Burren region, which includes Hag's Head (a superb walk with excellent views) and the Cliffs of Moher, one of Ireland's most spectacular natural features. From there the road dips downhill towards Doolin, a well known rest stop for backpackers and a centre of Irish music.

GETTING THERE & AWAY

This region has infrequent local bus service to the coastal towns and villages; some buses run from Limerick while others are from Galway, and services are more frequent in summer. Phone Ennis bus station (☎ 065-24177) for exact times and fares.

One express service has its terminus in Ennis or Ennistymon and runs through Lahinch, Miltown Malbay, Lisdoonvarna, Doolin, Kilrush and Kilkee. Another bus goes to Galway, Kilcolgan, Kinvara, Ballyvaughan, Lisdoonvarna, Doolin, the Cliffs of Moher, Lahinch, Miltown Malbay, Doonbeg, Kilkee and Kilrush. There's also a service to Limerick, Ennis, Ennistymon, Lahinch, Quilty, Doonbeg, Kilkee and Kilrush.

In summer, a bus runs three times daily (once on Sunday) between Limerick and Lisdoonvarna, passing through Ennis, Ennistymon, Lahinch, Liscannor, the Cliffs of Moher and Doolin en route. The rest of the year it goes once a day only.

KILLIMER

Killimer is a nondescript village, close to the Shannon Estuary and Moneypoint, Ireland's largest power station. At 915 megawatts, Moneypoint is capable of supplying 40% of the country's needs and burns two million tonnes of coal a year.

The Colleen Bawn ('white girl') was a woman called Eileen Hanly who was murdered in 1819 and thrown into the River Shannon by her husband, John Scanlon. Her body washed ashore and was buried in Killimer graveyard. Scanlon was hanged. The story has inspired novels, plays, songs and operas; unfortunately, her tombstone has been carried away by souvenir hunters.

Getting There & Away

A 20-minute car ferry (☎ 065-53124) runs from Killimer to Tarbert in County Kerry every hour on the hour across the Shannon Estuary year round (every half-hour in peak season). April to September, the schedule is from 7 am (9 am on Sunday) to 9 pm; during the rest of the year sailings are 7 am (10 am on Sunday) to 7 pm. The one-way/return fares are IR£2/3 for bikes and foot passengers, IR£7/10 for cars (IR£8/12 between June and September).

KILRUSH

This small town overlooks the Shannon Estuary and the hills of Kerry to the south, but it's not a particularly attractive place. Kilrush (Cill Rois) has the west coast's newest and biggest marina, the 120-berth Kilrush Creek. If you happen to be interested in stained glass, the Catholic church has some nice examples by well known craftsman Harry Clarke. East of town is Kilrush Wood, which has some fine old trees and a picnic area. The nearby harbour at Cappa is where you catch the boat to Scattery Island in the estuary.

Kilrush has banks, a post office on Frances St, and a tourist office (☎ 065-51577) in the town hall on Market Square open in July and August only. The Kilrush Heritage Centre (☎ 0615-51596) in the same building has an exhibition entitled 'Kilrush in Landlord Times' and opens June to August, Monday to Saturday, 10 am to 1 pm and 2 to 4 pm. Admission costs IR£2/1.

Among the places to stay is the IHH *Katie O'Connors Holiday Hostel* (☎ 065-51133) at 49-50 Frances St just off the square and open all year. Dorm beds are IR£6 or IR£7; the two doubles cost IR£15 to IR£18. *Kilrush Creek Lodge* (☎ 065-52595) at the marina is a new place charging IR£11 to IR£13 per person in shared accommodation or IR£9 for a dormitory bed. The *Central Restaurant* and the large *self-service café*, both on Market Square, are inexpensive places for a meal.

Bikes can be hired at Gleeson Wholesale

(☎ 065-51127) on Henry St for IR£7/35 per day/week plus deposit.

SCATTERY ISLAND

This island is 2.5km south-west of Cappa pier and is the site of a Christian settlement founded by St Senan in the 6th century. The windswept and treeless island has one of the tallest and best preserved round towers in Ireland. It's 36m high, and the entrance is at ground level instead of the usual position high above the foundation. There are the remains of five medieval churches, including a 9th century cathedral.

In order to build his monastery, St Senan had to rid the island of a monster. The Irish name for the island is Inis Cathaigh, Cathach being the sea serpent who had made his lair on the island. With the help of the archangel Raphael, Senan banished the monster and also excluded all women. A local, apparently very friendly, virgin named Cannera wanted to join Senan, provoking much speculation about how he withstood the temptation.

Legend hints that had the maid,
Until morning's light delayed,
And given the saint one rosy smile,
She'd ne'er have left his lonely isle.

Scattery was a beautiful but unfortunate site for a monastery, as it was all too easy for the Vikings to sail up the estuary and pillage the place, which they did repeatedly in the 9th and 10th centuries. They occupied the island for 100 years until 970 when they were dislodged by Brian Ború.

An exhibition on the history and wildlife of Scattery Island is housed in the OPW **Scattery Island Centre** (☎ 065-52144) on Merchant's Quay in Kilrush. It's open mid-June to mid-September daily 9.30 am to 6.30 pm (no admission charge).

During the summer, Scattery Island Ferries (☎ 065-51237) runs boats from Cappa pier to the island for about IR£3 return. There's no strict timetable as the trips are subject to demand. You can buy tickets at the small kiosk on Merchant's Quay.

KILKEE

During the summer, Kilkee's wide bay is thronged with day trippers and holiday-makers from all over Clare and Limerick. Kilkee first became popular in Victorian times when rich Limerick families built seaside retreats here. Today, Kilkee (Cill Chaoi) is a little too fat with guesthouses, amusement arcades and takeaways.

Visitors come for the fine sheltered beach and the Pollock Holes, natural swimming pools in the Duggerna Rocks to the south of the beach. St George's Head to the north has good cliff walks and scenery, while south of the bay the Duggerna Rocks form an unusual natural amphitheatre. Farther south is a huge sea cave. These sights can be reached by driving to Kilkee's West End section and following the coastal path.

Information

The seasonal tourist office (☎ 065-56112) is on O'Connell St just up from the seafront. It's open June to early September, 10 am to 6 pm, closed 1 to 2 pm and on Sunday. There are Bank of Ireland and Allied Irish Bank branches on O'Curry St.

The telephone code is ☎ 065.

Activities

Kilkee is a well known diving centre. There are shore dives from the Duggerna Rocks fringing the west side of the bay, or boat dives on the Black Rocks farther out. Right at the tip of the Duggerna Rocks is the small inlet of Myles Creek, and there is excellent underwater scenery out from it. Kilkee Diving & Watersports Centre (☎ 56707) by the harbour has tanks and other equipment for hire and gives five-day PADI courses for IR£350.

Places to Stay

Camping There are plenty of campsites. *Cunningham's Holiday Park* (☎ 56430) opens late April to late September and charges IR£8 to IR£11 for a tent plus IR£1/50p per adult/child. From the N67 on the Kilrush side of town, turn left, go through the roundabout and take the first left. *Green*

CLARE

Acres Caravan & Camping Park (☎ 57011), with a flat IR£7 charge (or IR£3 for cyclists/hikers), is 6km south of Kilkee on the R487.

Hostel The IHH *Kilkee Hostel* (☎ 56209) is clean, well run and open February to November. It's 50m from the seafront on O'Curry St, and costs IR£6 a night in a dorm (no private rooms). It rents bicycles and has a well equipped kitchen, a laundry room and a small coffee shop.

B&Bs There are countless guesthouses in Kilkee, usually a little more expensive than in other areas. There are some good ones at West End, including *Dunearn* (☎ 56545), charging IR£21/32, and *Harbour Lodge* (☎ 56090), with rooms from IR£19/28. At busy times, you may have to take whatever the tourist office can get you.

Hotels There are plenty of hotels in Kilkee, but for the extra money you don't get much extra luxury. *Halpin's Hotel* (☎ 56032), 2 Erin St, is a pleasant family-run hotel. B&B is from IR£45/70.

Places to Eat
There are plenty of fast-food joints. For good home cooking at reasonable prices try the *Pantry* (☎ 065-56576), half way up O'Curry St from the seafront on the left, or *Ryan's Restaurant & Bistro* next to Myles Creek pub. *Michael Martin's* pub on Erin St next to Halpin's Hotel has bar food. The *Strand* pub on the seafront is also worth trying. Meals at all these places are from around IR£5.

Almost 2km north of Kilkee is the popular *Manuel's Seafood Restaurant* (☎ 065-56211), open for dinner only, which costs IR£20 or more.

Entertainment
Opposite the hostel on O'Curry St is the *Myles Creek* pub, Kilkee's trendiest spot. The pub is on the band circuit and attracts many of Ireland's best young rock groups. *O'Mara's* on the same street and the popular *Strand* on the seafront have sessions during the week.

Getting Around
Bicycles can be hired at Williams (☎ 065-56041), on Circular Rd near the Catholic church, for IR£7.50/30 a day/week.

SOUTH OF KILKEE TO LOOP HEAD
The land from Kilkee south to Loop Head is poor and flat, but the cliff scenery is spectacular: the coast is peppered with sea stacks, arches and wave-sculpted rocks. It's a glorious day's bike ride down to the head and back. Better still, if you have the energy, is the 24km cliff walk between Loop Head and Kilkee. The cliffs compare with the more famous Cliffs of Moher to the north and are much less visited.

Intrinsic Bay
Just south of Kilkee is Intrinsic Bay, named after the ship that was wrecked here in 1856 en route to America. The summit shadowing the bay is Lookout Hill. To the north are Diamond Rock and **Bishop's Island**, the latter a remarkable pillar of rock with a medieval oratory perched on the summit. The oratory is attributed to the 6th century St Senan who also built the settlement on Scattery Island in the Shannon Estuary. Later, a selfish bishop is supposed to have lived here while his people starved in a famine; when the gap to the mainland widened in a storm, the bishop himself starved to death.

Kilbaha
At the end of the R487, 7km east of Loop Head, Kilbaha's tiny church contains an unusual relic of more repressive times. The 'little ark' is a small wooden altar used by Catholics in the 1850s. In order for the priest to celebrate Mass, the altar was wheeled below the high-tide mark where it was outside the jurisdiction of the local Protestant landlord. A stained-glass window above the church door depicts the ark in use. Father Michael Meehan, the courageous local priest who had the ark built, is buried in the church.

There's a 'submerged forest', a collection

of 5000-year-old tree stumps (probably pine) on the shore east of Rinvella Bay, near Kilbaha. They were originally preserved in peat bog, which was washed away as the sea level rose, leaving the stumps visible.

Carrigaholt

On 15 September 1588, seven tattered ships of the Spanish Armada took shelter off Carrigaholt, a tiny village inside the mouth of the Shannon Estuary. One, probably the *Annunciada*, was torched and abandoned, sinking somewhere out in the estuary. Today, Carrigaholt has a safe beach and the substantial remains of a 15th century McMahon castle with a square keep overlooking the water. Dolphinwatch (☎ 065-58156 or 088-584711), with an office opposite the post office on the harbour, runs two-hour trips (IR£8/4 for adults/children) in the estuary to view some of the 70 resident dolphins, one of only four resident groups of the aquatic mammals left in Europe.

The *Long Dock* (☎ 065-58106) on West St, open Easter to September, is a cosy pub-cum-restaurant, with bar food, seafood dinners and Irish music three times a week. The *Village Pub* nearby has traditional music and set dancing at the weekend. You might also try *Fennell's*, a dumpy little pub with music on some nights.

Loop Head

On a clear day, Loop Head, Clare's southernmost point, has magnificent views south to the Dingle Peninsula crowned by Mt Brandon (953m), and north to the Aran Islands and Galway Bay. There are bracing walks in the area and a long hike running along the cliffs to Kilkee.

NORTH OF KILKEE

North of Kilkee, the 'real' west of Ireland begins to reassert itself. The N67 runs inland for some 32km until it reaches Quilty. Take the occasional lane to the west and search out unfrequented places like Ballard Bay and White Strand, north of Doonbeg. Ballard Bay is 8km north of Doonbeg, where an old telegraph tower looks over some fine cliffs.

Donegal Point has the remains of a promontory fort.

There's good fishing for bass, pollock and mackerel all along the coast, and safe beaches at Seafield, Lough Donnell and Quilty.

Doonbeg

Doonbeg is a tiny fishing village half way between Kilkee and Miltown Malbay. Near the mouth of the River Doonbeg, another Armada ship, the *San Esteban*, was wrecked on 20 September 1588. The survivors were later executed at Spanish Point.

White Strand (signposted 'An Trá Ban') is a quiet beach, 2km long and backed by dunes. For campers the side roads around Doonbeg are good places to pitch a tent and watch the sun go down. There are two ruined castles nearby, Doonbeg and Doonmore.

Places to Stay & Eat The Igoe Inn in Doonbeg has the *Olde Kitchen Restaurant* (☎ 065-55039), which does steak and seafood (dinner only) from IR£12. *An Tinteán* ('the hearth'; ☎ 065-55036) is a seafood restaurant and guesthouse, with turf fires and good rooms with bathrooms. B&B costs from IR£15 per person. The *San Esteban* (☎ 065-55105) is 1km from Doonbeg in Rhynagonaught. B&B costs from IR£19/28.

Entertainment *Morrissey's* pub on Main St in Doonbeg often has music as does the shocking-pink *Tubridy's* pub on Thursday.

Quilty

The small village of Quilty lies on a particularly bleak stretch of coast. Quilty is a centre for seaweed production; kelp and other plants are collected, dried on the stone walls and sent for processing. The resulting alginates are used in toothpaste, beer, agar and certain cosmetics. Quilty has a good beach, and boats are available for deep-sea angling.

One of the most powerful ships of the Spanish Armada, the *San Marcos* was wrecked just off nearby Mutton Island in

CLARE

September 1588. It had taken a terrible battering, and only four of the 1000 sailors on board survived.

Local guesthouses include *Clonmore Lodge* (☎ 065-87020), some 3km from the village. B&B costs from IR£22/34 and it opens April to October.

Miltown Malbay

Like Kilkee, Miltown Malbay was a resort favoured by well-to-do Victorians, though the town isn't actually on the sea: the beach is 3km away at Spanish Point. Every year Miltown Malbay hosts a Willie Clancy Irish Music Festival as a tribute to one of Ireland's greatest pipers. The festival usually runs during the first week in July, when the town is overrun with wandering minstrels, and Guinness is consumed by the bucket. You can also find music in the surrounding villages. Excellent pubs here include *Clancy's* and *Queeley's*.

Spanish Point

There's a great beach at Spanish Point, and when the waves are running there's good surfing.

The beach gets its name from the execution of 60 Armada survivors on Cnoc na Crocaire ('hill of the gallows') nearby. They had swum ashore, only to be executed by the local head honcho, Boetius Clancy, the sheriff of Clare, and Turlough O'Brien, the local chief who was loyal to the English crown.

Lahinch

Lahinch is the archetypal seaside resort, full of fast-food joints, amusement arcades and places to stay. The town sits on a protected bay with a fine beach, and the surfing can be good. In 1943, a US bomber flying off course landed on the beach, and the 12 airmen were repatriated to Allied forces through Northern Ireland. Lahinch is very busy in the summer; you may prefer to move on to Ennistymon, Liscannor or Doolin.

The seasonal tourist office (open June to August, 10 am to 6 pm) is in the Lahinch Seaworld Leisure Centre (☎ 065-81900) on the Promenade. There's an Allied Irish Bank branch on Church St, at the southern end of Main St. Surfboards can be rented on the seafront from the Surf Shop. The Willie Daly Riding Centre (☎ 065-71385) en route to Liscannor has pony trekking.

The IHH *Lahinch Hostel* (☎ 065-81040), along Church St, has beds for IR£6.50 to IR£7, six doubles for IR£16 to IR£18, and there's a laundry. An excellent restaurant is *Mr Eamon's* (☎ 065-81050) on Kettle St open for lunch and dinner (from IR£17) March to November.

The bus running between Limerick and Lisdoonvarna three times a day in summer (and once daily on Sunday and during the rest of the year) stops at Lahinch outside O'Hanlon's newsagents. Contact Ennis bus station (☎ 065-24177) for exact times and fares.

ENNISTYMON

Ennistymon, a moderately attractive little town with essentially one long main street called Church St, is 3km inland from Lahinch on the banks of the River Inagh. The town started out as a settlement around a castle built by Turlough O'Brien in 1588. The town's appearance has scarcely changed over the past few decades, and its charm derives primarily from its many well maintained shops and old pubs.

The bridge over the River Inagh is just above the 200m rapids known as the Cascades, which can be impressive if the river is high. There's trout and salmon fishing here.

Things to See

The River Inagh runs directly behind and parallel to Church St. The **Cascades** are just down the lane beside the Archway Bar to the south of the square. It's a pleasant stroll around here in the evening. When the Inagh is in flood, though, the waters can rise almost to the houses. Down river, the **Falls Hotel** is a former residence of the McNamaras and has its own water-powered generator.

Places to Stay

The independent *White House Hostel*

(☎ 065-26793), just off Church St to the east above a violin bow maker's shop, is a very basic hostel with dormitory beds for IR£5 per person. In the town centre on Church St is *San Antone* (☎ 065-71078), part of McMahon's pub, with B&B from IR£14 per person and open March to October. *Station House* (☎ 065-71149) is about half a km south of the square on the Ennis road (N85) with singles/doubles from IR£21/32.

Falls Hotel (☎ 065-71004) is a comfortable old country house in 20 hectares of wooded gardens with rooms from IR£35/50 or, May to December, IR£54/88.

Places to Eat

Franco's Fast Foods, with pizza and other takeaways on Church St, is one of the very few decent low-priced eateries in Ennistymon. *Sugan Chair* is a modest restaurant on Main St. *Cooley's House* pub on Church St has reasonable bar food and music most evenings during the summer. The *Archway Bar*, just south of the square, serves run-of-the-mill food until 9 pm. For something more substantial – and upmarket – try the *Falls Hotel*, where dinner is IR£22.

Entertainment

Daly's Matchmaker's Shack is a cosy, traditional place and gets a good crowd. It's one of the best places in town for Irish music with sessions most nights in summer (on Thursday night in winter). *Phil's Place* across from the Archway Bar has music on Saturday and Sunday nights. *Cooley's House* pub has music at weekends, and *Carrigg's* is worth a look.

Getting There & Away

The bus that travels between Limerick and Lisdoonvarna also stops at Ennistymon in front of Aherne's on Church St. Contact Ennis bus station (☎ 065-24177) for times and fares.

LISCANNOR & AROUND

This small fishing village offers a fine view over Liscannor Bay and Lahinch as the road (R478) heads for the Cliffs of Moher and

Doolin. Liscannor (Lios Ceannúir) has given its name to a characteristic paving stone with ripples on the surface. The stone is widely used locally for floors, walls and even roofs.

John Philip Holland (1840-1914), the inventor of the submarine, was born in Liscannor. He emigrated to the USA in 1873, and he hoped his invention would be used to sink British warships.

Things to See

On the way to the Cliffs of Moher and close to Murphy's and Considine's pubs is the **Holy Well of St Brigid**, marked by a tall stone column topped with an urn. People with all sorts of physical problems come to pray and drink the healing waters. There is a collection of discarded crutches and walking sticks nearby, so it obviously works!

The well's significance probably predates Christian times, as its Irish name suggests a connection with a pre-Christian god, Crom Dubh. People from all over Clare and the Aran Islands make the pilgrimage to the well in July, particularly on the last weekend of the month, and there can be up to 400 people there on the Sunday.

Clahane Beach to the west of Liscannor is good and safe. A 'lost city' and church known as Kilstephen are supposed to sit on an underwater reef in Liscannor Bay. The Celtic hero Conan is buried on **Slieve Callan** to the south. He is said to lie with the key to the lost church.

The ruined square **castle** on the point just outside Liscannor was built by the O'Connors.

Places to Stay & Eat

The IHH *Liscannor Village Hostel* (☎ 065-81385), at the eastern end of the village behind the Captain's Deck craft shop and restaurant, is a big, well run place with dormitory beds for IR£6 to IR£8 and doubles for IR£16. It opens all year.

Coming from Lahinch, just before the village on the right, is *Sea Haven* (☎ 065-81385), with B&B for IR£21/32 and good, hard beds. Three km north-west of Liscannor, you'll find the closest B&B to the

Cliffs of Moher – the friendly *Moher Lodge* (☎ 065-81269), charging from IR£16 per person and open April to October.

For cheap meals, try the pubs on the main street such as *Vaughan's Bar* or the small coffee rooms at the Cliffs of Moher. There's good fresh seafood at the *Captain's Deck* (☎ 065-81666) in front of the hostel. It's open daily 10 am to 10 pm with main courses from IR£9 to IR£15. It has a simpler set dinner from 6 to 7.30 pm for IR£12. The *Cottage Restaurant* is a small seafood restaurant tucked away in a tiny cottage near the Holy Well of St Brigid.

Entertainment

There are a string of pubs in Liscannor on the main street, most with music. *Joseph McHugh's* is the best known and is as genuine an old Irish pub as you'll find anywhere, down to the groceries and other oddments piled on the shelves. For music, try *McHugh's* on Tuesday or the equally good *Egan's* two doors down. *Vaughan's Bar* has music almost every night during the summer.

Getting There & Away

The bus running between Limerick and Lisdoonvarna (three times a day in summer, once daily on Sunday and during the rest of the year) stops at Liscannor. Contact Ennis bus station (☎ 065-24177) for exact times and fares.

HAG'S HEAD

Hag's Head forms the southern end of the touristy but magnificent Cliffs of Moher. There's a superb walk to the head (see the following), where a signal tower was erected in case Napoleon tried to attack on the west coast. The tower is built on the site of an ancient promontory fort called Mothair, which has given its name to the famous cliffs to the north.

Hag's Head Walk

Hag's Head is an excellent place to view the Cliffs of Moher, and the walk out is well worth the effort. To get there, go just over 5km out of Liscannor towards the Cliffs of

Cúchulainn's Leap
Loop is a corruption of the word 'leap', and legend has it that the Celtic warrior Cúchulainn was being chased all over Ireland by the formidable Mal. Cornered on this headland, he leapt onto a seastack and when she tried to follow him, Mal fell to her death. The sea turned crimson and her body washed ashore at various points along the coast, giving Hag's Head and Malbay their names. Some say the headland looks like a seated woman looking out over the Atlantic. West of the lighthouse, you'll find the seastack in question; the gap is known as Cúchulainn's Leap. ■

Moher until, just past the Moher Lodge, you'll spot a rough track turning to the left. You can only drive a short distance, and then you'll have to walk along the path out towards the point and tower. There's a huge sea arch at the tip and another visible to the north. The return trip takes about three hours.

CLIFFS OF MOHER

One of Ireland's most spectacular sights, the Cliffs of Moher rise from Hag's Head to the south and reach their highest point (203m) just north of O'Brien's Tower before slowly descending farther north again. On a clear day, the views are tremendous: the Aran Islands stand etched on the waters of Galway Bay and beyond lie the hills of Connemara in western Galway.

From the cliff edge, you can just hear the booming far below as the waves eat into the soft shale and sandstone. Sections of the cliff often give way, and they're generally so unstable that few birds or plants make them their home. With a due-west exposure, sunset is the best time to visit, and there is a bracing 8km walk along the cliff edge down to Hag's Head. Part of the walk was walled off with Liscannor stone by the eccentric local landlord Cornelius O'Brien (1801-57), who built the lookout tower to impress lady visitors. Entry is 75p/50p.

The sea stack – covered with seabirds and

CLARE

TOM SMALLMAN

TOM SMALLMAN

TOM SMALLMAN

County Kilkenny
Top: The Marble City Bar, Kilkenny City
Middle: Kilkenny Castle & grounds, Kilkenny City
Bottom: House in Bennettsbridge

TOM SMALLMAN

TOM SMALLMAN

TOM SMALLMAN

TOM SMALLMAN

Central South
A: Emily Square, Athy, County Kildare
B: Market House & town square, Kildare Town
C: Ballaghmore Castle, County Laois
D: Clonmacnois monastic site, County Offaly

their guano – just below the tower is called Breanan Mor and is itself over 70m high.

Information

The information office in the visitors' centre (☎ 065-81171) opens March to October; the shop, and bureau de change there are open daily all year 10 am to 6 pm (9.30 am to 6.30 pm May to September and 9 am to 8.30 pm in July and August). Be warned: the cliffs are one of the most popular attractions in Ireland, and coaches roll up ceaselessly during the day. The car park costs IR£1.

The Liscannor-based Cliffs of Moher Pony Trekking & Riding Centre (☎ 065-81283) has ponies for hire.

A Risky Route

The cliffs just north of Moher are known as Aill na Searrach ('cliff of the foals') because a group of young fairy horses are supposed to have leapt into the sea at this point. There's a precipitous and dangerous path to the base of these cliffs, suitable only for the fittest of walkers and in dry weather. The beginning of the path is about 2km north of the Cliffs of Moher car park.

Where the road comes off the mountain, there is a small bridge and a rough track leading to a galvanised gate. Cross the field to the dip on the left, where the path begins. At the bottom, massive boulders have been worn smooth and piled high by the Atlantic rollers.

You can also reach this path by following the clifftop path north from O'Brien's Tower, as if walking to Doolin. You can clearly see the path, which zigzags down to the rocky beach.

Organised Tours

O'Neachtain Tours (☎ 091-553188) and Lally Coaches (☎ 091-562905), both based in Spiddal, County Galway, have day-long coach tours of the Burren and Cliffs of Moher leaving the Galway tourist office at 9.45 am (9.55 am from the Salthill tourist office branch) and returning at 4.30 pm. The price is IR£10/8/5 for adults/students/children.

Getting There & Away

The bus between Limerick and Lisdoonvarna stops at the Cliffs of Moher as does the bus from Galway to Kilrush. Contact Ennis bus station (☎ 065-24177) for exact times and fares.

The Burren

Between Corofin and Kinvara in northern Clare and stretching to the Atlantic coast is the Burren region, an extraordinary and unique place. *Boireann* is the Irish for 'rocky country' or 'karst', and when you see the km of polished limestone stretching in every direction you'll know why one of Cromwell's generals was moved to exclaim that there was 'neither water enough to drown a man, nor a tree to hang him, nor soil enough to bury him'.

Along the coast are a few settlements, including Doolin, a very popular Irish music centre with some wonderful caves in the vicinity, and Ballyvaughan, an attractive little village on the south coast of Galway Bay. East of Ballyvaughan the Burren peters out near Kinvara. This area has a lot of historical sites, notably Corcomroe Abbey and the churches of Oughtmama. The deeply indented coastline has plenty of wildlife and some fine walks.

INFORMATION

The nearest tourist information point to the Burren is at the Cliffs of Moher (☎ 065-81171). A must if you intend spending any time here is Tim Robinson's *Burren Map & Guide* (IR£3.60). It's available in many shops and shows just about every object and place of interest in the Burren. The *Book of the Burren* (IR£11.95) published by Tír Eolas is a delightful introduction to ecosystems, history and folklore of the region.

ARCHAEOLOGY

The Burren's bare limestone hills were once lightly wooded and covered in soil. Towards the end of the Stone Age, about 6000 years

CLARE

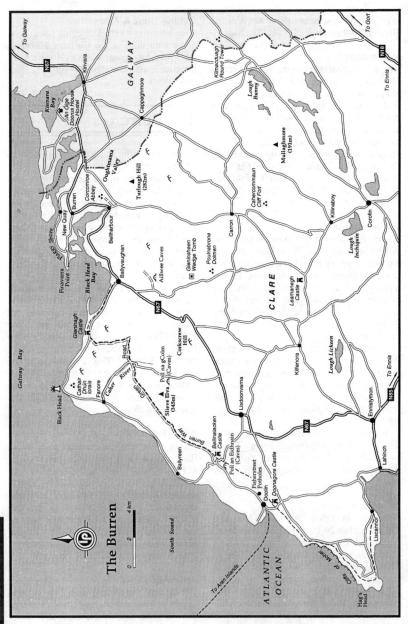

The Burren

ago, the first farmers arrived in the area. They began to clear the woodlands and use the upland regions for grazing. Over the centuries, the soil was eroded and the huge mass of limestone we see today began to emerge.

Despite its desolation, the Burren supported quite large numbers of people in ancient times and has over 2500 historic sites. Chief among them is the 5000-year-old Poulnabrone Dolmen, one of Ireland's finest ancient monuments.

There are at least 65 megalithic tombs erected by the Burren's first settlers. Many of these tombs are wedge-shaped graves, stone boxes tapering both in height and width and about the size of a large double bed. The dead were placed inside, and the whole structure was covered in earth and stones. Gleninsheen, south of Aillwee Caves, is a good example.

Ring forts dot the Burren in prodigious numbers. There are almost 500 in all, including Iron Age stone forts like Ballykinvarga and Cahercommaun near Carron.

In later times, many castles in the area were built by the region's ruling families, and these include Leamanegh Castle near Kilfenora, Ballinalacken Castle near Doolin and Gleninagh Castle on the Black Head road.

FLORA & FAUNA
Soil may be scarce here, but the small amount that gathers in the cracks is limey, well drained and rich in nutrients. This together with the soft Atlantic climate

---

Geology of the Burren
The Burren is the most extensive limestone region or karst (after the original Karst in Slovenia) in the British Isles. It is almost entirely limestone except for a cap of mud and shale that sits on the higher regions from Lisdoonvarna north to Slieve Elva.

During the Carboniferous period 350 million years ago, this whole area was the bottom of a warm and shallow sea. The remains of coral and shells fell to the seabed, and coastal rivers dumped sand and silt on top of these lime deposits. Time and pressure turned the layers to stone, with limestone below and shale and sandstone above.

Massive rumblings in the earth's crust some 270 million years ago buckled the edges of Europe and forced the seabed above sea level, at the same time bending and fracturing the stone sheets to form long, deep cracks. Wind, rain and ice have since removed most of the overlying shale, leaving these mountains of limestone.

The difference between the areas of porous limestone and nonporous shale is acute. Shale country is a depressing dull green, covered in acid bogs, marshes and reeds. On limestone the soil is sparse, water disappears and grey rock predominates.

Being slightly acidic, rainwater dissolves the limestone, widening the vertical cracks known as grikes. (The horizontal slabs are called clints.) Springs, rivers and even lakes (such as the turloughs around Corofin) appear and disappear. The water follows weak points (sinkholes) in the rock, carving out underground rivers and caverns. The calcium bicarbonate from the dripping water below creates stalactites (the ones that hang down) and stalagmites (the ones that shoot up). When these underground caverns collapse – and they do periodically – they form a depression. Rainwater is caught on top of the shale and eventually drains off at the edges into the limestone, which it erodes. A ring of caves appears along the shale/limestone boundary.

The southern boundary of the Burren is roughly where the limestone dips under the shale between Doolin and Lough Inchiquin. Underneath the limestone of the Burren is a huge mass of granite, which surfaces to the north-west in Connemara.

During numerous Ice Ages, glaciers have scoured the hills, rounding their edges and sometimes polishing the rock to a shiny finish. They also dumped a thin layer of rock and soil over the region. Huge boulders were carried by the ice, incongruous aliens on a sea of flat rock. Seen all over the Burren, these 'glacial erratics' are often a visibly different type of rock.

The only surface river in the Burren is the River Caher, which flows down the so-called Khyber Pass before meeting the sea at Fanore. The valley is lined with glacial sediments, which stop the water from leaking away. ■

support an extraordinary mix of Mediterranean, Arctic and Alpine plants.

The Burren is a stronghold of Ireland's most elusive mammal, the weasel-like pine marten. They are rarely seen, although there are certainly some living near Gleninagh Castle and up the Caher Valley. Badgers, foxes and even stoats are common throughout the region. Otters and seals live along the shores around Bellharbour, New Quay and Finavarra Point. The estuaries along this northern coast of the Burren are rich in birdlife and frequently attract brent geese during the winter. More than 28 of Ireland's 33 species of butterfly are found here, including one endemic species, the Burren green.

Unfortunately, modern farming and EU land-improvement grants have had their effect on the Burren. Weedkillers and fertilisers encourage grass and little else. Many ring forts and stone walls have been bulldozed into extinction.

WALKING
'Green roads' are the old highways of the Burren, crossing hills and valleys to some of the remotest corners of the region. Unpaved and possibly dating back thousands of years, they're now used mostly by hikers and the occasional farmer. Many are signposted.

Particularly good walks are the green road from Ballinalacken Castle to Fanore and back through a hidden valley, which forms part of the Burren Way, and the climb up Black Head to the Iron Age fort called Cathair Dhún Iorais. The 42km Burren Way (see the introductory Activities chapter) runs down through the Burren from Ballyvaughan to Doolin and then south to the Cliffs of Moher and Liscannor. The southern portions of this walk are described in more detail in the Fanore and Doolin sections.

Guided nature, history, archaeology and wilderness walks are available through Burren Hill Walks (☎ 065-77168 or ☎ 088-654810) based at Corkscrew Hill, Ballyvaughan, or Southwest Ireland Walks (☎ 061-19477) in Limerick.

CAVING
Serious caving is not for the faint-hearted. If you fancy trying it, take a course or at least find an experienced guide.

Tim Robinson's *Burren Map & Guide* has most of the cave entrances marked on it. Serious cavers should consult *The Caves of Northwest Clare* by Tratman.

ORGANISED TOURS
See Organised Tours in the Cliffs of Moher section for bus tours of the Burren.

GETTING THERE & AWAY
For precise times and other details of the buses to the Burren area, ring the bus stations in Ennis (☎ 065-24177), Limerick (☎ 061-313333), or Galway (☎ 091-562000).

Various buses pass through the Burren. A local service runs regularly between Ennis, Ennistymon, Lisdoonvarna, Doolin, Kilrush and Kilkee; another service connects Galway with Ballyvaughan, Lisdoonvarna, Lahinch, Kilkee and Tralee, three times a day (once on Sunday) Monday to Saturday from late May to late September; and a third runs from Galway to Kinvara, Ballyvaughan, Black Head, Fanore, Lisdoonvarna and Doolin. This last service has one bus a day between Monday and Saturday in winter and up to three buses a day (one on Sunday) in the summer months, late May to late September.

From Limerick, a bus to Doolin passes through Ennis, Lahinch, the Cliffs of Moher, Ennistymon and Lisdoonvarna, and this service consists of one bus a day in winter and three every day (one on Sunday) in summer.

GETTING AROUND
The best way to see the Burren is on foot (see the previous Walking section). Cycling comes next, and good mountain bikes are available from the Doolin Holiday Hostel (☎ 065-74006) or Burke's Garage (☎ 065-74022) on the square in Lisdoonvarna for IR£6 a day. You can easily ride a mountain bike along the green roads.

CLARE

DOOLIN

Doolin – or Fisherstreet on some maps – stretches for several km along the road, but despite appearances it has some of the best music pubs in the west, a couple of decent restaurants, and plenty of good cafés, hostels and guesthouses. It's also an excellent base for the Burren, which lies just to the north. There's a ferry to Inisheer, the smallest of the three Aran Islands, and the Cliffs of Moher are only a few km to the south.

Doolin's popularity among backpackers and music lovers has skyrocketed over the past few years, and at night the pubs are packed with a cosmopolitan crowd. In high season it can be difficult to get a bed, so try to book ahead. The place is particularly popular with German aficionados of traditional Irish music, who flock with all the zeal of medieval pilgrims to visit what was once the base of the Kellys, a popular German-Irish music family.

Orientation & Information

Doolin is made up of three parts. Coming from the north along the R479 you first hit the Catholic church on the left, then after less than 1km the upper village of Roadford area with a shop, restaurant and cafés, hostels, two pubs and the Doolin post office. Then there's a slightly bigger gap before reaching Fisherstreet, the lower village, which has the popular Doolin Holiday Hostel, more shops and O'Connor's pub. It's another 1.5km to the harbour and the ferry to Inisheer.

There are no banks in Doolin, but a mobile bank reaches town every Thursday, and you can change money and travellers' cheques in the Doolin Holiday Hostel as well as in O'Connor's pub just over the bridge. The post office is in Roadford.

The telephone code is ☎ 065.

Activities

A number of people operate excellent walking tours of the Burren. See the earlier Walking section. Doolin Pitch & Putt is half way between Fisherstreet and the harbour.

Places to Stay

Camping Down by the harbour two people can pitch a small tent at *Nagles Doolin Caravan & Camping Park* (☎ 74458) for IR£4 plus IR£1.50/1 per adult/child. It opens May to September. *O'Connors Riverside Camping & Caravan Park* (☎ 74314) nearby charges IR£4 to IR£6 for a tent and IR£1.50/1 per adult/child. It opens April to September.

Hostels Budget travellers are well catered for in Doolin, and all but the Aille River Hostel remain open all year. The IHH *Doolin Holiday Hostel* (☎ 74006), more commonly known as Paddy Moloney's, is in the lower village, Fisherstreet. A bed in this friendly place costs from IR£6.50 to IR£8; doubles are IR£15 to IR£18. Paddy's can get very busy so book ahead. *Fisherstreet House* (☎ same), under the same ownership and across the road, is usually reserved for groups.

In Roadford, the upper village, the *Rainbow Hostel* (☎ 74415) is near McGann's pub. It's smaller (only 16 beds) and older than the Doolin Holiday Hostel, and its front room has an open turf fire. Dormitory beds are IR£6.50 to IR£7 and two doubles IR£15 to IR£17. Also here is *Flanagan's Village Hostel* (☎ 74564) with dormitory beds (only) for the same price.

Off the road on the way down to O'Connor's pub from the upper village is the *Aille River Hostel* (☎ 74260) in a converted farmhouse with turf fires. The cost is IR£6.50 to IR£7 a night, with three doubles for IR£15 to IR£16. Aille River opens mid-March to mid-November.

B&Bs *Killilagh House* (☎ 74392) in the upper village is on the right going south past the post office. Excellent singles/doubles with bathrooms are from IR£25/32. Continuing on past McGann's pub and around the bend on the left is the equally good *Doolin House* (☎ 74259) at IR£36 for a double.

Between Roadford and Fisherstreet and fronting the little River Aille, *Cullinan's* (☎ 74183) has excellent singles/doubles

CLARE

from IR£17/30 or IR£27/36, depending on the season. Another good place nearby is *Doonmacfelim House* (☎ 74503) with singles/doubles for IR£17/30 or IR£22/38, depending on the season.

In Fisherstreet, *Moloney's Horseshoe Farmhouse* (☎ 74006) is near the Doolin Holiday Hostel, owned by the same family, and charges IR£28 to IR£32 for doubles only. The nearby *Sancta Maria* (☎ 74124) charges from IR£25 for a double. *Atlantic View* (☎ 74189), with rooms from IR£17.50/25, is closer to the harbour.

A good B&B outside Doolin is *Island View House* (☎ 74346), from IR£19/28, 3km from Doolin on the Lisdoonvarna road via Garrahy's Cross.

Hotel *Aranview House* (☎ 74061), with 19 rooms, is a comfortable, friendly country house hotel 1km north of town near the Catholic church. Singles/doubles here are IR£35/54 or, July to October, IR£45/70.

Places to Eat

Both *O'Connor's* in the lower village and *McGann's* in the upper village serve decent pub food all day; the latter has Irish stew for around IR£5 – and photographs of the singing Kellys on the walls.

The *Flagship Restaurant* at the Doolin Crafts Gallery 1km along the Lisdoonvarna road just before the church, does delicious snacks and light meals as well as dinner. *Doolin Café*, opposite the post office with vegetarian dishes, and the *Doolin Chipper* just next to MacDermott's pub. *Cullinan's* (☎ 74183) B&B also has an excellent restaurant.

If you feel like splashing out, there are several very good restaurants, including *Bruach na hAille* (☎ 74120), in the upper village next door to McGann's; the nearby *Lazy Lobster* (☎ 74390) and, in Fisherstreet, *Ilsa's Kitchen* in the Ivy Cottage just down from the Doolin Holiday Hostel. The restaurant at *Aranview House* does an excellent dinner for IR£18.

Entertainment

Doolin is renowned for Irish music, and you can hear it almost every night during the summer and occasionally during the winter. *O'Connor's* pub in Fisherstreet is the best known (note the international collection of police department badges behind the bar), but the staff at *McGann's* in Roadford can be friendlier. On a good night, the atmosphere in either pub is hard to beat. *McDermott's*, also in Roadford near the post office, is frequented by locals and is much quieter. Watch out for music sessions in nearby Lisdoonvarna or Kilfenora. Even if you're not staying at *Aranview House*, its bar provides a pleasant way to escape the tumult in the village.

Getting There & Away

Bus The Bus Éireann stop is outside Fisherstreet House opposite the Doolin Holiday Hostel. There are buses between Doolin and Ennis, Galway, Limerick and Dublin. For details, see the introductory Getting There & Away section to the Burren section.

Boat Doolin is the jumping-off point for the ferry to Inisheer, the smallest and the easternmost of the three Aran Islands. From April to September, there is also a single daily sailing to the largest island, Inishmór. Otherwise, you can make onward connections from Inisheer.

Doolin Ferries (☎ 74189 or 74455 at the pier kiosk) is the only line currently sailing and has four boats. It takes around 30 minutes to cross the 8km to Inisheer, and the return fare is IR£15. Ferries run April to September, and June to August there are around seven sailings a day beginning at 9.30 am. The last ferry returns from Inisheer at around 6 pm.

The daily ferry to Inishmór leaves Doolin Harbour April through September at 10 am and departs Inishmór for the return trip to Doolin at 4 pm. The trip takes 50 minutes, and the return fare is IR£20.

Getting Around

The Doolin Holiday and Aille River hostels have bikes for around IR£7/35 a day/week plus deposit. Burren Bike Tours (☎ 74429) opposite the post office also rents bikes, including ones for children.

AROUND DOOLIN

Caves

Doolin is very popular with spelunkers. The British seem particularly fond of this sport and use Doolin as a base, spending their days crawling blindly through dirty holes and their nights crawling blindly through Doolin's pubs. The Fisherstreet potholes are nearby, and **Poll na gColm**, 5km north-east of Lisdoonvarna, is Ireland's longest cave, with over 12km of mapped passageways.

Just a few hundred metres south of Ballinalacken Castle, you will see some low cliffs on the eastern (or inland) side across a field. These hide the entrance to **Poll an Eidhnain** (or Poll an Ionáin), a cave which, after a difficult and mucky passage, widens to a chamber containing a 6m stalactite said to be the tallest in Western Europe. The cavern is difficult to get to, and the farmer is not keen on trespassers, so ask permission first.

The rocks to the north of Doolin Harbour are honeycombed with an unusual system of undersea caves called the **Green Holes of Doolin**. They are the longest known undersea caves in temperate waters – one of them has been explored inland for a km. Non-divers can look into 'Hell', a large gash in the rocks, north of the harbour and about 50m from the sea. The gash is about 6m, and the heaving water at the bottom leads to a maze of submarine passages.

Doonagore Castle

If you follow the coastal road (R478) for about 3km south of Doolin you will come to Doonagore Castle, a restored 15th century tower with a surrounding walled enclosure (or *bawn*). There's a lovely view from here over Doolin and the Aran Islands, especially at sunset.

Ballinalacken Castle

Five km north of Doolin en route to Fanore is Ballinalacken Castle. Sitting astride a small cliff, this 15th century O'Brien tower house is in excellent repair. The stairway is intact and there are good views of the Burren from the top. Look out for an original fireplace perched half way up the interior with the date 1679 carved on it.

Just beside the gateway to the castle and the posh *Ballinalacken Castle Hotel* (☎ 065-74025; singles/doubles from IR£60/120), a minor road leads inland up into the Burren. After about a km, it meets one of the Burren's ancient green roads, and in good weather this route up to Fanore makes for a lovely walk. It also forms part of the Burren Way. See the Fanore section for a more detailed description of the return part of this route.

LISDOONVARNA

Lisdoon, as the town is generally called (its Irish name is Lios Dún Bhearna), is well known for its mineral springs, which people have been visiting for centuries to drink and to bathe in. The town also used to be the centre of matchmakers *(basadóiri)* who, for the appropriate fee, would fix you up with a mate. Most aspiring swains would hit town in September, after the hay was in.

Today, genuine matchmaking is a little thin on the ground, but the Matchmaking Festival is still a great excuse for drinking, merrymaking and music in the pubs. And with all those singles events, a few romances must blossom.

Orientation & Information

Lisdoonvarna is essentially a one-street town with a square in the middle where you turn west for Doolin and the coast. The town has plenty of shops, pubs and smart hotels with good restaurants. There's a Bank of Ireland branch behind the Ritz Restaurant on the square. The post office is on Main St to the north.

The telephone code is ☎ 065.

Spa Wells Centre

The centre (☎ 74023) is the only working

spa in Ireland. It has a sulphur spring, a Victorian pump house, massage room, sauna and mineral baths, all in a nice wooded setting. The iron, sulphur, magnesium and iodine in the water are supposed to be good for rheumatic and glandular complaints, so if you have a spot of hyperthyroidism or ankylotic spondylitis, this is the place for you. You can drink the water, but it's not a pleasant experience. The centre opens June to mid-October.

Burren Smokehouse Visitor Centre
If you've ever wanted to know more about the 'ancient Irish tradition of oak-smoking Atlantic salmon', an audiovisual display called 'The Salmon of Knowledge Experience' at the visitor centre (☎ 74432) will answer all your questions – and then some. Smoked salmon in all its guises is on sale, and there's local tourist information available. The centre, open daily year round 10 am to 7 pm, is just west of Lisdoonvarna on the Doolin road (N67).

Places to Stay & Eat
The IHH *Kincora & Burren Hostel* (☎ 74300) is just outside of town on the road to Ennistymon. Beds are IR£6.50 to IR£8, doubles IR£15 to IR£19. Meals are available at the attached Kincora pub, where there is often music at night, and bikes can be hired during the day. There are about a dozen hotels in Lisdoonvarna, all charging from IR£30 to IR£50 for singles and IR£40 to IR£70 for doubles, depending on the season. Among the best is the 84-room, baby-blue *Imperial Hotel* (☎ 74042) with high-season rates (May-October) of IR£42/60. The smaller *Carrigan Hotel* (☎ 74036), with 20 rooms, charges the same.

In town, the *Irish Arms* is a popular pub serving food and music at night; the *Matchmaker Bar* at the Imperial Hotel also has music. The *Dolmen* in the square specialises in seafood but also does excellent full Irish breakfasts. The *Orchid Restaurant* at Sheedy's Spa View Hotel (☎ 065-74026) in town has been recommended, and dinner ranges from around IR£10 for a vegetarian

choice to IR£15 for fish main courses. It opens May to September.

Getting There & Around
For information regarding bus services to Lisdoonvarna, see the introductory Getting There & Away section to the Burren. Burke's Garage (☎ 74022) on the square and opposite Sheedy's Spa View Hotel has bikes for hire.

BALLYREEN
Ballyreen is no more than a deserted stretch of coast about 5km south of Fanore, but it's a lovely spot and a good place to camp. There's a cliff called Ailladie, which boasts some of Ireland's finest rock climbing. For scuba divers, a barely visible track leads to a small inlet that has some excellent underwater scenery on the left, dropping quickly to a depth of about 20m, with vertical walls and gullies covered in jewel anemones.

Offshore after heavy rain you may see currents of brown water coming through the clear surface water. These are resurgences: fresh water flooding from an undersea cave. On land, glaciers have polished the limestone to a gloss. The incongruous stones and boulders were dumped here by glaciers.

Getting There & Away
There's no direct bus to Ballyreen. The coastal bus service that covers the Burren area starts in Galway and goes to Kinvara, Ballyvaughan, Black Head, Fanore, Lisdoonvarna and Doolin, returning by the same route. There's usually one bus daily Monday to Saturday in winter and up to three buses a day (one on Sunday) in the summer months, late May to late September.

FANORE
Fanore, 5km south of Black Head, could hardly be called a village. It's more like a stretch of coast, with a shop, a pub, and a few houses every now and then along the main road (R477). It has a fine sandy beach with an extensive backdrop of dunes; it's the only safe beach between Lahinch and Ballyvaughan.

CLARE

The remains of a Stone Age settlement were discovered near the small river that runs down through the dunes. Along the road south of the beach are a scattering of 10th and 11th century church ruins.

Information
Four km south of the beach on the ocean side of the road is Fitzpatrick's, a small grocery store/post office/newsagent/fishing tackle shop. O'Donoghue's pub almost opposite is a friendly place, with music on Saturday night. There are no other shops or bars along the coast. John McNamara at the Admiral's Rest Restaurant (☎ 065-76105) organises weekend 'safaris' of the Burren (see Places to Stay & Eat).

The telephone code is ☎ 065.

Things to See & Do
Just behind Fanore Beach, a road goes inland and up the **Khyber Pass**, or Caher River Valley. This is the only surface river in the Burren. The first few km are very pleasant, and there is a village up on the left, which has been deserted since the Famine. There are foxes, badgers and pine martens in the area, though you'll be lucky to spot any.

There are a couple of lovely **walks**. On the coast road about 400m south of the beach, a small road goes inland. After about a km, it meets an old green road that can be followed south to Ballinalacken Castle and is part of the Burren Way.

Alternatively, you can park at the Admiral's Rest Restaurant and go straight up through the fields to the green road. On top of this hill are two caves. **Poll Dubh** is a relatively easy cave for amateurs to explore, with delicate stalactites on view. The other, **Poll Mor**, is home to badgers, foxes, hares and rabbits.

There's a very well preserved **ring fort** and souterrain on top of a hill at the southern end of Fanore and about 1km inland.

There's another good walk south of here. Travelling south, just past the Fanore town sign, the dip before the last hill on the left turns out to be a wonderful hidden valley, which eventually debouches onto the green road to Ballinalacken Castle.

Places to Stay & Eat
At the northern end of Fanore, a few hundred metres inland from where the river crosses the road, is the IHO *Bridge Hostel* (☎ 065-76134). It's in an old police station, with 20 dorm beds at IR£6 or three doubles costing IR£8 per person. The hostel opens March to October.

At the southern end of Fanore is the *Admiral's Rest Seafood Restaurant* (☎ 065-76105) run by John McNamara, which also does B&B. Clean, tidy rooms cost IR£21/32. Dinner at the restaurant costs from IR£8 to IR£18. John organises a Burren Wildlife Weekend twice a year, in May and October. Those staying at the Admiral's rest for a week get a free boat ride on Galway Bay.

Getting There & Away
On Tuesday and Thursday only, one bus a day makes the run between Galway and Doolin, stopping at Ballyvaughan, Black Head, Fanore and Ballinalacken Castle en route.

BLACK HEAD & FORT OF IRGHUS
Black Head, Clare's north-westernmost point, is a bleak but imposing mountain of limestone dropping swiftly into the sea. The head has an unstaffed lighthouse and good shore angling for sea bass and cod. If you're lucky, you may see dolphins.

There's a great hike up the head to a large Iron Age stone fort called **Cathair Dhún Iorais**, the 'fort of Irghus'. The views across Galway Bay and the Aran Islands are exceptional, especially with the steep walls of the fort as a backdrop.

Inland, the hills rise to 318m and farther back is Slieve Elva (345m) capped with shale. Some of the intervening summits are marked with Bronze Age cairns. On your way up to the fort you cross an old green road.

BALLYVAUGHAN & AROUND
Ballyvaughan is a small pretty fishing

village on a quiet corner of Galway Bay. In the past few years it has been attracting well heeled visitors, and its nice pubs, restaurants and places to stay make it a good base for visiting the northern part of the Burren.

Just west of the village, past the holiday cottages and the Tea Rooms restaurant, is the quay and Monk's Bar. The harbour was built in 1829 at a time when boats traded with the Aran Islands and Galway, often bringing in turf – a scarce commodity in this area.

Ballyvaughan (Baile Uí Bheacháin) is a T-junction. Going south and inland on the N67 brings you to the centre of the Burren, Aillwee Caves, Poulnabrone Dolmen and Lisdoonvarna. Turning west leads you to the magnificent coast road (N477), Black Head and down towards Doolin. Going north-east on the N67 you reach Kinvara and County Galway.

Information

There are no banks in Ballyvaughan, but you can change money in Walsh's Craft Shop next to Claire's Restaurant on Main St or at the Whitethorn Craft & Visitor Centre, east of Ballyvaughan on the way to Kinvara. Alternatively, try Hyland's Hotel. The post office is on Main St.

The telephone code is ☎ 065.

Corkscrew Hill

Five km south of Ballyvaughan on the Lisdoonvarna road is a series of severe bends up Corkscrew Hill. The road was built as part of a famine-relief scheme in the 1840s. From the top there are spectacular views of the north Burren and Galway Bay with Aillwee Mountain and the caves on the right and Cappanawalla Hill on the left with the partially restored 16th century Newtown Castle, erstwhile residence of the O'Lochlains, at its base. From here, the route to Lisdoonvarna is through boggy and fairly boring country-side.

Gleninagh Castle

Down a narrow leafy lane and just off the coast road about 6km west of Ballyvaughan is Gleninagh, another 16th century

O'Lochlain castle. The O'Lochlains were chieftains in this region, and people lived here as late as 1840. In front of the castle is a holy well still in use, and the ruins of a medieval church. To the east you may find a small horseshoe-shaped mound of earth: a *fulacht fiadh*, or cooking place dating from the Bronze Age.

Places to Stay

You can *camp* in many of the fields around Ballyvaughan or along the coast just beyond the harbour. There are no hostels in Ballyvaughan. The closest ones are the *Bridge Hostel* to the west in Fanore (see previous section) or *Johnston's Hostel* (☎ 091-637164) on Main St in Kinvara, with dorm beds for IR£6, one double for IR£24 and open June to September only.

For B&B, *Meadowfield* (☎ 77083) is 200m along the road to Kinvara and costs from IR£18/32. Almost opposite is *Ocean-ville* (☎ 77051), with doubles for around IR£30. *Stonepark House* (☎ 77056) in Bishops Quarter, just over a km along the Kinvara road, costs IR£18/26. There are many more guesthouses out around Doorus and New Quay and they all get busy in season, so book ahead.

A particularly good B&B is *Rusheen Lodge* (☎ 77092), a little over 1km out on the inland road to Lisdoonvarna. At IR£25/40 or, May to October, IR£35/50, it's not cheap but the rooms and breakfasts are top-class. *Hyland's Hotel* (☎ 77037) in the middle of Ballyvaughan is a 19-room, family-run hotel with a cosy atmosphere, costing IR£46/58 or IR£53/72 in high season. They serve bar food and the restaurant (dinner IR£18) is good as hotels go.

Places to Eat

The *Tea Rooms* in an old cottage down towards the harbour, has top-notch soups, salads and home-cooked desserts. They are open till 6 pm. *Monk's Pub*, a popular place on the harbour, has melt-in-your-mouth mussels, seafood chowder and brown bread.

The *Tea Junction Café* in the village centre does a good breakfast and serves reasonable snacks all day. Most bars in town serve pub food. The restaurant at the *Aillwee Caves* is great for soups, salads and desserts. *Whitethorn Craft & Visitor Centre*, 3km north of town en route to Kinvara, has a good coffee shop-cum-restaurant. The tourist menu is IR£13.

Claire's Restaurant (☎ 77029) in the village is the best around and the food is superb. Dinner will cost you IR£20 or more a head.

Entertainment

Monk's Bar has traditional Irish music sessions on Tuesday and Friday to Sunday in summer. *Hyland's Hotel* has music at weekends while, a few doors down, *O'Brien's* has music Thursday to Sunday night. Poky little *O'Lochlain's*, on the left as you head down to the harbour, is a lovely old country pub, much less touristy than Monk's.

Getting There & Around

See the introductory Getting There & Away section to the Burren section for details of public transport to and from Ballyvaughan. Monk's Bar (☎ 77059) by the harbour has bikes for hire.

CENTRAL BURREN

The road through the heart of the Burren – the R480 and R476 – runs between Ballyvaughan and Corofin via Leamanegh Castle. Travelling south from Ballyvaughan, turn east before Corkscrew Hill at the sign for the Aillwee Caves. The road goes past Gleninsheen Wedge Tomb, Poulnabrone Dolmen and into some really desolate scenery.

To the south of the Burren, it's worth taking a diversion to Kilfenora to visit the Burren Centre and Kilfenora's cathedral and high crosses.

Aillwee Caves

The extensive limestone Aillwee Cave system (☎ 065-77036) is a good place to spend a rainy afternoon. The main passage penetrates for 600m into the mountain, widening into larger caverns, one with its own

waterfall. The caves were carved out by water some two million years ago. Near the entrance are the remains of a brown bear, extinct in Ireland for over 10,000 years.

Aillwee was discovered in 1944 by a local farmer, and today has a discreetly designed outer building with an excellent café. Behind the cave entrance there is a relatively easy scramble up 300m Aillwee Mountain, with fine views from the summit.

You can only go into the cave as part of a guided group, and tours are IR£3.95/2.25. Aillwee opens mid-March to early November, daily 10 am to 6 pm (7 pm in summer) and the last tour departs at 5.30 pm (6.30 pm in summer). Try and visit early in the day before the crowds arrive.

Gleninsheen Wedge Tomb

This tomb is known in folklore as the 'Druid's Altar', though the druids lived a long time after this was built. The tomb is beside the N480 just south of Aillwee Caves. It's thought to date from 4000 to 5000 years ago and, like most of the other tombs in the Burren, it's on high ground.

A magnificent gold torc was found nearby in 1930 by a boy hunting rabbits. It was in a crack in the limestone and at first the boy thought it was part of a coffin. Dating from around 700 BC, the torc is reckoned to be one of the finest pieces of prehistoric Irish craftwork and is now on display at the National Museum in Dublin.

Poulnabrone Dolmen

Poulnabrone Dolmen is one of Ireland's most photographed ancient monuments, the one you see on all the postcards with the sun setting behind it. The dolmen is a three-legged tomb, sitting in a sea of limestone without a house in sight. At quiet times of day, this is a truly lovely place. It's 8km inland from Aillwee and signposted from the N480.

Poulnabrone was built over 5000 years ago. It was excavated in 1989, and the remains of more than 25 people were found among pieces of pottery and jewellery. Radiocarbon dating suggests that they were

CLARE

buried between 3800 and 3200 BC. When the dead were originally entombed here, the whole structure was covered in a mound of earth, which has since worn away. *Poll na bró* in Irish means 'hole of the quern', and the capstone weighs five tons. Try and visit early in the morning or at sunset for good photographs. Better still, try a moonlit night.

Carron & Cahercommaun Cliff Fort

The Burren Perfumery (☎ 065-89102) in the tiny village of Carron (or Carran on some maps), a few km east of the N480, uses wildflowers of the Burren to produce its scents, and it's the only handicraft perfumery in Ireland. It's open daily.

Three km south of Carron and perched on the edge of an inland cliff is the great stone fort of Cahercommaun. It was inhabited during the 8th and 9th centuries by a group of people who hunted deer and grew a small amount of grain. There are the remains of a souterrain leading from the fort to the outer face of the cliff.

To get there, go south from Carron and take a left turn for Kilinaboy. After 1.5km a path on the left leads up to the fort.

East of Carron

If you turn east at Carron, you have two options. The first is to turn north after about 2km, which takes you on a magnificent drive through a valley to Cappaghmore in County Galway. If you continue directly east from Carron you come close to the lovely Mt Mullaghmore (191m). Later, just over the Galway border on the main road to Gort (R460), is Kilmacduagh, a monastic site with a splendid round tower.

KILFENORA

The tiny, windswept village of Kilfenora lies on the southern fringes of the Burren, 8km south-east of Lisdoonvarna. Most visitors come to see the monastic remains, five high crosses and a tiny 12th century cathedral. The village itself is a touch forlorn, but has some attractive shopfronts and pubs.

Burren Centre

The centre (☎ 065-88030) was built by the local community and has a fair amount of information on the Burren as well as guidebooks for sale. There's a display, a video presentation and a decent café attached. The centre opens daily March to October, 10 am to 5 pm (9.30 am to 6 pm, June to September). Entry is IR£2.50/1.25.

Kilfenora Cathedral

The pope has the honour of also being the bishop of the diocese of Kilfenora & Killaloe; in the past the ruined 12th century cathedral was an important place of pilgrimage. St Fachan (or Fachtna) founded the monastery here in the 6th century, and it later became the seat of Kilfenora diocese, the smallest in the country.

The cathedral is the smallest one you are ever likely to see. Only the ruined structure and nave of the more recent Protestant church are actually part of the cathedral. The chancel has two primitive carved figures on top of two tombs. One is a bishop (note the mitre), and it must be said that neither were very handsome gentlemen. The theory goes that after the Black Death in the 14th century there was a general decline in craft skills across the continent, and these poor carvings may be examples of this.

High Crosses

Kilfenora is best known for its high crosses, three in the churchyard and a large 12th century example in the field about 100m to the west.

The most interesting one is the 800-year-old **Doorty Cross**, standing prominently to the west of the church's front door. It differs significantly from the standard Irish high cross in that it's without the usual pierced disc or wheel. It was lying broken in two until the 1950s when it was re-erected.

The east face of the cross is the better preserved. One interpretation of the carvings has Christ on top ordering two figures in the middle to destroy the devil/bird at the bottom, which is misbehaving; another is that it portrays St Patrick. The west face is much less clear. Christ (?) still appears to be on top, this time surrounded by birds. Directly underneath are delicate designs and a man on horseback holding the ends of the patterns. Some say it's Christ's entry into Jerusalem. One theory suggests the cross may commemorate Kilfenora being made the diocesan seat in the 12th century.

Places to Stay
One km along the Lisdoonvarna road is the welcoming *Mrs Geraldine Howley's* B&B (☎ 065-88075), at IR£19/28 for singles/doubles. The *Burren Farmhouse* (☎ 065-71363), 2km along the Ennistymon road, is equally pleasant and charges the same for its three rooms.

Places to Eat
The *Burren Centre* has a reasonable tea room next door, open 9.30 am to 6 pm. The *Parlour Restaurant* at Vaughan's pub on the green also has bar food.

Entertainment
Vaughan's pub has regular Irish music sessions during weeknights and on Saturday. *Nagle's Lounge Bar* has music at weekends only.

COROFIN
Corofin is a small village on the southern fringes of the Burren. Commonly found in the area are turloughs (from the Irish *turlach*), small lakes that often disappear during dry summers. O'Brien castles abound in this boggy countryside, two of which are on the shores of nearby Lake Inchiquin.

Corofin is home to the intersting **Clare Heritage & Genealogical Centre** (☎ 065-37955), which has facilities for people researching their Clare ancestry and a display covering the period around the Potato Famine. Over a quarter of a million people lived in Clare before the Potato Famine; today the county's population stands at about 94,000 – a drop of some 62%. Opening hours are 9.30 am to 5.30 pm, May to September (though the genealogical

section can be contacted all year). Admission is IR£2/1.

About 4km north-west of Corofin, on the road to Leamanegh Castle and Kilfenora (R476), look for the small town of Kilinaboy. The ruined church here is worth seeking out for the sheila-na-gig over the doorway.

Places to Stay
The IHH *Corofin Village Hostel* (☎ 065-37683) is a fine hostel and campsite on Main St with good facilities. A bed in a dorm is IR£7, and the three doubles cost IR£17. Camping for two people is IR£8.

There are plenty of B&Bs in the area, many of them in Kilinaboy along the road to Kilfenora and Lisdoonvarna. Good ones include *Cottage View* (☎ 065-37662), 2km from Corofin, at IR£14 per person and open March to October, and *Clifden House* (☎ 065-37692) with four rooms at IR£35 for a double.

Places to Eat
Near the heritage centre is a reasonable *coffee shop* serving light meals all day. For pub food try the *Angler's Rest* on Main St. *Bofey Quinn's*, also on Main St, is a very popular pub and seafood restaurant serving simple but delicious snacks and meals to 10.30 pm between Easter and September.

Getting There & Away
There is one bus on Monday from Kilkee or Doonbeg to Ennis and Limerick stopping in Corofin. Check with the Ennis bus station (☎ 065-24177) or the Corofin Village Hostel for times.

LEAMANEGH CASTLE
Leamanegh is a well preserved castle-cum-fortified house 8km north-west of Corofin. The castle's name is pronounced 'lay-um-on-ay' and is from the Irish for 'deer's leap' or 'horse's leap'. If you look carefully, you will see that there are two parts joined together. The five-storey tower house on the right was built around 1480 by the O'Briens and is much more solid and better defended than the main house, which Conor O'Brien

added in 1640. This has four storeys, and its most appealing features are the largely intact stone window frames.

The whole building was originally surrounded by a high wall. Just above the tower house entrance is a vertical shaft or 'murder hole'. If this was the 15th century and you were an uninvited guest, all manner of unspeakable things could be dropped on top of you from here, including boiling oil, tar, arrows, dead animals – or anything else that came to hand. There's a fine view from the top of the tower.

Maire Rua McMahon

Conor O'Brien was killed in 1651 while fighting for the royalists against Cromwell. His wife, the infamous Maire Rua McMahon, reportedly refused to take his body back into Leamanegh Castle. After his death, she offered to marry one of Cromwell's soldiers to ensure that her son Donough didn't lose his inheritance. Marry Maire did, but they still lost the estate. Despite this setback, she and her new husband, John Cooper, stayed together. They regained their property in 1675, but later records show she was tried – and acquitted – for Cooper's subsequent murder. She died in 1686. ∎

NORTH-EAST CLARE

Low farmland stretches south from County Galway until it meets the bluff limestone hills of the Burren. The Burren begins just west of Kinvara and Doorus, where the road forks, going inland to Carron or along the coast to Ballyvaughan.

From Oranmore in County Galway all the way down to Ballyvaughan, the coastline wriggles along small inlets and peninsulas; some like Finavarra and New Quay are worth a detour.

Just inland near Bellharbour is the largely intact Corcomroe Abbey, and the three ancient churches of Oughtmama lie up a quiet side valley.

Galway Bay forms the backdrop to some outstanding scenery: bare stone hills shining in the sun, with small hamlets and rich patches of green wherever there is soil.

Getting There & Away

There's a bus service between Galway and Cork that passes through Kinvara and Ballyvaughan three or four times a day (once or twice on Sunday) late May to late September only. Another service running between Galway and Doolin also stops in those two places, and there is usually one bus daily Monday to Saturday in winter and up to three buses a day (one on Sunday) in the summer months. Details of these bus services are available from Galway bus station (☎ 091-562000) or Ennis bus station (☎ 065-24177).

New Quay & the Flaggy Shore

New Quay, on the Finavarra Peninsula, is about 2km off the main Kinvara to Ballyvaughan road (N67). There are a couple of thatched cottages on the peninsula and the ruins of a 17th century mansion.

Linnane's pub in New Quay serves seafood and is right next door to Ireland's largest oyster farm.

The Flaggy Shore, west of New Quay, is a particularly fine stretch of coastline. Layers of limestone march boldly into the sea, and behind the coastal path swans parade gently on Lough Muirí. There are otters in the area. On the way out to Finavarra Point is Mt Vernon Lodge, the summer home of Augusta Lady Gregory, playwright and friend of WB Yeats. She was prominent in the Anglo-Irish literary revival.

On Finavarra Point is one of the west coast's few **Martello towers**, built in the early 1800s to warn Galway in case Napoleon came sailing by and sneaked into Ireland through the back door. The road loops back and joins the main road beside a small lake, which is rich in birdlife, including ducks, moorhens and herons.

Bellharbour

Bellharbour is no more than a crossroads with some thatched holiday cottages about 8km east of Ballyvaughan. There's an excellent walk along an old green road that begins

The Legend of Corcomroe

In 1317, the Battle of Corcomroe was fought very near the abbey between two O'Brien clans trying to win control of Clare. Legend has it that one of the chieftains, Donough, was passing by Lough Rask on his way to battle, when he saw a witch washing a pile of bleeding limbs in the water. The witch told Donough that her name was Bronach Boirne and that the corpses would be those of his soldiers if he insisted on going into battle. To make matters worse, Donough's own head was in the pile.

Donough's men tried to capture the elusive witch, but she flew up in the air and rained curses on them. To reassure his men, Donough told them that Bronach was the lover of his arch rival Dermot O'Brien and her warnings merely a ploy to frighten them off. Unfortunately for Donough, by that night he and most of his army were lying dead in the abbey.

Incidentally, on nearby Moneen Mountain is a pass called Mam Catha, the 'pass of the battle', which could refer to the route taken by Donough and his army. Dermot, the victor, later defeated de Clare of Bunratty, halting the spread of Anglo-Norman influence in Clare for a couple of hundred years. ■

behind the modern Church of St Patrick, 1km north of Bellharbour, and threads north along Abbey Hill.

Just inland from here is Corcomroe Abbey, the valley and churches of Oughtmama, and the interior road that takes you right through the heart of the Burren.

Wildlife You can almost be guaranteed a sighting of seals along the coast west of Bellharbour. Go about 1km along the Ballyvaughan road until you spot a large dark-green farm shed on the right. Follow the path down to the shore, and you may see seals. This inlet is also thick with birds, and winter visitors include brent geese from northern Canada.

Corcomroe Abbey Corcomroe is a former Cistercian abbey 1km inland from Bellharbour. It lies in its own small valley surrounded by low hills and is a very peaceful place. It was founded in 1194 by Donal Mór O'Brien. His grandson, Conor O'Brien (died 1267),

king of Thomond, occupies the tomb in the north wall, and there is a crude carving of him below another effigy of a staring bishop armed with a crozier. Some fine Romanesque carvings are scattered throughout the abbey.

Oughtmama Valley Oughtmama is a lonely and deserted valley hiding some small and ancient churches. To get there turn inland at Bellharbour, left at the Y-junction, and up to a clump of trees and a house on the right. A rough track here will bring you east up a blind valley to the churches. St Colman MacDuagh, who also built churches on the Aran Islands, founded the monastery here in the 6th century. The three churches were built in the 12th century by monks in search of solitude.

It's a hardy walk up Turlough Hill behind the chapels, but the views are tremendous. Near the summit are the remains of an Iron Age hill fort.

County Galway

County Galway is one of the highlights of any visit to Ireland. Stretching from Ballinasloe in the midlands westward through the wilds of Connemara to the craggy Atlantic coastline beyond Clifden, Galway has just about everything packed into its 5940 sq km. It's the second-largest county in Ireland after Cork, and the city of Galway is the west coast's liveliest and most populous settlement.

Galway's neighbour to the south is County Clare, and the Burren limestone region peters out near Kinvara, a picturesque little coastal town just within the Galway border. However, the limestone surfaces out to sea in a long, grey reef; this forms the three Aran Islands, which are famous for their folklore, bleak but evocative scenery, Irish speakers and woollen sweaters.

Galway's landscape is extremely varied. Lough Corrib cuts off the rugged coastal region from the largely flat interior that makes up the bulk of the county.

Galway

The city of Galway is a delight, with its narrow streets, old stone and wooden shopfronts, good restaurants and bustling pubs. It's also the administrative capital of the county, and home to the local government, University College Galway, and a regional college to the east of town. There's a ferry to the Aran Islands from the docks, although you're better off travelling farther west along the Connemara coast and taking a boat from Rossaveal.

In marked contrast to most of the depopulated west coast, Galway is one of Europe's fastest-growing cities and ranks fourth in size after Dublin, Cork and Limerick. Large factories and a bustling energy underlie its relative economic security.

Galway is a gateway for Connemara and

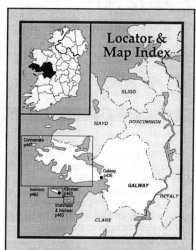

Highlights

- Walk in the Connemara National Park
- Take the scenic journey through the Lough Inagh Valley in Connemara
- Visit Inishmór (Aran Islands) and especially Dún Aengus perched on the edge of its southern cliffs
- Cycle or walk on Inishmaan & Inisheer (Aran Islands)
- Enjoy the pubs and cultural life of Galway city
- Walk or cycle the Sky Road west of Clifden in Connemara
- Explore Inishbofin and Inisturk islands

the west, as it sits at the southern tip of Lough Corrib, which forms a natural border to the region. The city is also a handy base for exploring the Burren, which begins some 30km to the south in County Clare.

Galway has always attracted a bohemian crowd of musicians, artists, intellectuals and young people. This mix is partly due to the

GALWAY

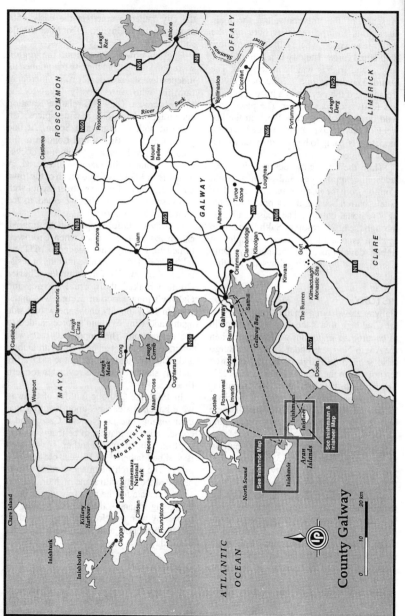

County Galway

presence of the university, but the main attractions for the traveller here are the nightlife and pubs, where talk and drink flow with equal force. The city is a major Gaelic centre, and Irish is widely understood. The Druid Theatre is one of the best in the Ireland, and the city hosts a hugely popular arts festival every summer. The place goes wild during Galway Race Week in the last week of July. If you haven't booked, accommodation is going to be very difficult to find at these times.

While the city centre deserves its accolades, the approaches and suburbs don't. Coming from the east, you pass huge modern hotels, barren housing developments and the ugly regional college. The coast road west through the beach resort of Salthill and on to Spiddal is one of the worst examples of ribbon development in the country. Only after Spiddal do the bungalows start to thin out.

HISTORY

Galway grew from a small fishing village in the Claddagh area at the mouth of the Corrib to become an important walled town when the Anglo-Normans under Richard de Burgo (also spelled de Burgh or Burke) captured territory from the local O'Flahertys in 1232. The Irish word for 'outsiders' or 'foreigners' is *gaill*, which may be the origin of the city's name in Irish, Gaillimh. The town walls were built by the Anglo-Normans from around 1270.

Galway became something of an outpost in the 'wild west'. In 1396, Richard II granted a charter to the city, which effectively transferred power from the de Burgos to 14 merchant families or 'tribes'. This led to the name 'City of the Tribes' by which Galway is still known. These powerful families were mostly English or Norman in origin, but there were tribes outside the walls as well as inside. Clashes with the leading Irish families of Connemara were frequent, and at one time the city's west gate bore the prayer and warning: 'From the fury of the O'Flahertys, good Lord deliver us.' To ensure the ferocity was kept on the outside,

the city fathers warned in the early 16th century that no uninvited 'O' or Mac' should show his face on Galway's streets.

English power throughout the region waxed and waned, but the city maintained its independent status under the ruling merchant families who were mostly loyal to the English crown. Galway's relative isolation encouraged a huge trade in wine, spices, fish and salt with Portugal and Spain. At one point, it rivalled Bristol and London in the volume of goods passing through its docks.

For a long while Galway prospered. A huge fire in 1473 destroyed much of the town but created space for a new street layout with many solid stone buildings erected in the 15th and 16th centuries.

Galway's faithful support of the English crown led to its downfall when Cromwell turned up. The city was besieged in 1651 and fell in April 1652 after nine months of resistance. Cromwell's forces under Charles Coote wreaked their usual havoc, and Galway's long period of decline was under way. In 1691 the city chose the wrong side again, and King William's forces added to the destruction. The important trade with Spain was almost at an end, and with Dublin and Waterford taking most of the sea traffic, Galway stagnated until its revival in modern times.

In 1992, the Catholic faithful of Galway were knocked sideways upon learning that their bishop, one Dr Eamonn Casey and a conservative on matters of celibacy, contraception, abortion and other sex-related issues, had fathered an 18-year-old son as a priest. The church's damage-control efforts provided the city with some high drama and serious debate for the next few weeks but – this being Ireland – the humour behind the hypocrisy won out. Jokes about the bishop and the bishopric (as it were) were the order of the day.

ORIENTATION

Galway's tightly packed town centre lies on both sides of the River Corrib, which connects Lough Corrib with the sea, though Eyre Square and most of the main shopping areas are on the river's east (left) bank. There are three main bridges; the northernmost, Salmon Weir Bridge, looks over a salmon trap and is overshadowed by Galway Cathedral.

Just west of the river mouth is the historic, but now totally redeveloped, district of Claddagh, while slightly farther west is the beach resort of Salthill, quite a popular area for accommodation and restaurants. Eyre Square is just west of the combined bus and railway station and near the tourist office.

From Eyre Square, the meandering main shopping street starts as Williamsgate St and becomes William St and then Shop St before splitting into Mainguard St and High St. High St then becomes Quay St and crosses the River Corrib over Wolfe Tone Bridge. Mainguard St leads to Bridge St and William O'Brien Bridge.

INFORMATION
The big Ireland West Tourism office (☎ 091-563081) is just east of Eyre Square and opens daily July and August 8.30 am to 7.45 pm. In June it opens 9 am to 6.45 pm and, in May, Monday to Saturday 9 am to 5.45 pm. The rest of the year the office opens weekdays 9 am to 5.45 pm, Saturday 9 am to 12.45 pm. At the height of the season it's busy, and there can be delays of an hour or more in making accommodation bookings. There's a tourist office branch (☎ same) in Salthill just off the Seapoint Promenade where it meets Upper Salthill Rd.

There's a USIT travel office (☎ 091-565177) at the Kinlay House hostel.

Money
All Irish banks have branches in the city centre. There's a Bank of Ireland at 43 Eyre Square, another one on the square's west side, and an Allied Irish Bank in Lynch's Castle on Shop St; all open weekdays 10 am to 4 or 5 pm and have ATMs. The many building societies based in Eyre Square have bureaux de change open Monday to Friday 9.30 am to 5 pm and sometimes Saturday 10 am to 1 pm. The main tourist office also

changes money. The bureau de change in the Eyre Square Shopping Centre opens Monday to Saturday 9 am to 5 pm and in summer daily 8 am to 10 pm. American Express was due to open an office on the north side of Eyre Square sometime in 1997; seek further details from the tourist office.

Post & Communication
The post office is on Eglinton St, north of William St. It's open Monday to Saturday 9 am to 6 pm. One World (☎ 091-569012), 3 Francis St, is a cyber-café where you can log on to the Internet.

The telephone code is ☎ 091.

Bookshops
Hawkins House at 14 Churchyard St, opposite St Nicholas Collegiate Church, and Charlie Byrne's in the Cornstore on Middle St are good bookshops. There's also an Eason's branch on Shop St. Kenny's Bookshop on High St is one of the leading antiquarian bookshops in Ireland.

Medieval Galway: A Rambler's Guide & Map, published by Tír Eolas, is available in most bookshops.

Laundry
There's a laundrette on Sea Rd, just off Upper Dominick St, and Bubbles laundrette is on Mary St. A more central one can be found in the Olde Malte Mall shopping arcade, off High St. It opens Monday to Saturday 8.30 am to 6 pm.

EYRE SQUARE
The square is the focal point for the eastern part of the city centre though it shows no great imagination in its design and layout. The bus/railway station is to the east while the tourist office is just off the south-east corner.

This side of the square is taken up almost entirely by the Great Southern Hotel, a large grey limestone pile. To the west of the square is Browne's Doorway of 1627, a fragment from the home of one of the city's merchant rulers.

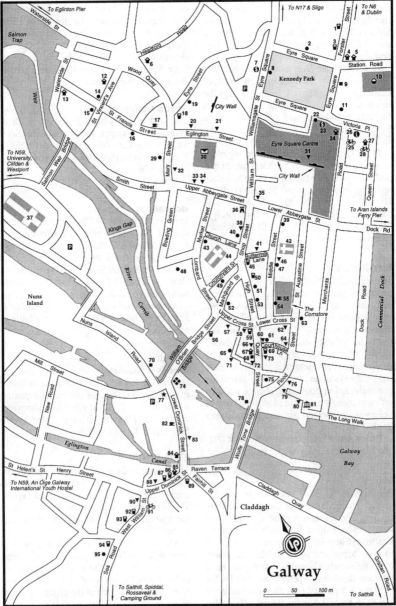

Galway

0   50   100 m

To Salthill

To Eglinton Pier

Waterside St

To N17 & Sligo

To N6
& Dublin

Salmon
Trap

Weir

Headford   Road

Waterside St

Wood Quay

St. Vincent's Ave

St Francis   Street

Mary   Street

Bowling Green

Eyre   Street

Forster   Street

Station   Road

Eyre   Square

Kennedy Park

Eyre   Square

Eyre   Square

Eglington   Street

Eglinton   Street

Williamsgate   St

William   St

Victoria   Pl

Eyre   Square   Centre

City Wall

City Wall

Eyre Square Centre

To Aran Islands
Ferry Pier

Dock   Rd

To N59,
University,
Clifden &
Westport

Salmon Weir   Bridge

Smith   Street

Kings Gap

Nuns
Island

River   Corrib

Nuns   Island   Road

William   Street

O'Brien   Bridge

Bridge   Street

Market   Street

Lombard   Street

Church Lane

Churchyard St

Mainguard St

High   Street

Shop   Street

Upper Abbeygate Street

Lower   Abbeygate   St

Middle   Street

Buttermilk
Lane

Quay   St

Upper Cross St

Lower Cross St

St Augustine   Street

Merchants   Road

The Cornstore

Courthouse Lane

Crn Ln

Quay   Street

Mill   Street

New   Road

Lower Dominick   Street

Wolfe Tone Bridge

Flood   Street

The Long Walk

Commercial   Dock

Dock   Road

Dock   Road

Commercial Dock

Eglington   Street

St Helen's St

Henry   Street

Canal

Raven   Terrace

Fairhill   St

Upper Dominick   St

Claddagh   Quay

Claddagh

Galway
Bay

Grattan   Road

To N59, An Oige Galway
International Youth Hostel

West   William   St

Sea   Road

To Salthill, Spiddal,
Rossaveal &
Camping Ground

PLACES TO STAY
4 Galway Hostel
5 Great Western House Hostel
6 Woodquay Hostel
9 Great Southern Hotel
12 Salmon Weir Hostel
13 Corrib Villa Hostel
24 Kinlay House Hostel & USIT Office
27 Celtic Tourist Hostel
67 Quay Street Hostel
68 Spanish Arch Hotel
70 St Martin's B&B
78 Jury's Galway Inn
84 Galway City Hostel
85 Arch View Hostel

PLACES TO EAT
17 One World Cyber-Café
20 Conlons Takeaway
21 Conlons Restaurant
31 Sails Restaurant
32 Fan Sune Chinese Restaurant
33 Couch Potatoes Restaurant
34 Brannagan's Restaurant
35 Food for Thought Café
38 McDonald's
41 Tulsi Indian Restaurant
46 Brasserie Restaurant
55 Macken's Café
57 Busker Brownes Restaurant
58 Hungry Grass
60 Quay West Restaurant
62 Café Uí Néill
64 Sev'nth Heav'n
66 Pierre Victoire Restaurant
71 Kirwan's Lane Creative Cuisine

72 Pasta Mista & McDonagh's Restaurant
73 Fat Freddy's Pizzeria
76 Shama Indian Restaurant
79 Hooker Jimmy's Seafood Bar
80 Lotus Inn Restaurant
82 Left Bank Café
83 Le Graal Restaurant
88 Kebab House
90 An Chistin Restaurant

PUBS
1 Rabbitt's Bar & Restaurant
3 An Púcán Pub
18 McSwiggan's Pub
45 Taafes Bar
50 King's Head Pub
56 Lisheen Bar
59 O'Neachtain's Bar
69 Quays Bar
86 Róisín Dubh Pub
87 Taylor's Bar
89 Monroe's Tavern
92 The Blue Note
93 Claddagh Ring Pub
94 Crane's Bar

OTHER
2 American Express Office
7 Bank of Ireland
8 Browne's Doorway
10 Bus & Train Station
11 Island Ferries
14 Town Hall Theatre
15 Town Hall
16 Franciscan Abbey
19 Corrib & Apollo Cabs

22 Eyre Square Centre Entrance & Bureau de Change
23 Bank of Ireland
25 Chieftain Cycle Hire
26 Tourist Office
28 Celtic Cycles
29 Bubbles Laundrette
30 Post Office
36 Lynch's Castle & Allied Irish Bank
37 St Nicholas Cathedral
39 Mulligan Records
40 Eason's Bookshop
42 Augustinian Church
43 Lynch Memorial Window
44 St Nicholas Collegiate Church
47 The Galway Theatre (Irish Language)
48 Nora Barnacle's House
49 Hawkins House Bookshop
51 Olde Malte Mall & Laundrette
52 Galway Taxis
53 Kenny's Bookshop
54 Charlie Byne's Bookshop
61 Druid Theatre
63 Mayoralty House
65 Design Concourse Ireland
74 Bridge Mill Shopping Centre
75 Punchbag Theatre & Club
77 Garda Station
81 Spanish Arch & Museum
91 Flaherty's Cycles
95 Laundrette

In the centre of the square is Kennedy Park. US President John F Kennedy visited Galway in 1963, and a stone tablet in the square marks the occasion. To the north of the square is a controversial statue to the Galway-born writer Pádraic O'Conaire (1883-1928), a noted hell-raiser. It's one of the better examples of modern sculpture in Ireland. Behind Browne's Doorway there's a curious object that is supposed to evoke the sails of a *húicéir* (or hooker), a traditional Galway vessel. It was designed by Eamon O'Doherty and erected during the city's quincentennial in 1984.

COLLEGIATE CHURCH OF ST NICHOLAS OF MYRA

This Protestant church on Shop St with its curious pyramidal spire dates from 1320 and is not only Galway's most important monument but also the largest medieval parish church in Ireland still in use. Although it has been rebuilt and enlarged over the centuries, much of the original form has been retained. After Cromwell's victory, the church suffered the usual indignity of being used as a stable. Much damage was done but at least it survived; 14 other Galway churches were simply knocked to the ground. Look for the

GALWAY

damaged stonework. The church has numerous finely worked stone tombs and memorials. The two church bells date from 1590 and 1630.

Parts of the floor are paved with gravestones from the 16th to the 18th centuries, and the Lynch Aisle holds the tombs of the powerful Lynch family. A large block tomb in one corner is said to be the grave of James Lynch, a mayor of Galway in the late 15th century who condemned his son Walter to death for killing a young Spanish visitor. None of the townsfolk would act as executioner, and the mayor was so dedicated to upholding justice that he personally acted as hangman, after which he went into seclusion – or so the story goes. A plaque, complete with skull and crossbones, on the **Lynch Memorial Window** on Market St north of the church tells the tale and claims to be the spot where the gallows stood.

At the end of the south transept is the 'empty frame' which once held an icon of the Virgin Mary. It was supposedly taken to Győr in western Hungary in the 17th century by an Irish bishop sent packing by Cromwell and is still an object of veneration there.

It's said that Christopher Columbus tarried in Galway to hear Mass and pray at the church. This Galway side-trip supposedly occurred either because one of the crew was a Galway man or because Columbus wished to investigate tales of St Brendan's earlier voyage to the Americas from here.

The church opens mid-April to September 9 am to 5.45 pm, and 9.30 am to 4.30 pm the rest of the year.

BOWLING GREEN

Across the road from Lynch's Memorial Window is Bowling Green. No 8 Bowling Green was once the home of Nora Barnacle (1884-1951), companion and later wife to James Joyce. The house is now a small museum dedicated to the couple, open mid-May to mid-September Monday to Saturday 10 am to 5 pm (IR£1). Joyce first visited the house in 1909 and again several times during the summer of 1912.

LYNCH'S CASTLE

On the corner of Shop and Abbeygate Sts, parts of the old stone town house called Lynch's Castle (now a branch of the Allied Irish Bank) date back to the 14th century. Most of the present building, said to be the finest town castle in Ireland, dates from around 1600, however. The Lynch family were the most powerful of the 14 ruling Galway 'tribes', and members of the family held the position of mayor no less than 80 times between 1480 and 1650 – including the son-slayer James Lynch.

Lynch's Castle has numerous fine stone features on its facade, including the coats of arms of Henry VII, the Lynches and the Fitzgeralds of Kildare, as well as gargoyles, unusual in Ireland.

THE SPANISH ARCH

A 1651 pictorial view of Galway clearly shows its extensive city walls. But since the visits of Cromwell in 1652 and King William in 1691, and the subsequent centuries of neglect, the walls have almost completely disappeared. Located near the river, the Spanish Arch (1584) appears to have been an extension of the walls through which ships unloaded their goods – often wine and brandy from Spain.

The small and unremarkable **Galway City Museum** is by the arch. It's open Monday to Saturday 10 am to 1 pm and 2.15 to 5.15 pm. Admission costs IR£1/50p.

ST NICHOLAS CATHEDRAL

From the Spanish Arch, a pleasant riverside path runs all the way up river and across the Salmon Weir Bridge to the second church in town dedicated to St Nicholas. The cathedral is a huge and imposing structure, dedicated by the late Cardinal Richard Cushing of Boston in 1965. Tasteful it's not, and critics vie for the most caustic descriptions of this monument to inelegance.

Inside things are a little less grandiose, but it's a mishmash of styles and intentions. Even the cathedral's proper name is a mouthful: the Catholic Cathedral of Our Lady Assumed into Heaven and St Nicholas.

SALMON WEIR

The Salmon Weir Bridge crosses the River Corrib just east of the cathedral. Upstream is the great weir where the waters of the Corrib cascade down one of their final descents before reaching the sea, 1km to the south. The weir controls the water levels above it, and when the salmon are running you can often see shoals of them waiting in the clear waters before making the rush upstream to spawn in Lough Corrib.

The earliest records of Galway include references to the de Burgo family owning the fisheries on the town's weirs. Today they're owned by the Central Fisheries Board. The salmon and sea trout seasons are usually from February to September, but most fish pass through the weir during May and June. Fishing licences are obtainable from the Fishery Office (☎ 562388), Nuns Island, Galway.

SALTHILL

Within walking distance of the city, is Salthill, an old-fashioned seaside resort. The beaches are often packed in hot weather but are not particularly good. Leisureland (☎ 521455) in Salthill Park, with several covered pools and a giant waterslide, opens daily year round from 8 am to 10 pm and costs IR£3.30/2.20 for adults/students & children. Family tickets are available from IR£7.70.

ORGANISED TOURS

The Spiddal-based O'Neachtain Tours (☎ 553188) has day-long coach tours of Connemara or the Burren and Cliffs of Moher leaving the Galway tourist office at 9.45 am (9.55 am from the Salthill tourist office branch) and returning at 4.30 pm. The price of each is IR£10/8/5 for adults/students/children. Lally Coaches (☎ 562905), also in Spiddal, has a similar tour of Connemara (including Cong). The departure points, times and prices are the same as the O'Neachtain ones.

April to September/October, the *Corrib Princess* (☎ 592447) does 1½-hour cruises at 2.30 and 4.30 pm on the Corrib River from Eglinton Pier, at the northern end of Waterside St, upriver from the Salmon Weir. Bookings (IR£5/2.50 for adults/children) can also be made at the tourist office.

SPECIAL EVENTS

The Jazz Festival in February is now well established. Around Easter there is the Cúirt

---

Claddagh

> If you ever go across the sea to Ireland
> It may be at the closing of the day
> You can sit and watch the moon rise over Claddagh
> And watch the sun go down on Galway Bay
> **Arthur Colahan, *Galway Bay*, (1947)**

A romantic icon in the hearts and songs of Irish-Americans for generations, Claddagh was once Galway's main commercial fishing area. Strictly speaking, the district begins at the western end of Wolfe Tone Bridge and up to 3000 people and 300 boats were based here at one stage. Among the boats were the traditional Galway sailing vessels with pitched black hulls and rust-coloured sails known as *púcáin* and *gleoitoige*, today collectively called Galway hookers.

Claddagh used to have its own characteristic costume and dialect, as well as its own king. Although the traditional Claddagh of thatched roofs, Irish speakers, and fishing boats has been gone for decades, you'll still see many people wearing Claddagh rings, with a crowned heart nestling between two outstretched hands signifying friendship (the hands), loyalty (the crown) and love (the heart). If the heart points towards the hand, the wearer is taken or married; towards the fingertip means that he or she is looking for a mate. It has been the wedding ring used throughout much of Connaught since the mid-18th century and is enjoying something of a renaissance today, judging from the well stocked jewellery shop windows. ∎

Festival of Literature which is growing in importance every year. The city parties with a vengeance at the Galway Arts Festival in late July/early August. The whole town turns out for this two-week extravaganza of theatre, music, art and a parade.

The last week of July is Galway Race Week, which is as much an event off the course as on it. The racecourse, 3km east of the city centre at Ballybrit, hosts a traditional Irish fair.

PLACES TO STAY

Galway has a huge variety of accommodation, but you may still have difficulty finding a bed in July and August. There's more accommodation in Salthill, a couple of km to the south-west.

Camping

Silver Strand Caravan & Camping Park (☎ 592040) is on the coast, just beyond Salthill. Large/small tents are IR£7/6 plus 50p per adult, and the site opens April to September. *Spiddal Caravan & Camping Park* (also signposted in Irish as Pairc Saoire an Spidéil) (☎ 553372) is 18km west of Galway on the same coastal road (R336). Large/small tents are IR£7/5 and adults/children pay IR£1.50/50p. It's open all year. *Ballyloughane Caravan & Camping Park* (☎ 755338) is at Ballyloughane Beach on the Dublin road (N6), 5km east of Galway. A site for a large/small tent here is IR£5/4 with the per-person charge IR£2/50p.

Hostels

There are legions of hostels in and around Galway. All are open year round except for the An Óige and Mary Ryan hostels.

Several hostels are extremely central. The large IHH *Great Western House* (☎ 561150) in Frenchville Lane adjacent to the bus and railway station has beds from IR£7.50 to IR£9.50 (IR£12.50 in four-bedded rooms), 22 private rooms costing IR£14 to IR£16 per person and a sauna. On the same street but closer to the square is the security-conscious IHO *Galway Hostel* (☎ 566959), with beds from IR£6 to IR£8 and six private rooms for

IR£8 to IR£9.50 per person. The modern 150-room *Kinlay House* (☎ 565244), opposite the tourist office, is well equipped, has a variety of rooms from IR£8 to IR£11.50 and includes a light breakfast. The 15 private rooms here cost IR£12 to IR£14 per person. Around the corner on Queen St the not-so-attractive IHO *Celtic Tourist Hostel* (☎ 566606) has beds for IR£6 to IR£6.90 and six doubles for IR£16 to IR£19.

The IHH *Quay Street House* (☎ 568644), 10 Quay St, has 98 beds and charges IR£6.50 to IR£7.50; doubles are IR£24 to IR£26. The IHH *Corrib Villa* (☎ 562892), 4 Waterside St, near the Salmon Weir Bridge, costs IR£6.50 to IR£7.50, and there are no private rooms. The independent *Woodquay Hostel* (☎ 562618) costs from IR£5.90 to IR£7.50 (IR£15 for one of two doubles) and has a decent kitchen and eating area but cramped washrooms and rickety bunks. It's just north of the city centre, in St Anne's House at 23-24 Woodquay. Around the corner in St Vincent's Ave is the IHO *Salmon Weir Hostel* (☎ 561133). Beds are IR£6.50 to IR£8.50, and the three private doubles cost IR£20 to IR£22.

On the other side of the river, the independent *Arch View Hostel* (☎ 586661), with 60 beds at IR£5 to IR£6, is hidden away at the junction of Upper and Lower Dominick Sts, west of Wolfe Tone Bridge. Close by, on the other side of the canal, is the IHO *Galway City Hostel* (☎ 566367) at 25-27 Lower Dominick St, with beds for IR£6 to IR£10. There are no doubles.

If you continue north-west from Upper Dominick St through the name changes Henry St and St Helen's St then turn left (south) onto St Mary's Rd, you'll come to An Óige's huge 200-bed *Galway International Youth Hostel* (☎ 527411). This is a summer hostel in St Mary's College, open late June to late August only. It's between central Galway and Salthill, and you can reach it on bus No 1 from Eyre Square. It costs IR£8.50, including a light breakfast, and also has family rooms.

In Salthill, the independent *Grand Holiday Hostel* (☎ 521150) is on the promenade and has rooms with four or six beds from IR£6.50 a night; private rooms cost IR£9. *Stella Maris* (☎ 521950), 151 Upper Salthill Rd, a member of both the IHH and IHO, costs IR£6.50 to IR£7.50 for a bed and IR£7.50 to IR£10 for a private room. The independent *Mary Ryan Hostel* (☎ 523303) is at 4 Beechmount Ave, Highfield Park, beyond Salthill to the south of the centre. It's about a 20-minute walk from the centre, or you could take bus No 2 from Eyre Square to Taylor Hill Convent. Mary Ryan Hostel has twin rooms only (IR£7.50 per person) and opens mid-June to mid-September. Ring before heading out to make sure there are rooms available.

B&Bs

In summer you may have to travel to the suburbs. There are not many B&Bs around the city centre, but it's worth trying Mrs Sexton's *St Martin's B&B* (☎ 568286), 2 Nuns Island Rd, which is delightfully situated right on the Corrib. The friendliness of the owners and proximity to the sights, restaurants and pubs in the centre put it head and shoulders above everything else in Galway. Expect to pay IR£15 to IR£18 per person for B&B accommodation in Galway.

There are plenty of places less than 10 minutes' walk away on Newcastle Rd, which runs parallel to the river to the west in a north-south direction, becoming the N59 to Clifden. *Villa Nova* (☎ 524849), 40 Lower Newcastle Rd, charges from IR£28 to IR£36 for doubles while the *Newcastle Lodge* (☎ 527888), at No 28, is more expensive at IR£27/34 for singles/doubles. At 4 Greenfields Rd is *Edelweiss* (☎ 524501), with singles/doubles for IR£18/32.

Salthill and adjacent Renmore are good hunting grounds for B&Bs; Upper and Lower Salthill Rds are packed with places. Particularly good B&Bs include *Norman Villa* (☎ 521131) at 86 Lower Salthill Rd for IR£31/46. *Devondell* (☎ 523617) is down a cul-de-sac at 47 Devon Park, Lower Salthill Rd. Singles/doubles here are IR£22/34. *Roncalli House* (☎ 584159), 24 Whitestrand Ave, Lower Salthill, has been recommended

by readers and charges IR£16 per person. It opens all year.

Along Upper Salthill Rd try *Mandalay by the Sea* (☎ 524177), 10 Gentian Hill, which costs from IR£18/28. Also in Gentian Hill is *Bay View House* (☎ 522116) in a cul-de-sac, which costs IR£21/32. *Clare Villa* (☎ 522520), 38 Threadneedle St near the water, charges IR£22/34 while Mrs Lally's *Bayview* (☎ 526008), off Threadneedle St at 20 Seamount, costs from IR£20/32.

Hotels

The charming *Spanish Arch* (☎ 569191), with 20 rooms on Quay St, costs from IR£40 to IR£65 per person, depending on the season. Just south on Quay St and overlooking the river and Wolfe Tone Bridge, the huge *Jury's Galway Inn* (☎ 566444), with 128 rooms, has a flat room rate of IR£70 to IR£85, depending on the season.

The sumptuous 114-room *Great Southern* (☎ 564041), Galway's 'face' hotel and taking up one complete side of Eyre Square, charges IR£106 to IR£120 per room.

PLACES TO EAT
Cafés & Takeaways

Hungry Grass on Upper Cross St has baguette sandwiches from IR£1.75 and lots of other possibilities, including salads for less than IR£4. A few doors down in the historic Slate House dating from 1615, *Busker Brownes* is a popular, almost 24-hour café and eatery with sandwiches and excellent seafood chowder (IR£2.25). *Food for Thought* is a wholefood (though it also serves chicken and fish) lunchtime possibility at Lower Abbeygate St, with sandwiches/main courses from IR£1.50/2.50. Another good choice is *Café Uí Néill* on Lower Cross St with lots of salads and a wholemeal breakfast for IR£4.

Couch Potatoes, on Upper Abbeygate St next to Brannagan's restaurant, is an appropriate place for a bite in this tuber-devouring land; spuds with a multiple of various fillings cost around IR£3.95, and Couch opens daily from noon to 9 or 10 pm. Nobody does fish & chips (from IR£3.95) better than *Conlons* on Eglinton St. It has a takeaway branch with a few tables on the same street a few doors to the west.

Macken's Café is in the Cornstore on Middle St, while *Sails*, a popular self-service restaurant, is in the Eyre Square Centre. *One World* (☎ 569012), a cyber-café at 3 Francis St, has soups/pasta for IR£1.95/4.75 – and lots of computers to log on to.

The choice isn't so good on the other side of the river, but the *Left Bank Café* (it's actually the right bank but we're not telling) on Lower Dominick St is another good sandwich place and open daily 8 am to 7 or 8 pm. For late-night eats, a good bet farther down on Upper Dominick St is the *Kebab House*.

Restaurants & Pubs

The Quay St area is awash with restaurants, but finding a quiet one can be difficult. *Sev'nth Heav'n*, beside the Druid Theatre on the corner of Courthouse Lane and Flood St, is an excellent place for pasta (around IR£3.95) and good vegetarian dishes. *Fat Freddy's* in the Halls on Quay St has a similar menu (pizzas from under IR£4) and likewise is popular. Two similar places are *Pasta Mista* on Quay St, with pasta and pizza for around IR£5 and Italian main courses from IR£10.50, and the *Brasserie*, 19 Middle St, with pizza and a great salad bar (IR£2.95).

McDonagh's, on Quay St, a Galway fixture for years, is excellent for seafood; be sure to try the 'wild' local mussels. *Quay West* (☎ 563015), diagonally opposite the hostel at 9 Quay St, is relatively trendy as it's name would imply and has a IR£14.75 set dinner. The very popular *Pierre Victoire* (☎ 566066) chain of French bistros has a branch at 8 Quay St and its usual three-course dinner for IR£9.90. *Brannagan's*, 36 Upper Abbeygate St, claims to serve 'Italian, French, Cajun, Mexican and Oriental food' with main courses from IR£6.95 (unless you want the alligator tail in Creole sauce, which costs IR£13). It's open every day from 5 pm.

On the other side of the Corrib *Le Graal*, 13 Lower Dominick St, is a charming choice for lunch or dinner, with mains from IR£6.95, including nightly vegetarian and fish specials. *An Chistin* ('the kitchen') on West William St has an all-day Irish breakfast for IR£3 and student menus for under IR£2.

Two Indian restaurants worth trying are the long-established *Shama* (☎ 566696) on Flood St, with tandoori and balti specialities from IR£7.50, and the new kid on the block, *Tulsi* (☎ 564831), which is tucked away in Buttermilk Lane off Middle St. For Chinese food there's the vegetarian-friendly *Fan Sune* on Mary St, with lots of meatless choices from around IR£6.50, or the *Lotus Inn* near the Spanish Arch just off Flood St, which serves lunch and dinner daily till 11.30 pm. Close to the latter and facing Flood St, *Hooker Jimmy's* (☎ 568351) is a seafood bar/restaurant, with a half-dozen Galway oysters costing IR£4.75 and fish main courses from around IR£10.95.

Galway's most astonishing restaurant – in every sense – is *Kirwan's Lane Creative Cuisine* (☎ 568266) at the end of Kirwan's Lane, the oldest street in the city. It's a place that could happily sit in the most stylish areas of New York or London and has the prices to match: appetisers/main courses start at IR£4.95/12.95, though there's an excellent-value lunch for IR£6.95.

One of the best restaurants in the country is *Drimcong House* (☎ 555115), 14km along the Clifden road (N59) past Moycullen. It cannot be recommended highly enough and has a very reasonable (for its bracket) set menu for around IR£20, including vegetarian choices. It opens daily for dinner 6.30 to 10.30 pm but closes late December to March.

ENTERTAINMENT
Pubs

The *Galway Edge*, with complete listings of what's on in Galway and surrounds and published on Thursday, is available free from the tourist office and other venues around town. The monthly *Tin Drum*, Galway's new independent magazine, takes a less commercial approach.

There's lots going on in Galway's pubs. At 17 Upper Cross St is the cosy, 100-year-old *O'Neachtain's*, which has a truly fabulous atmosphere and can attract a somewhat flamboyant crowd. Farther north on High St, the *King's Head* has music most nights in summer. The enormously popular *Taafes* is a music and sports bar almost next door. *McSwiggan's* on Daly's Place at the start of Eyre St is big and busy. The *Quays* on Quay St draws a great crowd at weekends and in summer. *Lisheen* at 5 Bridge St is one of the better traditional-music venues on this side of the Corrib.

There are some flashier but less atmospheric pubs around Eyre Square, including *O'Flaherty's* in the Great Southern Hotel on the square itself, *An Púcán* just off the square at 11 Forster St (music most nights) and *Rabbitt's Bar* at No 23 of the same street.

Across the river the choice spot for traditional music (and set dancing on Tuesday) is *Monroe's Tavern* on the corner of Upper Dominick and Fairhill Sts. The *Róisín Dubh* ('black rose') opposite on Upper Dominick St is good for alternative music. *Taylor's Bar* next door and, round the corner on Sea Rd, the *Claddagh Ring* and *Crane's Bar*, all have music. *The Blue Note*, 3 West William St, has live jazz and rock a few nights each week.

Theatre

Galway has three (or maybe four) good theatres. The long-established *Druid Theatre* (☎ 568617) on Courthouse Lane is famed for its experimental works while the new *Town Hall Theatre* (☎ 569777), in Courthouse Square just off St Vincent's Ave, is more middle-of-the-road. The most important theatre in Galway – but not of much interest to most travellers – is *An Taibhdhearc na Gaillimhe* (The Galway Theatre; ☎ 562024) on Middle St, which stages plays in Irish. The once celebrated *Punchbag Theatre* (☎ 565422) near the river is more of a club these days but may still put on the odd performance.

THINGS TO BUY

The purchase of choice for most visitors to Galway is a Claddagh ring in silver or gold. Price them at one of the many jewellery shops in the town centre, such as Fallers

(☎ 561226) on Williamsgate St. The Design Concourse Ireland (☎ 566927) on Kirwan's Lane is a wonderful place to look around; it displays (and sells) the cutting edge in Irish design – from furniture and tableware to high fashion in Donegal tweed (no less) – from all 32 Irish counties.

Mulligan Records (☎ 564961), 5 Middle St, is where you want to go if you're an aficionado of traditional Irish music. They do mail order. One of the better places around for outdoor gear like hiking boots and backpacks is Trek & Trail (☎ 568810), 15 Mainguard St.

The Eyre Square Centre is a big shopping centre right off Eyre Square by the tourist office. They've cunningly incorporated a reconstructed stretch of the old city wall in this modern centre. Other shopping centres are Bridge Mills, in an old mill building right by the river, and the Cornstore on Middle St.

Just outside town, the Royal Tara China factory (☎ 751301) at Mervue is worth a look. Take the N6 Dublin Rd and take the first left after Ryan's Hotel. The Galway Irish Crystal Heritage Centre (☎ 757311) at Merlin Park, a bit farther along the N6, will meet all your needs in the stemware department. If you're interested in how the local marble is worked, head for the factory and showroom of Connemara Marble Industries (☎ 555102) in Moycullen, 13km north-west of Galway on the N59.

GETTING THERE & AWAY
Air

Galway airport (☎ 755569) is in Carnmore, 10km east of the city. Take the main Dublin road to Oranmore and turn north, then watch out for the signs to the airport. A taxi to or from the airport costs IR£10 to IR£12. There are two Aer Lingus flights each day to and from Dublin. A bus runs once a day (IR£2.50) between the airport and Galway bus station.

Bus

The bus station (☎ 562000) is behind the Great Southern Hotel on Eyre Square and next to the railway station. There are regular

Bus Éireann services from Galway to all major cities in the Republic and the North – and points in between – and a lot of private companies are also represented.

Feda O'Donnell Coaches (☎ 761656) runs a service between Crolly, County Donegal, and Galway via Donegal and Sligo twice a day Monday to Saturday, with three buses on Friday and Sunday. The buses depart from in front of the cathedral except the last bus on Sunday (8 pm), which leaves from Eyre Square.

Nestor Travel (☎ 797144) runs between four and seven buses a day to Dublin via Dublin Airport. The first bus leaves Eyre Square at 7.40 am (8 am on Sunday), the last at 6 pm. The stop in Dublin is at the Tara St DART Station on George's Quay.

Edward Walsh Coach Operators (☎ 098-35165 in Westport) has a bus from Eyre Square to Westport on Sunday at 5.10 pm. McNulty Coaches (☎ 097-81016 in Belmullet) leave Eyre Square for Belmullet via Westport and Newport on Friday at 4, 5.30 and 6 pm.

Michael Nee Coaches (☎ 095-51082 in Clifden) runs private buses between Galway and Clifden in summer. June to September there are two daily expresses from Foster St in Galway to Clifden (three on Friday and Sunday), and the same number leave the Square in Clifden for Galway.

Train

From Ceannt railway station (☎ 564222) there are up to five trains to and from Dublin (2½ hours), Monday to Saturday, and four on Sunday. Connections with other train routes can be made at Athlone (one hour).

GETTING AROUND

You can walk to most everything in Galway and even out to Salthill, but there are regular buses from Eyre Square. Bus No 1 runs from Eyre Square to Salthill and sometimes on to Blackrock; bus No 2 goes from Knocknacarra and Blackrock through Eyre Square to Renmore; bus No 3 runs between Eyre Square and Castlepark and bus No 4 goes to Newcastle.

Drivers will need parking discs for parking on the street; these are available from newsagents. The car park just over O'Brien Bridge is next to the garda station, so it should be safe.

Taxi

Galway Taxi (☎ 561111) is on Mainguard St, Corrib & Apollo Cabs (☎ 564444) is on Eyre St north off Eglinton St, and there are also a couple of big taxi ranks on Eyre Square.

Bicycle

Most of the hostels, including Kinlay House, Salmon Weir, Stella Maris and Galway City, rent bikes. Chieftain Cycle Hire (☎ 561600), next to the tourist office on Merchants Road, and Celtic Cycles (☎ 566606) on Queen St rent bikes for IR£7/30 a day/week. On the west side of the river is Flaherty's Cycles (☎ 589230) on West William St.

South of Galway

Many visitors pass through the small area of County Galway south of the city on their way to or from the spectacular limestone Burren in County Clare. But there are many places worth visiting in the area, including the tranquil monastic settlement and round tower at Kilmacduagh.

CLARINBRIDGE & KILCOLGAN

Some 16km south of Galway, Clarinbridge and Kilcolgan are the focus for Galway's famous Clarinbridge Oyster Festival held during the second weekend in September. *Paddy Burke's Oyster Inn* (☎ 091-796107) in Clarinbridge is an old-fashioned place famous for its association with the festival. It's open daily for lunch and dinner till 10.30 pm, and a dozen oysters costs IR£10. A little farther south, signposted off the road in Kilcolgan, is *Moran's Oyster Cottage* (☎ 091-976113), a wonderful thatched pub and restaurant overlooking narrow Dunbulcaun Bay, where the famous Galway oysters are reared. During the festival, the world oyster-opening championships are held at Moran's.

Getting There & Away

Clarinbridge is on the main Galway to Gort, Ennis and Limerick road (N18) and is served by numerous Bus Éireann buses from Galway. Kilcolgan is also on the main road, and Moran's pub is about 1.5km to the west.

KINVARA

Kinvara is a delightful village tucked away on the south-east corner of Galway Bay. A small stone harbour is home to a number of the traditional sailing boats called Galway hookers. Kinvara is a quaint, relatively quiet spot and doesn't attract anything like the numbers of visitors that Ballyvaughan, 24km to the west, does. A few km west of Kinvara, you come to County Clare and the start of the Burren limestone region.

Dunguaire Castle

Dunguaire Castle is north of Kinvara on the shore and was erected around 1520 by the O'Hynes. It later passed into the hands of Oliver St John Gogarty (1878-1957), poet, writer, surgeon, Irish Free State senator and 'the wildest wit in Dublin'. The castle is supposedly built on the site of the 6th century royal palace of Guaire Aidhne, king of Connaught.

The castle is in excellent condition, and the displays on each floor are dedicated to a particular period in its history, right down to the last mildly eccentric owner, who lived here through the 1960s. It has a gift shop, guided tours, as well as medieval banquets (☎ 091-37108, or 061-360788 in Shannon), held at 5.30 and 8.45 pm daily May to September, though they're on a more intimate scale than the ones at Bunratty Castle near Shannon in County Clare and slightly cheaper at IR£29 per person. Just south of Dunguaire is a bare stone arch, the only remains of an older castle.

Dunguaire Castle opens daily mid-April to September 9.30 am to 5.30 pm. Entry is IR£2.50/1.40/1.30.

Special Events

Every August the village hosts the Cruinniú na mBáid ('gathering of the boats') festival in celebration of the Galway hookers.

Places to Stay & Eat

The IHH *Johnston's Hostel* (☎ 091-637164) is on Main St, open June to September only. Dorm beds are IR£6, a double IR£24, and there's a small campsite.

Six km to the north-west and signposted off the main road to Ballyvaughan (N67) is An Óige's *Doorus House* (☎ 091-637512). The hostel building was once owned by a count called Floribund de Basterot, who entertained such notables as WB Yeats, Lady Augusta Gregory, Douglas Hyde and Guy de Maupassant here. Yeats and Lady Gregory are said to have first mooted the idea of the Abbey Theatre in Dublin while visiting Doorus House. It's a good base for exploring the Burren and opens all year. Beds are IR£4.50 to IR£5 for those under 18 and IR£5.50 to IR£6.50 for everyone else.

Many B&Bs are scattered around the Doorus Peninsula, including *Burren View Farm* (☎ 091-637142), which charges IR£14 to IR£16 per person and opens April to October. Three km north of Kinvara is *Clareview House* (☎ 091-637170), with singles/doubles for IR£22/34 and open the same months.

The excellent little *Café on the Quay*, overlooking the harbour, has snacks and light meals available all day. *Partners* on Main St serves seafood meals and snacks and is pleasant enough.

Getting There & Away

From late May to late September, one Bus Éireann route serves Galway, Kinvara, Ballyvaughan, Lisdoonvarna, Doolin, the Cliffs of Moher, Lahinch, Miltown Malbay, Doonbeg, Kilkee, Kilrush, Tralee and Cork. The bus runs three or four times a day Monday to Saturday and twice on Sunday.

Another route serves the Burren coast, running to and from Galway via Kinvara, Ballyvaughan, Blackhead, Fanore, Lisdoonvarna and Doolin. There are usually three or four buses Monday to Saturday (two on Sunday) from late June to late September. The rest of the year, the service runs only once a day Monday to Saturday. For more details contact the Galway bus station (☎ 091-562000).

GORT, COOLE PARK & KILMACDUAGH

In Gort, 37km south-east of Galway and just off the N18, a 16th century Norman tower known as **Thoor Ballylee** (☎ 091-631436) was the summer home of Yeats from 1922. It opens daily May to September 10 am to 6 pm. Admission is IR£3/2.50/1 for adults/students/children.

About 5km to the north of Gort is Coole Park (☎ 091-631804). It was the home of Lady Augusta Gregory, co-founder of the Abbey Theatre and patron of Yeats; the exhibition focuses on the literary importance of the house and the natural history of the surrounding reserve. Coole Park is an OPW site and opens daily mid-June to August 9.30 am to 6.30 pm; mid-April to mid-June and in September it's closed Monday and the hours are 10 am to 5 pm. Admission is IR£2/1.

Five km south-west of Gort is the extensive monastic site of Kilmacduagh. Beside a small lake is a well preserved round tower, the remains of a small 14th century cathedral (Teampall Mór MacDuagh), an oratory dedicated to St John the Baptist and various other little chapels. The original monastery is thought to have been founded by St Colman MacDuagh at the beginning of the 7th century, and such was its importance that it became the focus for a new diocese in the 12th century. St MacDuagh founded the monastery under the patronage of King Guaire Aidhne of Connaught, who gave his name to Dunguaire Castle in Kinvara. The round tower is 34m tall and leans some 60cm from the perpendicular. The doorway is 8m above ground level. There are fine views over the Burren from here.

Connemara

Connemara (Conamara) is the wild and barren region north-west of the city of Galway. It's a stunning patchwork of bogs, lonely valleys, pale grey mountains and small lakes that shimmer when the sun shines. Its devotees – Irish, French, Americans, Germans – buy up remote cottages as holiday homes or spend a small fortune on a week's holiday in a castle hotel during the salmon-fishing season.

Connemara is not a distinct geographical region like the Burren. At its heart are the Maumturk Mountains and the grey, quartzite peaks of the Twelve Bens (or Pins), which offer some tremendous hill walking. They look south over a plain dotted with lakes and run southwards into the sea around Carna and Roundstone in a maze of rocky islands, tortuous inlets and sparkling white beaches. The coastal road west of Spiddal (R336) eventually enters this maze, and it's well worth losing yourself for a day around Carraroe, Roundstone, Lettermullan and Lettermore islands and Ballyconneely Bay. Pink Galway granite is the predominant rock in this lower country, while the mountains and northern part of the region are made of a mixture of quartzite, gneiss, schist and greenish marble. However, the best scenery is in the middle of the region. The journey from Maam Cross north-west to Leenane

Teampall Mór MacDuagh at Kilmacduagh

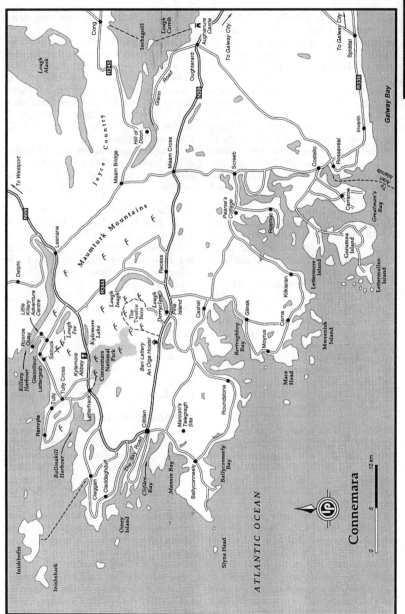

Connemara

0   5   10 km

(R336) or north-east to Cong (R345) takes you through Joyce Country, a stunning mountainous region. The trip up the Lough Inagh Valley past the Twelve Bens and around Kylemore Lake would be difficult to surpass anywhere in the country.

One of the most important Gaeltachtaí in the country begins just west of Galway around Barna and stretches westward through Spiddal and Inverin, and along much of the coast as far as Cashel. Ireland's national Irish-language radio station, Radio na Gaeltachta, is based at Costello and does much to sustain the language. The Irish-language weekly newspaper *Foinse* ('source'), is published in Spiddal.

Heading west from Galway you have two options: the coast road (R336) through Salthill, Barna and Spiddal, or the inland route (N59) through Oughterard, which leads directly to the heart of wild and beautiful Connemara.

The excellent *Connemara: A Map & Gazeteer* (IR£12) by Tim Robinson and published by Folding Landscape Maps is a must if you intend any detailed exploration. Their *Connemara: A Hill Walker's Guide* by Robinson and Joss Lynam is also invaluable. A series of five brochures in several languages called *Cósta Chonamara* that outline walks and treks in the area are available at the Galway and Salthill tourist offices as well as the Island Ferries office in Rossaveal.

GETTING THERE & AWAY

There are numerous Bus Éireann services serving most parts of Connemara, many of which originate in Galway, so check with the bus station (☎ 091-562000) there for times and fares. Services can be very sporadic, and many only operate in summer.

One service runs between Galway, Oughterard, Maam Cross, Recess, Roundstone, Ballyconneely and on to Clifden five times a day (twice on Sunday) mid-June to August; usually one of the buses on this service also carries on from Clifden to Kylemore, Leenane and Westport. At other times of the year this service runs only once a day from Galway to Clifden via Maam

Cross and Leenane but does not make all the above stops.

Galway, Cong, Leenane and Clifden are connected by an infrequent service Monday to Saturday only. Another runs between Galway, Spiddal, Inverin, Rossaveal, Carraroe, Lettermore and Lettermullen islands. Monday to Saturday year round one bus a day runs between Galway, Oughterard, Maam Cross, Rosmuc, Recess, Glinsk, Carna and Moyrus.

Many road signs in this area are posted only in Irish. See the Place Names Appendix at the back of this book for their English equivalents.

SPIDDAL

Just 17km from Galway, Spiddal (An Spidéal) is a lively little roadside settlement with some good pubs. East of the village is the Irish-language Coláiste Chonnacht (Connaught College; ☎ 091-553383), founded in 1910, and Standún (☎ 091-553108), a massive craft shop that also operates a bureau de change (open Monday to Saturday 9.30 am to 6.30 pm; closed January and February). Nearby, in front of the large Spiddal Craft Centre, is a good beach, which can get crowded during summer. If you're looking for open landscapes and wild coastlines, leave Spiddal behind and head west towards Roundstone.

SPIDDAL TO ROUNDSTONE

West of Spiddal, the scenery gets more dramatic and at Costello (Casla) you can turn west off the main road for Carraroe (An Cheathrú Rua) and into a maze of inlets and islands. Before Costello, you'll notice the signs for Rossaveal (Ros a' Mhíl), the main departure point for ferries to the Aran Islands. It's well worth heading out to Carraroe and back across a series of rugged islands, all connected to the mainland. **Carraroe** is famous for its fine beaches, including the Coral Strand, which is composed entirely of shell and coral fragments. Equally well known is the University College Galway's Irish Language Centre (☎ 091-595101), or Áras Mháirtín Uí

County Clare
Top: Cliffs of Moher
Middle: Ennis Abbey, Ennis
Bottom: Turlough (Temporary Lake), The Burren

MARK DAFFEY

MARK DAFFEY

MARK DAFFEY

County Galway & County Mayo
Top Left: Doolough Pass Road, Mweelrea Mountain, County Mayo
Top Right: Fly fishing, Eriff River, County Mayo
Bottom: Kylemore Abbey, Connemara, County Galway

Chadhain, which offers one/two week courses in the Irish language for IR£150/250 plus board of IR£17 to IR£26 per person a day. **Lettermore**, **Gorumna** and **Letter-mullen** islands are low and bleak, with a handful of farmers eking out an existence from tiny, rocky fields. Fish farming has become big business, and there are salmon cages floating in some of the bays.

From Screeb (Scriob) you can head up to Maam Cross or continue along the coast down to **Carna**, a small fishing village with a marine biology research station nearby. From Carna there are some good walks out to **Mweenish Island** or north to **Moyrus** and out to **Mace Head**. Back on the coast road, it's a lovely journey back up to Cashel and south again to Roundstone. There's a pleasant walk from Roundstone to the top of Mt Errisbeg (298m); just follow the small road past O'Dowd's pub in the centre of the village.

Cashel Equestrian Centre (☎ 095-31082), about 1.5km west of the centre of Cashel, has horses and Connemara ponies for hire and gives riding lessons.

Pearse's Cottage

Patrick Pearse (1879-1916) was one of the leaders of the Gaelic revival and in 1908 he founded the bilingual School of St Enda (Scoil Éanna) in Dublin. He was the least political of the 1916 rebels, being heavily imbued with an almost religious need for blood sacrifice, but nevertheless was the commander-in-chief of the insurgents and was named president of the provisional government. After the revolt he was executed by the British. He wrote some of his short stories and plays in this cottage, which is also called by its Irish name, Teach an Phiarsaigh.

Admission to the OPW cottage (☎ 091-574292) is IR£1/40p, and it opens mid-June to mid-September 9.30 am to 6.30 daily. It's near Gortmore, west of Screeb, on the R340.

Places to Stay

Camping *Spiddal Caravan & Camping Park* (also signposted as Pairc Saoire an Spidéil in Irish) is on the R336 coastal road

1.5km west of Spiddal. See Places to Stay in the Galway section for details. *Carraroe Caravan & Camping Park* (☎ 091-595266) is 1km south of Carraroe on the R343. It costs IR£5/5.50 to pitch a small/large tent and adults pay IR£1.50 each.

Hostels An Óige's *Inverin Hostel* (☎ 091-593154), by the R336 just west of Inverin, has 50 beds costing IR£4.50/5.50 or IR£5/6.50 for juniors/seniors, depending on the season, and there are bikes for hire. A bed at the IHO *Connemara Tourist Hostel* (☎ 091-593104) in Inverin costs from IR£5.50 to IR£6.50. Both hostels are open all year.

B&Bs & Hotels There are plenty of B&Bs along the road. One that has been recommended as a relaxing place is *Col Mar House* (☎ 091-553247), 2km west of Spiddal, and costing from IR£16 per person.

There are some exclusive hotels tucked away out here; they're also good places to stop for a sandwich, drink or meal if you can rise to their prices. The lovely *Ballynahinch Castle Hotel* (☎ 095-31006), south-west of Recess with 28 rooms, was formerly the home of Humanity Dick (1754-1834), a local landlord, MP and one of the chief forces behind the Royal Society for the Prevention of Cruelty to Animals (RSPCA). Bally-nahinch Castle is well worth a visit even if it's just for a drink in the bar and a quick scout around the delightful grounds. B&B is IR£63/92 or IR£77/120 for a single/double, depending on the season.

Near Cashel, the 19-room *Zetland Country House Hotel* (☎ 095-31111) has B&B for IR£82/134, while the *Cashel House Hotel* (☎ 095-31001), with 32 rooms, charges IR£49/98 or, April to September, IR£71/142. It has a stable of Connemara ponies, and riding lessons are available.

The 22-room *Carraroe Hotel* (☎ 091-595116) – also called Óstán An Cheathrú Rua – is a bit more down to earth, with singles/doubles from IR£40/70.

ROUNDSTONE

The small fishing village of Roundstone (Cloch na Rón) is 16km south-west of Recess on a western extension of Bertraghboy Bay. Looming behind the neat stone harbour is Errisbeg; at 298m, it's the only significant hill along this section of coastline. From the summit there are wonderful views across the bay to the distant humps of the Twelve Bens.

The village itself consists essentially of one main street of tall houses, shops and a couple of pubs overlooking the water. The small harbour is home to lobster boats and many a currach *(cúrach* in Irish), the featherweight rowing boat of black tar on hide or canvas laid over a wicker frame. At the head of the pier is the home of Tim Robinson, the man behind Folding Landscape Maps, attractive and informative maps of the Burren, the Aran Islands and Connemara that you will see for sale everywhere.

Just south of the village is an Industrial Development Agency (IDA) craft complex with various small factory shops selling everything from teapots to sweaters. One of the more interesting shops is Roundstone Musical Instruments (☎ 095-35808), which makes and sells the *bodhrán*, the goatskin drum beloved of traditional Irish musicians, as well as tin whistles, harps and Irish flutes. It opens year round Monday to Saturday 9 am to 7 pm and has a branch open April to September in Clifden. Farther south and off the road to Ballyconneely (R341) are the magnificent white beaches of Gorteen (or Gurteen) Bay and Dog's Bay.

Places to Stay & Eat

Gurteen Beach Caravan & Camping Park (☎ 095-35882) is 2km west of town near the beach and charges IR£7 a night for two people. For B&B, Mrs Lowry's excellent *St Joseph's* (☎ 095-35865) on Main St overlooking the harbour, costs IR£16 per person; it's almost worth coming to Roundstone just to stay at this friendly place, and they do an excellent evening meal for IR£11 in summer. *Roundstone House* (☎ 095-35864), a 13-room hotel on Main St, has good views over

the bay to Connemara and costs IR£64 to IR£78 for a double.

O'Dowd's Pub on Main St has good food in the bar and a restaurant with excellent oysters. Nearby *Beola Restaurant* (☎ 095-35871) serves seafood in the IR£12 range. They are open for lunch and dinner. There's a nice coffee shop in the *IDA Craft Park* just outside the village, open all day.

AROUND ROUNDSTONE

Some 12km west of Roundstone is **Ballyconneely**. If you detour south off the Clifden road (R341) towards the Connemara Golf Club, you pass the ruins of **Bunowen Castle** before reaching the shore at **Trá Mhóir** ('great beach'), a superb expanse of impossibly white sand.

OUGHTERARD

The small town of Oughterard, 27km along the main road from Galway to Clifden, calls itself the 'Gateway to Connemara'. And sure enough, just west of town, the countryside opens to sweeping panoramas of lakes, mountain and bog that get more spectacular the farther west you travel.

Oughterard (Uachtar Árd) itself is a pleasant little town and one of Ireland's principal angling centres. It has a number of good cafés, pubs, and restaurants as well as some fairly exclusive country house establishments hidden in the surrounding countryside.

The focus of the anglers' attention is Lough Corrib, just north of town. Nearby attractions include Aughanure Castle to the south-east and the lovely drive along the Glann Rd by Lough Corrib to a vantage point overlooking the Hill of Doon.

The telephone code is ☎ 091.

Information

The extremely helpful local tourist office (☎ 552808) on Main St opens April to September 9 am to 6 or 8 pm. During the rest of the year it opens on weekdays only 9 am to 5.30 pm.

There's an Allied Irish Bank on Main St next to Holland's supermarket, a Bank of

Ireland branch on Bridge St, and bureaux de change at Fuschia Crafts on Main St and Keogh & Sons Sweaters on the Square. The post office is on Main St next to the Mace supermarket. The Corrib Laundrette is on Bridge St just before the Corrib House Hotel.

Aughanure Castle

Three km east of Oughterard and off the main Galway road (N59) is the 16th century O'Flaherty fortress, Aughanure Castle, built on the site of earlier structures. The clan controlled the region for hundreds of years after they fought off the Normans, and the 'fighting O'Flahertys' were constantly at odds with the forces of Galway. The six-storey tower house stands on a rocky outcrop overlooking Lough Corrib and has been extensively restored. Surrounding the castle are the remains of an unusual double bawn or perimeter fortification. Underneath the castle, the lake washes through a number of natural caverns and caves.

The castle (☎ 552214), run by the OPW, opens daily mid-June to mid-September 9.30 am to 6.30 pm, and the entrance fee is IR£2/1.

Places to Stay

Hostels *Canrawer House Hostel* (☎ 552388) is at the Clifden end of town, just over 1km down a signposted turning. The bunk beds are IR£7.50 (IR£9.50 B&B), five regular beds with their own bathroom are IR£8.50, and the one double room ensuite is IR£18. Camping is IR£5. The kitchen is big, and boats can be hired.

The IHH *Lough Corrib Hostel* (☎ 552866) is on Camp St. From the centre of town, turn north for the Hill of Doon drive, and it's about 200m along on the left. They have two-person Canadian-style canoes for hire at IR£10 for half a day as well as bikes. There are tent sites and boat trips to Inchagoill Island in Lough Corrib. Beds are IR£6 to IR£7 and the two doubles cost IR£16.

B&Bs There are legions of B&Bs around Oughterard, but not many right in town. One

of the few is the *Jolly Lodger* (☎ 552682) on Bridge St with singles/doubles for IR£20/32. *Woodlawn House* (☎ 550198) in Doon, Rosscahill, on the Galway side of Oughterard, does B&B from IR£20/29. Farther east of Oughterard and travelling towards Portacarron and the lake, you'll see plenty of signposts.

If you turn north at the main crossroads in Oughterard and travel 5km along Glann Rd towards the Hill of Doon, you come to the excellent *Glann House* (☎ 552127), charging from IR£20/30.

Hotels The *Corrib House Hotel* (☎ 552329) on Bridge St is a comfortable old hotel with 26 rooms from IR£25 to IR£35 per person. *Currarevagh House* (☎ 552312), at least one of the authors' favourite hotel in Ireland, is a 19th century mansion just outside Oughterard on the shore of Lough Corrib and renowned for its exquisite evening meals (IR£19.50) and quality accommodation. Singles/doubles are from IR£45/90, and it's open April to mid-October. It's difficult to think of a more romantic place anywhere.

Places to Eat

On Main St, *Corrib County* is an excellent low to medium-priced restaurant with very good coffee, lunches and dinners. There's another cosy coffee shop-cum-restaurant, *O'Fatharta's*, farther east on Main St. For good pub food and meals, try the *Boat Inn* on the Square. *Keogh's Bar* on the Square also does reasonable pub food.

On Bridge St, the western extension of Main St, is the upmarket *Water Lily* right on the river. Also on Bridge St, the *Corrib House Hotel* does a good four-course dinner for around IR£13.95. Dinner at the *Lake Hotel* (☎ 552794) is IR£18.

Entertainment

The *Thatch Bar* on Main St often has music in summer as do *Faherty's* and the *Boat Inn* on the Square.

Getting Around

Bikes can be hired from Lough Corrib Hostel.

LOUGH CORRIB

The Republic's largest lake, Lough Corrib is over 48km long and covers some 200 sq km. It virtually cuts off western Galway from the rest of the country and has over 360 islands. The largest one, Inchagoill, has a monastic settlement and can be visited from Oughterard or Cong.

Lough Corrib is world-famous for its salmon, sea trout and brown trout, and the area attracts legions of anglers from all over the world in season. The highlight of the fishing year is the mayfly season, when zillions of the small lacy bugs hatch over a few days (usually in May) and drive the fish and anglers into a feeding and fishing frenzy. The hooks are baited with live flies, which join their cousins dancing on the surface of the lake. The main run of salmon does not begin until June. The owner of the Canrawer House Hostel is a good contact for information and boat hire. You can buy fishing supplies from Thomas Tuck (☎ 091-552335) on Main St in Oughterard.

Inchagoill Island

The largest island on Lough Corrib and some 7km north-west of Oughterard, Inchagoill is a lonely place hiding many ancient remains. Most fascinating is an obelisk called the **Lia Luguaedon Mac Menueh** ('stone of Luguaedon, son of Menueh') marking a burial site. It stands some 75cm tall near the Saints' Church, and some people claim that the Latin writing on the stone is the oldest Christian inscription in Europe apart from those in the catacombs in Rome. It certainly is the oldest Latin inscription in Ireland.

Teampall Phádraig (St Patrick's Church) is a small oratory of a very early design with some later additions. The prettiest church is the Romanesque **Teampall na Naoimh** (Saint's Church), probably built in the 9th or 10th centuries. There are carvings around the arched doorway.

The island can be reached by boat from Oughterard or from Cong in County Mayo. From May to October, Corrib Cruises (☎ 091-552644) sails from Oughterard to Inchagoill Island (IR£6) and on to Cong (IR£10). Departures are at 11 am and 2.45 and 5 pm.

MAAM CROSS TO LEENANE & DELPHI

West of Oughterard, Maam Cross (Crois Mám) is the first settlement along the road to Clifden (N59). *Peacockes* (☎ 091-552306) is a huge, touristy bar/shop/restaurant/petrol station, with a tacky model donkey and 'traditional' Irish cottage, by the turn-off for Leenane. The trip to Leenane is lovely, but if you have only one run through the region it's better to stay on the Clifden road and turn up north onto the R344 into the Lough Inagh Valley instead. It's also a nice journey south towards Screeb and the coast. *Tullaboy House* (☎ 091-552305) is an excellent farmhouse B&B 5km east of Maam Cross towards Oughterard on the N59. It costs from IR£18.50/27 for singles/doubles.

Leenane

Leenane's name in Irish, An Líonán, means 'ravine', referring to the way the sea edges its way into narrow, fjord-like Killary Harbour. Leenane itself makes a convenient stopover on the way north, and the road north-west to Louisburgh via Delphi is startlingly beautiful. Like nearby Cong, the village can boast a film connection, having been the location for *The Field*, which was shot in 1989 and based on a John B Keane poignant play about a tenant farmer's ill-fated plans to pass on a rented piece of land to his son. The dance and pub scenes were filmed in the village and the church scene at nearby Aasleagh. The village's name has also made it on the literary map with the runaway success in London of young dramatist Martin McDonagh's play *The Beauty Queen of Leenane*.

The **Sheep & Wool Museum** in the Leenane Cultural Centre (☎ 095-42323) focuses on the woollen industry and gives demonstrations of carding, spinning and weaving, with a 15-minute video every half hour that sets the historical and social scene. Locally made woollen garments are on sale. Admission is IR£2/1, and there's a coffee shop that serves dinner in the evening. There are several excellent walks from Leenane, including one to **Aasleagh Waterfall** at the eastern end of Killary Harbour.

The *Village Grill*, over the bridge and south of the centre, and the *Carraig Bar*, in the north-east corner of the harbour, are good choices for lunch or a snack.

Delphi

The Brownes of Westport were originally a Catholic family, but they converted to Protestantism in order to avoid the constraints of the penal laws. This allowed one of the family to be ennobled as the marquess of Sligo at the time of the Act of Union in 1801, and the 2nd marquess gave the unlikely name of Delphi to his fishing lodge in Galway. A friend of Byron, he had travelled in central Greece and returned home convinced that his fishing territory bore an uncanny resemblance to the area around Delphi.

At Delphi Lodge (☎ 095-42211) permits are available for fishing in the local waters, and the Delphi Adventure Centre (☎ 095-42246) has organised sports throughout the summer.

The IHH *Delphi Hostel* (☎ 095-42246), at the adventure centre and open July and August only, has beds from IR£6.50, four private rooms for IR£9 per person, camping space and bikes for hire. *Delphi Lodge* (☎ 095-42211), which caters to anglers, has accommodation from IR£35 to IR£55 per person.

RECESS & AROUND

Recess (Straith Salach) is nothing more than a few houses on the N59 between Clifden and Maam Cross. Turning north here brings you on a minor road through the wonderful Lough Inagh Valley. If you continue along the main road from Recess towards Clifden instead, there are some marvellous views over Lough Derryclare and Pine Island. The grassy layby overlooking the island is an excellent place to camp. About 1km west of here off the Clifden road is a dead-end road heading north into a great valley enclosed by a ring of six of the Twelve Bens. It's a beautiful drive up this road, and there's a challenging circuit hike of the six peaks.

Back on the main Clifden Rd and another 1km west is An Óige's *Ben Lettery Hostel* (☎ 095-51136). It's an excellent and popular base to explore the Twelve Bens and makes a good starting or finishing point for the walk mentioned previously. The hostel, open Easter to September, is 8km from Recess, 13km from Clifden. Beds are IR£4.50/5.50 or IR£5/6.50 for juniors/seniors, depending on the season.

Lough Inagh Valley

The journey north up the Lough Inagh Valley is one of the most scenic in the country. There are two fine approaches up valleys from the south, starting on either side of Recess, and the long sweep of Derryclare and Inagh loughs accompanies you for most of the way. On the west side are the brooding Bens, while just out of the valley on the north side is the picturesque drive along Kylemore Lake.

Half way up the Inagh Valley is the *Inagh Valley Lodge* (☎ 095-34706), an upmarket country house hotel with singles/doubles for IR£63/92 or IR£77/120, depending on the season. It's a worthwhile place to stop for a snack, particularly in good weather. The location is magnificent.

Towards the northern end of the valley, a track leads off the road west up a blind valley, which is also well worth exploring.

Kylemore Abbey & Lake

Just outside the northern end of the beautiful Inagh Valley is the almost equally scenic Kylemore Lake with its accompanying abbey. The road skirts the northern shore of the lake, winding through overhanging trees with magnificent views across the silent lake. South of the lake are the Twelve Bens and Connemara National Park, while the mountains behind the abbey are Dúchruach (530m) and Binn Fhraoigh (545m).

The lake passes under the road and extends to the north, where you will see the castellated towers of the 19th century neo-Gothic Kylemore Abbey among the trees. The abbey was built for a wealthy English businessman, Mitchell Henry, after he had spent his honeymoon in Connemara and had fallen in love with the region. During WWI, a group of Benedictine nuns left Ypres in Belgium and eventually set up in Kylemore, turning the place into an abbey.

Today, the nuns run an exclusive convent boarding school with some sections open to the public (April to October daily 9.30 am to 6 pm; November to March 10 am to 4 pm). There's also a craft shop and tearoom here. You can walk up behind the abbey to a statue overlooking Kylemore Lake. The abbey is 17km from Clifden.

CLIFDEN

Clifden (An Clochán), the capital of Connemara, is some 80km west of Galway at the head of narrow Clifden Bay. Astride the Owenglen River, the tightly packed houses and the needle-sharp spires of the town's churches are shadowed by the steep backdrop of the Twelve Bens to the east. A landlord, John D'Arcy, was the main force behind the establishment of the town around 1812, but the Famine ruined the family, and their estate along the Sky Rd is now deserted.

Information

The tourist office (☎ 095-21163) is at the bottom of Market St and opens mid-April to September. At other times enquire at the Clifden Walking Centre (☎ 095-21379) at Island House on Market St closer to the Square. There's a Bank of Ireland branch on Main St opposite Leo's Hotel. The post office is on Main St just up from the Square, where you'll also find a laundrette, the Shamrock Washeteria.

The telephone code is ☎ 095.

Activities

There are superb cycling possibilities, and if Map 31 in the Ordnance Survey Discovery Series is available at long last, this is all you

need to plan your tour of the area. Clifden Walking Centre runs guided walking trips to local geographical and natural-interest sites. A half-day walk is about IR£10, and longer ones are available. They also sell maps. See the following Around Clifden section for good local walks and cycle routes.

Errislannan Manor (☎ 21134), about 3.5km south on the Ballyconneely road (R341), has Connemara ponies for hire (IR£12 per hour) for riding along the beach and up into the hills. It opens Monday to Saturday.

Places to Stay

Camping & Hostels The IHH *Clifden Town Hostel* (☎ 21076) is in the centre of town on Market St and costs from IR£6 to IR£7 for a bed and IR£8 to IR£9 per person in one of three private rooms. *Leo's Hostel* (☎ 21429), belonging to both the IHH and IHO, is near the square; it costs IR£8 for a dorm bed in high season and also has camping space. The IHH/IHO *Brookside Hostel* (☎ 21812), down by the Owen Glin River in a quiet location on Hulk St, costs from IR£6 to IR£7 for a bed. All three hostels are open year round. There's another hostel in Cleggan to the north-west; see that section for details.

B&Bs & Hotels In town, *Kingston House* (☎ 21470) on Bridge St costs from IR£14 to IR£18 per person. Many B&Bs are to the south on the Ballyconneely road (R341). One km from Clifden and signposted off the road is *Mallmore House* (☎ 095-21460), with B&B for IR£17. *Actons* (☎ 44339), at Claddaghduff at the end of Sky Rd, has been warmly recommended. Singles/doubles are from IR£25/40.

Barry's Hotel (☎ 21287), with 18 rooms on Main St, charges from IR£35/56 summer while the 19-room *Alcock & Brown Hotel* (☎ 21206) in the town centre does B&B for IR£40/60. A better choice is *Foyle's* (☎ 21801), also on Main St. June to August its 28 rooms go for IR£62.50/85.

Places to Eat

My Tea Shop on Main St, two doors down

from Barry's Hotel, is a friendly, wholemeal café and serves meals for around IR£5.

For pub food, try *Mitchell's* on the Square. *EJ Kings* on the Square serves pub food all year round, with the entrance to its more formal restaurant round the corner on Market St. The food is good and reasonably priced. On Main St, the *D'Arcy Inn*, opposite Barry's Hotel, does similar fare with the accent on seafood; meals are under IR£10.

The *Salmon Leap Seafood Restaurant* three doors away has salmon main courses from IR£8.95. *O'Grady's Seafood Restaurant* (☎ 21450), on Market St and a sister restaurant of the highly recommended Kirwan's Lane Creative Cuisine in Galway, is one of the best restaurants in western County Galway and opens for lunch and dinner daily except Sunday till 10 pm. The cheaper *Fogerty's* (☎ 21427) on Market St is also worth trying.

Out at Claddaghduff on the road to Cleggan, the cliff-top *Acton's Restaurant* (☎ 095-44339) does good food, and exhilarating views of the Atlantic are thrown in for free. It's open late May to late September daily except Monday.

Things to Buy
Makers of the bodhrán, Roundstone Musical Instruments (☎ 21516) has a branch next to the Salmon Leap restaurant on Main St. It opens April to September.

Getting There & Away
The bus stop is outside Cullen's on Market St. For information phone the bus station in Galway (☎ 091-562000). Buses go between Galway and Clifden and Westport via Oughterard and Maam Cross or via Cong and Leenane. For more details, see the Getting There & Away section under Connemara.

Michael Nee Coaches (☎ 51082) runs private buses between Clifden and Galway in summer. From June to September there are two daily expresses from Foster St in Galway to Clifden (three on Friday and Sunday) and the same number leave the Square in Clifden for Galway. During the

same period, three daily buses (at 11.15 am, 1.35 and 5.45 pm) depart from Clifden for Cleggan, from where the ferry leaves for Inishbofin and Inishturk islands.

Getting Around
Mannions (☎ 21160/21155) Railway View, Clifden, hires out bicycles as does the Clifden Town and Leo's hostels.

AROUND CLIFDEN
The road south of Clifden (R341) passes the fine beach at **Mannin Bay** to **Ballyconneely**. Heading directly west from Clifden, the Sky Rd takes you on a loop out to a townland known as Kingston and back to Clifden through some rugged, stunningly beautiful coastal scenery. The round trip is about 12km and can easily be walked or cycled. The deeply indented coastline farther north brings you to the tiny village of **Claddaghduff**. Turning west here down by the Catholic church you come out on Omey Strand, and at low tide you can drive or walk across the sand to **Omey Island**, a low islet of rock, grass and sand with a few houses for the island's population of 20. During the summer there are horse races held on Omey Strand.

Back on the mainland to the north is Cleggan, the embarkation point for ferries to Inishbofin island.

CLEGGAN
Cleggan is a small fishing village 16km north-west of Clifden which many visitors pass through en route to Inishbofin Island. Boats also leave from here for Inishturk Island; for more details see that section in the Mayo & Sligo chapter.

There are a couple of B&Bs around Cleggan as well as the independent *Masters House Hostel* (☎ 095-44746), which also offers camping. Beds are IR£6 to IR£6.50, and doubles are IR£16 to IR£18.

There's a daily bus to Cleggan from Clifden at 8.30 am during the summer, and Cleggan is on an infrequent route from Galway to Clifden via Oughterard and Leenane.

GALWAY

INISHBOFIN ISLAND

Inishbofin Island, some 9km out in the Atlantic from Cleggan, is a haven of tranquillity. The island is compact – 6km long by 3km wide – with a population of only 180. Its highest point is a mere 86m above sea level. Good sheltered beaches, open grasslands, quiet lanes and a strong sense of isolation are what make Inishbofin so special.

The island is made of some of the oldest rocks in Ireland. The birdlife includes corncrakes, choughs, corn buntings and a variety of seabirds.

Just off the north beach is Lough Bó Finne from which the island gets its name. *Bó finne* means 'white cow'.

History

Inishbofin's main historical figure of note was St Colman, who at one stage was a bishop in England. He fell out with the English church in 664 over their adoption of a new calendar, and exiled himself to Inishbofin, where he set up a monastery. North-east of the harbour is a small 13th century church and hollowed stone, or bullaun, which are said to occupy the site of Colman's original monastery.

Grace O'Malley, the famous pirate queen who was based on Clare Island, also used Inishbofin as a base in the 16th century.

Cromwell's forces captured Inishbofin in 1652 and built a star-shaped prison for

---

The Legend of Inishbofin Island

According to legend, Inishbofin Island was once permanently enveloped in a thick blanket of fog. Some fishermen came upon the island, lit a fire near the lake and immediately the mist began to clear. Emerging from the mist was a woman with a long stick driving a white cow (or bó finne) in front of her. She hit the white cow with the stick, turning it to stone. Irritated at such behaviour, the fishermen grabbed the stick and struck her, upon which she also turned to stone.

Until the late 19th century, two white stones stood by the lake: the remains of the cow and its owner. ■

---

priests and clerics. Many died or were killed, and one bishop was reputedly chained to Bishop's Rock near the harbour and drowned as the tide came in.

Information

Inishbofin has a small post office and a grocery shop. The bars and hotels will usually change travellers' cheques.

The telephone code is ☎ 095.

Places to Stay & Eat

Hostel & Camping The IHH *Inishbofin Island Hostel* (☎ 45855), a fine hostel 500m up from the harbour, opens from March to October. It costs IR£6 to IR£7 for a bed and doubles are IR£16 to IR£18. Camping is also possible here, but you can pitch a tent on most unfenced ground and by the beaches too.

Hotels The modern and comfortable *Day's Hotel* (☎ 45803), open April to October, has turf fires and a dining room looking out over the sea. Rooms are from IR£17 to IR£25 per person. The food is creative, with excellent fresh fish; a four-course dinner is IR£16. *Day's Bar* next door has a lively atmosphere. There are bikes for hire.

Doonmore Hotel (☎ 45804) has B&B from IR£35/50. Seafood is the speciality and dinner is IR£15. They also have bikes for hire.

Getting There & Away

The *Queen* leaves Cleggan from April to October for Inishbofin at 11.30 am and 6.45 pm with an additional sailing at 2 pm in July and August. It departs from Inishbofin at 9 am and 5 pm (plus an extra sailing at 1 pm in July and August). The fare is around IR£12 return (bikes go free), and the trip takes 45 minutes. Ring ☎ 44642 for details.

LETTERFRACK

Letterfrack (Leitir Fraic), founded by the Quakers in the mid-19th century, is barely more than a crossroads with a few pubs some 15km north-east of Clifden on the N59. It lies at the head of Ballynakill Harbour, but the sea is only visible from west of the cross-roads and from the entrance to the Connemara National Park.

The small IHH *Old Monastery* hostel (☎ 095-41132), open all year, is recommended because of its free breakfast, friendliness, and IR£6 optional evening meal, which includes a vegetarian choice. There are also bikes for hire and camping (IR£4) is possible, so it's worth considering as a base for visiting Connemara National Park, which is literally next door. Dorm beds are IR£6.50, one of the four private rooms costs IR£9 per person.

North of the crossroads you come to Tully Cross, which has a line of neat, thatched holiday cottages for rent and some nice little pubs. West of here is Tully where *An Teach Ceoil* (☎ 095-43446) has regular music and Irish dancing sessions.

In Tully, both Diamond's (☎ 095-43431) and Renvyle Stores (☎ 095-43485) have bikes for rent.

CONNEMARA NATIONAL PARK

Connemara National Park, which is managed by the OPW, covers an area of 2000 hectares of bog, mountain and heath in the countryside south-east of Letterfrack. The headquarters and visitors' centre (☎ 095-41054) are housed in pleasant old buildings just south of the crossroads in Letterfrack.

The park encloses a number of the Twelve Bens, including Bencullagh, Benbrack and Benbaun. The heart of the park is Gleann Mór, the 'big glen' through which flows the River Polladirk. There's fine walking up the glen and over the surrounding mountains.

The visitors' centre will give you an insight into the park's flora, fauna and geology, as well as showing maps and various trails. Bog biology and the video 'Man and the Landscape' are interesting, so wandering round is not a waste of time. It has an indoor eating area and rudimentary kitchen facilities for walkers. The centre opens daily in July and August 9.30 am to 6.30 pm, in June from 10 am and in April, May and September 10 am to 5.30 pm. The entry fee is IR£2/1.

There are usually guided nature walks on Monday, Wednesday and Friday in July and August, leaving the centre at 10.30 am and taking two to three hours. Bring good boots ('knee-high ones', one reader recommends) and rainwear. There are also short, self-guided walks. If the Bens look too daunting, you can hike up Diamond Hill nearby.

NORTH OF LETTERFRACK

There's some fine coastal scenery along the coast north of Letterfrack, especially from Tully Cross east to Lettergesh and Salruck, home to the Little Killary Adventure Centre.

Just short of Salruck is Glassillaun Beach, a breathtaking expanse of pure white sand. There are other fine beaches at Gurteen and at Lettergesh, where the beach horse-racing sequences for John Ford's 1952 film *The Quiet Man* were shot. There are fine walks all along the coast and around Renvyle Point to Derryinver Bay. There's an excellent hill walk, which takes four to five hours each way, from the post office at Lettergesh up Binn Chuanna and Maolchnoc and then down to Lough Fee.

Things to See & Do

Focusing on the sea and marine life, **Oceans Alive** (☎ 095-43473) is a new aquarium and museum complex on Derryinver Bay. It opens May to September 9.30 am to 7 pm and 10 am to 4.30 pm the rest of the year. To get there from Letterfrack head north to Tully Cross and turn west for Renvyle. Oceans Alive is 2.5km beyond Renvyle.

The Little Killary Adventure Centre (☎ 095-43411) near Salruck is a well run place offering accommodation (dorm beds from IR£10.50, B&B from IR£12.50), plus courses in canoeing, sea kayaking, sailing, rock climbing, and just about every other adventure sport you can think of. On Glassillaun Beach to the north-west is Scubadive West (☎ 095-43922), offering courses and diving on the surrounding coast and islands.

For sea trips or deep-sea angling on the MV *Lorraine-Marie* contact John or Phil Mongan at Oceans Alive (☎ 095-43473) in

Derryinver and for horse trekking contact Joe O'Neill (☎ 095-42269).

Places to Stay & Eat

Camping *Renvyle Beach Caravan & Camping* (☎ 095-43462), open March to September, is west of Tully and they charge IR£4 to IR£4.50 a night for tents or IR£3 per hiker or cyclist. East of Tully Cross near Lettergesh Beach is the *Connemara Caravan & Camping Park* (☎ 095-43406). It costs IR£7 to pitch a two-person tent here (IR£3.50 for hikers), and each extra adult/child pays IR£3.50/1. The site opens May to September.

Hostel An Óige's *Killary Harbour Hostel* (☎ 095-43417), 13km north-east of Tully Cross on Rosroe Quay, 8km off the N59, charges IR£4.50/5.50 or IR£5/6.50 for juniors/seniors, depending on the season (open March to September). The Austrian philosopher Ludwig Wittgenstein (1889-1951) stayed here for seven months in 1948. Some food and supplies are available at the hostel, but the nearest shop is 5km away in Lettergesh, so stock up in advance. There's a fine hike from the hostel along an old road by the fjord to Leenane.

Hotels The 56-room *Renvyle House Hotel* (☎ 095-43511) is a converted country house in Renvyle and was once owned by the poet Oliver St John Gogarty. It's the best place in the area to have a drink or snack or relax after a walk but staying here would destroy most travellers' budgets: singles/doubles are IR£95/140. *Heather Island House* (☎ 095-41028), on a tiny offshore island accessible by rowing boat, does B&B at a much more down-to-earth IR£22 per person. It opens June to September.

Getting There & Away

There's a bus Monday to Saturday year round between Galway and Clifden, calling at Cong, Leenane, Salruck, Lettergesh, Tully Church, Kylemore, Letterfrack, Cleggan and Claddaghduff en route. The times change daily and according to the season so check

with Bus Éireann (☎ 091-562000) in Galway for the latest schedule.

KILLARY HARBOUR & AROUND

Mussel rafts dot long, narrow Killary Harbour, which looks like a fjord but may not actually have been glaciated. It's 16km long, over 45m deep in the centre and has a superb anchorage. Mt Mweelrea (819m) towers over its northern shores. From Leenane (see the earlier Maam Cross to Leenane & Delphi section) at the south-east end of the harbour, the road runs west for a couple of km along the southern shore before veering inland. However, you can continue walking along the shore to Rosroe Quay on an old road.

County Mayo begins just north-east of Leenane, and there is magnificent scenery around the northern side of Killary Harbour and up the R335 to Delphi and into the Doo Lough Valley, one of the most scenic in the country.

Aran Islands

The same stretch of limestone that created Clare's Burren region surfaces in the middle of Galway Bay to form the three Aran Islands (Oileáin Árainn): Inishmór, Inishmaan and Inisheer. The islands are like one long, undulating reef, with no significant hills or mountains – although on the western side of Inishmór and Inishmaan, the land rises high enough to create some very dramatic cliffs over the Atlantic. As in the Burren, the limestone and, below that, the older bluestone create a spectacular moonscape: sheets of grey and grey-blue rock with flowers and grass bursting from the cracks.

The islands have some of the most ancient pre-Christian and Christian remains in Ireland. Farming was once much easier to pursue here than on the densely forested mainland. The most significant ruins on the islands are massive Iron Age stone forts, such as Dún Aengus on Inishmór and Dún Chonchúir on Inishmaan. Almost nothing is known about the people who built these structures, partly because their iron implements quickly rusted away. In folklore, the forts are said to have been built by the Firbolgs, a Celtic tribe who invaded Ireland from Europe in prehistoric times.

Christianity reached the islands remarkably quickly, and some of the earliest monastic settlements were founded by St Enda (Éanna) in the 5th century. Any remains you see today are later, from the 8th century onward. Enda appears to have been an Irish chief who converted to Christianity and spent some time studying in Rome before seeking out a suitably remote spot for his monastery. Many great monks studied under him on Aran, including Colmcille (or Columba) who went on to found the monastery on Iona in Scotland.

From the 14th century on, control of the islands was disputed by two Gaelic families, the O'Briens and the O'Flahertys. During the reign of Elizabeth I, the English took control and in Cromwell's times a garrison was stationed here.

As Galway's importance waned so too did that of the islands. They became a quiet and windy backwater. The islands' isolation allowed Irish culture to survive when it had all but disappeared elsewhere. Irish is still very much the native tongue, and until recently people wore traditional Aran dress: bright red skirts and black shawls for women, baggy woollen trousers and waistcoats with a colourful belt (or *crios*) for men. The classic white sweater knitted in complex patterns originated here. You may still see old people wearing some elements of the traditional dress, particularly on Inishmaan. The other Aran trademark is the currach.

Even the smallest patches of rocky land are bordered by stone walls. Over the centuries, tonnes of seaweed were brought up from the beaches, mixed with sand and laid out on the bare rock to start walls. The walls may be hundreds or even thousands of years old so have respect for them, and replace any stones you dislodge. On Inishmaan and Inisheer many of the walls are up to eye level, and it's a joy to walk for hours along the

sandy lanes between them. The odd-looking seaweed you'll see drying atop the stone walls on the islands is sea rod collected at low tide. It's sent to the mainland where it's used in the production of certain cosmetics. A tonne of the slimy stuff earns the collector IR£150.

The elemental nature of life on the islands has always attracted writers and artists. The dramatist John Millington Synge (1871-1909) spent a lot of time on the islands, and his play *Riders to the Sea* (1905) is set on Inishmaan. His book *The Aran Islands* is the classic account of life here and is readily available in paperback. The American Robert Flaherty came to the islands in 1934 to shoot *Man of Aran*, a dramatic account of daily life. It became a classic and there are regular screenings of it in Kilronan on Inishmór. The islands have produced their own talent, particularly the writer Liam O'Flaherty (1896-1984) from Inishmór. His outstanding novels, including *Famine* (published by Wolfhound), make an appropriate introduction to an interesting writer who wandered around North and South America before returning to Ireland in 1921 and fighting on the Republican side in the Civil War.

The mapmaker Tim Robinson has written a wonderful, though not easily accessible, two-volume account of his explorations on Aran called *Stones of Aran: Pilgrimage* and *Stones of Aran: Labyrinthe* (Penguin). His *The Aran Islands: A Map & Guide* (IR£3, or IR£10 with a Companion Guide) is superb. Two other excellent publications in paperback are *The Book of Aran* (IR£15.95), edited by Anne Korf and published by Tír Eolas, consisting of articles by 17 specialists covering diverse aspects of the islands' culture, and *Aran Reader* (Lilliput Press) with essays on the islands' history, geography, culture etc by various scholars.

Today, the islands have become major attractions with quick and convenient travel connections to the mainland, a plethora of B&B and hostel accommodation, and a veritable armada of bicycles waiting to be hired. Inishmór – the largest of the three – is exceedingly busy during the summer with armies of day trippers and shuttle buses all over the island. At the busiest times, the 100 or so licensed vehicles on Inishmór actually get locked in traffic jams in the lanes.

If you have the time, try to get to the smaller islands, particularly Inishmaan – the least visited – and allow yourself a few days for exploration. Inisheer is the smallest and closest to land, just 8km from Doolin, in County Clare.

GETTING THERE & AWAY
Air
If time is important or seasickness a concern on the often rough Atlantic, you can fly to the islands and back with Aer Árann (☎ 091-593034) for IR£35/29/20 adults/students/children. For IR£29 you can fly one way and take the ferry the other. Flights operate to all three islands four times a day (hourly in summer) and take less than 10 minutes. The mainland departure point is Connemara regional airport at Minna, near Inverin, 38km west of Galway. A connecting bus from outside the Galway and Salthill tourist offices costs IR£4 return. A package that includes a return flight and one night's B&B accommodation costs IR£47.

Boat
Only one big ferry line makes the run to the islands daily year round. Island Ferries' services from Rossaveal, 37km west of Galway, are popular because the crossing is quick (about 40 minutes), and there are frequent sailings. The ferries operate up to six times in summer (two or three times daily in winter) with an adult/student/child return fare of IR£15/12/8 for the 40-minute trip. The return Galway to Rossaveal bus trip costs IR£4/3/2 and leaves the Island Ferries' Galway office (☎ 091-568903) off Victoria Place opposite the tourist office 1½ hours before the scheduled departure. The car park at Rossaveal opposite Island Ferries Rossaveal office (☎ 091-561767) costs IR£2 a day, IR£3 overnight.

Island Ferries also has direct services from Galway between June and September. This is a journey of about 46km to Inishmór,

taking 1½ hours, and costs about IR£18 return. There are usually two daily sailings in July and August, one a day in June and in September. O'Brien Shipping (☎ 091-567676 in Galway) operates a cargo boat service that takes on passengers to all three Aran Islands daily June to September and three times a week (Tuesday, Thursday and Saturday) the rest of the year. The boat usually departs from the Galway docks at around 10.30 am. It has a desk in the Galway tourist office in summer.

Doolin Ferries (☎ 065-74455 in Doolin) operates a service April to September from Doolin to Inisheer and (May to August) to Inishmór. It's only 8km to Inisheer, taking about 30 minutes and costing IR£15 return. See the Doolin section in the County Clare chapter for more details.

Inter-island services run by Island Ferries under the name Sunda Teo (☎ 091-561767) are not quite so regular. Between one and four boats a day from Rossaveal continue on to Inishmaan and Inisheer in summer, according to demand, but there are only about three a week in winter.

GETTING AROUND
Inisheer and Inishmaan are small enough to explore on foot, but on larger Inishmór, bikes are the way to go. You can also arrange transport on Inishmór with any of the small tour vans on the islands, and pony traps are also available for hire.

INISHMÓR
The island, which is called Inish Mór ('big island') or just Árainn in Irish, slopes up from its comparatively sheltered northern shores to the southern edge, then plummets straight into the tumultuous Atlantic Ocean. Once you have climbed the hill west of Kilronan, all you can see is rock, stone walls and boulders, with the odd patch of deep green grass and potato plants. There's a fine beach at Kilmurvey, west of Kilronan, and it's nice to stay out here away from the bustle of the island 'capital' (though transport can be a problem). Just before the beach, in a sheltered little bay of Port Chorrúch, up to

50 grey seals make their home, sunning and feeding in the shallows. Inishmór has a population of around 800.

Orientation

Inishmór is 14.5km long and a maximum 4km wide, running along a north-west to south-east axis. All ferries and boats arrive and depart from Kilronan (Cill Rónáin) on Cill Éinne Bay on the south-eastern side of the island. The airstrip is 2km farther south-east, on the other side of the bay, and faces Kilronan. One principal road runs the length of the island with many smaller lanes and paths of packed dirt and stone leading off of it.

Information

The small tourist office (☎ 099-61263), on the waterfront west of the ferry pier in Kilronan, opens May to mid-September. At other times, seek assistance from the Inishmore Island Co-operative (☎ 099-61354). A branch of the Bank of Ireland north of the centre opens on Wednesday only (and possibly Friday in July and August); many of the shops and the Ionad Árann (Aran Heritage Centre) will change money. The post office, which has a bureau de change, is next to the bank.

The telephone code is ☎ 099.

Things to See & Do

Inishmór has three impressive stone forts, probably about 2000 years old. Two thirds of the way down the island and perched on the edge of the sheer southern cliff, **Dún Aengus** is one of the most amazing archaeological sites in the country. It has a remarkable *chevaux de frise*; a defensive forest of sharp stone spikes around the exterior of the fort to help stop any would-be attackers.

Dún Aengus is a magical place and should not be missed; you won't soon forget the sight and sound of wild swells pounding the cliff face below. Try and go at a less busy time such as late evening when there are few visitors about. But be very careful when approaching the cliffs; there are no guard

---

Aengus, King of the Firbolgs

Folklore suggests that Aengus was a king of the Firbolgs, a legendary Celtic tribe from Europe who are said to have retreated to Aran and built the stone forts after falling out with the mainland chiefs. Other sources say that he was a 5th century Irish chief and pupil of St Enda, the islands' most important saint. ∎

---

rails and the winds can be very strong. In December 1996, a 25-year-old German tourist was blown off and killed on the rock shelf below.

Half way between Kilronan and Dún Aengus is the smaller **Dún Eochla**, a perfectly circular ring fort. Directly south of Kilronan and dramatically perched on a promontory is **Dún Dúchathair**. It's surrounded on three sides by cliffs and is less visited than Dún Aengus.

The ruins of numerous stone churches trace the island's monastic history. The small **Church of St Kieran** (Teampall Chiaráin), with a high cross in the churchyard, is near Kilronan. Past Kilmurvey is the perfect **Clochán na Carraige**, an early Christian stone hut, standing 2.5m tall and the ruins of various small early Christian remains known rather inaccurately as the **Seven Churches** (Na Seacht dTeampaill), consisting of a couple of ruined churches, monastic houses and some fragments of a high cross from the 8th or 9th century. To the south is **Dún Eoghanachta**, another circular fort. Near the airstrip are the sunken remains of a church said to be the site of **St Enda's Monastery** in the 5th century.

Ionad Árann (Aran Heritage Centre; ☎ 61355), just off the main road leading out of town, offers an introduction to the landscape and culture of the three islands. It opens daily 10 am to 7 pm April to October; admission is IR£2/1.50. It also has a coffee shop and bureau de change.

Enda Conneely at Aran Watersports (☎ 75073) can organise kayaks, paddle boats, currachs and angling.

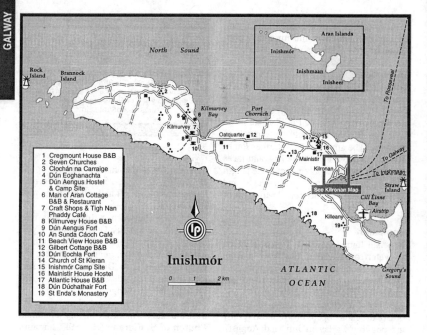

1 Cregmount House B&B
2 Seven Churches
3 Clochán na Carraige
4 Dún Eoghanachta
5 Dún Aengus Hostel
   & Camp Site
6 Man of Aran Cottage
   B&B & Restaurant
7 Craft Shops & Tigh Nan
   Phaddy Café
8 Kilmurvey House B&B
9 Dún Aengus Fort
10 An Sunda Cáoch Café
11 Beach View House B&B
12 Gilbert Cottage B&B
13 Dún Eochla Fort
14 Church of St Kieran
15 Inishmór Camp Site
16 Mainistir House Hostel
17 Atlantic House B&B
18 Dún Dúchathair Fort
19 St Enda's Monastery

Inishmór

0   1   2 km

ATLANTIC
OCEAN

Places to Stay

Camping *Inishmór Camp Site* (☎ 61185) has a fine setting near the beach in Mainistir, almost 2km north-west of Kilronan and about a 30-minute walk from the pier. Facilities are basic, and cost IR£2.50 per person. The Dún Aengus Hostel has a new campsite beside it costing the same, and there is a kitchen and separate showers.

Hostels In Kilronan, the *Aran Islands Hostel* (☎ 61255), which is also known as Tí Joe Mac's Hostel, is only a short walk from the pier and has dorm beds for IR£6 to IR£9. It's above Tí Joe Mac's pub but is owned by the people at the large Spar supermarket a few steps north around the corner so go there first off season. *St Kevin's Hostel*, between Tí Joe Mac's and the Spar, opens only in summer and charges about IR£7 for a bed; enquire at the Dormer House B&B (☎ 61125) opposite.

The small, basic *Aharla Hostel* (☎ 61305)

in Kilronan, just off the road leading to Kilmurvey, has two rooms with eight beds each and charges IR£6 to IR£7 per person.

North-west of Kilronan, the IHO *Mainistir House Hostel* (☎ 61169) has beds for IR£6.50 to IR£7.50 and doubles for IR£23, including a breakfast of porridge and scones. The hostel has a van meeting guests at the ferry pier.

Dún Aengus Hostel (☎ 61318) is near the beach on the west side of Kilmurvey Bay some 7km from Kilronan. This is a nice country house charging IR£5 to IR£6 a night, and there is free pick up and delivery from/to the ferry.

South-east of Kilronan, the small IHO *Killeany Lodge Hostel* (☎ 61393) has 14 beds costing IR£5 per person. It opens June to September only.

B&Bs The numerous B&Bs in and around Kilronan include the large *Dormer House* (☎ 61125) behind Tí Joe Mac's in Kilronan, with singles/doubles for IR£18/30 and open all year. *Bayview Guesthouse* (☎ 61260), open March to mid-November, enjoys an enviable position overlooking the harbour and charges from IR£17/32. Farther west is *St Brendan's* (☎ 61149) in a charming old house on Cill Éinne Bay with B&B for IR£12 to IR£15 per person and open all year. *Árd Éinne* (☎ 61126) is farther west still and has rooms from IR£22/27. It opens March to October.

Along the road to Kilmurvey, *Claí Bán* (☎ 61111) charges IR£13, or IR£15 with ensuite bathroom, and opens all year. To the north is *An Crúgán* (☎ 61150) costing IR£16 per person and opens March to November.

Atlantic House (☎ 61185) in Mainistir opposite the hostel opens March to October and charges IR£17/28. *Beach View House* (☎ 61141), in Oatquarter some 5km north-west of Kilronan, charges IR£19/28 for singles/doubles May to September. Nearby is the cosy *Gilbert Cottage* (☎ 61146), open May to September and costing IR£13 per person (dinner IR£12.50).

Overlooking Kilmurvey Bay, *Man of Aran Cottage* (☎ 61301), where some of the eponymous film was shot, does B&B March to October and charges from IR£19/34. *Kilmurvey House* (☎ 61218), in a lovely old mansion on the path leading to Dún Aengus, has 12 rooms with singles/doubles from IR£23/36. It opens April to September, and dinner costs IR£13.50.

At the north-west end of the island, 9km from Kilronan in Creggakeerain, is *Cregmount House* (☎ 61139), which overlooks Galway Bay and costs IR£14 per person. Cregmount opens April to October.

Places to Eat

In Kilronan there's a takeaway place called the *Old Pier* (or An tSean Chéibh in Irish) just up from the tourist office. *Café Veronica* at the Bayview Guesthouse is a nice place for coffee or a snack. About the best place for pub food is *Joe Watty's Bar*, farther north on the way out of Kilronan.

The *Aran Fisherman* (☎ 61104) has a wide range of meat, seafood and vegetarian

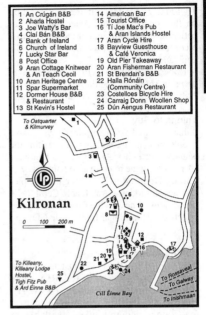

1 An Crúgán B&B	14 American Bar
2 Aharla Hostel	15 Tourist Office
3 Joe Watty's Bar	16 Tí Joe Mac's Pub
4 Claí Bán B&B	& Aran Islands Hostel
5 Bank of Ireland	17 Aran Cycle Hire
6 Church of Ireland	18 Bayview Guesthouse
7 Lucky Star Bar	& Café Veronica
8 Post Office	19 Old Pier Takeaway
9 Aran Cottage Knitwear	20 Aran Fisherman Restaurant
& An Teach Ceoil	21 St Brendan's B&B
10 Aran Heritage Centre	22 Halla Rónáin
11 Spar Supermarket	(Community Centre)
12 Dormer House B&B	23 Costelloes Bicycle Hire
& Restaurant	24 Carraig Donn Woollen Shop
13 St Kevin's Hostel	25 Dún Aengus Restaurant

Kilronan

dishes from around IR£9.50, though pizzas and burgers are about IR£6. Its sister restaurant, *Dún Aengus* (☎ same), to the south-west and overlooking Cill Éinne Bay, has a set dinner for around IR£12 and serves good grills, steaks, chips and lovely scones and fruitcake.

Mainistir House Hostel serves good buffet dinners at 8 pm (7 pm in winter) that include vegetarian dishes. They cost IR£7 for residents and IR£8 for non-residents.

Man of Aran Cottage is a tea shop and restaurant with dinner for IR£12.

Outside of Kilronan, at the start of the path leading to Dún Aengus fort and near several craft shops, is a small café called *Tigh Nan Phaddy*. The larger *An Sunda Cáoch* ('the blind sound') café is farther down the path.

Entertainment

There's music in most Kilronan pubs at night. For Irish music and crack at its best, try *Joe Watty's Bar* or, west of the village,

Tigh Fitz. Tí Joe Mac's in the centre is a bit on the rough side; the *American Bar* has better music and a friendlier crowd. Another nice option is the *Lucky Star* between the bank and post office.

Robert O'Flaherty's 1934 film *Man of Aran* is screened regularly (IR£3) at the Halla Rónáin, Kilronan's community centre.

Things to Buy

A hand-knitted Aran sweater is what most people are in the market for when visiting the islands, and either Aran Cottage Knitwear (☎ 61117) on the main road to Kilmurvey or Carraig Donn (☎ 61123) near the old pier can accommodate. An Teach Ceoil ('the music house') next to the former has a good selection of traditional Irish music CDs and tapes.

Getting Around

Aran Cycle Hire (☎ 61132), just up from the pier, has very good bikes for IR£5 a day (IR£3 for groups). Costelloes (☎ 61241), opposite the Old Pier takeaway, has just a few, rather decrepit bikes available in summer only for the same price. You can bring your own bicycle out on the ferry.

There are some two dozen small tour buses offering 2½-hour tours of the island's principal sights for IR£5. Bertie Faherty (☎ 61329) and Michael Hernon (☎ 61131) are two such operators and can be used for evening transfers to Kilronan. However, walking and cycling will give you more of a sense of the place. Pony traps with a driver are also available for an island trip from Kilronan to Dún Aengus for around IR£20.

INISHMAAN

Inishmaan (Inis Meáin, or 'middle island') is the least visited of the three Aran Islands and well worth the effort of getting there.

Inishmaan is lozenge-shaped and about 5km long by 3km wide. The fields are bordered by high stone walls, and it's a delight to wander along these boreens and take in some of the tranquillity that attracted the playwright JM Synge and the nationalist Patrick Pearse. **Synge's Chair** is a sheltered

spot where the writer is said to have spent much time reflecting. It's at the west of the island near the end of a path that leads to a sheer cliff.

Most of the houses on Inishmaan are in the centre of the island, while the principal boat landing stage is at An Córa on the east side. There's a reasonable beach (Trá Leitreach) just north of the slip. The airstrip is on the north-east corner of the island.

Inishmaan is not hell bent on attracting tourists, though Martin McDonagh's play *The Cripple of Inishmaan* has at least put the island's name on the world map. Inishmaan is home to a knitwear factory that exports fine woollen garments to some of the world's most exclusive shops. There's a factory shop (☎ 099-73009) on the island.

Information

The helpful Inishmaan Island Co-operative (☎ 099-73010) is north of the post office.

The telephone code is ☎ 099.

Things to See

The main archaeological site here is **Dún Chonchúir**, a massive oval-shaped stone fort built on a high point and offering good views of the island on a fine day. It's similar to Dún Aengus on Inishmór, but it's built inland overlooking a limestone valley. Chonchúir is said to have been a brother of Aengus. Dún Chonchúir's age is a bit of a puzzle; it's thought to have been built somewhere between the 1st and the 7th centuries AD. The thatched cottage on the road just before you head up to the fort is where JM Synge spent his summers between 1898 and 1902.

Cill Cheannannach is a rough 8th or 9th century church south of the pier. The well preserved stone fort **Dún Fearbhaigh**, a short distance to the west, dates from about the same time.

Places to Stay & Eat

One of the best B&Bs on the island is *Angela Uí Fátharta's* (☎ 73012) in Creigmore about 500m north-west of the pier, which costs IR£12 per person and opens March to

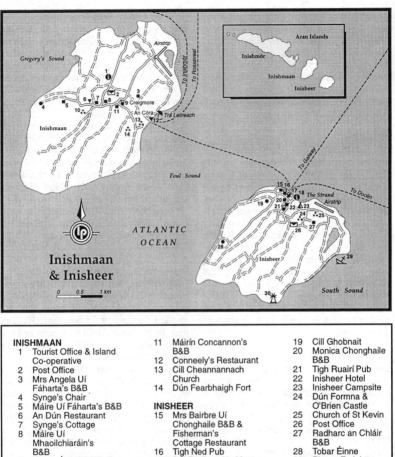

October. *Máire Uí Mhaoilchiaráin's*
(☎ 73016) is a good B&B on a corner south
of the post office, similarly priced. Another
good one in the village is *Máirín Con-
cannon's* B&B (☎ 73019), across the road
from the island's only pub, charging
IR£13.50 per person.

Máire Uí Fátharta's B&B (☎ 73027), in

Ard Alainn past the road up to Dún Chonchúir and open Easter to September, charges
from IR£13 per person.

Most B&Bs serve evening meals for
IR£10 to IR£12. The island has just one pub,
Teach Ósta Inis Meáin (☎ 73003) in Baile an
Mhothair, serving snacks, sandwiches, soups
and seafood platters between 11.30 am and

6 pm. This is a terrific little bar and hums with life on summer evenings.

There are only two restaurants here: *Conneely's* (☎ 73085) just up from the pier, and *An Dún* (☎ 73068), opposite the entrance to Dún Chonchúir. The latter offers reasonably priced omelettes, pasta for lunch for around IR£6 and dinner for around IR£10 per main course.

INISHEER

Inisheer (Inis Oírr, or 'eastern island') is the smallest of the three Aran Islands and only 8km off the coast from Doolin in County Clare. The view from the ferry is of a sheltered white beach backed by modern bungalows – few traditional thatched cottages and buildings survive – overlooked by a squat stone 15th century castle. To the south there's a maze of fields without a building in sight. The island has a timelessness about it, and a summer stroll through its sandy lanes is hard to beat. Despite a regular ferry service, the absence of major archaeological sites and tourist amenities keeps the number of visitors down, making Inisheer rather special.

Information

During the summer there is a tourist information desk at the harbour. You can also contact the Inisheer Island Co-operative (☎ 099-75008) for assistance. Bikes are available for hire at a couple of houses near the pier and at Rothair Inis Oírr (☎ 099-75033).

The telephone code is ☎ 099.

Things to See & Do

The 15th century **O'Brien Castle** (Caislea'n Uí Bhriain) overlooks the beach and harbour. It was built within the remains of a ring fort call **Dún Formna** dating from as early as the 1st century AD. Nearby is an 18th century signal tower. On the Strand (An Trá) is the 10th century **Teampall Chaoimháin** (Church of St Kevin), with some gravestones and shells from an ancient kitchen midden, or dumping ground. The **Inisheer Heritage House** (☎ 75021) is a typical stone built

thatched cottage with some interesting old photographs. It has a craft shop and a café.

Cill Ghobnait (Church of Saint Gobnait) is west of the main pier, and this small 8th or 9th century church is named after Gobnait, who fled here from Clare trying to escape an enemy who was in hot pursuit. A 2km walk south-west of the church leads to the **Tobar Éinne** (Well of St Enda).

The best parts of Inisheer are uninhabited and the signposted 10.5km Inisheer Way walk is recommended. The eastern road to the lighthouse is more popular, but the coast around the west side is wilder. On the eastern shore is the rusting hulk of the *Plassy*, a freighter wrecked in 1960 and thrown high up onto the rocks. The uninhabited lighthouse (1857) on the island's southern tip, with its neat enclosure, is off limits.

Places to Stay & Eat

Inisheer Camp Site (☎ 75008) by the strand opens May to September. It charges IR£2.50 per tent and have basic facilities. The *Brú Radharc Na Mara* (☎ 75087), the IHH hostel near the pier, costs IR£6.50 a night and has two double rooms for IR£18. It opens all year round and has bikes for hire.

Radharc an Chláir (☎ 75019), a B&B near the castle, charges from IR£15/26, does an IR£11 dinner, and opens all year. Other B&Bs have similar rates. Try *An Cladach* (☎ 75033) in West Village or there's *Mrs Bairbre Uí Chonghaile* (☎ 75025) or *Monica Chonghaile* (☎ 75034), also in West Village not far from the pier.

The modern *Inisheer Hotel* (Óstán Inis Oírr) (☎ 75020), just up from the Strand, offers B&B from IR£19/34.

The restaurant at the *Inisheer Hotel* serves reasonable seafood, and dinner is about IR£15. *Fisherman's Cottage* (☎ 75073), not far from the pier in the western part of the village, has very good seafood. Lunch is around IR£6, most main courses for dinner are around IR£12 and vegetarian meals are also available. Inisheer's two pubs are *Tigh Ned* just up from the Strand and *Tigh Ruairí* past the Inisheer Hotel in Baile Lurgan.

Eastern Galway

Eastern Galway is markedly different from the wild and bleak landscape of Connemara and the county's west coast. The two regions are divided by Lough Corrib. Eastern Galway is relatively flat, and its underlying limestone has given it a well drained, fertile soil. This is the largest section of the county, but it lacks any areas of significant interest. Country towns like Ballinasloe, Loughrea and Tuam serve relatively prosperous farming regions.

In the south-east corner of the county, the lakeside town of Portumna is an attractive place and a popular base for boating and fishing on Lough Derg in County Clare.

BALLINASLOE

The biggest town in eastern Galway, Ballinasloe (Béal Átha na Sluaighe) was a strategic crossing point over the River Suck. In the early 12th century, Turlough O'Connor, king of Connaught, built a castle to guard the river crossing, and this became the nucleus of the town's development. Around 6km south-west of town on the N6, Aughrim was the site of a crucial victory by the Protestant William of Orange over the Catholic forces of James II in 1691, the bloodiest battle ever fought on Irish soil. The **Battle of Aughrim Interpretive Centre** (☎ 0905-73939) helps to put it all in perspective, and there are signposts from the centre indicating the actual battle site. It opens Easter to October daily 10 am to 6 pm. Admission costs IR£3/2/1 for adults/students/children. *Hyne's Hostel* (☎ 0905-73734), almost next to the centre, charges IR£6 a night for a dorm bed or IR£8 to IR£8.50 per person for one of two private rooms.

Today, Ballinasloe is on the main Dublin to Galway road (N6), with most traffic diverted south around the town centre. The town is pleasant enough, but there is no real reason to stay except possibly over the eight days in October when the Ballinasloe Horse Fair attracts legions of horse buyers, horse sellers and merrymakers.

CLONFERT CATHEDRAL

Around 15km south-east of Ballinasloe is the tiny 12th century cathedral at Clonfert. The monastery is said to have been founded in the middle of the 6th century by St Brendan the Navigator and was ravaged by Vikings in 844 and 1179. The remarkable Romanesque doorway, with its human and animal heads dates from the 1160s, but much of the limestone carvings were badly restored in the 19th century.

LOUGHREA

Loughrea (Baile Locha Riach) is a large and busy market town 26km south-east of Galway. It gets its name from the little lake at the southern end of town. **St Brendan's Catholic Cathedral** (1903) is renowned for its Celtic Revival stained glass. Loughrea has Ireland's only functioning medieval **moat**, which runs from the lake at the Fair Green near the cathedral to the River Loughrea north of town.

Seven km north of Loughrea near Bullaun is the remarkable **Turoe Stone**, a phallic standing stone covered in delicate La Tène-style relief carvings. It dates from between 300 BC and 100 AD. There are similarly carved stones in Brittany associated with La Tène Celts. The stone was not set here originally but was found at an Iron Age fort a few km away.

PORTUMNA CASTLE

The castle was built in 1618 by Richard de Burgo (or Burke) and boasts a formal, geometrically laid-out garden of some pretension. The castle (☎ 0509-41658) is an OPW site, open daily mid-June to mid-September 9.30 am to 6.30 pm. Entrance is IR£1/40p.

Counties Mayo & Sligo

Despite Mayo's and Sligo's shared history of rural poverty, remoteness and underpopulation, County Sligo – the smaller of the two – is better known to most travellers, thanks largely to the poetry of WB Yeats. But the qualities of landscape and sense of place that inspired Yeats belong equally to both Mayo and Sligo. And, apart from a small number of towns like Sligo, Westport and Cong, both counties are ideal for anyone wishing to escape the well worn tourist trail. Mayo in particular is just waiting to be discovered by intrepid travellers.

County Mayo

Mayo (Maigh Eo) has an identity that distinguishes itself on many different levels: an introspective landscape, a Connaught accent with its own inflection, and a people who seem far removed from cosmopolitan Dublin or touristy Killarney. The relative poverty of the land meant that the invaders left it to last, but what delayed the English is what attracts today's visitors: lakes, mountains, boglands, and a population density among the lowest in Europe.

The more recent history of Mayo is one of massive and ongoing emigration and, apart from the small industries that sustain Castlebar's relative prosperity, there is a chronic lack of employment opportunities for young people.

The county was particularly hard-hit by the Famine, and the woeful refrain 'County Mayo, God help us!', still used among older Irish at home and abroad, probably dates from this sad time.

CONG

Blink your eyes while driving though the small town of Cong (Conga) and you won't see much, but there's a great deal hidden behind that ordinary main street. In 1951 the

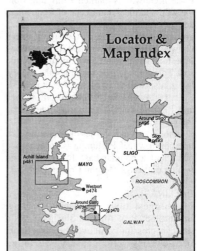

Highlights

- Cycle or drive from Louisburg to Leenane through the Doolough Valley
- Visit Achill Island off the coast of West Mayo
- Experience the lonely expanses of bogland in the Belmullet Peninsula
- Wander through North Mayo's historical and prehistoric sites
- See the museum and art gallery in Sligo Town
- Take in Carrowmore Megalithic Cemetery outside Sligo Town
- Discover WB Yeats' County Sligo
- Explore Inishmurray Island

American director John Ford, along with John Wayne and Maureen O'Hara, came here to film *The Quiet Man*, and there are still many reminders of that momentous event. True fans of the film will want to buy the *Complete Guide to the Quiet Man Locations* by Lisa Collins. Cong is just east of the border with County Galway and a km north of Lough Corrib.

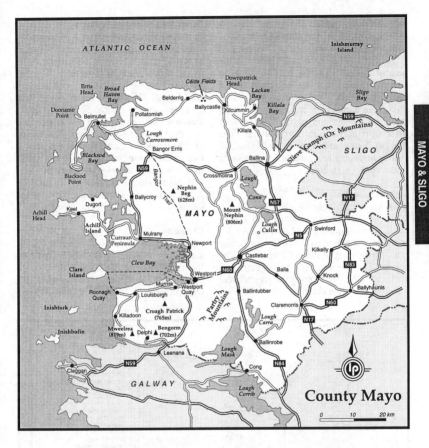

ATLANTIC OCEAN

Inishmurray Island

Erris Head
Broad Haven Bay
Doonamo Point
Belmullet
Pollatomish
Belderrig
Ballycastle
Céide Fields
Downpatrick Head
Kilcummin
Lackan Bay
Killala Bay
Sligo Bay

N59

Lough Carrowmore
Bangor Erris
Killala

Blacksod Bay
Blacksod Point

N59

Bangor Trail

Nephin Beg (628m)
Crossmolina
Ballina

Slieve Camph (Ox Mountains)

SLIGO

Achill Head
Keel
Dugort
Achill Island
Curraun Peninsula
Ballycroy
Mulrany
Newport

MAYO

Mount Nephin (806m)
Lough Conn
Lough Cullin
Swinford
Kilkelly

N57
N5
N17
N83

Clare Island
Clew Bay
Murrisk
Westport Quay
Westport
Castlebar
Balla
Knock
Ballyhaunis

Roonagh Quay
Louisburgh
N60

Inishturk
Killadoon
Croagh Patrick (765m)
Ballintubber
Claremorris
N60

Inishbofin
Mweelrea (819m)
Delphi
Bengorm (702m)
Partry Mountains
Lough Carra
N17

Leenane
Lough Mask
Ballinrobe

Cleggan

N59

GALWAY

Cong
N84

Lough Corrib

County Mayo

0   10   20 km

Information

Tourist information (☎ 092-46542) is available daily May to September, 10 am to 6 pm, in the old courthouse building opposite Cong Abbey in Abbey St. Get a copy of the Heritage Trail brochure to explore the town and discover the fascinating history of the 1123 Cong Cross, now in the National Museum in Dublin.

The local booklets *The Glory of Cong* and *Cong: Walks, Sights, Stories* have more information.

Guided tours focusing on *The Quiet Man* locations depart from the tourist office at 8.45 am each morning in season and last about 90 minutes.

There are no banks in Cong, but you can change money at the hostels and O'Connors craft shop on Main St, where you'll also find the post office.

The telephone code is ☎ 092.

Cong Abbey

This 12th century Augustinian abbey, founded by Turlough Mór O'Connor, high king of Ireland and king of Connaught, in 1120, occupies the site of a 6th century abbey. It has a carved doorway on the north side and fine windows and decorated medieval stonework in the **Chapter House** – some of the finest such work in Ireland. Just west of the abbey on a small island in the nearby river stands the **Monks' Fishing House**, where a bell was rung every time a fish was caught. The 1960s-style Catholic church, in a corner of the abbey site, is an unbelievable eyesore plonked down with utter disregard for its surroundings. The **Market Cross**, at the junction of Main and Abbey Sts, is the reconstructed remains of a 14th century high cross.

Ashford Castle

This Victorian castle (☎ 46003), once the home of the Guinness family and now a hotel, stands on the site of an early Anglo-Norman castle built by the de Burgos family after their defeat of the O'Connors of Connaught. The interior is strictly for guests, and it costs IR£2/1 just to enter the grounds and view the fairy-tale exterior.

Quiet Man Heritage Cottage

In a life-imitating-art exercise so twisted it begs a map, the Quiet Man Heritage Cottage (☎ 46089), on Abbey St just west of the tourist office, attempts to recreate the exact set John Ford used to film many of the interior shots of *The Quiet Man* in Hollywood. Of course, original cottages like this one – and their interiors – were his inspiration but, hey, they want real Hollywood. The cottage also contains the **Cong Archaeological & Historical Exhibition**, which rather ambitiously attempts to trace the story of Cong and its surrounds from 7000 BC to the 19th century in a very small space. The cottage opens daily 9.30 am to 6 pm.

Cruises

April to October, Corrib Cruises (☎ 46029) sails from the pier at Ashford Castle to Inchagoill Island (IR£6) and then on to Oughterard in County Galway (IR£10). Departures are at 10 and 11 am and 2.45 and

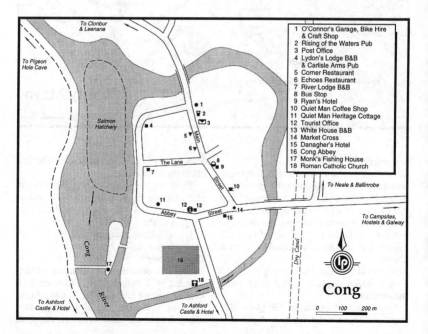

1 O'Connor's Garage, Bike Hire & Craft Shop
2 Rising of the Waters Pub
3 Post Office
4 Lydon's Lodge B&B & Carlisle Arms Pub
5 Corner Restaurant
6 Echoes Restaurant
7 River Lodge B&B
8 Bus Stop
9 Ryan's Hotel
10 Quiet Man Coffee Shop
11 Quiet Man Heritage Cottage
12 Tourist Office
13 White House B&B
14 Market Cross
15 Danagher's Hotel
16 Cong Abbey
17 Monk's Fishing House
18 Roman Catholic Church

Cong

5 pm. During the rest of the year, departures are at 11 am and 2.45 pm, weather permitting.

Places to Stay

Camping You can camp at *Cong Caravan & Camping Park* (☎ 46089), on Lake Rd 2km east of town in Lisloughrey off the road to Galway (R346), for IR£3.75/1 per adult/child; or at the *Courtyard Hostel* farther east at Cross. The sites are open year round.

Hostels The popular IHH *Cong Hostel* (☎ 46089) next to the campsite in Lisloughrey has good facilities and charges IR£6 to IR£7.50 for a bed and IR£17 for a double room. It screens *The Quiet Man* and Yves Boisset's 1971 film *Un Taxi Mauve*, also filmed in Ireland, every night. The *Courtyard Hostel* (☎ 092-46203), 3km farther east in Cross, has beds for IR£6 and two doubles for IR£15.

B&Bs Central B&Bs include *Lydon's Lodge* (☎ 46053), at the start of the circular road, charging IR£25/36 for singles/doubles with bath, and the *White House* (☎ 46358), across from the abbey on Abbey St and charging from IR£15 per person. Both are open March to September/October.

There are a few B&Bs down the Lane heading toward the river, including the *River Lodge* (☎ 46057) open April to September. Singles/doubles here are IR£23/34.

Hotels *Ryan's Hotel* (☎ 46243) on Main St has 10 rooms from IR£25 to IR£35 per person, depending on the season. *Danagher's* (☎ 46028) is an old-style, 11-room hotel on Abbey Street near the town's main junction, with singles/doubles for IR£30/60. That sounds like a positive give-away compared with the IR£430/510 charged between April and September at *Ashford Castle* (☎ 46003). In fact, some of the castle hotel's 83 rooms are boxy and disappointing – but they do provide *The Quiet Man* on the in-house video for viewing any time of the day or night.

Places to Eat

The *Rising of the Waters* pub in Main St has light meals as does the *Quiet Man Coffee Shop* at the southern end of the street. *Danagher's Hotel* has a fine old bar, a straightforward eating area and a fancier restaurant. Bar food in the IR£7 to IR£10 range is available at *Ryan's Hotel*, and set dinner is IR£16.50. Attached to Lydon's Lodge is the *Carlisle Arms* pub-restaurant; its tourist menu has been recommended.

If your credit card won't accommodate the *Ashford Castle restaurant*, where dinner is around IR£36 per person, consider unleashing it at *Echoes* (☎ 46059) on Main St, an award-winning restaurant that proves fine dining has arrived in rural Ireland. Starters average about IR£4.50 and main courses IR£12.95, so count on at least IR£50 for two with wine. A cheaper but still excellent alternative is the *Corner Restaurant* (☎ 46655) a few doors up, with starters/mains from IR£2.50/8.

Getting There & Away

There's a Bus Éireann connection with Galway Monday to Saturday in the late afternoon, and the bus from Galway to Clifden stops at Cong in the early evening. The bus stop is outside Ryan's Hotel.

If travelling by car or bike farther into County Mayo, eschew the main N84 to Castlebar and take the longer, but much more attractive, route west to Leenane (starting with the R345) and north to Westport via Delphi.

Getting Around

There are enough interesting sites close to Cong to make a bike worth having. They can be hired from O'Connor's (☎ 46008) on Main St; it's the combined Esso station, Spar supermarket and craft shop next to the Rising of the Waters pub. Both hostels have bikes for hire as well.

AROUND CONG

There's a surprising amount to see and do in the vicinity of Cong, including a collection of caves, a canal that never functioned, a

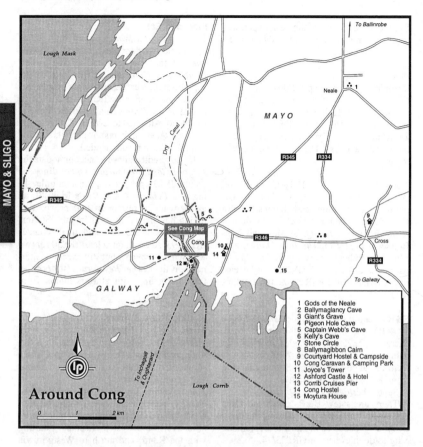

1 Gods of the Neale
2 Ballymaglancy Cave
3 Giant's Grave
4 Pigeon Hole Cave
5 Captain Webb's Cave
6 Kelly's Cave
7 Stone Circle
8 Ballymagibbon Cairn
9 Courtyard Hostel & Campside
10 Cong Caravan & Camping Park
11 Joyce's Tower
12 Ashford Castle & Hotel
13 Corrib Cruises Pier
14 Cong Hostel
15 Moytura House

Around Cong

0   1   2 km

stone circle and a curious folly. The limestone strata of the Cong area account for the numerous caves, for the failure of the canal and for the local phenomenon known as 'the rising of the waters', where water from Lough Mask to the north percolates through the limestone and emerges from the ground at Cong before flowing down to Lough Corrib.

Caves

The Cong area is peppered with caves, many of them only a short walk from the village. The **Pigeon Hole** is about 1.5km west of Cong and can be reached by road or by the walking track from across the river. Stone steps lead down into the cave, which is sometimes very wet. There's a local legend about two fairy trout who dwell in the cave.

From the Pigeon Hole, take the R345 west towards Clonbur, passing the **Giant's Grave** turn-off and on to a lane that turns south about 5km from Cong. A stream flows into the extensive **Ballymaglancy Cave**, which is off the road to the right. The cave has stalactites and stalagmites and has been explored for about 500m.

Two other caves are north-east of Cong,

near the road to Cross (R346). **Captain Webb's Cave** is just outside the village, a short distance beyond the dry canal and behind the school grounds. It's actually a deep, water-filled hole in the ground where, two centuries ago, a local villain is said to have hurled a succession of local women. Another 200m from Cong, a wide path leads to **Kelly's Cave**, which is usually locked up; the key is kept at the Quiet Man Coffee Shop, and a small deposit may be required. **Lady's Buttery** and **Horse's Discovery** are two other caves beside a road to the castle.

The Dry Canal

Lough Mask is about 10m higher than Lough Corrib, and in the mid-18th century it was decided to cut a canal between the two. The project started in 1848, using labourers who were desperate for work due to the deprivations of the famine years. In 1854, when construction was nearing completion, the economic basis for the canal was already coming into question as railways rapidly spread across the country. And then a much greater problem was discovered – the canal was not watertight. The porous limestone simply soaked up any water that flowed into the canal like a plughole. Although various schemes for sealing the canal bed were considered, the whole expensive project was abandoned in 1858. The dry canal, complete with locks for raising and lowering the water level, runs north-south to the east of Cong.

Circles & Graves

The stone slabs of the megalithic burial chamber known as the **Giant's Grave** can be easily visited between the Pigeon Hole and the Ballymaglancy Cave. A path leads into the forest to the south of the R345 road to Clonbur, about 3km from Cong. About 100m from the road take the turn-off to the left; the grave is off that path to the right.

There are several stone circles in the area, including an excellent one just to the east side of the road from Cong to Neale at Nymphsfield, about 1.5km north-east of Cong. Just north of the road from Cong to Cross is **Ballymagibbon Cairn**, supposedly

the site of a legendary Celtic battle. **Moytura House**, near the shores of Lough Corrib, takes its name from this battle and was a childhood home of Oscar Wilde.

Neale

The village of Neale, 5km north-east of Cong, has some interesting sites. Neale Park is on the east side of the road, and if you take the turn-off at the northern end of the village, the curious stone known as the **'Gods of the Neale'** is about 200m east of the main road, just inside the walls of the park. The slab, originally found in a nearby cave, is carved with figures of a human, an animal and a reptile in low relief and is dated 1757.

Inchagoill Island

In the centre of Lough Corrib, the island of Inchagoill (actually County Galway) has the ruins of the 5th century St Patrick's Church, the 12th century Church of the Saint, and an ancient obelisk in the graveyard. The island can be reached by boat from the jetty next to Ashford Castle (see the previous Boating section) and from Oughterard in County Galway.

WESTPORT

Westport (Cathair na Mairt), in the southern half of County Mayo, didn't acquire its postcard prettiness gradually like many other small Irish towns. It was designed that way, and the Mall, with the River Carrowbeg running right down the middle of it, is as nice a main street as you'll find anywhere. The present Westport House was built on the site of an O'Malley castle, which was once surrounded by about 60 hovels and the original settlement of Westport. These were moved when the house was planned, and the Brownes, who came here from Sussex during the reign of Elizabeth I, even had the course of the river altered to make the Mall a grand approach to the gates of the house. This wasn't entirely successful, as the Mall is still subject to occasional flooding.

Orientation & Information

Westport consists of two parts: the town

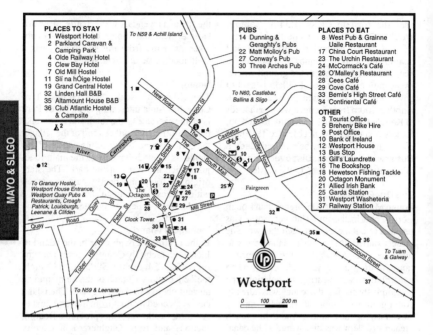

PLACES TO STAY
1 Westport Hotel
2 Parkland Caravan & Camping Park
4 Olde Railway Hotel
6 Clew Bay Hotel
7 Old Mill Hostel
11 Slí na hÓige Hostel
19 Grand Central Hotel
32 Linden Hall B&B
35 Altamount House B&B
36 Club Atlantic Hostel & Campsite

PUBS
14 Dunning & Geraghty's Pubs
22 Matt Molloy's Pub
27 Conway's Pub
30 Three Arches Pub

PLACES TO EAT
8 West Pub & Grainne Uaile Restaurant
17 China Court Restaurant
23 The Urchin Restaurant
24 McCormack's Café
26 O'Malley's Restaurant
28 Cees Café
29 Cove Café
33 Bernie's High Street Café
34 Continental Café

OTHER
3 Tourist Office
5 Breheny Bike Hire
9 Post Office
10 Bank of Ireland
12 Westport House
13 Bus Stop
15 Gill's Laundrette
16 The Bookshop
18 Hewetson Fishing Tackle
20 Octagon Monument
21 Allied Irish Bank
25 Garda Station
31 Westport Washeteria
37 Railway Station

Westport

0   100   200 m

---

proper and Westport Quay on the bay, just outside of town on the road to Louisburgh (R335). The tourist office (☎ 098-25711) on the Mall opens all year. Between April and September, the hours are Monday to Saturday, 9 am to 6 pm; in July and August it opens on Sunday as well. The rest of the year it's open Monday to Friday, 9 am to 5.15 pm and closes for lunch 12.45 to 2 pm. For information about fishing, enquire at Hewetson (☎ 098-26018) on Bridge St.

There's an Allied Irish Bank on Shop St and the Bank of Ireland is on the North Mall, next to the post office. The Bookshop on Bridge St has a good selection of OS maps.

Westport Washeteria, open Monday to Saturday, 9.30 am to 6 pm, is on Mill Street near the clocktower, but Gill's Laundrette on James St is more convenient to the hostel.

The telephone code is ☎ 098.

Westport House

The present house (☎ 25430) dates from 1730. Commercialisation is pushed to the hilt here, from a hokey 'dungeon' to tacky souvenirs for sale in the 'gifte shoppe'. Entry to the house is a pricey IR£6/3, but if you're planning to visit the zoo as well, the cost only rises to IR£6.50/3.25 (family tickets IR£18.50). The house and zoo are open Monday to Saturday, 10.30 am to 6 pm, and 2 to 6 pm on Sunday from late June to late August. During early June, the rest of August and early September it opens only in the afternoon 2 to 5 or 6 pm. Only consider a visit if your itinerary doesn't take in a stately home elsewhere in Ireland.

To reach Westport House in a vehicle, head out of town west on Quay Road towards Croagh Patrick and Louisburgh, and the entry road is on the right. An alternative approach is on foot via the Westport Hotel. Enter through the iron gates to the right of the hotel's entrance and follow the path until you reach the sign for the zoo on the right. Go down to the left, cross the small red bridge and follow the river to the right. It takes about 10 minutes.

Westport Heritage Centre
The heritage centre (☎ 26852) in Westport Quay has an interesting collection of local artefacts and documents, including the spinning wheel presented by the people of Ballina to Maud Gonne, the dynamic political rebel who was married briefly to Major John MacBride and was the object of Yeats' adoration. Also housed in this centre are the records of the trial of Patrick Egan, who commandeered Westport House during the 1798 Rising. The centre opens daily June to August, 10 am to 4 pm, and 11 am to 3 pm in May, September and October. Admission is IR£1.

The Octagon Monument
This memorial was erected in 1845 in honour of an eminently forgettable local banker, whose statue stood upon an octagonal podium at the top of the column. During the Civil War, Free State troops decapitated the statue, and it was later removed. In 1990 a Roman-looking statue of St Patrick complete with serpent-entwined staff replaced the unfortunate capitalist.

Places to Stay
Camping Camping is recommended at the *Club Atlantic Hostel*, where a riverside site costs IR£4. *Parkland Caravan & Camping Park* (☎ 27766) on the Westport House estate and accessible by the same road that leads to the house, charges an outrageous IR£17.50/13 for one night's pitch of a family/two-person tent. If the hostel sites are full, consider the *Old Head Forest campsite* 16km away near Louisburgh (see that section for details).

Hostels The well equipped IHH *Old Mill Hostel* (☎ 27045) is right in the centre in Barrack Yard just off James St and costs IR£6.50 a night. There's one double room for IR£13, four family rooms, and the hostel opens all year. The super IHH *Club Atlantic Holiday Hostel* (☎ 26644), on Altamount St

near the railway station, has even better facilities; dormitory beds are IR£5.50 to IR£6.50, singles are IR£8 to IR£14, and double rooms are IR£14 to IR£19. Although there's an enormous eat-in kitchen, you can order breakfast/packed-lunch/dinner (with vegetarian choices) for IR£2/3/5. It opens March to October.

Two other hostels in Westport are the IHO *Granary* (☎ 25903) at Westport Quay, just before the Westport House entrance. Beds are IR£5 and it opens January to November. The *Slí na hÓige* (Way of Youth hostel) (☎ 26459) on the Fairgreen opens June to October. It charges IR£5 for a bed and IR£7 per person in one private room.

The IHH *Country School Hostel* (☎ 41099) in Kilmeena, 5km north-west of Westport, has dorm beds for IR£7, private rooms for IR£8 per person and opens June to mid-September.

B&Bs The tourist office books rooms in the town's plentiful supply of B&Bs, but if you should arrive late, try *Linden Hall* (☎ 27005) on Altamount St, with rooms in two separate houses for IR£15 per person and open all year, or *Altamount House* (☎ 25226), a few doors up and closer to the railway station, with singles/doubles for IR£19/28. It opens March to mid-November.

Hotels *Clew Bay* hotel (☎ 25438) on James St has 29 rooms from IR£35/50 or IR£47.50/75, depending on the season. In this category, however, the 14-room *Grand Central* (☎ 25027) at the Octagon is better value at IR£30/50 or IR£35/70. The 15-room *Olde Railway Hotel* (☎ 25166), where Thackeray chose to stay on his tour around Ireland in the 19th century, is next to the tourist office. Singles/doubles in this Victorian showcase cost from IR£60/80 in the high season (June to October). The *Westport Hotel* (☎ 25122), with 74 rooms on New Rd, is functional by comparison but charges more during the same period: IR£67/104.

Places to Eat
Bridge St has a fair selection of cafés; try

McCormack's, where lunch is around IR£7, or the *Cove* farther down. Another good choice for lunch or a snack is *Bernie's High Street Café*, south of the clocktower, or the *Continental Café*, almost opposite with good vegetarian food. On the Octagon, *O'Cee's* is a popular soup-and-sandwich place open Monday to Saturday, 9 am to 7 pm.

The *Grainne Uaile* restaurant at the West pub on the corner of Bridge St and the South Mall opens for lunch and dinner daily to 10 pm and main courses are about IR£7.95.

The immensely popular *O'Malley's* upstairs on Bridge St has a vast and varied menu of pizza, steak and seafood (IR£7.50 to IR£10). Almost opposite is the charming *Urchin* restaurant, with *nouvelle* main courses in the IR£8.50 to IR£12 range. If you're in need of a fix of rice or noodles, you could do worse than at the *China Court* (☎ 28177), in Market Lane off Bridge St. It opens daily for dinner 5 to 11.30 pm and main courses start at IR£5.50.

At Westport Quay, just outside town on the road to Louisburgh (R335), there are a number of pubs and restaurants mostly specialising in seafood. Near the entrance to Westport House, *Quay Cottage* (☎ 26412) has a nautical theme and evening meals are around IR£15. On the quay itself the *Moorings* restaurant (☎ 25874) is in the house where Major John MacBride, briefly married to Maud Gonne and executed after the 1916 Rising, was born. Both these places open for dinner and Sunday lunch. Nearby, the *Asgard Tavern*, the *Towers Bar*, *Ardmore House* and still farther out toward Louisburgh, the *Shebeen* pub, all serve pub food, lunch and dinner.

Entertainment

There are a number of excellent pubs in Westport, including those on Quay Rd, with music most weekends and throughout the summer. *Matt Molloy's* on Bridge St is owned by Matt Molloy of the Chieftains; it's way overcrowded and they sometimes charge IR£5 when they have 'name' Irish music sessions. *Conway's* on Bridge St is a quieter, old-style place, and the *Three Arches*

near the clocktower sometimes has music. Two pubs rubbing shoulders and facing the Octagon, *Dunning* and *Geraghty's*, put tables out on the pavement on fine days. The *West* pub on the corner of Bridge St and the South Mall has music sessions on Sunday.

Getting There & Away

Buses running Monday to Saturday to/from the Octagon in Westport include: two to Achill; three to Ballina (one on Sunday); one to Belfast; three or four to Cork; five or six to Galway (one on Sunday); three or four to Limerick and Shannon (one on Sunday); and two to Sligo (one on Sunday). Edward Walsh Coaches (☎ 35165) runs buses from the town hall on Friday morning and early Sunday evening to Eyre Square in Galway.

The railway station (☎ 25253) is up Altamount St 500m from the Fairgreen and within easy walking distance. There are three daily connections (four on Friday) with Dublin (3½ hours) via Athlone.

Getting Around

You can call a taxi on ☎ 27171. Bicycles can be hired from Breheny Bike Hire (☎ 25020) on Castlebar St just east of the Mall or from the Club Atlantic Holiday Hostel for IR£6/30 a day/week. The latter also provides a trilingual pamphlet with seven suggested itineraries.

AROUND WESTPORT
Croagh Patrick

Croagh Patrick (also known as the Reek) towers to the west of Westport. It was from the top of this mountain that St Patrick performed his snake-expulsion act – Ireland has been free of venomous serpents ever since. Climbing the 765m holy mountain is an act of penance for thousands of pilgrims on the last Sunday of July (Reek Sunday); the truly contrite make the trek along Tóchar Phádraig (Patrick's Causeway), the original 40km route from Ballintubber Abbey, and ascend the mountain barefoot.

The trail for mortal folk begins at Campbell's pub in the village of Murrisk, west of Westport. There's a sign between the pub and the car park pointing the way, and there's no mistaking the route. If the weather is clear, the two-hour climb gives fine views at any time of year.

Louisburgh

The town got its name from the 1st marquess of Sligo, who laid it out and who had a relative fighting against the French at the Battle of Louisburgh in Canada. Louisburgh (Cluain Cearbán) is home to the **Granuaile Visitor Centre** (☎ 098-66195), dedicated to the life and times of Grace O'Malley (1530-1603), the pirate queen and the most famous of the O'Malley clan. The centre, in a disused church on Church St just past the fire station, also includes an exhibit devoted to the Famine. Admission is IR£2.50/1.50 and, during the summer, it's open 10 am to 7.30 pm, Monday to Saturday. There's a tourist information board in the centre of town on the corner of Long and Church Sts.

There are some excellent **beaches** in the vicinity; Old Head Beach (which has a Blue Flag) and the Silver Strand are particularly sandy and safe and are suitable for surfing and other water sports. About 4km from Louisburgh and just off the main road to Westport is the *Old Head Forest Caravan & Camping Park* (☎ 098-66021). Large/small tents cost IR£7/6 plus 50p per person. The beach is only 300m away.

Doolough Valley

There are two roads connecting Westport and Leenane but the one nearest the coast (the R335) via Delphi (see the County Galway chapter) and Louisburgh travels through the stunning Doolough Valley. It's wildly beautiful, not least because of the lonely expanse of Doo Lough – the Dark Lake – with the Mweelrea Mountains behind. At the southern end of the lake, Bengorm rises to 702m. The landscape changes from baize green and sparkling wet stone to a forbidding grey, as shadows envelop everything when cloudbanks spread in from the Atlantic.

During the Potato Famine, the valley was the scene of tragedy when some 600 men, women and children walked from Louisburgh to Delphi Lodge in the hope that the landlord would offer them food. Help was flatly refused, and on the return journey around 400 perished through hunger and exposure. There's a memorial to the unfortunate souls along the road.

Killadoon

Killadoon is a small village on the coast reached by a narrow coastal road heading south from Louisburgh or by turning west off the R335 at Cregganbaun. The main attractions here are the panoramic ocean views and the sandy beaches. An inexpensive hotel in the area is the 10-room *Killadoon Beach*

Grace O'Malley, the Pirate Queen

Grace O'Malley (1530-1603), also called Granuaile, was the daughter of a Connaught chief who established her own fleet and commanded her own army. From her Clare Island base she attacked the ships of those who had submitted to the English. In 1566 she married Richard Burke (her first husband had died years earlier), a neighbouring clan chief, and her power grew to such an extent that the merchants of Galway pleaded with the English governor to do something about her.

In 1574 her castle was besieged, but she turned the siege into a rout and sent the English packing. In 1577 she was held in prison but, mysteriously, managed to get herself released on a promise of good behaviour. Over the next few years she craftily entered a number of alliances, both with and against the English.

In 1593 she travelled to London and was granted a pardon after meeting Elizabeth I, who offered to make her a countess. Grace declined, for she already considered herself the queen of Connaught.

Back in Ireland she appeared to be working for the English, but the final recorded reference to her in the English State Papers of 1681 makes it seem likely that she was still fiercely independent. An English captain tells of meeting one of her pirate ships, captained by one of her sons, on its way to plunder a merchant ship. By that time she was more than 50 years of age. ∎

MAYO & SLIGO

Hotel (☎ 098-68605), charging between IR£14 and IR£20 per person, depending on the room category and season.

Getting There & Away
Between two and three buses a day link Westport and Louisburgh via Murrisk. On Thursday only the service continues on to Killadoon.

CLARE ISLAND
Clare Island (population 150) has the ruins of a Cistercian abbey and a castle, both associated with Grace O'Malley, the pirate queen. The tower castle was her stronghold, although it was altered considerably when the coast guard service took it over in 1831. Grace is supposed to be buried in the small abbey, which contains a stone with her family motto: 'Invincible on land and sea'.

The island is also one of the dwindling number of places where you can find choughs, which look like blackbirds but have red beaks.

The island has safe, sandy beaches and is perfect for walking and climbing on a clear day. The highest point, Mt Knockmore (461m) dominates the landscape. The island's only hotel (☎ 098-26307) has tourist information and attracts sea anglers, scuba divers and sailing folk.

Places to Stay & Eat
Free *camping* should not be a problem. The *Bay View Hotel* (☎ 098-26307) beside the harbour is the main accommodation here (open June to September) and singles/doubles are from IR£21/37. There are a number of B&Bs, the least expensive being *Ballytoughey Lodge* (☎ 098-25412) at IR£15 per person, which also offers organised treks and residential study tours. Mary O'Malley's *Cois Abhainn* (☎ 098-26216), 5km from the harbour, costs IR£16/28 for singles/doubles while the more unusual *Clare Island Lighthouse* (☎ 098-45120), which dates back to 1806, has all the comforts one would expect for IR£50/80.

If you're going for just one day, it's best to take your own lunch – though food is available at the Bay View Hotel and the B&Bs all do evening meals for residents and non-residents (from IR£9.50).

Getting There & Away
The *Pirate Queen*, run by Clare Island Ferry & Clew Bay Cruises (☎ 098-28288; mobile ☎ 087-414653) and Chris O'Grady (☎ 098-26307) make the 90-minute trip April to September from Westport Quay to Clare Island. In April and May there's a sailing from Westport Quay at 11 am and June to September at 11 am, noon and 6 pm; they depart Clare Island at 10 am in April and May, and at 10 and 11.30 am and 5 pm June to September. Return fares are IR£10/5 adults/children. When the tides are unsuitable, sailings are from Roonagh Quay, 8km west of Louisburgh.

INISHTURK ISLAND
Evidence of pre-Christian life has been found on this island, but it's believed that the ancestors of many of today's inhabitants were probably driven there in Cromwell's time.

This island does not receive many tourists, despite the two sandy beaches on its east side, wonderful flora & fauna and a rugged landscape ideal for random walking. B&B is available from a few of the farmhouses, including *Tranaun House* (☎ 098-45655) for IR£13/24 singles/doubles. Dinner is IR£8.

Contact the island's tourist association (☎ 098-45510) for details of transport from Roonagh Quay. The *Cahar Star* (☎ 098-45541) sails from Cleggan Pier in County Galway to Inishturk via Inishbofin in summer on Tuesday and Thursday at 11.30 am. It leaves Inishturk at 9.30 am.

NEWPORT
The small town of Newport (Baile Uí Fhiacháin) on the banks of the River Newport is often just passed through on the way to Achill, but it deserves a closer look.

From the end of the 19th century until 1937, the Great Western Railway ran a line from Westport to Achill Sound. Some 50 years later the route was pedestrianised and now offers an interesting walk, with views of the river.

On the western end of Main St, there is a mural on the gable end of a house depicting the arrest of Father Manus Sweeney who led the Achill contribution to the 1798 Rising and was later executed.

There's a tourist information office (☎ 098-41822) near this mural and opposite the Angler's Restaurant; it opens in summer only. Newport is also the beginning – or end – of the Bangor Trail. See the Bangor Erris section.

Places to Stay & Eat

In the centre is *Debille House* (☎ 098-41145) with singles/doubles for IR£21/32 and open mid-May to September. The *Nelphin View* (☎ 098-41481) on the Mulrany road (N59) charges IR£19/28 and opens all year. The poshest place in these parts is *Newport House* (☎ 098-41222), right in the centre, which charges from IR£76/132.

The *Bridge Inn* on Main St next to the entrance of Newport House serves light food for around IR£5, and the *Debille House Café* charges about the same. Across the river on the road to Westport, the *Black Oak Inn* has a small restaurant. Dinner at *Newport House* is a stiff IR£30, but the snug little bar is worth a visit any time.

Getting There & Away

In July and August the bus from Achill to Belfast stops at Newport and goes on through Ballina, Sligo, Enniskillen; another service continues on to Derry from Sligo during the same period. Throughout the year, one daily bus links Achill and Ballina via Newport from Monday to Saturday. The bus stop is outside Chambers' pub.

AROUND NEWPORT
Burrishoole Abbey

The abbey was founded in 1486 by the Dominicans. What remains is a solid tower and the east window of the cloisters. It's beside the river that drains Lough Furnace into the sea. About 2.5km beyond Newport

on the Newport-Achill road, a sign points the way down to the left.

Rockfleet Castle

Formerly known as Carrigahowley, this 15th century castle has a strong association with Grace O'Malley.

The story goes that after the death of her first husband, Grace married a second time – to Richard Burke – on the condition that at the end of the first year either party could summarily dissolve the marriage. When the year was up she shut herself up in her fortified castle and announced the divorce as he approached.

Whether the story is true or not, the castle does look impregnable. Grace O'Malley is supposed to have lived out the rest of her years here, and she successfully repulsed an English force besieging the castle. To get there, turn south at the sign about 5km beyond Newport on the road to Achill.

Mulrany

This small town (also called Mallaranny) stands on the isthmus between Clew Bay, with its (supposed) 365 islands, and Bellacagher Bay and boasts a lovely big beach. To get to it, either take the footpath opposite the defunct Mulrany Bay Hotel, a huge chocolate-and-cream pile on the N59, or continue a little way past the hotel and bear left following the Atlantic Drive sign and then left again where the sign points to Mallaranny Strand, another Blue Flag beach.

The Mulrany Bay Hotel may reopen one day and if it does the owners will hopefully retain the Lennon Suite, named after John Lennon when he came here for a visit and ended up purchasing one of the little islands in Clew Bay.

Places to Stay & Eat

An Óige's *Traenlaur Lodge* hostel (☎ 098-41358), charging IR£4.50/5.50 or IR£5/6.50 for juniors/seniors depending on the season, is on Lough Feeagh 8km from Newport and signposted on the road to Achill. Achill seems the obvious destination if you're travelling from Newport, but the wild Curraun

MAYO & SLIGO

Peninsula, joined to Achill Island by a bridge, has a couple of B&Bs where you can get away from it all. *Curraun House* (☎ 098-45228) is attached to the George Pub, which serves lunch and dinner, and B&B is IR£12.50 per person. To get there, follow the beautiful Atlantic Drive road from Mulrany; Curraun House, open June to September, is on the south-west corner of the peninsula, just before a sign pointing up to Achill Sound. Farther up this road, just before the Sound, Mrs Cannon's *Teach Mweewillin* (☎ 098-45134) charges IR£21/34 and opens April to September. The beach at Mulrany has a field marked out for *camping*, and there are public toilets nearby.

ACHILL ISLAND

Joined to the mainland by a bridge, Achill combines views, bogland and mountains on just one island – at 147 sq km, the largest off the Irish coast. For most of this century Achill (Acaill) was forgotten by tourists and, many of the islanders would assert, the Dublin government. The amount of arable land is limited here, and there are few employment opportunities to keep young people around. The deserted village of Slievemore is the most dramatic example of the process of decay in remote rural Ireland. But that may all start to change as the number of visitors increases dramatically every year.

Information

The tourist office (☎ 098-45384), open July and August only, is above Alice's Harbour Inn, just before the bridge over Achill Sound. A few km farther along on the road to Keel, an Esso garage (☎ 098-47242) also dispenses tourist information.

O'Malley's Spar supermarket at Keel doubles as a post office and will change money.

The telephone code is ☎ 098.

Slievemore Deserted Village

Different explanations have been given for the abandonment of Slievemore some time in the middle of the 19th century. The 'booley houses' here were the summer residences of cattle grazers. Years of famine may have forced them to seek a living nearer the sea, and the inhabitants, it seems, moved permanently down to the coast at Dooagh. There has been talk of renovating a couple of the ruins and establishing an interpretive centre here.

Beaches

Achill has some lovely beaches that are often all but deserted even in fine weather. Four of them – at Keel, Keem, and Dugort (Doogort on some maps) – are Blue Flag beaches and the ones at Dooega, Dooagh and Dooniver are just as sandy.

Activities

The island is perfect for walking and even the highest point (Mt Slievemore, 672m) presents no problems. It can be climbed from behind the deserted village and from the top there are terrific views of Blacksod Bay. A longer climb would take in Croaghaun (668m), Achill Head and a walk atop what are said to be the highest cliffs in Europe. The walk is covered in the *New Irish Walks: West & North* (Gill & Macmillan) by Whilde & Simms.

Sea angling gear is sold by O'Malley's Island Sports (☎ 43125) in Keel. It can also arrange boat hire.

Other activities include windsurfing, hang-gliding from the top of Mt Minaun (403m), rock climbing and surfing. If you're interested in any of these, it's worth calling in at the Activity & Leisure Centre on the road to Keel. McDowell's Hotel south-west of Dugort hires out canoes and surfboards.

Places to Stay

Camping The first campsite is at *Alice's Harbour Inn*, on the Curraun Peninsula just before the bridge to Achill Island. In the north, close by the Valley House Hostel and on the beach, is *Lavelle's Golden Strand Caravan & Camping Park* (☎ 47232), charging a combined IR£4.50/50p/25p per tent/adult/child and open April to October. To the west is the *Seal Caves Caravan & Camping Park* (☎ 43262) which charges

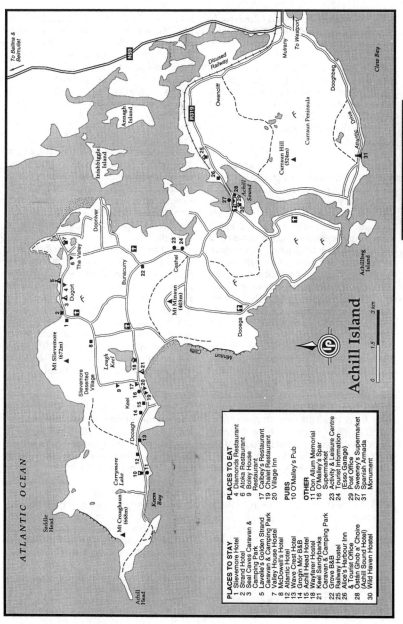

Achill Island

ATLANTIC OCEAN

Clew Bay

To Ballina &
Belmullet

To Westport

Saddle
Head

Achill
Head

PLACES TO STAY
1 Slievemore Hotel
2 Strand Hotel
3 Seal Caves Caravan &
 Camping Park
5 Lavelle's Golden Strand
 Caravan & Camping Park
7 Valley House Hostel
8 McDowell's Hotel
12 Atlantic Hotel
13 Wave Crest Hotel
14 Grogin Mór B&B
15 Achill Head Hotel
18 Wayfarer Hostel
21 Keel Sandybanks
 Caravan & Camping Park
25 Grove B&B
26 Railway Hostel
 Alice's Harbour Inn
 & Tourist Office
28 Óstán Ghob a' Choire
 (Achill Sound Hotel)
30 Wild Haven Hostel

PLACES TO EAT
4 Diamonds Restaurant
6 Atoka Restaurant
9 Boley House
 Restaurant
17 Calbey's Restaurant
19 Chalet Restaurant
20 Village Inn

PUBS
10 O'Malley's Pub

OTHER
11 Don Allum Memorial
16 O'Malley's Spar
 Supermarket
23 Activity & Leisure Centre
24 Tourist Information
 (Esso Garage)
29 Post Office
27 Sweeney's Supermarket
31 Spanish Armada
 Monument

IR£5/50p. At Keel there is *Keel Sandybanks Caravan & Camping Park* (☎ 43211) charging IR£6.

Hostels The IHO *Railway Hostel* (☎ 45187) is on the east side of Achill Sound bridge, just up from the tourist office. Beds are IR£6 and the one double is IR£14. The excellent IHO *Wild Haven Hostel* (☎ 45392) is over the bridge on the left behind the church. The basic rate is IR£6 and two-bed rooms cost IR£2 extra per person. Breakfast and evening meals can be ordered in advance at this welcoming hostel, which also has a bar. Both hostels are open year round.

The IHO *Valley House Hostel* (☎ 47204), also with a licensed bar and IR£6 beds, is in the north of the island, with some lovely sandy beaches within walking distance. It opens mid-March to October. To get there, take the road to Keel and turn right (northeast) at the Bunacurry junction signposted for Dugort. The IHH *Wayfarer Hostel* (☎ 43266), open mid-March to mid-October, is in the village of Keel. Beds here are IR£6 and the three private rooms are IR£7 per person.

B&Bs & Hotels At the Bunacurry junction, the *Grove* (☎ 47108) has rooms with shared bathrooms for IR£15/28. Farther west in Keel, Mrs Quinn's *Grogin Mór* (☎ 43385) charges from IR£20/30. The nearby *Achill Head Hotel* (☎ 43108) has 19 rooms from IR£18/30. The 36-room *Óstán Ghob a' Choire* (☎ 45245) – the Achill Sound Hotel in English – is on the west side of Achill Sound bridge and charges IR£24/44 in high season.

At Dugort, the *Slievemore Hotel* (☎ 43224), with 18 rooms, charges IR£20 per person, while the nearby 15-room *Strand Hotel* (☎ 43241), facing the sea and close to a small beach, costs the same. *McDowell's Hotel* (☎ 43148) on Slievemore Rd to the south-west has 10 rooms from IR£23 per person.

Out at Dooagh, the 12-room *Wave Crest Hotel* (☎ 43115) has singles/doubles in summer from IR£18/34. The other hotel

here, the *Atlantic* (☎ 43113) charges from IR£26/41 in summer for its 10 rooms. Opposite the hotel is the spot where Don Allum, the first person to row across the Atlantic Ocean in *both* directions, landed in his 6m-long plywood boat, the *QE3* after 77 days at sea in September 1982. O'Malley's Pub opposite has photos and other memorabilia of the feat.

Places to Eat
If you're camping or hostelling, stock up at Sweeney's supermarket, which is just across the bridge on Achill, or at O'Malley's Spar supermarket in Keel. Nearly all the hotels serve lunch or dinner to non-residents, with dinner costing from IR£14 at the *Strand* in Dugort to IR£17.50 at the *Atlantic* in Dooagh.

At Dugort the cosy little *Atoka Restaurant* has a conventional menu of grilled meat dishes for around IR£6 to IR£8. Farther along the road, *Diamonds* is worth a try. At Keel the most popular eating place is the *Boley House Restaurant* (☎ 43147); if this is full try farther down the road at the junction where *Calbey's* opens all day and serves breakfast. Also close by is the *Village Inn* serving pub food and dinner and the *Chalet* restaurant offering a seafood menu.

Entertainment
In summer most pubs and hotels have music. The best time of the year for traditional Irish music and dance is the first two weeks of August, when Irish culture is promoted through a number of workshops. Most bands end up in the pubs at night.

Getting There & Away
In July and August a bus runs from Dooagh, outside O'Malley's, to Keel, Achill Sound, Westport, Sligo, Enniskillen and eventually Belfast. It leaves Dooagh at 7.30 am and Achill Sound 20 minutes later. Coming from Westport the bus leaves at 5.45 pm. Another service continues on to Derry from Sligo during the same period.

Throughout the year Monday to Saturday, a bus runs across the island from Dooagh, taking in Keel, Dugort and Dooega before crossing to Mulrany, Newport, Westport and finally Ballina. Check with the tourist office for the schedule as it changes daily.

Getting Around

Bikes can be hired from the hostels, the Achill Sound Hotel or O'Malley's Island Sports (☎ 43125) in Keel.

BELMULLET PENINSULA & BANGOR

Probably the least visited corner of the whole of Ireland, this strange and remote land, popularly known as the Mullet (or Béal an Mhuirthead in Irish), has a population density of only 10 people per sq km. The peninsula is 30km in length, rarely rising to more than 30m above sea level, and the boggy land offers a poor livelihood. The peninsula is Irish-speaking.

Information

The Lorras Domhnann tourist office (☎ 097-81500) is on the left side of the main road (R313) and next to the Erris Credit Union as you enter the town of Belmullet. McIntyre's Travel (☎ 097-81147), an agency on Main St, also has local information, and there's a tourist information board opposite the Anchor Pub. The Ulster Bank (Banc Uladh) is on Main St and a Bank of Ireland branch is at the roundabout to the east. The post office is at the western end of the same street, opposite the Údarás na Gaeltachta (Gaeltacht Authority; ☎ 097-82382), which has a small exhibition on the peninsula open weekdays, 9.30 am to 5 pm.

The telephone code is ☎ 097.

Belmullet

Belmullet was founded in 1825 by the local landlord, William Carter, and built on an unimaginative plan, with one main street and side roads at right angles. Carter also designed a canal joining Broad Haven Bay with Trawmore and Blacksod bays to the south, and a bridge now crosses the narrow channel.

Blacksod Point

The road south from Belmullet curves around the tip of the peninsula before rejoining itself at Aghleam. Near the point are the remains of an old church, and the view across the bay takes in the spot where *La Rata Santa Maria Encoronada*, part of the 1588 Spanish Armada, came in and was later burned by the captain, who then left to join two other Spanish ships that had found refuge farther north in Elly Bay.

The road to Blacksod Point passes sandy Mullaghroe Beach on the east. In the early years of this century, a whaling station operated at Ardelly Point, just north of the beach. There's also a decent beach at Elly Bay.

Doonamo Point

This typical promontory fort is the main point of interest north of Belmullet and is built on a spit of land and defended by water on three sides. There are other forts farther north near Erris Head, but this one is the most accessible.

Bangor Erris

The main reason for being here is to begin or end the long-distance Bangor Trail that connects Bangor, as it's called, and Newport. This is an extraordinary walk that takes you through the bleakest and most remote landscape to be found anywhere in Ireland. The useful *County Mayo: The Bangor Trail* (IR£6) by Joe McDermott and Robert Chapman is available in Keohane's bookshop in Ballina and elsewhere. Unfortunately, you'll need more than one of the 1:50,000 Ordnance Survey maps to cover this trail.

Places to Stay & Eat

There's the usual run of bungalow B&Bs on the main road approaching Belmullet; singles/doubles are IR£15/25 at the *Western Strands Hotel* (☎ 81096) on Main St. If its 10 rooms are full, Mrs Gaughan's *Mill House* (☎ 81181) in nearby American St has four rooms for IR£16/26. It opens June to August. In Bangor, *Hillcrest House* B&B (☎ 83494) charges from IR£19/28 and opens all year.

MAYO & SLIGO

Some 16km east of Belmullet at Pollatomish, signposted on the road to Ballycastle (R314), the IHH *Kilcommon Lodge Hostel* (☎ 84621) has beds for IR£6 and four double rooms for IR£14. It opens mid-March to November and there's a sandy beach and headland walks nearby.

In Belmullet the *Appetiser Café* at the top end of Main St does soup, salads and sandwiches for under IR£2. There's also the *Anchor Bar* for pub food and *Paddy's Family Fare Restaurant* on the roundabout at the start of Main St. The *Western Strands* serves snacks and a set dinner for IR£15. Opposite Hillcrest House in Bangor, *Kitty's Tavern* serves pub food all day and has fresh and smoked local salmon for sale.

Getting There & Around

One bus runs Monday to Saturday from Ballina to Bangor (one hour) and Belmullet (1½ hours) then south to Blacksod Point. Contact the bus station in Ballina (☎ 096-71800) or the Lorras Domnhnann tourist office in Belmullet for the schedule. McNulty Coaches (☎ 81016), with an office on Chapel St in Belmullet, runs a bus to Galway and Ennis in County Clare via Newport and Westport on Sunday at 5.30 pm. There's also a daily service to Castlebar via Newport departing at 8.15 am and leaving from Castlebar at 5.30 pm. There's an additional service from Belmullet on Sunday at 5.30 pm.

In Belmullet, you can hire bikes from Walsh's Garage (☎ 82260) on Chapel St, opposite the McNulty's Coaches office.

BALLINA & AROUND

The largest town in the county, Ballina is renowned for its fishing and is a good base for exploring north Mayo and the North Mayo Sculpture Trail. The tourist office has free maps of interesting walks near the town. Ballina (Béal an Átha) is a not-unattractive Connaught town, with some decent pubs and fine restaurants. Its most famous progeny is Mary Robinson, the much missed former president of Ireland.

Information

The tourist office (☎ 096-70848) is across the River Moy from the centre on Cathedral Rd near West Bridge. It opens 10 am to 5.45 pm (closed 1 to 2 pm), Monday to Saturday, mid-April to September. There are several banks on Pearse St, including the Ulster Bank with an ATM and Bank of Ireland. The post office is at the top of O'Rahilly St.

Keohane's bookshop on Tone St has a decent selection of maps and walking guides. Opposite is the Jiffy Cleaners laundrette.

The telephone code is ☎ 096.

Rosserk Abbey

Situated close to the River Rosserk, a tributary of the Moy, this Franciscan abbey dates back to the middle of the 15th century. It's remarkably well preserved, and there is an interesting carved piscina (a perforated stone basin for carrying away the water used in rinsing the chalices) in the chancel. Like Rathfran Abbey near Killala, Rosserk was burned down by Richard Bingham, the English governor of Connaught in the 16th century.

To get there, leave Ballina on the R314 for Killala and after 6.5km turn right at the sign and take the first left at the next crossroads. Beware of the loose sign at this junction, which may point in any direction but the right one. Continue for another km and turn right at the next sign for the abbey.

Moyne Abbey

This abbey was established by the Franciscans around the same time as Rosserk. It, too, was burned down by Richard Bingham in the 16th century and perhaps he did a better job on this one, as it is in worse condition than its neighbour.

After leaving Rosserk Abbey go back to the main road and continue north for another 3km until you can see the abbey on the right across a field. After returning across the field continue north-west for 1.5km until the main R314 is reached. Turn right for Killala or left for Ballina.

North Mayo Sculpture Trail

This 'trail' of 15 outdoor sculptures essentially follows the R314 from Ballina (Point 'A', *Guest Space* by Peter Hynes) to Blacksod Point (Point 'O', *Deirble's Twist* by Michael Bulfin). The project was inaugurated to mark 5000 years of Mayo history and leading sculptors from eight countries were commission to create works of art reflecting the beauty and wilderness of the northern Mayo countryside.

Activities

The River Moy is one of the most prolific salmon rivers in Europe – 12,500 were caught here in the 1996 season alone – and a leaflet listing the fisheries and contacts for permits is available from the tourist office. From the large picture window of the lounge in the hostel, you can see the scaly critters jumping in the Ridge (or salmon pool), with otters and grey seals in famished pursuit. The season runs February to September, but the best fishing is June to August.

Lough Conn to the south-west of Ballina is also an important brown trout fishery, and there is no shortage of places with boats and ghillies available around the lake. Pontoon is a good base for trout fishing in both Lough Conn and Lough Cullin to the south, and again there are plenty of places hiring boats and dispensing advice. The daily rate for hiring a motor boat is around IR£25.

Woodpark Farm (☎ 70774) at Crofton Park 1.5km from Ballina has horses for hire (IR£8 to IR£10 per hour). Bakkina swimming pool (☎ 70506) near the tourist office on Cathedral Rd opens daily and costs IR£1.80/1.20.

Special Events

The two-week Ballina Street Festival (formerly the Salmon Festival), one of the best outdoor parties in the country, takes place in July; Heritage Day is when shop fronts – and Ballina townsfolk – take on a 19th century look during the festival. The popular Fleadh Cheoil na hÉireann (Music Festival of Ireland) was held here during the last weekend of August in 1997 and, as is tradi-tional, it will probably take place again in Ballina in 1998.

Places to Stay

The well equipped *Belleek Caravan & Camping Park* (☎ 71533) is 2.5km north of town off the road to Killala (R314). A tent costs IR£6, and there is a IR£1 charge per person. Hikers/motorcyclists pay IR£3.50/4

The IHH *Salmon Weir* (☎ 71903), one of the most attractive and best run hostels in Ireland, is housed in a converted timber and grain mill in Barrett St hard by the River Moy. Dorm beds cost IR£7.50 to IR£9, depending on the number in each room (four to six), and the eight private rooms, all ensuite, cost IR£9 to IR£11 per person.

Bartra House (☎ 22200) is an old-style hotel on Pearse St with 22 rooms costing IR£26.50 to IR£28 per person, depending on the season. Ballina's best hotel, complete with swimming pool, is the 50-room *Downhill* (☎ 21033) with singles/doubles in summer for IR£71.50/119. It's north of the centre on the Sligo road (N59).

An equally posh guesthouse, the *Mount Falcon Castle* (☎ 70811), 6.5km south of town on the Foxford road (N57), charges from IR£59/98 during the same period.

Places to Eat

Cafolla's is a café and takeaway on Bridge St and *Padraic's*, next to Keohane's bookshop, has a wide selection of quick meals from IR£5.95. There are lots of pubs on Pearse St serving lunch.

Salmon – poached, grilled, baked or smoked – is the speciality of Ballina and you could try it at the excellent *Old Bond Store* on Dillon St, which has a set salmon dinner for IR£12, or at *Murphy Bros*, a pub-restaurant on Clare St north of the tourist office. Another good choice for an over-budget meal is *Tullios* on Pearse St, with main courses averaging about IR£12 and set dinner for IR£19.

Entertainment

Ballina, with a population of just over 8000 people, counts some 60 pubs, and many of them have traditional music sessions on Wednesday and Friday evenings. Among the best are the *Broken Jug* at the top of O'Rahilly St, which also has *The Pulse* nightclub; *Brogan's* on Garden St; *Murphy Brothers* on Clare St; and *An Bolg Buí* ('the yellow belly') by the river on the corner of Bridge and Barrett Sts.

Getting There & Away
The bus and railway stations are on Kevin Barry St south-west of the centre and a short walk from the hostel. Bus Éireann buses (☎ 71800) go west to Achill, east to Sligo, to the North (Belfast, Enniskillen, Derry), and south to Limerick, Shannon and Cork.

There are also a couple of private bus companies running scheduled trips at cheaper rates though they basically operate to transport pupils and students to and from school. Treacy's (☎ 70968) runs a daily return service from outside Dunnes store on Pearse St to the Quay St car park in Sligo. Also, Barton Transport (☎ 01-628 6026) has a daily return service between Ballina and Dublin.

The Westport to Dublin train stops at Ballina up to three times daily. Connections to other routes can be made at Athlone.

Getting Around
Bicycles can be hired from Gerry's Cycle Centre (☎ 70455) on the Crossmolina road west of the centre. The Salmon Weir Hostel can arrange this for you.

CROSSMOLINA
The town of Crossmolina (Crois Mhaoiliona) itself is undistinguished, but it serves as a quiet retreat for anyone wishing to fish in Lough Conn or explore the lakes and scenery around Mt Nephin. The mountain (806m) takes under two hours to climb and is described, along with other walks in Mayo, in *New Irish Walks: West & North* (Gill & Macmillan) by Whilde and Simms.

North Mayo Family History Research & Heritage Centre
If you have a family connection with north-

ern Mayo, this is the place to contact (☎ 096-31809). An initial assessment will cost about IR£20 and if this looks promising, your full family record would be researched for between IR£50 and IR£100.

The heritage centre houses a collection of old farm machinery and domestic implements. It opens weekdays year round, 9 am to 4 pm (and Saturday and Sunday, 2 to 6 pm between June and September only).

Errew Abbey
The abbey is the remains of a house for Augustinian monks built around 1250 on the site of an earlier 7th century church. In common with other abbeys in Mayo, the monks wisely chose to live close to where they could fish, and the location of Errew Abbey is particularly picturesque.

To get there, take the road from Crossmolina that leads to the heritage centre, and 1km after the centre turn left at the sign and keep going for another 5km.

Places to Stay & Eat
Enniscoe House (☎ 096-31112) does B&B from IR£46/72, and dinner in this friendly 18th century home costs IR£22. It opens April to mid-October. *Shalom House* (☎ 096-31230) at Gortnor Abbey, open March to September, charges about IR£14 per person for B&B, and dinner is IR£12. The best food in Crossmolina is to be found in *Hiney's* pub in the town centre.

Getting There & Away
There are regular bus connections to Ballina and Castlebar. The bus stop is outside Hiney's pub.

KILLALA & AROUND
It's claimed that St Patrick founded Killala, and the 25m round tower is evidence of the role Killala (Cill Alaidh) played in early church history. The tower was struck by lightning in 1800 and the cap is a later reconstruction. The Church of Ireland cathedral is supposed to have been built on the site of the first Christian church, where St Patrick

installed Muiredach as the town's first bishop.

It's the French connection that has really put Killala on the map, however. On 22 August 1798, over 1000 troops under the command of General Humbert landed in Killala Bay, the plan being that Irish peasants would rise in rebellion and help Napoleon in his war against the English. At first there were dramatic successes, with Killala, Ballina and Castlebar falling. On 8 September, however, Humbert was defeated by Cornwallis at Ballinamuck in County Longford. The best account of Humbert's arrival in Killala was written by the Protestant Bishop Stock. He was put under house arrest by the French, and his *Narrative* is available in some bookshops in Ballina and Castlebar.

Information

Tourist information may be available during the summer from the Community Centre (☎ 096-32166) just beyond the turn-off for the hostel as you enter Killala on the Ballina road (R314).

The telephone code is ☎ 096.

Rathfran Abbey

The Dominicans came here in 1274 and built a friary; only the ruins remain. In 1590 the friary was closed down and burned by the English, but the monks remained in the community until the 18th century.

Take the R314 road that heads north out of Killala and after 5km turn right after crossing the Cloonaghmore River. After another couple of km turn right at the crossroads.

Breastagh Ogham Stone

The stone is 2.5m high, but the Ogham script is not easy to read. It's in a field by the left side of the R314 just past the crossroads with the turning for Rathfran Abbey (not the earlier crossroads, which has a sign for both the stone and the abbey). Cross the ditch just where the sign points to the stone.

Kilcummin

This is the place where General Humbert and his men landed in 1798. A right turn off the main R314 is signposted for Kilcummin. It's not a very dramatic spot.

The imagination is more easily kindled by the sculpture of the French revolutionary soldier helping a prostrate Irish peasant. It's on the main road just after the turning to Lacken Bay and marks the spot where the first French soldier died on Irish soil.

Lackan Bay & Downpatrick Head

Lackan Bay is wonderfully sandy and ideal for young children. Downpatrick Head has a fenced off blowhole that occasionally shoots up plumes of water. The rock stack just off the shore is Dun Briste.

Places to Stay & Eat

An Óige's *Cill Alaidh* hostel (☎ 32172), in an historic old stone building just off the Ballina road, is easily the best place for accommodation. Beds cost IR£4.50/5.50 or IR£5/6.50 for juniors/seniors, depending on the season, and the hostel opens March to October. The B&Bs are mostly outside town, such as *Rathoma House* (☎ 32035), which charges IR£21/32 and opens May to October, or *Beach View* (☎ 32023), reached by turning right at the sign to the beach. Singles/doubles at Beach View, which opens all year, are IR£19/28.

There are a couple of pubs in town, including the *Anchor Inn*, serving food and the *Country Kitchen*, one of the few restaurants around, has been recommended.

Getting There & Away

The Ballina to Ballycastle bus, which runs once or twice a day Monday to Saturday, stops outside the hostel and McGregor's.

BALLYCASTLE

Ballycastle (Baile an Chaisil) boasts some of the oldest and most extensive Stone Age archaeological excavations in Europe.

Information

A tourist information point (☎ 096-43256) may be open during the summer. If you're entering the town from Killala, it's on the right side of the main street at the bottom of

MAYO & SLIGO

town. Failing that, there is a tourist information board on the right side of the main street as you head west for Belmullet.

The telephone code is ☎ 096.

Céide Fields

Over 5000 years ago there was a wheat and barley farming community with domesticated cattle and sheep, just a few km west of Ballycastle at Céide Fields (Achaidh Chéide). The growth of the bog led to the decline and eventual end of the community and their stone walls and farm buildings disappeared into the bog. Perhaps the farmers, gradually diminishing the soil's fertility, contributed to the growth of the bog or maybe the wet climate made it inevitable. Whatever the cause, the farms lay buried for thousands of years but have now been excavated and opened to the public as the oldest enclosed landscape in Europe and the most extensive Stone Age monument in the world.

The OPW Interpretive Centre (☎ 43325), in a modern glass pyramid overlooking the site, incorporates an exhibition court and audiovisual room detailing aspects of the site's architecture, botany and geology (a script of the exhibition is available in French and German). There's also a panoramic viewing platform and tearooms. It opens daily, June to September, 9.30 am to 6.30 pm. Mid-March to May and in October and November, the hours are 10 am to 5 pm (4.30 pm in November). Admission is IR£2.50/1

Céide Fields is 8km west of Ballycastle on the main R314 road.

Places to Stay & Eat

B&B is available from *Sunatrai* (☎ 43040) on the road to Downpatrick Head for IR£18/30 from mid-June to mid-August. The *Céide House* pub (☎ 43105) in town also has similarly priced rooms.

Beyond Céide Fields at Belderrig, which has another prehistoric farm site, the *Hawthorns* (☎ 43148) does B&B all year from IR£16/24 as does the *Yellow Rose* (☎ 43125) for IR£16/26. *Tír Sáile* (☎ 21277), on the Killala side of Ballycastle, has attractive holiday cottages available for IR£90 to

IR£285 a week, depending on the size and season. It also has special weekend rates.

In town, the *Céide House* pub and the nearby *Castle Bar/Café* serve food from around IR£5. The other possibility is the more expensive *Doonferry House*, which is a few km west of town on the road to Céide Fields and has a restaurant and bar.

Getting There & Away

A bus runs between Ballina and Ballycastle once or twice a day, Monday to Saturday, stopping outside the Castle Bar & Café.

CASTLEBAR & AROUND

Although this is Mayo's county town and has a relatively large population (7650 people), Castlebar has far less appeal to travellers than Westport or even Ballina. The old shops have been replaced by modern stores, and there is little to evoke the history of the place. But Castlebar (Caisleán an Bharraigh) does have a place in history, for it was here in 1798 that General Humbert and his army of French revolutionary soldiers and dispossessed Irish peasants encountered the numerically stronger British forces under the command of General Lake. The defeat of the British and their ignominious cavalry retreat became known as the 'Castlebar Races'.

The attractive village green, known as the Mall, was once the cricket ground of the Lucan family who own a significant amount of property in the area. There's still a Lucan St close to the tourist office, and some tenants in Castlebar still pay rent to the Lucan estate, or at least they were until the notorious Lord Lucan disappeared after the murder of his children's nanny in London in 1974.

Information

The tourist office (☎ 094-21207) is on Linenhall St near the Castlebar Shopping Centre. To get there, turn left (west) at the northern end of Market St, the main thoroughfare. It opens mid-April to early September, 9.30 am to 5.30 pm (closed 1 to 2 pm).

There's an Allied Irish Bank next to the

Mandalay restaurant on Market St. Una's Laundrette is on New Antrim Rd, a short walk from the tourist office and hostel.

The telephone code is ☎ 094.

Turlough Round Tower

The 9th century tower stands next to a ruined 18th century church and a graveyard that is still in use. The tower is about 5km northeast of Castlebar on the main road to Ballina (N5).

Michael Davitt Memorial Museum

The museum (☎ 56488) in Straide (Strade on some maps) is attached to the church and houses a small collection of material relating to the life and times of Michael Davitt (1846-1906), a Fenian and founding member of the Irish National Land League, who is buried in the churchyard. The museum opens daily April to October.

Take the N5 Dublin road and turn left (north-east) onto the N58 to Straide. It's 16km from Castlebar.

Ballintubber Abbey

The only church in Ireland that was founded by an Irish king and is still in use, Ballintubber Abbey (☎ 30934) was over 250 years old when Columbus sailed to the New World. It was founded in 1216 next to the site of an earlier church founded by St Patrick after he came down from Croagh Patrick. It's one of the most impressive church buildings in Ireland and well worth a visit.

Features of the church include the 15th century west doorway and 13th century windows on the right side of the nave. The nave roof was erected in 1965 and is an Irish oak reproduction of the timber one burned down by Cromwell's soldiers in 1653. A leaflet available inside the church describes the church in detail.

Take the N84 heading south to Galway and after about 13km a signposted road on the left leads to the abbey.

Places to Stay & Eat

The immaculate IHH *Hughes House International Hostel* (☎ 23877), on Thomas St around the corner from the tourist office, opens May to September and has dorm beds from IR£6.50 to IR£8 and one private room for IR£8 to IR£10 per person, depending on the season. No connection with us, the delightfully named IHO *Lonely Planet Hostel* (☎ 24822) – watch it, guys! – at the Moreen roundabout just outside the centre charges IR£6 a bed and opens all year.

There are lots of B&Bs in and around Castlebar, but among the most central is *Ivy House* (☎ 21527), just off Market St on Castle St, with singles/doubles from IR£20/28 and open all year.

Davitt Restaurant on Thomas St near the tourist office has fish meals for around IR£6. Along Market St the *Mandalay* is OK for burgers, grills and salads. Nearby, the *Oriental* Chinese restaurant has main courses from around IR£4.50.

Two decent choices on New Antrim Rd are *Jay Dee's Restaurant & Coffee Shop* and *Café Rouge*, a branch of the popular UK-based bistro chain. The upmarket *Imperial Hotel* (☎ 21961) on the Mall has decent bar food, set lunch from IR£4 and dinner for IR£16.

Getting There & Away

An express bus connecting Westport (20 minutes) and Dublin (4½ hours) stops outside Flannelly's pub in Market St three times daily (once on Sunday) in each direction. There's also a direct bus south to Shannon and Cork and north to Ballina four times a day (twice on Sunday). The bus north-east to Sligo (2¼ hours) and Derry (4¼ hours) goes once a day Monday to Saturday in July and August only. McNulty Coaches (☎ 097-81016), based in Belmullet, runs a daily service from Castlebar to Belmullet at 5.30 pm. It returns from Belmullet at 8.15 am.

The Westport to Dublin (3¼ hours) train stops at Castlebar three times daily; the railway station is out of town on the road to Galway.

Getting Around

Taxis can be hired by ringing ☎ 097-26699.

Tommy Robinson's (☎ 21355) on Spencer St and Bike World (☎ 25220) on New Antrim Rd rent bikes. The latter charges IR£5 to IR£10 a day, depending on the make, and organises cycle tours of the area.

KNOCK
This once undistinguished village has been famous for over a century as the site of visions and miracles: Ireland's answer to Lourdes or Fatima.

Knock (Cnoc Mhuire) is at the junction of the N17 and the R323. Knock Marian Shrine consists of a number of churches and shrines, including the modern basilica and the Church of the Apparition. North of the latter are a number of shops, restaurants and the tourist office (☎ 094-88193), which opens daily May to September, 10 am to 6 pm. There's a Bank of Ireland branch nearby.

Church of the Apparition
On a wet evening in August 1879, two women of Knock were apparently struck by the sight of Mary, Joseph and St John the Evangelist standing in light against the south gable of the local church. Others were called to witness the apparition, and a church investigation quickly confirmed the apparition as a bona fide miracle. Other miracles followed as the sick and disabled claimed amazing recoveries after visiting the church, and another church commission upheld Knock's status in 1936. Today, the Knock industry continues unabated, and crowds of dutiful worshippers are always to be found praying here and at the modern Basilica of Our Lady, Queen of Ireland, which can accommodate 12,000 people.

Accompanying the fervent, almost medieval piety of the pilgrims is an astounding display of commercial exuberance that can seem unspeakably tacky. Wall thermometers, shake-up snow domes and plastic holy water bottles shaped like the Virgin are easy to mock; just remember that many people have spent much of their savings to come here and for many of the Catholic faithful, Knock is as sacred a place as the Wailing Wall in Jerusalem is to Jews, Mecca to

Muslims or the Ganges to Hindus. Knock was visited by Pope Paul VI in 1974, Pope John Paul II in 1979 and Mother Teresa in 1993.

Knock Folk Museum
This small museum (☎ 094-88100 for information) is one of the better ones of its type around and also serves as an ideal introduction to the Knock phenomenon. There's plenty of material on the apparition and subsequent church commissions of enquiry, including photographs of the display of crutches left behind by grateful pilgrims. The museum also houses an extensive collection of craft tools, costumes and various artefacts relating to rural life in the west of Ireland. It's all attractively presented.

The museum is in a separate building near the basilica and opens 10 am to 6 pm May to October (till 7 pm in July and August). Entry is IR£2/1.

Places to Stay
Knock Caravan & Camping Park (☎ 094-88100), a five-minute walk south of the shrine, costs IR£6 (IR£4 for hikers and motorcyclists) and opens March to October. The *Byrne Craft Shop* (☎ 094-88184) just behind the Church of the Apparition does B&B as does *Aisling House* (☎ 094-88558), near the entrance to the shrine on the Ballyhaunis road (R323) for IR£15.50 per person. The 10-room *Knock International Hotel* (☎ 094-88466), on Main St in the village, charges from IR£28/50.

Getting There & Away
The Knock airport (☎ 094-67222) is near Glentavraun, 15km to the north by the N17, and there is a daily flight from Dublin. There are bus connections to/from Castlebar on both Tuesday and Saturday; Westport and Athlone three times a day (once on Sunday); Sligo and Galway once daily; Dublin three times daily (once on Sunday); and Ballina and Cork (four times a day and once on Sunday).

County Sligo

The poet and dramatist William Butler Yeats (1865-1939) was educated in Dublin and London, but his poetry is inextricably linked with the county of his mother's family. He returned to Sligo (Sligeach) many times, becoming a close friend of the Gore-Booths who lived at Lissadell. (The most famous member of that family was Constance Markievicz (1868-1927), a participant in the 1916 Easter Rising.) There are many remind-ers of Yeats' presence in the county town of Sligo and in the rolling green hills around it.

SLIGO

One of the more interesting portrayals of Yeats is a sculpture outside the Ulster Bank on Stephen St, which has his poetry inscribed all over his body. Hard to find are two of his most famous lines, from *Easter 1916*:

All changed, changed utterly:
A terrible beauty is born...

The poem pays homage to the executed

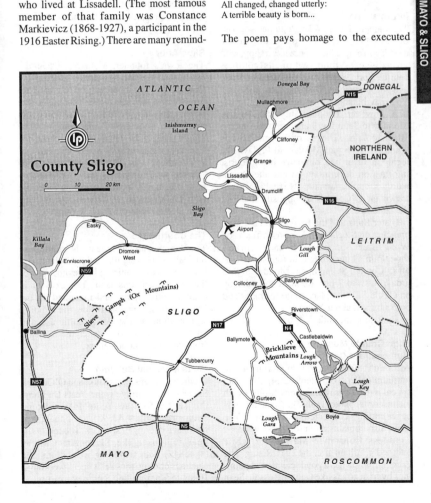

rebels of the Easter Rising, including John MacBride who was married to Maud Gonne. Yeats' unrequited love for Maud Gonne underlies many of his greatest poems. Politics divided them, for while she remained a rebel and a socialist all her life, Yeats ended up alarmingly close to fascism.

Yeats apart, the town's main attractions lie a few km outside at Carrowmore and Knocknarea.

Information

The modern North-West Regional Tourism office (☎ 071-61201), just south of the centre on Temple St, is more like a shop, with virtually everything within its confines bearing a price tag except a photocopied map and sheet titled 'A Walking Tour of Sligo'. You may be able to get some free information, however. It opens July and August, Monday to Saturday, 9 am to 8 pm (Sunday, 10 am to 2 pm). The rest of the year it opens 9 am to 5 or 6 pm, Monday to Friday. The local Chamber of Commerce has a tourist information desk in summer at the Quinsworth shopping arcade, which has an entrance on O'Connell St opposite the Ritz Restaurant.

Ulster Bank and the Bank of Ireland have branches on Stephen St. The post office is on Wine Street, opposite Michael Quirke's shop. Pam's Laundrette is in Johnston Court off O'Connell St and opens Monday to Saturday, 9 am to 7 pm. Keohane's Bookshop on Castle St is the place to go for maps and books by and about Yeats.

The telephone code is ☎ 071.

Sligo County Museum & Municipal Art Gallery

Although there is other material at the museum/gallery on Stephen St, the main appeal is the Yeats room, chock-a-block with manuscripts, photographs, letters and newspaper cuttings connected with the poet. The room also contains an apron dress worn by Countess Constance Markievicz while interned in Britain after the 1916 Rising. The gallery upstairs has a good selection of paintings by Irish artists like George Russell, Sean

Keating and Jack B Yeats, brother of the poet, who said he never did a painting without putting a thought of Sligo into it.

The museum opens year round Monday to Saturday, 10.30 am to 12.30 pm and 2.30 to 4.30 pm. The gallery keeps the same hours June to September but from Tuesday to Saturday. In April, May and October it opens in the morning only. Admission is free.

For some contemporary wood sculptures, look through the window of Michael Quirke's shop, a former butcher's on Wine St.

Sligo Abbey

The town's founder, Maurice FitzGerald, established the abbey around 1250 for the Dominicans, but it burned down in the 15th century and was rebuilt. It was put to the torch once again – and for the last time – in 1641, and ruins are all that remains. The oldest parts of the abbey are the choir, the 15th century east window and the altar.

The abbey is an OPW site and opens mid-June to mid-September, daily 9.30 am to 6.30 pm. If it's locked, a key is available from the caretaker, Mr Loughlin, at 6 Charlotte St. Admission is IR£1.50/60p.

The Courthouse

The Victorian architecture of the courthouse on Teeling St is very unusual for Ireland, and it stands out as a reminder of the other power that once ruled this land. The exterior is extravagantly Gothic and modelled on the Law Courts in London. Inside, the building still functions as a working courthouse, and on a busy day the foyer takes the overspill from the small public gallery.

Yeats Memorial Building

On the corner of Lower Knox and O'Connell Sts near Hyde Bridge is the Yeats Building, the centre for the Yeats International Summer School (☎ 42693), an annual international gathering of scholars. The rest of the year it houses the Sligo Art Gallery (☎ 45847) with travelling exhibitions and paintings often up for sale. It opens weekdays, 10 am to 5 pm, and on Saturday to 1 pm.

MAYO & SLIGO

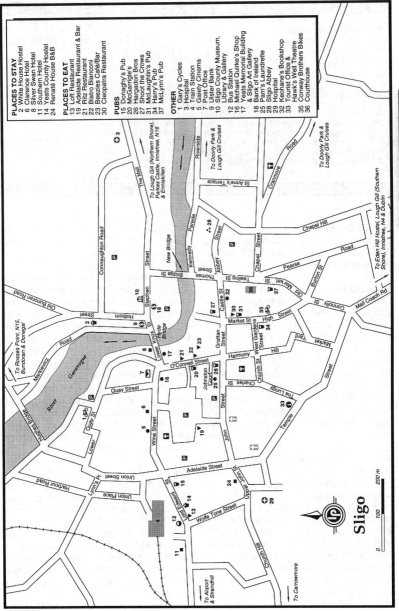

PLACES TO STAY
2 White House Hostel
6 Clarence Hotel
8 Silver Swan Hotel
11 Southern Hotel
14 Yeats County Hostel
24 Renaté House B&B

PLACES TO EAT
13 Loft Restaurant
19 Adelaide Restaurant & Bar
21 Ritz Restaurant
22 Bistro Bianconi
23 Beezies Café/Bar
30 Cleopatra Restaurant

PUBS
15 Donaghy's Pub
20 McGarrigle's
26 Hargadon Bros
27 Shoot the Crows
31 McLaughlin's Pub
34 Harry's Pub
37 McLynn's Pub

OTHER
1 Gary's Cycles
3 Hospital
4 Train Station
5 Gaiety Cinema
7 Post Office
9 Ulster Bank
10 Sligo County Museum,
   Library & Gallery
12 Bus Station
16 Michael Quirke's Shop
17 Yeats Memorial Building
   & Sligo Art Gallery
18 Bank of Ireland
25 Sam's Laundrette
28 Sligo Abbey
29 Hospital
32 Keohane's Bookshop
33 Tourist Office &
   Hawk's Well Theatre
35 Conway Brothers Bikes
36 Courthouse

Sligo

0   100   200 m

William Butler Yeats

The most celebrated of Irish poets was born in 1865 in a Dublin suburb. His mother was from Sligo, and Yeats spent a lot of time there as a child. At the age of nine he moved with his family to London, but six years later they were all back in Ireland. His early interest in the occult led him to help found the Dublin Hermetic Society, and the budding poet became more and more interested in Irish mythology.

As his poetry became better known, he counted among his friends William Morris, George Bernard Shaw and Oscar Wilde. His most important encounter, though, was with Maud Gonne (1866-1953), whose nationalism and socialism provided a healthy balance to his predilection for mysticism and an ill-defined romanticism. The story of their relationship has attracted a lot of speculation – especially the sexual side – with Maud Gonne finally refusing to marry him. She took the title role in his one-act play *Cathleen Ni Houlihan* (1904), which has been credited as the catalyst for the 1916 Easter Rising.

Yeats became a senator of the Irish Free State in 1922 and the following year he received the Nobel Prize for Literature. In 1928 he moved to Italy where, in the years to follow, his flirtation with fascism sat uneasily alongside his stature as a poet of world renown. He died in 1939. ■

Special Events

The Sligo Arts Festival takes place during the first two weeks in September. For information call ☎ 69802.

Places to Stay

Camping The closest campsite is the new *Gateway Caravan & Camping Park* (☎ 45618) in Ballinode, 3km north-east of Sligo on the N16. Charges are IR£7.50/50p for tents/adults; hikers and cyclists pay IR£5. Farther afield, the *Strandhill Caravan & Camping Park* (☎ 68120), 8km west of Sligo and off the road to the airport (R292), charges IR£5.50 to IR£6.50 for a tent and 50p per person. A third campground close to Sligo is the one at Rosses Point (see that section).

Hostels On Pearse Rd in Marymount, the excellent IHH *Eden Hill Holiday Hostel* (☎ 43204) is about a 10-minute walk south-east from the centre on the Dublin road and costs IR£6.50 for a bed or IR£15 for one of two doubles. It's open all year. Just north of the town centre on Markievicz Rd the IHH *White House Hostel* (☎ 45160) costs the same, but there are no private rooms. The smaller IHO *Yeats County Hostel* (☎ 46876) is just west of the centre, opposite the bus/railway station at 12 Lord Edward St, and costs IR£6.50.

There's also a *hostel* in Strandhill; see the West & South of Sligo section at the end of this chapter for details.

B&Bs & Hotels The less expensive B&Bs are to be found on the various approach roads into town, including the smoke-free *Lissadell* (☎ 61937) on Pearse St with singles/doubles for IR£18/32. *Renaté House* (☎ 62014), in the centre on Upper John St, is a traditional B&B costing from IR£19/28.

The *Silver Swan* (☎ 43231) is a comfortable and friendly hotel by the River Garavogue and close to the centre with 29 rooms from IR£48/76. The 11-room *Clarence Hotel* (☎ 42211) on Wine St charges from IR£36/60. The stately *Southern Hotel* (☎ 62101), with 68 rooms on Lord Edward St, charges from IR£52/80.

Places to Eat

The *Ritz Restaurant* on O'Connell St is a big place, likely to be crowded but good for lunch, snacks or coffee. Also on O'Connell St at No 44, *Bistro Bianconi* serves decent Italian dishes for around IR£10, salads and pizzas from IR£7. *Beezies*, a flashy, modern café/bar with food, is down the alleyway around the corner. It serves soups, sandwiches and pasta (IR£3.50) from 12.30 to 6 pm daily.

On the corner of John St and Harmony

Hill, the *Helm* is a popular self-service restaurant. In the Quinsworth shopping arcade car park, the *Adelaide Restaurant & Bar* is popular with townspeople at lunch.

One of the better restaurants around is the *Loft* (☎ 46770), upstairs at MJ Carr's pub at 17-19 Lord Edward Rd, with Mexican, fish and chicken dishes from IR£5.50 to about IR£10.50. The burgers are especially good here. Another decent place for similar fare is *Cleopatra* on Market St.

Entertainment

Sligo has the usual bevy of pubs, some with traditional music on certain nights, including *McLynn's* (Tuesday) on Old Market St, *McLaughlin's* (Wednesday) on Market St, the *Oak Tree* (Thursday) on Cranmore Rd and *Donaghy's* (Sunday) on Lord Edward St. *TD's Lounge* on Lynn's Place near Hughes Bridge has bands most nights of the week. *McGarrigle's* on O'Connell St has a good 'alternative music' bar upstairs.

No place in Sligo can beat *Hargadon Bros* on O'Connell St for atmosphere, however. While it doesn't have music, this old place is like a stage set with snugs, nooks, crannies and 19th century bar fixtures.

Shoot the Crows on Castle St at Market Square attracts a younger crowd while serious drinking is best conducted at *Harry's* pub on High St, where there are lots of special offers and the cheapest pint in town.

Theatre & Cinema The *Hawk's Well Theatre* (☎ 61526) is attached to the tourist office in Temple St, and it's always worth checking to see what is on. The four-screen *Gaiety Cinema* on Wine St has films daily at 8.30 and 10.30 pm.

Getting There & Away

Air From Sligo airport (☎ 68280) there is a daily nonstop Aer Lingus flight to/from Dublin. Flights to other parts of Ireland and Europe are all routed through Dublin.

Bus Bus Éireann (☎ 60066) has three daily services to and from Dublin (four hours). There's also a Galway-Sligo-Derry service

three times a day. The bus depot is just below the railway station to the west of the centre on Lord Edward St.

Feda O'Donnell Coaches (☎ 075-48114 in Fintown, ☎ 091-761656 in Galway) runs a service between Crolly, County Donegal, and Galway via Donegal and Sligo twice a day, Monday to Saturday, with three buses on Friday and Sunday. The buses arrive and depart from in front of Lyon's Café on Wine St.

Train Trains leave the railway station (☎ 69888) three times a day (four on Monday and Friday) for Dublin via Boyle, Carrick-on-Shannon and Mullingar.

Getting Around

There's a bus service from the airport into town while a taxi (☎ 44444 or ☎ 55555) costs about IR£8. Bike hire is available from Conway Bros (☎ 61370) on High St or Gary's Cycles (☎ 45418) on Lower Quay St. The Eden Hill Hostel also has bikes for hire.

AROUND SLIGO
Rosses Point

The scene of a battle between two Irish warlords in 1257, Rosses Point is now a picturesque seaside resort with a lovely Blue Flag beach and easily reached on a Sligo town bus.

Carrowmore Megalithic Cemetery

Carrowmore's megalithic cemetery has over 60 stone circles and passage tombs, making it one of the largest Stone Age cemeteries in Europe. Over the years, many of the stones have been removed – a survey in 1839 noted 23 more sites than now exist – and a complicating factor is that some of the best stones are on private land.

The dolmens were the actual tombs and were probably covered with stones and earth, so it requires some imagination to picture what this 2.5km-wide area might once have looked like.

The OPW site centre (☎ 071-61534) opens daily 9.30 am to 6.30 pm May to September. Entry is IR£1.50/60p.

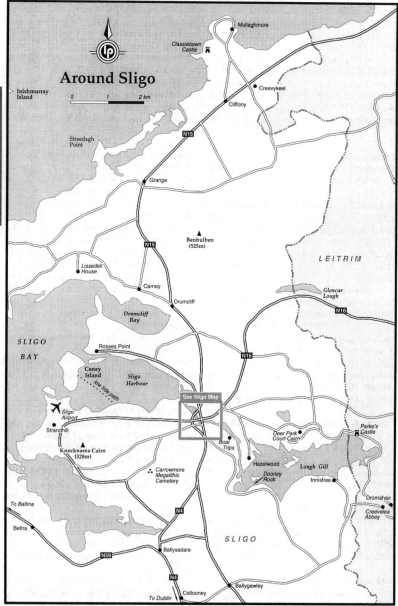

MAYO & SLIGO

Around Sligo

0   1   2 km

Inishmurray
Island

Mullaghmore

Classiebawn
Castle

Creevykeel

Cliffony

N15

Streedagh
Point

Grange

N15

Benbulben
(525m)

LEITRIM

Lissadell
House

Carney

Glencar
Lough

N16

Drumcliff

Drumcliff
Bay

SLIGO
BAY

Rosses Point

Coney
Island

low tide path

Sligo
Harbour

N16

See Sligo Map

Parke's
Castle

Sligo
Airport

Strandhill

Deer Park
Court Cairn

Boat
Trips

Knocknarea Cairn
(328m)

Hazelwood

Lough Gill

Carrowmore
Megalithic
Cemetery

Dooney
Rock

Innisfree

Dromahair

To Ballina

Creevelea
Abbey

Beltra

N4

SLIGO

N59

Ballysadare

N4

Collooney

Ballygawley

To Dublin

To get there, leave town by Church Hill and carry on for 5km; the site is clearly signposted.

Knocknarea

A couple of km north-west of Carrowmore is the hilltop (328m) cairn grave of Knocknarea. About 1000 years younger than Carrowmore, the huge cairn is supposed to be the grave of the legendary Queen Maeve (Queen Mab in Welsh and English folk tales). The 40,000 tons of stone have never been excavated, despite speculation that a tomb on the scale of the one at Newgrange in County Meath lies buried below.

Leave Sligo as for Carrowmore and a sign shows the way to Knocknarea. If leaving the Carrowmore OPW centre, continue down the road, and turn right at the junction with a church. At the next crossroads (signposted Mescan Meadhbha Chambered Cairn) turn left, and leave your vehicle at the car park. From here it is only half an hour to the summit and panoramic views.

Deer Park Court Cairn

This impressive court tomb (also called Magheraghanrush Court Cairn) stands on a wooded limestone hill with fine views of Lough Gill. The court area is not outside the front entrance but in the centre of the tomb with two burial chambers opening off at one end and another one at the other end. The site has been dated to around 3000 BC.

Take the N16 out of Sligo and turn off on the R286 for Parke's Castle. Almost immediately after joining this road turn left at the Y-junction on a minor road signposted for Manorhamilton, ignoring the road to the right that is signposted for Parke's Castle and Dromahair. Continue along the minor road for about 3km, park in the car park and follow the trail through the trees.

Places to Stay

Rosses Point *Greenlands Caravan & Camping Park* (☎ 071-77113) is next to the golf course near the beach. It opens at Easter and late May to mid-September and costs IR£7.50/50p per tent/person. The two hotels

at Rosses Point are quite different in character: the larger 79-room *Yeats Country* (☎ 071-77211) attracts families, while *Ballincar House* (☎ 071-45361), with 25 rooms, is relaxed and peaceful away from the beach. Rates at the Yeats Country are from IR£55/90, and at Ballincar House from IR£63/87.

B&Bs are not difficult to find although they can fill up quickly in season. Try Mrs Gill's *Kilvarnet House* (☎ 071-77202) or, among the closest to the sea, Mrs Brady's *Coral Reef* (☎ 071-77245). Both have doubles for IR£32 to IR£34.

Carrowmore & Knocknarea Two B&Bs close to the Carrowmore OPW centre are *Culbree House* (☎ 071-68189) and *Cillard* (☎ 071-68201), both with doubles for IR£32. Closer to Knocknarea, Mrs Carter's *Primrose Grange House* (☎ 071-62005), just along the road that leads to the Knocknarea car park, costs from IR£19/28.

Places to Eat

A day out to Carrowmore and Knocknarea requires a packed lunch, but there is no shortage of eating places at Rosses Point. The *Bunker* pub on the main road leading to the beach always has pub food, and the *Moorings Restaurant*, which serves mostly seafood, is close to the Yeats Country Hotel. Best of all, if your budget stretches to IR£20 to IR£25 a head, is the restaurant at the *Ballincar House Hotel*.

Getting There & Away

Apart from the Sligo town buses (☎ 071-60066) that go as far as Rosses Point, there is no public transport to the other places of interest in the area. A bicycle hired in Sligo would be the best way of getting around. While it's possible to walk to both Carrowmore and Knocknarea from town, it's a long day's trek on foot there and back.

LOUGH GILL

A round trip of 48km would take in most of this lough east of Sligo as well as Parke's Castle which, though inside the Leitrim border, is more likely to be visited on a day trip from Sligo than, say, Carrick-on-Shannon. There are legends associated with Lough Gill; one that can be put easily to the test is the old story that a silver bell from the abbey in Sligo was thrown into the lough and only those who are free from sin can still hear its pealing. We're all ears.

Dooney Rock

There are good views of the lough and its islands from the top of Dooney Rock. In *The Fiddler of Dooney*, Yeats immortalises the rock, although his poem about Innisfree is more famous.

Leave Sligo on the N4 going south and after half a km turn left at the sign to Lough Gill. Another left at the T-junction brings you onto the R287 road and the viewpoint of Dooney Rock.

Innisfree Island

If Yeats had not written *The Lake Isle of Innisfree*, this tiny island (Inis Fraoigh in Irish) near the south-east shore would not attract so many visitors, and it would probably have kept the air of tranquillity that so moved the poet:

I will arise and go now, and go to Innisfree,
And a small cabin build there, of clay and wattles made;
Nine bean rows will I have there, a hive for the honey bee,
And live alone in the bee-loud glade.

From the Dooney Rock car park turn left at the crossroads and after 3km turn left again for another 3km. A small road leads down to the lake.

Creevelea Abbey

This was the last Franciscan friary to be founded in Ireland before the orders were suppressed. The columns in the cloister have some interesting carvings of St Francis, one displaying his stigmata and another one showing him in a pulpit with birds perched on a tree. It was burned in 1590 by Richard Bingham but restored by the monks before

they were again ejected by Cromwell. They returned yet again and thatched the church roof, remaining here until the end of the 17th century.

From Innisfree, return to the R287 and continue east until the sign for the abbey is seen in the village of Dromahair.

Parke's Castle

The placid setting of Parke's Castle, with swans drifting by on Lough Gill, belies the fact that the early plantation architecture was created out of insecurity and fear by an unwelcome English landlord. The three-storey castle, which has been carefully restored, forms part of one of the five sides of the bawn, which also has two rounded turrets at the corners. This is an OPW site so try to join one of the guided tours after viewing the 20-minute video 'Stone by Stone', which gives a general introduction to the antiquities of the area.

The castle (☎ 071-64149) opens 9.30 am to 6.30 pm daily between June and September; in October, April and May the hours Tuesday to Sunday are 10 am to 5 pm. Admission is IR£2/1.

From Creevelea Abbey, continue east along the R287. To return to Sligo from Parke's Castle turn west onto the R286.

Places to Stay & Eat

There are not many eating places on a tour of Lough Gill, and a picnic lunch might be a good idea. *Parke's Castle* has a small café. In Dromahair's Main St, *Stanfords Village Inn* (☎ 071-64140) does a IR£15 dinner as does the *Breffni Centre* (☎ 071-64199).

Getting There & Away

Car & Bicycle Leave for the northern shore via the Mall (the continuation of Stephen St) past the hospital, and turn right off the N16 onto the R286. Following the signs to the right for Hazelwood leads to a parking area, where a 4km sculpture trail with a dozen works of art is situated. Ignoring the Hazelwood turn off and staying on the R286 leads to the northern shore of Lough Gill and around to Innisfree. The southern route is less interesting until reaching Dooney Rock.

Boat *The Wild Rose Water Bus* (☎ 071-64266) cruises Lough Gill twice daily mid-June to September from Doorly Park (a half-hour's walk east of town) and five times a day from Parke's Castle for IR£4.50/1.50 (Sunday only in April, May and October). There's also a IR£3.50/1.50 tour around Innisfree, and one-way trips between Parke's Castle and Sligo.

NORTH OF SLIGO
Drumcliff & Benbulben
WB Yeats died in 1939 in Roquebrune, France, but his wishes were that 'if I die here, bury me up there on the mountain (the cemetery in Roquebrune), and then after a year or so, dig me up and bring me privately to Sligo'. True to his wishes, his body was interred in the churchyard at Drumcliff in 1948 – where his great-grandfather had been rector – although it was hardly a private affair, as the photographs in the Sligo County Museum make clear. The grave is on the left near the Protestant church, and alongside Yeats is buried Georgie Hyde-Lees whom he married in 1917, when she was 15 and he was 52. The famous epitaph was his own composition:

Cast a cold eye
On life, on death.
Horseman, pass by!

Nearly 1300 years earlier, St Colmcille chose the same location for the foundation of a monastery, and the remains of the round tower, damaged by lightning in 1936, can still be seen. An 11th century high cross is nearby, depicting Adam and Eve, Cain's murder of Abel, Daniel in the Lions' Den and Christ in Glory on the east face. On the west side of the cross, the Presentation in the Temple and the Crucifixion can be made out.

Look for the round tower on the N15 road from Sligo. Going by bus you need to take the 8.45 am bus from Sligo (arriving 9.05 am) because the next one is at 4.15 pm,

The Battle of the Book
After Drumcliff, the first turn west goes to the village of Carney and just north of the village, in Cooldrumman, is where the 'Battle of the Book' took place in the year 561. At the time, St Colmcille borrowed a rare psalter from St Finian and made a pirate edition for his own use. When St Finian found out and demanded the copy, the resulting argument found its way to the high king of Ireland, who was asked to arbitrate. The delivered judgement was 'To every cow its calf and to every book its copy'. St Colmcille refused to accept the judgement, and in the battle that followed over 4000 people were slain. Struck with remorse and shame, St Colmcille built a monastery at Drumcliff before departing forever into voluntary exile on the remote Scottish island of Iona. ■

which means you'll miss the two daily return buses that pass through Drumcliff at 12.30 and 4.53 pm (though there is a 3 pm bus from Sligo to Drumcliff on Saturday only).

Glencar Lough
Fishing apart, the attraction of the lake is the scenic waterfall signposted from the car park. Yeats refers to this picturesque spot in *The Stolen Child*, and the surrounding countryside can be best enjoyed by walking east along the road and taking the steep trail that heads north to the valley.

From Drumcliff it's less than 5km to the lake, and there is also a bus service from Sligo.

Lissadell House
This is the ancestral home of the Gore-Booth family, among whose members was Constance Markievicz (1868-1927), a friend of Yeats and a participant in the 1916 Easter Rising. The death penalty she received for her involvement was later withdrawn and, in 1918, she became the first woman ever elected to the House of Commons. Like many Irish rebels since then, she refused to take her seat.

Constance's sister Eva was a poet, and Yeats' poem *In Memory of Eva Gore-Booth and Con Markievicz* is inscribed on a sign at the entrance to the house.

The light of evening, Lissadell,
Great windows, open to the south,
Two girls in silk kimonos....

Yeats was a frequent visitor to Lissadell and in 1894 he wrote of the interior: 'Great sitting room as high as a church and all things in good taste.'

Lissadell House (☎ 071-63150) opens June to mid-September, Monday to Saturday, 10.30 am to 12.15 pm and 2 to 4.15 pm. The entrance charge is IR£2.50/1, and the guided tour, which is informative and interesting, takes about 45 minutes.

To get there, follow the N15 north from Sligo and turn west at Drumcliff.

Mullaghmore

If you turn left at Cliffony, off the N15, the main road to Mullaghmore first passes **Streedagh Beach**, a grand stretch of sand that was the final resting place for many of the 1300 sailors who perished when three ships from the Spanish Armada were wrecked nearby.

The beach at Mullaghmore is also delightfully wide and safe. It was in this bay that the IRA assassinated Lord Mountbatten and members of his family in 1979 by blowing up his yacht. On the way to the Mullaghmore headland you pass **Classiebawn Castle**, built for Lord Palmerston in 1856 and later the home of Lord Mountbatten. The castle is not open to the public but the neo-Gothic pile can be viewed from the N15 and the R279 as you approach Mullaghmore.

Inishmurray Island

If access was easier to arrange, a visit to this uninhabited island would be a must. It contains the remains of three churches, beehive cells and open-air altars. The old monastery is surrounded by a stone wall with five separate entrances to the central area, which contains the churches and altars. The monastery was founded in the early 6th century by St Molaise, and a wooden statue of the saint

that once stood in the main church is now in the National Museum in Dublin.

The early monks on Inishmurray assembled some fascinating pagan relics. There's a collection of cursing stones; those who wanted to lay a curse did the stations of the Cross in reverse, turning over the stones as they went along. There were also separate burial grounds for men and women and a strong belief that if a body was placed in the wrong ground it would move itself during the night.

A distance of only 6km separates Inishmurray from the mainland, but there is no regular boat service and the lack of harbour makes landing subject to the weather. Trips can be arranged through Lomax Boats (☎ 071-66124) in Mullaghmore, from Streedagh Point through Joe McGowan (☎ 071-66267), or from Rosses Point through Tomas McCallion (☎ 071-42391). If you're lucky, a fishing group might be going out, and an arrangement could be made; otherwise you need a group of at least six to make it economical.

Creevykeel Court Cairn

North of Cliffony on the N15 is a court tomb with a wide high front tapering away to a narrow end. The unroofed court stands outside the front entrance, and at some later stage, chambers were added to the west side of the cairn. It was constructed around 2500 BC.

Places to Stay

The *Karuna Flame Hostel* (☎ 071-63337) at Celtic Farm, 1km north of Grange, is a useful base for the north of Sligo and opens all year. Beds are IR£6 and the one private room costs IR£7 per person. Connemara ponies can be hired for riding on the beaches nearby. *Shaddan Lodge* (☎ 071-63350) near Streedagh Beach does B&B from IR£19/28 and opens Easter to October. The German-owned *Horse Holiday Farm* (☎ 071-66152), at Mountemple 2km north of Grange, has week-long riding programmes including B&B and your own horse from IR£400 and four-night weekend specials from IR£300.

At Drumcliff there are a good number of B&Bs, including Mrs Hennigan's *Benbulben Farm* (☎ 071-63211) in Barnaribbon, where singles/doubles are from IR£22/28.

At Mullaghmore the *Beach Hotel* (☎ 071-66108) has an indoor swimming pool and opens April to September. Singles/double are IR£38/56 or IR£42/64, depending on the season, and fishing trips can be arranged.

Places to Eat

The *Yeats Tavern* restaurant in Drumcliff opens daily until 10 pm. Lunch specials are good value. The place is about 100m past Yeats' grave on the left of the main road. In Mullaghmore, the *Fishes' Circle* restaurant has excellent seafood.

Getting There & Away

There are regular bus connections between Sligo, Drumcliff, Grange and Cliffony as nearly all the buses to Donegal and Derry go along the N15. In Drumcliff the bus stop is outside the creamery, in Grange it's outside Rooney's shop and in Cliffony it's Ena's pub. The first bus stopping at all these places leaves Sligo at 8.45 am; the last bus from Cliffony is at 4.35 pm.

WEST & SOUTH OF SLIGO
Strandhill

The interesting places west of Sligo are Carrowmore and Knocknarea, mentioned earlier; Strandhill is the only other place close to town that might be worth a visit. There's a golf course, the *Dunes Tavern* pub with accommodation, and the IHO *Knocknarea Hostel* (☎ 071-68777), with beds for IR£7 or IR£8 and open all year. The beaches are sandy, though not always safe for swimming, and at low tide you can walk across to Coney Island. The story goes that New York's own Coney Island was named by a man from Rosses Point.

Collooney

The **Teeling Monument** can be found at the northern end of this village. It commemorates the daring of Bartholomew Teeling who was marching with Humbert's French-Irish army when it encountered stiff resistance from an English gunner. Teeling charged up to the gunner and killed him, thus allowing the army to march on to eventual defeat at the battle of Ballinamuck in Longford in September 1798. Although the French were treated as prisoners of war, Teeling and 500 other Irishmen were executed.

The other attraction near Collooney is **Markree Castle**, which is signposted off the main road on the left after leaving the village. The castle has remained in the same family since Cromwell's time. When Charles Kingsley stayed here in the 19th century he wrote that he cried over the misery inflicted on the local peasantry – while at the same time exalting in the excitement of fishing for salmon in the estate's river. And it's said that Mrs Alexander wrote the hymn *All Things Bright & Beautiful* after her stay here.

Markree Castle (☎ 071-67800) now functions as an 11-room hotel; singles/doubles start at IR£60/96. B&B at IR£15 or IR£16 per person is available at *Union Farm* (☎ 071-67136) 2km outside the village.

Ballymote

This small town, definitely off the tourist trail, has a couple of attractions. **Ballymote Castle**, which is on the road from town to Tubbercurry, might look like a designer's idea of a ruin but this is the real thing; an early 14th century castle contested among Irish chiefs before succumbing to the English in 1577 and now crumbling in obscurity. It was from here that O'Donnell marched to disaster at the Battle of Kinsale in 1601.

The **Protestant church** is also worth a glance, if only to read the plaque saying that the clock was paid for by the tenants of Ballymote estate as a mark of respect to Sir Robert Gore-Booth of Lissadell. Unlike many of these tributes this one was genuine; Robert Gore-Booth mortgaged Lissadell House during the Famine to raise money for food for the starving. Constance Markievicz, his daughter, received a minute-long ovation from the local peasants here after her release from a British jail in June 1917.

MAYO & SLIGO

There are a few B&Bs here including Mrs Mullin's *Millhouse* (☎ 071-83449) costing IR£21/32, and Mrs McGettrick's *Hillcrest* (☎ 071-83398), with rooms for IR£14 per person. More upmarket is *Temple House* (☎ 071-83329), an old Anglo-Irish home which gets its name from the Knights Templar, which costs from IR£43/76.

There are plenty of unpretentious pubs to choose from and the *Old Stand Pub* serves reasonable bar food. The *Stonepark* restaurant upstairs is good for an evening meal. *Corran's* is a takeaway place up the road.

Carrowkeel Passage Tomb Cemetery

Situated on a hilltop in the Bricklieve Mountains overlooking Lough Arrow, this place is uplifting, with panoramic views on a clear day, and also a little spooky, given the 14 cairns, various dolmens and scattered remnants of other graves. The place has been dated to the late Stone Age (3000-2000 BC).

The site, off the main N4 road, is closer to Boyle than Sligo. If you're coming from the latter, turn right at the sign in the village of Castlebaldwin and then left at the fork as indicated. The site is a couple of km uphill from the gateway. You can take an Athlone bus from Sligo and ask to be put off at Castlebaldwin.

Coopershill House (☎ 071-65108) in Riverstown is close to the Carrowkeel Passage Tomb Cemetery, half way between Sligo and Boyle, and is a handsome retreat for anyone wanting to relax in a Georgian family mansion. B&B is from IR£55/90, and there are facilities available for boating and fishing. A down-to-earth Irish meal with good wine and open log fires is IR£24.

Lough Arrow

Lough Arrow has its own small tourist office (☎ 079-66232) open daily July and August, 9.30 am to 5.30 pm. It's on the main N4 road just north of Boyle and a short distance from the border with County Roscommon.

Lough Arrow is of interest to anglers, particularly for its brown trout (season: May to September). Mayfly Holidays (☎ 071-65065), at Ballindoon near Riverstown, does

B&B at IR£13 per person a day; motor boat hire plus packed lunch for two is IR£10 plus another IR£25 if a ghillie is required. The 10-room *Rock View Hotel* (☎ 079-66073) on the lakeshore also caters to anglers. B&B costs IR£17 to IR£20 per person.

Tubbercurry

Sometimes spelled Tobercurry, this is another off-the-beaten-track town. It comes alive around the middle of July when a music summer school takes place. On the second Wednesday in August, the town's big Fair Day is held. Nearly all the pubs have music, and the first place to call in at is *Killoran's* (☎ 071-85111) on the main street, which functions as a combined pub/restaunt/takeaway/travel agent/off-licence/tourist office.

Easky & Enniscrone

The main route west to Mayo is pleasant enough, but there is little to detain the visitor. The town of Easky has the ruins of a 15 century castle, and the surfing possibilities are highly regarded. The sandy Blue Flag beach known as the Hollow at Enniscrone, farther west, is a popular holiday spot for families and the *Atlantic 'n' Riverside Caravan & Camping Park* (☎ 096-49001) is only 12km north-east of Ballina in County Mayo. An attraction here is **Kilcullen's Seaweed Baths** (☎ 096-36238). It opens daily May to October, 10 am to 9 pm (10 pm in July and August). The rest of the year the baths are open Saturday and Sunday only, 10 am to 8 pm.

West Coast Cycles (☎ 096-36593) in Enniscrone rents bicycles.

Getting There & Away

The Dublin to Sligo express bus stops outside Quigley's in Collooney as does the Galway-Derry express. The Sligo to Castlerea bus also stops at Collooney, Ballymote and Tubbercurry, and a local bus runs from Sligo to Collooney. Easky and Enniscrone are on the Sligo-Dooagh (Achill Island) bus route. The Dublin-Sligo train stops at Collooney and Ballymote three times daily (four times on Friday).

The Central North

Someone once described Ireland as a dull picture with a wonderful frame. Indeed, most visitors are attracted by the frame – the coast – and rarely venture inland to explore the picture. But while the six counties of the central north (Cavan, Monaghan, Roscommon, Leitrim, Longford and Westmeath) may never lure the same hordes as the west or south, they do have a number of places of great interest, and the smaller number of visitors can make them that much more attractive.

Cavan, Monaghan and Donegal all border Northern Ireland and, together with the six counties there, make up the province of Ulster. All border crossing points between the Republic and the North are now open though you will occasionally have to pass through a garda checkpoint when crossing back into the Republic.

County Cavan

The low, undulating county of Cavan (An Cabhán) is barely a two-hour drive from Dublin and lies just south of the border with Northern Ireland. Cavan is dominated by lakes (it's said there is one for every day of the year), bogs and drumlins, which are small round hills deposited and shaped by retreating glaciers during the last Ice Age. In the far north-west of the county, the wild and barren Cuilcagh Mountains are the source of the River Shannon, at over 300km long the mightiest river in Ireland or Britain.

Cavan is equally famous for its potholed roads, which are often twisty and badly signposted. The roads seem to go over the drumlins, whereas in neighbouring Monaghan they go round them.

Cavan was the birthplace of Percy French, the late 19th century songwriter responsible for *The Mountains of Mourne*.

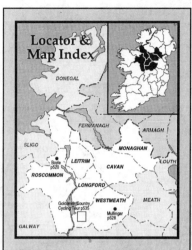

Locator & Map Index

Boyle p520

Goldsmith Country Cycling Tour p535

Mullingar p528

Highlights

- Enjoy the excellent fishing
- Visit Monaghan County Museum in Monaghan town, one of the best regional museums in Ireland and home to the Cross of Clogher
- See Boyle Abbey, just east of Boyle, one of the finer Cistercian abbeys in Ireland
- Explore the superb Drumanone Dolmen, just outside of Boyle, one of the largest in Ireland
- Experience the 24km Shannon–Erne Waterway with its 34 stone bridges and 16 locks

HISTORY

Archaeological evidence suggests that Cavan was inhabited as far back as Neolithic times. Magh Sleacht, a plain in the north-west of the county near the border village of Ballyconnell, was one of the most important druidic centres in the country in the 5th century, when St Patrick was winning the pagan Irish over to Christianity. The principal

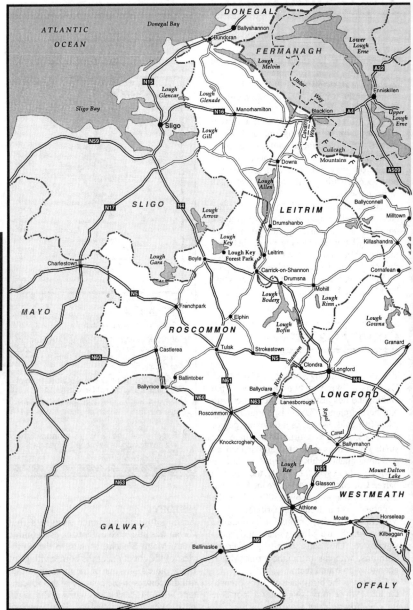

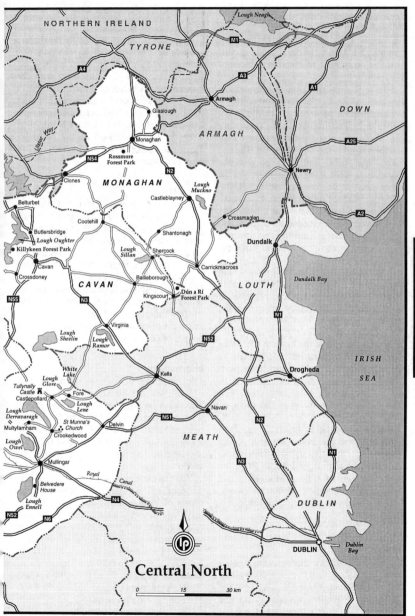

CENTRAL NORTH

Central North

0   15   30 km

Celtic deity was Crom Cruaich, whose significance swiftly diminished as the Christian teachings of Patrick spread. In the 12th century, the Anglo-Normans made a concerted effort to get a foothold in Cavan, but the landscape proved difficult to penetrate and the region remained under the control of the Gaelic O'Reilly clan for many years.

Their grip on power began to slip in the 16th century. The English 'shired' the county into baronies, dividing these among clan members loyal to the English crown. The end came when the O'Reillys joined with the other Ulster lords – the O'Donnells and the O'Neills – in the Nine Years War (1594-1603) against the English and were defeated.

As part of the plantation of Ulster after 1609, Cavan was divided up among English and Scottish settlers, and the new town of Virginia was created, named after Elizabeth I, the Virgin Queen.

In the 1640s, with Charles II in trouble in England, the Confederate Rebellion led by Owen Roe O'Neill took place in opposition to the plantation. O'Neill, a returned exile, had one major victory over the English at the Battle of Benburb in County Tyrone in 1646. Only with the end of the English Civil War and the arrival of Cromwell in 1649 were the English again able to take control. Owen Roe O'Neill died in suspicious circumstances in 1649 – poisoning was suspected – in Cloughoughter Castle near the town of Cavan.

The Irish population generally remained in poverty and the Potato Famine of the 1840s and '50s led to massive emigration. After the War of Independence in 1922, the Ulster counties of Cavan, Monaghan and Donegal were incorporated into the South. With the border so close, Republicanism is strong.

FISHING

Anglers from all over Europe converge on Cavan in season to fish the many lakes along the country's southern and western borders. The fishing is excellent; it's primarily coarse fishing for pike, perch, bream and roach but there's also some game angling for brown trout in Lough Sheelin.

Some of the lakes like Lough Sheelin are recovering after years of serious pollution from the numerous pig farms in the area. Most lakes are well signposted, with the types of fish available also marked. Some of the villages and guesthouses depend heavily on anglers, many of whom return every year. For more information, contact North West Tourism (☎ 049-31942) or the Northern Regional Fisheries Board (☎ 049-37174), both in Cavan town.

CAVAN

The most important settlement in the county is the rather drab town of Cavan. Its slightly peculiar layout centres around two parallel streets, Farnham St and Main St. Main St (and its continuation, Connolly St) has the feel of an Irish country town with typical shops and pubs on each side, while Farnham St more closely resembles a city avenue, with some elegant Georgian houses housing doctors' surgeries and lawyers' offices, a large courthouse and garda station and a couple of churches.

Information

The North West Tourism office (☎ 049-31942), on the corner of Farnham and Thomas Ashe Sts, opens June to September, 9 am to 5 pm Monday to Friday. It may be open 9 am to 1 pm weekdays in the late spring and early autumn, but you'll find it shut tight in winter – with a sign advising you to 'go to Sligo'.

You can change money at the ACC Bank, 91 Main St. The modern post office is on the corner of Main and Townhall Sts. You can leave your laundry at the Supaklene laundrette on Farnham St about 100m from the bus station or at the Laundry Basket at the southern end of Connolly St. It opens Monday to Saturday 8.30 am to 6.30 pm. There's also a small genealogical office (☎ 61094) in Cana House, signposted up the hill from the Presbyterian church on Farnham St.

The telephone code is ☎ 049.

Things to See & Do

Cavan developed around a 13th century Franciscan friary of which no traces remain. On the site in Abbey St is an 18th century **Protestant church tower** which marks the grave of Owen Roe O'Neill, though it's not very impressive.

Lifeforce Mill (☎ 62722), on Bridge St along the little Kennypottle River, is a fully operational flour mill dating from 1846 that still uses the centuries-old 'cool' method of milling wheat. Visitors actually prepare a loaf of wholemeal brown bread on arrival and pick it up hot from the oven at the end of their 40-minute tour. The mill opens daily 10 am to 5 pm May to September and costs IR£2.50/2/1.50 for adults/students/children (family ticket IR£6).

Two km south-east of the town centre on the Dublin road (N3) is the **Cavan Crystal Factory** (☎ 31800), Ireland's second-oldest crystal manufacturer. The showroom opens Monday to Friday 9.30 am to 5.30 pm, Saturday 10 am to 5 pm, and Sunday 2 to 5 pm. There are free factory tours (weekdays between 9.30 am and 3 pm) by arrangement where you can see the crystal being blown and cut by hand.

Courses in **canoeing** are given by local Irish Canoe Union instructors on the River Erne. Check out the notice board in Louis Blessing's pub. The large **County Cavan Swimming & Leisure Complex** (☎ 62888) in Drumalee north-east of town has swimming (from IR£2.50/1.50) and a number of other sporting facilities available weekdays 7.30 am to 10 pm, and 11 am to 6 pm at the weekend.

Places to Stay

B&Bs There's very little choice in the town centre. The most central place with B&B-style accommodation is the *Bridge Restaurant* (☎ 31538), 5 Coleman Rd, close to the bus station. It offers B&B in spacious rooms for IR£18 per person, plus a IR£3 key deposit. *Oakdene* (☎ 31698), 29 Cathedral Rd at the northern end of town, has four spotless rooms costing from IR£19.50/29 singles/doubles. *Halcyon* (☎ 31809), in

Drumalee 600m north-east along the Cootehill road and then right by McDonald's shop, has five rooms at almost the same rates. *Rose's Brough House* (☎ 30311), 4km southeast on the Dublin road, has three rooms for IR£17/28 with separate bathroom.

There are some real gems farther out of town. *Lisnamandra Farmhouse* (☎ 37196) is 7km west along the Crossdoney road (R198) and well signposted on the left-hand side. B&B is IR£21.50/33 with a shower, full dinner is about IR£15 and you should book ahead (open May to September).

Hotels In the centre of town on Main St almost opposite Market Square, you could try the very popular *Farnham Arms Hotel* (☎ 2577) with B&B for IR£30/50 and IR£32/60 a single/double, depending on the season. The *Kilmore Hotel* (☎ 049-32288), on the Dublin road just beyond the Cavan Crystal Factory, has B&B from IR£37/68 and IR£45/72.

Places to Eat

The town has fast-food places like *Uncle Sam's* near the bus station on College St, or *Una's Takeaway* at the start of Connolly St opposite the small market. *Galligan's*, just off Main St on Bridge St, is good for inexpensive lunches and early dinners. The *Melbourne Bakery* is a small restaurant-cum-coffee shop half way up Main St. The *Bridge Restaurant* is a good, reasonably priced place to eat, with chicken dishes from IR£2.50 and fish from IR£3. It's open 9 am to 9 pm. For Chinese, try the *Happy Valley Restaurant* where Main and Connolly Sts meet.

The *Farnham Arms Hotel* has a comfortable lounge with reasonable food, and the restaurant at the *Imperial Hotel* on Main St is popular with Cavanites.

The best place in town is the *Olde Priory* (☎ 61898), on Main St in an old convent basement opposite the Melbourne Bakery. It serves pizzas from IR£5 and also does seafood, kebabs and vegetarian dishes. It has a bar and is closed Monday and at lunch on Sunday.

Entertainment

McGinty's Corner Bar on College St has won a regional 'pub of the year' title and sometimes has music at weekends. There are heaps of pubs on Main St. The *Black Horse Inn* is popular with young locals and has pool tables. You will occasionally find jazz in *Louis Blessing's* rustic pub in a small courtyard off Main St; *An Crúiscín Lán* ('the bumper') at the top of Main St has Irish sessions on Friday. The most popular pub these days is the renovated *An Síbín* ('the speakeasy') on the corner of Townhall and Main Sts.

Getting There & Away

The small bus station (☎ 31353) is at the southern end of Farnham St near the bridge and roundabout. The ticket office opens daily 7.30 am (8.30 am on Sunday) to 8.30 pm

Cavan is on the Dublin to Donegal, Galway to Belfast and Athlone to Belfast bus routes. On weekdays there are five daily buses to Dublin (two hours), three buses to Belfast (three hours) and two to Galway (3¾ hours). Bus Éireann also has services running from Cavan through the county to Bawnboy, Ballyconnell, Belturbet, Virginia, Kells, Dunshaughlin, Navan and many other small towns, including Cootehill.

Wharton's (☎ 37114) has private buses leaving the nearby Mallard's Hotel for Parnell Square in Dublin Monday to Saturday at 8 am.

Getting Around

Taxis can be ordered either on ☎ 31172 or ☎ 32876. On Yer Bike Tours (☎ 31932), in the Abbeyset Printers building (a deconsecrated church) on Farnham St, rents bikes for IR£7/30 a day/week plus deposit. With advance notice, they can also organise day or week-long leisurely group cycling tours of the area.

AROUND CAVAN
Kilmore Cathedral

This modest Church of Ireland cathedral, built in 1860, is about 5km west on the R198

Crossdoney road to Killykeen Forest Park. On the west side of this relatively modern building is a fine 12th century Romanesque doorway brought here from an Augustinian monastery on Trinity Island in Lough Oughter. If you look closely, you'll notice that some of the stones have not been replaced in the correct order. In the churchyard is the grave of Bishop William Bedell (1571-1642), who commissioned the first translation of the Old Testament into Irish; there's a copy of it on display in the chancel.

Killykeen Forest Park

This forest park (☎ 049-32541) is 12km north-west of Cavan on the shores of Lough Oughter. Lough Oughter winds a tortuous path around the undulating landscape, and the park has some fine walks, nature trails, fishing spots and good chalets for rent among its 243 hectares of trees and inlets. Many of the low wooded islands in the lake are likely to have been *crannógs* – fortified, artificial islands.

Within the park to the north is the inaccessible **Clough Oughter Castle**, built in the 13th century by the O'Reillys on an island in the lake and the place where the rebel leader Owen Roe O'Neill died in 1649, reputedly from poisoning. The best way to get near it is from the south-east, along a narrow road running north from the village of Garthrattan.

Admission to the park is IR£1 for a car, IR£3 for a family. There are self-catering chalets on the shores of Lough Oughter that sleep four/six and can be rented by the week for IR£160/198 (IR£310/395 June to August) or IR£110/130 on weekends for three nights (IR£165/220 in summer).

Canadian-style **canoes** can be rented (☎ 049-32842) for a paddle on Lough Oughter or the Erne waterways, and there's coarse fishing and horse riding within the park.

Pighouse Folk Museum

From Crossdoney you'll see signposts for the Pighouse Folk Museum (☎ 049-37248) in Corr House, Cornafean. Its hodgepodge of artefacts dating from the 1700s is preserved in the original pighouse and barns. If you like rummaging through other people's attics, then you'll love this place. It's almost worth the trip just for the view it affords of the drumlins and valleys. The museum opens by appointment, so phone ahead to see if Mrs Faris is going to be there. Admission is IR£2.

Drumlane Monastic Site
One km south of Milltown, north of Killeshandra on the R201 road to Belturbet, is Drumlane, a monastic site dating from the 6th century. (The small church and peculiar round tower just over 11m high were built later.) The monastery was founded by St Mogue, and the site's location between two small lakes – Drumlane and Derrybrick – and the surrounding hills is its most attractive feature.

Butlersbridge
Six km north of Cavan is the pretty hamlet of Butlersbridge on the River Annalee. **Ballyhaise House** nearby was designed by Richard Castle (responsible for Dublin's Leinster House) and is worth a quick look for its fine brickwork. It's now an agricultural college.

Just near the river in Butlersbridge, *Ford House* (☎ 049-31427) has ensuite rooms for IR£18/32 a single/double; it opens May to October. The *Derragarra Inn*, a very attractive pub by the River Annalee, has good bar food available all day, a reasonably priced tourist menu and peat fires.

Belturbet
A small town on the River Erne 16km north-west of Cavan on the N3, Belturbet is an angling centre with cruises available on Upper Lough Erne during the summer. Turbet Tours (☎ 049-22360) has sailings on the Shannon-Erne Waterway from June to September aboard the *Erne Dawn* between Belturbet and Ballyconnell. The 2½-hour tour costs around IR£5/3.

A very central choice for accommodation is *Erne View* (☎ 049-22289), at 9 Bridge St in the centre of town, with singles/doubles

from IR£16/27. B&B at *Fortview House* (☎ 049-38185), 2km from the centre in Cloverhill, is IR£21/32 for singles/doubles. *Hilltop Farm* (☎ 049-22114), in Kilduff 5km south on the road to Cavan, has 10 rooms with B&B at IR£23/36. All three places have facilities for anglers.

Getting There & Around Bus Éireann (☎ 049-31353 in Cavan) stops here four times daily (three times on Sunday) in each direction on the route between Cavan and Donegal (2¼ hours). The bus stop is outside O'Reilly's Garage. You can rent bicycles – and seek advice about cycling routes – from Paddy Fitzpatrick's (☎ 049-22866) on Bridge St for IR£7/30 a day/week.

Lough Sheelin
Lough Sheelin, 24km south of Cavan, is noted for its game angling for brown trout, especially in May and June. The two main accommodation centres – at opposite ends of the 6km-long lough – are the villages of Finnea just over the border in County Westmeath and Mountnugent. There are several places in Mountnugent where you can stay and hire boats for fishing: the *Sheelin Shamrock Hotel* (☎ 049-40387), with singles/doubles from IR£22/38; *Ross House* (☎ 049-40218), from IR£23/36; and the *Crover House Hotel* (☎ 049-40206), from IR£32.50/55 and open between April and September.

WEST CAVAN
Sometimes known as the Panhandle because of its long, narrow shape, West Cavan is dominated by the starkly beautiful, but little visited, Cuilcagh Mountains. To the south-west, Magh Sleacht, the area around Kilnavert and Killycluggin, is supposed to have been a druidic centre dedicated to the deity Crom Cruaich. In the far north-west corner of the county, the road runs parallel to the Northern Irish border before dividing. The left fork heads west to Dowra and Blacklion, a desolate area with some interesting ancient sites. The right fork heads north to Swanlinbar and the border.

Getting There & Away

There are few buses serving this remote part of the county. The express Donegal-Dublin buses pass through Ballyconnell, Bawnboy and Swanlinbar four times daily (three on Sunday). Swanlinbar is also on the Athlone to Derry run, which runs once a day Monday to Saturday. The Galway to Belfast bus stops in Blacklion twice daily (once on Sunday); the Sligo (from Westport in summer) to Belfast bus stops two or three times daily (once on Sunday). Contact Bus Éireann (☎ 049-31353 in Cavan) for more information.

Ballyconnell

Ballyconnell, 29km north-west of Cavan and 7km west of Belturbet, is the gateway to the Cavan Panhandle. There's not a lot in the village itself, but it's a good base from which to explore. There are tours available on the Shannon-Erne Waterway; see the earlier Belturbet section for details.

Places to Stay The county's only hostel, the IHO *Sandville House* (☎ 049-26297), is 3km south-east of Ballyconnell, signposted off the Belturbet road (R200), in a peaceful rural two hectare setting. A dorm bed is IR£6, and there is an area to pitch a tent. The Dublin to Donegal bus stops at the Slieve Russell Hotel in Ballyconnell on request, and if you ring the hostel beforehand they can arrange to pick you up.

Ballyconnell has lots of B&Bs. *Snugborough House* (☎ 049-26346) has four rooms at IR£25/36 with bath. *Angler's Rest* (☎ 049-26391) is a pub-cum-guesthouse, which has ensuite rooms for IR£19/32 B&B.

The huge *Slieve Russell Hotel* (☎ 049-26444), 2km south-east of Ballyconnell, is something of a legend. Built by a local millionaire, it features marble, fountains, restaurants, bars, nightclubs, a swimming pool and an 18-hole golf course. B&B is normally around IR£85/160 a single/double, but there are frequent weekend and midweek specials.

Dowra & Black Pig's Dyke

Dowra is on the upper reaches of the River Shannon, and between the river and Mt Slievenakilla (545m) to the east is a 5km section of the mysterious Black Pig's Dyke, an earthworks that wriggles worm-like across much of the region. It's thought to have been built as a fortification and frontier of Ulster as early as the 3rd century AD.

Blacklion

Five km south of Blacklion are the remains of a **cashel** or ring fort with three large circular embankments. Inside is a sweathouse, a stone hut that served as a type of Turkish bath or sauna and was used mostly in the 19th century. Between Dowra and Blacklion there are the remains of quite a number of these curiosities.

Lough MacNean House (☎ 072-53022), on Main St, is one of the few B&Bs in or around Blacklion and costs from IR£23/40 a single/double. It also provides set dinner in the evening for IR£22.

The Galway to Belfast and Sligo to Belfast buses stop in Blacklion twice daily (once on Sunday). In summer, the latter bus originates in Westport once a day and stops in Blacklion. The bus stop is in front of Maguire's.

The Cavan & Ulster Ways

Blacklion and Dowra are the ends of the 16km Cavan Way, and Blacklion is also on the Ulster Way. See the Activities chapter.

EAST CAVAN

Heading east from the town of Cavan you move into the heart of drumlin country. The history of foreign settlement has left its mark on the fabric and layout of the main towns.

Getting There & Away

Four or five express Bus Éireann (☎ 049-31353 in Cavan) buses on the Donegal to Dublin route pass through Virginia (three on Sunday), and there are also three daily buses passing through between Cavan and Dublin. Cootehill is on a Dundalk to Cavan route, and two buses a day Monday to Saturday (four on Friday) link it with the county seat.

The Sweathouse

Sweathouses, built of stone with a small opening or doorway, were used to ease aches and pains, some of them alcohol-inflicted; readers of Leon Uris' epic novel *Trinity* will remember the well used sweathouse in the fictional town of Ballyutogue.

A turf fire would be lit inside for several hours and when the sweathouse was sufficiently hot the fire was removed. The patient would then go inside and sit or lie on a pile of rushes or straw until they felt they had sweated enough. They would then emerge and take a dip in a nearby running stream. ■

There's a daily bus on weekdays during the school year (September to June) from Cootehill to Monaghan.

A Dundalk to Cavan bus passes through Kingscourt on Tuesday only. There's also a Kingscourt-Navan-Dublin service which has two buses Monday to Saturday and one on Sunday.

Virginia

On the shores of Lough Ramor in the southeast corner of the county, the origins of Virginia (Achadh Lir) go back to the plantation of Ulster in the early 17th century. Like the US state first settled in 1607, it was named after Elizabeth I, the Virgin Queen. Six km to the north-west is **Cuilcagh House**, home of the Sheridan family, where Jonathan Swift is said to have come up with the idea for *Gulliver's Travels* while visiting in 1726.

Places to Stay & Eat Five km south of Virginia on the southern tip of Lough Ramor is the somewhat scruffy *Lough Ramor Camping & Caravan Park* (☎ 049-47447). It has only 13 tent sites, which cost IR£4 plus IR£1.50/75p per adult/child; motorcyclists pay IR£3 including tent, hikers and cyclists IR£2.50. It opens from mid-May to mid-September.

On the lake shore 1km from Virginia on the Dublin road, *St Kyran's* B&B (☎ 049-47087) opens April to September and costs

from IR£19/28 for a single/double without bathroom. Two km south-west along the Oldcastle road (R395) is the *White House* (☎ 049-47515), with four rooms for IR£15 to IR£18 per person.

In the centre of town on Main St is the 15-room *Ramor Lodge* (☎ 049-47003) with singles/doubles from IR£32/56. Just southeast of Virginia heading toward Dublin, the *Park Hotel* (☎ 049-47235) is an 18th century building overlooking a small lake, with 20 rooms at IR£80/140. It has a nine-hole golf course and good but pricey food (full dinner IR£25).

Sharkey's Hotel, on Main St, does teas, coffees and snacks all day and lunches in the bar.

Cootehill

Farther north, the small, neat market town of Cootehill (An Mhuinchille) is named after the Cootes, a planter family who, after acquiring some confiscated land from the O'Reillys, were instrumental in founding the town in the 17th century. This colourful clan had many interesting members, including Sir Charles Coote, one of Cromwell's most ruthless and effective leaders, and Richard Coote (1636-1701) who became governor of New York state, and then New Hampshire and Massachusetts.

The Coote mansion, **Bellamont House** (1729), was designed by Edward Lovett Pearce (architect of the Bank of Ireland in College Green, Dublin) and is described as one of the best Palladian villas in Ireland. It's open in the afternoons (no admission fee).

Places to Stay & Eat One of the most attractive B&Bs in town is the *Manse* (☎ 049-52322) on Bridge St, with singles/doubles with bathroom for IR£19.50/35. *Knockvilla* (☎ 049-52203), on Station Rd, a small cul-de-sac off the Shercock road, costs IR£14 to IR£15 per person. Also worth trying is *Beeches* (☎ 049-52307), on Station Rd, which has single/doubles for IR£21/32 with bathroom. One km out on the Cavan side of Cootehill is *Riverside House* (☎ 049-52150), an excellent B&B with rooms from

IR£22/34 and open all year. A central and affordable hotel is the 30-room *White Horse* (☎ 049-52124) on Main St, which charges IR£20 per person and has a popular nightclub.

The *Coffee Pot*, on Market St, has good coffee, cakes, sandwiches (IR£1.20) and lunches during the day. *Sean's Diner* is a decent café nearby. The *White Horse Hotel*, at the end of the same street, has a good carvery lunch and other dishes for around IR£6. Dinner here costs IR£15.

Shercock

Shercock (Searcóg) is a pretty little village on the shores of Lough Sillan, 13km southeast of Cootehill. The lake is noted for its pike fishing. The *Lakelands Caravan & Camping Park* (☎ 042-69488), about 1km west of the village in a tranquil setting beside the lake, charges IR£7 per tent plus 50p per person and opens Easter to mid-September. *Annesley Heights* (☎ 042-69667), a B&B east of town on the Carrickmacross road (R178), charges IR£18/28 and opens all year.

Kingscourt

In the far east of the County Cavan, Kingscourt (Dún an Rí) is a fairly drab village. **St Mary's Catholic Church** has some superb 1940s stained-glass windows by the artist Evie Hone. The church has views of the surrounding region, and just to the northwest is 225 hectare **Dún a Rí Forest Park** (☎ 042-67320), with wooded walks, picnic spots and a famous 'wishing well'.

Places to Stay & Eat *Mackin's Hotel* (☎ 042-67208), on Church St, is an ordinary country hotel with 15 rooms costing from IR£17 per person. *Cabra Castle* (☎ 042-67030), 3km out of Kingscourt on the Carrickmacross road, is an imposing structure with 29 rooms and its own nine-hole golf course, but it isn't cheap. B&B is IR£75/110 a single/double May to September. It's worth trying for a snack or meal at lunch or dinner (IR£21.95).

County Monaghan

Few visitors ever pass through Monaghan (Muineachán), a landscape of neat round hills, crisscrossed by unkempt hedgerows and scattered farms. The hills are drumlins, deposited by the glaciers of the last Ice Age in a belt stretching from Clew Bay in County Galway across the country to County Down. It's pleasant but never spectacular scenery; walkers and cyclists may enjoy the many peaceful country lanes if the weather is cooperative. Monaghan has fewer lakes than neighbouring Cavan, though the fishing is still good.

Patrick Kavanagh (1905-67), one of Ireland's most respected poets, was born in this county, in Inniskeen. *The Great Hunger* which he wrote in 1942, and *Tarry Flynn* written in 1948 evoke the atmosphere and often grim reality of life for the poor farming community.

The barren terrain has restricted the development of large-scale mechanised farming but, despite this, Monaghan's farming cooperatives are among the most active and forward-looking in the country. Monaghan is noted for its lace, and this eye-straining craft continues in Clones and Carrickmacross, the centre of the industry since the early 19th century.

HISTORY

The earliest traces of humans in this region go back to before the Bronze Age. None of the sites here measure up to the magnificent monuments of County Meath, though the Tullyrain Ring Fort close to Shantonagh in the south of the county is worth a look, as are Mannor Castle near Carrickmacross and the crannóg in Convent Lake in Monaghan, the county seat. Like Cavan, County Monaghan is lacking in religious remains despite its proximity to Armagh, the principal seat of St Patrick. The round tower and high cross in Clones in the west of the county are among the scant remains from this period of Irish history.

The Anglo-Normans were also less influential here than elsewhere. The county was controlled through the early Middle Ages by many Gaelic clans and septs, including the O'Carrolls, McKennas and MacMahons. Enemies for a long time of the O'Neills of Armagh, these families united with them on the losing side of the Nine Years' War (1594-1603) against the English.

Unlike Cavan and much of Ulster, Monaghan was largely left alone during the Ulster plantation. The transfer of Monaghan land to English hands came later – after the Cromwellian wars – and much of it was granted to soldiers and adventurers or bought by them from local chieftains (under pressure and often for a fraction of its true value). These new settlers levelled the forests and built numerous new towns and villages, each with their own Protestant church. The planning and architecture exemplified their tidy, no-frills approach to life. Disapproving of Irish pastoral farming methods, they introduced arable farming, and the linen industry later became very profitable.

Monaghan's historical ties with Ulster were severed by the partition of Ireland in 1922 and, though Republicanism is quite strong, it's not as visible as you might expect. A number of towns have Sinn Féin bookshops and advice centres.

MONAGHAN

The county town of Monaghan is 141km north-west of Dublin and just 8km south of the border with North Ireland. Though it has a population of less than 6000, it's the only town of any size in the county. Its design and buildings reflect the influence of the British newcomers of the 17th and 18th centuries and of the money generated by the linen industry in the 18th and 19th centuries. Compared to many Irish midland towns, Monaghan is a pleasant surprise; many of the town's important buildings are quite elegant limestone edifices.

History

Nothing remains of the ruling MacMahons' 1462 friary or their earlier forts, but in Convent Lake, just behind St Louis Convent, there is a small, overgrown crannóg that served as the headquarters for the family around the 14th century.

After the turbulent wars of the 16th and 17th centuries, the town was settled by Scottish Calvinists who built a castle using the rubble of the old friary, some fragments of which can be seen near the Diamond. The 19th century profits from the linen trade transformed the town and brought many sturdy new buildings.

Orientation & Information

Monaghan's principal streets form a roughly continuous arc, broken up by the town's three main squares – Church Square, the Diamond and Old Cross Square – where most of the sights and important buildings can be found. To the west of this arc at the top of Park St is Market Square. Here, the tourist office (☎ 047-81122) in Market House (1792) opens Monday to Saturday, 9 am to 1 pm in season only.

The post office is on Mill St, which runs between Hill St and North Rd. You can get your laundry done at Supreme Dry Cleaners on Park St just south of the tourist office on the left-hand side.

There are two small lakes, Peter's Lake to the north of the Diamond and Convent Lake with its crannóg at the south-west corner of town. A one-way traffic system operates through the centre of town.

The telephone code is ☎ 047.

Monaghan County Museum & Gallery

This excellent museum (☎ 82928) is just north-west of the tourist office at the start of Hill St and is one of the best regional museums in Ireland. Taking up two Victorian houses, it includes exhibits from the Stone Age to modern times and has displays on local lace-making, the linen industries, the abandoned Ulster Canal (which runs just to the south of the town and is being renovated) and, of course, the border with the North. The museum's prized possession, though, is the **Cross of Clogher**, a bronze 13th or 14th century altar cross.

Local and national artists have exhibits in the Art Gallery wing. The museum opens Tuesday to Saturday 11 am to 5 pm, closed 1 to 2 pm except June to September, and admission is free.

Other Sights

At the top of Dawson St is **Church Square**, the first of the three squares, with an 1857 **obelisk** for one Colonel Dawson, who was killed in the Crimean War. Overlooking the square is a fine Doric-style 1830 **courthouse**, the former Hibernian Bank (1875) and the Gothic St Patrick's Church.

In the centre of town, the **Diamond** is the town's original marketplace, with a Victorian sandstone fountain presented to the town in 1875 in honour of the Baron of Rossmore, a member of the area's former leading family. This spot was once occupied by the **Market Cross** (and sundial), which was moved to Old Cross Square at the end of Dublin St to accommodate the baron's memorial.

The birthplace of **Charles Gavan Duffy**, one of the leaders of the Young Ireland Movement and a founder of the *Nation* newspaper, is at 10 Dublin St. In the 1840s, the *Nation* set out to teach Irish people about their history and literature, as well as to present a non-sectarian view of Irish news. Later, Duffy moved to Australia, where he became a premier of Victoria. Nearby, the **Sinn Féin Advice Centre** has a display of Republican literature. A large bomb was found and defused outside the centre in March 1997 while this book was being researched.

South of the Ulster Canal on the Dublin road, the very imposing **St Macartan's Catholic Cathedral** with its slender spire was designed by JJ McCarthy (responsible for the College Chapel in Maynooth, County Kildare), and is said to be his finest building, though some feel it has been marred by the later addition of incongruous Carrara marble statues. It has good views of the surrounding area.

Convent Lake with its crannóg is at the bottom of Park St, over the canal. The **St**

Louis Convent Heritage Centre (☎ 83529) has exhibits on the convent, crannóg and local history. It opens Monday, Tuesday, Thursday and Friday 10 am to noon, and 2.30 to 4.30 pm, and Saturday and Sunday in the afternoon only. Admission is IR£1/50p adults/children.

Places to Stay

B&Bs The central *Ashleigh House* (☎ 81227), 37 Dublin St, has 12 rooms with singles/doubles at IR£20/34 with bath, IR£15/28 without bath. *Hilldene House* (☎ 83297) on Canal St charges IR£15/28 for rooms with shared bath.

On the Clones road south of the centre, the *Cedars* (☎ 82783) has three rooms from IR£20/30. *Lisdarragh House* (☎ 81473), 2km to the south on the Cootehill road (R188) charges IR£16 per person.

Hotels The fine, red-brick *Westenra Arms Hotel* (☎ 81517), in the Diamond in the centre of town, has 17 rooms with bathroom for IR£40/70. The Georgian-style *Lakeside Hotel* (☎ 835919), on North Rd beside Peter's Lake, is cheaper with 10 rooms for IR£30/55. The modern 40-room *Four Seasons Hotel* (☎ 81888), about 2km north on the Derry road in Coolshannagh, costs IR£48/90.

Places to Eat

Pizza d'Or, in Market Square behind the tourist office, turns out good takeaway pizzas from IR£4.50 and opens from 5 pm until late. The *Genoa* on Dublin St is a popular fast-food place serving pizzas, steaks and ice cream. Just down from the Genoa is the attractive *Mediterraneo*, which has pizzas (from IR£5.95), pasta (IR£6.50) and Italian main courses from IR£8.50. *Dinkin's Coffee Shop & Restaurant*, next to the courthouse on Church Square, has solid fare like hamburgers and chips downstairs and is busy at lunch times. The award-winning *Andy's Bar & Restaurant* on Market St, facing the tourist office, is one of the better places in town for food or a quiet drink. Lunch costs about IR£4; set dinner is IR£15.

There are two Chinese restaurants on Glaslough St running north from the Diamond: the *China Inn* and the *Treasure House*. The latter is more authentic.

Entertainment

Some of the best pubs are on Dublin St, including *McGinn's* and the popular *Shamrock Bar*. On Old Cross Square is *McConnon's Olde Cross Inn*. Another popular pub is *Terry's* on Market St, near the museum. *Jimmy's*, on Mill St across from the post office, is a quiet local.

The *Garage Theatre* (☎ 81597), north of town on the Derry road (N2) almost opposite the Four Seasons Hotel, hosts professional theatre companies as well as local amateur drama groups. The *Diamond Screen* (☎ 84755) is a three-screen cinema beside the car park in the Diamond Centre shopping mall.

Getting There & Away

From the bus station (☎ 82377) on North Rd beside the former railway station, there are numerous daily intercity services within the Republic and into the North. These include five or six a day (four on Sunday) to Dublin (two hours); four or five (two on Sunday) to Derry (two hours) via Omagh; and three (one on Sunday) to Belfast (two hours) and Armagh (40 minutes). There are also many daily local services to the nearby towns of Ardee, Ballybay, Castleblayney and Carrickmacross.

McConnon's private bus company (☎ 82020) has two daily buses from Church Square to Dublin's Parnell Square serving Carrickmacross, Castleblayney and Slane en route, and one daily bus to Clones.

Getting Around

Clerkin's Cycles (☎ 81113), next to Pizza d'Or on Market Square behind the tourist office, rents out bikes in summer for IR£5/20 a day/week. The closest other bike-rental place is the local Raleigh dealer Paddy McQuaid (☎ 88108) in Emyvale, about 12km north of Monaghan.

ROSSMORE FOREST PARK

This park (☎ 047-81968), 3km south-west of Monaghan on the Newbliss road (R189), was originally the home of the Rossmores, but only the buttresses to their castle's walls and the entrance stairway remain. Besides forest walks and picnic areas, the park has Californian sequoias, some of the tallest trees in Ireland. Other items include the Rossmores' pet cemetery as well as Iron Age wedge and court tombs. A gold collar (or lunula) from 1800 BC was found here in the 1930s and taken to the National Museum in Dublin. Fishing in the lakes here is popular. Admission to the park is free for pedestrians and IR£1.50 if you bring in a car.

GLASLOUGH

Glaslough, 9km north-east of Monaghan, is a neat little village of cut-stone cottages set beside its namesake, Glaslough (Green Lake). To get there from Monaghan, take the N2 Omagh road north, turn east onto the N12 for about 2km then turn north onto the R185.

Beside the village is the 500 hectare demesne of **Castle Leslie** (☎ 047-88109), a magnificent 19th century Italianate mansion overlooking the lake. The castle's attractions include a toilet used by Mick Jagger. Greystones Equestrian Centre (☎ 047-88100) has some fine hacks in the demesne, where there are 40km of trails.

The castle and gardens are open June to the end of August daily noon to 7 pm. Admission is IR£3/1.50, which includes a tour and coffee or tea. On Sunday afternoon only, teas of hot scones with cream and plenty of calorific desserts are served in the conservatory.

For the ultimate 'Victorian experience', you can stay in one of the castle's six bedrooms all with original decor for IR£50/76 a single double (or IR£57/90 for one of the enormous master bedrooms). Six-course dinners, prepared by the Swiss hotel-trained owner and descendent, Samantha Leslie, cost IR£23.50. For those whose budget is a bit more fragile, the *Pillar House Hotel*

(☎ 047-88125) at the entrance to the Castle Leslie estate, charges IR£18 per person.

CLONES & AROUND

The border town of Clones (Cluain Eois), 19km south-west of Monaghan, was the site of an important 6th century monastery that later became an Augustinian abbey. The bus stop, post office and banks, including a Bank of Ireland branch, are in the central Diamond, or square. Clones is the birthplace of the former world-featherweight-champion boxer, Barry McGuigan.

Things to See & Do

Along with the scant remains of the **abbey** founded by St Tiernach on Abbey St, there is a truncated 22m **round tower** in the old cemetery south of town; the layout suggests it may be an early, 9th century example. There's also a fine **high cross** in the town centre and the Protestant **St Tiernach's Church** overlooking the Diamond.

The Ulster Way in Northern Ireland runs through **Newtownbutler** in Fermanagh, 8km to the north-west of Clones. North of Newtownbutler, there is a **scenic drive** from Derrnawilt to Lisnaskea. South-east of Clones, the road from Newbliss to Cootehill is quite pretty and takes you to the edge of **Bellamont Forest**, which straddles the border with Cavan.

Places to Stay & Eat

Lennard Arms Hotel (☎ 047-51075) on the Diamond has 10 rooms with B&B for IR£20/36 with bathroom (IR£15/30 without). *Creighton Hotel* (☎ 047-51284) on Fermanagh St is popular with anglers. It has 16 simple but comfortable rooms with bathroom at a reasonable IR£20 B&B per person. This is also a nice place for a snack, lunch or full dinner (IR£9).

For a real treat, *Hilton Park* (☎ 047-56007) is an ideal place to forget the 20th century and blow any spare cash that may be weighing you down. Five km south along the L45 then L44 to Scotshouse, this country house has its own estate and serves top-class food in regal surroundings. Many of the

ingredients are grown on the estate's organic farm. B&B in six splendid rooms costs from IR£59/98 a single/double, and dinner is IR£25 or more. The grounds of Hilton Park are open to visitors (IR£3) May to September.

Getting There & Around

Bus Éireann (☎ 047-82377 in Monaghan) runs buses from Clones through Monaghan and on to Castleblayney, Carrickmacross, Slane and Dublin three to four times a day (twice on Sunday). Buses stop in the Diamond. Ulsterbus (☎ 01365-322633 in Enniskillen) has a number of daily buses on a route which takes in Monaghan, Clones, Enniskillen as well as Belfast. McConnon's (☎ 047-82020) has a daily bus between Clones, Monaghan, Castleblayney, Carrickmacross, Slane and Dublin.

You can rent bikes in Clones at Canal Stores (☎ 047-52125) on Cara St.

CARRICKMACROSS & AROUND

At one time a stronghold of the MacMahon clan, Carrickmacross (Carraig Mhachaire Rois) owes its origins to the third earl of Essex, who was a favourite of Elizabeth I and who built a castle here in the 1630s. The site is now occupied by the Convent of St Louis. An extensive lace industry helped the early English and Scottish planters to develop this pleasant little town, which consists of one wide street with some lovely Georgian houses and an old Protestant church.

Things to See & Do

The **Carrickmacross Lace Gallery** (☎ 042-62506) on Market Square, run by the local Lace Co-operative, has a some fine displays and lace for sale. It opens May to October 9.30 am to 12.30 pm and 1.30 to 5 pm (mornings only on Wednesday and Saturday; closed Sunday).

There's **fishing** in many of the lakes around Carrickmacross including Loughs Capragh, Spring, Monalty and Fea. Contact Jimmy McMahon at the Carrick Sports Centre (☎ 042-61714) for information on where to fish. Lough Fea also has an adjacent mansion (1827) and demesne with oak parkland. Five km south-west along the R179 Kingscourt road is **Dún a Rí Forest Park** (☎ 42-67320) with trails and picnic spots.

Mannan Castle is an enormous and heavily overgrown motte-and-bailey, about 5km north-west of Carrickmacross in Donaghmoyne. This fortified Norman mound has fragments of a stone castle dating from the 12th century. Both structures were built by the Pipard family, who were given an estate here in 1186 by England's King John.

Places to Stay

Carrickmacross has lots of B&B accommodation. The *Shirley Arms* pub (☎ 042-61209) on Main St has reasonable singles/doubles for IR£22/40 with bathroom. *Arradale House* (☎ 042-61941), a farmhouse on the Kingscourt road south of town, has eight rooms with bathroom for IR£18/32.

Things to Buy

The nuns of the Convent of St Louis revived the craft of lace-making at the end of the 19th century, and today the local lace cooperative runs the remaining small-scale industry. There is a display with some of their handiwork for sale in the Lace Gallery (☎ 042-62506) at the bottom of Main St. It opens May to October weekdays 9.30 am to 5.30 pm and Saturday mornings till noon.

Getting There & Away

Seven Bus Éireann (☎ 047-82377 in Monaghan) buses a day (five on Sunday) to/from Dublin (1¼ hours) pass through Carrickmacross, at least three on a Letterkenny to Dublin route, two on a Coleraine to Dublin route and one going between Clones and Dublin. Collins (☎ 042-61631), a private bus company, has four departures a day to Dublin, three on Sunday. McConnon's (☎ 047-82020) service includes Carrickmacross on its Dublin to Monaghan and Clones route, which also passes through Castleblayney, with two daily buses Monday to Saturday.

The bus stop is outside O'Hanlon's shop on Main St.

INNISKEEN

The village of Inniskeen (Inis Caoin), birthplace of the poet Patrick Kavanagh, is 10km north-east of Carrickmacross. Kavanagh is buried in the local graveyard where his cross reads: 'And pray for him who walked apart on the hills loving life's miracles'.

The **Patrick Kavanagh Rural & Literary Resource Centre** (☎ 042-78560), housed in the village's plain chapel and focusing on the poet's life and work as well as local and folk history, opens all year 11 am to 5 pm Monday to Friday, 2 to 6 pm on Saturday (June to September) and Sunday (mid-March to November). Nearby, the forlorn skeletal ruin of a **round tower** is all that is left of the 6th century **St Daig monastery**.

CASTLEBLAYNEY

Castleblayney (Baile na Lorgan), which is about half way between Carrickmacross and Monaghan on the N2, is nicely situated near Lough Muckno, the county's most expansive and scenic lake. This small town takes its name from Sir Edward Blayney and his family, who built a castle by the lake in 1622 and were responsible for the construction of the plain Georgian courthouse and both the Protestant and former Catholic churches – an uncommon gesture by a landowner at the time.

Blayney's castle was sold in the last century to the Hope family and was renamed after them. In the demesne is the 365 hectare **Lough Muckno Leisure Park** (☎ 042-46356), which has lakeshore and woodland trails as well as golf, tennis, cycling, canoeing, sailing, water-skiing, fishing and horse riding.

Places to Stay

The *Lough Muckno Leisure Park* (☎ 042-46356) has a 50-bed hostel for about IR£10 per person; it's open April to October. *Connolly's Guesthouse* (☎ 042-45162) in Castleblayney has rooms with shared bathroom for IR£12.50 per person and opens all year. The 27-room *Glencarn Hotel* (☎ 042-46666) on the Monaghan road charges IR£35/60 for singles/doubles.

Getting There & Away

Castleblayney is on the main Monaghan to Dublin route, with seven buses daily in each direction. McConnon's (☎ 047-82020) private bus service also has a number of daily buses from Clones and Monaghan through Castleblayney and on to Dublin.

County Roscommon

County Roscommon (Ros Comáin), much longer than it is wide, is more a transit route than a destination in itself. But besides the sleepy county town (population 3400), there are places well worth visiting. Strokestown has one of the better presented mansions in the country as well as the important Famine Museum. Just south of the Sligo boundary, the town of Boyle is also worth a stop, especially for the unique King House Interpretive Centre.

Much of Roscommon's western border follows the River Suck; about half way down, a few km inland from Ballyforan, is Dysart (Thomas St on some maps), ancestral stomping grounds of the illustrious Fallon sept. The remains of their castle are near the town as is a recently renovated church, parts of which date from the 12th century, in the middle of an ancient cemetery. Roscommon's eastern border is formed by a number of loughs, including the large Lough Ree (or Rea), and the River Shannon, which flows between them. Naturally, fishing is a major draw.

STROKESTOWN & AROUND

Strokestown (Béal na mBuillí), on the N5 between the town of Longford and Tulsk, is about 18km north-west of Roscommon.

A wide avenue leads to the arched entrance of **Strokestown Park House** (☎ 078-33013), built in the 1730s for Thomas Mahon, whose ancestors were granted a 12,000 hectare estate by Charles II after the Restoration.

The architect was Richard Castle, who introduced the Palladian style into Ireland, satisfying the Anglo-Irish gentry's desire for impressive (some might say ostentatious) family homes. By 1979, when the family sold up, the estate had been whittled down to 120 hectares. *Woodbrook* (see Books in the Facts for the Visitor chapter) is the perfect book to read after your visit and is available here.

Even children will enjoy the tour, which takes in a schoolroom and a child's bedroom, complete with 19th century toys and 'funhouse' mirrors. The 45-minute tour provides a fascinating glimpse into the whole Anglo-Irish ascendancy and costs IR£3/1 (students IR£2, families IR£7). The house opens May to September, noon to 5.30 pm Tuesday to Sunday.

The fascinating material on the Potato Famine is housed in the **Famine Museum** (☎ 078-33013) in the old stable yards. As well as depicting the famine and its causes, the material draws parallels with world hunger and poverty today. The Famine Museum opens Easter to October, 11 am to 5.30 pm Tuesday to Sunday. Admission is IR£2.70/1 (students IR£2, and families IR£6.50).

St John's Heritage & Genealogical Centre (☎ 078-33380), north of the centre in a disused Protestant church, has local history displays and one on Roscommon family names. The centre also offers a family research service for those whose families hail from County Roscommon, with records dating back to the 1660s. The initial charge is IR£20. The centre opens weekdays May to September 9 am to 1 pm and 2 to 5 pm (though genealogical enquiries can be made throughout the year).

Elphin, some 10km north-west of Strokestown, was an important bishopric from the time of St Patrick until 1961, when the seat was moved to Sligo. Ruins of the cathedral, parts of which date from about the 13th century, can be seen in the centre of town.

Famine, Suffering and Injustice
When the potato crop failed in the mid-1840s, Major Denis Mahon (landlord of Strokestown at the time) and his land agent simply evicted the hundreds of starving peasants who could no longer contribute to the estate's coffers and chartered ships to transport them away from Ireland. These overcrowded 'coffin ships', which carried emigrants to the USA and elsewhere, resulted in more suffering and deaths.

In 1847 Major Mahon was shot dead just outside the town, and one of the documents on display is a newspaper account of how Patrick Hasty and Owen Beirne committed the deed. Their signed confession looks as suspicious as the ones that convicted the Birmingham Six – exonerated in 1991 – of terrorism in Britain in the 1970s. ■

Places to Stay

Martin's (☎ 078-33247) is a B&B in the centre of Strokestown not far from the heritage centre charging about IR£15 per person. *Church View House* (☎ 078-33047), 5km east of town, has singles/doubles from IR£21/32. It opens April to October.

Getting There & Away

The Bus Éireann (☎ 071-60066 in Sligo) express bus from Sligo to Athlone (via Roscommon and Boyle) stops in Strokestown once a day Monday to Saturday between mid-July and August and daily on Sunday year round. The Ballina to Dublin bus via Longford and Mullingar stops in Strokestown three times daily (four on Sunday). The bus stop is outside Corcoran's on Main St.

BOYLE & AROUND

Boyle (Mainistir na Búille) is a garrison town in the north-west of the county at the foot of the Curlew Mountains and on the River Boyle between Lough Key and Lough Gara. It has many attractions, including the fine Boyle Abbey, the renovated King House Interpretive Centre and the impressive Drumanone Dolmen just outside town. Maureen O'Sullivan, the American film actress and mother of Mia Farrow, was born in a house on Main St opposite the Bank of Ireland building in 1911. The long-suffering Mia visits Boyle regularly and stays *en famille* at her mother's childhood home – now a B&B – in Knockvicar to the north-east

of Boyle near Lough Kee. Mention of actor/director Woody Allen, Mia's erstwhile partner, should be avoided at all costs in these parts.

Information

The tourist office (☎ 079-62145), in King House on the corner where Military Rd meets Main St, opens May to mid-September on weekdays 10 am to 5 pm. At other times seek assistance from the friendly staff at the interpretive centre or at the Úna Bhán Tourism Cooperative (see Organised Tours), both in King House, or from the tourism information board in front of the clocktower in the Crescent, the central square.

There's a National Irish Bank branch with an ATM on the corner of Bridge and Patrick Sts and a Bank of Ireland at the eastern end of Main St. The post office is on Carrick Rd, south of the river.

The telephone code is ☎ 079.

Boyle Abbey

Beside the N4, to the east of the town centre, is one of the finest Cistercian abbeys in Ireland, with remains dating back to the 12th century when it was founded by monks from Mellifont in County Louth. In 1659 military forces occupied the abbey and turned it into a fort. The western side of the abbey was originally set aside for the monks' sleeping quarters; later, the military forces had a dog kennel built into the left side of the gatehouse entrance.

The interesting 13th century nave in the

CENTRAL NORTH

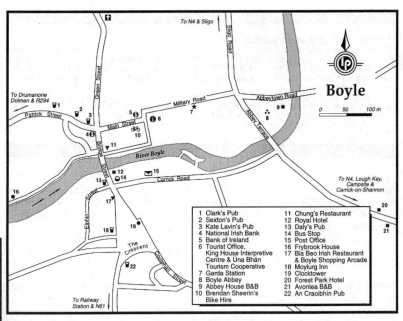

To N4 & Sligo

Sligo Road

Boyle

To Drumanone
Dolmen & R294

Military Road

Abbeytown Road

0   50   100 m

Green Street

Patrick Street

Main Street

Bridge Street

River Boyle

Abbey Terrace

Elphin Street

Carrick Road

To N4, Lough Key,
Campsite &
Carrick-on-Shannon

The Crescent

Cootehall Street

To Railway
Station & N61

1 Clark's Pub	11 Chung's Restaurant
2 Sexton's Pub	12 Royal Hotel
3 Kate Lavin's Pub	13 Daly's Pub
4 National Irish Bank	14 Bus Stop
5 Bank of Ireland	15 Post Office
6 Tourist Office,	16 Frybrook House
King House Interpretive	17 Bia Beo Irish Restaurant
Centre & Una Bhán	& Boyle Shopping Arcade
Tourism Cooperative	18 Moylurg Inn
7 Garda Station	19 Clocktower
8 Boyle Abbey	20 Forest Park Hotel
9 Abbey House B&B	21 Avonlea B&B
10 Brendan Sheerin's	22 An Craoibhín Pub
Bike Hire	

northern part of the abbey has Gothic arches on one side that are narrower than the Romanesque arches on the other. The capitals are also distinctive. On the southern side of the abbey, once the refectory area, there is a fine stone chimney built after the monks left and the abbey became a fortified home. Edward King, whose death by drowning in 1637 inspired the English poet John Milton to compose *Lycidas*, is buried here.

The abbey (☎ 62604), an OPW site, opens daily 9.30 am to 6.30 pm June to mid-September. Entry is IR£1/40p (families IR£3) and guided tours are available. It's possible to view the abbey at other times by asking for the keys from the neighbouring Abbey House B&B.

King House Interpretive Centre

This interpretive centre (☎ 63242), certainly one of the most inspired in the country, is in a lovely mansion built by Henry King in 1730. It subsequently served as a military

barracks for the Connaught Rangers and sat derelict for most of this century until the county council renovated it (1989-95) at a cost of IR£3 million. It contains audiovisual exhibits detailing the turbulent history of the Connaught kings and the chieftains like the MacDermots and the O'Conors, the town of Boyle and the King family, who settled here in 1603 and were later named earls of Kingston. Kids will especially enjoy King House; it's very much a hands-on museum where they can try on ancient Irish cloaks, brooches and leather shoes, write with a quill 'pen' and even 'build' a vaulted ceiling – King House has four floors of them – from specially designed blocks. A tour of King House is an excellent precursor to one of the Famine Museum in Strokestown.

The centre opens May to September daily 10 am to 6 pm and the same hours on Saturday and Sunday only in April and October. Admission is IR£3/2.50/8 for adults/children & students/families.

Frybrook House

This rather magnificent Georgian mansion (☎ 63513) was built in 1750 for Henry Fry, who came to Boyle at the invitation of Lord Kingston. The drawing room contains some of the finest Georgian plasterwork anywhere and an Adams fireplace. The house was noted for its hospitality, and local lore has it that a bell was sounded every day at 5 pm inviting anyone who wished to come and dine. A tent was set up in the garden to cope with the overflow.

Frybrook House opens to visitors June to August daily 2 to 6 pm. Admission costs IR£3/2/7 for adults/students/families.

Drumanone Dolmen

This superb dolmen is one of the largest in Ireland, measuring 4.5m by 3.3m, and was constructed before 2000 BC. To get there, follow Patrick St west out of town for 2km, bear left at the junction sign for Lough Gara for another km, passing under a railway arch. A sign indicates the path across the railway line.

Lough Key Forest Park

This 350 hectare park (☎ 62363), on the N4 3km east of Boyle, was part of the Rockingham estate, owned by the King family from the late 18th century until it was sold to the Land Commission in 1957. Rockingham House, designed by John Nash, was destroyed by a fire in the same year; all that remains are some stables and outbuildings and a tunnel leading from what was the house to the lake. The inexpensive café opens 12.30 to 6 pm and in summer a restaurant opens for lunch and dinner. The park opens daily year round and entry costs IR£1 (IR£3 for families).

Lough Key is at the northern limit for cruising on the Shannon. Rowing boats are available for a pricey IR£6 an hour, and fishing is a popular pursuit; a record-breaking 17.8-kg pike was caught here in 1992. The ruins of a 12th century abbey can be seen on tiny Trinity Island. On Castle Island, a 19th century castle stands on the site of 16th century MacDermot Castle.

Douglas Hyde Interpretive Centre

Frenchpark, some 12km south-west of Boyle on the R361, is home to the Douglas Hyde Interpretive Centre (☎ 0907-70016) in the former Protestant church where Hyde's father was rector. Hyde (1860-1949) was one of the founding members of the Gaelic League in 1893 and was later elected the first president of the Republic in 1937. This Renaissance man published many works of prose and poetry under the pen name 'An Craoibhín Aoibhinn' ('delightful little branch'), and he is buried in the churchyard. The centre, also known as the Gairdín an Craoibhín ('garden of the little branch'), opens May to September daily except Monday, 2 to 5 or 6 pm.

Organised Tours

The Úna Bhán Tourism Cooperative (☎ 63033), whose office is in the grounds of King House, organises week-long cycling, horse-riding and fishing tours which include accommodation on a working farm. There's an excellent craft shop here open daily 10 am to 6 pm year round.

Places to Stay

Camping The *Lough Key Forest Caravan & Camping Park* (☎ 62212) is in the park, so indicate your intention to camp to avoid the IR£1 entrance charge. Camping costs IR£8 for a family tent, or IR£3 per hiker, cyclist or motorcyclist; electricity is an extra IR£1.50.

B&Bs Beside the abbey and the River Boyle, *Abbey House* (☎ 62385) charges IR£22.50/32 for singles/doubles with bath and opens March to October. At *Avonlea* (☎ 62538), on the Carrick road (N4) just south-east of town and almost opposite the Forest Park Hotel, rates are IR£21/32 with bath. *Carnfree* (☎ 62516), almost next door to the hotel, charges from IR£16 per person and opens all year. About a km farther on is *Rosdarrig* (☎ 62040) charging IR£15 or IR£16 per person. Farther south on the N4, Mrs Kelly in *Forest Park House* (☎ 62227) offers B&B for IR£21/32.

Riversdale House (☎ 67012), which is in

Knockvicar, 12km north-east of Boyle on the R285, charges IR£24/35 and opens April to October.

Hotels In the town centre, the 18th century *Royal Hotel* (☎ 62016) has 16 rooms with bath for IR£37.50 per person, while the 12-room *Forest Park Hotel* (☎ 62229), just outside town on the N4, charges IR£50/65.

Places to Eat
The best place in town for a IR£3 or IR£4 pub lunch is at *An Craoibhín* in the Crescent, which is also the most popular pub in town. On Patrick St, reasonable pub food is available at *Sexton's*. For snacks and lunch the *coffee shop* in King House is a good bet. It's open daily 10 am to 6 pm.

Overlooking the river, *Chung's* serves passable Chinese food daily 5 to 11.30 pm. Main courses range from around IR£4.50 to IR£6.50. *Bia Beo* is a rare breed indeed – an Irish restaurant – upstairs in the Boyle Shopping Arcade on Bridge St. The *Royal* and *Forest Park* hotels do lunch and set dinners (IR£15.95 and IR£19.95 respectively).

Entertainment
The *Railway Bar* near the station, *Clark's* and *Kate Lavin's* in Patrick St, and the *Moylurg Inn* opposite the clocktower in the Crescent have music and a decent drop of Guinness.

Getting There & Away
From almost outside the Royal Hotel (and opposite Daly's pub) on Bridge St, the Bus Éireann (☎ 071-60066 in Sligo) express bus leaves three times daily for Sligo (40 minutes) and Dublin (3¼ hours). From Boyle, a train goes three times daily (four on Friday) between Sligo (40 minutes) and Dublin (3¼ hours) via Mullingar.

Getting Around
You can order a taxi on ☎ 63344 or ☎ 62119. Bikes are available from Brendan Sheerin's cycle shop (☎ 62010) in Main St for IR£7/35 daily/weekly. It's open daily except Wednes-

day and Sunday, 9.30 am to 1 pm and 2 to 6 pm.

ROSCOMMON
The small county town of Roscommon (Ros Comáin), sitting at the crossroads of several major highways, has a few sights of interest that make it worth a stopover. The town gets its name from *ros*, meaning 'wooded headland', and St Coman, who founded a monastery here in the 8th century.

Information
The local tourist office (☎ 0903-26342), in John Harrison Hall in Market Square, opens daily late May to early September. The post office is next door, and there is a Bank of Ireland opposite Gleeson's Guesthouse on the square.

The telephone code is ☎ 0903.

Things to See & Do
The Norman **Roscommon Castle** built in 1269 was almost immediately destroyed by Irish forces and rebuilt in 1280. The mullioned windows were added in the 16th century, and the massive walls and round bastions give it an impressive look, standing alone in a field at the northern end of town off Castle St.

At the southern end of town off Circular Rd are the remains of a 13th century **Dominican priory**, the most notable feature of which is an effigy of the founder, Felim O'Conor, carved around 1300. It's set in the north wall near where the altar once stood.

The **Roscommon County Museum** (☎ 63856) is in John Harrison Hall on Market Square, a former Presbyterian church with an unusual window in the form of a Star of David supposedly representing the Trinity. Though not yet completed, the museum contains some interesting pieces, including an inscribed slab from St Coman's monastery and a sheila-na-gig from Rahara. The museum opens April to October, Monday to Saturday 10 am to 5.30 pm.

Market Square's Bank of Ireland used to be the **courthouse**. Opposite is the enormous **old jail**, where executions were carried out by 'Lady Betty' in the mid-18th century. She herself had been condemned to death after confessing to the murder of a lodger in her house – who turned out to be her own son. She escaped death by offering to take over as executioner.

Ask the tourist office for a map of the new **Suck Valley Way**, a 75km walking trail. The river offers some of the best mixed fishing in Ireland, with rudd, tench, pike and perch in abundance.

Places to Stay

Gailey Bay Caravan & Camping Park (☎ 61058) is in Knockcroghery beside Lough Ree about 10km south-east of Roscommon on the N61 to Athlone; a sign points east just near the railway station and it's a couple of km up the road. Pitching a tent costs IR£4 plus IR£1 per person; hikers or cyclists pay IR£3.

In town, nothing could be more central than *Gleeson's Guesthouse* (☎ 26954), a friendly place in the former manse of the Presbyterian church (now John Harrison Hall) on Market Square. It has 22 rooms in a new and an old wing, and singles/doubles start at IR£20/36. *Regan's Guesthouse* (☎ 25339) just next door with 10 rooms costs about the same but is not as nice.

There are several B&Bs on the Galway road (N63) to the south-west, including Mrs Campbell's *Westway* (☎ 26927) which has singles/doubles for IR£15/24 with separate bathroom, and also Mrs O'Grady's *Villa* (☎ 25998) from IR£18/28. Westway opens March to November, the Villa all year.

The 19-room *Royal Hotel* (☎ 26317) in the centre of town on Castle St has singles/doubles with shower and toilet for IR£35/52. The poshest place in town is the 25-room *Abbey Hotel* (☎ 26250) south-west of Market Square at the start of the Galway road. Singles/doubles cost IR£40/70 or IR£50/80, depending on the season.

Places to Eat

There are a number of cafés and fast-food places on Main St, including the *Alpine Grill*. *Gleeson's Restaurant* on the square serves full Irish breakfast for IR£3.50 and lunch (from IR£3.95) daily. *Regan's* next door has a standard dinner menu with the usual main courses ('with chips') from about IR£5. *China Palace* is a Chinese restaurant upstairs on Main St open every evening except Tuesday, 5 pm to 12.30 am, and also for lunch on Sunday from 1 pm. The *Royal Hotel* serves an excellent set dinner for IR£15.

Entertainment

One of the best pubs in town is *Down the Hatch* on Church St. The *Central Bar* and *JJ Hagerty's* on Market Square are also worth a look.

Getting There & Around

Bus Éireann (☎ 071-60066 in Sligo) express buses between Westport (2¼ hours) and Dublin (three hours) stop in Roscommon three times daily (once on Sunday). Buses stop in front of Regan's Guesthouse on Market Square. Roscommon is also served by train three times daily (four on Friday) on the Dublin (two hours) to Westport (1½ hours) line.

You can order a taxi on ☎ 26096.

WEST ROSCOMMON

The village of Ballintober (Ballintubber on some maps; Baile an Tobair in Irish), about 15km north-west of Roscommon off the N60, is dominated by the 14th century **Ballintober Castle**, built in the early 14th century and was once home to the fierce O'Conors of Connaught. Cromwellian forces took the castle in 1652, but it was later restored – only to be lost again after the defeat of the Catholics at the Battle of the Boyne in 1690. The large central courtyard has polygonal towers at each corner, and the whole edifice is a good example of an early Irish castle. Also in Ballintober is the **Old Schoolhouse Museum** (☎ 0907-55397), which recreates a rural Irish classroom in the 1920s. It opens daily Easter to October, and entry is IR£1.50/1/50p for adults/stuents/ children.

To the north-west past Castlerea on the

N60, **Clonalis House** (☎ 0907-20014), built in 1878, opens to the public June to mid-September Tuesday to Sunday 11 am to 5 pm. Admission is IR£3/2/1 for adults/students/children. The house is rather cold and lacks atmosphere, but it does have the harp of Turlough O'Carolan (1630-1738), the great blind harpist and composer (see the following Around Carrick-on-Shannon section) as well as a copy of the last Brehon Law (Irish common law dating back to pre-Christian times) judgement handed down in 1580. Overnight guests are welcome at *Clonalis House* between mid-April and September. There are four bedrooms and singles/doubles cost IR£51/90.

County Leitrim

Leitrim (Liatroim) stretches 80km from the border with Longford to Donegal Bay in the north-west, with a short coastline of about 5km around Tulloghan. Lough Allen splits the county almost in two; the attractions in northern Leitrim with its mountains and glens are more accessible from Sligo and are covered in the Counties Mayo & Sligo chapter. The southern part of Leitrim's main interest is its lush scenery of lakes and drumlins but, while a walking or cycling tour of the area would be enjoyable, most visitors just speed through on their way north.

CARRICK-ON-SHANNON

Carrick-on-Shannon (known simply as Carrick, or in Irish as Cora Droma Rúisc), on the border with Roscommon and the main town in the county, marks the upper limit of navigation on the River Shannon. But apart from boating and fishing trips, there is little to keep the visitor here for long.

Information

The tourist office (☎ 078-20170), on West Quay at the Marina beside Carrick Bridge, opens May to September, 9 am to 1 pm Monday to Thursday, and 9.30 to 1 pm on Friday. A signposted walking tour takes in all the buildings and places of interest in town.

There's an Allied Irish Bank branch at the top of Main St. The post office is on Bridge St opposite Flynn's Corner House bar.

The telephone code is ☎ 078.

Costello Chapel

At the top of Bridge St, next to Flynn's Corner House, is the sombre little Costello Chapel. It measures only 5m by 3.6m and was built in 1877 by one distraught Edward Costello after the death of his wife. She is buried on the left side under a heavy slab of glass and her husband was interred on the other side in 1891. The chapel was built on the site of the old courthouse, where 19 men were hanged in the 19th century.

Boating & Fishing

Michael Lynch (☎ 20034), based on the quay near the tourist office, has rowing boats for hire at IR£6 an hour, or between IR£20 and IR£30 a day for one with an engine. More upmarket launches are available through Tara Cruisers (☎ 20736), which is based at the Rosebank Marina on the Dublin road (N4). Moon River (☎ 21777) runs cruises in season from the Marina. Contact the tourist office or check the information board on the quay.

For information on fishing, contact the Carrick-on-Shannon Angling Association (☎ 20489).

Places to Stay

Camping is free on the river bank near the tourist office. Tokens for the showers at the nearby Marina can be purchased from the Marina office. The IHH *Town Clock Hostel* (☎ 20068), in the town centre at the junction of Main and Bridge Sts, has dorm beds for IR£5.50 to IR£6.60 and one private room for IR£8 per person. It opens June to September.

Carrick has lots of B&Bs. On Station Rd, near the railway station on the Roscommon side of the river, *Villa Flora* (☎ 20338), open April to October, charges from IR£20/28 for singles/doubles, while *Ariadna* (☎ 20205), open all year, costs IR£14 per person. The

Bush Hotel (☎ 20114), in the centre of town, has B&B with private bathroom from IR£35/64.

Places to Eat

Flynn's is a fast-food joint on Main St next to the Corner House. *Coffey's Pastry Case* is a busy, inexpensive self-service coffee shop/bakery on the corner near the bridge and tourist office. Next door, *Cryan's Pub* does a IR£3.25 lunch and has traditional Irish music sessions most nights. Next door *Buadh* ('victory') at the Oarsman Pub is a more expensive place with main courses (mostly seafood) from IR£8 to IR£12.

Farther up Bridge St, the *Mariner's Reach* has lunch specials for about IR£3.50, but even better is the four-course bar special available until 9.30 pm for IR£5. *Chung's*, a branch of the Chinese restaurant in Boyle, County Roscommon, is on Main St and has dishes (with several vegetarian options) for around IR4.50 to IR£6.50.

Getting There & Away

The bus stop is outside Coffey's Pastry Case on the corner near the bridge and tourist office. The Bus Éireann (☎ 071-60066 in Sligo) main express bus between Dublin (2¾ hours) and Sligo (one hour) stops there three times daily in each direction. There are also buses to Boyle, Longford and Athlone.

The railway station (☎ 20036) is a 15-minute walk from the bridge on the Roscommon side of the river. Turn right over the bridge, then left at the service station. Carrick has three trains daily to Dublin (three hours) and Sligo (50 minutes) with an additional one on Friday.

Getting Around

You can hire bicycles from Geraghty's (☎ 21316) on Main St for IR£7/30 per day/week; it also rents out rods and tackle on a daily or weekly basis. The *Visitors' Guidebook* from the tourist office includes details of suggested cycling tours.

AROUND CARRICK-ON-SHANNON

The countryside around Carrick with its quiet lanes and gently undulating landscape is tailor-made for cycling.

Turlough O'Carolan Country

There are three places to visit in the area that are connected with the famous blind poet, composer and harpist, Turlough O'Carolan (1670-1738). He spent most of his time in **Mohill** where his patron, Mrs MacDermot Roe, resided, and a sculpture on the main street of the town commemorates the association. To reach Mohill from Carrick-on-Shannon, follow the N4 to Dublin then turn east onto the R201 shortly after passing Drumsna.

O'Carolan is buried in **Kilronan church**, which preserves a 12th century doorway, just over the border in County Roscommon. To reach the church, take the R280 north from Carrick-on-Shannon and at the village of Leitrim turn west on the R284 to Keadue (Keadew on some maps). In Keadue turn west on the R284 to Sligo. Keadue – a coal-mining town at the foot of the Arigna Mountains until the 1980s and now a spruced up 'tidy-town competition' winner – also has strong associations with the musician and hosts the annual O'Carolan Harp Festival during the first week in August.

Lough Rynn Estate

Lough Rynn, south of Mohill, was the home of the Clements family, the earls of Leitrim, and the various 19th century buildings put up during the time of the third earl are open to the public. Within the wooded estate (☎ 078-31427) there's a picnic site and restaurant, and guided tours of the principal buildings are available. It's open daily late April to mid-September, 10 am to 7 pm. Admission to the grounds is IR£3.50 per car, IR£1.50 per person and the tour is another IR£1.

Drumshanbo

Drumshanbo (Droim Seanbhó), about 9km north of Carrick-on-Shannon on the southern shores of Lough Allen, is mainly a centre for coarse fishing. The Sliath an Iarainn Visitors' Centre (☎ 078-41522) has an interesting audiovisual display (IR£1/50p) on the history and culture of the locality, and a non-functioning replica of an ancient Irish sweathouse not unlike a sauna. The centre opens April to September, 10 am to 6 pm Monday to Saturday, 2 to 6 pm Sunday.

Mrs Mooney at the *Drumshanbo Holiday Centre* (☎ 078-41013), 2 Carrick Rd at the southern end of town, does B&B for IR£13/22 singles/doubles and provides local tourist information.

SHANNON-ERNE WATERWAY
The Shannon-Erne Waterway stretches from the River Shannon beside the village of Leitrim 4km north of Carrick-on-Shannon, through north-west County Cavan to the southern shore of Upper Lough Erne, just over the Northern Irish border in County Fermanagh. The 258km waterway is a series of rivers and lakes linked by canals. The original canal, named the Ballinamore-Ballyconnell Canal, was completed in 1860, but soon fell into disuse with the coming of the railway. Today, the waterway with its 34 stone bridges and 16 locks is busy with boats and pleasure cruisers. Emerald Star (☎ 01-679 8166), 47 Dawson St, Dublin 2, rents cruisers on the waterway. Pre-paid Smart Cards to operate the locks, showers, washing machines, chemical toilets and pumpouts at each mooring can be purchased from Waterway Rangers and local shops along the Shannon-Erne.

The waterway is jointly operated by the OPW in the Republic and the Department of Agriculture in Northern Ireland.

LEITRIM WAY
The Leitrim Way begins in Drumshanbo and ends in Manorhamilton, a distance of 48km. See the introductory Activities chapter for details.

County Longford

The history of County Longford (An Longfort) dates back to prehistoric times; St Patrick visited here and for centuries it was the centre of power of the O'Farrell family, who arrived in the 11th century. During the 1798 Rising, the British army under Lord Cornwallis defeated a combined Irish and French army at Ballinamuck, 16km north of Longford. The Potato Famine of the 1840s and 50s saw massive emigration; many Longford migrants went to Argentina, where one of their descendants, Edel Miro O'Farrell, became president in 1914.

Longford, the county town, is solidly agrarian and prosperous but of little interest to the tourist; many people pass through travelling between Dublin and Mayo or Sligo. **Carriglass Manor** (☎ 043-45165), 5km north-east, has been the home of the Huguenot Lefroy family since 1810. The manor has an interesting collection of furnishings and memorabilia, including Victorian costumes and hand-made lace, and opens to the public June to September.

The 150km **Royal Canal** from Dublin passes through the county to meet the River Shannon near Clondra (or Cloondara) west of Longford. The canal's towpath provides an interesting walking route through the county.

The main attraction for most visitors to County Longford, however, is the fishing around Lough Ree and Lanesborough.

LANESBOROUGH
Also spelt Lanesboro in English (or, in Irish, Béal Átha Liag), this small town is the site of one of Ireland's first turf-fired generating stations, which dominates the skyline. It's close to the banks of the River Shannon and provides a flow of warm water into a channel. The river divides County Longford from County Roscommon, and Lanesborough is linked by bridge to Ballyclare on the Roscommon side.

Information
There's an National Irish Bank branch on Main St a few doors down from MJS Motorcycles. The post office is farther east on Main St and opposite Samantha's Restaurant & Coffee Shop.

The telephone code is ☎ 043.

Fishing

When the mayfly appears in May, then again in August and September, this stretch of water becomes prime angling territory. Bream and tench are caught early in the morning and at night, while roach are available throughout the day. The water is only just over a metre deep. This isn't the only place to fish and enquiries should be made at Pricewyse tackle shop in the middle of Lanesborough. You can hire boats for about IR£25 from the affable Mark Shields at MJS Motorcycles (☎ 21510) on Main St.

Places to Stay

B&B is available above *Samantha's Restaurant & Coffee Shop* (☎ 21558) on Main St for IR£13 per person. *Dunamase House* (☎ 21201), on Rathcline Rd south-east of the centre, charges from IR£19/28 a single/double and opens April to September. The only hotel in town is the run-down, rather unfriendly *Sliabh Bán* (☎ 21790), also known as the Anchor, with B&B at IR£15 per person. Self-catering accommodation is available through the *Lough Ree Arms* pub (☎ 21145) on Main St.

Places to Eat

The *Flagship*, a restaurant in a converted barge on the Shannon, is a good and friendly place, open 8 am to 10 pm; fish with salad and chips is IR£6.95 and it does snacks as well. *Samantha's* is good for sandwiches and light lunches.

The *Lough Ree Arms* and the thatched *Máirtín's Cottage Bar* attached to the Sliabh Bán Hotel do reasonable pub food. Another decent pub is the *Shannon Princess* on a barge moored by the bridge.

Getting There & Around

Lanesborough is on the N63, half way between the towns of Longford and Roscommon. The nearest bus and railway stations are at these two towns, and there is a bus service to both from Lanesborough twice daily Monday to Saturday. The Belfast to Galway express via Sligo and Longford stops in Lanesborough on Friday and Sunday only.

Harrison's Supermarket at the Statoil petrol station just over the bridge rents out bicycles.

County Westmeath

Characterised by lakes and rich pasture land, Westmeath (An Iarmhí) is noted more for its beef than its scenic splendour or historic sites. An exception to the generally monotonous landscape is the area north of Athlone known as Goldsmith Country, while the places of genuine interest in Westmeath – and there are a few – are mostly in the vicinity of Mullingar.

MULLINGAR

Mullingar (An Muileann gCearr) is a prosperous marketing town – with a well used commuter train service each morning and evening to and from Dublin – and much of the surrounding area is rather like the rich English countryside. There are some fine fishing loughs in the vicinity and a preserved bog that delights naturalists. The town itself is one of the few places outside Dublin that James Joyce visited.

The Royal Canal, linking Dublin with the River Shannon via Mullingar, was constructed in the 1790s as a rival to the Grand Canal. It never managed to compete successfully and, by the 1880s, passenger business had ceased. There was a slight revival during WWII with a turf trade to Dublin, but it finally closed in 1955. Restoration work west of Mullingar is in progress, with walkways and cycle trails under construction.

Information

The Midlands-East Tourism (☎ 044-48650), on the Dublin road east of the centre, opens all year 9.30 am to 1 pm and 2 to 5.30 pm Monday to Friday. June to September it's also open on Saturday 10 am to 6 pm with an hour lunch break. It will move to Market House in the centre sometime in 1998.

CENTRAL NORTH

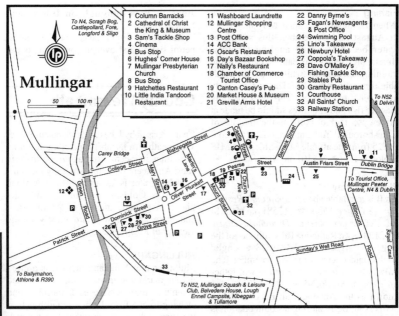

Mullingar

0   50   100 m

1	Column Barracks	11	Washboard Laundrette	22	Danny Byrne's

1 Column Barracks
2 Cathedral of Christ the King & Museum
3 Sam's Tackle Shop
4 Cinema
5 Bus Stop
6 Hughes' Corner House
7 Mullingar Presbyterian Church
8 Bus Stop
9 Hatchetes Restaurant
10 Little India Tandoori Restaurant
11 Washboard Laundrette
12 Mullingar Shopping Centre
13 Post Office
14 ACC Bank
15 Oscar's Restaurant
16 Day's Bazaar Bookshop
17 Nally's Restaurant
18 Chamber of Commerce Tourist Office
19 Canton Casey's Pub
20 Market House & Museum
21 Greville Arms Hotel
22 Danny Byrne's
23 Fagan's Newsagents & Post Office
24 Swimming Pool
25 Lino's Takeaway
26 Newbury Hotel
27 Coppola's Takeaway
28 Dave O'Malley's Fishing Tackle Shop
29 Stables Pub
30 Gramby Restaurant
31 Courthouse
32 All Saints' Church
33 Railway Station

Another tourist office (☎ 044-44044), operated by the local chamber of commerce, is in town next to Market House, but it does little more than distribute pamphlets and brochures. It's open year round Monday to Friday 9.30 am to 5.30 pm, and on Saturday in summer.

There are a number of banks on the main street, which changes names five times, including an ACC Bank branch at the start of Oliver Plunkett St. You can also change money at Day's Bazaar Bookshop on the same street; it opens Monday to Saturday 8 am to 6 pm.

The post office is to the west on Dominick St.

The Washboard laundrette is on Austin Friars St, just before Dublin Bridge.

The telephone code is ☎ 044.

Cathedral & Ecclesiastical Museum

The Cathedral of Christ the King was built just before WWII and has large mosaics of St Anne and St Patrick by the Russian artist Boris Anrep.

There's a small museum of liturgical objects over the sacristy, entered from the side of the church, which contains vestments worn by St Oliver Plunkett (see Drogheda in the Meath & Louth chapter).

Guided tours (IR£1/50p) operate June to September between 3 and 4 pm on Wednesday, Saturday and Sunday. Otherwise call at the church house to the right of the cathedral inside the gates or phone ☎ 48338.

Market House Museum

This museum (☎ 48152), in Market House on Pearse St, has an odd collection of artefacts, including axe-heads, fossils, a German army helmet, a rubber bullet from North Ireland, a shillelagh, a stone hot-water bottle and a great butter churn. It's open July to September, 2 to 5.30 pm Tuesday to Saturday. Entry is 50p/20p, but call first to make an appointment.

Mullingar Bronze & Pewter Visitors' Centre

Mullingar is known for its pewterware, and the visitors' centre (☎ 44948) allows you to watch craftspeople turning the silvery-grey metal into cups, bowls and *objets d'art*. The shop and showroom are open March to October, Monday to Saturday, 9.30 or 10 am to 6 pm, and on weekdays only the rest of the year. Guided tours are available weekdays, 9.30 am to 4 pm (last tour on Friday at 12.30 pm). The centre is in The Downs, about 6km south-east of Mullingar on the Dublin road (N4).

Activities

The Mullingar Squash & Leisure Club (☎ 40949), Lynn Industrial Estate, offers squash, sauna, snooker and indoor bowls for IR£3. You can go swimming at the local swimming pool (☎ 40488) off Austin Friars St for about IR£2. Mullingar Equestrian Centre (☎ 48331), south-west of Mullingar on the Athlone road (R390), has riding packages available.

Special Events

The Mullingar Festival (☎ 44044) is held in the second week of July. It's a low-key affair, the highlight of which is the election of the queen and the bachelor of the festival.

Places to Stay

Camping Camping at *Lough Ennell Caravan & Camping Park* (☎ 48101), 8km south of town on the N52 road to Tullamore, costs a whopping IR£10/8 for a family/two-person tent and IR£1 per adult; motorcyclists with a tent pay IR£4 while hikers and cyclists are charged IR£3. The site opens April to September, and it can get busy on sunny weekends.

Hostel The closest hostel is the IHH *Farragh House* (☎ 71446) in Bunbrosna, 12km north-west of Mullingar on the N4 and near Lough Owel. It costs from IR£6.50 to IR£7.50 for a dorm bed, IR£8.50 per person for one of the two private rooms, and opens February to November. It rents boats and bicycles.

B&Bs Most B&Bs are on the approach roads from Dublin and Sligo. *Woodside* (☎ 41636) has singles/doubles from IR£18/30, and *Moorland* (☎ 40905) charges IR£21/34 for rooms with bath. Both are on the Dublin road.

Hotels The very friendly *Newbury Hotel* (☎ 42888), with 12 rooms on Dominick St, costs IR£25/36 for B&B, or there's the more expensive *Greville Arms Hotel* (☎ 48563) on Pearse St, which costs from IR£40/70.

Places to Eat

The best takeaways in town are available at *Lino's* on Austin Friars St; those from *Coppola's*, across Grove St from the Newbury Hotel, are vastly inferior. At *Nally's Restaurant*, 9 Oliver Plunkett St, main meals are around IR£5 during the day, but the

The Joyce Connection

James Joyce came to Mullingar in his late teens in 1900 and 1901 to visit his father, John Joyce, a civil servant who had been sent to the town to compile a new electoral register. John Joyce worked in the courthouse on Mount St, and the Joyces stayed at Levington Park House near Lough Owel.

Parts of *Stephen Hero*, an early version (1904) of what would be published as *A Portrait of the Artist as a Young Man*, are set in Mullingar. The Greville Arms Hotel is mentioned, as are the *Westmeath Examiner* office, the Royal Canal and the Colum Barracks on Green Rd.

In *Ulysses*, Leopold Bloom's daughter, Millie, is working in Mullingar, employed in a photographer's shop. This is now Fagan's newsagent and sub-post office on Pearse St near the junction with Castle St, but at the time of Joyce's visits it was owned by a photographer, Phil Shaw. Mullingar also gets a few brief mentions in *Finnegans Wake*. ■

evening à la carte menu is a little more expensive; there is also a decent vegetarian selection. The *Gramby Restaurant* on Dominick St is a little more upmarket and opens daily 8 am to 10 pm (à la carte meals from 3 pm). The bar food in the *Greville Arms Hotel*, on Pearse St, is good and it has a *James Joyce Restaurant* with dinner for around IR£16.

The *Little India Tandoori* restaurant on Austin Friars St has reasonable takeaways, but main courses in the small restaurant are expensive at IR£7 to IR£9 (vegetarian dishes from IR£5). The Italian-ish *Oscar's* on Oliver Plunkett St has so-so pasta (IR£5.95) and main dishes (from IR£7.95), but the service is so cavalier as to be almost rude. It's closed on Monday. A much better choice in this category is *Hatchettes* (☎ 49755), 54 Austin Friars St, with starters from IR£2.50, main courses from IR£9.50 and an excellent four-course dinner for IR£20. Hatchettes opens for lunch and dinner daily till 10.30 pm.

Entertainment
Hughes' Corner House, at Castle and Pearse Sts, has traditional music on Wednesday night and jazz on Thursday, while the *Stables* in Dominick St attracts blues bands. *Danny Byrne's* on Pearse St has music on Thursday and Sunday nights and a wide selection of beers. The *Greville Arms Hotel* has dancing on Sunday night, and country & western line dancing on Monday night. *Canton Casey's* is a museum-quality old-style pub on Pearse St.

Getting There & Away
Bus Éireann (☎ 01-836 6111 in Dublin) runs two daily buses (one on Sunday) from Galway (three hours) to Dundalk (2¼ hours); three (four on Sunday) from Dublin (1½ hours) to Ballina (2¾ hours); three (seven days a week) from Dublin to Sligo (2½ hours); and one from Monday to Saturday from Dublin to Longford (one hour). All stop at Mullingar, and they arrive and depart from opposite the cinema in Castle St.

Trains stop at Mullingar (☎ 48274) three

or four times daily in each direction on the Dublin (one hour) to Sligo (two hours) line.

AROUND MULLINGAR
Belvedere House & Gardens
Belvedere was the scene of a tale that finds its way into Joyce's *Ulysses*.

Belvedere House was built around 1740 for the recently remarried Lord Belfield, 1st earl of Belvedere. He soon accused his young wife of adultery with his younger brother Arthur and imprisoned her here. She remained under house arrest for 31 years. When the earl's death finally released her, she was still dressed in the fashion of three decades earlier. She died still protesting her innocence. Belvedere also sued his brother and had him jailed in London for the rest of his life.

Not far from the house, the **Jealous Wall** was deliberately built by the cantankerous Lord Belfield as a ready-made 'ruin' to block a view of the neighbouring house of a second brother, George, with whom he also fell out. Belvedere House & Gardens (☎ 044-40861) are 5.5km south of Mullingar on the N52 road to Tullamore, just before Lough Ennell Caravan & Camping Park. The house itself, which is undergoing extensive renovations, is closed; entrance to the gardens is IR£1/50p. Opening hours are May to October, noon to 4.30 pm Monday to Friday, and to 6 pm on Saturday and Sunday.

Locke's Distillery
Some 16km south-west of Mullingar on the N52 road to Tullamore past Belvedere House & Gardens, Locke's Distillery (☎ 0506-32134) in the small town of Kilbeggan still has a working mill wheel. The 35-minute tour of the distillery, which opens April to October, 9 am to 6 pm daily, 10 am to 4 pm the rest of the year, costs IR£3/2. Lunch and snacks are served at the adjoining coffee shop, whiskey at the bar.

Crookedwood & Around
Crookedwood, about 5km north-east of Mullingar off the R394, is a small village on the shores of Lough Derravaragh. The lough is

associated with the tragic legend of the Children of Lir who were transformed into swans by a jealous stepmother.

Two ecclesiastical sites near Crookedwood are worth a visit. Three km to the west is the **Multyfarnham Franciscan Friary**. In the present church, parts of a 15th century church remain, and there are outdoor stations of the Cross set beside a stream.

East of Crookedwood, a small road leads up 2km to the ruins of **St Munna's Church**. It dates from the 15th century, replacing a 7th century church founded by St Munna. This fortified church has a lovely location, and there is a grotesque figure over the north window. Keys to the church are available from the nearby bungalow.

Scragh Bog

Scragh Bog is a nature reserve and home to a rare wintergreen, *Pyrola rotundifolia*, which flowers around willow and beech trees in midsummer. Other, less rare, plants include members of the sedge family, orchids and sphagnum species, and there is a profusion of insects. This small bog is 7km north-west of Mullingar near Lough Owel on the N4 road to Longford. The Wildlife Service does not recommend unaccompanied visits, and waterproof boots are a necessity.

Tullynally Castle & Gardens

This family seat of the Pakenham family and the earldom of Longford is another 'pretend' castle. The original fortress was converted into a house in the first half of the 18th century, and various additions were made over the next 150 years. The most notable feature is the extensive Gothic facade. The laundry is wonderfully preserved, and there are many workaday items worth examining.

The house opens daily mid-June to mid-August, 2 to 6 pm with the first tour beginning at 2.30 pm. The charge is IR£3.50/2 and this includes admission to the 12 hectares of gardens and parkland, which are open separately May to September, 2 to 6 pm for IR£2/1. It might be worth telephoning (☎ 044-61159) at other times.

Take the N4 north-west out of Mullingar then follow the R394 road north-east to Castlepollard. From there the castle and gardens are signposted 2km to the north-west.

Fishing

Trout fishing is popular in the loughs around Mullingar, including Lough Owel, Lough Derravaragh, Lough Glore, White Lake, Lough Lene, Lough Sheelin, Mt Dalton Lake, Pallas Lake and Lough Ennell – where in 1894 an 11.9-kg trout was landed, still the largest trout ever caught in Ireland. The fishing season runs from 1 March or 1 May (depending on the lake) to 12 October, and all the lakes except Lough Lene are controlled by the Shannon Regional Fisheries Board (☎ 044-48769 in Mullingar).

For further information contact the Midlands-East Tourism office in Mullingar, Dave O'Malley's (☎ 044-48300), 33 Dominick St, or Sam's Tackle Shop (☎ 044-40431) on Castle St. Sam's can provide boats on Lough Owel or Lough Ennell, ghillies and permits. For Lough Derravaragh contact Mr Newman (☎ 044-71206); for Lough Owel, Mrs Doolan (☎ 044-42085); for Lough Sheelin, Mr Reilly (☎ 043-81124); and for Lough Ennell, Mrs Hope (☎ 044-40807) or Mr Roache (☎ 044-40314).

Swimming

Swimming is possible in loughs Lene, Ennell and Owel, but Derravaragh is very deep and has no shallows.

FORE VALLEY

Just outside the small village of Fore, in the north-east of the county near the shores of Lough Lene, are a group of early Christian sites that date back to 630 AD when St Fechin founded a monastery here. There are no visible remains of this early settlement, but there are three later buildings still standing in the valley plain, and they're closely associated with a legend that 'seven wonders' occurred here.

The Fore Valley is a great area to explore by bicycle or on foot. For a guided tour that

Adolphus Cooke, Eccentric

Mullingar was home not only to the paranoiac Lord Belvedere, but also to one bizarre Adolphus Cooke. This character served under the Duke of Wellington and survived a shipwreck and a desert island before becoming convinced that his grandfather had been reincarnated as a turkey. Later, he sentenced his dog to death for its loose morals, but when the executioner was attacked by the turkey he realised that the dog was probably also related to him and granted it a reprieve. He wanted his library and favourite chair to be buried with him, and his extraordinary grave is tucked away in a fading Protestant churchyard outside Mullingar. He thought he might be reborn as a bee.

To get to the grave, take the N52 road to Devlin for 12km until, after passing a small number of houses, you come to a junction with a sign pointing straight on to Kells. Follow this road for another half km and turn into the fancy arched entrance on the left to the Bee Hive Nite Club. Pass the first sheep gate immediately on the right, but cross over the second black gate just after it. Follow the side of the field under the trees and the old church is about 200m along. Cooke's grave is hard to miss – it's shaped like a beehive. ■

---

takes in the early Christian sites, see Lough-crew Cairns in the Counties Meath & Louth chapter.

The Seven Wonders of Fore

The oldest of the three buildings is **St Fechin's Church**, which may well mark the original monastery. The chancel and baptismal font inside are early 13th century, and over the unusually large entrance there is a huge lintel stone carved with a Greek cross. It was supposed to have been put into place through the divine power of St Fechin's prayers and, as such, counts as one of the Seven Wonders.

A path runs up from the church to the attractive little **Anchorite Cell**, which dates back to the 15th century and is another of the Seven Wonders. The Seven Wonders pub in the village holds the key to the hermit's cell.

Down on the plain, on the other side of the road, there are extensive remains of a 13th century **Benedictine priory**, built on what was once bog (another Wonder). In the next century it was turned into a fortification; hence the castle-like square towers, each of which formed a separate residence, and loophole windows. The west tower is in a dangerous state – keep clear. Two other Wonders are a mill without a race and water that flows uphill. The mill site is marked, and legend has it that St Fechin caused water to flow uphill, towards the mill, by throwing his crozier against a rock near Lough Lene, about 1.5km away.

The last two Wonders are water that will not boil and a tree with only three branches that will not burn. Both are associated with St Fechin's well, which can be seen on the way to the friary from the road.

To get to the Fore Valley from Mullingar take the N4 north-west out of town and then follow the R394 road north-east to Castlepollard. From there the road to Fore is signposted.

ATHLONE

Despite its historic importance, due mainly to its strategic position midway on the River Shannon, the county town of Athlone (Baile Átha Luain) is an unattractive, rather unwelcoming garrison town; there's much more life and interest in Mullingar to the northeast. Although Athlone does have a few attractions, most of them are out of town. A visit to the castle is worth considering, and there are fishing and boat trips along the river to Lough Ree or to the Clonmacnois monastic site in County Offaly.

Orientation & Information

Athlone is in the far south-west of County Westmeath on the border with Roscommon. It's on the main Dublin to Galway road (N6), and the River Shannon flows north through town into Lough Ree. The landmarks here are Athlone Castle and Sts Peter & Paul Cathedral, prominently located on the west bank of the river by the Town Bridge and overlooking Market Square. The castle houses the tourist office, a museum and a heritage centre.

The tourist office (☎ 0902-94630) opens May to mid-October, 9.30 am to 5.30 pm Monday to Saturday; mid-June to August the hours are 9 am to 6 pm. It has a Tourist Trail booklet that offers the reader a choice of three different walks. The local chamber of commerce has a good information office (☎ 0902-73173) with brochures and pamphlets open year round at the Jolly Mariner Marina in Coosan, north of the centre on the east bank of the Shannon beyond the railway bridge.

The Bank of Ireland is at the start of Northgate St, just up from Costume Place. The post office is on Barrack St beside the cathedral.

The telephone code is ☎ 0902.

Athlone Castle & Museum

The Normans probably had an encampment by the ford over the river before they built a castle here in 1210. In 1690 the castle held out for James II, but the following year the bridge came under Protestant attack again, and this time the Jacobite city fell to the troops under William of Orange's Dutch commander, Ginkel. The Jacobites retreated to Aughrim and were decisively defeated there by Ginkel. Major alterations to the castle took place between the 17th and 19th centuries, and the ramp that forms the present entrance is a relatively recent addition. The oldest surviving part is the central keep where the museum is now housed.

Athlone Museum (☎ 92192) has two floors: upstairs is the folk collection, and downstairs has artefacts from prehistoric times. There's also an old gramophone that belonged to John McCormack (1884-1945), a native of Athlone and one of the greatest tenors of all time. It's still in working order, and there are records of his songs which you can ask to be played.

The museum opens daily May to Septem-ber, 10 to 4.30 pm Monday to Saturday, noon to 4.30 pm Sunday. Entry is IR£2.50/80p (students IR£1.75, family IR£6). The price includes a visit to the **heritage centre**, which has an audiovisual presentation of the town's history and flora & fauna.

Fishing

Just below the Church St end of Town Bridge on the east bank of the river opposite the castle, the Strand Tackle Shop (☎ 76729) is the place to go for information, boats and rods. A day's hire of boat and guide for mostly pike fishing will cost around IR£60. You can fish for free along the Strand. The hostel can also organise fishing trips.

River Cruises

Several companies offer cruises from Athlone. Between July and September, Rossana Cruises (☎ 73383) has a Wednesday cruise on its Viking ship south to Clonmacnois, an important early monastic site in County Offaly. It costs IR£9/4/7 for adults/children/students and departs at 10 am on Wednesday and Thursday. Every day of the week there are cruises north to Lough Ree for IR£4.50/3.50. The boats usually depart from the Strand at 2.30 and 4.30 pm; a timetable is available from the tourist office.

The MV *Ross* (☎ 72892) has 90-minute cruises on Lough Ree for IR£4.50/3/13 adults/children/families. The boats depart from the Strand most weekdays in summer at noon and 3.30 pm, and on Sunday from the Jolly Mariner Marina in Coosan at 3.30 pm.

Places to Stay & Eat

The IHH *Athlone Holiday Hostel* (☎ 73399), one of the more chaotically run and expensive hostels in Ireland, is on the Crescent next to the railway and bus stations. It has dormitory beds for between IR£8 and IR£10 and one private room for IR£10 to IR£12 per person, depending on the season. It opens all year and also rents bicycles.

Most of the B&Bs are east of Athlone on the Dublin road, including the *Auburn*

(☎ 74323) with singles/doubles from IR£19/28 and open April to October. The 73-room *Prince of Wales Hotel* charges from IR£43/70.

Attached to the Athlone Holiday Hostel on the Crescent is the reasonably priced *Crescent Restaurant*.

Getting There & Away

The bus depot (☎ 73300) is beside the railway station, and express buses stop there on many routes from the east to the west coast. There are nine buses daily (eight on Sunday) to Dublin (two hours) and Galway (1¼ hours), three (one on Sunday) to Westport (2¾ hours) and two (one on Sunday) to Mullingar (one hour).

From Athlone railway station (☎ 73300), there are three daily trains (four on Friday, two on Sunday) to Westport (2¼ hours) in County Mayo, five to seven (four on Sunday) to Galway (1¼ hours) and up to 11 (seven on Sunday) to Dublin (1½ hours).

The railway station is on the east bank on Southern Station Rd. To get there, follow Northgate St up from Costume Place. Its extension, Coosan Point Rd, joins Southern Station Rd near St Vincent's Hospital.

Getting Around

You can order a taxi on ☎ 74400. Bicycles can be hired for IR£7/30 per day/week from Hardiman's (☎ 78669), opposite the Athlone Shopping Centre on Dublin road.

AROUND ATHLONE
Lough Ree

Just north of Athlone is Lough Ree, one of the three main lakes formed by the River Shannon. It's celebrated for the early monastic ruins on its many islands and for some excellent trout fishing. The lough is also home to many migratory birds who come here to nest, particularly swans, plovers, mallard ducks and curlews.

Sailing is popular and the Lough Ree

Goldsmith Country Cycling Tour

The following tour pretty much follows the one in *The Lough Ree Trail: A Signposted Tour* by Gearoid O'Brien and published by Midlands-East Tourism. It's available from the tourist offices in Athlone and Mullingar. The tour takes in places associated with 18th century writer Oliver Goldsmith.

Five km north-east of Athlone, the road comes to the village of Ballykeeran to the west of which is the Lough Ree East Caravan & Camping Park. About 3km farther is the village of Glasson (or Glassan), which Swift called Auburn in his poem *The Deserted Village*. Just north of the village a left turning goes to the Killinure Spur on the shore of Lough Ree. The turning is marked by No 8 on the Lough Ree Trail road sign and it's 2.5km to a junction, marked as No 11 on the tourist trail road sign. From there, another left goes down to the marina at Killinure where you can rent boats.

Back at the No 11 junction, the road continues north for another 2.5km to a junction, No 14 on the tourist trail signs. Turning left leads to the Portlick Inn pub by the shore opposite Inchmore Island. Turning right at No 14 leads after 3km to the village of Tubberclair (or Tuberclare), which takes its name from a holy well, on the N55.

Continuing north the road leads into Goldsmith Country proper, with the reminders and remains of:

The never-failing brook, the busy mill,
The decent church that topt the neighbouring hill.

Only the site remains of the schoolhouse where the young Goldsmith and his fellow pupils wondered at the wisdom of their teacher:

And still they gazed, and still the wonder grew
That one small head could carry all he knew.

From Tubberclair northward Goldsmith Country extends into County Longford. From the site of the schoolhouse, it's about 15km back south to Athlone via the N55. The whole tour takes a couple of hours. ■

Lough Club (☎ 0902-75976), established around 1720, is one of the world's oldest yacht clubs. The Wineport Sailing Centre (☎ 0902-85466) has a dozen different boats for hire – from a 12m cruiser to dinghies – and does sailing courses in the day and evening.

Goldsmith Country

From Athlone, the N55 north-west to County Longford runs close to the eastern side of Lough Ree and through Goldsmith Country, so-called because of the area's associations with the 18th century poet, playwright and novelist, Oliver Goldsmith. The gentle aspect of the landscape makes it ideal for cycling.

Places to Stay Camping is possible at *Lough Ree East Caravan & Camping Park* (☎ 0902-78561) in Ballykeeran where tent sites are only 50p though adults/children pay IR£2.50/1 and hikers and cyclists pay IR£2.50 including tent. The *Portlick Inn* pub (☎ 0902-85204) near Killenmore has a nearby guesthouse with B&B for IR£12 to IR£15 per person. There are self-catering chalets available at Killinure, Glasson and

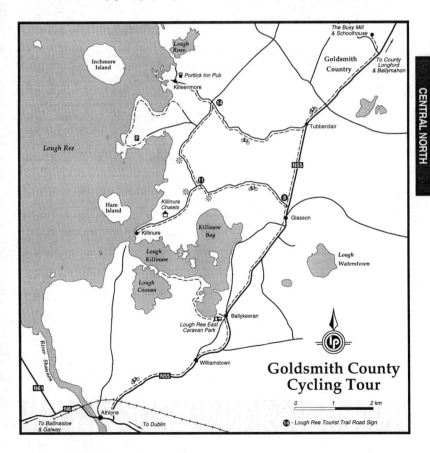

Goldsmith County Cycling Tour

0   1   2 km

14 - Lough Ree Tourist Trail Road Sign

The Busy Mill & Schoolhouse
Lough Ross
Inchmore Island
Goldsmith Country
To County Longford & Ballymahon
Portlick Inn Pub
Killeenmore
Tubberclair
N55
Lough Ree
P
Killinure Chalets
Hare Island
Glasson
Killinure
Killinure Bay
Lough Waterstown
Lough Killinure
Lough Coosan
Ballykeeran
Lough Ree East Caravan Park
Williamstown
N55
River Shannon
N61
N6
Athlone
To Ballinasloe & Galway
To Dublin

Tubberclair; enquiries should be made at the tourist office in Athlone.

Moate

The village of Moate, half way between Athlone and Kilbeggan on the N6, about 40km south-west of Mullingar, gets its name from a nearby motte. The **Dún na Sí Heritage Park** (☎ 0902-81183) ('fairy mound castle') is a small folk museum with displays of 19th century farm tools, kitchenware and the like; it also functions as a genealogical centre for those researching their Westmeath ancestors.

The museum opens April to October and entry is IR£1/50p. There's a traditional Irish session of music, dance and storytelling here every Friday at 9 pm in July and August.

County Donegal

County Donegal outdoes anywhere else in Ireland for bleakness, dramatic cliffs and hectares of peat bogs – all of which can be great if the weather isn't equally bleak, dramatic and, well, boggy. County Donegal extends farther north than anywhere in Northern Ireland; it's virtually separated from the rest of the Republic by the westward projection of County Fermanagh.

Roughly one third of Donegal lies in the Gaeltacht, where Irish is more widely spoken than English. You'll see signs pointing to offices of the Údarás na Gaeltachta, a government agency that promotes the social, economic and cultural well-being of Irish-speaking areas. Around Gweedore in particular, it has been instrumental in creating an industrial zone where hundreds of people are employed in the production of yarn, plastics, radiators and so on.

Tourism in Donegal is extremely seasonal, and many attractions and almost all the tourist offices close except between June (interpreted pretty narrowly here) and September – at the latest. Arrive in, say, March and you'll find most of the county shut down and fast asleep.

Unless you are entering Donegal from the North you will be travelling there from Sligo on the N15, passing by Bundoran and Ballyshannon on the way to the town of Donegal.

Although you can get round County Donegal by bus, it's a time-consuming endeavour, especially in winter. This is very much walking and cycling country. When driving, be prepared for switchback roads, suicidal sheep, directions only in Irish, signs hidden behind vegetation or no signs at all.

Donegal

The town's name in Irish, Dún na nGall ('fort of the foreigner') refers to the Vikings, who

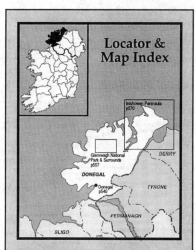

Locator & Map Index

Highlights
- Get drenched in Glenveagh National Park
- Stay up till all hours enjoying pub music sessions in Donegal town
- Gaze down on Slieve League cliffs
- Enjoy the view from Grianán of Aileach
- Walk the Bloody Foreland and Horn Head
- Visit Glebe House and Gallery
- Relax in Ramelton village

DONEGAL

had a fort here in the 9th century. Donegal's later importance developed as it was the main seat of the O'Donnell family, which controlled this part of Ireland before the 17th century.

Donegal is the principal jumping-off point for the rest of the county and is a pleasant and very popular little place where time can be well spent enjoying the town. The triangular Diamond, the centre of Donegal, is often choked with traffic in summer; there are some good shops selling quality souvenirs and garments here.

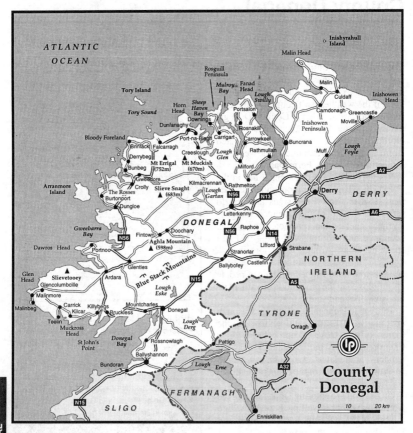

County Donegal

INFORMATION

The tourist office (☎ 073-21148) is south of the Diamond by the River Eske on the Quay, but it's only open Monday to Friday, from 9 am to 4 pm in season. If you find it open, ask for *A Signposted Walking Tour of Donegal Town* to take in all the sights. There's a Bank of Ireland branch on the southern side of the Diamond. The post office is on Tirchonaill St north of the Diamond. The Four Masters on the Diamond is the only bookshop in Donegal. It has a so-so selection of maps. There's a laundrette in the Mill Court Shopping Mews, a mall off the Diamond.

Permits are required for fishing in many of the local rivers and one for the River Eske, along with licences for salmon and sea trout, are available from Doherty's (☎ 073-21119) on Main St. Don't expect much help otherwise from the staff here, however.

The telephone code is ☎ 073.

DONEGAL CASTLE

Built on a rocky outcrop over the River Eske, what remains of this recently restored castle is impressive. It was built by the O'Donnells in the 15th century and may well have been burned down by Hugh Roe O'Donnell at the end of the 16th century rather than see it fall into the hands of the English. Sir Basil Brooke, the Englishman who took possession of the castle about 1623, rebuilt it in Jacobean style. Notice the floral decoration on the corner turret and the decorated fireplace on the 1st floor. Brooke also built the three-storey manor house adjoining the castle.

Donegal Castle, an OPW site (☎ 22405), opens daily June to October, 9.30 am to 6.30 pm. The admission fee is IR£2/1.

THE DIAMOND OBELISK

In 1474, Red Hugh O'Donnell and his wife Nuala O'Brien founded a Franciscan monastery by the shore in the south of town. It was accidentally blown up in 1601 by Hugh Roe O'Donnell while laying siege to an English garrison, and very little of it now remains. What makes it famous is that four of its friars, realising that the arrival of the English meant the end of Celtic culture, chronicled the whole of known Celtic history and mythology from 40 years before the Flood to AD 1618 in 'The Annals of the Four Masters'. The obelisk in the Diamond commemorates the work, copies of which are on display in the National Library in Dublin. The Four Masters remains an important source for early Irish history.

SPECIAL EVENTS

Donegal has a three-day Arts Festival in late June/early July, featuring song, dance and story-telling, with arts and crafts thrown in for good measure. The tourist office should have details.

PLACES TO STAY
Hostels

The comfortable and friendly *Donegal Town Independent Hostel* (☎ 22805), registered with both the IHH and IHO, is 1km northwest of town on the Killybegs road (N56). Dormitory beds cost R£6 and IR£7.50 per person in private rooms. You can also camp in the grounds for IR£3.50 per person. The hostel opens all year.

An Óige's *Ball Hill Hostel* (☎ 21174) in Ball Hill south-west of Donegal has an absolutely stunning setting at the end of a quiet road, right on the shores of Donegal Bay. To get there, continue along the Killybegs road and look out for the signs on the left-hand side of the road about 5km out. Beds here cost IR£4.50/5.50 or IR£5/6.50 for juniors/seniors, depending on the season, and it's open Easter to September. The location is pretty remote, so stock up on food before arriving.

B&Bs

There are plenty of B&Bs within walking distance of the centre. *Drumcliffe House* (☎ 21200) on Coast Rd off the road to Killybegs (N67) is a pleasant old place with singles/doubles from IR£19/28. Waterloo Place, north of the castle and beside the river, has a couple of guesthouses close by one another. *Riverside House* (☎ 21083) charges IR£18/28 while at *Castle View House* (☎ 22100), singles/doubles are IR£14/28. On Main St the *Atlantic Guesthouse* (☎ 21187) has decent singles/doubles from IR£18/28. The *Tourist Lodge* (☎ 23060), opposite the tourist office on the quay, has five triple rooms, which are good value at IR£35. If these are all full, there are plenty of others about town, including two on Ballyshannon Rd: *Hillcrest* (☎ 21837), with doubles from IR£28, and *Ardlenagh View* (☎ 21646), from IR£19.50/29.

Hotels

The 49-room *Abbey Hotel* (☎ 21014) and the *Hyland Central Hotel* (☎ 21027), with almost twice as many rooms, are both in the Diamond; singles/doubles at the former are from IR£41/80, at the latter from IR£45/75.

For something rural, try *Arches Country House* (☎ 22029) on the Lough Eske ring road. It has six rooms for IR£21/32. More expensive (from IR£35 per person) is the nearby *Ardnamona House* (☎ 22650), a late 18th century house with five rooms and a splendid garden. Beautifully sited on the shores of Lough Eske and signposted from the Killybegs road is the 20-room *Harvey's*

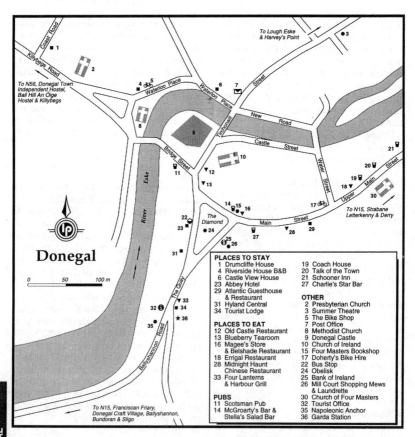

Donegal

0   50   100 m

PLACES TO STAY
1 Drumcliffe House
4 Riverside House B&B
6 Castle View House
23 Abbey Hotel
29 Atlantic Guesthouse
   & Restaurant
31 Hyland Central
34 Tourist Lodge

PLACES TO EAT
12 Old Castle Restaurant
13 Blueberry Tearoom
16 Magee's Store
   & Belshade Restaurant
18 Errigal Restaurant
28 Midnight Haunt
   Chinese Restaurant
33 Four Lanterns
   & Harbour Grill

PUBS
11 Scotsman Pub
14 McGroarty's Bar &
   Stella's Salad Bar

19 Coach House
20 Talk of the Town
21 Schooner Inn
27 Charlie's Star Bar

OTHER
2 Presbyterian Church
3 Summer Theatre
5 The Bike Shop
7 Post Office
8 Methodist Church
9 Donegal Castle
10 Church of Ireland
15 Four Masters Bookshop
17 Doherty's Bike Hire
22 Bus Stop
24 Obelisk
25 Bank of Ireland
26 Mill Court Shopping Mews
   & Laundrette
30 Church of Four Masters
32 Tourist Office
35 Napoleonic Anchor
36 Garda Station

Point Country Hotel (☎ 22208) with singles/doubles from IR£50/80.

PLACES TO EAT

There are at least a half-dozen places to eat within 100m or so of the Diamond. *Stella's Salad Bar* at McGroarty's Bar on the Diamond offers lunches with a healthy twist. The *Atlantic Restaurant* on Main St and the renovated *Errigal Restaurant* farther east are inexpensive, with meals from IR£4. The *Midnight Haunt*, upstairs in Main St, has almost unrecognisable Chinese food, with main courses from IR£6 to IR£8. The recom-

mended *Belshade Restaurant* on the 1st floor of Magee's store does breakfast for IR£3.95 and lunches with vegetarian possibilities.

Round the corner by the *Old Castle*, one of the fancier places in town with a good-value lunch for IR£5, is the *Blueberry Tearoom* over a lamp shop. It does quiches, soups and sandwiches.

Opposite the tourist office on the quay there's *Four Lanterns* for fast food, with the *Harbour Grill* restaurant doing seafood, pizzas and steak right next door.

For a real treat, try the restaurant at *Harvey's Point Country Hotel* (☎ 22208),

6km north-east of Donegal on the small road to Lough Eske and the Blue Stack Mountains. A five-course dinner costs IR£25. Reservations and dressy attire are in order here.

ENTERTAINMENT

Numerous music pubs can be found on Main and Upper Main Sts, within a stone's throw of the Diamond, including the *Coach House* at the western end of Upper Main St and the *Schooner Inn* just beyond it. *Talk of the Town Lounge* between the two has music most nights as well as pool tables. The *Scotsman* on Bridge St attracts a friendly, local crowd ready to sing or strum at the drop of a pint. *Charlie's Star Bar* is another lively place, with somewhat more modern music and a younger crowd.

The *Summer Theatre* is run by a local theatre group and presents Irish plays in O'Cleary Hall by the junction north-east of the castle three times a week at 9 pm in July and August. Posters will be in the shops and tourist office.

THINGS TO BUY

Well worth a browse is Magee's in the Diamond. It has its own garment factory and sells its tweed rolls at IR£16 per metre. A mailing service is available. Tweed jackets cost around IR£150, skirts IR£60 and there are lots of Aran sweaters for around IR£80. It opens daily except Wednesday and Sunday, 9.45 am to 6 pm.

Also worth visiting is the Donegal Craft Village (☎ 22228), a complex of small art and craft workshops by the side of the N15 en route to Ballyshannon about 1.5km from town. Pottery, crystal, batik, garments and jewellery are all made on the premises. Its coffee shop opens daily 9 am to 6 or 7 pm.

GETTING THERE & AWAY

There are frequent Bus Éireann connections with Derry, Enniskillen and Belfast in the North, Sligo, Galway and Killybegs to the west, Limerick and Cork in the south and Dublin in the south-east. The bus stop is outside the Abbey Hotel, and information is available by phoning ☎ 21101.

Feda O'Donnell (☎ 075-48114, 091-761656 in Galway) runs private coaches to and from Galway every day, via Ballyshannon, Bundoran and Sligo. They leave from in front of the tourist office in Donegal at 9.45 am and 5.15 pm every day and reach Galway Cathedral (or Eyre Square on Sunday evening) at 1.10 and 8.45 pm. There's an additional departure on Friday at 1.15 pm, and on Sunday they leave at 9.45 am and 4.15 and 8.15 pm.

It's also worth checking out McGeehan's Coaches (☎ 075-46150), which does a Donegal to Dublin return trip three to four times a day (more in summer) for IR£15 and departs from outside the garda station opposite the tourist office.

GETTING AROUND

Doherty's (☎ 073-21119), on the corner of Main and Water Sts, hires out bikes for £6/25 a day/week. The far superior Bike Shop (☎ 073-22515), across from the castle on Waterloo Place, charges IR£6/30 a day/week and IR£15 for a three-day weekend. The owner of the Bike Shop is very friendly and knowledgeable and will help you plan a cycling itinerary.

Around Donegal Town

DONEGAL

LOUGH DERG

June to mid-August, this small lake due east of Donegal is alive with pilgrims who spend three days on a small island in the middle of the lake where St Patrick is believed to have stayed and fasted. Anyone over the age of 14 is welcome, and some 30,000 turn up every year – but be warned: the penitential aspect is taken seriously. The pilgrimage starts with a 24-hour vigil; only one meal a day is allowed; and everyone is expected to complete the stations of the Cross in bare feet on the first day, having fasted from the preceding midnight. The pilgrims reach the island by boat, but outside the pilgrim season, there is no regular service to the island.

The **Lough Derg Visitors' Centre** (☎ 072-61546), on Main St in Pettigo 7km south of the lake, details Lough Derg's Celtic past and recounts the story of St Patrick. It's open April to September, 10 am to 5 pm Monday to Saturday, and noon to 5 pm Sunday. Admission is IR£2/1.

Places to Stay & Eat

There's no need to book if making the pilgrimage to the island; just turn up at Pettigo and pay on the spot for accommodation and the boat fare, which is around IR£2. In Pettigo, *Avondale* (☎ 072-61520) on the Lough Derg road, and *Hilltop View* (☎ 072-61535) at Billary just before Pettigo on the road from Donegal offer B&B from IR£17/28.

Getting There & Away

Pettigo and Lough Derg are extremely remote, at the end of a road across the moors. During the pilgrim season (1 June to 15 August), a special Bus Éireann service leaves Dublin's Busáras station at 10 am each day, arriving at Lough Derg shore at 1.45 pm. During the same period a bus leaves Galway at 9 am, stopping at Sligo and Ballyshannon – but not Donegal – before reaching Lough Derg at 2.15 pm. The first boat leaves at around 11 am, the last at 3 pm. Further information is available from the Priory (☎ 072-61518), St Patrick's Purgatory, Pettigo.

LOUGH ESKE

This is a place for fishing or for cycling or walking over the Blue Stack Mountains. If you're walking, consider using the guide *New Irish Walks: West & North* (Gill & Macmillan) or *Hill Walkers' Donegal* by David Herman (Shanksmore Press), available from the Four Masters Bookshop in the Diamond in Donegal. There's also an interesting walk around the hills of Lough Derg.

Getting There & Away

Leave Donegal on the N56 to Killybegs and turn right just past the bridge following the signs to *Harvey's Point Country Hotel*. The ring road eventually joins the N15 to the north-east of Donegal so it makes a convenient cycling trip. If you hire a bike from the Bike Shop in Donegal, they'll give you a photocopied map.

ROSSNOWLAGH

If you want a beach holiday without the amusement arcades, then Rossnowlagh, south-west of Donegal, is the place to visit. The sandy Blue Flag beach is stunning, extends for nearly 5km and mostly attracts surfers.

Places to Stay & Eat

Camping is available at *Manor House Caravan & Camping Park* (☎ 072-51477). It costs about R£7 per night to camp (IR£3.50 for cyclists), and there's a shop, takeaway-food outlet and restaurant at the campsite, which opens July and August.

Ard-na-Mara (☎ 072-51141) has B&B available all year from IR£25/39. Dinner here is IR£15. The *Sand House* (☎ 072-51777) is a 45-room beach hotel, charging IR£70/110 mid-May to September. The front rooms have magnificent sea views.

BALLYSHANNON

This is a busy, hilly little town set above the River Erne with a small adjunct of shops and houses south of the river and connected by a bridge. Ballyshannon (Béal Átha Seanaidh) could be more appealing than Bundoran as a base for exploring the coastline before heading up to Donegal. It's also very convenient for trips into the North, with regular buses to Derry and Enniskillen.

Orientation & Information

The centre of Ballyshannon, north of the river, has two main streets converging below the very distinctive clocktower of Gallogley Jewellers: Main St runs to the north-west and Market St to the north-east. There's a Bank of Ireland branch at the start of Main St. The post office is at the start of Market St just up from Gallogley Jewellers. There's a laundrette next to Seán Óg's Pub.

The telephone code is ☎ 072.

Allingham's Grave

The poet William Allingham (1824-89), best remembered for *The Fairies*, which begins 'Up the airy mountains/Down the rushy glen', was born in Ballyshannon and is buried in the graveyard. It's signposted at the first left up Main St after Dorrian's Imperial Hotel. The tombstone is on the left side of the churchyard.

Donegal Parian China Visitors' Centre

Parian china is lighter and more translucent than bone china. All the pieces manufactured by Donegal Parian China are on display (and for sale) at the centre (☎ 51826), which is about 1.5km south-west of Ballyshannon on the Bundoran road (N15). Prices range from around IR£10 for small pieces to IR£250 for a full tea set. Free guided tours, a tearoom, a bureau de change and mail order service are all laid on here. The centre opens daily 9 am to 6 pm June to September, and 9 am to 5.30 pm Monday to Saturday the rest of the year.

Water Wheels

Water Wheels (☎ 51580) is a heritage centre with an audiovisual display, craft shop and café in the restored mills of Assaroe Abbey, founded in the late 12th century by Cistercian monks from Boyle in County Roscommon. To get there, turn left off Main St onto Bridge St and past the Thatch Pub on the road to Rossnowlagh (R231). After about 2km, signs indicate 'Water Wheels' and 'Abbey Mill' on the left. It opens daily May to September, 10.30 am to 6.30 pm. The rest of the year, it's only open on Sunday, 1.30 to 6 pm. There are fine views of the Erne Estuary and Donegal Bay.

Places to Stay

The IHH *Duffy's Hostel* (☎ 51535), less than 1km north of town on the road to Donegal, has a dozen beds for IR£6 each and opens March to October. You can camp in the

garden for £3.50 a head, and they have bikes for rent.

There are lots of B&Bs, including *Macardle House* (☎ 51846), 55 Assaroe View, Knather Rd, signposted on the corner opposite the Seán Óg's Pub on Market St. Singles/doubles are IR£18/28. The best hotel in town is the grand *Dorrian's Imperial* (☎ 51147), with 26 rooms in Main St. Singles/doubles are IR£33/62 or, May to September, IR£46/79.

Places to Eat

Kitchen Bake, where the two main streets meet, serves cakes and coffee. A great place for breakfast and sandwiches (from IR£1.95) is the *Dead Poet's Café* just opposite.

Cúchulainn's, on the corner diagonally opposite Seán Óg's, is a pub and takeaway place with a restaurant upstairs. Across the road, *Embers* in Paddy Donagher's pub does seafood, pasta and a few vegetarian options at lunch and dinner to 9 pm. The bar at *Dorrian's Imperial Hotel* serves pub food at lunch time, and dinner is around IR£16, depending on what's on.

There's a *coffee shop* in the Water Wheels heritage centre at Assaroe Abbey north-west of town.

Entertainment

Pubs have live music throughout the summer, but the perfect time to be entertained in Ballyshannon is during the August bank holiday weekend music festival, the first weekend of August. The pubs to check out are *Seán Óg's* in Market St and the lovely little *Thatch Pub* on Bridge St, just off the top of Main St as you turn towards Rossnowlagh. Across the River Erne are *Owenroe's*, *Fergie's* and the *Commercial*. The *Abbey Centre* (☎ 51375) at the northern end of Main St on Tirconaill St has one cinema screen and occasional plays.

Getting There & Away

The bus station is between the bridge and the Gallogley Jewellers clocktower. There are daily Bus Éireann buses (☎ 074-21309 in Letterkenny) to Bundoran, Derry, Sligo,

Galway, Donegal and Dublin (via Enniskillen, Cavan and Navan).

The Feda O'Donnell bus (☎ 075-48114) departs from outside the Green Lady pub opposite the bus station for Donegal, Letterkenny, Dunfanaghy, Gweedore and Crolly at 12.45 and 6.35 pm, Monday to Saturday (with extra departures on Friday at 4.10 and 8.30 pm), and at 5.45 and 11 pm on Sunday. The fare for anywhere in Donegal is IR£3 or IR£4. It leaves for Sligo and Galway from in front of Maggie's Bar, which is south of the river at the roundabout, at 10 am and 5.30 pm Monday to Saturday (also at 1.30 pm on Friday), and 10 am, 4.30 and 8.30 pm on Sunday.

BUNDORAN

Bundoran is one of the most popular seaside resorts in Ireland. It comes alive during the summer but is generally just passed by during the rest of the year. It's not hard to see why: the main street – East End and West End – is a series of games arcades, including some real antique shove ha'penny games, fish & chips shops, and tacky souvenir stands. Bundoran (Bun Dobhráin) is frequented mainly by Catholic Northerners, and at nights the traditional music in the pubs favours the rebel over the folk song.

Information

The tourist office (☎ 072-41350) is a kiosk opposite the Holyrood Hotel, on the left as you come into town from Sligo on the N15. It's open June to mid-September, 10 am to 1 pm and 2 to 6 pm daily. Outside peak season, you'd be lucky to find it open even at the times posted on the door.

The telephone code is ☎ 072.

Activities

Just north of the town centre, Tullan Strand is a handsome Blue Flag beach with waves big enough to deter swimmers. The strange cliffside rock formations have whimsical names like the Fairy Bridges and the Puffing Hole.

Children enjoy Waterworld (☎ 41172) where a slide pool, wave pool and restaurant

pack them in by the hundred. The noise level in here probably breaks several EU standards. Tickets cost IR£1 for the under-sixes, IR£3.50 for those seven to 16 and IR£4.50 for wrinklies. It's open 11 am to 7 pm daily over Easter and late May to August, weekends only in September.

Stracomer Riding School (☎ 41787) organises hourly sessions as well as residential courses.

Places to Stay

Should you decide to give Bundoran a whirl, there's the IHH *Homefield Hostel* (☎ 41288) in Bayview Ave, with 38 dorm beds for £7 to IR£10 a head and a few private rooms for IR£8 to IR£12 per person. Going for B&B you're spoiled for choice, though little stands out. Waterworld keeps a handy list for when the tourist office is closed. *Aughrus* (☎ 41556), on Tullan Strand Rd, has rooms from IR£15 per person and opens June to September. Going upmarket, *Holyrood Hotel* (☎ 41232), at the southern end of the main street, has 58 rooms for IR£50/76 in high season.

The 96-room *Great Northern Hotel* (☎ 41204) by the beach charges IR£66/104 during the same period.

Places to Eat

There's no shortage of cafés and fast-food places along the main street; try *Blazing Saddles* just north of the Holyrood Hotel. During the summer months the *Kitchen Bake*, half way along the street in a converted 19th century church, does at least offer light lunches in more imaginative surroundings. *Hoy Kwong* is a Chinese restaurant in the southern part of the main street with dishes for around IR£3 to IR£4.

Getting There & Away

Bus Éireann buses (☎ 074-21309 in Letterkenny) stop on the patch of land known as Railway Yard; turn down beside the Railway Tavern and Blazing Saddles restaurant to find it. There's a direct daily service to Dublin, Derry, Sligo, Galway and Westport. Ulsterbus (☎ 01232-333000 in Belfast) has services to Belfast and Enniskillen twice a day (once on Sunday). The Feda O'Donnell bus (☎ 075-48114) from Crolly to Galway stops in Bundoran outside the Holyrood Hotel at 10.05 am and 5.35 pm Monday to Saturday, with an extra bus on Friday at 1.35 pm, and on Sunday at 10.05 am and 4.30 and 8.30 pm.

Getting Around
The Hire & Sell Centre (☎ 072-41526) at the southern end of town has bikes for about IR£5 a day plus IR£20 deposit.

MOUNTCHARLES TO BRUCKLESS
The first town you'll hit travelling along the coastal road (N56) west of Donegal, Mountcharles has a safe and sandy beach, angling possibilities, and an interesting story-telling festival. Four of the eight pubs have live music on weekends. The road west to Bruckless passes through the village of Inver, which has its own small beach. A little farther west at Dunkineely, a minor road runs down the promontory to St John's Point, but there is no sand here.

Activities
Michael O'Boyle (☎ 073-35257) has a boat called the *Martin Óg* available for deep-sea angling at IR£15 to IR£20 a day, including rod and tackle. The boat leaves from the Mountcharles pier; take the first turning on the left as you come into the village from the east.

There's horse riding and pony trekking available at Deane's Open Farm (☎ 073-73160) near Gallagher's Farm Hostel in Bruckless.

Special Events
Seamus MacManus was a local story-teller (*seanchaí*) who regaled locals with tales around the village pump in the 1940s and 1950s. In the past, the festival organised by the Seamus MacManus Society consisted of lectures, walks and sessions with modern story-tellers. It hasn't taken place in a few years, but there are hopes of reinstating it soon.

The Donegal tourist office (☎ 073-21148) should be able to help you, or try the Tannery (☎ 073-35533), a craft shop and information centre on the main road just west of Mountcharles.

Places to Stay
Mountcharles The *Coast Road* guesthouse (☎ 073-35018) on the main street has rooms for IR£15 per person and opens all year. Near the church on Station Rd, *Clybawn* (☎ 073-35076), open April to September, has singles/doubles from IR£19/28.

Bruckless The attractive IHH *Gallagher's Farm Hostel* (☎ 073-37057), with 18 beds in converted farm outbuildings, is half way between Dunkineely and Bruckless on the N56. Beds cost IR£6.50 with another IR£3 for breakfast. Camping is also possible here at IR£3 a head, and there are separate kitchen facilities. The hostel supplies guests with a list of walks in the area. *Bruckless House* (☎ 073-37071), just past the hostel, is a cut above the usual B&B, and a night in this 18th century home costs from IR£25.

Dunkineely The IHO *Blue Moon Hostel* (☎ 073-37264) on Main St in Dunkineely charges IR£5 per person for a dormitory bed or one in a private room. It opens all year.

Places to Eat
Apart from the few pubs and cafés in Mountcharles and Dunkineely, there is little choice, so stock up before leaving Donegal or Killybegs.

Getting There & Away
Three times a day (five in July and August) Monday to Saturday, a Bus Éireann bus leaves Donegal for Killybegs, stopping outside Mulhern's in Mountcharles, the Inver post office and McGinley's shop in Dunkineely.

DONEGAL

South-Western Donegal

KILLYBEGS

Killybegs (Ceala Beaga) is Ireland's most important fishing port, and some travellers may be put off by the smell cast by the large fishmeal processing plant on the eastern outskirts; those of us who grew up by the sea find it positively aromatic! The wild-looking and secluded Fintra Beach, a couple of km to the west, is more fun to explore than to swim from.

Information

The tourist information point – a board with maps – is in the car park by the harbour.

The telephone area code is ☎ 073.

MacSweeney's Tomb

A right turn in town up the steep hill brings you to St Catherine's Church, which also contains the tomb slab of Niall Mór MacSweeney, with its Celtic-style carved gallowglasses. Gallowglasses were Scottish mercenaries who first came to the north and west of Ireland in the late 13th century. At first they were only hired by the big chiefs, but by the late 15th century, their descendants were being employed around the country as personal bodyguards and constables.

Fishing

In summer the *Michelle* departs Blackrock Pier daily at 10 am, returning at 6 pm, with the opportunity to fish for pollock, cod and whiting. For details phone Anthony Doherty on ☎ 31079. Inclusive B&B and angling deals can be arranged for groups of eight people or more.

Places to Stay

If you decide to stay in Killybegs and don't like the smell of fish, pick a guesthouse along Fintra Rd on the western outskirts. Clean and friendly is the recommended *Oileán Roe House* (☎ 31192), 1km west on Fintra Rd, with B&B from IR£12.50 to IR£15 per person. It opens May to September. Alternatively, there's *Glenlee House* (☎ 31026) just across the road, charging IR£19/30. Other nearby places on Fintra Rd include *Bannagh House* (☎ 31108), charging IR£32 for doubles and open Easter to October, and the ambitiously named *Lismolin Country House* (☎ 31053), a bungalow B&B open all year and charging IR£21/32.

Tullycullion House (☎ 31842) is a lovely place east of the centre and open April to September. Singles/doubles are IR£21/32.

The 38-room *Bay View Hotel* (☎ 31950) in the centre of Killybegs, with a leisure centre and pool, charges £60/100 in high season (June to September).

Places to Eat

You can pick up fish & chips opposite the car park at *Baywatch*. A better place for seafood takeaway though is *Killybeg's Catch-West* near the Sail Inn pub.

Cope House on Main St houses the *Ship's Inn* pub with bar food and the *Peking Chef* restaurant with Asianesque specialities. *Barnacles* in the Lone Star pub, down a side street opposite, is a seafood restaurant with meals from about IR£10. The *Sail Inn* farther west on Main St has cheap pub grub and a restaurant upstairs.

Bayview Hotel has a downstairs pub-brasserie and a lovely upstairs restaurant specialising, not surprisingly, in seafood. The excellent three-course set dinner is IR£17.50.

Getting There & Away

The Bus Éireann service from Donegal to Killybegs runs three times daily (five times in July and August) Monday to Saturday. The bus stop is outside Hegarty's shop. There's also a service to Portnoo via Ardara and Glenties twice daily Monday to Saturday in July and August (as far as Glenties only on Tuesday, Thursday and Friday during the rest of the year). Another bus heads west to Kilcar, Glencolumbcille and sometimes Malinmore once daily Monday to Saturday (twice a day in July and August).

McGeehan's Coaches (☎ 075-46150)

from Glencolumbcille to Dublin stops at the Pier bar daily at 8.10 am, with additional buses at 5.40 pm on Friday and 3.45 pm on Sunday. Extra buses are laid on in summer.

KILCAR

Kilcar and neighbouring Carrick are good bases for exploring the indented coastline of south-west Donegal and the Slieve League cliffs. Just outside Kilcar (Cill Chathaigh) is a small, sandy beach.

Information

Tourist information is available from the Craft Shop (☎ 073-38002) in the centre, which opens daily in summer. They can provide details of two local walks, which take in many prehistoric sites.

The telephone code is ☎ 073.

Donegal Tweed

Opposite the Craft Shop is a small tweed factory (☎ 38002) offering free guided tours on weekdays. In the Craft Shop itself, the tweed can be bought by the metre for under IR£10; you're unlikely to get better prices than this anywhere else in Donegal.

Slieve League

Carrick, 5km from Kilcar, is where you turn off for Teelin and the Bunglas viewing point for Slieve League, a cliff face dropping some 300m straight into the sea. To drive to the cliff edge, be sure to take the turn-off signposted Bunglas from the Killybegs-Glencolumbcille road (R263) at Carrick, and continue beyond the narrow track signposted Slieve League to the one which is signposted Bunglas.

Another way to view the changing colours of the rock face is by boat from Teelin Pier (☎ 39117) south of Carrick. June to September, provided the weather's good, the boat leaves at 11.30 am and 2.30 pm and costs around IR£6/3. It only operates with a minimum of six people.

Starting from Teelin, experienced walkers can spend a day walking via Bunglas and the somewhat terrifying One Man's Path to Malinbeg, near Glencolumbcille.

Places to Stay

There are two hostels in Kilcar, both on the western side of the village. The welcoming *Dún Ulún House* (☎ 38137) on the Coast Rd charges IR£7.50 to IR£9.50 per person for hostel beds and IR£13.50 to IR£14.50 for B&B. Singles are IR£18.50 to IR£19.50, and camping across the road costs IR£3 per person. It also has a cottage nearby for rent (IR£175 per week). The equally friendly IHH *Derrylahan Hostel* (☎ 38079), some 3km west of the village, charges IR£6 in six-bed dorms and IR£16 for its two doubles; camping costs IR£3. There's a small shop, plentiful cooking facilities and a group house accommodating 19 people; a phone call from Kilcar village or Carrick will get you a lift to the hostel.

For B&B, *Kilcar Lodge* (☎ 38156) in Main St charges IR£14.50 to IR£16 per person. It opens April to September.

In Carrick, the *Slieve League* pub (☎ 073-39041) in the centre has hostel accommodation for about IR£6 per person.

Places to Eat

The thatched *Piper's Rest* pub in Kilcar serves light food while the *Village Restaurant* on Main St opens during July and August with meals for around IR£10. On the road between Kilcar and Killybegs the panoramically situated *Blue Haven* (☎ 073-38090) serves lunch and dinner, with a more imaginative menu than you might expect; a full meal might cost about IR£15, but there are main courses for around IR£5.

Getting There & Away

Buses connect Kilcar and Carrick with Killybegs and Glencolumbcille once a day Monday to Saturday (twice daily in July and August). McGeehan's Coaches (☎ 075-46150) from Glencolumbcille to Dublin stops at Carrick daily at 7.40 am with an additional bus at 5.10 pm on Friday and 3.15 pm on Sunday; they stop in Kilcar outside John Joe's pub about 10 minutes later. There are extra buses in summer.

DONEGAL

GLENCOLUMBCILLE

The name of this village in Irish – Gleann Cholm Cille (meaning the 'glen of Columba's church') – suggests that the 6th century St Columba (alias Colmcille) lived in the valley here, and the remains of his church can still be seen. Every year at midnight on 9 June – the saint's feast day – the village becomes the focal point of a penitential walkabout.

The village appears as Glencolmcille on some maps.

Information

The Lace House (☎ 073-30116) in the centre of the village dispenses information and sells a useful archaeological guide to the area entitled *A Guide to 5000 Years of History in Stone*.

The telephone code is ☎ 073.

Beaches

The beach opposite the Folk Village can be dangerous due to the undercurrents, and it's worth making the short journey west of Glencolumbcille to Doonalt where there are two sandy beaches. Another beach can be found at the end of the road to Malinbeg, where steps descend to a lovely sheltered cove.

Folk Village

This heritage centre (☎ 30017), established by Father James McDyer 1967, comprises several replicated thatched cottages as lived in by people from the 18th and 19th centuries, with genuine period fittings. The shebeen house sells local wine alongside marmalade and fudge. The old National School is also open to visitors, and there's a short nature trail up the hill behind.

The museum opens Easter to September 10 am to 6 pm Monday to Saturday, noon to 6 pm on Sunday. There's a IR£2.50/1.75 admission fee, including a tour of the site's buildings and entry to the museum.

Malinmore Adventure Centre

Overlooking Malin Bay, this sports centre (☎ 30123) offers scuba diving, canoeing, snorkelling, fishing, orienteering, boat trips and other activities.

Courses

Late March to October, Oideas Gael (☎ 30248) at the Foras Cultúir Uladh (Ulster

---

DONEGAL

A Tale of Two Priests

While it's the sexual improprieties of the clergy in Ireland that grab the headlines, most of the Catholic faithful like to think of their priests and nuns as 'living saints' who perform corporal works of mercy and contribute to the development of the community. County Donegal can claim two such men.

When Father James McDyer came to Glencolumbcille from Tory Island in 1952, he was galvanised into action by a community with an emigration rate of 75%. He organised cooperatives and diversified farming practices as well as promoting tourism. By 1964 emigration had dropped to 20%.

The Folk Village established by Father McDyer in 1967 – long before such heritage centres became trendy and there were substantial EU grants to help pay for the expense of setting them up – is the most tangible evidence of the work of a priest who played a remarkable role in the development of a community.

Another cleric who made his mark on a remote part of rural Donegal was Father Diarmuid Ó Péicín. When the then retired Jesuit missionary visited Tory Island for a day trip in 1980, he encountered a totally dispirited people. They were convinced that the government was going to move the total population of 200 islanders to the mainland, and the 'lonely rock' they called home would go the way of the Blasket Islands (see the Kerry chapter), abandoned in the 1950s. Father Ó Péicín took up the fight and campaigned both in Ireland and abroad for an electrification and water scheme for Tory, proper sanitation and a regular ferry. All of this has been achieved and a new harbour is under construction.

You can read all about Father Ó Péicín's work in his new autobiography, *Islanders: The True Story of One Man's Fight to Save a Way of Life* (Harper Collins). ■

Cultural Foundation) in Glencolumbcille offers a number of adult courses in the Irish language and ones on traditional culture – from Donegal dancing and marine painting to bodhrán playing and tapestry weaving. For the language courses (absolute beginners welcome) fees range from IR£45/95 for a three-day weekend/week-long course; cultural courses cost around IR£80 and last a week.

Rental accommodation sharing with other course participants can also be arranged at IR£55 per person a week or IR£115 in a B&B.

Places to Stay

The friendly *Dooey Hostel* (☎ 30130), the flagship property of the IHO, is about 1.5km beyond the village and offers everything from camping space (IR£3.50 per person) and 32 dormitory beds (IR£6) to four private rooms (IR£6.50 per person) and a group house for 20 people with superb views out over Glen Bay. The hostel has six kitchens and, rather surprising for somewhere as remote as this, it offers wheelchair access. If driving, take the turn beside the Glenhead Tavern; if walking or cycling, take a short cut up a track beside the Folk Village.

A nice B&B next to the hostel is Anne Ward's *Atlantic Scene* (☎ 30186) charging IR£12 per person and open June to September. The *Ulster Cultural Foundation* (☎ 073-30248) offers B&B year round for IR£15/26.

At Malinmore, about 2km past the Folk Village, *Ros Mór* (☎ 30083) is a pleasant place charging IR£16/28 for B&B. Nearby is the renovated *Glencolumbcille Hotel* (☎ 30003), with 35 doubles for IR£60.

Places to Eat

There's a restaurant and afternoon tea shop above *Lace House*, open daily until 9.30 pm and offering soups, sandwiches and burgers for under IR£2. The café at the *Folk Village* sells excellent Irish cakes, apple tart and bread. *An Chistin* ('the kitchen') at the Ulster Cultural Foundation specialises in seafood and opens for lunch and dinner March to October.

Things to Buy

The Glencolumbcille Woollen Market (☎ 39377), 3km south-east of the village on the R263, has a large selection of Donegal tweed jackets, caps and ties alongside lambswool scarves and shawls. Also available are Aran sweaters and handwoven rugs. At Lace House, Rossan sells knitted garments, jackets and rugs. You can also buy handmade sweaters at the Dooey Hostel.

Getting There & Away

A Bus Éireann bus (☎ 074-21309 in Letterkenny) leaves for Killybegs daily Monday to Saturday at 8.30 am, with an extra bus on Saturday at 11.35 am. There's another bus daily in July and August at 12.35 pm.

McGeehan's Coaches (☎ 075-46150) leave daily for Donegal and Dublin. From Dublin the bus leaves the Royal Dublin Hotel on O'Connell St at 6 pm (extra buses on Friday at 4.30 pm and on Monday at 10 am), arriving at Glencolumbcille at 11 pm. Departure from Glencolumbcille is at 7.30 am (extra buses on Friday at 5 pm and on Sunday at 3 pm) from outside Biddy's Pub. McGeehan's Coaches runs to Letterkenny (two hours) via Killybegs, Ardara and Glenties, and also leaves at 7.30 am Monday to Saturday. It leaves Letterkenny for Glencolumbcille at 4.45 pm.

ARDARA

The road from Glencolumbcille to Ardara goes via the scenically stunning Glengesh Pass, a glaciated valley that suddenly opens up before you, with long winding bends carrying the road down to the river. Before entering Ardara (Árd na Rátha), a small road to the left runs down to the tiny village of Maghera and its attractive beach with caves that can be explored. Be careful as some of them flood when the tide comes in. The long, narrow peninsula that extends from Ardara and separates Loughros More Bay from

Loughros Beg Bay is also worth walking or cycling.

There's an Ulster Bank on the Diamond in the centre of Ardara. The post office is just opposite.

Ardara Heritage Centre

This heritage centre (☎ 075-41704) tells the story of Donegal's role in the tweed-weaving industry and gives you the chance to watch a handloom weaver. A video upstairs describes the surrounding area, and there's a tea shop. It's open daily Easter to September, 10 am to 6 pm, Sunday 2 to 6 pm. Admission costs IR£2 and children usually get in free.

Ardara Weavers Fair

The Ardara Weavers Fair had its origins in the 18th century but went into decline early this century. It has been recently revived and now takes place over the first weekend in June.

Places to Stay

The *Drumbarron Hostel* (☎ 075-41200) charges IR£6 for a dormitory bed and IR£14 for its one double. It opens April to October.

Drumbarron House (☎ same), next to the hostel on the Diamond, has four rooms costing IR£13 to IR£16 per person. It opens all year. *Laburnum House* (☎ 075-41146), also on the Diamond on corner of the Portnoo road, does B&B for IR£12.50. At the east end of Main St, *Homeward Bound* (☎ 075-41246) has singles/doubles for IR£21/32 and opens Easter to October.

Places to Eat

The best place for snacks or a meal is *Nancy's*. This small, dark place has lots of atmosphere and serves burgers, various seafood dishes (including garlic oysters) and a ploughman's lunch. *Charlie's West End Café* at the Killybegs end of Main St can do you breakfast, as well as soups, sandwiches and steak.

Entertainment

The *Central Bar* has live music nightly and invites all musicians to join in. Another place to try is the *Corner Bar* on the Diamond.

Things to Buy

There are a few shops specialising in locally made knitwear, and prices are competitive. Aran cardigans and sweaters are between IR£35 and IR£75, scarves around IR£12, and tweed jackets from IR£90 to IR£150. Compare prices and styles at Kennedy's (☎ 075-41106) and Bonner & Son (☎ 075-41303), almost side by side on Front St, and John Molloy (☎ 075-41133), 1km out on the Killybegs road and open daily 9 am to 8 pm.

Getting There & Away

The Bus Éireann express (☎ 074-21309 in Letterkenny) from Dublin to Donegal is extended to Ardara on Friday, and a Sunday bus leaves Ardara for Dublin at 4.30 pm. In July and August, the Killybegs bus for Portnoo departs at 10 am and 5.05 pm, reaching O'Donnell's in Ardara in about half an hour. At 1.07 and 7.07 pm buses leave for Killybegs. The rest of the year, these buses run on Tuesday, Thursday and Friday only. McGeehan's Coaches (☎ 075-46150) also run to Dublin each morning from the post office at 8.30 am (extra Friday bus at 5.45 pm and one on Sunday at 3.45 pm). The Glencolumbcille to Letterkenny bus via Glenties also stops in Ardara, Monday to Saturday at 8.30 am.

DAWROS HEAD

The two camping and caravan sites here are packed out every summer with holiday-makers from the North and consequently the area is busier than you might expect. The Blue Flag beach at Narin is a big crowd-puller, and at low tide you can walk out to Iniskeel Island to the remains of a monastery founded by St Connell, a cousin of St Colmcille.

Doon Fort

Signposts off the road from Narin to Rosbeg lead 3km to a lake in the centre of which sits 2000-year-old Doon Fort, a fortified oval settlement. To reach it, you need to hire a

DONEGAL

rowing boat. The signs lead you to the site and a boat will cost you about IR£3 for an hour.

Armada Site

In 1588 the *Duquesa Santa Ana* ran aground off Tramore Beach. The survivors temporarily occupied O'Boyle's Island in Kiltoorish Lake but then marched south through Ardara to Killybegs, where they set sail again in the *Girona*. The *Girona* met a similar fate that year off the Antrim coast in Northern Ireland, with the loss of over 1000 crew.

Places to Stay

Dunmore Caravans (☎ 075-45121) is on the Strand Rd at Portnoo and accepts tents for IR£5 – call first to check whether there's a space available. It's open mid-March to November. The other campsite, the *Tramore Beach Caravan & Camping Park* (☎ 075-51491) at Rosbeg, charges about IR£7 for a two-person tent. Take the road from Ardara to Narin and turn off to the left following the signposts.

There are a few B&Bs at Narin and Portnoo that open for the season (generally April to September). *Carnaween House* (☎ 075-45122) charges IR£15/28 and *Thalassa Country Home* (☎ 075-45151) costs IR£16 per person.

Getting There & Away

In July and August from Monday to Saturday, Bus Éreann buses leave Killybegs for Portnoo at 10 am and 5.05 pm. They leave Portnoo for the return journey at 12.15 and 6.15 pm. The rest of the year, these buses run on Tuesday, Thursday and Friday only.

GLENTIES

There are a number of pubs in the small town of Glenties (Gleannta) that offer music at night, and the place is usually hopping with Northerners. The town was home to Patrick McGill (1891-1963), the 'navvy poet', and a small festival in his honour takes place in mid-August. There's a board with tourist information beside the garda station in the main street. Glenties has won the coveted title of 'Ireland's Tidiest Town' more times than it can count.

St Connell's Museum & Heritage Centre

The local history museum beside the old courthouse has a small collection of local artefacts, including an impressive set of early 20th century bathroom fixtures in the basement and reminders of the old railway Glenties-Fintown line that ran through the town. It's open April to September, 10 am to 12.30 pm and 2 to 4.30 pm Monday to Friday, and 10.30 am to 12.30 pm Saturday. Admission is under IR£2.

Places to Stay

Clean, spacious IHH *Campbell's Holiday Hostel* (☎ 075-51491) is on the left beside the museum as you enter from Ardara on the N56. A bed in a dorm with ensuite facilities is IR£6 and there are seven twin rooms for IR£16. There's also a big kitchen-cum-common room, with a welcoming fire. Two B&Bs are along Glen Rd about 1km out of town: *Claradon* (☎ 075-51113) and *Avalon* (☎ 075-51292), both of which have singles/doubles for IR£19/28. The 20-room *Highlands Hotel* (☎ 075-51111) on the main street has singles/doubles from IR£30/48.

Places to Eat

The *Highlands Hotel* serves substantial meals even on a Sunday evening; dinner is IR£14. Otherwise, there are several fast-food places like *McGuinness Café* and a chips shop called *Nighthawks* on the main street.

Getting There & Away

In July and August from Monday to Saturday a Bus Éireann bus (☎ 074-21309 in Letterkenny) connects Killybegs with Portnoo, stopping outside the post office in Glenties at 10.45 am and 5.50 pm. From Portnoo bound for Killybegs the bus stops in Glenties at 12.40 and 6.40 pm. The rest of the year, these buses run Tuesday, Thursday and Friday only.

On Friday an express bus leaving Dublin for Donegal at 5.15 pm extends its service to Glenties, arriving at 10.20 pm. On Sunday

DONEGAL

the bus leaves Glenties at 4.15 pm and reaches Dublin at 9.45 pm.

McGeehan's Coaches (☎ 075-46150) from Glencolumbcille to Dublin stops outside the Highlands Hotel at 8.15 am (extra bus on Friday at 5.30 pm and on Sunday at 3.30 pm). There's also a bus to Letterkenny, Monday to Saturday at 8.40 am.

Getting Around
You can rent a bike from Glenties Tool Hire (☎ 075-51122) on the main street for IR£5 a day.

INLAND TO THE FINN VALLEY
This part of Donegal is not well travelled – a blessing if you want to get away on your own for some fishing, hill walking or cycling. The River Finn is a good salmon river, especially if there has been heavy rain before the middle of June. There's also sea trout, and fishing gear is available from McElhinneys (☎ 074-31217) in Ballybofey.

There's good **hill walking** on the Blue Stack Mountains and along the Ulster Way, but you need to be equipped with maps and provisions. The Finn Farm Hostel (see Places to Stay) dispenses maps and advice and will even arrange a pick-up at the beginning or end of a walk. A long, one-day trek could start from the hostel and end at Campbell's Holiday Hostel in Glenties or the hostel in Fintown.

Horse riding is best arranged through the Finn Farm Hostel which organises lessons at IR£7 an hour. Experienced riders can take a horse for the whole day for IR£30. Six-day trips across the border can also be arranged.

The main town is **Ballybofey** (pronounced 'Bally-boh-fay'), which is linked to Stranorlar by an arched bridge over the River Finn. In Ballybofey's Protestant church is the grave of Isaac Butt (1813-79), founder of the Irish Home Rule movement. **Fintown**, 30km to the north-west and also on the River Finn, is a much smaller settlement, just a cluster of houses, a hostel, shop, post office, garage and pubs. Nevertheless, a renovated part of the **narrow-gauge railway** (☎ 075-46280) between Fintown and Glenties runs

excursions alongside Lough Finn on 5km of track. July to September, trains leave the station weekdays 11 am to 5 pm, Saturday and Sunday 2 to 5 pm. In June the schedule is 1 to 4 pm on weekdays and to 5 pm on Saturday. Fares are IR£2/1/6 for adults/children/families.

Places to Stay
The wonderful IHH *Finn Farm Hostel* (☎ 074-32261), a member of the IHH and the IHO, is 2km from Ballybofey, and the left turn off the road is signposted on the road to Glenties (R253). When you think you're lost and there can't possibly be a hostel this far down the old green road you're on, it will appear in front of you. A bed is IR£6, while camping costs IR£3 (IR£2 if you can manage without the hostel's indoor facilities). There's a new building in front with five double ensuite rooms costing IR£10 to IR£15 per person. Finn Farm opens all year. *Fintown Hostel* (☎ 075-46244), also open all year, charges IR£5.50 for a bed and is beautifully situated above Lough Finn, with the Finnian's Rainbow pub at the end of the drive.

There are B&B possibilities in both Ballybofey and Stranorlar. *Finn View House* (☎ 074-31351), on the Lifford road in Ballybofey, has rooms for IR£19/28, while Maureen Fahey's *Ashburn* (☎ 074-31312) on the Letterkenny road in Stranorlar charges from IR£28 for doubles. *Kee's Hotel* (☎ 074-31018) in Stranorlar, where the mail horses were changed on the Derry-Sligo run in the 19th century, has singles/doubles in high season for IR£42/72, which includes use of the leisure club's swimming pool and sauna. *Jackson's Hotel* (☎ 074-31021) is more expensive with high season (July to October) singles/doubles for IR£50/80.

Places to Eat
The big hotels will be able to do you dinner for about IR£18. Otherwise, there's the small *Red Rose Café* in Ballybofey, or the equally small *Caife na Locha* run by a women's co-operative in Fintown; both do tea and

light meals. Caife na Locha opens seven days a week in summer.

Entertainment

There's the small *Balor Theatre* (☎ 074-31840) in Ballybofey, but you'll have more fun checking out the area's traditional music outlets. The *Finn Farm Hostel* is a centre for a community work scheme aimed at reviving dying musical traditions, so if you stay during the week you'll be able to hear the musicians practising between 10 am and 6 pm; at weekends you'll have to make do with a tape of their best efforts. They practise in the two Ballybofey pubs – the *Claddagh* and the *Bonner's Corner Bar* – on Wednesday and Thursday nights. In Fintown, *An Teach Ceoil* ('the music house') is the venue of choice. The *Glen Tavern*, midway between Glenties and Fintown, is renowned for its traditional music on Saturday night.

Getting There & Away

The Bus Éireann express (☎ 074-21309 in Letterkenny) from Galway to Derry via Sligo and Letterkenny stops outside the shopping centre in Ballybofey three times a day, Monday to Saturday. There's also one or two buses a day to Donegal. Local buses connect Ballybofey with Killybegs and Letterkenny.

McGeehan's Coaches (☎ 075-46150) run a Glencolumbcille to Letterkenny bus Monday to Saturday that stops in front of the Fintown post office at 9 am (at 5.35 pm heading for Glenties, Ardara, Killybegs, Kilcar and Glencolumbcille). There's also a McGeehan's Coaches bus from Fintown to Ballyfoley at 1.15 pm Monday to Saturday, mid-July to August. It stops in Ballybofey en route to Fintown, Killybegs and Glencol-umbcille at 5 pm.

The Feda O'Donnell bus (☎ 075-48114) from Crolly to Galway stops in Ballybofey outside McElhinneys at 9.15 am and 4.45 pm Monday to Saturday, with an extra bus on Friday at 12.45, and on Sunday at 9.15 am and 3.45 and 7.45 pm.

Getting Around

Bicycles can be rented from the Finn Farm Hostel and Kee's Hotel for IR£6 a day.

North-Western Donegal

The various monikers which are bestowed on Donegal's scenery – wild, spectacular, dramatic etc – are nowhere more applicable than in the north-west of the county. Despite the absence of large towns, you're rarely far from a village or pub, and the area around Gweedore claims to be one of the most densely populated rural regions in Western Europe.

The stretch of land between Dungloe in the south and Crolly in the north is a bleak and rocky Gaeltacht area known as the Rosses. The main attraction here is the island of Arranmore, reached by ferry from the village of Burtonport.

The other accessible island, the visually distinctive Tory Island farther to the north, is even more appealing. The coast around here, the area between Bunbeg and Dunfanaghy, is absolutely superb, and there are wonderful cycling tours around the Bloody Foreland and Horn Head.

DUNGLOE
Information

In theory, the tourist office (☎ 075-21297) on Main St in Dungloe (An Clochán Liath) opens 10 am to 1 pm and 2 to 6 pm Monday to Saturday, June to August. If it's closed the nearby festival office (☎ 075-21254) may be able to help. The nearest good beach is just north of Maghery.

The telephone code is ☎ 075.

Special Events

In late July/early August, Dungloe plays host to the 10-day Mary of Dungloe festival, named after a popular song. Thousands of people crowd into town for a series of events culminating in a contest to pick the year's 'Mary'. Supposedly, she's selected on the basis of personality, but the fact that only women aged 18 to 25 are eligible to enter rather puts the lie to this. The festival is a big, raucous and boozy affair, and although it's sometimes graced by big names like singers Christy Moore or 'the-boy-next-door' Daniel O'Donnell, some people might want to avoid Dungloe at this time. If you do want to attend, book a bed well ahead. For more details phone ☎ 21254.

Places to Stay

The very well run IHH *Greene's Hostel* (☎ 21021), in Carnmore Rd and open all year, charges IR£6 a bed in six and eight-bed dorms and IR£8 per person in a half-dozen private rooms. There's also space for tents: IR£5 if you're hitching or cycling. You can also hire a bike here for IR£5 a day. An Óige's *Crohy Head Hostel* (☎ 21950), 8km west of Dungloe at scenic Crohy Head, charges IR£4/4.50 or IR£5/6 for juniors/ seniors, depending on the season, and it's open Easter to September.

The 16-room *Delaney's Hotel* (☎ 21033) on Main St charges from IR£22/40. If singer Daniel O'Donnell is your man, you might want to make a pilgrimage to his home village, Kincasslaugh, on the Rosses Peninsula and stay at the 15-room *Viking House Hotel* (☎ 43295), owned by Daniel and run by his family. Singles/doubles are IR£31/50 and it's open all year.

Places to Eat

The *Bridge Inn* pub near the tourist office does light snacks, or there's the nearby *Courthouse Restaurant* for cheap seafood meals. For a quiet spot, seek out the *Scrumptious Café* in the otherwise uninspiring Dungloe Centre shopping mall. Other possibilities in the evening include *Delaney's Hotel* (dinner IR£17.50), the nearby *Riverside Bistro* or the *Evergreen* Chinese restaurant, up the hill from the Riverside. Egg rolls and other starters are from IR£3, noodles and other main dishes from IR£5.50.

Annagry is a small village 4km west of Crolly and 10km north of Dungloe, where you will find the snazzy *Danny Minnies Restaurant* (☎ 48201). It does good seafood

dinners for about IR£17 and lunches from around IR£8.

Getting There & Away

Dungloe isn't served by Bus Éireann but there are plenty of private companies. McGeehan's Coaches (☎ 46150) from Glencolumbcille to Dublin stop at Greene's Hostel in Dungloe, Monday to Saturday at 7.45 am (extra bus on Friday at 5 pm and on Sunday at 3 pm). Mid-July to August it also has a daily bus from Dungloe to Fintown at 11.50 am.

O'Donnell Buses (☎ 48356) run from Dungloe to Belfast (4½ hours) via Burtonport, Bunbeg, Dunfanaghy, Letterkenny and Derry. Buses leave from in front of Delaney's Hotel on Main St, Monday to Saturday at 7.15 am and 4.30 pm on Sunday. Derry-based Lough Swilly (☎ 01504-262017, ☎ 074-29400 in Letterkenny) has a Dungloe to Derry service via Bunbeg, Dunfanaghy and Letterkenny three times a day Monday to Friday.

Twice a week, Feda O'Donnell (☎ 075-48114) runs a bus from Annagry to Killybegs via Burtonport, Dungloe (8.10 am on Monday, 2.40 pm on Sunday), Glenties and Ardara. It goes in the other direction two times on Friday only, stopping in Dungloe at 8.15 and 10 pm.

BURTONPORT

The otherwise uninteresting port village of Burtonport does have two claims to fame: it's the embarkation point for spectacular Arranmore Island and, back in 1974, the Atlantis commune was established here by one Jenny James, who practised a form of primal therapy. Her followers soon became known as 'the Screamers'.

Eventually the commune relocated to the Columbian jungle and another group arrived to take its place. 'The Silver Sisters' chose to live a Victorian lifestyle, complete with Victorian dress, and soon bizarre stories were circulating about them. They, too, have now moved on, allowing Burtonport (Ailt an Chórrain) to sink back into anonymity.

ARRANMORE

The small island of Arranmore (Árainn Mhór), 14km by 5km, has some spectacular cliff scenery and sandy beaches, as well as pubs and a small festival held each August. The island has been inhabited for thousands of years, and a prehistoric fort can be seen on the south side. The western and northern parts are wild and rugged with hardly any houses to disturb the sense of isolation. For fishing trips in the area ring ☎ 075-42077.

Places to Stay

Glen Hotel (☎ 075-20505) has 10 rooms costing from IR£15 to IR£18 per person, depending on the season. *Bonner's Ferry Boat Restaurant* (☎ 075-20532) does B&B for IR£14 per person.

Places to Eat

Bonner's Ferry Boat Restaurant is near the ferry pier at Kilrannan, and there are a number of pubs elsewhere on the island doing food, including *O'Donnell's Atlantic Bar* in Aphort and *Phil Bans Bar* in Leabgarrow.

Getting There & Away

Throughout the year, the ferry run by the Bonners (☎ 075-20532) plies the 1.5km from Burtonport to Kilrannan; the trip takes 20 minutes and costs IR£5 return. In July and August, there are some nine daily ferry crossings, usually starting at 8.30 am (noon on Sunday). Count on at least five sailings in winter.

GWEEDORE, DERRYBEG & BUNBEG
Orientation & Information

Derrybeg (Doirí Beaga) and Bunbeg (Bun Beag) virtually run into each other along the R257; Gweedore (Gaoth Dobhair) is a few km to the east on the R258. The post office on the main road between Derrybeg and Bunbeg has a bureau de change, and there's an Allied Irish Bank with a tourist information point in the car park.

The telephone code is ☎ 075.

Places to Stay

The IHO *Backpackers Ireland Seaside Hostel* (☎ 32244) at Magheragallon near Derrybeg has beds for IR£7 per person and one twin for IR£14. It opens mid-March to October. The wonderfully remote and friendly IHO *Screag an Iolair* ('eagle's nest') hostel (☎ 48593) is signposted up in the hills above Crolly to the south-west of Gweedore on the N56. It charges IR£6 to IR£7.50, has two private rooms and offers a free pick-up service if you don't fancy the 5km walk from the main road.

Bunbeg has plenty of B&Bs, with *Atlantic View* (☎ 31550) on Strand Rd offering singles/doubles from IR£20/32, and *An Teach Ban* (☎ 31569) beside the Allied Irish Bank from IR£16/28.

There are a couple of prettier places beside Bunbeg Harbour, including *Bunbeg House* (☎ 31305), charging IR£17/32. In summer, heavy traffic to the harbour might detract a bit from the charm here, though. *Fernfield* (☎ 31258), farther away at Middletown, charges from IR£14.50 per person.

The 36-room *Óstán Gweedore* (☎ 31177), right by Bunbeg beach, has the best facilities, including a leisure complex. B&B for two is IR£70. *Óstán Radharc na Mara* (☎ 31076), also in Bunbeg, charges from IR£35/50.

Places to Eat

There are lots of cafés in Bunbeg, including *An Chislenach* opposite the Hudí Beag pub. *Mooney's Restaurant* is opposite the Radharc na Mara, but it only opens during summer evenings. The *Radharc na Mara* itself does grills and steak meals. *Bunbeg House* by Bunbeg harbour has dinner for IR£15 and also serves afternoon tea.

Entertainment

For traditional pub music it would be hard to beat the Monday night sessions at *Tábhairne Hudí Beag* (☎ 31016) in Bunbeg high street.

Getting There & Away

Feda O'Donnell Coaches (☎ 48114) has buses leaving Gweedore for Letterkenny, Donegal, Sligo and Galway. They depart at

7.30 am and 2.55 pm Monday to Saturday (with an extra bus on Friday at 10.30 am), and on Sunday at 7.30 am and 2 pm. They depart from the Bunbeg crossroads and the Radharc na Mara Hotel. In Galway the bus leaves the cathedral at 10 am and 4 pm daily (also at 5.30 pm on Friday), and at 3 pm and 8 pm (from Eyre Square) on Sunday.

Getting Around
You can hire a bike for IR£5 a day from McFadden's Tool Hire (☎ 31066) in Bunbeg.

LAKESIDE CENTRE
Beside Lough Dunlewy, Dunlewy (Dún Lúiche) is a small village at the foot of Mt Errigal (752m), Donegal's highest peak. Here the Lakeside Centre (Ionad Cois Locha; ☎ 075-31699) reconstructs the home of Manus Ferry, the last of the local weavers, who died in 1975. Visitors can watch all the stages of weaving in operation and then go outside to see assorted farm animals, walk along the lake shore or take a boat ride with a storyteller on board to fill them in on local history, geology and folklore. There may well be music at the centre as well. There's an excellent café with a turf fire for cold days and a big shop selling everything from sweaters to traditional music tapes.

A ticket for the house and grounds costs IR£2.20; for a boat trip it's IR£2.50; combined it's IR£4. A combined family ticket is particularly good value at IR£10. The centre opens weekends only in April and May. It's open June to September, 11.30 am to 6 pm Monday to Saturday, and 12.30 to 7 pm Sunday.

MT ERRIGAL & THE POISONED GLEN
You don't need to be an experienced mountaineer to climb Mt Errigal, but it can be tough going and you should always be wary of damp, misty days when visibility can drop with little warning. There are two paths up to the summit: the easier tourist route, which covers 5km and takes roughly two hours to complete; and the more difficult 3.25km walk along the north-west ridge, which involves scrambling over scree for about 2½ hours. Details of both routes are available at the Lakeside Centre.

There are all sorts of stories about how the Poisoned Glen got its name. The more prosaic ones suggest it's because poisonous Irish spurge used to grow here or because the original name – An Gleann Neamhe ('the heavenly glen') became corrupted to An Gleann Nimhe ('the poisoned glen'). Another story has it that the British were once camped here, and Irish rebels poisoned the water to kill their horses. Most imaginative of all is the tale that says the ancient giant Balar was killed here by his exiled grandson Lughaidh, whereupon the poison from his eye split the rock and poisoned the glen.

Whichever story you choose to believe, it's possible to walk through the glen, although some of the ground is rough and boggy. From the Lakeside Centre a return walk along the glen is about 12km and takes two to three hours.

Places to Stay
The IHO *Backpackers Ireland Lakeside Hostel* (☎ 075-32133) at the old Dunlewy Hotel charges IR£7 for a bed and an expensive IR£12.50 per person in eight private rooms. It's open mid-March to October. There's An Óige *Errigal Hostel* (☎ 075-31180) at Errigal, a simple place between Dunlewy and Gweedore on the R251. Beds cost IR£4.50/5 or IR£5.50/6.50 for juniors/seniors, depending on the season, and it's open all year.

GLENVEAGH NATIONAL PARK
The Dunlewy Lakeside Centre is right beside the 10,000 hectare Glenveagh National Park (Pairc Naísúnta Ghleann Bheatha), in a lake-filled valley overlooked by the Derryveagh Mountains. Much of the land comprising the park was once farmed by tenants, 244 of whom were evicted by landowner John George Adair in the winter of 1861. A plaque on a gable end at Ardaturr farm commemorates their fate. Adair was responsible for the building of Glenveagh Castle in 1870. After the mysterious disappearance of the second

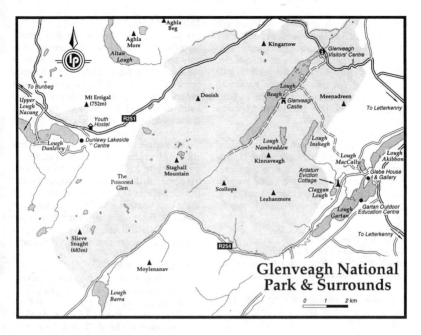

Glenveagh National Park & Surrounds

0   1   2 km

DONEGAL

owner, the land was bought in 1937 by American Henry McIlhenny, who eventually sold it to the state and later donated the castle and gardens.

Adair's wife Cornelia introduced two things that define the appearance of the national park: the herd of red deer, and the rhododendrons. The latter, despite their beauty in blossom, are seen as a pest, preventing broad-leafed trees from seeding themselves and running riot in the landscape.

Features of the park include a nature trail through woods of Scots pine and oak to a stretch of blanket bog, and a viewing point, just a short walk behind the castle.

The **Glenveagh Visitors' Centre** (☎ 074-37090) is excellent and has a useful audio-visual display on the ecology of the park and the infamous Adair. There's also an extremely imaginative toy theatre representation of the story. The restaurant serves hot food and snacks, and the reception sells the necessary midge repellent, which is as vital in summer as walking boots and waterproofs are in winter.

The park opens all year, and the visitors' centre opens daily mid-April to early November, 10 am to 6.30 pm. June to early September it's open until 7.30 pm on Sunday, while in October/early November it closes on Friday. The charge is IR£2/1; a family ticket is IR£5. Camping is not allowed in the park.

Glenveagh Castle

The castle built by John George Adair in 1870 was modelled on Balmoral in miniature, but Henry McIlhenny restored it as a comfortable gentleman's home with lots of reminders of the deer hunting once so important to upper-class society life. A guided tour takes in a series of rooms that look as if McIlhenny just left them. Some of the nicest ones, including the tartan-draped music room and the guest room for female visitors, are in the round tower. The drawing room also has a splendid 300-year-old Adams-style fireplace bought by McIlhenny from the Ards estate near Dunfanaghy.

On a dry day the gardens are spectacular. They were nurtured for decades and include a variety of features: a terrace, an Italian garden, a walled kitchen garden and the Belgian Walk built by Belgian soldiers who stayed here during WWI.

The castle keeps the same hours as the visitors' centre, although the last guided tours leave about 45 minutes before closing time. Admission costs IR£2. Free minibuses run from the centre to the castle roughly every 15 minutes. The pleasant tearoom in the castle does sandwiches and cold snacks.

BLOODY FORELAND
This headland – Cnoc Fola in Irish – gets its name from the colour of the rocks, and the road to it is wonderfully remote and ideal for cycling. The tiny village of Brinlack, about 1km past the viewing point, has a thatched cottage selling tea and cakes (mid-June to August only).

Places to Stay
There's a small, 12-room hotel, the *Foreland Heights* (☎ 075-31785), near the viewing point, which is open April to September. Singles/doubles are IR£32/47 in July and August.

TORY ISLAND
Not so long ago a visit to Tory Island (Oileán Thóraigh) was a precarious venture; visitors could be stranded for days due to bad weather. With modern boats, this is no longer a problem, and the island is trying to attract visitors.

Tory Island has its own indigenous school of painters, whose work has been exhibited around Europe. The most accomplished of them, James Dixon, didn't start painting until he was in his 60s, when he was inspired by the English landscape artist Derek Hill. He died in 1970. There's a permanent exhibition in the island's community hall.

Things to See
St Colmcille is said to have founded a monastery on the island in the 6th century. The only remains of this monastic era are near West Town: the **Tau Cross**, a small undecorated T-shaped cross on the pier, and a **round tower**, with a circumference of nearly 16m, built of rounded beach-stones and rough granite with a round-headed doorway some distance above the ground.

The north-eastern side of the island has cliffs with colonies of puffins. The south-west is quite different – very flat but with dangerous offshore rocks. It was here that the British gunboat *Wasp* was wrecked in 1884 while on a mission to collect taxes from the islanders. There's just one pebbly beach, but the cliff walks and a visit to the island's pub at night make a stay here well worthwhile.

Places to Stay & Eat
The accommodation situation has improved dramatically over the last few years. The IHO *Radharc na Mara Hostel* (☎ 074-65145), in West Town and open April to October, has beds for IR£7, and there are a few B&Bs in the two villages, including *Grace Duffy's* (☎ 074-35136) in East Town with singles/doubles from IR£15/26 and open all year. The 14-room *Óstán Thóraigh* (☎ 074-35920) has beds from IR£35/54 in high season.

There's a small café on the island. Otherwise you can get pub food or full meals (dinner IR£15) at the *Óstán Thóraigh*.

Getting There & Away
Donegal Coastal Cruises (Turasmara Teo; ☎ 075-31340) operates a boat service from Bunbeg (☎ 075-31991), which is just west of Gweedor, and Magheraroarty (☎ 074-35061), which is reached by turning off the N56 at the western end of Gortahork near Falcarragh. The road is signposted 'Coastal Route/Bloody Foreland'. Twice a week in July and August, and once in June and September, there is also a boat service from Port-na-Blagh and Downings near Dunfanaghy.

Daily between June and September the

boat leaves Bunbeg at 9 am and returns from Tory at 7 or 9 pm. The boat from Magheraroarty leaves at 11.30 am and returns from Tory at 3.30 and 4.30 pm. On Wednesday from June to September, the boat leaves Portna-Blagh at 2 pm and returns at 6.30 pm. Each Saturday (Sunday in June and September) there is also a 2 pm departure from Downings, returning at 6.30 pm. There are several extra services in July and August. No matter where you leave from, the fare is IR£12 return. Bicycles are carried free on all the boats.

FALCARRAGH

This rather uninspiring village (An Fál Carrach), along with neighbouring Gortahork (Gort an Choirce), has a significant Irish-speaking community. During the summer the pubs come alive at night, many with traditional music.

Beach

You can reach the beach by following signs marked An Trá from either end of the main street. At the eastern end turn left beside the supermarket opposite the Bank of Ireland. At the T-junction turn right until another sign marked Trá points down to the left and you're there. The beach is superb for walking but not for swimming. From the supermarket, it's 4km.

Places to Stay & Eat

The IHH *Shamrock Lodge Hostel* (☎ 074-35859) has 14 beds in the village pub of the same name and charges IR£6 a bed (or IR£8 per person in two private rooms). It's perfect for people who want a lively nightlife close by, but not for anyone wanting to get to sleep before 1 am. *Baile Conaill* (☎ 074-35363), a huge place on the Ballyconnell Easte in Falcarraigh some 10 minutes from the beach has hostel accommodation (88 beds) for IR£7.50 as well as B&B from IR£12.50. It opens all year. *Sea View* (☎ 074-35552) is 2km off the road going to Dunfanaghy (N56) and charges from IR£19/28 for B&B.

The *Gweedore Bar* has a restaurant

upstairs, and *Coyle's Café* is almost next door. For fast food, try *Mighty Mac's Café*.

Getting There & Away

The Feda O'Donnell bus (☎ 075-48114) from Crolly to Galway stops in front of the phone box on Main St in Falcarragh at 7.50 am and 3.15 pm Monday to Saturday, reaching Letterkenny about an hour later and Galway at 1.10 and 8.45 pm. There's an extra bus on Friday at 10.50 am, and on Sunday they leave at 7.50 am and 2.20 pm.

The Anthony McGinley bus (☎ 075-48167) leaves for Dublin daily at 7.25 am.

Derry-based Lough Swilly (☎ 01504-262017, ☎ 074-29400 in Letterkenny) has a bus from Dungloe to Derry stopping at Falcarragh at 10.35 am and 5 pm on weekdays only, and at noon Monday to Saturday. This bus stops on Main St near the hostel.

DUNFANAGHY

Dunfanaghy (Dún Fionnachaidh) is a popular holiday resort in a small and discreet way; the vast sandy stretches of virtually empty beach are a big draw, and there are a couple of smart hotels as well as a hostel. Dunfanaghy makes a good base for trips south to Letterkenny or west to Tory Island.

Information

There's no tourist office but the post office has a bureau de change facility, open until 5.30 pm on weekdays. The Allied Irish Bank has a branch opposite the Carrig Rua Hotel.

The telephone code is ☎ 074.

Dunfanaghy Workhouse & Gallery

After the passage of the Poor Law in 1838, workhouses were set up around Ireland to accommodate and employ the destitute in conditions that were deliberately intended to be uncomfortable. Men, women, children and the sick were all separated from one other, and their lives were rigorously governed, with hard work the order of the day. Dunfanaghy's workhouse opened in 1845, just before the onset of the Famine, which caused the number of residents to multiply. By 1847 it was expanded to accommodate

DONEGAL

some 600 people, double the number originally planned.

The workhouse has now been opened as a small heritage centre (☎ 36540), with information about local history in general as well as its own. It's open March to October, 10 am to 5 pm weekdays, noon to 5 pm weekends. Admission is IR£2/1.

Dunfanaghy Gallery (☎ 36224) next door started life as a fever hospital. Nowadays it houses art and crafts and opens Monday to Saturday, 10 am to 7 pm.

Horn Head

Horn Head (Corrán Binne) has some of Donegal's most spectacular coastal scenery, with a welcome absence of ugly residential development. The towering headland, with quartzite cliffs over 180m high, could be reached by continuing on from the end of the walk described in the following section, but the route can be perilous at times. Consult the guide *New Irish Walks: West & North* (Gill & Macmillan) or *Hill Walkers' Donegal* by David Herman (Shanksmore Press) for details.

An alternative route is to go by bike or car from the Falcarragh end of Dunfanaghy. The road circles the headland and offers tremendous views on a fine day: the islands of Tory, Inishbofin, Inishdooey and tiny Inishbeg to the west, Sheep Haven Bay and the Rosguill

Peninsula to the east, Malin Head to the north-east, and even the coast of Scotland. You could easily spend a day walking this area, with breaks for a swim and a bite to eat.

Walking

For an exhilarating walk, follow the road west to Falcarragh for about 4km and turn right at the first track past the Corcreggan Mill Cottage Hostel. Continue along the track down to the dunes by first passing a farm and then crossing a field on a clearly indicated pathway. The vast and lovely Tramore Beach opens up below the sand dunes, and you may well be the only person here. Turn to the right and follow the beach to the end where you can find a way up onto a path that leads north to Pollaguill Bay. From the bay you can continue to the cairn at the end of the bay and follow the coastline for a stupendous view of the 20m Marble Arch, carved out by the sea.

Organised walks are offered by Donegal Walking Holidays (☎ 36376), Sessiagh Cottage, Woodhill, Dunfanaghy.

Other Activities

Horse riding can be arranged at the Stracomer Riding School through Arnold's Hotel (☎ 36208), which also offers a programme of birdwatching, painting and photography holidays. You can organise sea-angling trips

---

The Corncrake Crisis

Not so long ago, nights in the Irish countryside were punctuated by the distinctive 'crek, crek' cry of the lovelorn male corncrake. But in 1988 an all-Ireland survey found only 903 birds still calling, and by the mid-1990s this number had fallen to just 130. Nowadays, corncrakes survive only in northern Donegal and in the Shannon Callows, Mayo and small areas of the west coast.

The corncrake is a dowdy, secretive bird that winters in south-east Africa before arriving in Ireland to breed in April each year. But, like so many endangered species, it has habits that render it peculiarly vulnerable to modern life. Having laid their eggs in long grass, the females will stay with their chicks even as a mowing tractor's blades descend on them. Even if they realise the danger, long centuries of programming make them reluctant to rush for the safety of open ground.

With the hands at two minutes to midnight for the corncrake, the Irish Wildbird Conservancy (IWC) now offers grants to farmers who will delay mowing until August when the nesting season is over, or cut the grass in 'corncrake-friendly' fashion. A 24-hour Corncrake Hotline (☎ 074-65126 in County Donegal, ☎ 096-51326 in County Mayo) has been set up and you'll see notices in shop windows inviting people to ring it if they hear one. An IWC officer will then visit the site and decide if a nest is in need of protection. ■

from Port-na-Blagh on the *Cricket* through Pat Robinson (☎ 36280).

Places to Stay

Close to a large deserted beach, the IHH *Corcreggan Mill Hostel* (☎ 36409) is a place 4km from Dunfanaghy on the road to Falcarragh (N56). Beds in dorms cost IR£6 to IR£8, a couple of private rooms cost IR£9 per person, and camping is also possible at IR£3 per person.

The biggest hotel is the 32-room *Arnold's* (☎ 36208) with singles/doubles from IR£55/80 in high season. The 22-room *Carrig Rua Hotel* (☎ 36133) opposite charges the same for single/doubles. Both *Rosman House* (☎ 36273) and the *Whins* (☎ 63481) do B&B for IR£21/32.

Places to Eat

Dunfanaghy has a couple of fast-food places on the main street. For coffee and cake, try the café attached to *Dunfanaghy Workhouse* on the N56. The restaurant at *Arnold's Hotel* has good views over the sea and serves hearty dinners from IR£18; the menu at the *Carrig Rua Hotel* is very much the same. *Danann's Seafood Restaurant* (☎ 36150), next to McAuliffe's craft shop on the main street, is popular, with main courses from IR£7. It's open from 6 pm, and reservations will often be necessary. The more expensive *Danny Collins Restaurant* (☎ 36205), a few doors to the west, is also worth a visit. Nearby at Port-na-Blagh, the *Cove* restaurant (☎ 36300) comes highly recommended and reservations are likely to be necessary. Reckon on about IR£20 a head.

Getting There & Away

The Anthony McGinley bus (☎ 075-48167) for Letterkenny and Dublin leaves Annagry daily at 7 am and reaches Dunfanaghy at 7.35 am. There are extra buses on Sunday, Monday and Thursday at 3.55 pm and on Friday at 11.45 am and 3.55 pm. From Dublin the buses leave at 5.45 pm daily with extra buses on Monday and Saturday at 9.30 am, Sunday at 12.30 and 8.30 pm, and on Friday at 12.30 and 4.30 pm.

Buses run by Feda O'Donnell Coaches (☎ 075-48114) from Crolly to Galway stop in the square Monday to Saturday at 8 am and 3.25 pm with an extra bus on Friday at 11 am. They leave on Sunday at 8 am and 2.30 pm.

Derry-based Lough Swilly (☎ 01504-262017, ☎ 074-29400 in Letterkenny) has a bus from Dungloe to Derry that stops in Dunfanaghy at 10.55 am and 5.15 pm on weekdays only, and at 12.20 pm Monday to Saturday.

AROUND DUNFANAGHY
Ards Forest Park

The park, 5km north of Creeslough off the N56, has marked nature trails, varying in length from about 2km to 13km, and is also a wildfowl sanctuary. It covers the northern shore of the Ards Peninsula, which was once an estate of over 800 hectares. In 1930 the southern part was taken over by Capuchin monks; the grounds of their friary buildings are open to the public. The park opens until 9 pm in summer (4.30 pm in winter).

Creeslough

This small village (An Craoslach), on the N56 near an inlet of Sheep Haven Bay, has an interesting modern church, best viewed against the outline of distant Mt Muckish (670m).

Mt Muckish is a distinctive landmark, visible after leaving Letterkenny on the N56 and dominating the coast between Dunfanaghy and the Bloody Foreland. The hardest climb is from the Creeslough side; a road turns off to the left 2km north-west of Creeslough, by a small derelict shop, on the N56. After 6km along here a rough track begins the ascent. The easier route to the top is by way of Muckish Gap, off the inland road from Falcarragh. Consult *New Irish Walks: West & North* (Gill & Macmillan) for details of both routes.

Doe Castle

The castle (Caisléan na dTuath) was once the stronghold of the Scottish MacSweeney family, who were actually employed by the

DONEGAL

O'Donnells. It was built in the early 16th century and was constantly fought over by the MacSweeney brothers. Early in the 17th century it passed into English hands and was repaired and lived in until well into the 19th century. The curious slab that rests against the tower near the entrance is thought to be the tomb of one of the MacSweeneys. It's picturesquely located on a very low promontory with water on three sides and a moat hewn out of the rock on the land side. The best view is from the Carrigart to Cresslough road.

The castle is 5km from Creeslough on the Carrigart road and is clearly signposted. Admission is free and, if the gate is locked, a key is available from the nearby house.

Places to Stay

The 45-room *Hotel Port-na-Blagh* (☎ 074-36129) has singles/doubles for IR£55/90 in July and August. There are a couple of B&Bs in the Creeslough area, including *Hillcrest* (☎ 074-38145), 2km north toward Ards, charging from IR£16/28 and open April to September. *Creeslough Holiday Cottages* (☎ 074-38101) has a number of modern detached cottages that sleep seven adults and cost around IR£325 per week in July and August. Cottages for two can be as cheap as IR£100 in the low season.

Places to Eat

You'll do better in Dunfanaghy or Letterkenny than along the N56 that joins them, but the inexpensive *Red Roof Restaurant* is convenient at the southern approach to Creeslough. Creeslough has a couple of cafés, and if you're hostelling or camping, there are supermarkets at Creeslough, Dunfanaghy and Falcarragh. During the day *Lurgyvale Thatched Cottage* opens as a tea shop (see that section for details).

Letterkenny & Around

Letterkenny is Donegal's largest town and could be used as a base for exploring the surrounding areas as an alternative to staying in smaller Dunfanaghy in the north or Dungloe in the west.

LETTERKENNY

Letterkenny (Leitir Ceanainn) is the county town and has grown considerably since Derry, 34km to the north-east, was cut off from its hinterland by the partition of Ireland. There's not a great deal to detain a tourist here, although it makes a pleasant enough place to spend the night en route to or from Derry.

Information

Main St, said to be the longest high street in Ireland, runs from Dunnes Stores at one end to the courthouse at the other end and divides into Upper and Lower Main Sts. At the top of Upper Main St there is a junction with High Rd veering to the left and Port Rd going right and down to the bus station and the road out to Derry and Dublin.

The tourist office (☎ 074-21160), on the main Derry road outside town, is geared towards the motorist; you could walk there from the roundabout where the buses stop, but it wouldn't be a very enjoyable experience, and you'd probably find it closed outside the peak season. In the town itself, there's an excellent Chamber of Commerce visitors' centre (☎ 074-24866) with all manner of free literature and advice. They also have an inexpensive signposted walking tour booklet of the town that will help you focus on the highlights. The centre opens Monday to Friday 9 am to 5 pm and closes for lunch (1 to 2 pm) in winter.

Allied Irish Bank has a branch at 2 Port Rd. The post office is on Upper Main St almost opposite the Central Bar. Browse-A-While is a bookshop on Upper Main St with a decent map selection. They stock *Hill Walkers' Donegal* by David Herman (Shanksmore Press; IR£3.99). There's a rather glamorous Duds 'n' Suds laundrette on Pearse Rd east of the high street.

The telephone area code is ☎ 074.

Donegal County Museum

This small modern museum (☎ 24613) has a collection of local archaeological finds including some interesting Iron Age stone heads and early Christian material upstairs. Downstairs there are temporary displays, often on the local tweed-making and weaving industries, and some very telling photos about the realities of life in 19th century rural Ireland to counterbalance the rather rosy model on display upstairs. The museum is on High Rd, past the Manse Hostel, and opens Tuesday to Friday 11 am to 12.30 pm and 1 to 4.30 pm, and afternoons only on Saturday. Entrance is free.

Fishing

There are a number of salmon and trout rivers in the area surrounding Letterkenny as well as at various lakes. The Letterkenny Anglers Association opens to visitors and there are shops in town where membership and permits are available, including McCormick's Sports & Leisure (☎ 27833), 56 Upper Main St, and McGrath's newsagent, 50 Port Rd.

Other Activities

The Letterkenny Leisure Centre (☎ 25251) opposite the Manse Hostel has swimming for IR£2/1, family IR£6, including use of the sauna and steam room before 3 pm. A ticket valid for all the facilities in the evening costs IR£3.50/2.50.

There's 10-pin bowling, pool tables and a pitch & putt at Letterkenny Bowling Centre (☎ 26000), north of the tourist office on the road to Rathmelton.

Special Events

A four-day international festival of music and dance (☎ 27856 for information) is held at the end of August. It features a variety of music from Celtic rock to folk and jazz and includes a crafts day, street music and competitions.

Places to Stay

Manse Hostel (☎ 25238), which belongs to the IHH and the IHO, is on High Rd at the top of Upper Main St with beds for IR£6 and a half-dozen private rooms for IR£7. Family rooms are also available. It's friendly, with lots of info on what to see and do locally, and opens all year. The IHO *Rosemount Hostel* (☎ 26284), at 3 Rosemount Terrace just off Upper Main St, has beds for IR£5.50 and opens June to October. There's also a third (but less-than-salubrious) *hostel* (☎ 25315/26288) at 24 Port Rd. It has dorm beds for IR£5.75, and singles/doubles/triples for IR£8/14/19.50.

For B&B you could try *Covehill House* (☎ 21038) set back from Port Rd and therefore likely to be fairly quiet. Singles/doubles cost £19/28. Near the Manse Hostel, *Carmel's* (☎ 21332) above a newsagent's on High Rd is better than it looks from the outside and has B&B for IR£13 per person. In the centre of town the 27-room *Gallagher's Hotel* (☎ 22066), 110 Upper Main St, charges IR£30/50. If you arrive late and everything's full, the modern *Hotel Clanree* (☎ 24369) is on the outskirts as you approach from Derry and charges the same as Gallagher's.

Places to Eat

Four Lanterns has standard fast food next to McGrath's newsagent on Port Rd. The *Dolphin*, 58 Upper Main St, does fish & chips.

The best place for a pizza or pasta is *Pat's Pizza* in Market Square; *Pat's Too* midway along Main St sells part-cooked pizzas to take away as well as kebabs and sandwiches. Close to Pat's Too is the *Central Bar*, which does pub food. *Bakersville* in Church St is pleasant enough for coffee and snacks, or there's the *Quiet Moment* tearoom in Upper Main St for baps and salads. *Yellow Pepper*, also on Main St, opens for breakfast (IR£3) and has excellent sandwiches from IR£3.50. Inside the new Courtyard Shopping Centre in Main St, opposite Market Square, there's a good coffee shop, and *Galfee's Restaurant* in the basement has a few tables outside looking onto a mural so you can appreciate the Donegal scenery even when it's raining outside.

DONEGAL

New Music from Old Roots

The true origins of traditional Irish music are lost in the proverbial mists of time. However, clues to its humble origins lie in the very instruments themselves. The *bodhrán*, the simple drum that resembles nothing as much as a giant cymbal, for example, was originally probably shaken to separate the corn from the chaff, while the small knuckle-ended 'beater' was banged against it to frighten wrens away from the fields.

Celtic traditional music may have found its way overland from Asia and India some 2000 years ago. The Irish harp may even have been developed in Egypt.

Until around 1700, this harp was the most important instrument in Irish music, although it was a smaller version than the one played today. It was wooden-framed and had wire strings that were sounded with the fingernails rather than the fingertips. Just as the great painters of the Renaissance in Italy depended on the patronage of wealthy

merchants, so the harpists found support and patronage among Ireland's Gaelic chieftains. Consequently, music suffered a serious setback in 1607 when the episode known as the Flight of the Earls saw the chieftains flee to the continent, leaving the harpists to turn to teaching music to support themselves. The most famous of these itinerant musicians was Turlough O'Carolan, some of whose tunes are still played today.

Traditionally, music was performed as a background to dancing, so the 17th-century Penal Laws did nothing to help by banning all expressions of traditional culture, including dancing. Music was forced underground, which goes some way towards explaining the homely feel of much Irish music today. Until the late 18th century, Irish music was largely unwritten. In 1762, a book of 49 airs was published in Dublin. Then in 1792 Edward Bunting attended a Belfast harp festival and recorded the tunes he heard. His manuscripts are still housed in the library of Queen's University in Belfast.

In 1847 the Potato Famine dealt traditional music another blow as musicians either died or emigrated in search of a better life. However, within the Irish diaspora the traditions lived on. To the standard repertoire of songs new themes were added, as musicians sang nostalgically of the homeland and celebrated their new lives. Piano backing was added to some tunes while others were speeded up.

Eventually the tide turned. Recordings of the music being made in America in the 1920s travelled back across the Atlantic and sparked renewed interest in what had been lost. Copying the Irish-Americans, musicians at home also began to experiment by adding new instruments to the traditional line-up of fiddle, whistle, pipes and drum.

In the 1960s, Seán O'Riada (1931-71) of Cork set up Ceoltóirí Chualann, a band featuring a fiddle, flute, accordion, bodhrán and uilleann pipes, and began to perform music to listen to rather than dance to. When his band performed at the Gaiety Theatre in Dublin, they gave a whole new credibility to traditional music. Members of the band went on to form the Chieftains, who played an important role in introducing Irish music to an international audience. Others who followed on and helped develop 'traditional' music into its current forms included Planxty, the Bothy Band (who introduced the bazooki), Moving Hearts and the Horslips, who added a very 1970s rock twist. ■

For dinner, *Gallagher's Hotel* (☎ 22066) in Upper Main St has a set menu for IR£12.95; it serves bar food at the pub (from IR£3) till 9 pm. *Taj Mahal* (☎ 27554) in Main St does standard Indian and Pakistani food with mains from IR£6.

Entertainment

One of the better pubs for music is the *Central Bar* close to Pat's Too on Main St; the emerald-green *Cottage Bar* on Upper Main St has music sessions on Thursday night. The *Pulse* is a big disco in the Port Centre on Port Rd; the *Downtown Pub* on Upper Main St hosts a disco on some weekends.

There's a four-screen cinema (☎ 21976) in Port Rd.

Getting There & Away

Letterkenny is a major bus transport hub for north-west Ireland. The bus station (☎ 22863) is by the roundabout down Port Rd east of the centre where the road to Derry begins.

Bus Éireann (☎ 21309) runs an express service from Dublin four times a day Monday to Saturday (three on Sunday) to Letterkenny via Omagh and Monaghan. The Derry-Galway bus stops at Letterkenny three times a day Monday to Saturday (twice on Sunday) before travelling on to Donegal, Bundoran, Sligo, Knock and Galway. The Derry-Cork express goes via Letterkenny, Sligo, Galway and Limerick. It runs twice a day and once on Sunday. There's also a daily service from Derry to Westport via Donegal, Sligo and Ballina.

Anthony McGinley (☎ 48167) has a daily service from Letterkenny to Dublin, with an extra two buses on Friday. Derry-based Lough Swilly (☎ 29400) runs a regular service from Derry to Dungloe, via Letterkenny and Dunfanaghy, as well as a more direct route between Letterkenny and Derry.

The John McGinley bus (☎ 35201) runs daily from Annagry to Dublin through Letterkenny and Monaghan. There's a Feda O'Donnell bus (☎ 075-48114 in Donegal) from Crolly to Galway through Letterkenny. It goes on to Donegal, Bundoran, Sligo and Galway.

McGeehan's Coaches (☎ 075-46150) runs a Letterkenny-Glencolumbcille service from Monday to Saturday. Doherty's Travel (☎ 075-21105) has a coach to Glasgow that leaves from outside Dunnes store; it's a daily service in July and August.

Getting Around

You can order a taxi on ☎ 27400 or ☎ 27000. In summer, bikes can be hired from Church Street Cycles (☎ 25041), 11 Church St.

COLMCILLE HERITAGE CENTRE

Colmcille – or Columba – was born in Gartan, 17km north-west of Letterkenny, and the heritage centre (☎ 074-37306) is devoted to his life and times, with a lavish display on the production of illuminated manuscripts.

Gartan clay is associated with the birth of Colmcille. The clay is only found on a townland belonging to the O'Friel family, whose oldest son is the only one allowed to dig it up. The story is that Colmcille's mother, on the run from pagans, haemorrhaged during childbirth and her blood changed the soil's colour from brown to pure white. Ever since, the clay has been regarded as a charm. Ask nicely and the staff may produce some from under the counter.

The centre opens over Easter and early May to late September, 10.30 am to 6.30 pm and Sunday from 1 to 6.30 pm. The charge is IR£1.50/50p.

On the way to the heritage centre you'll also see signs to the ruins of Colmcille's Abbey and to the site of the saint's birthplace, marked by a cross erected by Cornelia Adair in 1911.

Getting There & Away

Leave Letterkenny on the R250 road to Glenties and Ardara and a few km out of town turn right on the R251 to the village of Churchill. Alternatively, from Kilmacrennan on the N56 turn west and follow the signs.

GLEBE HOUSE & GALLERY

The early 19th century Glebe House was once a rectory and then a hotel. It was bought by the artist Derek Hill in 1953 for IR£1000. A fascinating guided tour of the house takes about 40 minutes.

Derek Hill was born in England in 1916 and worked in Germany before travelling to Russia. He visited Armenia with the intrepid explorer Freya Stark and became interested in Islamic art. The kitchen is done up in a wonderfully folksy style and is full of paintings by the Tory Island artists, including a bird's-eye view of West Town by James Dixon (see the Tory Island section). There's some original William Morris wallpaper in several rooms. Don't miss the unusual bathroom with the forward-flushing loo.

Glebe House would be worth visiting for

DONEGAL

its works of art alone. Landseer, Pasmore, Hokusai, Picasso, Augustus John, Jack B Yeats and Kokoschka are all represented. The gardens are also wonderful.

The house (☎ 074-37071) opens over Easter and mid-May to September, 11 am to 6.30 pm daily except Friday. The charge is IR£2/1, family IR£5. It's on the shore of Lough Gartan close to the Colmcille Heritage Centre.

DOON WELL & ROCK

During penal times it was believed that wells had curative properties, and some people still believe this to be the case at Doon Well, judging from the bits of cloth left hanging on the nearby bushes. There are good views from the top of the rock, which is where the O'Donnell kings were inaugurated.

Getting There & Away

There are a number ways of reaching the well. The most straightforward route is to take the signposted turn-off from the N56 just north of Kilmacrennan. Doonwell is 1.5km north of Kilmacrennan.

GARTAN OUTDOOR EDUCATION CENTRE

The centre, 18km north-west of Letterkenny, is set in its own 35-hectare estate and conducts a variety of courses throughout the summer, such as rock climbing, sea canoeing, windsurfing and hill climbing. Courses are run for both adults and children and the full details are available from the Gartan Outdoor Education Centre (☎ 074-37032), Churchill, Letterkenny, County Donegal. Including hostel accommodation, a weekend multi-skill course for adults costs about IR£60, a five-day course about IR£155.

NEWMILLS VISITORS' CENTRE

In the village of Newmills, 6km north-west of Letterkenny just off the N56 between Creeslough and Kilmacrennan, an old flax and corn mill has been restored and opened to the public with a visitors' centre explaining the role of these products and how they were produced. The centre (☎ 074-25115) is

relatively new, and there are plans for a riverside walk to a two-room 19th century scutcher's cottage and a village forge. The waterwheels attached to the mill will also start turning again. The mills are open daily mid-June to mid-September, 10 am to 6.30 pm (last tour 5.45 pm). Admission is IR£2/1, family tickets IR£5.

LURGYVALE THATCHED COTTAGE

In a flagstone-floored cottage (☎ 074-39216) filled with rural artefacts, staff at this early 19th century cottage dispense tea and scones with home-made jam in the kitchen for under IR£2. On Thursday evening from 8.30 pm, traditional music sessions are held with dancing and singing. During the summer there are demonstrations of traditional crafts on the first Sunday of the month.

Getting There & Away

The cottage is next to the road bridge on the N56 in the village of Kilmacrennan, easily spotted because of the large numbers of old farming implements scattered about.

LIFFORD

About 22km south of Letterkenny, along the N14, is the small town of Lifford (Leifear). It was once the judicial capital of County Donegal, a position now held by Letterkenny.

Lifford Old Courthouse Visitors' Centre

This fine 17th century courthouse has been given a new lease of life as a heritage centre (☎ 074-41733), looking at both the historic role of Donegal's Gaelic chieftains and at some of the cases tried in the court and their verdicts.

For those who can't tell their O'Neills from their O'Donnells, some of the information provided in the Clans Room can be pretty heavy going. Descend into the court room, though, and the stories of 'Napper' Tandy, 'Half-hanged' McNaughten and other 'criminals' are riveting, and it's amazing how often they ended up being transported to Australia!

Downstairs again and you end up in the

chilly cells where there are models of some of the prisoners you've already heard about. Now you hear their side of the story. Down here there's also a small café serving soup, sandwiches and teas. The courthouse opens Easter to October, Monday to Saturday 10 am to 6 pm, and Sunday noon to 6 pm. Admission costs IR£2.50/1.

Cavanacor House
At Rossgier, 3km north of Lifford off the N14, Cavanacor House (☎ 074-41143) is an attractive 18th century building, once inhabited by Magdalen Tasker, who was the great-great-great-grandmother of James Knox Polk, 11th president of the USA from 1845 to 1849. King James II is said to have dined beneath a sycamore in the front garden during the Siege of Derry in 1689. Three rooms in the house are now open to visitors, although the gallery at the back housing the paintings and sculptures created by its current owners is probably more interesting.

Cavanacor opens from Easter to September, Tuesday to Saturday noon to 6 pm, and Sunday 2 to 6 pm. Admission is IR£2/1.

Places to Stay
B&B is available in Sligo Rd at *Rossborough House* (☎ 074-41132), open March to October and charging IR£21/32, and *Haw Lodge* (☎ 074-41397), open the same months and costing IR£19/28. Both are in Sligo Rd.

North-Eastern Donegal

ROSGUILL PENINSULA
From Carrigart it's a 15km journey around this small peninsula along a road marked Atlantic Drive. Carrigart itself has a lovely beach, which is relatively deserted because the campsite at Downings draws the crowds to the other end. The best beach for swimming is Trá na Rossan, and An Óige's hostel nearby is an added attraction. On no account should you go swimming in Boveeghter Bay or Mulroy Bay; both have had drownings in the recent past.

There are no tourist attractions to detract from the scenery on the peninsula, but there is plenty of social life at night in the Downings pubs, which are often packed with holidaymakers from the North staying at the campsite.

Places to Stay
Casey's Caravan Park (☎ 074-55376), open April to September, has limited camping space so it's best to ring first and check. A family tent is IR£10 a night, and a small tent IR£8.

An Óige's *Trá na Rosann Hostel* (☎ 074-55374), east of the beach, opens Easter to September and costs IR£4/4.50 or IR£5/6 for juniors/seniors, depending on the season. It's 6km from Downings and hitching is the best bet if you're without wheels.

Accommodation at the oddly designed 48-room *Hol-Tel Carrigart* (☎ 074-55114) costs IR£42 per person, and there's an indoor pool. Nearby in Dunmore, *Hill House* (☎ 074-55221) has B&B from IR£17.50/29.

There's a little more choice in Downings: *Baymont* (☎ 074-55395) and *An Crosóg* (☎ 074-55498) both do B&B for about IR£15 a head. The 20-room *Beach Hotel* (☎ 074-55303) costs from IR£18/32.

Places to Eat
Carrigart itself is the best bet for food. The *North Star* pub has bar food, and *Weavers Restaurant & Wine Bar* has meals for around IR£5.

Getting There & Away
There's a local bus between Carrigart and Downings, but it's of limited use for visitors from elsewhere. You really do need your own transport for this area.

FANAD HEAD PENINSULA
Western Side
On the western side of the Fanad Peninsula, Carrowkeel (Kerrykeel on some maps) has an attractive location overlooking Mulroy Bay and also nearby is the 19th century

DONEGAL

Knockalla Fort, built to warn of any approaching French ships. There's also the **Kildooney More portal tomb** to visit, but that's about it. The small villages of Milford and Rosnakill have little to offer visitors, and there are no particularly good beaches.

Getting There & Away The Lough Swilly bus (☎ 074-29400 in Letterkenny) leaves Letterkenny at 10.05 am and 6.05 pm and reaches Milford an hour later. From Milford it takes a further 10 minutes to Carrowkeel and 35 minutes to Portsalon, handy for the campsite.

Eastern Side

The eastern side of the Fanad Peninsula is far more interesting, and both Rathmelton (Ramelton on some maps) and Rathmullan make good bases for a quiet break. Accommodation is relatively limited so it would be wise to book ahead.

Rathmelton

The first town you come to is pretty Rathmelton (Ráth Mealtain), founded in the early 17th century by William Stewart and boasting some fine Georgian houses and stone warehouses. When the railway was routed to Letterkenny instead of Rathmelton, a hush descended on the town. Rathmelton was the location for *The Hanging Gale*, the 1995 TV series set during the Famine. You'll see signposts indicating various location sites along the R245 from Letterkenny.

In Back Lane the old Meeting House dating from around 1680 now houses the **Donegal Ancestry Family Research Centre** (☎ 074-51266), open weekdays 9 am to 4 pm (to 3 pm on Friday). The ruined **Tullyaughnish Church** is also worth a visit because of the Romanesque carvings in the east wall, which were taken from a far older church on nearby Aughnish Island. Shops in the main square sell the useful *Rathmelton: An Illustrated Guide to the Town* for around IR£2.

Places to Stay & Eat At the quiet northern end of Rathmelton is *Crammond House* (☎ 074-51055), where singles/doubles from IR£19/28 come with a warm welcome. Near the town centre, *Clooney House* (☎ 074-51125) charges IR£15 per person.

A couple of km out of Letterkenny, before reaching Rathmelton, *Carolina House Restaurant* (☎ 074-22480) is a smart establishment specialising in fish. It only opens during the evenings, Tuesday to Saturday, and dinner is in the IR£20 bracket.

In Rathmelton itself *Fish House* is attractively placed in an old stone building by the river and serves tea and light meals 10 am to 7 pm. For something more substantial *Mirabeau Steak House* (☎ 074-51138) cooks gigantic steaks with home-made sauces. The fish dishes are good but vegetarians would need to put in a special order.

Getting There & Away There are Lough Swilly buses (☎ 074-29400) leaving Letterkenny at 10.05 am and 4.20 and 6.05 pm, taking 25 minutes to reach Rathmelton.

Rathmullan

Just like Rathmelton, Rathmullan (Ráth Maoláin) feels as if it has been bypassed by the modern age, although in the 16th and 17th centuries it was the scene of momentous events. In 1587, Hugh O'Donnell, the 15-year-old heir to the powerful O'Donnell clan, was tricked into boarding a ship at Rathmullan and taken to Dublin as prisoner. He escaped four years later on Christmas Eve and, after unsuccessful attempts at revenge, died in Spain, aged only 30.

In 1607, despairing of fighting the English, Hugh O'Neill, the earl of Tyrone, and Rory O'Donnell, the earl of Tyrconnel, boarded a ship in Rathmullan harbour and left Ireland for good. This decisive act, known as the Flight of the Earls, marked the effective end of Gaelic Ireland. In the aftermath of the earls' departure, large-scale confiscation of their estates took place, preparing for the plantation of Ulster with settlers from Scotland and England.

Rathmullan Heritage Centre This small, rather wordy centre (☎ 074-58229) focuses on the Flight of the Earls and will mainly appeal to those with a deep interest in Irish history. It's housed in an early 19th century fort built by the British fearing Napoleon's intentions and opens 10 am to 6 pm (noon to 6.30 pm on Sunday) Easter to September. Admission costs IR£2/1. In lieu of a tourist office, the heritage centre can help with enquiries about local accommodation, sights in the surrounding area etc.

The sandy area near the pier outside the centre is the only clean part of the town's beach, but there's a strong smell of fish from the quayside warehouse.

Rathmullan Priory This Carmelite friary was founded around 1508 by the Mac-Sweeneys, and it was still in use in 1595 when an English commander named George Bingham raided the place and took off with the communion plate and priestly vestments. The fact that it looks so well preserved is due to Bishop Knox's renovation in 1618; he wanted to use it as his own residence. The earls left Ireland forever in 1607 from just outside the priory.

Places to Stay The IHO *Bunnaton Hostel* (☎ 074-50122) in Glenvar, north-west of Rathmullan, has dorm beds for IR£6 and three private rooms for IR£7.50 to IR£8.50 per person. It opens all year.

The *Water's Edge Inn* (☎ 074-58182) does B&B for IR£25 per person. It's just south of town and most of the rooms have fine views of Lough Swilly. The *Coachman's Inn* (☎ 074-58178) next to the Pier Hotel charges from IR£14 per person.

Rathmullan has three hotels, all quite different in appearance and style. The 10-room *Pier Hotel* (☎ 074-58178), originally a 19th century coaching inn, charges from IR£25/40 and is very much a family establishment. A couple of km north of town, *Rathmullan House* (☎ 074-58188) is a swanky 20-room country house with its own indoor heated swimming pool and sauna. Singles/doubles are IR£82.50/125. The 15-room *Fort Royal* (☎ 074-58100) has its own private beach and

organises sporting activities; singles/doubles are from IR£63/87.

Places to Eat *Water's Edge Inn*, just south of town, does bar food as well as full à la carte meals with lovely lake views. The *Beachcomber Pub* just up from the Pier Hotel does bar food. Dinner at the three hotels costs IR£15 at the *Pier Hotel*, IR£22.50 at *Rathmullan House*, and IR£24 at the *Fort Royal*.

Getting There & Away The Lough Swilly bus from Letterkenny via Rathmelton arrives in Rathmullan at 10.45 am and 6.45 pm and departs straight away for Milford, Carrowkeel and Portsalon (morning bus only).

Portsalon & Fanad Head

Portsalon (Port an tSalainn), once a popular holiday resort with Northern Irish, has little to offer except a long stretch of golden sand that is safe for swimming. It's another 8km to Fanad Head, which also has little to detain the traveller other than the scenic drive to get there.

INISHOWEN PENINSULA

The Inishowen Peninsula, with Lough Foyle to the east and Lough Swilly to the west, reaches out into the Atlantic and at Ireland's northernmost point: Malin Head. The landscape is typically Donegal: rugged, desolate and mountainous. Ancient sites abound, but there are also some wonderful beaches and plenty of places where travellers can go off alone. Tourist offices in Donegal, Letterkenny or Derry have free leaflets about walks for the Inishowen (Inis Eoghain) area, complete with maps.

The route below follows the road out of Derry up the coast of Lough Foyle to Moville and then north-west to Malin Head before travelling down the western side down to Buncrana. If coming from Donegal the peninsula could be approached from the Lough Swilly side by turning off for Buncrana on the N13 road from Letterkenny to Derry. Leaving from Derry, though, the first village in the Republic is Muff. A scenic drive, the

DONEG

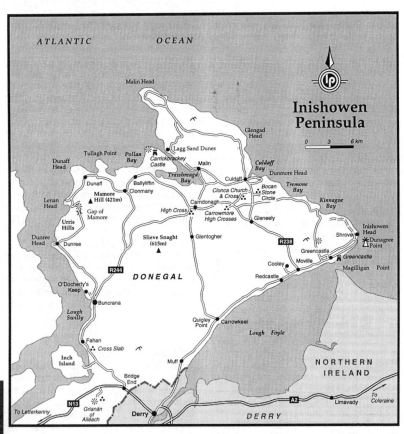

ATLANTIC OCEAN

Inishowen Peninsula

0   3   6 km

DONEGAL

'Inis Eoghain 100', is clearly signposted round the peninsula.

Muff to Moville

The tiny village of Muff (Mugh) is only 8km from Derry. At night the pubs have their fair share of Northerners, and north-east of Muff along the coast there are larger pubs catering to the same market.

Places to Stay The IHH *Muff Independent Hostel* (☎ 077-84188), charging IR£6 a night for a bed and IR£7.50 per person in a private room, is in the village at the northern

end just before the Renault garage; turn left if you're coming from Derry. The hostel, open March to September, is up this narrow road on the left. Camping is possible, but it's best to phone ahead. *Mrs Reddin* (☎ 077-84031), next to the post office on Main St, runs the only B&B in the village. Renovated rooms cost only IR£14 a head.

Beyond Muff and just before Moville there is a hotel and a bunch of B&Bs at Redcastle. Next to the village post office, *Fernbank* (☎ 077-83032) does B&B from IR£14. Overlooking Lough Foyle, the lovely 31-room *Redcastle Country Hotel* (☎ 077-

82073) has all the facilities of a big hotel, including a nine-hole golf course and the Bailey Gothic Nightclub. Singles/ doubles cost IR£45/60 or IR£60/90, depending on the season.

Places to Eat There are a few pubs serving sandwiches and the *Village Café* does takeaways, but no restaurants. More substantial meals are available at the *Redcastle Country Hotel* farther up the coast before Moville; their tourist menu has three-course meals from IR£9, served 11 am to 6.30 pm. After 7 pm, dinners starts at IR£14.95. There are a couple of cafés at scenic Quigley Point, a few km out of Muff and also on the coast road.

Getting There & Away Lough Swilly (☎ 01504-262017 in Derry, ☎ 074-29400 in Letterkenny) runs up to nine buses a day from Derry on the Cardonagh service that stops at Muff, with almost as many buses to Shrove that also pass through Muff. There's no Sunday service on either route. Worth considering is Lough Swilly's eight-day unlimited travel pass for IR£18/12/9 for adults/students/children.

Moville

Now a sleepy seaside town, Moville (Bun an Phoball) was once a busy port where emigrants set sail for America. The coastal walkway from Moville to Greencastle takes in the stretch of coast where the steamers used to moor. The Foyle Oyster Festival is held in late September here. For information ring ☎ 077-82042.

Cooley Cross & Skull House

By the gate of the Cooley gravehouse is a 3m high cross, unusual because of the ringhole in its head through which the hands of negotiating parties are said to have clasped to seal an agreement. (We wonder how they could reach so high ...) In the graveyard itself there is a small building known as the Skull House, which still contains some old bones. It may be associated with St Finian, the monk who accused Colmcille of plagiarising one of his

manuscripts in the 6th century. He lived in a monastery here that was founded by St Patrick and survived into the 12th century.

Approaching Moville from the south, look out for a turning on the left (if you pass a church, you've gone too far) which has a sign on the corner for the Cooley Pitch & Putt. The graveyard is just over 1km up this road on the right.

Places to Stay The IHH *Moville Holiday Hostel* (☎ 077-82378), on Malin Rd, charges IR£6 for a dorm bed, IR£10 per person in a private room. There are also a few B&Bs in and around Moville. *Gulladuff House* (☎ 077-82378), on Malin Rd, charges from IR£15/27 while *Barron's Café* (☎ 077-82472) in town has beds from IR£12. On the road out of town, *Iona House* (☎ 077-82173) is a small homely place charging IR£30 for doubles. The large *McNamara's Hotel* (☎ 077-82010), with 51 rooms, charges IR£36/68 in high season.

Places to Eat *Barron's Café* and *McNamara's Hotel* are the best bets; dinner at the latter costs IR£16. The *Point* also serves food until 11 pm (10 pm on Sunday).

If you have your own transport, nearby Greencastle is worth the trip. *Greencastle Fort* (☎ 077-81279) is inside a Napoleonic fort, and you can dine either in the officers' mess bar (from IR£16) or the soldiers' canteen.

Greencastle

In 1305 the castle was built by Richard de Burgo, known as the Red Earl because of his florid complexion. The Green Castle functioned as a supply base for English armies in Scotland and for this reason was attacked by the Scots under Robert Bruce in the 1320s. In 1555 the castle was demolished, and little of it survives.

Five Lough Swilly buses travel daily between Derry and Shrove, passing through Greencastle, but there is no Sunday service.

Inishowen Head

A right turn outside Greencastle leads to

Shrove; a sign indicating Inishowen Head is 1km to the left. It's possible to drive or cycle part of the way, but it's also an easy walk to the headland from where views take in the Antrim coast as far as the Giant's Causeway on a clear day. A more demanding walk continues to the sandy beach of Kinnagoe Bay. At Shrove, where the road left goes to the headland, a right turn goes to Dunagree Point and back to Greencastle, but this loop has little to recommend itself.

Carndonagh

Information Inishowen Tourism (☎ 077-74933), south-west of the main square at the top of Bridge St, opens Monday to Friday 9.30 am to 5.30 pm, and daily mid-June to September. They also sell fishing licences for all of Donegal. There are two banks on the main square; the post office is on Bridge St.

The telephone code is ☎ 077.

Things to See On Bridge St in a small church by the post office, a collection of local folk items are on display in the **Inishowen Heritage Centre & Folk Museum**. It only opens in July and August, Monday to Saturday 2 to 4 pm.

At the Buncrana end of Carndonagh, the 8th century **Carndonagh High Cross** has been re-erected against the wall of an Anglican church. Next to the cross are two small pillars, one said to show a man with a sword and shield, possibly Goliath, next to David and his harp. In the graveyard there is a pillar with a carved marigold on a stem. On the other side of the stone there's a Crucifixion scene.

Places to Stay & Eat *Radharc na Coille* (☎ 74471) at Teirnaleague, not far from Carndonagh High Cross, costs IR£21/30 for B&B.

In the main square there's *Trawbreaga Bay House* for main meals, but for something lighter, head down Malin St to the *Corncrake Restaurant* (☎ 74534), which opens 10 am to 5 pm on weekdays (later in summer) and until 9 pm at weekends. Here you can tuck

into dishes like mussels in garlic or sea trout for lunch (from IR£4) and dinner (from IR£12). The *Quiet Lady* opposite has good pub lunches.

If you're off to Malin Head for the day or going on to the campsite at Clonmany, stock up with victuals at the Centra supermarket in Malin Rd.

Getting There & Away A Lough Swilly bus leaves Buncrana for Carndonagh on weekdays at 8.40 am, on Monday and Thursday at 1 and 5.45 pm and on Friday at 1.45 and 6.15 pm. On Saturday the buses go at 12.15, 2.15 and 6.15 pm. On weekdays they return from Carndonagh at 7.25 and 10 am and 4 pm. They also run a bus between Derry and Malin Head via Carndonagh three times a week.

North West Busways (☎ 82619) operates a service between Letterkenny and Moville via Carndonagh and Buncrana.

Around Carndonagh

There are several ancient sites in the area that can be visited from the main Moville-Carndonagh road (R238).

Clonca Church & Cross The carved lintel over the door of this 17th century building is thought to come from an earlier church. In the north-east corner, the rather interesting tombstone was erected by one Magnus MacOrristin and has a sword and hurling stick carved on it. The remains of the cross show the Miracle of the Loaves and Fishes on the east face and geometric designs on the sides.

Look for the turn-off to Culdaff, on the right if coming from Moville, on the left after about 6km if coming from Carndonagh. The Clonca Church and Cross are 1.5km on the right behind a couple of farm buildings.

Bocan Stone Circle There are better stone circles in Ireland than this one, which has only a few of some 30 original stones left, but the surrounding views help to conjure up the kind of significance the place must have held some 3000 years ago.

From Clonca Church, continue along the road until a T-junction is reached with a modern church and a cemetery facing you. Turn right here and after about half a km turn left (no sign). The stone circle is inside the first heather-covered field on the left.

Carrowmore High Crosses Like the Bocan Stone Circle, these high crosses may prove a little disappointing to some. One is basically a decorated slab showing Christ and an angel, while on the other side of the road there is a taller cross with stumpy arms.

From Bocan Stone Circle and Clonca Church, retrace the route back to the main Carndonagh-Moville road and turn left and then almost immediately right. The sign to the crosses will be pointing in the wrong direction; ignore it.

Malin Head
At the top of the Inishowen Peninsula is Malin Head, the northernmost point of Ireland and a familiar name to listeners of radio weather forecasts throughout the island. The tower on the cliffs was built in 1805 by the British admiralty and later used as a Lloyds signal station. The huts were used by the Irish army in WWII as lookout posts.

Above Ballyhillion Beach nearby, the *Cottage* serves tea and food all week, June to September.

The pretty plantation village of Malin is centred round a triangular green. One of the Inishowen walk leaflets outlines an interesting circular route from the village green that takes in a local hill with terrific views as well as Lagg Presbyterian Church, which is the oldest church still in use on the peninsula. Children will love the massive sand dunes by the church.

Places to Stay There are two IHO hostels at Malin Head: the *Malin Head Hostel* (☎ 077-70309), open March to October, and the larger *Sandrock Holiday Hostel* (☎ 077-70289), open all year. Both charge IR£6.50 for a dormitory bed, and there are no private rooms.

There's one small hotel, the 12-room *Malin* (☎ 077-70645), in the village. Singles/doubles are from IR£25/46 in high season. B&B at *High View* (☎ 077-70283) costs IR£21/32. At Malin Head there are also a few B&Bs, including Mrs Doyle's *Barraicin* (☎ 077-70184) charging from IR£18/21. *McGrory's* (☎ 077-79104) in Culdaff is a popular music pub with B&B from IR£15 per person.

Getting There & Away The best way to approach Malin Head is by the R238/242 from Carndonagh, rather than up the eastern side from Culdaff. Lough Swilly runs a bus Monday, Wednesday and Friday at 11 am between Derry and Malin Head via Carndonagh; on the same days a bus leaves Carndonagh at 3 pm for Malin Head. There are three buses from Derry to Malin Head on Saturday.

Ballyliffin & Clonmany
The small resort of Ballyliffin (Baile Lifin) attracts more Irish than overseas visitors. There's plenty of accommodation in the area.

About 1km north of Ballyliffin is the lovely expanse of Pollan Bay Beach; unfortunately, it's not safe for swimming. A walk to the north brings you to the ruins of Carrickbrackey Castle (also spelt Carrickabraghy), dating from the 16th century. To reach the beach, turn down the road in Ballyliffin by the thatched cottage and the Atlantic ballroom. There's one sign on the road, but it's only visible from the Clonmany side.

The other beach is at Tullagh Bay, immediately behind the campsite. It's great for an exhilarating walk, but the current can be strong and swimming is not recommended when the tide is going out. Someone drowned here in 1992.

Places to Stay & Eat *Tullagh Bay Camping & Caravan Park* (☎ 077-76289) is near the bear at Tullagh Bay. There are legions of B&Bs on the 2km stretch of road between Ballyliffin and Clonmany, including *Ard Doon* (☎ 077-76156), open all year, and

Swilly View (☎ 077-76137), open May to September. Both charge IR£20/32.The two hotels here are the 13-room *Ballyliffin* (☎ 077-76101), with singles/doubles for IR£24/40, and the 12-room *Strand*, which costs IR£35/60 in high season.

The *Strand Hotel* does lunch for about IR£8 as well as bar food, while in the evening, dinner costs from IR£14. The *Ballyliffin Hotel* also does pub food and dinner from IR£13.

Entertainment Most of the pubs and hotels have music sessions throughout the summer. In Clonmany, *McFeeley's* and the *Square Bar* are popular pubs and *Mackey's Tavern*, near the campsite, has lively music sessions at the weekend.

Getting There & Away A Lough Swilly bus leaves Buncrana for Carndonagh on weekdays at 8.40 am, on Monday and Thursday at 1 and 5.45 pm, and on Friday at 1.45 and 6.15 pm. On Saturday the buses go at 12.15, 2.15 and 6.15 pm. On weekdays they return from Carndonagh at 7.25 and 10 am and 4 pm, arriving in Clonmany 20 minutes later.

Clonmany to Buncrana

There are two routes from Clonmany to Buncrana: the scenic coastal road via the Gap of Mamore and Dunree Head, or the speedier inland road (R238). The Gap of Mamore (262m) descends dramatically between Mamore Hill and the Urris Hills into a valley where the road follows the River Owenerk most of the way to Dunree.

The main reason to pause in Dunree would be to visit the interesting **Fort Dunree Military Museum**. In 1798 Wolfe Tone, with the help of the French, planned to arrive at Lough Swilly and march on Derry. The British constructed six forts to guard the lough and the museum tells the whole story. The museum (☎ 074-24613) opens June to September, Monday to Saturday 10 am to 6 pm, and noon to 6 pm Sunday. The charge is IR£2/1, and there's a small café at the site. Fulmars nest on the rocks below the fort, so close you can see them easily.

Buncrana

After Bundoran this must be the most popular resort in Donegal for holidaymakers from Derry and elsewhere in the North, but unlike Bundoran it contrives to suggest there is life beyond tourism. In fact, Fruit of the Loom has two knitting mills here, something for which Buncrana (Bun Cranncha) is very proud. The resort has a long sandy beach that is safe for swimming, all the pubs you could hope for, and several places of interest to while away your spare hours.

Information Despite the huge signs trumpeting the tourist information office (☎ 077-62600) in Swilly Terrace opposite the leisure centre as you come in from Letterkenny, you'll be lucky to find it open outside July and August.

Ulster Bank has a branch on Upper Main St, where you'll also find the post office. The laundrette on Maginn St opens Monday to Saturday 8.30 am to 7 pm.

The telephone code is ☎ 077.

Tullyarvan Mill This community-run exhibition (☎ 61613), craft shop and café is well worth a visit. The exhibition is devoted to the restoration of the mill, local history, flora & fauna, and is attractively presented. The place is also worth checking out for its lively traditional music evenings that take place regularly throughout the summer.

The centre opens in summer Easter to September, 10 am to 6 pm Monday to Saturday, and noon to 6 pm on Sunday. Admission to the exhibition costs IR£1.50/75p.

To find the place, take the road out to Dunree and the mill is signposted on the right after the bridge.

O'Docherty's Keep At the north end of the seafront an early 18th century six-arched bridge leads to a tower house built by the O'Dochertys, the local chiefs, in the early 15th century. It was burned by the English and then rebuilt for their own use. The big house nearby was built in 1718 by John Vaughan, who also constructed the bridge.

Places to Stay There's no shortage of B&Bs around town, but they can fill up quickly during August. *Golan View* (☎ 62644) is close to the town centre and charges IR£20/32. *Kincora* (☎ 61174) in Cahir O'Doherty Ave charges from IR£18 single, IR£28 double.

The *White Strand* (☎ 61059) hotel has 12 rooms from IR£25 per person, and the *Lake of Shadows Hotel* (☎ 61902), in Grianán Park with 23 rooms, costs IR£28 per person in high season.

Places to Eat At the Clomany end of town, the *Roadside Café* lives up to its name, and a takeaway service is also available. The café at the *Tullyarvan Mill* serves cakes and drinks at sensible prices, but the best place in terms of choice is probably the *Ubiquitous Chip* (☎ 62530) at 47 Upper Main St, with main courses from IR£5.95.

Across the road at No 40 is *Wing Tai House*, a Chinese restaurant that serves chips with almost everything. The *Four Lanterns* next door dishes up fast food. Despite its old-fashioned name, *Dorothy's Kitchen* at 3 Church St, off Upper Main St, stays open dishing out burgers and kebabs until late. The *Town Clock*, 6 Upper Main St, does good lunch; a four-course one on Sunday costs IR£5.95.

Entertainment The main entertainment is found, unsurprisingly, in the town's many pubs strung out along the main street. The *Atlantic Bar* can be relied on for live music at weekends, as can *McCallion's* nearby on Market Square. Attached is the popular *Chino's Disco Bar*. For somewhere quiet and relaxing, try *Rodden's Crana Bar*. There's a one-screen cinema at the end of Upper Main St (with bingo on Friday night).

Getting There & Around From Buncrana, Lough Swilly (☎ 01504-262017 in Derry, 074-29400 in Letterkenny) runs a daily service to Derry and to Carndonagh. Taxis are available from the Roadside Café (☎ 61366) or Crana Taxis (☎ 62200).

South of Buncrana
Fahan Cross Slab A monastery was founded in Fahan by St Colmcille in the 6th century, and the stone slab in the graveyard beside the Anglican church has been dated to the century after. Each face is decorated with a cross, and the Greek inscription, which is not easily made out, is the only one known from this early Christian period.

Grianán of Aileach This impressive hilltop stone fort offers panoramic views of the surrounding countryside: Swilly and Foyle loughs, Inch Island and distant Derry. The walls are 4m thick and enclose an area 23m in diameter. The fort may be at least 2000 years old, but the site has pagan associations that go back much further. Between the 5th and 12th century it was the seat of the O'Neills before being demolished by Murtogh O'Brien, king of Munster. You might be wondering how a fort that was demolished 800 years ago could possibly look so complete. The answer is that between 1874 and 1878 an amateur archaeologist from Derry set about reconstructing the fort, and this is mostly what you see today.

The design of the attractive circular **church** at the foot of the hill was modelled on the fort. It's by Derry architect Liam McCormack and was built in 1965-67.

Grianán of Ailéach Visitors' Centre The 19th century church of Christchurch at Burt, at the bottom of the hill with the fort, houses a small display on the church's history up among the roof rafters. There's a life-size model of Muirchertach na gCochall Craicinn, a 10th century ancestor of the O'Neills and king of Aileach from 938 to 943. In 942 he went on an extended tour of Ireland, recorded in verse by Cormacan Eigean. There are also models of members of Christchurch's Victorian congregation and information about the local flora & fauna. The centre (☎ 077-68512) opens daily 10 am (from noon in winter) to 6 pm, and admission is IR£2/1.10.

Inch Island Few tourists make it to Inch

DONEGAL

Island, connected to the mainland by a causeway, but it does have an old **Napoleonic fort** open to the public and the **O'Dochartaigh Geneology Centre** (☎ 077-60488) open year round 9 am to 6 pm.

Places to Stay & Eat On Inch Island, *O'Doherty's* (☎ 077-60488) charges IR£15 per person for B&B and opens all year. It's to the right of the pier, just past the sign to the beach, and there is usually a US flag flying outside next to an Irish one.

The restaurant at the *Grianán of Aileách Visitors' Centre* has a lot of character – the bar counter is created out of a Boer war memorial slab, the reservations book resting in the pulpit etc – and opens 10 am to 10 pm in summer, noon to 10 pm in winter.

The restaurant offers plenty of choice, including several vegetarian options. If you don't fancy such formality, however, there are a few tables on the ground floor for coffee, open-face sandwiches and other snacks.

TOM SMALLMAN   TOM SMALLMAN

TOM SMALLMAN

Central North
Top Left: Lough Key, County Roscommon
Top Right: Saints Peter & Paul Cathedral and Market Square, Athlone, County
     Westmeath
Bottom: Main Street, Mullingar, County Westmeath

GUINNESS
FOR
STRENGTH

ní neart
go
Guinness

County Donegal
Top Left: Tree festooned with offerings beside Doon Well
Top Right: Bilingual Guinness ad
Bottom: Garden gnomes

Counties Meath & Louth

Heading north from Dublin along the coast takes you through counties Meath and Louth before crossing the border with Northern Ireland into County Down. This low, coastal landscape is the opposite of the hilly country to the south of the capital, rising only slightly inland to the plain known in folklore as Murtheimne, where many events mentioned in the Iron Age saga 'The Cattle Raid of Cooley' took place. The epic's dramatic climax occurred on Louth's beautiful Cooley Peninsula, and many places there owe their names to the legendary heroes and battles of that time.

The scenery in Meath and Louth is reminiscent of the English countryside: verdant, settled farmland with fine old farmhouses throughout. And here lie some of the most remarkable legacies of the ancient Irish people: the tombs of Newgrange and Loughcrew as well as the fine monasteries at Monasterboice, Mellifont and Kells, built by early Irish Christians.

County Meath

Meath (An Mhí), Dublin's immediate neighbour to the north and north-west, has long been one of Ireland's leading farming counties, a plain of extremely rich soil stretching north to the lakes of Cavan and Monaghan and west before running into the bleak Bog of Allen. Among the huge fields and old stands of trees are the solid houses of Meath's former settlers and today's prosperous farmers – many of whom are even wealthier since EU farming policies started offering subsidies for letting land lie fallow.

For a large county, Meath has surprisingly few major settlements. Navan, Trim and Kells are no more than medium-sized towns, while places like Ashbourne, Dunshaughlin and Dunboyne on the southern fringe have become commuter suburbs of Dublin. The

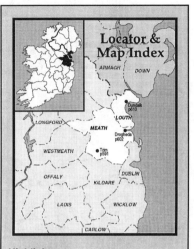

Highlights

- Explore the prehistoric remains at Newgrange and Knowth
- Track the remains of medieval Trim
- Climb the Hill of Tara
- Visit Mellifont Abby and Monasterboice
- Circumnavigate the Cooley Peninsula
- Eat oysters in Carlingford

county's principal attractions are its ancient sites, and the isolated hills of Tara and Slane have immense historical significance. Also be sure to visit Butterstream Gardens in Trim which are some of the finest in Ireland.

HISTORY

Meath's rich soil, laid down during the last Ice Age, attracted settlers as early as 8000 BC, who worked their way up the banks of the River Boyne transforming the landscape from forest to farmland. Brugh na Bóinne, an extensive prehistoric necropolis dating

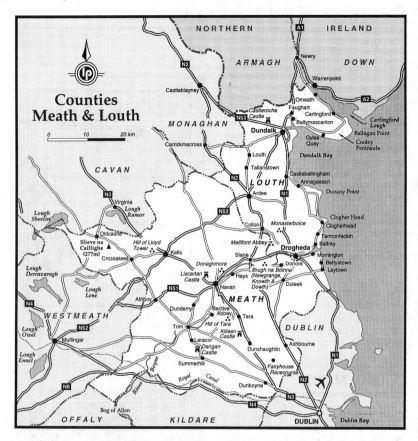

Counties Meath & Louth

from around 3000 BC, lies on a meandering section of the Boyne between Drogheda and Slane. There's a group of smaller passage graves in the Loughcrew Hills near Old-castle.

For 1000 years the Hill of Tara in Meath had been the seat of power for Irish high kings until the arrival of St Patrick in the 5th century. Later, Kells became one of the most important and creative monastic settlements in Ireland and lent its name to the famed 'Book of Kells', a 9th century illuminated manuscript now displayed in Trinity College, Dublin.

THE COAST

Meath's mere 10km of coastline includes a number of small resorts with wide expanses of sand dunes and safe beaches. From the Elizabethan **Maiden Watch Tower** in Mornington at the mouth of the Boyne there are fine views of Drogheda, 5km to the west, and the Boyne estuary.

Laytown is a busy little place with golf, tennis and good windsurfing (boardsailing). It hosts annual horse races on the beach in mid-August. Outside Laytown on the road to Julianstown (the R150), is the **Sonairte National Ecology Centre** (☎ 041-27572), beside the River Nanny. It has an organic garden, a nature trail and exhibits displaying the use of wind, water and solar power. In the gift shop you can buy its own wine made from organically grown grapes. The centre opens Monday to Friday 10 am to 5 pm, Saturday noon to 6 pm and entry costs IR£2/50p.

Barely 1km north of Laytown is **Bettystown**, whose claim to fame is that the magnificent 8th-century Tara Brooch was found on the beach here in 1850. It's now on display in the National Museum, Dublin.

Bus Éireann runs buses regularly along the coast from Drogheda.

Places to Stay & Eat

Ardilaun (☎ 041-27033), 41 Beach Park, Laytown, is near the beach, and a single/double costs IR£19/28, or IR£21/32 with bathroom. It's open April to September. *Tara Guesthouse* (☎ 041-27239) overlooks the beach and costs IR£13 per person, IR£15 with bathroom. Breakfast is extra. It also does dinner for IR£10.

Hotel Neptune (☎ 041-27107) in Bettystown is an ordinary, medium-priced hotel with B&B for IR£26.

In Bettystown, *Annabel Lee's* near the beach does coffees and snacks while *Fast Alfie's* nearby produces fast food of the burger and chips variety. *Bacchus Restaurant* (☎ 041-28251), on the main road, is one of the best in the region. It's beside the shore, and the early-bird dinner (6 to 7.30 pm) costs IR£12.50, thereafter it's à la carte. It's open Tuesday to Saturday from 6 pm, and Sunday noon to 7 pm. You have to book at weekends.

Battle of the Boyne

On 1 July 1690, the forces of the Catholic James II were defeated by those of the Protestant William III of Orange at the Battle of the Boyne. It was the decisive battle of the War of English Succession, confirming a Protestant monarch. The victory is still celebrated by Protestants in Northern Ireland as the Glorious Twelfth – the date having been adjusted in 1752 when the Gregorian calendar was adopted.

There's little left of the battle site itself except green fields. Nevertheless, a visit may give some understanding of the forces that shaped Ireland then and now. See History in the Facts about Ireland chapter.

The site is near Oldbridge, 4km west of Drogheda, and is clearly marked with a huge orange billboard. A trail leads to a slight rise overlooking the battlefield. Before the battle, William's army camped just west of Oldbridge in what is now Townley Hall demesne and Forest Park. The Jacobite camp was stretched out along the slopes of Donore Hill, 4km south of Oldbridge. James's command post was near the ruined church on the summit.

On 1 July, William's men crossed the river near Slane and Oldbridge, and despite the death of the able Marshal Schomberg in an Irish cavalry charge (an obelisk at the base of the bridge marks the spot), they outflanked James's forces and in the face of brave resistance routed them. The vanquished retreated to Donore and Duleek, where they spent the night, and then to the Shannon and Dublin.

James himself fled south to Dublin and then to Waterford, from where he crossed back to France and ignominious exile. Remnants of the Catholic forces regrouped and fought on for another year, but symbolically and politically the struggle was over. ■

King William III

Next door is *Tea & Talent*, an art gallery with coffee, teas and light meals during the day.

DULEEK

Duleek claims to have had one of Ireland's first stone churches, and the town's name comes from *damh liag* or 'stone house'. No trace of the church remains, however. The church's founder was the omnipresent St Patrick, and it was built by his disciple St Cianán somewhere around 450. On its way to Armagh for interment, Brian Ború's body lay in state here after his death in 1014 at the Battle of Clontarf, where the Vikings were defeated.

Duleek's abbey and tower ruins date from the 12th century and contain a number of excellent effigies and tombstones, while outside there is a 10th or 11th century high cross. The town square of Duleek has a wayside cross, erected in 1601 by Lady Jennet Dowdall in memory of her husband William Bathe and herself.

Annesbrook House (☎ 041-23293), open March to September, is a comfortable country house surrounded by extensive wooded grounds 9km south of Duleek, but it's rather expensive at IR£30/50 singles/doubles. The house is a 17th century building with Georgian additions, and George IV paid a visit in 1821. There are a couple of pubs in the centre serving lunch, including the *Greyhound Inn* on Main St.

BRUGH NA BÓINNE

There was extensive settlement along the Boyne Valley in prehistoric times, and the necropolis known as Brugh (or Brú) na Bóinne was built in the area. This consists of many different sites, the three principal ones being Newgrange, Knowth and Dowth. They were the largest artificial structures in Ireland until the construction of the Anglo-Norman castles.

Over the centuries these tombs decayed, were covered by grass and trees and were plundered by everybody from Vikings to Victorian treasure hunters, whose carved initials can be seen on the great stones of Newgrange. The countryside around them is littered with countless other ancient mounds (or tumuli) and standing stones.

Newgrange

Newgrange is a huge, flattened, grass-covered mound about 80m in diameter and 13m high. The mound covers the finest Stone Age passage tomb in Ireland and is one of the most prehistoric sites in Europe. It dates from around 3200 BC, pre-dating the great pyramids of Egypt by some six centuries. The purpose for which it was constructed remains uncertain. It may have been a burial place for kings or a centre for ritual – although the alignment with the sun at the time of the winter solstice might also suggest it was designed to act as a calendar.

Over the centuries Newgrange, like Dowth and Knowth, deteriorated and was even quarried at one stage. There was a standing stone on the summit until the 17th century. The site was extensively restored in 1962 and again in 1975.

A superbly carved kerbstone with double and triple spirals guards the tomb's main entrance. The front facade has been recon-

Detail of the Threshold Stone at Newgrange, Ireland's finest Stone Age passage tomb

structed so that tourists don't have to clamber in over it. Above the entrance is a slit or roof box, which lets light in. Another beautifully decorated kerbstone stands at the exact opposite side of the mound. Some experts say that a ring of standing stones encircled the mound, forming a Great Circle about 100m in diameter, but only 12 of these stones remain – with traces of some others below ground level.

Holding the whole structure together are the 97 boulders of the kerb ring, designed to stop the mound from collapsing outwards. Eleven of these are decorated with motifs similar to those on the main entrance stone, although only three of these have extensive carvings.

The white quartzite was originally brought from Wicklow, 80km to the south, and there is also some granite from the Mourne Mountains in Northern Ireland. Over 200,000 tonnes of earth and stone also went into the mound.

You can walk down the narrow 19m passage, lined with 43 stone uprights, some of them engraved, which leads into the tomb chamber, about a third of the way into the colossal mound. The chamber has three recesses, and in these are large basin stones that held cremated human bones. Along with the remains would have been funeral offerings of beads and pendants, but these must have been stolen long before the archaeologists arrived.

Above, the massive stones, many with intricate engravings, support a 6m-high corbel-vaulted roof. A complex drainage system means that not a drop of water has penetrated the interior in 40 centuries.

At just before 9 am during the winter solstice (19 to 23 December), the rising sun's rays shine through the slit above the entrance, creep slowly down the long passage and illuminate the tomb chamber for 17 minutes.

Places to experience this annual event are booked up well into the next century, and the waiting list is now closed. However, for the legions of daily visitors – Newgrange is Ireland's most visited site – there is a simulated winter sunrise for every group taken into the mound.

A couple of things puzzled the archaeologists when studying the phenomenon. The light comes all the way down the passageway a few minutes after sunrise, not at the precise moment, and surprisingly it stops short of illuminating the centre of the back wall. Recent studies by cosmic physicists have found that the earth's position has shifted; when the mound was built, the sunlight would have illuminated the whole chamber precisely at sunrise.

According to Celtic legend, the god Aengus lived at Newgrange, and the hero Cúchulainn was conceived here.

In the past, visitors could go directly to Newgrange or Knowth for guided tours but now they must assemble at the new **Brú na Bóinne Visitors' Centre** (☎ 041-24488), south of the River Boyne and 2km west of Donore, from where they will cross the footbridge over the Boyne and be bused to the sites. Tours of Newgrange and the centre take place daily 9 am to 7 pm, June to mid-September (to 6.30 pm in May). Mid-March to April and again in October, the hours are 9.30 am to 5.30 pm. November to February the site closes at 5 pm. The last tours of the monuments leave 1½ hours before closing time though you can enter the visitors' centre 45 minutes before closing. Entry to the centre and Newgrange is IR£3/1.25/7.50 for adults/students & children/families, IR£2/1/5 for just the centre, and IR£5/2.25/12.50 for the centre, Newgrange and Knowth.

In summer, particularly at weekends, and during school holidays, Newgrange is very crowded and it's best to come during the week and/or first thing in the morning. Large groups must be booked in advance – because of this and the limited space inside the tomb, individual visitors may find themselves with a long wait at peak times.

There's a seasonal tourist office (☎ 041-24274) across from the entrance to Newgrange. It's usually open April to October but may close now that the visitors' centre has been completed. There has even been talk of closing the tomb to visitors altogether in order to protect the fragile carvings. If that happens, visitors will have to make do with a reproduction.

A few hundred metres down the hill to the west of the tomb is **Newgrange Farm** (☎ 041-24119), a 135 hectare working farm with a large collection of animals on view, displays, a picnic area and a coffee shop. The farm opens for tours 10 am to 5.30 pm Monday to Friday, and 2 to 5.30 pm on Sunday, April to September; in July and August, it's also open on Saturday afternoons. Admission is IR£2 per person or from IR£8 for a family ticket.

Knowth

The burial mound of Knowth (Cnóbha) north-west of Newgrange was built around the same time and seems set to surpass its better known neighbour, both in the extent and importance of the discoveries made here. It has the greatest collection of passage grave art ever uncovered in Western Europe, but it's still under excavation and the interior remains closed to visitors.

Modern excavations started at Knowth in 1962 and soon cleared a 34m passage to the central chamber, much longer than the one at Newgrange. In 1968 a second 40m passage was unearthed on the opposite side of the mound. Although the chambers are separate, they're close enough for archaeologists to hear each other at work. Also in the mound are the remains of six early Christian souterrains built into the side. Some 300 carved slabs and 17 'satellite graves' surround the main mound.

Human activity at Knowth continued for thousands of years after its construction and accounts for the site's complexity. The 'beaker people', so called because they buried their dead with drinking vessels, occupied the site in the Bronze Age (circa 1800 BC), as did the Celts in the Iron Age around 500 BC. Remnants of bronze and iron workings from these periods have been discovered. Around 800 to 900 AD it was turned into a ráth or earthen ring fort, a stronghold of the very powerful Uí Néill (O'Neill) sept (or clan). In 965, it was the seat of Cormac MacMaelmithic, later Ireland's high king for nine years. The Normans built a motte-and-bailey here in the 12th century. In about 1400 the site was finally abandoned. Excavations are likely to continue at least for the next decade.

Partly because of the archaeological work and partly because the later buildings on the site weakened the internal structures, making it difficult for anyone to walk along the passage, only the exterior opens for guided tours, which you must join at the Brú na Bóinne Visitors' Centre (see Newgrange). Knowth keeps the same hours as Newgrange but *only* from May to October. Admission to the visitors' centre and the site is IR£2/1/5 for adults/students & children/families. If you want to visit Newgrange as well, the tour costs IR£5/2.25/12.50.

Dowth

The circular mound at Dowth (Dubhadh) is similar in size to Newgrange – about 63m in diameter – but is slightly taller at 14m high. It has suffered badly at the hands of everyone from road builders and treasure hunters to amateur archaeologists, who scooped out the centre of the tumulus in the 19th century. For a time, Dowth even had a teahouse ignobly perched on its summit. Relatively untouched by modern archaeologists, Dowth shows what Newgrange and Knowth looked like for most of their history. Because it's unsafe, Dowth is closed to visitors though the mound can be viewed from the road.

There are two entrance passages leading to separate chambers (both sealed), and a 24m early Christian souterrain at either end which connect up with the west passage. This 8m-long passage leads into a small cruciform chamber, in which a recess acts as an entrance to an additional series of small compartments, a feature unique to Dowth. To the south-west is the entrance to a shorter passage and smaller chamber.

North of the tumulus are the ruins of **Dowth Castle** and 18th century **Dowth House**.

A native of Dowth was one John Boyle O'Reilly (1844-90). For his part in the Irish

Republican Brotherhood, O'Reilly was deported to a penal colony in Australia from where he later escaped to the USA. As editor of the *Boston Pilot* newspaper he made an influential contribution to liberal opinion and supported the cause of minorities. The people of Boston erected a memorial to him in their city centre while the locals did the same here in the churchyard beside the castle.

Getting There & Away
Newgrange, Knowth and Dowth are all well signposted. Newgrange lies just north of the River Boyne, about 13km south-west of Drogheda, while Slane is 5km to the north-west. Dowth is between Newgrange and Drogheda, while Knowth is about 1km north-west of Newgrange or almost 4km by road.

There are no direct buses to any of the sites; during most of the week the closest you'll get is Slane, which is served by up to six buses a day Monday to Saturday from Drogheda. On Saturday only the Drogheda-Slane bus stops at Donore, closer to the new visitors' centre, at 10.15 am and 2.10 pm. Alternatively, Dublin-based Mary Gibbons Tours (☎ 01-283 9973) take in Newgrange (or Knowth, according to demand) and parts of the Boyne Valley on Monday, Wednesday and Friday, leaving the Shelbourne Hotel on St Stephen's Green at 1.10 pm and the Dublin Tourism Centre on Suffolk St 10 minutes later. The IR£15 cost includes the admission fee. Bus Éireann's Newgrange and Boyne Valley tour, which costs IR£15/8 for adults/children, departs from the Busáras in Dublin, Saturday to Thursday, May to September, returning at 5.45 pm. In April the tour runs on Saturday and Sunday only and in October on Thursday and Sunday.

SLANE
Built as a manorial village for an important castle, Slane (Baile Shláine) is a charming little place with stone houses and cottages and mature trees. Just south-west of the centre is the massive grey gate to the privately owned Slane Castle.

Four identical houses face each other at the junction of the main roads. Local lore has it that they were built for four sisters who had taken an intense dislike to one other and kept watch from their individual residences.

Orientation & Information
Slane is perched on a hillside overlooking the River Boyne, at the junction of the N2 and N51, some 15km west of Drogheda. At the bottom of the hill to the south, the Boyne glides by under a narrow bridge.

The helpful community-run tourist office (☎ 041-24010) on Main St opposite the Conyngham Arms Hotel opens April to October, daily 9 am to 6 pm. During the rest of the year the hours are Monday to Friday 9.30 am to 5 pm.

The telephone code is ☎ 041.

The Hill of Slane
Just above the village, about 1km to the north, is the Hill of Slane. Tradition holds that St Patrick lit a paschal (Easter) fire here in 433 – just a year after his arrival in Ireland – to proclaim Christianity throughout the land. This act was in direct contravention of a decree issued by Laoghaire, the pagan high king of Ireland, that no flame should be lit within sight of Hill of Tara. The king was furious but was restrained by his druids, who warned that 'the man who had kindled (the flame) would surpass kings and princes'. Instead, Laoghaire set out to meet Patrick and question him and all but one of the king's attendants – a man called Erc – greeted him with scorn.

During the encounter, Patrick killed one of the guards and summoned an earthquake to subdue the rest. He then plucked a shamrock and used its three leaves to explain the paradox of the Trinity – the union of the Father, the Son and the Holy Spirit in one Godhead. The king made peace and, while he refused to be converted, he allowed Patrick to continue his missionary work. Erc was baptised and later named as the first bishop of Slane. On Holy Saturday the local parish priest still lights a fire on the hill.

The Hill of Slane originally had a church

MEATH & LOUTH

associated with St Erc and, later, a round tower and monastery, but only an outline of the foundation remains. Later a motte-and-bailey was constructed and is still visible on the west side of the hill. A ruined church, tower and other buildings once formed part of an early 16th century Franciscan friary. On a clear day from the top of the tower, which is always open, you can see the Hill of Tara and the Boyne Valley as well (it's said) as seven Irish counties.

St Erc is believed to have become a hermit in old age, and the ruins of a small Gothic church marks the spot where he is thought to have spent his last days around 512 to 514. It's on the north river bank, behind the Protestant church on the Navan road, and lies within the private Conyngham estate. It only opens to the public on 15 August.

Slane Castle

Slane Castle, the private residence of Lord Henry Conyngham, earl of Mountcharles, is west of the centre along the Navan road and is best known in Ireland as the setting for major outdoor rock concerts. Bruce Springsteen, Bob Dylan, the Rolling Stones and Guns 'n' Roses have appeared here, but events have dwindled of late due to local antipathy to hordes of young rock fans. There's usually only one concert each summer now.

Built in 1785 in Gothic Revival style by James Wyatt, the building was altered later by Francis Johnson for the visit of George IV to Lady Conyngham. She was allegedly his mistress, and it's said the road between Dublin and Slane was built especially straight and smooth to speed up the randy king's journeys.

Unfortunately, much of the castle, including some valuable furnishings, was destroyed by fire in 1991, whereupon it was discovered that the earl – a Lloyd's name – was underinsured. Money is now being raised for restoration. The castle and grounds are closed to the public.

Ledwidge Museum

Just about 1km east of the village on the Drogheda road is the Ledwidge Museum (☎ 24544). This labourer's cottage was the birthplace of Francis Ledwidge, a poet who died on the battlefield of Ypres in Belgium in 1917 just short of his 30th birthday. Admission is IR£1, and it opens daily 9 am to 1 pm and 2 to 7 pm, April to September (to 4.30 pm the rest of the year).

Places to Stay

Hostel The nearest hostels are at Kells and Trim (summer only). See those sections for details.

B&Bs The lovely *Ye Old Post House* (☎ 24090) on Main St, a few doors east of the tourist office, charges from IR£20 per person for its three ensuite rooms. *Castle View House* (☎ 24510) on the Navan road almost opposite the entrance to Slane Castle costs from IR£19/28. The *Boyne View* (☎ 24121), down by the river near the bridge, charges from IR£28 to IR£32 for doubles.

Hotel The lovely old *Conyngham Arms Hotel* (☎ 24155) is near the crossroads in Slane village and has 15 rooms costing IR£59/79 in summer (June to September). They have a reasonable restaurant, and you can get good snacks in the bar 10.30 am to 7 pm.

Places to Eat

Ye Old Post House B&B is also a coffee shop and restaurant with main courses (some of them vegetarian) from IR£3.95. It's open till about 9 pm. Pubs on Main St serving food include *Slane House* and *Knowth Tavern*.

The *Roadrunner Café* is attached to a petrol station and shops about a km north of the centre on the Derry road just beyond the turn to the Hill of Slane. It does generous servings of straightforward food.

The *Mary McDonnell Craft Studio* in Newgrange Mall on the Drogheda road has a nice coffee shop in summer where you can also get lunches. For a serious meal try the *Conyngham Arms*, which has a menu for IR£17.50.

Getting There & Away

Bus From Dublin, Slane is on the Letterkenny (three to five buses a day) and Armagh (up to six daily) routes as well as the less busy routes to Portrush (one or two) and Derry (two to four), which sometimes requires a change at Omagh. The stop is in front of the sweet shop on the Derry road. There's bus service between Slane and Drogheda and Slane and Navan about six times a day. The stop is at Conlon's shop near the crossroads. For information ring Bus Éireann (☎ 01-836 6111) in Dublin.

Train Only the coast is served by the Dublin (Connolly Station) to Belfast line, with several stops a day between late May and early September at Mosney, a holiday centre 2km south of Laytown, and Laytown itself just before Drogheda.

SLANE TO NAVAN

The 14km journey on the N51 south-west from Slane to Navan follows the Boyne Valley past a number of manor houses, ruined castles, round towers and churches; they're only of moderate interest compared to the fine sites elsewhere in County Meath, though.

Dunmoe Castle lies down a badly signposted cul-de-sac to the south 4km before reaching Navan. This D'Arcy family castle is a 16th century ruin with good views of the countryside and of the impressive red-brick **Ardmulchan House** on the opposite side of the River Boyne. Cromwell is supposed to have fired at the castle from the riverbank in 1649, and local legend holds that a tunnel used to run from the castle vaults under the river. Near Dunmoe Castle is a small overgrown chapel and graveyard, with a crypt containing members of the D'Arcy family. Ardmulchan House, though somewhat dilapidated, is still used as a private residence.

You can't miss the fine 30m round tower and 13th century church of **Donaghmore**, on the right 2km nearer Navan. The site has a profusion of modern gravestones, but the 10th century tower with its Crucifixion scene

above the door is interesting, and there are carved faces near the windows and the remains of the church wall.

NAVAN

The county town of Navan (An Uaimh) at the confluence of the Boyne and Blackwater rivers is disfigured by the busy N3 Dublin-Cavan road, which cuts off the rivers from the town. Navan was the birthplace of Sir Francis Beaufort of the British Navy, who in 1805 devised the internationally accepted scale for wind strengths. The town has a carpet factory and Europe's largest lead and zinc mine, Tara, is 3km along the Kells road.

Orientation & Information

Market Square is the town hub, with Ludlow, Watergate and Trimgate Sts leading off from it in the direction of the former town gates.

The local tourist office (☎ 046-21581) is in the town library on Railway St, about 500m south-west of Market Square. There's a map and information point in the town hall car park at the northern end of Watergate St.

The modern post office is past the big shopping centre on Kennedy Rd, which runs off Trimgate St, and there's an Allied Irish Bank branch on the corner of these two streets. The Bizzy Laundry is two doors down from the defunct Lyric Cinema on Brews Hill, the continuation of Trimgate St.

The telephone code is ☎ 046.

Places to Stay

Hostels The nearest hostels are in Kells and Trim (summer only). See those sections for details.

B&Bs *Riverside Lodge* (☎ 28762), 19 Watergate St, has singles/doubles with shared bath for £18/30 above a decent restaurant. *Tower View* (☎ 23358), open April to October, 3km along the Slane road, costs from IR£18/28. *Lios na Gréine* (☎ 28092), almost 2km south of Navan on the R153 Kentstown road, has three rooms priced from IR£19/28.

Highfield House (☎ 27809), 3km from Navan in Balreask Old, has rooms from

IR£19/28; go 2km south along the N3 Dublin road until the Old Bridge Inn, then turn right and it's 1km along. *Swynnerton Lodge* (☎ 21371), 1km from Navan on the main road to Slane, is a 19th century fishing lodge overlooking the Boyne and open April to September. It caters for fishing and shooting aficionados and charge from IR£23/36. Dinner is IR£15.

Hotels The *Ardboyne* (☎ 23119) is a first-class hotel on the Dublin road, charging from IR£45.50/75 for B&B. The *Beechmount Hotel* (☎ 21553), just outside Navan on the Trim road, costs IR£27 per person.

In Kilmessan, 10km south of Navan and close to the Hill of Tara, the delightful little *Station House* (☎ 25239) costs IR£25 to IR£35 for a single and IR£40 to IR£50 for a double. Light meals are available at lunch times, and it has a good restaurant open Monday to Saturday 6 to 9.30 pm. Dinner is IR£15.95.

Places to Eat

Cafés & Takeaways *Susie's Cookhouse* in Watergate St does good light lunches as does the *Valley Café* opposite from IR£3.60. The *Pepper Pot* (with full Irish breakfast for IR£2.60), the cosy *Coffee Dock* and *Tasty Bites*, all in Trimgate St, are other good bets. The fast-food chain *Abrakebabra* has a outlet on Trimgate St.

Pubs Try the comfortable *O'Flaherty's*, on the corner of Railway St and Brews Hill or *Bernard Reilly's* on Trimgate St. *Smyth's Flat House* at the roundabout opposite the tourist office/town library also serves good, solid food.

Restaurants One of the best places around is *The Loft* opposite O'Flaherty's and upstairs at 26 Trimgate St with 'funky food, art and music' every night to 11 pm and an early-bird special before 7 pm for IR£6.95. More upmarket is the pan-Pacific *Hudson's Bistro* (☎ 29231) in Railway St with main courses from IR£8.95. Hudson's opens for dinner 6.30 to 11 pm Tuesday to Saturday.

At 15 Ludlow St just across from Birmingham's Pub and next to the Palace Cinema is *Vivaldi's*, offering a predictable menu of pasta dishes (from IR£5.95) and Italian main courses (from IR£8.95). On Brews Hill, the popular *China Garden* (☎ 23938) does decent Chinese with main courses from IR£7 and limited European food.

Entertainment

O'Flaherty's and *Bernard Reilly's* are popular, modern, comfortably furnished pubs on Trimgate St and its extension, Brews Hill. *Robbie O'Malley's* on Watergate St is similar and has music on Monday.

The tiny *Birmingham's Pub* on Ludlow St has an old wooden frontage and faded posters inside. They have music on Thursday. The *Lantern Lounge* at the bottom of Watergate St has an Irish music night on Wednesday as does *Henry Loughran's* in Trimgate St. There's a nightclub in the Beechmount Hotel with line dancing at weekends.

The *Palace Cinema* in Ludlow St still rakes up enough of an audience for its two screens.

Getting There & Away

Buses stop in front of the Mercy Convent on Railway St and in Market Square. Destinations and times are posted, or call Bus Éireann (☎ 01-836 6111) in Dublin for information. There are four or five daily buses (three on Sunday) to/from Dublin and the same number to/from Donegal via Kells and Cavan. Other destinations include Galway, Drogheda, Trim and Slane.

Getting Around

You can order a taxi from Navan Cabs (☎ 23053), and there are ranks on Market Square and in front of the shopping centre on Kennedy Rd. Clarke's Sports (☎ 21130), in the back of the Navan Indoor Market at 39 Trimgate St, is the local Raleigh dealer, with bikes for IR£7/20 a day/week plus a deposit of IR£50.

AROUND NAVAN

There are some nice walks in the area, particularly the one following the towpath that runs along the old River Boyne Canal towards Slane and Drogheda. On the south bank, you can go out about 7km as far as Stackallen and the Boyne bridge with ease, passing Ardmulchan House and, on the opposite bank, the ruins of Dunmoe Castle. (See the earlier Slane to Navan section for details.) Going beyond the bridge towards Slane is trickier as the path is rough and in some places switches to the opposite side of the bank, with no bridge for you to cross over.

Just west of town is the **Motte of Navan**, a scrub-covered mound that tradition holds to be the burial site of Odhbha, the wife of a Celtic prince who had abandoned her for Tea (pronounced 'Tay-ah'), the lady who gave her name to Tara. Odhbha followed her husband to Navan and died of a broken heart. In reality, the 16m-high mound was probably formed naturally – a deposit of gravel from the Ice Age – and was then adapted by the Normans as a motte-and-bailey.

Two km south-east of town are the impressive remains of **Athlumney House**, built by the Dowdall family in the 16th century with additions made 100 years later. This relatively intact castle was said to have been set alight in 1690 by Sir Lancelot Dowdall, after James' defeat at the Battle of the Boyne. Dowdall vowed that the conqueror, William of Orange, would never shelter or confiscate his home. He watched the blaze from the opposite bank of the river before leaving for France and then Italy.

Close to the Kells road (N3), 5km northwest of Navan, is the large ruin of another castle that once belonged to the Talbot family. **Liscartan Castle** is made up of two 15th century square towers joined by a hall-like room.

TARA

The Hill of Tara has occupied a special place in Irish legend and folklore for millennia, although it's not known exactly when people first settled on this gently sloping hill with its commanding views over the plains of Meath. One of the many mounds on the hill was found to be a Stone Age passage grave from about 2500 BC, and during the Bronze Age people of high rank and status were certainly being buried here.

Much of the pagan significance of Tara (Teamhair) seems to have derived from its associations with the goddess Maeve (or Medbh) and the mythical powers of the druids or priest-rulers who reigned over part of the country from here. By the 2nd and 3rd centuries AD, Tara was the seat of the most powerful rulers in Ireland, a place where the high king (*ard rí*) and his royal court had their ceremonial residence, feasted and watched over the realm. While Tara's kings may have been more powerful than the others, they would by no means have held sway over all Ireland as there were countless other petty kings (*rí tuaithe*) controlling many smaller areas.

Tara's remains are not visually impressive. Only mounds and depressions in the grass mark where the Iron Age hill fort and surrounding ring forts once stood, but it remains an evocative, somewhat moving place especially on a warm summer's evening.

As the focus of Irish political influence and a centre of pagan worship, Tara was targeted by the early Christians. A great pagan *feis* (festival) is thought to have been held around what is now Halloween. On Tara – if not on the Hill of Slane – St Patrick supposedly used the shamrock and its three leaves to explain the Christian canon of the Trinity. Hence the adoption of the shamrock as the Irish national symbol.

After the 6th century, once Christianity had taken hold and Tara's pagan significance had waned, the high kings began to desert Tara. The kings of Leinster continued to be based here until the 11th century, however.

In August 1843, Tara saw one of the greatest crowds ever to gather in Ireland. Daniel O'Connell, the 'Liberator' and leader of the opposition to union with Great Britain, held one of his 'monster rallies' at Tara, and up to 750,000 people came to hear him speak.

MEATH & LOUTH

The Hill of Tara is an open site, accessible at any time and is free.

Tara Visitors' Centre

The former Protestant church (with a window by well known artist Evie Hone) houses the Tara Visitors' Centre (☎ 046-25903), where a 20-minute audiovisual presentation on the site called 'Tara: Meeting Place of Heroes' is shown. During the summer the tour from here is a must, as the anecdotes really bring the mounds and relics to life. Admission to the centre and the tour costs IR£1/40p/3 for adults/students & children/families. It's open – and tours are available – mid-June to mid-September, daily 9.30 am to 6.30 pm, and May to mid-June and mid-September to October, 10 am to 5 pm.

Ráth of the Synods

The names applied to Tara's various humps and mounds were adopted from ancient texts, and mythology and religion intertwine with the historical facts. The Protestant church grounds and graveyard spill onto the remains of the Ráth of the Synods, a triple-ringed fort supposedly where some of St Patrick's early meetings (or synods) took place. Excavations of the ráth suggest it was used between 200 and 400 AD for burials, rituals and living quarters. Originally the ring fort would have contained wooden houses surrounded by timber palisades.

During a digging session in the graveyard in 1810, a boy found a pair of gold torcs (necklaces of twisted gold bands), now in the National Museum in Dublin. Later excavations brought a surprise when Roman glass, shards of pottery and seals were discovered, showing links with the Roman Empire, even though the Romans never extended their power into Ireland.

The poor state of the ráth is due in part to a group of British 'Israelites' who in the 1890s dug the place up looking for the Ark of the Covenant, much to the consternation of the local people. The Israelites' leader claimed to see a mysterious pillar on the ráth, but unfortunately it was invisible to every-

one else. After they failed to uncover anything, the invisible pillar moved to the other side of the road, but before the adventurers had time to start work there, the locals chased them away.

The Royal Enclosure

To the south of the church, the Royal Enclosure (Ráth na Ríogh) is a large, oval Iron Age hill fort, 315m in diameter and surrounded by a bank and ditch cut through solid rock under the soil. Inside the Royal Enclosure are smaller sites.

Mound of the Hostages This bump in the north corner of the ráth (known as Dumha na nGiall in Irish) is the most ancient known part of Tara and the most visible of the remains. Supposedly a prison cell for hostages of the 3rd century King Cormac MacArt, it is in fact a small Stone Age passage grave dating from around 1800 BC and later used by Bronze Age people. The passage contains some carved stonework, but it's closed to the public.

The mound produced a treasure trove of artefacts including some ancient Mediterranean beads of amber and faïence (glazed pottery). More than 35 Bronze Age burials were found here, as well as a mass of cremated remains from the Stone Age.

Cormac's House & Royal Seat Two other earthworks found inside the enclosure are Cormac's House (Teach Cormaic) and the Royal Seat (Forradh). Although they look similar, the Royal Seat is a ring fort with a house site in the centre, while Cormac's House is a barrow, or burial mound, in the side of the circular bank. Cormac's House commands the best views of the surrounding lowlands of the Boyne and Blackwater valleys.

Atop Cormac's House is the phallic **Stone of Destiny** (Lia Fáil), originally located near the Mound of the Hostages and representing the joining of the gods of the earth and the heavens. It's said to be the inauguration stone of the high kings of Tara. The would-be king stood on top of it, and if the stone let out three roars, he was crowned. The mass grave of 37 men who died in a skirmish on Tara during the 1798 Rising is next to the stone.

Enclosure of King Laoghaire

South of the Royal Enclosure is the Enclosure of King Laoghaire (Ráth Laoghaire), a large but worn ring fort where the king – a contemporary of St Patrick – is supposedly buried dressed in his armour and standing upright.

Banquet Hall

North of the churchyard is Tara's most unusual feature, the Banquet Hall or Teach Miodhchuarta, which translates as the 'House of Mead-circling' (mead, which was a popular tipple, is fermented from honey). This rectangular earthwork measures 230m by 27m along a north-south axis. Tradition holds that it was built to cater for thousands of guests during feasts like the feis. Much of this information about the hall comes from the 12th century 'Book of Leinster' and the 'Yellow Book of Lecan', which even includes drawings of it.

Opinions vary as to the site's real purpose. Its orientation suggests that it was a sunken entrance to Tara, leading directly to the Royal Enclosure. More recent research has uncovered graves within the compound, and it's possible that the banks are in fact the burial sites of some of the kings of Tara.

Gráinne's Fort

Gráinne's Fort (Ráth Gráinne) and the north and south Sloping Trenches (Claoin Fhearta) off to the north-west are burial mounds. Gráinne's Fort was named after the daughter of King Cormac who was betrothed to Fionn McCumhaill (Finn McCool). She eloped with Diarmuid ÓDuibhne, one of the king's warriors, on her wedding night and they became the subjects of the epic 'The Pursuit of Diarmuid and Gráinne'.

Getting There & Away

Tara is 10km south-east of Navan just off the N3 Dublin-Cavan road. Buses linking Dublin and Navan pass within 1km of the site; ask to be dropped off at Tara Cross and follow the signs.

From April to October, Bus Éireann sometimes includes the Hill of Tara in their day-long Newgrange and Boyne Valley tour (£15/8 for adults/children). To check whether it will be included on a particular day call Bus Éireann (☎ 01-836 6111) in Dublin.

AROUND TARA

Five km south of Tara on the Dunshaughlin-Kilmessan road is **Dunsany Castle** (☎ 046-25198), the residence of the lords of Dunsany, former owners of the lands around Trim Castle. The Dunsanys are related to the Plunkett family, the most famous Plunkett being St Oliver, who was executed and whose head is kept in a church in Drogheda.

The present Lord Dunsany opens his house to visitors in July and August Monday to Saturday 9 am to 1 pm daily, but it's best to ring ahead and check. Admission is IR£3, and they prefer people to come as part of group tours organised by the Drogheda tourist office and the Irish Georgian Society. There's an impressive private art collection and many other treasures related to important figures in Irish history, such as Oliver Plunkett and Patrick Sarsfield, leader of the Irish Jacobite forces at the siege Limerick in 1691.

About 1.5km north-east of Dunsany is the ruined **Killeen Castle**, the seat of another line of the Plunkett family. The 1801 mansion was built around a Hugh de Lacy original dating from 1180 and comprises a neo-Gothic structure between two 12th century towers.

According to local lore, the surrounding lands were divided at one point among the two Plunkett branches by a foot race. Starting at the castles, the wives had to run towards each other and a fence was placed where they met. Luckily for the Killeen womenfolk, their castle was on higher ground and they made considerable gains as they ran downhill toward their Dunsany's counterparts.

Another 5km south-east on the Dublin

road is the town of **Dunshaughlin** with Fairyhouse Racecourse 7km beyond. The Easter holiday races of 1916 attracted a large contingent of British officers from Dublin while the Rising began.

TRIM

Trim (Baile Átha Troim or 'town at the ford of the elder trees') is a rather sleepy little town on the River Boyne, with several interesting ruins. The medieval town was a jumble of streets and once had five gates. At one stage, there were also seven monasteries in the immediate area. In the past, few visitors have paused to inspect the impressive ruins of Trim Castle, Ireland's largest Anglo-Norman structure, though this will almost certainly change when word gets out that the storming of York Castle by the Scots in Mel Gibson's Oscar-winning film *Braveheart* (1996) was filmed here.

According to local history, Elizabeth I considered Trim as a possible site for Trinity College, which eventually ended up in Dublin. The Duke of Wellington went to school for a time in St Mary's Abbey (Talbot Castle), which served as a Protestant school in the 18th century. There's a local (and unlikely) belief that he was born in a stable south of the town, which probably arose from the duke's observation that being born in a stable didn't make one a horse, and thus his birth in Ireland didn't make him Irish! A Wellington column stands at the junction of Patrick and Emmet Sts. After defeating Napoleon at the Battle of Waterloo, the Iron Duke went on to become prime minister of Great Britain and in 1829 passed the Catholic Emancipation Act, which repealed the last of the repressive penal laws.

Trim was once home to the county jail, giving rise to the ditty: 'Kells for brogues, Navan for rogues and Trim for hanging people'.

Information

The tourist office (☎ 046-37111) in Mill St opens daily 9.30 am to 5 pm (to 6 pm May to September) but in winter the Sunday hours are only noon to 4 pm. Among the brochures

for sale is the handy little *Trim Tourist Trail* (60p) walking tour booklet. The post office is at the junction of Emmet and Market Sts, where you'll also find an Allied Irish Bank branch.

In the same building as the tourist office on Mill St is Meath Heritage Centre (☎ 046-36633) with an extensive genealogical database for people trying to trace Meath ancestors. It opens weekdays 9 am to 1 pm and 2 to 5 pm, and the minimum charge is IR£20. Noel French at the centre also runs group tours (from IR£1.50 per person per site) of Trim and other places of interest in Meath.

The telephone code is ☎ 046.

The Power & the Glory

Immediately next door to the tourist office in Mill St is the informative **Trim Heritage Centre** (☎ 37227) with an exhibit known as The Power and the Glory, which outlines the medieval history of Trim in audiovisuals. It makes a good starting point for a tour of the town and opens daily 10 am to 6 pm, April to September. Admission is IR£2/1.25 for adults/students and children.

Trim Castle

Hugh de Lacy founded Trim Castle in 1173, but Rory O'Connor, said to have been the last high king of Ireland, destroyed this motte-and-bailey within a year. De Lacy did not live to see the castle's replacement, and the building you see today was begun around 1200. It has hardly been modified since then.

Although King John visited Trim in 1210 to bring the de Lacy family into line – giving the castle its alternative name of King John's Castle – he never actually slept in the castle. On the eve of his arrival, Walter de Lacy locked it up tight and left town, forcing the king to camp in the nearby meadow.

De Lacy's grandson-in-law, Geoffrey de Geneville, was responsible for the second stage of the keep's construction in the mid to late 13th century. De Geneville was a crusader who later became a monk at the Dominican abbey he founded in 1263 just

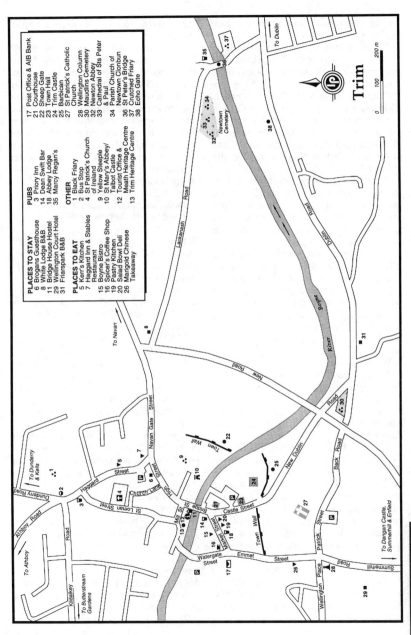

Trim

PLACES TO STAY
6 Brogans Guesthouse
8 White Lodge B&B
11 Bridge House Hostel
29 Wellington Court Hotel
31 Friarspark B&B

PLACES TO EAT
5 Kerr's Kitchen
7 Haggard Inn & Stables Restaurant
15 Boyne Bistro
16 Spicer's Coffee Shop
19 Pastry Kitchen
20 Salad Bowl Deli
26 Magpie Chinese Takeaway

PUBS
3 Priory Inn
14 Dean Swift Bar
18 Abbey Lodge
35 Marcy Regan's

OTHER
1 Black Friary
2 Bus Stop
4 St Patrick's Church of Ireland
9 Yellow Steeple
10 St Mary's Abbey/Talbot Castle
12 Tourist Office & Meath Heritage Centre
13 Trim Heritage Centre
17 Post Office & AIB Bank
21 Courthouse
22 Sheep Gate
23 Town Hall
24 Trim Castle
25 Barbican
27 St Patrick's Catholic Church
28 Wellington Column
30 Maudlins Cemetery
32 Newton Abbey
33 Cathedral of Sts Peter & Paul
34 Parish Church of Newtown Clonbun
36 St Peter's Bridge
37 Crutched Friary
38 Echo Gate

MEATH & LOUTH

outside the northern wall of the town near Athboy Gate.

In 1399 Henry of Lancaster, later Henry IV, was imprisoned in the Dublin Gate at the southern part of the outer wall by his cousin King Richard II.

Trim was conquered by Silken Thomas in 1536 and again in 1647 by Catholic Confederate forces, opponents of the English parliamentarians. In 1649 it was taken by Cromwellian forces, and the castle, town walls and Yellow Steeple were badly damaged.

The grassy two hectare enclosure is dominated by a massive stone keep, 25m tall and mounted on a Norman motte. Inside are three lofty levels, the lowest one divided in two by a central wall. Just outside the central keep are the remains of an earlier wall.

The principal outer curtain wall, some 500m long and for the most part still standing, dates from around 1250 and includes eight towers and a gatehouse. The finest stretch of the outer wall runs from the River Boyne through Dublin Gate to Castle St. The outer wall has a number of sally gates from which defenders could exit to confront the enemy.

Within the north corner was a church and, facing the river, the Royal Mint which produced Irish coinage (called 'Patricks' and 'Irelands') into the 15th century. The Russian cannon in the car park is a trophy from the Crimean War and bears the tsarist double-headed eagle.

In 1465, Edward IV ordered that anyone who had robbed or 'who was going to rob' should be beheaded and their heads mounted on spikes and publicly displayed as a warning to other thieves. In 1971, excavations in the castle grounds near the depression south of the keep revealed the remains of 10 headless men, presumably the hapless criminals (or criminal wannabes).

Talbot Castle/St Mary's Abbey
Across the river from the castle are the ruins of the 12th century Augustinian St Mary's Abbey, rebuilt after a fire in 1368 and once home to a miraculous wooden statue of the Virgin Mary, which was destroyed during the Reformation.

Part of the abbey was converted in 1415 into a fine manor house by Sir John Talbot, then viceroy of Ireland, which came to be known as Talbot Castle. The Talbot coat of arms can be seen on the north wall. Talbot went to war in France, where in 1429 he was defeated by none other than Joan of Arc at Orleans. He was taken prisoner, released and went on fighting the French until 1453. He was known as 'the scourge of France' or 'the whip of the French', and Shakespeare wrote of this notorious man in *Henry VI*:

Is this the Talbot so much feared abroad
That with his name the mothers still their babes?

Talbot Castle was owned in the early 18th century by Esther 'Stella' Johnson, the mistress of Jonathan Swift. She bought the manor house for £65 and lived there for 18 months before selling it to Swift for a tidy £200. He lived there for a year. Swift was rector of Laracor, 3km south of Trim, from around 1700 until 1745, when he died. From 1713 he was also – and more significantly – dean of St Patrick's Cathedral in Dublin.

Just north of the abbey building is the 40m **Yellow Steeple**, once the bell tower of the abbey, dating from 1368 but damaged by Cromwell's soldiers in 1649. It takes its name from the colour of the stonework at dusk.

A part of the 14th century town wall stands in the field to the east of the abbey, and includes the **Sheep Gate**, the lone survivor of the town's original five gates. It used to be closed daily between 9 pm and 4 am, and a toll was charged for sheep entering to be sold at market.

Trim Castle has been under renovation for some time and may not be accessible during your visit.

Newtown
About 1.5km east of town on Lackanash Rd, Newtown Cemetery contains an interesting group of ruins.

What had been the **parish church of**

Newtown Clonbun contains the late 16th century tomb of Sir Luke Dillon, chief baron of the Exchequer during the reign of Elizabeth I, and his wife Lady Jane Bathe. The effigies are known locally as 'the jealous man and woman', perhaps because of the sword lying between them.

Rainwater that collects between the two figures is claimed to cure warts. Place a pin in the puddle and then jab your wart. When the pin becomes covered in rust your warts will vanish. Some say you should leave a pin on the statue as payment for the cure.

The other buildings here are Newtown's **Cathedral of Sts Peter & Paul** and the 18th century **Newtown Abbey**, or the Abbey of the Canons Regular of St Victor of Paris, to give it its full name. The cathedral was founded in 1206 and burned down two centuries later. Parts of the cathedral wall were flattened by a storm in January 1839, which also damaged sections of the Trim Castle wall. The abbey wall throws a superb echo back to **Echo Gate** across the river.

South-east of these ruins and just over the river is the **Crutched Friary**. There are ruins of a keep and traces of a watchtower and other buildings from a hospital set up after the crusades by the Knights of St John of Jerusalem, who wore a red crutch, or cross, on their cassocks. **St Peter's Bridge** beside the friary is said to be the second-oldest bridge in Ireland. *Marcy Regan's*, the small pub beside the bridge, claims to be Ireland's second-oldest pub.

Other Attractions

The site of the 13th century Dominican **Black Friary** lies north of the town, near the junction of the Athboy and Dunderry roads. Only a few mounds remain.

At the other end of town, **Maudlins Cemetery** has a bronze statue of Our Lady of Trim, a later version of a wooden statue put in St Mary's Abbey after its 1368 restoration. The statue, which was reputed to have miraculous powers, survived the abbey's suppression in 1540 and later came into the possession of a powerful local family. After the sacking of Drogheda in 1649, Crom-

well's commander lodged in the house and the statue was burned as firewood.

On the western outskirts of Trim, signposted from the centre of town, are the award-winning **Butterstream Gardens** (☎ 36017), open April to September, daily 11 am to 6 pm. Admission costs IR£3.

Places to Stay

Hostel The IHH *Bridge House Hostel* (☎ 31848), next to the tourist office and facing Bridge St, has dormitory beds for IR£10 and two private rooms for IR£12 per person. It opens June to August only.

B&Bs *Brogans Guesthouse* (☎ 31237), in the centre of Trim on High St, has an old-world flavour and costs from IR£17.50/30 singles/doubles. It has an adjoining bar that serves lunch. *White Lodge* (☎ 36549) is 500m east of the centre at the northern end of New Road. B&B is IR£20/28, or IR£25/32 with bathroom, and it opens March to October.

Linda O'Brien's *Friarspark* (☎ 31745) on Dublin Rd costs from IR£15 per person. *Crannmór* (☎ 31635) is a converted farmhouse about 2km along the road to Dunderry costing IR£21/32 with bathroom. Both open April to September.

Hotel Trim's only hotel is the 18-room *Wellington Court* (☎ 31516) in Summerhill Rd. Well equipped singles/doubles cost from IR£35/50.

Places to Eat

Emmet St has takeaway places including *Marigold* for Chinese food. *Spicer's Coffee Shop* in Market St is good for a snack. For a more substantial lunch, try the *Salad Bowl Deli* or the *Pastry Kitchen* next door on the same street. Almost opposite, the *Boyne Bistro* also does soups and sandwiches as well as more substantial lunches. The *Dean Swift Bar* in Bridge St, the *Abbey Lodge* on Market St and the *Priory Inn* on Haggard St are fine for bar food and lunches.

Stables (☎ 31110), the restaurant at the Haggard Inn on Haggard St is one of the best

MEATH & LOUTH

places to eat in town and has a three-course menu for around IR£12. Nearby is *Kerr's Kitchen*, where the service is a bit iffy, but the cakes look fine.

Getting There & Away

Buses stop in front of Tobin's newsagent at the top end of Haggard St. Buses running between Dublin's Busáras and Granard pass through Trim four times daily (twice on Sunday) in each direction. Some of these buses continue on to Athboy and Navan.

AROUND TRIM

Some 7.5km north-east of Trim on the way to Navan is **Bective Abbey** founded in 1147 and the first Cistercian offspring of magnificent Mellifont Abbey in Louth. The remains seen today are 13th and 15th century additions and consist of the chapter house, church, ambulatory and cloister. After the suppression of the monasteries in 1543, it was used as a fortified house, and the tower was built.

In 1186, Hugh de Lacy, lord of Meath, began demolishing the abbey at Durrow in County Offaly in order to build a castle. A workman, known both as O'Miadaigh and O'Kearney, was offended by this desecration, lopped off de Lacy's head and fled. Although de Lacy's body was interred in Bective Abbey, his head went to St Thomas Abbey in Dublin. A dispute broke out over who should possess all the remains, and it required the intervention of the Pope to, well, pontificate on the matter, with a ruling in favour of St Thomas Abbey.

Some 12km north-west of Trim on the road to Athboy is **Rathcairn**, the smallest Irish-speaking (or Gaeltacht) district in Ireland. Rathcairn's population is descended from a group of Connemara Irish speakers, who were settled on an estate here as part of a social experiment in the 1930s.

Six km south of Trim on the road to Summerhill stands **Dangan Castle**, built by the Wellesley family and the boyhood home of the Duke of Wellington. The castle is also supposed to have been the birthplace of Don Ambrosio O'Higgins (1720-1801), the

Spanish viceroy of Peru and Chile at the end of the 18th century. His son Bernardo O'Higgins went on to become the liberator of Chile, and Santiago's main thoroughfare is named after him. The mansion's current state is the result of the efforts of Roger O'Conor, its last owner, who set it alight on a number of occasions in 1808-09 for the insurance money.

Summerhill, another 5km farther south, is a pleasant, sleepy little village with a large, tidy green, but there's nothing much to do here except have lunch at *John Shaw's*, a pub-restaurant at the northern edge of the village. Jonathan Swift's connection with the area includes a curious folly in **Castle-richard**, a hamlet 10km west of Summerhill. By the church over the old bridge is a large stone pyramid inscribed with the word 'Swifte'.

KELLS

While almost every visitor to Ireland pays homage to the magnificent 'Book of Kells' in Dublin's Trinity College, few come to see where it originated and perhaps with good reason: present-day Kells (Ceanannas Mór) is an uninspiring place and little remains of the monastic site established here in the 6th century. Still, there are some fine high crosses in various states of preservation, a 1000-year-old round tower, the even older St Colmcille's House, and an interesting display in the gallery of the local church.

After establishing monasteries at Derry, Durrow and, in 559, at Kells, St Colmcille (also known as St Columba) went into exile on the remote Scottish island of Iona. In 807, monks from the Iona monastery arrived here after 68 of their brethren were killed in a Viking raid. It's thought that they brought both the remains of their revered saint and the 'Book of Kells' with them. The book was stolen two centuries later, but the thief was only after its gold case, and the manuscript was later found buried in a bog. Kells proved to be no safer than Scotland for the monks, however, as Viking raids soon spread to Ireland. Kells was plundered on no less than five different occasions between the 9th and 11th centuries.

Orientation & Information

The N3 from Dublin to Cavan and the border with Northern Ireland almost bypasses the town. Turning south at Cross St brings you down to Farrell St, where you'll find most of the pubs and shops (including Maguire's, a newsagent and grocery with disposable mousetraps among other useful items). There's no tourist office at present though one will open at the new heritage centre behind the town hall on Headfort Place when it's completed. For further information, ring the Kells Heritage Trust (☎ 40064). The hostel is also helpful with queries.

There's a Bank of Ireland branch on John St. The post office is in Farrell St.

The telephone code is ☎ 046.

Round Tower & High Crosses

The Protestant Church of St Columba west of the town centre stands on the grounds of the old monastic settlement. The church gallery has an exhibit on the settlement and its illuminated manuscript, with a facsimile on display. It opens weekdays 10 am to 5 pm, and on Saturday to 1 pm.

A square belfry dating from the 15th century stands beside the church. Above the doorway is an inscription detailing the addition of the neo-Gothic spire in 1783 by the earl of Bective from a design by Thomas Cooley, the architect of Dublin's City Hall.

The churchyard has a 30m-high, 10th century round tower on the south side. It's minus its conical roof but is known to date back to at least 1076, when Muircheartach Maelsechnaill, the high king of Tara, was murdered in its confined apartments.

Inside the churchyard are four 9th century high crosses in various states of repair. The **West Cross** at the far end of the compound from the entrance is the stump of a decorated shaft with scenes of the Baptism of Jesus, the Fall of Adam and Eve, and the Judgement of Solomon on the east face, and Noah's Ark on the west face. All that is left of the **North Cross** is the bowl-shaped base stone.

Detail of an illustration from the 'Book of Kells'

Near the tower is the best preserved of the crosses, the **Cross of Patrick & Columba**, with its semi-legible inscription 'Patrici et Columbae Crux' on the east face of the base. Above it are scenes of Daniel in the Lions' Den, the Fiery Furnace, the Fall of Adam and Eve and a hunting scene. On the opposite side of the cross are the Last Judgement, the Crucifixion, and riders with a chariot and a dog on the base. The council has plans to move this cross into the new heritage centre when completed to protect it from the elements.

The other surviving cross is the unfinished **East Cross**. On the east side is a carving of the Crucifixion and a group of four figures on the right arm. The three blank, raised panels below these were prepared for carving, but the sculptor apparently never got around to the task.

St Colmcille's House

From the churchyard exit on Church St, St Colmcille's House is left up the hill, among the row of houses on the right side of Church Lane. It usually opens June to September; otherwise, pick up the keys from the brown-coloured house at No 1 Lower Church View as you ascend the hill.

This squat, solid structure is a survivor from the old monastic settlement. The original entrance to the 1000-year-old building was over 2m above ground level and, inside, a very long ladder leads to a low attic room under the roof line.

MEATH & LOUTH

Market High Cross

Until recently the Market Cross had stood for centuries in Cross St in the town centre, marking the farthest extent of the 10th century monastery. It's said that it was moved here by Jonathan Swift, and in 1798 the British garrison executed rebels by hanging them from the crosspiece, one on each arm so the cross wouldn't fall over. Alas, in 1996 the cross met its ignoble fate – in a crass, modern manner. A motorist – local wags like to point out it was a woman driver – took a tight turn, reversed and toppled the 1000-year-old thing. It has now been repaired and will take pride of place in the new heritage centre. A replica will be placed in Cross St.

On the east side of the Market Cross are Abraham's sacrifice of Isaac, Cain and Abel, the Fall of Adam and Eve, guards at the tomb of Jesus, and a wonderfully executed procession of horsemen. On the west face, the Crucifixion is the only discernible image. On the north side is a panel of Jacob wrestling with the angel.

Places to Stay

The IHH *Kells Hostel* (☎ 40100) is next to Monaghan's pub on the Cavan road, 200m uphill from the bus stop. A bed in a dorm costs IR£6 to IR£7.50 depending on the season, and the two private rooms IR£7 to IR£9 per person. There's a full kitchen and other facilities. Camping in the garden costs IR£3 per person. You may have to check in at Monaghan's.

Headfort Arms Hotel (☎ 40063), in John St, has 18 rooms costing IR£30/58 for singles/doubles. Breakfast is IR£6.50 extra. It has a nightclub and restaurant attached.

The wonderful 200-year-old *Lennoxbrook House* (☎ 45902) is in Carnaross, 5km north of Kells on the N3, and costs from IR£21/32 for B&B. It's open all year.

Places to Eat

Penny's Place in Market St is an excellent café with home-made food; their brown bread has few equals. It's open until 6 pm, Monday to Saturday. *O'Shaughnessy's* pub farther west on Market St does reasonable sandwiches and lunches. Next to the post office in Farrell St, the *Round Tower* (☎ 40144) has a good restaurant and does substantial pub lunches. On the same street, *McGee's* on the corner opposite Maguire's does sandwiches, soups and afternoon teas. *Monaghan's* pub next to the hostel does lunch for around IR£5 and dinner with main courses from IR£6.

Entertainment

O'Shaughnessy's features lots of rustic timber, while the nearby *Blackwater Pub* has regular Irish music sessions. *Monaghan's* attracts a young crowd and often has music at weekends.

Getting There & Away

Buses stop in front of the church on John St and near the hostel (request stop only). Times are posted at the stop or phone Bus Éireann (☎ 01-836 6111) in Dublin. Buses run from Dublin to Kells and Cavan and back almost hourly from 7 am to 10 pm. Two of the buses are express coaches on their way to and from Donegal. There are also regular services to Navan, Dunshaughlin and Drogheda.

AROUND KELLS
Hill of Lloyd Tower

The 30m tower on the Hill of Lloyd is visible from behind the hostel in Kells, and it's easy to see why it became known as the 'inland lighthouse'. Built in 1791 by the earl of Bective in memory of his father, it has been renovated and if it's open you can climb to the top for IR£1/50p adults/children, or picnic in the surrounding park. The tower is 3km north-west of Kells, off the Crossakeel road.

Crosses of Castlekeeran

Two km farther down the Crossakeel road, signposted to the right, are the Crosses of Castlekeeran. Access is through a farmyard. Three plainly-carved, early 9th century crosses, one in the river, are surrounded by an overgrown cemetery, while at the ruined church in the centre are some early grave slabs and an Ogham stone.

LOUGHCREW CAIRNS

Northwest of Kells and near Oldcastle, the Loughcrew Hills – of which Slieve (or Sliabh) na Caillighe is the highest peak (277m) – give marvellous views east and south to the plains of Meath and north into the lake country of Cavan. On the summit of three of the hills – Slieve na Caillighe, Carnbane East and Carnbane West – are the remains of 30 Stone Age passage graves built around 3000 BC but used up to the Iron Age. In some cases, a large mound is surrounded by numerous, smaller satellite graves. Like Newgrange, larger stones in some of the graves are decorated with spiral patterns. Archaeologists have unearthed bone fragments and ashes, stone balls and beads. Some of the graves look like large piles of stones while others are less obvious, the cairn having been removed.

To get there from Kells, head north-west on the R163. About 5km from Oldcastle you'll see a sign for 'Sliabh na Caillighe'. Turn right, and at the first house on the right collect the keys to the cairn entrances from Basil Balfe (but ring ☎ 049-41256 first).

If anybody is there to collect it, a deposit of IR£5 (hikers can leave their backpacks as collateral!) is required, and a leaflet about the sites is available. A torch (flashlight) is useful on dull days. Coming from the east, the first group of hills – Patrickstown Cairns – is of little interest; the most interesting and intact remains are on the next two, Carnbane East and Carnbane West.

The owners of the Kells Hostel have a guided tour, available between June and September, of the Slieve na Caillighe cairns which also takes in the Hill of Lloyd tower and the early Christian sites at Fore Valley in County Westmeath. The tour costs IR£12 per person, with discounts for hostel residents. Raingear is provided, but you should wear suitable hiking shoes or boots.

Carnbane East

Carnbane East has a cluster of sites; Cairn T is the biggest at about 35m in diameter and has numerous carved stones. One of its outlying kerbstones is called the Hag's Chair and is covered in gouged holes, circles and other markings. You need the gate key to enter the passageway and a torch to see anything in detail. It takes about half an hour to climb Carnbane East from the car park. From the summit on a reasonably clear day, you should be able to see the Hill of Tara to the south-east while the view north is into Cavan with Lough Ramor to the north-east and Lough Sheelin and Oldcastle to the north-west.

Carnbane West

From the same car park, it takes about an hour to the summit of Carnbane West where Cairn D and L are both some 60m in diameter. Cairn D has been disturbed in an unsuccessful search for a central chamber. Cairn L, north-east of Cairn D, is also in poor condition, though you can enter the passage and chamber where there are numerous carved stones and a curved basin stone where human ashes were placed.

County Louth

Although the smallest county in Ireland, Louth is home to the two principal towns of Ireland's north-eastern region. Drogheda makes a good base for exploring the Boyne Valley, with its prehistoric sites to the west and the monastic relics to the north. Dundalk is a border town to the north and a gateway to the lonely but scenic Cooley Peninsula.

HISTORY

Humans have lived in this region since about 7000 BC, but Louth's Stone Age relics – like the Proleek dolmen and passage grave near Dundalk – pale in comparison with the Brugh na Bóinne relics in County Meath. Only with the coming of the Iron Age did Louth rival its neighbour.

The north of the county and the Cooley Peninsula are the setting for legends of

MEATH & LOUTH

Cúchulainn, one of the most famous heroes of ancient Ireland, who was born and raised around Faughart, just north of Dundalk. Cúchulainn was the lead player in the story of the Táin Bó Cúailnge (The Cattle Raid of Cooley), one of the great Celtic myths. *The Táin* by Thomas Kinsella (Dolmen Press) is a modern version of this compelling and bloody tale.

St Patrick introduced Christianity in the 5th century, and numerous religious communities sprang up in the region. The monastery at Monasterboice and the later Cistercian abbey at Mellifont, both near Drogheda, are Louth's most interesting archaeological sites.

Irish society underwent a huge upheaval with the arrival of the Anglo-Normans in the 12th century. Hugh de Lacy's reward for his Irish conquests was the fertile land of Meath and Louth. Mottes, such as the one at Millmount in Drogheda, were first built around this time to defend Anglo-Normans against the hostile Irish.

The Normans' stone castles came later, and smaller satellite castles such as Termonfeckin, north-east of Drogheda, dot the countryside. The Norman invaders were responsible for the development of Dundalk, and for the two towns, on opposite banks of the Boyne, which united in 1412 to become what is now Drogheda.

These new settlers would become some of the staunchest defenders of Ireland in later centuries, particularly against the English parliamentarians. In 1649, Cromwell's forces massacred the native Irish and old English Catholic defenders of Drogheda for refusing to surrender.

Ireland succumbed to English control in 1690, after the Battle of the Boyne where the Protestant William of Orange defeated his father-in-law, the English Catholic king, James II. James had enlisted the help of the Irish in return for greater religious and political freedom, and his defeat resulted in a new influx of Protestant settlers.

DROGHEDA

The historic town of Drogheda hugs a bend on the River Boyne, 5km from the sea. It's a compact settlement, with a small village-like adjunct to the south of the river around Millmount. Unfortunately, the city centre is congested and distinctly run-down in places, though restoration and redevelopment is taking place.

Once fortified, Drogheda still has one town gate in fine condition, together with some interesting old buildings and the curious hump of Millmount, south of the river. The embalmed head of the Catholic martyr St Oliver Plunkett (1629-81) is housed in St Peter's Roman Catholic Church.

The town's name comes from Droichead Átha, the Bridge of the Ford, after the bridge built by the Normans to link the two earlier Viking settlements. Drogheda featured in novelist Colleen McCullough's blockbuster *The Thornbirds*.

History

There was probably a rough settlement here before the 10th century, but Drogheda really began to take shape around 910, when the Danes built defences to guard a strategic crossing point on the River Boyne. In the 12th century, the Normans built a bridge and expanded the two settlements forming on either side of the river. They also built a large defensive motte-and-bailey castle on the south side at Millmount.

By the 15th century, Drogheda was one of Ireland's four major walled towns. Many Irish parliament sessions were held here, and Poyning's Law, passed in 1494, is the most famous piece of legislation from Irish medieval times. It diminished prospects of home rule or independence for Ireland by granting the English crown the right to veto any measures the Irish proposed to enact.

In 1465, the Irish parliament conferred on Drogheda the right to a university, but the plan foundered in 1468, when the earl of Desmond was executed for treason. During the period of the Pale, when only a small portion of the country around Dublin was fully controlled by the English, Drogheda was a frontier town. Farther north were the fractious Ulster folk, definitely beyond the Pale.

In 1649, the town was the scene of Cromwell's most notorious Irish slaughter. Marching north from Dublin he met with stiff resistance at Drogheda and when his forces overran the town on the third assault, the defenders were shown no mercy. The order went out to kill every man who had borne arms: an estimated 3000 were massacred, including civilians and children.

The defenders were a combination of native Irish and old English Catholic Royalists led by Sir Arthur Aston, who was beaten to death with his own wooden leg. Some of the survivors were shipped to Barbados. When 100 people hid in the steeple of St Peter's Church of Ireland, Cromwell's men simply burnt the church down. Drogheda also plumped for the wrong side at the Battle of the Boyne in 1690, but surrendered the day after James II was defeated.

It took many years for the town to recover from these events, but in the 19th century a number of Catholic churches were built. The massive railway viaduct and the string of quayside buildings hint at the town's brief Victorian industrial boom, when it was a centre for cotton and linen manufacture, and brewing.

For trivia buffs, it was a Drogheda man called Finlay who blew the bugle signalling the start of the Charge of the Light Brigade at Balaclava during the Crimean War (1853-56).

Orientation & Information

Drogheda sits astride the River Boyne with the principal shopping area on the north bank along the main street, called West St and Laurence St. The area south of the river is residential, dull and dominated by the mysterious Millmount mound. The main road to Belfast skirts around the town to the west.

The tourist office (☎ 041-37070) is currently housed in an office at the bus station on the south side of the river; there are plans to move to another location but it depends on funding. It opens Monday to Saturday 9.30 am to 5.30 pm, Sunday 11.45 am to 5 pm.

The main post office is on the middle of West St, next to the Westcourt Hotel. Most of the main banks are also on West St.

There's terrible traffic congestion in the city centre and disc parking is in operation throughout the town. Discs can be bought in newsagents and other shops.

The Wise Owl bookshop, on the corner of Shop St and North Quay, has a good range of books.

The telephone code is ☎ 041.

St Peter's Church

On West St, the Gothic-style St Peter's Catholic Church, dating from 1791, dominates the centre of town. In a glittering brass and glass case in the north transept you can see the head of St Oliver Plunkett (1629-81), executed by the perfidious English and now surrounded by flowers, candles and the attentions of the devout.

St Laurence's Gate

Astride Laurence St, the eastward extension of the town's main street, is St Laurence's Gate, the finest surviving portion of the city walls and one of only two surviving gates from the original 11.

The 13th-century gate was named after St Laurence's Priory which once stood outside the gate; no traces of it now remain. It consists of two lofty towers, a connecting curtain wall and the entrance to the portcullis. This imposing pile of stone is not in fact a gate but a barbican, a fortified structure used to defend the gate, which was farther behind it. When the walls were completed in the 13th century, they ran for 3km around the town, enclosing 52 hectares.

Millmount & Museum

Across the river from the town centre, in a village-like enclave amid a sea of dull suburbia, is Millmount, an artificial hill overlooking the town. Although it may have been a prehistoric burial mound along the lines of nearby Newgrange, it has never been excavated. There is a tale that it was the burial place of a warrior-poet who arrived in Ireland from Spain around 1500 BC.

MEATH & LOUTH

A Moving Head

In the north transept of Drogheda's St Peter's Church, a relic lurks inside a soaring reliquary of solid brass and unbreakable glass. Closer inspection reveals the leathery head of St Oliver Plunkett, hanged by the English in 1681 for his supposed part in the 'Popish Plot'.

Plunkett was born at Loughcrew, near Oldcastle, in 1629, a descendant of Brian Ború who had defeated the Danes at Clontarf in 1014. In 1645 he was sent to Rome to complete his education and stayed in Italy for 25 years. Ordained in 1654, he became Archbishop of Armagh and Primate of all Ireland in 1670. Following his consecration, he returned to Ireland in 1670. In the first three years of his mission he confirmed 48,655 people, ordained many priests and set up what may have been the first integrated Roman Catholic and Protestant school in Drogheda.

Oliver Plunkett

But Plunkett lived during a time when the English were particularly paranoid about the supposed threat from Roman Catholicism, and in 1679 he was seized and imprisoned in Dublin, accused of involvement in the 'Popish Plot'. This was an entirely fabricated conspiracy dreamt up by Titus Oates, a ne'er-do-well with a long history of dubious dealings, who claimed in 1678 that he had uncovered a plot to kill Charles II and turn the country over to the Jesuits. Despite Oates' past, he was believed and about 35 men were put to death for supposed involvement. Plunkett was accused of planning the invasion of Ireland by foreign powers and in 1680 he was moved to London's Newgate Prison. Tried and convicted of treason, he was hanged at Tyburn on 1 July 1681. The very next day the plot was revealed as a sham. Oates himself was flogged, pilloried and imprisoned for perjury, only to be pardoned and granted a pension after the revolution of 1688.

At the time of Plunkett's execution, the custom was to quarter the body and then burn the parts. Plunkett's friends obtained permission to remove the body, but only just managed to snatch the head from the fire; scorch marks are still visible on the left cheek and nose. The head and forearms were placed in tin boxes, and the rest of the body buried in St Giles Cemetery. Later it was exhumed and sent first to a Benedictine monastery in Germany, then to Downside in England. The head, meanwhile, was taken to Rome, then to Drogheda where the Sisters of Sienna looked after it for the next 200 years.

In 1920 Plunkett was beatified and the head was given to the new parish church of St Peter's, 'the Oliver Plunkett Memorial Church'. Following a miraculous cure in a Naples hospital which was attributed to Plunkett's intervention, the pope canonised him in October 1975.

In 1990 the priest of St Peter's decided to have the head examined since it was showing signs of decay. At the same time a living descendant of the saint provided a blood sample so that Turin Shroud-style DNA tests could be carried out to verify its authenticity. The tests having proved satisfactory, the saint's head was replaced in its reliquary inside an inner capsule containing silica gel which would make it easier to maintain the correct humidity level. The reliquary was then enclosed in a pedestal shrine over a metre high and with a soaring 9m stone spire. Beside it is displayed the original certificate of authenticity, dated 1682. ■

Throughout Irish history, poets have held a special place in society and have been both venerated and feared.

The Normans constructed a motte-and-bailey on top of this convenient command post overlooking the bridge. It was followed by a castle, which in turn was replaced by a Martello tower in 1808.

It was at Millmount that the defenders of Drogheda made their last stand before surrendering to Cromwell. Later, an 18th century English barracks was built around the base, and today this has been converted to house craft shops, museums and a restaurant, though the courtyard retains the flavour of its former life.

The tower played a dramatic role in the 1922 Civil War and the Millmount Museum has a colourful (and somewhat romanticised) painting of its bombardment. The top of the tower offers a fine view over the centre of Drogheda, on the opposite side of the river.

Millmount Museum A section of the army barracks is now a museum (☎ 33097) with interesting displays about the town and its history. They include three wonderful late-18th century guild banners, perhaps the last in the country. The pretty, cobbled basement is full of gadgets and kitchen utensils from bygone times, including a cast-iron pressure cooker and an early model of a sofa bed. There's an excellent example of a coracle, a tiny boat from earliest times. Across the courtyard, the **Governor's House** opens for temporary exhibitions.

The museum opens Tuesday to Saturday 10 am to 6 pm, Sunday 2.30 to 6 pm and entry is IR£1.50/75p. You can drive up to the hilltop or climb Pitcher Hill via the steps from St Mary's Bridge.

Butter Gate The 13th-century Butter Gate, just north-west of the Millmount, is the only genuine town gate to survive. This tower, with its arched passageway, predates the remains of St Laurence's Gate by about a century. St Mary's Churchyard to the south-east contains some of the original town wall and is reputedly where Cromwell breached the walls in 1649.

Other Buildings
On the corner of West and Shop Sts is the **Tholsel**, an 18th century limestone town hall, now occupied by the Bank of Ireland. Off Hardmans Gardens is the rather charming and more recent **Church of Our Lady of Lourdes**.

North of the centre on William St is **St Peter's Church of Ireland**. This contains the tombstone of Oliver Goldsmith's uncle Isaac, as well as another on the wall depicting two skeletal figures in shrouds, dubiously linked to the Black Death. This is the church whose spire was burnt by Cromwell's men, resulting in the death of 100 people seeking sanctuary inside. Today's church (1748) is the second replacement of the original destroyed by Cromwell. It stands in an attractive close approached through lovely wrought-iron gates. Note the old 'Blue School' of 1844 on one side.

On Fair St the modest 19th century **Courthouse** is being renovated and is home to the sword and mace presented to the town council by William of Orange after the Battle of the Boyne.

Topping the hill behind the main part of town is the **Magdalene Tower**, dating from the 14th century, the belltower of a Dominican friary founded in 1224. Here, England's King Richard II, accompanied by a great army, accepted the submission of the Gaelic chiefs with suitable ceremony in 1395; but peace lasted only a few months and his return to Ireland led to his overthrow in 1399. The earl of Desmond was beheaded here in 1468 because of his treasonous connections with the Gaelic Irish. The tower is reputed to be haunted by a nun.

Organised Tours
The Drogheda Historical Society occasionally runs summer tours of the town; phone the Millmount Museum (☎ 33097) to check if anything is scheduled. Harpur House (☎ 32736) helps organise tours of Drogheda and the Boyne Valley.

Places to Stay
Hostel The family run *Harpur House* (☎ 32736) on William St is near the centre of town. A dorm bed costs IR£7 or IR£10 in the double rooms. Breakfast is an extra IR£3.

B&Bs It's advisable to book ahead during the summer months.

Near town, south of the river, *Orley House* (☎ 36019), 100m off the main Dublin road in a housing estate, costs from IR£18/28. Nearby, on the main Dublin road near the railway station, is *St Gobnait's* (☎ 37844), costing IR£20/33 with bathroom.

Harbour Villa (☎ 37441) is 2km along the river towards the sea on the Mornington road. It overlooks the estuary and has small but pleasant rooms at IR£20/32 with shared bathroom. Further up the scale is *Boyne Haven* (☎ 36700), on the Dublin road opposite the Rossnaree Hotel. Its three rooms all have showers and cost IR£33/42.

Drogheda

PLACES TO STAY
14 Harpur House Hostel
24 Westcourt Hotel
36 St Gobnait's B&B
37 Orley House B&B

PLACES TO EAT
6 Ming Garden
12 Burke's Restaurant
13 La Pizzeria
17 Swan House
19 Moorland Café
23 Ger's
28 A Little Mouthful
33 Buttergate Restaurant

PUBS
8 Branagan's Pub
16 C Ní Cairbre
18 Weavers Pub

OTHER
1 Our Lady of Lourdes Hospital
2 Church of Our Lady of Lourdes
3 Cottage Hospital
4 Magdalene Tower
5 PJ Carolan Bike Hire
7 Courthouse
9 St Peter's Church of Ireland
10 Presbyterian Church
11 Police/Garda Station
15 St Laurence's Gate
20 St Peter's Catholic Church
21 Abbey Centre Cinema
22 Post Office
25 Drogheda Arts Centre
26 Tholsel
27 Wise Owl Bookshop & Coffee Shop
29 Bus Station & Tourist Office
30 St Mary's Catholic Church
31 Butter Gate
32 Millmount & Museum
34 Railway Station
35 St Mary's Church of Ireland

Hotels The more upmarket *Westcourt Hotel*
(☎ 30965) in West St is right in the town
centre, and normally costs IR£60/90 a
single/double, but it's worth asking about
special weekend bargain breaks. Both Mary
Robinson and Jack Charlton have visited
here.

Boyne Valley Hotel (☎ 37737) is a 19th century mansion set way back from the road and
has rooms at IR£49/90. It's just along the
main Dublin road. Farther out on the same
road you'll find the cheaper *Rossnaree Hotel*
(☎ 37673), just over the border in Meath,
which is good and costs IR£30/50.

Places to Eat
Cafés & Fast Food At the river end of Shop
St, on the corner of North Quay, *A Little
Mouthful* (☎ 42887) does excellent sand-
wiches (IR£1.75) and soup. Wednesday to
Sunday it opens from 7 pm as an Italian
restaurant and wine bar. *Moorland Café* on
West St does good coffee, snacks and light
meals. A chicken burger with chips is
IR£2.95.

The busy, Italian-owned *La Pizzeria*
(☎ 34208) on Peter's St features pizzas for
under IR£6, from 6 to 11 pm. It also does
pasta dishes. Down an alley on the other side

of the road, *Burke's Restaurant* does soups for IR£1.10 and main courses for IR£3.50. *Ger's* is another possible lunch stop for coffee and sandwiches in Peter's St.

The popular *Swan House* (☎ 35838) is a Chinese restaurant in West St; chicken dishes are around IR£7 and it does takeaways. The *Ming Garden* on Trinity St, also does Chinese food.

Pub Food & Restaurants The popular *Weavers* pub (☎ 32816), on West St, does some tasty pub food; lasagne with chips is IR£3.95. *Branagan's* (☎ 35607), on Magdalene St, is also popular, with a varied menu; main courses are IR£6.50 to IR£12 and Thai chicken is IR£8.85. About a km along the Dublin road, the *Black Bull Inn* (☎ 37139) was once winner of the 'regional pub of the year' title, and gets the local vote. Most mains are IR£7 to IR£12; Chinese-style duck is IR£8.90.

The excellent *Brasserie* at Rossnaree Hotel does an early-bird, three-course dinner 6 to 7.30 pm for IR£11.95; thereafter it's à la carte.

The rather cosy *Buttergate Restaurant* (☎ 34759), upstairs beside Millmount Museum has excellent food, with meals before 7 pm at IR£8 and after at IR£15 to IR£21. It opens Tuesday to Saturday for dinner and on Sunday for lunch and dinner.

Entertainment
Weavers on West St always has a youngish crowd and has live music Wednesday night, DJs at weekends. *Bridie Macs*, attached to the Westcourt Hotel, also offers a wide range of musical possibilities Thursday, Friday and Saturday. The *Black Bull Inn*, about 1km along the Dublin road, also has music on weekends.

C Ní Cairbre (Carberry's) pub, on North Strand near Laurence St, is a traditional old pub with Irish music sessions on Tuesday. In theory it's open from 7.30 am; in reality, opening hours vary depending on who's expected! It gets busy weekend nights.

The *Earth* nightclub, downstairs in the Westcourt Hotel, is popular. The Rossnaree

and the Boyne Valley hotels on the Dublin Rd also host *Place* and *Luciano's* nightclubs, respectively. Entry is about IR£5.

The two screen *Abbey Centre Cinema* (☎ 30188) is at the back of the Abbey shopping centre off West St. In the municipal building on Stockwell St, the *Drogheda Arts Centre* (☎ 33946) stages theatrical and musical events.

Getting There & Away
Bus Drogheda is only 48km north of Dublin, on the main N1 route to Belfast. The Bus Éireann station (☎ 35023), on the corner of John St and Donore Rd just south of the river, has numerous connections (6.15 am to 9 pm) with Dublin and Dundalk as well as to Belfast and other centres. The one-way fare to Dublin is IR£4.50. There's a handy expressway service from Drogheda to Galway once each morning; you can get off at Athlone for connections to Limerick, Sligo and Donegal.

Cheaper is Capital Coaches (☎ 042-40025) which has a daily Dundalk to Dublin service through Drogheda; its one-way fare from Drogheda to Dublin is IR£3.50.

Train Drogheda railway station (☎ 38749) is just south of the river and east of the town centre, off the Dublin road. Drogheda is on the main Belfast to Dublin line and there are five or six express trains (and many more slower ones) daily each way, with four on Sunday.

The train crosses the river just downstream from Drogheda on Sir John McNeill's mid-19th century Boyne Viaduct, a fine piece of engineering which dominates the seaward view.

Getting Around
Drogheda itself is infinitely walkable, and many of the surrounding region's interesting sites are within easy cycling distance. PJ Carolan (☎ 38242), 77 Trinity St, is part of the Raleigh Rent-a-Bike scheme and has good bikes for IR£7 a day. Bridge Cycles (☎ 3742), on North Quay near the bridge, rents bikes for IR£5 a day.

There's a small taxi rank (☎ 51839) on Duke St, just off West St. There's a larger cab rank on Laurence St near St Laurence's Gate.

AROUND DROGHEDA

Drogheda makes an excellent base for exploring the Boyne Valley sites to the west – see the County Meath section of this chapter for more details. In Louth itself, Mellifont and Monasterboice are two famous and picturesque monastic sites a few km north of Drogheda. Travelling to or from Northern Ireland there's a coastal route; the faster and duller N1 main road route; and a more circuitous inland route via Collon and Ardee which can include Mellifont and Monasterboice.

Beaulieu House

Five km east of Drogheda on the Baltray road is Beaulieu House, built between 1660 and 1666. The land, which had belonged to the Plunkett family since Anglo-Norman times, was confiscated under Cromwell. This lovely red-brick mansion, with distinctive steep roof and tall chimneys, is thought to have been designed by Sir Christopher Wren (architect of St Paul's Cathedral in London).

In 800 years the estate has been in the possession of only two families, first the Plunketts and then the ancestors of Lord Tichbourne. There's an impressive art collection, but it's a private residence, not open to the public.

Mellifont Abbey

Mellifont Abbey (☎ 041-26459), 8km northwest of Drogheda beside the River Mattock, was Ireland's first Cistercian monastery. The name comes from the Latin 'melli-fons' or 'honey fountain'. In its prime, Mellifont was the Cistercians' most magnificent and important centre in the country but, while the remains are well worth seeing, they don't really match the site's former significance.

In 1142 St Malachy, bishop of Down, brought in a new troop of monks from Clairvaux in France to combat the corruption and lax behaviour of the Irish monastic orders. These strait-laced new monks were deliberately established at this remote location, far from any distracting influences. The French and Irish monks failed to get on, and the visitors soon returned to the continent. However, within 10 years nine more Cistercian monasteries were established and Mellifont was eventually the mother house for 21 lesser monasteries. At one point, as many as 400 monks lived here.

Mellifont not only brought fresh ideas to the Irish religious scene, it also heralded a new style of architecture. For the first time in Ireland, monasteries were built with the formal layout and structure that was being used on the continent. Only fragments of the original settlement remain, but the plan of the extensive monastery can easily be traced. Like many other Cistercian monasteries, the buildings clustered around an open cloister or courtyard.

To the northern side of the cloister are the remains of a principally 13th century cross-shaped church. To the south, the chapter house, probably used as a meeting hall by the monks, has been partially floored with medieval glazed tiles, originally found in the church. Here also would have been the refectory or dining area, the kitchen and the warming room – the only place where the austere monks could enjoy the warmth of a fire. The east range would once have held the monks' sleeping quarters.

Mellifont's most recognisable building, and one of the finest pieces of Cistercian architecture in Ireland, is the *lavabo*, an octagonal washing house for the monks. It was built in the 13th century and used lead pipe to bring water from the river. A number of other buildings would have surrounded this main part of the abbey.

After the dissolution of the monasteries, a fortified Tudor manor house was built on the site in 1556 by Edward Moore, using materials scavenged from the demolition of many of the buildings. In 1603, this house was the scene of a poignant and crucial turning point in Irish history. After the disastrous Battle of Kinsale, the vanquished Hugh O'Neill, last of the great Irish chieftains, was given shelter here by Sir Garret Moore until he surrendered to the English Lord Deputy Mountjoy. After his surrender, O'Neill was pardoned but, despairing of his position, fled to the continent in 1607 with other old Irish leaders in the Flight of the Earls. In 1727 the site was abandoned altogether.

The visitor's centre next to the site describes monastic life in detail. Entry is IR£1.60/60p and the grounds are open daily, May to mid-June, 10 am to 5 pm; mid-June to mid-September, 9.30 am to 6.30 pm; and mid-September to the end of October, 10 am to 5 pm. A back road connects Mellifont with Monasterboice.

Monasterboice

Just off the N1 road to Belfast, about 10km north of Drogheda, is Monasterboice (Mainistir Bhuithe), an intriguing monastic site containing a cemetery, two ancient church ruins, one of the finest and tallest round towers in Ireland and two of the best high crosses.

Down a leafy country lane and set in sweeping farmland, Monasterboice has a special atmosphere, particularly at quiet times. The site can be reached directly from Mellifont via a winding route along narrow country lanes.

The original monastic settlement at Monasterboice is said to have been founded by St Buithe, a follower of St Patrick, in the 4th or 5th century, although the site probably had pre-Christian significance. St Buithe's name somehow got converted to Boyne, and the river is named after him. It's said that he made a direct ascent to heaven via a ladder lowered from above. An invading Viking force took over the settlement in 968, only to be comprehensively expelled by Donal, the Irish high king of Tara, who killed at least 300 of the Vikings in the process.

Entrance to Monasterboice is free and there's a small gift shop outside the compound. There are no set hours but come early or late in the day to avoid the crowds.

High Crosses Monasterboice's high crosses are superb examples of Celtic art. The crosses had an important didactic use, bringing the gospels alive for the uneducated – cartoons of the Scriptures, if you like. Like Greek statues, they were probably brightly painted, but all traces of colour have long disappeared.

Muiredach's Cross, the one nearest to the entrance, dates from the early 10th century. The inscription at the foot reads 'Or do Muiredach Lasndernad i Chros' – 'A prayer for Muiredach for whom the cross was made'. Muiredach was abbot here until 922.

The subjects of the carvings have not been positively identified. On the east face, from the bottom up, are thought to be: on the first panel, the Fall of Adam and Eve and the murder of Abel; on the second, David and Goliath; on the third, Moses bringing forth water from the rock to the waiting Israelites; and on the fourth, the Three Wise Men bearing gifts to Mary and Jesus. The Last Judgement is at the centre of the cross with the risen dead waiting for their verdict, and farther up is St Paul in the desert.

The west face relates more to the New Testament and from the bottom depicts the arrest of Christ; Doubting Thomas; Christ giving a key to St Peter; the Crucifixion in the centre; and Moses praying with Aaron and Hur. The cross is capped by a representation of a gabled-roof church.

The West Cross is near the round tower and stands 6.5m high, making it one of the tallest high crosses in Ireland. It's much more weathered, especially at the base, and only a dozen or so of its 50 panels are still legible.

The more distinguishable ones on the east face include David killing a lion and bear; the sacrifice of Isaac; David with Goliath's head; and David kneeling before Samuel. The west face shows the Resurrection; the crowning with thorns; the Crucifixion; the baptism of Christ; Peter cutting off the servant's ear in the garden of Gethsemane; and the kiss of Judas.

A third, simpler cross in the north-east corner of the compound is believed to have been smashed by Cromwell's forces and has only a few, straightforward carvings. Photographers should note that this cross makes

MEATH & LOUTH

a great evening silhouette picture, with the round tower in the background.

The round tower, minus its cap, stands in a corner of the complex. It's still over 30m tall but is closed to the public. In 1097, records suggest, the tower interior went up in flames, destroying many valuable manuscripts and other treasures. The church ruins are later and of less interest.

COLLON

Collon, a small village 10km north-west of Drogheda, was planned along English lines in the 18th century. It's now home to the newer Mellifont Cistercian monastery, founded in 1958, which is housed in the former landlord's residence north of the village.

The highly recommended but expensive *Forge Gallery Restaurant* (☎ 041-26272), near the parish church, features meat, fish, game and some vegetarian dishes; a set dinner costs £24. It's in an old forge building and exhibits paintings by local artists. It's closed Sunday and Monday.

ARDEE

How many towns can claim to have two castles in their main street? The sleepy market town of Ardee (Baile Átha Fhirdhia) on the narrow River Dee is 10km north of Collon on the N2. Its long, tidy main street – divided into Bridge, Market and Irish Sts – is dominated by Ardee Castle to the south and Hatch's Castle to the north.

History

For a small town, Ardee has a colourful history. It takes its name from Áth Fhír Diadh, or Fear Diadh's ford, inspired by the well-known tale of the combat between Cúchulainn and Fear Diadh or Ferdia, as recorded by the ancient tale of the Cattle Raid of Cooley.

In the 12th century, the area was turned into a barony and the town remained in English hands until being taken by the O'Neills in the 17th century. James II had his

headquarters here for two months in 1689, prior to the Battle of the Boyne.

Things to See

A square tower dating from the 13th century, **Ardee Castle** was an important outpost on the edge of the English Pale. It later became a courthouse and is now under restoration and will eventually house a museum. The smaller **Hatch's Castle** also dates from this time and it remained, from Cromwellian times until 1940, in the hands of the Hatch family. It's still a private residence.

The river bank can be explored around the ford, where there's a well-tended **riverside walk**.

Places to Stay

The *Railway Bar* (☎ 041-53279) in Market St does B&B for £15 a head. *Carraig Mor* (☎ 041-53513), 2km south of Ardee on the main Dublin to Donegal road, has rooms at IR£19 single or IR£28 to IR£32 double. *Gable's Restaurant* (☎ 041-53789), in Dundalk Rd, has rooms for IR£23/38.

For a real treat, try the elegant Georgian *Red House* (☎ 041-53523), which stands in its own demesne. Take the Dundalk road past Gable's Restaurant and it's about 500m along on the left. B&B costs IR£42.50/65, or IR£50/80 with bathroom. Dinner is another IR£20.

Places to Eat

Caffrey's bakery and coffee shop in the centre does sandwiches, light meals and cakes. *Sizzlers Cafe* does the full Irish breakfast all day for IR£3.50. Chinese takeaways are available from *Chinese Palace* (☎ 041-53998) near the bridge. *Auberge*, further along on Market St, is a restaurant and bar; mixed grill is IR£6.50. Similar is *Brian Muldoon & Sons*, where you can get a good steak, on Bridge St. At the other end on Irish St, a popular pub for meals is the *Lemon & Clove*.

The *Gable's Restaurant* (☎ 041-53789) charges IR£19.50 for a set dinner (its desserts are particularly memorable), and is

The Táin Bó Cúailnge – The Cattle Raid of Cooley

This remarkable tale of greed and war is one of the oldest stories in any European language and the closest thing Ireland has produced to the Greek epics. Queen Maeve, the powerful ruler of Connaught, was jealous because she couldn't match the white bull owned by her husband Ailill. She heard tales of the finest bull in Ireland, the brown bull of Cooley, and became determined to rectify the situation.

Maeve gathered her armies and headed for Ulster, where she conspired with her druids to place the Ulster armies under a spell. A deep sleep descended on them, leaving the province undefended. The only obstacle remaining was the boy warrior Cúchulainn, who tackled Maeve's soldiers as they tried to ford the river at Ardee in County Louth. Cúchulainn killed many of them and halted their advance. Maeve eventually persuaded Cúchulainn's half-brother and close friend, Ferdia, to take him on, but he was defeated after a momentous battle and died in Cúchulainn's arms.

The struggle continued across Louth and on to the Cooley peninsula, where many place names echo the ensuing action. Sex rears its head regularly in the Táin, for Maeve was more interested in her chief warrior Fergus than in her husband Ailill. At various spots in the saga, they sneak off to make love and in one instance Ailill steals the sword of the distracted Fergus, to shame him and show how careless he was.

While Maeve's soldiers were being despatched in all sorts of ways by Cúchulainn, Maeve had managed to capture the brown bull and spirit it away to Connaught. The wounded Cúchulainn defeated her armies, but the bull was gone. In the end, the brown bull killed Ailill's white bull and thundered around Ireland leaving bits of his victim all over the place. Finally, spent with rage, he died near Ulster at a place called Druim Tarb, the ridge of the bull. Cúchulainn and Ulster then made peace with Maeve and thus the saga ended. ∎

open Tuesday to Saturday. Bookings are advisable.

AROUND ARDEE
The Jumping Church of Kildemock

Three km south-east of town are the remains of the area's oddly named landmark, the Jumping Church of Kildemock. On a thunderous night in February 1715, a storm caused a wall of St Catherine's Church to shift inward from its foundations. However, rather than settle for this straightforward explanation, locals decided the church had miraculously jumped to exclude the remains of an excommunicated member of the flock who had been buried within its walls. Thus was born the 'jumping church'.

Tallanstown

North of Ardee, the main road forks to Monaghan and Dundalk. The slightly more interesting route to Dundalk is via Tallanstown (Baile an Tallúnaigh), with nearby Louth Hall, once belonging to the Plunkett family, barons of Louth. Oliver Plunkett took shelter here among his relations in the 1670s. It's not open to the public.

Louth Village

North of Tallanstown (but the turn-off is just south of town), the county's namesake is an insignificant little place with some mildly interesting remains. **St Mochta's** is a small 11th or 12th century church with enclosure and stone roof. St Mochta, a British follower of St Patrick, founded a monastery here in the early 6th century. Nearby is the church of a 15th century Dominican friary, sometimes called Louth Abbey.

Ardpatrick

To the east of Louth village is Ardpatrick and Ardpatrick House, home of Oliver Plunkett. There's a mound here where he is supposed to have illegally ordained priests. It was also a good vantage point to spot any advancing English soldiers.

THE COAST ROAD

While the most visually rewarding route between Drogheda and Dundalk is the minor inland road via Mellifont and Collon, the coastal route is also scenic. The latter heads off north under the railway viaduct, passes Baltray with its championship golf course

MEATH & LOUTH

and continues on quiet country roads to Termonfeckin.

Termonfeckin

A 6th century monastery was founded in Termonfeckin (Tearmann Féichín) by St Féichín of Cong, County Mayo. All that remains are some gravestones and a 10th century high cross, on the left as you enter the churchyard.

There's also a well-preserved 15th century **castle** or tower house (you can get the key from across the road, 10 am to 6 pm) which has two small corbel-vaulted alcoves and an anticlockwise spiral staircase (most go clockwise). From the village, follow the road to Seapoint Golf Club, take the first left, then the first right.

Clogherhead

A couple of km farther north is the busy seaside and fishing centre of Clogherhead (Ceann Chlochair), with a good, shallow Blue Flag beach. Around the town there are enjoyable walks along the coast (partially marred by vistas of caravan parks) or out to **Port Oriel**, an attractive little harbour with views of the Cooley Peninsula and the Mourne Mountains farther north. During the summer, Port Oriel is home to a fleet of trawlers and smaller fishing boats.

On the south side of the headland is **Red Man's Cave**. At low tide a reddish fungus becomes visible, covering the cave walls. According to folklore, a group of people fleeing from Cromwell hid in the cave. A barking dog then revealed the hide-out and the people were slaughtered, their blood splashing on the walls, where it remains to this day. The cave is hard to find so it's sensible to ask a local for directions, but even if you don't find it the walk is satisfying enough.

Annagassan

A minor road (R166), providing picture-book views, continues 12km north to Annagassan (Áth na gCasan), a town on the north side of Dunany Point, at the junction of the Dee and Glyde rivers. It's claimed locally that Annagassan is the site of the Vikings' first settlement in Ireland. Records suggest they sacked a monastery here in 842 and may have been responsible for the promontory fort, which is now a low mound overlooking the village.

Castlebellingham

North of Annagassan, the coast road joins the busy main N1 at Castlebellingham, only 12km from Dundalk. The village grew up around its 18th century mansion, which is something of a disappointment after the imposing castellated entrance. The mansion is on the site of an earlier castle burnt down by James II's troops; the owner, Thomas Bellingham, worked as a guide to William of Orange during his visit to Ireland in 1689-90. The building is now a hotel and restaurant (☎ 042-72176), with rooms from IR£19/28.

Buried in the local graveyard is Dr Thomas Guither, a 17th century physician supposed to have reintroduced frogs to Ireland by releasing imported frog spawn into a pond in Trinity College, Dublin. Frogs, along with snakes and toads, had supposedly received their marching orders from St Patrick 1000 years earlier.

Places to Stay

The coast road doesn't have too many places to stay but *Cross Garden* (☎ 041-22675), 1km south of Clogherhead on the Termonfeckin road, overlooks the sea and has very comfortable rooms for IR£20/30.

Places to Eat

The excellent *Triple House Restaurant* (☎ 041-22616) at the top of the hill in Termonfeckin serves a lot of fish and some meat. There's a three-course menu 6.30 to 7.30 pm for IR£11.50; after that it's IR£17.50. It's closed Monday. For cheaper food, try the nearby *Waterside Inn* which does soup and sandwiches.

Clogherhead's pubs are pretty ordinary but the *Sail Inn* has a large restaurant with an open fire.

PAT YALE

PAT YALE

TONY WHEELER

TONY WHEELER

TONY WHEELER

Counties Meath & Louth

A: Village pub/store, Carlingford, Louth
B: Harbour & castle, Carlingford, Louth
C: Church ruins, Slane, County Meath
D: West Cross, Monasterboice, County Louth
E: Drogheda, County Louth

TONY WHEELER

PAT YALE

PAT YALE

PAT YALE

TOM SMALLMAN

TONY WHEELER

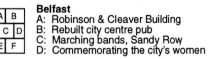

A	B
C	D
E	F

Belfast
A: Robinson & Cleaver Building
B: Rebuilt city centre pub
C: Marching bands, Sandy Row
D: Commemorating the city's women

E: Queen Victoria statue in front of City Hall
F: Grand Opera House

DUNDALK

Half way between Dublin and Belfast, Louth's charmless county town of Dundalk (Dún Dealgan) is only 13km from the border and widely regarded as a Republican stronghold.

Its name is derived from Dún Dealgan, a prehistoric fort which was reputedly the home of the hero Cúchulainn. The town grew under the protection of a local estate controlled by the de Verdon family who were granted lands here by King John in 1185. In the Middle Ages, Dundalk was at the northern limits of the English-controlled Pale, strategically located on one of the main highways heading north.

Orientation & Information

Northbound traffic sweeps round to the east of the town centre. The main commercial streets are Cambrassil and Park Sts. The tourist office (☎ 042-35484) is on Jocelyn St next to Louth County Museum. It's open Monday to Friday, 9.30 am to 5.30 pm (closed from 1 to 2 pm); in July and August it opens till 6 pm and on weekends. At other times there are boards and maps with tourist information dotted around town. The main post office is on Clanbrassil St.

The telephone code is ☎ 042.

Things to See

The **Courthouse** on the corner of Crowe and Clanbrassil Sts is a fine neo-Gothic building with large Doric pillars, designed by Richard Morrison who also designed the courthouse in Carlow. In the front square is the stone **Maid of Éireann**, commemorating the Fenian Rising of 1798.

At the top of Church St, **St Nicholas' Church**, or the Green Church, is the burial site of Agnes Burns, elder sister of Robert, the Scottish poet. She married the local rector, and the monument was erected by the townspeople to honour them both. The 15th century tower to the right of the church entrance is the oldest structure on the site.

The richly decorated **St Patrick's Cathedral** was modelled on King's College Chapel in Cambridge and in front of it on Jocelyn St is the **Kelly Monument**, in memory of a local captain drowned at sea in 1858. Also in Jocelyn St is the interesting **County Museum** (☎ 27056), with displays depicting the growth of industry in Louth since 1750. It opens Monday to Saturday, 10.30 am to 5.30 pm, Sunday 2 to 6 pm. Admission costs IR£2/60p.

At the east end of Jocelyn St is the Seatown area of Dundalk with its **castle** (really a Franciscan friary tower) and a derelict, sail-less **windmill**, the tallest in Ireland. If you arrive in Dundalk by train you pass the 1820 **Garda station** on St Dominick's Place on the way into town. Its first prisoner is believed to have been its architect, who misappropriated funds and was arrested for non-payment of bills.

Places to Stay

Camping The nearest camping is at *Gyles Quay Caravan & Camping Park* (☎ 76262), 16km west on the Cooley Peninsula. It's open March to October, has excellent facilities and charges IR£6.

B&Bs An excellent B&B is *Fáilte House* (☎ 35152) on the corner of Hill St and The Long Ave, which charges from IR£16/28 for singles/doubles. Just as good is *Rosemont* (☎ 35878), run by Mrs Meehan, near the Carroll's cigarette factory about 2km south of town on the main Dublin road. B&B is IR£20/30 or £21/32 with bathroom.

Innisfree (☎ 34912) in Carrick Rd close to the railway station is a pleasant, large Victorian house with rooms at IR£22/30, or IR£25/36 including bathroom. *Krakow* (☎ 37535), on Ard Easmuinn St, north of the railway station, has rooms for IR£19/28 or IR£21/32 with bathroom; dinner is available for IR£12.

Hotels *Imperial Hotel* (☎ 32241), on Park St, has a better interior than the outside would suggest. Singles/doubles with bathroom are IR£50/70. The *Fairways Hotel* (☎ 21500) on the Dublin road is modern, plush and costs IR£50/80.

Ballymascanlon Hotel (☎ 71124) is a

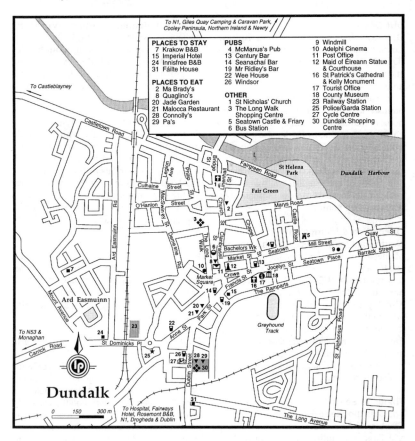

PLACES TO STAY
7 Krakow B&B
15 Imperial Hotel
24 Innisfree B&B
31 Fáilte House

PLACES TO EAT
2 Ma Brady's
8 Quaglino's
20 Jade Garden
21 Malocca Restaurant
28 Connolly's
29 Pa's

PUBS
4 McManus's Pub
13 Century Bar
14 Seanachaí Bar
19 Mr Ridley's Bar
22 Wee House
26 Windsor

OTHER
1 St Nicholas' Church
3 The Long Walk
    Shopping Centre
5 Seatown Castle & Friary
6 Bus Station
9 Windmill
10 Adelphi Cinema
11 Post Office
12 Maid of Éireann Statue
    & Courthouse
16 St Patrick's Cathedral
    & Kelly Monument
17 Tourist Office
18 County Museum
23 Railway Station
25 Police/Garda Station
27 Cycle Centre
30 Dundalk Shopping
    Centre

Dundalk

manor-house hotel with a swimming pool, squash courts, nine-hole golf course and other sporting facilities. It's 6km north of Dundalk on the way to Carlingford and costs IR£58/80 for B&B.

Places to Eat

Dundalk has plenty of cheap eateries. Try *Connolly's*, a small cafe and delicatessen on the ground floor of the Dundalk Shopping Centre south of the town centre and just off Dublin St. It serves mostly sandwiches and cakes. Upstairs, *Pa's* is a large restaurant and bar where you can get sandwiches and light

meals all day, including some vegetarian ones. Burgers are IR£2.50 to IR£3.75.

The busy *Malocca Restaurant* (☎ 34175), on Park St, serves curries, burgers, pizzas and sandwiches. Braised liver and onions cost IR£2.75. *Ma Brady's*, 7 Church St, is a homely place where a substantial dinner costs IR£5 to IR£10. Sirloin is IR£8.50. The *Windsor* pub on Dublin St, does light meals all day.

More upmarket places in town include *Quaglino's* (☎ 38567), an Italian restaurant near the post office where a five-course dinner costs IR£19. Back on Park St, the

Jade Garden (☎ 30378) is an excellent Chinese restaurant with dinners IR£8 to IR£15.

Entertainment

Several good pubs are found around Park St. *Mr Ridley's* has pop/rock most nights while *Seanchaí Bar* has Irish music on Tuesday night, jazz/blues on Sunday night. *Century Bar* at Roden Place, the *Wee House* in Anne St and *McManus's* in Seatown are popular watering holes.

The three-screen *Adelphi Cinema* (☎ 34843) is just off Market Square.

Getting There & Away

Bus Bus Éireann runs an almost hourly service to Dublin and a less-frequent one to Belfast. The bus station (☎ 34075) is on The Long Walk near the shopping centre. There are plenty of local buses and daily connections to centres nationwide. The one-way fare to Dublin is IR£6.

Train Clarke railway station (☎ 35521), a few hundred metres west of Park St on Carrick Rd, has 10 trains daily (four on Sunday) on the Dublin to Belfast line.

Getting Around

The Cycle Centre (☎ 37159), 44 Dublin St opposite Dundalk Shopping Centre south of the town centre, rents bikes for IR£4 a day.

Local taxi companies include A-1 Cabs (☎ 26666), 9 Crowe St, and Five Star Cabs (☎ 36000), 74 Canbrassil St.

AROUND DUNDALK
Into Northern Ireland

If you're heading for Derry, take the N53 to the west of town, while for Belfast continue north on the main N1 route. If you're hiking or cycling and want to go directly to the Mourne Mountains you can, June to September, get a ferry from Omeath to Warrenpoint in County Down.

The border is about 13km north of Dundalk. It's staffed by a garda and a British soldier (during the day anyway) but you probably won't be stopped. North of the border there are a couple of places where you can eat and change money.

Castleroche

Five km north-west of Dundalk on the Castleblayney road, Baron de Verdon's 1230 Castleroche Castle is impressively situated on a pinnacle of rock. The triangular remnants of the building include a twin-towered entrance house and protective wall. One of the windows on the west side is called 'Fuinneóg an Mhurdair', the Murder Window, because the baroness was said to have had the architect thrown from it to prevent similar castles ever being built.

Faughart

Faughart (Fochaird), about 4km north-east of Dundalk, has fine views and is reputed to be the birthplace of St Brigid, Ireland's most revered saint after St Patrick. She was the daughter of a local chieftain and settled in Kildare in the 6th century. The grotto and church here mark the spot of a monastery associated with her, and devotions are still carried out on 1 February, her feast day.

In the west corner of the graveyard is the grave of Edward Bruce, a king of Ireland who died in 1318. As part of the Gaelic revival he was invited to Ireland from Scotland and crowned by the Ulster lords, who hoped he would create trouble for the English in Ireland. He accepted the job, hoping this would relieve English pressure at home on his brother, Robert Bruce of Scotland. The hero Cúchulainn is said to have been born near here.

Proleek Dolmen & Gallery Grave

Heading north from Dundalk, turn right after 3km towards Ballymascanlon Hotel, the start of the Cooley Peninsula ring route. In the grounds of the hotel, up by the 5th green of the golf course (there's a signposted trail for non-golfers) is the fine Giant's Load Proleek Dolmen and Gallery Grave.

Local legends say it's the grave of Para Buí Mór MhacSeóidín, a Scottish giant who came here to challenge Fionn MacCumhaill, leader of the fabled Fianna warriors. It dates from 3000 BC, and the 47 tonne capstone sits precariously on three uprights. The pebbles on top are later additions and come from the belief that if you can land a stone on top, any wish will be granted. Single women who achieve this are guaranteed marriage within a year.

COOLEY PENINSULA

East of Dundalk, the lonely moorlands of the Cooley Peninsula are the setting for a large part of Ireland's most famous fable, the Táin Bó Cúailnge or the Cattle Raid of Cooley. The low mountains are really a part of Northern Ireland's Mourne Mountains, but are cut off from them physically by the flooded valley of Carlingford Lough and politically by the border which runs up the centre of the lough. The peninsula is a world of its own and has strong Republican traditions.

The best way to explore the peninsula is by first circumnavigating it on the ring road, perhaps detouring closer to the sea at **Gyles Quay** which has a safe beach, before arriving in Carlingford and Omeath. There's camping at *Gyles Quay Caravan Park* (☎ 042-76262), off the road to Greenore. Open March to October, it has excellent facilities and charges IR£6 per tent for up to two people.

Carlingford is probably the best base from which to venture inland over the peninsula's hilltops, soaked in the legends of the Cattle Raid of Cooley, through Windy Gap to the **Long Woman's Grave** and beyond to the picturesque country roads and forests which make the place a haven for walkers.

Carlingford

Near Carlingford (Cairlinn), the peninsula's mountains and views display themselves to dramatic effect. This pretty village, with its cluster of narrow streets and whitewashed houses, nestles on Carlingford Lough, beneath Slieve Foye (587m). After visiting in 1914, the Reverend Laurence Murray wrote of its 'medieval suggestiveness'; that suggestiveness survives today in the street plan and the crumbling walls and towers dotted around the village. Hard though it is

to believe, not much of this was appreciated until the late 1980s, when the villagers got together to show what can be done to revive a dying community. The story of their efforts is vividly told in the heritage centre.

The Mourne Mountains are just a few km north across the lough.

Information There's a small tourist office near the heritage centre. It's open Monday to Friday 9 am to 5 pm; on weekends you can get information from the heritage centre itself.

The telephone code is ☎ 042

Holy Trinity Heritage Centre The heritage centre (☎ 73454) in Churchyard Rd is in the former Holy Trinity Church. The information boards are encased within closeable doors so that the centre can double as a concert hall outside visiting hours. A fine mural shows what the village looked like in its medieval heyday when the Mint and Taafe's Castle were right on the waterfront. A short video describes the village history and explains what has been done to give it new life in recent years.

The centre opens daily noon to 5 pm. Admission costs IR£1/50p.

King John's Castle Carlingford was first settled by the Vikings, and in the Middle Ages became an English stronghold under the protection of the castle. It was built on a pinnacle in the 11th to 12th centuries to control the entrance to the lough. On the western side, the entrance gateway was constructed to allow only one horse and rider through at a time. King John's name stuck to a remarkable number of places in Ireland, given that he spent little time in or near any of them! In 1210 he spent a couple of days here en route to a nine day battle with Hugh de Lacy at Carrickfergus Castle in Antrim. It's suggested that the first few pages of the Magna Carta, the world's first constitutional bill of rights, were drafted while he was here.

Other Attractions Near the disused railway station is **Taafe's Castle**, a 16th century tower house which stood on the waterfront until the land in front was reclaimed to build the shortlived railway line. The **Mint**, in front of the hostel near the square, is of a similar age, but although Edward IV is thought to have granted a charter to a mint in 1467 no coins were produced here. The building has some interesting Celtic carvings around the windows. Near it is the **Tholsel**, the only surviving gate to the original town, although much altered in the 19th century when its defensive edge was softened in the interests of letting traffic through.

West of the village centre are the remains of a **Dominican Friary**, built around 1305 and used as a storehouse by oyster fishermen after 1539.

Carlingford is the birthplace of Thomas D'Arcy McGee (1825-68), one of Canada's founding fathers. A bust commemorating him stands opposite Taafe's Castle.

The Táin Trail Carlingford is the starting point for the 40km Táin Trail, making a circuit of the Cooley Peninsula, through the Cooley Mountains. The route is a mixture of surfaced roads, forest tracks and green paths. For more information contact the local tourist office or the office in Dundalk.

Cruises The Carlingford Pleasure Cruises (☎ 73239) run one-hour and all-day cruises between May and September. The one-hour cruises cost IR£3/1.50 per person; there's no set time, as departure depends on the tides.

Special Events In mid-August, the pubs are packed morning to midnight when the village is overrun by 20,000 visitors to the Oyster Festival, with funfairs, live bands and buskers alongside the official oyster-opening competitions and tastings.

Almost every weekend June to September, Carlingford goes event-crazy with summer schools, medieval festivals, leprechaun hunts and homecoming festivals.

Places to Stay Carlingford is a nicer place to stay than Dundalk and it has the bulk of accommodation on the peninsula, but it's limited and the village gets busy in summer, especially on weekends.

Hostel The IHH *Carlingford Adventure Centre & Hostel* (☎ 73100) is on Tholsel St just off the main street. Dorm beds cost IR£8.50 to IR£9.50 in rooms for two to eight people, and bedding costs IR£1 extra. The adventure centre exists to teach rock climbing, orienteering, hill walking and windsurfing to groups, so it's a good idea to check whether any large and potentially noisy gaggles of school kids will be staying at the same time as you.

B&Bs Carlingford's B&Bs are of a high standard, but there aren't many of them, so in summer and at weekends it's wise to book ahead. In the middle of the village, *Carlingford House* (☎ 73118) charges IR£35/40 and has a big drawing room with an open turf fire. *Viewpoint Guesthouse* (☎ 73149) overlooks the harbour in the village on the Omeath road. The motel-style rooms cost IR£26/40, including an excellent breakfast.

Mourneview farmhouse (☎ 73551), a km out of Carlingford in Belmont, costs IR£20/30. *Shalom* (☎ 73151) is along the road toward the pier, and has rooms with bathroom for IR£16 per person.

Hotels *McKevitt's Village Hotel* (☎ 73116) on Market Square has rooms at IR£40/70, and boasts a good bar and restaurant. *Jordan's* (☎ 73223) also has some comfortable, spacious rooms for IR£45/75.

Places to Eat The *Carlingford Arms* serves hefty helpings of pub food; two people could manage perfectly well with one serving of fish & chips. A three-course dinner costs IR£12.50. *PJ's* pub, the rear extension of O'Hare's grocery store, does half-a-dozen Carlingford Lough oysters with brown bread for £3.

Jordan's Restaurant (☎ 73223) in Newry St is a cosy place overlooking the water, and serves surprisingly sophisticated food. The menu ranges from oysters to unusual Irish dishes like crubeens (pig's trotters). There's a set dinner for IR£23.50; for à la carte count on around IR£30 per person with drinks. It's a good idea to make reservations in summer.

When everything else in town is closed, *McKevitt's* may still be serving food; salmon is IR£8.95. You can also get breakfast here for IR£5.50, even if you're not staying.

Entertainment Popular pubs include the *Carlingford Arms* and the *Central Bar* opposite, which has Irish music on weekends. *PJ's* pub, next door, is a traditional Irish bar where there's Irish music every Wednesday.

Getting There & Away Monday to Saturday, Bus Éireann has buses five times daily to Dundalk, twice daily to Newry. There are no Sunday services.

Omeath

Omeath (Ó Méith), smaller and less busy than Carlingford, lies across Carlingford Lough from County Down's Warrenpoint.

Facilities at the family-oriented *Táin Holiday Village* (☎ 042-75385), 2km south of Omeath on the Carlingford road, include a jacuzzi and indoor pool; tent sites cost £14.50. Nearby is the An Óige *Omeath Hostel*, beside the Táin Trail.

Farther south is the friendly *Delamare House* (☎ 042-75101), opposite St Jude's Shrine. It's run by Eileen McGeown and B&B in the large clean rooms costs IR£19/28, or IR£21/32 with bathroom.

Weather permitting, a passenger ferry (☎ 016937-72001), crosses the lough to Warrenpoint in County Down, May to September, daily 1 to 6 pm for £2/1 return.

Northern Ireland

A quarter of a century of bad publicity had rendered much of Northern Ireland a tourism no-go area. In 1995, following the declaration of the first ceasefire, the numbers of visitors from abroad and the South jumped dramatically. Although the numbers fell in 1996 after hostilities resumed, they were still higher than in 1994. Now that peace has broken out for a second time those figures are set to rise once more. Despite the apprehension engendered by news of bombings and shootings, tourists to Northern Ireland had always faced more danger from erratic Irish drivers – and probably still do – than from the Troubles.

In the North, the accent is distinctly different, the currency is pounds sterling and distances are measured in miles, but otherwise the changes across the border are insignificant. If anything, the Northern Irish are more friendly to foreign visitors than their compatriots in the South – perhaps to compensate for that bad publicity.

The rewards of a foray to the North are certainly worthwhile – the Antrim Coast road follows a stunning stretch of coastline, there are some fascinating early Christian remains around Lough Erne, and Derry has one of the best preserved old city walls in Europe. But even with the coming of peace and the ending of the military roadblocks, the signs of the Troubles can't be ignored: the street murals in Belfast and Derry, fortified police stations, armoured cars and circling helicopters are still as much a part of Northern Ireland as green fields and noisy pubs.

HISTORY

With the industrial revolution, Belfast and the surrounding counties became the major industrial centre on the island, but the wealth of Belfast's industrial expansion went primarily to the Protestant community. In the late 19th and early 20th centuries, when Home Rule for Ireland became a possibility, the Protestant citizens of Belfast joined the Ulster Volunteer Force (UVF) in large numbers to resist any such move. The Catholic minority felt increasingly alienated and there were occasional sectarian attacks.

Partition

Northern Ireland's relationship with the South was fraught with problems from the moment of partition. In the Government of Ireland Act of 1920 Lloyd George split Ireland into two and allowed for parliaments both north and south of the border. The division of the island was a rough and ready one. The Ulster Unionist leaders demanded only the six of Ulster's nine counties where they were supported by half or more of the population. While the South was overwhelmingly Catholic with a small Protestant minority (5%), the balance was very different in the North, with a substantial Catholic minority (over 30%) and many areas, especially in South Armagh, where Catholics were actually in the majority.

The Anglo-Irish Treaty of 1921 which partitioned the country and granted Ireland its independence was less than completely clear on the future of the North. A Boundary Commission was supposed to reconsider the borders and make adjustments as necessary, something it never did.

On 22 June 1921 the Northern Ireland parliament came into being, with James Craig as the first prime minister. In 1923 the Civil War in the South ground to an exhausted halt with reluctant acceptance of Ireland's division. In the North, Catholic nationalists elected to the new Northern Ireland parliament took up their seats with equal reluctance, but only in 1925, after the Boundary Commission had collapsed. The politics of the North became increasingly divided on religious grounds.

Protestant Dominance

The Northern Ireland parliament sat from 1920 until 1972 and the Protestant majority made sure their rule was absolute by systematically excluding Catholics from power. There was widespread discrimination against Catholics in housing, employment and social welfare. The Protestant reluctance to share the country with Catholics was exacerbated by the shortage of things to share out anyway. The effects of the 1930s depression were even more severe in Northern Ireland than elsewhere in the UK, with unemployment averaging 25%. Per capita income was only about 60% of the level in Britain, and indicators in every area from housing to public health were considerably worse than in Britain.

The government at every level from local councils to the Stormont parliament was Protestant-dominated and consistently followed a 'jobs for the (Protestant) boys' mentality. In the early 1970s when Belfast's population was 25% Catholic, only 2.5% of Belfast Corporation jobs were held by Catholics. In 1922, the bitter struggle going on in the South spilled over the border and serious rioting broke out in Belfast. In 1935, 11 people died in further riots in Belfast. But in spite of all this, Northern Ireland remained relatively peaceful for many years after partition.

In WWII, Belfast was heavily bombed, with many deaths and large areas of the city flattened. The first US army forces to land in Europe passed through Belfast on 26 January 1942. The strong support given to Britain's war effort further entrenched British backing for Northern Ireland's continued existence and independence. In 1949 the creation of the Republic of Ireland cut the South's final links, via the British Commonwealth, with the North. Even though the new republic's constitution enshrined its eventual goal of regaining the North, this caused little stir. Not until the 1960s did Northern Ireland's basic instability begin to show itself.

Civil Rights

In the 1960s the government, under Prime Minister Terence O'Neill, took the first tentative steps towards dealing with the problems of the North's Catholics. A meeting with the South's prime minister and a visit to a Catholic girls' school were hardly earth-shattering moves. But the reaction to these symbolic initiatives propelled Reverend Ian Paisley to the front of the stage as the ranting personification of Protestant extremism.

The next innocent addition to what was soon to become a messy stew was the creation of the Northern Ireland Civil Rights Association in 1967, to campaign for fairer representation for the North's Catholics. It was in Derry (Londonderry) that Protestant political domination was at its most outrageous, and in Derry that 50 years of Catholic anger at the rigging of council elections finally boiled over in the late 1960s.

Derry's population was split approximately 60% Catholic to 40% Protestant, yet the city's council was consistently elected with exactly the reverse ratio. This was accomplished not only by a long-running gerrymander of the electoral boundaries, but also by handing out more votes to the Protestants via residency and home-ownership requirements. In October 1968 a civil rights march in Derry was violently broken up by the Royal Ulster Constabulary and the Troubles, as they became euphenistically known, were under way.

In January 1969 People's Democracy, another civil rights movement, organised a Belfast to Derry march to demand a fairer division of jobs and housing and an end to unfair voting practices. Just outside Derry a Protestant mob attacked the marchers. The police stood to one side and then compounded the problem with a sweep through the predominantly Catholic Bogside area of Derry. Further marches and protests followed but, increasingly, exasperation on one side was met with violence from the other, and far from keeping the two sides apart the police were becoming part of the problem.

Finally in August 1969 British troops were sent into Derry and, two days later, Belfast, to maintain law and order. Though the British army was initially welcomed by the Catholics, it soon came to be seen as a tool of the Protestant majority. The peaceful civil rights movement lost ground and the IRA, which had been hibernating, found itself with new and willing recruits for an armed struggle for independence from among the beleaguered Catholic minority. Socialists like Bernadette Devlin provided a brief flash of leadership, but it was 'the men with the guns' who soon called the tune.

The Troubles

For 25 years the story of the Troubles was one of lost opportunities, intransigence on both sides and fleeting moments of hope. Suspected IRA sympathisers were interned without trial, and on 'Bloody Sunday' (30 January 1972) 13 civilians were killed by troops in Derry. Northern Ireland's increasingly ineffective parliament was abolished in 1972, although substantial progress had been made towards meeting the original civil rights demands. A new power-sharing arrangement was worked out in the 1973 Sunningdale agreement, but it was first rejected by the Protestants, then killed stone dead by the massive and overwhelmingly Protestant Ulster Workers' Strike of 1974. Northern Ireland has been ruled from London ever since.

Whilst continuing to target people in Northern Ireland, the IRA also moved their campaign of violence and terror to mainland Britain, bombing pubs and shops and killing many civilians. Their activities were increasingly criticised by citizens on all sides of the political spectrum, and by all mainstream political parties in Britain and the Republic. Meanwhile Loyalist paramilitaries were running a sectarian murder campaign against Catholics. The Troubles rolled back and forth throughout the 1970s, and although they slowed down during the 1980s an answer to the Irish problem seemed nowhere nearer. Passions reached fever pitch in 1981 when Republican prisoners in the North went on a hunger strike, demanding the right to be recognised as political prisoners. Ten of them fasted to death, the best known being an elected MP, Bobby Sands.

The waters were further muddied by an incredible variety of parties, groups, splinter groups and even splinters of splinter groups,

each with its own agenda. The Royal Ulster Constabulary (RUC) was reorganised and retrained, while the IRA split into 'official' and 'provisional' wings from whom sprang even more extreme republican organisations like the Irish National Liberation Army (INLA). Protestant loyalist paramilitary organisations sprang up in opposition to the IRA, and violence was frequently met with violence, indiscriminate outrage with indiscriminate outrage.

In 1985 the Anglo-Irish Agreement gave the Dublin government an official consultative role in Northern Ireland affairs for the first time. The idea was to make Northern nationalists feel that someone was looking out for their interests. However, the Unionist politicians were outraged by what they saw as meddling by the Republic and protested against and boycotted anything to do with the agreement. From 1985 onwards there was a steady increase in the level and professionalism of violence from the loyalist side of the divide.

It's easy to line up the 'if onlys' when it comes to the problems of Ireland. If only the Home Rule movement hadn't encountered such violent opposition to Irish independence in the early part of this century, Ireland might be one country today and the problem would simply not exist. Northern fears might have been reduced if only the Republic hadn't pandered to them by allowing the Catholic church's prejudices (on sex, marriage, censorship and the position of the church) to insinuate themselves into so many corners of the country.

Northern Catholics' antipathy to Northern Protestants might have been less if only they had been treated with some fairness between the 1920s and 1970s. Northern fears of Southern impoverishment might have been lower if only the Republic's government had not pursued its vision of a rural arcadia for longer than was sensible. The British army's unpopularity might have been far less if only it hadn't over-reacted to IRA provocation. And the North's unwillingness to countenance any agreement with the South might have been less if only the IRA hadn't been so callously indiscriminate in its violence or, equally frequently, so callously inept.

In 1970 the British home secretary, the hapless Reginald Maudling, was castigated for observing that the best hope for Northern Ireland was to achieve 'an acceptable level of violence'. Twenty years later that was precisely what had been achieved.

Today

However, in the 1990s some external circumstances started to alter the picture. Membership of the EU had reduced the differences between North and South, while economic progress in Ireland shrunk the disparity between Northern and Southern standards of living. The importance of the Catholic church in the South had also diminished.

In 1991, the various factions had met for talks under Peter Brooke, the British government's representative in Northern Ireland. Further talks were held in 1992. On the surface nothing much seemed to come of all this, but behind the scenes individuals, and particularly the Social Democratic & Labour Party (SDLP) leader John Hume, continued to beaver away, trying to persuade the mouthpieces of the main groups that something had to give.

Then, 25 years after the Troubles began, seemingly out of the blue, on 31 August 1994 the Sinn Féin leader Gerry Adams announced a 'cessation of violence' on behalf of the IRA. In October 1994 the Combined Loyalist Military Command also announced a ceasefire. Most British troops were then withdrawn to barracks and roadblocks were removed. There followed an edgy peace while all the parties restated their conflicting agendas.

In 1995 the British and Irish governments published two Framework documents intended to act as a basis for discussion on the way forward. The first, *A Framework for Accountable Government in Northern Ireland*, set out the British government's proposals for restoring democracy through a new 90-member Assembly to be elected by proportional representation and with 'sub-

stantial legislative and administrative powers'. In the second, *A New Framework for Agreement*, the British and Irish governments put forward their joint proposals for relationships within the island and between the two different governments.

Although it was stressed that these were discussion documents and that nothing would be imposed on anyone without a referendum first, both sides dug their heels in. The main sticking point was the issue of 'decommissioning' – the requirement by Unionists that the IRA show good faith on a final peace settlement by surrendering its weapons before talks begin. For their part Sinn Féin and the IRA argued that no arms could be given up until the British troops withdrew and political prisoners were freed, and that decommissioning should be part of the final settlement. With the peace process stalled, the IRA declared the ceasefire over when it exploded bombs in Canary Wharf in London on 9 February 1996, killing two people.

John Major's government, with a small majority in the House of Commons, had depended on the support of Unionist MPs. But in the British general election of May 1997, Tony Blair's Labour Party won a landslide victory enabling it to act with a much freer hand. In the same election, Sinn Féin's Gerry Adams and Martin McGuinness won two of Northern Ireland's seats in Westminster. In June, in the Irish Republic's general election, Fianna Fáil's Bertie Ahern, who had declared that he would be willing to talk to Sinn Féin about a new ceasefire, was elected as Taoiseach.

In the same month British officials, led by the Northern Ireland Secretary Dr Mo Mowlam, promised to admit Sinn Féin to all-party talks in Stormont Castle following any new ceasefire. In the meantime the British and Irish governments had accepted the proposal by George Mitchell, the former US senator brokering the talks, on how to get round the decommissioning impasse. Talks on the future of Northern Ireland would take place parallel with the talks on decommissioning.

The Public Faces of Conflict

Gerry Adams

The *Daily Telegraph* once claimed that the bearded, bespectacled Sinn Féin president, Gerry Adams, could be mistaken for a Liberal Democrat candidate canvassing in Oxford. Elsewhere he's been described as resembling a sociology lecturer at one of the old polytechnics. A glance at his CV quickly dispels any such illusions.

Adams was born in Belfast in 1948 into a staunchly Republican family and by the age of 16 had already joined Fianna, the IRA's youth wing. A year later, allegedly, he joined the IRA itself, rising rapidly through its ranks until, it is thought, he became chief of staff. Throughout the 1970s he was in and out of jail on a variety of charges and non-charges, but on his release he was elected to the Northern Ireland Assembly. In December 1982 he was excluded from Britain following a bomb outrage. Elected to the House of Commons as MP for West Belfast in 1983, he refused to take up his seat in a 'foreign Parliament'. He lost his seat at the 1987 general election but regained it in 1997.

Gerry Adams

It was Gerry Adams who articulated the belief that Irish freedom could only be bought by someone with a bullet in one hand and a ballot paper in the other. Throughout the Troubles, Adams was regularly featured in news broadcasts, organising and participating in paramilitary funerals. However, by 1988, when he met SDLP leader John Hume for talks, the tone of his public utterances had begun to soften.

In 1994 and 1997 it was Adams, as Sinn Féin president, who announced the IRA ceasefires. The end of the first ceasefire led to a lifting of the absurd British broadcasting ban which had meant his words could only be read on TV by an actor. Since then Adams has walked the world stage, meeting the likes of presidents Clinton and Mandela, and tirelessly expounding the Republican cause. He's the author of several books, including *Free Ireland: Towards a Lasting Peace*, in which he sets out his vision for the future, and an autobiography *Gerry Adams: Before the Dawn*.

Ian Paisley

If Gerry Adams is the man to set the hackles rising on one side, Reverend Ian Paisley, leader of the Democratic Unionist Party, has much the same effect on the other. Paisley, however, with his white hair, burly build and habit of throwing off microphones and stomping out of TV interviews, could never be mistaken for anything other than what he is, namely the extremist face of Protestant Unionism.

Born in Ballymena in 1926, Paisley took longer than Adams to get into his political stride. Motivated by a desire to exclude Catholics from power, he established the Protestant Unionist Party in 1970, later leaving and founding the Democratic Unionist Party. Although some of Paisley's views are unexpected (he opposed internment without trial, for example), he has been astonishingly persistent in opposing virtually every attempt at a settlement. He resigned his parliamentary seat in protest at the 1985 Anglo-Irish Agreement, only to win it back again with an increased majority in the ensuing by-election.

It's easy to parody Paisley (the man who wanted *The Sound of Music* banned because it featured a novice nun, the man who called Mrs Thatcher a liar from the House of Commons gallery and showered the Northern Ireland minister, Nicholas Scott, with bits of torn-up order paper in one of his more mature protests) but that would be to understate his importance. In *The Independent* David McKittrick once wrote that 'it seemed impossible to conceive of an arrangement which included him since he was more interested in protest than power – but it also seemed impossible to establish a workable arrangement without him, since he had the capacity to bring it down'. Even the normally open-minded travel writer Dervla Murphy was moved to write that she had recognised an 'evil influence' after listening to Paisley preach a sermon of pure hatred at his Matryrs' Memorial Free Presbyterian Church in Belfast at the height of the Troubles. ■

Encouraged by this, and by the decision of Ulster's Loyal Orange lodges to reroute or cancel some potentially violent 12 July marches celebrating the Battle of the Boyne, the IRA declared another ceasefire from 20 July. This cleared the way for Sinn Féin to take part in talks. Not surprisingly, extreme Unionists, led by Ian Paisley, responded by walking out, but more moderate Unionists, including the influential Ulster Unionist Party, led by David Trimble, have so far remained.

A timetable for negotiations, in which Tony Blair has declared that no outcomes are predetermined, has been set. It's intended that the results of their deliberations will be taken to the people of Northern Ireland to vote on in a referendum. Given Ireland's history and the conflicting aims of the protagonists it's clear that there's still a long way to go, but the faltering peace process may at last be moving forward.

GOVERNMENT & POLITICS

Together with Britain, Northern Ireland is part of the United Kingdom and is governed from Westminster, to which it sends 17 MPs to sit in the House of Commons.

The main Protestant/Loyalist party in the North is the Ulster Unionist Party (UUP), founded by Edward Carson. The largest political party in the province, it favours union with Britain, aligns itself with the British Tory Party and is led by David Trimble. The Democratic Unionist Party (DUP), led by the controversial Reverend Ian Paisley, not only wants to maintain ties with Britain, but also Unionist dominance of government institutions. Other Loyalist parties are the Progressive Unionist Party (PUP), the political wing of the Ulster Volunteer Force; the Ulster Democratic Party (UDP); and the United Kingdom Unionist Party (UKUP).

Trying to occupy the middle-of-the-road Catholic and Nationalist ground is the Social Democratic & Labour Party (SDLP), led by John Hume. Its aim is peaceful unification by consent of the majority of people in Northern Ireland, and over the years has been the main recipient of Nationalist votes. Sinn Féin ('Ourselves Alone') is the political wing of the IRA and attracts hard-line Nationalist voters. Its leader is Gerry Adams, with Martin McGuinness as his deputy.

ECONOMY

The region is heavily subsidised by Britain and, increasingly, by the European Union. It has also been receiving investment through the International Fund for Ireland (IFI), of which the US is one of the largest contributors. The aim of the fund is to promote the economy of the North and of the counties in the Republic that border it, emphasising cooperation between the two communities.

Traditionally, the North has been regarded as an economic black hole for Britain and much of the spending has been on defence and security. But things are improving.

Northern Ireland's unemployment rate has fallen to around 10%, from a high of 17% in the early 80s. Unemployment has largely been a result of the region's de-industrialisation during the 1970s and 80s; arguably it would have been much worse without the attention and money which has poured in during the last 20-odd years. Unemployment used to be far greater amongst the Catholic community, but the imbalance has narrowed.

About 32% of the working population is employed in one way or another by the government and there are many departments doing work for Britain. Agriculture employs around 6% of the labour force and manufacturing and construction 24%.

The first ceasefire in 1994 brought an almost instant dividend in the shape of a 20% boom in tourism, especially from Britain and the Republic, and the second one may produce similar results. If so, it could lead to the creation of thousands of jobs, and not just in tourism. On the other hand, jobs will be lost amongst security guards, glaziers and others who managed to earn a living out of the conflict.

Even before the second ceasefire was declared, the economy was doing well. The GDP was growing at a steady rate of 3% to 4% which forecasters expect to continue. Foreign investment in 1996 was a record £432 million and British retailers, like Sainsbury and Tesco, were expanding into Northern Ireland. There was also a big rise in shoppers from the South, taking advantage of the North's lower prices. With peace and the end of political uncertainty these changes could accelerate.

Belfast

Had the Troubles never happened, the capital of Northern Ireland would simply have been a big, rather ugly industrial city, pleasantly situated and with some imposing and impressive Victorian architecture but well past its prime. As it is, the strife which has torn Belfast apart for over 25 years has given it quite another edge. If your only view of the city has been through the media's lens, you may be surprised to find it's actually busy and bustling, clean and even prosperous in parts, with more glossy shopping centres and shiny new cars than Dublin.

However, a 'black taxi' ride through the strictly divided working-class areas of the Falls and Shankill Rds in West Belfast will show you the flip side of the coin. Much of the city centre is pedestrianised for security reasons, and reminders of the Troubles linger on in the grey armoured Land-Rovers ('tangis'), the heavily fortified police stations and the occasional helicopters buzzing overhead.

You may be reassured to know that no tourists have been killed or injured since the Troubles began in the early 1970s. In fact, statistically Belfast is a much safer city for a visitor than even the most touristically inclined US metropolises.

Another feature of Belfast is its size; the centre is compact, the traffic relatively light and most points of interest are within easy walking distance of each other. To the west are the Belfast Hills, visible from the town centre. The rocks and green slopes of Cave Hill, with the outline of 'Napoleon's Nose', loom over the city to the north, while the sweep of Belfast Lough cuts into the city centre from the north-east.

HISTORY

Compared with many other cities, Belfast is relatively new, with few reminders of its pre-19th century existence. The city's name comes from Beál Feirste, or 'mouth of the sandy ford', a reference to the River Farset

Highlights

- Eat out along the 'Golden Mile'
- Learn about the Troubles on the 'Living History' tour
- Watch the animals in Belfast Zoo and stroll through nearby Cave Hill Country Park
- Rub shoulders with the crowds in the Crown Liquor Saloon
- Take a (free) City Hall tour

which used to flow through the town centre but is now contained inside an underground pipe. In 1177, the Norman John de Courcy built a castle by the River Lagan, and a small settlement grew up around it.

Both were destroyed 20 years later, and the region was controlled for a long time afterwards by the Irish O'Neill family. In 1613, James I gave Belfast a charter as a city for the first time, but even during the late 17th century it was hardly more than a village; the population was a mere 550 in 1657. The first significant wave of foreign settlers were Huguenots: French Protestants, fleeing from persecution in France, who laid the foundations for a thriving linen industry. More Scottish and English settlers arrived, and other industries such as rope-making, tobacco, engineering and shipbuilding were also developed.

A strong antagonism between Protestants and Catholics only really developed during the 19th century. Prior to this, Belfast had produced many Protestant supporters of an independent Ireland and a fairer society. The United Irishmen, who pushed for increasing independence from England, were actually founded in Belfast in 1791, and the struggle for fairer trading terms enjoyed Protestant and Catholic support. The 1798 Rising, for example, was not purely religious. In Belfast a number of Protestant ministers who supported the revolt were hanged.

During the 18th and 19th centuries Belfast was the one city in Ireland which really experienced the industrial revolution. Sturdy rows of brick terraced houses were built for the factory and shipyard workers. A population of around 20,000 people in 1800 grew steadily to around 400,000 at the start of WWI, by which time Belfast had nearly overtaken Dublin in size. Some suspected that the frequent adjustments to the Dublin city boundaries were made partly in order to ensure the city's population remained a step ahead of the northern upstart.

Queen Victoria visited Belfast in 1849 and her brief foray through the city has been immortalised by a large number of streets and monuments named after her. Belfast was granted city status by Victoria in 1888.

The division of Ireland after WWI and independence in the South gave Belfast a new role as the capital of Northern Ireland. It also marked the end of the city's industrial growth, although the decline didn't really set in until after WWII. For nearly 50 years from 1922 until the late 1960s, Northern Ireland was a comparatively quiet place and as a result was studiously ignored by the British government. The Protestant-dominated Unionist government was left to run things as it saw fit, and since Catholic complaints

were relatively subdued, and were generally suppressed when they did get too loud, the underlying instability of the region was not noticed.

Since the initial outbreak of rioting in 1969, Belfast has seen more than its fair share of violence and bloodshed, and shocking pictures of extremist bombings and killings, often matched by security force brutality, have made the city a household name around the world. The mayhem reached its peak in the 1970s, and through the 80s and into the 90s Belfast appeared to have simmered down to an 'acceptable' level of violence. The ceasefire in 1994 briefly raised hope that things might at last improve, but after the bombing of Canary Wharf in London in 1996, there was a return to the tit-for-tat killings. The 1997 ceasefire has been met with more caution.

Greater Belfast's population of around 500,000 is about one-third of Northern Ireland's. While unemployment is relatively high, there's a burgeoning middle class which benefits from the reasonable tax rates and the relative cheapness of housing. Belfast has plenty of new cars and neat suburban houses, the city restaurants always seem full, and huge expenditure on public housing has smartened up even some of the bleak areas of West Belfast. The city is much livelier and more cheerful than its grim reputation leads visitors to expect.

ORIENTATION

The city centre is a compact area with the imposing City Hall in Donegall Square as a convenient central landmark. North of the square is Donegall Place/Royal Ave which leads to Donegall St and St Anne's Cathedral. This is Belfast's principal shopping district. Reminders of the Victorian era can be found in the stately buildings surrounding City Hall, in the narrow alleys known as the Entries off Ann and High Sts and in the museum-like Crown Liquor Saloon on Great Victoria St.

If you're looking for restaurants or accommodation head south from the square down Great Victoria St or Dublin Rd to University

Rd, where you'll find Queen's University, the Botanic Gardens and the Ulster Museum. This stretch is called the Golden Mile, and at night it's the most energetic and cheerful area of a generally hard-working city.

The Europa Buscentre is behind the rebuilt Europa Hotel, in Glengall St, and connected with the Great Victoria St train station. The new Laganside Buscentre is on Oxford St opposite Queen Elizabeth Bridge.

A cross-harbour rail link, the Dargan Bridge, runs alongside the Lagan Bridge north of Queen Elizabeth Bridge.

To the east of Donegall Square is Chichester St which runs down to Oxford St where you'll find the Royal Courts of Justice, the Laganside Buscentre, the River Lagan and Belfast Waterfront Hall a large conference and concert centre. East of the river are Samson and Goliath, the giant cranes dominating the Harland & Wolff shipyards. Short's aircraft factory is beside the Belfast city airport.

West of the centre, the Westlink Motorway divides the city from West Belfast and does nothing to improve the appearance of the place. The (Protestant) Shankill Rd and the (Catholic) Falls Rd run west into West Belfast. The 'Peace Line' built between the two was intended as a safety measure to discourage extremists of either ilk from creating mayhem then scuttling quickly back to their side of the tracks. It's now possible to cross from one side to the other. Beyond the Falls Rd lie even more run-down, deprived areas like Andersonstown and the Ardoyne.

It's worth remembering that Belfast grew out of the industrial revolution and, like cities in England's depressed north, has fallen on hard times, particularly in areas like West Belfast. Nevertheless, a great deal of renovation and reconstruction, much of it part-funded by the European Regional Development Fund (ERDF) or the International Fund for Ireland (IFI), is going on.

Maps

Tourist brochures contain reasonable maps of the city centre, but these are usually limited in scope or legibility. Ordnance Survey of Northern Ireland publishes the large fold-out *Greater Belfast Street Map* which is good for an overall view of the city and includes bus routes. It's rather unwieldy for use in a car, in which case you might want to consider a street atlas like Bartholomew's *Belfast Streetfinder*.

INFORMATION
Tourist Offices

The Northern Ireland Tourist Board office (☎ 246609) is at St Anne's Court, 59 North St. Most of the year it opens Monday to Saturday 9 am to 5.15 pm. In June, July and August, the peak of the summer season, it has extended opening hours which may vary depending on the number of visitors. In those months it's usually open Monday to Friday 9 am to 7 pm, Saturday 9 am to 5.15 pm, Sunday 10 am to 4 pm. Outside these hours, a computerised database outside gives details of accommodation etc. You can pick up information about the whole of Northern Ireland here, and book accommodation both within Northern Ireland and in Britain. There's also a bureau de change and souvenir shop. The tourist information office also stocks four *Civic Festival Trails* to guide you round the best of the city centre's buildings.

There are also tourist information offices in Belfast city and international airports; the city airport branch opens daily 5.30 am to 10 pm, while the international airport branch opens more or less round the clock except November to February when it closes between 11 pm and 7 am.

The Irish Tourist Board, or Bord Fáilte (☎ 01232-327888), 53 Castle St, opens Monday to Friday 9 am to 5 pm, Saturday 9 am to 12.30 pm from March to the end of September only. The head office of the Youth Hostel Association of Northern Ireland (YHANI; ☎ 315435) is at 22-32 Donegall Rd, off Shaftesbury Square.

Foreign Consulates

Some countries with consular representation in Belfast are:

Denmark, Sweden
c/o G Heyn & Sons Ltd, Head Line Buildings, 10 Victoria St, Belfast BT1 3GP (☎ 01232-230581)
Greece, Norway, Portugal
c/o M F Ewings (Shipping) Ltd, Hurst House, 15-19 Corporation Square, Belfast BT1 3AJ (☎ 01232-242242)
Italy
7 Richmond Park, Belfast BT9 5EP (☎ 01232-668854)
USA
Consulate General, Queen's House, 14 Queen St, Belfast BT1 6EQ (☎ 01232-328239)

Other consulates in Northern Ireland are:

Belgium
c/o John Preston & Company, Flax House, 29-31 Lisburn St, Hillsborough, County Down (☎ 01846-682671)
Netherlands
Old Glenarm Rd, Larne, County Antrim BT42 2ST (☎ 01574-261300)

Money
There are branches of the major Northern Irish banks in the centre of Belfast and numerous cash machines which dispense money to Visa, MasterCard (Access) and other customers.

The tourist office in St Anne's Court has a bureau de change, as does the GPO in Castle Place and the post office in Shaftesbury Square.

There's a branch of Thomas Cook (☎ 550232) with exchange facilities at 11 Donegall Place, and another at the international airport (☎ 01849-422536) which stays open until 8 pm.

Post & Communications
The GPO, on Castle Place at the junction of Donegall Place and Royal Ave, opens weekdays 9 am to 5.30 pm, Saturday 9 am to 7 pm. Other convenient post offices are in Shaftesbury Square and at the junction of University and Malone Rds.

There are plenty of public telephones and these are divided into coin only, phone card only, and those that accept both.

You can log onto the Internet at the Revelations cafe (☎ 320337; email info@revelations.co.uk) on Bradbury Place near

Roscoff restaurant, south of Shaftesbury Square.

Belfast's telephone code is ☎ 01232.

Useful Organisations
The AA (☎ 0990-989 989), 108-10 Great Victoria St, sells maps and travel guides; for breakdowns phone ☎ 0800-887766. For the RAC call ☎ 0345 331133; for breakdowns phone ☎ 0800 828282.

Northern Ireland Women's Aid (☎ 249041), 129 University St, will help with inquiries about specific women's issues.

Travellers with disabilities can call Disability Action (☎ 491011), 2 Annadale Ave, for advice; the tourist office also produces a useful free brochure, *Accessible Accommodation in Northern Ireland*.

Cara-Friend, PO Box 44, Belfast BT1 1SH, is able to advise you on gay and lesbian matters. Otherwise, evenings only, men can call the mensline (☎ 322023) Monday to Wednesday 7.30 to 10.30 pm; women can call the lesbian line (☎ 238668) Thursday 7.30 to 10.30 pm.

Travel Agencies
The USIT/Belfast Student Travel office (☎ 324073) is at 13B Fountain Centre, College St. Queen's University Travel Centre (☎ 241830), in the Student Union Building in University Rd, is also run by USIT and opens to non-students of Queen's too.

For more conventional travel information there's Thomas Cook (☎ 550232) at 11 Donegall Place.

Bookshops
Mainstream bookshops include Waterstone's (☎ 247355), 8 Royal Ave, Eason's (☎ 328566), 16 Ann St, and Dillon's (☎ 240159), 42 Fountain St. Queen's University also has a bookshop at University Terrace off University Rd beside Elmwood Hall and opposite Queen's College.

For a wide selection of books on Ireland and good advice on what to read, try Familia (☎ 235392), 64 Wellington Place on the

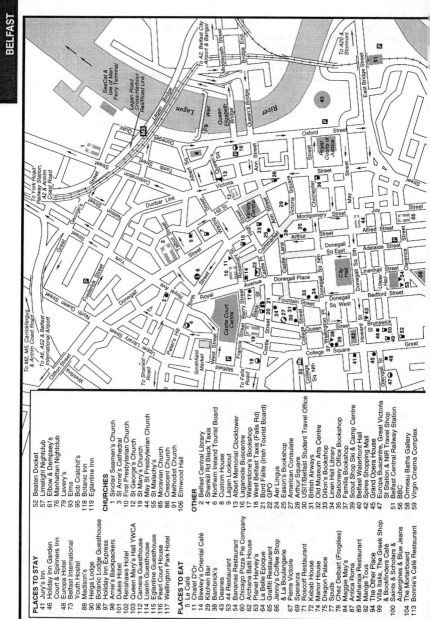

PLACES TO STAY
41 Jury's Inn
46 Holiday Inn Garden
   Court & Spinners Inn
48 Europa Hotel
73 Belfast International
   Youth Hostel
88 Madison's
90 Helga Lodge
96 Botanic Lodge Guesthouse
97 Holiday Inn Express
98 Arnie's Backpackers
101 Dukes Hotel
102 Renshaws Hotel
103 Queen Mary's Hall YWCA
112 Camera Guesthouse
114 Liserin Guesthouse
115 Eglantine Guesthouse
116 Pearl Court House
117 Wellington Park Hotel

PLACES TO EAT
5 Le Café
11 Chalet D'Or
14 Bewley's Oriental Café
29 Kitchen Bar
38 Bambrick's
43 Deanes
53 44 Restaurant
54 Bananas Restaurant
60 Chicago Pizza Pie Company
62 Archana Balti House
63 Planet Harvey's
64 La Belle Epoque
65 Graffiti Restaurant
66 Jenny's Coffee Shop
   & La Boulangerie
67 Pierre Victoire
69 Speranza
72 Roscoff Restaurant
74 Kebab House
75 Dragon Palace
77 Spuds
78 Chez Delbart (Froglies)
84 Maggie May's
87 Antica Roma
89 Maharaja Restaurant
92 Mange Tous
94 The Other Place
99 Villa Italia, The Greek Shop
   & Bookfinders Café
100 Saints & Scholars &
   Aubergines & Blue Jeans
104 The Mortarboard
113 Bonnie's Café Restaurant

52 Beaten Docket
57 Limelight Nightclub
61 Elbow & Dempsey's
76 Manhattan Nightclub
79 Lavery's
93 Elms
95 Bob Cratchit's
118 Botanic Inn
119 Eglantine Inn

CHURCHES
1 Sinclair Seamen's Church
3 St Anne's Cathedral
10 First Presbyterian Church
12 St George's Church
19 St Mary's Church
44 May St Presbyterian Church
55 St Malachy's
85 Moravian Church
86 Crescent Church
91 Methodist Church
106 Elmwood Hall

OTHER
2 Belfast Central Library
4 Shankill Rd Black Taxis
6 Northern Ireland Tourist Board
8 Custom House
9 Lagan Lookout
13 Albert Memorial Clocktower
16 Laganside Buscentre
17 Waterstone's Bookshop
18 West Belfast Taxis (Falls Rd)
21 Bord Fáilte (Irish Tourist Board)
22 GPO
24 Aer Lingus
25 Eason's Bookshop
27 American Consulate
28 Arthur Square
30 USIT/Belfast Student Travel Office
31 British Airways
32 NI Museum Arts Centre
33 Dillon Bookshop
34 Linen Hall Library
35 Stationery Office Bookshop
37 Familia Bookshop
39 Scout Shop Ski & Camp Centre
40 Belfast Waterfront Hall
42 Spires Shopping Mall
45 Grand Opera House
47 Europa Buscentre, Great Victoria
   St Station & NIR Travel Shop
51 Belfast Central Railway Station
56 BBC
58 Ormeau Baths Gallery
59 Virgin Cinema Complex

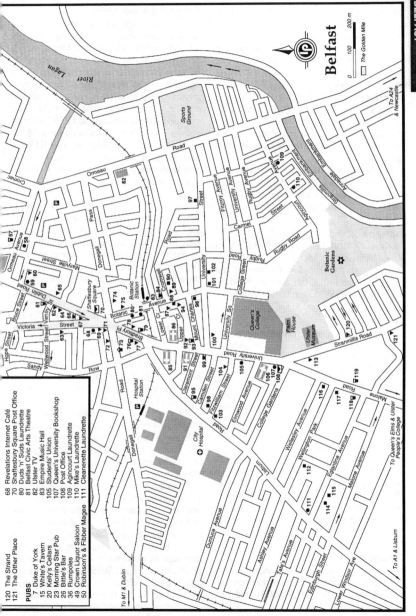

BELFAST

120 The Strand
121 The Other Place

PUBS
7 Duke of York
15 White's Tavern
20 Kelly's Cellars
23 Morning Star Pub
26 Bittle's Bar
36 Rumpoles
49 Crown Liquor Saloon
50 Robinson's & Fibber Magee

68 Revelations Internet Café
70 Shaftesbury Square Post Office
80 Duds 'n' Suds Laundrette
81 Belfast Civic Arts Theatre
82 Ulster Hall
83 Empire Music Hall
105 Students' Union
107 Queen's University Bookshop
108 Post Office
109 Agincourt Laundrette
110 Mike's Laundrette
111 Cleanerette Laundrette

Belfast

The Golden Mile

River Lagan

Sports Ground

To A24 & Newcastle

To M1 & Dublin

To A1 & Lisburn

To Queen's Elms & Ulster People's College

City Hospital

Botanic Gardens

Queen's College

Ulster Museum

Palm House

corner of College Square East. The Green Cross Art Shop (☎ 243371), 51-3 Falls Rd, has a range of books on Irish issues, mainly giving the Republican perspective. It's run by the wives of Republican prisoners. The government-run Stationery Office Bookshop (☎ 235041), 16 Arthur St, has a selection of maps and guides.

Bookfinders (☎ 328269), 47 University Rd, is a second-hand bookshop with a popular café at the back. Roma Ryan's (☎ 242777), 73 Dublin Rd, stocks prints and rare books.

See Books & Bookshops in the Facts for the Visitor chapter for books on Northern Ireland's turbulent history, visitors' accounts and fiction by Northern Irish writers.

Libraries

Belfast Central Library (☎ 243233), in Royal Ave, opens Monday and Thursday 9.30 am to 8 pm; Tuesday, Wednesday and Friday 9.30 am to 5.30 pm; Saturday 9.30 am to 1 pm. See also the Linen Hall Library later.

Laundry

In the university area there's Mike's Laundrette and Agincourt Laundrette at 46 and 120 Agincourt Ave, and Cleanerette Laundrette at 160 Lisburn Rd. More fun is Duds 'n' Suds, 37 Botanic Ave, which incorporates a snack bar. It's open Monday to Friday 8 am to 9 pm, Saturday 8 am to 6 pm, Sunday noon to 6 pm.

Medical Services

Shaftesbury Square Hospital (☎ 329808) is at 16-20 Great Victoria St near the city centre. Further south, Belfast City Hospital (☎ 329241) is on Lisburn Rd; bus Nos 58 and 59 pass by. Royal Victoria Hospital (☎ 24053) is on Grosvenor Rd west of the city centre; bus Nos 80 and 81 stop nearby.

Emergency

For police, ambulance or fire services phone ☎ 999. Other emergency numbers are the Rape Crisis Centre (☎ 326803) and the Samaritans (☎ 664422).

Dangers & Annoyances

Even at the height of the Troubles Belfast wasn't a particularly dangerous city for tourists. The callous violence between the IRA (and its various offspring) and the equivalent Loyalist paramilitaries was usually aimed at specific people. Nevertheless, security precautions used to affect tourists as much as anyone. If the present ceasefire holds, you can expect to see the army and RUC security patrols scaled down. You're no more likely to be stopped and asked for your ID on a Belfast street than on a London one and you're probably safer from 'normal' criminal activity in Belfast than you are in London.

It continues to make sense to be careful where you park your car though. Cars illegally (or suspiciously) parked can expect rough treatment. In practice this isn't quite as fearsome as it sounds; even in the bad times you were unlikely to come back to find the bomb squad in action just because you'd overstayed a parking meter for 10 minutes! Parking isn't allowed in the prominently marked Control Zones. Indeed it's still wise to use proper car parks wherever possible, whatever the cost, if only because Belfast has a problem with 'joy-riding'; the police view is that guarded multi-storey car parks are the best bet. The tourist office has a leaflet showing all the car parks, or for information you can phone ☎ 253031.

As anywhere, you should always lock your car when you leave it and take anything valuable with you. If you leave it in the car, make sure it's out of sight and bear in mind that many insurance policies exclude items stolen from cars.

From the visitor's point of view one of the irritating legacies of the Troubles is the absence of luggage storage facilities at bus or train stations. You may need to open your bag for inspection before going into some public buildings, but this type of security measure is now more commonplace in Dublin than Belfast! Some letterbox slits are also partially closed to prevent anything bulkier than a letter being posted. To outsiders police stations can also look offputtingly fortified. Take heart though. If you need to report a 'normal' crime like a stolen camera, just march up to the door and press the buzzer. Someone will emerge to help you out.

It's still a good idea to carry some form of identification on you; a passport is particularly good as it proves you're a real visitor. If you want to take photos of fortified police stations, army posts or other military or quasi-military paraphernalia, ask first to be on the safe side.

You're unlikely to get into furious political or religious arguments in Belfast pubs because both topics are usually avoided with outsiders. In staunchly single-minded pubs of either persuasion, outsiders are often studiously avoided!

AROUND THE CENTRE

Donegall Place runs north from Donegall Square then changes its name to Royal Ave. The city's busy and mainly pedestrianised shopping centre spreads out on either side of this important avenue. The pedestrianisation of the centre is in part a by-product of the Troubles. At their height in the 1970s, terrorist activities turned the whole centre into a heavily militarised zone, but the security presence is very low-key now, and modern city planning would probably have got around to excluding cars in any case.

The **Cornmarket** (William St South), just east of Donegall Place, takes its name from an older agricultural Belfast but is still a popular, if scruffy, meeting place. Two modern shopping centres, the Castle Court in Royal Ave and the Variety Centre in High St, are symbols of the vibrant Belfast that has grown up in spite of the Troubles.

Belfast City Hall

The industrial revolution transformed Belfast, and that rapid rise to muck-and-brass prosperity shows to this day. The Portland-stone City Hall in Donegall Square was completed in 1906. Built in the Classical Renaissance style, much to the disdain of architectural purists, it has some fine Italian marble inside and a great deal of pomp and splendour outside. The first meeting of the Northern Ireland parliament was held here in 1921, but it subsequently met at the Union Theological College until Stormont was completed in 1932.

The most noticeable feature of the exterior used to be the huge 'Belfast Says No' banner displayed along the top of the building. It was placed there by the Unionist city fathers to show their objections to the Anglo-Irish Agreement, which was signed in 1985 and formed the basis of ongoing consultations between Britain and the Republic over the North. Most Unionist city councillors also refused to take part in council affairs while the agreement was in force. In 1988 the City Hall was bombed and the stained glass windows in the Great Hall were destroyed. When the building was uncovered after cleaning in 1994, the banner had disappeared, a small symbol of a greater willingness to negotiate

The hall is fronted by a statue of a rather dour Queen Victoria. Statues of city mayors also guard the building on the Donegall Square North side. At the north-east corner of the City Hall grounds is a statue of Sir Edward Harland, the Yorkshire-born marine engineer who founded the Harland & Wolff shipyards. In its prime, the shipyard was one of Belfast's biggest businesses and it still survives, if in much quieter form. The yard's most famous construction was the ill-fated *Titanic*, which sank in 1912 after colliding with an iceberg on its maiden voyage to America. A memorial to the disaster and its victims stands on the east side of the City Hall.

The Marquess of Dufferin (1826-1902), whose career included postings as ambassador to Constantinople in Ottoman Turkey, St Petersburg in Tsarist Russia, Paris and Rome, and as governor-general to Canada and viceroy to India, has an extremely ornate temple-like memorial on the west side of the City Hall. He was responsible for adding Burma to the British Empire in 1886. Look out, too, for monuments to the United States of America Expeditionary Force which

The Red Hand of Ulster

The symbol of the province of Ulster is a striking red hand which you'll see displayed on coats of arms, in stained-glass windows and, vividly, above the entrance to the Linen Hall Library in Donegal Square North. The story goes that way back in the Middle Ages when Viking raids were a regular occurrence, a group of Vikings had already settled the land and looked on in horror as another raiding vessel approached. The chief announced that the land would belong to whoever put their hand on it first, whereupon he sliced off his own hand and threw it forward, thus beating the raiders to it. Impressed by this, the O'Neill clan later adopted the red hand as their emblem, and it went on to become the symbol of Ulster. ∎

arrived in Belfast in January 1942, and to the Boer War.

June to September, Monday to Friday at 10.30, 11.30 am and 2.30 pm there are free one-hour tours of the City Hall (☎ 320202, ext 2346); the rest of the year they're available Monday to Friday at 2.30 pm and Wednesday at 10.30 am. Among other things, you get to see the Council Chamber with red and blue flashing lights to tell councillors when they've overtalked their allotted 10 minutes; a painting of the proclamation of Edward VII outside City Hall (slashed by a visitor in 1991 and now behind glass); and some highly fanciful images in the grey and white marble of the hall.

Linen Hall Library

At 17 Donegall Square North, looking across the square to the City Hall, the Linen Hall Library (☎ 321707) was established in 1788 (although not in this building), and has a major Irish collection, most of which survived an IRA incendiary device planted inside. It includes the most complete collection of early Belfast and Ulster printing, and key research collections in Irish and local studies.

Thomas Russell, the first librarian, was a founding member of the United Irishmen and a close friend of Wolfe Tone – a reminder that this movement for independence from Britain had its origins in Belfast. Russell was hanged in 1803 after Robert Emmet's abortive rebellion. For over a century the library was in the White Linen Hall, which was built from 1784 but demolished to make way for

the City Hall. The entrance doorway to the present library is draped with stone linen and topped by the red hand of Ulster.

You can visit the library Monday to Wednesday and Friday 9.30 am to 5.30 pm, Thursday to 8.30 pm, and Saturday to 4 pm. Only library members may borrow books though.

Other Donegall Square Buildings

Donegall Square, with the City Hall squarely in the middle, is undoubtedly the centre of Belfast. If you come into town by local bus you're likely to be dropped here as most local bus services arrive and depart from around the square.

It has a number of interesting buildings, but easily the most magnificent is the wonderfully ornate **Scottish Provident Building**, built from 1899 to 1902, overlooking the City Hall from Donegall Square West. It's decorated with a veritable riot of fascinating statuary, including several allusions to the industries that assured Victorian Belfast's prosperity, as well as sphinxes, dolphins and a variety of lions' heads. Nowadays it houses a gift shop.

The building was the work of the architectural partnership of Young & MacKenzie who counterbalanced it in the same year with the **Pearl Assurance Building** on the Donegall Square East corner. Between these two examples of turn-of-the-century extravagance is the equally fine **Robinson & Cleaver Building**, once the Royal Irish Linen Warehouse and then Belfast's finest department store.

The Entries

The area immediately north of High St was the oldest part of Belfast but it suffered considerable damage during WWII bombing. The narrow alleyways known as the **Entries** run off High St and Ann St in the pedestrianised shopping centre. At one time they were bustling commercial and residential centres: Pottinger's Entry had 34 houses in 1822. Today pubs are just about all that survive down these reclusive hideaways. The **Morning Star** on Pottinger's Entry is one of the most attractive of these wonderful old Belfast bars.

Joy's Entry commemorates the Joy family. In 1737 Francis Joy founded the *Belfast News Letter*, the first daily newspaper in Britain. It's still in business today. One of his grandsons, Henry Joy McCracken, was executed for supporting the 1798 United Irishmen's revolt.

The United Irishmen were founded in 1791 by Wolfe Tone in Peggy Barclay's tavern in **Crown Entry**. They used to meet in **Kelly's Cellars** (1720) on Bank St off Royal Ave. **White's Tavern** (1630) on Wine Cellar Entry is the oldest pub in the city and is still a popular lunch-time meeting spot.

Albert Memorial Clocktower

WJ Barre's 1867 Albert Memorial Clocktower, located in Queen's Square at the junction of High St and Victoria St, is not so dramatically out of kilter as the famous tower in Pisa, but it is, nevertheless, a leaning tower.

Around the Clocktower

Looking across the River Lagan from the clocktower, west Belfast is dominated by the huge cranes of the Harland & Wolff shipyards. Many of the buildings around the clocktower are the work of Sir Charles Lanyon, the pre-eminent architect of Belfast in its prime. The modern Queen Elizabeth Bridge crosses the Lagan just to the south, but immediately south again is **Queen's Bridge** with its ornate lamps. Completed in 1843, this was Lanyon's first important Belfast construction. Immediately north of the clocktower is a disused white stone building originally completed in 1852 by Lanyon as a head office for the Northern Bank.

Further north stands **Clifton House**, built in 1774 as a poorhouse and the finest surviving 18th-century building in Belfast. East towards the river is the renovated **Custom House**, built by Lanyon in Italianate style in 1854-7. On the waterfront side the pediment carries sculptured portrayals of Britannia, Neptune and Mercury.

Follow the waterfront round to the SeaCat and Isle of Man ferry terminal beside the **Harbour Office**. The office has exhibits relating to the city's maritime history but is only rarely open to the public. The intriguing Sinclair Seamen's Presbyterian Church next door is dealt with later in this chapter.

Lagan Lookout Visitor Centre

A weir built across the River Lagan makes it possible to control the flow of water and keep ugly mudflats covered up. The Lagan Lookout Visitor Centre (☎ 315444) offers a state-of-the-art explanation of how the weir works and why it was needed, with interactive computers to bring things to life. Through the windows of the circular building you can view not just the weir but also the distant Harland & Wolff shipyard. Each Sunday there's a guided tour through a tunnel under the river from Donegall Quay to Queen's Quay.

April to September it opens Monday to Friday 11 am to 5 pm, opening at noon on Saturday and 2 am on Sunday. October to March it closes at 3 pm Monday to Friday and opens 1 to 4 pm Saturday, 2 to 4 pm Sunday. Admission is £1.50/75p.

Crown Liquor Saloon

Across from the Europa Hotel on Great Victoria St, the Crown Liquor Saloon was built by Patrick Flanagan in 1885 and displays Victorian architectural flamboyance at its most extravagant. Owned by the National Trust, who have removed some of the newer embellishments, and operated by Bass Ireland, this pub is on every visitor's itinerary; you need to get there early to have any hope of standing space, let alone a seat. The exterior is decorated with myriad different coloured and shaped tiles, while the interior has a mass of stained and cut glass, marble, mosaic and mahogany furniture. 'Gas' mantles provide atmospheric lighting.

A long, highly decorated bar dominates one side of the pub while on the other is a row of ornate wooden snugs topped by stirring mottoes. The snugs come equipped with brass plates for striking matches and with bells which were once connected to the bell board behind the bar, enabling drinkers to demand top-ups without leaving their seats. The bells have since been disconnected and you'll have to take your chances in the crush around the bar; men appear to take precedence over women when it comes to getting served.

The Crown was lucky to survive the 1993 bomb which devastated the Opera House and destroyed Robinson's, a couple of doors away. Above the Crown is the **Britannic Bar** which displays memorabilia from the *Titanic*; the entrance is around the corner in Amelia St.

Grand Opera House

One of Belfast's great landmarks is the Grand Opera House (☎ 241919), across the road from the Crown Liquor Saloon on Great Victoria St. Opened in 1895, the Opera House was closed for a considerable part of the 1970s before a restoration project completely refurbished both the interior and the red-brick exterior.

It suffered grievously at the hands of the IRA. A 450kg truck bomb was their 1991 Christmas gift to Belfast culture, and a multi-million-pound reconstruction had barely been completed before they parked another well-loaded truck outside on 20 May 1993. The interior has been restored to over-the-top Victoriana, with purple satin in abundance and swirling wood and plasterwork. It's constantly busy with music shows, operas and plays.

WALKING TOURS
Walking Tour 1 – Prince Albert to Queen Victoria

This walking tour takes you from a memorial to Prince Albert, Queen Victoria's husband, to another to Queen Victoria herself, exploring the city's Victorian heartland on the way. Sadly, many of the grand 19th-century buildings stand empty and boarded-up. The leaning (1) **Albert Memorial Clocktower** on Queen's Square makes an easily located start for the walk. Immediately north of the clocktower is (2), the 1852 building Sir Charles Lanyon designed for the **Northern Bank**, now owned by the First Trust Bank but disused.

This walk passes by several other Lanyon buildings, including the grand 1857 (3) **Custom House**; restoration work should have given this a new lease of life by the time you read this. From the waterfront side you can see the sculptured pediment at the front of the building. Across the road is the now disused Calder Fountain, erected in memory of a naval commander who installed cattle troughs in Belfast in the 1840s and founded the local Society for the Prevention of Cruelty to Animals.

Turn down Albert Square and cross Victoria St to Waring St where the grandiose 1860 (4) **Ulster Bank** survived wartime bombing that obliterated much of this area. The imposing building has iron railings decorated with the red hand of Ulster, cast-iron lamp standards, soaring columns and sculptured figures of Britannia, Justice and Commerce. The rooftop figures were by Thomas Fitzpatrick who was also responsible for the carvings on the nearby Custom House. Inside it's even more impressive, with cute blue cherubs playing instruments to customers queuing to access their bank accounts.

At the junction of Waring St with Donegall St is the deserted 1822 (5) **Commercial Building**, easily identified by the prominent name of the Northern Whig Printing Company. Opposite is the (6) **Belfast Bank Building**, now occupied by the Northern Bank and the oldest public building in

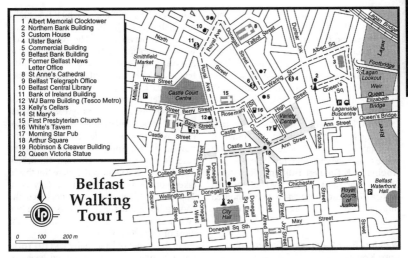

1 Albert Memorial Clocktower
2 Northern Bank Building
3 Custom House
4 Ulster Bank
5 Commercial Building
6 Belfast Bank Building
7 Former Belfast News
  Letter Office
8 St Anne's Cathedral
9 Belfast Telegraph Office
10 Belfast Central Library
11 Bank of Ireland Building
12 WJ Barre Building (Tesco Metro)
13 Kelly's Cellars
14 St Mary's
15 First Presbyterian Church
16 White's Tavern
17 Morning Star Pub
18 Arthur Square
19 Robinson & Cleaver Building
20 Queen Victoria Statue

Belfast
Walking
Tour 1

0   100   200 m

the city (although bearing little relationship to its original design). The building started life as a single-storey market house in 1769, became the Assembly Rooms, with the addition of an upper storey, in 1777 and in 1845 was remodelled by Charles Lanyon to become the bank buildings.

Turn up Donegall St, looking for Commercial Court, a narrow laneway hiding the Duke of York pub. The former home of the (7) *Belfast News Letter* at No 59 is an 1873 building decorated with bas-relief portraits of literary figures. The imposing (8) **St Anne's Cathedral** was built from 1899 but has little of interest inside apart from the grave of Edward Carson. At Royal Ave turn left, noting the modern offices of the (9) *Belfast Telegraph* and then the red sandstone (10) **Belfast Public Library**. Continue along Royal Ave as it bends to the left, but look back to the (11) **Bank of Ireland Building**, a fine example of 1920s Art Deco and elegantly placed at the junction of North St and Royal Ave.

Past the Castle Court Centre and the Virgin Megastore is the 1868 (12) **WJ Barre Building**, designed by the man who was also responsible for the Albert Memorial Clock-

tower at the start of this walk. The building is now owned by Tesco Metro and has been imaginatively restored, with the supermarket extension at the rear. Turn right by the bank into Bank Place and (13) **Kelly's Cellars**, a whitewashed 18th-century pub where the United Irishmen once met. Just beyond the pub is the elaborate grotto of (14) **St Mary's**, the first Catholic church in Belfast, which opened in 1784. Return to Royal Ave and backtrack to the Virgin Megastore then turn right into Rosemary St, past the 1783 (15) **First Presbyterian Church** with its curious elliptical interior.

A few steps further, a right turn leads into Winecellar Entry where Belfast's oldest pub, (16) **White's Tavern**, lurks. It's been here since 1630 although it was rebuilt in 1790. Turn right, then left down High St with its narrow 'entries'. On the right is Pottinger's Entry sheltering the (17) **Morning Star Pub**. Pottinger's Entry emerges on to pedestrianised Ann St: note the arm holding up an umbrella which emerges from the building opposite the entry.

Turn right down Ann St to (18) **Arthur Square**, where five pedestrianised streets meet with a bandstand, newsstands, buskers, preachers, hawkers and all sorts of other activities. This was once the central traffic junction in the city but the traffic has long been diverted. It was also the site of the Abercorn, a popular café before the Troubles, until one crowded Saturday lunch time in 1972 when a terrorist bomb destroyed it; redevelopment has removed all trace of the place. Continue along Castle Lane and turn left down Donegall Place with the City Hall towering in front of you. At the corner of Donegall Place and Donegall Square North is the ornate carved stone facade of the (19) **Robinson & Cleaver Building**. Resolutely guarding the front of the City Hall, the (20) **statue of Queen Victoria** in time-honoured 'not amused' pose marks the end of this walk.

Walking Tour 2 – Queen Victoria to Lord Kelvin

The (1) **statue of Queen Victoria** in front of the City Hall concluded Walk 1 and marks the beginning of this walk south of the city centre to the university area, botanic gardens and the restaurant-studded Golden Mile. See the City Hall section for information about this symbol of Belfast at the height of the industrial revolution. Standing in front of the Victoria statue and looking, like her, down Donegall Place, you can see the (2) **Robinson & Cleaver Building** on the corner of the square and Donegall Place. To the right on the corner of the square is the magnificent redbrick (3) **Pearl Assurance Building**. To the left is the even more magnificent (4) **Scottish Provident Building**, now housing a gift shop.

Bid Victoria farewell and turn left along Donegall Square North noting the (5) **Linen Hall Library** whose history, though not all at this site, dates back to 1788. Continue down Wellington Place towards the (6) **statue of Dr Henry Cooke** (1788-1868). It's typical that this prickly character should stand not beside the road but right in the middle of it. Behind his statue is the (7) **Technical Institute** of 1907 and the (8) **Royal Belfast Academical Institution** or 'Inst' of 1814. The Inst is a story of frustrated plans – it

stands on College Square, which is actually only half a square because the west and south sides were never built. The building itself wasn't completed to its original plans due to a shortage of funds and the Technical Institute was plonked in front of it due to another college cash shortage.

Turn left down College Square past the bulk of the ornate (9) **Presbyterian Church House**, which dates from 1905 and is decorated with angels, eagles and dragons and now houses the Spires Shopping Mall and a café. Turn left on to Howard St, which shortly becomes Donegall Square South and takes you along the back of the City Hall. The White Linen Hall once occupied the City Hall site and as a result the surrounding area was crowded with linen warehouses, most of them long gone.

On the corner of Linenhall St is (10) **Yorkshire House**, with 16 sculptured heads of various personages, real and imaginary. Donegall Square South changes names to become May St and passes the (11) **May St Presbyterian Church**, built in 1829 and also known as Cooke Memorial Church. Yes, it's named after the same Dr Henry Cooke who stands resolutely in the middle of the street on College Square. Continue along May St to Joy St. Across the road is a car park, of zero interest except for the (12) **Dunlop plaque** on the east wall which explains that this was the former site of John Boyd Dunlop's workshop, where he developed the first pneumatic tyre in the 1880s.

Turn down Joy St and then right on to Russell St and left past (13) **St Malachy's Church**. Another right takes you on to Clarence St and past the (14) **Robinson Patterson architectural office**, an intriguing redevelopment of a 19th-century warehouse which sliced the end off the building and glassed it over to produce a design which won a 'Building of the Year' architectural award. Turn right into Bedford St, past the (15) **Ulster Hall**, dating from 1862; on the opposite side of the road murals painted to look as if they were done on damask linen illustrate scenes of linen manufacture.

Turn left into Franklin St to Brunswick St,

passing Surf Mountain, a reminder to surfing enthusiasts that Northern Ireland has some good waves, then backtrack past the Drury Lane pub and down Amelia St to the wonderful (16) **Crown Liquor Saloon**. Across the road are the (17) **Europa Hotel** and the (18) **Grand Opera House**, which could also qualify for a 'much bombed' accolade. Turn south down Great Victoria St, noting the memorial statue to working women just south of the Europa Hotel.

Further south, Shaftesbury Square marks the start of the university area. Glance back at the junction to the (19) **statuary** tacked on the front of the **Ulster Bank Building**; the figures are known locally as Draft and Overdraft. Continue across Shaftesbury Square, more a road junction than a square in the conventional sense. Donegall Pass, which runs off the junction to the left (east), is the only remaining 'pass' into Belfast, a reminder that the city was once bounded on this side by private land belonging to Lord Donegall, and the passes through Cromac Woods were the only access to the city. Today Donegall Pass is guarded at the Shaftesbury Square end by a typically forbidding (20) **RUC guardpost**.

Bradbury Place runs south from the junction; a narrow alley (Albion Lane) disappearing down the back of the buildings was once used as a discreet back entry to (21) **Lavery's Gin Palace**. Today it's just a popular student pub, but Lavery's has a long bohemian and literary tradition in Belfast. Bradbury Place becomes University Rd and on the right side of the road is the 1887 (22) **Moravian Church**. A left turn takes you into Lower Crescent, beside the 1887 (23) **Crescent Church**, with its instantly recognisable skeleton-like bell tower.

The green behind the church is enclosed by Lower Crescent, Crescent Gardens and Upper Crescent. Walking round the green takes you past mid-19th century, neoclassical-style terraces, built by Robert Corry, a local entrepreneur, and possibly designed by Charles Lanyon. Across University Rd, WJ Barre's (24) **Methodist Church** of 1865 completes the happy trio of University Rd

Belfast Walking Tour 2

1	Queen Victoria Statue	15	Ulster Hall
2	Robinson & Cleaver Building	16	Crown Liquor Saloon
3	Pearl Assurance Building	17	Europa Hotel
4	Scottish Provident Building	18	Grand Opera House
5	Linen Hall Library	19	Ulster Bank Statues
6	Dr Henry Cooke Statue	20	RUC Guardpost
7	Technical Institute	21	Lavery's Gin Palace
8	Royal Belfast Academical Institution	22	Moravian Church
9	Presbyterian Church House	23	Crescent Church
10	Yorkshire House	24	Methodist Church
11	May St Presbyterian Church	25	Mount Charles Villas
12	Dunlop Plaque	26	Queen's College
13	St Malachy's Church	27	Student's Union
14	Robinson Patterson Office	28	Elmwood Hall
		29	Gate Lodge
		30	McArthur's Hall
		31	Methodist College
		32	Lord Kelvin Statue

churches. Continuing along University Rd the next street left is Mt Charles with a group of (25) stylish **villas** dating from 1842. University Square, also to the left from University Rd, has another fine group of terraced houses. Queen Victoria herself laid the foundation stone for (26) **Queen's College** in 1845. It's the principal building of Queen's University and was yet another Charles Lanyon design.

Across University Rd from the college building is the modern (27) **Student's Union**, a stark contrast to the exotic (28) **Elmwood Hall**. Built by John Corry, the architect son of Robert Corry whose crescents were seen earlier on this walk, the Italian-inspired church building is now used as a university concert hall. Walk along Elmwood Ave beside Elmwood Hall, then left on to Lisburn Rd and left again beside a toy-like (29) **gate lodge** into College Gardens. The road takes you past (30) **McArthur's Hall** and the grandiose (31) **Methodist College**, built in High Victorian style in 1865-8.

Cross University Rd to enter the Stranmillis Rd gate of the Botanic Gardens. Just inside the gate is a (32) **statue of Lord Kelvin** (1824-1907) who invented the Kelvin temperature scale and patented inventions for underwater submarine cables. By now you will probably be ready to collapse in one of the Golden Mile's many eateries.

SOUTH OF THE CENTRE
Sandy Row
Just a block west of Great Victoria St, the road which leads from the city centre to the university, is the curving Sandy Row. This used to be the main road south out of the city, and it's still a working-class Protestant enclave, wedged in beside the wealthier Golden Mile area. Here you'll find red, white and blue kerbstones and Unionist murals, just like on the Shankill Rd in West Belfast. Van Morrison fans may remember that he wandered 'up and down the Sandy Row' in his 1968 album *Astral Weeks*.

Ulster Museum
The Ulster Museum (☎ 383000) is beside the Botanic Gardens near the university. As well as a quick rundown on Irish history, there are good displays on Irish art, wildlife, dinosaurs, steam and industrial machines, minerals and fossils; allow several hours to see everything properly. Items from the 1588 Spanish Armada wreck of the *Girona* (see Dunluce Castle in the County Antrim chapter) are a highlight, especially the gold jewellery which includes a ruby-encrusted salamander and an inscribed gold ring. Many of the Armada ships were wrecked along the west coast of Ireland, but the *Girona* came to grief on the north-east coast, off the Giant's Causeway. The wreck was investigated by the Belgian marine archaeologist Robert Stenuit in 1968, 380 years later.

The museum was designed in 1911 but not completed until late in the 1920s. An extension was added in 1971, and the complex includes a shop and the Collections Café, overlooking the Botanic Gardens. Entry to the museum is free and it opens Monday to Friday 10 am to 5 pm, Saturday 1 to 5 pm, Sunday 2 to 5 pm. Bus No 69 or 71 will get you there from the centre.

Botanic Gardens
The somewhat tatty Botanic Gardens are a restful oasis away from the busy main road and worth a wander about. The gardens date from 1827 and their centrepiece is the fine Palm House with its cast-iron and curvilinear glass construction, built between 1839 and 1852 and housing palms and other hot-house flora. Even though Belfast's pre-eminent architect Charles Lanyon played a part in its creation, the Palm House was essentially the work of Richard Turner of Dublin who also built glasshouses in the Dublin Botanic Gardens and at Kew Gardens in London, and worked on the 1851 Crystal Palace in London. Just inside the gardens at the Stranmillis Rd gate is a statue of Belfast-born Lord Kelvin who invented the Kelvin Scale which measures temperatures from absolute zero (-273°C or 0°K). The gardens are open daily from 8 am to sunset.

From April to September the Palm House opens Monday to Friday 10 am to 5 pm, Saturday and Sunday 2 to 5 pm. In winter it's open weekdays 1 to 4 pm, weekends 2 to 4 pm. The unique Tropical Ravine tucked in beside the Ulster Museum was designed by Charles McKimm of Donaghadee in 1887 as an enclosed sunken glen with balconies for visitors to look down on the plants. Ferns, cycads, bananas and lilies all grow here. It keeps the same opening hours as the Palm House.

Belfast has a number of other parks and gardens, and the Belfast City Council (☎ 320202), 4-10 Linenhall St, produces a booklet titled *Parks of Belfast* describing parks in and around the city.

Queen's University

Just over 1km south of Donegall Square and the City Hall is the muted red and yellow brick Queen's College building of Queen's University, Northern Ireland's most prestigious university. It caters for around 8000 students and has a particularly strong reputation in medicine, engineering and law. Although the plan of the college building is based on Magdalen College in Oxford, once again Charles Lanyon was responsible for the design. Queen Victoria was present for the laying of the foundation stone in 1845, and the building was completed in 1849.

The lofty entrance hall leads into the quadrangle. On the south side a chimney has brickwork spelling out VR 1848 (Victoria Regina). Beyond the college building is Old Library, designed by Lanyon's assistant WH Lynn and built in 1864, then extended in 1913.

Surrounding the university are quiet tree-lined streets with small cafés full of students. University Square, on the north side of the campus, dates from 1848-53 and is one of the finest terraced streets in Ireland. It was once known as the Harley St of Belfast, and is now owned by the university. Behind the Queen's College building, across Botanic Ave, is the colonnaded Union Theological College, originally the Presbyterian College. It opened in 1853 and it too was a Lanyon

design. From the partition of Ireland it served as the Northern Ireland parliament, until 1932 when Stormont Castle took over for the next 40 years.

ART GALLERIES

The Ulster Museum has a collection of Irish art on the top floor, but Belfast's principal modern art gallery is the **Ormeau Baths Gallery** (☎ 321402), near the BBC building on Ormeau Ave; it's open Tuesday to Saturday 9 am to 5 pm. The **Old Museum Arts Centre**, 7 College Square North, a fine building dating back to 1831, houses temporary exhibitions of modern art. It's open Monday to Friday 10 am to 5.30 pm; ring the doorbell for admission. **Malone House** (☎ 681246) has exhibitions on Belfast parks and an art gallery. It's well to the south of the centre in Barnett's Demesne on Upper Malone Rd and opens Monday to Saturday 10 am to 4.30 pm. Bus Nos 70 and 71 pass by.

Private galleries in Belfast include the Crescent Arts Centre (☎ 242338), 2 University Rd, the Fenderesky Gallery (☎ 235245) at the same address, the Bell Gallery (☎ 662998), 13 Adelaide Park, and the Eakin Gallery (☎ 668522), 237 Lisburn Rd.

FALLS & SHANKILL RDS

The Catholic Falls Rd and the Protestant Shankill Rd have been battlefronts for the Troubles, and apart from the occasional bright flash of a wall mural they're grey and rather dismal. For visitors they're quite safe, and more modern (and enlightened) public housing is not only replacing the old Victorian slums but also the 1960s tower blocks. These areas are worth venturing into, if only to see the large murals expressing local political and religious passions. King Billy riding to victory in 1690 on his white steed and hooded IRA gunmen are two of the more memorable images. Less noticeable to first-time visitors are the red, white and blue painted pavement kerbs which adorn staunch Protestant loyalist areas, and the green, white and orange kerbs in the Catholic areas.

West Belfast grew up around the linen

mills which propelled the city into its industrial revolution prosperity. It was an area of low-cost working-class housing, and even in the Victorian era was divided along religious lines. The advent of the Troubles in 1968 solidified the sectarian division, and the construction of the Westlink Motorway neatly divided the area – and its problems – from central Belfast. Since the start of the Troubles, working-class religious segregation has grown steadily and West Belfast is now almost wholly Catholic. Although the Shankill Rd is the Protestant flip side of the Catholic Falls Rd, it's actually in retreat. Were it not for its strong symbolic importance, the shrinking proportion of Protestants in West Belfast would undoubtedly be even smaller.

There are other Protestant working-class enclaves around the city, such as along the Newtownards Rd to the east of the centre, where you'll also see the brightly painted sectarian murals. If you don't fancy a tour (see Organised Tours), the ideologically sound way to visit the sectarian zones of the Falls and Shankill Rds is by what is known locally as the 'people taxi'.

These recycled London cabs run a bus-like service up and down their respective roads from terminuses in the city. Shankill Rd taxis go from North St, Falls Rd taxis from Castle St, both sites close to the modern Castle Court Centre. The Falls Rd taxis occupy the first line at the Castle St taxi park, with signs up in Gaelic. They're used to doing tourist circuits of the Falls and typically charge £10 (the cabs hold up to five people) for a one-hour visit which takes in the main points of interest from republican murals to British army bases.

If you simply want to share a black taxi down the Falls Rd, the fare is 45p to 75p depending on the distance, and your fellow passengers are likely to be women and children returning from a city shopping trip or men coming back from the pubs. Fares are similar on the Shankill Rd taxis. Alternatively bus Nos 12, 13, 14 or 15 will take you down the Falls Rd; bus Nos 39, 55, 63 or 73 go down the Shankill.

Falls Rd

The Falls Rd taxis start from the taxi park beside the Smithfield Market, a pale reflection of the bustling market which used to operate here. Separated from the city centre by the Westlink Motorway, but actually a very short distance west of the centre, the ugly and infamous Divis Flats take their name from Divis Mountain, the highest summit in the hills which surround Belfast. They were constructed in the late 1960s during the world-wide mania for high-rise public housing, and as elsewhere in the world they quickly became 'vertical slums'. During their planning and construction they were actually welcomed by local residents as both an alternative to substandard housing and as a way of retaining the local community. Extremely fearful of losing their congregations, the Catholic churches in the vicinity were particularly enthusiastic backers.

The Divis Flats were as disastrous in Belfast as elsewhere, and the Troubles quickly turned them into the scene of many confrontations between residents and the army. Today most of the flats have been replaced with modern housing. Divis Tower, a single block of high-rise flats, still overlooks the other buildings and the motorway. At the start of the Troubles the Irish Republican Socialist Party colonised its roof, winning it the nickname 'The Planet of the IRPS'. When the British army took their place, this was changed, predictably, to 'The Planet of the Apes'. The top storeys are still occupied by the British army who come and go by helicopter. Taking pictures without permission might not be a particularly bright idea.

Across Divis Rd a huge blue-and-white mural of the Madonna and Child decorates what was once the Brickfields Barracks, the first purpose-built police barracks in Belfast, now a refuge for homeless men.

From Divis Tower, Divis St runs west, becoming the Falls Rd which runs in a south-westerly direction through the area known as the Lower Falls. On the right are a swimming pool and the heavily protected Sinn Féin offices; the massive boulders are to deter car bombers. If you turn right (north) off the Falls Rd into the side streets you'll quickly come up against the 'Peace Line', a rough corrugated iron wall separating Catholics from their Protestant neighbours. In places you could almost lean out of a back window and touch the wall.

On the other side of the Falls Rd in the Lower Falls, the old slums which stood here before the Troubles have been replaced with neat rows of houses, a reminder of the huge sums spent to improve public housing in the 1970s and 1980s; even at the height of the Thatcher era, Northern Ireland remained relatively immune to public spending cutbacks. The Falls Rd passes the Royal Victoria Hospital, which developed a well-earned reputation for dealing with medical emergencies at the height of the Troubles in the 1970s.

The area's famous murals are found along the Falls and in adjacent streets. It's a constantly changing art show, with new murals appearing over old, and demolition and reconstruction removing and replacing the canvases. Along the Falls Rd itself you're unlikely to have problems taking pictures but be warned that there have been stories of gangs of small boys extorting cash for photos in quieter side streets. Beyond the Lower Falls the road is less interesting until it reaches the Milltown Cemetery, the main site for republican burials, housing the graves of numerous noted republicans who have died in shoot-outs, hunger strikes and other events of the Troubles.

The junction of Glen Rd and Andersonstown Rd marks the end of the Falls Rd with a strongly fortified army base looking down the Falls from its position in the fork. It's one of four 'forts' in West Belfast. Andersonstown (Andytown) is about 3km from the centre and beyond here is Twinbrook, another staunchly republican suburb and the former home of Bobby Sands, the first 1981 hunger striker to die. In the surprisingly neat, tidy and modern development where he lived, one end of a block has been turned into a memorial. More murals, slogans and graf-

fiti can be found in the Ballymurphy area by taking Whiterock Rd or Springfield Rd, north of the Falls, but these are thoroughly impoverished areas where a stranger will be very noticeable.

Shankill Rd

The Shankill Rd begins not far west of Belfast Cathedral and runs north-west towards the Crumlin Rd. Although the Shankill has been given less media and tourist attention than the Falls, it's also of interest. The street's name comes from *sean chill*, the old church, and once again the brightly painted murals, including some of the Derry apprentice boys slamming the city gates in 1689, are the central attraction. Here the villains and heroes have switched roles, and the hooded and menacing paramilitaries are members of the UDA and other Protestant groups, instead of the IRA or INLA.

At the far end of Shankill Rd, look out for **St Matthew's**, a church built in shamrock shape in 1872.

AROUND BELFAST
Harland & Wolff Shipyards

Although you can't easily visit the Harland & Wolff shipyards, they certainly dominate East Belfast, separated from the city centre by the River Lagan. The giant cranes known as Samson & Goliath, one of them over 100m high and 140m long, straddle a 550m-long shipbuilding dock. The shipyard was founded in 1833 but it was under the Yorkshire engineer Edward Harland, who recruited the German marine draughtsman Gustav Wolff in 1858, that it assumed its leading role in Victorian shipbuilding. There's a statue of Sir Edward Harland by the City Hall. The good ship *Titanic* was built here and more recent constructions have included oil tankers and passenger vessels, including the *Canberra* in 1960.

The Harland & Wolff dry dock is one of the biggest in the world, capable of handling ships of up to 200,000 tons. With substantial British government support the shipyard managed to continue through the 1970s and 1980s, when most European shipbuilding

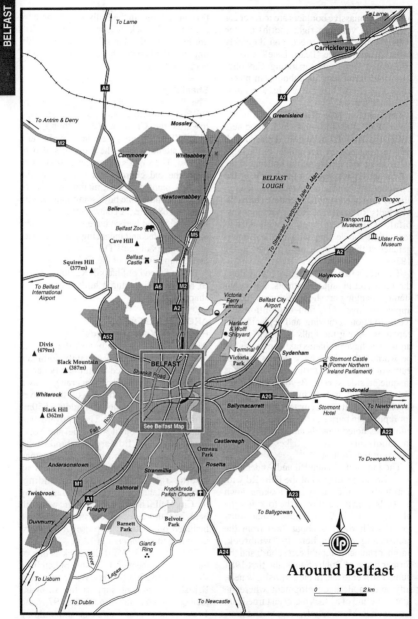

Around Belfast

0   1   2 km

crumbled before Asian competition. Current employment is at a fraction of its former levels. In its heyday 60,000 people worked here; by the 1970s it had fallen below 10,000; by the mid-1980s it was down to 5000; and by the early 1990s below 2000. Work at the yards today is primarily maintenance and repair rather than new construction.

Stormont Castle

The former home of the Northern Ireland parliament is 8km east of the centre, off the A20. The regal 1932 building in Neoclassical style stands at the end of an imposing avenue, fronted by a defiant statue of Lord Carson, the Dublin-born architect of the fierce Ulster opposition to union with Ireland. This is where the Northern Ireland parliament met until 1972 when power was transferred to London. Now it's home to the Northern Ireland Secretary. You can walk in the extensive grounds, but visits to the parliament buildings must be arranged in advance (☎ 760556). At the time of research Stormont was undergoing extensive restoration work which may be finished by the time

you read this. Citybus Nos 22 and 23 run directly to Stormont from Donegall Square West in the city centre.

Belfast Zoo

Belfast Zoo (☎ 776277) is an exceptionally good one and has pursued an aggressive policy of building new and large enclosures for its exhibits. The sealion and penguin pool with its underwater viewing is particularly good. Some of the more unusual animals include tamarins, spectacled bears and red pandas, but children flock to the meerkats and to the ring-tailed lemur colony. The zoo enjoys a splendid location on the slopes below Cave Hill with views out over Belfast Lough. The animal enclosures are laid out down the hillside, making for some strenuous walking.

April to September opening hours are daily 10 am to 6 pm, with last admissions at 5 pm; October to March it opens 10 am to 3.30 pm (to 2.30 pm on Friday). Entry is £4.80/2.40. Senior citizens and children under four get in free. Bus Nos 2, 3, 4, 5, 6 or 45 take you to the zoo from Donegall Square West.

Edward Carson

It was Edward Carson (1854-1935), a Protestant lawyer from Dublin, who spearheaded the Ulster opposition to Home Rule and led the movement which eventually resulted in Ireland's partition. Carson's career in law included numerous successful prosecutions of Irish tenants on behalf of British absentee landlords, and he played a leading role in the conviction of Oscar Wilde for homosexuality in 1895.

Carson was elected to the British House of Commons in 1892 and was solicitor general for Britain from 1900 to 1905. He was in line for the leadership of the Conservative Party until, in 1910, his fervent distaste for Home Rule and Irish independence led him to take the leadership of the Irish Unionists. Carson believed that without Belfast's heavy industries, an independent Ireland would be economically unviable, and that he could frustrate Irish independence simply by keeping the North separate. The British Liberal government's determination to enact Home Rule was frustrated by Carson's parliamentary manoeuvres in 1912, and a year later he actually established a provisional government for the North in Belfast.

Carson threatened an armed struggle for a separate Northern Ireland if independence was granted to Ireland. By 1913 he had established a private Ulster army, and weapons were landed from Germany at Larne in 1914, shortly before the outbreak of WWI. The British began to bend before this Ulster opposition and, in July 1914, Carson agreed that Home Rule could go through for Ireland so long as Ulster was kept separate. The events of WWI and the 1916 Easter Rising in Dublin shifted the whole question from Home Rule to complete independence. By 1921, however, the Ulster opposition which Carson had nurtured was so strong that the country was carved up.

A statue of Carson fronts Stormont Castle, the former parliament building, where talks on the future of Northern Ireland are taking place. Carson is buried in St Anne's Cathedral in central Belfast. ■

Cave Hill Country Park

Cave Hill Country Park (☎ 776925) covers 300 hectares of northern Belfast on the shores of Belfast Lough. Walks through the grounds are waymarked (make sure you've noted which colour arrows you need to follow for any specific route), and it's a pleasant stroll from the zoo back as far as Belfast Castle. Cave Hill itself is 355m high; from the top there are panoramic views over Belfast, Belfast Lough and even parts of Scotland on a clear day.

The park contains evidence of prehistoric occupation in the form of several raths and a *crannóg*. On top of Cave Hill one such ringfort is known as McArt's Fort, a prominent spot from which members of the United Irishmen, including Wolfe Tone, looked down over the city in 1795 and pledged to struggle for independence for Ireland.

The peak was originally named after a 9th-century Ulster king, Matudhain, a name that gradually corrupted to Ben Madigan. One look at its profile, which dominates the Belfast skyline, and you'll understand why it's known as 'Napoleon's Nose' in popular parlance. In previous centuries Cave Hill was a popular site for lighting Hallowe'en bonfires and for rolling hand-painted eggs downhill at Easter. To the north of McArt's Fort are five man-made caves, some of them accessible. To the south side there's a disused limestone quarry.

The country park encompasses two nature reserves, at Ballyaghagan and Hazelwood. There are five park entrances: beside Belfast Castle and the zoo; at Carr's Glen Linear Park, Ballysillan Rd; at Upper Cave Hill Rd; and in the Upper Hightown Rd. Admission is free.

To get there take Citybus Nos 45 to 51 from Donegall Square.

Belfast Castle

On the slopes of Cave Hill stands Belfast Castle (☎ 776925). There has been a 'Belfast Castle' since the late 12th century, but this particular model was only built, in the then fashionable Scottish Baronial style, in 1870. The castle was presented to the City of Belfast in 1934 and became a fashionable venue for weddings after WWII. From 1978 to 1988 the council undertook extensive renovation of the castle, parts of which are now open again as a posh restaurant (see Places to Eat) and for social functions. The cellars also house a bistro, tavern and shop. Upstairs, there's a small Cave Hill Heritage Centre with details of the history, flora & fauna of the area. It's open daily 9 am to 6 pm. Admission is free and you may have to ask for the key at reception.

Legend has it that the castle's residents will only experience good fortune as long as a white cat lives there, a tale commemorated in the formal gardens with nine portrayals of cats in mosaic, painting, sculpture and garden furniture.

ORGANISED TOURS

There's a 3½-hour, £7.50/5 Citybus tour (☎ 458484) taking in all the city sights including Stormont, the shipyards and Belfast Castle. It begins at Castle Place outside the GPO at 1.30 pm every Wednesday and Friday during the summer months.

This is supplemented with a popular 'Living History' tour, taking in the sites and areas associated with the Troubles; if you feel nervous about walking up and down the Falls or Shankill Rds or venturing into the Ardoyne or Andersonstown alone, this tour fits the bill, although some might have qualms about ghoulish voyeurism. During the summer, tours leave Castle Place at 2 pm on Thursday and Saturday. Tickets cost £7.50 and the tour lasts 2½ hours with a short break for tea. The souvenir booklet alone almost justifies the tour price. These tours also take place during the rest of the year, but are subject to demand.

Pub walking tours take place in the summer. Contact the tourist office for information. Itineraries are likely to include the Duke of York, White's Tavern, Kelly's Cellars, Robinson's and the Crown Liquor Saloon.

SPECIAL EVENTS

Every May Belfast hosts a Civic Festival

when music, dance, theatre and sports events take place all over the city. Some buildings which may otherwise be closed become accessible then. The tourist office is able to supply a programme.

The Belfast Folk Festival takes place in mid-June, while on the last weekend of the month there's a Taste Fest when different restaurants from across Belfast set up stalls in the Botanic Gardens

For two weeks from mid-November, the Belfast Festival at Queen's hosts drama, dance and music performances and movies at various places around town.

PLACES TO STAY
Accommodation in Belfast is both scarce and expensive, particularly in the better guesthouses and hotels. Fortunately, the YHANI hostel is ideally situated in Donegall Rd, just off Shaftesbury Square, within walking distance of the city centre. Most B&Bs are clustered together in the Golden Mile area near the university. At the other end of the scale, expensive hotels are either right in the centre or well out of it.

Camping
Camping possibilities close to Belfast are very restricted. The Northern Ireland Tourist Board produces a *Camping & Caravanning* brochure but the two sites close to Belfast are small and intended only for caravans or campervans. Tent sites can be found along the coast beyond Bangor towards Portaferry.

The *Jordanstown Lough Shore Park* (☎ 868751) is 8km north of central Belfast on Shore Rd in Newtownabbey. Although this is a well-equipped site, costing £6.50 per night and mainly intended for caravans, it's still very small and there's a maximum stay of two consecutive nights. *Dundonald Leisure Park* (☎ 482611), 111 Old Dundonal Rd off Upper Newtownards Rd, is a new, larger park 8km south-east of the centre.

Hostels
The cheapest place to stay in Belfast is *Arnie's Backpackers* (☎ 242867), 63 Fitzwilliam St, where beds cost £7.50. Arnie's

has laundry and cooking facilities but, with only 19 beds, demand for space far exceeds supply. It makes sense to book ahead. Bus Nos 70 and 71 pass the end of Fitzwilliam St.

The YHANI *Belfast International Youth Hostel* (☎ 315435) is at 22-32 Donegall Rd, between Shaftesbury Square and Sandy Row. Beds cost £10, or £11 with breakfast. It organises cheap train tickets to Dublin. There's a laundry and a Backpackers Coffee House, but no cooking facilities. You can get there by train to Botanic Station or by bus from Donegall Square; bus Nos 69, 70 and 71 pass nearby, while Nos 89 and 90 stop outside.

June to the end of September *Queen's Elms* (☎ 381608), 78 Malone Rd, run by the university, offers excellent accommodation. The rooms cost £8.50 for UK students, £10 for international students and £13 for non-students. Twin rooms cost £21. Rates include bed linen but not towels and there are cooking and laundry facilities. Rooms may also be available for short periods over Christmas and Easter. *Queen Mary's Hall* (☎ 240439) is the YWCA at 70 Fitzwilliam St. In theory it has single and double rooms at £14.50 per person including breakfast, but in practice it's usually full of long-term resident students. Further south, off Malone Rd, is *Ulster People's College* (☎ 665161), 30 Adelaide Park, which does bed and continental breakfast for £13, bed and cooked breakfast for £15. It offers accommodation all year.

B&Bs
The tourist office makes B&B reservations in return for a minimal booking fee; credit card bookings can be made on freefone number ☎ 0800-317153. Many B&Bs are in the university area with prices around £20 to £22. This area is close to the centre, safe and well stocked with restaurants and pubs. Botanic Ave, Malone Rd, Wellington Park and Eglantine Ave are good hunting grounds.

Botanic Ave near Queen's University is a pleasant residential street. The large, and very comfortable *Helga Lodge* (☎ 324820),

7 Cromwell Rd, just off Botanic Ave, costs from £22/32 to £27/50 for singles/doubles. Note the colourful orange frontage. Most rooms have their own bathroom, TV and phone. Nearby is the handsome *Botanic Lodge Guesthouse* (☎ 327682), 87 Botanic Ave, where the rooms all have TV and cost £22/40. Bus Nos 83, 85 or 86 will get you to these two.

Also in this popular university area, the *Queen's University Common Room* (☎ 665938), 1 College Gardens, offers B&B for £37.50/55 all year.

Eglantine Ave, just 2km south of the city centre, is quiet and packed with guesthouses and B&Bs. To reach them catch a bus along Lisburn Rd from Donegall Square.

The George (☎ 683212), 9 Eglantine Ave, has six rooms for £19/42 and is open all year. At No 17 is *Liserin Guesthouse* (☎ 660769), costing £19/38. *Eglantine Guesthouse* (☎ 667585) at No 21 has B&B for £20/38. At No 30 is *Marine House* (☎ 662828) at £28/45. *East Sheen House* (☎ 667149) at No 81 charges £17.50/35. Near Queen's University, *Pearl Court House* (☎ 666145), 11 Malone Rd, has B&B for £20.50 per person. More expensive places include the Edwardian *Camera Guesthouse* (☎ 660026), 44 Wellington Park, where B&B for singles/doubles costs £35/55.

Along the Antrim Rd, good cheapies include *Drumragh House* (☎ 773063) at No 647. It's 3km north from the city centre, close to the zoo and costs £20/36. Also out here is *Aisling House* (☎ 771529), 7 Taunton Ave off the Antrim Rd, in a quiet residential area with B&B at £18.50/36; the breakfasts come highly recommended.

Hotels

There's no shortage of hotel beds in Belfast, but prices are comparatively high, except at weekends when business travellers go home and prices drop accordingly.

Great value (especially for couples and families) given its location so close to the university is the *Holiday Inn Express* (☎ 205000), 106A University St, which charges £49.95 for a room including conti-

nental breakfast. It was built to accommodate people attending the conference centre next door, so it's worth booking ahead.

Madison's (☎ 330040; fax 328007), 59-63 Botanic Ave, claims to be Belfast's trendiest hotel, and probably is. It's well designed and rooms come complete with hair dryer and trouser press. Rates are £59/69 including continental breakfast.

In the city centre, Belfast's newest hotel is *Jury's Inn* (☎ 533 5000), in College Square opposite Spires Shopping Mall. It's a moderately priced three-star hotel with rooms for only £55 (not including breakfast).

The much-bombed *Europa Hotel* (☎ 327000) is a Belfast landmark – many city directions begin with 'Do you know the Europa?' Now part of the Hastings Group, it's one of the city's best hotels and costs from £125/165 a single/double. The modern *Holiday Inn Garden Court* (☎ 333555), 15 Brunswick St, another victim of bombing, is behind the Crown Liquor Saloon and only a short stroll from the Europa. Rooms cost £75/85 including breakfast.

Wellington Park Hotel (☎ 381111), 21 Malone Rd, is another smaller hotel close to the Ulster Museum and Queen's University. Rooms cost £75/90 including breakfast, but the setting is nothing special. *Malone Lodge* (☎ 382409), 60 Eglantine Ave, has rooms including breakfast at £79/92. In University St, at No 75 *Renshaws Hotel* (☎ 333366) has rooms for £70/85, while *Dukes Hotel* (☎ 236666) at No 65 is pricier at £87.50/105.

Opposite the Empire Music Hall, the *Regency Hotel* (☎ 323349; fax 320646), 13 Lower Crescent on the corner of Botanic Ave, has rooms for £55/70 including breakfast. Rates drop to £40/60 on weekends.

Belfast's glossiest hotel (there's even an external glass lift) is the four-star *Stormont Hotel* (☎ 658621), directly across from the Stormont parliament building on Upper Newtownards Rd. It's some distance from the centre and costs £104/143, but you do get a rubber duck to float in the bathtub.

Immediately opposite the terminal at the Belfast international airport, in Aldergrove, the recommended *Aldergrove Airport Hotel*

Europa Hotel – a Blast from the Past

A mid-1993 article on war zone hotels in *The Guardian* gave the Europa the blue riband as 'the world's most bombed hotel', ahead of such strong contenders as the Holiday Inn, Sarajevo, and the Commodore, Beirut. When the Europa opened in the late 1960s it was several stars better than anything Belfast had previously seen, but with the start of the Troubles it quickly took on a new role as the nerve centre for a nervous city, as well as the most visible target for bomb-happy terrorists.

During the 1970s the Europa was bombed no less than 29 times, but every single time the broken glass was swept up, new drinks appeared on the bar and life continued. The Europa was where journalists from around the world gathered to interview paramilitary spokespeople from both religious extremes, who often left by the back door just as military personnel entered by the front to conduct yet another press briefing.

However, two big blasts – the latter in May 1993 – almost brought the Europa to its knees. The British government once again picked up the repair bill, new owners took over, and the Europa reopened for business in 1994. Today, there's little sign of the considerable structural repairs that were needed to keep the hotel operating or of any security cameras or guards. ■

(☎ 01849-422033) has excellent rooms and facilities at £82.50/90.

Country Houses

The lovingly restored *Cottage* (☎ 01247-878189), 377 Comber Rd, Dundonald, about 16km south-east of the city has two bedrooms with B&B for £20/35. Off the main road to Carrickfergus is the pleasant *Glenavna House Hotel* (☎ 01232-864461), 588 Shore Rd, Newtownabbey, standing in quiet parkland, with rooms at £75/90.

PLACES TO EAT

Belfast has a surprising number and variety of restaurants, including one of the very best restaurants in all of Ireland. More than one journalist has noted that the Troubles seemed to have given the citizens of Belfast a positive passion for eating out! Although there are plenty of pubs, cafés and fast-food places around the centre, Belfast's best eating is found south of the city centre along the Golden Mile towards the university, where there are eating houses to suit all purses.

Cafés & Fast Food

The Donegall Rd youth hostel's decent *Backpackers Café* opens to non-residents too. Food is reasonably priced and you can fill up on the Ulster fries, but service can be slow and the café closes at 7.30 pm. After

that the *Kebab House* across the road from the hostel does a mix and match assortment of tasty kebabs, Indian dishes and fish and chips. Curries are £2 to £3.

The streets around the hostel are prime hunting ground for cheap meals and the cafés in Botanic Ave, in particular, are usually crammed with students from Queen's. Immediately round the corner, Bradbury Place can seem like one solid fast food shop, with everything from filled potatoes for £1.95 at *Spuds* to excellent fish & chips at *Bishops*.

Jenny's Coffee Shop, 81 Dublin Rd, is a pleasant little café cum sandwich bar with snacks like lasagne for £2.75, next door to *La Boulangerie* where you can get an after-lunch pastry.

At 50 Botanic Ave, near the Botanic railway station, the friendly *Maggie May's* serves tasty healthy food, with the emphasis on vegetarian dishes but also with meat options. Vegetarian cottage pie is £3.50. It opens daily for breakfast until late. Across the road in *Queen's Espresso* at No 17 you can get a cheap breakfast or lunch in more sedate surroundings. It's closed Sunday. Further up the road at No 79 there's a branch of the extremely popular *The Other Place* where burgers and chips for £3.95 come to an accompaniment of popular music tracks and lots of student jollity. It also does more substantial meals for around £7 and you can bring your own wine. There's a second, equally popular branch in Stranmillis Rd.

Heading up University Rd towards Queen's College, *Bookfinder's Café* at the back of the bookshop at No 47 is an excellent place for a quick lunch. Mushroom pasta is £3.40. The *Beech Restaurant* on the 1st floor of the Student Union building directly opposite Queen's College is good for rock-bottom meals if in large, soulless surroundings. *The Mortarboard*, 3 Fitzwilliam St, serves good coffee and snacks until late, provided you don't mind the slightly religious overtones.

The city centre has its representatives of the international fast-food chains. There's also a food hall offering fish & chips, Chinese, pizzas and more in the *Variety Centre* in High St. There's also a branch of the popular *Bewley's Oriental Café* chain in Donegall Arcade off Rosemary St. If that looks too pricey, *Delaney's* nearby in Rosemary St offers food at reasonable rates; quiche or lasagne costs £3.95. Across the road the *Chalet d'Or* is a rougher and readier lunch spot with cod & chips for £3.

For good lunches at modest rates head for *Spires Restaurant* in Spires Shopping Mall on College Square; a soup and a roll costs £1.99, light meals £3. The very friendly *Bambrick's*, 58 Wellington Place near the corner of College Square, also does light lunches at similar prices. Both also open for breakfast.

Near St Anne's Cathedral, *Le Café*, 38-42 Hill St, is an enterprise worth supporting. It's a training centre for people studying for National Vocational Qualifications and does lunches prepared by students. Dishes such as cajun chicken or tagliatelli cost £4 to £5.

Should everything else fail, Belfast is famous for its excellent bread (don't miss the soda farls) and you'll find innumerable bakeries around the city centre and along Botanic Ave near the university.

Pub Food

At the *Crown Liquor Saloon* (☎ 249476) on Great Victoria St in the centre you can get oysters and Irish stews, and at the same time take in the magnificent décor. They serve food from 11 am to 3 pm, but you'll need to get there early to get a seat.

Keeping a low profile at 81 Chichester St, on the corner of Victoria St near the Royal Courts of Justice, *Rumpole's* (☎ 232840) is good for steak-type lunches. A block further north *Bittle's Bar* (☎ 311088) is a small pub in a rather interesting triangular building; although its address is 103 Victoria St, it's entered from 70 Upper Church Lane. It specialises in traditional dishes like sausages and champ (an Ulster speciality consisting of mashed potatoes and spring onions). *White's Tavern* (☎ 243080), at Winecellar Entry between Rosemary and High Sts, is one of Belfast's most historic taverns and a popular lunch time meeting spot.

The *Duke of York* (☎ 241062) is another oldie, popular with journalists from the nearby local papers and stuffed with printing memorabilia. It serves sandwiches for £1 and excellent solid lunches for around £5. It's hidden away down Commercial Court, an alleyway leading off Donegall St just south of St Anne's Cathedral. The *Kitchen Bar* (☎ 324901) in Victoria Square is another popular lunch time rendezvous where you'll be lucky to get a seat. If you do, you can tuck into the house speciality, Paddy pizza (£2.95) on a toasted soda bread base, and other more traditional dishes.

Restaurants

Bottom End Deep pan pizzas and other American food can be found at the *Chicago Pizza Pie Factory* (☎ 233555) at the back of the Virgin Cinemas on Dublin Rd, for £6.95 to £9.95.

There are numerous cheaper restaurants south of the centre in the Golden Mile area and around the university. *Planet Harvey's* (☎ 233433), 95 Great Victoria St, does good pizzas for £3.85 to £7.75 and Tex-Mex dishes.

Italian restaurants are popular. *Graffiti* (☎ 249269), 50 Dublin Rd, serves excellent, filling pasta dishes for under £7, while there are often queues to get into *Villa Italia* (☎ 328356), 37-41 University Rd, a vibrant

Italian restaurant and pizzeria. In Shaftesbury Square *Speranza* (☎ 230213) does good pizzas for £4 to £7 and even better desserts. *Deanes*, 10 Brunswick St, also turns out excellent Italian dishes as well as more traditional Irish ones including roast cod with mushy peas for £7.95.

There's also a branch of *Pierre Victoire* (☎ 559911), 89 Dublin Rd, which serves delicious seafood; swordfish steak is £8.60. Midweek it also does a good-value three-course set lunch for £5.90.

Chez Delbart (also known as *Frogities*) (☎ 238020) is a fairly cheap and cheerful French restaurant at 10 Bradbury Place where you can get good crêpes for £4.95. *Mange Tous* (☎ 315151), serves a French influenced menu with three-course set lunches for only £3.90, and à la carte from 6 pm.

If you can stand the frenetic atmosphere, *Aubergines and Blue Jeans* (☎ 233700), 1 University St next to Saints and Scholars (see Restaurants – Top End), serves all sorts of interesting goodies in a crazy décor with blue jeans much in evidence. Mains are £6 to £13. During the day you can get a light meal (eg cheese burger) and a pint of beer or glass of wine for £5.50. Don't drop by between 7 and 9.30 pm at weekends unless you've reserved a table in advance.

There are plenty of Indian and Chinese restaurants in the university area. The *Archana Balti House* (☎ 323713), upstairs at 53 Dublin Rd, offers balti curries (£4 to £8) named after the metal balti in which it's cooked and served. It says everything for Belfast's recent troubled history that this is the Archana's third incarnation; the previous two were both lost to bomb blasts.

The *Maharaja* (☎ 234200), upstairs at 62 Botanic Ave near Helga Lodge, is a more traditional Indian restaurant in the heart of the university area and does tandoori chicken for £7.25. In the same area, the *Dragon Palace* (☎ 323869), 16 Botanic Ave, offers Chinese food, or you can turn the corner past the forbidding police station to *Manor House* (☎ 238755), 47 Donegall Pass, which has excellent Cantonese food. Beef dishes are

£6.50 to £9. There are other Indian and Chinese restaurants around Belfast, many of them further from the centre along Lisburn Rd and Ormeau Rd.

Finally, the *Greek Shop* (☎ 333135), 43 University Rd next to Bookfinders, does pleasing if not especially cheap Greek meals. Moussaka is £6.50.

Middle & Top End Close to the centre the tropical ambience at *Bananas* (☎ 339999), 4 Clarence St, may feel a trifle odd, but the adventurous international mix of dishes (kebabs, mussels, tiger prawns, chicken kiev) is well done and reasonably priced. Mains are £6 to £13. It's open Monday to Friday for lunch, Monday to Saturday for dinner. It shares a kitchen with the more formal *44 Restaurant* (☎ 244844), which is next door but in Bedford St at No 44; mains include baked salmon or roast pork. You'll need to book to get into either on a Saturday night.

Bonnie's Café Restaurant (☎ 664914), 11A Stranmillis Rd, is perfect for a meal after inspecting the Ulster Museum opposite. Nearby, *The Strand* (☎ 682266), at 12 Stranmillis Rd, offers traditional dishes and a popular lunch special at £4.50; at dinner mains like baked stuffed aubergine cost £12 to £18. Surprisingly for a fairly upmarket restaurant it doesn't have a non-smoking area.

French cuisine can be sampled in *La Belle Epoque* (☎ 323244), 61 Dublin Rd, Belfast's most authentic French restaurant; escalope de veau (pan-fried veal) is £10.95. It's closed Sunday.

The stylish *Antica Roma* (☎ 311121), 67 Botanic Ave near the university, serves pasta for £7 to £8, and is open for lunch and dinner. Also near the university is *Saints and Scholars* (☎ 325137), 3 University St, where advance booking is essential. This is where John Major and Peter Brooke dined while negotiating the 1994 ceasefire arrangements. Roast pig is £8.25.

Behind an anonymous frosted glass facade, *Roscoff* (☎ 331532), 7 Lesley House, Shaftesbury Square, serves superb food in modern surroundings. Paul Rankin has a tremendous reputation (and his own TV programme) and this is one of only three restaurants in Ireland with a Michelin star; the other two are in Dublin. A complete dinner could set you back £40 per person but lunch is cheaper (set 'business lunches' cost £14.50) and on some nights there's a set dinner for £21.50.

You can also eat in the *Belfast Castle Restaurant* (☎ 776925), provided you remember to book ahead and allow £12 to £18 a main course. Cream tea in the basement café might be nearly as satisfying.

ENTERTAINMENT
The Buzz is Belfast and Northern Ireland's commercial 'what's on' magazine, but the fact that it comes out every two months renders it useless for rapidly changing events and cinema programmes. What's more, it's appallingly written and costs £1.95. *That's Entertainment* is a better bet for listings, not least because it's free. Pick it up in Belfast's tourist offices, the youth hostel or pubs.

Theatre & Music
Belfast's newest and largest concert venue is the impressive *Belfast Waterfront Hall*, on Oxford St near the corner of East Bridge St. It hosts local, national and international performers from pop music artists to symphony orchestras. For credit card bookings call ☎ 334455; for a programme call ☎ 334400.

The Belfast *Grand Opera House* (☎ 241919) on Great Victoria St is host to a mixture of good theatre, opera and music shows. The booking office at 17 Wellington Place opens Monday to Saturday from 9.45 am to 5.30 pm (☎ 241919) or you can get recorded details of the current programme on ☎ 249129. On Botanic Ave in the university area, the *Belfast Civic Arts Theatre* (☎ 316900), 41 Botanic Ave, chiefly puts on popular plays or comedies. Further out from the centre, the *Lyric Theatre* (☎ 381081), 55 Ridgeway St, has a more serious bent and includes Irish plays in its repertory. Performances also take place at *Whitla Hall* in Queen's University.

Northern Ireland's excellent Ulster Orchestra often plays in the *Ulster Hall* (☎ 323900) on Bedford St , and this is also the venue for larger rock music events (and for lunch time organ recitals and even boxing bouts). The *Group Theatre* (☎ 329685) next door stages plays by local playwrights.

King's Hall (☎ 665225) at Balmoral is another centre for big rock events; get there by bus down Lisburn Rd or by train to Balmoral Station. Performances also take place at *Elmwood Hall*, the church building now used as a concert hall on University Rd directly opposite Queen's College. The *Crescent Arts Centre* (☎ 242338), at 2 University Rd, is another smaller music venue. *St Anne's Cathedral* (☎ 328332), Lower Donegall St, also hosts occasional lunch time organ recitals. Both the *Factory* (☎ 244000), 52 Hill St, and *The Old Museum Arts Centre* (☎ 235053), in College Square North, host 'arty' live events including drama and comedy.

Pubs
At lunch times many of the city centre pubs are crammed to overflowing. In the evenings, the same is equally so, but many pubs here and along the Golden Mile have bouncers on the door and operate an ad hoc dress code: look too scruffy and you'll be turned away. Large groups of men without accompanying women are not looked on favourably; conversely, lone women can often find service to be slow and frosty.

Belfast has some pubs which are as much museums as drinking places, particularly the wonderful old *Crown Liquor Saloon* opposite the Opera House, which even teetotallers should have a look at. The *Britannic Bar* upstairs opens at 5 pm and, with its plush seating and soft lighting, has been described as the pub to which local men bring their mistresses!

The narrow alleys known as the Entries shelter a plethora of older pubs. Good ones to sample include the rough-edged *Morning Star* on Pottinger's Entry, the historic *White's Tavern* on Winecellar Entry and the *Globe Tavern* on Joy's Entry. Other older pubs in the centre include *Kelly's Tavern* (1720) on Bank St, or the *Duke of York*, hidden away down Commercial Court near St Anne's Cathedral. Also popular are the linked *Kitchen* and *Parlour* bars at the junction of William St and Victoria Square.

On Blackstaff Square and completely rebuilt after it was destroyed by a bomb, is *Fibber Magee's*, heavily disguised as a grocer's shop. Inside, it's a bit like plunging into a heritage centre, with salamis and hot-water bottles supposedly for sale hanging from the beams, a draper's counter at the back and a model man asleep in front of the range. Don't be fooled by any of this – it really is a pub. Push through the doors at the back and you'll emerge in *Robinson's*, with a mock-up library among other distractions. Upstairs is the *Shoe Shine*, a themed Manhattan speakeasy bar. Upstairs again and you'll emerge in *Spot Robinson's* (☎ 247447 for details) where bands play. In the basement is the *Rock Bottom* where Belfast's beautiful bikers and their molls hang out.

In front of Fibber Magee's is the sculpture of a butterfly emerging from a chrysalis symbolising rebirth after yet another bombing incident.

In the same square is the *Spinner's Inn*, below the Holiday Inn Garden Court, named after a spinner of yarns who stands in effigy in one of the many alcoves.

On Great Victoria St, opposite the Crown Liquor Saloon, the *Beaten Docket* is equally popular with younger Belfastians.

In the university area, *Bob Cratchit's* on Lisburn Rd is a trendy, modern pick-up joint. Somewhat less trendy *Lavery's* on Bradbury Place is popular with an extraordinary range of clients, from students to bikers to hardened drinkers, and has a long and colourful history as Lavery's Gin Palace. In the evenings there's a cover charge just to go in for a beer. On the corner of Dublin Rd and Ventry St, the *Elbow* is a quiet spot for a drink, while *Dempsey's* nearby focuses on a younger clientele. The *Elms*, 36 University Rd, is another popular student pub. Further south the *Eglantine Inn* and the *Botanic* are institutions, packed at weekends with

crowds of students. Known as the Egg and Bott, they face each other across Malone Rd.

Discos & Nightclubs
Music, either disco or live, features in many of Belfast's pubs including the *Eglantine Inn* (☎ 381994), 32 Malone Rd; the *Botanic* (☎ 660460), 23 Malone Rd; *Spot Robinson's* (☎ 247447), upstairs at Fibber Magee's; the *Duke of York* (☎ 241062), 11 Commercial Court; the *Kitchen Bar* (☎ 324901), 16 Victoria Square; and also *Bob Cratchit's* (☎ 332526). The *Elms* (☎ 322106), 36 University Rd, and the *Chicago Pizza Pie Factory* (☎ 233555), 1 Bankmore Square, also have live music. Further out from the centre the *Rosetta Bar* (☎ 649297), 75 Rosetta Rd, is one of Northern Ireland's main rock venues.

The *Errigle Inn* (☎ 641410), 320 Ormeau Rd, south of the centre, is also popular. Nightclub-style discos can be found at the *Limelight* (☎ 325968), 17 Ormeau Ave, and the *Manhattan* (☎ 233131) at Bradbury Place close to the university. Popular gay hangouts include the mixed *Crow's Nest*, on the corner of Skipper and High Sts, and *Parliament Bar* in Dunbar St with a disco upstairs. Monday night is also gay night at the *Limelight*.

When there's music, most places levy entry charges, typically £2 to £8 depending on the night and the venue.

The *Empire Music Hall* (☎ 328110), 42 Botanic Ave, a barn-like pub inside a redundant church, with *Titanic* memorabilia lining its walls, has live music three nights a week.

Comedy
The basement of the Empire Music Hall is the in place for stand-up comedy, when it presents the *Empire Laughs Back* every Tuesday night at 9 pm. Be there by 7.30 pm if you want to get a seat. Acts consist of a local warm-up followed by a more established comedian. Tickets cost £4.

Cinema
Belfast's biggest cinema complex, the 10-screen *Virgin Cinemas* (☎ 243200 for

recorded programme details), is at the north end of Dublin Rd, just south of the city centre and five minutes walk from the youth hostel; admission is £4.25 except before 5 pm Monday to Friday and all day Tuesday when it's £3. The *Movie House* (☎ 755000), with five screens, is north of the centre in the Yorkgate Shopping Centre. The *Queen's Film Theatre* (☎ 244857), 21 University Square Mews near the university, is the closest Belfast has to an art house cinema; tickets are £3.80, or £2.20 for students.

That's Entertainment lists what's on but without the times.

THINGS TO BUY

Two modern shopping centres are Castle Court in Royal Ave and the Variety Centre in High St. Another is Spires Shopping Mall on College Square in the converted Presbyterian Church House. Donegall Arcade, off Rosemary St, is popular with Belfast trendies.

The Craftworks Gallery (☎ 236334), 13 Linenhall St, specialises in Northern Irish crafts with work by craftspeople from all over Ulster, but you're unlikely to find many bargains. For Irish linen and all things tackily Irish (shamrocks, leprechauns etc), try Smyth's Irish Linens (☎ 242232), 65 Royal Ave, which runs a VAT-free scheme for foreign visitors.

For camping gas cylinders, other camping equipment or for surfing gear, Surf Mountain (☎ 248877), 12 Brunswick St in the centre, is excellent. There's also the Scout Shop Ski & Camp Centre (☎ 320580), 12-14 College Square East near Wellington Place.

For music, try the Vintage Record Store (☎ 314888), 54 Howard St. St George's Market (near the central station) takes place Tuesday and Friday 7 am to 3 pm. It's a depressing undercover jumble-sale of a place, but plans exist to revamp it as part of the Laganside development.

Many shops open until 9 pm on Thursday.

GETTING THERE & AWAY

Belfast has that rare thing – an integrated public transport system, with buses and trains linking both airports to the central railway stations and bus stations, and to the ferries.

See the introductory Getting There & Away chapter for international flights and ferries to Belfast.

Air

There are flights from some regional airports in Britain to the convenient Belfast city airport (☎ 457745), Airport Rd, but everything else goes to Belfast international airport (☎ 01849-422888), 30km north of the city in Aldergrove by the M2.

There are tourist offices at both airports. There's a branch of Thomas Cook in the departure hall of the international airport; it opens until 8 pm daily and you can change Northern Irish banknotes into more familiar sterling notes.

For more details see the introductory Getting There & Away chapter.

Ferry

Ferries to and from Northern Ireland come into one of three terminals. Closest to the centre is the SeaCat and Isle of Man terminal on Donegall Quay. About 5km further north is the Victoria terminal (for Liverpool) on West Bank Rd, while the Larne terminal is 30km north along the coast. There are trains from Larne to Belfast's Central station. Ulsterbus services to and from Belfast's Europa Buscentre also connect with the Larne ferries.

Norse Irish Ferries (☎ 779090) has a service between Belfast and Liverpool, and operates from the Victoria terminal. The Isle of Man Steam Packet Company (☎ 01624-661661) operates between the Isle of Man and Belfast from the SeaCat terminal on Donegall Quay; it's linked to Donegall Square and the bus and train stations by a 90p bus run.

SeaCat (☎ 01345-523523) runs huge catamaran car ferries that make a 1½-hour crossing between Belfast and Stranraer. Conventional ferries to and from Scotland dock at Larne; for more information see Larne in the Counties Derry & Antrim chapter and the Sea section in the Getting There & Away chapter.

Bus
Belfast has two separate modern bus stations. The smaller of the two is the Laganside Buscentre in Oxford St near the river, with bus connections to Counties Antrim, Down and Derry (the eastern side).

Buses to everywhere else in Northern Ireland, the Republic, the international airport and the Larne ferries leave from the bigger Europa Buscentre in Glengall St, behind the Europa Hotel. Buses to Larne Town, as opposed to the harbour, leave from the Laganside Buscentre.

Pick up regional bus timetables for 25p each at the bus stations or phone ☎ 333000 for timetable information; phone ☎ 320011 for tickets. Ulsterbus produces an excellent free *Exploring Ulster* booklet with information on bus services and fares to major attractions accessible by bus from Belfast.

There are four Belfast-Dublin services daily (three on Sunday) taking about three hours and costing £10.50 one-way. For connections to Derry and Donegal contact the Lough Swilly Bus Company (☎ 01504-262017) in Derry.

For security reasons there are no left-luggage facilities at Belfast train and bus stations.

Students are eligible for 15% reductions on Ulsterbus fares of more than £1.15 on production of their ISIC card.

Train
For tickets and information the NIR Travel Shop (☎ 230671) is at the new Great Victoria St station next to the Europa Buscentre; it opens weekdays 9 am to 5 pm, Saturday 9 am to noon. Information about local trains is also available from Belfast Central station (☎ 899411). Great Victoria St is now the most central station while Belfast Central is east of the city centre on East Bridge St.

Trains to all destinations including Larne, Derry, Dublin, Newry, Portadown and Bangor arrive and depart from Belfast Central. A free Linkline bus to Donegall Square in the city centre leaves from outside every 10 minutes. A local train also connects with Great Victoria St.

Trains also leave Great Victoria St station for Portadown, Lisburn, Bangor, Larne Harbour and Londonderry.

Dublin-Belfast trains run up to six times a day (three on Sunday) and take about two hours at a cost of £15 one-way. All stop at Portadown or Dundalk, and some stop at Lisburn and Newry as well.

On Sunday you can buy a £3 go-as-you-please-ticket, allowing you to travel all over the Northern Irish rail network.

The nearest train station to the university/YHANI hostel area is Botanic, which you can reach direct from Belfast city airport.

Car
The principal motorways out of Belfast are the M1 heading south-east towards Fermanagh, the M2 which runs north-west past Belfast airport to the A6 and on to Derry, and the M5 north-east towards Carrickfergus. If you're heading for Dublin take the M1 then branch off onto the A1, which becomes the N1 south of the border.

GETTING AROUND
The Airports
The Belfast international airport (☎ 01849-422888) is 30km north of the city. Buses connect it with the Europa Buscentre behind the Europa Hotel for £4/7 one way/return. There are two services an hour, 19 daily even on Sunday. A taxi costs about £20.

The more convenient Belfast city airport (☎ 457745) is only 6km from the centre, and you can cross the road from the terminal to the Sydenham Halt train station from which a train to Botanic costs 80p. Citybus No 21 services Belfast city airport also for 80p. Services run roughly every half-hour on weekdays, less frequently on weekends. A taxi fare to the city centre is about £4.50 to £5.

Bus
Citybus (☎ 246485) operates the bus system

in Belfast, which is divided into zones. Very short trips in the centre are just 50p, but in general around the city the standard bus fare is 80p. The fare increases by zones as you travel further, but 80p gets you all the way to Cave Hill or Belfast Zoo. A multitrip ticket costs £2.50 and gives you four rides at slightly lower cost and much greater convenience.

A Day Ticket gives you unlimited travel within the City Zone from 9.30 am on weekdays or all day on weekends for £2.20. A seven-day bus pass costs £10.50.

Most local bus services depart from Donegall Square, near the City Hall. Timetables are available from the kiosk on Donegall Square West. Single tickets are bought from the driver, but multiple tickets need to be purchased in advance from kiosks in Castle Place or Donegall Square West.

Belfast has a good system of night buses on Friday and Saturday to enable people to join in the nightlife. Most buses leave from Shaftesbury Square at midnight, 1 and 2 am. You buy tickets (£2) in advance from a mobile ticket booth between 9 pm and 1.50 am. There are even buses to outlying towns like Antrim, Carrickfergus, Lisburn, Bangor and Newtownards so, if you wished, you could stay in any of these places and still take advantage of the Belfast nightlife. These buses leave between 12.15 am and 1.30 am and tickets cost £3 single. For information call ☎ 233933.

Car

If you're driving, be fastidious about where you park. Although things have eased you still shouldn't park within the well-marked Control Zones. Tales of foolish tourists coming back to find their car about to be blown up by a bomb demolition squad are, however, essentially urban myths. Terrorism aside, Belfast has a bad reputation for joyriding.

There are plenty of car parks in Belfast, and it's wise to use them, even though they're often rather expensive. Multi-storey car parks are probably the safest places to leave your vehicle.

Rental The car rental agencies in Belfast include:

Avis
    69 Great Victoria St (☎ 240404); city airport (☎ 452017); international airport (☎ 01849-422333)
Budget
    96-102 Great Victoria St (☎ 230700); city airport (☎ 451111)
CC Economy Car Hire
    2 Ballyduff Rd (☎ 840366)
Europcar
    City airport (☎ 450904); international airport (☎ 01849-423444)
Hertz
    International airport (☎ 01849-422533)
McCausland Car Hire
    21-31 Grosvenor Rd (☎ 333777); city airport (☎ 454141); international airport (☎ 01849-422022)

McCausland is one of the cheapest, with prices starting from £24/95 per day/week for a Ford Fiesta to £70/350 for Ford Granada; VAT is extra.

Taxi

Black taxis operate bus-like services down the Shankill Rd from North St and down the Falls Rd from Castle St. Fares are 45p to 75p. Regular taxis are pricey with a £2 minimum price (flagfall) and £1 per mile. For security reasons, hailing taxis on the street isn't normal in Belfast. Companies to call include Fon A Cab (☎ 233333), 104 Great Victoria St, or Jet Taxis (☎ 323278), 12 Donegall Rd, near the youth hostel.

Bicycle

McConvey Cycles (☎ 491163), 467 Ormeau Rd, rents bicycles for £7/40 a day/week. A deposit of £30 is required. The tourist office has a leaflet outlining four possible cycle routes in Northern Ireland.

Counties Down & Armagh

County Down

County Down is Northern Ireland's sunny south-east, being relatively dry. Neighbouring Belfast delivers hordes of day trippers to the many seaside resorts on the coast from Bangor to Newcastle and beyond. The shoreline runs from the flat Ards Peninsula, encompassing the drowned drumlins and nature reserves of Strangford Lough, to the Mourne Mountains which coax the traveller farther south. In the famous lyrics by Percy French, the Mournes 'sweep down to the sea'; they're the highlight of Down. Besides tourists, more permanent visitors reside in the numerous retirement homes in the seaside towns – look out for elderly pedestrians! The interior of the county is well past its booming Industrial Revolution heyday but Hillsborough retains much of its Georgian splendour. The main Belfast to Dublin road crosses into the Republic just south of Newry.

HISTORY
The history of Down goes back 7000 years. The county has its fair share of early monuments; the Giant's Ring near Belfast and the Legananny Dolmen near Ballynahinch are two of the best examples. St Patrick landed in Strangford Lough in 432, and died in the area in 461. The whereabouts of his remains is disputed, though Downpatrick Cathedral is the favoured site.

By the time of St Patrick's death, the crusade he had started in Ulster had made Ireland Christian and turned him into one of the few genuinely national heroes. After St Patrick's death, Irish monasteries flourished and multiplied, surviving repeated Viking attacks.

They were finally to lose out to the Normans, who ousted the Irish monks and built Grey Abbey on the Ards Peninsula and

Locator & Map Index

DOWN & ARMAGH

Highlights
- Walk in the Mourne Mountains and the Silent Valley
- Explore a 'reconstructed' Ireland at the Ulster Folk & Transport Museum
- Experience the wonderful Mount Stewart House & Gardens
- Travel the coastal roads of the Ards and Lecale peninsulas and South Down
- Cruise Carlingford Lough
- Spend time in historic Armagh City
- Visit Down Cathedral

Inch Abbey near Downpatrick. Castles were their main priority, however, and many along the coast survive today. The Scottish and English settlers who arrived with the plantation of Ulster in the 17th century were given large tracts of land previously occupied by the native Irish. They built towns and roads, and were responsible for the development of the linen industry in the 17th and 18th centuries.

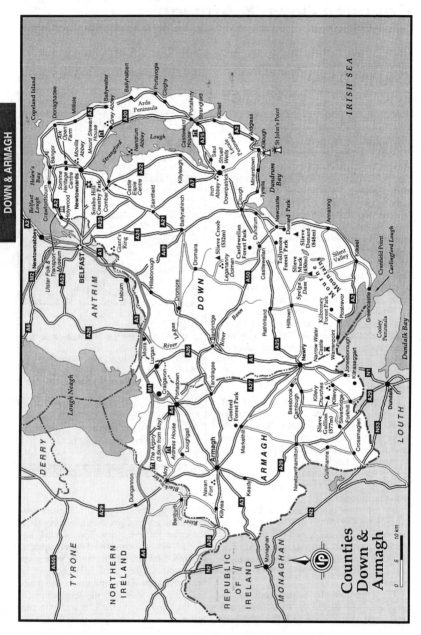

DOWN & ARMAGH

Counties
Down &
Armagh

0   5   10 km

BELFAST TO BANGOR

Belfast creeps north-eastward along the southern shores of Belfast Lough towards the Irish Sea. The A2 road out of Belfast follows the railway line and is a pleasant route to the Ards Peninsula.

Ulster Folk & Transport Museum

This is one of the finest museums in Ireland, 11km north-east of Belfast, near Holywood. Farmhouses, forges, churches and mills (almost 30 buildings in all) have been very carefully reconstructed on the wooded 60-hectare site, with plenty of human and animal extras combining to give strong impressions of Irish life over the last few hundred years. From industrial times, there are complete terraces of 19th century Belfast and Dromore houses. During the summer, activities such as thatching and horse ploughing are displayed for visitors.

On the opposite side of the road the new transport museum is a sort of automotive zoo. The Dalchoolin Transport Galleries display horse carts, donkey *creels* (baskets), carriages, bicycles and one of the prototypes for a VTOL – a vertical take-off and landing aircraft. Particularly popular is the section which records the sinking of the Belfast-built *Titanic* in 1912.

Included in the large automobile collection is a gull-wing stainless steel car, built in Belfast after former American General Motors whiz kid John de Lorean persuaded the British government that to invest £80 million in manufacturing a flash new car would help reduce Northern Ireland's horrifyingly high unemployment figures. Unfortunately the new car was launched into a market suffering from recession and much of the development money simply vanished into numbered Swiss bank accounts. One de Lorean car put in a starring role as the time machine in *Back to the Future*. (A warrant remains out for John de Lorean.)

A separate railway gallery looks at the history of Irish railways, with lots of preserved locomotives, videos and sound effects.

The park and museum (☎ 01232-428428)

open year round: July and August, Monday to Saturday 10.30 am to 6 pm, Sunday noon to 6 pm; April to June and during September, 9.30 am to 5 pm, Saturday 10.30 am to 6 pm, Sunday noon to 6 pm; October to March, 9.30 am to 4 pm, weekends 12.30 to 4.30 pm. Admission is £3.60/2.40.

Trains and buses to Bangor stop nearby; get off the train at Cultra station. Bear in mind, though, that the site has been designed for drivers; it's hilly and spread out and you'll need a good half day to do it justice.

There's a fine coastal walk of some 6km from Holywood to Helen's Bay, with more pleasant seashore trails continuing north-east to Grey Point.

Crawfordsburn Country Park

Just over 3km west of Bangor, off the B20 at Helen's Bay, this country park has a number of wooded and coastal walks, and a 20th century gun emplacement. The large-calibre artillery have been trained on Belfast Lough since before WWI, though a shot has never been fired in anger. The command post and lookout station also remain.

The park opens 9 am to dusk all year and admission is free; phone the visitors' centre (☎ 01247-853621) for details of occasional free guided walks; it opens 10 am to 5 pm in winter, April to September 10 am to 6 pm. The park is accessible on Belfast-Bangor bus No 2 or also by train to Crawfordsburn (unstaffed) or Helen's Bay station, the latter a wonderful little Victorian railway station dating from 1865 and built by the marquess of Dufferin, who owned the surrounding estate.

The 17th century *Old Inn* (☎ 01247-853255), 15 Main St, in the pretty black and white village of Crawfordsburn has bags of character but isn't cheap; B&B is £70/80. It also serves dinner for around £20.

BANGOR

It's barely 21km from Belfast to Bangor (Beannchar), a seaside resort and dormitory town for Belfast commuters. The Belfast to Bangor railway line was built in the late 19th century to connect the capital with what was

DOWN & ARMAGH

then a flourishing resort. What little survives of the original Victorian charm is now under siege from amusement arcades and cheap restaurants, and Main St contrives to look like any British high street. At the bottom of Main St, however, a marina, with fountains, landscaped parking, promenades and a modern outsize public toilet block, gives it a touch of glamour. The Pickie Fun Park, with mute-swan pedaloes, continues the more kitsch tradition of British seaside resorts.

History

The town dates back to the 6th century, when the Abbey of St Comgall made Bangor one of the great centres of the early church. St Comgall was a teacher and friend of St Columbanus and St Columcille, two of Ireland's most famous saints. Because Bangor was close to the sea and so often the first landfall after their journey from Scandinavia, the Vikings repeatedly attacked Bangor Abbey, which was abandoned by the 10th century; only one wall remains today. The one priceless surviving relic – 'The Antiphonary of Bangor', a small 7th century prayer-book, the oldest surviving Irish manuscript – is now housed in Milan's Ambrosian Library.

Orientation & Information

Unusually, Bangor has a Main St and a High St, both busy commercial centres. The bus and railway stations are side by side in Abbey St, at the top of Main St, near the post office. At the bottom of Main St is the marina, with B&Bs clustered to east and west on Queen's Parade and Seacliff Rd.

For information on Bangor and the North Down region, call in to the helpful Tower House tourist office (☎ 270069), in Quay St, housed in a tower originally built as a fortified customs post in 1637. It's open June to September, Monday to Friday 9 am to 5 pm (to 7 pm in July and August), Saturday 10.30 am to 4.30 pm (10 am to 7 pm July and August), Sunday 1 to 5 pm (noon to 6 pm July and August); October to May, Monday to Friday 9 am to 4 pm, Saturday 10 am to 4 pm.

The telephone code is ☎ 01247.

North Down Heritage Centre

Surrounded by Castle Park, this small museum (☎ 271200) is in the converted laundry, stables and stores of Bangor Castle in Castle Park Ave. It contains an early 9th century handbell, some ancient swords, a milepost with distances in Irish miles, and a facsimile of 'The Antiphonary of Bangor', as well as details of the North Down Coastal Path. It's open Tuesday to Saturday 10.30 am to 4.30 pm (5.30 pm in July and August), and Sunday 2 to 4.30 pm (5.30 pm in July and August). Admission is free.

Places to Stay

Accommodation can be hard to get even outside the busy summer months, so it's wise to book ahead.

B&Bs A cluster of virtually identical guest-houses lining Seacliff Road offer B&B from £14 to £18 a head; amongst the cheapest are *Bayview* (☎ 464545), at No 140, *Pierview* (☎ 463381), at No 28, and *Snug Harbour* (☎ 454238), at No 144.

More guesthouses are grouped in Queen's Parade overlooking the marina; try the *Battersea Guesthouse* (☎ 461643), at No 47, for £18.50, or the friendly *Ashley House* (☎ 473918), at No 50, for £16, doubles with en suite £42. The *Emmaus* (☎ 456887) on Holborn Ave has rooms for as little as £12/22.

A little farther out and likely to have a room when others don't is *Kildara Guest-house* (☎ 461245), 51 Prospect Rd (between Main St and Hamilton Rd), which has rooms with shared bathroom for £16.

There's another group of B&Bs on Prince-town Rd, past Queen's Parade.

Hotels The modern *Marine Court Hotel* (☎ 451100), 18-20 Quay St, offers B&B for £75/50, while the *Sands Hotel* (☎ 270696), 72 Seacliff Rd, does B&B for £52.50/72.50, or less at weekends.

Places to Eat

Main St has plenty of takeaways and cheap restaurants. At 94 Main St, the *Heatherlea*

Tea Rooms (☎ 453157) serves terrific light meals all day.

In High St, *Wolsey's* is an eating house and bar worth trying for lasagne (£4.95) and pizza. It has a good vegetarian selection. Up the hill, *Jenny Watt's* offers Chinese chicken pitta (£4.25) and chilli (£4.95) with cask-conditioned ales and musical accompaniment on Tuesday. On Crosby St, round the corner from the tourist office, the *Dragon Palace* does reasonably priced Cantonese food, and at the *Simply Indian* you can bring your own wine. The popular *Vesuvio*, on the 1st floor of 8 Quay St, offers marina views and cheap pizzas (£3.85 to £6.95). For lunch in attractive surroundings, head for the *Castle Garden Restaurant* attached to the North Down Heritage Centre.

The best places for more expensive meals are the *Sands Hotel* (☎ 270696) on Seacliff Rd (dinner is £14), and the *Royal Hotel* (☎ 271866) on Quay St, where the unappealing exterior belies the good food (salmon fillet is £12.45) to be had inside. The stylish *Café Brazilia*, (☎ 272763), in Bridge St overlooking the marina serves filled baguettes (from £2.60) and cakes to kill for, from 9 am to 5 pm Monday to Saturday; Wednesday to Sunday it also opens for dinner 6.30 to 9 pm. Even more stylish is the cavernous, Art Deco *Café Ceol*, on High St opposite Wolsey's which opens from lunch time till late. Lasagne is £3.25 and the menu has vegetarian options.

Outside Bangor, near Groomsport on the A2 Donaghadee road, is the excellent *Abelboden Lodge* (☎ 464288). Lunch mains are £4.50 to £5.50, and there are always good vegetarian dishes. It also does high teas but closes Monday and Sunday.

Getting There & Away
Bus Ulsterbus Nos 1 and 2 from Belfast depart from the Laganside Buscentre (☎ 01232-320011) for Bangor. There's a bus each way every 20 minutes or so on weekdays (and every 30 minutes on the weekends) and the one-way fare is £2. From Bangor, bus No 6 heads for Newtownards, while bus Nos 3 and 7 travel across the north

of the Ards Peninsula to Donaghadee and Millisle. These services run roughly hourly. For timetable details ring ☎ 271143.

Train There's a regular half-hourly service to Bangor (and the Ulster Folk & Transport Museum) from Belfast Central railway station (☎ 01232-899400). Bangor station (☎ 474143) is in Abbey St.

Car & Motorcycle The A21 runs south from Bangor to Newtownards and Strangford Lough, while the A2 links it to Belfast to the west and to Donaghadee to the east.

Getting Around
Ulsterbus operates a network of local buses from the bus station Monday to Saturday.

A1 Car Hire (☎ 464447), 14 Dufferin Ave, has a small fleet, as does *Low Cost Car & Van Hire* (☎ 271535), 12 Church St.

SOMME HERITAGE CENTRE
Near Newtownards on the A21 is the Somme Heritage Centre (☎ 01247-823202), which relates the circumstances leading up to the WWI Somme campaign of 1916 from the perspective of men of the 10th (Irish), 16th (Irish) and 36th (Ulster) divisions. It's a high-tech show, with short films, a talking model of a wandering preacher and costumed interpreters to explain everything on a 25-minute guided tour. You even walk through a mock-up trench, although inevitably health and safety requirements make this a pretty sanitised experience. There's nothing at all celebratory about the displays, intended as a memorial to the men who died.

It's open July and August, Monday to Friday 10 am to 5 pm, Sunday noon to 5 pm; April to June and September, Monday to Thursday 10 am to 4 pm, and weekends noon to 4 pm; and the rest of the year Monday to Thursday 10 am to 4 pm, Saturday noon to 4 pm. Admission costs £3.50/2.50. Bus No 6 passes the entrance but you have to dash across a busy dual carriageway. There's ample parking space outside.

ARK OPEN FARM

Opposite the Somme Heritage Centre, on the other side of the dual carriageway, is the Ark (☎ 01247-812672), an open farm with displays of rare breeds of sheep, cattle and poultry, alongside a few llamas and a solitary donkey. It's open 1 March to 31 October, Monday to Saturday 10 am to 6 pm, Sunday 2 to 6 pm; entry is £2.10/1.50.

NEWTOWNARDS

Newtownards (Baile Nua na hArda), like Bangor, was founded as a 6th century ecclesiastical centre and can easily be visited on a day trip from Belfast or Bangor. The tourist office (☎ 826846), 31 Regent St, next to the bus station, opens Monday to Friday 9.15 am to 5 pm, Saturday 9.30 to 5 pm. The post office is also on Regent St whose western and eastern extensions are Church St and Frances St respectively.

The telephone code is ☎ 01247.

Scrabo Hill Country Park

The park (☎ 811491), 2km south-west of town, was once the site of extensive prehistoric earthworks, but these were largely removed during construction of the 1857 Memorial Tower in honour of the 3rd marquess of Londonderry. The summit (after 122 steps) of the 41m tower offers some expansive views of Strangford Lough. The park opens year-round, while the tower opens June to September, Saturday to Thursday 11 am to 6.30 pm. Admission to both is free.

Other Attractions

There's a ruined 13th century **Dominican friary**, on Court St, currently closed for renovations, and the scant remains of **Movilla Abbey** and its 13th century church 1.5km to the east. There's some fine 18th and 19th century architecture in town, especially along Church St. Most striking is the 18th century **Market House** on High St which once housed the town's prison, but is now the local arts centre; a bustling **market** takes place in Conway Square in front of it every Saturday. The **Market Cross** in High St dates back to the 17th century.

Places to Stay

B&Bs There's no budget accommodation in central Newtownards. The attractive modern *Cuan Chalet* (☎ 812302), 41 Milecross Rd west of town, offers B&B for £15 single or sharing, and opens year round. *Greenacres* (☎ 816193), 5 Manse Rd near the Ards Shopping Centre is in lovely gardens overlooked by the Memorial Tower; B&B costs £22/36 with bathroom.

Hotel The neat, three-star *Strangford Arms Hotel* (☎ 814141), at the far end of Church St, does B&B for £72/84.

Places to Eat

For cheap meals *Smyth's Café* is a typical greasy spoon, in West St behind the bus station. A better bet is *Knott's Coffee Shop*, 45 High St, where the café at the rear is bigger and more attractive than the facade suggests; it's open Monday to Saturday until 5 pm. The *Regency Restaurant & Coffeeshop* (☎ 814347), 5 Regent St, does good breakfasts and lunches; its Ulster fry costs £1.35.

On Court St the *Ming Court* (☎ 815073) does Cantonese food for around £6 to £7. The nearby Indian *Ganges* (☎ 811426) is also good. There are Chinese and Indian takeaways a short walk away in Castle St. For Italian food try *Giuseppe's Ristorante* (☎ 812244), 33 Frances St, or *Roma's* (☎ 812841), 4 Regent St opposite the Regency; it also has other cuisines and its honeyed chicken costs £8.25.

The *Strangford Arms Hotel* (see Places to Stay) has a respectable à la carte menu; roast duckling costs £11.50.

Getting There & Away

Bus The Ulsterbus station is on Regent St. There are buses roughly every half hour to Bangor and Belfast (£1.50 one way), and less-frequent services along the east and west sides of the Ards Peninsula.

Getting Around

The Strangford Arms Hotel (see Places to Stay) rents bikes for £7.50 a day.

STRANGFORD LOUGH

Cut off from the sea by the Ards Peninsula (see below), except for a km-wide strait at Portaferry ('The Narrows'), Strangford Lough (Loch Cuan) is almost a lake. It's 25km long, about 6km wide on average and up to 45m deep. Large colonies of grey seals live in and around the lough, particularly at the southern tip of the peninsula where the exit channel widens out into the sea. Birds abound on the shores and mudflats, including brent geese wintering from Arctic Canada, eider ducks and many species of wader. Underwater the muddy lough has a diverse marine biology, which can be studied at closer quarters at Exploris in Portaferry (see Things to See & Do in the Portaferry section, following). Killer whales have occasionally come into the lough, spent a few days there, and caused a sensation. The lough is a great leisure resource, with boats and yachts plying their way up and down its sheltered waters.

At Portaferry, however, 400,000 tonnes of tidal water surge through the strait four times a day; you can get some idea of the current's remarkable strength just by watching the Portaferry/Strangford ferry being whipped sideways by the riptide.

There are boat trips around the lough; see under Strangford in the Lecale Peninsula section later.

The western side of Strangford Lough isn't as scenic or interesting as the east, although it's the route followed by the Ulster Way walking trail. The main roads between Belfast and Downpatrick (A7) and Comber and Killyleagh (A22) are both remarkably straight, considering the number of drumlins locally.

ARDS PENINSULA

The Ards Peninsula (An Aird) slots in between the eastern side of Strangford Lough and the Irish Sea, with Newtownards and Donaghadee acting as gateways. From Newtownards the A20 heads south, following the lough shore, passing Mt Stewart and Grey Abbey, before arriving at Portaferry, linked by ferry across 'The Narrows' to Strangford on the western shore of the lough. The A2 heads back north along the peninsula's seaward side, passing through the fishing port of Portavogie (fallen on hard times in the 1990s as EU fishing quotas bite) to Millisle and Donaghadee. Relatively flat, the peninsula is about 6km wide and 35km long, with some good beaches. Dotted the length of the peninsula are the remains of tower-houses, built after Henry VI offered a £10 subsidy to anyone constructing a tower to protect the border in 1429; most date from the 16th century.

Nowadays the Ards is an agricultural region where farmers have diversified into ostrich-rearing and daffodil-bulb cultivation. It's a world away from the tension and industrial grittiness of Belfast, but you'll still spot red, white and blue kerbstones testifying to strong sectarian feeling. Watch out for dried *dulse*, Ards edible seaweed, on sale in greengrocers; it tastes much as you'd expect – strong, salty, very much an acquired taste.

Due to the shortage of accommodation in Newtownards, Portaferry and Donaghadee, it may be best to explore the Ards using Bangor as a base for day trips.

Mount Stewart House & Gardens

Eight km south of Newtownards, on the A20, is Mount Stewart. The magnificent 18th century house and gardens were the home of the Marquess of Londonderry, though much of the landscaping was carried out early this century by Lady Edith, wife of the 7th marquess, for the benefit of her children. The 35 hectares form one of the finest gardens in Ireland or Britain and are now in the charge of the National Trust.

The gardens are a cosmopolitan affair, with gardens, woodlands and lakes, elegantly populated by a vast collection of plants and statues. Unusual creatures from history (dinosaurs and dodos) and myth (griffins and mermaids) join forces with giant frogs and duck-billed platypuses, to provide a world of adventure for children. The 18th century owners constructed the **Temple of the Winds**, a folly in the classical Greek style built on a high point above the lough.

The classical house still has lavish plasterwork, marble nudes and valuable paintings (including works by George Stubbs, the painter of animals). Kings have stayed here in bedrooms dedicated to the great European cities. Viscount Castlereagh was born here; he went on to become British foreign secretary and was responsible for the passing of the Act of Union in 1801, dissolving the Dublin Parliament and making Ireland legally a part of Britain. Another member of the family was a general under the Duke of Wellington.

The opening hours are unusually complicated. The gardens are open March on Sunday 2 to 5 pm; April to September daily 10.30 am to 6 pm and at the weekends during October. The house (☎ 012477-88387) is open May to September, Wednesday to Monday and at weekends during April and October 1 to 6 pm. The temple opens the same days as the house but only 2 to 5 pm. Access to the gardens, house and temple costs £3.50/1.75. Bus Nos 9, 9A and 10 pass the gate except on Sunday.

Places to Stay About 7km south-east of Newtownards, off the A20, near Mount Stewart Gardens, is the idyllically situated *Ballycastle House*, (☎ 012477-88357) an 18th century farmhouse. B&B is £18 per person with full facilities and top-class breakfasts. It also has a self-catering cottage. Take the first turning left after you pass the Newtownards Sailing Club.

Grey Abbey

In the village of Grey Abbey, 3km south-east of Mount Stewart, are the fine ruins of a Cistercian abbey founded in 1193 by Affreca, wife of the Norman John de Courcy. The abbey was a daughter house of Holm Cultram Abbey in Cumbria and was used for worship as late as the 18th century. What remains is a characteristic 12th century

The ruins of Grey Abbey

Cistercian ground plan, consisting of a large cruciform church, two chapels and parts of a refectory, chapter house and rest rooms.

The church was built in early Gothic style even though Romanesque still reigned supreme elsewhere in Ireland. At the far end of the church is a carved tomb possibly depicting Affreca; her husband may be represented by the effigy in the north transept. The grounds, overlooked by 18th century Rosemount House, are awash with trees and flowers on spreading lawns, making this an ideal picnic spot. A sweet-smelling physic (herb) garden has been replanted, and there's a small visitors' centre.

April to September, the grounds are open Tuesday to Saturday, 10 am to 7 pm, Sunday 2 to 7 pm. Admission is £1/50p.

In the village of Grey Abbey are a number of antique shops.

Places to Stay *Mervue* (☎ 012477-88619), 28 Portaferry Rd, has B&B at £17.50/35; all rooms have their own bathroom. At 4 Cardy Rd, *Brimar* (☎ 012477-88681) offers B&B for £25; all rooms are ensuite.

Portaferry

Portaferry (Port an Pheire) is the most substantial settlement on the Ards Peninsula. A neat huddle of streets, it was originally called Ballyphilip; its new, duller name relates to its position as the terminus for the short ferry ride across the lough to Strangford. The renowned marine biology station on the waterfront uses the lough as an outdoor laboratory. The town itself is a sleepy place that feels like the end of the road, which of course it is. In good weather, you can sit outside the pubs on the waterfront and watch the lough and the ferry go by.

The tourist office, opposite the ferry wharf, is open Monday to Friday 10 am to 5 pm.

Things to See & Do There's a small 16th century **towerhouse** on Castle Lane, which isn't open to the public yet, though you can see a film about it in the tourist office. Next to the towerhouse is the state-of-the-art aquarium, **Exploris** (☎ 012477-28062), concentrating on marine life from Strangford Lough and the Irish Sea. Exploris opens March to August, Monday to Friday, 10 am to 6 pm, Saturday 11 am to 6 pm, Sunday 1 to 6 pm. The rest of the year it closes at 5 pm. Admission is £3.60/2.50 and it's hellishly overcrowded during school holidays.

Diving is a popular pastime in the lough. Des Rogers (☎ 12477-28297) takes out dive charters and the youth hostel has a compressor and special drying room.

Places to Stay At the YHANI-affiliated *Barholm Hostel* (☎ 012477-29598), 11 The Strand, opposite the ferry slipway, beds cost £9.95; there's no curfew and food can be provided if you book in advance. On the square, in the centre of the village, Mrs Adair's modest signless and nameless guesthouse at *No 22* (☎ 012477-28412) offers B&B at £15/28. At 15 High St, *White's* (☎ 012477-28580) charges £15 per person. At *Lough Cowey Lodge* (☎ 012477-28263), 9 Lough Cowey Rd, a few minutes out of Portaferry, B&B is £20/30. Moving more upmarket, the seafront *Portaferry Hotel* (☎ 012477-28231), 10 The Strand, does B&B for £55/90.

Places to Eat In the square, *Christine's* is OK for sandwiches and snacks. More inviting is *Harlequin*, across from the tourist office, offering good, cheap lunches. Nearby, *The Cornstore* offers meals till 9 pm; the pasta is £5.50.

The *Portaferry Hotel* serves delicious seafood in its restaurant and in the bar, with snacks available 12.30 to 2.30 pm. High teas are served 5.30 to 7 pm for £13.50.

Getting There & Away Ulsterbus Nos 9 and 10 go to Portaferry, Grey Abbey and Ballywalter from Belfast or Newtownards every hour or so. You can also pick up buses around the peninsula in Newtownards.

The ferry (☎ 01396-86637) sails every half hour from Portaferry to Strangford and back between 7.45 am and 10.45 pm Monday to Friday, 8.15 am to 11.15 pm on Saturday, and 9.45 am to 10.45 pm on Sunday. The journey time is only around five minutes. The fare is £4 for a car and driver, £2.50 for motorcyclists and their bikes, and 80/40p for car passengers and those on foot.

Millisle & Around
Below the high street in Millisle (Oileán an Mhuilinn) lies a pretty shoreline, with a stone wall running out to sea, handy for watching the eider ducks and brent geese bobbing offshore. About 1.5km north-west along Moss Rd (the B172 to Newtownards) is **Ballycopeland Windmill** (☎ 01247-861413), an 18th century tower mill which was in commercial use until 1915. It's been restored to working order, and has an adjacent visitors' centre. It's open June to August, Tuesday to Saturday, 10 am to 7 pm, Sunday 2 to 7 pm. Admission is £1/50p. Bus No 7 from Donaghadee passes the entrance.

Places to Stay *Ballywhiskin Caravan & Camping Park* (☎ 01247-862261), 216 Ballywalter Rd, has pitches for only £4.50 and opens mid-March to the end of October.

Crossdoney (☎ 01247-861526), 216 Abbey Rd, does B&B for £15 per person, while *Mount Erin House* (☎ 01247-861979), 46 Ballywater Rd, charges £17/30.

Donaghadee
Donaghadee (Domhnach Daoi) is a pretty, small port, encircled by harbour walls designed by John Rennie in 1819 and completed by his son, Sir John Rennie, who

designed several of London's bridges. In summer it's possible to get a boat out to the **Copeland Islands**, which were abandoned to the birds at the turn of the century; enquire at the Harbour Office at the southern end of the harbour toward the lighthouse.

In the village, **Grace Neill's** dates from 1611 and claims to be Ireland's oldest pub. Among its 17th century guests were Peter the Great, tsar and later emperor of Russia, who popped by for lunch in 1697 on his grand tour of Europe. In the 19th century, John Keats found the place 'charming and clean' but was 'treated to ridicule, scorn and violent abuse by the local people ... (who) objected to my mode of dress and thought I was some strange foreigner'.

Places to Stay *Donaghadee Caravan Park* (☎ 01247-882369), 183 Millisle Rd, has lots of tent sites for £5 a night.

Two of the cheapest B&Bs are *Waterside Shanaghan* (☎ 01247-888167), 154 Warren Rd, and *Bridge House* (☎ 01247-883348), 93 Windmill Rd, 3km from Donaghadee; both do B&B for £15. *Deans* (☎ 01247-882204), 52 Northfield Rd, has beds for £18/30 for singles/doubles; it also offers high tea for £8.50.

Places to Eat *Dunallen Hotel*, 27 Shore St, offers lunches with views of the bay. Farther around, *The Captain's Table*, 6 The Parade, does fish & chips, and is open daily for both lunch and dinner. *Moorings Restaurant* (☎ 012477-882239), nearby, does simple meals until 9 pm except on Sunday; roast of the day is £3.90. At No 35, *The Olde Seafarers Tavern* does lunches noon to 2.30 pm, with bistro meals 5.30 to 9 pm on Thursday to Saturday; a meal for two including wine is £25.

In the Market House on New St, *Coffee Plus* offers light meals and coffee breaks in daytime (closed Sunday); filled baked potato is £1.95. Finally, for a pint and a bite in historic surroundings, the *Grace Neill's* pub, 33 High St, fits the bill perfectly (it doesn't serve meals Sunday or Monday).

Western Shore of Strangford Lough

Castle Espie Centre Two km south-east of Comber is a haven for fledgling ornithologists, and for a large gathering of geese, ducks and swans, in the hands of the Wildfowl & Wetlands Trust. The interesting centre (☎ 01247-874146) opens March to October, Monday to Saturday, 10.30 am to 5 pm, Sunday 11.30 am to 6 pm; November to February, it opens Monday to Saturday 11.30 am to 4 pm, Sunday to 5 pm. Admission is £3/1.90. Best time to visit is May/June when the grounds are overrun with goslings, ducklings and cygnets.

Trench Farm (☎ 01247-872558) is almost 4km from Comber on the Ringcreevy Rd, with B&B at £17.50 a head. Comber's *Old School House Inn* (☎ 01238-541182), near the turning to Castle Espie, is the area's best known restaurant. It concentrates on seafood, serves fresh oysters from its own oyster farm, has game in winter and a set dinner for £16.95. It also does B&B for £45/65 with each room named after a US president connected with Ulster.

Six km south of Comber on the A22, in the hamlet of Lisbane, is *Lisbarnett House* (☎ 01238-541589) for good, inexpensive and familiar food like bangers and mash for £4.45.

Nendrum Monastic Site The site is on Mahee Island, connected to the lough's western shore by a causeway; the remains of 15th century Mahee Castle guard the causeway. Nendrum is earlier than Grey Abbey on the opposite shore; it was built in the 5th century under the guidance of St Mochaoi (St Mahee). The scant remains provide a clear outline of its early plan. Foundations exist from a number of churches, a round tower, beehive cells and other buildings, as well as three concentric stone ramparts and a monks' cemetery, all in a wonderful country setting. A particularly interesting relic is the vertical stone sundial, which has been reconstructed with some of the original pieces. The ruins were only uncovered in 1844, even though the island has long been inhabited.

Access to the site is free although there's a small visitors' centre which charges 75/40p. An excellent video compares Nendrum to Grey Abbey, and there's some interesting material about the concept of time and how we measure it, presented in child-friendly fashion. The centre opens April to September, Tuesday to Saturday, 10 am to 7 pm, Sunday 2 to 5 pm; October to March it only opens Saturday 10 am until 4 pm, Sunday 2 to 4 pm.

In Killinchy, *Burren Cottage* (☎ 01238-541475), 19 Main St, does B&B for £18 per person. *Barnageeha* (☎ 01238-541011), 90 Ardmillan Rd, charges £25/40; all rooms have a bathroom and dinner costs £15. Near Killinchy, *Tides Reach* (☎ 01238-541347) in Whiterock Bay, on the lough shore, is a small restaurant serving mostly seafood; fillet of cod is £4.95.

Killyleagh The A22 continues south to Killyleagh (Cill O Laoch), an old fishing village dominated by the impressive hilltop **castle** of the Hamilton family. Built originally by the Norman John de Courcy in the 12th century, this partly 14th and 17th century structure sits on the original motte-and-bailey and was heavily restored in 1850 to create the romantic version we see today. It's in private hands but the gates are left open so you can peer through. Outside the gatehouse a plaque commemorates Sir Hans Sloane, the naturalist born in Killyleagh in 1660, whose collection was the basis for the founding of the British Museum. He also gave his name to Sloane Square in London. The parish church has the tombs of members of the Dufferin family, some of whom lost their lives in the battles of Trafalgar and Waterloo.

The *Dufferin Arms* (☎ 01396-828229), 35 High St near the castle, provides B&B in spacious rooms with ensuite for £35/60 and its restaurant is good value for meat and fish dishes.

LECALE PENINSULA
East of Downpatrick at the southern end of Strangford Lough is the Lecale Peninsula.

From Clough, the A2 follows the coast east then north to Strangford, from where you have the option of taking the ferry across to Portaferry and the Ards Peninsula. St John's Point, the southern tip of the Lecale Peninsula, is surmounted by an automatic lighthouse. It's a wonder that St John managed to get a mention around this part of the world, because the Lecale Peninsula is unequivocally St Patrick's territory.

St Patrick (as you'll probably know by now) was originally kidnapped from Britain by Irish pirates and spent six years tending sheep on Slemish Mountain in County Antrim before escaping back to Britain. After religious training, he returned to Ireland to preach the faith in 432 and is said to have landed near the mouth of the Slaney Burn river. Patrick's first church was in a sheep shelter near Saul, to the north-east of Downpatrick. Using Saul as his base, he made forays out into the country, returning to Saul after some 30 years of evangelising. He's buried nearby, or so the locals believe.

Strangford
The small, quaint fishing village of Strangford (Baile Loch Cuan) is 16km north-east of Downpatrick. The Vikings sailed into the lough and noted the strong tidal currents through the strait – hence 'strong fjord'. Most of the village is in a conservation area dominated by **Strangford Castle**, another 16th century tower-house; the keys are available from Mr Seed, 39 Castle St, 10 am to 7 pm daily. Steps up at the end of Castle St (opposite the castle) lead to a network of paths and a fine view of the lough. There's a large and noisy colony of nesting terns on Swan Island, just off the slipway.

Ninety-minute tours around the lough on the *Islander Marine* (☎ 01396-881303) leave from the slip, operating from April to October on Wednesday, Saturday and Sunday at 3.30 pm. The fare is £6. For details of the car ferry to Portaferry, see Getting There & Away in the Portaferry section above.

Accommodation is rather scarce in Strangford. The *Strangford Caravan Park*

(☎ 01396-881888), 87 Shore Rd, has tent sites for £5. Otherwise, there's *Strangford Cottage* (☎ 01396-881208), 41 Castle St, with B&B for £30/50.

The *Lobster Pot* (☎ 01396-881288) is a bar and restaurant on the square serving excellent seafood; half a lobster is £14.95, bar snacks much cheaper. The *Cuan Bar & Restaurant* (☎ 01396-881222), also on the square, does hot and cold buffet lunches; a three-course Sunday lunch is £11.95. The *Cottage Grill* next door does takeaways.

Castleward

This huge estate stretches away from the inlet to the west, with the house 2km along the Downpatrick road. It was built in the 1760s by Lord and Lady Bangor – Bernard Ward and his wife Anne who were quite a pair. Their tastes were poles apart, and diverging all the time. The result was Castleward House (and a subsequent divorce). Bernard favoured the neoclassical Palladian approach, and was victorious in the design of the front facade and the classical staircase.

Anne had leanings towards the Strawberry Hill Gothic style, which she implemented on the back facade and in her Gothic boudoir with its incredible fan vaulting. The rest of this great house is a mixture of their different aesthetic tastes.

Around the grounds are some decent walks with vistas of the lough, a Greek folly, a fine 16th century Plantation tower-house, Castle Audley by the lough, a Victorian laundry museum, and tearooms (open the same hours as the house) which also do light lunches. The garden lakes have plenty of birds. Castleward Estate (☎ 0139-6881204) is in the hands of the National Trust.

The house is open May to August, Friday to Wednesday 1 to 6 pm and at the same time at weekends during April, September and October. Admission to the house is £2.50/1.50. The grounds are open all year until dusk and admission is £3.50 for a car in summer, £1.75 in winter or after the house has closed for the day.

Castleward Estate has a *campsite* (☎ 0139-6881680) for caravans and tents at

The Osebery, a Viking long ship similar to those that first sailed into Strangford Lough

£6 a night; the entrance is separate from the main entrance and closer to Strangford. Otherwise, accommodation in the area is scarce and you're better off heading for Portaferry or even Newcastle.

Strangford to Dundrum

A string of castles stretches from Strangford to Dundrum along the A2 road, the majority of them are large and in good condition.

Kilclief Castle Only 4km south of Strangford, Kilclief Castle guards the seaward mouth of the strait. This is the oldest towerhouse castle in the county, built in the 15th century by the adulterous bishop of Down. It has some elaborate details and is viewed as the prototype for other castles in the region. It opens July and August, Tuesday to Saturday 10 am to 7 pm, Sunday 2 to 7 pm. Admission is £1/50p.

Ardglass Thirteen km south of Strangford is Ardglass (Ard Ghlais), a fishing village with no less than seven castles or fortified houses from the 14th and 16th centuries. Ardglass Castle (now the clubhouse for the local golf club) and Gowd Castle adjoining it, have Horn and Margaret Castle towers nearby, while King's and Queen's Castles reside on a hilltop above the village. The only one open to the public is **Jordan's Castle** on Low Rd, a four-storey tower near the harbour. Like the others this was built by wealthy merchants at the dawn of economic development in Ulster. The castle now houses a local museum and a collection of antiques gathered together by its last owner.

It's open July and August, Tuesday to Saturday 10 am to 7 pm, Sunday 2 to 7 pm. Admission is 75/40p. On the hill north of the village is a 19th century **folly** built by Aubrey de Vere Beauclerc as a gazebo for his disabled daughter.

Just outside Ardglass on the Killough Rd is *Coney Island Park* (☎ 01396-841210) with tent spaces at £3. It's open late March to late November. On the B1 road from Ardglass to Downpatrick is *Strand Farm* (☎ 01396-841446), a small B&B with two

rooms at £15 per person. *Aldo's* (01396-841315) on Castle Place in Ardglass serves seafood or à la carte dinners for under £10, Tuesday to Sunday 5 to 10 pm; pepper steak is £8.90.

Killough Four km west of Ardglass is the seaside village of Killough, planned by Castleward's Lord Bangor, who constructed the road which runs dead straight from here to his estate 12km to the north. The harbour has long silted up but the village still has a picturesque, vaguely continental feel, the tree-lined streets and buildings around Palatine St and Palatine Square exemplifying this. The Palatines were 17th century German refugees escaping the Thirty Years War (1618-48).

A worthwhile walk is south to the 10th century church ruins and nearby lighthouse of St John's Point, a return trip of about 4km. From the point, the path heads north-west to Minerstown and Tyrella Strand. The 7km stretch of firm sand along here is privately owned and you must pay to use it.

Clough This small town lies at the northern end of a long and narrow inlet, at the crossroads of east and south Down and is home to the ruins of yet another castle. Clough Castle, at the junction of the A24 and A25, is a good example of a 13th century Norman motte-and-bailey with a small stone keep. About 2km north of Clough, on the A24, is the village of **Seaforde**, with a large demesne containing a maze and butterfly house.

Dundrum The final castle on this trip is 4km south of Clough on the shore of Dundrum (Dún Droma) Bay. Dundrum Castle was built in 1177 by de Courcy on the site of an earlier Irish fortification. The extensive ruins dominate the village, a rugged fortress on a rocky outcrop amidst the trees. De Courcy's castle was made of wood, and his successor, de Lacy, was probably responsible for most of the walls in the first years of the 13th century. King John confiscated the castle in 1210 and added the donjon at the highest point, its thick walls still containing the accessible stairway to the top. After a few changes in ownership it was captured from the Magennises by Cromwell, who blew it up in 1652.

You can walk up to the castle from the village centre or there's a car park just before it. April to September, opening hours are Tuesday to Saturday, 10 am to 7 pm, Sunday 2 to 7 pm. It closes at 4 pm the rest of the year and lunch times 1 to 1.30 pm all year. Admission is 75/40p.

Mourneview House (☎ 01396-51457) is at 16 Main St but the entry is off the street; it has B&B for £13 and overlooks the quay. There's pub food in places like the *Murlough Tavern* or the *Road House Inn*. The *Bucks Head Restaurant* (☎ 01396-755 1868) is the best place to eat and does good seafood lunches and dinners; it does a popular three-course Sunday lunch for £11.50.

DOWNPATRICK

Downpatrick's name (Dún Pádraig) comes from Ireland's patron saint who is associated with numerous places in this corner of Down. From Saul and Downpatrick Cathedral, he developed the island into what was to become the 'land of saints and scholars'. St Patrick had tried to land in Wicklow but was blown ashore at Strangford Lough near Saul.

Downpatrick is the county's administrative centre and capital, 32km south of Belfast. It was settled long before the saint's arrival, his first church here being constructed inside the dún or fort of Rath Celtchair, an earthwork still visible to the south-west of the cathedral. The place later became known as Dún Padraic, anglicised to Downpatrick in the 17th century.

In the 11th century, St Malachy moved the diocesan seat to Bangor, but the transfer was short-lived. In 1176 the Norman John de Courcy claimed to have brought the relics of St Columcille and St Brigid to Downpatrick to rest with the remains of St Patrick. This may have been a ploy to protect the churches of the town from the native Irish, who were disgruntled because the Irish clergy had been

removed and replaced with Benedictines and Cistercians. Later the town declined along with the cathedral until the 17th and 18th centuries, when the Southwell family developed it into more like what we see today. Much of the Georgian work is centred around English, Irish and Scotch Sts, which radiate from the town centre, although the best is in the Mall leading up to the cathedral. The street names derive from the ethnic ghettoisation of Downpatrick in the 17th century.

Information

The tourist office (☎ 612233) is in Market St opposite the bus station. Mid-June to mid-September, it's open Monday to Saturday 9 am to 6 pm, Sunday 11 am to 6 pm. The rest of the year it opens Monday to Saturday 9 am to 5 pm.

The telephone code is ☎ 01396.

Down Cathedral

Over the past 1600 years a cathedral has been created that is a conglomerate of reconstructions. Repeated Viking attacks wiped away all trace of the earliest churches and monasteries here, while the Irish Augustinians produced little before being evicted by the Norman Benedictines. Their cathedral and settlements were destroyed by Edward Bruce in 1315. The rubble of those times was used in the 15th century construction, which was finished in 1512 and lasted until 1538; after the dissolution of the monasteries it fell into ruins. Today's structure is an 18th and 19th century reconstruction with a few additions. Down Cathedral is also called the Cathedral of the Holy and Undivided Trinity.

In the grounds are a 9th century high cross in poor condition and, to the south, a turn-of-the-century monolith with the inscription 'Patric'. It has been believed since de Courcy's time that the saint is buried somewhere nearby. The legend goes that Patrick died in Saul, where his followers were told by angels to place his body on an ox-cart and that the angels would guide the cart to the spot where the saint was to be buried. They supposedly halted at the church on the hill of

Down, now the site of the cathedral. The interior (open Monday to Friday 9 am to 5 pm, weekends 2 to 5 pm) reveals a bygone era of churchgoing. The private pews are the last of their kind still in use in Ireland. Note the pillar capitals, the east window representing the Apostles, and the fine 18th century church organ.

There's a memorial to an Oliver Cromwell, though not 'the' Cromwell. All the treasured relics of St Patrick wouldn't save a church in Ireland from destruction if it housed that man's body!

Inch Abbey

This abbey, built by de Courcy for the Cistercians in 1180 over an earlier Irish monastic site, is visible across the river from the cathedral. The Cistercians arrived from Lancashire in England with a strict policy of non-admittance to Irishmen and managed this for nearly 400 years before closing in 1541. Much of the remains consists of foundations and low walls only; the groomed setting in the marshes of the River Quoile is its most memorable feature.

The grounds are open all year. April to September, the abbey's open Tuesday to Saturday 10 am to 7 pm (closed lunch times 1 to 1.30 pm), Sunday 2 to 7 pm. The rest of the year it closes at 4 pm. Admission is 75/40p. To get here head out of town for about 1.5km on the Belfast road, then turn left just before the Abbey Lodge Hotel.

Down County Museum/
St Patrick Heritage Centre

Down the Mall from the cathedral is the county museum (☎ 01396-615218), housed in an extensive 18th century jail complex. The gatehouse contains exhibits on the life of St Patrick, while the main buildings deal with the history of the county. In the cell block at the back are models of some of the prisoners incarcerated here. Perhaps the biggest exhibit of all is outside – a short signposted trail from here leads to the **Mound of Down**, a good example of a Norman motte-and-bailey.

The museum opens June to August,

Monday to Friday, 11 am to 5 pm, weekends 2 to 5 pm. September to May, it opens Tuesday to Friday, 11 am to 5 pm, weekends 2 to 5 pm. Admission is free.

The Mall itself is the most picturesque street in Downpatrick, with some marvellous 18th century architecture, including Soundwell School built in 1733 and a courthouse with a finely decorated pediment.

Quoile Countryside Centre

Signposted off the Strangford Rd is the small Quoile Countryside Centre (☎ 01396-615520), an educational centre with lots of info on the local flora & fauna. It's beside the ruins of **Quoile Castle**, a 17th century tower-house which stood on the shores of the River Quoile when it was first built. Access to the lower floors is via the Countryside Centre which opens free from 1 April to 30 September daily 11 am to 5 pm, shorter hours the rest of the year.

Places to Stay

B&Bs Accommodation in Downpatrick is very thin on the ground. *Hillcrest* (☎ 01396-612583), 157 Strangford Rd, charges £16/30. Farther afield is the 200-year-old *Havine Farm* (☎ 01396-851242), 51 Bally-donnell Rd, about 7km south-west of Downpatrick and 3km north of Tyrella in Ballykilbeg. It has four bedrooms and B&B is £16/31 in a truly rural environment.

Hotels Near Inch Abbey, the not very inviting two-star *Abbey Lodge Hotel* (☎ 01396-614511) has rooms at £45/60 including breakfast.

Places to Eat

By far the best place to eat is in the *Arts Café* (☎ 01396-615283) in the Down Arts Centre. It's a fine red-brick Victorian building with a clocktower, hard to miss at the centre of town, at the junction of English, Irish and Scotch Sts. It opens Monday to Saturday 9 am to 5 pm (to 9 pm on Thursday).

The *Golden Dragon*, Scotch St, combines Chinese and European menus; chow mein is £6.40. Arriving by bus it's difficult to miss

Harry Afrika's Diner & Restaurant (☎ 01396-617161) immediately opposite the station. It opens for breakfast and Sunday lunch, and from 6 pm has an à la carte menu. *Denvir's Pub*, Mall St, a good choice for pub grub, was closed for renovations but should be open by the time you read this. The *Abbey Lodge Hotel* has a good seafood-orientated restaurant with a set dinner for £13.

Getting There & Away

Ulsterbus Nos 15 and 215 depart regularly from Europa Buscentre (☎ 01232-320011) for Downpatrick station (☎ 01396-612384), Market St, every half hour or so (less on Sunday).

AROUND DOWNPATRICK

Saul

Saul is 3km north-east of Downpatrick off the A2 Strangford road. Upon landing near here in 432, St Patrick made his first convert, Díchú, the local chieftain, who gave St Patrick a sheep barn ('sabhal' meaning barn in Irish) from which to preach. This was the saint's favourite spot and he returned here regularly. West of the village is the supposed site of the barn, with a mock 10th century church and round tower built in 1932 to mark the 1500th anniversary of his arrival. Beside the church is the surviving wall of a medieval abbey where St Patrick is said to have died. Also in 1932, a massive 10m statue was erected on nearby Slieve Patrick, with Stations of the Cross along its ascent.

Struell Wells

Two km east of Downpatrick, on a back road behind the hospital, is the final pilgrimage site associated with the saint. Since the Middle Ages, the waters from these wells have been popular cures for all ills, with one well specially set aside for eye ailments. The site's popularity was at its peak in the 17th century, and the men's and women's bath houses date from this time.

CENTRAL COUNTY DOWN

South of Belfast is pastoral countryside, with towns like Craigavon, Lurgan, Saintfield,

Ballynahinch, Hillsborough, Moira and Banbridge servicing the region. Hillsborough is a particularly attractive little town, but Moira too has a quiet charm. Craigavon is an ugly sprawl, best avoided although many bus services connect here. Only Slieve Croob, south-west of Ballynahinch, breaks the flatness of the terrain. Down's greatest megalithic monuments are in this region, including the Giant's Ring and the Legananny Dolmen.

Giant's Ring

This earthwork is within easy reach of Belfast, only 8km south of the city centre, west of the A24 in Ballynahatty. The ring is a huge prehistoric enclosure nearly 200m in diameter, enclosing nearly three hectares. In the centre is the **Druid's Altar**, a dolmen from around 4000 BC. Prehistoric rings were commonly believed to be the home of fairies, and consequently treated with respect, but this one was commandeered in the last century as a racetrack. The 4m embankment was a natural grandstand and course barrier.

Legananny Dolmen

This is perhaps Ulster's most famous Stone Age monument, and features extensively in tourist literature. Situated just west of Slieve Croob (532m), the tripod dolmen is less bulky than most, and its elevated position has the great backdrop of the Mournes to the south. The source of Belfast's River Lagan is on Slieve Croob, and the mountain is crowned with the remains of a court cairn. Farther up, the summit also presents a much wider panorama of the county.

To reach the mountain, head west from Ballynahinch along the B7 to Dromara, from where there are roads leading south-east across the slopes.

Ballynahinch

Ballynahinch (Baile na hInse), 20km south of Belfast, was once a spa town and is now a plain market and agricultural centre. It has a small tourist office (☎ 01238-561950) in the Ballynahinch Leisure Centre, 55 Windmill St off the square. About 12km south of

Ballynahinch on the A24, **Seaforde Tropical Butterfly House** (☎ 01396-811225) has hundreds of free-flying tropical butterflies and many safely caged tropical insects and reptiles. It might make a good place to break a journey south to Newcastle. It opens Easter to September, Monday to Saturday 10 am to 5 pm, Sunday 1 to 6 pm. Admission costs £2/1.20.

Moira

Moira (Maigh Rath), near the County Antrim border, owes much of its attractive appearance to the Rawdon family from Yorkshire who settled here in the 17th century and built a huge mansion in a demesne which is now a public park. The broad main street was laid out in the 18th century and retains many elegant buildings like the town hall and St John's Parish Church.

If you want to get away from the main tourist route through Northern Ireland, you can camp in the *Moira Demesne Transit Caravan Park* (☎ 01846-619974) for just £2 a night. *Albany House* (☎ 01846-612211), 35 Main St, does B&B for £25/40.

Hillsborough

The gracious small town of Hillsborough (Cromghlinn), 15km south-west out of Belfast, was founded in the 1640s by a Colonel Hill who built a fort here to quell Irish insurgents. Fine Georgian architecture rings the square and runs down Main St where there are several antique shops.

At the top of Main St, the most notable building is **Hillsborough House**, built in the 1780s; as the official royal residence in Northern Ireland, and the official residence of the Secretary of State for Northern Ireland (the British government's main representative), it hosts official receptions and isn't open to the public. The most notable exterior feature is the elaborate wrought-iron gates dating from 1745 which were designed for Richhill Castle near Armagh and brought here when the house was restored after a fire.

Nearby are the Georgian **Market House** and **Court House**, while just at the bottom of Main St stands **St Malachy's Parish Church**, one of Northern Ireland's most splendid churches, with twin towers at the ends of its transepts and a graceful spire at the west end. Originally dedicated in 1663, St Malachy's was restored and improved in 1774 by the first marquis of Downshire, who was also responsible for its fine Snetzler organ. Inside, the nave and transepts are filled with box pews and there are some impressive 18th and 19th century wall tablets as well as a 17th century copy of the Bible in Irish.

Beside the church, only the ramparts of **Hillsborough Fort** date from Colonel Hill's day; the structures dotted around them mostly date from the 19th century. The fort (☎ 01846-683285) opens April to September, Tuesday to Saturday 10 am to 7 pm, Sunday 2 to 7 pm. Admission is free.

There are fine views over Hillsborough forest and lake from the ramparts.

Places to Stay *Growell House* (☎ 01238-532271), 207 Dromore Rd (past Hillsborough House) has two rooms with B&B for £15 per person. *Avoca Lodge* (☎ 01846-682343), at No 53, lets out rooms for £18.50 a head.

Places to Eat The *Plough Inn*, at the top of Main St, boasts that it has been offering 'beer and banter' since 1758; upstairs is *Clouseau's* wine bar, with excellent food available for lunch and dinner. The *Hillside Bar*, farther down on Main St, serves good bar food until 8 pm and nouvelle cuisine and seafood in its more formal restaurant until 9 pm. Steak is £10.25. *Ritchies*, on the corner of Ballynahinch St, does above average bar meals: home-made burgers for £3.95, steaks and lasagne. In the square, *La Glacerie*, offers coffee and snacks as well as ice cream.

The *Lapis Lazuli* restaurant in the White Gables Hotel (☎ 01846-682755), 23 Dromore Rd, relies on the best of local produce for its à la carte menu. Roast salmon is £13.50, and there are several vegetarian dishes. The hotel also serves food in the bar and has tea rooms for the less hungry.

Getting There & Away There are frequent daily services on bus Nos 38 and 238 to Belfast's Europa Buscentre. Bus No 38 also runs back and forth to Lisburn.

Banbridge & Around

Fifteen km south-west of Hillsborough is Banbridge (Droíchead na Banna), another Industrial Revolution town. The Gateway Tourist Information Centre (☎ 23322), 200 Newry Rd, is out of the town centre at the roundabout. It's open July and August, Monday to Saturday 9 am to 7 pm, to 5 pm the rest of the year; Easter to October it also opens Sunday 2 to 6 pm.

The telephone code is ☎ 018206.

Things to See Near the centre at the bottom of the hill is the **statue of Captain Francis Crozier**, complete with polar bears which look like no other polar bears you're likely to encounter. A native of Banbridge, Captain Crozier was commander of HMS *Terror* in the 1840s, and explored the uncharted Antarctic continent. Later he went with Sir John Franklin in search of the elusive North-West Passage. Franklin died on that voyage in 1847, and Crozier and his crew starved to death a year later, their bodies remaining lost in the Arctic for 10 years. Crozier lived in the fine blue and grey Georgian house, now colonised by solicitors, across the road from the statue.

Banbridge is the start of a **Brontë Homeland Drive** which travels the River Bann valley to Rathfriland 12km to the south-east. Patrick Brontë, father of the famous literary sisters, was born here and taught in a local school. The locals like to think that her father's tales of the Mourne Mountains inspired the bleak setting for Emily's *Wuthering Heights*. Milking this tenuous connection for all it's worth, is the **Brontë Homeland Interpretive Centre** (☎ 018206-31152) in what was Drumballyroney church, 13km south-east of Banbridge; it's open March to October Tuesday to Friday 11 am to 5 pm, weekends 2 to 6 pm; admission is £1, children 50p.

Organised Tours The tourist office is the 'gateway' for the so-called Linen Homelands (Banbridge, Craigavon and Lisburn). It's here that you can join tours of the linen towns on Wednesday and Saturday from May to the end of September. Tours begin at 10 am and take in the Irish Linen Centre in Lisburn, a flax farm in Dromore and a linen factory still in production, returning to Banbridge around 4 pm. The charge is £10, children £8.50, and advance booking is essential; phone ☎ 23122.

Places to Stay *Lisdrum* (☎ 22663) is on the main road to Newry, in well over 10 hectares of nicely tended gardens. Its flatlets, each with a small lounge, cost £16/30 for B&B. It's open year-round.

Places to Eat Banbridge is something of a culinary wasteland. *Rosamar's Restaurant*, 14 Bridge St, does sandwiches and soups; toasted sandwiches with salad cost £2.25. Fast food is available from *Friar Tuck's*, near the bottom of Bridge St; burgers are £1.55. For more substantial food try the Chinese *Lotus Garden* opposite; duck with cashew nuts costs £5.80.

Getting There & Away Bus Nos 38 and 238 run regularly from Belfast's Europa Buscentre, through Dromore, Hillsborough and Lisburn; bus No 238 also goes to Newry.

SOUTH DOWN & MOURNE MOUNTAINS

The relatively compact yet rather impressive Mourne Mountains have long resisted human settlement. Today they're surrounded on all sides by towns and villages, but are crossed only by the B27 road between Kilkeel and Hilltown. The reservoirs of the Silent Valley and Spelga are among the few intrusions on nature. The steep and craggy granite peaks have suffered less from glaciation than other similar ranges. There are no low polished hills to be found here.

The highest, most accessible peak is **Slieve Donard** (848m). In its shadow, the town of Newcastle is the best base for exploring this or other peaks, as the Mourne

Countryside Centre here provides detailed information. The less adventurous can visit the numerous forest parks around Newcastle. For walkers, Newry and Downpatrick tourist offices stock *St Patrick's Vale: The Land of Legend* which describes 31 possible walks and costs £1.

The **Silent Valley Park** plunges into the range's heart, surrounded by most of the peaks. **Ben Crom**, **Slieve Muck** and **Slievelamagan** are good for strenuous hiking. Westwards is the B27 road which passes **Spelga Dam**, a picturesque drive in the evening, when the sun goes down behind **Eagle Mountain** and **Pigeon Rock Mountain**. There's good rock climbing in this area.

As in Connemara, the farmers here have produced the characteristic patchwork of small fields with dry-stone walls out of the boulder-strewn landscape. The biggest of the walls, the **Mourne Wall**, is a different kettle of fish; it was built early this century to provide employment and to enclose the catchment area of the Silent Valley reservoir; it stretches for 35km over numerous peaks.

Newcastle

All along the coast from the north of the county the Mournes beckon. If you stick to the coastline you'll eventually end up in Newcastle (An Caisleán Nua), 46km from Belfast. Despite its marvellous setting with the huge Slieve Donard stretching up behind the town as a backdrop, Newcastle itself is fairly dreary, the Bangor of south Down, with fast-food joints, amusement arcades and general seaside tackiness. To be fair, it also boasts 5km of beaches. If the peace process continues Newcastle is well positioned to catch the Southern holiday market.

Information The tourist office (☎ 22222), in the Newcastle Centre & Tropicana Complex on Central Promenade, opens Monday to Saturday 10 am to 5 pm, Sunday 2 to 6 pm (longer hours in summer). For more details on the Mournes, drop into the Mourne Countryside Centre (☎ 24059), 91 Central Promenade, beside the Avoca Hotel. June to September (weekdays 9 am to 7 pm, week-

ends noon to 6 pm), it provides more information on history and scenery in the form of exhibitions, brochures and maps of suggested walks. Free guided walks of varying distances (four to 14km) into the mountains leave from the centre Monday and Saturday at 10 am.

The telephone code is ☎ 013967.

Places to Stay The YHANI *Newcastle Youth Hostel* (☎ 22133), 30 Downs Rd, near the bus station and Slieve Donard Hotel, charges £6.50 a night including bed linen, and opens all year.

For value for money there are few B&Bs better than *Glenside Farmhouse* (☎ 22628), about 1km from Tollymore Forest Park on Tullybrannigan Rd, with simple rooms available for £14. There are several, more-central B&Bs on or near Bryansford Rd including *Arundel Guesthouse* (☎ 22232), at No 23, which is non-smoking and has rooms with shared bathroom for £15 per person and private parking.

Briers Country House (☎ 24347), 39 Middle Tollymore Rd, is a delightful old farmhouse almost 1km from Newcastle; B&B is £35/50 a single/double.

If all you want to do on reaching Newcastle is to get out again, *Old Town Farm* (☎ 22740), 25 Corrigs Rd, could fit the bill nicely. Turn right immediately after the Burrendale Hotel (see below) and take the first right down a country lane to the far end. Beds cost £18 per person. At £35/60 including breakfast, the *Donard Hotel* (☎ 22203), 27 Main St, is the cheapest hotel. It's not to be confused with the large, dominating *Slieve Donard Hotel* (☎ 23681; fax 24830) on Downs Rd beside the beach, which offers rooms for £75/110 but has all the extras and special deals.

Bryansford Rd has some good-value hotels such as the *Brook Cottage Hotel* (☎ 22204), with pleasant rooms at £42.50/68 including breakfast. Finally, the *Burrendale Hotel & Country Club* (☎ 22599), a three-star establishment, has spacious rooms for £55/80 with breakfast and reputedly the best restaurant in Newcastle.

Places to Eat Main St and its extension, Central Promenade, have plenty of fast-food outlets. On the seafront, the *Strand Restaurant* is marginally more upmarket but with main courses for around £5; it's in the back past the ice-cream parlour, and there's a coffee shop upstairs. Next door at the *Mariner Restaurant* (☎ 23473) dinners come with musical accompaniment, and there are also bar meals. The *Pavilion* on Downs Rd, opposite the entrance to the Slieve Donard Hotel, is more seafood-orientated with grilled trout for £4.95.

If you're prepared to venture farther afield, the *Tea House* in Tollymore Forest Park (see the Around Newcastle section, following) is designed to resemble a treehouse and has fine views of the park. It's open 10.30 am to 6.30 pm daily (closed November/December). You can get a decent light lunch for under £5 here. The *Burrendale Hotel* has a high-quality restaurant with a set dinner at £18. Bar snacks and restaurant meals (sirloin steak £7.25) are also available in the *Brook Cottage Hotel*.

The *Oak Restaurant* at the Slieve Donard Hotel (☎ 23681) isn't bad either with four-course dinner specials for £19; booking is essential. Life is less formal (and cheaper) at the *Percy French Grill Bar & Restaurant* by the gates, where poached salmon costs £7.95 and there's a vegetarian selection.

Getting There & Away The bus station (☎ 22296) is in Railway St and there's an hourly service from Belfast (1¼ hours, £6.80 return) on Ulsterbus Nos 18 and 20 through Ballynahinch. Alternatively, you can go from Belfast to Downpatrick and from there take Ulsterbus No 17 to Newcastle (20 minutes).

Getting Around During July and August, Ulsterbus No 34A (the Mourne Rambler) runs from Newcastle (☎ 22296) to Silent Valley and the Spelga Dam, with four buses on weekdays, three on Saturday.

Wiki Wiki Wheels (☎ 23973), 10B Donard St, near the main roundabout, rents bikes, as does Ross Cycles (☎ 78029), on Clarkhill Rd in nearby Castlewellan, the region's main Raleigh dealer. Bikes are £7/30 a day/week.

Around Newcastle
Newcastle is an ideal base from which to explore the Mournes, and there are three forest parks close by, for walks, hikes and pony treks. **Donard Park** at the southern edge of town is the best place from which to ascend Slieve Donard. On a good day the three-hour effort is well rewarded, with Down's patchwork of fields, Scotland, Wales and the Isle of Man all on show at varying splendid perspectives. Two cairns can be found near the summit and were long believed to have been cells of St Donard, who retreated here to pray in early Christian times.

Tollymore Forest Park (☎ 22428) is 3km north-east of town. Its 500 hectares offer lengthy walks along the Shimna River and the north slopes of the Mournes. The park opens daily, 10 am to sunset and admission is £3 per car, £1.50 for a motorcycle. The visitor centre is in a 19th century barn, designed to look like a church, and displays the single plaster plaque that survives from Tollymore House as well as info on the flora, fauna and history of the park. June to August, it opens daily noon to 5 pm, the rest of the year weekends only. Guided walks leave from outside at 2 pm on summer weekends. **Tollymore Outdoor Centre** (☎ 22158), part of the park but with a separate entrance, runs group courses on hill walking, rock climbing and canoeing; call in advance if you'd like to join a course to see what's offered when. Bus No 34 runs from Newcastle bus station to Tollymore but there's no Sunday service except June to August.

Farther north-east is the finest but slightly smaller park, **Castlewellan Forest Park** (☎ 22428), and its lovely lake. Trout fishing is allowed (daily permit £8) and there's also boat hire. The internationally known **Arboretum** is well established, dating from 1760, with a wide variety of fine shrubs and trees. It's open 10 am to dusk and the admission fee is the same as for Tollymore. The park

PAT YALE

PAT YALE

TONY WHEELER

TOM SMALLMAN

TONY WHEELER

PAT YALE

A	B
C	D
E	F

Counties Down & Armagh
A: Commemorative statue,
   Crossmaglen, County Armagh
B: Boating, Bangor, County Down
C: Bangor, County Down

D: Inch Abbey, County Down
E: Abbey ruins in Grey Abbey,
   County Down
F: Donaghadee harbour, County Down

VITA · VERITAS · VICTORIA

County Derry
Top Left: Mural, Derry youth hostel
Top Right: Derry Coat of Arms
Bottom: Symbol of hope, Derry

entrance is off the main street in the village of Castlewellan and you could leave your vehicle there and walk in.

Outside the park is **Mount Pleasant Horse Trekking Centre** (☎ 78651), which caters both to the experienced rider and to the beginner, with various treks into the park for £8 an hour inclusive of guide.

Places to Stay There are plenty of campsites on offer though they can fill up at the height of summer. Both *Castlewellan* (☎ 78664) and *Tollymore* (☎ 22428) have spaces for tents from £6 to £9.50 depending on the season. Nearer the town is the similarly priced *Lazy BJ Park* (☎ 23533) on the Dundrum road.

Mournes Coast Road

The coastal drive along the A2 south and around the sweeping Mourne slopes is the most memorable journey in Down. Annalong, Kilkeel, Rostrevor and Warrenpoint offer convenient stopping points, from which you can detour into the mountains. If you take the Head Rd, following the sign for the Silent Valley 1km north of Annalong, you go through the beautiful stone-wall countryside, past the Silent Valley, and back to Kilkeel.

Annalong The busy little tourist spot of Annalong (Áth na Long), with its shingle beach, is 12km south of Newcastle. Overlooking the harbour is the nicely preserved **Annalong Corn Mill** (☎ 013967-68736), an 1830 watermill which still mills flour. The mill opens February to November, Tuesday to Saturday, 11 am to 5 pm; admission is unusually priced at £1.44/72p.

For B&B in the £14 to £16 range, on Kilkeel Rd there are *Four Winds* (☎ 013967-68345), which is at No 237, and *Kamara* (☎ 013967-68072) at No 106A. Annalong's *Glassdrumman Lodge* (☎ 013967-68451) is an expensive guesthouse (£85/110 for singles/doubles) which also serves up French cuisine for £27.50. It has the *Kitchen Garden* for more moderately priced meals. More down to earth is the *Harbour Inn*

(☎ 013967-68678) by Annalong's waterfront, serving up fish, steaks and pub food daily.

Kilkeel Kilkeel (Cill Chaoil), 9km farther south, is bigger than Annalong, with a quayside fish market stocked by Northern Ireland's largest fishing fleet. From Kilkeel the B27 ventures north into the mountains. The friendly tourist office (☎ 016937-62525), on Newcastle St, the main street, opens April to September, Monday to Saturday 9 am to 5.30 pm, the rest of the year Monday to Friday 9 am to 5.30 pm.

Chestnutt Caravan Park (☎ 016937-62653), beside a Blue Flag beach is good, with pitches at £8.50 a night. B&Bs within the £16 range are *Mourne Abbey* (☎ 016937-62426), 16 Greencastle Rd south of town, and *Sharon Farm House* (☎ 013967-62521), 6 Ballykeel Rd, about 5km north-west in Ballymartin. Mourne Abbey only opens April to September. *Hill View House* (☎ 016937-64269), 6km north of Kilkeel, just off the B27, opens all year and does B&B at £17/31 a single/double. The homely *Kilmorey Arms Hotel* (☎ 016937-62220), 41 Greencastle St, costs £28.50/47. It also does a medium-priced menu of familiar à la carte dishes.

Silent Valley Just east of Kilkeel is the Head Rd, which leads to the beautiful Silent Valley 6km north. In the valley the Kilkeel River has been dammed to provide water for Belfast. The dry-stone **Mourne Wall** surrounds the valley and climbs over the summits of 15 of the nearby peaks. Two metres high and over 35km long, it was built in 1910-22 and outlines the watershed of the springs which feed the two lakes.

At the south end of the valley is the Silent Valley information centre (☎ 01232-746581), behind the grey stone building. From near the car park (admission £3 for cars, £1.50 motorcycles, £1.50/50p pedestrians) there's a bus up the valley to the top of Ben Crom. This operates daily July and August and costs £1.20 return; but in May, June and September it runs weekends only.

Otherwise it's a fine walk. The centre opens 10 am to 6 pm April to September, until 4 pm the rest of the year.

Greencastle Six km south-west of Kilkeel, on the tip of a promontory across Carlingford Lough, is Greencastle (Caisleán na hOireanaí). The first castle was built in 1261 as a companion to Carlingford Castle on the opposite side of the lough in County Louth. However, the square, turreted remains date from the 14th century. Once the property of the earls of Kildare, it was seized by the crown and given to the Bagenal family of Newry in the 1550s. They maintained it as a royal garrison until it was destroyed by Cromwell's forces in 1652. The rooftop provides a good vantage point west up the lough. The interior opens July and August, Tuesday to Saturday 10 am to 7 pm (closed for lunch 1 to 1.30 pm), Sunday 2 to 7 pm. Admission is 75/40p.

Cranfield Point, to the south-east, is the most southerly tip of Northern Ireland.

Rostrevor From Kilkeel the journey is westward along Carlingford Lough. Thirteen km to the west, Rostrevor (Caislean Ruairi) is a pretty Victorian seaside resort of a couple of streets at the base of Slievemartin. Just before entering the town from the north, the road passes a large **obelisk** to Major General Ross.

A British commander in the American War of 1812, Ross's achievement was the capture of Washington DC and the burning of the White House. Up until then the presidential residence had been stone grey, but was painted white to cover the smoke and scorch marks left by Ross's men.

Kilbroney Forest Park From the park (☎ 016937-38134), to the north-east of the town, there's a forest drive and then a footpath to the top of Slievemartin, or a strenuous trek up the steepest side of the mountain. The Kilbroney Forest Park *campsite* on Shore Rd costs only £5.25 per tent.

Near Rostrevor, 2km inland by the Fairy Glen riverside walk, is the attractive early 18th century *Forestbrook House* (☎ 016937-38105) on Forestbrook Rd. It charges £16 for B&B.

Most eateries are on Bridge St. The best place to eat in Rostrevor is *Goodfellows*. It's a delicatessen with a café at the back, and does good pies, sandwiches, snacks and cakes. Quiche is £2.60. Its staff all wear chefs outfits. The *Corner House* offers substantial pub food. For takeaway there's the *Wok Way* Chinese and the *La Pinta* for burgers. The *Glenside Inn* in Bridge St is a pleasant watering hole.

Warrenpoint & Around At the head of the lough, on the way to Newry, is Warrenpoint (An Pointe), another spacious and picturesque resort around the large central Diamond. It's one of the livelier towns around, with an active nightlife in the pubs and halls, although for many people it will always be associated with an incident in 1979 when the IRA detonated a bomb hidden in a haycart, killing 15 soldiers and seriously injuring eight others.

The tourist office (☎ 01637-52256), in the Church St town hall, opens weekdays year-round 9 am to 5 pm, plus weekends during summer.

Just over 3km west of Warrenpoint is the small **Burren Heritage Centre** which has information about the court tombs and crannógs of the area, along with a collection of embroidery, tools and bits and pieces rescued from local churches. It has a craft shop and teashop attached. Opening hours are April to September, Tuesday to Saturday, 11 am to 6 pm, Sunday 2 to 6 pm; weekdays 10 am to 5 pm the rest of the year. Admission is £1.50.

On the main road from Warrenpoint to Newry, you'll see **Narrow Water Castle**, a medieval tower-house, standing on the shores of the lough and the round tower of **Clonallan** monastic settlement on the opposite shore.

For somewhere to stay you could try *Fernhill House* (016937-72677), 90 Clonallon Rd, where B&B is £18.50, or the cheaper *Glen Rosa* (☎ 016937-72589), 40

Great Georges St South, for £15. For pub food, try *Bennett's* on Church St, or the *Victoria* on the Diamond which has a Tandoori Indian restaurant upstairs. Alternatively *Diamonds* (☎ 016937-52053) nearby has an extensive menu with something to suit most tastes including vegetarians. Lasagne is £3.95.

April to September there's a 90-minute cruise around the lough on the *Maiden of Mourne* (☎ 016937-72950) which costs £3 (children £2). For sailing timetables and tickets you could also call into the tourist office.

Weather permitting, a passenger ferry (☎ 016937-72001), crosses the lough to Omeath in County Louth, May to September, daily 1 to 6 pm for £2/1 return.

Newry

Newry (An tIúr) has long been a frontier town, guardian of the Gap of the North which lies between the Mourne Mountains to the east and Slieve Gullion to the south-west. Its name derives from a yew tree planted here by St Patrick in an early monastery, of which nothing remains.

A stone castle was first built in the town in 1180 by de Courcy, but it was repeatedly attacked. Cistercian monks came to shelter near the castle, until their abbey was taken over by Nicholas Bagenal in the 1570s. As Grand Marshal of all English forces in Ireland, the powerful Bagenal attracted the attention of some of the local rulers. One, Seán 'the Proud' O'Neill, completely destroyed the castle and house in 1566. In 1575 Bagenal used the rubble to construct the first Protestant church built in Ireland since the Reformation. He is buried in the grounds of St Patrick's Church of Ireland on Stream St which may eventually become a museum.

Newry Canal, built in 1740, preceded the English network which led that country into the Industrial Revolution. The canal brought trade, and later its decline led to the decline of the town.

Always too close to the borders to be popular with tourists, Newry is starting to

find its feet. Its location makes it a good base from which to explore the Mourne Mountains, Slieve Gullion Forest Park and the Cooley Peninsula. Its position on the main Dublin-Belfast road (the A1/M1) also makes it a magnet for shoppers, in particular for Southerners who come for the cheaper merchandise, especially around Christmas. But traffic congestion is a year-round problem.

Information There's a small helpful tourist office (☎ 68877) inside the town hall. June to September it opens Monday to Friday 9 am to 5 pm, Saturday 10 am to 4 pm; the rest of the year it opens weekdays only and closes 1 to 2 pm.

The telephone code is ☎ 01693.

Newry Museum The small Newry Museum (☎ 66232), in the Arts Centre on Bank Parade, presents a detailed historical account of the town, and has some intriguing exhibits, including Admiral Nelson's cabin table from HMS *Victory*. This piece sits near the base of the entrance stairs, its glass case bearing only a small plaque naming the benefactor. The museum opens weekdays 9 am to 5 pm, 10 am to 1 pm on Saturday. Admission is free.

Town Hall The red-brick town hall was built in 1893 on the border of Counties Down and Armagh. So fierce was the rivalry between the two counties that it was erected right on the border, which meant building it on a three-arched bridge over Clanrye River. The cannon outside was captured during the Crimean War (1853-56) and given to the town in memory of the men who volunteered to fight in the war.

Newry Canal You can hardly miss Newry Canal in the centre of town where it parallels Clanrye River, separated from it by a narrow strip of land. It runs 29km north to Lough Neagh, and 9.5km south to Carlingford Lough. Victoria Lock, south of the town centre, has been restored for visitors as part of the long term Newry Canal Restoration

Project to restore the whole canal and reopen it to leisure traffic.

Newry Town Trail While it's certainly not a pretty town, Newry repays a bit of foot-slogging, especially if you pick up a copy of the town trail map from the tourist office. There are two versions, a long and a short trail, both starting from the town hall.

Places to Stay *Ashton House* (☎ 62120) is on Fathom Line on Omeath Rd, close to town. It does B&B for £20/35, and all rooms have their own bathroom. The modern *Hillside* (☎ 65484), 1 Rock Rd, is 8km north of Newry off the Belfast road and charges £18/30 for B&B. More central, *Millvale House* (☎ 63789), 8 Millvale Rd, charges £16/20 with shared bathroom. The large modern *Mourne Country Hotel* (☎ 67922), 52 Belfast Rd, has rooms for £32.50 per person including breakfast.

Places to Eat There are numerous places to stop for a bite. The *Friar Tuck* fast-food outlets on Monaghan St and Sugar Island are good for their kind. *Snaubs*, on Monaghan St, has a range of healthier possibilities including vegetarian options (spinach and onion tart £4.50) and good bread and cakes.

The *Ambassador*, on Hill St, is good for familiar fare at reasonable prices: shepherd's pie is £3.50, cod and chips £4. It accepts punts for pounds on a one for one basis. For good steaks the *Brass Monkey*, on Trevor Hill, is a bar and grill and relatively inexpensive; Dover sole is £9.50.

Entertainment The two-screen *Savoy Cinema* (☎ 67549) is in Merchants Quay on the corner of Monaghan St.

Getting There & Away From Belfast's Europa Buscentre (☎ 01232-320011), bus Nos 38, 45 and 238 run regularly to Newry station (☎ 63531) on Edward St. From the Mall in Newry, bus No 39 leaves once or twice an hour for Kilkeel, passing through Rostrevor and Warrenpoint.

Trains between Dublin and Belfast stop at Newry; the station (☎ 69271) is a fair way from the centre but there are bus connections.

County Armagh

County Armagh could be – should be – a major tourist attraction. Quite apart from the venerable town of Armagh, there are some wonderful prehistoric sites, and sights, in the surrounding countryside and you could easily spend a week or more here. Unfortunately, modern history came very close to rendering the county a no-go area. Apart from small Protestant outposts such as Bessbrook, County Armagh is strongly Catholic and its nationalist identity is keenly felt. The resolve of its people to refuse incorporation into the UK is steadfastly maintained; nowhere else is there so strong a sense of Ireland being occupied by a foreign force. The evidence of barely suppressed conflict is apparent everywhere, but Armagh is also beautiful and deserves to have more visitors.

ARMAGH

Armagh (Ard Mhacha), one of the towns most worth visiting in the North, has suffered badly from the social and political unrest; witness the huge army post on the edge of town and the boarded-up courthouse, destroyed by a bomb in 1993, but being rebuilt. Here, as elsewhere, there's cautious optimism that the peace process will continue and bring a tourism dividend. The St Patrick's Trian and Navan Fort developments are indicative of an effort to turn things round.

History

This compact little city lays claim to being one of Ireland's oldest settlements. Legend has it that the hill now home to the Church of Ireland cathedral was once the power base of Queen Macha, wife of Nevry, some time during the first millennium BC. She gave her name to the city, whose Irish form, Ard

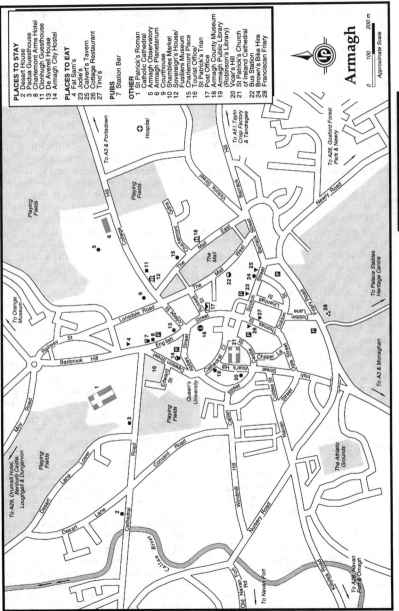

PLACES TO STAY
2 Desart House
3 Padua Guesthouse
8 Charlemont Arms Hotel
11 Clonhugh Guesthouse
13 De Averell House
14 Armagh City Hostel

PLACES TO EAT
4 Fat Sam's
23 Jodie's
25 Calvert's Tavern
26 Cottage Restaurant
27 Tino's

PUBS
7 Station Bar

OTHER
1 St Patrick's Roman
   Catholic Cathedral
5 Armagh Observatory
6 Armagh Planetarium
9 Courthouse
10 Shambles Market
12 Sovereign's House/
   Fusiliers Museum
15 Charlemont Place
16 Charlemont Place
17 Tourist Office/
   St Patrick's Trian
18 Post Office
19 Armagh County Museum
19 Armagh Public Library
   (Robinson's Library)
20 Vicar's Hill
21 St Patrick's Church
   of Ireland Cathedral
22 Bus Station
24 Brown's Bike Hire
28 Franciscan Friary

Armagh

0   100   200 m

Approximate Scale

DOWN & ARMAGH

Macha, means 'Macha's height'. St Patrick set up the first Christian church in Ireland here, on a site at the base of the hill. Later the local chieftain, a convert to the new religion, gave Patrick the hilltop, and a church of some kind has stood on that spot for over 15 centuries, predating Canterbury as a Christian religious site. By the 8th century Armagh was one of Europe's best known centres of religion, learning and craftwork.

However, its fame was its undoing, as the Vikings raided the city 10 times between 831 and 1013, taking slaves and valuables, and leaving many dead in their wake. Brian Ború, who died in 1014 near Dublin during the last great battle to defeat the Vikings, was buried on the north side of the cathedral.

With the Vikings gone, the Irish clans fought each other for the city, and the Norman settlement in the 12th and 13th centuries saw more attacks. But the religious life continued, with the conversion from Celtic Christianity to Catholic customs in the 12th century and the establishment of a Franciscan friary in 1263. What the Vikings and Normans hadn't managed, the Reformation did. The monasteries and educational establishments were destroyed by either English or Irish forces fighting yet again for control of the city. By the 17th century little was left of a once flourishing city.

During the plantation, Irish landowners were thrown off their lands, and settlers from England and Scotland took their place. Today's Armagh is a largely Georgian construct and owes its distinctive architecture to Richard Robinson, a Church of Ireland primate. By the time of his arrival in 1765 the town had recovered, economically at least, from the many invasions and had a flourishing linen industry. In 1995 its old city status was restored again.

Information

The helpful tourist office (☎ 527808), 40 English St inside the building housing St Patrick's Trian, opens Monday to Saturday, 9 am to 5 pm, Sunday 2 to 5 pm all year. The car park next door charges 30p for two hours, 80p for four. If you're intending to spend just

one day here don't do it on Sunday when, like the rest of Northern Ireland, Armagh more or less closes down.

The telephone code is ☎ 01861.

St Patrick's Church of Ireland Cathedral

The core of the building dates right back to medieval times while the rather dull sandstone-clad exterior is the result of a 19th century restoration by Primate Beresford. Around the exterior are a series of carved heads, and inside, along with the chilly wooden pews of established religion, are some interesting plaques and an 11th century Celtic cross. The chapter house has assorted paraphernalia from the ancient city. Every time anyone has knocked down a house or rebuilt a wall and found some ancient object, it has been deposited here, unexamined and unexplained. There's usually someone around who can tell you what's known about the collection.

On the west wall of the north transept a plaque commemorates the burial of Brian Ború. Near the cathedral, **Vicar's Hill** is one of the oldest terraces in Ireland, built in the 18th century by Richard Castle in the Palladian style. The ghost of a green lady is said to haunt the area. Beside St Patrick's Cathedral on the corner of Abbey St, **Armagh Public Library** (☎ 523142), which is also known as Robinson's Library, opens daily 9 am to 5 pm. It has several ancient manuscripts, a set of 1838 Ordnance Survey maps and a first edition of *Gulliver's Travels*, annotated by Swift himself.

St Patrick's Roman Catholic Cathedral

From the Church of Ireland cathedral you can walk down Dawson St and Edward St to the other St Patrick's Cathedral, built between 1838 and 1873, with the Famine interrupting building work for a while. It's built in the Gothic Revival style, with huge twin towers dominating the approach up flight after flight of steps. Inside it seems almost Byzantine, with every piece of wall and ceiling covered in brilliantly coloured mosaics. The sanctuary was modernised in 1981 by Liam McCormick and has a very distinctive tabernacle holder and crucifix which seem out of place among the mosaics and statues of the rest of the church.

The Mall

Back along English St (stopping to admire the Shambles at the corner of English St and Cathedral Rd) and Russell St, you come to the Mall. It's not a collection of supermarkets and dress shops, but a pleasantly laid out park which once held horse races, cock fighting and bull baiting sessions, until Richard Robinson decided it was a bit low-class for a city of learning. Now several war memorials stand sentinel over the flowerbeds.

At the top of the Mall, behind wire mesh fences, barbed wire and video cameras, used to stand the **courthouse**, built in 1809 by Armagh man Francis Johnston, who later became one of Ireland's most famous architects. It was destroyed by a huge bomb in 1993 and the site is still under restoration. On the opposite corner the **Sovereign's House**, built for the Armagh equivalent of the mayor, was also damaged by the explosion.

Farther along the Mall East, away from the courthouse, is a series of Georgian terraces. **Charlemont Place** is a creation by Francis Johnston, and so is the Armagh County Museum's portico, fronting a more workaday building originally put up as a school.

Armagh County Museum

In the Mall East, Armagh has one of Ireland's nicer small museums (☎ 523070). Its showcases are pleasantly filled with prehistoric axe heads, items found in bogs, old clothes, corn dollies and strawboy outfits, plus some very dead stuffed wildlife, and military costumes and equipment. It opens Monday to Friday, 10 am to 5 pm, Saturday 10 am to 1 pm, 2 to 5 pm, but sometimes closes on bank holidays. Admission is free.

Royal Irish Fusiliers Museum

The museum (☎ 522911), which is in the old Sovereign's House near the courthouse, consists of much paraphernalia of war: polished silver and brass, medals and the little personal items that survived from the many

battles the fusiliers fought. It opens weekdays 10 am to 5 pm and entry costs £1.50 (children 75p).

Armagh Observatory & Planetarium

A healthy walk up College Hill from the Mall brings you first to the 200 year old observatory, which still contributes to astronomical research. It isn't open to the public but you can walk around the grounds weekdays 9.30 am to 4.30 pm.

Farther up the hill, Armagh Planetarium (☎ 523689) has the interesting Hall of Astronomy displaying astronomical instruments, with lots of hands-on stuff, and an Eartharium Gallery designed to give visitors 'a global view of our home'. Both stand in Astropark, laid out to show the relationships of the different planets to each other.

The planetarium opens September to March weekdays 10 am to 5 pm (with daily shows at 3 pm), Saturday 1.30 to 5 pm (shows at 2 and 3 pm); April to June it also opens Sunday 1.30 to 5 pm (with shows at 2 and 3 pm); July and August there are hourly shows on weekdays. Admission to everything costs £3.50/2.50.

Palace Stables Heritage Centre

The heritage centre (☎ 529629), 10 minutes walk out of town off Friary Rd, stands in the grounds of the Palace Demesne, built by Archbishop Robinson when he was appointed primate of Ireland in 1769. As you turn into the demesne, you'll see the ruins of the Franciscan friary dating back to the 13th century. Much of its stonework was taken to build the demesne walls.

The stables house a set of tableaux meant to illustrate how a guest was entertained in the days of Richard Robinson, but as there are no real artefacts except in the coachman's kitchen downstairs, it's of fairly limited interest. There's a nice coffee shop, craft shop and a children's play room. The centre opens April to September, Monday to Saturday 10 am to 5.30 pm, Sunday 1 to 6 pm; October to March, Monday to Saturday 10 am to 5 pm, Sunday 2 to 5 pm. You have to go round with a guide; admission and tour cost £2.90/1.80. The palace itself houses council offices, but the ground floor lobby retains some of the grandeur of earlier days, with fine portraits of George III and his wife.

Next to the palace, the Primate's Chapel, designed by Thomas Cooley with a little help from Francis Johnston, is now deconsecrated. Inside are fine oak carvings, an elaborate coffered ceiling and stained-glass windows. Beside it steps lead down to a tunnel. Archbishop Robinson didn't like the smell of cooking, so the kitchen was in an outside building connected to the palace by a tunnel. There's also an interesting ice house which would have once been filled with ice, which didn't melt as long as it wasn't exposed to outside air.

St Patrick's Trian

The old second Presbyterian church behind the tourist office has been turned into a heritage centre (☎ 521801), focusing on the theme of 'faith' in a city so associated with St Patrick. For children there's also a Land of Lilliput exhibition with a rather wonderful model of Gulliver tied down on the ground while the Lilliputians climb all over him. The story of his adventures there is then retold by a gigantic, seemingly real, model of Jonathan Swift's famous creation.

It opens April to September, Monday to Saturday, 10 am to 5.30 pm, Sunday 1 to 6 pm; October to March, Monday to Saturday, 10 am to 5 pm, Sunday 2 to 5 pm. Admission costs £3.25/1.60, family £8.50.

Places to Stay

Camping You can camp at *Gosford Forest Park* (☎ 551277) about 11km south of town on the A28 near Markethill. It has a good campsite with lots of facilities and you don't need to get an advance permit. Camping costs £5.50 to £8.50 a night.

Hostel The new YHANI *Armagh City Hostel* is being built at 36 Abbey St, near St Patrick's Trian, and should be open by the time you read this. Beds will cost from £8, and it'll have a kitchen, TV lounge and a

currency exchange facility. Call ☎ 01232-324733 for information.

B&Bs Beyond the cathedral in Cathedral Rd are *Padua Guesthouse* (☎ 522039) at No 63, with rooms at £12 per person, and the slightly more expensive *Desart House* (☎ 522387), at No 99, with beds at £15. On College Hill, a few doors up from the Fusiliers Museum, is pleasant *Clonhugh Guesthouse* (☎ 522693), charging £20/35 a single/double.

Hotels *Charlemont Arms Hotel* (☎ 522028), 63 Lower English St, charges £28/50 with bathroom. In the nearby newer *De Averell House* (☎ 511213), 47 English St Upper, the rooms, which have TV, telephone and ensuite, go for £32.50/59. It has a restaurant downstairs. On Moy Rd the small *Drumsill Hotel* (☎ 522009) offers rooms with ensuite at £49.50/74 and has a nightclub at weekends.

Rates at all these places includes breakfast.

Places to Eat

There are lots of places to get snacks or lunch but evening meals are more of a problem. In St Patrick's Trian, *Pilgrim's Table Restaurant* does pleasant lunches, including vegeburgers; chicken and leek crumble is £3.15. *Tino's*, on Thomas St, does fairly inexpensive food; the ham salad costs £3. Despite its rather off-setting name, *Fat Sam's*, on Lower English St, is a bright, stylish place doing tasty jacket potatoes with assorted fillings from £2.25. In Gazette Arcade off Thomas St, *Cottage Restaurant*, with muzak and single flowers in vases on the table, looks nothing like a cottage. It has a good selection of lunches at around £3.50.

For evening meals at reasonable prices there's *Jodie's* in Scotch St, which also does filling lunch specials from £3 and afternoon coffee. *Charlemont Arms Hotel*, *De Averell House* and *Drumsill Hotel* all offer evening meals. De Averell House has a varied menu; cauliflower balti costs £7.95. *Calvert's Tavern*, on the corner of Scotch and Barrack

Sts, provides reasonable pub food and serves meals weekdays until 9 pm, weekends to 9.30 pm.

Entertainment

Armagh has plenty of pubs. The unpretentious *Station* bar, Lower English St, is good for a quiet pint. *Rafferty's* bar, beside Wellworth's in town, has traditional music Saturday night. Out of town, *McAleavey's*, 7.5km south in Keady, has traditional music, set dancing and singing on Wednesday.

Getting There & Away

The bus terminal (☎ 522266) is in Mall West. There are daily connections with Belfast (roughly hourly) and to Enniskillen (Monday to Saturday), and a service to Dublin that involves a change of bus at Slane. The Belfast-Galway bus No 270 also stops in Armagh. A return fare to Belfast is £7.50. Bus Nos 40 and 44 run frequently (no Sunday service) to Newry.

Getting Around

Bikes can be hired from Brown's Bikes (☎ 522782), 21A Scotch St, for £4/24 per day/week.

AROUND ARMAGH
Navan Fort

A little over 3km west of Armagh is Navan Fort or Emain Macha, an Irish Camelot and the principal archaeological site in Ulster. The Egyptian geographer Ptolemy marked this site on his map of the known world in the 2nd century AD, naming it Isamnion.

Legend has it that a pregnant woman called Macha was forced to race against the king's horses here; at the end of the race she died giving birth to twins, and the name Emain Macha means 'twins of Macha'. Another legend says that it was the great Queen Macha who began this place, marking out the area with her brooch.

Whatever its origins, the hill was the site for homes and a huge temple during both the Iron and Bronze Ages. At one stage an enormous timber structure was filled with lime and deliberately burnt, suggesting that it was

sent on its way to heaven rather than sacked by its enemies. Close by is a Bronze Age pond now called the King's Stables where remains of bronze castings have been found.

An impressive visitor centre (☎ 01861-525550), in the shape of a Bronze Age building, details the excavation of the site and retells the legends associated with it. It's just a 10 minute walk behind the centre to the site itself which can seem uninspiring on a dull day, but offers magnificent views on a good one.

The centre opens October to March, Monday to Friday 10 am to 5 pm, Saturday from 11 am, Sunday from noon. April to June and September it stays open till 6 pm weekdays; July and August it opens Monday to Saturday 10 am to 7 pm, Sunday 11 am to 7 pm. Admission costs £3.90/3. It's just about walkable or you can take bus No 73 from Mall West, Armagh.

Orange Museum

This Orange Order museum, 10km north of Armagh at Loughgall, was created in 1961 on the premises of what was then a pub. It's open on request during office hours; enquire in the building next door. It contains sashes and banners, and weapons from the Battle of the Diamond in 1795 between the Protestant 'Peep o' Day Boys' and the Catholic 'Defenders'. This took place at Diamond Hill 5km north-east of the village and led to the founding of the Orange Order.

Ardress House

The 17th century Ardress House (☎ 01762-851236) started life as a farmhouse and was upgraded to a manor house in 1760. Much of the original neoclassical interior remains and the farmyard still functions, with a piggery and smithy. There are pleasant walks around the wooded grounds. April, May and September it opens weekends and on bank holidays, 2 to 6 pm; June to August it opens Wednesday to Monday 2 to 6 pm. May and September the farm opens Monday, Wednesday and Friday, noon to 4 pm. Admission is £2.20/1.10, family £5.50. Ardress House,

The Orange Order

Wherever there's a sizeable Protestant population in Northern Ireland, you'll come across buildings, ranging from sheds like scout huts to imposing mansions, designated as 'Orange Lodges'. The Orange Order is a secretive Irish Protestant political society named after King William III of Orange, the 'hero' of the Battle of the Boyne. It owes its origins to a quarrel between Protestants and Catholics in County Armagh in 1795 which blew up into the 'Battle of the Diamond' as the Protestant 'Peep o' Day Boys' and the Catholic 'Defenders' slogged it out for supremacy.

The battle over, the Protestants determined to set up what was originally called the Orange Society to defend Protestantism and the Protestant succession to the English throne from what they saw as a creeping tide of green Catholicism. Lodges quickly spread through Ireland, into Britain and thence to the colonies. Secret societies always make governments twitchy (viz the Freemasons) and this one was no exception. In 1835 the House of Commons petitioned the king to abolish all secret societies and those excluding people on grounds of their religion. The target was clearly the Orange Order, but the petition wasn't successful.

Since then the Orange Order has flourished, bearing much responsibility for strengthening the resistance to the granting of Home Rule in 1912 and objecting to almost any proposal that didn't leave Protestants politically dominant in the North. There have been sporadic efforts to stop its provocative 'marching season' which extends from Easter through to the 12 July when they round things off with a giant celebration of 'their' victory in 1690, complete with pipes, drums and outsize bonfires.

To an outsider, these marches may look like colourful, quirky variations on carnival floats and Salvation Army bands, but many of these middle-aged 'apprentice boys' in their sashes and bowler hats represent the intractable 'No Surrender' face of Irish politics which made it so difficult to make any headway over the years.

That intractability may be showing signs of mellowing (or of coming to terms with political reality), at least in some quarters of the Orange Order. In 1997, in the face of potential major unrest between the Protestant and Catholic nationalist communities, it cancelled or rerouted disputed 12 July parades in Armagh, Belfast, Derry and Newry. This unprecedented conciliatory gesture may have helped persuade Sinn Féin and the IRA to declare their subsequent ceasefire. ■

14km north-east of Armagh, is reached by taking the B77 to Loughgall off the A29.

The Argory

A fine country house in 125 hectares of woodland, The Argory (☎ 01868-784753) retains most of its 1824 fittings; some rooms are lit by acetylene gas from the house's private plant. It opens the same hours as Ardress House and admission costs £2.40 (£1.20 children) or £1.50 if you just want to see the grounds. It's on Derrycaw Rd off the B28, 3.5km north-west of Moy.

Benburb Valley Park

The park straddles the Blackwater River which is popular for salmon fishing and canoeing. In the park is **Benburb Castle**, founded by Shane O'Neill, who had a stronghold here long before the English arrived though nothing remains of it. In 1611 Sir Richard Wingfield added a barn which does still stand. In the 19th century, floors were raised and a private house was incorporated into the building. During WWII, US troops used the place as a hospital and the towers were altered to allow access to the roofs. The castle has been restored along 17th century lines.

About 800m from the castle is **Benburb Valley Heritage Centre** in a restored linen mill. The centre and castle open April to September, Monday to Saturday, 10 am to 5 pm. Admission is £1.50.

The village of Benburb in County Tyrone is 11km north-west of Armagh; take the A29 and then turn left onto the B128. The centre is on the left and clearly marked, and the castle is a short distance farther along.

Gosford Forest Park

At this relaxing picnic spot children will enjoy the weird and wonderful poultry on display. Nature trails work their way around the park and through the trees and in the middle of it all is a vast mock-Norman castle that isn't open to the public. Admission to the park (☎ 01861-551277) is £2.50 if you're in a car, £1 (children 50p) if you're on foot. The park is beside the A28, south-east of town near Markethill. Town buses to Markethill stop outside.

SOUTH ARMAGH

The notoriety of south Armagh earned it the forbidding epithet of Bandit Country. The intensity of the armed conflict between the IRA and the British army was nowhere more evident or dramatic. At the height of the Troubles many small towns were effectively sealed off by the British military, and army helicopters buzzed overhead. Even now wreaths by the roadside bear silent homage to the many victims of the fighting. It would be hard to venture into the remoter areas without being made aware of the demands of the Nationalist side for any peace settlement: the disbanding of the RUC, the freeing of all political prisoners, demilitarisation (by which they mean the total withdrawal of the British army) and a united Ireland.

The area is strongly Catholic with small Protestant communities living a beleaguered existence amid more Irish tricolours than ever graced the Republic. There's nothing to stop you visiting what is a lovely part of Ireland with some interesting archaeological and ecclesiastical places to see. It's unlikely that anyone will ask any questions even though helicopters still buzz overhead, and the hilltops still sprout listening posts and watchtowers.

To our knowledge, no tourist has been attacked in south Armagh, but you should still exercise caution. If you have a British accent, don't assume a warm welcome awaits in local pubs even now.

Most places worth seeing could be taken in on a half-day trip by car from Armagh City or Newry. On a bicycle give yourself the whole day.

Bessbrook

Army posts guard the roads in and out of the small town of Bessbrook (An Sruthán) founded in the mid-19th century by a Quaker

industrialist. The layout of the houses and shops gave the Cadbury family the idea of building Bournville near Birmingham in England. Most buildings are made from local granite and arranged around two squares. Originally, everyone worked in the manufacturing of linen, and because of the Quaker influence no pubs were built. Even now there's only a fish & chip shop in town. From Newry, take the A25 west and turn right onto the B133 to Bessbrook. From Armagh, take the B31 south to Newtownhamilton and turn left onto the A25 and then, before Newry, left again onto the B133.

Camlough

Camlough is only a short distance from Bessbrook but quite different in character and political allegiance, as the flying tricolours make plain. There's a Chinese restaurant, *Happy Villa*, the *Two Roses* café serving pizza and a couple of pubs serving bar food. To get to Camlough, don't return to the B133, but leave Bessbrook from the other end that you came in and turn left immediately after the army control box. Continue down to the main road and turn right back onto the A25. Camlough is a short distance along this road.

Killevy Churches

Surrounded by beech trees, these ruined Siamese-twin churches were built on the site of a 5th century nunnery founded by St Monenna and plundered by the Vikings in 923. During the Middle Ages a convent of Augustinian nuns was founded, but it was dissolved in 1542. The eastern church dates from the 15th century, the western one from the 12th century; the massive lintel on the western door with the granite jambs may be 200 years older still. Originally, the two churches were nearly a metre apart but became joined at an unknown date.

To the north, the traditional site of St Monenna's grave is marked by a granite slab, and a signed walkway leads to a holy well. Heading west out of Camlough, turn left at the crossroads, keeping the lough on the right. A junction on the road points right to the churches and left to Bernish Rock Viewpoint. The churches are 5km from Camlough and can be visited at any time.

Slieve Gullion Forest Park

The coniferous forest, on the B113 about 8km south-west of Armagh, covers the lower slopes of Slieve Gullion (577m) and a gorgeous 13km drive takes in a walk to a lake. The drive emerges from the trees to picturesque views of the Ring of Gullion, a circle of small hills around Slieve Gullion. Slieve Gullion can be climbed from the south or north. The south approach has a forest road for the first part of the journey, while the north approach is made a little easier because of a rough path all the way. On the summit there are two early Bronze Age cairns.

The visitor centre (☎ 016937-38284) and the park open daily Easter to September 10 am to dusk. Admission is £2 per car.

Crossmaglen

Crossmaglen (Crois Mhic Lionnáin) is a small town with a fierce reputation – more than 20 soldiers have been killed in the town square alone. The square is dominated by a sprawling, ugly army-cum-police post built right against the houses. Notwithstanding this, people go about their daily business apparently oblivious to the helicopters and the listening devices. Except for a prehistoric grave about 2km north of town, there are no real attractions in what would otherwise be a sleepy little backwater. The army post makes a visit here educational, not to mention sobering if you're British.

Places to Stay & Eat

In Crossmaglen, *Murtagh's Bar & Lounge* (☎ 01693-861378), 13 North St, offers B&B £20/32 a single/double plus dinner for £8. On the B30 toward Newry, just after the junction with the A29, *Lima Country House* (☎ 01693-861944), 16 Drumalt Rd, Silverbridge, charges £18 a head with another £9 for dinner.

In Crossmaglen the pleasant *Glen Café* in the square does light meals like burgers and curried chips. There are also a couple of pubs in the square offering bar food including *Chums*, close to Glen Café, while *McConville's* is across the other side.

Getting There & Away

Bus No 42 runs regularly Monday to Saturday (no Sunday service) between Newry and Crossmaglen via Camlough.

Counties Derry & Antrim

Ireland isn't short of fine stretches of coast, but the Causeway Coast from Portstewart in County Derry to Ballycastle in County Antrim, and the Antrim Coast from Ballycastle to Belfast, are as magnificent as you could ask for. Most spectacular of all is the surreal landscape of the Giant's Causeway. It's familiar from many a postcard and calendar, and looks like some weird image from a Magritte painting.

GETTING AROUND

In winter it's difficult to explore the Causeway and Antrim coasts using public transport, but in summer there are two regular Ulsterbus services.

The Antrim Coaster – bus No 252 – operates between Belfast and Coleraine twice daily, Monday to Saturday late May to late September. It leaves Belfast at 9.10 am and 2 pm, and Coleraine at 9.50 am and 4.10 pm. The trip takes about four hours. The open-topped Bushmills Bus – bus No 177 – is a double-decker that runs (weather permitting) from the Giant's Causeway to Coleraine five times daily in July and August. The trip takes just over an hour.

Year round, bus No 162 runs along the Antrim coast between Larne and Cushendun, calling at Ballygally, Glenarm, Carnlough, Waterfoot and Cushendall.

County Derry

The chief attraction of the county is the town of Derry (Doire) itself, nestled poetically by the wide sweep of the River Foyle. There's a terrible sadness in the contrast between the cosy feel of the town itself and its recent past, scarred by injustice and bitterness. After the defeat of Hugh O'Neill in 1603, the part of the county inland from Derry was systematically planted with English and Scottish settlers. The dour, staunchly Protestant

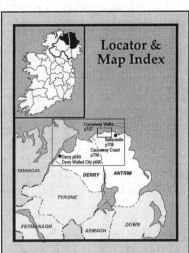

Locator & Map Index

Causeway Walks p707
Ballycastle p709
Causeway Coast p706
Derry p689
Derry Walled City p690
DONEGAL
DERRY ANTRIM
TYRONE
FERMANAGH DOWN
ARMAGH

Highlights

- Travel along the Antrim Coast road
- See the Giant's Causeway 'in the flesh'
- Walk around Murlough Bay
- Totter across Carrick-a-rede Rope Bridge
- Visit ruinous Dunluce Castle
- Taste some whiskey after a tour through Bushmills Distillery
- Explore the walled city of Derry
- Discover the history of Derry in the Tower Museum
- Learn more than you ever dreamt of knowing about linen at Lisburn's Irish Linen Centre

towns continue to evoke and live out the history of sectarian apartheid and there's little to attract the tourist. On the coast in the resort town of Portstewart, the atmosphere is more relaxed.

DERRY

Although Derry (Doire) is more peaceful now than at any time since the 1960s, there

DERRY & ANTRIM

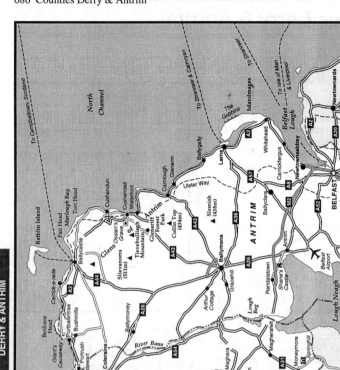

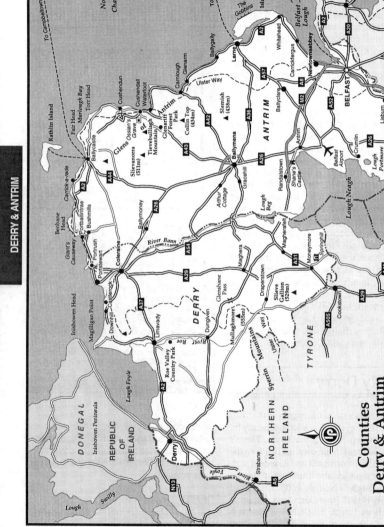

Counties
Derry & Antrim

can still be a sharp edge to its atmosphere. Derry is as safe to visit as anywhere else in Northern Ireland, although it might not be wise to hang around some nationalist pubs in the Bogside or Creggan late at night if you have a British accent. The walled city area retains a slightly schizophrenic air, the Shipquay St side being lively and relaxed while the Bishop's Gate end is blighted by the forbidding army post. Outside the city, the murals in places like the Bogside are reminders of the Troubles.

Things are changing however. The military keep a low profile, the control zones have all but gone, and the historic courthouse near Bishop's Gate is being restored. Marks & Spencer has opened a store and outside the city walls the Foyleside Shopping Centre when completed will be the largest in Northern Ireland. Also being built is a new entertainment, commercial and retail centre, the Millennium Complex.

History

Although you sometimes get the feeling that Derry's history started in 1688, in fact there has been a settlement on the site since the 6th century AD when St Columba (otherwise known as St Columb, Columcille or Colm-

cille) founded a monastic community on the hillside, probably where the Church of Ireland chapel of St Augustine stands today. In the Middle Ages Derry seems to have escaped the worst of the Viking raids and had a burst of independent prosperity in the 12th and 13th centuries under the Mac Lochlainn dynasty.

In the late 16th century Elizabeth I became determined to conquer troublesome Ulster, and an English garrison arrived in Derry in 1566. In 1600 a second, more lastingly successful attempt to secure the town was made during the Nine Years War (1594-1603) against the O'Neills and O'Donnells. In 1603 an English trading colony was established and given city status. Sir Cahir O'Doherty attacked this settlement in 1608 and virtually wiped it out, but in 1609 James I determined to settle matters for good by granting land to English and Scottish settlers. The wealthy London trade guilds were put in charge of 'planting' Derry and were responsible for the present layout of the walled city and for the walls themselves.

In 1688 the gates of Derry were slammed shut by 13 apprentice boys before the Catholic forces of James II, and some months later the great Siege of Derry began. For 105

DERRY & ANTRIM

What's in a Name?

Derry's original name was Daire Calgaigh, meaning 'oak grove of Calgach'. In the 10th century it was renamed Doire Colmcille, or 'the oak grove of St Columba', in remembrance of the 6th century saint who had established the first monastic settlement on the site. However, in 1609 when the English government decided to 'plant' Derry properly, it signed an agreement with the Corporation of London to provide the necessary settlers. To commemorate this fact the new city's name was lengthened to Londonderry.

Until the Troubles, people readily abbreviated the town's name to 'Derry'. At that point, however, what anyone called it suddenly became a touchstone for their political views, with Protestant Unionists dogmatically asserting the full Londonderry and Catholic Republicans equally firmly shortening it to Derry. Although the city is still officially called Londonderry, in 1984 the city council was renamed Derry City Council.

The naming controversy persists today, turning the normally straightforward business of buying a bus ticket into a political minefield; you can easily judge someone's position on the conflict by noting whether they react to your Derry with an emphatic *London*derry or vice versa. All over the country, but especially in the border areas, you'll see the word 'London' scratched off offending signposts.

On the radio, to avoid offending anyone, you may hear announcers say both names together – 'DerrystrokeLondonderry' – almost as one word.

Luckily, not everyone takes the Derry/Londonderry controversy too seriously. In Belfast, for example, wags have dropped both possibilities, opting instead for the simple 'Stroke City'! ∎

days the Protestant citizens of Derry withstood bombardment, disease and starvation. Rejecting proffered peace terms, they declared that they would eat the Catholics first, then each other before surrendering. By the time a relief ship burst through the boom on the River Foyle and broke the siege, an estimated quarter of the city's 30,000 inhabitants had died. It wasn't the final victory for the Protestant forces, but the long distraction gave King William time to increase his army's strength, and it thus played an important role in his victory at the Battle of the Boyne on 12 July 1690.

In the 19th century Derry was one of the main ports from which the Irish emigrated to the USA, a fact commemorated by the statue of a departing family standing in Waterloo Place. It also played a vital role in the transatlantic trade in shirts and collars; supposedly, local factories provided uniforms for both sides in the American Civil War. To this day Derry still supplies the US president with 12 free shirts every year.

More recently, Derry has been a flashpoint for the Troubles. Resentment at the long-running domination and gerrymandering of the council by Protestants boiled over in the civil rights marches of 1968. Simultaneously, attacks on the Catholic Bogside district began, but by the time of the 12 July celebrations in 1969 the people there were prepared. Confrontation between Catholics and Protestants led to a veritable siege of the Bogside, and for over two days the community withdrew behind barricades. It was as if the Bogside had seceded from the UK, and even the government in the South talked of Ireland's duty to protect its own. It seemed that open warfare and disintegration could only be prevented by military intervention, and on 14 August 1968 British troops entered Derry.

In January 1972, 'Bloody Sunday' saw the deaths of 13 unarmed Catholic civil rights marchers at the hands of the army. Today, the old Bogside estate has been rebuilt, giving a curiously modern, neat feel to what was once a violent ghetto.

After a 1981 survey discovered that almost 30% of the inner city was bombed out, abandoned or derelict, the Inner City Trust began work to make good the damage – work that is still continuing. Consequently much of what you see inside the city walls now is fairly recently restored.

Orientation

The old centre of Derry is the small walled city on the west bank of the River Foyle. At its heart is the square called the Diamond, with Shipquay, Ferryquay, Butcher and Bishop Sts converging on it. The train station is on the east side of the River Foyle, while buses stop on the west bank, just outside the walled city. The Craigavon Bridge and farther downstream the Foyle Bridge link the two banks of the river. The Catholic Bogside area is below the walls to the west while to the south is a Protestant estate known as the Fountain.

Information

The tourist office in Pittsburgh House, at 8 Bishop St in the walled city, houses both the Northern Ireland Tourist Board (☎ 01504-267284) and Bord Fáilte (☎ 01504-369501). It opens Monday to Thursday 9 am to 5.15 pm, Friday to 5 pm, and weekends 10 am to 6 pm. The tourist office is scheduled to move to 44 Foyle St, outside the city walls.

The Calgach Centre (☎ 01504-373177), 4-22 Butcher St, just up from Oakgrove Manor hostel, houses the genealogy centre; it's open weekdays 9 am to 5 pm for anyone wishing to trace their ancestors.

The banks change punts into pounds and vice versa. Outside banking hours there's a bureau de change (☎ 01504-260636) on the top floor of the Richmond Centre, and in the tourist office and GPO. The latter is on Custom House St, just north of the city walls.

The USIT travel office (☎ 01504-371888), 33 Ferryquay St, opens weekdays 9.30 am to 5.30 pm, Saturday 10 am to 1 pm.

The telephone code is ☎ 01504.

Bookshops The Bookworm (☎ 261616), 16-18 Bishop St, is excellent for material on the Troubles, Derry and Ireland generally.

There's also Shipquay Books & News
(☎ 371747) at 10 Shipquay St, and a branch
of Eason's (☎ 377133) in the Foyleside
Shopping Centre.

Laundry Oakgrove Manor hostel has a
laundry room downstairs. Alternatively, visit
Duds 'n' Suds, 141 Strand Rd, which is about
as glamorous as a laundrette can get – it has
a pool table, electronic games and a snack
bar! It's open 8 am to 9 pm Monday to Friday,
to 8 pm Saturday. A wash, dry and fold costs
£6.

City Walls

Until the mid-1990s, the presence of the
army and protective iron gates made Derry's
magnificent city walls hard to appreciate and
impossible to walk round. The gates are still
there, but now they're open and it's possible
to walk all round the walls.

The walls were built between 1613 and
1618 making Derry the last walled city to be
built in Ireland. They're about 8m high, 9m
thick, and go around the old city for a length
of 1.5km.

Gunner's Bastion, Coward's Bastion and
Water Bastion have all been demolished and
the four original gates (Shipquay, Ferryquay,
Bishop's and Butcher's) rebuilt, while three
new gates (New, Ferry and Castle) have been
added. Derry's sobriquet, the Maiden City,
derives from the fact that the walls have
never been breached. The south-west end,
overlooking the cathedral on the inside and
the Bogside to the north-west, is wired up
and provides an army lookout point for the
Bogside. Behind the wall that runs beside the
cathedral is the Fountain estate, a fenced and
battered area that suggests the Protestants
there have a lot in common with their Catholic neighbours.

An excellent overview of the Bogside and
its defiant murals can be had by going up on
to the city walls between Butcher's Gate and
the army post. There you'll also see behind
you in Society St the Apprentice Boys' Hall.
Cannons, given by the London livery companies and reminders of the siege of 1689,
still point out over the Bogside. An ugly

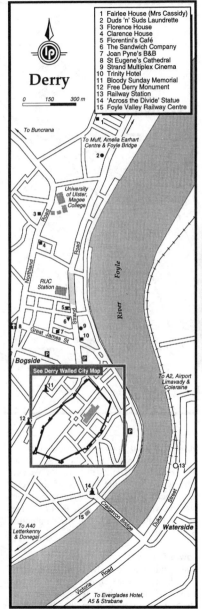

Derry

0   150   300 m

1 Fairlee House (Mrs Cassidy)
2 Duds 'n' Suds Laundrette
3 Florence House
4 Clarence House
5 Fiorentini's Café
6 The Sandwich Company
7 Joan Pyne's B&B
8 St Eugene's Cathedral
9 Strand Multiplex Cinema
10 Trinity Hotel
11 Bloody Sunday Memorial
12 Free Derry Monument
13 Railway Station
14 'Across the Divide' Statue
15 Foyle Valley Railway Centre

To Buncrana

To Muff, Amelia Earhart
Centre & Foyle Bridge

University
of Ulster,
Magee
College

RUC
Station

River Foyle

Great James St

Bogside

See Derry Walled City Map

To A2, Airport
Limavady &
Coleraine

Waterside

Craigavon Bridge

Duke Street

To A40
Letterkenny
& Donegal

Victoria Road

To Everglades Hotel,
A5 & Strabane

DERRY & ANTRIM

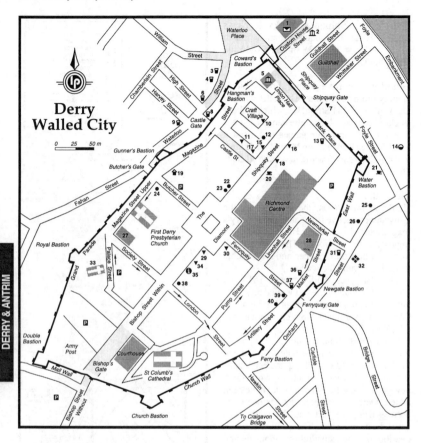

Derry
Walled City

0   25   50 m

DERRY & ANTRIM

pillar, that used to be topped by a statue of the Reverend George Walker, stands on Royal Bastion. The 2.7m statue of Walker, who was one of the leaders of the 1698 resistance and who kept a diary of the siege, was blown off by the IRA in 1973. The restored statue stands beside the Apprentice Boys' Hall.

Tower Museum

Just inside Coward's Bastion, the modern O'Doherty's Tower houses the excellent Tower Museum which tells the story of Derry right through from the days of St

Columcille to the present through traditional exhibits and audiovisuals; allow a good two hours to do it justice. It's open Tuesday to Saturday 10 am to 5 pm year round, and Monday to Saturday 10 am to 5 pm, Sunday 2 to 5 pm in July and August. Admission costs £3.25/1.

St Columb's Cathedral

Standing within the walls of the old city, St Columb's Cathedral dates from 1628. It shares the austerity of many Church of Ireland cathedrals, with dark, carved wooden pews, an open timbered roof resting on the carved heads of past bishops and deans, and a gruesome skull-and-crossbones wall tablet in the north aisle. Beside the pulpit is a cross of nails donated by Coventry Cathedral. Unusually, the bishop's throne is placed in the nave; the 18th century mahogany chair inside the canopy is a beautifully carved example of what is known as Chinese Chippendale.

In the porch is a mortar shell lobbed into the city during the siege by the Jacobites, which carried the terms of surrender. The Chapter House, now designated a museum, contains some drums, paintings, old photos and huge padlocks used to close the city gates in the 17th century. Built in a style known as Planter's Gothic with an embattled exterior, the cathedral now sits rather forlornly surrounded by the barbed wire and surveillance cameras of a more recent siege. Walk around the building to admire the architecture. April to October it opens from Monday to Saturday 9 am to 5 pm, November to March Monday to Saturday 9 am to 4 pm. Visitors are asked to donate £1 towards its upkeep.

Other Churches

The Catholic **St Eugene's Cathedral** in Great James St was dedicated to St Eugene in 1873 by Bishop Keely, and the handsome east window is a memorial to the bishop.

St Columba's Church (aka Long Tower Church) was Derry's first post-Reformation Catholic church. It stands on the site of the older Tempull Mor church, the cathedral church of the Derry diocese during the Middle Ages. St Columba's Church was erected in 1784 in neo-Renaissance style and stands off Bishop St outside the city walls in the Bogside.

Guildhall

Just outside the city walls, the red-brick Guildhall (☎ 365151) was originally built in 1890 and rebuilt after a fire in 1908. As the seat of the old Londonderry Corporation, which institutionalised the policy of discriminating against Catholics over housing and jobs, it incurred the wrath of nationalists and was bombed twice by the IRA in 1972. One of the convicted bombers was elected to the new council in 1985! The Guildhall is noted for its fine stained-glass windows, including one of George V's coronation upstairs; others on the stairs commemorate the various London livery companies that played so divisive a role in the city's development. It's open Monday to Friday 9 am to 5.30 pm.

Bogside & the Free Derry Monument

As you step out of Butcher's Gate, the Bogside comes into view, and down on the

DERRY & ANTRIM

left is the famous 'You Are Now Entering Free Derry' monument. This was once the end wall of a row of old houses, but the area was rebuilt with low-level flats, and it now stands in the centre of a dual carriageway. During the early 1970s, until the army's Operation Motorman smashed the barricades in July 1972, this was a no-go area as far as the military authorities were concerned. It took 5000 soldiers with Chieftain tanks to bring down the barriers. The monument, with its much repainted slogan, remains as a defiant response to the army watchtower that continues to look down from the walled city on the Bogside.

Bloody Sunday Memorial

On Sunday, 30 January 1972, some 20,000 civilians marched through Derry in protest at the policy of internment without trial. It now seems clear that the 1st Battalion of the Parachute Regiment opened fire on the unarmed marchers. By the end of the day 13 unarmed people were dead, some shot through the back, and a 14th subsequently died of his injuries. None of those who fired the 108 bullets, or those who gave the order to fire, were ever brought to trial or even disciplined. The subsequent enquiry was a whitewash. To reach the monument, leave the walled city by Butcher's Gate; it's a little to the right down near the roadside. The actual incident happened in the enclosed square across the road.

Craigavon Bridge

The double-decker bridge spanning the River Foyle was erected in 1933 and used to carry trains on the lower deck and cars on the upper. Since Northern Ireland's railways were pruned back in 1965, it has carried cars on both decks.

Foyle Valley Railway Centre

Just outside the walled city by Craigavon Bridge, the centre stands on what was once the junction of four railway lines. Exhibits inside tell the story of the railways, and you can take a 20 minute, 4km excursion on a train with diesel engine. The museum opens

April to September, Tuesday to Saturday 10 am to 4.30 pm, Sunday 2 to 5.30 pm. Admission is free but the excursion, at 2.30 pm each day, costs £2.50/1.25.

Harbour Museum

A small, old-fashioned maritime museum (☎ 377331), with models of ships and the figurehead of the *Minnehaha*, takes up two rooms of the old Londonderry Port Building on Guildhall St. It's open Monday to Friday 10 am 1 pm, 2 to 4.30 pm, and is free.

Amelia Earhart Centre

In 1932 when Amelia Earhart became the first woman to fly solo across the Atlantic she mistook Derry for Paris and landed in a field in what is now the suburb of Ballyarnett (5km north-west of Derry) where a small cottage contains pictures and memorabilia. The centre (☎ 354040) opens Monday to Thursday 9 am to 4 pm, Friday 9 am to 1 pm; admission is free.

The Fifth Province

There have been some teething problems in getting this exhibition up and running in the Calgach Centre (☎ 373177), on Butcher St near Oakgrove Manor hostel, but it should be ready by the time you read this. The exhibition tells the interesting story of the Celtic warrior, Calgach, and his people, who once lived where Derry stands today. It's planned to open daily 9.30 am to 4.30 pm; admission will be £3/1.

Organised Tours

July to September walking tours depart Monday to Friday from the tourist office at 10.30 am and 2.30 pm. They cost £3/1.75 and last about 1½ hours. Macnamara Tours (☎ 265536) offers one-hour historical walking tours of the city mid-April to September daily for £2.50/2. They leave from Guildhall Square in front of Guildhall.

Every Tuesday during July and August, Ulsterbus (☎ 262261) runs its 1½-hour Foyle Civic Tour of the city departing from the bus station at 2 pm; it costs £3/2.

The Derry Skeleton

Round about town you'll soon spot the Derry skeleton, a mournful figure usually with his skull leant to one side, adorning the city's coat of arms. There are several stories to explain how he came to be there. One suggests that he's associated with the 1689 Siege of Derry; another that he represents Sir Cahir O'Doherty who had sacked Derry in 1608 to avenge an insult. Neither explanation is likely to be right though, because the skeleton was already gracing the arms in 1600 when the first plantation of Derry took place.

The most convincing suggestion is that the skeleton represents Walter de Burgo, an Anglo-Norman knight and nephew of the Red Earl, Richard de Burgo. He's said to have fallen out with his cousin William de Burgo, the Earl of Ulster, who had him imprisoned in a dungeon in Greencastle in County Donegal. There, he eventually starved to death in 1332. If this story is true, the castle also shown on the coat of arms would probably be Greencastle. In 1311 Edward II granted the Inishowen Peninsula and the island of Derry to Richard de Burgo, thus explaining how his nephew ended up immortalised on the city's coat of arms. ■

Places to Stay

If the peace process continues, albeit falteringly, Derry is likely to find the number of visitors putting pressure on available accommodation. However, there's already one new hotel and a Holiday Inn is being built. Booking ahead is advisable, especially in July when an annual gathering of O'Dohertys from around the world puts even greater strain on the accommodation supply.

Hostels The YHANI hostel is in the renovated *Oakgrove Manor* (☎ 372273), 4-6 Magazine St, inside the city walls near Butcher's Gate just 150m from the bus station. Dorm beds cost £7.50, or £8 with bathroom; singles/twins cost £15 per person including breakfast. Cooking, laundry and currency exchange facilities are available. If it's full, the IHH *Aberfoyle Independent Hostel* (☎ 370011), 29 Aberfoyle Terrace, Strand Rd, 1.5km north of the centre costs £7.50.

July to September you may be able to stay at the University of Ulster's *Magee College* (☎ 371371), 26 Northland Rd, at £12 a head without breakfast.

B&Bs Within walking distance of the bus station, the friendly *Joan Pyne* (☎ 69691),

36 Great James St, offers a bed and a big breakfast for £24/40 in a lovely 19th century Victorian house. Farther north, there's the slightly officious (but well-run) *Clarence House* (☎ 265342), 15 Northland Rd, charging £16.50 a head. Farther along at No 16, *Florence House* (☎ 268093) is just slightly cheaper at £16 per person. Farther north again, at *Fairlee House* (☎ 374551), 86 Duncreggan Rd, Mrs Cassidy charges £17/32. You can get to these places on Bus No D6 or by shared black taxi from Foyle St.

Farmhouse accommodation costs about the same as B&B and there are quite a few places out at Eglinton on the A2 to Limavady. For example, *Longfield Farm* (☎ 810210), 122 Clooney Rd, has rooms for £16/28, and *Greenan Farm* (☎ 810422), 25 Carmoney Rd, charges £15 per person. Rates at both include breakfast. The tourist office has a complete list and makes bookings.

Hotels Derry's newest and most central hotel, *Trinity Hotel* (☎ 27121), 22-24 Strand Rd, is just north of the city centre. It has rooms for £70/85 including breakfast and there are special deals available.

South of the city and on the east side of the river, *Everglades Hotel* (☎ 46722, fax 49200) is on Prehen Rd, just off the A5

(Victoria Rd); from the city turn right after crossing Craigavon Bridge. It charges £69/89.

There are three other hotels on the east side of the river but north of the city. *Broomhill Hotel* (☎ 47995, fax 49304) costs £45/60 and is easy to find on the Limavady Rd. A little farther out the *White Horse Hotel* (☎ 860606, fax 860371), 68 Clooney Rd, costs £50/60. Nearby and beside the Caw Roundabout at 14 Clooney Rd, the circular *Waterfoot Hotel* (☎ 45500, fax 311006) has rooms for £62/75. Rates at all these hotels include breakfast.

Places to Eat

Fast Food & Cafés Inside the walled city there's plenty of choice along Shipquay St. *Loui's Select Café*, isn't so select but the food, served cafeteria style, is OK; bacon and eggs cost £1.40. Across the road the *Galley Restaurant* boasts home cooking at reasonable prices.

A little farther down Shipquay St, *Wheeler's*, part of a small chain, dishes up fast food for £2 to £5. *Marlene's Diner*, opposite, offers slightly more substantial offerings; beef and Guinness casserole is £3.29. Handy lunch stops are *The Sandwich Company*, on the corner of the Diamond, which does some excellent sandwiches and baguettes, and *Malibu Restaurant* (sandwiches £1.35), beside the tourist office. More upmarket, the *Boston Tea Party* in the Craft Village off Shipquay St, offers sandwiches, quiche, lasagne and good cakes but is only open until 5.30 pm.

The *Tower Coffee Shop* is a large cafeteria in Austin's department store on the Diamond; it serves Irish breakfast for £3 as well as cakes and sandwiches and provides fine views over the city centre. Across from the Guildhall, *Open Oven* does good sandwiches, as does *Cappuccino's* opposite the bus station which opens at 7 am.

In the Foyleside Shopping Centre is a branch of Dublin's *Kylemore Café*.

Heading along Strand Rd, inexpensive places include *Fiorentini's* and another branch of *The Sandwich Company* which

doubles as a Mexican restaurant, *Jalapenos*, Wednesday to Saturday from 5.30 pm, Sunday from noon.

Pub Food & Restaurants On Shipquay St, the *Townsman* (☎ 260820) is particularly popular at lunch time. Pub food is also available at the *Anchor Inn* and the *Linen Hall* by Ferryquay Gate. The *Dungloe* on Waterloo St is pleasantly untarted up, with photographs of the old Bogside on the walls.

A bit more expensive, *Thra'n Maggies* (☎ 264267) in the Craft Village off Shipquay St is one of the few places to dine in the walled city; it's open till 9.15 pm weekdays and Saturday, till 10 pm Sunday. A meal won't make too big a hole in the budget, grilled salmon is £8.90, and there's a wide selection of international wines.

Reasonably priced meals can be enjoyed at the *Satchmo* restaurant (☎ 46722) in the Everglades Hotel which offers four-course dinners for £19.50. The *Trinity Hotel* also has a large restaurant; fillet of plaice costs £8.95 and there's a good vegetarian selection.

Entertainment

Performance *Bridie's Cottage* in the Craft Village holds music and dance sessions on Wednesday evenings in summer. Classical music shows are scheduled during summer at the University of Ulster's *Magee College* and the *Guildhall*. The tourist office has details. The *Orchard Gallery* (☎ 269675) in Orchard St has regular exhibitions, concerts and drama. Theatrical events take place regularly throughout the summer at the *Playhouse* (☎ 264481), in Artillery St, the *Rialto Entertainment Centre* (☎ 260516) nearby in Linenhall St and *St Columb's Hall* (☎ 262880) in Orchard St.

The new *Millennium Complex* will house an auditorium for dance, drama and music performances.

Pubs Derry does a fine line in themed pubs, many of them masquerading as shops. The liveliest are those along Waterloo St, like the *Gweedore*, which hosts regular music and quiz functions, the *Bound for Boston*, the *Dungloe* and the *Castle Bar*. *Peadar O'Donnell's* is also good for traditional music. The *Metro Bar* on Bank Place, just inside the walls, is very popular.

Others include the *Anchor Inn* and the *Linen Hall* by Ferryquay Gate, *Badger's Place* on the corner of Newmarket and Orchard Sts just outside the walls, and the *Forum* beside the bus station and looking like a tea merchant's.

Pick up the *Good Pub Guide to Derry* free in the *The Townsman* in Shipquay St for more suggestions.

Cinemas You can see films at the *Hall Cinema* (☎ 267789), Orchard St, or the *Strand Cinema Complex* (☎ 373938), Quayside Centre.

Things to Buy
The two main shopping centres are the Richmond Centre within the city walls, and the new, enormous Foyleside Shopping Centre, just outside.

Derry Craft Village, tucked away in one of the corner blocks of the walled city, contains a number of craft shops selling Derry crystal (with a mail service), handwoven cloth and other items crafted by local people. Most shops open Monday to Saturday 9.30 am to 5.30 pm and some open Sunday during summer.

If you're interested in traditional music, Soundsaround (☎ 374511), 22A Waterloo St, has an excellent selection.

Close to the Diamond in Shipquay St, the Donegal Shop (☎ 266928) sells garments, tweeds and souvenirs. Austin's (☎ 261817), 2-6 The Diamond, is also worth a look as it is Ireland's oldest department store.

Getting There & Away
Air About 13km east of Derry along the A2 past Eglington is the City of Derry airport (☎ 810784). It has direct British Airways Express (☎ 0345-222111) flights to Glasgow (from £69 return) and Manchester (from £63 to £94 return). A return ticket is often cheaper than a one-way fare. Jersey European (☎ 01232-457200) offers direct flights to Belfast, Dublin and Paris, with connections via Belfast to Birmingham, Blackpool, Bristol, Exeter, Guernsey, the Isle of Man, Jersey, Leeds and London; for more information call ☎ 01232-457200.

Bus No 143 to Limavady stops near the airport; otherwise a taxi costs about £7.

Bus The Ulsterbus station (☎ 262261) is just outside the city walls, on Foyle St near the Guildhall.

There are frequent services between Belfast and Derry. Bus No 212, the Maiden City Flyer, is the fastest (1 hour 40 minutes), followed by bus No 272 that goes via Omagh; a single ticket costs £6.10. A bus to Portstewart and Portrush leaves at 2.15 pm on Thursday and Sunday for most of June, and on Thursday, Friday and Saturday in most of July and August. Each day at 8.20 am a bus leaves Derry for Cork, arriving at 7.15 pm. The bus from Cork leaves at 9.15 am and arrives in Derry at 8.30 pm.

Bus Éireann operates a Derry-Galway service three times daily, via Donegal and Sligo. It's £14 single to Galway, although midweek you can get a return for the same price.

Lough Swilly Bus Service (☎ 262017) has an office upstairs at the Ulsterbus station, and connects with Buncrana, Dunfanaghy, Dungloe, Letterkenny and Malin Head in County Donegal, across the border.

Feda O'Donnell's private buses (☎ 075-48114, 0141-631 3696 in Glasgow) include a service from Letterkenny to Glasgow via Derry. It leaves from the bus station at 8.45 am, reaching Glasgow around 4 pm. The coach from Glasgow leaves at 8 am from the Citizens' Theatre in Gorbals St and reaches Derry around 3 pm. Services run daily in July and August, four times weekly the rest of the year. The return fare is IR£60.

Train From the Northern Ireland Railways station (☎ 01504-42228), on the east side of the River Foyle, there are frequent Derry-Belfast services taking about three hours. The earliest train for Portrush departs at 6.10

am (11.10 am on Sunday), the last one at 7.10 pm. With a valid train ticket there's a free Linkline bus into the town centre from outside the station.

Getting Around

Local buses leave from Foyle St in front of the bus station, where there are also share-able black cabs to outlying suburbs like Shantallow. Auto Cabs (☎ 45100) and Foyle Taxis (☎ 263905) operate from the city centre and go to all areas.

There are street-level car parks on Butcher St, behind the Richmond Centre and beside the station and a multi-storey one beside Foyleside Shopping Centre.

COLERAINE

Although it stands on the banks of the River Bann, Coleraine (Cúil Raithin) isn't particularly attractive, and the pedestrianised town centre could be any British shopping area. But Coleraine is an important transport hub for County Derry and you could well find yourself waiting here for a bus or train connection. There are plenty of shops catering to the largely Protestant population, who first arrived in 1613 when the land was given by James I to loyal Londoners. The University of Ulster was established just north of town in 1968, much to the chagrin of Derry which had lobbied hard to win it. Efforts are being made to brighten things up, with the town hall, St Patrick's church and the birthplace of the obscure 19th century illustrator Hugh Thomas in Church St all having undergone renovation.

Information

The tourist office (☎ 01265-44723), near the railway station on Railway Rd and next to Coleraine Leisure Centre, opens Monday to Saturday 9 am to 5 pm, closing at 6 pm Friday and Saturday in summer.

The telephone code is ☎ 01265.

Mountsandel Mount

The age and purpose of this large oval mound south of Coleraine is something of a mystery. It may have been an early Christian strong-

hold or a later Anglo-Norman fortification. Just to the north-east of the mound, a Mesolithic site dating back to the 7th millennium BC has been excavated; post-holes, hearths and pits bear testimony to the early inhabitants of the area. The site is signposted from the Lodge Rd roundabout. At the T-junction after the roundabout turn right. There's parking at the heavily fortified courthouse on the right; from there cross over the road where a sign points the way. From here it's a 15-minute walk through the forest. Bicycles aren't allowed.

Places to Stay

July to September, you can get B&B with shared bathroom for £18.68 per person at the *University of Ulster at Coleraine* (☎ 44141, ext 4567), on Cromore Rd, but it's often full and cannot be relied on.

In the *Lodge Hotel* (☎ 44848) on Lodge Rd, which joins Railway Rd, singles/doubles are £50/76 including breakfast. The *Town House* (☎ 44869), 45 Millburn Rd, charges £28/35 for B&B, while *Coolbeg* (☎ 44961), 2E Grange Rd on the outskirts of town, charges from £20/38.

All the other B&Bs are out of town; the tourist office has a complete list. The 17th century *Camus House* (☎ 42982), 27 Curragh Rd off the A54, 5km south of town, is worth the £25/40. *Tullan's Farm* (☎ 42309), 46 Newmills Rd, is a working farm just one mile from Coleraine, where B&B costs £17/30.

Places to Eat

There are plenty of eating places around the pedestrianised precinct. *Twenty Two*, opposite Woolworth's, does breakfast for £1.95 and hearty lunches for around £3.50. Beside Woolworth's, *The Forum* has a morning special of coffee or tea with croissant or scone for £1.65; it also serves reasonably priced lunches. *Kitty's of Coleraine* in Church Lane beside St Patrick's, does good cheap coffee and cakes.

If you're just passing through, you could do worse than patronise the *Whistlestop Café* in the train station, which is next to the bus station; Irish stew is £1.50. It's closed Sunday though. *Eileen's Diner*, opposite the train station entrance, does open on Sunday, however; until lunchtime anyway.

Getting There & Away

The Belfast-Derry trains stop at Coleraine and there's a branch line to Portrush. The Ulsterbus No 218 travels express between Portrush, Portstewart and Belfast via Coleraine and Antrim. Bus No 234 takes an hour to reach Derry for £4.20. See Getting Around at the start of this chapter for information on the Antrim Coaster and Bushmills Bus services.

LIMAVADY & AROUND

You're unlikely to want to linger in Limavady (Léim an Mhadaidh), a pitstop of a town with a handful of attractive 19th century houses. Its only claim to fame is that one Jane Ross (1810-79) heard a travelling fiddler playing the *Londonderry Air* – aka *Danny Boy*, probably the most famous Irish song of all – and noted it down; a blue plaque on the wall of 51 Main St where she lived commemorates the fact.

Information

The tourist office (☎ 015047-22226), in the council building at 7 Connell St, opens Monday to Friday 9 am to 12.30 pm and 1.30 to 5 pm, and weekends 10 am to 5 pm. Outside those hours there's a computerised database in the wall.

The telephone code is ☎ 015047.

Roe Valley Country Park

The park stretches for 5km either side of the River Roe, south of Limavady. The area is associated with the O'Cahans, who ruled the valley until the Plantations. The 17th century settlers saw the flax growing potential of the damp river valley and the area became an important linen manufacturing centre. In the visitors' centre, called the Dogleap Countryside Centre (☎ 22074), there are some excellent old photographs of the flax industry and around the park are relics of that time. The weaving shed houses a small museum

near the main entrance. The scutch mill, where the flax was pounded, is a 45 minute walk away, along the river, past two watch towers built to guard the linen when it was spread out in the fields for bleaching.

The park also contains Ulster's first domestic hydro-electric power station, opened in 1896. The plant opens to visitors free of charge on request at the visitors' centre next door.

The park itself is always accessible and the visitors' centre opens daily 9 am to 5 pm all year. The café keeps the same hours but only Easter to September. The park is clearly marked off the B192 road between Limavady and Dungiven. Bus No 146 from Limavady to Dungiven will drop you on the main road, but there's no weekend service.

Places to Stay

There's camping at *Roe Valley Country Park* (☎ 22074), just off the B192 to Dungiven; you'll be charged £6 for a tent. *Gorteen House Hotel* (☎ 22333), 187 Roe Mill Rd, charges £28/42 for B&B. If you're coming in from Derry on the A2 turn right just after crossing the bridge and follow Roe Mill Rd down until it turns to the left past a cemetery; the hotel is off to the right. Otherwise, the pistachio coloured 19th century *Alexander Arms* (☎ 63443), 34 Main St, offers B&B for £18 a head.

Places to Eat

The *Alexander Arms* on Main St is OK for bar food and it offers a four-course high tea for £6.95. It's open until 10 pm weekdays and Saturdays, till 9 pm Sundays. Open daily for dinner, *Gentry's* (☎ 22017), on the same street, offers a choice between Indian food and pizzas; balti dishes cost from £4.95. At 54 Main St *McNulty's* has been efficiently wrapping up fish & chips for over half a century.

Getting There & Away

Bus Nos 134 and 234 travel to Coleraine, bus No 146 to Dungiven. Bus No 143 runs to Derry almost hourly. There's no direct bus to

DERRY & ANTRIM

The Flax About Linen

The manufacture of linen, probably the earliest textile made from plants, was once of vital significance to the Ulster economy. Linen was made in ancient Egypt and introduced into Britain by the Romans. The real boost to linen-making in Ulster though, came with the arrival of Huguenot weavers seeking sanctuary in the late 17th century.

The flax plant was sown in the north of Ireland from March to May and harvested in mid-August. The first stage in the harvesting was the pulling of the flax plants and bundling them into stacks for open-air drying. The seeds were removed and crushed for linseed oil or kept for the following year's planting. The second stage was a messy and smelly one, entailing the soaking of the bundles of flax in freshwater ponds, or 'lint holes', for up to two weeks. This process of 'retting' softened the outer stem and the 'scutching' could begin.

Scutching separated the dried flax stem; with the introduction of water wheels in the 18th century, large wooden blades pounded and loosened the flax. The fibres were then ready for spinning on a wheel before being woven into lengths of cloth. Some of this unbleached linen was sold as 'brown linen', hence the number of Brown Linen Halls that used to exist.

The next stage was the bleaching, carried out in the open air after the cloth had been soaked in water for hours. Huge lengths were stretched out across fields and left in the sunlight. The moisture in the material reacted with the sunlight to produce hydrogen peroxide which bleached the cloth. The final stage involved the hammering of the cloth by wooden hammers, or beetles, which smoothed out the material and made it ready for selling to the public. Bleached linen was sold through the many White Linen Halls.

At its height the linen industry was so important that Belfast was sometimes referred to as 'Linenopolis'. Flax growing died out in the North towards the end of the 19th century but was reborn during WWI with the demand for parachute material. There was a similar resurgence during WWII, but most of the linen now purchased is made in Scandinavia with the aid of chemicals. In recent years there has been an attempt to reintroduce flax growing in Ulster, and you may spot the occasional field of blue flax.

You can visit a beetling mill at Wellbrook outside Cookstown in County Tyrone. For a complete picture of the linen industry and its history, visit the impressive Irish Linen Centre in Lisburn, County Antrim, near Belfast. ■

Belfast but connections can be made at Coleraine or Dungiven.

DUNGIVEN & AROUND

Despite the defiant Irish flags flying on the bridge, Dungiven (Dún Geimhin) exudes an air of desolation, with many shops in the high street boarded up and abandoned. Its only attractions are nearby ecclesiastical sites and one of the North's few independent hostels, which could make it a better base than Limavady if you're travelling between Belfast and Derry or if you want to explore the Sperrin Hills.

The telephone code is ☎ 015047.

Dungiven Priory

The remains of this Augustinian priory,

signposted off the A6 road to Antrim, date back to the 12th century, when they replaced a pre-Norman monastery.

The church contains the ornate tomb of Cooey-na-Gal, a chieftain of the O'Cahans who died in 1385. On the front of the tomb are figures of six kilted gallowglasses, mercenaries from Scotland hired by Cooey O'Cahan as minders and earning him the nickname na-Gal ('of the foreigners'). In the 17th century another foreigner, Sir Edward Doddington, who built the walls of Derry, remodelled the priory and an adjacent small castle built by the O'Cahans. He constructed a private dwelling of which only the foundations remain.

Nearby is a bullaun, a hollowed stone originally used by the monks for grinding grain but now collecting rainwater and used by people seeking cures for illnesses.

Maghera Old Church

The church site goes back to a 6th century monastery that was plundered by the Vikings in 832. The present ruined nave is 10th century while the Romanesque door on the west side is two centuries younger. There are interesting motifs on the door jambs, and the lintel carries a fine Crucifixion scene that's as good as the carvings on the celebrated high crosses. In the churchyard there's an unmistakable pillar stone, carved with a ringed cross, which is said to mark the grave of the 6th century founder, St Lurach.

The town of Maghera is on the A6 Derry to Belfast road and the best approach is from Dungiven via the Glenshane Pass. Rising to 555m the road through the Sperrin Mountains offers dramatic views. In town turn right at the north end of the main street into Bank Square and then left to the car park. Bus No 116 runs regularly between Coleraine and Maghera, bus No 278 less frequently.

Places to Stay

The *Flax Mill Hostel* (☎ 42655), Mill Lane, Derrylane, Dungiven, generates its own electricity and charges £5 for a dorm bed, £3 to camp. The hostel is 5km from Dungiven. Take the A6 to Derry and after crossing the river take the first road on the right, signposted for Limavady and the Roe Valley Country Park. Then take the third road on the left, Altmover Rd, and the hostel is (unsigned) down the first lane on the right. The German-run hostel is sometimes full with groups from Germany but every effort is made to accommodate other travellers.

In town, at *Bradagh* (☎ 41346), 132 Main St, Mrs McMacken does B&B for £13.50 per person with shared bathroom and large breakfasts.

Places to Eat

When it comes to food, Dungiven hits rock bottom. The *Carraig Rua* pub, 40 Main St, serves evening meals but in less than inviting surroundings. If you're travelling on to Maghera on the A6, the *Ponderosa Bar & Restaurant* at the top of the Glenshane Pass does steaks, chicken and seafood; haddock is £4.50.

Getting There & Away

Express bus No 212 between Derry and Belfast operates 10 times daily (five times on Sunday) and stops on Main St in Dungiven. Ulsterbus No 146 travels between Limavady and Dungiven.

PLANTATION TOWNS

The rest of inland Derry, to the south of Dungiven, is strong Protestant territory made up of towns planned and created by London companies with gracious thanks to William of Orange for the grants of land. In Draperstown, Magherafelt and Moneymore the kerbstones are often painted red, white and blue, and for weeks after 12 July, when the victory of King Billy over the Catholics is celebrated, flags and banners proclaim the diehard patriotism of the locals.

Springhill

Springhill (☎ 016487-48210), 1.5km south of Moneymore on the B18, is an interesting example of early Plantation architecture. The original house was built about 1695 by the Conynghams who came here from Scotland after acquiring the 120-hectare Springhill estate. It was built at the same time as Hezlett House near Portstewart but has little in common with that more humble abode. The central block has a high pitched roof, enlarged by the addition of the wings in the 18th century which give a more solid air of Baroque assurance to the house. The barn is also late 17th century and was built to accommodate a warning bell. The Williamite war was over but then, as now, a certain siege mentality remained. Inside the house is some old oak furniture, a library, a collection of weapons and many costumes.

The house opens 2 to 6 pm weekends April, May, June and September, daily July and August. Admission is £2.40, children £1.20.

PORTSTEWART

When the English novelist Thackeray visited Portstewart (Port Stíobhaird) in 1842, he noted the 'air of comfort and neatness'; nearly 160 years later this still rings true and the place has an air of superiority that distinguishes it from the more proletarian Portrush, only 6km farther down the coast in County Antrim. A day could easily be passed visiting the excellent beaches in the vicinity, and the town makes a convenient base for the Giant's Causeway and other coastal attractions.

Orientation & Information

Portstewart consists of one long promenade. To the east it heads along the coast to Portrush and Ballycastle, and to the west to a fine beach, Portstewart Strand. The castle-like building perched at the end of the promenade is a Dominican school. Attractions west of town can only be reached by first going inland to Coleraine, then north again up the other side of a narrow inlet.

The tourist office (☎ 01265-832286), in the library in the lower level of the red-brick town hall at the western end of town, only opens in July and August, 10 am to 1 pm, 1.30 to 4 pm Monday to Saturday.

The telephone code is ☎ 01265.

Things to See & Do

This wide, sweeping **Portstewart Strand** is about 20 minutes' walk or a short bus ride west of town along Strand Rd. Despite the fact that the strand is a National Trust site, vehicles are allowed onto the firm sand which can accommodate over 1000 cars. When someone is on duty (unlikely out of season or in the evening) there's a £2.50 charge to take cars on the beach.

In summer you can hire speedboats and try parascending; phone ☎ 824099 for details.

Special Event

In May the North-West 200 motorcycle race is run on a road circuit between Portrush, Portstewart and Coleraine. This classic race is one of the last to be run on closed public roads anywhere in Europe; most such events

are now considered too dangerous. It attracts up to 70,000 spectators.

Places to Stay

Camping Camp sites are plentiful along the coast road. The council-run *Juniper Hill Caravan Park* (☎ 832023), 70 Ballyreagh Rd, about a mile east, has a few tent sites for £9. At Benone Beach, *Benone Complex* (☎ 015047-50555) has sites for £5.25, while the larger *Golden Sands Caravan Park* (☎ 015047-50324) charges £6.50.

Inland toward Coleraine, *Portstewart Holiday Park* (☎ 833308) charges £9 for tent sites.

For other nearby caravan parks see Portrush.

Hostel The *Causeway Coast Hostel* (☎ 01265-833789), 4 Victoria Terrace at the eastern end of town, charges £6 per person in four, six or eight-bedded dorms, £7 in private rooms. It has its own kitchen and laundry, and welcoming fires in winter. Real baths also make a nice change from showers.

B&Bs There are a number of B&Bs at the eastern end of town at the junction of Victoria Terrace, Hillcrest and Atlantic Circle. Typically, *Forty Winks* (☎ 834584), 5 Atlantic Circle, charges £15 for B&B with shared bathroom. At 26 The Promenade, the central *Craigmore* (☎ 832120) costs £32 for a double plus £6 each for dinner. *Mount Oriel* (☎ 832516), at No 74, charges £15 per person, and *Akaroa* (☎ 832067), next door at No 75, charges £18.

Hotels The very pleasant, lemon-coloured *Windsor Hotel* (☎ 832523), 8 The Promenade, charges £27.50/55 a single/double. Farther out, *Edgewater Hotel* (☎ 833314), 88 Strand Rd overlooking Portstewart Strand, is also pleasant, with rooms for £55/85.

Self-Catering Describing themselves as 'exclusively adult', the cottages at *Rock Castle* (☎ 01265-832271) overlook Portstewart Strand and vary from £130 a week for a one-bedroom unit in the low season to £485 for a two-bedroom unit in the high season.

Places to Eat

For reasonably priced hot or cold lunches, try *Squires*, 18 The Promenade, which also does early evening meals. A mixed grill costs £6.95. The *Heathrhon Diner* at No 31 is similar. You can hardly miss neon-lit *Morelli's*, midway along the Promenade, which dispenses mouth-watering ice creams from as little as 60p. Next door, but part of the same complex, is *Nino's* which does hot meals as well as ice cream and usually has a vegetarian special for around £3. Up some stairs and round the back, the *Outback*, yet another part of the same complex, serves steaks in the evenings.

Montagu Arms (☎ 834146), 68-9 The Promenade, has a carvery but does toasted sandwiches (called 'toasties') as well, as does *Shenanigans* up the hill. Farther up, *Ashiana*, 12 The Diamond, has a mixed menu of Indian and European dishes and kebabs. Chicken Madras is £4.95.

Dinner costs around £9 to £12 in the *Windsor Hotel* restaurant on the Promenade or at the *Edgewater Hotel* where the bar and restaurant have great views of the broad Portstewart Strand.

Out of town toward Portrush, *Some Plaice Else* (☎ 824945), 21 Ballyreagh Rd, is a large seafood restaurant on the sea side of the coast road.

Getting There & Away

Bus Buses leave from The Promenade. Ulsterbus No 218 leaves Portstewart for Belfast eight times daily on weekdays, four times on Saturday and twice on Sunday, stopping at Coleraine, Ballymoney and Antrim. This is the express route and takes two hours. Bus No 218 also does the scenic coastal route and takes four hours.

Bus No 234 leaves several times daily Monday to Friday for Derry (once daily on weekends), and takes an hour. Bus No 140 plies between Coleraine and Portstewart (17 minutes) roughly every half hour (fewer on Sunday); a one-way fare is £1.25.

See Getting Around at the start of this chapter for information on the summertime Antrim Coaster and Bushmills Bus services.

Train The nearest station is at Portrush, with connections to the Derry-Belfast train at Coleraine. See Portrush for details.

WEST OF PORTSTEWART

To reach the attractions west of Portstewart take the A2 from Coleraine and head west.

Hezlett House, Castlerock

This house (☎ 012565-848567) was built in the late 17th century. It is a single-storey thatched cottage noted for its cruck truss roof gables of stone and turf strengthened with wooden crucks or crutches. The interior decoration is Victorian. The house is owned by the National Trust and opens July and August, Wednesday to Monday 1 to 6 pm. April to June and September it's open the same hours on weekends and bank holidays only. Admission is £2/1 and there's a car park across the road. The house is 8km west of Coleraine at Liffock on the A2.

Downhill & Mussenden Temple

An eccentric, rich bishop of Derry was also the earl of Bristol, and his fine home at Downhill was built in 1774. It was burnt down in 1851, rebuilt in 1870 and abandoned after WWII. The roof was removed for its scrap value and the remains of the small castellated building now stand forlornly in a field.

The major attraction, a short walk from the house, is the curious little Mussenden Temple, perched on the cliff edge and built by the energetic bishop to house either his library or his mistress – opinions differ! He conducted an affair with the mistress of Frederick William II of Prussia well into his old age.

Even though you have to pick your way through sheep droppings, it's a pleasant walk to the temple and the reward is some fine views of the sand at Portstewart and also

DERRY & ANTRIM

Benone/Magilligan, the railway line below and the hills of Donegal across the water. The beach immediately below is where the bishop set his own clergy to race on horseback, rewarding the winners by appointing them to the more lucrative parishes. In the distance shadowy outlines of the Scottish mountains are visible. The bishop inscribed a quotation from Lucretius on a frieze:

It is pleasant to see from the safe shore
The pitching of ships and hear the storm's roar.

The inscription is thoroughly appropriate on a windy day. The site is about 20km west of Portstewart by road, much closer as the crow flies. It's owned by the National Trust but there's no admission charge. The temple opens daily July and August noon to 6 pm; April, May, June and September it's open the same hours on weekends and bank holidays only. There are also short walks in **Downhill Forest** on the other side of the road.

B&B is available down the hill at the *Downhill Inn* (☎ 01265-848598) which also has bar food all day and opens its restaurant at 6 pm.

Immediately past Downhill Inn, Bishop's Rd forks up to the left, leading over the mountains to Limavady, with terrific views from **Gortmore** picnic area.

Benone/Magilligan Beach

Some 10km in length and hundreds of metres wide at low tide, this huge Blue Flag beach – called both Benone and Magilligan – is worth a visit. It sweeps out to Magilligan Point where a Martello tower stands and from where sailplanes and hang-gliders can be seen riding the wind. Look for the sign to the Benone Tourist Complex & Strand on the A2.

County Antrim

East of Ballycastle the distinctive cliffs of Fair Head mark the point where the coast turns southwards and the Antrim coast

makes its way down to Larne before turning inland for Carrickfergus and Belfast Lough. This coastal strip is known as the Glens of Antrim after the series of nine valleys which cut across the range of hills between Ballycastle and Larne. The A2 road runs along the coast for most of the way and it's an exciting route for cyclists. The short run between Waterfoot and Carnlough is particularly fine.

Inland, Antrim (Aontroim) is perhaps the least interesting part of Northern Ireland, and Antrim Town has little to recommend it. To the south of nearby Lisburn the infamous Long Kesh prison was the scene of the hunger strikes in 1981 which led to the deaths of 10 men who were campaigning for the right to be recognised as political prisoners.

Most visitors pass along Antrim's coast where there's little to remind one of the Troubles. The scenery is delightful and everyone is drawn towards the northern coastline that bears the distinctive geological formation, the Giant's Causeway.

PORTRUSH

The busy little resort of Portrush (Port Rois), bursts at the seams with holidaymakers from all round the North in summer and on bank-holiday weekends. Not surprisingly, many of its attractions are unashamedly focused on families.

Information

The tourist office (☎ 01265-823333) is in the Dunluce Centre on Dunluce Ave. It opens daily 9 am to 8 pm June to September, 9 am to 5 pm Monday to Friday April and May, noon to 5 pm weekends only March and October and closes altogether November to the end of February.

The telephone code is ☎ 01265.

Things to See & Do

In summer, **boat trips** depart regularly for cruising or fishing; contact the tourist office for a list of operators. For **pony trekking** contact the Maddybenny Riding Centre (☎ 823394, or 823603 after hours); it has lessons for £8. Also try Hillfarm Riding & Trekking Centre (☎ 848629), 47 Altikeragh Rd.

Portrush is carving out a name for itself as a **surfing** paradise. There are several surf shops including the friendly Troggs (☎ 823923), 8 Bath St, which does board and wetsuit hire, surf reports and general advice. It also offers some basic accommodation upstairs.

Waterworld (☎ 822001) by the harbour has pools, waterslides and spa baths for children to play in. The **Dunluce Centre** (☎ 824444) has a 'turbo tour', a hands-on nature trail with lots of buttons to press, and animated shows on local myths and legends. In summer it's open daily 10 am to 8 pm, but usually closes at 5 pm in winter; an inclusive ticket costs £4.50 March to September, £4 at other times.

Places to Stay

Camping The Bushmills Bus (bus No 177) runs to *Margoth Caravan Park* (☎ 822531), 126 Dunluce Rd, which charges £9 for a site. The smaller *Carrick Dhu Caravan Park* (☎ 823712), 12 Ballyreagh Rd, charges the same. *Golf Links Holiday Home Park* (☎ 823539), on Bushmills Rd, offers sites for £8 including power.

There's also *Portrush Caravan Park* (☎ 823537) on the Portrush-Coleraine road, opposite the Magherabuoy Hotel; a tent for up to four people costs £9.

Hostel *Macools* is an unusually clean 20-bed independent hostel with sea views at 5 Causeway View Terrace (☎ 01265-824845). Beds in single-sex dorms cost £5 a head (£7.50 in the one private room), and there are laundry and cooking facilities.

B&Bs B&Bs fill up quickly during summer and it's advisable to book in advance through the tourist office. Guesthouses with sea views on Landsowne Crescent include *Clarmont* (☎ 822397) at No 10, *Alexandra* (☎ 822284) at No 11 and also *Belvedere* (☎ 822771) at No 15, all charging £25 to £36 a double in the high season.

With more character, there's the *Old Manse* (☎ 824118), 3 Main St, which dates from 1850 and charges £21/40 a single/double. If you arrive late, there are also a few B&Bs immediately opposite the station in Eglinton St, including *Atlantic View* (☎ 823647), *Glenshane* (☎ 824839) and *An Uladh* (☎ 822221).

June to August, the *Northern Ireland Hotel & Catering College* (☎ 823768), Ballywilliam Rd, offers B&B in its halls of residence for £18 per person, or £20 with bathroom. The college trains many of Ireland's chefs and guests can eat at the restaurant here.

Hotels Rooms at *Magherabuoy House* (☎ 823507), 41 Magherabuoy Rd, are £50/80, while at the *Eglinton Hotel* (☎ 822371), 49 Eglinton St, they're £49/69; rates at both include breakfast. The *Langholm Hotel* is closed for renovation and when it reopens will probably have a name change.

Places to Eat

Cafés and fast-food places jostle with amusement arcades all the way along Main St and you need to head for the harbour end to find better.

Ramore (☎ 823444), next to Waterworld and overlooking the harbour, is Portrush's premier eating place; it can get unbelievably busy. The wine bar downstairs opens for lunch 12.30 to 2.15 pm (there are good value lunch specials from £4.95), and again from 5 pm, while the pricier restaurant upstairs doesn't open until 7 pm.

Rowland's, 92 Main St, near the harbour, does mains including salmon steak for £6 to £9.50. Around the corner *Hidden Cove* in Bath St is fine for snacks. Open daily, *Don Giovanni's Ristorante* on Causeway St near the junction with Eglington and Main Sts, isn't as expensive as it looks. Pasta dishes are £4.90 to £6.50.

Some hotels are also reliable eating places. At *Magherabuoy House* generous helpings make the Sunday lunch particularly good value at £9.50. It also offers high tea and dinner.

Entertainment

The *Harbour Bar*, unsurprisingly by the harbour, is immensely popular at night. About 1.5km out of town, the flashiest local entertainment complex is still known as *Kelly's*, although its various sections have each been given their own name. The nightclub is called *Lush*, while two of the bars are called *God's* and *Armani*. A taxi charges about £4 to get you there.

Getting There & Away

Bus The bus terminal is near the Dunluce Centre. Bus No 218 leaves daily from Portrush for Belfast, travelling inland via Portstewart, Coleraine, Ballymoney, Ballymena and Antrim; there are only three or four services on Saturday and two on Sunday. Bus Nos 139 and 140 run weekdays to Coleraine (£1.25). In summer bus No 278 runs daily to Dublin.

See Getting Around at the start of this chapter for information on the Antrim Coaster and Bushmills Bus services.

Train Portrush is served by train from Coleraine roughly every hour for the 12-minute journey. The earliest train leaves Coleraine at 8.02 am, the latest at 10.25 pm; from Portrush the times are 6.35 am and 8.20 pm respectively. At Coleraine connections can be made for Belfast or Derry. To Dublin from here, changing at Coleraine and Belfast, takes nearly five hours. Contact Portrush station (☎ 822395) for details.

Getting Around

For taxis call Andy Brown's (☎ 822223) or North West Taxis (☎ 824446). They're both near the red-brick town hall. A taxi to the Giant's Causeway costs about £6 or £7.

PORTBALLINTRAE

Portballintrae ('the port of the town of strand') is little more than a small harbour ringed with houses and a couple of seaside-style hotels. During WWI it was the only place in the UK to be shelled by a German submarine. Luckily, the result was no worse than a crater on the outskirts of town and the downing of the electric tram lines.

Dunluce Castle

The site, beside the A2 just west of Portballintrae, was used for defensive purposes long before a stone castle was constructed, as shown by the existence of a 1000-year-old souterrain. Parts of the castle date from the 14th century. In the 16th century it came into the hands of the Scottish Sorley Boy MacDonnell family, who ex-tended the buildings and tried to strengthen its walls after a serious artillery attack by the English. In the 17th century a manor house with medieval floorplan and Renaissance embellishments was built inside the walls.

The south wall, facing the mainland, has two openings cut into it which were made to hold cannons salvaged from the wreck of the *Girona*, a Spanish Armada vessel that foundered nearby. Perched 30m above the sea, the castle was of obvious military value, and there are extensive remains inside the walls, giving a good idea of life here.

The palatial hall needed two fireplaces, while the kitchen area has ovens, storage space and a drainage system all built into the stone. The lower yard retains the original cobbling and was surrounded by service rooms, some of which collapsed into the sea in 1639; servants and a night's dinner were lost.

The castle opens April to the end of September, 10 am to 7 pm Monday to Saturday, 2 to 7 pm Sunday. The rest of the year it opens 10 am to 4 pm Monday to Saturday, 2 to 4 pm Sunday. Entry is £1.50/75p which includes an audiovisual display telling the castle's history.

Places to Stay & Eat

Portballintrae Caravan Park (☎ 012657-31478), on Ballaghmore Rd, has space for 11 tents at £6 a night. The accommodating *Keeve-Na* (☎ 012657-32184), beside the caravan park on Ballaghmore Rd, does B&B for £17/32. The sea-facing *Bayhead Guest*

TOM SMALLMAN

PAT YALE

PAT YALE

PAT YALE

MARK DAFFEY

MARK DAFFEY

County Antrim
A: The Diamond, Ballycastle
B: Orange Hall, Lisburn
C: Clough Williams-Ellis houses, Cushendun
D: Ireland's smallest church, Portbradden

E: Rugged coast, Giant's Causeway
F: Rainbow over Dunluce Castle, Portrush

TONY WHEELER

TOM SMALLMAN

Counties Tyrone & Fermanagh
Top: Beaghmore Stone Circles, County Tyrone
Bottom: Rural scene near Enniskillen, County Fermanagh

House (☎ 012657-31441), 8 Bayhead Rd, charges £30/39. *Bayview Hotel* (☎ 012657-31453), 2 Bayhead Rd, has an indoor heated swimming pool and costs £45/70 while the better *Beach House Hotel* (☎ 012657-31214), 61 Beach Rd, charges £48/76.

Sallies Coffee Shop, on Seaport Ave, serves satisfying snacks during the day. Decent, substantial meals are available from *Beach House Hotel* and cost around £5.50, but don't eat here if you're in a hurry.

Getting There & Away

Weekdays bus No 132 between Portrush and Ballymoney stops here twice daily. Bus No 138 runs regularly (except Sunday) to Coleraine and Portrush, while bus No 172 runs several times daily to Portrush and Ballycastle. See Getting Around at the start of this chapter for information on the Antrim Coaster and Bushmills Bus services.

BUSHMILLS

On the River Bush, Bushmills (Muileann na Buaise) is a small town off the A2 between Portrush and Ballycastle. At its centre is the Diamond, with a grim grey circular clocktower and war memorial from which Main St makes its way half a km west to the famous Bushmills Distillery.

Bushmills Distillery

This is the only place in the world where Bushmills whiskey is distilled, and it is the world's oldest legal distillery. Whiskey was first officially distilled here in 1608, but records indicate that the activity was going on for hundreds of years before that. After a noisy tour of the industrial process (they're quieter on weekends when production is halted), you're rewarded with a whiskey-tasting session where you get to compare Bushmills' whiskeys with other brands. These sessions take place in the 1608 Bar, where an exhibition area has been created in what were once malt kilns.

The distillery (☎ 012657-31521) opens April to October, Monday to Saturday 9.30 am to 5.30 pm, Sunday noon to 5.30 pm (the last tour is at 4 pm). November to March it

opens weekdays 10 am to 5 pm (the last tour is at 3.30 pm). Admission costs £2.50, children free.

Places to Stay

The spectacularly sited YHANI hostel at White Park Bay is 6km east of Bushmills (see Giant's causeway to Ballycastle).

Ardeevin (☎ 012657-31661), 145 Main St, on the way to the distillery, does B&B for £16 a head. The clean rooms have views of the weir at the back. The pleasantly quiet *Bushmills Inn* (☎ 012657-32339), on Main St, charges £55/88 a single/double. *Pineview* (☎ 012657-41527), 111 Castlecatt Rd (the B66), is a farmhouse 5km south of Bushmills and charges £14 per person.

Places to Eat

The *Coffee Shop* in the Diamond serves snacks and sandwiches, but you'll do better at *Valerie's Pantry* where cream tea costs £1.50 and roast beef lunch £3.80. It's on Main St as you walk to the distillery and you can pay in punts if you want to. The *Bushmills Inn* has an attractive restaurant serving everything from toasted sandwiches, to full à la carte dinners (£17.50).

Strangely, in a place synonymous with Irish whiskey, the *Scotch House Tavern* on Main St boasts a wide range of Scotch whisky.

Getting There & Away

Bus No 172 connects Bushmills with Ballycastle, the Giant's Causeway and Portrush, as does bus No 254 which also goes to Coleraine, Larne and Belfast. See Getting Around at the start of this chapter for information on the Antrim Coaster and Bushmills Bus services. Buses drop you off in the Diamond.

GIANT'S CAUSEWAY

The chances are you've seen pictures of the Giant's Causeway (Clochán an Aifir), the North's number one tourist attraction, long before getting here. A bishop of Derry, who became interested in geology after seeing Vesuvius erupt, commissioned the paintings

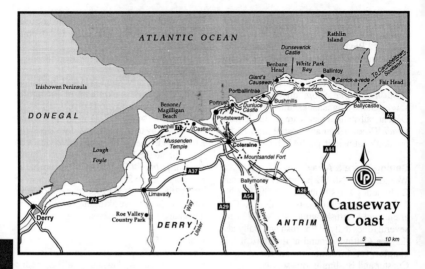

ATLANTIC OCEAN

Rathlin Island

Dunseverick Castle

Benbane Head White Park Bay Ballintoy

Giant's Causeway

Portballintrae

Inishowen Peninsula

Portbradden

To Campbeltown, Scotland

Carrick-a-rede

Fair Head

Portrush Dunluce Castle Bushmills

Ballycastle

Benone/ Magilligan Beach

DONEGAL

Portstewart

Downhill Castlerock

Mussenden Temple

Coleraine

Lough Foyle

Mountsandel Fort

A2

A44

A37

Ballymoney

A26

Derry

Roe Valley Country Park

Limavady

DERRY

Ulster Way

A2

A29

A54

River Bann

ANTRIM

Causeway Coast

0   5   10 km

DERRY & ANTRIM

of the site that led to its fame. The hexagonal basalt columns are impressive and do look as if a giant might have playfully tipped out all 37,000 of them, if you count the ones under the water. According to legend the giant in question, Finn McCool, fancied a female giant on the Scottish island of Staffa and built some stepping stones to the island where, indeed, similar rock formations are found.

The modern, more prosaic explanation is that red hot lava erupted from an underground fissure and crystallised some 60 million years ago into the shapes that we see today. The phenomenon is very clearly explained in the Causeway Visitors' Centre (☎ 012657-31855), alongside the surprising fact that the Causeway only came to general notice as late as 1740. The audiovisual section, however, is more of an animated tourist brochure, debatably worth the charge of £1 (children 50p). It costs nothing to make the pleasant 1.5km pilgrimage to the actual site. From mid-March to the end of October minibuses with wheelchair access ply the route every 15 minutes (£1/50p return).

Different areas of the rock formations have their own names, most invented by the many Victorian guides who made a summer living by escorting the tourists who arrived on the electric tram from Coleraine. Past the main spill of columns, the pathway brings into view a formation that does deserve its own name. Chimney Tops was identified by ships of the Spanish Armada in 1588 as part of Dunluce Castle, and consequently fired upon.

Two well-established footpaths at different levels start from outside the visitors' centre and form a circular walk. The less strenuous route is to follow the clifftop path out then down to the Causeway, then take the lower walk back to the visitors' centre.

From the clifftop at Hamilton's Seat, there's one of the best views of the Causeway and headlands to the west, including Malin Head and Inishowen. If you want to go farther, the path continues around Benbane Head and the sandy beach of White Park Bay comes into view. On the right is Portmoon House. The headlands become lower and lower until the path reaches the main road near Dunseverick Castle. The walk from the visitors' centre to the castle and back is 16km.

From below the remains of the castle a

path winds up and round to the east, ending at Ballintoy. It crosses a number of small wooden bridges before reaching the beach at White Park Bay. There's a YHANI hostel here, so the whole 16km journey from the Giant's Causeway could be done in one day.

These walks follow the North Antrim Cliff Path, which actually begins west of the visitors' centre at Blackrock, a short walk of about 2.5km. A useful 75p map from the visitors' centre details the walks, including the various rock formations that can be seen along the way.

The Giant's Causeway can be visited free of charge any time but the car park costs £2.50. July and August the visitors' centre opens daily 10 am to 7 pm. September to June it opens 10 am to 5 pm. It only closes on Christmas Day and Boxing Day. There's a National Trust shop and a café in the same building but they close earlier.

Next to the visitors' centre, and mainly of interest to children, the **Causeway School Museum** opens daily July and August, 11 am to 5 pm; 75/50p, or £2 for a family.

Places to Stay

If you want to stay close to the Causeway, the *Causeway Hotel* (☎ 01267-31226) is within spitting distance and charges £50/70 including breakfast. The nearest hostel is in White Park Bay (see below). Otherwise, you could stay in Bushmills or Portballintrae, or even in Portrush or Ballycastle, and still visit the Causeway perfectly easily.

Lochaber (☎ 012657-31385), on the coast road at 107 Causeway Rd, just 1.5km from the Causeway, charges £13 per person, while at 23 Causeway Rd *Carnside Guest House* (☎ 012657-31337) charges £15/34.

Places to Eat

The *Giant's Pantry* café in the Causeway Visitors' Centre is OK and you can buy sandwiches etc in two small shops outside. You'll get a more substantial meal though at the nearby *Causeway Hotel*. Its restaurant is extremely popular, so it's wise to book in advance.

Getting There & Away

The B146 Causeway to Dunseverick road runs parallel to the A2 but closer to the coast and can be joined just east of Bushmills or near White Park Bay. Bus Nos 172 and 254 between Portrush and Ballycastle pass the

DERRY & ANTRIM

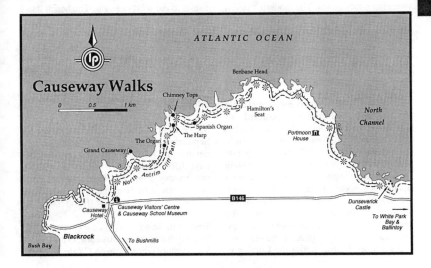

site. See the introduction to this chapter for information on the Antrim Coaster and Bushmills Bus services. It's only five minutes by bus from the Giant's Causeway to the Diamond in Bushmills and another five minutes to Portballintrae.

GIANT'S CAUSEWAY TO BALLYCASTLE

Spectacularly sited by the side of the B146 (which is reached off the A2 coast road) is **Dunseverick Castle**, though unfortunately little remains of it. Older than Dunluce, it was once the home of Conal Cearnac, a famous wrestler and swordsman said to have been present at Christ's crucifixion; he reputedly moved the stone at Christ's sepulchre. St Patrick is also said to have visited the castle and a road was laid from here to Tara, the headquarters of the pagan high kings of Ireland.

Signposted off the A2 is **Portbradden**, a hamlet of half a dozen pretty harbourside houses. Tiny, blue-and-white St Gobban's church is said to be the smallest in Ireland, and it's easy to believe it.

Visible from Portbradden and accessible via the next road junction off the A2 is the spectacular **White Park Bay** with its wide, sweeping sandy beach. The modern YHANI *White Park Bay Hostel* (☎ 012657-31745) has a common room positioned to soak up the view. Four-bed dorms cost £8.50/10 for members/non-members, twins £10.50/12 per person. Rates include bed linen. The hostel has a bureau de change, and residents can hire bikes for £6 a day.

A few km farther along is **Ballintoy** (Baile an Tuaighe), another picture postcard village, set around a harbour. Look out for the idiosyncratically designed house on the right on the way down. B&B is available at *Ballintoy House* (☎ 012657-62317), 9 Main St, for £12 a single, or £28 a double with ensuite. It's open all year. By the harbour, *Roark's Kitchen* serves teas, coffees and light lunches in summer. Bearing in mind the minuscule size of the place, though, it's best to avoid visiting at the peak of the season.

It's a scary traipse across the **Carrick-a-rede Rope Bridge** to a small island with a salmon fishery and hundreds of nesting fulmars and razorbills. Carrick-a-rede means 'rock in the road' and the 20m bridge sways some 25m above the rock strewn water. It's especially frightening if it's windy, but there are secure handrails to help steady your nerves and your balance; stout footwear is advised and no more than two people should cross simultaneously. The bridge is put up every spring by workers at the fishery. Once on the island there are good views of Rathlin Island and Fair Head to the east. You can cross the bridge free, but the National Trust car park costs £2; it's a 1.25km walk from there to the bridge.

The small National Trust Information Centre (☎ 012657-62178) has a café and opens daily 10 am to 6 pm April, May and September; 10 am to 8 pm June, July and August.

BALLYCASTLE

Ballycastle (Baile an Chaisil), where the Atlantic Ocean meets the Irish Sea, also marks the end of the Causeway Coast. It's a pretty, small town, with plenty of 18th and 19th century architecture, and its location makes it a natural base for exploring the coasts to the west or south. The beach itself may be nothing special but there's a seaside feel to the harbour area which is being expanded. The Giant's Causeway, Bushmills distillery and the rope bridge are all less than 16km away and the Glens of Antrim are due south.

Information

The tourist office (☎ 012657-62024) is in the Moyle District Council Office on Mary St; September to June it opens weekdays 9.30 am to 5 pm; July and August it opens weekdays 9.30 am to 7 pm, Saturday 10 am to 6 pm, Sunday 2 to 6 pm. Pick up a free copy of the Ballycastle Heritage Trail leaflet here.

The telephone code is ☎ 012657.

Things to See

The tiny **Ballycastle Museum**, in the town's 18th century courthouse on Castle St, opens

Monday to Saturday 2 to 6 pm in July and August, free of charge. The **lookout** on North St has views of the harbour and the cliffs to the east, while down near the harbour is a **memorial** to Guglielmo Marconi (see Rathlin Island).

The remains of the Franciscan **Bonamargy Friary** are 1km east of town on the A2 to Cushendun, on the Ballycastle golf course. The friary was founded around 1500 and used for two centuries. South of the friary a vault contains the bodies of the MacDonnells, the earls of Antrim, including Sorley Boy MacDonnell from Dunluce Castle. Entry is free.

Special Events

In late May, the Northern Lights Festal is a three day celebration of Ulster culture. Mid-June there's the three day music and dance festival known as Fleadh Amhrán agus Rince.

The bigger Ould Lammas Fair, on the last Monday and Tuesday of August, is one of the oldest fairs in Ireland, dating back to 1606, and is associated with the sale of two traditional foods, yellowman and dulse.

Yellowman is a hard chewy toffee, while dulse is a dried seaweed that's sold salted and ready to eat, although some people toast it. Always available during the Ould Lammas Fair, dulse is on sale generally June to September while yellowman is available throughout the year. The Fruit Shop at the Diamond often stocks both delicacies.

Places to Stay

Camping *Silvercliffs Holiday Village* (☎ 62550), 21 Clare Rd, is a big, noisy caravan park and campsite, north-west of town and within walking distance. It's also expensive at £10 per tent. Comfortable four-berth caravans can be hired for £22 a night. On the A2 to Cushendun, 10km from Ballycastle, *Watertop Open Farm* (☎ 62576) has space for a few tents (£8 each) and is a

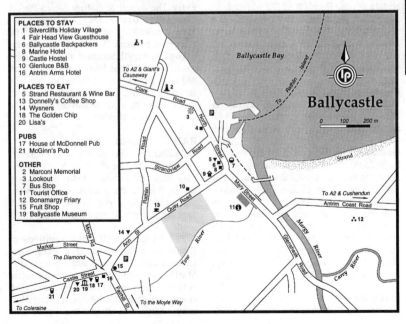

PLACES TO STAY
1 Silvercliffs Holiday Village
4 Fair Head View Guesthouse
6 Ballycastle Backpackers
8 Marine Hotel
9 Castle Hostel
10 Glenluce B&B
16 Antrim Arms Hotel

PLACES TO EAT
5 Strand Restaurant & Wine Bar
13 Donnelly's Coffee Shop
14 Wysners
18 The Golden Chip
20 Lisa's

PUBS
17 House of McDonnell Pub
21 McGinn's Pub

OTHER
2 Marconi Memorial
3 Lookout
7 Bus Stop
11 Tourist Office
12 Bonamargy Friary
15 Fruit Shop
19 Ballycastle Museum

Ballycastle Bay

Ballycastle

0   100   200 m

To A2 & Giant's Causeway

To A2 & Cushendun
Antrim Coast Road

To Coleraine

To the Moyle Way

DERRY & ANTRIM

good place for children, with pony trekking and farm tours. *Fair Head Caravan Park* (☎ 62077), 13 Whitepark Rd, also has limited camping space at £9 a tent.

Hostels The IHH *Castle Hostel* (☎ 62337), 62 Quay Rd just past the Marine Hotel, charges £6 a night. It's clean, welcoming and unusually spacious. *Ballycastle Backpackers* (☎ 63612), 4 North St, near the seafront and main bus stop, has accommodation in five-bed dorms for £7.50 (including linen).

B&Bs If you want to be close to the sea, *Fair Head View* (☎ 62822), 26 North St, is above the harbour; rooms cost £16 per person. *Glenluce* (☎ 62914), 42 Quay Rd, painted white with blue trim, charges £34 a double. Other possibilities along Quay Rd include *Fragens* (☎ 62168), at No 34, *Ammiroy* (☎ 62621), at No 26, and *Silversprings House* (☎ 62080), at No 20, charging £15 to £18 a person.

Hotels *Marine Hotel* (☎ 62222), 1 North St, is right on the seafront and costs £52/70 a single/double. The smaller *Antrim Arms Hotel* (☎ 62284), 75 Castle St inland, charges £35 a double. Rates at both include breakfast.

Places to Eat
On the seafront the *Strand Restaurant & Wine Bar* does all-day breakfasts for £3.80 and opens for evening meals until 10.30 pm. Nearby the *Marine Hotel* also serves dinner until 10.30 pm; the roast of the day sets you back £5.90. In the streets leading off the Diamond there are the usual small cafés. For fish & chips, try the *Golden Chip*, or *Lisa's*, both on Castle St. *Wysners* (☎ 62372), 16 Ann St, good for lunch or afternoon tea, serves sausages and champ for £4.95; there's also a restaurant upstairs which opens Friday and Saturday evenings. *Donelly's Coffeeshop*, 28 Ann St, is another good lunch stop; roast chicken is £4.25.

Entertainment
The *Marine Hotel* has live music at week-

ends during summer and a disco Saturday nights. There's more live music on Castle St at *McGinn's* pub and the popular *House of McDonnell*, which has traditional music sessions Friday nights. The *Central Bar* on Anne St has lively traditional sessions Wednesday nights.

Getting There & Away
Bus Bus Nos 131 and 217 link Ballycastle with Belfast, and bus No 171 links the town with Coleraine, but there are no Sunday services on these routes. Bus No 172 provides daily connections with Bushmills and Portrush.

McGinns (☎ 63451), the local private bus, runs to Belfast's Europa Buscentre from the Diamond on Friday at 4 pm and Sunday at 8 pm. It takes 1½ hours and costs £6 (children £4) return.

See the introduction to this chapter for information on the summertime Antrim Coaster bus.

Ferry The Argyll & Antrim Steam Packet Company (☎ 0345 523523) has begun operating a new ferry service aboard the MV *Claymore* between Ballycastle and Campbeltown in Argyll, Scotland. It leaves Ballycastle twice daily at 10.45 am and 7.15 pm and takes three hours. The standard one-way fare is £25/57/172 for either a foot passenger, motorcyclist or a car containing up to two adults and three children.

RATHLIN ISLAND
Only 22km from Scotland's Mull of Kintyre, Rathlin Island (Reachlainn) is itself only 6km long and nowhere more than 1.5km across. It has a pub, a restaurant, two shops, a campsite and a guesthouse, along with approximately 100 inhabitants and thousands of seabirds.

The island, which Pliny mentions as Ricnia, was raided by Vikings in AD 795 and suffered again in 1595 when Sorley Boy MacDonnell sent his family here for safety only to have them massacred by the English along with all the inhabitants. Its most illustrious visitor was Robert the Bruce who spent some time in 1306 in a small cave on the north-east point learning a lesson about fortitude. Watching a spider's resoluteness in repeatedly trying to spin a web gave him the courage to have another go at the English, whom he subsequently defeated at Bannockburn.

Another claim to fame is the fact that Rathlin Island was the first place to have a wireless. Marconi's assistant contacted Rathlin by radio from Ballycastle in 1898 to prove to Lloyd's of London that the idea worked.

The birdlife at **Kebble Nature Reserve** at the western end of the island is the chief attraction. Guillemots, kittiwakes, razorbills and puffins can be seen around West Lighthouse, but by late summer they're no longer nesting or rearing their young and are difficult to spot from the land. During summer a minibus (☎ 012657-63905) takes you there from the ferry harbour for £2.50 return (children £1.25). The service doesn't run to a timetable so check your return time. You can go **scuba diving** at various points around the island; contact Tommy Cecil (☎ 012657-63915) for organised dives.

Places to Stay

Camping space is provided by the owner of the one pub, in a field a short distance east of the harbour. The *Richard Branson Activity Centre* (☎ 012657-63915) offers dorm beds for £10 but call first to see if there's space. *Rathlin Guesthouse* (☎ 012657-63916/7), by the harbour, does B&B for £15 per person.

Getting There & Away

In theory a ferry service (☎ 01880-730253) operates daily year round from Ballycastle, but boats may not sail when the weather's bad. It's wise to show up well in advance of the scheduled sailing time.

November to March boats leave Ballycastle at 10 am and 4 pm (on Friday the second ferry leaves at 5 pm) and leave Rathlin at 9 am and 3 pm. April to June and September to October boats leave Ballycastle at 10 am and 5 pm, and leave Rathlin at 9 am and 4 pm. July and August they leave Ballycastle at 10 am, 12.15, 5 and 6.45 pm, and leave Rathlin at 9 and 11.15 am, 4 and 6 pm. The fare is £3.50/1.75 one way.

MURLOUGH BAY

The scenic coast between Ballycastle and Cushendun is best covered not by the main A2 but by the Cushendun Scenic Route (to Torr Head) that takes in Murlough Bay. This is the most stupendous part of the Antrim coastline. The A2 goes inland between Cushendun and Ballycastle and cannot compete with the grandeur of the coastal route.

Leave your transport at the first car park – there are three altogether – where a map display sets out the walking possibilities. From the first car park walk No 1 is to Coolanlough, a 3.5km return trip. The views from Fair Head are magnificent. From a vantage point 186m above the sea, Rathlin Island is to the left, while out to sea the peaks of the Isle of Arran can be seen on a clear day beyond the Mull of Kintyre. The walk also takes in Lough na Cranagh, in the middle of which is an ancient crannóg.

The second walk begins from the second car park farther down the road; follow the clear pathway to the west. It leads to some abandoned coal mines, indicated only by arches in the rock, which are probably not safe to explore. By following the main road down past the second car park you come to a third parking area on the right. From there the road down becomes a green track and ends in a cul-de-sac by a small house.

Between the first and second car parks, the remains of a cross can be seen, a memorial to Roger Casement whose family came from this area. Casement, who was hanged in London in 1916 for enlisting the aid of Germany in the nationalist struggle, made a last request to his cousin: 'Take my body back with you and let it lie in the old churchyard in Murlough Bay.' It was 50 years before the British consented to release the body.

DERRY & ANTRIM

CUSHENDUN

Much of Cushendun (Bun Abhann Duinne) is owned by the National Trust and any new buildings must match existing ones. The distinctive black and white houses at the southern end are the work of Clough Williams-Ellis, designer of Portmeirion in North Wales, who came here to work for Lord Cushendun.

The telephone code is ☎ 012667.

The village, on a bay with a small beach, is on the **Ulster Way** (see the Activities chapter) and part of the walk can be undertaken from here. North from Cushendun the walk goes inland before heading down to Murlough Bay and then along the coast to Ballycastle. Going south the walk travels inland nearly all the way to Cushendall.

Places to Stay

Camping is available at *Cushendun Caravan Park* (☎ 61254), 14 Glendun Rd, run by the local council. The only hotel is the *Bay Hotel* (☎ 61267), 20 Strandview Park, with rooms at £18 per person. A few doors away, the largish *Cushendun* (☎ 61266) calls itself a guesthouse, perhaps because it's only open during July and August. B&B here is £20 per person. North of the village, the *Villa* (☎ 61252), 185 Torr Rd, has a great view over the bay and does B&B for £18/36.

Self-catering houses and flats around Cushendun go for around £180 to £380 a week. One of the cheaper ones is *Strand House Annexe* (☎ 01648-27077), but it only has one unit, or else try *Mullarts Apartments* (☎ 61221), 114 Tromra Rd, inside a converted church.

Places to Eat

Cushendun Village Tearooms, on the corner near the bridge, serves hot snacks and salads. Bar food and evening meals are available at the *Bay Hotel* and the *Cushendun*. If you phone beforehand, the *Villa* does homemade meals until 7.30 pm for around £10.

Entertainment

Near Cushendun guesthouse is *McBride's* pub, reputed to be the smallest pub in

Ireland. At the time of research it was closed for refurbishment.

Getting There & Away

Ulsterbus Nos 120 and 150 link Cushendun with Ballymena, from where a connection to Belfast can be made. They don't run on Sunday. Bus Nos 156, 162 and 252 travel to Larne five times daily on weekdays, three times daily on weekends. From Larne it's a short hop to Belfast.

See the introduction to this chapter for information on the summertime Antrim Coaster bus.

CUSHENDALL

The red sandstone tower at the crossroads of this picturesque little village was built in the early 19th century by Francis Turnly. From the village the B14 road runs inland to Glenariff Forest Park, in the loveliest of Antrim's nine glens, whence the A43 rejoins the A2 south of Cushendall (Bun Abhann Dalla) at Glenariff, also called Waterfoot. The bay that the village overlooks is known as the Moyle. On a clear day you can see across to the Mull of Kintyre and the Scottish mainland.

About 5000 years ago, stone from nearby Tievebulliagh Mountain, was the basis of an important stone-axe industry.

Information

The tourist office (☎ 012667-71180), in Mill St, is run by the Glens of Antrim Historical Society. It opens February to May, Monday to Saturday 10 am to 1 pm; June to September it also opens 2.30 to 5 pm. Boats and tackle can be hired for sea fishing from Red Bay Boats (☎ 012667-71331/71373) signposted off the main coast road.

The telephone code is ☎ 012667.

Layde Old Church

This ruined church and churchyard stand beside a fast-flowing stream that heads down to the sea. The church is believed to have been founded by Franciscans but was used as a parish church from the early 14th century until 1790. The tombstones in the graveyard include MacDonnell memorials, and there's a rather pagan-looking one with a hole through it, immediately on the left after you enter the grounds. The church is over 1km up a steep coast road (not the A2) which goes north to Cushendun and passes the YHANI hostel. There's a car park outside and a coastal footpath nearby.

Ossian's Grave
Romantically, but inaccurately, named after the legendary warrior-poet of the 3rd century AD, this Neolithic court tomb consists of a two chambered burial ground once enclosed by an oval cairn. The site is signposted off the A2 outside Cushendall on the Cushendun side. You can park at the farm and walk up.

Glenariff Forest Park
Over 800 hectares of woodland make up the park, and the main attraction is Ess-na-Larach Waterfall, about half an hour's walk from the visitors' centre. There are various other walks, not all clearly marked; the longest is a three hour circular mountain trail. Views of the valley led the writer Thackeray to exclaim that it was a 'Switzerland in miniature'. There's a £2.50 charge for cars, £1.50 for motorcycles and £1 (children 50p) for pedestrians. If you park at the Manor Lodge Restaurant, on the road to the forest park, you only need to pay the pedestrian fee.

Opposite the entrance to the park is the start of **The Moyle Way**, which leads 32km north to Ballycastle.

Places to Stay
Camping & Hostel Camping is possible at *Glenariff Forest Caravan Park* (☎ 58232), outside the forest park, while *Glenville Caravan Park* (☎ 71520) on the Layde road has a small camping area, charging £3 for a tent for two. *Cushendall Caravan Park* (☎ 71699) on the coast road and overlooking the Moyle, is bigger and pricier at £4.40 a tent site.

The YHANI *Cushendall Hostel* (☎ 71344) costs £7 and is on the Layde road that leads from Cushendall village up to Layde Old Church. It sometimes gets booked out by large groups so ring ahead.

Hotels & B&Bs *Thornlea Hotel* (☎ 71223), 6 Coast Rd, has singles/doubles for £35/55 including breakfast. Next door, *Tros-ben-villa* (☎ 71130), at No 8, does B&B for £20/35. Farther up, at 1 Kilnadore Rd off Coast Rd, *Mountain View* (☎ 71246) is cheaper, with beds at £14/28. In the centre is *Riverside Guest House* (☎ 71655), 14 Mill St, with singles/doubles for £17/30. Closer to Waterfoot, at *Moyle View* (☎ 71580), 2 Ardmoyle Park, Moira makes you feel very much at home; B&B costs £16.

Places to Eat
Gillans Coffee Shop, in Mill St, does a great Ulster fry and snacks all day. Midweek, *Thornlea Hotel*, 6 Coast Rd, has a set dinner menu for £9.50; at weekends it's à la carte only. *Harry's Restaurant* (☎ 72022), in the village centre, looks more like a pub that does meals; it has bar snacks for around £3 while mains like Mexican chicken are £6.95. Glenariff Forest Park has its own *Glenariff Tea House*, open for snacks daily March to October. On the road to the park *Manor Lodge* (☎ 58221), 120 Glen Rd, does steaks and seafood; lemon cod is £9.95. In Waterfoot, pub food is available from *Glenariff Inn*.

Entertainment
On Friday nights, *Joe McCollam's* bar is the place to go for traditional Irish music.

Getting There & Away
The buses serving Cushendall are the same as for Cushendun: bus Nos 120 and 150 go to Ballymena and Belfast daily except Sunday; bus Nos 156, 162 and 252 go to Larne daily; bus No 252 also goes to Portrush.

Getting Around
YHANI Cushendall Hostel hires out bikes for £6 a day.

CARNLOUGH

The good beach attracts holidaymakers, and there are many buildings made of the fine local limestone, commissioned to be built by the marquess of Londonderry in 1854. The limestone quarries were in use until the early 1960s, with the white stone bridge across the village carrying trains that brought the stone down to the harbour to be loaded on to ships for export.

The tourist office is in McKillop's store on Harbour Rd.

The telephone code is ☎ 01574.

Places to Stay

Camping Both *Bay View Caravan Park* (☎ 885685), 89 Largy Rd, and *Whitehill Caravan Park* (☎ 885233), 30A Whitehill Rd, have limited camping space and charge £5 per night.

Hotel The prosperous, solid *Londonderry Arms Hotel* (☎ 885255), 20 Harbour Rd, was built as a coaching inn by the marchioness of Londonderry in 1848. It was eventually inherited by a distant relation of hers, William Churchill, who sold it to the present owners. Singles/doubles cost £45/75, but there are specials worth enquiring about.

Places to Eat

The *Londonderry Arms Hotel* serves up locally caught fish, and a wild salmon steak for £9 is difficult to resist. The *Arkle Bar* in the hotel, named by loyal followers of the Irish horse that won 27 of its 35 races before being put down in 1970, is decorated with photographs of the famous horse. *Glencloy Inn* (☎ 885226), at the junction of Harbour Rd and Bridge St, does food; steak burgers cost £4.95. The *Harbour House Tea Rooms* (☎ 885056), by the harbour, serves teas and light meals until 9 pm.

Getting There & Away

Bus No 128 travels to and from Ballymena five times a daily Monday to Saturday, with connections to Belfast; bus No 252 also goes to Belfast. Bus No 162 between Cushendun and Larne stops at Carnlough.

See the introduction to this chapter for information on the summertime Antrim Coaster bus.

GLENARM

Glenarm (Gleann Arma), the oldest village in the glens, is 5km south of Carnlough and the first one you come to if you're travelling north from Belfast or Larne. The pavements are made from attractive black and white pebbling and many of the buildings are coated white from the limestone dust of the local quarries. In the glen stands **Glenarm Castle** dating from the early 17th century; it was remodelled in the 19th century and is privately owned.

Places to Stay & Eat

If you're coming from Carnlough, turn right at the crossroads for *Margaret's House* (☎ 01574-841307), 10 Altmore St, which does B&B for £14 a head and also has a café. *Mrs Dempsey* (☎ 01574-841640), 35 The Cloney, charges £16 per person for B&B. *Drumnagreagh Hotel* (☎ 01574-841651), 408 Coast Rd, has singles/doubles for £40/60, The hotel is the best place for a meal, though the *Poacher's Pocket* is OK for grills and salad; sausage and champ costs £2.95. There's often live music here at weekends.

Getting There & Away

Bus Nos 162 and 252 go daily to Belfast, Carnlough and Cushendun.

LARNE

Arriving from Scotland, Larne (Lutharna) offers a poor introduction to the spectacular Antrim coast and the rest of Northern Ireland. Conversely, if you've travelled down the coast, you might almost have forgotten the North's troubles until the sectarian graffiti around Larne brings it back again. There's not much to linger for in Larne.

Orientation & Information

It's about 15 minutes' walk from the ferry terminal to the town centre; take Fleet St on the right as you leave the terminal, then turn right again along Curran Rd, which becomes Main St and runs through the centre of town.

Inside the ferry terminal there's a small tourist information office with a helpful list of B&B phone numbers beside the phone booths. The main tourist office (☎ 01574-260088), is in Narrow Gauge Rd. October to Easter it opens weekdays 9 am to 5 pm; Easter to June and September it opens Monday to Saturday 9 am to 5 pm; July and August it opens Monday to Wednesday 9 am to 5 pm, Thursday and Friday to 7.30 pm, Saturday to 6 pm. As you leave Larne Town station, it's in the car park on the far side of the roundabout.

The telephone code is ☎ 01574.

Things to See

Crumbling away at the end of a row of terraced housing, **Olderfleet Castle** is an uninspiring example of a ruined 16th century tower-house; to get there from the ferry terminal, take Olderfleet Rd along the seafront and turn right following the signpost at the roundabout. More imposing is the 19th century round **Chaine Memorial Tower**, north of the ferry terminal in Chaine Memorial Rd. It was built to commemorate James Chaine, an MP from 1855 to 1874. Chaine played an important role in getting Larne Harbour expanded to handle traffic with North America.

Heading along Curran Rd into town you'll pass two other reminders of Larne's American links. A statue of a family group commemorates the 52 people who emigrated to Boston from Larne on the *Friend's Goodwill* in 1717, while a plaque commemorates the arrival of the first Americans into Larne during WWII in 1942.

Places to Stay

Camping The most convenient campsite, if you're just off a ferry or you want to stay near the terminal, is *Curran Caravan Park* (☎ 273797), five minutes from the harbour, on the left of Curran Rd, and reached by following the sign to the town centre. It costs £6.50 a night. One of Ireland's better little campsites is at *Carnfunnock Country Park*

(☎ 270541), nearly 5km north of town off the A2. It's a modest place but well run and pleasantly situated. A tent costs £5.50 a night. There's also *Browns Bay Caravan Park* (☎ 260088) on Islandmagee (see the following section).

B&Bs Closest to the harbour are a couple of B&Bs in Olderfleet Rd: *Manor Guesthouse* at No 23 (☎ 273305) with rooms for £24/30 a single/double, and the *Bellevue* at No 35 with beds for £13.50/27.50. Along Curran Rd, also within walking distance of the harbour, are *Moneydara* (☎ 272912), 149 Curran Rd, with rooms for £16/30, and the very comfortable *Seaview Guest House* (☎ 272438), across the road at No 156, charging £19/36. Even cheaper is *Killyneedan* (☎ 274943), 52 Bay Rd, with beds at £15 per person.

Hotels *Curran Court Hotel* (☎ 275505), 84 Curran Rd near the harbour and just past the campsite, charges £45 a double, while *Kilwaughter House* (☎ 272591), 61 Shanes Hill Rd, charges £40. *Magheramorne House Hotel* (☎ 279444), 59 Shore Rd, is a classy Victorian establishment on the A2 south of Larne, at £48.50/66. On Donaghy's Lane, just 1.5km from town, *Highways Hotel* (☎ 272272) has rooms for £45/67.50.

Places to Eat

The cafeteria-style *Captain's Kitchen* in the ferry terminal makes a good fallback for hot and cold food at odd hours. Inexpensive places are at the harbour end of Main St. *The Bailie*, at No 111-13, does reasonably priced bar meals; braised steak and onions are £4.25. *Lotus Flower* Chinese takeaway, popular with taxi drivers, is next door. *Carriages*, at No 105, does reasonable pizzas, kebabs and seafood (grilled salmon costs £9.95) and opens noon to 11 pm Monday to Saturday. *Upper Crust* cafe, at No 28, has steak meals for only £4.

More typically Irish meals – meat-dependent and substantial – are available at the hotels.

Getting There & Away

Bus Bus No 156 is the regular service to and from Belfast. The earliest bus leaves the bus station (☎ 272345) on Circular Rd, without calling at the harbour, at 7.15 am and the last one goes at 7.20 pm. It takes just over an hour and there are only three buses on a Sunday. Bus No 162 to Cushendun usually operates only from the bus station; late May to late September, it also operates twice daily via the harbour.

See Getting Around at the start of this chapter for information on the Antrim Coaster bus.

Train Larne has two stations: the main Larne Town station (☎ 260604) for the town centre and Larne Harbour (the end of the line) for the ferries. The journey from Belfast Central takes about 50 minutes.

Ferry P&O and Stena Sealink share Larne's ferry terminal, beside a train station and bus stop and with car hire and foreign exchange facilities inside. P&O handles the route from Larne to Cairnryan and Stena Sealink the route from Larne to Stranraer, both in Scotland; crossings take just over two hours. Note that the ferries get very busy over public holidays, when advance booking is advisable.

For details of P&O's sailings contact the P&O Travel Centre (☎ 274321), Passenger Terminal, Larne Harbour, BT40 1AQ. For Stena Sealink details contact the Sealink Travel Centre (☎ 273616), Passenger Terminal, Larne Harbour, BT40 1AW. For more information, including fares, see the Sea section in the Getting There & Away chapter.

ISLANDMAGEE

A day trip to Islandmagee (or Island Magee; Oileán Mhic Aodha in Irish) makes a pleasant excursion. The name is deceptive in that this is an 11 by 3km peninsula, not an island – but you get there by ferry from Larne. Close to the ferry landing point is the **Ballylumford Dolmen** in the front garden of a private home. Also at this north end of the peninsula is **Brown's Bay**, which has a

sandy beach. Open April to September, *Brown's Bay Caravan Park* (☎ 01574-260088) has tent sites for £4.50.

Taking the picturesque east coast road (B150) brings you to the **Gobbins**: over a mile of basalt cliffs with a path cut into the rock. During the 1641 rebellion, the garrison at Carrickfergus, seeking to revenge their fellow Protestants, massacred the Catholic inhabitants of the peninsula, throwing live and dead bodies over the cliffs.

Getting There & Away

The first Islandmagee ferries leave Larne at 7.30, 8 and 8.30 am, then hourly on the hour until 3 pm, and then every half hour until 5.30 pm; contact Larne Harbour Office (☎ 01574-279221) for more details.

CARRICKFERGUS & AROUND

Carrickfergus (Carraig Fhearghais) is a commuter suburb just north of Belfast, noted for its wonderfully situated castle, overlooking the harbour where William III landed on 14 June 1690; there's a commemorative blue plaque on the site and a statue of the king on the seaward side of the castle. The town centre has some attractive 18th century houses, and you can still trace a good part of the 17th century city walls. Touches of kitsch abound; look out for the painted depiction of medieval life on a gable wall opposite the town hall at the end of High St.

Orientation & Information

The train station is at the northern end of North St. Turn left outside the station and pass under North Gate; the castle is five minutes' walk downhill to the seafront. Ulsterbuses stop on Joymount Parade behind the town hall on the seafront.

The tourist information centre (☎ 01960-366455) is on Antrim St inside the Heritage Plaza housing the Knight Ride and open the same hours (see below).

The telephone code is ☎ 01960.

Carrickfergus Castle

Theatrically sited on a rocky promontory, commanding the entrance to Belfast Lough, this fine castle was built by John de Courcy soon after his 1177 invasion of Ulster. Besieged by King John in 1210 and Edward Bruce in 1315, and briefly captured by the French in 1760, the castle also witnessed an attack on a British vessel in 1778 by the American John Paul Jones in the *Ranger* (the Americans won). The oldest part of the castle, going back to its Anglo-Norman origins, is the inner ward which is enclosed by a high wall. The keep houses a museum telling the castle's history, and the site is dotted with life-size figures illustrating the castle's history and adding colour to what is undoubtedly Ireland's finest (and first) Norman castle.

The castle (☎ 351273) opens April to September, Monday to Saturday 10 am to 6 pm, Sunday 2 to 6 pm; October to March it closes at 4 pm. Entry is £2.70/1.35, but joint tickets covering the Knight Ride as well cost £4.85/2.40.

Knight Ride
Inside the glistening, glassy Heritage Plaza on Antrim St is a smells-and-all ride through Carrickfergus's past. Seated in a giant knight's helmet hanging beneath a monorail you swing out over the atrium and then run back through time, catching quick glimpses of Mary Dunbar's haunted house and the hanging corpses of members of the 18th century O'Haughan gang. There's also more serious stuff about the castle narrated from the point of view of a child and his grandfather. Afterwards, you can recap the details on descriptive charts and examine a model of Carrickfergus in 1690 on the way out.

The Knight Ride (☎ 366455) opens April to September Monday to Saturday 10 am to 6 pm, Sunday noon to 6 pm; the rest of the year it closes at 5 pm. Admission costs £2.70/1.35; or £4.85/2.40 for a combined ticket for the castle too.

St Nicholas' Church
The pillars in the nave date back to the church's establishment immediately after de Courcy's invasion of Ulster. Most of the rest dates to 17th century restoration work, a

particularly fine example of which is the Chichester memorial in the transept known as the Donegal aisle. It's probably the work of an English master mason who was influenced by the Renaissance style of northern Europe. Stained glass in the south side and the nave's west end is 16th century Irish work.

To gain admission call at or telephone the church office (☎ 360061), 3 Market Place, between 9.30 am and noon.

Andrew Jackson Centre
The parents of the 7th US president left Carrickfergus in the second half of the 18th century, hence the Andrew Jackson Centre (☎ 366455), a reconstructed dwelling of that era complete with fireside crane and earthen floor. It has displays on the life of Jackson, the Jackson family in Ulster and Ulster's connection with the USA.

Also here is the **US Rangers Centre** with a small exhibition on the first US rangers, who were trained during WWII in Carrickfergus before heading for Europe.

April and May the centre opens 10 am to 1 pm and 2 to 4 pm weekdays, 2 to 4 pm weekends; June to September it stays open till 6 pm. Admission is £1.50/75p. The centre is in Boneybefore, 3km north of Carrickfergus; there's a signposted right turn to the centre in Donaldson's Ave. The actual site of the ancestral home is indicated by a blue plaque just down the road from the centre. On weekdays you can get a bus to Downshire Rd from where it's a short walk.

Places to Stay
The least expensive B&B at £13 per person is the charming two-storey *Marathon House* (☎ 01232-862475), 3 Upper Station Rd, in the village of Greenisland south of town. In Carrickfergus, *Marina House* (☎ 364055), 47-49 Irish Quarter South, does B&B for £20 a head, while the *Langsgarden* (☎ 366369), 70-72 Scottish Quarter, charges £17. *Dobbin's Inn Hotel* (☎ 351905), 6-8 High St, has been around for over three centuries and has a priest's hole and 16th century fireplace

to prove it; it charges £44/64 for a single/double.

Places to Eat

For snacks and coffee, *Number 10* along the pedestrianised West St is OK; breakfast specials cost only £1.90. Similar is *Old Tech Griddle*, farther up from Dobbin's Inn Hotel; it also bakes good bread. Monday to Saturday, *Courtyard Coffee House*, 38 Scotch Quarter, serves light lunches as well as rich cakes; it has a smaller branch inside Carrickfergus Castle. The restaurant at *Dobbin's Inn Hotel* serves bar meals plus a set lunch and dinner; cajun chicken is £6.95.

Getting There & Away

Ulsterbus No 165 takes 15 minutes to Belfast's Laganside Buscentre; bus No 163 takes 30 minutes. There are also regular daily trains from Belfast Central/Botanic stations (£1.80 one way).

ANTRIM

Antrim (Aontroim) is no more interesting than the rest of inland County Antrim. In 1649 the town was burnt by General Monro, and in 1798 it resisted an attack by the United Irishmen. Modern Antrim Town is dominated by its shopping centre, but there are a few older buildings, including the fine courthouse which dates back to 1762.

Belfast airport is handy, only 6km to the south.

Information

The very helpful tourist office (☎ 01849-428331), at Pogue's Entry off Church St, the main street, opens May to September, Monday to Saturday 9.30 am to 6 pm, and provides a free heritage trail guide.

The telephone code is ☎ 01849.

Things to See

In **Pogue's Entry**, a narrow alley at the end of Church St, a blue plaque marks the tiny, mud-floored home of Alexander Irvine (1863-1941), missionary and writer. His *My Lady of the Chimney Corner* tells the story of his mother's brave struggle to rear nine children in grinding poverty. **Antrim Castle Gardens**, behind the courthouse, alongside Sixmilewater River, were originally laid out in the 17th century. Antrim Castle burnt down many years ago but the gardens are open to the public. Although some parts are a bit neglected this is a good place for a summer picnic.

A 10th century **round tower**, 27m high, in Steeple Park about 1.5km north of town, is all that remains of a monastery that once stood on the site. The walls are over 1m thick and the 10th century dating is strong evidence for linking this and other towers with the Viking raids. Follow the signs for Steeple Industrial Estate, then for the Antrim Borough Council offices.

Places to Stay

It's best to avoid having to stay a night in Antrim if possible. *Sixmilewater Caravan Park* (☎ 463113), is near the Antrim Forum sports complex south-west of town. Washing facilities are a long walk away at the Forum which is locked outside office hours. The campsite itself is only an open field and there's no security. Tent sites cost £3.

There are a few B&Bs in town, which include *Springhill* (☎ 469117), 37 Thornhill Rd, with rooms for £16.50 per person. Down the road at No 23, *Mr & Mrs Dennison* (☎ 462964) have rooms for £15 per person. More B&Bs are found in nearby Crumlin which is convenient for early morning flight departures. The tourist office has a complete list.

There's only one hotel, *Deerpark Hotel* (☎ 462480), 71 Dublin Rd, with singles/doubles for £40/60 including breakfast.

Places to Eat

Antrim is hardly filled with gourmet restaurants but for a light lunch you could try *Lisa's Kitchen* in Church St, down the hill from the tourist office. Farther down, the *Old Rogue* pub near the courthouse would do nicely for a drink afterwards. *Morwood's Sandwich Bar & Bakery* does home-made sandwiches and cakes.

Entertainment

Clotworthy Arts Centre (☎ 428111) in Antrim Castle Gardens has a small theatre and hosts changing exhibitions. The gallery opens weekdays 9.30 am to 4.30 pm, Saturday to 1 pm, Sunday to 9.30 pm; admission is free. To find out what's on at the theatre without calling in try the tourist office or the local paper.

Getting There & Away

Bus No 120 from Ballymena to Belfast stops in Antrim. There's also bus No 109 to Belfast via Lisburn.

AROUND ANTRIM CITY
Lough Neagh

The largest lake in Britain and Ireland, Lough Neagh (Loch nEathach) covers 400 sq km, and legend has it that the giant Finn McCool created it by scooping out a lump of earth and throwing it into the Irish Sea, thus also creating the Isle of Man (which does bear a resemblance in shape and size to the lough). Of Northern Ireland's six counties, only County Fermanagh doesn't border the lake.

The *Maid of Antrim* (☎ 463113, 465961 recorded information) cruises the lough but the schedule varies according to demand and weather conditions; it's best to phone or check with the tourist office. One-hour trips cost £3/1.80 and leave at 2, 3.30 and 5 pm. The boat leaves from the marina just past the Antrim Forum.

Shane's Castle

The castle, once the seat of the O'Neills of Clandaboy, is on the western outskirts of Antrim on the A6. The castle isn't open to the public but you can visit the well-maintained demesne, part of which is a nature reserve.

Patterson's Spade Mill

The National Trust owns Ireland's last surviving water-driven mill (☎ 01849-433619) for making spades. There are continuous demonstrations of the processes involved in spade manufacture and a chance to buy your own spade should you have a spare £25 or so. June to August the mill opens Wednesday to Monday 2 to 6 pm. In April, May and September it opens weekends 2 to 6 pm. Admission is £2.50/1.25. To get there, follow the A6 through Templepatrick towards Belfast and it's 3km along on the left.

Randalstown

Six km west of Antrim the River Main flows under an aqueduct through Randalstown (Baile Raghnaill). The town has a 1790 **Presbyterian church** that's worth a second look – a magnificent oval building with an octagonal porch. You can only get inside during services. On the A6 toward Toome is **Randalswood Forest**, which extends to the shore of Lough Neagh and has walking trails, wildfowl and a herd of deer.

BALLYMENA & AROUND

As you enter the town of Ballymena (An Baile Meánach), a large sign proclaims it the 'City of the Seven Towers'. The story goes that one Sir Alexander Shafto Adair, owner of the Ballymena Estate, was standing on raised ground looking at the town when it occurred to him that you could see the towers of the old and new Episcopalian churches, the First Ballymena Presbyterian church, the Roman Catholic church, the town hall, the Braidwater spinning mill and the castle. The castle has since been demolished and the mill only ever had a chimney, not a tower, but you can pick up a tower trail for £1 in Morrow's Shop Museum (see below).

This is the home town of Ian Paisley, founder leader of the Free Presbyterian Church and the stridently anti-Catholic Democratic Unionist Party. The town council was the first in the North to fall under control of the Democratic Unionist Party in 1977 and voted unanimously to remove all mention of Darwin's theory of evolution from religious education in Ballymena's schools, for, as the mayor explained, 'if you believe you come from a monkey you'll act like a monkey'. For those for whom politics is a closed book, it's also the birthplace of actor Liam Neeson of *Schindler's List* and *Michael Collins* fame.

While Ballymena is a pleasant enough small town, there's not much reason to linger. The tourist office (☎ 653663), 80 Galgorm Rd, opens May to October 10.30 am to 5 pm Monday to Friday, Saturday 10 am to 4 pm. At other times contact Ballymena Borough Council (☎ 01266-44111).

The telephone code is ☎ 01266.

Morrow's Shop Museum

In this museum, 13-15 Bridge St, there's a small and not very inspiring exhibition of local historical bits and bobs. It opens weekdays 10 am to 1 pm and 2 to 5 pm, Saturday 10 am to 1 pm.

Arthur Cottage

The ancestors of Chester Alan Arthur, the 21st president of the USA, lived in a simple cottage about 6km north-west of Ballymena, near the village of Cullybackey. It's open to visitors May to September weekdays 10.30 am to 5 pm, Saturday 4 pm. Interpreters in traditional costume demonstrate baking and quilting throughout June, July (except on the 12th) and August; call the tourist office for dates and times. Admission is £1.10/55p. Take bus No 113 or 115 from Ballymena.

Gracehill

In the mid-18th century many Moravians fled their homeland to escape religious persecution and some of them settled in Gracehill (Baile Uí Chinnéide), 2km east of Ballymena, where they became part of the larger Protestant community persecuting the Catholics. The Georgian architecture of their elegant village square includes a church (on the right as you enter the square) with separate entrances for men and women worshippers. If you'd like to see inside, visitors are welcome to Sunday services at 11 am. Even the graveyard at the back of the church is laid out for men on the left and women on the right, with the numbered tombstones lying flat either side of the walkway! Man

and woman alike, they're rapidly vanishing beneath a coating of moss and grass.

Bus No 127 from Ballymena stops at Gracehill. If you're driving, take the A42 past Ballymena's bus and rail station; look for a brown sign with a church marked on it and take the turning to the left.

Places to Eat

If you're passing through and just want somewhere for lunch, the *Rendezvous Coffee Shop*, Balleymoney St near the car park, does an Ulster fry (£1.95) and good soup-style lunches. Alternatively, try the *Fern Room* in McKillen's department store, in Church St uphill from the tourist office; roast salmon is £4.50.

Getting There & Away

Bus Nos 120, 149, 219 and 220 run south to Belfast, while bus Nos 115, 175 and 143 head north to Derry. Ballymena sits at the junction of a number of A roads. From Belfast, take the A52 then A26, a journey of 18km.

LISBURN & AROUND

The small town of Lisburn (Lios na gCearrbhach) is about a 30 minute bus ride south-west of Belfast, and is most noted today as the location of Long Kesh (aka the Maze) prison.

In the early 1600s the Crown gave the Conways a lease to settle Lisburn. In 1627 they were also given permission to hold a Tuesday market which continues to this day (beside the bus terminal), making Tuesday the best day for a visit. A disastrous fire in 1707 destroyed much of Lisburn but the 17th century Market House survived to become an assembly hall in the 18th century.

In the 18th and 19th centuries Lisburn grew rich on the proceeds of the linen industry; the modern post office in Linenhall St stands on the site of the old Brown Linen Hall where unbleached linen used to be sold. In the 18th century John Wesley came here several times, preaching in 1789 at Lisburn's first Methodist church in Market St.

Nowadays the main reason to come here

is to see the Irish Linen Centre & Lisburn Museum, a visit to which is included in Irish Linen Tours (see Information under Banbridge, County Down).

Information

The tourist office (☎ 01846-663377) is in the same building as the Lisburn Museum, on Market Square. It opens April to September Monday to Saturday 9.30 am to 5.30 pm, Sunday 2 to 5.30 pm, closing half an hour earlier the rest of the year. It has a bureau de change and can book accommodation.

The telephone code is ☎ 01846.

Irish Linen Centre & Lisburn Museum

The Irish Linen Centre, inside what was once a drapery shop, is beside Lisburn Museum, itself housed in the fine old Market House where brown linen was sold in the 18th century.

Visits start in the Lisburn Museum on the ground floor where there are models of 18th century linen traders in action. Upstairs in the Irish Linen Centre are temporary exhibits in what were the old Assembly Rooms; you then proceed through a series of rooms which explain the creation and use of linen, with hand-loom damask weavers in period costume to illustrate their trade. There are plenty of audiovisuals and hands-on exhibits to keep everyone amused. Finally you descend to the basement to see an audiovisual presentation about life in the 19th century linen factories.

Entry to Lisburn Museum is free but admission to the Irish Linen Centre costs £2.75/1.75. Both open the same hours as the tourist office.

Other Attractions

Opposite a fine 19th century building in Castle St which has had Lisburn College tacked onto it, **Castle Gardens Park** contains a monument to Sir Richard Wallace, a large cannon, some pieces of city wall and fountains springing from stone birds.

With your own transport you could visit **Ballance House** (☎ 648492), 118A Lisburn Rd, Glenavy, 8.5km north-west of Lisburn. It's the birthplace of former New Zealand prime minister John Ballance (1839-1893). The farmhouse has been restored to its assumed appearance in 1850 and opens April to September, Tuesday to Friday 11 am to 5 pm, weekends 2 to 5 pm. Entry is £2/50p.

Places to Stay & Eat

You can easily visit Lisburn from Belfast but if you do want to stay, *Strathearn House* (☎ 601661), 19 Antrim Rd, has rooms for £20/36 a single/double. *Overdale House* (☎ 01846-672275) at 150 Belsize Rd charges £20/30.

Probably the best place to eat is *Café Crommelin* in Lisburn Museum which does sandwiches and baguettes for £2.35 to £3.15, or a wonderful selection of filled pastries. *Toffs*, 6 Railway St, is owned by the same people and does curries and lasagnes for under £4. *Jeffers Home Bakery & Coffee House* near the museum entrance, does good coffee and cakes.

Getting There & Away

Bus Nos 38, 51, 109, 523 and 525 leave frequently from Belfast's Europa Buscentre. From Lisburn you can catch onward buses to Hillsborough, Banbridge and Newry. For more information contact the local Ulsterbus office (☎ 662091), 2A Smithfield Square.

Counties Tyrone & Fermanagh

While Tyrone is the larger of these two counties (in fact, it is the biggest county in Northern Ireland), Fermanagh attracts more visitors with its lakes, rivers and medieval sites. In Tyrone the Sperrin Mountains are still relatively unspoiled and offer good hiking opportunities. No trains operate in this part of Ireland, but Ulsterbus has services to most towns and the larger villages.

County Tyrone

The attractions of County Tyrone – forest parks, prehistoric sites, the lonely Sperrin Mountains – are sprinkled among some less-than-interesting towns in a way that makes it difficult for visitors to get a feel for the county as a whole. But it's worth the effort of trying to get to know Tyrone for the county has an illustrious history, and its unspoiled countryside is ideal for those wanting to 'get away from it all'.

For centuries County Tyrone had been the territory of the O'Neills, until March 1603 when Hugh O'Neill, earl of Tyrone, finally submitted to the English at Mellifont. This marked the end of Gaelic Ireland. The English and Scottish planters moved in, introducing linen in the 18th century. Many local people subsequently migrated to America, and there are still strong links with the USA today. The huge Ulster-American Folk Park near Omagh, sufficient reason in itself for visiting Tyrone, tells the story.

OMAGH
The county town of Tyrone, Omagh (An Óghmagh) is pleasantly situated at the confluence of the Camowen and Drumragh rivers, which join to form the River Strule. Although there are no special attractions in the town itself, Omagh serves as a useful base for the surrounding area, and there are plenty of restaurants and shops. It's also a

Locator & Map Index

Highlights

- Visit the Ulster-American Folk Park, 8km north of Omagh, one of the best museums in Ireland

- Explore the lonely Sperrin Mountains, 64km from east to west, which straddle the border with Derry

- Enjoy fishing and relaxing cruises on Upper and Lower Lough Erne, which stretches for 80km from the North to the South

- Spend time on the islands of Lough Erne, which contains many Celtic and early Christian archaeological sites

- View the Janus figure on Boa Island, one of the oldest stone statues in Ireland

- Discover the round tower on Devenish Island, one of the best in the country

useful start or finish to a trip to the Sperrin Mountains or a section of the Ulster Way.

Information
From the confluence of the rivers, Market St and then High St lead west to the neoclassical 19th century courthouse. The tourist office

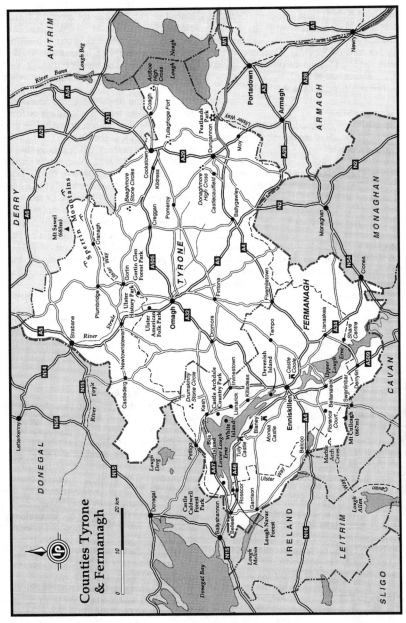

Counties Tyrone & Fermanagh

TYRONE & FERMANAGH

(☎ 01662-247831) is in the Sperrin Centre at 1 Market St. It opens from 9 am to 5 pm Monday to Friday and, from April to September, also on Saturday. There are several banks on High St, and the post office is next to the courthouse at No 7.

The telephone code is ☎ 01662.

Places to Stay

There's little accommodation in the centre of town. For details of the nearest campsite see Around Omagh.

Hostel The IHH *Omagh Independent Hostel* (☎ 241973), 9A Waterworks Rd, is 4km north-east of town on the B48 to Gortin. From the bus station walk north on Mountjoy Rd, turn east at Killybrack Rd and follow the signs. It has 29 beds (three of which are adapted for wheelchair users) and charges £6.50; the one private room costs the same per person. It rents bikes and opens all year. If you ring from the station, they'll come and pick you up.

B&Bs A standard B&B close to the centre and charging £15 per person, is *Ardmore* (☎ 243381), 12 Tamlaght Rd. Go up High St from the tourist office, heading for the courthouse at the top of the street and take the left turn in front of the church into John St. Follow its continuation (James St) south and Tamlaght Rd is the second turning on the right. Farther south at 63 Dromore Rd is the *Four Winds* (☎ 243554), which charges £17 per person for each of its three rooms. *Arleston House* (☎ 241719), 1 Arleston Park off the Cookstown road to the east, has two rooms at £15 per person.

Hotels Omagh's oldest hotel – it dates from 1787 – is the 21-room *Royal Arms* (☎ 243262), 51-53 High St, just west of the tourist office. Singles/doubles cost £40/75 for B&B. The *Silverbirch Hotel* (☎ 242520), 5 Gortin Rd, has 46 rooms, all with bathroom, and charges £35/60 for B&B.

Places to Eat

The *Memory Lane Lounge* in the Royal Arms hotel has pub lunches for around £4 and dinners for a couple of pounds more. The *Hunting Lodge*, also in the hotel, is a coffee lounge with tempting home-made snacks and sandwiches. The hotel's restaurant, the *Village Gossip*, has dinner for two for about £25.

Opposite the Royal Arms, the *Shoppers' Restaurant* does lunches and salads as does the *Salad Bowl* on Market St just before the turn on Dublin Rd. The *Carlton* on High St does excellent pastries and breads and has a coffee shop at the back. Next to the courthouse at 2 High St, *Dragon Castle* is a Chinese restaurant that also serves European food, with main dishes between £4 and £6.

On Bridge St toward the bus station *Joe's* is suitable for fast-food fans and the nearby *Bridge* has breakfasts for around £2. The *Clock Pub* in the shopping mall off Bridge St has decent lunches for less than £4, and the *Expressway* opposite the bus station has a carvery and coffee shop.

Out of town, on the A5 road to Newtownstewart about 1.5km from the Ulster-American Folk Park, is the *Mellon Country Inn* (☎ 61224), 134 Beltany Rd. It serves good food, with reasonable buffet lunches from £6.

Getting There & Away

Ulsterbus services connect Omagh with a number of towns in the North and in the Republic. Bus No 273 runs eight times daily (five on Sunday) to Belfast (1¾ hours) and nine times (five on Sunday) to Derry (1¼ hours). Bus No 274 runs six times daily (four on Sunday) from Omagh to Dublin (three hours) via Monaghan (50 minutes) and Slane. A number of other buses leave Omagh for Dungannon (bus No 78) and Enniskillen (bus No 94), where you change for Donegal, Killybegs and Glenties. Bus No 296 leaves Omagh for Cork (9¼ hours) once a day Monday to Saturday at 10 am and travels via Longford, Athlone and Cahir.

The bus station (☎ 242711), 3 Mountjoy Rd, is a short walk north of the town centre along Bridge St and across the River Strule.

Getting Around

Bicycles can be hired from Conway Cycles (☎ 246195), 1 Old Market Place, for £7/30 a day/week. Apart from the hostel, there are no bike-hire places closer to the Sperrin Mountains.

AROUND OMAGH
Ulster-American Folk Park

This is one of the best museums (☎ 01662-243292) in Ireland and well worth a visit. Thousands of Ulster people left their country to forge a new life across the Atlantic in the 18th and 19th centuries; 200,000 emigrated in the 1700s alone. The American Declaration of Independence was signed by several Ulstermen, and the Exhibition Hall is able to offer many more examples of this transatlantic link.

The real appeal of the folk park, though, is the outdoor museum. The number of life-size exhibits is impressive: a forge, weaver's cottage, Presbyterian meeting house, schoolhouse, log cabin, a 19th century Ulster street, an early street from western Pennsylvania, a typical one-room cottage dating from before the Potato Famine, and a ship and dockside gallery with reconstructed parts of an emigrants' ship.

Costumed guides and craftspeople are on hand to chat and explain the art of spinning, weaving, candle making and so on. There's almost too much to absorb in one visit, and at least half a day is needed to do the park justice.

Admission is £3.50/1.70/10 for adults/children/families. It opens April to September, 11 am to 6.30 pm Monday to Saturday, and 11.30 am to 7 pm Sunday and public holidays. The rest of the year it's open 10.30 am to 5 pm weekdays only.

The park is 8km north-west of Omagh on the A5 to Newtownstewart. Bus No 97 to Strabane and Derry stops outside the park. On Tuesday and Thursday in July and August only, bus No 213 (the Sperrin Sprinter) leaves Omagh at 1.45 pm and stops at the park 20 minutes later, but you'd need to catch bus No 97 back.

Ulster History Park

The theme of this park is the story of settlements in Ireland from the Stone Age to the 17th century plantation. Full-scale models are on show of a Mesolithic encampment, Neolithic houses, a late Bronze Age crannóg, a 12th century church settlement complete with a stone round tower, and a Norman motte-and-bailey. There's also a reception building (☎ 016626-48188) with a cafeteria, shop and audiovisual theatre and a model plantation settlement from the 17th century. But the park is over-reliant on models and reconstructions, giving it a rather phoney feel.

It's open April to September, Monday to Saturday, 10.30 am to 6.30 pm, and Sunday 11.30 am to 7 pm. October to March the weekday hours are 10.30 am to 5 pm. Admission is £3/1.75.

Ulster History Park is about 10km northeast of Omagh off the B48 road to Gortin. Bus No 92 between Omagh and Gortin stops outside, but there's no Sunday service.

Gortin Glen Forest Park

Over 400 hectares of Gortin Glen Forest form this park, mostly planted with conifers and containing a herd of Japanese Sika deer as well as other wildlife. It's a park suited for cars and motorbikes, and a breathtaking 8km tarmac drive through the forest is the main way to get around. Near the main car park there are some wildlife enclosures, an indoor exhibit, a small nature trail and a café. An entry ticket costs £2.50 for a car (£2 for a motorbike) from the ranger on duty or from the ticket machine.

There's a manageable day's walk from Gortin Forest Park to the Ulster-American Folk Park along a section of the **Ulster Way**. The 16km trip is mostly over small roads, forest roads and tracks, and from the folk park bus No 97 can be caught back to Omagh. The last bus leaves the folk park at 7.30 pm.

A leaflet entitled *The Ulster Way: North-West Section* (£2) covers this area with a map and should be available from the Omagh tourist office or by post from the Sports

Council for Northern Ireland (☎ 01232-381222), House of Sport, Upper Malone Rd, Belfast BT9 5LA.

Fishing

There is fishing along stretches of the three rivers around Omagh – mainly for brown and sea trout and salmon in season (April to mid-October). Permits, advice and information are available in Omagh from CA Anderson (☎ 01662-242311), 64 Market St (entrance on Drumragh Ave) or Chism Fishing Tackle (☎ 01662-244932), above the butcher shop at 2 Bridge St.

Places to Stay

Camping The closest campsite is at *Gortin Glen Caravan Park* (☎ 016626-48108), 10km north-east of Omagh on the B48 Omagh-Gortin road. Tent sites are £4 to £7; caravans are £7. Bus Nos 92 and 213 (July and August only) stop nearby. The campsite is a few minutes from the Ulster Way, and campers get a discount at the Omagh Leisure Centre.

Some 12km north-west of Omagh in New-townstewart on the A5 past the Ulster-American Folk Park is *Harrigan Caravan Park* (☎ 016626-62414). There's only room for half a dozen pitches, and you have to arrive before 5 pm, but it costs just £2/3.50 per tent/caravan and it's open all year.

B&Bs If you want to make a day of it visiting both the Ulster History Park and Ulster-American Folk Park, *Camphill Farm* (☎ 01662-245400) is just south of the latter at 5 Mellon Rd, Mountjoy, and costs £14 per person. Another place charging £13/25 for singles/doubles is *Daleview* (☎ 01662-241182) at 96 Beltany Rd on the A5 just past the folk park. *Derrylynn* (☎ 01662-244256), with four rooms at 13 Beltany Rd, costs £18 per person. Dinner is £12.50.

SPERRIN MOUNTAINS

In the north-east of the county, the gentle contours of the Sperrin Mountains, some 64km from east to west, straddle the border with County Derry. The blanket bog and heather of the open moorland in the upper reaches contrast with the farmland and wooded valleys on the lower slopes. Wildlife is plentiful, and fishing for trout is a popular activity.

The mountains reach their highest point at Mt Sawel (683m) just behind the **Sperrin Heritage Centre** (☎ 016626-48142), 274 Glenelly Rd in Cranagh. In the centre, computer presentations and other displays are devoted to the historical, social and ecological aspects of the region. Gold has been found in the mountains, and part of the exhibition is devoted to it. Barry McGuigan, the Irish world-featherweight-champion boxer, had his first gold medal made from this local precious metal.

The centre opens March to October, 11 am to 6 pm Monday to Friday, Saturday 11.30 am to 6 pm, and Sunday 2 to 7 pm; admission is £1.80/80p. For 65p/35p extra you can try your luck at prospecting for gold in a nearby stream. The centre has a restaurant and café called the *Glenelly Kitchen*.

The centre is on the B47. To get there from Omagh, follow the B48 north-east through Gortin to Plumbridge. From there it's about 13km east on the B47 to Cranagh. Buses from Omagh go only as far as Plumbridge.

While the Sperrin Heritage Centre can be easily reached from Cookstown via the B162 and B47, **An Creagán Visitors' Centre** (☎ 016627-61112) in Creggan is closer, about 20km to the west on the A505. It has an interpretive exhibition, rambling and cycling routes, bikes for rent and a licensed restaurant. Admission is £2/1 and the centre opens April to September, daily 11 am to 6.30 pm, weekdays only the rest of the year 11 am to 4.30 pm.

If you're thinking of **walking** up Mt Sawel, enquire at the centre about the best route to take. The climb is easy, but some farmers are more accommodating than others when hikers cross their land. The Ulster Way comes in this direction, and it could be joined at Leagh's Bridge 6km away. This point is roughly half way along the 55km Dungiven (County Derry) to Gortin section of the trail. Another outdoor trip through the Sperrins is on **horseback**. Edergole Riding Centre (☎ 016487-62924), 70 Moneymore Rd in Cookstown, is a horse-riding school that organises three-day trekking trips through the mountains, or hourly hire for about £8 (see Places to Stay in the Cookstown section).

COOKSTOWN

Until just recently Cookstown (An Chorr Chríochach) represented Northern Ireland at its most forbidding. The town, founded in 1609 by planter Alan Cooke, has a wide, 2.5km-long main street (William St then James St), with Catholics living at one end and Protestants at the other. There's still an army base next to the Catholic school, and the courthouse remains heavily barricaded. But the two heavily guarded army checkpoints, nicknamed the 'daleks', that once stood at both approaches to the main street, have been removed, and the most visible display of authority on the streets these days is the traffic warden.

Information

The tourist office (☎ 016487-66727), 48 Molesworth St, opens April to September, 9 am to 5 pm Monday to Friday, and to 1 pm Saturday. Molesworth St, which runs east off the main street (James St), is the beginning of the B73 road to Coagh on the border with County Derry. During the rest of the year, seek tourist information from the Cookstown District Council Development Office (☎ 016487-62205) on Burn Rd, which runs west off James St. It opens weekdays 9 am to 5 pm.

There's a Bank of Ireland branch on the corner of Molesworth and James Sts. The post office is directly opposite on James St. Near the tourist office, the Laundrette at 45 Molesworth St opens Monday to Saturday 9 am to 5.30 pm.

The telephone code is ☎ 016487.

Places to Stay

The nearest campsite is *Drum Manor Forest Park*; see Around Cookstown for details. The least expensive B&B is the *Central Inn*

(☎ 62255), 27 William St, at £16 per person. *Edergole* (☎ 62924), 70 Moneymore Rd, costs £18 per person and has a horse-riding school. Both B&Bs are open all year.

Hotels in town are the upmarket 53-room *Glenavon House* (☎ 64949), 52 Drum Rd (which is the road to Omagh), at £47.50/75 a single/double for B&B; the cheaper *Greenvale* (☎ 62243) nearby at 57 Drum Rd with a dozen rooms for £35/60; and the *Royal* (☎ 62224), 68 Coagh St, with 10 rooms for £30 per person. All are open year round.

Places to Eat

For takeaways and café cuisine try *Jo Mac's Diner* on Molesworth St. Inexpensive Chinese and European food, with main courses for under £5, is available at *Golden Crown*, 9 William St, and the *Dragon Palace*, at the southern approach to town. The nearby *Taj Mahal* on James St is acceptable for curry. *Rossiter's*, also on the main street 50m from the Central Inn, is good for cheap standard meals (around £3) during the day. A similar place is *Jack's*, a diner-like establishment at 18 James St. A favourite lunch spot (under £5) among locals is the *Courtyard*, upstairs at 56A William St.

Lunch and dinner are available at the three hotels; the *Greenvale* is the most expensive at around £18 for dinner, while *Glenavon House* charges £13 and the *Royal* £15.

Getting There & Away

Bus No 110 connects Cookstown eight to nine times a day with Belfast (1¾ hours) via Antrim, Monday to Saturday (three times on Sunday). The No 278 service runs once or twice a day Monday to Saturday to Dungannon (20 minutes), Armagh (50 minutes) and, in the Republic, Monaghan (1½ hours) and Dublin (four hours). Bus No 80 shuttles regularly between Cookstown and Dungannon, where you can connect with bus No 273 to Belfast, Omagh or Derry. Bus No 89 makes three to five daily trips to Coagh from Monday to Saturday.

The bus station (☎ 66440), which is on

Like Mother, Like Daughter

Bernadette Devlin was born at the Catholic end of Cookstown in 1947. As a student she became involved in the Civil Rights movement, and was elected from the Mid-Ulster constituency to Westminster in 1969 as the youngest-ever MP.

She was imprisoned for her part in the 1969 Bogside confrontation in Derry, and after Bloody Sunday in 1972 her notoriety reached its peak when she physically attacked the British Home Secretary in the House of Commons.

After withdrawing from parliamentary politics, Bernadette McAliskey, as she became known, worked on issues of human rights and social justice.

When an IRA mortar bomb was defused outside Osnabruck barracks in Germany in June 1996, there were few clues to indicate who was responsible. Then later the same year the German police applied to extradite Roisin McAliskey to face charges.

The daughter of Bernadette McAliskey, Roisin was no stranger to controversy. Her staunchly Nationalist family had been attacked in their Cookstown home by a Protestant assassination squad in 1981, an attack which left her mother partially disabled. Roisin herself had been filmed helping to carry the coffin of a leading Republican.

At the time of her arrest Roisin was pregnant. Despite this she was held as a Category A prisoner in a jail designed for men. After determined protest, her security rating was eventually reduced and she was moved to Holloway and then into a prison hospital where she gave birth to a daughter.

It remains to be seen whether the fingerprint evidence that the German police claim to have can justify the charges against McAliskey. ■

Molesworth St near the tourist office, opens weekdays 9 to 11 am, and 1.30 to 5.30 pm.

AROUND COOKSTOWN

No public transport goes directly to the following sights though buses do pass close by. For bus numbers, times and fares check with the bus station (☎ 016487-66440) in Cookstown.

Wellbrook Beetling Mill

Beetling, the final stage in the making of linen, is when the cloth is beaten with wooden hammers, or beetles, to give it a smooth sheen. There were once six such mills at Wellbrook. The hammers were driven by water, and one of the mills (☎ 016487-51735) is maintained by the National Trust and can be seen in operation. It was literally deafening for those employed here.

The beetling mill opens July and August, 2 to 6 pm Wednesday to Monday, while April to June and in September it opens Saturday, Sunday and bank holidays only 2 to 6 pm. Admission is 1.50/75p. Take the A505 Omagh road 5km west to Kildress and turn

right at the church; it's about a km from there.

Cregganconroe Chambered Cairn

This cairn is ancient but not spectacular. The lintel stone has collapsed onto the two portal stones that led into the burial gallery, and the huge capstone has also slipped. The site has not been excavated. To get there, take the A505 west from Cookstown and after a few km look for the signpost for Cregganconroe on the left. From there it is about 6km to the site.

Beaghmore Stone Circles

On the fringe of the Sperrin Mountains, set on desolate moorland near Davagh Forest Park, this series of Bronze Age (2000 to 1200 BC) circles, cairns and stone alignments are a mystery to archaeologists. Preserved in peat, the monuments were only discovered in the mid-1950s. Especially intriguing is the 'Dragon's Teeth', one of the larger of the seven circles. It's filled with closely set stones that jut out of the ground in an apparently random manner. Various explanations have been suggested for these monuments –

religious, astronomical, social – but no one knows for sure.

The circles, 14km north-west of Cookstown, are signposted off the A505 road to Omagh.

Tullaghoge Fort

This hill fort was the burial ground of the O'Hagans, chief justices of early Ireland, and the coronation place of the O'Neills as kings of Ulster in the 11th century. A map dated 1601 marks the spot on the hillside to the south-east where the stone coronation chair stood. The following year the chair was destroyed by General Mountjoy while in pursuit of Hugh O'Neill, the last of the clan to be crowned.

To reach Tullaghoge, leave Cookstown on the A29 Dungannon road south then turn left onto the B520; the fort is 4km south-east of Cookstown. From the car park a path leads to the site.

Ardboe High Cross

The 10th century Ardboe (the 'd' is not pronounced) high cross stands 5.5m high in front of a 6th century monastery site, now housing the ruins of a 17th century church, and with Lough Neagh – the largest lake in Ireland or Britain – in the background, it should be more dramatic than it is. The cross is one of the best preserved in Ulster, with the east face showing Old Testament scenes and the west one New Testament ones. On the east side try to make out Adam and Eve, the sacrifice of Isaac, Daniel and the Lions, the Burning Fiery Furnace, a bishop with people around him, and Christ in glory. The New Testament side has the Magi, the Miracle at Cana, the Miracle of the Loaves and Fishes, the entry into Jerusalem, the arrest of Christ and the Crucifixion. A lot easier to decipher are some of the 18th century tombstones in the churchyard.

Ardboe (Ard Bo) is 16km east of Cookstown on the shore of Lough Neagh. To get there take the B73 through Coagh and turn south just before Newtown Trench.

Places to Stay

Drum Manor Forest Park (☎ 01868-759664), a pleasant place 4km west of Cookstown on the A505 road with a couple of lakes, a butterfly farm and arboretum, has a small camping area for tents only costing £1.60 per person a night and open all year. A new caravan site (from £5.50 to £8.50), with all the mod cons and 30 pitches, is also open year round. If you have a car be sure to arrive before 4 pm when a barrier goes down, and collect a key if you're intending to leave early in the morning.

DUNGANNON

Until 1602, when the castle and town were burned to prevent them falling into the hands of the English, Dungannon (Dún Geanainn) was one of the chief seats of the O'Neill family. Plantation of English and Scottish settlers took place in the 17th and 18th centuries. In 1969 the town entered the history books when the Civil Rights Association, formed a year earlier to protest against the rampant social and political inequalities suffered by Catholics in Northern Ireland, organised its first march from Coalisland south-west to Dungannon. The crowd of 4000 was met by a police cordon outside the town, and although there was no serious violence, it was the beginning of a new era.

Information

The local tourist office – the so-called Killymaddy Tourist Amenity Centre (01868-767259) – is inconveniently located some 10km south-west of Dungannon on the A4 Ballygawley road. It opens all year. In town you might be able to pick up a few brochures at the council office (☎ 01868-725311) in Circular Rd next door to the large Dungannon Leisure Centre. The office opens weekdays 9 am to 1 pm and 2 to 5 pm.

The Control Zone in the town centre is enforced, which is why parked cars have at least one person inside; if you're driving, leave your car farther out or use the pay-and-display car parks close to Market Square, which will cost a lot less than the £20 fine for leaving a vehicle unattended.

The Heritage Centre (☎ 01868-724187), 26 Market Square, claims to have the largest computerised genealogical database in Ireland, with more than 8 million records.

You'll find several banks and the post office in the centre on Market Square.

The telephone code is ☎ 01868.

Tyrone Crystal

At the Tyrone Crystal factory (☎ 725335), just north-east of town, tours cover the different stages in the production of crystal, starting with a visit to the furnace where the molten glass is prepared and then hand-blown. The glass pieces are then checked for faults, bevelled, marked, cut and polished.

The showroom contains examples of all the crystal, including slightly imperfect pieces that do not bear the Tyrone Crystal insignia but cost about 25% less. Tyrone Crystal may not have the lustrous reputation of Waterford glass, but it makes a splendid gift or souvenir. Prices range from £13 for a tumbler to £100 (and up) for vases and bowls.

The tour costs £2, which you get back if you buy something. The factory opens 9.30 am to 3.30 pm Monday to Saturday, April to October, and weekdays only the rest of the year. To get there take the A45 toward Coalisland for about 2.5km – it is clearly signposted – or catch bus No 80 heading for Cookstown.

Places to Stay

Camping The *Killymaddy Tourist Amenity Centre* (☎ 767259; see the Information section) has a campsite with full facilities and costs £6/4 for caravans/tents. The entrance to Parkanaur Forest Park is about 3km from here. Though larger, *Dungannon Park* (☎ 727327), about 1.5km south of town on Moy Rd and signposted off the A29, is in a quiet location, has good facilities and costs the same. To get there, take the A29 south towards Armagh for 2.5km and turn left (west) at the signpost.

B&B & Hotels The *Town House* (☎ 723957), 32 Northland Row, is one of the least expensive B&Bs at £15/28 for singles/doubles. *Glengannon Hotel* (☎ 727311) at Drumgormal on the A4 Ballygawley road charges from £30 per room for B&B, while the *Inn on the Park* (☎ 725151) on Moy Rd charges £55/80. *Grange Lodge* (☎ 784212), 7 Grange Rd south-east of Dungannon toward Moy, does B&B for £49/69 and opens all year except January.

Places to Eat

Just down from Market Square on the corner of Scotch and George Sts, the *Northland Arms* serves pub food and set meals as does the *Fort* on Scotch St. Farther down Scotch St is the *Jasmine House* Chinese restaurant and *Paradise Kebab House*. *Number 15*, a café-restaurant at 15 Church St, has a salad bar and lunches for under £5 as well as home-made scones and cakes. The restaurant at the *Inn on the Park* serves decent steaks and fish for around £10; set dinner is £18.

For something fancy in the £20-a-head range, try the award-winning restaurant at the *Grange Lodge* (see Places to Stay), which specialises in locally reared duckling.

Getting There & Away

Bus No 80 shuttles regularly between Dungannon and Cookstown (20 minutes) to the north. The No 278 service runs once or twice a day Monday to Saturday south to Armagh (30 minutes) and, in the Irish Republic, Monaghan (one hour) and Dublin (3½ hours). The journey between Dungannon and Belfast (50 minutes) or Enniskillen (1½ hours) is possible on bus No 261 up to 10 times a day (five on Sunday). Bus No 273 links Dungannon with Belfast, Omagh and Derry up to eight times a day (four on Sunday).

The bus station (☎ 722251) is at the bottom of Scotch St, over the bridge and to the left.

AROUND DUNGANNON
Peatlands Park

Peatlands Park visitors' centre (☎ 01762-851102) has an informative display about peat, aimed at a young audience. The bog garden is worth a visit if only to familiarise yourself with the sundew, one of two carnivorous plants indigenous to Ireland. It's a tiny thing, easily missed. Pitcher plants also thrive in the garden, but these were introduced into Ireland over a century ago from Canada. Also in the park are two lakes, a small forest and an orchard.

An open-top, narrow-gauge railway, once used for transporting peat, does a 15-minute circuit of the park for children. From Easter to the end of September trains run from 2 to 6 pm Saturday and Sunday (daily in July and August) for 70p/30p. The visitors' centre has the same hours.

To get to Peatlands Park, which is at The Birches some 13km south-east of Dungannon, take Exit 13 off the M1 motorway heading toward Belfast.

Donaghmore High Cross

The cross is a hybrid, being made of the base and shaft of one cross and the head and part of the shaft of another with the join clearly visible. The carved biblical scenes are similar to those on the Ardboe Cross. On the east side are the Angel and Shepherds, the Adoration of the Magi, the Miracle at Cana, the Miracle of the Loaves and Fishes and the arrest of Christ and the Crucifixion. On the west side are Adam and Eve, Cain and Abel, and Abraham and Isaac. The nearby heritage centre (☎ 01868-767039), in a converted 19th century school, opens weekdays 9 am to 5 pm and, May to August, Saturday 11 am to 4 pm.

The cross is 8km north-west of Dungannon on the B43 road to Pomeroy, easily spotted at a road junction.

Castlecaulfield

Not a castle as such but the remains of what was once a substantial Jacobean house, Castlecaulfield was built in the early 17th century by Sir Toby Caulfield on the site of an earlier fort belonging to the O'Donnellys. Over the gatehouse, the Caulfield coat of arms can be made out, and this survived the O'Donnellys' act of revenge in 1641 when the house was burned down. It was rebuilt and, in 1767, hosted a church service by John Wesley, the founder of Methodism.

To get to Castlecaulfield, take the A4 west out of Dungannon and after about 6km a small road is signposted to the right.

Parkanaur Forest Park

About 1.5km from Castlecaulfield, an oak forest is being developed on what was once the Burgess family estate; the Victorian dwelling is now used as a training centre for the disabled. The old farm buildings display farm and forest machinery, and there are some short nature trails. The park has four colour-coded walking trails.

The white fallow deer in the park are descended from the oldest deer herd in Ireland, going back to 1595 when a doe and a hart, a gift from Elizabeth I to her goddaughter, were raised at Mallow Castle. The park brought five deer from Mallow in 1978 and there are now about 25.

The park has a *campsite* (☎ 01868-759664) for £4 to £7 a night plus a deposit for the barrier key, but there are no facilities. An entry ticket to the park, available from the ranger on duty, costs £2 for cars and motorbikes. The park entrance is 11km west of Dungannon on the A4.

Grant Ancestral House

Ulysses S Grant led Union forces to victory in the American Civil War and was later elected the 18th US president for two terms (1869-77). The home of his mother's family has been restored in the style of a typical 19th century Irish small farm. The furniture is not authentic, but the original field plan of this four-hectare farm is still there, together with various old farming implements.

The visitors' centre has an exhibition and café and opens April to September, noon to 5 pm Monday to Saturday, and 2 to 6 pm Sunday. Admission is £1/50p. The site is 20km west of Dungannon. Take the A4 west and turn left at the sign just before the village of Ballygawley.

The Argory

This neoclassical house (☎ 01868-784753)

dates from 1824 and the National Trust touts it as a 'time capsule' because of its complete turn-of-the-century furnishings. There's no electricity; the central stove and the acetylene gas plant help define the late-Victorian and Edwardian character of the house. Tours of the building and grounds take in the drawing room, with its rosewood Steinway piano, the study and billiard room, the dining room and the organ lobby with its unique pipe organ contemporary with the house. The courtyards house more displays as well as a shop and tearoom.

The Argory opens April, May and September, 2 to 6 pm Saturday and Sunday, while in June, July, August and Easter it opens 2 to 6 pm daily except Tuesday. Admission is £2.30/1.15 plus £1 for the car park.

The Argory is on Derrycaw Rd in Moy, 9km south-east of Dungannon: take the A29 south, then turn left (west) onto the B106 and right (south) onto the B34.

County Fermanagh

The River Erne wends its way through County Fermanagh – one of the smallest counties in Ireland – into a lake that is 80km long. The point at which Lough Erne constricts is the town of Enniskillen, in the centre of Fermanagh and a good base for exploration. The town's efficient tourist office serves the whole county.

Lower Lough Erne, the more developed of the lake's 'halves', attracts people for varying reasons: the fishing is superb; there are good facilities for water sports outside Enniskillen; and Devenish and White islands have remarkable ecclesiastical remains. A third island, Boa, has a cemetery with a unique stone statue dating back around 2000 years.

Early Christian missionaries settled in Fermanagh, but the religion penetrated the local pagan culture slowly; Viking and Norman invaders couldn't subdue the region and even the Tudors were unable to do so until after 1600, when Enniskillen finally fell

to the English. Planters then moved in and quickly established a series of castles around Lough Erne. The town of Enniskillen was transformed into a centre of colonial power, and its strategic importance to the British led to its unparalleled boast of possessing two royal regiments.

At the time of Partition, Fermanagh was reluctantly drawn into Northern Ireland – despite the fact that most of its people were Catholic – and its nationalist spirit has not diminished. Parliament does not like to be reminded that one of its members was allowed to starve himself to death in an effort to establish political recognition for IRA prisoners. Bobby Sands was elected as MP for Fermanagh and South Tyrone in the spring of 1981, and he died 66 days after beginning his fast, without ever taking up his seat in Westminster.

ENNISKILLEN

The town of Enniskillen (Inis Ceithleann) is a useful centre for activities on Upper and Lower Lough Erne and the antiquities around them. Oscar Wilde and Samuel Beckett were both pupils at the Portora Royal School north-west of the centre. The town is predominantly Catholic, close to the border, and lacks the dourness of some of the North's other towns.

In November 1987 an IRA bomb exploded at a Remembrance Day service in Enniskillen, killing 11 innocent people.

Orientation & Information

The town centre is on an island in the waterway connecting the upper and lower loughs. The main street changes several times, but the clocktower marks the centre. The other principal thoroughfare through town is Wellington Rd, which runs south of and parallel to the main street. Vehicles should not be left unattended in the town centre, but there are plenty of car parks around.

The helpful, well run Fermanagh Tourist Information Centre (☎ 01365-323110) just south of Wellington Rd opens year round on weekdays 9 am to 5 pm. In May, June and September, the office closes a half-hour later

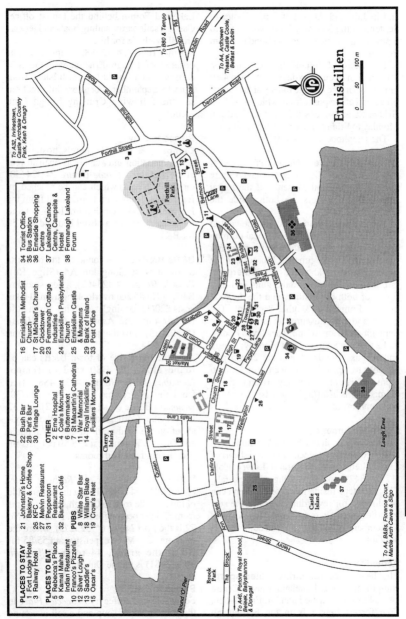

Enniskillen

0   50   100 m

PLACES TO STAY
1 Fort Lodge Hotel
3 Railway Hotel

PLACES TO EAT
5 Rebecca's Place
9 Kamal Mahal
   Indian Restaurant
10 Franco's Pizzeria
12 Silver Lough
13 Saddler's
15 Oscar's

21 Johnston's Home
   Bakery & Coffee Shop
26 KFC
27 Melvin Restaurant
31 Peppercorn
   Restaurant
32 Barbizon Café

PUBS
8 White Star Bar
18 William Blake
19 Crow's Nest

22 Bush Bar
28 Pat's Bar
30 Vintage Lounge

OTHER
2 Erne Hospital
4 Cole's Monument
6 Buttermarket
7 St Macartin's Cathedral
11 War Memorial
14 Royal Inniskilling
   Fusiliers Monument

16 Enniskillen Methodist
   Church
17 St Michael's Church
20 Clocktower
23 Fermanagh Cottage
   Industries
24 Enniskillen Presbyterian
   Church
25 Enniskillen Castle
   Museums
29 Bank of Ireland
33 Post Office

34 Tourist Office
35 Bus Station
36 Emeside Shopping
   Centre
37 Lakeland Canoe
   Centre, Campsite &
   Hostel
38 Fermanagh Lakeland
   Forum

TYRONE & FERMANAGH

and in July and August at 7 pm. Easter to September the Saturday hours are 10 am to 6 pm and the office opens on Sunday 11 am to 5 pm.

The Bank of Ireland has a branch on Townhall St open weekdays 9.30 am to 4.30 pm. You can also change money at the tourist office and at the post office, which is on East Bridge St and opens 9.30 am to 5.30 pm Monday to Friday and to 12.30 pm Saturday.

The telephone code is ☎ 01365.

Enniskillen Castle & Museums

The Fermanagh History & Heritage Centre and the Regimental Museum of the Royal Inniskilling Fusiliers are both inside the castle (☎ 325000).

The heritage centre occupies the central keep and contains artefacts on local farming and manufacturing, but it is not particularly interesting. The Regimental Museum, in the turreted building known as the **Watergate**, is crammed full of medals, guns and uniforms of both the fusiliers and the dragoon guards, Enniskillen's other regiment. The centre and the museum are open May to September, 10 am to 5 pm Tuesday to Friday, and 2 to 5 pm Saturday and Monday; in July and August, Sunday hours are 2 to 5 pm. October to April they're open Monday 2 to 5 pm and Tuesday to Friday 10 am to 5 pm. Admission is £2/1/5 for adults/students & children/families.

Cole's Monument

The monument, in Forthill Park at the eastern end of town, was named after the 1st earl of Enniskillen's son, Galbraith Lowry Cole (1772-1842), one of Wellington's generals. The 108 steps inside this Doric column can be climbed for rewarding views of the surrounding area. It opens mid-May to mid-September, daily 2 to 6 pm, and admission is 60p/30p.

Activities

The best place for hiring **water sports** equipment is the Lakeland Canoe Centre (☎ 324250) on Castle Island in Enniskillen. Free ferries depart from the Fermanagh

Lakeland Forum behind the tourist office. Canoes, sailboards, sailing boats and jet skis are all available for hire.

Erne Tours (☎ 322882) runs 1¾-hour **cruises** of Lough Erne aboard the MV *Kestrel* with a stop at Devenish Island from June to September. For more information, see the following Cruising Lough Erne section.

Places to Stay

Camping & Hostel There's hostel-style accommodation and a campsite open all year at the *Lakeland Canoe Centre* (☎ 324250) on Castle Island, which can be reached by ferry (free) from 9 am to midnight from the Fermanagh Lakeland Forum. It costs £8 to pitch a tent, £9 for a hostel bed and £10.50 for B&B.

B&Bs B&Bs can be found on the outskirts of town west along the A4 (Sligo Rd). *Rossole House* (☎ 323462), a non-smoking B&B at No 85 and overlooking a small lake, costs £20/32 for singles/doubles. Just a little farther out, the *Ashwood Guest House* (☎ 323019) is well appointed, spacious and costs £18/34.

At the other side of town B&Bs can be found along the B80 road to Tempo. *Lackaboy Farm House* (☎ 322488), 1km from the centre, has rooms for £17/30. *Drumcoo House* (☎ 01365-326672) is at 32 Cherryville, Cornagrade Rd, by the roundabout on the road north to Castle Archdale and Omagh. Rooms cost £18.50 per person, and all four have bathrooms.

Hotels The 150-year-old *Railway Hotel* (☎ 322084), 34 Forthill St, at the eastern side of town on the road to Omagh, has 19 rooms from £33 per person for B&B. Nearby at No 72 is the *Fort Lodge* (☎ 323275), where the rates are £25. More expensive at £55/85 for B&B, the grand, 44-room *Killyhevlin* (☎ 323481) is on the Dublin road.

Places to Eat

For snacks and coffee try *Rebecca's Place* in the Buttermarket; soup and a roll is around

£1.50. There's a *KFC* fast-food outlet west of the tourist office on Wellington Rd.

The popular *Franco's Pizzeria*, on Queen Elizabeth Rd on the north side of town, has pizzas from £5.95, pasta dishes from £6.65 (including vegetarian lasagna for £7.75) and a seafood bar. It's closed on Sunday.

Along East Bridge St the *Barbizon Café* is OK for snacks, salads and set lunches but closes at 6 pm. *Johnston's Home Bakery & Coffee Shop*, on Townhall St just east of the clocktower in the centre, has good sandwiches (from £1.50) and pies. The *Crow's Nest* pub, in High St, is aimed at tourists, with menus in French and German.

Back along Townhall St the *Peppercorn* is pleasant, serving breakfast and lunch for about £4. Just a few doors away the upstairs *Melvin* restaurant has lunch specials for around £5; it closes at 6 pm Monday to Thursday, and at 9.30 pm Friday and Saturday.

By the roundabout at the end of Belmore St, *Saddler's* is a steakhouse (£10 to £13) open daily. *Oscar's* (☎ 327037), one of Enniskillen's best restaurants both for food and atmosphere, is nearby at 29 Belmore St. It has quite a varied menu, including at least three vegetarian options, and main courses range from £7.95 to £12.95. For Chinese food, try the *Silver Lough* on Belmore Rd with dishes (including a large choice of vegetarian ones) from £6 and open until midnight every day. *Kamal Mahal* on the corner of Water and Cross Sts serves Indian food at dinner only daily until 11.30 pm.

Entertainment
The main street through town has a number of popular pubs. These include the Victorian *William Blake* (also called Blake's of the Hollow) on Church St with music on Thursday evening; the *Crow's Nest*, 12 High St, with good food and music most evenings (traditional Irish sessions on Monday in summer); the *Vintage Lounge* on Townhall St; the *Bush Bar* on East Bridge St, with music (including Irish sessions) on Monday, Wednesday, Friday and Saturday; and *Pat's Bar*, next to the Melvin Restaurant, which occasionally has music at night. The *White Star Bar* on Church St is popular with Enniskillen's young bloods.

During the year just about every kind of performance takes place at the *Ardhowen Theatre* (☎ 325440), about 2km south of the town centre on Dublin Rd (A4). The programme includes concerts, local amateur and professional drama and musical productions, pantomime and films.

Things to Buy
The best place for shopping in Enniskillen is the Buttermarket (☎ 324499), off Queen Elizabeth Rd. The refurbished buildings of the old marketplace house a variety of craft shops making and selling their wares; ceramics and jewellery are the best buys. Another good outlet for crafts is Fermanagh Cottage Industries next to the Presbyterian church on East Bridge St. The Erneside Centre is a modern complex of shops, cafés and a supermarket across the waterway south of Wellington Rd.

Getting There & Away
Ulsterbus No 261 runs up to 10 times daily (five on Sunday) via Dungannon to Belfast (two hours). Bus No 296 runs to Derry (2½ hours) via Omagh (one hour) and, in the other direction, to Cork (8¼ hours) via Athlone (three hours). The No 262 service runs to Sligo (1½ hours), Ballina (1¼ hours) and Westport (4½ hours). There's also a service from Enniskillen to Bundoran via Belleek. Bus Éireann's bus No 30 between Dublin (three hours) and Donegal (1¼ hours) calls at Enniskillen four times daily (three times on Sunday).

The bus station (☎ 322633) is conveniently opposite the tourist office on Shore Rd.

Getting Around
Bicycles can be hired at the Lakeland Canoe Centre (☎ 324250) for £10 a day or from Erne Tours (☎ 322882) at the Round 'O' Quay at Brook Park.

AROUND ENNISKILLEN
Castle Coole
This mansion (☎ 01365-322690) designed by James Wyatt ranks as probably the purest expression of late 18th century neoclassical architecture in Ireland. The house was completed in 1798. Over the following two centuries the Portland stone exterior absorbed water to the point that the walls started to crumble.

The National Trust embarked on an expensive rebuilding of the outside walls and an extensive redecoration of the interior. (The present earl still lives on the estate.) The result is that now the house displays the pristine elegance of its original conception. The austerity of the design borders on the sterile; the obsession with symmetry is almost neurotic; and the guided tour takes in many examples of form triumphing over substance: fake doors balancing real ones, hollow columns painted to resemble marble ones, keyhole covers on doors that have no keyholes.

The tour first visits the male sanctuary of the library where, as the guide points out, once locked the doors could only be opened from the inside. Most of the furniture is original, and the curtain rail is typical of the extravagance of the 2nd earl of Belmore, who decorated the house. The 1st earl spent so much money having the place built that he had nothing left for decorations.

The castle is in a 600-hectare demesne and its lake is home to a colony of greylag geese.

The castle opens May to August, daily except Thursday 1 to 6 pm. In April and September it opens 1 to 6 pm Saturday, Sunday and public holidays only, while over Easter it also opens daily the same hours. Admission is £2.60/1.30/6.50 for adults/children/families. Castle Coole is on Dublin Rd (the A4), 2.5km south-east of Enniskillen.

Florence Court
This Palladian mansion (☎ 01365-348249) is named after the wife of John Cole, who settled in the area in the early 18th century. His son built the present central block and the wings were added by his grandson, although the architect is unknown. The house was acquired by the National Trust in the 1950s and partly rebuilt after a fire in 1955. It's said that every Irish yew tree has its origin from one in the garden of Florence Court.

Unlike Castle Coole, Florence Court has a lived-in feel to it, and despite the fire much of the original rococo plasterwork remains – the staircase is the best example of it.

In the grounds there is a walled garden and a forest park which has a number of walking trails; one of the trails leads to the top of Mt Cuilcagh (667m).

May to August, Florence Court opens daily (except Tuesday) 1 to 6 pm, while in April and September it's open 1 to 6 pm weekends and public holidays only. It's also open daily 1 to 6 pm during Easter. Admission is £2.60/1.30/6.50 for adults/children/families. The house is almost 13km southwest of Enniskillen; take the A4 Sligo road and turn left (south) onto the A32 Swanlinbar road.

Marble Arch Caves
The extensive Marble Arch Caves (☎ 01365-348855) are very popular and very commercialised; it's wise to phone ahead and book on the 1½-hour tour. The caves open mid-March to September from 10.30 am daily, with the last tour at 4.30 pm. The cost is £5/2 for adults/children (students £3.50, families £12) and starts with a boat trip on the river running through the caves.

During the summer there are occasional free guided walks through the surrounding limestone hills conducted by the Department of the Environment. Enquire at the tourist office in Enniskillen or contact the Nature Reserve Office (☎ 013656-21588) at Castle Archdale Country Park in Lisnarick.

The Marble Arch Caves are 16km southwest of Enniskillen near the border via the A4 (Sligo road) and the A32 (Swanlinbar road). The site is well signposted.

LOUGH ERNE
Stretching for 80km, Lough Erne is made up

of two sections: the Upper Lough in the south and the Lower Lough in the north. The loughs are joined by the River Erne, which begins its journey in County Cavan and flows out to Donegal Bay west of Ballyshannon. The lakes have numerous islands, many containing Celtic and early Christian archaeological sites (see Around Lough Erne). Coarse and game fish are plentiful, and birdlife, especially on Upper Lough Erne, is abundant.

Fishing

The lakes of Fermanagh are renowned for coarse fishing, but trout are found in the northern part of Lower Lough Erne, close to Boa Island and Kesh Bay. Lough Melvin, near the town of Garrison, is home to the Gillaroo trout. The Lough Erne trout fishing season runs from the beginning of March to the end of September. Salmon fishing begins in June and also continues to the end of September. The mayfly season usually lasts a month from the second week in May. There's no closed season for bream, eel, pike, perch, roach or rudd.

A coarse fishing licence or permit is required for Lough Erne and a game permit or licence for fishing in Lower Lough Erne other than from the shore. These can be purchased from the Fermanagh Tourist Information Centre (☎ 01365-323110) in Enniskillen or the marina (☎ 013656-28118) at Castle Archdale County Park, which also hires day boats. A three-day joint licence and permit is £6.55 for coarse fishing; you'll pay £11.60 for an eight-day one. An eight-day joint licence and permit for game fishing is £22.85. Most of the rivers in County Fermanagh are privately owned, and information on those rivers where permission need not be sought is available from the tourist office in Enniskillen. It also has a list of ghillies available.

Cruising Lough Erne

The MV *Kestrel* (☎ 01365-322882) is a 56-seater waterbus that cruises the lough for 1¾ hours, calling at Devenish Island along the way. It departs from the Round 'O' Quay

at Brook Park, a short distance out of Enniskillen on the A46 to Belleek. During May and June it departs at 2.30 pm Sunday and public holidays only; in July and August it departs at 10.30 am, 2.15 and 4.15 pm daily and, via the Upper Lough, at 7.15 pm Tuesday, Thursday and Sunday; in September it departs at 2.30 pm on Tuesday, Saturday and Sunday. The cost is £5/2.50 (or £4/2 if you take the morning cruise).

There are Viking Voyages (☎ 013657-22122) departing at 3 pm from the Share Centre on the Derrylin road about 7km from Lisnaskea. The replica of a Viking longboat does 90-minute cruises on Upper Lough Erne over Easter, April to June and in September on Saturday and Sunday; July and August, they run Monday and Wednesday and Friday to Sunday. The cost is £4/3/10 for adults/children/families.

There are about eight companies in Fermanagh that hire out cruisers on a weekly basis. The rates vary from about £400 for a four-berth to about £1100 for an eight-berth. Just as many companies also rent out day boats at Belleek, Enniskillen, Garrison, Kesh, Killadeas and Newtownbutler. Prices start at about £25 for a four-person rowing boat with outboard engine and £50 for six-seater with front cabin and diesel inboard engine. The tourist office in Enniskillen has a full list of the companies and costs.

AROUND LOUGH ERNE

There are a number of ancient religious sites and other antiquities around Lough Erne. In early Christian times the lough was an important highway providing a route from the Donegal coast to inland Leitrim. Churches and monasteries acted as staging posts, and in medieval times there was an important pilgrim route to Station Island in Donegal that went via Lough Erne.

The village of Belleek, famous for its chinaware, is just inside the Northern Irish border and easily reached from either side of the lough.

The places below are set out in an anti-clockwise tour north from Enniskillen.

TYRONE & FERMANAGH

Devenish Island

The most extensive of the ancient sites at Lough Erne is Devenish Island (Daimh Inis). A monastery here, founded by St Molaise in the 6th century, was sacked by Vikings in 837 AD in just one of the many incidents of its colourful history. There are church and abbey ruins, some fascinating old gravestones, an unusual 15th century high cross, an excellent small museum and one of the best round towers in Ireland. The 25m tower dates from the 12th century and is in perfect condition; you can climb to the top for 75p (including museum entry).

A ferry runs across to the site from Trory Point landing, some 6.5km north of Enniskillen. To get there, take the A32 heading for Irvinestown and after 5km look for the sign on the left. It's just after a Burmah service station and before the junction where roads fork left to Kesh and right to Omagh. The ferry runs April to September continuously from 10 am to 6.30 pm Tuesday to Saturday, and 2 to 7 pm Sunday. The return fare is £2.25/1.20 adults/children and the crossing takes 10 minutes.

Killadeas Churchyard

Tucked away in a small graveyard stands the **Bishop's Stone**, a remarkable stone carving dating from between the 7th and 9th centuries that encapsulates the transition from Celtic paganism to Christianity. The face that stares out from the front seems quite at odds with the side engraving of a bishop with bell and crozier.

Just after the turn off for Devenish Island on the A32, follow the B82 along the shoreline toward Kesh and look for the sign to the Manor House Country Hotel. Continue past this sign for just over a km and look for the small church on the left side of the road.

White Island

White Island, close to the eastern shore of the lough, has the remains of a small 12th century **church** containing a line of eight statues thought to date from as early as the 6th century. Nothing remains of the earlier monastic settlement except the boundary bank that can still be made out on the far side of the church. The most impressive surviving part of the church is the Romanesque door on the south side.

The eight **stone figures** are intriguing. The first resembles a sheila-na-gig, while the next is of someone reading a book or holding some object. Number three is obviously ecclesiastical, and while the next one has been identified as the young David, the meaning of his hand pointing to his mouth has been lost. Number five is a curly-haired figure holding the necks of two griffin-like birds. Number six has a military appearance, number seven is unfinished and the last one is a single frowning face that resembles a death mask.

Places to Stay There's a good YHANI hostel at *Castle Archdale Country Park* (☎ 013656-28118). A bed is £5.50/6.50 for juniors/seniors, and family rooms are available. It opens March to December. The park also has a *campsite* (☎ 013656-21333), which is huge and dominated by on-site caravans, but it has good facilities. A site for a two-person tent is £9; a caravan costs £1 more. Ulsterbus No 194 from Enniskillen to

The sheila-na-gig figure on White Island

Sheila-na-Gig

The term sheila-na-gig is probably an anglicisation of *Síle na gcíoch* ('Sheila of the teats'). It refers to crude carvings of women displaying exaggerated genitalia on the outside of certain medieval churches and buildings. One theory traces their origin back to the exhibitionist figures found in French Romanesque churches that illustrated the ungodly powers threatening men.

Another theory is that they're representations of Celtic war goddesses. Early Irish sagas like the epic *Táin Bó Cúailnge (The Cattle Raid of Cooley)* refer to women using overt genital display as a weapon to subdue the hero Cúchulainn. This may have encouraged the belief that the 'Sheilas' could ward off evil and hence explain their incorporation into early Christian architecture.

Another theory is that they may have been connected with some sort of fertility cult or used as a fetish against the evil eye. ■

Pettigo stops outside the park, from where the hostel is a 15-minute walk, but it runs only when school is in session. At other times take the bus to Lisnarrick Corner (four departures daily), which will drop you off about 1.5km from the park.

Getting There & Away From April to September a ferry runs across to the island from the marina in Castle Archdale Country Park, which is 16km north of Enniskillen on the Kesh road (B82). The ferry operates every hour on the hour daily 10 am to 7 pm and costs £3/2. The sailing takes 15 minutes.

Drumskinny Stone Circle & Alignment

This circle is made up of 39 stones with a small cairn and an alignment of two dozen stones and dates back to the Bronze Age. The circle is 7km north-east of Kesh and sign-posted just beyond the junction with the road to Boa Island.

Boa Island

At the north end of the Lower Lough is narrow Boa Island, which is connected at both ends by bridges to the shore. The **Janus figure** (also known as the 'Lusty Man') in Caldragh graveyard could be 2000 years old, one of the oldest stone statues in Ireland and quite unparalleled. Another, more recent stone figure stands beside it.

There's just a small sign to the cemetery, about a km from the bridge at the west end of the island, 6km from the east-end bridge.

Castle Caldwell Forest Park

At the entrance to the park, the **Fiddler's Stone** is a memorial to a musician who fell off a boat in a drunken stupor and drowned in 1770. The castle itself was built between 1610 and 1619, but all that remains is a ruin that is not safe to explore. It's a few minutes walk from the café and small visitors' centre. The park is a nature reserve full of birdlife and the main breeding ground of the common scoter duck.

The park is about 5km west of Boa Island along the A47.

Belleek

The only reason for stopping at this drab border village is to visit the world-famous Belleek pottery works (☎ 013656-58501),

The Janus figure on Boa Island in Lough Erne

which has provided employment here since 1857.

There are regular tours every 20 minutes, from 9 am Monday to Friday, the last tour beginning at 4.30 pm (except on Friday, when the last one is at 3.30 pm). The tour costs £1. The small museum at the visitors' centre, showroom and café are open March through June, and also September, 9 am to 6 pm Monday to Friday, 10 am to 6 pm Saturday, 2 to 6 pm Sunday; July and August, 9 am to 8 pm Monday to Friday, 10 am to 6 pm Saturday and 11 am to 8 pm Sunday; and October to February, 9 am to 5.30 pm Monday to Friday only.

Lough Navar Forest
In this coniferous forest, on the western shore of Lough Erne, an 11km scenic road leads up to a viewing point overlooking the lough and the mountains to the north. A section of the Ulster Way passes through the forest. An entry ticket costs £2 for a car. The park is signposted off the A46.

Tully Castle
A signposted left turn off the A46 some 16km south-east of Belleek leads to Tully Castle. The castle was built in 1613 as a fortified home for a Scottish planter's family, but it was captured and burned by Roderick Maguire in 1641. The bawn (cattle enclosure) has four corner towers and retains a lot of the original paving. The vaulted ground floor has a large fireplace with an equally large staircase leading to the 2nd floor and attics above that.

The castle opens April to September, 10 am to 7 pm Tuesday to Saturday, and 2 to 7 pm Sunday; admission is £1/50p.

Monea Castle
Continuing south on the A46 toward Enniskillen there is a signposted turn to the right to the B81 and Monea Castle. This was built as the best of Fermanagh's plantation castles around the same time as Tully Castle. It too was captured in the 1641 rising but remained in use until the mid-18th century when it was gutted by fire. The main en-trance has two imposing circular towers topped with built-out squares in a style that can be found in contemporary Scottish castles. There's no charge for viewing the remains. A crannóg sits in the nearby lake.

Places to Stay
Camping At Blaney, 13km north-west of Enniskillen on the A46 to Belleek and behind the Blaney service station, *Blaney Caravan Park* (☎ 013656-41634) has tent/caravan sites for £5/8.50. On the other side of the lough outside Kesh, *Lakeland Caravan Park* (☎ 013656-31578) also has caravan and tent sites. South of Enniskillen and about 2km north-west of Lisnaskea near Upper Lough Erne, camping is possible at *Mullynascarthy Caravan Park* (☎ 013657-21040) for £5.50/9 and *Share Holiday Village* (☎ 013657-22122) in Shanaghy for £6/11.

B&Bs There are plenty of B&Bs along the roads that skirt either side of Lough Erne. *Lakeview Farm House* (☎ 013656-41263) is on the A46 at Blaney, with singles/doubles for £16/30, and on the other side of the lough at Killadeas, *Beeches* (☎ 013656-21557) has two rooms for £18/34 and boats for hire. *Manville House* (☎ 013656-31668), at Letter, 13km from Kesh on the road to Belleek, is well situated for the angler, with boat hire available and four rooms at £16/30. In Belleek itself, *Moohan's Fiddlestone* (☎ 013656-58008), 15 Main St, is a friendly place with five rooms costing £18 per person and a bar downstairs.

Hotels The grandly situated *Manor House Country Hotel* (☎ 013656-21561), over-looking Lough Erne about 11km from Enniskillen in Killadeas on the B82 to Kesh, has 46 rooms costing £65/90 for singles/doubles. At the 18-room *Mahon's Hotel* (☎ 013656-21656), on Mill St in the centre of Irvinestown, the rates are £35/65, and the bar is packed with local people at weekends. *Drumshane Hotel* (☎ 013656-21146), in Lisnarick due west of Irvinestown, is a good 10-room hotel with a restaurant, a grand piano in the bar and rooms from £32.50/65.

On the main street in Lisnaskea the *Ortine Hotel* (☎ 013657-21206) has 18 rooms for £28.50/47.

Places to Eat

Open daily, the restaurant at the *Manor House Country Hotel* (see Places to Stay) has à la carte and set dinners for around £20 per person. There's traditional and country music at weekends in summer.

In Irvinestown, 13km due north of Enniskillen, the *Hollander* (☎ 013656-21231), 15 Main St, is a family-run pub-restaurant with a reputation for good food at reasonable prices. Reservations are recommended, vegetarian meals are always featured, and you should count on spending £12 to £15 per person. The restaurant opens for lunch and dinner in winter and continuously 11 am to 11 pm in summer. The pub has some interesting photographs of the Catalina and Sunderland flying boats that operated from the nearby army base at Castle Archduke during WWII. There's even a model of the plane that flew from here and spotted the *Bismarck*.

Across the road from the Hollander, the *Central Bar* serves food during the day and was a popular watering hole for US pilots; only the TV sets and security monitor detract from the 1940s feel of the place.

North-west of Kesh on Boa Island, reservations are recommended for the *Drumrush Lodge* (☎ 013656-31578) on Boa Island Rd or *Mullynaval Lodge* (☎ 013656-31995), where dinner is £10. Pub food is available at the *May Fly* on the main street in Kesh or at *Cleary's Corner Bar*, 5 Main St, in Belleek; the latter has traditional Irish music on Friday night. The *Carlton Hotel* opposite serves meals daily for £5 to £10.

Getting There & Away

From Enniskillen, Ulsterbus No 64 runs on Tuesday, Thursday and Saturday to Belleek (1¼ hours) via Garrison on the western side of Lower Lough Erne. Bus No 99 also goes to Belleek, following the western shoreline through Blaney (15 minutes) past Tully Castle and Lough Navar Forest. On the eastern side bus No 194 runs daily to Irvinestown (35 minutes), Lisnarick (50 minutes) and Kesh (one hour).

Getting Around

Cycle-Ops (☎ 013656-31850), Mantlin Rd in Kesh, hires bikes for £7.50 a day (or £5 a half-day). It also has tandems, and child seats are available.

TYRONE & FERMANAGH

Glossary

An Óige – Irish youth hostel association (meaning 'The Youth').

Anglo-Norman – Norman, English and Welsh peoples who invaded Ireland in the 12th century.

Ard – Irish place name, meaning 'high'.

ard rí – Irish 'high king'

bailey – the space enclosed by castle walls.

bawn – enclosure surrounded by walls outside the main castle, acting as a defence as well as a place to keep cattle in time of trouble.

beehive hut – circular stone building, shaped like an old-fashioned beehive.

Black & Tans – British recruits to the Royal Irish Constabulary shortly after WWI, noted for their brutality.

Blarney Stone – bending over backwards to kiss this sacred rock in Blarney Castle, County Cork, is said to bestow the gift of the gab or allow you to 'gain the privilege of telling lies for seven years'.

bodhrán – (pronounced 'bore-run') hand-held goatskin drum.

Bord Fáilte – Irish Tourist Board, 'Welcome Board'.

botharin or **boreen** – a small lane or roadway.

Bronze Age – the earliest metal-using period, around 2000 BC to 500 BC in Ireland, after the Stone Age and before the Iron Age.

B-specials – Northern Irish auxiliary police force, disbanded in 1971.

bullaun – stone with a depression, probably used as a mortar for grinding medicine or food and often found on monastic sites.

CAC IRA – the Continuity Army Council of the IRA, another breakaway group

caher – a stone-walled enclosed circular area.

cairn – a mound of stones heaped over a prehistoric grave.

cashel – stone-walled circular fort; see *ráth*.

Cath – Irish place name, meaning 'battle'.

ceilí – a session of traditional music and dancing.

Celts – Iron Age warrior tribes which arrived in Ireland around 300 BC and controlled the country for 1000 years.

chancel – the east end of a church where the altar is situated, reserved for the clergy and choir.

Cill or **Kill** – Irish place name, meaning 'church'.

Claddagh ring – the ring used throughout much of Connaught from the mid-18th century with a crowned heart nestling between two hands; if the heart points towards the hand then the wearer is taken or married, towards the fingertip means he or she is looking for a mate.

clochán – dry-stone beehive hut from the early Christian period.

control zone – area of a town centre, usually the main street, where parked cars must have at least one person inside.

craic or **crack** – conversation, gossip, fun, good times.

crannóg – an artificial island, made in a lake to provide habitation in a good defensive position.

creel – basket.

crios – a multicoloured woven woollen belt traditionally worn in the Aran Islands.

cromlech – see *dolmen*.

currach – rowing boat made of framework of laths covered with tarred canvas; spelled *cúrach* in Irish.

Dáil – lower house of the Irish parliament.

dairtheach – an oratory, a small room set aside for private prayer.

demesne – landed property close to a house or castle.

diamond – town square.

dolmen – tomb chamber or portal tomb made of vertical stones topped by a huge capstone. From around 2000 BC.

drumlin – rounded hill formed by retreating glacier.

Dúchas – formerly known as the Office of Public Works, it's a government department in charge of parks, monuments and gardens in the Republic.

dún – a fort, usually constructed of stone.

DUP – Democratic Unionist Party, hard-line Northern Irish Protestant loyalist party founded by Ian Paisley.

Éire – Irish name for the Republic of Ireland.

esker – gravel ridge.

Fianna – a mythical band of warriors who feature in many tales of ancient Ireland.

Fianna Fáil – 'Warriors of Ireland', major political party in the Republic of Ireland, originating from the Sinn Féin faction opposed to the 1921 treaty with Britain.

Fine Gael – 'Tribe of the Gael', the other major political party, originating from the Sinn Féin faction which favoured the 1921 treaty with Britain. Formed the first government of independent Ireland but has subsequently only gained power as part of a coalition.

fir – men (singular *fear*), sign on men's toilets

fulacht fiadh – Bronze Age cooking place.

Gaeltacht – Irish-speaking area.

garda – Irish Republic police (plural *gardaí*).

ghillie or **ghilly** – a fishing or hunting guide.

Gort – Irish place name, meaning field.

Gothic – style of architecture characterised by pointed arches, from the 12th to the 16th centuries AD.

Hibernia – the Roman name for Ireland and meaning 'the land of winter' (the Romans had confused Ireland with Iceland).

hill fort – usually dating from the Iron Age, hill forts are formed by a ditch that follows the contour of the hill to surround and fortify the summit.

INLA – Irish National Liberation Army, extremist IRA splinter group.

IRA – Irish Republican Army, dedicated to the removal of British troops from the North and the reunification of Ireland.

IRB – Irish Republican Brotherhood, a secret society also called the Fenians, believed in independence through violence if necessary; originally founded in 1858 and revived in the early 20th century; precursor to IRA.

Iron Age – in Ireland the Iron Age lasted from around the end of the Bronze Age in 500 BC to the arrival of Christianity in the 5th century.

jaunting car – Killarney's traditional horse-drawn transport.

jarvey – the driver of a jaunting car.

keep – the main tower of a castle.

Lambeg drum – a very large drum associated with Protestant loyalist marches.

leprechaun – a mischievous elf or sprite from Irish folklore.

lough – Irish word for lake, or a long narrow bay or arm of the sea.

Loyalist – person, usually a Northern Irish Protestant, insisting on the continuation of Northern Ireland's links with Britain.

Mesolithic – Middle Stone Age, the time of the first human settlers in Ireland.

mná – women, sign on women's toilets.

motte – early Norman fortification consisting of a raised, flattened mound with a keep on top. When attached to a bailey it is known as a motte-and-bailey, many of which were built in Ireland until the early 13th century.

naomh – Irish for 'holy' or 'saint'.

Nationalists – proponents of a united Ireland.

Neolithic – also known as the New Stone Age, a period characterised by a settled agriculture and lasting until around 2000 BC in Ireland.

North, The – the term refers to the political entity of Northern Ireland, not the northernmost geographic part of Ireland (not Donegal, for example).

NITB – Northern Ireland Tourist Board.

Ogham stones – Ogham (pronounced 'o-am') was the earliest form of writing in Ireland, using a variety of notched strokes placed above, below or across a keyline, usually on stone.

OPW – Office of Public Works, former name of *Dúchas*.

Orange Order – loyalist Protestant organisation in Northern Ireland which takes its name from William of Orange, the Protestant victor of the Battle of the Boyne. Members of the Orange Order are known as Orangemen and they meet in Orange Lodges.

Palladian – a style of architecture developed by Andrea Palladio (1508-80), based on ancient Roman architecture.

Partition – the division of Ireland in 1921.

passage grave – Celtic tomb with chamber reached by a narrow passage, typically buried in a mound.

penal laws – laws passed in the 18th century forbidding Catholics to buy land, hold public office etc.

plantation – the settlement of Protestant migrants in Ireland in the 17th century.

poteen – (pronounced 'potcheen'), illegally brewed potato-based firewater.

Prod – slang for Northern Irish Protestant.

Provisionals – the Provisional IRA, formed after a break with the Official IRA who are now largely inconsequential. The Provisionals, named after the provisional government declared in 1916, have been the main force combating the British army in the North.

ráth or **rath** – ring fort with earth banks around a circular timber wall (see *cashel*).

Republic of Ireland – twenty-six counties of the South.

Republican – supporter of a united Ireland.

ring fort – used from the Bronze Age right through to the Middle Ages, particularly in the early Christian period. Basically a circular habitation area surrounded by banks and ditches.

Romanesque – a style of architecture which dominated Europe until the arrival of Gothic in the 12th century. Characterised by rounded arches and vaulting.

round tower – tall circular tower from around the 9th to 11th century, built as a lookout and as a sanctuary during the period when monasteries were frequently subject to Viking raids.

RUC – Royal Ulster Constabulary, armed Northern Irish police force.

SDLP – Social Democratic Labour Party of Northern Ireland. The party represents predominantly liberal, middle-class opinion opposed to violence. Mostly Catholic.

seisún – a music session.

shamrock – clover, a plant with three leaves said to have been used by St Patrick to illustrate the Holy Trinity: the union of the Father, the Son and the Holy Spirit in one Godhead.

sept – a clan.

shebeen – from the Irish *síbín*, an illicit drinking place or speakeasy.

sheila-na-gig – 'Sheila of the teats'; a female figure with exaggerated genitalia, carved in stone on the exteriors of some churches and castles. Various explanations have been offered for the iconography, ranging from male clerics warning against the perils of sex to the idea that they represent Celtic war goddesses.

shillelagh – a stout club or cudgel, especially one made of oak or blackthorn.

Sinn Féin – 'We Ourselves', political wing of the IRA.

Six Counties – the six out of nine counties of the old province of Ulster which form Northern Ireland.

slí – a 'way' or (hiking) 'trail'.

snug – partitioned-off drinking area in a pub.

souterrain – an underground chamber usually associated with ring forts and hill forts. The purpose may have been to provide a hiding place or an escape route in times of trouble and/or a storage place for goods.

South, The – The Republic of Ireland

standing stone – upright stone set in the ground. Such stones are common across Ireland and date from a variety of periods.

Usually the purpose is obscure, though some are burial markers.

Tánaiste – Irish deputy prime minister.

Taoiseach – Irish prime minister.

TD – 'teachta Dála', member of the Irish parliament.

teampall – church.

Tinkers – derogatory term used to describe Irish gypsies, itinerant communities that roam the country (see *Travellers*).

trá – Irish word for 'beach' or 'strand'.

Travellers – today's politically correct term to denote Ireland's itinerant communities (see *Tinkers*).

Treaty – the Anglo-Irish Treaty of 1921, which divided Ireland and gave relative independence to the South. Cause of the Civil War of 1922-23.

Tricolour – green, white and orange Irish flag. It was designed to symbolise the hoped-for union of the green Catholic southern Irish with the orange Protestant northern Irish.

turloughs – small lakes which often disappear in dry summers; from the Irish *turlach*.

Twenty Six Counties – the Republic of Ireland, the South.

UDA – Ulster Defence Organisation, legal Northern Irish paramilitary organisation.

UDF – Ulster Defence Force, illegal Northern Irish paramilitary organisation.

UFF – Ulster Freedom Fighters, another illegal Northern Irish paramilitary organisation.

Ulster – one of the four ancient provinces of Ireland sometimes used to describe the six counties of the North, but also including Cavan, Monaghan and Donegal in the Republic.

Unionists – Northern Irish who want to retain the links with Britain.

United Irishmen – organisation founded in 1791 aiming to reduce British power in Ireland, which led a series of unsuccessful risings and invasions.

UUP – Ulster Unionist Party, the principal Northern Irish Protestant political party, founded by Edward Carson.

UVF – Ulster Volunteer Force, and yet another illegal Northern Irish paramilitary organisation.

Volunteers – an offshoot of the IRB that came to be known as the IRA.

way – a long-distance trail.

YHANI – Youth Hostel Association of Northern Ireland.

Appendix – Place Names

Place	Irish Name	County
Achill	Acaill	Mayo
Adare	Áth Dara	Limerick
Annalong	Áth na Long	Down
Antrim	Aontroim	Antrim
Aran Islands	Oileáin Árainn	Galway
Ardara	Árd na Rátha	Donegal
Ardboe	Ard Bo	Tyrone
Ardee	Baile Átha Fhirdhia	Louth
Ardfert	Ard Fhearta	Kerry
Ardglass	Ard Ghlais	Down
Ardmore	Ard Mór	Waterford
Ards Peninsula	An Aird	Down
Arklow	An tInbhear Mór	Wicklow
Arlow	Eatharlach	Tipperary
Armagh	Ard Mhacha	Armagh
Arranmore	Árainn Mhór	Donegal
Athlone	Baile Átha Luain	Westmeath
Athy	Áth Í	Kildare
Avoca	Abhóca	Wicklow
Ballina	Béal an Átha	Mayo
Ballinasloe	Béal Átha na Sluaighe	Galway
Ballinspittle	Béal Átha an Spidéil	Cork
Ballintober	Bail an Tobair	Roscommon
Ballintoy	Baile an Tuaighe	Antrim
Ballybunion	Baile an Bhuinneánaigh	Kerry
Ballycastle	Baile an Chaisil	Antrim, Mayo
Ballyliffin	Baile Lifin	Donegal
Ballymena	An Baile Meánach	Antrim
Ballynahinch	Baile na hInse	Down
Ballyshannon	Béal Átha Seanaidh	Donegal
Ballyvaughan	Baile Uí Bheacháin	Clare
Banbridge	Droíchead na Banna	Down
Bangor	Beannchar	Down
Bantry	Beanntrai	Cork
Belfast	Beál Feirste	Belfast
Bessbrook	An Sruthán	Armagh
Blemullet	Béal an Mhuirthead	Mayo
Birr	Biorra	Offaly
Blarney	An Bhlarna	Cork
Bloody Foreland	Cnoc Fola	Donegal
Boyle	Mainistir na Búille	Roscommon
Bunbeg	An Bun Beag	Donegal

Place	Irish Name	County
Buncrana	Bun Cranncha	Donegal
Bundoran	Bun Dobhráin	Donegal
Bunratty	Bun Raite	Clare
Burren, The	Boireann	Clare
Burtonport	Ailt an Chórrain	Donegal
Bushmills	Muileann na Buaise	Antrim
Cahir	An Cathair	Tipperary
Carlingford	Cairlinn	Louth
Carlow	Ceatharlach	Carlow
Carraroe	An Cheathrú Rua	Galway
Carrickfergus	Carraig Fhearghais	Antrim
Carrick-on-Shannon	Cora Droma Rúisc	Leitrim
Carrickmacross	Carraig Mhachaire Rois	Monaghan
Cashel	Caiseal Mumhan	Tipperary
Castleblayney	Baile na Lorgan	Monaghan
Cavan	An Cabhán	Cavan
Castlebar	Caisleán an Bharraigh	Mayo
Céide Fields	Achaidh Chéide	Mayo
Charleville	Rath Luirc	Cork
Clare	An Clár	Clare
Clifden	An Clochán	Galway
Clones	Cluain Eois	Monaghan
Clonmacnois	Cluain Mhic Nóis	Offaly
Clonmel	Cluain Meala	Tipperary
Clontarf	Cluain Tarbh	Dublin
Cobh	An Cobh	Cork
Coleraine	Cúil Raithin	Derry
Cong	Conga	Mayo
Connemara	Conamara	Galway
Cookstown	An Chorr Chríochach	Tyrone
Cootehill	An Mhuinchille	Cavan
Costello	Casla	Galway
Cork	Corcaigh	Cork
Creeslough	An Craoslach	Donegal
Crossmaglen	Crois Mhic Lionnáin	Armagh
Crossmolina	Crois Mhaoiliona	Mayo
Cushendall	Bun Abhann Dalla	Antrim
Cushendun	Bun Abhann Duinne	Antrim
Dalkey	Deilginis	Dublin
Derry/Londonderry	Doire	Derry
Derrybeg	Doirí Beaga	Donegal
Devenish Island	Daimh Inis	Fermanagh
Dingle	An Daingean	Kerry
Donaghadee	Domhnach Daoi	Down
Donegal	Dún na nGall	Donegal

Place	Irish Name	County
Downpatrick	Dún Pádraig	Down
Dowth	Dubhadh	Meath
Drogheda	Droichead Átha	Louth
Drumshanbo	Droim Seanbhó	Leitrim
Dublin	Baile Átha Cliath	Dublin
Duleek	Damh Liag	Meath
Dundrum	Dún Droma	Down, Tipperary
Dunfanaghy	Dún Fionnachaidh	Donegal
Dungannon	Dún Geanainn	Tyrone
Dungarvan	Dún Garbhán	Waterford
Dungiven	Dún Geimhin	Derry
Dungloe	An Clochán Liath	Donegal
Dunlewy	Dún Lúiche	Donegal
Ennis	Inis	Clare
Enniscorthy	Inis Coirthaidh	Wexford
Enniskillen	Inis Ceithleann	Fermanagh
Falcarragh	An Fal Carrach	Donegal
Galway	Gaillimh	Galway
Giant's Causeway, The	Clochán an Aifir	Antrim
Glenarm	Gleann Arma	Antrim
Glencolumbcille	Gleann Cholm Cille	Donegal
Glendalough	Gleann dá Loch	Wicklow
Glengarriff	An Gleann Garbh	Cork
Glenties	Gleannta	Donegal
Glenveagh	Gleann Beatha	Donegal
Gracehill	Baile Uí Chinnéide	Antrim
Greencastle	Caisleán na hOireanaí	Down
Gortahork	Gort an Choirce	Donegal
Gweedore	Gaoth Dobhair	Donegal
Hillsborough	Cromghlinn	Down
Holy Island	Inis Cealtra	Clare
Howth	Binn Éadair	Dublin
Inishmore/Inishmór	Inis Mór or Árainn	Galway
Inishmaan	Inis Meáin	Galway
Inishowen	Inis Eoghain	Donegal
Innisfree	Inis Fraoigh	Sligo
Inisheer	Inis Oírr	Galway
Inniskeen	Inis Caoin	Monaghan
Islandmagee	Oileán Mhic Aodha	Antrim
Kells	Ceanannas Mór	Meath
Kilcar	Cill Chathaigh	Donegal

Place	Irish name	County
Kildare	Cill Dara	Kildare
Kilkee	Cill Chaoi	Clare
Kilkeel	Cill Chaoil	Down
Kilkenny	Cill Chainnigh	Kilkenny
Killala	Cill Alaidh	Mayo
Killaloe	Cill Dalua	Clare
Killarney	Cill Airne	Kerry
Killybegs	Ceala Beaga	Donegal
Killyleagh	Cill O Laoch	Down
Kilmainham	Cill Mhaigneann	Dublin
Kilmallock	Cill Mocheallóg	Limerick
Kilrush	Cill Rois	Clare
Kilronan	Cill Rónáin	Galway
Kingscourt	Dún an Rí	Cavan
Kinsale	Cionn tSáile	Cork
Knock	Cnoc Mhuire	Mayo
Knowth	Cnóbha	Meath
Lanesborough	Béal Átha Liag	Longford
Larne	Lutharna	Antrim
Leenane	An Líonán	Galway
Leitrim	Liatroim	Leitrim
Letterfrack	Leitir Fraic	Galway
Letterkenny	Leitir Ceanainn	Donegal
Lifford	Leifear	Donegal
Limavady	Léim an Mhadaidh	Derry
Limerick	Luimneach	Limerick
Lisburn	Lios na gCearrbhach	Antrim
Liscannor	Lios Ceannúir	Clare
Lisdoonvarna	Lios Dún Bhearna	Clare
Lismore	Lios Mór	Waterford
Longford	An Longfort	Longord
Lough Neagh	Loch nEathach	Antrim
Loughrea	Baile Locha Riach	Galway
Louisburgh	Cluain Cearbán	Mayo
Maam Cross	Crois Mám	Galway
Malahide	Mullach Ide	Dublin
Mallow	Mala	Cork
Maynooth	Maigh Nuad	Kildare
Mayo	Maigh Eo	Mayo
Meath	An Mhí	Meath
Millisle	Oileán an Mhuilinn	Down
Moira	Maigh Rath	Down
Monaghan	Muineachán	Monaghan
Monasterboice	Mainistir Bhuithe	Louth
Monasterevin	Mainistir Eimhín	Kildare

Place	Irish name	County
Mountshannon	Baile Uí Bheoláin	Clare
Moville	Bun an Phoball	Donegal
Muff	Mugh	Donegal
Mullingar	An Muileann gCearr	Westmeath
Naas	An Nás	Kildare
Navan	An Uaimh	Meath
Nenagh	An tAonach	Tipperary
Newbridge	Droichead Nua	Kildare
Newcastle	An Caisleán Nua	Down
Newport	Baile Uí Fhiacháin	Mayo
New Ross	Rhos Mhic Triúin	Wexford
Newry	An tIúr	Down
Newtownards	Baile Nua na hArda	Down
Omagh	An Omaigh	Tyrone
Oughterard	Uachtar Árd	Galway
Portaferry	Port an Pheire	Down
Portarlington	Cúil an tSúdaire	Laois
Portlaoise	Port Laoise	Laois
Portrush	Port Rois	Antrim
Portsalon	Port an tSalainn	Donegal
Portstewart	Port Stíobhaird	Derry
Randalstown	Baile Raghnaill	Antrim
Rathfarnham	Ráth Fearnáin	Dublin
Rathlin Island	Reachlainn	Antrim
Rathmelton	Ráth Mealtain	Donegal
Rathmullan	Ráth Maoláin	Donegal
Recess	Straith Salach	Galway
Roscommon	Ros Comáin	Roscommon
Roscrea	Ros Cré	Tipperary
Rossaveal	Ros a' Mhíl	Galway
Rosslare	Ros Láir	Wexford
Rostrevor	Caislean Ruairi	Down
Roundstone	Cloch na Rón	Galway
Scattery Island	Inis Cathaigh	Clare
Screeb	Scriob	Galway
Shercock	Searcóg	Cavan
Skellig Islands	Oileáin na Scealaga	Kerry
Slane	Baile Shláine	Meath
Sligo	Sligeach	Sligo
Spiddal	An Spidéal	Galway
Strabane	An Srath Bán	Tyrone
Strangford	Baile Loch Cuan	Down

Place	Irish Name	County
Strangford Lough	Loch Cuan	Down
Strokestown	Béal na mBuillí	Roscommon
Swords	Sord	Dublin
Tara	Teamhair	Meath
Thurles	Durlas	Tipperary
Tipperary	Tiobraid Árann	Tipperary
Tory Island	Oileán Thóraigh	Donegal
Tralee	Trá Lí	Kerry
Trim	Baile Átha Troim	Meath
Tuam	Tuaim	Galway
Tullamore	Tulach Mór	Offaly
Virginia	Achadh Lir	Cavan
Warrenpoint	An Pointe	Down
Waterford	Port Láirge	Waterford
Westmeath	An Iarmhí	Westmeath
Westport	Cathair na Mairt	Mayo
Wexford	Loch Garman	Wexford
Wicklow	Cill Mhantáin	Wicklow
Youghal	Eochaill	Cork

Index

Thanks

Many thanks to the travellers who used the last edition and wrote to us with helpful hints, useful advice and interesting anecdotes:

Francesca, Richard & Dagmar Abbotts, Olives Albrecht, Frank Aschmann, Geraldine Bailie, Pam Baker, D L & D C Baker, P R Birch, Peter Birch, Phil Booth, Deborah Bourner, Stan Bowen, Charles Brod, Jenny Brown , Liz Burke , J Burt , Roy H C Byrne, Laurie & Olivier Cacault, James Cadman, Annette Campion, Maurice Carroll, Stephanie Lynn Carta, Thomas Carver, Bill & Pat & The 8 Cunningham Children, Richard Cole, Declan Connar, M Rosaria Contestabile, Helen Corry, Jane Cosgrave, Nancy Couto, Fiona Cowie, Jocelyn Craib, Tom Craig Elaine Crowe, Andets Dahlsjo, Amy & Ross Dalgleish, A Dallas, J F Davies, Christopher Davis, Annette de Graaf, Ann De Schryver, Deborah Diers, Ed Diggle, Alison Diver, Fiona Dodd, Emma Dods, Michaela Dohnalkova, Joseph Donnelly, Stewart & Marie Dougan, Clark Downs, Leslie Drake, Stephen Draper, James Earl, Bibi Eng, Urs Federer, Sylvia Fieres, Mat Fitzwilliam, Tracey Flynn, D Fooney, J Forsberg, Susan Fraiman, Shiela Francis, Kathy Furman, Caroline Furze, Markus Fussel, Miriam Gallacher, Martin Giblin, Juliet Gill, Danielle Glosser, Helen Graves, Germain Groll, Verita Gulati, Bernard Hampsey Jnr, Robyn Harper, L Harris, Shane Harrison, Jane Headley, Alain Herman, Bridget Herold, Dr Harriet Hiscock, Michael Hofschuster, Pauline Holder, Charlotte Holmes, Tomas Homann, Wendy Hughes, J J Hunt, Frank Jansen, Gene Jemail, Betty Jo Harper, Dr John Dorling, Marilyn Karasopoulos, Daniel Kavanaugh, Zoe Kavel, Philippa Kay, Nigel Keane, Rachel Kemsley, B & P Kennedy, John Kenyon, Birgitt Kleimann, Sharon Lane, T Lee, Robert Lew, Michael Lintner, Stefan Livens, Eric Lord, Jeanne Loughlin, Noreen MacMahon, Sue Magee, John Maher, Karen & Martin Makes, Rita Maloney, Jim Marshall, Gary & Jane Martin, Gary Mayne, Claire McCombie, Laura McGuinness, Helen McKelleher, J McKenzie, Paulo Mendonca, Julie Mitchell, Alice Morden, George von der Muh, Mr & Mrs Mulley, Alan & Cathie Murdey, Niall Murphy, Han Nabben, Shona Nairn, Nancy Newark, Arno Nolte, Seamus O'Brien, Hugh O'Reilly, Chris Olsen, Staly Omniewski, P Onnekink, Jolien Ophof, Simone Ostmeier, Richard Owen, Richard Parry, Terry Parsons, Chris & Linda Perry, John Peters, Jeffrey Pierce, Helen Pinoft, Wendy Porter, Margaret Powell, Rita Prusinski, C Ratkovic, Mary Reynolds, Thea Risby, A Rozema, A Rzepa, Tobi Sanger, M Santamaria, Malcolm Savage, Shirley Schaaf, Mr Scheuring, Oliver Schmidt, Corinna Schmolhe, Marie-Rose Schwizer, Lynda Sekora, Dr Madeleine Shataugh, Joan Sheldrick, Kathleen Simmons, R J Sims, J Smith, F Stewart, Peter Stewart, John & Janie Stewart, Martin Sudeberg, Janice & Robin Tausig, Pam & Dave Tindall, D Tishel, Mr & Mrs R Tocknell, Margaret Toohey, Neil Toyn, D Valk, J Veenboer, Cla Walsh, S Watt, Ken Weilerstein, Kevin Wenlock, Mary White, H Williams, Stephen Wilson, Sonja Wolf, Jim Woodfin, Nancy Woods, Caroline Wright, Mary Wright-Smith, C Wymberry, I A Zwematra

LONELY PLANET PHRASEBOOKS

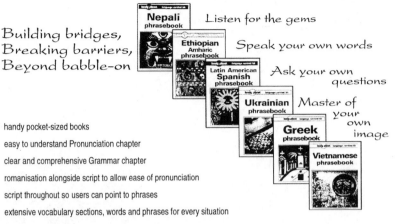

Building bridges,
Breaking barriers,
Beyond babble-on

Listen for the gems

Speak your own words

Ask your own
questions

Master of
your
own
image

- handy pocket-sized books
- easy to understand Pronunciation chapter
- clear and comprehensive Grammar chapter
- romanisation alongside script to allow ease of pronunciation
- script throughout so users can point to phrases
- extensive vocabulary sections, words and phrases for every situation
- full of cultural information and tips for the traveller

'...vital for a real DIY spirit and attitude in language learning' – Backpacker

'the phrasebooks have good cultural backgrounders and offer solid advice for challenging situations in remote locations' – San Francisco Examiner

'...they are unbeatable for their coverage of the world's more obscure languages' – The Geographical Magazine

---

Arabic (Egyptian)
Arabic (Moroccan)
Australia
  Australian English, Aboriginal and Torres Strait languages
Baltic States
  Estonian, Latvian, Lithuanian
Bengali
Burmese
Brazilian
Cantonese
Central Asia
Central Europe
  Czech, French, German, Hungarian, Italian and Slovak
Eastern Europe
  Bulgarian, Czech, Hungarian, Polish, Romanian and Slovak
Egyptian Arabic
Ethiopian (Amharic)
Fijian
French
German
Greek

Hindi/Urdu
Indonesian
Italian
Japanese
Korean
Lao
Latin American Spanish
Malay
Mandarin
Mediterranean Europe
  Albanian, Croatian, Greek, Italian, Macedonian, Maltese, Serbian, Slovene
Mongolian
Moroccan Arabic
Nepali
Papua New Guinea
Pilipino (Tagalog)
Quechua
Russian
Scandinavian Europe
  Danish, Finnish, Icelandic, Norwegian and Swedish

South-East Asia
  Burmese, Indonesian, Khmer, Lao, Malay, Tagalog (Pilipino), Thai and Vietnamese
Spanish
Sri Lanka
Swahili
Thai
Thai Hill Tribes
Tibetan
Turkish
Ukrainian
USA
  US English, Vernacular Talk, Native American languages and Hawaiian
Vietnamese
Western Europe
  Basque, Catalan, Dutch, French, German, Irish, Italian, Portuguese, Scottish Gaelic, Spanish (Castilian) and Welsh

LONELY PLANET JOURNEYS

JOURNEYS is a unique collection of travel writing – published by the company that understands travel better than anyone else. It is a series for anyone who has ever experienced – or dreamed of – the magical moment when they encountered a strange culture or saw a place for the first time. They are tales to read while you're planning a trip, while you're on the road or while you're in an armchair, in front of a fire.

JOURNEYS books catch the spirit of a place, illuminate a culture, recount a crazy adventure, or introduce a fascinating way of life. They always entertain, and always enrich the experience of travel.

THE GATES OF DAMASCUS
Lieve Joris

Translated by Sam Garrett

This best-selling book is a beautifully drawn portrait of day-to-day life in modern Syria. Through her intimate contact with local people, Lieve Joris draws us into the fascinating world that lies behind the gates of Damascus. Hala's husband is a political prisoner, jailed for his opposition to the Assad regime; through the author's friendship with Hala we see how Syrian politics impacts on the lives of ordinary people.

Lieve Joris, who was born in Belgium, is one of Europe's leading travel writers. In addition to an award-winning book on Hungary, she has published widely acclaimed accounts of her journeys to the Middle East and Africa. *The Gates of Damascus* is her fifth book.

'Expands the boundaries of travel writing' – Times Literary Supplement

---

KINGDOM OF THE FILM STARS
Journey into Jordan
Annie Caulfield

Kingdom of the Film Stars is a travel book and a love story. With honesty and humour, Annie Caulfield writes of travelling in Jordan and falling in love with a Bedouin. Her book offers fascinating insights into the country – from the traditional tent life of nomadic tribes to the first woman MP's battle with fundamentalist colleagues. *Kingdom of the Film Stars* unpicks some of the tight-woven Western myths about the Arab world, presenting cultural and political issues within the intimate framework of a compelling love story.

Annie Caulfield, who was born in Ireland and currently lives in London, is an award-winning playwright and journalist. She has travelled widely in the Middle East.

'Annie Caulfield is a remarkable traveller. Her story is fresh, courageous, moving, witty and sexy!' – Dawn French

LONELY PLANET TRAVEL ATLASES

Lonely Planet has long been famous for the number and quality of its guidebook maps. Now we've gone one step further and in conjunction with Steinhart Katzir Publishers produced a handy companion series: Lonely Planet travel atlases – maps of a country produced in book form.

Unlike other maps, which look good but lead travellers astray, our travel atlases have been researched on the road by Lonely Planet's experienced team of writers. All details are carefully checked to ensure the atlas corresponds with the equivalent Lonely Planet guidebook.

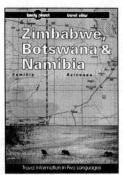

The handy atlas format means no holes, wrinkles, torn sections or constant folding and unfolding. These atlases can survive long periods on the road, unlike cumbersome fold-out maps. The comprehensive index ensures easy reference.

- full-colour throughout
- maps researched and checked by Lonely Planet authors
- place names correspond with Lonely Planet guidebooks
  – no confusing spelling differences
- legend and travelling information in English, French, German, Japanese and Spanish
- size: 230 x 160 mm

Available now:
Chile & Easter Island • Egypt • India & Bangladesh • Israel & the Palestinian Territories •Jordan, Syria & Lebanon • Kenya • Laos • Portugal • South Africa, Lesotho & Swaziland • Thailand • Turkey • Vietnam • Zimbabwe, Botswana & Namibia

---

LONELY PLANET TV SERIES & VIDEOS

Lonely Planet travel guides have been brought to life on television screens around the world. Like our guides, the programmes are based on the joy of independent travel, and look honestly at some of the most exciting, picturesque and frustrating places in the world. Each show is presented by one of three travellers from Australia, England or the USA and combines an innovative mixture of video, Super-8 film, atmospheric soundscapes and original music.

Videos of each episode – containing additional footage not shown on television – are available from good book and video shops, but the availability of individual videos varies with regional screening schedules.

Video destinations include: Alaska • American Rockies • Australia – The South-East • Baja California & the Copper Canyon • Brazil • Central Asia • Chile & Easter Island • Corsica, Sicily & Sardinia – The Mediterranean Islands • East Africa (Tanzania & Zanzibar) • Ecuador & the Galapagos Islands • Greenland & Iceland • Indonesia • Israel & the Sinai Desert • Jamaica • Japan • La Ruta Maya • Morocco • New York • North India • Pacific Islands (Fiji, Solomon Islands & Vanuatu) • South India • South West China • Turkey • Vietnam • West Africa • Zimbabwe, Botswana & Namibia

The Lonely Planet TV series is produced by:
Pilot Productions
The Old Studio
18 Middle Row
London W10 5AT UK

For video availability and ordering information contact your nearest Lonely Planet office.

Music from the TV series is available on CD & cassette.

PLANET TALK

Lonely Planet's FREE quarterly newsletter

We love hearing from you and think you'd like to hear from us.

When...is the right time to see reindeer in Finland?
Where...can you hear the best palm-wine music in Ghana?
How...do you get from Asunción to Areguá by steam train?
What...is the best way to see India?

For the answer to these and many other questions read PLANET TALK.

Every issue is packed with up-to-date travel news and advice including:

- a letter from Lonely Planet co-founders Tony and Maureen Wheeler
- go behind the scenes on the road with a Lonely Planet author
- feature article on an important and topical travel issue
- a selection of recent letters from travellers
- details on forthcoming Lonely Planet promotions
- complete list of Lonely Planet products

To join our mailing list contact any Lonely Planet office.

Also available: Lonely Planet T-shirts. 100% heavyweight cotton.

LONELY PLANET ONLINE

Get the latest travel information before you leave or while you're on the road

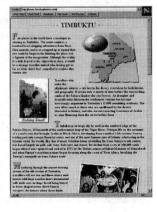

Whether you've just begun planning your next trip, or you're chasing down specific info on currency regulations or visa requirements, check out Lonely Planet Online for up-to-the minute travel information.

As well as travel profiles of your favourite destinations (including maps and photos), you'll find current reports from our researchers and other travellers, updates on health and visas, travel advisories, and discussion of the ecological and political issues you need to be aware of as you travel.

There's also an online travellers' forum where you can share your experience of life on the road, meet travel companions and ask other travellers for their recommendations and advice. We also have plenty of links to other online sites useful to independent travellers.

And of course we have a complete and up-to-date list of all Lonely Planet travel products including guides, phrasebooks, atlases, Journeys and videos and a simple online ordering facility if you can't find the book you want elsewhere.

www.lonelyplanet.com
or
AOL keyword: lp

LONELY PLANET PRODUCTS

Lonely Planet is known worldwide for publishing practical, reliable and no-nonsense travel information in our guides and on our web site. The Lonely Planet list covers just about every accessible part of the world. Currently there are eight series: *travel guides*, *shoestring guides*, *walking guides*, *city guides*, *phrasebooks*, *audio packs*, *travel atlases* and *Journeys* – a unique collection of travel writing.

EUROPE

Amsterdam • Austria • Baltic States phrasebook • Britain • Central Europe on a shoestring • Central Europe phrasebook • Czech & Slovak Republics • Denmark • Dublin • Eastern Europe on a shoestring • Eastern Europe phrasebook • Estonia, Latvia & Lithuania • Finland • France • French phrasebook • German phrasebook • Greece • Greek phrasebook • Hungary • Iceland, Greenland & the Faroe Islands • Ireland • Italian phrasebook • Italy • Mediterranean Europe on a shoestring • Mediterranean Europe phrasebook • Paris • Poland • Portugal • Portugal travel atlas • Prague • Russia, Ukraine & Belarus • Russian phrasebook • Scandinavian & Baltic Europe on a shoestring • Scandinavian Europe phrasebook • Slovenia • Spain • Spanish phrasebook • St Petersburg • Switzerland • Trekking in Spain • Ukrainian phrasebook • Vienna • Walking in Britain • Walking in Switzerland • Western Europe on a shoestring • Western Europe phrasebook

Travel Literature: The Olive Grove: Travels in Greece

NORTH AMERICA

Alaska • Backpacking in Alaska • Baja California • California & Nevada • Canada • Florida • Hawaii • Honolulu • Los Angeles • Mexico • Miami • New England • New Orleans • New York City • New York, New Jersey & Pennsylvania • Pacific Northwest USA • Rocky Mountain States • San Francisco • Southwest USA • USA phrasebook • Washington, DC & the Capital Region

CENTRAL AMERICA & THE CARIBBEAN

Bermuda • Central America on a shoestring • Costa Rica • Cuba • Eastern Caribbean • Guatemala, Belize & Yucatán: La Ruta Maya • Jamaica

SOUTH AMERICA

Argentina, Uruguay & Paraguay • Bolivia • Brazil • Brazilian phrasebook • Buenos Aires • Chile & Easter Island • Chile & Easter Island travel atlas • Colombia • Ecuador & the Galápagos Islands • Latin American Spanish phrasebook • Peru • Quechua phrasebook • Rio de Janeiro • South America on a shoestring • Trekking in the Patagonian Andes • Venezuela

Travel Literature: Full Circle: A South American Journey

ANTARCTICA

Antarctica

ISLANDS OF THE INDIAN OCEAN

Madagascar & Comoros • Maldives • Mauritius, Réunion & Seychelles

AFRICA

Africa - the South • Africa on a shoestring • Arabic (Moroccan) phrasebook • Cape Town • Central Africa • East Africa • Egypt • Egypt travel atlas• Ethiopian (Amharic) phrasebook • Kenya • Kenya travel atlas • Malawi, Mozambique & Zambia • Morocco • North Africa • South Africa, Lesotho & Swaziland • South Africa, Lesotho & Swaziland travel atlas • Swahili phrasebook • Trekking in East Africa • West Africa • Zimbabwe, Botswana & Namibia • Zimbabwe, Botswana & Namibia travel atlas

Travel Literature: The Rainbird: A Central African Journey • Songs to an African Sunset: A Zimbabwean Story